Business & Company
RESOURCE CENTER

Business and Company Resource Center (BCRC)

Gitman and McDaniel keep you up-to-date and continually interacting with the business world by providing online exercises that point you to current articles located in our BCRC. These exercises, part of ThomsonNOW, ask you to read the articles and answer questions, encouraging you to apply your knowledge of concepts to the ideas discussed in the article. When you purchase ThomsonNOW for *The Future of Business, 6e* you will automatically receive access to the BCRC database. This access will not only allow you to answer gradable homework questions tied to articles found in BCRC, but will also open up an entire database in which you can research a wide variety of global business information, including competitive intelligence, career and investment opportunities, business rankings, company histories, and much more. View a guided tour of the Business & Company Resource Center at

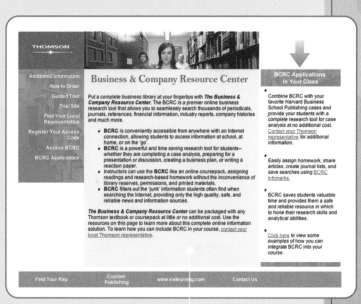

http://bcrc.swlearning.com.

The Future of Business

6e

Lawrence J. Gitman
San Diego State University

Carl McDaniel
University of Texas, Arlington

THOMSON

™

SOUTH-WESTERN

Australia · Canada · Mexico · Singapore · Spain · United Kingdom · United States

The Future of Business, Sixth Edition
Lawrence J. Gitman and Carl McDaniel

VP/Editorial Director:
Jack W. Calhoun

Publisher:
Neil Marquardt

Acquisitions Editor:
Erin Joyner

Senior Developmental Editor:
Mary H. Draper

Marketing Manager:
Nicole C. Moore

Content Project Manager:
Robert Dreas

Technology Project Manager:
Kristen Meere

Marketing Communications Manager:
Sarah Greber

Sr. 1ˢᵗ Print Buyer:
Diane Gibbons

Production House:
Pre-Press Company, Inc.

Printer:
Courier Corporation
Kendallville, Indiana

Art Director:
Stacy Jenkins Shirley

Internal and Cover Designer:
Liz Harasymczuk

Cover Images:
© Getty Images/Image Bank

Photography Manager:
Deanna Ettinger

Photo Researcher:
Terri Miller
E-Visual Communications

Library of Congress Control Number:
2006907297

For more information about our products, contact us at:

Thomson Learning Academic Resource Center

1-800-423-0563

Thomson Higher Education
5191 Natorp Boulevard
Mason, OH 45040
USA

Dedicated to the memory of my mother, Dr. Edith Gitman, who instilled in me the importance of education and hard work.

—Lawrence J. Gitman

To Michelle, Mimi, and Eric

—Carl McDaniel

AUTHORS

Lawrence J. Gitman

Lawrence J. Gitman is an emeritus professor of finance at San Diego State University. He received his Bachelor's Degree from Purdue University, his M.B.A. from the University of Dayton, and his Ph.D. from the University of Cincinnati. Professor Gitman is a prolific textbook author and has over 50 articles appearing in *Financial Management, Financial Review, Financial Services Review, Journal of Financial Planning, Journal of Risk and Insurance, Journal of Financial Research, Financial Practice and Education, Journal of Financial Education*, and other publications.

His singly authored major textbooks include *Principles of Managerial Finance: Brief*, Fourth Edition, *Principles of Managerial Finance*, Eleventh Edition, and *Foundations of Managerial Finance*, Fourth Edition. Other major textbooks include *Personal Financial Planning*, Tenth Edition, and *Fundamentals of Investing*, Ninth Edition, both co-authored with Michael D. Joehnk. Gitman and Joehnk also wrote *Investment Fundamentals: A Guide to Becoming a Knowledgeable Investor*, which was selected as one of 1988's ten best personal finance books by *Money* magazine. In addition, he co-authored *Introduction to Finance* with Jeff Madura and *Corporate Finance*, Second Edition, with Scott B. Smart and William L. Meggison.

An active member of numerous professional organizations, Professor Gitman is past president of the Academy of Financial Services, the San Diego Chapter of the Financial Executives Institute, the Midwest Finance Association, and the FMA National Honor Society. In addition he is a Certified Financial Planner (CFP)© and a Certified Cash Manager (CCM). Gitman served as Vice-President, Financial Education of the Financial Management Association, as a Director of the San Diego MIT Enterprise Form, and on the CFP© Board of Standards. He and his wife have two children and live in La Jolla, California, where he is an avid bicyclist.

Carl McDaniel

Carl McDaniel is a professor of marketing at the University of Texas—Arlington, where he is Chairman of the Marketing Department. He has been an instructor for more than 20 years and is the recipient of several awards for outstanding teaching. McDaniel has also been a District Sales Manager for Southwestern Bell Telephone Company. Currently, he serves as a board member of the North Texas Higher Education Authority, a 1.5 billion member organization that provides immediate financing for student loans across America.

In addition to this text, McDaniel has also co-authored a number of textbooks in marketing. McDaniel's research has appeared in such publications as *Journal of Marketing, Journal of Business Research, Journal of the Academy of Marketing Science*, and *California Management Review*.

McDaniel is a member of the American Marketing Association, Academy of Marketing Science, Society for Marketing Advances, and Southwestern Marketing Association.

Besides his academic experience, McDaniel has business experience as the co-owner of a marketing research firm. Recently, McDaniel served as senior consultant to the International Trade Center (ITC), Geneva, Switzerland. The ITC's mission is to help developing nations increase their exports. McDaniel also teaches international business each year in France. He has a Bachelor's Degree from the University of Arkansas and his Master's Degree and Doctorate from Arizona State University.

BRIEF CONTENTS

CONTENTS

Part 6 >

Finance 597

Your Future is Our Business

What is in your future?

What we know:

The Future of Business, 6e prepares you for a successful career in business by equipping you with the knowledge, skills, and competencies you need to prepare for tomorrow's competitive workplace. The authors present business principles and highlight emerging business trends in fields such as management, leadership, production, marketing and finance.

What you will want to know:

In this edition, Gitman and McDaniel offer multiple resources to help you prepare for your future business careers.

- Trends in Business
- ThomsonNOW™
- SCANS Integration
- Integrated Learning System
- Exploring Business Career Videos

The Future with
our New Features

This edition is packed with new features and cases to help you stay excited about the business world. Each new feature, case, or activity is designed to help you understand how real business problems are solved, determine what business careers are right for you, and evaluate the role of ethics. All of these are in place to prepare you for the future business world.

continuing case on Apple, Inc.

Part 1 • The Evolution of Apple, Inc.

In the 1970s, the United States business environment was volatile with unpredictable swings in inflation and recession. The political and social environments were unstable due largely to the country's continued presence in Vietnam. Price controls, oil embargos, high unemployment, highly publicized labor disputes, and rapid rates of change in consumer prices all contributed to a decade of pessimism. Such economic issues contributed to the productivity slowdown of the 1970s. The largest slowdowns were in pipelines, motor vehicles, oil/gas extraction, utilities, and air transportation—all industries affected by the energy crisis of the 1970s. Interestingly, this environment proved ripe for innovation and was the backdrop for the inception of Apple, Inc. and a new product category that would ultimately become a way of life
society.

____ed a new product category when it offered the
_____t the market's needs. This

designed for fun to take to the Homebrew Computer Club meeting, not to be a product for a company. Diagrams of the Apple I were shared at the club meetings. Thus, the Apple computer was being demonstrated as it was being developed. In this manner, the product was receiving critical technical review from experts who were dabbling in computers as a hobby. The Homebrew Computer Club was one of the first steps in the development of today's multibillion dollar personal computer industry.

THE WOZNIAK AND JOBS DUO

Stephen Wozniak and Steve Jobs met in 1969 and developed their first commercial product in 1971. Unfortunately, their first invention was not a viable product offering. The two had developed and packaged a "blue box" that could hack into the phone system. Product development was shut down,
____ when the developer of the original phone hacking
_____fraud charges.

New Apple, Inc. Continuing Case

Brand new to this edition, the Apple Computer, Inc. continuing case is located at the end of each part, providing an in-depth look at the company's tumultuous evolution and demonstrating how chapter concepts are applied in an actual business.

New Exploring Business Careers Videos

New opening vignettes and videos highlight the careers of successful business leaders from a variety of service and manufacturing firms, providing insight into many business careers.

Exploring Business Careers
Natalie Tessler
Spa Space

If you happen to catch her, Natalie Tessler will be trying simultaneously to find the company checkbook, prepare for a 100-person party, and talk to several employees about clients they are assisting. Her first career, as a lawyer for some of the country's most prestigious firms, required a great deal of educational training. None of that training, however, prepared her for running her own business. "People think that, owning a spa, I'm able to live this glamorous lifestyle," she laughs. "Owning a spa is ____ like going to one—my nails always are ____ my back is usually in

presentation. Seeking an outlet for that flair, she found the spa industry, an industry where attending to the client is key to success. And after much research, the idea for Spa Space was born.

Tessler wanted to design a spa that focused on something new: creating a comfortable, personalized environment of indulgence while not neglecting the medical technology of proper skin care. "My father's a dermatologist, so we discussed the importance of making this more than a spa where you can get a frou-frou, smell-good treatment that might actually harm your skin. We both thought it was important to
____beneficial for people's

Concept in Action Photo Essays

"Concept in Action" photo essays speak to today's visual learners by illustrating chapter concepts using interesting companies and business leaders. Each photo is accompanied by captions that provide detailed information about the person or business profiled, followed by a critical thinking question.

China's exports have boomed largely thanks to foreign investm_____ low labor costs, big manufacturers have surged into China to expand_____ tion base and push down prices globally. Now manufacturers of al_____

CONCEPT in Action

Giant-screen movie exhibitor Imax is taking its trademark big film presentations to an even bigger market: India. The Canadian theater chain recently expanded into Mumbai and New Delhi where it is dazzling Indian audiences with mega-screen adaptations of today's blockbuster movies. With crystal clear images up to eight stories high and rumbling digital surround sound, the Imax system delivers an unparalleled film experience. *What factors make India an attractive market for Imax?*

© ARCHIVBERLIN FOTOAGENTUR GMBH/ALAMY

New Ethics Activities

These new ethics activities at the end of each chapter present real-world ethical challenges and prompt you to choose the most ethical course of action.

research its infrastructure to determine how it will help or hinder_____
variety of countries, ranging from the most highly developed to_____
oped. (Resources, Interpersonal, Information, Technology)

Ethics Activity

The executives of a clothing manufacturer want to outsource some of their manufacturing to more cost-efficient locations in Indonesia. After visiting several possible sites, they choose one and begin to negotiate with local officials. They discover that it will take about six months to get the necessary permits. One of the local politicians approaches the executives over dinner and hints that he can speed up the process, for an advisory fee of $5,000.

Using a Web search tool, locate articles about th_____
write responses to the following questions. Be sure_____
arguments and cite your sources.

Ethical Dilemma: Is paying the advisory fee a_____
ceptable cost of doing business in that area of t_____
should the executives do before agreeing to pay th_____

Sources: Jane Easter Bahls, "Illicit Affairs? If You Do Business Overseas_____ 'Administrative Fees' Aren't Really Illegal Bribes," *Entrepreneur*, Septe_____ Paul Burnham Finney, "Shaking Hands, Greasing Palms," *New York* _____ p. C10; Phelim Kyne, "Freeport-McMoRan Indonesia Payments Not _____ *Financial News*, January 18, 2006.

Working the Net

1. Go to the Trade Compliance Center site at **http://tcc.mac.doc.g_____
   search Your Country Market" and then "Search Reports." Pick a_____
   terests you from the index, and read the most current available_____
   country. Would this country be a good market for a small U.S. m_____
   ufacturer interested in expanding internationally? Why or why n_____
   main barriers to trade the company might face?

2. While still at the Trade Compliance site, **http://tcc.mac.doc.gov_____
   Agreements" and then "List All Agreements." Select one that i_____
   summarize what you learn about it.
   _____ exchange rates between the U._____ up chart_____

Preparing for Tomorrow's Workplace: **SCANS**

1. Suppose you are considering two job offers for a computer programming position at: a two-year-old consulting firm with 10 employees owned by a sole proprietor, or a publicly traded software developer with sales of $500 million. In addition to comparing the specific job responsibilities, consider the following:
   - Which company offers better training? Do you prefer the on-the-job training you'll get at the small company, or do you want formal training programs as well?

SCANS Integration

The Secretary's Commission on Achieving Necessary Skills (SCANS) recommends students develop five workplace competencies: using and allocating resources, working with others, acquiring and using information, understanding systems, and working with technology. The "Preparing for Tomorrow's Workplace" activities are designed to develop these skills and are included in the homework section of each chapter.

The Future with

our Technology

ThomsonNOW™ with BCRC for Gitman/McDaniel's *The Future of Business, 6e*

Designed BY instructors and students FOR instructors and students, *ThomsonNOW* for **Gitman/McDaniel's *The Future of Business, 6e*** gives you what you want to do, how you want to do it.

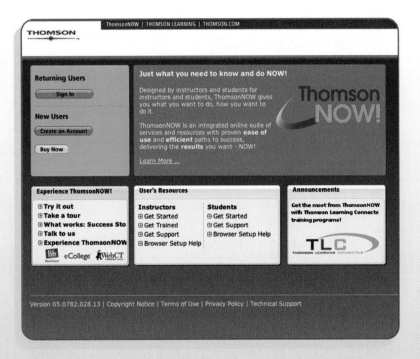

Access to a Unique Database

When you purchase *ThomsonNOW* for the Gitman/McDaniel text you will automatically receive access to the BCRC database (see the next page for more details). This access will not only allow you to answer gradable homework questions tied to articles found in BCRC, but will also open up an entire database in which you can research company histories, articles, industry data, company financials and more!

Personalized Study Plan

ThomsonNOW gives you a person-alized study plan that helps you focus on what you still need to learn, as well as the opportunity to select activities, videos, animations, web links, text pages, and audio lectures that best match your learning style.

Delivering the Results You Deserve

Students report that they are more efficient studying and feel more confident taking exams. Instructors report that students do better on exams and come to class better prepared when using *ThomsonNOW*. *ThomsonNOW* gets the results you want FAST.

For more information on *ThomsonNOW*, please visit **www.thomsonedu.com/thomsonnow.**

Business & Company
RESOURCE CENTER

Business and Company Resource Center (BCRC)

Gitman and McDaniel keep you up-to-date and continually interacting with the business world by providing ethics activities that point you to current articles located in our BCRC. These activities, part of ThomsonNOW, ask you to read the articles and answer questions, encouraging you to apply your knowledge of concepts to the ideas discussed in the article. When you purchase ThomsonNOW for *The Future of Business, 6e* you will automatically receive access to the BCRC database. This access will not only allow you to answer gradable homework questions tied to articles found in BCRC, but will also open up an entire database in which you can research a wide variety of global business information, including competitive intelligence, career and investment opportunities, business rankings, company histories, and much more. View a guided tour of the Business & Company Resource Center at

http://bcrc.swlearning.com.

The Future with

New Video Cases

Exploring Business Careers
Natalie Tessler
Spa Space

If you happen to catch her, Natalie Tessler will be trying simultaneously to find the company checkbook, prepare for a 100-person party, and talk to several employees about clients they are assisting. Her first career, as a lawyer for some of the country's most prestigious firms, required a great deal of educational training. None of that training, however, prepared her for running her own business. "People think that, owning a spa, I'm able to live this glamorous lifestyle," she laughs. "Owning a spa is nothing like going to one—my nails always are broken from fixing equipment; my back is usually in ...tting hunched over a computer trying to ...keting promo-

presentation. Seeking an outlet for that flair, she found the spa industry, an industry where attending to the client is key to success. And after much research, the idea for Spa Space was born.

Tessler wanted to design a spa that focused on something new: creating a comfortable, personalized environment of indulgence while not neglecting the medical technology of proper skin care. "My father's a dermatologist, so we discussed the importance of making this more than a spa where you can get a frou-frou, smell-good treatment that might actually harm your skin. We both thought it was important to create an experience that is as beneficial for people's skin as it is for their emotional well-being." To ...ical advisory

NEW Exploring Business Careers Videos

New opening vignettes and videos highlight the careers of successful business leaders from a variety of well-known companies such as:

- JP Morgan Chase
- Navistar International
- Caterpillar
- BP
- Domino's Pizza

Trends in Business

To better prepare you for tomorrow's business world, Gitman and McDaniel believe students need to be aware of the latest trends and emerging issues in management, leadership, production, marketing, finance, and more. Therefore, each chapter covers both the principles of business and devotes the last learning goal of each chapter to emerging business trends.

Discuss the laws that govern wages, pensions, and employee compensation.

Describe the Americans with Disabilities Act.

How do the Wagner and Taft-Hartley Acts impact labor-management relations?

persuasion. In conciliation the specialist assists management and the union to focus on the issues in dispute and acts as a go-between, or communication channel through which the union and employer send messages to and share information with each other. The specialist takes a stronger role in mediation by suggesting compromises to the disputing organizations.

Trends in Human Resource Management and Labor Relations

 What trends and issues are affecting human resource management and labor relations?

Some of today's most important trends in human resource management are using employee diversity as a competitive advantage, improving efficiency through outsourcing and technology, and hiring employees who fit the organizational culture. Although overall labor union enrollment continues to decline, a possible surge in membership in service unions is anticipated.

Employee Diversity and Competitive Advantage

competitive advantage
A set of unique features of an organization that are perceived by customers and potential customers as significant and superior to the competition.

American society and its workforce are becoming increasingly more diverse in terms of racial and ethnic status, age, educational background, work experience, and gender. A company with a demographic employee profile that looks like its customers may be in a position to gain a competitive advantage, which is a set of unique features of a company and its product or service that are perceived by the target market as superior to those of the competition. Competitive advantage is the factor that causes customers to patronize a firm and not the competition. Many things can be a source of competitive advantage: for Southwest Airlines it is route structure and high asset utilization; for the Ritz-Carlton it is very high quality guest services; for Toyota it is manufacturing efficiency and product durability; and for Starbucks it is location, service, and outstanding coffee products. For these firms, a competitive advantage is also created by their HR practices. Many firms are successful because of employee diversity which can produce more effective problem solving, a stronger reputation for hiring women and minorities, greater employee diversity, quicker adaptation to change, and more robust product solutions because a diverse team can generate more options for improvement.[16]

In order for an organization to use employee diversity for competitive advantage, top management must be fully committed to hiring and developing women and minority individuals. An organization that highly values employee diversity is the United States Postal Service (USPS). In 1992 the Postal Service launched a diversity development program to serve as the organization's "social conscience and to increase employees' awareness of and appreciation for ethnic and cultural diversity both in the ...rkplace and among customers." Within about ten years, 36 percent of postal ...black, 7.6 percent Hispanic,

The Future of
Your Career

In order to demonstrate how business concepts are applied in real business settings, Gitman and McDaniel have created these special boxed features. Each boxed feature includes a series of critical thinking questions to prompt you to consider the implications of each business strategy that's presented.

Customer Satisfaction and Quality

Because customer satisfaction and quality are essential to attracting and keeping customers, the Customer Satisfaction and Quality box adresses how these concepts are illustrated and applied in actual companies.

Expanding Around the Globe

Upon entering today's workplace, you are very likely to conduct business with colleagues, clients, and vendors from around the world. The Expanding Around the Globe feature offers insights into the global economy and highlights the strategies firms take to expand their business and improve their productivity by utilizing global resources.

Catching the Entrepreneurial Spirit

Because you will either open your own business or go to work for a small organization, this feature highlights the challenges and opportunities available in small businesses.

Managing Change

The turbulent business climate requires companies to adapt their business strategies in response to a variety of forces, including economic, social, competitive, and technological. The Managing Change feature highlights how businesses have altered their business strategies in response to these forces.

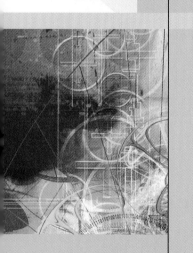

Your Future is Our Business

PREFACE

Welcome to the exciting, sometimes crazy, fun, and challenging world of business. The story that we are about to tell you is about your future. If you plan to be an engineer, medical doctor, social worker, or any other of professional person, business will impact you. Even though a doctor will devote the bulk of her day to treating patients, she also needs the skills and understanding of business to make her office run smoothly and profitably. So enjoy reading this exciting, easy-to-read, story-filled book because it will help you navigate the tricky waters that make up the future of business and prepare you for success!

Features That Help You Learn

We are thrilled that you have joined us on the journey to the future of business. We have made many changes in the Sixth Edition that make it by far the best ever. In this preface, we describe the hallmark features that make this text a success with both students and instructors. We also spotlight the new features and content of this dynamic edition.

Each Chapter Offers Dual Coverage: Business Principles and Business Trends

You told us that you wanted a crisp, innovative chapter structure, and that's what we deliver in the Sixth Edition. With the dual coverage of business principles and business trends in every chapter, *The Future of Business* prepares you for tomorrow's business world.

Principles of Business Each chapter delivers a comprehensive overview of current business principles and practices. You will learn what is happening in today's businesses with examples from the largest global corporate giants, such as General Electric and Procter and Gamble, to the smallest family start-ups.

Trends in Business The last learning goal of every chapter explores new business trends and how they are reshaping today's business and altering tomorrow's competitive environment. Technology and the global economy are covered extensively in every trends section. We expose you to the fundamental factors that are reshaping the business world in which you will soon begin professional careers. With this preview of the future, you gain a keen advantage when entering the workplace.

The Integrated Learning System Ties Everything Together

The Integrated Learning System helps you learn quickly by driving home key chapter concepts and providing a framework for studying. We tie all instructor and student materials to each chapter's learning goals. The learning goals provide a common link to the text and all of the great supplements that accompany the Sixth Edition. Learning goals are listed at the beginning of each chapter and then repeated throughout the chapter in the margins of the text. After reading each section, you can test your retention by answering the questions in the Concept Checks. Every learning goal is further reinforced by the chapter summary.

The Integrated Learning System also helps instructors easily prepare their lectures. Learning goals at the beginning of each chapter outline the key concepts in the chapter and provide structure for lesson plans and help in exam preparation. Test questions, the PowerPoint Slides, and the Instructor's Manual lecture outline are all organized by the Integrated Learning System.

Hundreds of Business Examples Bring Business Concepts to Life

This book is about you—the typical student. We have done a lot of research about your needs, abilities, experiences, and interests and then shaped the text around them. We have used our experiences both inside and outside the classroom to create a book that is both readable and enjoyable. We believe that the real business applications that are found throughout *every* chapter set the standard for readability and understanding of key concepts.

Videos Cases Offer a Behind-the-Scenes Tour of Interesting Companies

Twenty video cases, found at the end of every chapter, give you a glimpse inside interesting businesses including Toyota, ESPN, P. F. Chang's, and Geek Corporation, and highlight the topics from each chapter. Learning is made fun and interesting through the study of real business issues and strategies implemented by a variety of service and manufacturing firms.

Learning Business Terminology Is Made Easy

As you begin your study of business, you will begin to explore new words and concepts like *entrepreneurship, venture capital, competitive advantage, relationship management, the European Union, strategic alliance*, and more. To help you learn this language of business, we define each new term in the chapter, print them in red type, list the word and its definition in the margin, and offer a complete glossary at the end of the book. When you finish this book, you will be able to speak the language of business!

Activities and Cases Put Knowledge to Work

The Future of Business, Sixth Edition helps you develop a solid grounding in skills like those you will apply in the workplace. These skill-building activities and resources help you build and polish competencies that your future employer will value.

- **Preparing for Tomorrow's Workplace and Team Activities**. These activities are designed to help build your business skills and practice teamwork. These highly practical exercises give you a meaningful advantage over fellow graduates in the workplace. New team activities in every chapter give you an opportunity to work with other students, building communication skills and interpersonal skills.
- **Working the Net Activities**. These activities guide you through a step-by-step analysis of actual e-business practices and give you opportunities to build online research skills.
- **Critical Thinking Cases**. Along with the Video Cases, the Critical Thinking cases invite you to explore business strategies of various companies, analyze business decisions, and prepare comments.
- **Hot Links Address Book**. These activities, found at the end of every chapter, take you to the Web sites of well-known companies and show you how to find the Web's most reliable and valuable business resources. These Hot Links demonstrate actual e-commerce practices and policies, covering issues as diverse as online security, new distribution systems, mass customization, and more.

Student-Friendly Writing Makes *Future of Business, Sixth Edition* Accessible

Our objective is for you to finish this text and feel like this is absolutely the best college textbook that you have ever read! You will find that our writing style is friendly and very conversational—like two friends speaking together. Instead of formal language that can often be stilted, chapter titles, headings, and chapter text are written in a relaxed, inviting manner.

New Features in the Sixth Edition

The Sixth Edition has been thoroughly updated with new learning tools and content to offer a complete, creative learning experience.

A Concise Format Creates a Sharper Focus

The number of chapters in the Sixth Edition has been reduced from 22 to 20. Although the labor relations chapter has been eliminated, key concepts from that chapter have been retained and folded into the human resources management chapter. This new chapter informs you of the latest trends and theories in human resource management. "Managing Your Personal Finances" has been updated and moved to the companion Web site as an enrichment chapter. You will also find a second, very helpful enrichment chapter called "Using the Internet for Business Success." This material gives you the latest techniques and strategies to conquer the world of e-commerce. These online enrichment chapters can be found at **http://www.thomsonedu.com/introbusiness/gitman**.

Apple, Inc. Continuing Case Illustrates Chapter Concepts

What company could be more exciting and fun than Apple? Apple, Inc. is featured in a continuing case at the end of each part, providing an in-depth look at the company's tumultuous evolution and demonstrating how chapter concepts are applied in a real business. By presenting the strategies that helped Apple rebound from a business slump in the mid-1980s to success today, you gain an insider's look at the organization's problems and solutions over an extended period of time.

Exploring Business Careers Offers an Insider's Look

You told us that you wanted to know more about successful people in business. *Exploring Business Careers*, featured on the first page of each chapter and in the new *Exploring Business Careers* videos, offers an insider's look at a variety of business careers. Begin each chapter by reading the stories of these successful business leaders and watching the professionally produced, fast-paced video to gain quick insight into business careers and the chapter topics.

Concept in Action Photo Essays Demonstrate Concepts at Work

In each chapter you will find interesting companies and business leaders profiled in our new "Concept in Action" photo essays. The photos and accompanying essays are fun, contemporary, insightful, and a super learning tool for the visual learner. Each photo essay concludes with a critical thinking question to spark further discussion and study about a business topic.

Ethic Activities Explore Right and Wrong

Ethics activities at the end of each chapter present real-world ethical challenges and prompt students to choose the most ethical course of action. Scenarios include the Enron collapse, teenage obesity and fast food, executive compensation, outsourcing jobs to foreign countries, whistle-blowing, and more. Each gives you a chance to decide the most ethical course of action in these challenging situations.

New Content in the Sixth Edition

This edition has been completely updated so that you are prepared you for tomorrow's competitive workplace. Below is a description of some of the new content in the Sixth Edition.

The Prologue offers sage advice on getting the most out of your college experience along with practical tips for landing your first job. Not only will you find up-to-date guidelines for finding a job using the Internet, you can gain insights into your own readiness for the job market. Fun Self-Tests explore the following topics:

- Can You Persuade Others?
- Can You Play the Political Game?
- How Well Do You Manage Your Time?
- Are You Good at Managing Money?
- Do You Need to Improve Your Study Habits?
- How Assertive Are You?
- Are You Really a Good Listener?

Chapter 1 (Participating in the Dynamic Business Environment) has been restructured to present more thorough coverage of the economic, political and legal, demographic, social, competitive, global, and technological sectors of the business environment. New material focuses on the impact on businesses of changes in these sub-environments. For example, the aging of the population calls for different marketing strategies, and human resource departments must find ways to handle the brain drain as large numbers of Baby Boomers retire. The chapter also covers the emergence of China and India as new global economic powers, the challenges of managing the multigenerational workplace, and the convergence of telecommunications technologies.

Chapter 2 (Understanding Evolving Economic Systems and Competition) has been updated to reflect the latest economic conditions. New material includes the resilience of the United States economy, concern over the increasing demand for energy worldwide and disruptions in energy supply, the importance of new business creation and entrepreneurship to economic growth in developing countries, and the changing attitudes toward socialism in many European countries.

Chapter 3 (Making Ethical Decisions and Managing a Socially Responsible Business) contains new material on understanding the nature of an ethical issue and ethical philosophies. The "Best Corporate Citizens" and "The Best Places to Work" have been updated and a new section added on "Making the Right Decision."

Appendix to Chapter 3 (Understanding the Legal and Tax Environment) adds new material on federal regulatory agencies and offers an in-depth discussion of the new Bankruptcy Abuse Prevention and Consumer Protection Act. Two other new laws covered are the Children's Online Privacy Protection Act and the Can Spam Anti-Spam law. The appendix concludes with new material on privacy.

Chapter 4 (Competing in the Global Marketplace) discusses outsourcing and whether it is good or bad for workers and the economy. The section on the benefits of globalization has been completely rewritten as well as the discussion of the European Union's antitrust actions. The new Central America Free Trade Agreement is introduced. The World Trade Organization and the material on the European Union have been thoroughly revised. A new section on governmental aid to exporters has been added along with the opportunities and pitfalls of doing business in China and India. The section on multinationals has also been thoroughly revised.

Chapter 5 (Forms of Business Ownership) offers new student-friendly examples and case studies such as the Pacific Sun retail store chain and Organic Valley Farming Co-operative to illustrate the relative merits of sole proprietorships, partnerships, corporations, and other alternative forms of business organization. An expanded section on franchising highlights the benefits and pitfalls of this increasingly popular business entity.

Chapter 6 (Entrepreneurship: Starting and Managing Your Own Business) invites students to put themselves in the shoes of entrepreneurs like 16-year-old Baruch Shemtov and his handmade neckties; brothers Fernando and Santiago Aguerre, the creators of Reef Brazil sandals, who began their entrepreneurial activities at the ages of 8 and 9 years old; young Miho Inagi who introduced bagels to Japan; or Harvard University student Apollonia Poilane who turned the tragic death of her parents into an opportunity to shine by taking over the family business—in Paris. Students will be inspired by the fascinating stories of these dynamic young entrepreneurs.

Chapter 7 (Management and Leadership in Today's Organizations) has been heavily revised and begins with a discussion on the efficiency and effectiveness of organizations. New examples are found throughout the chapter. We have revised the discussion on participative leaders, employee empowerment, and corporate culture. There is a new section on teams, crisis management, outside directors, and using technology such as dashboard software.

Chapter 8 (Designing Organizational Structures) offers new insights on aligning organization structure and goals. This chapter has a new section on informal communication channels and outsourcing.

Chapter 9 (Managing Human Resources and Labor Relations) is a new chapter. We begin with the latest challenges in effectively managing employees and a revised model of human resource management. The discussion of the management process and labor relations management has been updated and streamlined. There are new sections on employee diversity and competitive advantage, outsourcing HR and technology, executive compensation, and organizational culture and hiring for fit.

Chapter 10 (Motivating Employees) reworks the definition of motivation and offers new examples. There are also new sections on reinforcement theory and pay-for-performance, employee ownership, the paid sabbatical, and communities of practice.

Chapter 11 (Achieving World-Class Operations Management) focuses on the way technology and robotics, competitive forces, and changes in consumer expectations are shaping production and operations management. The trend section highlights a looming United States workforce crisis and suggests America may be losing its edge in the innovation race.

Chapter 12 (Creating Marketing Strategy To Meet Customers' Needs) begins with new material on how marketing plays a key role in creating revenue—the lifeblood of the firm. This chapter includes new material on eliminating unprofitable customers and Internet marketing research.

Chapter 13 (Developing Quality Products at the Right Price) provides new insights into brand loyalty, cobranding, and better nutritional labeling. A new section on the impact of the Internet on pricing goods and services has been added, and the coverage of products and packages has been thoroughly reworked.

Chapter 14 (Distributing Products in a Timely and Efficient Manner) offers new material on multiple channels of distribution, nontraditional channels, and strategic channel alliances. The material on channel functions has been reworked and expanded. There are new sections on inventory control, outsourcing of logistics, manufacturers' opening retail stores, and the rapid growth of Internet retailing.

Chapter 15 (Using Integrated Marketing Communications To Promote Products) has a completely new section on the impact of advertising. We also discuss the growing impact of technology and the Internet on traditional advertising. There are new sections on Internet advertising, creating an advertising campaign, couponing and product placement, and creating buzz. Blogging as a form of promotion, new technology applied to sales promotion, and podcasting are covered in new sections.

Chapter 16 (Using Technology to Manage Information) presents the latest developments in information technology and knowledge management, including networking trends and advances in software-on-demand services. The chapter also discusses digital forensics, a new field that provides tools for cyber-sleuthing; the shift to a distributed workforce model; and the rise in grid computing.

Chapter 17 (Using Financial Information and Accounting) provides updates on the latest issues in accounting. These include the collaboration between United States and international accounting boards to develop global accounting standards, the costs and challenges of implementing the provisions of the Sarbanes-Oxley Act, and the changing relationship between accountants and their clients. The chapter also discusses the ongoing efforts of the Financial Accounting Standards Board (FASB) to simplify the complexity of Generally Accepted Accounting Principles (GAAP), which include the possible shift from rules-based to principles-based accounting and a different version of GAAP for small companies.

Chapter 18 (Understanding Money and Financial Institutions) highlights the changing structure of the financial services industry. Financial institutions face new regulatory and compliance issues while striving to maintain and increase market share. Competitive pressures are pushing firms to look for new target markets such as Ivy League Moms and to once again focus on the personal touch through branch banking and similar services.

Chapter 19 (Managing the Firm's Finances) highlights the shift in finance from a relatively isolated, inward-looking function to a unit that is heavily involved in shaping and implementing a company's overall strategic objectives. CFOs are taking a more visible, active role, and financial managers must work closely with other business units. The chapter also provides new coverage of the role technology plays in improving the efficiency of financial processes and operations, and the importance of developing adequate risk management procedures.

Chapter 20 (Understanding Securities and Securities Markets) features extensive new material on the changes taking place in the securities markets. New sections explain the distinction between broker markets and dealer markets, discuss how major stock exchanges in both the United States and global securities markets are responding to competitive pressures, and describe ways that online brokerage firms are broadening the services they offer to investors.

Key Themes That Highlight Today's Latest Topics

Ethics

The business world has been rocked in the past few years by ethics scandals that led to bankruptcies for major organizations and jail terms for top executives. Well-publicized scandals have touched off a wave of reform and renewed emphasis on ethical business behavior. *A paramount theme of this text will always be that business must be conducted in an ethical and socially responsible manner.*

Chapter 3 (Making Ethical Decisions and Managing a Socially Responsible Business) is completely devoted to business ethics and social responsibility. We discuss techniques for setting personal ethical standards, how managers influence organizational ethics, tools for creating employee ethical awareness, and the concept of social responsibility. The Sixth Edition features new ethics activities at the end of each chapter. All ethical dilemmas are taken right out of today's business world!

Customer Satisfaction and Quality

We believe that delivering superior customer value, satisfaction, and quality are essential to attracting and keeping customers. Because customer satisfaction and quality are the foundation of all business principles, we have addressed these important topics in most chapters. Each chapter stresses that satisfied customers who experience quality products and services become loyal customers. We now offer a box in every chapter called "Customer Satisfaction and Quality," that demonstrates how these concepts are applied in actual companies.

Managing Change

If there is one truth in the business world it is that it is constantly changing. Failure to keep up with change can create huge problems such as those experienced by Ford, General Motors, Pier One, and Radio Shack. On the other hand, change can offer great opportunities for firms such as Apple, Inc. and Exxon. Our new "Managing Change" box describes how companies have recognized and responded to changes in technology, competition, economic forces, demographics, and culture.

Entrepreneurship and Small Business Management

Because many of you will either open your own businesses or go to work for small organizations, entrepreneurship and small business principles are covered throughout the text. Chapter 6 (Entrepreneurship: Starting and Managing Your Own Business) delivers interesting discussions on starting and managing a small business, including the advantages and disadvantages of small business ownership.

In addition, each chapter contains a feature called "Catching the Entrepreneurial Spirit" that offers practical insights into the challenges and rewards of actually owning and managing a small business. In Chapter 12 (Understanding the Customer and Creating Marketing Strategy) you will learn how two innovative young men created PenAgain, a company that manufactures a writing pen with a wishbone design. You will follow their struggles and gain insights into how to get the world's largest retailer, Wal-Mart, to carry your product.

Global Business Economy

Chapter 4 (Competing in the Global Marketplace) offers a thorough and exciting picture of competition in the global marketplace. We discuss why global trade is important to the United States, why nations trade, barriers to international trade, how companies enter the global marketplace, and a host of other international concepts and topics.

Because globalization impacts all of us today, it is covered throughout the text. The Trends section of each chapter frequently includes a discussion of how globalization will affect specific business activities. In addition, our global business box demonstrates how businesses are expanding their workforce, products, and customer base throughout the world in order to grow. In Chapter 14 (Distributing Products in a Timely and Efficient Manner) the "Expanding Around the Globe" features Selfridges, the world's most exciting and innovative department store. Each of Selfridges' four huge outlets has been radically redesigned to feel more like a collection of quirky boutiques. Selfridges is known for its "happenings" that run the gamut from having a group of 100 "Elvises" that gather to sing "Viva Las Vegas" to temporarily setting up a tattoo and body-piercing parlor called Metal Morphosis next to a women's fashion department. Selfridges is all about creating buzz.

Careers in Business

Many of you will launch your business careers in the near future. It is our responsibility to help you find the field that is right for you. The Sixth Edition is a rich source of career guidance. As mentioned before, all business people know that the only thing certain about business is that it always changes. With this in mind, Chapter 1 (Participating in the Dynamic Business Environment) describes the business trends altering the business landscape. The value for you is not only learning what trends influence business, but how these trends will influence business and careers within it. The Sixth Edition features the following valuable career information:

- **The Prologue.** A new prologue, *Fast Forward to the Future: Strategies for Success in School and Business*, explores the interpersonal, time management, and planning skills every student needs for success in school. In the prologue, we also offer career advice and recommendations for finding and landing that first professional job. The prologue addresses how to use the Internet to jump-start a job search, prepare a cyber résumé, and research potential employers. In addition, the prologue shows you how to discover economic, demographic, and climatic information about cities in which you might work. We close the prologue with tips on interviewing and winning that first promotion.
- **Career Material for Each Part.** You can explore the career opportunities in small businesses, management, marketing, technology and information, and finance at the companion Web site. This career material describes the different types of employment available, positions in demand, skills required, salary expectations, and employment outlook through the next several years.
- **Exploring Business Careers.** New opening vignettes and videos highlight the careers of successful business leaders from a variety of service and manufacturing firms. In addition to giving you insight into a variety of business careers, the opening vignettes and videos help spark an interest in the chapter topics through professionally produced videos.

The Best Instructor Resources Available

Our research tells us that you want a comprehensive, easy-to-use instructor resource package that helps you bring the text concepts and principles to life. You also want a great test bank and attention-grabbing videos. For us, this was just "starters." We place all the necessary tools in your hands to help you save time and be a great instructor!

Each component of the comprehensive supplements package has been carefully crafted by outstanding teachers, with guidance from the textbook authors, to ensure this course is a rewarding experience for instructors and students. The supplements package includes excellent time-tested teaching tools as well as new supplements designed for the electronic classroom.

Comprehensive Instructor's Manual. (*Available on the Instructor's Web site:* **http://www.thomsonedu.com/introbusiness/gitman** *and Instructor's Resource Guide CD-ROM:* ISBN: 0-324-53822-7) At the core of the integrated learning system for *The Future of Business* is the instructor's manual. Developed in response to numerous suggestions from instructors teaching this course, each chapter is designed to provide maximum guidance for delivering the content in an interesting and dynamic manner. Each chapter begins with learning goals that anchor the integrated learning system. The Instructor's Manual also includes an in-depth lecture outline that is interspersed with lecture "tidbits" that allow instructors to add timely and interesting enhancements to their lectures. In addition, we know that it's hard to generate class discussion. So the lecture outline also includes questions to be asked of the class to generate discussion and debate. A comprehensive video guide includes the running time of each video, concepts illustrated in the video, teaching objectives for the case, and solutions for video case study questions. A complete set of transparency masters includes exhibits from the textbook and key terms and concepts.

Teaching SCANS Competencies. A few years ago the Department of Labor created the Commission on Achieving Necessary Skills (SCANS) to encourage a high-skills, high-wage economy. From this came the SCANS competencies which define know-how that students need for workplace success. Many colleges and universities are now charged with teaching to these competencies. We make your job easier by identifying those skills in the Preparing for Tomorrow's Workplace activities. The core SCANS competencies are resource skills (allocating time, money, etc.), interpersonal skills (teamwork, negotiating), information ability (acquiring and evaluating data, using computers), systems understanding (operating within an organization or social system), and technology ability (selecting equipment, tools, and applying technology to specific tasks).

Test Bank and ExamView Testing Software. (*Available on the Instructor's Resource Guide CD-ROM:* ISBN: 0-324-53822-7) To ensure your total confidence in the accuracy of the test bank, it has been certified for accuracy. The comprehensive test bank is organized by learning goal to support the integrated learning system. With over 2,000 true/false, multiple-choice, fill-in-the-blank, and short answer questions, tests can be customized to support a variety of course objectives. The test bank is available in both Word and ExamView Testing software formats. This test bank is just one more way the Gitman author team is making instructors feel comfortable and at ease with their support materials. Custom tests can be ordered through the Thomson Learning Academic Resource Center (1-800-423-0563) or through Career Schools Support (1-800-477-3692) between 8:30 A.M. and 7 P.M., EST.

PowerPoint Slides Lecture. (*Available on the Instructor's Web site:* **http://www. thomsonedu.com/introbusiness/gitman** *and Instructor's Resource Guide CD-ROM:* ISBN: 0-324-53822-7) The PowerPoint Lecture System includes hundreds of slides that illustrate key chapter concepts and explain business vocabulary. As part of the integrated learning system, each slide is identified by the appropriate learning goal. These professionally designed slides help improve lecture organization and reduce classroom preparation time.

Transparency Acetates. Color acetate transparencies, available from your publisher's representative, feature key concepts, business terms, and exhibits from the textbook.

Instructor Web Site. (**http://www.thomsonedu.com/introbusiness/gitman**) Designed to support your course objectives, the Instructor Web site is a source of downloadable supplements and other valuable resources. **Intro to Business News**, for example, provides summaries of the latest business news stories, indexed by topic for your convenience. Each Intro to Business News summary contains a headline, subject category, key words, three- to five-paragraph summary of a news article, article source line, and questions to spur further thought. In addition, an Online Instructor's Resource Guide provides a guide for using all of *The Future of Business* resources to teach your course.

Instructor's Resource CD-ROM. (ISBN: 0-324-53822-7) For maximum convenience, the Instructor's Manual, Test Bank, ExamView Testing System, and PowerPoint Lecture System are all available on CD.

Comprehensive Video Package. (ISBN: 0-324-53826-X) Designed to enrich and support chapter concepts, each video presents real business issues faced by a variety of service and manufacturing organizations. The video cases challenge students to study business issues and develop solutions to business problems. The instructor's video guide, included in the Instructor's Manual, outlines the key teaching objectives of each video case and suggests answers to the critical thinking questions. New Exploring Business Career videos are an insightful way to begin the study of a new chapter and to illustrate the numerous career opportunities in business.

Resources for Students

ThomsonNOW for *The Future of Business*, **Sixth Edition**. ThomsonNOW is an integrated online suite of services and resources with proven ease of use and efficient paths to success, delivering the results you want—NOW! ThomsonNOW provides a customized learning path and tutorial to help you grasp chapter concepts and achieve success in the course. Through diagnostic pretests, students identify areas that require additional study. Tutorials provide additional guidance and direction on challenging topics.

- **Ease of use:** Developed through intensive student and instructor usability testing, this release of ThomsonNOW put customers at the center of the redesign effort, literally directing the redesign. And we aren't stopping now! We are working behind the scenes to take the program to the next level by consistently listening to what you want and need!
- **Efficient paths to success:** Time-saving and efficient, ThomsonNOW makes the path from assignment through grading and reporting quick and easy for instructors. Student-personalized learning plans lead them efficiently through textbook material, focusing on what each student still needs to learn—making every minute of study pay off! For an interactive introduction to ThomsonNOW, visit **http://www.thomsonedu.com/thomsonnow**.
- **Results:** Students using ThomsonNOW overwhelmingly report that it helps them understand their course content better and score better on tests. Instructors love the effect assigning ThomsonNOW has on classroom participation and performance!

Companion Web Site (**http://www.thomsonedu.com/introbusiness/gitman**). Developed to maximize student success in the course and build online skills, the student portion of the text's Web site includes quizzes for each chapter, links to related Web sites, online enrichment chapters, Intro to Business News, and career information.

Acknowledgements

We are exceedingly grateful to the many reviewers who have offered suggestions and recommendations for enhancing the coverage, pedagogy, and support package of *The Future of Business*. The insightful feedback from these instructors helped guide our efforts and ensured that this text surpassed expectations for customer satisfaction and quality.

We are deeply appreciative of the insight from the following reviewers of the current and past editions of this textbook:

Maria Zak Aria, Camden County College
Joseph H. Atallah, Devry Institute of Technology
Herm Baine, Broward Community College
Dennis R. Brode, Sinclair Community College
Harvey Bronstein, Oakland Community College
Mark Camma, Atlantic Cape Community College
Bonnie R. Chavez, Santa Barbara City College
M. Bixby Cooper, Michigan State University
Evelyn Delaney, Daytona Beach Community College
Kathryn E. Dodge, University of Alaska, Fairbanks
Jonas Falik, Queensborough Community College
Janice M. Feldbauer, Austin Community College–Northridge
Dennis Foster, Northern Arizona University
James Giles, Bergen Community College

Mary E. Gorman, University of Cincinnati
Carnella Hardin, Glendale College
Elizabeth Hastings, Business Department, Middlesex Community College
Frederic H. Hawkins, Westchester Business Institute
Melvin O. Hawkins, Midlands Technical College
Charlane Bomrad Held, Onondaga Community College
Merrily Joy Hoffman, San Jacinto College
Ralph F. Jagodka, Mount San Antonio College
Andrew Johnson, Bellevue Community College
Connie Johnson, Tampa College
Jerry Kinskey, Sinclair Community College
Raymond T. Lamanna, Berkeley College
Carol Luce, Arizona State University
Tom McFarland, Mt. San Antonio College
Carl Meskimen, Sinclair Community College
Andrew Miller, Hudson Valley Community College
H. Lynn Moretz, Central Piedmont Community College
Linda M. Newell, Saddleback College
Joseph Newton, Bakersfield College
David Oliver, Edison College
Teresa Palmer, Illinois State University
Jude A. Rathburn, University of Wisconsin–Milwaukee
Robert F. Reck, Western Michigan University
Carol Rowey, Community College of Rhode Island
Ann Squire, Blackhawk Technical College
Richard E. T. Strickler, Sr., McLennan Community College
Susan Thompson, Palm Beach Community College
David L. Turnipseed, Indiana-Purdue University
Ron Weidenfeller, Grand Rapids Community College

This book could not have been written and published without the generous expert assistance of many people. First, we wish to thank Marlene Bellamy, Writeline Associates, for her major and outstanding contributions to numerous aspects of this text. Special appreciation goes to Carolyn Lawrence, Linda Ravden, and Renee Barnow for their contributions to the Sixth Edition. We wish to thank Linda Hefferin, Elgin Community College, for her creative work on the Instructor's Manual; Deb Baker, Texas Christian University, for developing highly comprehensive, professionally designed PowerPoint™ slides; Jonas Falik and Brenda Hersh, Queensborough Community College, for their innovative ideas in developing the ThomsonNOW content; Jim Hess for his creative development of quizzes for ThomsonNOW; and Tom and Betty Pritchett, Kennesaw State University, for designing a highly accurate and extensive variety of test bank questions.

A special word of appreciation goes to the editorial team at South-Western, including Erin Joyner, Acquisitions Editor; Kimberly Kanakes, Marketing Manager; Bob Dreas, Content Project Manager; Deanna Ettinger, Photo Manager; Mary Draper, Senior Developmental Editor; and Stacy Shirley, Art Director.

Lawrence J. Gitman
Carl McDaniel

PROLOGUE

A Quick Guide to Your Future Success in Business

You Are a Winner Because You Elected to Go to College!
Never Quit until You Have Your Degree in Hand.

What makes someone a winner in life? A winner is someone who goes through the various stages of life content in knowing that they have done their best: their best at work, home, and in all pursuits of life. A big part of having a happy life is pursuing a career that offers job satisfaction and financial rewards. If you are going to "be all that you can be," you need a good education.

A college degree unlocks doors to economic opportunity.
Why get a degree?

- **Get and keep a better job.** Because the world is changing rapidly, and many jobs rely on new technology, more jobs require education beyond high school. With a college education, you will have more jobs from which to choose.
- **Earn more money.** People who go to college usually earn more than those who do not. Currently, a bachelor's degree is worth a minimum of $25,000 a year more than a high school diploma. If your career spans 45 years, you will earn $1,125,000 more than a high school graduate!
- **Get a good start in life.** A business college education helps you acquire a wide range of knowledge in many subjects as well as an advanced understanding of your specialized area of business. College also trains you to express your thoughts clearly in speech and in writing and to make informed decisions.

Simply stated, a degree in business gives you the chance to achieve the quality of life you deserve. The lifestyle, the new friends, the purchasing power of a degree won't guarantee happiness but will put you well on the road to finding it.

Learn the Basics of Business

You might want to pursue a career as a physician, florist, game warden, systems analyst, or any of a thousand other opportunities. One thing that all careers have in common is that you need to have a basic understanding of business. We hope that you will consider a career in business, but if not, your success in whatever you choose will partially depend on your basic business skills. And that is why this text is so important.

There is no other book that presents all the fundamental areas of business and then links them together like this textbook. This is where you get the big picture as well as an introduction to fundamental components of business. Learn it well because it will be invaluable throughout your life.

CONCEPT *in Action*

Finding one's dream job requires combing through job descriptions, researching salary information, taking career-assessment tests, and shadowing others in the workplace. Now career seekers can also "test-drive" an occupation. Career-trial services like VocationVacations place job hunters in engaging apprenticeship positions, from sports announcer and fashion designer to aquarium manager. As demonstrated on the Travel Channel's *This Job's a Trip*, taking a "working vacation" can change a life forever. *What can individuals learn by test-driving a job?*

Choose a Career

Because this introductory business course gives you a detailed overview of all of the areas of commerce, it will guide you in selecting a major should you select to get a degree in business. Choosing a major in college is one of life's true milestones. Your major essentially determines how you will spend the next four decades of your life! A marketing major will find a career in sales, marketing research, advertising, or other marketing-related field. An accounting major will become (you guessed it) an accountant. *Never* take selecting a major lightly. If you work 40 hours a week for the next 45 years (less vacations), you will put in about 90,000 hours on the job. Don't you think that you should choose something that you will enjoy?

Developing Interpersonal Skills Is Key to Your Success

A degree in business is going to offer you many great career opportunities. Once you take your first job, how rapidly you move up the ladder is up to you. People with great interpersonal skills will always do better on and off the job than those who lack them. It has been estimated that up to 95 percent of our workplace success depends on an understanding of other people.[1] Here's how to enhance your interpersonal skills:

1. **Build your people skills.** Learn to build alliances in a group and establish harmony. Make a concerted effort to know what is happening in the lives of those on your team at school and work. About once a month get together with your group and pass out a list of issues, concerns, fears, and potential problems. Then invite everyone to give input to solve little problems before they become big. If something goes wrong, try to find out where things are not running smoothly and improve them. Be sure to compliment someone in your group who is doing an exemplary job.

    Become a good listener. When you listen well, you are in effect telling the other person that he or she is worth listening to. Listening well includes listening to both what is said and not said. Learn to read unspoken gestures and expressions. When giving feedback, plan what you will say in advance. Be positive and be specific. Ask the person receiving the feedback if they would like to discuss your comments further.

2. **Understand how to persuade others.** Remember, we all must sell ourselves and ideas to get ahead in life and business. Influencing others means overcoming objections, igniting passions, or changing minds. The first step is to build *esprit de corps,* a shared enthusiasm and devotion to the group. Make your vision their vision so that everyone is working toward a common goal. Praise the team as a whole, but recognize the unique contributions different team members have made. The trick is to praise everyone, yet for different reasons. When you and your team successfully solve a problem, change will result.

    Persuasion rests on trust. You can build trust by being honest, fulfilling your commitments, being concerned about others, and minimizing problems and pain for others whenever possible. In short, if you have integrity, building trust becomes a simple task.

    When people raise objections to your plans or ideas, try to fully understand their comments and the motivation for making them. When you feel that you understand the true objection, answer the objection in the form of a benefit: "Yes, you will need to work next Saturday, but then you can have compensatory time off anytime you wish next month." Determine your persuasion skills by taking the quiz in Exhibit P.1.

3. **Learn to think on your feet.** Top executives, like former Chrysler Chairman Lee Iacocca, say that "speaking well on your feet" is the best thing that you can do for your career. If you cannot quickly express yourself with confidence, others will lose confidence in you.

Rate your level of agreement with the statements below using the following scale:

Strongly Agree	Agree	Neither Agree nor Disagree	Disagree	Strongly Disagree

1. I prefer to work in a team rather than individually.
2. I enjoy motivating others to help accomplish objectives.
3. I avoid working with difficult people or trying to resolve group differences.
4. I can learn more working in a team rather than working by myself.
5. I would prefer to work with individuals I have known previously.
6. I give up if my team members do not agree with me.
7. I may not always convince my team members to agree with my opinions, but I will go ahead and do what I feel is correct.
8. I think people who can persuade others always possess sound judgement.
9. I will do the work myself if others do not agree to do it.
10. To get the work done, I will listen to a person to understand how he/she wants it to be done.
11. I can get people to voluntarily make commitments and get the work done.[2]

See the scoring guidelines at the end of this textbook to obtain your score.

It will not happen overnight, but you can become an outstanding thinker and speaker. A simple technique is to set a timer for two minutes and ask a friend to begin speaking. When the timer goes off, your friend stops speaking and you begin talking. The challenge is to use the final thought that your friend spoke as the first word of your two-minute talk. Another technique is to have someone supply you with a series of quotes. Then, without hesitation, give your interpretation.

4. **Empower yourself.** No matter who you are, what position you will hold, or where you will work, you probably will have to report to somebody. If you are fortunate enough to work in a culture of empowerment, you are allowed control over your job (not complete control, but enough control to make you feel your opinion matters). When you are not given an opportunity to provide input, you will eventually lose interest in your job. When empowered, you have the confidence to do something to alter your circumstances. On the job, empowerment means that you can make decisions to benefit the organization and its customers.

If you want to gain empowerment in your life and work, here are a few tips: Be assertive, ask for credit for yourself when it is due, propose ideas to your group and your supervisor, initiate projects without being asked, tie your personal goals to those of the organization, develop your leadership skills, plan to learn on a continuous basis, be informed, don't let others intimidate you, and don't complain about a bad situation. Instead, take action to improve it.

5. **Acquire political savvy.** Politics is an inevitable part of every organization in the United States, including your school. Politics has always been a part of the workplace and always will be. The trick is to learn to play the political game to your own advantage *and* to the advantage of others without causing harm to anyone else. Being political means getting along with others in order to move them toward accomplishing a specific goal. It does not mean maneuvering for selfish purposes, manipulating in order to deceive, or scheming so others lose while you win.

Here are some tips and techniques to be an effective player in the political game:

- *Think about what you say.* Understand the effect your words will have on others before you say or write them.
- *Empathize.* Try to think of a situation from the other person's perspective.
- *Suggest a trial period, if you meet opposition to an idea you're proposing.* If you are as successful as you are confident, you can then ask to have the trial period extended.

● *Learn about the political climate in which you are working.* This means knowing, among other things, what actions have led to failure for others, knowing who is "in" and why, determining who is "out" and why, and learning what behaviors lead to promotion.

● *Volunteer to do the jobs no one else wants to do.* Occasionally pitching in shows your willingness to get the job done. However, do not make this your trademark; you do not want others to think they can take advantage of you.

● *Work hard to meet the needs of those in authority.* Make certain you fully understand management's requirements; then go out of your way to meet them. If in time you do not think you are getting the recognition or respect you deserve, make your own needs known.

● *Give credit.* You never know who may be in a position to hurt or harm you. Consequently, the best policy is to treat everyone with respect and dignity. Show your appreciation to everyone who has helped you. Do not steal credit that belongs to someone else.

● *Learn your supervisor's preferences.* The more you are in sync with your supervisor's style, wishes, and preferences, the better you can do your job. However, do not be a rubber stamp. Rather, work the way your manager works. When necessary, suggest better ways of doing things.

● *Keep secrets—your own and others'.* Resist the temptation to tell all. Not only do you run the risk of being labeled a gossip, but if you share too much about yourself, your words can come back to haunt you. If you are revealing information told to you in confidence, you are bound to lose the trust and respect of those who originally confided in you.

Find out how well you play the political game by taking the quiz in Exhibit P.2.

6. **Become a team builder.** Throughout your college and business career you will participate on teams. Ninety-five percent of U.S. business organizations employ teamwork. An effective team is one that meets its goals on time and, if a budget is involved, within budget. The first step in creating an effective team is to have goals that are clear, realistic, supported by each team member, and parallels the larger organization goals. Exhibit P.3 lists the questions that teams should answer to ensure their success.

Exhibit P.2 > Fun Self-Test—Can You Play the Political Game?

Rate your level of agreement with the statements below using the following scale:

Strongly Agree	Agree	Neither Agree nor Disagree	Disagree	Strongly Disagree

1. To be successful, you should have a strong relationship with your boss and subordinates.
2. Office politics is not very challenging.
3. Tough people give you a tough time but also teach you tough lessons.
4. Networking and observation plays a major role in being good at office politics.
5. There is no ethics or morals in office politics.
6. Corporate politics is not about the individuals, it is about the survival of the corporation.
7. Office politics is the only way; you gain real access to your boss's ear.
8. Those who avoid being political at work may not move forward in their careers, may find themselves resentful and frustrated and run the risk of being isolated.
9. If you do all of the work on a project, you won't tell the boss because you don't want your coworkers to get in trouble.
10. When faced with gossip and rumors, you prefer to be silent but aware.
11. To master office politics, you should seek a win-lose situation.
12. If a person in authority is out to get rid of you, a good tactic would be to establish allies and position yourself for another job in the company.
13. If you have made any significant contribution to a project, you always make sure that others know about it which, in turn, adds to your reputation.[3]

See the scoring guidelines at the end of this textbook to obtain your score.

1. What are the goals?
2. Who provides the mission statement?
3. What are our limits?
4. Where will support come from? Who will be our sponsor?
5. Who will be team leader? How is he or she selected?
6. What are the deadlines we face?
7. What resources are available?
8. What data will we need to collect?
9. For how long will our team exist?
10. Who are the customers for our team results? What do they expect of us?
11. Will our team responsibilities conflict with our regular jobs?
12. What is the reward for success?
13. How will decisions be made?
14. How will our efforts be measured?
15. Will our intended success be replicated? If so, how and by whom?

See the scoring guidelines at the end of this textbook to obtain your score.

7. **Handle conflict well.** The world is not a perfect place and there are no perfect people inhabiting it. The best we can hope for is people's willingness to improve life's circumstances. If we are truly committed to the idea of reducing school and workplace conflict, there is much we can do to inspire such willingness in others. Bringing conflict into the open has its advantages. Talking about conflict often helps to clear the air, and thinking about the possibility of conflict often helps to avoid it.

When conflicts occur, try the K-I-N-D technique. The letters stand for:

K = Kind
I = Informed
N = New
D = Definite

The technique involves your requesting a meeting with the difficult person, whether he or she is having a conflict with you or with others. Start off with kind words, words that encourage cooperation, words that show your determination to make the conflict situation better. Next, demonstrate that you have taken the time to learn more about the person, what is important to him or her, what he or she prefers in terms of work. Show by your words that you have taken the time to become informed about the individual.

The third step requires you to do something novel, something you have not tried before. Put your creativity to work, and discover a plan to which you can both subscribe (for example, keeping a journal regarding the problem and possible solutions).

Finally, do not permit the exchange to conclude until you have made a definite overture to ensure future success. What can you promise the other person you will do differently? What are you asking him or her to do differently? Set a time to meet again and review your individual attempts to achieve collective improvement.

Make Your Future Happen: Learn to Plan[4]

There is a natural conflict between planning and being impulsive, between pursuing a long-range goal and doing what you feel like doing right now. If you have ever had to study while the rest of the family was in the living room watching television, you know what that conflict feels like. If you have ever been invited to go to the mall to eat pizza and hang out with friends, but stayed home to work on a class assignment, you know that sticking to a plan is not easy.

CONCEPT *in Action*

Life requires planning, and the more important one's goals, the more important planning is to achieve those goals. Whether the objective is to graduate from college, develop a professional career, or build a brighter future for one's family and community, personal success depends on a good plan. *How can the six steps of the planning process help individuals achieve their educational, personal, and career dreams?*

STOCKBYTE PLATINUM/GETTY IMAGES

Of course, planning and being impulsive are both good. They both have a place in your life. You need to balance them. Having a plan does not mean that you can't act on the spur of the moment and do something that was not planned. Spontaneous events produce some of the happiest, most meaningful times of your life. Problems arise when you consistently substitute impulsive actions for goal-oriented planning. Success in life requires a balance between the two.

If you do not engage in long-range planning and lack the discipline for it, you may limit your opportunities to be impulsive. You are not going to take a weekend fun trip just because you need a break, if you have not saved the money to do it. In the short run, planning involves sacrifice, but in the long run, it gives you more options.

What Is a Plan?

A **plan** is a method or process worked out in advance that leads to the achievement of some goal. A plan is systematic, which means it relies on using a step-by-step procedure. A plan also needs to be flexible so that it may be adapted to gradual changes in your goal.

The Planning Process

Whether choosing a college or finding financial aid, you should understand how the planning process helps you accomplish your goals. The following steps outline the planning process.

Step 1: Set a Goal. Identify something you want to achieve or obtain, your goal. The goal, which is usually longer term in nature, will require planning, patience, and discipline to achieve. Just living in the present moment is not a goal.

Step 2: Acquire Knowledge. Gain an understanding of your goal and what will be required to achieve it. Gather information about your goal through research, conversation, and thought.

Step 3: Compare Alternatives. Weigh your options, which are the different paths you might take to achieve your goal. Analyze the pluses and minuses of each—the costs, the demands, the likelihood of success.

Step 4: Choose a Strategy. Select one option as the best plan of action. The choice is based on sound information, the experience of others, and your own interests and abilities.

Step 5: Make a Commitment. Resolve to proceed step-by-step toward achieving your goal. Keep your eyes on the prize.

Step 6: Stay Flexible. Evaluate your progress, and when necessary, revise your plan to deal with changing circumstances and new opportunities.

An Example of Planning

The following example illustrates the process of buying a new stereo using this planning process.

Step 1: Set a Goal. Purchase a stereo system.

Step 2: Acquire Knowledge. Visit friends to hear their systems. Study standards and specifications. Check on dealers, brands, models, and prices. Consult *Consumer Reports*.

Step 3: Compare Alternatives.

Alternative 1: Purchase a stereo from an online auction like e-Bay.

Pro: Affordable high-end equipment. Can buy right now.

Con: Uncertain condition of equipment. Limited warranty.

Alternative 2: Buy a compact shelf system for $325.

    Pro: Can afford now. New equipment with warranty.

    Con: Not suitable for adding extra speakers or using with television. Not the best sound quality.

Alternative 3: Buy a high-quality component system for $775.

    Pro: Excellent sound. Greatest flexibility. New equipment with warranty.

    Con: Costs more than prepared to pay now.

Step 4: Choose a Strategy. Decide to buy the high-quality system, but rather than using a credit card and paying interest, will delay the purchase for six months in order to save for it.

Step 5: Make a Commitment. Give up going to the movies for the six-month period, carry a lunch and stop eating out, and place the savings in a stereo fund.

Step 6: Stay Flexible. Four months into the plan, a model change sale provides an opportunity to buy comparable equipment for $550. Make the purchase, paying cash.

Planning for Your Life

Using the planning process to make a buying decision is a simple exercise. Making a decision about major parts of your life is far more complex. You will see that no part of life is exempt from the need for planning. It is important to apply thought, creativity, and discipline to all the interrelated phases of our lives. These phases include the following:

- **Career** Choosing a field of work and developing the knowledge and skills needed to enter and move ahead in that field. We will offer you some tips to get started on a great career later in the Prologue.
- **Self** Deciding who you are and what kind of person you want to be, working to develop your strengths and overcome your weaknesses, refining your values.
- **Lifestyle** Expressing yourself in the nature and quality of your everyday life, your recreation and hobbies, how you use your time and money.
- **Relationships** Developing friendships and learning to get along with people in a variety of contexts. Building family and community ties.
- **Finances** Building the financial resources and the economic security needed to pursue all the other dimensions of your life. We will give you some tips in the online chapter "Managing Your Personal Finances" on planning for financial security. You can find this chapter at **http://www.thomsonedu.com/introbusiness/gitman**.

Dreams and Plans

People are natural dreamers. Dreams give us pleasure. They are also part of making a future. If you do not have dreams or think that you are not worthy of dreaming, something very important may be missing from your life. You have a right to your dreams, and you need them—even if there is little possibility that they will ever come true.

Planning is not the same as dreaming, but it uses dreams as raw materials. It translates them into specific goals. It tests them. It lays out a course of action that moves you toward realizing these goals and sets up milestones you need to achieve. Planning brings dreams down to earth and turns them into something real and attainable. For example, assume you have a dream to visit Spain as an exchange student. To translate this dream into a specific goal, you will need to follow the planning process—gather information about the exchange process, discuss the program with parents and teachers, and improve your Spanish-language skills.

Directions for Your Life

One of the best things about pursuing our dreams is that, even when you fall short, the effort leads to growth, and opens a path to other opportunities. The person who practices the piano every day may not achieve the dream of becoming a concert pianist but may eventually put appreciation of music to work as the director of an arts organization. A basketball player may not make it to a professional team but may enjoy a satisfying career as a coach or a sports writer. Without a plan, dreams simply dissolve. With a plan, they give shape and direction to our lives.

Planning involves a lot of thinking and finding answers to lots of questions. The answers and even the plan will change over time as you gain more knowledge and life experience. Planning is a skill that is useful in every area of your life. It is something you have to pursue consciously and thoughtfully. When you plan, you translate your goals and dreams into step-by-step strategies, specific things you can do to test your goals and bring them to reality. You often have to revise your plans, but even when your plans are not fulfilled, planning will have a positive effect on the course of your life.

Going to College Is an Opportunity of a Lifetime—Never Drop Out[5]

You have already had one of your dreams come true—you are in college. It is indeed a rare privilege because far less than 1 percent of traditional college-age people around the world get to attend college. You're lucky! So make the best of it by finishing your degree and learning the following college skills.

Learn to Concentrate

Concentration is the art of being focused, the ability to pay attention. Without concentration, you have no memory of what you hear, see, and read. Concentration is a frame of mind that enables you to stay centered on the activity or work you are doing. You know when you're concentrating because time seems to go by quickly, distractions that normally take you off task don't bother you, and you have a lot of mental or physical energy for the task.

You are ultimately in charge of how well you concentrate. Here are some ways to make it happen:

- *Choose a workplace.* Avoid the bed—you associate it with relaxing or sleeping. Try a desk or table for studying; you will concentrate better and accomplish more in less time. You will also have a convenient writing space and plenty of space to spread out. Be sure to have good lighting.
- *Feed your body right.* What you eat plays an important role in how well or how poorly you concentrate. Protein foods (such as cheese, meat, fish, and vegetables) keep the mind alert, while carbohydrates (such as pasta, bread, and processed sugars) make you sleepy. Caffeine (commonly found in coffee, tea, soft drinks, and chocolate) acts as a stimulant in low doses.
- *Avoid food.* Food and serious learning don't mix well. Think about it. When you try to eat and study at the same time, which gets more of your concentration? The food, of course! You will be more effective if you eat first, then study.
- *Listen to your own thoughts.* Listening to anything but your own thoughts interferes with good concentration. Eliminating distractions such as music, television, cell phones, e-mail beeps, and other people can greatly increase the amount of studying you can accomplish. Hold all calls and let e-mail wait.
- *Make a to-do list.* If you are trying to study but get distracted by all of the things you need to do, take time to make a to-do list. Keeping track of your thoughts on paper and referring to the paper from time to time can be very effective for clearing your mind and focusing on your task.
- *Take short, frequent breaks.* Since people concentrate for about 20 minutes or less at a time, it would make sense to capitalize on your natural body rhythms and take a short break every 20 to 30 minutes. If you feel you are fully concentrating and involved in a task, then work until a natural break occurs.

Learn to Manage Your Time

There are two ways to make sure you have more time in a day. *The first and most important way to gain more time is to plan it!* It's like getting in a car and going somewhere. You need to know where you are going and have a plan to get there. Without a plan, you will waste your time and take longer to get to your destination—if you get there at all!

A **weekly project planner** will allow you to keep track of your assignments in more detail. It contains a to-do list specific to one day. It looks like a calendar but is divided into five, one-day periods with plenty of space to write. Using a weekly project planner is an effective way to keep track of assignments and plan study time according to the school calendar. Free calendars are available at **http://www.calendar.yahoo.com**.

A second way to gain more time in a day is to do more in less time. This can be as simple as doubling up on activities. For example, if you have three errands, you might try to combine them instead of doing one at a time, making one round-trip instead of three. If you commute on a bus or train or carpool, you can study during your ride. At lunch, you can review notes. Use your imagination as to how you can get more done in less time.

Here are some ideas to help you master your time:

- *Prepare for the morning the evening before.* Put out your clothes; make lunches; pack your books.
- *Get up 15 minutes earlier in the morning.* Use the time to plan your day, review your assignments, or catch up on the news.
- *Schedule a realistic day.* Avoid planning for every minute. Leave extra time in your day for getting to appointments and studying.
- *Leave room in your day for the unexpected.* This will allow you to do what you need to do, regardless of what happens. If the unexpected never happens, you will have more time for yourself.
- *Do one thing at a time.* If you try to do two things at once, you become inefficient. Concentrate on the here and now.
- *Learn to say "No!"* Say no to social activities or invitations when you don't have the time or energy.

How well do you manage your time? Take the quiz in Exhibit P.4 to find out.

Use your Money Wisely

You can get college money from three different sources:

- **Grants and Scholarships.** This refers to aid you do not have to repay. Grants are usually based on need while scholarships are frequently based on academic merit and other qualifying factors.
- **Educational Loans.** These are usually subsidized by federal and state governments or by the colleges themselves. Generally the loans carry lower interest rates than commercial loans, and you do not have to pay them off until after graduation.
- **Work Aid.** This is financial aid you have to work for, frequently 10 or 15 hours a week on campus.

There are many ways to cut the cost of going to college. Consider these:

- going to a community college for the first two years and then transferring to a four-year institution
- attending a nearby college and living at home
- enrolling in one of the 1,000 college and universities with cooperative educational programs that alternate between full-time studies and full-time employment
- taking a full-time job at a company that offers free educational opportunities as a fringe benefit

CONCEPT *in Action*

Personal digital assistants (PDAs) were originally designed as computerized personal organizers. As technology matured, the handheld devices came to include e-mail, phone, Internet and other wireless functionality. The introduction of PDAs like the BlackBerry, Treo, and iPAQ put even more desktop computing power at consumers' fingertips, providing users with personal information managers, to-do lists, and Microsoft Windows-based software. *How might college students utilize PDAs to accomplish more and make better use of time?*

Rate your level of agreement with the following statements using the scale below:

Strongly Agree	Agree	Neither Agree nor Disagree	Disagree	Strongly Disagree

1. I rarely feel driven by the urgencies that come my way.
2. I keep a log of each activity to be performed in a day. I prioritize them accordingly.
3. I prioritize not by the importance of the work but by its nature.
4. I can manage my schedule without preparing a weekly plan that includes specific activities.
5. I always want to do all the work myself, thinking I can do it better than anyone else.
6. I plan my weekends with my family and friends.
7. I can delegate work to people so that the work gets done on time and the people feel they are a part of the team.
8. I allow time for the unexpected things I cannot control.
9. If something doesn't happen as per my schedule, it doesn't get done.
10. To accomplish a set of objectives doesn't mean to avoid other unexpected problems.
11. I seldom work after office hours.
12. I would never work by hand if a machine could do it faster.
13. I feel it is easier and time-saving to try new ways of doing things.
14. I always find time to do what I want to do and what I should do.[6]

See the scoring guidelines at the end of this textbook to obtain your score.

To learn about college costs and financial aid, the first source to consult is *The College Board College Costs and Financial Aid Handbook*, which is probably available in the reference section of your local library. The handbook contains extensive tables outlining expenses and financial-aid programs at approximately 3,000 colleges and universities. It describes various kinds of financial aid, and because most financial aid is determined by need, it provides information for calculating your financial-aid eligibility. It also contains bibliographical information. The Web also offers information on financial aid, such as these sites:

- **http://www.fastweb.com** Fastweb has a database of more than 180,000 private sector scholarships, grants, and loans.
- **http://www.ed.gov** This is the U.S. Department of Education information site for federal aid programs.

Gain some insight into your money management skills by taking the quiz in Exhibit P.5.

Study Well

The first key to doing well in a subject is to complete your assignments on time. Most instructors base their assignments on what they will be discussing in class on a given day. So, if you read the pages you are assigned for the day they are due, you will better understand the day's lecture. If you don't complete an assignment when it is due, not only will you be at a disadvantage in the class, but you will have twice as much work to do for the following class.

Second, know what material to study. This may sound simple, but all too often students do not ask what material they should study and find out too late that they studied the wrong information. The easiest and most accurate way to learn what will be covered on a test is to ask your instructor or read the syllabus.

Tests measure your working memory and knowledge base. To help yourself remember, you can use several memory devices to recall the information you need to study. Here are a few memory devices that have been proven to work:

Rate your level of agreement with the following statements, using the scale below:

Strongly Agree	Agree	Neither Agree nor Disagree	Disagree	Strongly Disagree

1. I eagerly wait for the day I get my paycheck, because my bank balance is generally below the minimum.
2. I have set my savings and spending priorities and have a budget.
3. When I go shopping, I don't buy anything unless it is on sale or is required.
4. I can easily spend money when I am in school.
5. I can differentiate between what I want and what I truly need.
6. I always max out my credit cards.
7. I don't need to plan for my child's education because there will be plenty of government programs.
8. I don't plan to open or have a savings account.
9. I was raised in a family where I always felt that money was quite tight.
10. Credit cards have been useful to me during times of emergency.
11. It is easy for me to resist buying on credit.[7]

See the scoring guidelines at the end of this textbook to obtain your score.

- *Recite information using your own words.* You will learn more when you reinforce your learning in as many ways as possible. You can reinforce your learning through hearing, writing, reading, reviewing, and reciting.
- *Develop acronyms.* Acronyms are words or names formed from the first letters or groups of letters in a phrase. Acronyms help you remember because they organize information according to the way you need or want to learn it. For example, COD means "cash on delivery," and GDP refers to "gross domestic product." When you study for a test, be creative and make up your own acronyms.
- *Try mnemonic sentences, rhymes, or jingles.* Mnemonic sentences are similar to acronyms; they help you organize your ideas. But, instead of creating a word, you make up a sentence. Creating a rhyme, song, or jingle can make the information even easier to remember. The more creative and silly the sentence, the easier it is to remember. Take, for example, the nine planets listed in order according to their distance from the sun:

Mercury Venus Earth Mars Jupiter Saturn Uranus Neptune Pluto
The first letters of these words are: M V E M J S U N P.

An acronym using these letters would be difficult to remember. But if you create a sentence using the letters in order, you will remember the sequence better. For example: My Very Educated Mother Just Served Us Nine Pizzas

- *Visualize.* Visualization refers to creating or recalling mental pictures related to what you are learning. Have you ever tried to remember something while taking a test and visualized the page the information was on? This is your visual memory at work. Approximately 90 percent of your memory is stored visually in pictures, so trying to visualize what you want to remember is a powerful study tool.

Exhibit P.6 helps you evaluate your study skills.

Become a Master at Taking Tests

Taking a formal test is like playing a game. The object is to get as many points as possible in the time that you are allowed. Tests are evaluations of what you know and what you can do with what you know. Here are the rules of the test-taking game:

Rule 1: Act as If You Will Succeed. Thought is powerful. When you think negative thoughts, your stress level rises. Your confidence level may drop, which often

Answer "yes" or "no" to the following questions:

1. Do you usually spend too much time studying for the amount that you are learning?
2. Do you spend hours cramming the night before an exam?
3. Do you find it easy to balance your social life with your study schedule?
4. Do you prefer to study with sound (TV or radio) around you?
5. Can you sit for long periods and study for several hours without getting distracted?
6. Do you always borrow notes/materials from your friends before the exam?
7. Do you review your class notes periodically throughout the semester while preparing for the tests?
8. Is it easy for you to recall what you studied at the beginning of the semester?
9. Do you need to change your reading/learning style in response to the difficulty level of the course?
10. Do you normally write your papers or prepare for your presentations the night before they are due?
11. Do you feel comfortable contacting the instructor and asking questions or for help whenever you need it?
12. Do you prefer to study lying on a bed or couch rather than at a desk or table?[8]

See the scoring guidelines at the end of this textbook to obtain your score.

leads to feelings of failure. When this happens, think about success. Smile and take deep, slow breaths. Close your eyes, and imagine getting the test back with a good grade written at the top.

Rule 2: Arrive Ahead of Time. Being on time or early for a test sets your mind at ease. You will have a better chance of getting your favorite seat, relaxing, and preparing yourself mentally for the game ahead.

Rule 3: Bring the Essential Testing Tools. Don't forget to bring the necessary testing tools along with you, including extra pens, sharpened pencils, erasers, a calculator, laptop computer, dictionary, and other items you may need.

Rule 4: Ignore Panic Pushers. Some people become nervous before a test and hit the panic button, afraid they don't know the material. **Panic pushers** are people who ask you questions about the material they are about to be tested on. If you know the answers, you will feel confident; however, if you don't, you may panic and lose your confidence. Instead of talking with a panic pusher before a test, spend your time concentrating on what you know, not on what you don't know.

Rule 5: Preview the Playing Field. Here's how to do a preview:

- Listen to instructions, and read directions carefully.
- Determine the point spread. Look at the total number of questions and the point value of each. Decide how much time you can spend on each question and still finish the test on time.
- Budget your time. If you budget your time and stick to your time limits, you will always complete the test in the amount of time given.
- Use the test as an information tool. Be on the lookout for clues that answer other questions. Frequently, instructors will test you on a single topic in more than one way.

Rule 6: Write in the Margin. Before you begin the test, write key terms, formulas, names, dates, and other information in the margin so you won't forget them.

Rule 7: Complete the Easy Questions First. Answering easy questions first helps build your confidence. If you come across a tough question, mark it so you can come back to it later. Avoid spending so much time on a challenging question that you might run out of time to answer the questions you do know.

Rule 8: Know If There Is a Guessing Penalty. Chances are your tests will carry no penalty for guessing. If your time is about to run out and there is no penalty, take a wild guess. On the other hand, if your test carries a penalty for guessing, choose your answers wisely, and leave blank the answers you do not know.

Rule 9: Avoid Changing Your Answers. Have you ever chosen an answer, changed it, and learned later that your first choice was correct? Research indicates that three out of four times your first choice is usually correct; therefore, you should avoid changing an answer unless you are *absolutely sure* the answer is wrong.

Rule 10: Write Clearly and Neatly. If you are handwriting your test (versus using a computer), imagine your instructor reading your writing. Is it easy to read or difficult? The easier your test is for the instructor to read, the better your chances of getting a higher grade.

Here are some Web sites to help you learn more about taking tests:

> *Essay tests and a checklist for essay tests*
> http://www.calpoly.edu/~sas/asc/ael/tests.essay.html
> *Checklist for essay tests*
> http://www.mtsu.edu/~studskl/essay.html
> *General test taking*
> http://www.calpoly.edu/~sas/asc/ael/tests.general.html
> *Posttest analysis*
> http://www.calpoly.edu/~sas/asc/ael/tests.post.test.analysis.html

Get Your Career Off on the Right Track

Mark this section of the text with a permanent bookmark because you are going to want to refer back to it many times during the remainder of your college career. Yes, we are going to give you a road map to find, keep, and advance in that job that is perfect for you.

Think Positively

To be successful in life and in a career you need to be positive. *Positive thinking* is making a conscious effort to think with an optimistic attitude and to anticipate positive outcomes. *Positive behavior* means purposely acting with energy and enthusiasm. When you think and behave positively, you guide your mind toward your goals and generate matching mental and physical energy.

Positive thinking and behavior are often deciding factors in landing top jobs: your first job, a promotion, a change of jobs—whatever career step you are targeting. That's because the subconscious is literal; it accepts what you regard as fact.

Follow these steps to form the habit of positive thinking and to boost your success:

1. **Deliberately motivate yourself every day.** Think of yourself as successful, and expect positive outcomes for everything you attempt.
2. **Project energy and enthusiasm.** Employers hire people who project positive energy and enthusiasm. Develop the habit of speaking, moving, and acting with these qualities.
3. **Practice this positive-expectation mind-set until it becomes a habit.** Applicants who project enthusiasm and positive behavior generate a positive chemistry that rubs off. Hiring decisions are influenced largely by this positive energy. The habit will help you reach your peak potential.
4. **Dwell on past successes.** Focusing on past successes to remind yourself of your abilities helps in attaining goals. For example, no one is ever born knowing how to ride a bicycle or how to use a computer software program. Through training, practice, and trial and error, you master new abilities. During the trial-and-error phases of development, remind yourself of past successes; look at mistakes as part

of the natural learning curve. Continue until you achieve the result you want, and remind yourself that you have succeeded in the past and can do so again. You fail only when you quit trying![9]

Take a Good Look at Yourself

Once you've developed a positive, "can do" attitude, the next step is to better understand yourself. Ask yourself two basic questions: "Who am I?" and "What can I do?"

Who Am I? The first step is to ask "Who am I?" This question is the start of *self-assessment*, examining your likes and dislikes and basic values. You may want to ask yourself the following questions:

- Do I want to help society?
- Do I want to help make the world a better place?
- Do I want to help other people directly?
- Is it important for me to be seen as part of a big corporation?
- Do I prefer working indoors or outdoors?
- Do I like to meet new people, or do I want to work alone?

Are you assertive? Assess your assertiveness by taking the quiz in Exhibit P.7.

What Can I Do? After determining what your values are, take the second step in career planning by asking "What can I do?" This question is the start of *skill assessment*, evaluating your key abilities and characteristics for dealing successfully with problems, tasks, and interactions with other people. Many skills—for instance, the ability to speak clearly and strongly—are valuable in many occupations.

Be sure to consider the work experience you already have including part-time jobs while going to school, summer jobs, volunteer jobs, and internships (short-term jobs for students, related to their major field of study). These jobs teach you skills and make you more attractive to potential employers. It's never too early or too late to take a part-time job in your chosen field. For instance, someone with an interest in accounting would do well to try a part-time job with a CPA (certified public accountant) firm.

CONCEPT *in Action*

Aligning one's lifestyle interests with one's career trajectory is essential to long-term career satisfaction. If the idea of working in the big city captivates the imagination, it can become a guide to the types of jobs to pursue. If one is motivated to work with people or animals, then charity organizations or zoos might be a good place to look. *What jobs do you visualize yourself doing, and how can that vision guide your career search?*

BLENDIMAGES/GETTY IMAGES

Exhibit P.7 > Fun Self-Test—How Assertive Are You?

Rate your level of agreement with the following statements using the scale below:

Strongly Agree	Agree	Neither Agree nor Disagree	Disagree	Strongly Disagree

1. I don't easily agree to work for others.
2. There are some people who make jokes about the way I communicate and put me down repeatedly.
3. I speak up without fear of what others will think of me.
4. I rarely have to repeat my thoughts to make people understand.
5. I sound like I am asking a question, when I am making a statement.
6. I'm more reluctant to speak up on the job than in other situations.
7. I can always think of something to say when faced with rude remarks.
8. I tend to suffer in silence when unfairly criticized or insulted.
9. I tend to respond aggressively when criticized unfairly.
10. People don't listen when I am speaking.
11. If I say "no," I feel guilty.
12. When I have a conflict with someone, the results seem to always go their way.
13. When I speak, people listen.[10]

See the scoring guidelines at the end of this textbook to obtain your score.

In addition to examining your job-related skills, you should also look at your leisure activities. Some possible questions: Am I good at golf? Do I enjoy sailing? Tennis? Racquetball? In some businesses, transactions are made during leisure hours. In that case, being able to play a skillful, or at least adequate, game of golf or tennis may be an asset.

It's hard to like your job if you don't like the field that you're in. Most career counselors agree that finding work you're passionate about is one of the critical factors behind career success. That's why so many career counselors love all those diagnostic tools that measure your personality traits, skill levels, professional interests, and job potential.

The Web is virtually exploding with tests and assessments that you can take. Try, for example, **http://www.self-directed-search.com**. This test is based on the theory that people and work environments can be classified into six basic types: realistic, investigative, artistic, social, enterprising, and conventional. The test determines which three types best describe you, and it suggests occupations that could be a good match. The **Keirsey Character Sorter** (**http://www.keirsey.com**) is a first cousin of Myers-Briggs. It sorts people into four temperaments: idealists, rationals, artisans, and guardians. Like Myers-Briggs, it not only places you in an overall category, but it also offers a more detailed evaluation of your personality traits. To find a bunch of tests in one place, visit **Yahoo!** and type "online personality tests" in the search field.

Understand What Employers Want[11]

Employers want to hire people who will make their businesses more successful. The most desirable employees have the specific skills, transferable career competencies, work values, and personal qualities necessary to be successful in the employers' organizations. The more clearly you convey your skills as they relate to your job target, the greater your chance of landing your ideal job.

Job-Specific Skills. Employers seek job-specific skills (skills and technical abilities that relate specifically to a particular job). Two examples of job-specific skills are using specialized tools and equipment and using a custom-designed software program.

Transferable Skills and Attitudes. Change is a constant in today's business world. Strong transferable career skills are the keys to success in managing your career through change. The most influential skills and attitudes are the abilities to:

- Work well with people.
- Plan and manage multiple tasks.
- Maintain a positive attitude.
- Show enthusiasm.

Employers need workers who have transferable career competencies—basic skills and attitudes that are important for all types of work. These skills make you highly marketable because they're needed for a wide variety of jobs and can be transferred from one task, job, or workplace to another. Examples include these:

- Planning skills
- Research skills
- Communication skills
- Human relations and interpersonal skills
- Critical thinking skills
- Management skills

Take, for example, a construction supervisor and an accountant. Both must work well with others, manage time, solve problems, read, and communicate effectively—all transferable competencies. They both must be competent in these areas even though framing a house and balancing a set of books (the job-specific skill for each field, respectively) are not related. In every occupation, transferable competencies are as important as technical expertise and job-specific skills.

Find Your First Professional Job

The next step is landing the job that fits your skills and desires. You need to consider not only a general type of work but also your lifestyle and leisure goals. If you like to be outdoors most of the time, you might be very unhappy spending eight hours a day in an office. Someone who likes living in small towns may dislike working at the headquarters of a big corporation in Los Angeles or New York City or Chicago. But make sure that your geographic preferences are realistic. Some parts of the country will experience much greater growth in jobs than others.

You will find these cities as having more good job prospects than many others:

1. Fort Myers-Cape Coral, FL
2. Las Vegas, NV
3. Phoenix-Mesa, AZ
4. West Palm Beach-Boca Raton, FL
5. Daytona Beach, FL
6. Sarasota-Bradenton, FL
7. Fayetteville-Springdale-Rogers, AR
8. Riverside-San Bernardino, CA
9. Fort Lauderdale, FL
10. Monmouth-Ocean, NJ[12]

You may notice that half of the cities are in Florida. This is due to an economy that has been creating new jobs at a brisk pace, the result of the return of tourists, and a growing elderly population that has fueled the job growth in health care and other services. Good smaller cities for job seeking include: Missoula, Montana; Las Cruces, New Mexico; Santa Fe, New Mexico; Dover, Delaware; and Casper, Wyoming. The best prospect among America's ten largest metropolitan areas is Washington, DC.

You might start answering the question "What will I do?" by studying the *Career Employment Opportunities Directory—Business Administration*. The directory lists several hundred up-to-date sources of employment with businesses, government agencies, and professional organizations.

Another important source of job information is the *Occupational Outlook Handbook*, published every two years by the U.S. Department of Labor. The introduction in the current *Handbook* projects job opportunities by industry through the year 2008. The *Handbook* is divided into 19 occupational clusters describing 200 jobs (with a section on military careers). Among the clusters are education, sales and marketing, transportation, health, and social services. Each job description tells about the nature of the work, working conditions, required training, other qualifications, chances for advancement, employment outlook, earnings, related occupations, and sources of more information. Two other good sources of job information are *Changing Times Annual Survey: Jobs for New College Graduates* and *Peterson's Business and Management Jobs*. If you are a member of a minority group, you might want to check out **http://www.black-collegian.com**, or **http://www.saludos.com**.

The career information provided at the book's companion Web site is another good source of career information. It contains short job descriptions and explains what parts of the country are most likely to have openings in certain fields, the skills required, the employment outlook through 2012, and salary information.

Use the Internet to Find a Job

There are about 100,000 job-related sites and over 5 million résumés on the Internet. To break through the clutter, you must start with a great résumé—a written description of your education, work experience, personal data, and interests. Professional web résumé software (available through **http://www.web-resume.org**) can make your résumé preparation task a lot easier. WebResume software not only helps you format your résumé but also lets you control who sees it. A "confidential" option enables you to create a two-tiered résumé. The first tier offers professional information but doesn't include your name or address. The second tier contains contact information but is password protected—and you decide who can get the password. WebResume understands what's different about looking for a job online. Its "Search Engine Keywords" function inserts the "tags" that major search engines use to index résumés. And Web-Resume will submit your résumé to over 350 Internet career sites and over 14,000 professional recruiters and staffing firms.

There are three kinds of electronic résumés. The first is a paper résumé that becomes an electronic version when it is scanned into a computer. Second is a generic computer file that you create especially to send through cyberspace without ever printing it onto paper—an e-mailable version. The third type of electronic résumé is a multimedia résumé that is given a home at a fixed location on the Internet for anyone to visit at will. Let's look at each kind in turn.[13]

The Scannable Résumé

Here's the scenario. You create a paper résumé and mail it to a potential employer. Unknown to you, the company has implemented a computerized system for scanning résumés as they arrive in the human resources department. Instead of a human reading your résumé and deciding how to forward it along or file it, a clerk electronically scans your résumé which is then stored in a computerized résumé database. The paper is either filed or thrown away.

Also falling into this class is your paper résumé when it is faxed to a potential employer. Instead of receiving a printout of your résumé, a potential employer allows your fax to sit in a computer's queue until a clerk can verify and summarize the information into the same computerized database where the scanned paper résumés have been stored.

More than 1,000 unsolicited résumés arrive every week at most Fortune 500 companies, and before the days of applicant tracking systems and résumé scanning, 80 percent were thrown out after a quick review. It was simply impossible to keep track of that much paper. Applicant tracking systems electronically search for key words that, if found, sends the resume to a human resources clerk for further review. Nearly half of all mid-sized companies and almost all Fortune 1000 companies scan résumés and use computerized applicant tracking systems. Smaller companies turn to service bureaus and recruiters to find potential employees for them, and these same service bureaus and recruiters scan résumés.

The E-Mailable Résumé

When you type words onto a computer screen in a word processing program, you are creating what is called a "file" or "document." When you save that file, it is saved with special formatting codes like fonts, margins, tab settings, etc., even if you didn't add these codes. Each word processing program (Microsoft Word, WordPerfect, etc.) saves its files in its own native format, making the file readable by anyone else with the same software or with some other software that can convert that file to its own native format.

Only by choosing to save the document as a generic ASCII text file can your document be read by anyone, regardless of the word processing software used. This is the type of file you must create in order to send your résumé via e-mail. An ASCII text file is simply words—no pictures, no fonts, no graphics—just plain words. If you print this text, it looks very boring, but all the words are there that describe your life history, just like in the handsome paper résumé you created to mail to a potential employer. This computer file can be sent to a potential employer in one of two ways.

First, you can send the file directly to a company's recruiters via an e-mail address. Always choose to e-mail your résumé when an ad publishes an e-mail address. When you e-mail your résumé directly to a company, you have total control over whether or not your information is correct. You are not at the whim of a scanner's ability to read your font or formatting. This is also the fastest way to get your résumé into the hands of a hiring manager.

Second, you can use this file to post your résumé onto the Internet (to the home page of a company, to a job bank in answer to an online job posting, or to a newsgroup), an online service (like America Online), or a newsgroup service. In any case, the file ends up in the same type of computerized database where the scanned paper résumés have been stored. Your résumé will be accessible every time the hiring manager searches the résumé database using keywords.

You can also try posting your résumé on the "big 10" job sites. They are so large that they are worth checking out first. They tend to have more jobs listed, represent more companies, and have larger résumé databases, which attract even more companies.

- Adams JobBank Online (**http://www.adamsonline.com**)
- America's Job Bank (**http://www.ajb.dni.us**)
- CareerMosaic J.O.B.S. (**http://careermosaic.com**)
- CareerPath (**http://www.careerpath.com**)
- E-Span (**http://www.espan.com**)
- JobTrak (**http://www.jobtrak.com**)
- JobWeb (**http://www.jobweb.org**)
- MedSearch America (**http://www.medsearch.com**)
- Monster Board (**http://www.monster.com**)
- Online Career Center (**http://www.occ.com**)

The Multimedia Résumé

If you are going to become a computer programmer, home page developer, graphics designer, artist, sculptor, singer, dancer, actor, model, animator, cartoonist, or anyone who would benefit by the photographs, graphics, animation, sound, color, or movement inherent in a multimedia résumé, then this résumé is for you. For most people, however, a multimedia résumé and home page on the Internet isn't necessary. Most Internet service providers and commercial online services provide some space on their computers for subscriber home pages at no extra charge. American Online even offers free software that makes creating your home page easy.

Getting Your E-Résumé into the Short Pile

Applicant tracking systems screen for keywords which either reject your résumé or move it on to the short list. Your task is to use keywords that will produce as many "hits" as possible. Keywords tend to be more of the noun or noun phrase type (Total Quality Management, Wal-Mart, Sales Manager) as opposed to power action verbs often found in traditional resumes (developed, coordinated, organized). Every occupation and career field has its own jargon, acronyms, and buzzwords. There are also general keywords that apply to transferable skills important in many jobs, such as teamwork, writing, and planning.

Use these tips for adding effective keywords to your résumé:

- The best source of keywords is the actual job listing, which is likely to contain many, if not all, of the keywords that an employer will use to search the résumé database.
- Include plenty of keyword nouns and noun phrases throughout your résumé. If you have a "Summary of Qualifications" section at the beginning of your résumé, try not to repeat verbatim the contents of this section.
- If you are applying for technical positions, you can list your skills, separating each noun or phrase by a comma.

- In some fields, a simple list of skills does not sufficiently describe the job seeker's background. Where appropriate, include accomplishments, as well, but be sure to include enough keywords to satisfy the computer searches.[14]

There are several ways to determine what keywords are appropriate for your industry and job.

- Look through recent job ads online. Certain words will reappear consistently. Those are your "key" words.
- Make sure your résumé contains the keywords and concepts used in the *particular job listing* you are applying to.
- Talk to people in the career field you are targeting, and ask them what keywords are appropriate to the positions you are applying to.
- Visit professional association Web sites, and read the content carefully. Many of these are loaded with industry-related jargon that may be appropriate for your résumé.[15]

If you are *still in college*, try to get at least one internship in the career field you're targeting. Even if your internship lasts only a few weeks, you will significantly increase your keyword count. You should have a minimum of four industry- or job-specific keywords; the ideal is to have at least 12 keywords.[16]

Oh My Gosh—I've Got a Job Interview

If some of the companies you contacted want to speak with you, your résumé achieved its goal of getting you a job interview. Look at the interview as a chance to describe your knowledge and skills and interpret them in terms of the employer's specific needs. To make this kind of presentation, you need to do some research on the company. A great place to start looking is **http://www.hoovers.com**. This site offers profiles and financial data on more than 12,000 companies worldwide. It also provides links to other sites where you can dig further. Hoovers.com allows you to search for companies using the following categories:

- Company name
- Geographic location
- Industry
- Stock index
- News stories

Another great place to get company information is **http://www.wetfeet.com**. You can check out hundreds of companies in over 35 different industries. Want to know what it's really like to work in the automobile industry? Check out its **Industry Profiles** section. You'll find out who the major players are and what they do. The site's **What's Great and What's to Hate** section tells you just that. And the **Real People Profile** section offers an interview with—you guessed it—a real person in a specific industry. Interviews provide valuable insights from those with experience: how they got their job, what a typical day is like for them, what career aspirations they have for the future, and the biggest misconceptions about their business.

As you do your information search, you should build your knowledge in these three areas:

1. **General Information About the Occupational Field.** Learn about the current and predicted industry trends, general educational requirements, job descriptions, growth outlook, and salary ranges in the industry.
2. **Information About Prospective Employers.** Learn whether the organization is publicly or privately owned. Verify company names, addresses,

CONCEPT *in Action*

For today's wired college grads, preparation for a job interview should include taking time out to Google oneself. The Internet is an easy way for recruiters to learn about prospective employees, and what job candidates post on blogs or on social networking sites could convey an undesirable impression. Do a thorough search on popular search engines to make sure the Web is free of unflattering self-revelations. *What can employers learn about you online?*

products, or services (current and predicted, as well as trends); history; culture; reputation; performance; divisions and subsidiaries; locations (U.S. and global); predicted growth indicators; number of employees; company philosophies and procedures; predicted job openings; salary ranges; and listings of managers of your targeted department within the organization. Also learn about the competitors and customers.

3. **Information About Specific Jobs.** Obtain job descriptions; identify the required education and experience; and determine prevalent working conditions, salary, and fringe benefits.

Interview Like a Pro

An interview tends to have three parts: icebreaking (about five minutes), in which the interviewer tries to put the applicant at ease; questioning (directly or indirectly) by the interviewer; and questioning by the applicant. Almost every recruiter you meet will be trying to rate you in 5 to 10 areas. The questions will be designed to assess your skills and personality.

Many firms start with a *screening interview*, a rather short interview (about 30 minutes) to decide whether to invite you back for a second interview. Only about 20 percent of job applicants are invited back. The second interview is a half day or a day of meetings set up by the human resource department with managers in different departments. After the meetings, someone from the human resource department will discuss other application materials with you and tell you when a letter of acceptance or rejection is likely to be sent. (The wait may be weeks or even months.) Many applicants send follow-up letters in the meantime to show they are still interested in the firm.

For the interview you should dress conservatively. Plan to arrive about 10 to 15 minutes ahead of time. Try to relax. Smile and make eye contact with (but do not stare at) the interviewer. Body language is an important communicator. The placement of your hands and feet and your overall posture say a good deal about you. Here are some other tips for interviewing like a pro:

1. **Concentrate on being likable.** As simplistic as it seems, research proves that one of the most essential goals in successful interviewing is to be liked by the interviewer. Interviewers want to hire pleasant people others will like working with on a daily basis. Pay attention to the following areas to project that you are highly likable:

    - Be friendly, courteous, and enthusiastic.
    - Speak positively.
    - Smile.
    - Use positive body language.
    - Make certain your appearance is appropriate.
    - Make eye contact when you speak.

2. **Project an air of confidence and pride.** Act as though you want and deserve the job, not as though you are desperate.

3. **Demonstrate enthusiasm.** The applicant's level of enthusiasm often influences employers as much as any other interviewing factor. The applicant who demonstrates little enthusiasm for a job will never be selected for the position.

4. **Demonstrate knowledge of and interest in the employer.** "I really want this job" is not convincing enough. Explain why you want the position and how the position fits your career plans. You can cite opportunities that may be unique to a firm or emphasize your skills and education that are highly relevant to the position.

5. **State your name and the position you're seeking.** When you enter the interviewer's office, begin with a friendly greeting and state the position you're interviewing for: "Hello, Ms. Levine, I'm Bella Reyna. I'm here to interview for the accounting position." If someone has already introduced you to the interviewer, simply say, "Good morning, Ms. Levine." Identifying the position is important because interviewers often interview for many different positions.

6. **Focus on how you fit the job.** Near the beginning of your interview, as soon as it seems appropriate, ask a question similar to this: "Could you describe the scope of the job and tell me what capabilities are most important in filling the position?" The interviewer's response will help you focus on emphasizing your qualifications that best match the needs of the employer.

7. **Speak correctly.** Grammatical errors can cost applicants the job. Use correct grammar, word choice, and a businesslike vocabulary, not an informal, chatty one. Avoid slang. When under stress, people often use pet phrases (such as *you know*) too often. This is highly annoying and projects immaturity and insecurity. Don't use *just* or *only*. "I just worked as a waiter." Don't say "I guess." Avoid the word *probably* because it suggests unnecessary doubt. Ask a friend or family member to help you identify any speech weaknesses you have. Begin eliminating these speech habits now.

Also, you should avoid the following "disqualifiers" at all costs. Any one of these blunders could cost you your dream job:

1. Don't sit down until the interviewer invites you to; waiting is courteous.
2. Don't bring anyone else to the interview; it makes you look immature and insecure.
3. Don't smoke.
4. Don't put anything on or read anything on the interviewer's desk; it's considered an invasion of personal space.
5. Don't chew gum or have anything else in your mouth; this projects immaturity.
6. If you are invited to a business meal, don't order alcohol. When ordering, choose food that's easy to eat while carrying on a conversation.
7. Don't offer a limp handshake; it projects weakness. Use a firm handshake.[17]

Select the Right Job for You

Hard work and a little luck may pay off with multiple job offers. Your happy dilemma is deciding which one is best for you. Start by considering the FACTS:

- *Fit.* Do the job and the employer fit your skills, interests, and lifestyle?
- *Advancement and growth.* Will you have the chance to develop your talents and move up within the organization?
- *Compensation.* Is the employer offering a competitive salary and benefits package?
- *Training.* Will the employer provide you with the tools needed to be successful on the job?
- *Site.* Is the job location a good match for your lifestyle and your pocketbook?

A great way to evaluate a new location is through HOMEFAIR (**http://www.homefair.com**). This site offers tools to help you calculate the cost of moving, the cost of living, and the quality of life in various places. The **Moving Calculator** helps you figure out how much it will cost to ship your worldly possessions to a particular city. The **Relocation Crime Lab** compares crime rates in various locations. The **City Snapshots** feature compares demographic, economic, and climate information for two cities of your choosing. The **Salary Calculator** computes cost-of-living differences between hundreds of U.S. and international cities and tells you how much you'd need to make in your new city to maintain your current standard of living.

Start Your New Job

No time is more crucial, and possibly nerve-racking, than the first few months at a new job. During this breaking-in period, the employer decides whether a new employee is valuable enough to keep and, if so, in what capacity. Sometimes the employee's whole future with the company rides on the efforts of the first few weeks or months.

Most firms offer some sort of formal orientation. But generally speaking, they expect employees to learn quickly—and often on their own. You will be expected to become familiar with the firm's goals; its organization, including your place in the company; and basic personnel policies, such as coffee breaks, overtime, and parking.

Here are a few tips on making your first job rewarding and productive:

- *Listen and learn:* When you first walk into your new job, let your eyes and ears take everything in. Do people refer to one another by first names, or is the company more formal? How do people dress? Do the people you work with drop into one another's open offices for informal chats about business matters? Or have you entered a "memo mill," where anything of substance is put on e-mail and talks with other employees are scheduled through their administrative assistants? Size up where the power lies. Who seems to most often assume a leadership role? Who is the person others turn to for advice? Why has that person achieved that position? What traits have made this person a "political leader"? Don't be misled by what others say, but also don't dismiss their evaluations. Make your own judgments based on what you see and hear. Effective listening skills help you learn your new job responsibilities quickly. Take the quiz in Exhibit P.8 to see if you are a good listener.

- *Do unto others:* Be nice. Nice people are usually the last to be fired and among the first to be promoted. Don't be pleasant only with those who can help you in the company. Be nice to everyone. You never know who can help you or give you information that will turn out to be useful. Genuinely nice people make routine job assignments, and especially pressure-filled ones, more pleasant. And people who are dealt with pleasantly usually respond in kind.

- *Don't start out as a maverick:* If every new employee tried to change tried-and-true methods to suit his or her whims, the firm would quickly be in chaos. Individual needs must take a back seat to established procedures. Devote yourself to getting things done within the system. Every manager realizes that it takes time for a new person to adjust. But the faster you start accomplishing things, the faster the boss will decide that you were the right person to hire.

CONCEPT *in Action*

Finding a mentor can be especially helpful when starting a new career. Whether assigned through a corporate mentorship program or sought out on one's own, mentors have inside access to the company and can help protégés learn the ropes. A good mentor is a seasoned veteran who offers insight and advice, boosts morale, and makes networking contacts—while steering mentees away from pitfalls. *What lessons can a mentor pass on that aren't necessarily taught in school but are essential to career success?*

© IMAGE SOURCE/GETTY IMAGES

Exhibit P.8 > Fun Self-Test—Are You a Good Listener?

Rate your level of agreement with the statements below using the following scale:

Strongly Agree	Agree	Neither Agree nor Disagree	Disagree	Strongly Disagree

1. A person who takes time to ask for clarification about something that might be unclear is not a good listener.
2. While listening I am distracted by the sounds around me.
3. I try to understand not only what is being said but also analyze the strength of any ideas that are being presented.
4. I ask questions, make observations, or give opinion when necessary for clarifications.
5. While I am listening, I avoid eye contact but am polite.
6. I am tempted to judge a person whether or not he or she is a good speaker.
7. I feel more comfortable when someone talks to me about a topic that I find interesting.
8. I always jot down key phrases/points that strike me as important points of concern that require a response.
9. My listening style varies from the speaker's style of communication.
10. A good listener requires a good speaker.[18]

See the scoring guidelines at the end of this textbook to obtain your score.

- *Find a great mentor:* The leading cause of career unhappiness is working for a bad boss. Good jobs can easily be ruined by supervisors who hold you back. In contrast, your career will soar (and you will smile every day) when you have a great mentor helping you along the way. If you find a job with a super mentor, jump at the chance to take it.

Movin' On Up

Once you have been on the job for a while, you will want to get ahead and be promoted. Exhibit P.9 offers several suggestions for improving your chances of promotion. The first item might seem a bit strange, yet it's there for a practical reason. If you don't really like what you do, you won't be committed enough to compete with those who do. The passionate people are the ones who go the extra mile, do the extra work, and come up with fresh out-of-the-box ideas.

So there you have it! In the next chapter we will begin our journey through the world of business so that you can determine what areas of business are most interesting to you. Remember, it's never too early to begin planning your career—the future is now.

Exhibit P.9 > How to Move Up

- Love what you do, which entails first figuring out who you are.
- Never stop learning about new technologies and new management skills.
- Try to get international experience even if it is only a short stint overseas.
- Create new business opportunities—they could lead to a promotion.
- Be really outstandingly terrific at what you're doing now, this week, this month.

PART 1

The Business Environment

CHAPTER 1

Participating in the Dynamic Business Environment

Learning Goals

After reading this chapter, you should be able to answer these questions:

1 How do businesses and not-for-profit organizations help create our standard of living, and what benefits does the study of business provide?

2 What are the primary features of the world's economic systems?

3 What are the sectors of the business environment, and how do changes in the economic and political and legal environments influence business decisions?

4 What demographic shifts are creating both challenges and new opportunities for business?

5 What current social factors have the greatest impact on business?

6 How can businesses remain competitive in today's global marketplace?

7 How can implementing technological advances help a firm reach its goals?

8 What major trends do managers face today?

Exploring Business Careers
Karen Beal
Urban Gateways

Accounting for over one-fourth of all economic activity in the United States, not-for-profits are an undeniable force in the business world, even though their focus on goals other than profit falls outside the traditional model of a for-profit business. But it is this shift away from a focus on profit that allows them to pursue missions of social improvement. To be truly effective in a not-for-profit organization, a person must share the organization's vision. Karen Beal, who has worked with several not-for-profit organizations as volunteer, board member, even executive director, recognizes this: "I cannot stress enough the importance of the mission. You have to be in it for the mission—that has to be your reason for choosing *this* organization and not the one just down the block. Without that connection, there cannot be success."

Beal often begins her relationship with a not-for-profit as a volunteer because it allows her to get a feel for an organization without the level of commitment required by board membership. "Being a volunteer is an excellent way to determine firsthand if you espouse the mission of an organization. By volunteering for a committee or two, I am able to determine whether the organization and I are a good fit. This may lead to a more involved commitment, and frequently does, but that spark of connection needs to exist first."

Urban Gateways is one organization where she felt that spark immediately. Beal began working on a planning committee for a gala fundraising event, and quickly recognized that the organization was something special. Soon, the organization asked her to join its board, and she readily agreed. "When you are engaged with an organization for the mission, you can sell it better, you can talk about, make it come to

fruition. With Urban Gateways, I felt that way. I loved Urban Gateways because it was created by the community to fulfill a need they saw."

Indeed, Urban Gateways, like many not-for-profits, grew out of the community it serves. Its mission, posted clearly on their Web site (http://www.urbangateways.org), is simply: "To use art to educate and change children's lives." Created in 1961 as a response to inequities in arts education, especially in inner-city schools, Urban Gateways strove to expose children to the arts in an effort to awaken their potential to recognize the beauty and power of both creating and experiencing the arts. This awareness of the surrounding social trends and forces is important to any organization's success, whether it is for-profit or not. For organizations such as Urban Gateways, however, Beal feels it is even more critical. "You need to be intimately aware of the community you serve—much as in the for-profit world, you seek to please your shareholders. In a not-for-profit, community members are your shareholders, and they pay not with money but with their happiness, their opportunities to succeed, their time and commitment, and often their quality of life. In the end, their stake in what you are doing is so incredibly high that to disregard them would be a huge disservice both to them and to the organization." Urban Gateways actively engages the community in every level of their organization, from volunteer to board, and in every step of the process, from planning to implementation, to ensure they are keenly aware of their community's needs.

This chapter provides the basic structures upon which the business world is built: how it is organized, what outside forces influence it, and where it is heading.

Each day in America, thousands of new businesses are born. Only a rare few will become the next Apple, Microsoft, Google, or eBay. Unfortunately, many others will never see their first anniversary. The survivors understand that change is the one constant in the business environment. These businesses, both large and small, profit and not-for-profit, prosper because they track environmental shifts and trends and use them to identify potential opportunities. Urban Gateways survives and prospers because it capitalizes on evolving trends such as the use of art to educate and change children's lives.

We begin our study of business by introducing you to the primary functions of a business, the relationship between risk and profits, and the importance of not-for-profit organizations. You will also learn about the factors of production and how the study of business will help you succeed in whatever career you choose. Next we'll compare the key economic systems in place around the world today. Then we'll examine the major components of the business environment, demographic factors, and the social environment. Finally, we'll examine the challenges that a global marketplace creates, analyze the impact of technology, and look at key trends that face today's managers.

The Nature of Business

 How do businesses and not-for-profit organizations help create our standard of living, and what benefits does the study of business provide?

business
An organization that strives for a profit by providing goods and services desired by its customers.

goods
Tangible items manufactured by businesses.

services
Intangible offerings of businesses that can't be held, touched, or stored.

standard of living
A country's output of goods and services that people can buy with the money they have.

quality of life
The general level of human happiness based on such things as life expectancy, educational standards, health, sanitation, and leisure time.

Take a moment to think about the many different types of businesses you come into contact with on a typical day. As you drive to class you may stop at a gas station that is part of a major national oil company and grab lunch from a fast food chain like Taco Bell or McDonald's or the neighborhood pizza place. Need more cash? You can do your banking while you are grocery shopping, at an in-store branch that your bank opened. You don't even have to visit the store anymore: Online shopping brings the stores to you, offering everything from clothes to food, furniture, and concert tickets.

A **business** is an organization that strives for a profit by providing goods and services desired by its customers. Businesses meet the needs of consumers by providing movies, medical care, autos, and countless other goods and services. **Goods** are tangible items manufactured by businesses, such as desks. **Services** are intangible offerings of businesses that can't be held, touched, or stored. Physicians, lawyers, hairstylists, car washes, and airlines all provide services. Businesses also serve other organizations, such as hospitals, retailers, and governments, by providing machinery, goods for resale, computers, and thousands of other items.

Thus, businesses create the goods and services that are the basis of our standard of living. The **standard of living** of any country is measured by the output of goods and services people can buy with the money they have. The United States has one of the highest standards of living in the world. Although several countries such as Switzerland and Germany have higher average wages than the United States, their standard of living isn't higher because prices are so much higher in those countries. As a result, the same amount of money buys less in those countries. For example, in the United States we can buy a "Real Meal Deal" at McDonald's for less than $4, while in another country, a similar meal might cost as much as $10!

Businesses play a key role in determining our quality of life by providing jobs and goods and services to society. **Quality of life** refers to the general level of human happiness based on such things as life expectancy, educational standards, health, sanitation, and leisure time. Building a high quality of life is a combined effort of businesses, government, and not-for-profit organizations. Exhibit 1.1 shows how selected major cities around the world rank on a 39-factor quality of life survey that includes political, social, economic, and environmental factors, personal safety and health, education, transportation, and other public services. It may come as a surprise that the world's top cities for quality of life are not in the United States. Of the top 25 cities in the survey, 68 percent are in Europe, whereas Canada and Australia/New Zealand have 20 percent each. At the other end of the scale, Baghdad is the city scoring lowest on the survey.[1]

Exhibit 1.1 > Quality of Life Rankings for Selected Major Cities

City, Country	Rank
Amsterdam, Netherlands	12
Auckland, New Zealand	8
Boston, MA, U.S.	36
Frankfurt, Germany	5
Geneva, Switzerland	1
Honolulu, HI, U.S.	25
London, England	39
Melbourne, Australia	14
Munich, Germany	5
New York, NY, U.S.	39
Osaka, Japan	46
Ottawa, Canada	20
Paris, France	31
Portland, OR, U.S.	42
San Francisco, CA, U.S.	25
Seattle, WA, U.S.	46
Singapore, Singapore	34
Sydney, Australia	8
Tokyo, Japan	34
Toronto, Canada	14
Vancouver, Canada	3
Vienna, Austria	3
Zurich, Switzerland	1

Source: "Overall Quality of Living—Ranking," Mercer Human Resources Consulting, March 2005, http://www.mercerhr.com (September 28, 2005).

risk
The potential to lose time and money or otherwise not be able to accomplish an organization's goals.

revenue
The money a company earns from providing services or selling goods to customers.

costs
Expenses incurred in creating and selling goods and services.

profit
The money left over after all costs are paid.

Risk and Profits

Creating a quality of life is not without risks, however. **Risk** is the potential to lose time and money or otherwise not be able to accomplish an organization's goals. Without enough blood donors, for example, the American Red Cross faces the risk of not meeting the demand for blood by victims of disaster. Businesses like Microsoft face the risk of falling short of their revenue and profit goals. **Revenue** is the money a company receives by providing services or selling goods to customers. **Costs** are expenses for rent, salaries, supplies, transportation, and many other items that a company incurs from creating and selling goods and services. For example, some of the costs incurred by Microsoft in developing its software include expenses for salaries, facilities, and advertising. If Microsoft has money left over after it pays all costs, it has a **profit**. A company whose costs are greater than revenues shows a loss.

When a company like Microsoft uses its resources intelligently, it can often increase sales, hold costs down, and earn a profit. Not all companies earn profits, but that is the risk of being in business. In American business today, there is generally a direct relationship between risks and profit: the greater the risks, the greater the potential for profit (or loss). Companies that take too conservative a stance may lose out to more nimble competitors who react quickly to the changing business environment.

Take Sony, for example. The electronics giant, once a leader with its Walkman music players and Trinitron televisions, steadily lost ground—and profits—to other consumer technology companies by not embracing new technologies like the MP3 digital music format and flat-panel television screens. Sony misjudged what the market wanted and stayed with proprietary technologies such as MiniDiscs rather than create cross-platform options. Apple—an upstart in personal music devices—quickly grabbed the lion's share of the digital music market with its iPod players and iTunes music service. "The world in which this company operates has undergone seismic change," said Sony's chief executive officer Michael Stringer in September 2005, as he announced a major restructuring plan designed to revitalize the company's electronics business.[2]

Not-for-Profit Organizations

Not all organizations strive to make a profit. A **not-for-profit organization** is an organization that exists to achieve some goal other than the usual business goal of profit. Charities such as Habitat for Humanity, the United Way, the American Cancer Society, and the Sierra Club are not-for-profit organizations, as are most hospitals, zoos, arts organizations, civic groups, and religious organizations. Over the last 20 years, the number of nonprofit organizations—and the employees and volunteers who work for them—has increased considerably. Government is our largest and most pervasive not-for-profit group. In addition, more than 1.4 million non-governmental non-profit entities operate in the United States today and account for more than 28 percent of the country's economic activity.

Like their for-profit counterparts, these groups set goals and require resources to meet those goals. However, their goals are not focused on profits. For example, a not-for-profit organization's goal might be feeding the poor, preserving the environment, increasing attendance at the ballet, or preventing drunk driving. Not-for-profit organizations do not compete directly with each other in the same manner as, for example, Ford and Honda, but they do compete for talented employees, people's scarce volunteer time, and donations.

The boundaries that formerly separated not-for-profit and for-profit organizations have blurred, leading to a greater exchange of ideas between the sectors. As we will learn in Chapter 3, for-profit businesses are now addressing social issues. Successful not-for-profits apply business principles to operate more effectively. Not-for-profit managers are concerned with the same concepts as their colleagues in for-profit companies: developing strategy, budgeting carefully, measuring performance, encouraging innovation, improving productivity, and demonstrating accountability.

For example, Los Angeles County and the Cleveland Museums of Art were among several major museums looking for new directors in the summer of 2005. In addition to pursuing the museum's artistic goals, the top executive manages the administrative and business side of the museum: human resources, finance, and legal concerns—for example, the ramifications of purchasing art from other countries. Ticket revenues cover a fraction of the museum's operating costs of about $80 per visitor, so the director spends a great deal of time seeking major donations. Today's museum boards of directors include both art patrons and business executives who want to see sound fiscal decision making. Therefore, a museum director must tread a fine line between the institution's artistic mission and financial policies.[3]

CONCEPT *in Action*

Following Hurricane Katrina's devastation of the Gulf Coast region, Americans assisted storm victims by donating nearly $3 billion to disaster-relief efforts. Some not-for-profit charities focused aid towards the people of New Orleans, but others delivered care to a different group of sufferers: animals and pets. The American Society for the Prevention of Cruelty to Animals (ASPCA) funded dozens of shelters dedicated to the rescue of over 8,000 dogs, cats, horses, and other animals left homeless by the flood. *Why are tasks such as animal rescue managed primarily through not-for-profit organizations?*

© MARIO TAMA/GETTY IMAGES

Why Study Business?

Regardless of the career path you choose, understanding how businesses function, the environment in which they operate, and the interrelationship of business functions will contribute to your success in any type of organization. In your personal lives, too, knowledge of business organizations will make you a better consumer.

Perhaps your first position is as a marketing representative for a natural foods company. To accomplish your objectives, you must understand how changes in demographics and social trends affect the demand for natural food products and how you identify your target market segments. Is the economy doing well so that people have jobs and can afford your specialty products? You also need good management skills as you interact with employees in other departments or lead and participate in team projects. Familiarity with the manufacturing process and its cycle time are essential if you are selling a product for delivery by a certain date. Technology will help you communicate electronically with customers and provide systems for many purposes, from developing targeted marketing campaigns to evaluating buying patterns. You'll put your knowledge of accounting and finance to work tracking sales against goals and preparing the departmental budget.

If at some point you start your own business, you will discover that business owners wear many hats. The more you know about operations across the entire enterprise, the better prepared you will be to manage your company. If you become an attorney or family therapist, you will need to operate in a businesslike manner, using marketing skills to attract clients, as well as using information technology, accounting, and financial management to run your practice profitably.

These are just a few examples of how the topics covered in this Introduction to Business course apply across an organization and in different enterprises. Don't worry if you don't understand all the terms; you will by the end of the course!

Factors of Production: The Building Blocks of Business

factors of production
The resources used to create goods and services.

To provide goods and services, regardless of whether they operate in the for-profit or not-for-profit sector, organizations require inputs in the form of resources called **factors of production**. Four traditional factors of production are common to all productive activity: *natural resources, labor, capital,* and *entrepreneurship.* Many experts now include *knowledge* as a fifth factor, acknowledging its key role in business success. By using the factors of production efficiently, a company can produce more goods and services with the same resources.

CONCEPT *in Action*

The acquisition and development of land is vital to business, but accessing land also can be controversial. For years the U.S. government has denied oil companies access to the pristine Arctic National Wildlife Refuge (ANWR) in Alaska. Energy firms say the land can be excavated safely and without harm. Environmentalist groups believe oil excavation would hurt wildlife and disturb the region's immaculate beauty. *Can you think of situations where the needs of businesses to use land might conflict with the public interest?*

It Takes a (Sundance) Village

When you think of Robert Redford, you probably think of him as a movie star first. But Redford is also an entrepreneur with a vision: creating a community where nature's beauty would inspire artists and attract outdoor enthusiasts. From that dream came the Sundance Group, formed in 1988 to manage his interests in a variety of independent not-for-profit and profit-focused enterprises.

Sundance Group began small, with Redford's 1969 purchase of 6,000 acres in Utah's Provo Canyon. His goals were to preserve this wilderness area and provide a retreat for artists in different media. Redford funded his enterprise with earnings from one of his first big hits, *Butch Cassidy and the Sundance Kid.* Banks wouldn't lend him money, so he found investors who shared his vision: supporting independent artists and showcasing their work.

Since then, the Provo Canyon site has become a premier place to visit for vacationers and artists. Common values—independence, creative risk-taking, and discovery—link the separate Sundance Group units:

- *Sundance Village:* A cultural mecca with a top-rated mountain resort, art exhibitions, literary events, and musical concerts ranging from leading symphony orchestras to rising songwriters.
- *Sundance Institute:* A multidisciplinary, not-for-profit arts organization that promotes the artistic development of filmmakers, writers, playwrights, actors, and composers. It sponsors the foremost festival for independent films, the annual Sundance Film Festival. Ongoing Institute programs include the Documentary Film, Feature Film, Theatre, and Film Music Programs.

- *Sundance Channel:* A commercial-free cable television channel devoted to all aspects of independent filmmaking, a joint venture between Redford, Showtime Networks, and Universal Studios.
- *Sundance Catalog:* A for-profit mail-order company offering a diverse mix of jewelry, apparel, gift, and home decor items inspired by the American West. The catalog business was sold in 2005, with Redford keeping a minority share.
- *Sundance Cinema:* Redford's latest for-profit venture, a chain of theaters showing independent, documentary, and foreign-language films, quality studio films, and original programming, including shorts, filmmaker interviews, and forums.

What's next for Redford, and what drives him? "Anything which helps new and interesting voices in the cultural realm reach more people can only enrich the experience of artists, audiences, and communities, and this makes the effort worth it," he says.[4]

Critical Thinking Questions
- Why did Redford choose not-for-profit status for the Sundance Institute and organize some of his other ventures as for-profit businesses?
- What led Redford, a successful film star and producer, to pursue entrepreneurial activities? How did Redford's reputation help his entrepreneurial ventures?

---

natural resources
Commodities that are useful inputs in their natural state.

Commodities that are useful inputs in their natural state are known as **natural resources.** They include farmland, forests, mineral and oil deposits, and water. Sometimes natural resources are simply called *land,* although, as you can see, the term means more than just land. Companies use natural resources in different ways. International Paper Company uses wood pulp to make paper, and Pacific Gas & Electric Company may use water, oil, or coal to produce electricity. Today urban sprawl, pollution, and limited resources have raised questions about resource use. Conservationists, ecologists, and government bodies are proposing laws to require land-use planning and resource conservation.

labor
Economic contributions of people.

Labor refers to the economic contributions of people working with their minds and muscles. This input includes the talents of everyone—from a restaurant cook to a nuclear physicist—who performs the many tasks of manufacturing and selling goods and services.

capital
The inputs, such as tools, machinery, equipment, and buildings, used to produce goods and services and get them to the customer.

The tools, machinery, equipment, and buildings used to produce goods and services and get them to the consumer are known as **capital.** Sometimes the term *capital* is also used to mean the money that buys machinery, factories, and other production and distribution facilities. However, because money itself produces nothing, it is *not* one of the basic inputs. Instead, it is a means of acquiring the inputs. Therefore, in this context, capital does not include money.

entrepreneurs
People who combine the inputs of natural resources, labor, and capital to produce goods or services with the intention of making a profit or accomplishing a not-for-profit goal.

Entrepreneurs are the people who combine the inputs of natural resources, labor, and capital to produce goods or services with the intention of making a profit or accomplishing a not-for-profit goal. These people make the decisions that set the course for their firms; they create products and production processes or develop services. Because they are not guaranteed a profit in return for their time and effort, they must be risk takers. Of course, if their firms succeed, the rewards may be great.

Today, many Americans want to start their own businesses. They are attracted by the opportunity to be their own boss and reap the financial rewards of a successful firm. Many start their first business from their dorm rooms, like Michael Dell of Dell

Computers, or while living at home, so their cost is almost zero. Entrepreneurs include people like Bill Gates, the founder of Microsoft, who is now one of the richest people in the world, and Sergey Brin and Larry Page, Google's founders. Some entrepreneurs are known for other achievements as well, as described in the Catching the Entrepreneurial Spirit box. Many thousands of individuals have started companies that, while remaining small, make a major contribution to America's economy. We'll meet many more enterprising business people throughout this book, especially in Chapter 6 and other Catching the Entrepreneurial Spirit boxes.

knowledge
The combined talents and skills of the workforce.

A number of outstanding managers and noted academics are beginning to emphasize a fifth factor of production—knowledge. **Knowledge** refers to the combined talents and skills of the workforce and has become a primary driver of economic growth. The new competitive environment places a premium on knowledge and learning over physical resources. For example, the Organization for Economic Cooperation and Development (OECD) estimates that knowledge-based industries added about 50 percent in total value to the economies of Germany and Great Britain from 1985 to 1997. Companies that want to reap similar benefits are investing more heavily in areas that emphasize knowledge, such as research and development, licensing, and marketing.[5]

knowledge workers
Workers who create, distribute, and apply knowledge.

"**Knowledge workers** are going to be the primary force determining which economies are successful and which aren't," says Thomas Davenport, Babson College professor of information technology and management. "They are the key source of growth in most organizations. New products and services, new approaches to marketing, new business models—all these come from knowledge workers." Davenport estimates that knowledge workers, whom he defines as "people whose primary job is to do something with knowledge: to create it, distribute it, apply it," already comprise between 25 percent and 33 percent of the U.S. workforce.[6]

concept check

Explain the concepts of revenue, costs, and profit.

What career do you see yourself pursuing, and how will the study of business help you succeed?

What are the five factors of production, and what is the role of an entrepreneur in society?

Global Economic Systems

 2 **What are the primary features of the world's economic systems?**

economic systems
Combination of policies, laws, and choices made by its government to determine what goods and services are produced and how they are allocated.

Businesses and other organizations operate according to the **economic systems** of their home countries. An economic system is a combination of policies, laws, and choices made by its government to determine what goods and services are produced and how they are allocated. Today the world's major economic systems fall into two broad categories: free market, or capitalism, and planned economies, which include communism and socialism. However, in reality many countries use a mixed market system that incorporates elements from more than one economic system.

The major differentiator among economic systems is whether the government or individuals decides how to:

- Allocate limited resources—the factors of production—to individuals and organizations to best satisfy unlimited societal needs
- Choose what goods and services to produce, and in what quantities
- Determine how and by whom to produce these goods and services
- Distribute goods and services to consumers

Companies that do business internationally may discover that they must adapt production and selling methods to accommodate the economic system of another country.

Capitalism

capitalism
An economic system based on competition in the marketplace and private ownership of the factors of production (resources); also known as the *private enterprise system.*

In recent years, more countries have shifted toward free market economic systems and away from planned economies. Sometimes, as in the case of the former East Germany, the transition to capitalism was painful but fairly quick. In other countries, such as Russia, the movement has been characterized by false starts and backsliding. **Capitalism,**

© FORREST ANDERSON/GETTY IMAGES

also known as the *private enterprise system,* is based on competition in the marketplace and private ownership of the factors of production (resources). In a competitive economic system, a large number of people and businesses buy and sell products freely in the marketplace. In pure capitalism all the factors of production are owned privately, and the government does not try to set prices or coordinate economic activity.

A capitalist system guarantees certain economic rights: to own property (a central tenet), to make a profit, to make free choices, and to compete. Profit, the main incentive in a capitalist system, encourages entrepreneurship and is necessary for producing goods and services, building plants, paying dividends and taxes, and creating jobs. People in a capitalist economy can decide whether to become an entrepreneur or to work for someone else based on their own drive, interest, and training. The government does not create job quotas for each industry or give people tests to determine what they will do.

Competition benefits businesses and consumers in a capitalist system by leading to better and more diverse products, keeping prices stable, and increasing the efficiency of producers. Companies strive to produce goods and services at the lowest possible cost and sell them at the highest possible price. When profits are high, more firms enter the market to seek those profits. The resulting competition among firms tends to lower prices. Producers must then find new ways of operating more efficiently if they are to keep making a profit—and stay in business.

Communism

communism
An economic system characterized by government ownership of virtually all resources, government control of all markets, and economic decision making by central-government planning.

The complete opposite to capitalism is **communism**. In a communist economic system, the government owns virtually all resources and controls all markets. Economic decision making is centralized: The government, rather than the market's competitive force, decides what and how much to produce, where to locate production facilities and to acquire raw materials and supplies, who will get the output, and what the prices will be. This form of centralized economic system offers little if any choice to a country's citizens. In the 20th century, countries such as the former Soviet Union and China chose communism, believing that it would raise their standard of living. In practice, however, the tight controls over most aspects of people's lives, such as what careers they can choose, where they can work, and what they can buy, led to lower productivity. Workers had no reasons to work harder or produce quality goods, because there were no rewards for excellence. Errors in planning and resource allocation led to shortages of even basic items.

These factors were among the reasons for the 1991 collapse of the Soviet Union into multiple independent nations. Recent reforms in Russia, China, and most of the Eastern European nations have moved these economies toward more capitalistic, market-oriented systems. North Korea and Cuba are the best remaining examples of communist economic systems.

Socialism

socialism
An economic system in which the basic industries are owned either by the government itself or by the private sector under strong government control.

Socialism is an economic system in which the basic industries are owned by the government or by the private sector under strong government control. A socialist state controls critical, large-scale industries such as transportation, communications, and utilities. Smaller businesses and those considered less critical, such as retail, may be privately owned. To varying degrees the state also determines the goals of businesses, the prices and selection of goods, and the rights of workers. Socialist countries typically provide their citizens with a higher level of services, such as health care and unemployment benefits, than do most capitalist countries. As a result, taxes and unemployment may also be quite high in socialist countries. For example, the top individual tax rate in France is 48 percent, compared to 35 percent in the United States. These high rates have, however, dropped considerably and further rate reductions are anticipated as many socialist countries seek to stimulate their economies.

Many countries, including Great Britain, Denmark, Israel, and Sweden, have socialist systems, but the systems vary from country to country. In Denmark, for example, most businesses are privately owned and operated, but two-thirds of the population is sustained by the state through government welfare programs.

Socialism is proving to be surprisingly resilient in Western Europe. Tony Blair, Great Britain's prime minister, is a member of the Labour Party, which favors preeminence of government, nationalized industry, extraordinary social regulation, and massive taxation to support it all. Across the English Channel, France under Jacques Chirac is inching toward a capitalistic form of government. In July 2005, the French government sold 20 percent of Gaz de France, the nationalized gas utility, to the public and also planned to privatize Electricité de France. The French government owns 32 percent of France Telecom, 30 percent of Thales, a defense contractor, 18 percent of Air France, and 15 percent of automobile manufacturer Renault.[7]

Mixed Economic Systems

Pure capitalism and communism are extremes; real-world economies fall somewhere between the two. The U.S. economy leans toward pure capitalism, but it uses government policies and laws to promote economic stability and growth and to transfer money to the poor, the unemployed, and the elderly. American capitalism has produced some very powerful organizations in the form of huge corporations, such as General Motors and Microsoft. To protect smaller firms and entrepreneurs, the government has passed legislation that requires that the giants compete fairly against weaker competitors.

mixed economies
Economies that combine several economic systems; for example, an economy where the government owns certain industries but others are owned by the private sector.

Canada, Great Britain, and Sweden, among others, are also called **mixed economies** and use more than one economic system. Sometimes, the government is basically socialist and owns basic industries. In Canada, for example, the government owns the communications, transportation, and utilities industries, as well as some of the natural-resource industries. It also supplies health care to its citizens. But most other activity is carried on by private enterprise, as in a capitalist system.

The few factors of production owned by the government in a mixed economy include some public lands, the postal service, and some water resources. But the government is extensively involved in the economic system through taxing, spending, and welfare activities. The economy is also mixed in the sense that the country tries to achieve many social goals—income redistribution and Social Security, for example—that may not be attempted in purely capitalist systems. Exhibit 1.2 summarizes and compares key factors of the world's economic systems.

concept check

What is capitalism and why is it growing?

Describe the differences between communism and socialism. Why is communism in decline yet socialism is still popular?

Why are most economies mixed?

Exhibit 1.2 > The Basic Economic Systems of the World

	Capitalism	Communism	Socialism	Mixed Economy
Ownership of Business	Businesses are privately owned with minimal government ownership or interference.	Government owns all or most enterprises.	Basic industries, such as railroads and utilities, are owned by government. Very high taxation as government redistributes income from successful private businesses and entrepreneurs.	Private ownership of land and businesses but government control of some enterprises. The private sector is typically large.
Control of Markets	Complete freedom of trade. No or little government control.	Complete government control of markets.	Some markets are controlled and some are free. Significant central-government planning. State enterprises are managed by bureaucrats. These enterprises are rarely profitable.	Some markets such as nuclear energy and the post office are controlled or highly regulated.
Worker Incentives	Strong incentive to work and innovate because owners retain profits.	No incentive to work hard or produce quality products.	Private-sector incentives are the same as capitalism and public-sector incentives are the same as in a planned economy.	Private-sector incentives are the same as capitalism. Limited incentives in the public sector.
Management of Enterprises	Each enterprise is managed by owners or professional managers with little government interference.	Centralized management by the government bureaucracy. Little or no flexibility in decision making at the factory level.	Significant government planning and regulation. Bureaucrats run government enterprises.	Private-sector management similar to capitalism. Public sector similar to socialism.
Forecast for 2020	Continued steady growth.	No growth and perhaps disappearance.	Stable with probable slight growth.	Continued growth.
Examples	United States	Cuba, North Korea	Finland, India, Israel	Great Britain, France, Sweden, Canada

Understanding the Business Environment

3 What are the sectors of the business environment, and how do changes in the economic and political and legal environments influence business decisions?

Businesses do not operate in a vacuum but rather in a dynamic environment that has a direct influence on how they operate and whether they will achieve their objectives. This external business environment is composed of numerous outside organizations and forces that we can group into seven key sub-environments, as Exhibit 1.3 depicts: economic, political and legal, demographic, social, competitive, global, and technological. Each of these sectors creates a unique set of challenges and opportunities for businesses.

Business owners and managers have a great deal of control over the internal environment of business, which covers the day-to-day business decisions. They choose the supplies they purchase, which employees they hire, the products they sell, and where they sell those products. They use their skills and resources to create goods and services that will satisfy existing and prospective customers. However, the external environmental conditions that affect a business are generally beyond the control of management and change constantly. To compete successfully, business owners and managers must continuously study the environment and adapt their businesses.

Other forces, such as acts of nature, also have a major impact on businesses. For example, in September 2005, Hurricane Katrina devastated large areas of Louisiana and Mississippi. The city of New Orleans suffered major damage as its levees broke. Businesses in the affected areas experienced tremendous losses, with many destroyed completely. Residents were left homeless and without jobs. In the aftermath of the

Exhibit 1.3 > The Dynamic Business Environment

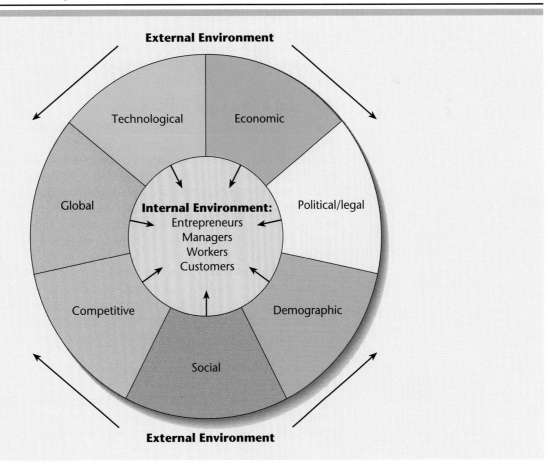

storm, which left behind damages estimated at $60 billion, many corporations reported additional costs directly attributable to the storm. For instance, Walgreen Co., the leading drugstore chain in the United States, took a $55 million charge for store closures related to the storm.[8] Other businesses, however, will benefit from the disaster. Manufacturers of recreational vehicles (RVs) such as Thor Industries and Fleetwood Enterprises supplied RVs to use as temporary shelters. Demand rose significantly for manufactured homes from Champion Enterprises and Palm Harbor Enterprises, because of the quick construction time.[9]

No one business is large or powerful enough to create major changes in the external environment. Thus, managers are primarily adapters to, rather than agents of, change. Global competition is basically an uncontrollable element in the external environment. In some situations, however, a firm can influence external events through its strategies. For example, efforts by the major U.S. pharmaceutical companies were successful in getting the Food and Drug Administration to speed up the approval process for new drugs. In October 2005, Google opened a lobbying office in Washington, DC to focus on the Internet and telecommunications and copyright laws.[10]

Let's now take a brief look at economic and political and legal influences, which are covered in detail later in Part 1, and then focus on demographic, social, competitive, global, and technological forces.

Economic Influences

As you'll learn in Chapter 2, which focuses on the economic environment, this category is one of the most important external influences on businesses. Fluctuations in the level of economic activity create *business cycles* that affect businesses and individuals in many ways. When the economy is growing, for example, unemployment rates are low and income levels rise. Inflation and interest rates are other areas that change according to economic activity. Through the policies it sets, such as taxes and interest rate levels, a government attempts to stimulate or curtail the level of economic activity. In addition, the forces of supply and demand determine how prices and quantities of goods and services behave in a free market.

Political and Legal Influences

The political climate of a country is another critical factor for managers to consider. The amount of government activity, the types of laws it passes, and the general political stability of a government are three components of political climate. For example, a multinational company such as General Electric will evaluate the political climate of a country before deciding to locate a plant there. Is the government stable, or might a coup disrupt the country? How restrictive are the regulations for foreign businesses, including foreign ownership of business property and taxation? Import tariffs and quotas and export restrictions also must be taken into account. We'll return to this important topic in Chapter 4.

In the United States, too, laws passed by Congress and the many regulatory agencies cover such areas as competition, minimum wages, environmental protection, worker safety, and copyrights and patents. For example, Congress passed the Telecommunications Act of 1996 to deregulate the telecommunications industry. As a result, competition increased and new opportunities arose as traditional boundaries between service providers blurred. Today we have telephone companies offering Internet services and cable television companies offering phone and Internet services.

Federal agencies play a significant role in business operations. When Pfizer wants to bring a new medication for heart disease to market, it must follow the procedures set by the Food and Drug Administration (FDA) for testing and clinical

CONCEPT *in Action*

Shock jock Howard Stern rocked the entertainment world in 2006 by taking his bawdy on-air freak show to Sirius Satellite Radio. The self-proclaimed King of All Media inked a deal with Sirius while under fire from federal regulators for the content of his show, which many consider lewd. Stern fled Viacom and terrestrial radio to avoid an imminent crackdown by the FCC, and he boisterously declared the "death of FM radio" after signing with his new broadcast partner. *How does the political-legal environment affect content standards for traditional and satellite radio programming?*

© SHANNON STAPLETON/REUTERS/CORBIS

---

concept check

Define the components of the internal and the external business environments.

What factors within the economic environment affect businesses? Choose one factor and give a specific example of how it would influence a business decision.

Why is the political climate in a country important to companies that do business abroad? Discuss how the laws Congress passes can change the way a business operates.

trials and secure FDA approval. Before issuing stock, Pfizer must register the securities with the Securities and Exchange Commission. The Federal Trade Commission will penalize Pfizer if its advertisements promoting the drug's benefits are misleading. These are just a few ways the political and legal environment affect business decisions.

States and local governments also exert control over businesses—imposing taxes, issuing corporate charters and business licenses, setting zoning ordinances, and similar regulations. We'll discuss the legal environment in greater detail in the Appendix to Chapter 3.

Demographic Factors

4 **What demographic shifts are creating both challenges and new opportunities for business?**

demography
The study of people's vital statistics, such as their age, gender, race and ethnicity, and location.

Demographic factors are an uncontrollable factor in the business environment and extremely important to managers. **Demography** is the study of people's vital statistics, such as their age, gender, race and ethnicity, and location. Demographics help companies define the markets for their products and also determine the size and composition of the workforce. You'll encounter demographics as you continue your study of business. For example, later in this chapter and in Part 3, we'll examine the challenges of managing a diverse work force. In Part 4, you'll learn how marketers use demographics to segment markets and select target markets.

The Digital Kids of Generation Y

Generation Y
Americans born between about 1977 and 1997.

Those designated by demographers as **Generation Y** were born between about 1977 and 1997 (demographers have reached no consensus as to exact dates, with some starting in 1979 and some ending as late as 2000). Also called the Echo Boomers or the Millennium Generation, they number about 74 million and represent about 26 percent of the U.S. population. According to Neil Howe and William Strauss, authors of *Millennials Rising: The Next Great Generation*, Generation Y is the most ethnically and socially diverse generation in American history. One-third of its members identify themselves

CONCEPT *in Action*

With the launch of its red-hot iPod player, Apple Computer revitalized the tech industry and set the standard for digital music. The ultra-hip trademark-white gadgets hold over 15,000 songs and store hundreds of hours of video for display on a stunning 2.5-inch color screen. Pulsating silhouette ads featuring pop-music icons like U2 and Eminem heighten iPod's mystique and further the player's cultural world-domination. *What characteristics of Generation Y make it the ideal target demographic for Apple's ubiquitous iPod?*

as non-Caucasian, about 25 percent live with just one parent, and 75 percent have mothers who work. As a result they tend to be more tolerant of multiculturalism and internationalism than their parents.[11] They are ambitious, independent, and have a generally positive outlook on life. Although they are willing to work to get ahead, they also place a high value on volunteering and helping others. Most are pragmatic, like convenience, and are value oriented.

The marketing impact of Generation Y has been immense—and they haven't yet reached their peak income and spending years. These prosperous young people have hundreds of billions of dollars to spend—and spend they do. In the first three months of 2005, this group outspent all others in the United States. In addition to their own purchases, they have a major influence on what their parents buy.[12]

These technologically sophisticated consumers are the first to grow up with digital technology and the Internet. "They actually go online to be with each other," comments Melissa Payner, chief executive of Bluefly Inc., an online retailer. "It's a different kind of life."[13] By 2009, the youth market will spend an estimated $500 billion on high-tech gear, and companies are designing their products and ad pitches to attract this group. Cell phones and MP3 players are loaded with features and come in many color combinations, allowing Gen Yers to keep up with their peers yet express their individuality through their gadgets.[14] Their spending habits reflect their love of technology, so electronic commerce—for example, Web sites with online ordering capabilities, e-mail newsletters and sale announcements—becomes an important tool to reach them. The best marketing approaches position brands as cutting-edge, fashionable, and popular, but avoid the hard sell.

As the older members of Generation Y enter the work force and approach 30, they are catching the eye of other types of companies. Banks and credit card issuers have already targeted these eager-to-spend consumers. American Express, which for years considered older executives its primary market, is using a very different marketing strategy to court Gen Yers who use debit cards. The result is a new line of no-fee credit cards with award points, including city-specific cards. Its ads tout "the über-glam lifestyle," and the city cards offer points towards discounts at hip restaurants, bars, and other trendy local spots.[15]

Generation X Reaches Middle Age

Generation X
Americans born between 1964 and about 1977.

Generation X—people born between 1964 and 1977—consists of about 50 million consumers. Although they are highly educated, until recently they have been overshadowed by the very large Baby Boomer generation that preceded them. As the first GenXers turn 40, they are finding their place and entering the mainstream. In the process, they are exhibiting different characteristics than earlier generations.

It is the first generation of latchkey children—products of dual-career households or, in roughly half of the cases, of divorced or separated parents. This influences their decisions to marry and start families later than their parents. Family and friends, rather than the career success and wealth accumulation that drove their parents, come first. Bombarded by multiple media since their cradle days, Gen Xers are savvy and cynical consumers. "The Xers are the first generation that will not live as well as their parents," says one marketing researcher. They've lived through several rounds of corporate downsizings and spend cautiously, planning for retirement.[16]

As they move into their peak income years, however, they are buying more high-end items—an important trend for marketers to note. A 2005 survey revealed that Generation X now outspends Baby Boomers by 18 percent each year as they accumulate big-ticket items. Boomers have made their major purchases and are preparing to retire.[17]

© KRISTA KENNELL/ZUMA/CORBIS

Other types of retailers are also responding to the aging of Generation X. In 2005 Gap Inc. introduced a new store concept called Forth & Towne that targets the over-35 female shopper, an underserved market sector for the company and one that has grown in importance. Its four clothing lines are designed to be contemporary and fashionable while flattering changing figures that may no longer fit into trendier styles of stores like Gap and Banana Republic. The new brand will also emphasize customer service to win over customers.[18]

Prime Time for Baby Boomers and Beyond

Baby Boomers
Americans born between 1946 and 1964.

In 2006 the first **Baby Boomers**, born between 1946 and 1964, turned 60, and currently more than half are over 50. This powerful age demographic represents 27 percent of the U.S. population and 42 percent of all households, about 78 million people, and has significant spending power—more than $2 trillion a year. Because some Boomers are in their peak earning years while others are nearing retirement, it's useful to divide Boomers into two subgroups:

- *Younger Boomers* in their 40s and early 50s, whose spending is still directed by their children and have the highest average household incomes and spending of any group
- *Older Boomers*, ages 55 and above, most of whom are empty nesters. Because over-50 Boomers have fewer people per household, they actually spend about 30 percent more per household member than under-50 households.[19]

Shifting Priorities The two groups exhibit different spending patterns. For Younger Boomers, home and family are still priorities. Two-thirds of this group own their homes and allocate a larger share of their budgets to home-related expenditures than other ages. Spending on kids and financing their college educations is a high priority for Young Boomers.

Older Boomers have a life expectancy averaging 78 for men and 82 for women. They have money and are willing to spend it on their health, their comforts, leisure pursuits, and cars. Vespa, the Italian motor scooter company, discovered that 25 percent of its U.S. sales were to buyers 50 and older. "The Boomers are particularly attractive because they tend to have free time," says Paolo Timoni, CEO of Piaggio USA, Vespa's parent company. "They're less likely to be raising young children, and their careers are established and stable."[20]

CONCEPT *in Action*

As Baby Boomers race toward retirement age, businesses rush to develop products and services that connect with Boomers' lifestyle interests. For marketers, this means reaching an over-50s crowd that is going on 35. Fidelity Investments, for example, advertises financial services to Older Boomers who grew up rocking with Paul McCartney and the Beatles. *What makes the ex-Beatle the ultimate Boomer icon, and what does Fidelity hope to achieve by associating its services with the perennially youthful frontman?*

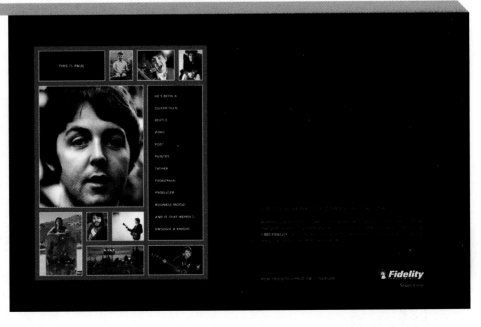

Marketers who chased after the youth market are now catering to the needs of this wealthy and diverse generation of consumers. Research from Home Depot indicates that those over 50 will account for half the growth in home-improvement spending as they remodel their existing homes and buy second homes for investment and retirement purposes. In response, the company introduced in-store kiosks in many of its Florida stores to provide information on making improvements that accommodate the needs of older people. Other industry sectors are courting the older consumer as well. Revlon recently launched a new line of makeup designed for women over 50 and called Vital Radiance. L'Oreal followed suit with its own products for older women.[21]

The automotive industry is also taking notice of the over-50 group, which makes more than half of all automobile purchases and will drive auto sales for the next 10 to 15 years. Boomers value quality finishes, safety features and luxury touches, and stylish rather than stodgy vehicles. Muscle cars such as the Ford Mustang are gaining in popularity. "They still are caught up in a car-culture mentality where a vehicle is really a primary means of defining who you are," says Art Spinella, president of CNW Marketing Research.[22]

Other industry sectors will be heavily influenced by the extended life spans and active lives of the Boomers and their parents. Many are pursuing new passions as they look forward to another 20 to 30 years of life, from hobbies to travel and even new careers. The aging population also places increased demands on health care and related services, and companies are already preparing to meet these needs.

Although many seniors live on fixed incomes, they are still a force in the marketplace. They like convenience and will pay for services, such as home delivery of groceries. About one-third of Safeway's online grocery-delivery service customers are over 50 years. The grocery chain has expanded this service to more states and improved the quality to meet Boomers' discerning tastes. Among the added features are custom-cut meats and the ability to include prescriptions and party platters with grocery deliveries.[23]

Not Over the Hill Yet

As the huge Baby Boomer generation ages, so does the workforce.[24] By 2010, 25 percent of all employees will be of retirement age—but the number of people who choose to retire at age 62 or 65 has been declining. Health advances make it possible for them to continue working if they so desire. As a result, this generation's extended work careers and rising productivity is expected to contribute 9 percent—about $3 trillion in today's dollars—to the economy by 2045. No longer is retirement an all-or-nothing proposition. As Exhibit 1.4 shows, a surprising number of Americans expect to work

---

Exhibit 1.4 > Reluctant Retirees

Surveys reveal the following attitudes toward aging and work among U.S. workers:

- The definition of "old age" depends on whom you ask: for the under-40 set, it begins at 58; from age 60 on, it starts at 74.
- 93 percent believe in allowing people to continue working as long as they can do the job satisfactorily.
- 46 percent like the option of shifting between work and recreation after age 65.
- 39 percent consider financial security a key factor to happiness as they age.
- 21 to 40 percent favor working part-time (depending on the survey).
- 19 percent do not want to work for pay anymore.
- 10 percent plan to work full-time.

Source: Adapted from information in Peter Coy, "Old. Smart. Productive." *Business Week*, June 27, 2005, http://www.businessweek.com (October 9, 2005). Copyright © 2005 by The McGraw-Hill Companies Inc. The McGraw-Hill Companies Inc.; and Sharon Linstedt, "Our Dreams for Retirement Often Include Another Job," *Buffalo News*, October 3, 2005, p. B7. Copyright © 2005 by The Buffalo News.

full- or part-time after "retirement," and most would work longer if phased retirement programs were available at their companies.

Financial reasons motivate some of these older workers, who worry that their longer life expectancies will mean outliving their money. Fewer companies offer traditional pension plans, so workers need to supplement social security benefits and retirement funds. For many, however, the satisfaction of working and feeling productive is more important than money alone. Some stay on with their former companies as consultants or with part-time schedules. But many are making major career changes in their 60s, in search of more satisfying work and even entrepreneurship, as we'll learn in Chapter 6.

In addition, the number of new entrants to the labor market is not sufficient to replace the retirees, creating resource shortages. Younger workers have different approaches and attitudes to work than their elders, as we'll discuss later in the chapter.

These converging dynamics create major challenges as companies must focus not only on recruiting employees to replace retiring workers and also track where employees fall in their career lifecycles, but to determine when, whether, and how to replace them. Many companies are developing special programs to retain older workers and benefit from their practical knowledge and problem-solving abilities:

- United Technologies Corp. offers flexible hours and an Employee Scholar Program to reimburse workers who take courses, regardless of age. The free tuition incentive has increased retention of the most motivated employees.
- Employers such as CVS and Home Depot actively seek out older workers because they are disciplined, reliable, and loyal. "They're doing their jobs, and they're doing them well," says Patty O'Connell, the head of human resources at People's Alliance Federal Credit Union in Hauppauge, New York.

When older employees do choose to retire, companies discover that they are taking with them vast amounts of knowledge that is difficult—if not impossible—to replace. The Managing Change box on page 46 describes how companies are planning for this new brain drain.

The Challenges of Diversity

America's growing ethnic diversity is having a profound impact on business. Minority populations, especially Hispanics and Asians, will drive 90 percent of the population growth in the United States between 1999 and 2050. By 2010 minorities will represent about 35 percent of the total U.S. population; by 2030, that figure will reach 42.5 percent, and by 2050, about half the population will be minority. Exhibit 1.5 on page 47 shows the current distribution of population groups in the United States, as well as the projections for 2030 and 2050.

Hispanics are the largest minority group, numbering about 41 million—14 percent of the total U.S. population—in 2004, followed by African Americans (39 million) and Asians (14 million). Minority population groups are also younger, in part because of immigration (discussed below), and higher birth rates. The median ages for all major minority groups except Asians is between 27 and 31 and is 34 for Asians, compared to 40 for whites.[25]

These age differences are creating another type of generation gap: The older generation is mostly white, while younger generations are more ethnically and racially diverse. By 2050, there will be more minorities under age 34 than whites. "(Age) 40 is a monumental dividing line," explains Brookings Institution demographer William Frey. "The white-dominated society that we had in the 1950s is being faded out." The younger age groups tend to be more Hispanic. In addition, people who are under 40 have grown up with diversity and are comfortable with our multicultural society.[26]

Along with their numbers, minorities' buying power is growing significantly as well. Minorities now control about $1.6 trillion in annual spending—up from about $541 billion in 1990, according to the Selig Center for Economic Growth at the

MANAGING CHANGE

Plugging the Brain Drain

At the National Energy Technology Laboratory in Morgantown, West Virginia, Hugh Guthrie is a full-time technical adviser to other chemical engineers. "My experience gives me a perspective which may not always be right but nearly always will be different," he says. "The greatest service I provide is in stimulating the thinking of people involved in a project." And at 86, Guthrie has lots of experience to share.

But what about the millions of workers who decide to retire, instead of staying on like Guthrie? Much of their collective knowledge will leave along with them and could be forever lost. A recent study revealed that almost half of the companies surveyed had no strategies for preserving essential technological, procedural, and practical knowledge, placing them at a significant competitive disadvantage.

"Most of American business is totally in denial," warns David DeLong, author of *Knowledge: Confronting the Threat of an Aging Workforce* and a leading researcher at MIT's AgeLab, "The situation is scary. People don't know what to do. But we can't give up just because it looks hard." Some recommended techniques include succession planning, mentoring initiatives, training and education, phased retirement programs, and creating a culture of retention that supports knowledge sharing.

"Companies are doing something they've never had to do at this level before—actually plan that migration and that transition of people, of knowledge, of information and networks," says Kathy Battistoni, a partner in Accenture's Human Performance Global Service. For example, Delta Airlines videotaped debriefings and exit interviews to preserve the expertise of the employees who took early retirement as part of a voluntary staff reduction program. It then used this information to train other employees.

Johnson & Johnson Co. (J&J), which has a strong culture supporting knowledge sharing and retention, is well prepared for the "brain drain." It documents effective operating procedures so that all employees can benefit. Teamwork facilitates knowledge transfer. "We work in concert with others on projects, so knowledge is shared rather than hoarded by any individual," explains Robert J. Darretta, chief financial officer at the drug and health care products corporation. Unlike companies where employees follow specialized career paths, J&J moves employees around to different departments every few years. This provides a pool of flexible generalists who can take jobs in various areas of the organization as the need arises.

Darretta emphasizes leadership development and succession planning in his finance organization. He and other J&J executives review key positions annually, ensuring that the department has well-trained employees ready to step in as vacancies occur. "You don't want knowledge to simply reside with the individual; you want knowledge to reside with the organization," he says "We make sure that knowledge is a consequence of the way we do things."[27]

Critical Thinking Questions

* What potential problems do companies need to address as large numbers of employees reach retirement age?
* You are a member of a task force that is developing knowledge transfer programs at a large financial services corporation. Describe two programs you would recommend. Would your recommendations differ, and how, if you worked at a large technology company? At a small retail business?

University of Georgia. By 2009, Hispanics will wield almost $1 trillion in spending power, an increase of 347 percent since 1990. By that same year, African Americans' spending will approach $965 billion, and Asians' spending power will have soared 347 percent since 1990, to $528 billion—far outpacing total U.S. growth in buying power for that period of 159 percent.[28]

More than ever, diversity is emerging as a priority goal for visionary leaders who embrace the incontestable fact that the United States is becoming a truly multicultural society. Marketers recognize that they must customize their products and promotional materials to each of these very different market segments. No longer can they assume that all minorities are concentrated in metropolitan areas—or that one strategy for a particular ethnic group will be effective in reaching all members of the same group. For example, advertising to Hispanics has proven to be very complex. Simply creating a Spanish language ad is not enough. Significant cultural differences characterize different segments of the Hispanic community. An ad designed to attract Mexican consumers may not be appropriate for Cubans or Puerto Ricans. Companies are also actively courting Hispanics. For example, cable television providers are offering more complete Spanish language channel line-ups.[29]

The Impact of Immigration

Part of the reason for the tremendous shift in American demographics is immigration. Each year more than 1 million newcomers enter the United States—about 15 million immigrants from 1990 to 2004. Today about 12 percent of the total population is foreign-born. The majority of the foreign-born population (53 percent) comes from Latin America, with 25 percent from Asia, 14 percent from Europe, and the remaining 8 percent from other regions, such as Africa and Oceania (Australia, New Zealand, and the Pacific island nations).[30]

Exhibit 1.5 > Our Changing Population: 2004 to 2050

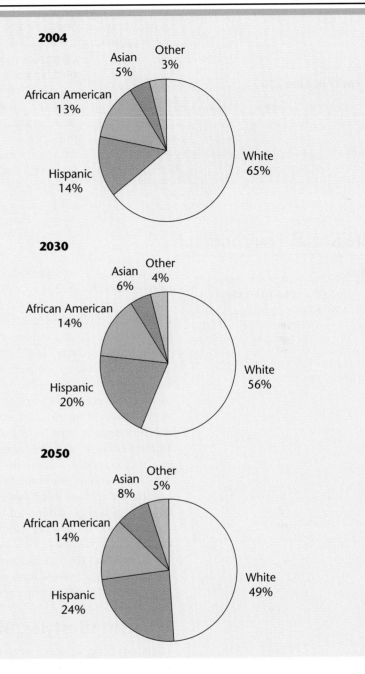

2004

Asian 5%
Other 3%
African American 13%
Hispanic 14%
White 65%

2030

Asian 6%
Other 4%
African American 14%
Hispanic 20%
White 56%

2050

Asian 8%
Other 5%
African American 14%
Hispanic 24%
White 49%

Source: "U.S. Interim Projections by Age, Sex, Race, and Hispanic Origin, 2004" *U.S. Census Bureau*, http://www.census.gov (October 9, 2005).

Immigration flows are influenced by many factors, especially the performance of the U.S. economy. When jobs are plentiful, immigration rises, as it did during the boom years at the end of the century. In both 1999 and 2000, 1.5 million people came to the United States. The rate dropped after 2001, when economic activity slowed. The largest single group comes from Mexico, which accounts for about one-third of the immigration flow.[31]

The United States is reaping the benefits of immigration. Immigrant entrepreneurs, from the corner grocer to the local builder, are creating jobs. Vibrant immigrant communities are revitalizing cities and older suburbs that would otherwise be suffering from a shrinking tax base. And the immigrants' links to their old countries are boosting U.S. exports to such fast-growing regions as Asia and Latin America.

High-tech industries, from semiconductors to biotechnology, depend on immigrant scientists, engineers, and entrepreneurs to remain competitive. In Silicon Valley, California, much of the technical workforce is foreign-born. The next generation of scientists and engineers will be dominated by immigrants. The number of native-born citizens getting science Ph.D.s has remained about the same, but the number of foreign-born students receiving science doctorates more than doubled between 1980 and 2005.

Until recently, immigrants tended to join their peers in large coastal cities and certain states. California, New York, Texas, Hawaii, New Mexico, and the District of Columbia already are "majority-minority" states, and Maryland, Mississippi, Georgia, New York, and Arizona currently have minority populations of about 40 percent. However, since 2001, many immigrants are seeking new places to call home, among them North Carolina and Iowa.[32]

concept check

Explain how Generation X, Generation Y, and Baby Boomers differ.

How is diversity changing the marketplace?

What is the impact of immigration on American businesses?

The Social Environment

5 **What current social factors have the greatest impact on business?**

Social change is perhaps the most difficult environmental factor for owners and managers to forecast, influence, or integrate into business plans. Social factors include our attitudes, values, and lifestyles. Attitudes include our beliefs about such varied topics as religion, family, and the role of government in providing social services. Whereas some attitudes have an indirect impact on business, others—for example, how we feel about work—directly affect businesses. Examples of values include honesty, job satisfaction, materialism, convenience, and simplicity. Lifestyles are the ways in which consumers and families live, use time, and spend money. Because such social factors are very subjective, they are often difficult to define and measure. They change as we move through different life stages. Recent college graduates may value job success most for several years until they establish their careers. Family often becomes their primary concern after they marry.

Social factors influence the products people buy, the prices they pay, the effectiveness of specific promotions, and how, where, and when people expect to purchase products. They are closely tied to and affected by demographics. For example, the living and spending patterns of the young single and empty nester lifestyles relate to those specific age groups. Young singles may spend a higher proportion of their income on entertainment, such as eating out, while empty nesters may travel more.

Companies that track customer attitudes, values, and interests have a competitive advantage. They can use their knowledge of what's in or out to develop goods and services that address changing consumer needs and desires.

Different Lifestyles, Different Choices

component lifestyle
A lifestyle made up of a complex set of interests, needs, and choices.

The lifestyles we choose have a significant impact on business decisions. If we choose the simple life as a way to reduce stress, we will buy less. If we choose a **component lifestyle**, one made up of a complex set of interests, needs, and choices, we become multidimensional rather than following a stereotype. Whereas in the past a person's profession—for instance, banker—defined that person's lifestyle, today a person can be a banker as well as a gourmet, fitness enthusiast, dedicated single parent, and conservationist—all at once. Each of these component lifestyles is associated with different goods and services and represents a unique market, increasing the complexity of consumers' buying habits. For example, this banker may respond to advertisements for cookware, wines, and exotic foods in magazines like *Bon Appétit* and *Gourmet*, and for mutual funds in business and finance magazines. She may buy Adidas equipment and special jogging outfits to suit her fitness needs and read *Runner's World* magazine, eat fast-food for lunch but drink French wine for dinner, own sophisticated photographic equipment but listen to a low-priced home stereo, and shop for hosiery at Wal-Mart and suits at Ann Taylor.

Today's fast paced lifestyles create a "poverty of time." Overworked, tired, and stressed out, we look for ways to gain control of our time. For example, more employees are asking for flextime and part-time schedules. On-site day care and fitness centers are popular employee benefits. Consumers place a high priority on convenience and healthier lifestyles—and some products meet both needs. Frozen dinners from Healthy Choice, Lean Cuisine, and South Beach Diet make it easy to stay on a low-fat diet. Recently Nabisco introduced 100-calorie "packages of cookies and chips to help calorie-counters limit their portions of snack foods." They were an immediate hit. "We live harried lives," says Stephanie Childs of the Grocery Manufacturers Association. "It's much easier to have somebody else count for you."[33]

Women in the Workforce

A contributing factor to the evolution of component lifestyles is the number of women in the workforce, including those in dual-income families, and the resulting increase in purchasing power. Approximately 60 percent of all females between 16 and 65 years old are now in the workforce, down from a high of 64.5 percent in 1999. Among women with children under 18, the figure is higher, about 70 percent. Currently both the husband and wife work in about half of all married couples, although about 67 percent of families with children under 18 have two incomes.[34] Today, there are almost 11 million women-owned businesses in the United States, and women are pursuing independent business ventures at twice the rate of men.[35]

The phenomenon of working women has probably had a greater effect on marketing than has any other social change. As women's earnings grow, so do their levels of expertise, experience, and authority. Working-age women are not the same group businesses targeted 30 years ago. They expect different things in life—from their jobs, from their spouses, and from the products and services they buy—and they want a say in major economic decisions. Trend expert Faith Popcorn believes that women influence or make 80 percent of all purchasing decisions. "If men and women are different (mentally), why do we market to them in the same way?" she asks. She adds that businesses must target their marketing to women and build relationships, regardless of the type of product they sell.[36] We'll return to this important idea of tailoring promotional strategies to different market segments in Part 4's marketing management chapters.

concept check

Briefly define the three factors that influence the social environment. Why are social changes the most difficult environmental factor to predict?

How do component lifestyles make it more difficult to predict a consumer's buying habits?

What social factor has had the greatest impact on business? Give an example of how a company has responded to this change.

CONCEPT *in Action*

The tremendous influx of women into the workforce has created a new class of female consumers with enormous purchasing power and unique lifestyle characteristics. Today's working women are busy multitaskers that must balance home, career, and personal needs—they are as preoccupied with home decorating and school supplies as with PDAs and personal fitness. *Why do companies that tailor their promotional messages directly to women gain a competitive advantage over those that don't?*

© PHOTODISC RED/GETTY IMAGES

Competition and the Global Environment

 6 How can businesses remain competitive in today's global marketplace?

The competitive and global environments are two critical and complex external elements that drive changes in the way companies conduct business. In recent years competition has become increasingly intense, and companies must work that much harder to maintain and grow their market share. With the growing interdependence of the world's economies, businesses must look beyond just domestic competition to the global marketplace.

Maintaining a Competitive Edge

productivity
The amount of goods and services one worker can produce.

Good planning and efficient use of resources have made American companies world-class competitors. American businesses are among the most productive and competitive in the world. During the 1990s many American businesses downsized—terminated or laid off employees—to reduce costs and increase efficiency. Personnel reductions can improve **productivity**, the amount of goods and services one worker can produce. When companies produce as many or more goods and services with fewer employees, productivity rises. Overall productivity in the United States has been rising steadily since 1995, with recent annual increases of about 4 percent for business and 5 percent for manufacturing.[37]

Another contributor to increased productivity is greater use of technology. For example, technological improvements in the U.S. retail and wholesale trade sectors have significantly boosted labor productivity, giving us a considerable lead over European competitors.[38] The relentless drive for efficiency has made many American firms leaders around the globe. Coca Cola, Procter & Gamble, Microsoft, Wal-Mart, McDonald's, and Exxon are truly world leaders in their fields. As we'll see in many examples in subsequent chapters, American firms of all sizes are just as effective in their markets against global competitors.

Companies also recognize that delivering excellent customer service and quality provides a significant competitive advantage and dramatically increases their chances of achieving their goals. As the Customer Satisfaction and Quality box explains, even an airline facing bankruptcy must continue to offer first-rate customer service.

When we speak of quality, we are not simply referring to product quality or service quality. We are also talking about having the highest quality personnel operations, financial operations, sales activities, and anything else with which the organization is involved. You'll learn more about quality programs in Chapter 11.

Taking the Global View

Although American companies lead the way in the world marketplace, one thing is certain—competition from domestic and foreign competitors is only going to get tougher. Currently the United States ranks second on the Growth Competitiveness Index compiled by the World Economic Forum (WEF). Exhibit 1.6 lists the countries ranking highest on the WEF's Growth Competitive Index, which considers such factors as productivity rates, exchange rates, technology, economic activity levels, and national policies and organizations that influence the competitive environment. The United States' technological superiority is a major factor in its ranking. Although the economies of China and India are growing rapidly, the WEF ranks them 49 and 50, respectively, based on high levels of government bureaucracy and the need for better infrastructure.[39]

exports
Goods and services sold outside a firm's domestic market.

gross domestic product (GDP)
The total market value of all final goods and services produced within a nation's borders in a year.

Agreements among nations and laws of individual countries have generally been supportive of global competition and trade. According to the World Trade Organization, world **exports** (goods and services sold outside a firm's domestic market) reached $11 trillion in 2004, an increase of 9 percent, and represented 20 percent of global output, or gross world product.[40] *Gross world product (GWP)* is the sum of all countries' **gross domestic product (GDP)**, which is the total market value of all final goods and services produced within a nation's borders in a year.[41]

CUSTOMER SATISFACTION AND QUALITY

Customer Service Still Flies at Delta

Passengers with reservations to fly on Delta Airlines were concerned to learn on September 14, 2005, that the U.S.'s third largest airline had filed for bankruptcy. Delta was not grounded, however, and its flights continued as scheduled in the near term. It joined three other major U.S. air carriers—United, US Airways, and Northwest—who had also filed bankruptcy as high fuel and labor costs and competition from low-cost carriers had cut deeply into their revenues. Soon after announcing its bankruptcy, Delta reported plans to downsize by up to 9,000 jobs, cut executive salaries, and reduce domestic flights. It also began to focus more heavily on international routes, such as Latin America and Europe, which provide higher passenger revenues. Yet one area that did not suffer cutbacks was customer service.

Customer service has become a key differentiator now that passengers can search the Internet for the lowest fares. Often the smallest price difference determines their choice. "Low fares may get customers on the plane the first time," says Lee Macenczak, executive vice president and chief customer service officer. "But it's service that's predictable, fast, and convenient that keeps them coming back. As a customer myself, when my service expectations are not met, I remember how I was treated more than what I received. This is what makes me return again."

Delta monitors customer attitudes and values to anticipate and then deliver the right services to meet travelers' needs. For example, passengers get very frustrated with flight delays. Delta gives employees the authority to make on-the-spot decisions to resolve problems. Other customer service initiatives include improving traffic flow at Delta's huge Atlanta hub ticketing area, increasing the number of self-service kiosks to shorten check-in lines, offering a selection of free snacks, and installing special phone lines in airports to connect passengers directly to customer service representatives. Its Web site, Delta.com (**http://www.delta.com**), has been upgraded and redesigned in line with customer requests for greater functionality and ease of use.

Customer service alone won't solve Delta's problems, of course. But listening to customers and doing what it takes to make it easier for them to fly Delta is a component of the airline's reorganization strategy. "Outstanding customer service has been Delta's hallmark for more than 75 years," Macenczak explains. "It's as important today as when we started out, if not more important, since customers have more travel choices than ever."[42]

Critical Thinking Questions
- Why has Delta continued to make customer service a priority despite financial constraints? Based on your own travel experiences, suggest other ways Delta can improve its customer service.
- You are a customer service manager for Delta Airlines. Develop a program to learn about customer perceptions of the airline and the service it provides. Why is it important to listen to customers?

Because global competition is fiercer than ever, businesses must be aware of competitors around the world as well as across town. Challenges to U.S. dominance are evident in many industries, from appliances to financial services. Korea's LG brand washers sit next to Whirlpool and Maytag. Branches of the London-based HSBC, which began in 1865 as the Hongkong Shanghai Banking Corporation, sit across the street from Bank of America's branches. With an international network of almost 10,000 offices in 77 countries, HSBC has adopted the slogan "the world's local bank."

Competition comes in a variety of forms. Not only do companies buy goods from and sell goods to other nations, but they also locate business operations, from sales offices to manufacturing facilities, in foreign countries to be near major markets,

Exhibit 1.6 > World Economic Forum's Growth Competitiveness Index, 2005

Rank	Country
1	Finland
2	United States
3	Sweden
4	Denmark
5	Taiwan
6	Singapore
7	Iceland
8	Switzerland
9	Norway
10	Australia
11	Netherlands
12	Japan
13	United Kingdom
14	Canada
15	Germany

Source: "Growth Competitiveness Index Rankings 2005 and 2004 Comparisons" *World Economic Forum* http://www.weforum.org. Copyright © World Economic Forum. All rights reserved. Reproduced by permission.

labor, and natural resources. Large U.S.-based multinational corporations have operations in many countries. For example, Procter & Gamble has operations in 80 countries and markets its 300 brands to consumers in over 160 countries. Today, BMW, Honda, Hyundai, Mercedes, Subaru, Toyota, and other foreign automotive firms manufacture more of their cars in the United States than they import, resulting in major savings in shipping costs. Toyota chose San Antonio, Texas, as the location for a huge plant to produce Tundra pickup trucks. "Texas is the biggest pickup market in the country, probably making it the biggest in the world, and to have a truck built by Texans can only make it better" says Toyota spokesman Dan Sieger.[43]

New countries are joining established ones as forces in the competitive marketplace. The economies of China and India are booming: China's GDP growth has been averaging 8 percent to 9 percent a year, and India is not far behind at 6 percent to 7 percent—compared to about 4 percent for the United States. Chinese companies are becoming major global competitors as economic reforms have unfolded. In addition, businesses must often seek out suppliers and contract with manufacturers and service providers (a process called *outsourcing*) from around the world to create world-class products. We will return to these and other topics relating to the global business environment in Chapter 4.

> **concept check**
>
> What is the relationship between productivity and competition, and how have U.S. companies improved productivity?
>
> Why must businesses consider both domestic and global markets critical to compete effectively today?
>
> Describe several different ways that companies compete in global markets.

The Impact of Technology

 7 **How can implementing technological advances help a firm reach its goals?**

technology
The application of science and engineering skills and knowledge to solve production and organizational problems.

The application of technology can stimulate growth under capitalism or any other economic system. **Technology** is the application of science and engineering skills and knowledge to solve production and organizational problems. New machines that improve productivity and reduce costs can be one of a firm's most valuable assets. Our ability as a nation to maintain and build wealth depends in large part on the speed and effectiveness with which we use technology. Technology can be used to invent and adapt more efficient machines to improve manufacturing productivity, to develop new products, and to process information and make it instantly available across the organization and to suppliers and customers.

High-Tech Tools

Technological advances are transforming every industry, from heavy manufacturing and farming to health care and financial services. For example, at the W. R. Johnson and Sons farm near the New Mexico–Mexico border, a new mechanical chili thinner run by one employee replaced 80 workers in the 600-acre chili fields. No jobs were lost when the new equipment arrived, however; workers were reassigned to other crops, which avoided chronic labor problems.[44]

American business is becoming better at using technology to create change. The development pipelines at many high-tech companies already showcase a whole new breed of miniaturized inventions with capabilities well beyond today's computer chips. These microelectromechanical systems (MEMS)—which combine sensors, motors, and digital smarts on a single sliver of silicon—are complete systems on a chip that can be manufactured at relatively low costs. MEMS are beginning to replace more expensive components in computer hardware, automobile engines, factory assembly lines, and dozens of other processes and products, so that companies can develop "smart" products that can sense, respond to, and control the environment.[45]

High-tech visionaries foresee far more radical developments in the next 15 to 20 years using nature's own creative machinery. In medicine, this means replacing the body's failing organs. In manufacturing, it means creating innovative, new devices that will save time and money. The coming wave of miniaturization and molecular

CONCEPT *in Action*

PDAs (personal digital assistants) are revolutionizing how, when, and where people work. Tops among them is Research in Motion's Black-Berry, a wireless handheld device used by over 3 million U.S. consumers to access phone, Web, e-mail, and other applications from any location—and all within the palms of their hands. The gadgets represent a giant leap forward in wireless innovation, combining hardware, software, and network technologies in a stylish, lightweight handheld. *How do BlackBerry's enhanced telecommunications features shatter the limitations of the traditional office?*

electronics—sometimes called "nanotechnology"—is taking shape at the intersection of chemistry, physics, biology, and electrical engineering. Among the new products coming from nanotechnology companies are a cochlear implant for the deaf and hearing-impaired, new types of drug delivery systems, and nano lithium-ion batteries. These are just the beginning of what could be another technological revolution.[46]

Digital Links

In today's digital age, information technology and telecommunications make it easy for workers to collaborate with colleagues across town or an ocean away. The Internet and other electronic networks have changed the way companies conduct their business and the way many people shop. Online communication, from e-mail to real-time chats, facilitates teamwork within companies and makes it easy to connect with suppliers, customers, and stockholders. Many large companies use the Internet to order materials and have special sites to keep suppliers updated about future requirements. By developing a Web site that describes its products, a small business can reach a global audience, 24 hours a day; with online ordering capabilities it becomes a global storefront.

Throughout this book we'll provide many other examples of how all types of businesses are using technology and the Internet in manufacturing, marketing, and finance. Chapter 16 focuses on information technology, and the online chapter, "Using the Internet for Business Success," which you'll find at **http://www.thomsonedu.com/introbusiness/gitman**, covers the world of electronic commerce and its impact on business.

concept check

What is technology, and how does its application benefit businesses?

List at least three examples of how technology can improve productivity for businesses.

What technology is having the most impact on business today, and in what ways is it changing how businesses operate?

Trends for Today's Managers

8 What major trends do managers face today?

Because organizations must identify trends and take appropriate actions to remain competitive, "trend spotting" has become one of the most valuable skills for today's managers. Sources for trends are plentiful. Many magazines, from business periodicals like *Fortune* and *Business Week* to general news magazines like *Time* and *Newsweek*, feature articles on trends. *Red Herring* (**http://www.redherring.com**) and *Wired* (**http://www.wired.com**) are among the best sources for technology-related trends.

Let's now look at several major business trends: the shift to a more human-centered work environment, the challenge of the multigenerational workforce, converging technologies, and the impact of technology on homeland security.

Focusing on the "Human" of Human Capital

More than ever we are experiencing a shift in focus—from the "capital" in human capital to the "human." At the center are employees and customers. For the past three decades, human capital was measured according to such "capital" variables as the cost of women in the workforce. Now human capital is being measured according to such "human" variables as fun in the workplace and valuing employees.

Businesses are focusing on what's right rather than what's wrong, on what works rather than what doesn't, on strengths rather than weaknesses, and on capitalizing on who you are rather than fixing who you are not. Having fun in the workplace may translate into something as readily seen as wearing costumes on Halloween or as readily experienced as a team-building Murder Mystery event, where staff members collaborate to solve the "who done it." The latter is an example of *action learning*, which is training to work on real business challenges. Another less obvious and more difficult to measure example of fun is a shared sense of "what a great place this is to work," where you work according to your strengths, do what you like to do, and are appreciated.

For example, Cisco Systems is consistently ranked as one of *Fortune's* "100 Best Companies to Work For." Employees applaud the company's fun-based initiatives, which include "nerd lunches" featuring technology discussions, special lunch menus such as movie-related dishes when the Academy Awards are given, and family movie nights with catered dinners.[47]

Appreciation, while certainly not a new concept in business, is getting more attention in the face of competition and high turnover. Complimenting employees, especially in writing, translates into friendlier customer service, employee retention, and company loyalty. At Wegmans Food Markets, for example, president Danny Wegman visits stores regularly, praising staffers for performing even routine tasks well.[48] (In Chapter 10 we'll learn more about why Wegmans consistently ranks among the top firms on the *Fortune* Best Companies list.)

The "Appreciative Inquiry" method is another way to enhance job satisfaction. Managers show employees that their ideas matter with such questions as, "What

CONCEPT *in Action*

The madcap days when tech firms lured young professionals with foosball tables and Frisbee courses faded with the bursting of the dot-com bubble. But the spirit of fun lives on, as many businesses sponsor offsite team-building retreats to improve worker morale and increase productivity. Some companies send workers on recreational getaways with ropes courses and whitewater rafting, but others incorporate fun with real-world problem-solving tasks. *How can workplace fun stimulate creativity and encourage teamwork among employees?*

© DIGITAL VISION/GETTY IMAGES

works well here? What would you like to see more of?" For example, the chief executive officer of CarMax, a chain of used car superstores, often asks his employees, "What are we doing that is stupid, unnecessary, or doesn't make sense?"[49]

Once working for a company, a good way to succeed is by continually enhancing your strengths or those of the people you manage. According to research conducted by Marcus Buckingham, senior vice president, The Gallup Organization, the best managers spend 80 percent of their time trying to amplify their people's strengths.[50] They are skilled in deep listening and value and encourage individual creativity. "The bottom line for a great manager is: Don't try to put in what God left out, try and draw out what God left in," Buckingham says, "Management isn't about transformation, it's about release . . . The judgment of the employee has value."[51]

Working with Kids Takes on a New Meaning

Today's workforce spans four generations. Recent college graduates (Generation Y), people in their 30s and 40s (Generation X), Baby Boomers (the first of which are of retirement age), and Traditionals (the generation that preceded the Baby Boomers) work together in most businesses in greater numbers than before. It's not unusual, therefore, to find a worker who is 50, 60, or even 70 working for a manager who is not yet 30. The largest group in the four-generation workforce is the Baby Boomers, at 41 percent, followed by Generation X (30 percent), Generation Y (21 percent), and Traditionals (8 percent).

Conflict across generations is not new; meeting the challenge of working with multiple generations is. Each generation brings its own attitudes and skill sets, as Exhibit 1.7 demonstrates. People in their 60s and 70s offer their vast experience of "what's worked in the past," which can upset those in their 20s and 30s who tend to be experimental, open to options, and greater risk takers. While this poses a challenge, experience and well-honed skills have value from which younger workers can benefit. Older workers increase their chances for successful relationships if they let go of the idea that they have the only answers. Well-suited to the faster pace of today's business environment, younger workers offer expertise about technology

---

Exhibit 1.7 > Generation Gaps

Generation Y	Generation X	Baby Boomers	Traditionals
• Quick studies • Multitaskers • Technologically literate • Want varied job responsibilities • Need better interpersonal skills • Expect to be asked for their opinions despite inexperience • Eager for coaching • Value exposure, recognition • Family takes priority over job • Prefer informal work environment and casual dress	• Personal career development favored over loyalty to one company • Fast learners • Comfortable with technology • Family takes priority over job • Willing to trade-off career advancement for more family time • Prefer informal work environment and casual dress	• Spent careers with one or just a few companies • Comfortable with management hierarchy and formal work environments • Paid their dues—and expect younger generations to do the same • Jobs take priority over families, although now finding themselves in sandwich generation with responsibility for children and aging parents • Keeping skills current a priority	• Spent careers with one or just a few companies • Known for their discipline, reliability, loyalty, respecting the system • Comfortable with management hierarchy and formal work environments • Paid their dues—and expect younger generations to do the same • Jobs take priority over families • Many working beyond traditional retirement age

---

and different ways of approaching issues from which older workers can benefit. The best managers will be ones that recognize the differences and use them to the company's advantage.[52]

Converging Industries

As the amount and types of information continue to escalate, businesses are discovering new ways to use information technology. The ability to convert video, audio, and data into digital formats easily transmitted by multiple media allows the convergence of what were once separate industries. The Center for the Study of Technology and Society defines *convergence* as the intersection of broadcasting, computers, telephones, video, and more. Examples include:

- Cell phones that also receive text messages and e-mail and surf the Internet.
- Internet and cable television companies offering long distance phone services at rates that often undercut traditional providers, and phone companies offering broadband Internet access
- Computers that are now multimedia broadcast centers, with radio broadcasts, videos of movies and television shows, and special Webcasts.

At the same time, the ability to send so much information digitally is overcrowding the current broadband transmission capabilities.[53]

This is just the beginning, however, as companies discover more ways to take advantage of convergence. AT&T (formerly SBC) and Verizon, the largest major telecommunications companies, are upgrading their networks to offer television services in direct competition with cable providers. In November 2005, cable operators Cox Communications, Time Warner, Comcast, and Advance/Newhouse responded with a joint venture with phone company Sprint Nextel to launch new services that bring together wireless, voice, and data services. Customers will be able to go to their cable company for both wired and wireless telecommunications. The service launched in seven pilot markets during the second half of 2006. Such mergers of phone, cable, Internet, and wireless technologies will allow consumers access to a variety of new services, such as having one voice mail for home and mobile phones, watching streaming video on cell phones, and more.[54]

Security Explosion

In response to the horrendous events of September 11, 2001, and subsequent terrorist attacks worldwide, the business of security has flourished. The Department of Home-

CONCEPT *in Action*

The ongoing terrorist threat has spurred the rapid growth of businesses specializing in transit security and surveillance. Airport security systems in particular have faced new challenges since 9/11, and both government and private-sector agencies have increased the development of technology designed to intercept potentially deadly attacks. *Do you think travelers are willing to surrender their privacy to the government to gain greater protection in public transit?*

© ASSOCIATED PRESS, AP

concept check

Describe strategies managers can use to improve the work environment and effectively manage a multi-generational workforce.

How will convergence affect competition in the telecommunications and media industries?

How have companies responded to the threat of global terrorism?

land Security, the military, and local law enforcement agencies have increased their budgets for improved technology to identify potential threats to the country. Private sector businesses, too, have increased their security-related spending. These steps create major opportunities for companies—from major corporations to small technology firms—to develop and share intelligence technology and other products such as surveillance devices and biometric identification methods. In-Q-Tel, formed in 1999 as a non-for-profit unit of the Central Intelligence Agency (CIA), provides funding for the development of intelligence-related technology and helps small companies bring their ideas to the attention of the appropriate federal agencies.[55]

Summary of Learning Goals

1 **How do businesses and not-for-profit organizations help create our standard of living, and what benefits does the study of business provide?**

Businesses attempt to earn a profit by providing goods and services desired by their customers. Not-for-profit organizations, though not striving for a profit, still deliver many needed services for our society. Our standard of living is measured by the output of goods and services. Thus, businesses and not-for-profit organizations help create our standard of living. The basic skills you gain by studying business will contribute to your success in any type of organization and make you a better consumer.

Businesses require the factors of production—natural resources, labor, capital, entrepreneurship, and knowledge—to produce goods and services and manage the business. The companies that will succeed in this new era will be those that learn fast, use knowledge effectively, and develop new insights.

2 **What are the primary features of the world's economic systems?**

Today there is a global trend toward capitalism. Capitalism, also known as the private enterprise system, is based on marketplace competition and private ownership of the factors of production. Competition leads to more diverse goods and services, keeps prices stable, and pushes businesses to become more efficient.

In a communist economy, the government owns virtually all resources, and economic decision making is done by central-government planning. Governments have generally moved away from communism because it is inefficient and delivers a low standard of living. Socialism is another centralized economic system in which the basic industries are owned by the government or by the private sector under strong government control. Other industries may be privately owned. The state is also somewhat influential in determining the goals of business, the prices and selection of products, and the rights of workers. Most national economies today are a mix of socialism and capitalism.

3 **What are the sectors of the business environment, and how do changes in the economic and political and legal environments influence business decisions?**

The external business environment consists of economic, political and legal, demographic, social, competitive, global, and technological sectors. Managers must understand how the environment changes and the impact of those changes on the business. When economic activity is strong, unemployment rates are low and income levels rise. The political environment is shaped by the amount of government intervention in business affairs, the types of laws it passes to regulate both domestic and foreign businesses, and the general political stability of a government.

4 **What demographic shifts are creating both challenges and new opportunities for business?**

Demographics, or the study of people's vital statistics, are central to many business decisions. Businesses today must develop different marketing approaches, goods, and services to meet the unique preferences of Generations X and Y and the Baby Boomers.

Because the population is growing older, businesses must develop strategies to manage a graying workforce. In addition, by 2010 minorities will represent 35 percent of the total U.S. population. Immigration has brought millions of new residents to the United States. Companies recognize the value of hiring a diverse workforce that reflects our society. Minorities' buying power has increased significantly as well, and companies are developing products and marketing campaigns that target different ethnic groups.

5 What current social factors have the greatest impact on business?

Social factors—our attitudes, values, and lifestyles—influence what, how, where, and when people purchase products. They are difficult to predict, define, and measure because they can be very subjective. They also change as people move through different life stages. Several social trends are currently influencing businesses. People of all ages have a broader range of interests, defying traditional consumer profiles. They also experience a "poverty of time" and seek ways to gain more control over their time. Changing gender roles have brought more women into the workforce. This development is increasing family incomes, heightening demand for time-saving goods and services, and changing family shopping patterns.

6 How can businesses remain competitive in today's global marketplace?

Exports continue to rise as a percentage of world gross domestic product. As countries open their markets, U.S. firms are finding greater opportunities abroad, but free trade also means that U.S. firms will face tougher competition at home. The economies of China and India are growing much faster than the United States. Nevertheless, efficient U.S. companies are meeting the global challenge by improving productivity and providing better customer service.

7 How can implementing technological advances help a firm reach its goals?

The application of technology by a firm can increase efficiency, lower costs, and help the firm grow by producing higher-quality goods and services. New technologies such as microelectromechanical systems and nanotechnology are changing the world as we know it. The Internet and other forms of electronic communication are changing how companies sell and communicate and how and what consumers buy. Technology enables continuous improvement.

8 What major trends do managers face today?

To remain competitive, businesses must identify and respond to trends in the various sectors of the business environment. Managers are taking a more people-centered approach and focusing on employee strengths to create a more satisfying work environment, as well as learning to manage a multigenerational workforce. Convergence of communications technologies creates business opportunities and increases competition. Spending on and development of security-related technology has increased since the September 11 terrorist attacks.

Key Terms

Baby Boomers 43	Generation X 42
business 30	Generation Y 41
capital 34	goods 30
capitalism 35	gross domestic product (GDP) 50
communism 36	knowledge 35
component lifestyle 48	knowledge workers 35
costs 31	labor 34
demography 41	mixed economies 37
economic systems 35	natural resources 34
entrepreneurs 34	not-for-profit organization 32
exports 50	productivity 50
factors of production 33	profit 31

quality of life   30
revenue   31
risk   31
services   30

socialism   37
standard of living   30
technology   52

Preparing for Tomorrow's Workplace: **SCANS**

1. **Team Activity** Form small groups with three or four members each. Each group should then go to a small business that has opened in the past two years. Ask the owner to describe (1) the most important lesson learned since opening the business, (2) unexpected pitfalls the business encountered, and (3) the information that helped the most prior to opening the business. (Interpersonal, Information, Systems)

2. Every country has its own customs, beliefs, and social trends. Talk to several international students at your college. Ask them to identify five customs that make doing business in their country different from the United States. (Interpersonal, Information)

3. **Team Activity** Create two teams of four people each. Have one side choose a communist economy and the other capitalism. Debate the proposition that "capitalism/communism is good for developing nations." (Interpersonal, Information)

4. Select a not-for-profit organization whose mission interests you. What are the organization's objectives? What resources does it need to achieve those goals? Select a for-profit business that provides a similar service and compare the differences between the two organizations. How does each use the factors of production? (Resources, Information, Systems)

5. Your local middle school is so bad that many of the parents are considering forming an alternative school for their children. Each parent is willing to put up $5,000 and to raise other funds to start the school. List and compare the advantages and disadvantages of organizing the school as a for-profit corporation or a not-for-profit corporation. Include parents, employees, and students in your comparisons. (Information, Systems)

6. **Team Activity** Form seven teams and assign each team one of the external business environment sectors (economic, political-legal, demographic, social, competition, global, and technology). Your boss, the president of Boeing Corp., has asked each team to report on the changes in that area of the external environment and how they will affect Boeing over the next five years. Each group should use the library, Internet, and other data sources to make its projections, with each member examining at least one data source. The team should then pool the data and prepare a report to present to the class. (Interpersonal, Resources, Information)

Ethics Activity

As top executives at Enron, Kenneth Lay and Jeffrey Skilling often were in the public eye, discussing the energy company's dynamic growth and climbing profits. Underneath the surface, however, the company was engaging in multiple schemes to manipulate financial data and inflate profits. In December 2001, Enron filed bankruptcy, sending shock waves through corporate America. Among the big losers were the company's employees, whose jobs and retirement savings disappeared, and investors in the company's stock, which became worthless. Many Enron executives, including Andrew Fastow, Enron's former chief financial officer, pleaded guilty to conspiracy and other charges and were sentenced to prison terms.

The trial of Kenneth Lay, Enron's former chief executive, began in Houston in January 2006. He was charged with multiple counts of fraud and conspiracy to deceive investors and employees about Enron's financial troubles. Lay continued to maintain that he was unaware of the crimes and placed the major blame on Fastow, saying he could not be expected to know everything that was happening at Enron. In late May 2006, a jury determined that Lay was guilty of all Enron-related charges in two trials. Skilling was found guilty on 19 of 28 counts. Before their scheduled sentencing, Kenneth Lay died at age 64 on July 5, 2006.

Using a Web search tool, locate articles about this topic and then write responses to the following questions. Be sure to support your arguments and cite your sources.

Ethical Dilemma: Do you agree with the verdict in the Lay and Skilling cases, and on what do you base your opinion? Was ignorance a valid defense for Kenneth Lay? How much can top executives be expected to know about the details of their companies' operations?

Sources: Alexei Barrionuevo, "Two Enron Chiefs Are Convicted in Fraud and Conspiracy Trial," *New York Times*, May 26, 2006, http://www.nytimes.com; Alexei Barrionuevo, "Witness Says Enron Hid Huge Loss From Investors," *New York Times*, February 3, 2006 p. C3(L); Greg Burns, "Enron Case Big Test of the 'Idiot Defense': Ex-Chief Vows to Say He Was Blind to Crimes," *Chicago Tribune*, January 2, 2006, p. 1; Anthony Bianco, "Ken Lay's Audacious Ignorance," *Business Week*, February 6, 2006, p. 58; Kate Murphy, "Ken Lay's Very Public Appeal," *Business Week Online*, December 15, 2005, http://www.businessweek.com.

Working the Net

1. Knowledge is an important asset in today's business environment. Go to the Intellectual Property Owners' site, **http://www.ipo.org/**. What is intellectual property? What kinds of information does the site provide, and how might a business use it? Be sure to provide an example.

2. How do you find what you need from among the billions of Web pages on the Internet? You'll need to use search engines and Internet directories to identify sites that contain the terms you enter in the search box. However, each search engine/directory takes a different approach to your query. Knowing how several present information and rank searches will help you decide which work best for your various information needs. In addition, there are meta-search engines that compile search results from several individual engines.

   From the following search and directory sites, choose two regular and one meta-search sites. (If you already have a favorite search engine, choose two new ones.) Research one of these topics from the chapter: GDP, Generation Y, or Baby Boomers. Compare your search experience, including the following: design of the opening screen, ease of use, presentation of results. Which made it easiest to find what you needed, and why? Do you prefer any of these to the search site you generally use?

   Altavista: **http://www.altavista.com**
   Excite: **http://www.excite.com**
   Google: **http://www.google.com**
   Teoma: **http://www.teoma.com**
   Yahoo!: **http://www.yahoo.com**
   Lycos: **http://www.lycos.com**
   MSN: **http://search.msn.com**
   Dogpile: **http://www.dogpile.com** (meta-search)
   Metacrawler: **http://www.metacrawler.com** (meta-search)
   All the Web: **http://www.alltheweb.com** (meta-search)

3. North Korea is probably the best example of communism in the world. Go to one of the Internet search engines listed in Activity 2 and look up the "North Korean economy." Write a report on the current economic conditions in North Korea.

4. The Bureau of Labor Statistics compiles demographic data. Visit its site, **http://www.bls.gov/bls/demographics.htm** and describe the different types of information it provides. What kinds of changes are likely to occur in the United States over the next 25 years? Click on Time Use and read about the American Time Use Survey, which shows how people spend their time. What trends can you identify?

5. Using the Internet search engine you liked best after your research in Activity 2, look up one of the topics discussed in the Social Influences section. Prepare a report summarizing your findings for the class. Also include the different categories of sites you visited and recommend the ones you found most helpful.

6. Go to either the *Red Herring* (**http://www.redherring.com**) or *Wired* (**http://www.wired.com**) site and research technology trends. Compile a list of three trends that sound most promising to you and describe them briefly. How will they affect businesses? What impact, if any, will they have on you personally?

Nordstrom Plays a New Tune

Long known for traditional quality clothing and unsurpassed customer service, upscale department store chain Nordstrom is "going interactive" as a way to reach younger customer demographics. "The goal," says Linda Finn, executive vice president for marketing at Nordstrom, "is to build the relationship with our multi-channel shopper, primarily women in their 30's and 40's who buy at the Nordstrom Web site, (**http://www.nordstrom.com**), as well as at the company's stores.

Nordstrom sent e-mail messages to 2.5 million customers, inviting them to download Nordstrom Silverscreen software from the Internet. Developed by Nordstrom's advertising agency Fallon Worldwide, the media player offers customers a branded entertainment channel, with video clips of popular music groups, a "mixing room" to create a personalized remix of the song with different fashions, merchandise previews, and, of course, opportunities to shop online. Customers who do not wish to download the software can enjoy a less elaborate version at a separate Silverscreen Web site. Those who download the software will receive messages alerting them to new content each month.

"We've been talking to some of Nordstrom's online users, who are very, very important customers, and they talk about how when they go online sometimes they shop and sometimes they look for fashion inspiration," said Rob White, president of Fallon. "This (campaign) isn't going to be judged on whether we sell a lot of tops over the Web for the holiday season," he said. "It will be judged on long-term feedback and bringing more people into Nordstrom stores, as well as (to) the Web site. And there is always the hope that Nordstrom customers will invite their friends and family to download the Silverscreen software too."

What began as a single downtown Seattle shoe store in 1901 has grown into a nationwide fashion specialty chain with renowned services, generous size ranges, and a selection of the finest apparel, shoes, and accessories for the entire family. And despite tapping into today's trends, Nordstrom never loses sight of its original philosophy which has remained unchanged since its establishment by John W. Nordstrom over 100 years ago: offer customers the best possible service, selection, quality, and value.

Critical Thinking Questions

- Why did Nordstrom take the dramatic step of designing a branded entertainment channel? What risks are there to this strategy?
- What impact is Nordstrom's new media player likely to have on customer demographics and sales?
- What unique philosophy and features have helped Nordstrom survive and thrive for more than 100 years in the notoriously difficult world of department store retailing?

Sources: Stuart Elliott, "Eager Retailers Can't Wait for Thanksgiving; They're Starting Christmas Now," *The New York Times,* November 12, 2005, http://www.nyt.com; Nordstrom corporate Web site, http://www.nordstrom.com (May 23, 2006); Nordstrom Silverscreen Web site, http://www.nordstromsilverscreen.com (November 12, 2005), John Vomhof Jr., "Fallon Takes Nordstrom to the Silverscreen," *Minneapolis/St. Paul Business Journal,* November 3, 2005, http://www.bizjournals.com/twincities.

Burton Snowboards Rides the Peak of Success

A 12-foot tall yeti, made from old catalogs, greets visitors to the 4,600-square-foot Burton Snowboards flagship retail store, which re-creates the feeling of a ski country lodge in the heart of Manhattan. The store features products from all Burton's brands, which in addition to its own boards now include several other company-owned lines of snowboards and accessories brands.

Burton Snowboards (**http://www.burton.com**), founded by Jake Burton in the winter of 1978–1979, is a successful, privately held manufacturer and distributor of snowboards, snowboarding accessories, and apparel. The Burton name is synonymous with premier-quality snowboarding products, and the Burton Way emphasizes "knowing and respecting the consumer while keeping one eye on the market and another on the product," both key components in the company's formula for success.

Burton played a pivotal role in the development of snowboarding as a sport, spearheading the effort to legalize snowboarding at ski resorts in the 1980s. "While other companies were saying 'our boards are great,' we were saying 'snowboarding is great,'" says Jake Burton. By focusing on the sport, Burton Snowboards helped create a growth market for snowboarding equipment. Traditionally, snowboarding appealed to males in their teens and early 20s. Now the market includes middle-aged enthusiasts and women, who buy almost half the snowboards sold. "We are developing more women's-specific merchandise, including boards and boots that are not just scaled-down versions of the men's," says Laurent Potdevin, Burton's president. Women's products now account for about 30 percent of the company's estimated $350 million annual sales. Jake Burton also founded Chill, a not-for-profit organization that brings snowboarding to kids who otherwise wouldn't have the opportunity.

Will the Burton Way enable Burton Snowboards to continue being successful as a privately held company? Jake Burton thinks so as he continues to acquire new brands to build the business and sponsors teams to advance the sport.

Critical Thinking Questions

Using information from the case and the video, answer the following critical thinking questions:

- Describe some of the key external environmental conditions that are influencing Burton Snowboards.
- How does the Burton Way address the environmental factors identified in question 1?
- Has Burton been able to shape the external environment in which it operates? Cite specific examples that support your answer.

Sources: Adapted from material in the video: "A Case Study in the Business Environment: Burton Snowboards" and Burton Snowboards corporate Web site, http://www.burton.com (May 23, 2006); Alex Kuczynski, "Preparing for Snow In the Ski-Free Zone," *New York Times*, October 27, 2005, p. G4; "Snowboarders Drop In and Take Off," *Concord Monitor*, February 27, 2005, p. C6; and Reed Tucker, "The 25 People We Envy Most: Jake Burton," *Fortune*, October 17, 2005, p. 152.

Hot Links Address Book

Interested in the current status of companies mentioned in our book's examples? Get business headlines, reports on individual businesses, and industry overviews at Hoover's, Inc., http://www.hoovers.com

Knowledge gives businesses a competitive edge. Brint.com, a business technology portal, offers insight into how companies are turning themselves into knowledge-based organizations, http://www.brint.com

Be inspired by reading stories of up-and-coming entrepreneurs in *Entrepreneur* magazine, http://www.entrepreneur.com

What makes a company good to work for or most admired? Find out by checking *Fortune's* special lists at http://www.fortune.com

Which country has the largest GDP? the most people? The answer is at http://www.zurich-base-line.com

Get the scoop on the latest technology trends affecting our lives from News.com, CNET's news portal at http://www.news.com; for product reviews, how-tos, and price comparisons, visit its sister site http://cnet.com

Fast Company bills itself as a magazine for a new, bold generation of businesses. Find out how businesses are approaching the future at http://www.fastcompany.com

CHAPTER 2

Understanding Evolving Economic Systems and Competition

Learning Goals

After reading this chapter, you should be able to answer these questions:

1 What is economics, and how are the three sectors of the economy linked?

2 How do economic growth, full employment, and price stability indicate a nation's economic health?

3 What is inflation, how is it measured, and what causes it?

4 How does the government use monetary policy and fiscal policy to achieve its macroeconomic goals?

5 What are the basic microeconomic concepts of demand and supply, and how do they establish prices?

6 What are the four types of market structure?

7 Which trends are reshaping the micro- and macroeconomic environments and the competitive arena?

Exploring Business Careers
Horst Köhler
International Monetary Fund

Imagine you are considering a large purchase—a new car or even your first house—but you do not have the money to pay for it up front. What will you do? Most likely, you will go to the bank to take out a loan. Now, imagine you are the leader of a country. You wish to implement programs to improve the quality of life of your citizens. Where do you turn?

Horst Köhler and the International Monetary Fund (IMF) may provide the answer. The IMF may not be a traditional bank as you think of one used for personal banking, but many of its functions are similar to those of personal banks. As Köhler, managing director of the IMF from 2000 until 2005, describes it, "The major goals of the IMF are, first, to provide financial stability in the international financial system and, second, to make a contribution to the international effort to fight poverty, which is far too high."

To achieve that second goal, the IMF established a program to assist developing countries. The program was designed to provide large loans to the developing countries, which they could use to foster growth— similar to the bank that provides you a loan for your car or house purchase discussed previously. Although the loans were intended to build a country's infrastructure (roads, harbors, airports, utility companies, etc.), the program came under criticism in the 1990s when it was discovered that as little as 30 percent of the money actually was used as intended. The rest was either embezzled or squandered. Borrowing countries were still responsible for the interest and repayment of the loans, so their economic burdens only increased.

Köhler became managing director of the IMF on May 1, 2000, and immediately sought to address these challenges. One of the most respected people in the field, he came to the job with experience as the president of the European Bank for Reconstruction and Development, the president of the German Savings Bank Association, and Germany's deputy minister of finance. Köhler saw an opportunity to correct the problems of the IMF's program to assist developing countries. He instituted a new Poverty Elimination program to concentrate more of the IMF's efforts on humanitarian issues, focusing on the people behind the economy. For this to be successful, though, he knew that the illegal uses of the loan money needed to stop. He insisted on the development of controls to guarantee that the monies were used as intended. In addition, he felt that, along with providing money, the IMF needed to provide training to recipient countries to teach budgeting and fiscal responsibility. In this way, the IMF would be able to greatly influence the economic systems of countries in crisis, creating stability, and, eventually, the potential for growth and entrance into the international economic marketplace.

With the implementation of these policies, Köhler and the IMF have seen great success in developing countries around the world. One such example, Tanzania, set the ambitious goal of cutting the poverty rate from 38 percent to less than 24 percent by 2010. Currently, Tanzania is ahead of schedule and provides the model for other countries looking to plot a course out of poverty.

By examining economic systems, both at the macroeconomic level—how the economy works as a whole—and at the microeconomic level—individual parts of the economy, such as businesses and consumers, this chapter illustrates the forces that the IMF attempts to control through their economic policies and programs.

economic system
The combination of policies, laws, and choices made by a nation's government to establish the systems that determine what goods and services are produced and how they are allocated.

A business's success depends in part on the economic systems of the countries where it is located and where its sells its products. As we learned in Chapter 1, a nation's **economic system** is the combination of policies, laws, and choices made by its government to establish the systems that determine what goods and services are produced and how they are allocated. Capitalism and planned economies, which we discussed in Chapter 1, are examples of economic systems. If you live in the United States and invent a new type of portable music player, you have the freedom to manufacture and market it. Your success or failure will be determined by several factors: Does it fill a customer need, is it priced correctly, and how much competition is there for the product? In a planned economy, however, you would have to get approval from government bureaucrats to build your product. Historically, planned economies with their high degree of control have done a much worse job of stimulating economic growth and creating a higher standard of living for their citizens than capitalist economies have.

Economics is an analytical science that will help you understand the world around you. As you study this chapter, remember that economics is not something you should learn for an exam and then forget. It can help you be more imaginative and insightful in everyday life. You will understand why prices are going up or down, when interest rates will fall, and when and why the unemployment rate will fall. A knowledge of basic economic concepts can help you decide whether to change jobs (and how much money to ask for) and whether to buy a car now or wait until next year. When you hear that Ford Motor Co. has 115 days of inventory, your understanding of the forces of supply and demand will tell you that now may be the time to buy that new car.

Similarly, economics will help you become a better-informed citizen. Almost every political issue is, in some way, grounded in economic concepts. Economics can also help you understand what is happening in other countries and raise your awareness of opportunities in those countries. As more countries have moved away from communist economies, American and foreign multinational firms are taking advantage of ground-floor investment opportunities.

This chapter will help you understand how economies provide jobs for workers and a competitive environment for businesses to create and deliver products to consumers. You will also learn how governments attempt to influence economic activity through policies such as lowering or raising taxes. Next, we discuss how supply and demand determine prices for goods and services and free-market competition. We conclude by examining trends in evolving economic systems and competition.

How Business and Economics Work

 What is economics, and how are the three sectors of the economy linked?

economics
The study of how a society uses scarce resources to produce and distribute goods and services.

Economics is the study of how a society uses scarce resources to produce and distribute goods and services. The resources of a person, a firm, or a nation are limited. Hence, economics is the study of choices—what people, firms, or nations choose from among the available resources. Every economy is concerned with what types and amounts of goods and services should be produced, how they should be produced, and for whom. These decisions are made by the marketplace, the government, or both. In the United States the government and the free-market system together guide the economy.

You probably know more about economics than you realize. Every day many news stories deal with economic matters: a union wins wage increases at General Motors; the Federal Reserve Board lowers interest rates; Wall Street has a record day; the president proposes a cut in income taxes; consumer spending rises as the economy grows; or retail prices are on the rise, to mention just a few examples.

CONCEPT *in Action*

The successful introduction of the 787 Dreamliner by American aerospace giant Boeing demonstrates that it pays to keep an eye on economic trends. Made from lightweight composites, the jet aircraft's ultraefficient design reduces fuel consumption by 20 percent per flight. The timing couldn't be better for Boeing's breakthrough design, as airlines overburdened by rising energy prices are in desperate need of cost-saving solutions. *How does the economy affect the types of goods and services that are produced?*

Macroeconomics and Microeconomics

The state of the economy affects both people and businesses. How you spend your money (or save it) is a personal economic decision. Whether you continue in school and whether you work part-time are also economic decisions. Every business also operates within the economy. Based on their economic expectations, businesses decide what products to produce, how to price them, how many people to employ, how much to pay these employees, how much to expand the business, and so on.

Economics has two main subareas. **Macroeconomics** is the study of the economy as a whole. It looks at *aggregate* data, data for large groups of people, companies, or products considered as a whole. In contrast, **microeconomics** focuses on individual parts of the economy, such as households or firms.

Both *macroeconomics* and *microeconomics* offer a valuable outlook on the economy. For example, Ford might use both to decide whether to introduce a new line of cars. The company would consider such macroeconomic factors as the national level of personal income, the unemployment rate, interest rates, fuel costs, and the national level of sales of new cars. From a microeconomic viewpoint, Ford would judge consumer demand for new cars versus the existing supply, competing models, labor and material costs and availability, and current prices and sales incentives.

macroeconomics
The subarea of economics that focuses on the economy as a whole by looking at aggregate data for large groups of people, companies, or products.

microeconomics
The subarea of economics that focuses on individual parts of the economy such as households or firms.

Economics as a Circular Flow

Another way to see how the sectors of the economy interact is to examine the **circular flow** of inputs and outputs among households, businesses, and governments as shown in Exhibit 2.1. Let's review the exchanges by following the red circle around the inside of the diagram. Households provide inputs (natural resources, labor, capital, entrepreneurship knowledge) to businesses, which convert these inputs into outputs (goods and services) for consumers. In return, households receive income from rent, wages, interest, and ownership profits (blue circle). Businesses receive revenue from consumer purchases of goods and services.

The other important exchange in Exhibit 2.1 takes place between governments (federal, state, and local) and both households and businesses. Governments supply many types of publicly provided goods and services (highways, schools, police, courts,

circular flow
The movement of inputs and outputs among households, businesses, and governments; a way of showing how the sectors of the economy interact.

Exhibit 2.1 > Economics as a Circular Flow

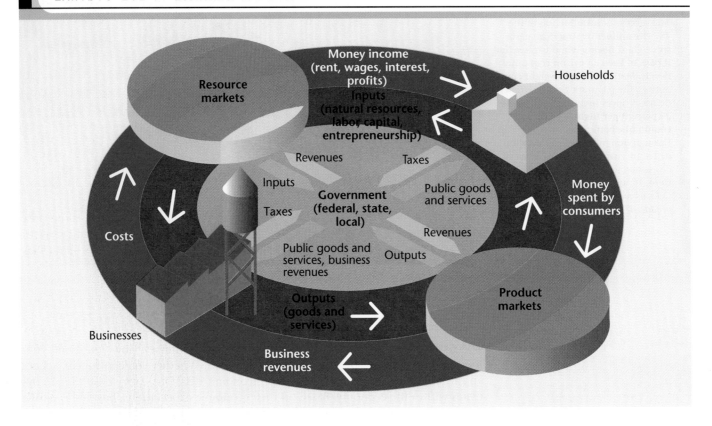

Resource markets

Money income (rent, wages, interest, profits)

Households

Inputs (natural resources, labor capital, entrepreneurship)

Revenues   Taxes

Inputs

Public goods and services

Taxes

Government (federal, state, local)

Money spent by consumers

Costs

Public goods and services, business revenues

Outputs

Revenues

Outputs (goods and services)

Product markets

Businesses

Business revenues

health services, unemployment insurance, Social Security) that benefit consumers and businesses. Government purchases from businesses also contribute to business revenues. When a construction firm repairs a local stretch of state highway, for example, government pays for the work. As the diagram shows, government receives taxes from individuals and businesses to complete the flow.

Changes in one flow affect the others. If government raises taxes, households have less to spend on goods and services. Lower consumer spending causes businesses to reduce production, and economic activity declines; unemployment may rise. In contrast, cutting taxes can stimulate economic activity. Keep the circular flow in mind as we continue our study of economics. The way economic sectors interact will become more evident as we explore macroeconomics and microeconomics.

concept check

What is economics, and how can you benefit from understanding basic economic concepts?

What is the difference between macroeconomics and microeconomics?

How do resources flow among the household, business, and government sectors?

Macroeconomics: The Big Picture

2 **How do economic growth, full employment, and price stability indicate a nation's economic health?**

Have you ever looked at CNN's Headline News on the Internet or turned on the radio or television and heard something like, "Today the Labor Department reported that for the second straight month unemployment declined"? Statements like this are macroeconomic news. Understanding the national economy and how changes in government policies affect households and businesses is a good place to begin our study of economics.

Let's look first at macroeconomic goals and how they can be met. The United States and most other countries have three main macroeconomic goals: economic growth, full employment, and price stability. A nation's economic well-being depends on carefully defining these goals and choosing the best economic policies for achieving them.

Striving for Economic Growth

Perhaps the most important way to judge a nation's economic health is to look at its production of goods and services. The more the nation produces, the higher its standard of living. An increase in a nation's output of goods and services is **economic growth**.

Economic growth is usually a good thing, but it also has a bad side. Increased production yields more pollution. Growth may strain public facilities, such as roads, electricity, schools, and hospitals. Thus, the government tries to apply economic policies that will keep growth to a level that does not reduce the quality of life.

As we saw in Chapter 1, the most basic measure of economic growth is the *gross domestic product (GDP)*. GDP is the total market value of all final goods and services produced within a nation's borders each year. The Bureau of Labor Statistics publishes quarterly GDP figures that can be used to compare trends in national output. When GDP rises, the economy is growing.

The *rate* of growth in real GDP (GDP adjusted for inflation) is also important. Recently, the U.S. economy has been growing at between 4 percent and 5 percent annually, up from just 2 percent in 2001. This growth rate has meant a steady increase in output of goods and services and relatively low unemployment. When the growth rate slides toward zero, the economy begins to stagnate and decline.

One country that continues to grow more rapidly than most is China. As we learned in Chapter 1, China's GDP has been growing at 8 to 9 percent per year. Today there are few things in the global marketplace that are not or cannot be made in China. The primary contributor to China's rapid growth has been technology. For example, most laptop computers are now produced in China, as the Expanding Around the Globe box on the next page explains.

The level of economic activity is constantly changing. These upward and downward changes are called **business cycles**. Business cycles vary in length, in how high or low the economy moves, and in how much the economy is affected. Changes in GDP trace the patterns as economic activity expands and contracts. An increase in business activity results in rising output, income, employment, and prices. Eventually,

economic growth
An increase in a nation's output of goods and services.

business cycles
Upward and downward changes in the level of economic activity.

CONCEPT *in Action*

In recent years, a meteoric rise in new home construction has played an important role in the growing U.S. economy. But as long-term interest rates bounce off 40-year lows and house prices retreat from frenzied highs, many analysts predict a cooldown in the market or even a bursting of the housing bubble. *What kinds of businesses have benefited from the recent housing boom, and how might these be affected by an economic slowdown?*

Your Laptop: Citizen of the World

Your new laptop computer has already traveled across the world—before you even open the box! Probably assembled in China by a Taiwanese company, it contains parts from many countries. The power supply may have come from China, the microprocessor from the United States, the hard drive and display from Japan, and the memory chips from South Korea. The graphics processor was probably designed in the United States—but manufactured in Taiwan.

Laptops, the best selling segment of the computer industry, are a good example of how companies and countries cooperate in today's global economic environment. Taiwanese companies manufacture 80 percent of the world's laptops, counting major U.S. manufacturers among their customers. Dell, Apple, Gateway, and Acer outsource 100 percent of their laptop production (Dell does final assembly in its own offshore factories), and Hewlett-Packard outsources 95 percent. Japanese companies such as NEC, Sony, and Toshiba also outsource, but to a lesser degree—between 35 percent and 60 percent.

Moving laptop production offshore is not a new strategy for U.S. computer companies, who needed to reduce costs and find more efficient production methods to stay competitive. Until the 1990s, many laptops were assembled in Japan and Singapore. In the 1990s, Taiwanese firms became the major recipients of U.S. business because of their lower labor costs and high quality.

The rising demand for laptops brought new companies into the market. Although total industry revenues are still rising due to higher demand, profits on laptops have fallen sharply. Low-cost-producers such as Acer and Averatec are willing to accept low profit margins to gain market share. With increased competition came sharply lower prices: between 2000 and 2005, the average price dropped 50 percent, from $2,100 to $1,050. International Data Corp. (IDC) expects prices will drop even further—as the result of high demand from price-sensitive Chinese consumers—to about $700 by 2008.

To stay competitive despite continuing cost pressures, most Taiwanese contract manufacturers shifted their production facilities to China after Taiwan's government lifted a ban on manufacturing in China in 2001. Quanta, the world's largest laptop manufacturer, employs 20,000 workers at its factory complex in Shanghai, China. Even though revenues increased 400 percent from 1999–2004, profit margins fell from 12.2 percent to 3.6 percent in that period.

Today China assembles 68 percent of the world's laptops, followed by Taiwan with 17 percent, and Japan with 8 percent. The Chinese government recognizes the importance of foreign investment to its economic future, especially in technology, and is encouraging companies to locate production facilities there. Producers of hard drives, displays, memory chips, and other components are already setting up shop in China.[1]

Critical Thinking Questions

- What are the benefits and disadvantages to U.S. computer companies of using offshore contract manufacturers to produce their laptops? Are there any risks in this strategy?
- How would you describe the market structure of the laptop industry (see the section "Competing in a Free Market" later in this chapter), and why?

---

recession
A decline in GDP that lasts for at least two consecutive quarters.

these all peak, and output, income, and employment decline. A decline in GDP that lasts for two consecutive quarters (each a three-month period) is called a recession. It is followed by a recovery period when economic activity once again increases. The most recent recession was in 2001 and 2002.

Businesses must monitor and react to the changing phases of business cycles. When the economy is growing, companies often have a difficult time hiring good employees and finding scarce supplies and raw materials. When a recession hits, many firms find they have more capacity than the demand for their goods and services requires. During the recession of the early 1990s, many firms operated at 75 percent or less of their capacity. When plants use only part of their capacity, they operate inefficiently and have higher costs per unit produced. Let's say that Mars Corp. has a huge plant with large, expensive machines that can produce one million Milky Way candy bars a day, but because of a recession Mars can sell only half a million candy bars a day. Producing Milky Ways at 50 percent capacity does not efficiently utilize Mars's investment in the plant and equipment.

Keeping People on the Job

full employment
The condition when all people who want to work and can work have jobs.

Another macroeconomic goal is **full employment**, or having jobs for all who want to and can work. Full employment doesn't actually mean 100 percent employment. Some people choose not to work for personal reasons (attending school, raising children) or are temporarily unemployed while they wait to start a new job. Thus, the government defines full employment as the situation when about 94 to 96 percent of those available to work actually have jobs. During the early 2000s, the economy operated at less than full employment.

Maintaining low unemployment levels is of concern not just to the United States but also to countries around the world. A contributing factor to the riots in France in the fall of 2005 was extremely high youth unemployment. The French government has made jobless and health benefits a higher priority than job creation. As a result, almost 22 percent of French youths under 25 were unemployed, compared to 13 percent in the United States and 11 percent in Great Britain. When jobs are limited and competition for jobs intense, discrimination is more likely to occur. One 21-year-old rioter of Moroccan origin described his life as, "Violence, unemployment, discrimination." Large numbers of idle youth, discontented and with no productive outlets for their energy, were easily angered and willing participate in destructive activities.[2]

Some economists point to the very different situation in the United States, where economic growth has contributed to low unemployment. Young workers get to know people of other races and ethnicities in the workplace, reducing the barriers between them and promoting tolerance and understanding.[3]

Measuring Unemployment

unemployment rate
The percentage of the total labor force that is not working, but is *actively looking for work*.

To determine how close we are to full employment, the government measures the **unemployment rate**. This rate indicates the percentage of the total labor force that is not working but is *actively looking for work*. It excludes "discouraged workers," those not seeking jobs because they think no one will hire them. Each month the Department of Labor releases statistics on employment. These figures help us understand how well the economy is doing. In the past two decades, unemployment rose as high as 9.7 percent in 1982, which was a recession year. It then declined steadily through the remainder of the 1980s and most of the 1990s. In 2000, the rate fell to under 4 percent, which was the lowest rate in almost 30 years, but the 2001–2002 recession drove unemployment to over 6 percent. Unemployment then declined steadily and was 4.7 percent in April 2006.

Types of Unemployment

Economists classify unemployment into four types: frictional, structural, cyclical, and seasonal. The categories are of small consolation to someone who is unemployed, but they help economists understand the problem of unemployment in our economy.

frictional unemployment
Short-term unemployment that is not related to the business cycle.

Frictional unemployment is short-term unemployment that is not related to the business cycle. It includes people who are unemployed while waiting to start a better job, those who are reentering the job market, and those entering for the first time such as new college graduates. This type of unemployment is always present and has little impact on the economy.

structural unemployment
Unemployment that is caused by a mismatch between available jobs and the skills of available workers in an industry or region; not related to the business cycle.

Structural unemployment is also unrelated to the business cycle but is involuntary. It is caused by a mismatch between available jobs and the skills of available workers in an industry or a region. For example, if the birthrate declines, fewer

CONCEPT *in Action*

The labor market's rebound after 9/11 surprised many observers, especially since challenges ranging from political instability and global competition to hurricanes and unionization have been ongoing. Yet despite 10-year lows in the U.S. unemployment rate, not all industries have fared well. Homebuilding, energy, and Internet firms have thrived in recent years, but U.S. automotive, newspaper, and airline businesses continue to announce layoffs. *What type of unemployment is common to slumping industries?*

teachers will be needed. Or the available workers in an area may lack the skills that employers want. Retraining and skill-building programs are often required to reduce structural unemployment.

cyclical unemployment
Unemployment that occurs when a downturn in the business cycle reduces the demand for labor throughout the economy.

Cyclical unemployment, as the name implies, occurs when a downturn in the business cycle reduces the demand for labor throughout the economy. In a long recession, cyclical unemployment is widespread, and even people with good job skills can't find jobs. The government can partly counteract cyclical unemployment with programs that boost the economy.

In the past, cyclical unemployment affected mainly less skilled workers and those in heavy manufacturing. Typically, they would be rehired when economic growth increased. Since the 1990s, however, competition has forced many American companies to downsize so they can survive in the global marketplace. These job reductions affected workers in all categories, including middle management. Firms continue to reevaluate workforce requirements and downsize to stay competitive with Asian, European, and other U.S. firms. Together the Big 3 U.S. automotive manufacturers have slashed 100,000 hourly and salaried workers from their payrolls since 2000—40,000 positions at Chrysler alone. In 2006, Ford Motor Company planned to cut almost 7,000 white-collar jobs, over 15 percent of its salaried workforce in North America. The announcement of the downsizing and other cost-reduction strategies came after Ford posted major losses in 2005. "The best of the competition is more competitive than we are on quality and costs, more efficient than us in their operations, and they're achieving market-share growth and sizable profitability all at the same time," said Mark Fields, Ford's executive vice president for the Americas. "We must do the same."[4]

seasonal unemployment
Unemployment that occurs during specific seasons in certain industries.

The last type is **seasonal unemployment**, which occurs during specific seasons in certain industries. Employees subject to seasonal unemployment include retail workers hired for the Christmas buying season, lettuce pickers in California, and restaurant employees in Aspen during the summer.

Keeping Prices Steady

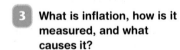

3 What is inflation, how is it measured, and what causes it?

The third macroeconomic goal is to keep overall prices for goods and services fairly steady. The situation in which the average of all prices of goods and services is rising is called **inflation**. Inflation's higher prices reduce **purchasing power**, the value of what money can buy. Purchasing power is a function of two things: inflation and income. If incomes rise at the same rate as inflation, there is no change in purchasing power. If prices go up but income doesn't rise or rises at a slower rate, a given amount of income buys less and purchasing power falls. For example, if the price of a basket of groceries rises from $30 to $40 but your salary remains the same, you can buy only 75 percent as many groceries ($30 ÷ $40) for $30. Your purchasing power declines by 25 percent ($10 ÷ $40). If incomes rise at a rate faster than inflation, then purchasing power increases! So you can, in fact, have rising purchasing power even if inflation is increasing. Typically, however, inflation rises faster than incomes, leading to a decrease in purchasing power.

inflation
The situation in which the average of all prices of goods and services is rising.

purchasing power
The value of what money can buy.

Inflation affects both personal and business decisions. When prices are rising, people tend to spend more—before their purchasing power declines further. Businesses that expect inflation often increase their supplies, and people often speed up planned purchases of cars and major appliances.

From the late 1990s to 2004, inflation in the United States was in the 1.5 to 4 percent range; for 2005, it was 3.4 percent. Because of a spike in the energy index, which increased 16.6 percent in both 2004 and 2005, the inflation rate for the first four months of 2006 rose to 5.1 percent.

These levels are generally considered quite low. In the 1980s we had periods of inflation in the 12 to 13 percent range. Some nations have had high double- and even triple-digit inflation in recent years. From 1998 to 2003, the average annual inflation rate in Zimbabwe was 77 percent; in Belarus, 94 percent; Angola, 185 percent; and the Congo, 277 percent.[5]

CONCEPT *in Action*

Buyers of Nespresso coffee, KitKat chocolate bars, and Purina pet food are paying more at the checkout lately, as food giant Nestlé has upped its prices since 2005. Rising input costs, such as the costs of raw materials and energy, have been hard on food firms, increasing the price of food production, transport, and packaging. *How might fluctuations in the producer price index (PPI) affect the consumer price index (CPI) and why?*

demand-pull inflation
Inflation that occurs when the demand for goods and services is greater than the supply.

cost-push inflation
Inflation that occurs when increases in production costs push up the prices of final goods and services.

consumer price index (CPI)
An index of the prices of a "market-basket" of goods and services purchased by typical urban consumers.

producer price index (PPI)
An index of the prices paid by producers and wholesalers for commodities such as raw materials, partially finished goods, and finished products.

concept check

What is a business cycle? How do businesses adapt to periods of contraction and expansion?

Why is full employment usually defined as a target percentage below 100 percent?

What is the difference between demand-pull and cost-push inflation?

Types of Inflation

There are two types of inflation. **Demand-pull inflation** occurs when the demand for goods and services is greater than the supply. Would-be buyers have more money to spend than the amount needed to buy available goods and services. Their demand, which exceeds the supply, tends to pull prices up. This situation is sometimes described as "too much money chasing too few goods." The higher prices lead to greater supply, eventually creating a balance between demand and supply.

Cost-push inflation is triggered by increases in production costs, such as expenses for materials and wages. These increases push up the prices of final goods and services. Wage increases are a major cause of cost-push inflation, creating a "wage–price spiral." For example, assume the United Auto Workers union negotiates a three-year labor agreement that raises wages 3 percent per year and increases overtime pay. Car makers will then raise car prices to cover their higher labor costs. Also, the higher wages will give auto workers more money to buy goods and services, and this increased demand may pull up other prices. Workers in other industries will demand higher wages to keep up with the increased prices, and the cycle will push prices even higher.

How Inflation Is Measured

The rate of inflation is most commonly measured by looking at changes in the **consumer price index (CPI)**, an index of the prices of a "market basket" of goods and services purchased by typical urban consumers. It is published monthly by the Department of Labor. Major components of the CPI, which are weighted by importance, are food and beverages, clothing, transportation, housing, health, recreation, and education. There are special indexes for food and energy. The Department of Labor collects about 80,000 retail price quotes and 5,000 housing rent figures to calculate the CPI.

The CPI sets prices in a base period at 100. The base period, which now is 1982–1984, is chosen for its price stability. Current prices are then expressed as a percentage of prices in the base period. A rise in the CPI means prices are increasing. For example, the CPI was 201.5 in April 2006, meaning that prices more than doubled since the 1982–1984 base period.

Changes in wholesale prices are another important indicator of inflation. The **producer price index (PPI)** measures the prices paid by producers and wholesalers for commodities such as raw materials, partially finished goods, and finished products. The PPI, which uses 1982 as its base year, is actually a family of indexes for many different product categories, including crude goods (raw materials), intermediate goods (which become part of finished goods), and finished goods. For example, the PPI for chemicals was 203.7 in April 2006. Examples of other PPI indexes include processed foods, lumber, containers, fuels and lubricants, metals, and construction. Because the PPI measures prices paid by producers for raw materials, energy, and other commodities, it may foreshadow subsequent price changes for businesses and consumers.

The Impact of Inflation

Inflation has several negative effects on people and businesses. For one thing, inflation penalizes people who live on fixed incomes. Let's say that a couple receives $1,000 a month retirement income beginning in 2004. If inflation is 10 percent in 2005, then the couple can buy only about 91 percent (100 ÷ 110) of what they could purchase in 2004. Similarly, inflation hurts savers. As prices rise, the real value, or purchasing power, of a nest egg of savings deteriorates.

Achieving Macroeconomic Goals

 4 How does the government use monetary policy and fiscal policy to achieve its macroeconomic goals?

monetary policy
A government's programs for controlling the amount of money circulating in the economy and interest rates.

Federal Reserve System (the *Fed*)
The central banking system of the United States.

contractionary policy
The use of monetary policy by the Fed to tighten the money supply by selling government securities or raising interest rates.

expansionary policy
The use of monetary policy by the Fed to increase the growth of the money supply.

fiscal policy
The government's use of taxation and spending to affect the economy.

CONCEPT *in Action*

As Chairman of the Board of Governors of the Federal Reserve System for two decades, Alan Greenspan was the face of U.S. monetary policy. But when Greenspan stepped down in 2006, Ben Bernanke, the head of the U.S. President's Council of Economic Advisers, took over as chairman. As a White House chief economist and former chair of Princeton's economics department, Bernanke has earned a reputation for being scholarly and independent-minded. *What are the responsibilities of the chairman of the Board of Governors of the Federal Reserve System?*

© TIM SLOAN/AFP/GETTY IMAGES

To reach macroeconomic goals, countries must often choose among conflicting alternatives. Sometimes political needs override economic needs. For example, bringing inflation under control may call for a politically difficult period of high unemployment and low growth. Or, in an election year, politicians may resist raising taxes to curb inflation. Still, the government must try to guide the economy to a sound balance of growth, employment, and price stability. The two main tools it uses are monetary policy and fiscal policy.

Monetary Policy

Monetary policy refers to a government's programs for controlling the amount of money circulating in the economy and interest rates. Changes in the money supply affect both the level of economic activity and the rate of inflation. The Federal Reserve System (the Fed), the central banking system of the United States, prints money and controls how much of it will be in circulation. The money supply is also controlled by the Fed's regulation of certain bank activities.

When the Fed increases or decreases the amount of money in circulation, it affects interest rates (the cost of borrowing money and the reward for lending it). The Fed can change the interest rate on money it lends to banks to signal the banking system and financial markets that it has changed its monetary policy. These changes have a ripple effect. Banks, in turn, may pass along this change to consumers and businesses that receive loans from the banks. If the cost of borrowing increases, the economy slows because interest rates affect consumer and business decisions to spend or invest. The housing industry, business, and investments react most to changes in interest rates.

For example, in March 2006, the Fed raised the target for the federal-funds rate, the interest rate charged on overnight loans between banks, to 4.75 percent from 4.5 percent. The 15th consecutive increase since the middle of 2004, when the rate was 1 percent, the higher rate indicated the Fed's ongoing desire to keep inflation in check. Although the Fed was optimistic about the economy's growth, it also had concerns about rising inflation because of elevated energy prices and disruptions in economic activity related to Hurricane Katrina that put a temporary damper on production output and employment. As expected, this change had a ripple effect: 11 of the 12 regional federal reserve banks agreed to increase the discount rate they charge commercial banks for short-term Fed loans to 5.75 percent from 5.5 percent, and many commercial banks raised the interest rates they charge their best customers by .25 percent as well. These actions were designed to slow down the U.S. economy.[6]

As you can see, the Fed can use monetary policy to contract or expand the economy. With contractionary policy, the Fed restricts, or tightens, the money supply by selling government securities or raising interest rates. The result is slower economic growth and higher unemployment. Thus, contractionary policy reduces spending and, ultimately, lowers inflation. With expansionary policy, the Fed increases, or loosens, growth in the money supply. An expansionary policy stimulates the economy. Interest rates decline, so business and consumer spending go up. Unemployment rates drop as businesses expand. But increasing the money supply also has a negative side: More spending pushes prices up, increasing the inflation rate.

Fiscal Policy

The other economic tool used by the government is fiscal policy, its program of taxation and spending. By increasing spending or by cutting taxes, the government can stimulate the economy. Look again at Exhibit 2.1. The

CONCEPT *in Action*

President George W. Bush cut taxes numerous times after winning the White House in 2000. Moreover, he repeatedly urged Congress to make those tax-cuts permanent, although federal codes require tax provisions to expire at a certain date. Proponents of tax cuts argue that lower taxes stimulate economic growth and job creation; opponents say tax breaks favor the rich and increase the national debt. *What are pros and cons to making tax cuts permanent?*

more government buys from businesses, the greater the business revenues and output. Likewise, if consumers or businesses have to pay less in taxes, they will have more income to spend for goods and services. Tax policies in the United States therefore affect business decisions. High corporate taxes can make it harder for U.S. firms to compete with companies in countries with lower taxes. As a result, companies may choose to locate facilities overseas to reduce their tax burden.

Nobody likes to pay taxes, although we grudgingly accept that we have to. Although most U.S. citizens complain that they are overtaxed, we pay lower taxes per capita (per person) than citizens in many countries similar to ours. In addition, our taxes represent a lower percentage of gross income and GDP compared to most countries, as Exhibit 2.2 demonstrates.

Taxes are, of course, the major source of revenue for our government. Every year the president prepares a budget for the coming year based upon estimated revenues and expenditures. Congress receives the president's report and recommendations and then, typically, debates and analyzes the proposed budget for several months. The president's original proposal is always modified in numerous ways. Exhibit 2.3 shows the sources of revenue and expenses for the U.S. budget.

Exhibit 2.2 > Taxation Around the World: Percentage of Gross Income and GDP

	Taxes as a Percentage of Gross Income*	Taxes as a Percentage of GDP
Japan	17.4%	25.3%
United States	24.2	25.4
Australia	24.3	31.6
Canada	24.7	33.0
Germany	40.5	34.6
United Kingdom	24.1	36.1
The Netherlands	39.4	39.3
France	26.7	43.7
Norway	28.7	44.9
Belgium	40.5	45.6
Italy	27.8	47.2
Denmark	41.2	49.6
Sweden	31.0	50.7

* Total of income taxes and employee Social Security contributions, based on single individual without children at the income level of the average production worker.

Source: "Tax Policies Vary Widely from Country to Country, OECD Study Shows," http://www.oecd.org, more information: Revenue Statistics 1965–2004—2005 Edition, © OECD 2005, http://www1.oecd.org/scripts/publications/bookshop/redirect.asp?pub=232005063PI

Exhibit 2.3 > Revenue and Expenses for the Federal Budget

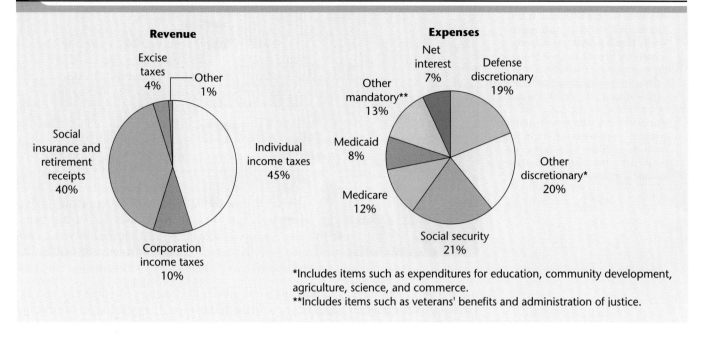

Revenue

Excise taxes 4%

Other 1%

Social insurance and retirement receipts 40%

Individual income taxes 45%

Corporation income taxes 10%

Expenses

Net interest 7%

Defense discretionary 19%

Other mandatory** 13%

Medicaid 8%

Other discretionary* 20%

Medicare 12%

Social security 21%

*Includes items such as expenditures for education, community development, agriculture, science, and commerce.
**Includes items such as veterans' benefits and administration of justice.

While fiscal policy has a major impact on businesses and consumers, continual increases in government spending raise another important issue. When government takes more money from businesses and consumers (the private sector) and uses these funds for increased government spending (the public sector), a phenomenon known as crowding out occurs. Here are three examples of crowding out:

crowding out
The situation that occurs when government spending replaces spending by the private sector.

1. The government spends more on public libraries, and individuals buy fewer books at bookstores.
2. The government spends more on public education, and individuals spend less on private education.
3. The government spends more on public transportation, and individuals spend less on private transportation.

In other words, government spending is crowding out private spending.

If the government spends more for programs (social services, education, defense) than it collects in taxes, the result is a federal budget deficit. To balance the budget, the government can cut its spending, increase taxes, or do some combination of the two. When it cannot balance the budget, the government must make up any shortfalls by borrowing (just like any business or household).

federal budget deficit
The condition that occurs when the federal government spends more for programs than it collects in taxes.

In 1998, for the first time in a generation, there was a federal budget surplus (revenue exceeded spending) of about $71 billion. By 2002, there was once again a deficit ($159 billion), and for fiscal year 2005 the deficit was more than $318 billion. Whenever the government finds itself with a surplus, Congress begins an often-heated debate about what to do with the money. Some members of Congress, for example, want to spend more on social programs or for defense. Others say that this money belongs to the people and should be returned in the form of tax cuts. Another alternative is to reduce the national debt.

national debt
The accumulated total of all of the federal government's annual budget deficits.

The U.S. government has run budget deficits for many years. The accumulated total of these past deficits is the national debt, which now amounts to about $8.5 trillion or about $28,555 for every man, woman, and child in the United States. Total interest on the debt is more than $360 billion a year. To cover the deficit, the U.S. government borrows money from people and businesses in the form of Treasury bills, Treasury notes, and Treasury bonds. These are federal IOUs that pay interest to their owners.

The national debt is an emotional issue debated not only in the halls of Congress, but by the public as well. Some believe that deficits contribute to economic growth, high employment, and price stability. Others have the following reservations about such a high national debt:

- **Not Everyone Holds the Debt:** The government is very conscious of who actually bears the burden of the national debt and keeps track of who holds what bonds. If only the rich were bondholders, then they alone would receive the interest payments and could end up receiving more in interest than they paid in taxes. In the meantime, poorer people, who held no bonds, would end up paying taxes that would be transferred to the rich as interest, making the debt an unfair burden to them. At times, therefore, the government has instructed commercial banks to reduce their total debt by divesting some of their bond holdings. That's also why the Treasury created **savings bonds**. Because these bonds are issued in relatively small denominations, they allow more people to buy and hold government debt.

- **Crowding out Private Investment:** The national debt also affects private investment. If the government raises the interest rate on bonds to be able to sell them, it forces private businesses, whose corporate bonds (long-term debt obligations issued by a company) compete with government bonds for investor dollars, to raise rates on their bonds to stay competitive. In other words, selling government debt to finance government spending makes it more costly for private industry to finance its own investment. As a result, government debt may end up crowding out private investment and slowing economic growth in the private sector.

savings bonds
Government bonds issued in relatively small denominations.

---

concept check

What are the two kinds of monetary policy?

What fiscal policy tools can the government use to achieve its macroeconomic goals?

What problems can a large national debt present?

Microeconomics: Zeroing in on Businesses and Consumers

5 What are the basic microeconomic concepts of demand and supply, and how do they establish prices?

Now let's shift our focus from the whole economy to *microeconomics,* the study of households, businesses, and industries. This field of economics is concerned with how prices and quantities of goods and services behave in a free market. It stands to reason that people, firms, and governments try to get the most from their limited resources. Consumers want to buy the best quality at the lowest price. Businesses want to keep costs down and revenues high to earn larger profits. Governments also want to use their revenues to provide the most effective public goods and services possible. These groups choose among alternatives by focusing on the prices of goods and services.

CONCEPT *in Action*

Microsoft's strategy to get a leg up on Sony's PlayStation 3 hit a glitch in 2005 when the worldwide rollout of the company's next-generation Xbox 360 game console became bogged down in a production-related quagmire. Suppliers of the console's memory chips and other components failed to keep up with high demand, leaving retailers' shelves empty and customer orders on hold for months. *How do businesses determine the optimum quantity of products or services to make available to consumers?*

© FRED PROUSER/REUTERS/LANDOV

As consumers in a free market, we influence what is produced. If Mexican food is popular, the high demand attracts entrepreneurs who open more Mexican restaurants. They want to compete for our dollars by supplying Mexican food at a lower price, of better quality, or with different features such as Santa Fe Mexican food rather than Tex-Mex. This section explains how business and consumer choices influence the price and availability of goods and services.

The Nature of Demand

demand
The quantity of a good or service that people are willing to buy at various prices.

demand curve
A graph showing the quantity of a good or service that people are willing to buy at various prices.

Demand is the quantity of a good or service that people are willing to buy at various prices. The higher the price, the lower the quantity demanded, and vice versa. A graph of this relationship is called a **demand curve**.

Let's assume you own a store that sells jackets for snowboarders. From past experience you know how many jackets you can sell at different prices. The demand curve in Exhibit 2.4 depicts this information. The *x*-axis (horizontal axis) shows the quantity of jackets, and the *y*-axis (vertical axis) shows the related price of those jackets. For example, at a price of $100, customers will buy (demand) 600 snowboard jackets.

In the graph the demand curve slopes downward and to the right, because as the price falls, people will want to buy more jackets. Some people who were not going to buy a jacket will purchase one at the lower price. Also, some snowboarders who already have a jacket will buy a second one. The graph also shows that if you put a large number of jackets on the market, you will have to reduce the price to sell all of them.

Understanding demand is critical to businesses. Demand tells you *how much you can sell* and *at what price*—in other words, how much money the firm will take in that can be used to cover costs and hopefully earn a profit. Gauging demand is difficult even for the very largest corporations, but particularly for small firms.

The Nature of Supply

supply
The quantity of a good or service that businesses will make available at various prices.

supply curve
A graph showing the quantity of a good or service that businesses will make available at various prices.

Demand alone is not enough to explain how the market sets prices. We must also look at **supply**, the quantity of a good or service that businesses will make available at various prices. The higher the price, the greater the number of jackets a supplier will make available and vice versa. A graph of the relationship between various prices and the quantities a manufacturer will supply is a **supply curve**.

Exhibit 2.4 > Demand Curve for Snowboarder Jackets

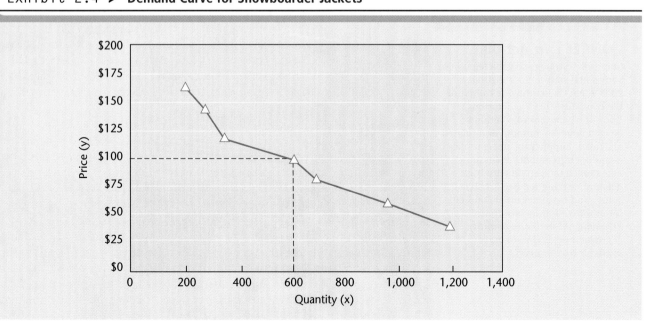

Exhibit 2.5 > **Supply Curve for Snowboarder Jackets**

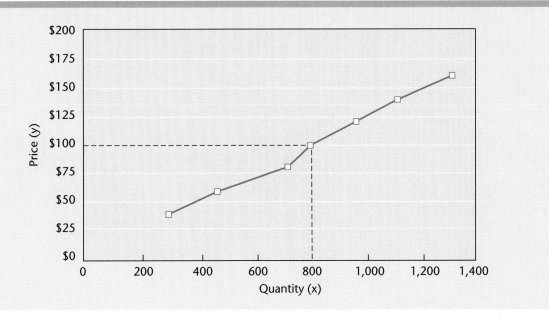

We can again plot the quantity of jackets on the *x*-axis and the price on the *y*-axis. As Exhibit 2.5 shows, 800 jackets will be available at a price of $100. Note that the supply curve slopes upward and to the right, the opposite of the demand curve. If snowboarders are willing to pay higher prices, suppliers of jackets will buy more inputs (Gore-Tex® fabric, dye, machinery, labor) and produce more jackets. The quantity supplied will be higher at higher prices, because suppliers can earn higher profits.

How Demand and Supply Interact to Determine Prices

In a stable economy, the number of jackets that snowboarders demand depends on the jackets' price. Likewise, the number of jackets that suppliers provide depends on price. But at what price will consumer demand for jackets match the quantity suppliers will produce?

To answer this question, we need to look at what happens when demand and supply interact. By plotting both the demand curve and the supply curve on the same graph in Exhibit 2.6, we see that they cross at a certain quantity and price. At that point, labeled E, the quantity demanded equals the quantity supplied. This is the point of **equilibrium**. The equilibrium price is $80; the equilibrium quantity is 700 jackets. At that point there is a balance between the quantity consumers will buy and the quantity suppliers will make available.

Market equilibrium is achieved through a series of quantity and price adjustments that occur automatically. If the price increases to $160, suppliers produce more jackets than consumers are willing to buy, and a surplus results. To sell more jackets, prices will have to fall. Thus, a surplus pushes prices downward until equilibrium is reached. When the price falls to $60, the quantity of jackets demanded rises above the available supply. The resulting shortage forces prices upward until equilibrium is reached at $80.

The number of snowboarder jackets supplied and bought at $80 will tend to rest at equilibrium unless there is a shift in either demand or supply. If demand increases, more jackets will be purchased at every price, and the demand curve shifts to the right (as illustrated by line D_2 in Exhibit 2.7). If demand decreases, less will be bought at every price, and the demand curve shifts to the left (D_1). When demand decreased, snowboarders bought 500 jackets at $80 instead of 700 jackets. When demand increased, they purchased 800 jackets.

equilibrium
The point at which quantity demanded equals quantity supplied.

Exhibit 2.6 > Equilibrium Price and Quantity

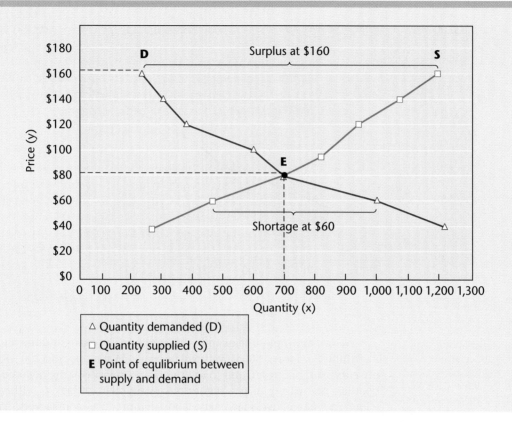

△ Quantity demanded (D)
□ Quantity supplied (S)
E Point of equlibrium between supply and demand

Exhibit 2.7 > Shifts in Demand

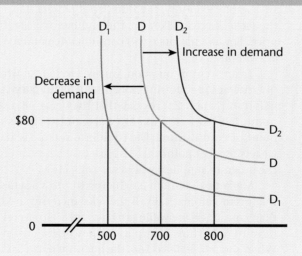

Changes in Demand

A number of things can increase or decrease demand. For example, if snowboarders' incomes go up, they may decide to buy a second jacket. If incomes fall, a snowboarder who was planning to purchase a jacket may wear an old one instead. Changes in fashion or tastes can also influence demand. If snowboarding were suddenly to go out of fashion, demand for jackets would decrease quickly. A change in the price of related

products can also influence demand. For example, if the average price of a snowboard rises to $1,000, people will quit snowboarding and jacket demand will fall.

Another factor that can shift demand is expectations about future prices. If you expect jacket prices to increase significantly in the future, you may decide to go ahead and get one today. If you think prices will fall, you will postpone your purchase. Finally, changes in the number of buyers will affect demand. Snowboarding is a young person's sport, and the number of teenagers will increase in the next few years. Therefore, the demand for snowboarding jackets should increase.

Changes in Supply

Other factors influence the supply side of the picture. New technology typically lowers the cost of production. For example, North Face, a supplier of ski and snowboarder jackets, purchased laser-guided pattern-cutting equipment and computer-aided pattern-making equipment. Each jacket was cheaper to produce, resulting in a higher profit per jacket. This provided an incentive to supply more jackets at every price. If the price of resources such as labor or fabric goes up, North Face will earn a smaller profit on each jacket, and the amount supplied will decrease at every price. The reverse is also true. Changes in the prices of other goods can also affect supply.

Let's say that snow skiing becomes a really hot sport again. The number of skiers jumps dramatically and the price of ski jackets soars. North Face can use its machines and fabrics to produce either ski or snowboard jackets. If the company can make more profit from ski jackets, it will produce fewer snowboarding jackets at every price. Also, a change in the number of producers will shift the supply curve. If the number of jacket suppliers increases, they will place more jackets on the market at every price. If any suppliers stop making jackets available, the supply will naturally decrease. Taxes can also affect supply. If the government decides, for some reason, to tax the supplier for every snowboard jacket produced, then profits will fall and fewer jackets will be offered at every price. Exhibit 2.8 summarizes the factors that can shift demand and supply curves.

CONCEPT in Action

Cigarette manufacturers are facing an uncertain future, as sales of smokes have plummeted to their lowest numbers since the 1950s. Causes of the slide are headline news: State and local legislatures have enacted smoking bans for public places, and federal regulations and taxes imposed on the industry restrict tobacco marketing and inflate prices. Anti-smoking groups say declining demand for cigarettes is evidence that health-awareness campaigns are working. *How does government intervention affect the market equilibrium for tobacco products?*

Exhibit 2.8 > Factors That Cause Demand and Supply Curves to Shift

Factor	Shift Demand	
	To the Right If	**To the Left If**
Buyers' incomes	increase	decrease
Buyers' preferences/tastes	increase	decrease
Prices of substitute products	increase	decrease
Expectations about future prices	will rise	will fall
Number of buyers	increases	decreases
	Shift Supply	
Technology	lowers cost	increases cost
Resource prices	fall	rise
Changes in prices of other products that can be produced with the same resources	profit of other product falls	profit of other product rises
Number of suppliers	increases	decreases
Taxes	lowered	increased

To better understand the relationship between supply and demand across the economy, consider the impact of Hurricane Katrina on U.S. energy prices. Oil and gas prices were already at high levels before Hurricane Katrina disrupted production on the Gulf Coast. Most U.S. offshore drilling sites are located in the Gulf of Mexico, and almost 30 percent of U.S. refining capacity is in Gulf States that were hit hard by the storm. Prices rose almost immediately as supplies fell while demand remained at the same levels.

The storm drove home the vulnerability of the U.S. energy supply to not only natural disasters but also terrorist attacks and price increases from foreign oil producers. Many energy policy experts questioned the wisdom of having such a high concentration of oil facilities—about 25 percent of the oil and natural gas infrastructure—in hurricane-prone states. Refiners were already almost at capacity before Katrina's devastation.[7]

High energy prices affect the economy in many ways. With oil at the time costing $50 to $60 a barrel—more than double the 2003 price—both businesses and consumers across the U.S felt the pinch in their wallets. Midwestern agricultural businesses export about 70 percent of their grain production through Gulf of Mexico port facilities. With fewer usable docking spaces, barges couldn't unload and return for more crops. The supply of both transportation services and grain products was inadequate to meet demand, pushing up transportation costs. Higher gas prices also contributed to rising prices, as 80 percent of shipping costs are related to fuel.

The Conference Board estimated that a sustained 50-cent increase in the price of gasoline translates to a 1 percent to 1.5 percent reduction in consumer spending. Higher oil prices are passed through to consumers in the cost of not only gasoline for vehicles but also any products that use petrochemicals (plastics, for example) and create inflationary pressure.[8]

> ### concept check
>
> What is the relationship between prices and demand for a product?
>
> How is market equilibrium achieved? Describe the circumstances under which the price for gasoline would have returned to equilibrium in the United States after Hurricane Katrina.
>
> Draw a graph that shows an equilibrium point for supply and demand.

Competing in a Free Market

 What are the four types of market structure?

market structure
The number of suppliers in a market.

One of the characteristics of a free-market system is that suppliers have the right to compete with one another. The number of suppliers in a market define the **market structure**. Economists identify four types of market structures: (1) perfect competition, (2) pure monopoly, (3) monopolistic competition, and (4) oligopoly. Exhibit 2.9 summarizes the characteristics of each of these market structures.

Perfect Competition

perfect (pure) competition
A market structure in which a large number of small firms sell similar products, buyers and sellers have good information, and businesses can be easily opened or closed.

Characteristics of **perfect (pure) competition** include:

- A large number of small firms are in the market.
- The firms sell similar products; that is, each firm's product is very much like the products sold by other firms in the market.
- Buyers and sellers in the market have good information about prices, sources of supply, and so on.
- It is easy to open a new business or close an existing one.

In a perfectly competitive market, firms sell their products at prices determined solely by forces beyond their control. Because the products are very similar and each firm contributes only a small amount to the total quantity supplied by the industry, price is determined by supply and demand. A firm that raised its price even a little above the going rate would lose customers. In the wheat market, for example, the product is essentially the same from one wheat producer to the next. Thus, none of the producers has control over the price of wheat.

Exhibit 2.9 > Comparison of Market Structures

Characteristics	Perfect Competition	Pure Monopoly	Monopolistic Competition	Oligopoly
Number of firms in market	Many	One	Many, but fewer than perfect competition	Few
Firm's ability to control price	None	High	Some	Some
Barriers to entry	None	Subject to government regulation	Few	Many
Product differentiation	Very little	No products that compete directly	Emphasis on showing perceived differences in products	Some differences
Examples	Farm products such as wheat and corn	Utilities such as gas, water, cable television	Retail specialty clothing stores	Steel, automobiles, airlines, aircraft manufacturers

Perfect competition is an ideal. No industry shows all its characteristics, but the stock market and some agricultural markets, such as those for wheat and corn, come closest. Farmers, for example, can sell all of their crops through national commodity exchanges at the current market price.

Pure Monopoly

pure monopoly
A market structure in which a single firm accounts for all industry sales and in which there are *barriers to entry*.

barriers to entry
Factors, such as technological or legal conditions, that prevent new firms from competing equally with an existing firm.

At the other end of the spectrum is **pure monopoly**, the market structure in which a single firm accounts for all industry sales of a particular good or service. The firm *is* the industry. This market structure is characterized by **barriers to entry**—factors that prevent new firms from competing equally with the existing firm. Often the barriers are technological or legal conditions. Polaroid, for example, has held major patents on instant photography for years. When Kodak tried to market its own instant camera,

CONCEPT *in Action*

A 1984 antitrust decision that split up AT&T into multiple entities came full circle when a 2006 merger between AT&T and BellSouth transformed the San Antonio–based firm into the largest telecommunications company in the United States. In addition to giving AT&T full control of cellphone giant Cingular Wireless, the mega-billion dollar deal put the heat on rival Verizon and positioned the company to respond to cable's triple-threat of television, Internet, and telephone services. *Does the merger with BellSouth raise the specter of another AT&T monopoly?*

Polaroid sued, claiming patent violations. Polaroid collected millions of dollars from Kodak. Another barrier may be one firm's control of a natural resource. DeBeers Consolidated Mines Ltd., for example, controls most of the world's supply of uncut diamonds.

Public utilities like gas and water companies are pure monopolies. Some monopolies are created by a government order that outlaws competition. The U.S. Postal Service is currently one such monopoly.

Monopolistic Competition

Three characteristics define the market structure known as **monopolistic competition:**

- Many firms are in the market.
- The firms offer products that are close substitutes but still differ from one another.
- It is relatively easy to enter the market.

Under monopolistic competition, firms take advantage of product differentiation. Industries where monopolistic competition occurs include clothing, food, and similar consumer products. Firms under monopolistic competition have more control over pricing than do firms under perfect competition because consumers do not view the products as perfect substitutes. Nevertheless, firms must demonstrate product differences to justify their prices to customers. Consequently, companies use advertising to distinguish their products from others. Such distinctions may be significant or superficial. For example, Nike says "Just Do It," and Tylenol is advertised as being easier on the stomach than aspirin.

Oligopoly

An **oligopoly** has two characteristics:

- A few firms produce most or all of the output.
- Large capital requirements or other factors limit the number of firms.

Boeing and Airbus Industries (aircraft manufacturers) and USX (formerly U.S. Steel) are major firms in different oligopolistic industries.

With so few firms in an oligopoly, what one firm does has an impact on the other firms. Thus, the firms in an oligopoly watch one another closely for new technologies, product changes and innovations, promotional campaigns, pricing, production, and other developments. Sometimes they go so far as to coordinate their pricing and output decisions, which is illegal. Many antitrust cases—legal challenges arising out of laws designed to control anticompetitive behavior—occur in oligopolies.

The market structure of an industry can change over time. Take, for example, telecommunications. At one time, AT&T had a monopoly on long distance telephone service nationwide. Then the U.S. government divided the company into seven regional phone companies in 1984, opening the door to greater competition. Other companies such as MCI and Sprint entered the fray and built state-of-the-art fiber optic networks to win customers from the traditional providers of phone service. The 1996 Telecommunications Act changed the competitive environment yet again by allowing local phone companies to offer long-distance service in exchange for letting competition into their local markets. Today, as we learned in Chapter 1, the broadcasting, computer, telephone, and video industries are converging as companies consolidate through merger and acquisition. The Managing Change box discusses how AT&T (formerly SBC) and Verizon are meeting the competitive challenges created by convergence.

concept check

What is meant by market structure?

Compare and contrast perfect competition and pure monopoly. Why is it rare to find perfect competition?

How does an oligopoly differ from monopolistic competition?

MANAGING CHANGE

Cutting the Wires

AT&T (formerly SBC) and Verizon Communications became the country's largest telecommunications companies by acquiring other companies and investing many billions of dollars in telecommunications infrastructure. Together they controlled 60 percent of the residential phone market—until upstart cable television and Internet companies siphoned off customers with low-cost Internet long distance service. "They don't have any fiber out there . . . any wires . . . anything," fumes AT&T chief executive Edward Whitacre. "They use my lines for free. . . . For Google or a Yahoo! or a Vonage or anybody to expect to use these pipes for free is nuts!"

In response, AT&T and Verizon moved quickly into broadband, wireless, and video services. Corporations were another major target market for the two firms. The old AT&T and MCI, with their large rosters of corporate clients, were logical acquisitions for SBC and Verizon, respectively. "We're not sitting back and waiting for the world to kill us," says Ivan Seidenberg, Verizon CEO. "We need to apply some adult thinking to this. It's not the death of anything. It just forces us to change faster."

Change is the name of the game at both corporations as they reduce their reliance on dwindling traditional phone service revenues. They will go head to head in many markets, especially for corporate customers. Each is rolling out new offerings at a fast clip, many of which link wireless, landline, and Internet services. Consumers could benefit from lower prices and more choices as competition increases for their telecommunications dollars.

Television will be a huge challenge for AT&T and Verizon. In early 2006 AT&T began offering IPTV, or Internet-delivered television, in selected areas. Verizon is building fiber-optic networks at a cost exceeding $10 billion to enter the broadband Internet and television markets. With the value of those media industries estimated at $120 billion, Seidenberg is confident his investment will pay off. The rivals hope to beat cable companies at their own game by offering customers packages of phone, Internet, and television services, all from one provider at lower prices—much as the cable companies did with phone service. The more types of services a consumer gets from one company, the harder it becomes to switch to a new provider. AT&T can therefore offer its customers what Whitacre calls a "quad"—a package of four services: landline phone, mobile phone, Internet, and video.

Because Whitacre sees cable companies as a more serious threat than Verizon, he is re-creating AT&T as a media-oriented company. For example, Comcast and other major cable providers are partnering with rival phone company Sprint to add cell phone services and bundle more phone, broadband Internet, and TV services. Verizon's strategy is to put customers first as it works with suppliers and partners to drive quicker changes. "As we go into 2006 we'll be able to spend less capital to do the same thing," says Seidenberg. "In the final analysis, beating my peers doesn't get us any points to go to heaven. Winning their customers gets us points to go to heaven."[9]

Critical Thinking Questions
- Describe the market structure of the telecommunications industry today.
- How are AT&T and Verizon responding to the changes in their competitive environment?

Trends in Economics and Competition

 7 **Which trends are reshaping the micro- and macroeconomic environments and the competitive arena?**

Trends in the economic environment occur at several levels. Each month the government releases new statistics that indicate the changes in macroeconomic trends and the direction of the economy. Tracking these statistics at the Bureau of Labor Statistics Web site (**http://www.bls.gov**) shows trends over short- and long-term periods.

Economic and competitive trends also occur on a broader level. For example, in Chapter 1 we discussed how U.S. companies compete effectively in the face of increased global competition by maintaining a productive workforce, applying technology, and focusing on quality and customer service. We will revisit these topics in later chapters. Now let's look at the continuing resilience of the U.S. economy, the growing demand for energy, staying competitive in the global economy, the increase in entrepreneurship outside the United States, and shifts in economic policies in Europe.

The U.S. Economy Weathers Many Storms

When Hurricane Katrina hit the Gulf Coast in August 2005, economists and others made dire predictions of its impact to the economy. As devastating as this natural disaster was in terms of lives lost and damaged property, the U.S. economy proved that it could weather this storm—just as it has other tests in recent years. Events such as the collapse of the stock market in 2000, the 2001 recession, terrorist attacks, numerous corporate scandals, wars in Afghanistan, Iraq, and Lebanon, and rising crude oil prices could have battered the U.S. economy and started the country on a downward spiral of reduced economic activity, higher unemployment rates, and rising inflation.

Instead, the economy has shown considerably less volatility than in the past and recorded steady growth with low inflation. Because the economy was in good shape when Katrina hit, the United States was better able to rebound despite significant disruptions to the energy supply (see the following section, "Running Out of Gas") and to business operations in the affected area.[10] It posted growth of 4.1 percent in the third quarter of 2005, only slightly down from the pre-Katrina estimate of 4.3 percent. "The economy has its own natural inertia that will carry it forward," said University of Maryland economist Peter Morici.[11]

For example, from 1997 to 2004, the trend in the CPI was a steady upward pattern, but the rate of growth was quite low, averaging about 2.4 percent. This low inflation rate is a contributor to the U.S. economy's resilience. Even though energy prices spiked in 2005 and early 2006, due in part to Hurricane Katrina, and pushed the CPI significantly higher than in prior years, productivity remained strong.

As noted earlier, the Federal Reserve Board increased interest rates to keep inflation under control. As a result, rates on both business and consumer loans edged upward. On a positive note, savers benefited from higher interest rates. Unemployment rates during that period show a different trend. They dropped from 5.6 percent in 1995 to 3.9 percent in 2000, climbing to 6.0 percent in the recession of 2002 before heading downward again to 4.7 percent by April 2006.

Running Out of Gas

As standards of living improve worldwide, the demand for energy continues to rise. Emerging economies such as China and India need energy to grow. Their demands are placing pressure on the world's supplies and driving up prices, as the laws of supply and demand would predict. By 2005, Chinese energy consumption had already moved beyond the Department of Energy's projections for 2010. State-supported energy companies in China, India, Russia, Saudi Arabia, Venezuela, and other countries will place additional competitive pressure on privately owned oil companies such as BP, Chevron Texaco, ExxonMobil, and Shell.[12]

Countries worldwide worry about relying too heavily on one source of supply for energy. The United States imports a large percentage of its oil from the Mideast and South America. Europeans get 25 percent of their natural gas from Russia's state-controlled gas utility OAO Gazprom. This gives foreign governments the power to use energy as a political tool. For example, in late December 2005 a disagreement over pricing caused Russia to stop supplying the Ukraine with gas. European gas supplies flow through Ukrainian pipelines, and Gazprom believed much of the gas was diverted and never made it to European customers, who reported shortages of as much as 50 percent. "Thirty percent of our gas comes from Russia at the moment. That should be increased," said Germany's Economy Minister Michael Glos. "But it can only be increased if we know that deliveries from the east are dependable." Added U.S. State Department spokesman Sean McCormack, "Such an abrupt step creates insecurity in the energy sector in the region and raises serious questions about the use of energy to exert political pressure."[13]

Countries and companies worldwide are seeking out additional sources of supply to prevent being held captive to one supplier. For example, in December 2005 ConocoPhillips agreed to purchase Burlington Resources Inc., an oil and natural-gas producer, for $35 billion—almost 10 percent more than Burlington's stock price. Conoco is betting that high demand and tight supplies will keep natural gas prices high. According to James Mulva, ConocoPhillips chairman and CEO, Burlington was especially attractive because 80 percent of its reserves are in the United States, providing a balance to Conoco's overseas ventures in politically risky countries such as Venezuela and Russia.[14]

Meeting Competitive Challenges

Companies are turning to many different strategies to remain competitive in the global marketplace. One of the most important is relationship management,

relationship management
The practice of building, maintaining, and enhancing interactions with customers and other parties to develop long-term satisfaction through mutually beneficial partnerships.

CONCEPT *in Action*

Apple didn't waste any time in touting a new alliance that places Intel microprocessors inside Mac products. A television ad trumpeting the development proclaimed that the Intel chip, formerly "trapped in PCs, inside dull little boxes performing dull little tasks," was finally "set free to live inside a Mac." The switch effectively ended Apple's 14-year relationship with IBM and eased longstanding resentment over Windows-Intel domination. *Why is the Apple-Intel alliance important to each firm in light of computing and digital-entertainment trends?*

strategic alliance
A cooperative agreement between business firms; sometimes called a *strategic partnership*.

which involves building, maintaining, and enhancing interactions with customers and other parties to develop long-term satisfaction through mutually beneficial partnerships. Relationship management includes both *supply chain management*, which builds strong bonds with suppliers, and *relationship marketing*, which focuses on customers. (We'll discuss supply chain management in greater detail in Chapter 11 and return to relationship marketing in Chapter 12.) In general, the longer a customer stays with a company, the more that customer is worth. Long-term customers buy more, take less of a company's time, are less sensitive to price, and bring in new customers. Best of all, they require no acquisition or start-up costs. Good long-standing customers are worth so much that in some industries, reducing customer defections by as little as five points—from, say, 15 percent to 10 percent per year—can double profits.

Another important way companies stay competitive is through **strategic alliances** (also called *strategic partnerships*). The trend toward forming these cooperative agreements between business firms is accelerating rapidly, particularly among high-tech firms. These companies have realized that strategic partnerships are more than just important—they are critical. Strategic alliances can take many forms. Some companies enter into strategic alliances with their suppliers, who take over much of their actual production and manufacturing. Nike, the largest producer of athletic footwear in the world, does not manufacture a single shoe. Gallo, the largest wine company on earth, does not grow a single grape.

Others with complementary strengths team up. For example, computer manufacturer Hewlett-Packard (H-P) and retail giant Wal-Mart partnered to improve sales at both. H-P provided Wal-Mart with low-cost electronic products. The two companies worked together to develop special products for Wal-Mart, such as desktop and notebook computers for about $400, digital cameras for $100, and all-in-one printers for $50. H-P was eager to satisfy Wal-Mart, one of its biggest retail partners. For Wal-Mart, H-P's products would lure customers who might otherwise shop for electronics at Best Buy and Circuit City into Wal-Mart where they could spend more of their holiday gift dollars.[15]

Companies in the same industry often form alliances. Smaller companies with unique products or technology may partner with larger companies who can provide wider distribution in exchange for access to the technology. Even rivals find strategic alliances advantageous. South Korean electronics manufacturer Samsung competes with Sony and a few other companies for the top spot in global television sales. Yet since 2003, the two companies have worked together on producing television display panels. Sony, in search of a supplier for its new line of flat-panel televisions, arranged to become a partner in Samsung's new liquid crystal display factory. The result has benefited both companies in many ways. Their engineers now cooperate on panel technologies, leading to speedier improvement cycles. With Samsung's approval, Sony introduced some of Samsung's LCD technologies before Samsung did—and sold significantly more models equipped with the new technology than Samsung. Why would Samsung want to continue working with Sony? Whereas Samsung had the edge in developing LCD technologies, Sony excelled at applying technology to consumer products, especially televisions. Teaming up with and at the same time competing with Sony has pushed Samsung to new technological breakthroughs and better product design. "If we learn from Sony, it will help us in advancing our technology," says Jang Insik, a Samsung engineer. Other Asian electronics manufacturers are pooling resources to their mutual benefit, despite struggles to overcome concerns about helping rivals and working with companies in other countries.[16]

Entrepreneurship Spreads Worldwide

A key trend in macroeconomics and competition is the rising entrepreneurial spirit in former communist economies and other developing nations such as India. As Russia and China have shifted away from centralized economic controls towards greater competitive freedom, many people have embraced the opportunity to start businesses that meet the needs of local consumers. A recent study conducted by Paul Reynolds, director of Florida International University's Entrepreneurship Research Institute, indicates that Asian entrepreneurs are beginning to challenge the U.S dominance in entrepreneurship. In China and India alone, 100 million people are already pursuing entrepreneurial ventures. "Most Asians feel they should take care of their own economic well-being," he says. "They will become a very major challenge to the U.S."[17]

China itself has been called "the world's largest start-up" as it goes through many of the same eras in the history of business that the United States experienced—but in a greatly compressed time frame. The development of modern business occurred over about 150 years in the United States; China is attempting to accomplish the same thing in about 25 years. A key element in China's economic transformation is setting free the as-yet-untapped entrepreneurial power of its citizens. The Chinese government recognizes the potential of this huge untapped resource and its role in creating new products and a world-class economy that will rival the United States.[18] The Catching the Entrepreneurial Spirit box introduces us to some of the new breed of Chinese entrepreneurs.

CATCHING THE ENTREPRENEURIAL SPIRIT

Ge-ti-hu *on the Go*

The Dacheng Mall is a prime example of a new generation of Chinese entrepreneurship in action. Located in Nanjing, capital of Jiangsu Province in eastern China, most of the stores are student-owned. City-sponsored programs helped students overcome economic and political obstacles to business ownership. These included business consultants to advise students about start-up procedures, special loans to finance their efforts, and rent and utility subsidies.

These policies and a loan of 30,000 yuan (about $3,750) helped Lu Jun, a 21-year-old student at Nanjing Agriculture University, open her own fashion store in November 2005. Daily sales at Freedom, her boutique, average about 200 yuan ($25). Lu hopes to be profitable by May 2006. However, her goals focus on career more than wealth. "Making money is not the sole aim," she says. "The job market is so disappointing these days. I have to do something to get myself better prepared. Otherwise I will probably become jobless immediately after my graduation."

About 30 percent of China's university students would like to join Lu and start their own companies. This low rate of new job creation is occurring at a time when the number of graduates is soaring: 3.4 million students received university degrees in 2005, compared to 1.15 million in 2001. China added only 9 million new jobs in 2005, and 5 million of those were set aside for workers who lost their jobs at state factories. With such intense competition for jobs, graduates must seek alternatives to traditional jobs.

"Under the previous planned economy, university graduates used to be [the] elite of the society," says Shen Jie, a sociologist at the Chinese Academy of Social Sciences. "They simply waited for the government to assign them jobs and they would get decent jobs and preferable pay right after graduation." The increasing market orientation of both the economy and the education system means that graduates must become involved in job creation through entrepreneurship.

Government incentive programs at national and local levels are encouraging more students to become *ge-ti-hu* (entrepreneurs). Exemption from first-year registration fees and tax revenues and low-interest-rate loans are among the initiatives offered to graduates who opt for business ownership. Another important step is the addition of entrepreneurship courses at Chinese universities. "We should acquaint our students with more market spirit and specific skills to run a business," says Wang Sheping, who edited the first Chinese book on student entrepreneurship. He also advises students that business ownership is not just about "ambition and professional skills. They also should consider the social responsibilities." Gao Zhijun is one student who fulfilled both profit and social objectives with a waste-collection business at his school, Tongjii University in Shanghai. Gao expects to net 300,000 yuan ($38,000) in profits. "I will give back part of the profit to help some impoverished students in Tongji, he says. He also employs students with financial needs to help him run his business.[19]

Critical Thinking Questions
- What economic conditions are contributing to Chinese students' interest in becoming business owners?
- Why is entrepreneurship an important component in the shift away from the communist economic system in China?

Another indication of entrepreneurial activity in China is the rising level of investments by major U.S. venture capital firms—$1.3 billion in 2004 alone, a 29 percent increase over 2003. Local government agencies provide startup funding for Chinese businesses, especially in technology. Shanghai Dingjia Ventures is a government fund that has invested in about 30 early-stage companies at Shanghai's Zhangjiang Science Park. Because the amount of funding from these sources is generally small, U.S. venture capital investors are welcomed eagerly by Chinese companies in need of additional financing to expand operations and compete globally. To date U.S. venture investments have included 51Job, an online job site that is now a public company; Baidu, a Chinese search company; and Worksoft, a rapidly growing technology firm that handles outsourced software development and testing for U.S. companies such as Qualcomm and PeopleSoft.[20]

Shifting Economics in Europe

The riots in France described earlier in this chapter were just one example of spreading dissatisfaction with the socialist economic policies in many Western European countries. Like France, Germany and other countries continued to believe that the government should play a key role in taking care of its citizens—providing them with generous pension, unemployment, healthcare, and other benefits—rather than adopt policies that promoted economic growth and created jobs. With short workweeks (35 hours are typical in France and Germany) and long vacations (five to six weeks for most workers), European companies were falling behind their American counterparts. Productivity suffered, and Western Europe's annual growth rate was only about 1.5 percent, compared to the world average of 4 percent.

Changing well-entrenched policies is not easy, but reforms are now appearing. France is working towards pension reform, and in Germany new restrictions are limiting unemployment benefits. Unions are agreeing to concessions such as longer workweeks in exchange for promises not to shift jobs overseas.[21]

> **concept check**
>
> What underlying economic trends helped the U.S. economy withstand the potentially devastating impact of Hurricane Katrina?
>
> Why is the increasing demand for energy worldwide a cause for concern?
>
> What strategies are companies using to remain competitive in the global economy?
>
> Explain the reasons for changes in attitudes toward business ownership in former communist countries and in economic policies in socialist countries.

Summary of Learning Goals

1 **What is economics, and how are the three sectors of the economy linked?**

Economics is the study of how individuals, businesses, and governments use scarce resources to produce and distribute goods and services. The two major areas in economics are macroeconomics, the study of the economy as a whole, and microeconomics, the study of households and firms. The individual, business, and government sectors of the economy are linked by a series of two-way flows. The government provides public goods and services for the other two sectors and receives income in the form of taxes. Changes in one flow affect the other sectors.

2 **How do economic growth, full employment, and price stability indicate a nation's economic health?**

A nation's economy is growing when the level of business activity, as measured by gross domestic product (GDP), is rising. GDP is the total value of all goods and services produced in a year. The goal of full employment is to have a job for all who can and want to work. How well a nation is meeting its employment goals is measured by the unemployment rate. There are four types of unemployment: frictional, structural, cyclical, and seasonal. With price stability, the overall prices of goods and services are not moving very much either up or down.

3	**What is inflation, how is it measured, and what causes it?**	Inflation is the general upward movement of prices. When prices rise, purchasing power falls. The rate of inflation is measured by changes in the consumer price index (CPI) and the producer price index (PPI). There are two main causes of inflation. If the demand for goods and services exceeds the supply, prices will rise. This is called demand-pull inflation. With cost-push inflation, higher production costs, such as expenses for materials and wages, increase the final prices of goods and services.
4	**How does the government use monetary policy and fiscal policy to achieve its macroeconomic goals?**	Monetary policy refers to actions by the Federal Reserve System (the Fed) to control the money supply. When the Fed restricts the money supply, interest rates rise, the inflation rate drops, and economic growth slows. By expanding the money supply, the Fed stimulates economic growth. The government also uses fiscal policy—changes in levels of taxation and spending—to control the economy. Reducing taxes or increasing spending stimulates the economy; raising taxes or decreasing spending does the opposite. When the government spends more than it receives in tax revenues, it must borrow to finance the deficit. Some economists favor deficit spending as a way to stimulate the economy; others worry about our high level of national debt.
5	**What are the basic microeconomic concepts of demand and supply, and how do they establish prices?**	Demand is the quantity of a good or service that people will buy at a given price. Supply is the quantity of a good or service that suppliers will make available at a given price. When the price increases, the quantity demanded falls but the quantity supplied rises. A price decrease leads to increased demand but a lower supply. At the point where the quantity demanded equals the quantity supplied, demand and supply are in balance. This equilibrium point is achieved by market adjustments of quantity and price.
6	**What are the four types of market structure?**	Market structure is the number of suppliers in a market. Perfect competition is characterized by a large number of buyers and sellers, very similar products, good market information for both buyers and sellers, and ease of entry and exit into the market. In a pure monopoly, there is a single seller in a market. In monopolistic competition, many firms sell close substitutes in a market that is fairly easy to enter. In an oligopoly, a few firms produce most or all of the industry's output. An oligopoly is also difficult to enter and what one firm does will influence others.
7	**Which trends are reshaping the micro- and macroeconomic environments and the competitive arena?**	The U.S. economy displayed ongoing resilience despite the devastation of Hurricane Katrina. The government's use of macroeconomic policies to control inflation was effective, and GDP growth continued. Worldwide demand for energy, especially from China and India, is challenging oil companies to increase supplies. U.S. vulnerability to disruptions in energy supply became painfully apparent when Katrina put Gulf Coast refineries and offshore drilling rigs out of commission. Companies are using relationship management and strategic alliances to compete effectively in the global economy. Entrepreneurship is on the rise around the world as emerging economies recognize the importance of new business creation to economic growth. In Europe governments are realizing that socialist economic policies are not supporting economic growth and passing new regulations that promote increased productivity.

Key Terms

barriers to entry   83
business cycles   69
circular flow   67
consumer price index (CPI)   73
contractionary policy   74
cost-push inflation   73
crowding out   76
cyclical unemployment   72
demand   78
demand curve   78
demand-pull inflation   73
economic growth   69
economic system   66
economics   66
equilibrium   79
expansionary policy   74
federal budget deficit   76
Federal Reserve System (the Fed)   74
fiscal policy   74
frictional unemployment   71
full employment   70

inflation   72
macroeconomics   67
market structure   82
microeconomics   67
monetary policy   74
monopolistic competition   84
national debt   76
oligopoly   84
perfect (pure) competition   82
producer price index (PPI)   73
purchasing power   72
pure monopoly   83
recession   70
relationship management   86
savings bonds   77
seasonal unemployment   72
strategic alliance   87
structural unemployment   71
supply   78
supply curve   78
unemployment rate   71

Preparing for Tomorrow's Workplace: SCANS

1. If a friend claimed, "Economics is all theory and not very practical," how might you counter this claim? Share your rationale with the class. (Interpersonal, Information)

2. Use the Internet or go to the library and determine the current trends in GDP growth, unemployment, and inflation. What do these trends tell you about the level of business activity and the business cycle? If you owned a personnel agency, how would this information affect your decision-making? (Interpersonal, Information, Technology)

3. What are the latest actions the federal government has taken to manage the economy? Has it used monetary policy or fiscal policy to achieve its macroeconomic goals? Summarize your findings. Choose one of the following industries and discuss how the government's actions will affect that industry: airlines, automobile manufacturers, banking, biotechnology, chemical manufacturing, home building, oil and gas, publishing, retail stores, telecommunication equipment, and telecommunication services. (Information, Systems)

4. As a manufacturer of in-line roller skates, you are questioning your pricing policies. You note that over the past five years, the CPI increased an average of 3 percent per year, but the price of a pair of skates increased an average of 8 percent per year for the first three years and 2 percent for the next two years. What does this information tell you about demand, supply, and other factors influencing the market for these skates? (Resources, Information)

5. Use a search engine or article database to identify three recent strategic alliances. Include alliances between companies in the same and in different industries. Describe the benefits and risks of the relationships for each company. (Information, Technology)

6. **Team Activity** Divide the class into three groups, each with two teams to debate the pros and cons of deregulation and its impact on the competitive environment. One group will debate the effect of airline deregulation; another will focus

on electric-utility deregulation; and the third group will cover the telecommunications industry. One team should take the pro and the other the con for each industry. Use the Internet to obtain current articles on the subjects. After the debates, have a general discussion comparing the industries and how they have responded to deregulation. (Information, Interpersonal, Systems)

Ethics Activity

In July 2005, Wal-Mart filed an application in Utah to form an industrial loan corporation (ILC). ILCs are classified as limited-service financial entities rather than banks, so under current regulations nonfinancial companies are allowed to own ILCs. They fall under state regulation, and the Federal Deposit Insurance Corp. (FDIC) supervises and insures them. Wal-Mart says it plans to use the ILC to process its stores' electronic payments (credit and debit card transactions) in-house, to save millions of dollars a year in processing fees. Wal-Mart emphasized that this ILC would not deal with consumers; Wal-Mart would be the only customer.

A flood of letters from community bankers soon began pouring into the FDIC, opposing the application. The local bankers worried that the giant retailer would use the ILC as a first step to move into financial services. They cite the example of small retailers being driven out of business when a Wal-Mart, which can buy in huge volume and offer lower prices, opens in their community. Their

concerns may be justified: Wal-Mart has tried to buy banks in the past. In recent years Wal-Mart has chosen to partner with banks and has leases for more than 1,100 branches inside its stores. It also has a history of aggressively expanding into new businesses and now sells groceries, pharmaceuticals, and gasoline at many of its stores.

Using a Web search tool, locate articles about this topic and then write responses to the following questions. Be sure to support your arguments and cite your sources.

Ethical Dilemma: Should Wal-Mart's application for an ILC be approved? Is the community bankers' worry that Wal-Mart will use its clout to reduce competition valid?

Sources: Michael Barbaro, "Bankers Oppose Wal-Mart as Rival," *New York Times*, October 15, 2005, p. C1(L);"Regulators Foresee a Hearing On Wal-Mart's Plan for a Bank," *New York Times*, January 21, 2006, p. C13(L); Tom Shean, "Wal-Mart's Bank Effort Sparks Concern," *Virginian-Pilot* (Norfolk, Virginia), December 21, 2005, p 1.

Working the Net

1. Point your browser to the Bureau of Economic Analysis (BEA) at **http://www.bea.doc.gov**. Navigate to the Regional Accounts Data (under Regional /Gross State Product). Find the historical information for your state's gross domestic product (GDP). What trends do you see? Can you identify any reasons behind these trends? Compare your state's GDP to the U.S. GDP overall, which you will find on the National/Gross National Product page (link is on the BEA home page).

2. Read more about how the Consumer Price Index (CPI) is computed at the Bureau of Labor Statistics site, **http://stat.bls.gov/cpi/**. Look at the relative importance of each category included in the CPI. How well do these weightings match your own expenditures in each of these categories? What are some of the drawbacks of computing the CPI this way? Do you think these categories give a realistic picture of how most Americans spend their money? Explain your answer.

3. What's the latest economic news? Go to the ABC News site's Business section (**http://abcnews.go.com/sections/business/**) and scroll to "Money 101." Read the various articles. Then do the same for Consumer Confidence. Prepare a summary of what you learned and use it to discuss where you think the economy is headed for the next 6 to 12 months.

4. Ever think about what you'd do if you were president? Here's your chance to find out how your ideas would affect the federal budget. The National Budget Simulator, at **http://www.budgetsim.org/nbs/**, lets you see how government officials make trade-offs when they prepare the federal budget. Experiment with your own budget ideas at the site. What are the effects of your decisions?

5. In early 2006, when the Managing Change box was written, AT&T, Verizon, and BellSouth (now part of AT&T) announced their intention of charging Google, Vonage, and similar companies that want to send content over telecommunications networks. The Internet companies claimed this was unfair and restricted competition, with the consumer losing the most. Using Internet article databases and search engines, investigate whether the phone companies were able to get these charges approved and also who's winning the race for telecommunications

customers. Summarize your findings and present them to the class. Compare your views of who's leading the pack with your classmates. Is there a clear winner among the companies?

Wipeout in the Surfboard Industry

Clark Foam, a plastics factory in Laguna Niguel, California that produces foam blanks for surfboards, closed its doors on December 5, 2005. Founder Gordon "Grubby" Clark cited lawsuits, alleged violations of environmental and fire codes—and also admitted that the company had a poor safety record.

Normally the closure of a small plant would not attract worldwide attention. But Clark Foam supplied the basic part for about 90 percent of the world's custom surfboards. The United States produces 750,000 to 1 million custom boards (75 percent of all surfboards sold) each year at prices ranging from $300 to $900 and more.

Grubby Clark, a leader in surfboard design, pioneered the use of foam cores as a replacement for balsa wood. Founded in 1961, Clark Foam soon outclassed its competition with high quality products and outstanding customer service. Clark was also a ruthless businessman. When new competitors tried to enter the market, he lowered prices and essentially forced them out. "He had a monopoly, basically," says Tim Bessel, a San Diego board shaper. "Nobody could compete. The prices have been artificially suppressed for 30 years."

What some surfers called "Hurricane Clark" set an entire industry adrift. The ripple effect started with the 100 workers of Clark Foam, who lost their jobs. Another 1,500–2,000 workers in Southern California alone were at risk. Without Clark's 700 to 1,000 foam blanks a week, workers at independent board manufacturers, most of whom are small businesses, companies that make the fins attached to the boards and apply the fiberglass coating, and foam core distributors could be out of work. Surfers, worried that they would not be able to get new boards, rushed to buy whatever was available. Prices jumped $100 to $200 per board the day after Clark closed. Some feared that the custom surfboard industry was in danger of wiping out and being replaced by molded boards machine-made in Asia.

Meanwhile, board manufacturers scrambled to find foam cores from other sources in the United States, Australia, South Africa, Brazil, and New Zealand. In the near term, severe shortages resulted, because these companies were already at capacity. Surfboard shapers were also concerned that quality would suffer, because Clark had the superior product.

The capitalist model was alive and well, however, and companies like Walker Foam, another California foam blank company, geared up to fill the gap left by Clark. Walker had been pushed out by Clark in 1973 but reopened in 1990. The company moved quickly to increase domestic production to meet demand and speed up construction of a manufacturing facility it was building in China. Other companies see Clark's demise as an opportunity to strengthen the industry, and welcome the opportunity to use newer materials like closed-cell Styrofoam, epoxy, and other types of resins, which were more expensive than foam until now.

"When it comes right down to it, this is healthy," said Matt Biolos of Lost Surfboards. "It's like Daddy telling us to all grow up and become more self-reliant. It's going to hurt in the short term, but in a few years we may have a healthier surfboard industry because of it."

Critical Thinking Questions

- How did Clark Foam develop a monopoly in surfboard foam cores?
- Show how the laws of supply and demand affect the custom surfboard industry with the closure of Clark Foam.

● Describe the change in the competitive environment for surfboards that will result from Clark's exit from the industry.

Sources: Penni Crabtree, "Board Industry Adrift," *San Diego Union-Tribune*, December 9, 2005, pp. C1, C4; Penni Crabtree, "Surfboard Biz Fears Wipeout," *San Diego Union-Tribune*, December 8, 2005, pp. A1, A14; Travis Hunter, "Surfboard Shapers Relatively Unfazed by Loss of Clark Foam," *La Jolla Light*, December 22, 2005, p. 8; Stephanie Kang and Peter Sanders, "Wipeout for Key Player in Surfboard Industry," *Wall Street Journal*, December 8, 2005, p. B1; Chris Mauro, "Clark Foam Apocalypse: Some Board Builders See Light Ahead While Clamoring to Fill Clark Foam Void," *Surfermag.com*, http://www.surfermag.com (January 12, 2006); Chris Mauro, "Surf World Shocker: Clark Foam Shuts Down," *Surfermag.com*, http://www.surfermag.com (December 15, 2005); "Surfboard Foam Maker Catches a Lucky Break," *San Diego Union-Tribune*, January 3, 2006, p. A3.

Video Case >

Demand Drives the Toyota Prius

Higher gas prices and concerns about global energy supplies are driving the demand for hybrid automobiles, which combine small, fuel-efficient gas engines with electric motors to boost fuel economy. Although they accounted for only 1.5 percent of all U.S. auto sales in 2006, many analysts predict that sales will triple by 2012.

One of the most popular hybrid cars is Toyota's Prius, which was launched in Japan in 1997 and introduced to the United States in 2000. Car enthusiasts have snapped up the egg-shaped Prius, which gets up to 60 miles to the gallon in city driving. With sales of about 100,000 vehicles in 2005, the Prius represents 2.4 percent of Toyota sales and 50 percent of the U.S. hybrid markets.

According to Paul Daverio, Prius product manager, customers look at hybrids for three main reasons: fuel economy, environmental performance, and the desire for the latest automotive technology. Purchase price and cost to operate and maintain are also factors. "If you don't bring a product that's going to be reliable and that's going to be of great value for them, it doesn't matter how great the technology is, it doesn't matter how clean it is, it doesn't matter if you get 100 miles per gallon, it won't sell," says Ed LaRocque, Toyota's national manager for Advance Technology Vehicles.

Building relationships with its Prius customers is an important part of Toyota's competitive strategy for its hybrid cars. Many buyers are willing to try this new technology because of Toyota's solid reputation for producing reliable, high-quality cars and providing excellent customer service. A large number of Prius owners have never owned a Toyota before, opening up new market segments for the company. Loyalty programs such as "Prius Pioneers" gave the owners of the early Prius models the first opportunity to buy the second generation Prius.

With hybrid vehicle prices about $4,000 to $5,000 more than a traditional gasoline car, the economics don't add up. Even at today's high gasoline prices, the savings over the life of the car won't offset the extra cost. So Toyota has improved the quality of the driving experience by adding more horsepower to make its hybrids more appealing to customers who want to make a statement about reducing dependency on foreign oil and show their concern for the environment.

Toyota also recognizes the importance of hybrid technology to its overall competitive strategy. In 2006 it introduced more hybrid models, including a version of its popular Camry sedan and a Lexus RX400h luxury sport utility vehicle. With its strong sales, reputation for high-quality, fuel-efficient vehicles, and excellent customer service, in mid-2006 it overtook General Motors to become the leader of the global automotive industry. At the same time, Toyota recognizes the importance of strategic alliances and works closely with competitors such as Nissan, which will license Toyota's hybrid technology for use in its vehicles.

Critical Thinking Questions

Using information from the case and the video, answer the following critical thinking questions:

- Explain the relationship between energy supplies, gas prices, and demand for hybrid vehicles. What might happen if more customers wanted to buy Prius cars than Toyota expected?
- How do Toyota's relationship-building strategies for the Prius brand enhance the company's competitive position?
- What benefits does Toyota achieve by sharing its hybrid technology with competing auto manufacturers?

Sources: Adapted from video "Toyota and the Toyota Prius;" Dee-Ann Durbin, "Hybrids Take Center Stage," *San Diego Union-Tribune*, January 6, 2006, p. C3; "U.S. Hybrid Sales in April Back over 21,000," *Green Car Congress*, May, 2, 2006, http://www.greencarcongress.com; Martin Fickler, "Toyota Asks: What Slump?" *San Diego Union-Tribune*, November 5, 2005, p. C3; Jathon Sapsford, "Toyota's Chief Bets on Hybrids, Squeezing Rivals," *Wall Street Journal*, July 13, 2005, pp. B1, B2; Noriko Slurouzu, "Toyota Studies Hybrid Switch," *Wall Street Journal*, January 11, 2006, p. D7

Hot Links Address Book

The Federal Reserve Board issues a variety of statistical information about the state of the U.S. economy. Find it at the Federal Reserve's site by clicking on the Economic Research and Data link: **http://www.federalreserve.gov**

Where does the federal government get its money, and where does it go? Learn about the federal budget at the Office of Management and Budget Web site: **http://www.whitehouse.gov/omb**

Want to know the current public debt per citizen, or even what it was in 1790? Go to **http://www.publicdebt.treas.gov** and click on The Public Debt.

The U.S. Bureau of Economic Analysis tracks national and regional economic statistics, including the GDP. To find the latest GDP statistics, visit the BEA at **http://www.bea.doc.gov**

How are the job prospects in your area? Your region's unemployment statistics can give you an idea of how hard it will be to find a job. Find the most recent unemployment statistics from the Bureau of Labor Statistics at **http://www.bls.gov**

Where does the consumer price index stand today? Go to **http://stats.bls.gov/cpi**

How do the PPI and the CPI differ? Get the answers to this and other questions about the PPI by visiting the Bureau of Labor Statistics PPI site at **http://www.bls.gov/ppi**

CHAPTER 3

Making Ethical Decisions and Managing a Socially Responsible Business

Learning Goals

After reading this chapter, you should be able to answer these questions:

1 What philosophies and concepts shape personal ethical standards?

2 How can organizations encourage ethical business behavior?

3 What is social responsibility?

4 How do businesses meet their social responsibilities to various stakeholders?

5 What are the trends in ethics and social responsibility?

APPENDIX: UNDERSTANDING THE LEGAL AND TAX ENVIRONMENT

6 How does the legal system govern business transactions and settle business disputes?

7 What are the required elements of a valid contract; and what are the key types of business law?

8 What are the most common taxes paid by businesses?

Exploring Business Careers
Lord John Browne
BP

Although stories of greedy and unscrupulous business executives have dominated the business news during the last few years, one innovative leader for British Petroleum (BP) has been at the forefront of social responsibility by demonstrating a commitment to preserving the world's fragile environment. Lord John Browne, group chief executive to the world's second largest company, is consistently recognized as one of the 100 most influential British executives, according to the British Newspaper *The Times*. But there's a good reason he's so newsworthy: Browne is keenly aware of BP's responsibility to protect and preserve the earth's fragile environment, and he uses his influence and position to make BP more environmentally responsible.

Environmental issues are a growing concern among businesses worldwide. In particular, energy companies face tough scrutiny by their customers and stakeholders to make socially and ethically responsible decisions. Recognizing a rapidly increasing demand for energy worldwide, Browne is committed to taking BP "beyond petroleum," although the burden of this increased demand still falls to hydrocarbon-based sources, such as oil and natural gas. And although Browne has confidence that the world's oil and natural gas supplies are sufficient, his concerns are clear: "The real challenge is the potential impact of burning ever greater volumes of hydrocarbons on the world's climate."

However, he is not satisfied simply to state the problem and head home. "Business is at heart of the process of taking scientific advances and transforming them into technology . . . which can alter the lives of individuals and whole communities, and which can protect the environment." And he is putting his—and BP's—money where his mouth is.

The Kyoto Protocol, a 1997 United Nations treaty on climate change, seeks to reduce the levels of carbon dioxide (CO_2), a harmful byproduct of hydrocarbon use, by 5.2 percent below a 1990 baseline. BP immediately sought to reduce their emissions by twice that amount, a goal they reached by 2002. At the same time, BP increased profitability by almost $650 million, dispelling the belief that environmental concerns cannot coincide with good business sense. They did this by increasing efficiency and eliminating waste in their manufacturing processes.

Additionally, BP has begun several innovative initiatives to help preserve the environment:

- BP built China's first natural gas terminal and pipeline for distribution, which will save approximately 16 million tons of CO_2 emissions over coal.
- In Algeria, BP has started to use a process called carbon sequestration in which carbon, produced by natural gas production, is trapped before it can be released into the atmosphere. It is then injected back into reservoirs below the ground where it does not harm the environment. BP estimates this project will prevent the release of 17 million tons of CO_2.

This chapter will examine further how ethical and socially responsible decisions, such as those concerning the environment, are a part of every business and will discuss the role of ethics in a successful business career.

Every day, managers and business owners make business decisions based on what they believe to be right and wrong. Through their actions, they demonstrate to their employees what is and is not acceptable behavior and shape the moral standard of the organization. Ethics is a set of moral standards for judging whether something is right or wrong. As you will see in this chapter, personal and professional ethics are important cornerstones of an organization and shape its ultimate contributions to society. First, let's consider how individual business ethics are formed.

ethics
A set of moral standards for judging whether something is right or wrong.

Understanding Business Ethics

 What philosophies and concepts shape personal ethical standards?

ethical issue
A situation where a person must choose from a set of actions that may be ethical or unethical.

The first step in understanding business ethics is learning to recognize an ethical issue. An ethical issue is a situation where someone must choose between a set of actions that may be ethical or unethical. Many times ethical issues are very clear-cut. Scott Livengood, chief executive of Krispy Kreme doughnuts, fudged financial results and profited greatly from questionable accounting practices.[1] Few people would call that ethical behavior. But consider the actions of the stranded, hungry people in New Orleans who lost everything in the aftermath of Hurricane Katrina. They broke into flooded stores, taking food and bottled water without paying for them. Was this unethical behavior? Or what about the small Texas plastics manufacturer that employed over 100 people and specialized in the Latin American market? The president was distraught because he knew the firm would be bankrupt by the end of the year if it didn't receive more contracts. He knew that he was losing business because he refused to pay bribes. Bribes were part of the culture in his major markets. Closing the firm would put many people out of work. Should he start paying bribes in order to stay in business? Would this be unethical? Let's look at the next section to obtain some guidance on recognizing unethical situations.

Recognizing Unethical Business Activities

Researchers from Brigham Young University tell us that all unethical business activities will fall into one of the following categories:

1. *Taking things that don't belong to you.* The unauthorized use of someone else's property or taking property under false pretenses is taking something that does not belong to you. Even the smallest offense, such as using the postage meter at your office for mailing personal letters or exaggerating your travel expenses, belongs in this category of ethical violations.

2. *Saying things you know are not true.* Often, when trying for a promotion and advancement, fellow employees discredit their coworkers. Falsely assigning blame or inaccurately reporting conversations is lying. Although "This is the way the game is played around here" is a common justification, saying things that are untrue is an ethical violation.

3. *Giving or allowing false impressions.* The salesperson who permits a potential customer to believe that cardboard boxes will hold the customer's tomatoes for long-distance shipping when the salesperson knows the boxes are not strong enough has given a false impression. A car dealer who fails to disclose that a car has been in an accident is misleading potential customers.

4. *Buying influence or engaging in a conflict of interest.* A conflict of interest occurs when the official responsibilities of an employee or government official are influenced by the potential for personal gain. Suppose a company awards a construction contract to a firm owned by the father of the state attorney general while the state attorney general's office is investigating that company. If this construction award has the potential to shape the outcome of the investigation, a conflict of interest has occurred.

5. *Hiding or divulging information.* Failing to disclose the results of medical studies that indicate your firm's new drug has significant side effects is the ethical violation of hiding information that the product could be harmful to purchasers. Taking your firm's product development or trade secrets to a new place of employment constitutes the ethical violation of divulging proprietary information.

6. *Taking unfair advantage.* Many current consumer protection laws were passed because so many businesses took unfair advantage of people who were not educated or were unable to discern the nuances of complex contracts. Credit disclosure requirements, truth-in-lending provisions, and new regulations on auto leasing all resulted because businesses misled consumers who could not easily follow the jargon of long, complex agreements.

7. *Committing improper personal behavior.* Although the ethical aspects of an employee's right to privacy are still debated, it has become increasingly clear that personal conduct outside the job can influence performance and company reputation. Thus, a company driver must abstain from substance abuse because of safety issues. Even the traditional company Christmas party and picnic have come under scrutiny due to the possibility that employees at and following these events might harm others through alcohol-related accidents.

8. *Abusing another person.* Suppose a manager sexually harasses an employee or subjects employees to humiliating corrections in the presence of customers. In some cases, laws protect employees. Many situations, however, are simply interpersonal abuse that constitutes an ethical violation.

9. *Permitting organizational abuse.* Many U.S. firms with operations overseas, such as Levi Strauss, The Gap, and Esprit, have faced issues of organizational abuse. The unfair treatment of workers in international operations appears in the form of child labor, demeaning wages, and excessive work hours. Although a business cannot change the culture of another country, it can perpetuate—or stop—abuse through its operations there.

10. *Violating rules.* Many organizations use rules and processes to maintain internal controls or respect the authority of managers. Although these rules may seem burdensome to employees trying to serve customers, a violation may be considered an unethical act.

11. *Condoning unethical actions.* What if you witnessed a fellow employee embezzling company funds by forging her signature on a check that was to be voided? Would you report the violation? A winking tolerance of others' unethical behavior is itself unethical.[2]

After recognizing that a situation is unethical, the next question is what do you do? The action that a person takes is partially based upon their ethical philosophy. The environment in which we live and work also plays a role in our behavior. This section describes personal philosophies and legal factors that influence the choices we make when confronting an ethical dilemma.

Justice—The Question of Fairness

justice
What is considered fair according to the prevailing standards of society; an equitable distribution of the burdens and rewards that society has to offer.

Another factor influencing individual business ethics is justice, or what is fair according to prevailing standards of society. We all expect life to be reasonably fair. You expect your exams to be fair, the grading to be fair, and your wages to be fair, based on the type of work being done.

In the 21st century, we take justice to mean an equitable distribution of the burdens and rewards that society has to offer. The distributive process varies from society to society. Those in a democratic society believe in the "equal pay for equal work" doctrine, in which individuals are rewarded based on the value the free market places on their services. Because the market places different values on different occupations, the rewards, such as wages, are not necessarily equal. Nevertheless, many regard the rewards as just. A politician who argued that a supermarket clerk should receive the same pay as a physician, for example, would not receive many votes from the American people. At the other extreme, communist theorists have argued that justice would be served by a society in which burdens and rewards were distributed to individuals according to their abilities and their needs, respectively.

Utilitarianism—Seeking the Best for the Majority

utilitarianism
A philosophy that focuses on the consequences of an action to determine whether it is right or wrong; holds that an action that affects the majority adversely is morally wrong.

One of the philosophies that may influence choices between right and wrong is **utilitarianism**, which focuses on the consequences of an action taken by a person or organization. The notion that "people should act so as to generate the greatest good for the greatest number" is derived from utilitarianism. When an action affects the majority adversely, it is morally wrong. One problem with this philosophy is that it is nearly impossible to accurately determine how a decision will affect a large number of people.

Another problem is that utilitarianism always involves both winners and losers. If sales are slowing and a manager decides to fire 5 people rather than putting everyone on a 30-hour workweek, the 20 people who keep their full-time jobs are winners, but the other 5 are losers.

A final criticism of utilitarianism is that some "costs," although small relative to the potential good, are so negative that some segments of society find them unacceptable. Reportedly, the backs of up to 3,000 animals a year are deliberately broken so that scientists can conduct spinal cord research that could someday lead to a cure for spinal cord injuries. To a number of people, however, the "costs" are simply too horrible for this type of research to continue.

Following Our Obligations and Duties

deontology
A person who will follow his or her obligations to an individual or society because upholding one's duty is what is ethically correct.

The philosophy that says people should meet their obligations and duties when analyzing an ethical dilemma is called *deontology*. This means that a person will follow his or her obligations to another individual or society because upholding one's duty is what is considered ethically correct. For instance, people who follow this philosophy will always keep their promises to a friend and will follow the law. They will produce very consistent decisions, because they will be based on the individual's set duties. Note that this theory is not necessarily concerned with the welfare of others. Say, for example, a serviceman for Orkin Pest Control has decided that it's his ethical duty (and very practical!) to always be on time to meetings with home owners. Today he is running late. How is he supposed to drive? Is the serviceman supposed to speed, breaking his duty to society to uphold the law, or is he supposed to arrive at the client's home late, breaking his duty to be on time? This scenario of conflicting obligations does not lead us to a clear ethically correct resolution, nor does it protect the welfare of others from the serviceman's decision.

Individual Rights

In our society, individuals and groups have certain rights that exist under certain conditions regardless of any external circumstances. These rights serve as guides when making individual ethical decisions. The term *human rights* implies that certain rights—to life, to freedom, to the pursuit of happiness—are conveyed at birth and cannot be arbitrarily taken away. Denying the rights of an individual or group is considered to be unethical and illegal in most, though not all, parts of the world. Certain rights are guaranteed by the government and its laws, and these are considered *legal rights*. The U.S. Constitution and its amendments, as well as state and federal statutes, define the rights of American citizens. Those rights can be disregarded only in extreme circumstances, such as during wartime. Legal rights include the freedom of religion, speech, and assembly; protection from improper arrest and searches and seizures; and proper access to counsel, confrontation of witnesses, and cross-examination in criminal prosecutions. Also held to be fundamental is the right to privacy in many matters. Legal rights are to be applied without regard to race, color, creed, gender, or ability.

How Organizations Influence Ethical Conduct

 2 **How can organizations encourage ethical business behavior?**

People choose between right and wrong based on their personal code of ethics. They are also influenced by the ethical environment created by their employers. Consider the following newspaper headlines:

- James Beard Foundation president forced to resign after spending hundreds of thousands of dollars on excessive salaries and meals.
- Dennis Kozlowski, former top executive of Tyco, International, convicted of grand larceny, conspiracy, securities fraud, and falsifying business records.
- Bernie Ebbers, ex-WorldCom chief executive, sentenced to 25 years in prison for his role in corporate fraud.
- Ex-Adelphia CEO, John Rigas, sentenced to 15 years for looting the company and cheating investors.[3]

As these actual headlines illustrate, poor business ethics can create a very negative image for a company, can be expensive for the firm and/or the executives involved, and can result in bankruptcy and jail time for the offenders. Organizations can reduce the potential for these types of liability claims by educating their employees about ethical standards, by leading through example, and through various informal and formal programs.

Leading by Example

Employees often follow the examples set by their managers. That is, leaders and managers establish patterns of behavior that determine what's acceptable and what's not within the organization. While Ben Cohen was president of Ben & Jerry's ice cream, he followed a policy that no one could earn a salary more than seven times the lowest-paid worker. He wanted all employees to feel that they were equal. At the time he resigned, company sales were $140 million and the lowest-paid worker earned $19,000 per year. Ben Cohen's salary was $133,000 based on the "seven times" rule. A typical top executive of a $140 million company might have earned 10 times Cohen's salary. Ben Cohen's actions helped shape the ethical values of Ben & Jerry's.

Offering Ethics Training Programs

In addition to providing a system to resolve ethical dilemmas, organizations also provide formal training to develop an awareness of questionable business activities and practice appropriate responses. Many American companies have some type of ethics training program. The ones that are most effective, like those created by Levi Strauss, American Express, and Campbell Soup Company, begin with techniques for solving ethical dilemmas such as those discussed earlier. Next, employees are presented with a series of situations and asked to come up with the "best" ethical solution. One of these ethical dilemmas is shown in Exhibit 3.1. Some companies have tried to add a bit of excitement and fun to their ethics-training programs by presenting them in the form of games. Citigroup, for example, has created The Work Ethic, a board game in which participants strive to correctly answer legal, regulatory, policy-related, and judgment ethics questions.

Exhibit 3.1 > An Ethical Dilemma Used for Employee Training

Bill Gannon was a middle manager of a large manufacturer of lighting fixtures in Newark, New Jersey. Bill had moved up the company ladder rather quickly and seemed destined for upper management in a few years. Bill's boss, Dana Johnson, had been pressuring him about the semiannual reviews concerning Robert Talbot, one of Bill's employees. Dana, it seemed, would not accept any negative comments on Robert's evaluation forms. Bill had found out that a previous manager who had given Robert a bad evaluation was no longer with the company. As Bill reviewed Robert's performance for the forthcoming evaluation period, he found many areas of subpar performance. Moreover, a major client had called recently complaining that Robert had filled a large order improperly and then had been rude to the client when she called to complain.

Discussion Questions
1. What ethical issues does the situation raise?
2. What courses of action could Bill take? Describe the ethics of each course.
3. Should Bill confront Dana? Dana's boss?
4. What would you do in this situation? What are the ethical implications?

---

code of ethics
A set of guidelines prepared by a firm to provide its employees with the knowledge of what the firm expects in terms of their responsibilities and behavior toward fellow employees, customers, and suppliers.

CONCEPT in Action

Better known as trustworthy gatekeepers than purveyors of scandal, news organizations rarely face scrutiny over internal ethical lapses. But in a spectacular journalistic misstep during a presidential campaign, CBS News anchor Dan Rather delivered a potentially election-swaying report based upon spurious, unauthenticated documents. The event drew harsh criticism from *60 Minutes* colleague Andy Rooney and led to executive firings and Rather's early retirement from CBS. *How might the "front page of the newspaper" test help journalists make ethical decisions?*

© CBS/LANDOV

Establishing a Formal Code of Ethics

Most large companies and thousands of smaller ones have created, printed, and distributed codes of ethics. In general, a code of ethics provides employees with the knowledge of what their firm expects in terms of their responsibilities and behavior toward fellow employees, customers, and suppliers. Some ethical codes offer a lengthy and detailed set of guidelines for employees. Others are not really codes at all but rather summary statements of goals, policies, and priorities. Some companies have their codes framed and hung on office walls or printed on cards to be carried at all times by executives. The code of ethics for Costco Wholesale, the chain of membership warehouse clubs, is shown in Exhibit 3.2.

Do codes of ethics make employees behave in a more ethical manner? Some people believe that they do. Others think that they are little more than public relations gimmicks. If senior management abides by the code of ethics and regularly emphasizes the code to empoyees, then it will likely have a positive influence on behavior.

All of the "Top 100 Best Corporate Citizens" listed by *Business Ethics* magazine, in a recent year, had formal codes of ethics. The top corporate citizens in 2006 were:

1. Green Mountain Coffee Roasters
2. Hewlett-Packard
3. Advanced Micro Devices
4. Motorola
5. Agilent Technologies
6. Timberland Company
7. Salesforce.com
8. Cisco Systems
9. Dell
10. Texas Instruments[4]

Cummins is one of 19 companies to be named every year since the list was created in 2000.

Making the Right Decision

In many situations there may be no simple right or wrong answers. Yet there are several questions that you can ask yourself and a couple of

Exhibit 3.2 > Costco Wholesale's Code of Ethics

COSTCO WHOLESALE

CODE OF ETHICS

By Jim Sinegal

OBEY THE LAW

The law is irrefutable! Absent a moral imperative to challenge a law, we must conduct our business in total compliance with the laws of every community where we do business.

Comply with all statutes.

Cooperate with authorities.

Respect all public officials and their positions.

Avoid all conflict of interest issues with public officials.

Comply with all disclosure and reporting requirements.

Comply with safety and security standards for all products sold.

Exceed ecological standards required in every community where we do business.

Comply with all applicable wage and hour laws.

Comply with all applicable anti-trust laws.

Protect "inside information" that has not been released to the general public.

TAKE CARE OF OUR MEMBERS

The member is our key to success. If we don't keep our members happy, little else that we do will make a difference.

Provide top-quality products at the best prices in the market.

Provide a safe shopping environment in our warehouses.

Provide only products that meet applicable safety and health standards.

Sell only products from manufacturers who comply with "truth in advertising/packaging" standards.

Provide our members with a 100% satisfaction guaranteed warranty on every product and service we sell, including their membership fee.

Assure our members that every product we sell is authentic in make and in representation of performance.

Make our shopping environment a pleasant experience by making our members feel welcome as our guests.

Provide products to our members that will be ecologically sensitive.

> Our member is our reason for being. If they fail to show up, we cannot survive. Our members have extended a "trust" to Costco by virtue of paying a fee to shop with us. We can't let them down or they will simply go away. We must always operate in the following manner when dealing with our members:
> Rule #1 – The member is always right.
> Rule #2 – In the event the member is ever wrong, refer to rule #1.
>
> "There are plenty of shopping alternatives for our members. We will succeed only if we do not violate the trust they have extended to us. We must be committed at every level of our company, with every ounce of energy and grain of creativity we have, to constantly strive to bring goods to market at a lower price."

> If we do these four things throughout our organization, we will realize our ultimate goal, which is to REWARD OUR SHAREHOLDERS.

TAKE CARE OF OUR EMPLOYEES

To claim "people are our most important asset" is true and an understatement. Each employee has been hired for a very important job. Jobs such as stocking the shelves, ringing members' orders, buying products and paying our bills are jobs we would all choose to perform because of their importance. The employees hired to perform these jobs are performing as management's "alter egos." Every employee, whether they are in a Costco warehouse or whether they work in the regional or corporate offices, is a Costco ambassador trained to give our members professional, courteous treatment.

Today we have warehouse managers who were once stockers and callers and vice presidents who were once in clerical positions for our company. We believe that Costco's future executive officers are currently working in our warehouses, depots, buying offices and accounting departments, as well as in our home offices.

To that end, we are committed to these principles:

Provide a safe work environment.

Pay a fair wage.

Make every job challenging, but make it fun!

Consider the loss of any employee as a failure on the part of the company and a loss to the organization.

Teach our people how to do their jobs and how to improve personally and professionally.

Promote from within the company to achieve the goal of a minimum of 80% of management positions being filled by current employees.

Create an "open door" attitude at all levels of the company that is dedicated to fairness and listening.

RESPECT OUR VENDORS

Our vendors are our partners in business, and for us to prosper as a company, they must prosper with us. It is important that our vendors understand that we will be tough negotiators but fair in our treatment of them.

Treat all vendors and their representatives as you would expect to be treated if visiting their places of business.

Pay all bills within the allocated time frame.

Honor all commitments.

Protect all vendor property assigned to Costco as though it were our own.

Always be thoughtful and candid in negotiations.

Provide a careful review process with at least two levels of authorization before terminating business with an existing vendor of more than two years.

Do not accept gratuities of any kind from a vendor.

> These guidelines are exactly that - guidelines, some common sense rules for the conduct of our business. Intended to simplify our jobs, not complicate our lives, these guidelines will not answer every question or solve every problem. At the core of our philosophy as a company must be the implicit understanding that not one of us is required to lie or cheat on behalf of Costco. In fact, dishonest conduct will not be tolerated. To do any less would be unfair to the overwhelming majority of our employees who support and respect Costco's commitment to ethical business conduct.
>
> If you are ever in doubt as to what course of action to take on a business matter that is open to varying ethical interpretations, take the high road and do what is right.
>
> If you want our help, we are always available for advice and counsel. That's our job, and we welcome your questions or comments.
>
> Our continued success depends on you. We thank each of you for your contribution to our past success and for the high standards you have insisted upon in our company.

97HR1005

self-tests to help you make the right ethical decision. First, ask yourself, "Are there any legal restrictions or violations that will result from the action?" If so, take a different course of action. If not, ask yourself, "Does it violate my company's code of ethics?" If so, again find a different path to follow. Third, ask "Does this meet the guidelines of my own ethical philosophy?" If the answer is "yes," then your decision must still pass two important tests.

The Feelings Test You must now ask, "How does it make me feel?" This enables you to examine your comfort level with a particular decision. Many people find that after reaching a decision on an issue they still experience discomfort that may manifest itself in a loss of sleep or appetite. Those feelings of conscience can serve as a future guide in resolving ethical dilemmas.

Front Page of the Newspaper Test The final test is the "front page of the newspaper." The question to be asked is how a critical and objective reporter would report your decision in a front-page story. Some managers rephrase the test for their employees: How will the headline read if I make this decision? This test is helpful in spotting and resolving potential conflicts of interest.

> ### concept check
>
> What is the role of top management in organizational ethics?
>
> What is a code of ethics?

Managing a Socially Responsible Business

3 What is social responsibility?

CONCEPT *in Action*

Originally an erectile-dysfunction (ED) treatment, Viagra has moved beyond impotence and found broader use as a sex-enhancing drug—a development that has rankled the Food and Drug Administration. The shift became apparent when Pfizer dumped elder Viagra-spokesman Bob Dole for a devil-horned poster boy known as "Wild Thing." *Is it socially responsible for Pfizer to promote recreational use of ED drugs, or is such marketing, as critics say, akin to peddling aphrodisiacs and encouraging risky behavior?*

AP PHOTO/PFIZER LABS

Acting in an ethical manner is one of the four components of the pyramid of corporate social responsibility. **Social responsibility** is the concern of businesses for the welfare of society as a whole. It consists of obligations beyond those required by law or union contract. This definition makes two important points. First, social responsibility is voluntary. Beneficial action required by law, such as cleaning up factories that are polluting air and water, is not voluntary. Second, the obligations of social responsibility are broad. They extend beyond investors in the company to include workers, suppliers, consumers, and communities.

Exhibit 3.3 portrays economic performance as the foundation for the other three responsibilities. At the same time that a business pursues profits (economic responsibility), however, it is expected to obey the law (legal responsibility); to do what is right, just, and fair (ethical responsibility); and to be a good corporate citizen (philanthropic responsibility). These four components are distinct but together constitute the whole. Still, if the company doesn't make a profit, then the other three responsibilities are moot.

Many companies are already working to make the world a better place to live. Consider these examples:

- Starbucks sponsors literacy programs as well as a holiday gift drive for seriously ill children.
- Each year, the accounting firm PricewaterhouseCoopers sends at least 20 partners to the developing world, for several months, to help local aid programs.
- Home Depot refuses to purchase wood from endangered forests and actively works to protect the South American rain forest.

Understanding Social Responsibility

Peter Drucker, the late globally respected management expert, said that we should look first at what an organization does *to* society and second at what it can do *for* society. This idea suggests that social responsibility has two basic dimensions: legality and responsibility.

Exhibit 3.3 > The Pyramid of Corporate Social Responsibility

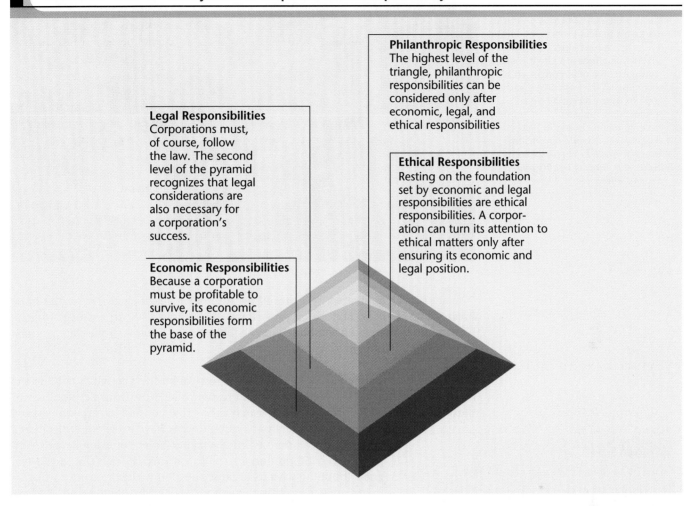

Legal Responsibilities Corporations must, of course, follow the law. The second level of the pyramid recognizes that legal considerations are also necessary for a corporation's success.

Economic Responsibilities Because a corporation must be profitable to survive, its economic responsibilities form the base of the pyramid.

Philanthropic Responsibilities The highest level of the triangle, philanthropic responsibilities can be considered only after economic, legal, and ethical responsibilities

Ethical Responsibilities Resting on the foundation set by economic and legal responsibilities are ethical responsibilities. A corporation can turn its attention to ethical matters only after ensuring its economic and legal position.

social responsibility
The concern of businesses for the welfare of society as a whole; consists of obligations beyond those required by law or contracts.

Illegal and Irresponsible Behavior The idea of social responsibility is so widespread today that it is hard to conceive of a company continually acting in illegal and irresponsible ways. Nevertheless, such actions do sometimes occur. Of course, the acts of managers of Enron, WorldCom, and Tyco created financial ruin for their organizations, extreme financial hardships for many former employees, and general hardships for the communities in which they operated. Yet top executives walked away with millions. Some, however, will ultimately pay large fines and have been sentenced to jail. Federal, state, and local laws determine whether an activity is legal or not. The laws that regulate business are discussed in the appendix to this chapter.

Irresponsible but Legal Behavior Sometimes companies act irresponsibly, yet their actions are legal. The federal government is pressuring the advertising industry and the automobile industry for more responsible advertising. The government is concerned about advertisements that place an emphasis on speed and that show vehicles engaging in dangerous driving practices. "It seems that some ads work against road safety rather than for it," according to one spokesperson.

Consumer Reports magazine, which tests consumer products and then reports the results, found that Sharper Image's Ionic Breeze air cleaner was "ineffective" and produced "almost no reduction in airborne particles." Sharper Image, in turn, sued Consumers Union, publisher of *Consumer Reports*. Consumers Union's attorney said,

"We are confident that we will prevail because our magazine's review of the Ionic Breeze is . . . fully accurate, as Sharper Image well knows."[5] Sharper Image lost the lawsuit. But is Sharper Image still selling the Ionic Breeze? Their Web site claims, "Ionic Breeze for every room in every price range."[6]

Legal and Responsible Behavior The vast majority of business activities fall into the category of behavior that is both legal and responsible. Most firms act legally, and most try to be socially responsible. Research shows that consumers, especially those under 30, are likely to buy brands that have excellent ethical track records and community involvement. Target, for example, gives approximately $2 million a week to various causes. "Our guests feel good shopping with us because they know they're contributing to many great causes as they shop," says John Remington, Target's vice-president of event marketing and communications.[7]

Responsibilities to Stakeholders

4 **How do businesses meet their social responsibilities to various stakeholders?**

What makes a company admired or perceived as socially responsible? Such a company meets its obligations to its stakeholders. Stakeholders are the individuals or groups to whom a business has a responsibility. The stakeholders of a business are its employees, its customers, the general public, and its investors.

Responsibility to Employees

stakeholders
Individuals or groups to whom a business has a responsibility; include employees, customers, the general public, and investors.

An organization's first responsibility is to provide a job to employees. Keeping people employed and letting them have time to enjoy the fruits of their labor is the finest thing business can do for society. Enron is an example of a company that violated this responsibility. Beyond this fundamental responsibility, employers must provide a clean, safe working environment that is free from all forms of discrimination. Companies should also strive to provide job security whenever possible.

Enlightened firms are also empowering employees to make decisions on their own and suggest solutions to company problems. Empowerment contributes to an employee's self-worth, which, in turn, increases productivity and reduces absenteeism.

CONCEPT *in Action*

Occupational disasters make national headlines and turn job safety into a pressing issue for industry leaders. A dramatic incident at West Virginia's Sago Mine exposed breakdowns in mining safety when coal miners trapped by an explosion were later found dead of carbon monoxide poisoning—hours after news media had reported their miraculous survival. Factors in mining accidents range from outdated equipment and unheeded warnings to cutbacks at the Mine Safety and Health Administration. *How might industry better fulfill its safety responsibility to workers?*

Each year *Fortune* conducts an extensive survey of the best places to work in America. The top 10 are shown in Exhibit 3.4. Some companies offer unusual benefits to their employees. CMP Media gives employees $30,000 for infertility treatments and adoption aid. FedEx allows free rides in the jump seats of company planes. Steelcase has a 1,200-acre camping and recreational area for employee use.

Responsibility to Customers

A central theme of this text is that to be successful today a company must satisfy its customers. A firm must deliver what it promises. It must also be honest and forthright with its clients. We will discuss this in the "Customer Satisfaction and Quality" boxes in most chapters.

Responsibility to Society

A business must also be responsible to society. A business provides a community with jobs, goods, and services. It also pays taxes that go to support schools, hospitals, and better roads. Most companies, such as Target as previously discussed, try to be good citizens in their communities.

Responsibility to society doesn't end at our shores. Global enterprises are attempting to help the around the public world as explained in the Expanding Around the Globe box.

Environmental Protection Business is also responsible for protecting and improving the world's fragile environment. The world's forests are being destroyed fast. Every second, an area the size of a football field is laid bare. Plant and animal species are becoming extinct at the rate of 17 per hour. A continent-size hole is opening up in the earth's protective ozone shield. Each year we throw out 80 percent more refuse than we did in 1960; as a result, more than half of the nation's landfills are filled to capacity.

To slow the erosion of the world's resources, many companies are becoming more environmentally responsible. Toyota is now using "renewable" energy sources to power its facilities, making it the largest single user of clean power in the world. Toyota's first step in the United States was to turn to renewable sources such as solar, wind, geothermal, and water power for the electricity at its headquarters in Torrance and Irving, California.

CONCEPT *in Action*

An impassioned debt-relief advocate and promoter of the Live 8 international rock festival, U2 frontman Bono has joined forces with corporate America to fight AIDS through a branding program called Product RED. As part of the charitable program, companies like American Express, Converse, and Gap develop and market "red-themed" products and donate the proceeds to disease-prevention agencies in Africa. *In what ways does the creation of global brand Product RED exemplify trends in corporate philanthropy?*

Exhibit 3.4 > America's Top Ten Best Places to Work

Rank Company Headquarters Website	**What makes it so great?**
1 Genentech South San Francisco http://www.gene.com	**What's better than being a valued member** of a cancer-fighting team? Having a great time while you're at work. (It doesn't hurt that 95% of workers are shareholders—and they've benefited handsomely from the soaring stock.)
2 Wegmans Food Markets Rochester, N.Y. http://www.wegmans.com	**Work really is a family affair** at this privately held grocery chain. Before it opened two new stores last year, Wegmans chartered jets to fly all new full-timers to Rochester to be welcomed by CEO Danny Wegman.
3 Valero Energy San Antonio http://www.valero.com	**When disaster strikes,** this team pulls together. After hurricanes Katrina and Rita hit, Valero dispatched trucks filled with supplies, set up temporary housing for employees, fed volunteers—and donated $1 million to the Red Cross.
4 Griffin Hospital Derby, Conn. http://www.griffinhealth.org	**Money isn't everything.** Despite pay scales 5% to 7% lower than hospitals in its area, Griffin received 5,100 applications for a range of 160 open positions in 2005, largely due to its top-notch reputation for patient care.
5 W.L. Gore & Associates Newark, Del. http://www.gore.com	**To encourage innovation** at the maker of Gore-Tex fabrics, Elixir guitar strings, and Glide dental floss, there are no bosses, job titles, or organization charts, just sponsors, team members, and leaders.
6 Container Store Coppell, Texas http://www.containerstore.com	**At this storage retailer,** even part-timers can receive bonuses, and drivers are rewarded for long service and safe driving records. In 2004 one driver took home $5,000 for ten years of perfect driving.
7 Vision Service Plan Rancho Cordova, Calif. http://www.vsp.com	**Ever wonder** if your boss could handle your job? At this not-for-profit eye-care-insurance firm, managers get into the trenches and work rank-and-file jobs on annual In Touch Day. Plus, monthly cake day celebrates employee birthdays.
8 J.M. Smucker Orrville, Ohio http://www.smuckers.com	**This 109-year-old** jam and food company has a family feeling that's still sweet. Two brothers, Tim and Richard Smucker, are at the helm. And employees interview job applicants to make sure future colleagues will fit the culture.
9 Recreational Equip. (REI) Kent, Wash. http://www.REI.com	**A shared passion for roughing it** unites employees with consumers at this outdoor-goods maker and retailer, which regularly hosts environmental-service projects. Says one worker: "REI is a way of life."
10 S.C. Johnson Racine, Wash. http://www.scjohnson.com	**They just won't budge.** The family-owned consumer products manufacturer has a devoted workforce, witnessed by an incredibly low turnover rate of 2%. Part of the reason: profit-sharing that added 19% to pay last year.

Source: Robert Levering and Milton Moskowitz, "The 100 Best Companies to Work For," *Fortune* (January 11, 2006), pp. 89–90. Copyright © 2006 by Time, Inc. All rights reserved. Reproduced by permission.

Clean Water, No Profit

Like plenty of multinationals, Procter and Gamble (P&G) rushed to offer aid to tsunami victims in Asia, shipping 15 million packets of water purifier to affected countries and pledging 13 million more if needed. What's different is that the product P&G airlifted was a commercial bust.

Called Pur, the powder was envisioned as a revolutionary way to clean the world's drinking water. P&G spent four years and $10 million for research and development before launching Pur in September 2002. But the packets of chlorine salt and iron sulfate are relatively complicated to mix and, at about 10 cents each, expensive for many of the world's poor.

By November of 2003, Pur still hadn't caught on as a profitable venture. In virtually every market where it was available, Pur gained early interest but not broad acceptance. By late 2004, P&G abandoned plans to sell the product for profit in developing countries and dramatically cut back its water-purification ambitions.

P&G wondered how it would unload the millions of packets of Pur sitting in the company's factory in Manila. Then, shortly after the December 26, 2004 tsunami, the phone started ringing with calls from AmeriCares, UNICEF, and the International Federation of the Red Cross with orders for Pur.

The company added a third shift to its factory and had orders to ship 15 million packets of the product to areas hit by the tsunami. Initially, P&G sold the packets to aid organizations at cost—3½ cents, but later decided to donate them because of the enormity of the disaster.

In order to keep the product going, management has examined a list of 40 countries with the highest rates of infant mortality due to unsafe drinking water. P&G had pledged to introduce Pur to two new countries a year. P&G is selling Pur in Haiti and Uganda for 8 or 9 cents a packet and Kenya is the next market to be served.[8]

Critical Thinking Questions
* After the tsunami, should P&G have given Pur away at the beginning?
* Should Pur be given away in Haiti, Uganda, and Kenya? Why?

---

corporate philanthropy
The practice of charitable giving by corporations; includes contributing cash, donating equipment and products, and supporting the volunteer efforts of company employees.

Corporate Philanthropy Companies also display their social responsibility through corporate philanthropy. **Corporate philanthropy** includes cash contributions, donations of equipment and products, and support for the volunteer efforts of company employees. Corporate philanthropy totals about $9 billion a year.[9] American Express is a major supporter of the American Red Cross. The organization relies almost entirely on charitable gifts to carry out its programs and services, which include disaster relief, armed-forces emergency relief, blood and tissue services, and health and safety services. The funds provided by American Express have enabled the Red Cross to deliver humanitarian relief to victims of numerous disasters around the world.

When Hurricane Katrina hit the Gulf Coast, Bayer sent 45,000 diabetes blood glucose monitors to the relief effort. Within a week of the disaster, Abbott, Alcoa, British Petroleum, Dell, Disney, Intel, Motorola, UPS, Walgreens, and other major corporations had contributed over $100 million for hurricane relief.[10] Small businesses can't match the charitable budgets of large companies, but that doesn't mean their impact can't be just as vital, as discussed in the Catching the Entrepreneurial Spirit box.

CONCEPT in Action

From the Toyota Prius to the Lexus RX400 SUV, hybrid cars are turning heads and promising to change the way the world drives. Petrol-electric vehicles are more eco-friendly and fuel-efficient than traditional gas-guzzlers, but they are also more expensive to own. Analysts project that, after fueling, insurance, and maintenance expenses, hybrid models cost thousands more than conventional models over a five-year period. *Do the environmental benefits associated with hybrid vehicles justify the higher cost of ownership?*

Small Companies but Big Hearts

In the wake of the deadly Asian tsunami in December 2004, New York restaurateur William Jack Degel felt compelled to help with the massive relief effort in any way he could. So the owner of Uncle Jack's Steakhouses decided to donate the proceeds from all his January and February dessert sales to benefit survivors. Alone, he expected to give about $20,000. But eventually, he began reaching out to other restaurants, and Sweet Relief was born. Now 50 restaurants in eight states have earmarked between 25% and 50% of their dessert sales in an effort to raise $250,000 for CARE, a global poverty group. "A big company can afford to give $30 million," Degel says. "But if small businesses collaborated as a whole throughout the U.S., we could beat out the big business donations."

When tragedy strikes, giving tends to strike back even harder. At large corporations, there are deep pockets to tap. Following the tsunami, corporate donations—among them, Pfizer's $10 million, ExxonMobil's $5 million, and Cisco's $2.5 million—threatened to outpace the U.S. government's initial pledge of $35 million, which was later bumped up to at least $350 million.

But away from the headline-making multimillion-dollar checks—as well as the headline-making tragedies—small-business owners continue to dream up their own creative ways to contribute. Without their own foundations, employee gift-matching plans, and in some cases, entire philanthropy departments, individual small businesses cannot flex the same kind of charitable muscle as corporate giants. But their collective impact does make a difference, particularly within the communities they operate. Countless small businesses in the South gave food, money, and merchandise to the victims of Hurricane Katrina in New Orleans. Most of them have found such acts of kindness to be an important part of doing business. Besides engendering good will among clients and employees, it helps raise visibility, burnish reputations, and can even bring in new business.

A national survey sponsored by the Better Business Bureau Wise Giving Alliance found that 91% of all small businesses with between 4 and 99 employees support charitable organizations on some level, whether it's outright cash gifts, fundraising for the local hospital, or sponsoring a Little League team. "They recognize the importance in supporting causes in their communities," says Bennett Weiner, the alliance's chief operating officer.

One of the most traditional ways that small businesses have contributed is by giving their time and expertise. Owen Cleaners, a family dry-cleaning business in Paducah, Kentucky, started collecting used winter coats 18 years ago, cleaning them for free and then distributing them to needy children. "We've probably cleaned more than 84,000 coats," says David Perry, who owns and operates the 85-year-old company, which boasts eight locations and 55 employees. "It's like an annual ritual here." Perry estimates that he spends about $7,500 a year on the Cal's Coats for Kids coat drive. Some employees volunteer their time while others get paid overtime. But, he says, "I don't really consider the tax deduction as part of the equation." His philosophy? "Every gift obviously adds up."[11]

Critical Thinking Questions

- Do small businesses have the same social responsibilities as large corporations?
- Should the federal government change tax laws and offer other incentives to encourage small businesses to be more socially responsible?

Responsibilities to Investors

Companies' relationships with investors also entail social responsibility. Although a company's economic responsibility to make a profit might seem to be its main obligation to its shareholders, some investors increasingly are putting more emphasis on other aspects of social responsibility.

Some investors are limiting their investments to securities that fit within their beliefs about ethical and social responsibility. This is called **social investing**. For example, a social investment fund might eliminate from consideration the securities of all companies that make tobacco products or liquor, manufacture weapons, or have a history of polluting. Not all social investment strategies are alike. Some ethical mutual funds will not invest in government securities because they help to fund the military; others freely buy government securities, with managers noting that federal funds also support the arts and pay for AIDS research. Today, about $100 billion is invested in social investment funds.

This decade has been among the worst ever, in modern times, of companies failing to meet responsibilities to investors. Scandals at WorldCom, Krispy Kreme, HealthSouth, Enron, and others so disturbed the investment community that they had a negative impact on the stock market. Investigators found companies claiming huge assets that never existed; falsified financial statements; huge loans by companies that could not be justified (or paid back); executives selling massive amounts of stock at high prices, then announcing several months later that the earnings were being restated at a much lower level, thus sending the stock crashing; and analysts making "buy" recommendations to the public while sending internal e-mails to coworkers stating that the stock was worthless. The Securities and Exchange Commission and many state attorneys

social investing
The practice of limiting investments to securities of companies that behave in accordance with the investor's beliefs about ethical and social responsibility.

concept check

How do businesses carry out their social responsibilities to consumers?

What is corporate philanthropy?

Is a company's only responsibility to its investors to make a profit? Why or why not?

MANAGING CHANGE

Citigroup Attempts to Create a New Culture

Citigroup, the world's largest financial firm, earns about $47 million in net profits every day! The firm has more than $1 trillion in assets, with Citibank being the largest. The former Chief Executive Officer (CEO), Sandy Weill, has now stepped up to chairman of the board, and Chuck Prince is the new CEO.

Chuck Prince says he has found his purpose. He wants to be the chief executive officer who brings a new culture of ethics to Citigroup. This may seem an odd effort for a man who earned his stripes as a close adviser to Sandy Weill. Although few would charge Mr. Weill with being unethical—"tough but honest" is a phrase used by those who know him—he built Citigroup's financial empire with a ruthless focus on cost-cutting, deal-making, and financial performance. He didn't spend much time talking about "values," "ethics," or "shared responsibilities."

But now, those have become Mr. Prince's watchwords, and his campaign is not just a paste-a-values-statement-on-the-Web-site effort. He predicts it will consume at least half of his executive time and energy in the next few years. "This is job one," Mr. Prince says. "If I don't own this, I don't think it will succeed."

It won't be easy. Citigroup played a pivotal role in financing fraud-ridden Enron, WorldCom, Adelphia, and Parmalat. Its private bank in Japan spent three years flouting the directives of regulators. And bond traders in Europe developed a trading strategy so extreme that they dubbed it "Dr. Evil." The company, under both Mr. Weill and Mr. Prince, has been caught misbehaving multiple times, on multiple continents. Mr. Prince says Citigroup isn't a company out of control. "We don't have a bad culture. We don't have a corrupt culture." Instead, he argues that Citigroup's leaders—himself included—have failed to make their own values and ethics part of the fabric of the corporation. "We emphasized the short-term performance side of the equation

exclusively," he said. "We didn't think we had to say: 'And by the way, don't violate the law.' There were unspoken assumptions that need to be spoken."

The first sign Mr. Prince was serious about all this came when he fired three senior executives for failing to manage the Japan problem. That got the attention of everyone at the company, including some top executives who thought he had overreacted. Since then, he's been quietly constructing a plan to remake the company culture. He chose three chief executives who he thought worth emulating—Jeff Immelt of General Electric, Michael Dell of Dell, and Bill Weldon of Johnson & Johnson—and paid a long visit to each.

The result is a massive campaign that has begun at Citigroup. Many of the company's 300,000 employees in 100 countries gathered to watch a movie that traced the company's history and called on employees to make Citigroup "the most respected global financial-services company." Citigroup's top executives have been told to expect a host of changes that include annual ethics training for all employees, expanded training for top managers, anonymous appraisal of managers by their employees ("That one came from Dell," Mr. Prince says), a 30 percent increase in resources for compliance and audit, and changes in the way management compensation is calculated. In addition, Mr. Prince plans a global tour each year to reinforce the effort.[12]

Critical Thinking Questions

- Should the Board of Directors at Citigroup have taken action earlier to alter the culture created by Sandy Weill? If so, why do you think that they didn't?
- What else could Chuck Prince do to make Citigroup employees more ethical and socially responsible?

general, particularly New York's, which is America's financial center, are working to enact new laws to curb these abuses.

One company that decided to quickly alter the way it did business around the globe was Citigroup, as discussed in the Managing Change box above.

Trends in Ethics and Social Responsibility

 5 **What are the trends in ethics and social responsibility?**

Three important trends related to ethics and social responsibility are changes in corporate philanthropy, a new social contract between employers and employees, and the growth of global ethics and social responsibility.

Changes In Corporate Philanthropy

Corporate philanthropy has typically involved seeking out needy groups and then giving them money or company products. Today, the focus is shifting to **strategic giving**, which ties philanthropy more closely to the corporate mission or goals and targets donations to regions where a company operates.

strategic giving
The practice of tying philanthropy closely to the corporate mission or goals and targeting donations to regions where a company operates.

Stan Litow, IBM's vice president of corporate community relations, notes that the company knows it takes more than just money—checkbook philanthropy (the old model)—to have a successful giving program. "With checkbook philanthropy you could contribute a lot of money and accomplish very little," he says. "I think that in the new model, being generous is incredibly important, but the most important aspect of this new model is using our many resources to achieve something of lasting value in the communities where we live, work and do business."[13]

IBM knows throwing money at something isn't good enough, because money, in and of itself, does not do the good. It's the people, products, and programs supported by cash donations that do the worthwhile work. IBM's philanthropic donations in 2006 totaled over $175 million. Of that, only 25 percent was cash. The remainder was technology and technical services—the best of what IBM has to offer.

Corporate philanthropy has also become a target for special-interest groups. AT&T, General Electric, and Eastman Kodak have come under attack by abortion foes for their donations to Planned Parenthood. The conservative Capital Research Center has criticized Anheuser-Busch, Hewlett-Packard, and other manufacturers for supporting what the center claims are radical groups seeking to undermine the capitalist system. When Philip Morris gave money to conservative political causes, the gay activist group ACT-UP encouraged consumers to stop buying its products.

A Social Contract Between Employer and Employee

Another trend in social responsibility is the effort by organizations to redefine their relationship with their employees. Many people have viewed social responsibility as a one-way street that focuses on the obligations of business to society, employees, and others. Now, companies are telling employees that they also have a responsibility when it comes to job security. The new contract goes like this: "There will never be job security. You will be employed by us as long as you add value to the organization, and you are continuously responsible for finding ways to add value. In return, you have the right to demand interesting and important work, the freedom and resources to perform it well, pay that reflects your contribution, and the experience and training needed to be employable here or elsewhere." Coca-Cola, for example, requires extensive employee retraining each year. The idea, according to a Coke executive, is to become a more valuable employee by adding 25 percent to your existing knowledge every year.

Global Ethics and Social Responsibility

As noted in the Managing Change box, when American businesses expand into global markets, they must take their corporate codes of ethics and policies on social responsibility with them. As a citizen of several countries, a multinational corporation has several responsibilities. These include respecting local practices and customs, ensuring that there is harmony between the organization's staff and the host population, providing management leadership, and developing a cadre of local managers who will be a credit to their community. When a multinational makes an investment in a foreign country, it should commit to a long-term relationship. That means involving all stakeholders in the host country in decision making. Finally, a responsible multinational will implement ethical guidelines within the organization in the host country. By fulfilling these responsibilities, the company will foster respect for both local and international laws.

Multinational corporations often must balance conflicting interests of stakeholders when making decisions regarding social responsibilities, especially in the area of human rights. Questions involving child labor, forced labor, minimum wages, and workplace safety can be particularly difficult. A report issued by Gap, Inc. conceded that working conditions are far from perfect at many of the 3,000 factories worldwide that make its clothing.

While documenting a wide variety of workforce violations at the mostly developing-country plants that make Gap clothing, the report paints a bleaker picture of the hundreds of factories that are vying to win Gap contracts. Of these, the report said, about 90 percent fail the retailer's initial evaluation.[14]

The Gap report details the exact code violations it found. For example, between 10 percent and 25 percent of its factories in China, Taiwan, and Saipan use psychological coercion or verbal abuse, Gap says. More than 50 percent of the factories visited in sub-Saharan Africa run machinery without proper safety devices. The giant retailer contracts with plants in about 50 countries to supply its Gap, Old Navy, and Banana Republic clothing-store chains. The report card indicates just how many roadblocks stand in the way of better factory conditions. Sometimes, factory managers oppose changes because their other customers don't demand the same requirements—say, a 60-hour workweek rather than an 84-hour workweek.[15]

concept check

Describe strategic giving.

What role do employees have in improving their job security?

How do multinational corporations demonstrate social responsibility in a foreign country?

Summary of Learning Goals

1 **What philosophies and concepts shape personal ethical standards?**

Ethics is a set of moral standards for judging whether something is right or wrong. A utilitarianism approach to setting personal ethical standards focuses on the consequences of an action taken by a person or organization. According to this approach, people should act so as to generate the greatest good for the greatest number. Every human is entitled to certain rights such as freedom and the pursuit of happiness. Another approach to ethical decision making is justice, or what is fair according to accepted standards.

2 **How can organizations encourage ethical business behavior?**

Top management must shape the ethical culture of the organization. They should lead by example, offer ethics-training programs, and establish a formal code of ethics.

3 **What is social responsibility?**

Social responsibility is the concern of businesses for the welfare of society as a whole. It consists of obligations beyond just making a profit. Social responsibility also goes beyond what is required by law or union contract. Companies may engage in illegal and irresponsible behavior, irresponsible but legal behavior, or legal and responsible behavior. The vast majority of organizations act legally and try to be socially responsible.

4 **How do businesses meet their social responsibilities to various stakeholders?**

Stakeholders are individuals or groups to whom business has a responsibility. Businesses are responsible to employees. They should provide a clean, safe working environment. Organizations can build employees' self-worth through empowerment programs. Businesses also have a responsibility to customers to provide good, safe products and services. Organizations are responsible to the general public to be good corporate citizens. Firms must help protect the environment and provide a good place to work. Companies also engage in corporate philanthropy, which includes contributing cash, donating goods and services, and supporting volunteer efforts of employees. Finally, companies are responsible to investors. They should earn a reasonable profit for the owners.

5 **What are the trends in ethics and social responsibility?**

Today, corporate philanthropy is shifting away from simply giving to any needy group and is focusing instead on strategic giving, in which the philanthropy relates more closely to the corporate mission or goals and targets donations to areas where the firm operates. Corporate philanthropy is coming under increasing attacks from special-interest groups, however.

A second trend is toward a new social contract between employer and employee. Instead of the employer having the sole responsibility for maintaining jobs, now the employee must assume part of the burden and find ways to add value to the organization.

As the world increasingly becomes a global community, multinational corporations are now expected to assume a global set of ethics and responsibility. Global companies must understand local customs. They should also involve local stakeholders in decision making. Multinationals must also make certain that their suppliers are not engaged in human rights violations.

Appendix: Understanding the Legal and Tax Environment

6 **How does the legal system govern business transactions and settle business disputes?**

Laws are the rules governing a society's conduct that are created and enforced by a controlling authority. The U.S. court system governs the legal system and includes both federal and state courts, each organized into three levels. The courts settle disputes by applying and interpreting laws. Most cases start in trial courts. Decisions can be appealed to appellate courts. The U.S. Supreme Court is the nation's highest court and the court of final appeal. To avoid the high costs of going to court, many firms now use private arbitration or mediation as alternatives to litigation.

7 **What are the required elements of a valid contract; and what are the key types of business law?**

A contract is an agreement between two or more parties that meets five requirements: mutual assent, capacity, consideration, legal purpose, and legal form. If one party breaches the contract terms, the remedies are damages, specific performance, or restitution. Tort law settles disputes involving civil acts that harm people or their property. Torts include physical injury, mental anguish, and defamation. Product-liability law governs the responsibility of manufacturers and sellers for product defects. Bankruptcy law gives businesses or individuals who cannot meet their financial obligations a way to be relieved of their debts. Some laws are designed to keep the marketplace free from influences that would restrict competition such as price fixing and deceptive advertising. Laws protecting consumer rights are another important area of government control.

8 **What are the most common taxes paid by businesses?**

Income taxes are based on the income received by businesses and individuals. Congress determines the income taxes that are to be paid to the federal government. In addition to income taxes, individuals and businesses also pay property taxes (assessed on real and personal property), payroll taxes (the employer's share of Social Security taxes and federal and state unemployment taxes), sales taxes (levied on goods), and excise taxes (levied against specific products such as gasoline, alcoholic beverages, and tobacco).

Key Terms

1. Many CEOs have sold shares of their company's stock when prices were near their high points. Even though their actions were legal, it soon became apparent that they knew that the stock was significantly overpriced. Was the CEO ethically obligated to tell the public that this was the case—even knowing that doing so could cause the stock price to plummet, thereby hurting someone who bought the stock earlier that day? (Systems)

2. Jeffrey Immelt, chairman and CEO of General Electric, the world's most admired company according to *Fortune* magazine, says that execution, growth, and great people are required to keep the company on top. Immelt said that these are predictable, but a fourth factor is not—virtue; and virtue was at the top of his list. Using BCRC or another articles database, find articles on what GE is doing to enhance its corporate citizenship. Report your findings to the class. Could GE do more or are they already doing too much? Why? (Systems, Technology)

3. Boeing Corp. makes business ethics a priority, asking employees to take refresher training every year. It encourages employees to take the Ethics Challenge with their work groups and to discuss the issues with their peers. You can take your own ethics challenge. Go to **http://www.ethics.org** and click on the "Ethics Effectiveness Quick Test." Summarize your findings. Were there any answers that surprised you? (Information)

4. Identify the potential ethical and social responsibility issues confronting the following organizations: Microsoft, Pfizer, Nike, American Cancer Society, and R.J. Reynolds. Make recommendations on how these issues should be handled. (Systems)

5. **Team Activity** Divide the class into teams. Debate whether the only social responsibility of the employer to the employee is to provide a job. Include a discussion of the employee's responsibility to bring value to the firm. Also, debate the issue of whether the only social responsibility of a firm is to earn a profit. (Interpersonal)

Ethics Activity

Too Delicious to Resist

We are constantly bombarded with media reports claiming that as a nation Americans are becoming dangerously overweight. A recent medical study also just classified obesity as a disease in its own right, unconnected to such symptoms as high blood pressure, cholesterol, or heart problems. So perhaps it is not surprising that a recent lawsuit claimed that McDonald's is responsible for the obesity of two teenagers by "getting them hooked" on their burgers and fries.

You are the attorney approached by the teens' parents to bring suit against McDonald's. You ask yourself some soul-searching questions. Does McDonald's market and sell food in such a manner that it poses a health danger to unsuspecting consumers? And what about personal accountability? Shouldn't the teens and/or their parents be held responsible for their food choices? You wonder whether if this were a local mom and pop restaurant, would the teens' parents be suing? Or are the deep pockets of McDonald's too delicious to resist?

Using a Web search tool, locate articles about this topic and then write responses to the following questions. Be sure to support your arguments and cite your sources.

Ethical Dilemma: Do you tell the teens' parents to go home, cook healthy, and put their kids on a diet? Or do you take the case, believing that McDonald's has not acted in a socially responsible way and recognizing the potential for some serious money?

Sources: Dave Carpenter, "DIET: McDonald's to post nutrition facts on packaging next year," The America's Intelligence Wire, October 26, 2005, http://galenet.thomsonlearning.com; Pallavi Gogoi, "McDonald's New Wrap," *Business Week Online*, February 17, 2006, http://www.businessweek.com.; Richard Martin, "Revived McD Obesity Lawsuit Still Suggests Personal-Responsibility Defense—for Now," *Nation's Restaurant News*, February 14, 2005, http://galenet.thomsonlearning.com; Wendy Melillo, "Bringing Up Baby: Where's the Line, and Who Should Draw It, In Advertising to Children?" *ADWEEK*, February 13, 2006, p.14+; Libby Quaid, "House Votes to Block Lawsuits Blaming Food Industry for Obesity," *The America's Intelligence Wire*, October 19, 2005, http:// galenet. thomsonlearning.com.

Working the Net

1. You'll find a comprehensive list of business ethics sites at **http://www.web-miner.com/busethics.htm.** Once at the site, go to the section on Corporate Codes of Ethics. Look at three examples of codes in different industries. What elements do they have in common? How are they different? Suggest how one of the codes could be improved.

2. Richard S. Scrushy, former CEO of HealthSouth Corporation, was charged with $1.4 billion in fraud. He was acquitted. Bernie Ebbers, former CEO of WorldCom, was found guilty of helping mastermind an $11 billion accounting fraud. Go to the Internet and read several articles about the charges against both men. Find articles on why one was guilty on all counts and the other acquitted on all counts. Explain the ethical issues involved with each. Were they completely different or the same? Also, read about the latest charges against Scrushy and comment on them. Begin your search at **http://money.cnn.com** and then **http://www.forbes.com.** You can find more articles on **http://www.google.com.**

3. Visit the Fur Is Dead Web site of the people for Ethical Treatment of Animal (PETA), **http://furisdead.com.** Read about PETA's view of the fur industry. Do you agree with this view? Why or why not? How do you think manufacturers of fur clothing would justify their actions to someone from PETA? Would you work for a store that sold fur-trimmed clothing? Explain your answer.

4. Green Money Journal, **http://www.greenmoneyjournal.com,** is a bimonthly online journal that promotes social responsibility investing. What are the current topics of concern in this area? Visit the archives to find articles on socially responsible investing and two areas of corporate social responsibility. Summarize what you have learned.

5. A global resource not-for-profit professionals is **http://www.onphilanthropy. com.** The site lists trends and best practices in corporate giving. Read several articles, then report to the class on trends in corporate giving. Also, give an example of a "best practice" in philanthropy.

Creative Thinking Case >

Timbuk2 Gets the Message

It all started in 1989 with one product: a custom messenger bag designed for San Francisco's bicycle couriers. That unique carrier became popular with not just cyclists, but also students and professionals, who loved its stylish yet durable features. Today Timbuk2 manufactures 30 products, including messenger bags, computer cases, totes, duffles, iPod sleeves, and yoga bags that generate more than $10 million in annual revenues. Loyal customers buy Timbuk2 cases at REI, EMS, Apple, and 1,200 independent specialty retail stores. The messenger bags cost from $60 to $90, depending on size; for $10 more customers can select custom color combinations.

Although other companies have shifted production to low-cost manufacturing centers overseas, Timbuk2 still produces its messenger bags at its original San Francisco factory. To preserve its local presence and retain jobs while maintaining a financially sound company, Timbuk2 took steps to boost the plant's productivity. Originally Timbuk2 made its bags "on demand" as customer orders came in. Converting to predetermined color combinations allowed the factory to operate independent of demand and to build inventory, greatly improving productivity. "That change alone saved our San Francisco factory from going out of business," says Mark Dwight, Timbuk2's president and chief executive officer. "There is value in the made-in-USA products, and locally produced bags can be customized to customer requests on a very short lead time. That quick response is a unique advantage."

The company discovered, however, that manufacturing its new lines was more complex than the messenger bags and called for specialized machinery. These factors and the resulting high labor costs led Timbuk2 to explore off-shore manufacturing options. Keeping the headquarters operation and design team in San Francisco but shifting production to a carefully selected factory in China enabled Timbuk2 to continue offering top quality products while keeping prices affordable.

Timbuk2 is proud of its commitment to ethical working conditions and fair wages at all its facilities. Executives visit the China factory every month or two to monitor the work environment and make sure that product quality remains high. The new products have been well-received, increasing Timbuk2's reputation as a lifestyle brand. As a result of its higher sales volume, the company has expanded the San Francisco factory, doubled its production staff, and added employees in all departments. It continues to roll out new products. "Our goal is to create a solid growth company, to continue delighting our customers with great products, to contribute to our local community, and to make the Timbuk2 swirl as recognizable as the Nike swoosh," says Dwight.[16]

Critical Thinking Questions

- Mark Dwight faced considerable resistance from existing managers when he assumed control of Timbuk2 and wanted to move the production of new products overseas. He has asked for your help in preparing a presentation to win their support. Summarize the arguments in favor of off-shore production.
- Now list the arguments against using foreign manufacturers and develop answers to help Dwight counter charges that it is not socially responsible to take jobs outside the United States.
- How did Dwight's decision to manufacture new products in China support the company's desire to be a good corporate citizen for San Franscisco?

Video Case >

Fair Trade Sweetens the Coffee

When sipping your morning coffee you probably don't wonder who grew the beans, but Rink Dickinson did. And when he learned that agents and middlemen were paying small coffee growers the lowest possible prices—forcing them to flee their farms and seek jobs in overcrowded cities, or plant illegal crops like marijuana or cocaine to generate enough cash for their next coffee crop—he decided to do something about it.

Co-founded in Boston in 1986 with partner Rob Everts, Equal Exchange changed these unfair practices by eliminating middlemen and buying direct from growers. The company, which now also offers organic gourmet tea, sugar, cocoa, and chocolate, occupies its fourth home, a 77,000 square foot building in West Bridgewater, Massachusetts, where it plans to take its roasting in-house.

Its mission is to build long-term trade partnerships that are economically just and environmentally sound. Equal Exchange also works hard to foster mutually beneficial relations between farmers and consumers and to demonstrate the viability of worker cooperatives and fair trade through its successful business model.

Now the oldest and largest for-profit fair trade company in the United States, Equal Exchange trades directly with democratically organized small farmer cooperatives, supporting sustainable farming practices and providing producers with advance credit for crop production. It also pays producers a guaranteed minimum price that provides them with a stable source of income as well as improved social services.

All this has significantly affected the economy and lifestyle of the region. Coffee-growing provides jobs for people who would otherwise be unemployed, and receiving a guaranteed minimum for their beans, even when the market is lower, assures farmers of a living wage during downturns. "We used to live in houses made of corn husks," recalled Don Miguel Sifontes, a farmer in El Salvador. "Now we have better work, better schools, homes of adobe, and a greater brotherhood of decision makers."

Following strict fair trade guidelines, Equal Exchange enters into long-term relationships with growers, buying directly from cooperatives owned and run by farmers who govern the even distribution of income and services—such as education and health care. The growers' entire region also benefits from projects the farm cooperatives undertake with their additional income—from reforestation programs to building new schools, day care centers, and carpentry workshops.

Fair trade underscores the idea that businesses are accountable to employees, customers, and the general public, and it encourages companies to engage in ethically and socially responsible ways of doing business. Under exclusive agreements with farming cooperatives, Equal Exchange growers receive better prices and customers are guaranteed award-winning coffee at a fair price.

Making credit available to farmers helps them avoid the cycle of debt. Up to 50 percent of a contract may be paid six months in advance, and the company also pays a premium price for certified organic and shade-grown coffee. By helping growers use environmentally friendly farming methods, both the environment and consumers are protected from toxic chemicals. When specialty coffee giants Starbucks and Green Mountain announced they were entering into fair trade agreements with coffee farmers, Equal Exchange congratulated them. "We know these farmers and their struggles. They need importers to pay a just price so we encourage our fellow roasters."

With that statement Dickinson raised the bar of ethical standards in the coffee business, knowing that his company cleared it with ease. And with 3 million pounds of coffee sold in 2006, generating over $20 million in revenues, he has the support of many coffee-loving consumers who do care where their beans come from.[17]

Critical Thinking Questions

- What are the key components of Equal Exchange's fair trade agreement with coffee growers?
- How has this fair trade agrement affected the coffee growers' regions and lifestyles?
- How has Equal Exchange gone beyond other organizations to be socially and ethically responsible?

Hot Links Address Book

Find out which companies test their products on animals and which don't in the campaign section of the People for the Ethical Treatment of Animals (PETA) Web site, http://www.peta.org

How is the International Business Ethics Institute working to promote business ethics worldwide? Find out at http://www.business-ethics.org

Ben & Jerry's ice cream has always taken its responsibilities as a corporate good citizen seriously. Learn about the company's positions on various issues and products that support social issues at its Web site, http://www.benjerry.com

Discover what the Texas Instruments employee "Ethics Quick Test" includes, as well as the company's overall ethics policies, by searching for "Ethics at TI" on the corporate home page, http://www.ti.com

What does IBM Corp require from its employees in terms of ethical business conduct? It's all presented in the Conduct Principles you will find on IBM's Web site, under Corporate Responsibility—Our Company—Management System—Global Employment Standards, http://www.ibm.com

Levi Strauss' unique corporate culture rewards and recognizes employee achievement. To learn about its Employee Community Involvement Program, go to the Levi Strauss Web site at http://www.levistrauss.com

Want to see how the global environment is changing and learn the latest about global warming? Check out http://www.climatehotmap.org

General Motors is committed to continuous improvement in product, environmental, social, and economic performance. Check out GM's Performance Scorecard at http://www.gm.com

Before donating to any charity, check out its credentials at http://charitywatch.org

Learn how U.S. businesses gain competitive advantage through corporate social responsibility programs at the Business for Social Responsibility site, http://www.bsr.org

A P P E N D I X

Understanding the Legal and Tax Environment

 How does the legal system govern business transactions and settle business disputes?

Our legal system affects everyone who lives and does business in the United States. The smooth functioning of society depends on the law, which protects the rights of people and businesses. The purpose of law is to keep the system stable while allowing orderly change. The law defines which actions are allowed or banned and regulates some practices. It also helps settle disputes. The legal system both shapes and is shaped by political, economic, and social systems. As Judge Learned Hand wrote in *The Spirit of Liberty,* "Without [the law] we cannot live; only with it can we insure the future which by right is ours."

laws
The rules of conduct in a society, created and enforced by a controlling authority, usually the government.

In any society **laws** are the rules of conduct created and enforced by a controlling authority, usually the government. They develop over time in response to the changing needs of people, property, and business. The legal system of the United States is thus the result of a long and continuing process. In each generation new social problems occur, and new laws are created to solve them. For instance, in the late 1800s corporations in certain industries, such as steel and oil, merged and became dominant. The Sherman Antitrust Act was passed in 1890 to control these powerful firms. Eighty years later, in 1970, Congress passed the National Environmental Policy Act. This law dealt with pollution problems, which no one had thought about in 1890. Today new areas of law are developing to deal with the Internet and the recent financial scandals.

The Main Sources of Law

common law
The body of unwritten law that has evolved out of judicial (court) decisions rather than being enacted by a legislature; also called *case law.*

Common law is the body of unwritten law that has evolved out of judicial (court) decisions rather than being enacted by legislatures. It is also called case law. It developed in England and came to America with the colonists. All states except Louisiana, which follows the Napoleonic Code inherited from French settlers, follow the English system. Common law is based on community customs that were recognized and enforced by the courts.

statutory law
Written law enacted by a legislature (local, state, or federal).

Statutory law is written law enacted by legislatures at all levels, from city and state governments to the federal government. Examples of statutory law are the federal and state constitutions, bills passed by Congress, and ordinances, which are laws enacted by local governments. Statutory law is the chief source of new laws in the United States. Among the business activities governed by statutory law are securities regulation, incorporation, sales, bankruptcy, and antitrust.

administrative law
The rules, regulations, and orders passed by boards, commissions, and agencies of government (local, state, and federal).

Related to statutory law is **administrative law**, or the rules, regulations, and orders passed by boards, commissions, and agencies of federal, state, and local governments. The scope and influence of administrative law have expanded as the number of these government bodies has grown. Federal agencies issue more rulings and settle more disputes than all the courts and legislatures combined. Some federal agencies that issue rules are the Civil Aeronautics Board, the Internal Revenue Service, the Securities and Exchange Commission, the Federal Trade Commission, and the National Labor Relations Board.

Business Law

business law
The body of law that governs commercial dealings.

Business law is the body of law that governs commercial dealings. These laws provide a protective environment within which businesses can operate. They serve as guidelines for business decisions. Every businessperson should be familiar with the laws governing his or her field. Some laws, such as the Internal Revenue Code, apply to all businesses. Other types of business laws may apply to a specific industry, such as Federal Communications Commission laws that regulate radio and TV stations.

Uniform Commercial Code (UCC)
A model set of rules that apply to commercial transactions between businesses and between businesses and individuals; has been adopted by all states except Louisiana, which uses only part of it.

In 1952 the United States grouped many business laws into a model that could be used by all the states. The **Uniform Commercial Code (UCC)** sets forth the rules that apply to commercial transactions between businesses and between individuals and businesses. It has been adopted by 49 states; Louisiana uses only part of it. By standardizing laws, the UCC simplifies the process of doing business across state lines. It covers the sale of goods, bank deposits and collections, letters of credit, documents of title, and investment securities. Many articles of the UCC are covered later in this appendix.

The Court System

judiciary
The branch of government that is responsible for settling disputes by applying and interpreting points of law; consists of the court system.

The United States has a highly developed court system. This branch of government, the **judiciary**, is responsible for settling disputes by applying and interpreting points of law. Although court decisions are the basis for common law, the courts also answer questions left unanswered by statutes and administrative rulings. They have the power to assure that these laws do not violate the federal or state constitutions.

Trial Courts

trial courts
The lowest level of courts, where most cases begin; also called courts of general jurisdiction.

Most court cases start in the **trial courts**, also called courts of general jurisdiction. The main federal trial courts are the U.S. district courts. There is at least one federal district court in each state. These courts hear cases involving serious federal crimes, immigration, postal regulations, disputes between citizens of different states, patents, copyrights, and bankruptcy. Specialized federal courts handle tax matters, international trade, and claims against the United States.

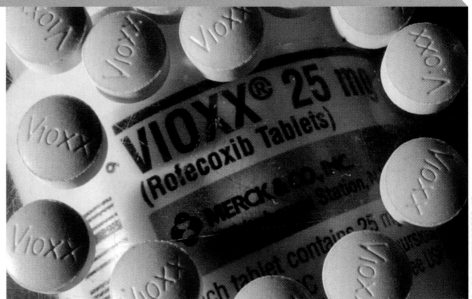

CONCEPT in Action

Big Three pharmaceutical firm Merck & Co. pulled Vioxx off the market after studies linked the drug to increased heart attacks and strokes. An osteoarthritis painkiller with annual sales of $2.5 billion, Vioxx is alleged to have caused up to 160,000 health failures nationwide. Refusing global settlement, Merck boldly opted to defend Vioxx in state courts, where corporate liability was estimated at $50 billion. *What is the appeals process for product-liability cases filed in U.S. courts?*

Appellate Courts

appellate courts (courts of appeals)
The level of courts above the trial courts; the losing party in a civil case and the defendant in a criminal case may appeal the trial court's decision to an appellate court.

The losing party in a civil (noncriminal) case and a losing defendant in a criminal case may appeal the trial court's decision to the next level in the judicial system, the **appellate courts (courts of appeals)**. There are 12 U.S. circuit courts of appeals. Cases that begin in a federal district court are appealed to the court of appeals for that district. These courts may also review orders from administrative agencies. Likewise, the states have appellate courts and supreme courts for cases tried in state district or superior courts.

No cases start in appellate courts. Their purpose is to review decisions of the lower courts and affirm, reverse, or modify the rulings.

The Supreme Court

The U.S. Supreme Court is the highest court in the nation. It is the only court specifically established by the U.S. Constitution. Any cases involving a state or in which an ambassador, public minister, or consul is a party are heard directly by the Supreme Court. Its main function is to review decisions by the U.S. circuit courts of appeals. Parties not satisfied with a decision of a state supreme court can appeal to the U.S. Supreme Court. But the Supreme Court accepts only those cases that it believes will have the greatest effect on the country, only about 200 of the thousands of appeals it gets each year.

Administrative Agencies

Administrative agencies have limited judicial powers to regulate their special areas. These agencies exist at the federal, state, and local levels. For example, in 1998 the Federal Trade Commission enacted the "Federal Universal Service Fund," which subjects each pager phone to an 18 cent fee. This fund was created by the Federal Trade Commission to ensure that all citizens, schools, libraries, and hospitals in rural areas have access to telecommunications service (like the Internet) at prices comparable to those charged in urban and suburban areas. A list of selected federal agencies is shown in Exhibit 3A.1.

Nonjudicial Methods of Settling Disputes

Settling disputes by going to court is both expensive and time consuming. Even if the case is settled prior to the actual trial, sizable legal expenses can be incurred in preparing for trial. Therefore, many companies now use private arbitration and mediation firms as alternatives to litigation. Private firms offer these services, which are a high growth area within the legal profession.

arbitration
A method of settling disputes in which the parties agree to present their case to an impartial third party and are required to accept the arbitrator's decision.

mediation
A method of settling disputes in which the parties submit their case to an impartial third party but are not required to accept the mediator's decision.

With **arbitration**, the parties agree to present their case to an impartial third party and are required to accept the arbitrator's decision. **Mediation** is similar, but the parties are not bound by the mediator's decision. The mediator suggests alternative solutions and helps the parties negotiate a settlement. Mediation is more flexible than arbitration and allows for compromise. If the parties cannot reach a settlement, they can then go to court, an option not available in most arbitration cases.

In addition to saving time and money, corporations like the confidentiality of testimony and settlement terms in these proceedings. Arbitration and mediation also allow businesses and medical professionals to avoid jury trials, which can result in large settlements in certain types of lawsuits, such as personal injury, discrimination, medical malpractice, and product liability.

Agency	Function
Federal Trade Commission (FTC)	Enforces laws and guidelines regarding unfair business practices and acts to stop false and deceptive advertising and labeling.
Food and Drug Administration (FDA)	Enforces laws and regulations to prevent distribution of adulterated or misbranded foods, drugs, medical devices, cosmetics, veterinary products, and hazardous consumer products.
Consumer Products Safety Commission	Ensures compliance with the Consumer Product Safety Act and seeks to protect the public from unreasonable risk of injury from any consumer product not covered by other regulatory agencies.
Federal Communications Commission (FCC)	Regulates wire, radio, and TV communication in interstate and foreign commerce.
Environmental Protection Agency (EPA)	Develops and enforces environmental protection standards and researches the effects of pollution.
Federal Energy Regulatory Commission (FERC)	Regulates rates and sales of natural gas products, thereby affecting the supply and price of gas available to consumers; also regulates wholesale rates for electricity and gas, pipeline construction, and U.S. imports and exports of natural gas and electricity.
Federal Aviation Administration (FAA)	Oversees the policies and regulations of the airline industry.
Federal Highway Administration (FHA)	Regulates vehicle safety requirements.

Contract Law

 7 **What are the required elements of a valid contract; and what are the key types of business law?**

contract
An agreement that sets forth the relationship between parties regarding the performance of a specified action; creates a legal obligation and is enforceable in a court of law.

Linda Price, a 22-year-old college student, is looking at a car with a sticker price of $16,000. After some negotiating, she and the salesperson agree on a price of $15,000, and the salesperson writes up a contract, which they both sign. Has Linda legally bought the car for $15,000? The answer is yes, because the transaction meets all the requirements for a valid contract.

A **contract** is an agreement that sets forth the relationship between parties regarding the performance of a specified action. The contract creates a legal obligation and is enforceable in a court of law. Contracts are an important part of business law. Contract law is also incorporated into other fields of business law, such as property and agency law (discussed later in this appendix). Some of the business transactions that involve contracts are buying materials and property, selling goods, leasing equipment, and hiring consultants.

A contract can be an *express contract*, which specifies the terms of the agreement in either written or spoken words, or an *implied contract*, which depends on the acts and conduct of the parties to show agreement. An example of an express contract is the written sales contract for Linda Price's new car. An implied contract exists when you order and receive a sandwich at Jason's Grill. You and the restaurant have an implied contract that you will pay the price shown on the restaurant's menu in exchange for an edible sandwich.

Contract Requirements

Businesses deal with contracts all the time, so it's important to know the requirements of a valid contract. For a contract to be legally enforceable, all of the following elements must be present:

- *Mutual assent.* Voluntary agreement by both parties to the terms of the contract. Each party to the contract must have entered into it freely, without duress. Using physical or economic harm to force the signing of the contract—threatening injury or refusing to place another large order, for instance—invalidates a contract. Likewise, fraud—misrepresenting the facts of a transaction—makes a contract unenforceable. Telling a prospective used-car buyer that the brakes are new when in fact they have not been replaced makes the contract of sale invalid.
- *Capacity.* Legal ability of a party to enter into contracts. Under the law, minors (those under 18), mental incompetents, drug and alcohol addicts, and convicts cannot enter into contracts.
- *Consideration.* Exchange of some legal value or benefit between the parties. Consideration can be in the form of money, goods, or a legal right given up. Suppose that an electronics manufacturer agrees to rent an industrial building for a year at a monthly rent of $1,500. Its consideration is the rent payment of $1,500, and the building owner's consideration is permission to occupy the space. But if you offer to type a term paper for a friend for free and your offer is accepted, there is no contract. Your friend has not given up anything, so you are not legally bound to honor the deal.
- *Legal purpose.* Absence of illegality. The purpose of the contract must be legal for it to be valid. A contract cannot require performance of an illegal act. A contract to smuggle drugs into a state for a specified amount of money would not be legally enforceable.
- *Legal form.* Oral or written form, as required. Many contracts can be oral. For instance, an oral contract exists when Bridge Corp. orders office supplies by phone from Ace Stationery Store and Ace delivers the requested goods. Written contracts include leases, sales contracts, and property deeds. Some types of contracts must be in writing to be legally binding. In most states, written contracts are required for the sale of goods costing more than $500, for the sale of land, for contract performance that cannot be carried out within a year, and for guarantees to pay the debts of someone else.

As you can see, Linda Price's car purchase meets all the requirements for a valid contract. Both parties have freely agreed to the terms of the contract. Linda is not a minor and presumably does not fit any of the other categories of incapacity. Both parties are giving consideration, Linda by paying the money and the salesperson by turning over the car to her. The purchase of the car is a legal activity. And the written contract is the correct form because the cost of the car is over $500.

Breach of Contract

breach of contract
The failure by one party to a contract to fulfill the terms of the agreement without a legal excuse.

A breach of contract occurs when one party to a contract fails (without legal excuse) to fulfill the terms of the agreement. The other party then has the right to seek a remedy in the courts. There are three legal remedies for breach of contract:

- *Payment of damages.* Money awarded to the party who was harmed by the breach of contract, to cover losses incurred because the contract wasn't fulfilled. Suppose that Ajax Roofing contracts with Fred Wellman to fix the large hole in the roof of his factory within three days. But the roofing crew doesn't show up as promised. When a thunderstorm four days later causes $45,000 in damage to Wellman's machinery, Wellman can sue for damages to cover the costs of the water damage because Ajax breached the contract.

patent
A form of protection established by the government for inventors; gives an inventor the exclusive right to manufacture, use, and sell an invention for 17 years.

- *Specific performance of the contract.* A court order requiring the breaching party to perform the duties under the terms of the contract. Specific performance is the most common method of settling a breach of contract. Wellman might ask the court to direct Ajax to fix the roof at the price and conditions in the contract.
- *Restitution.* Canceling the contract and returning to the situation that existed before the contract. If one party fails to perform under the contract, neither party has any further obligation to the other. Because Ajax failed to fix Wellman's roof under the terms of the contract, Wellman does not owe Ajax any money. Ajax must return the 50 percent deposit it received when Wellman signed the contract.

Warranties

copyright
A form of protection established by the government for creators of works of art, music, literature, or other intellectual property; gives the creator the exclusive right to use, produce, and sell the creation during the lifetime of the creator and for 50 years thereafter.

trademark
A design, name, or other distinctive mark that a manufacturer uses to identify its goods in the marketplace.

Express warranties are specific statements of fact or promises about a product by the seller. This form of warranty is considered part of the sales transaction that influences the buyer. Express warranties appear in the form of statements that can be interpreted as fact. The statement "This machine will process 1,000 gallons of paint per hour" is an express warranty, as is the printed warranty that comes with a computer or a telephone answering machine.

Implied warranties are neither written nor oral. These guarantees are imposed on sales transactions by statute or court decision. They promise that the product will perform up to expected standards. For instance, a man bought a used car from a dealer, and the next day the transmission fell out as he was driving on the highway. The dealer fixed the car, but a week later the brakes failed. The man sued the car dealer. The court ruled in favor of the car owner because any car without a working transmission or brakes is not fit for the ordinary purpose of driving. Similarly, if a customer asks to buy a copier to handle 5,000 copies per month, she relies on the salesperson to sell her a copier that meets those needs. The salesperson implicitly warrants that the copier purchased is appropriate for that volume.

Patents, Copyrights, and Trademarks

The U.S. Constitution protects authors, inventors, and creators of other intellectual property by giving them the rights to their creative works. Patents, copyrights, and registration of trademarks and servicemarks are legal protection for key business assets.

A **patent** gives an inventor the exclusive right to manufacture, use, and sell an invention for 17 years. The U.S. Patent Office, a government agency, grants patents for ideas that meet its requirements of being new, unique, and useful. The physical process, machine, or formula is what is patented. Patent rights—pharmaceutical companies' rights to produce drugs they discover, for example—are considered intangible personal property.

The government also grants copyrights. A **copyright** is an exclusive right, shown by the symbol ©, given to a writer, artist, composer, or playwright to use, produce, and sell her or his creation. Works protected by copyright include printed materials (books, magazine articles, lectures), works of art, photographs, and movies. Under current copyright law, the copyright is issued for the life of the creator plus 50 years after the creator's death. Patents and copyrights, which are considered intellectual property, are the subject of many lawsuits today.

A **trademark** is a design, name, or other distinctive mark that a manufacturer uses to identify its goods in the marketplace. Apple Computer's multicolored apple logo (symbol) is an example of a trademark.

CONCEPT *in Action*

Gangsta rapper 50 Cent, aka Curtis James Jackson, was embroiled in controversy when a copyright lawsuit alleged that the Jamaica, Queens, New York recording artist stole lyrics for his chart-topping hit "In Da Club." According to legal briefs, lyrics to "In Da Club" originally appeared in "It's Your Birthday," a song by former 2 Live Crew frontman Luther Campbell. *What legal protections are offered to songwriters and composers in the United States and why?*

© ASSOCIATED PRESS, AP

servicemark
A symbol, name, or design that identifies a service rather than a tangible object.

A **servicemark** is a symbol, name, or design that identifies a service rather than a tangible object. The Travelers Insurance umbrella logo is an example of a servicemark.

Most companies identify their trademark with the ® symbol in company ads. This symbol shows that the trademark is registered with the Register of Copyrights, Copyright Office, Library of Congress. The trademark is followed by a generic description: Fritos corn chips, Xerox copiers, Scotch brand cellophane tape, Kleenex tissues.

Trademarks are valuable because they create uniqueness in the minds of customers. At the same time, companies don't want a trademark to become so well known that it is used to describe all similar types of products. For instance, Coke is often used to refer to any cola soft drink, not just those produced by the Coca-Cola Company. Companies spend millions of dollars each year to keep their trademarks from becoming *generic words,* terms used to identify a product class rather than the specific product. Coca-Cola employs many investigators and files 70 to 80 lawsuits each year to prevent its trademarks from becoming generic words.

Once a trademark becomes generic (which a court decides), it is public property and can be used by any person or company. Names that were once trademarked but are now generic include *aspirin, thermos, linoleum,* and *toll house cookies.*

Tort Law

tort
A civil, or private, act that harms other people or their property.

A **tort** is a civil, or private, act that harms other people or their property. The harm may involve physical injury, emotional distress, invasion of privacy, or *defamation* (injuring a person's character by publication of false statements). The injured party may sue the wrongdoer to recover damages for the harm or loss. A tort is not the result of a breach of contract, which would be settled under contract law. Torts are part of common law. Examples of tort cases are medical malpractice, *slander* (an untrue oral statement that damages a person's reputation), *libel* (an untrue written statement that damages a person's reputation), product liability (discussed in the next section), and fraud.

A tort is generally not a crime, although some acts can be both torts and crimes. (Assault and battery, for instance, is a criminal act that would be prosecuted by the state and also a tort because of the injury to the person.) Torts are private wrongs and are settled in civil courts. *Crimes* are violations of public law punishable by the state or county in the criminal courts. The purpose of criminal law is to punish the person who committed the crime. The purpose of tort law is to provide remedies to the injured party.

For a tort to exist and damages to be recovered, the harm must be done through either negligence or deliberate intent. *Negligence* occurs when reasonable care is not taken for the safety of others. For instance, a woman attending a New York Mets baseball game was struck on the head by a foul ball that came through a hole in the screen behind home plate. The court ruled that a sports team charging admission has an obligation to provide structures free from defects and seating that protects spectators from danger. The Mets were found negligent. Negligence does not apply when an injury is caused by an unavoidable accident, an event that was not intended and could not have been prevented even if the person used reasonable care. This area of tort law is quite controversial, because the definition of negligence leaves much room for interpretation.

Product-Liability Law

product liability
The responsibility of manufacturers and sellers for defects in the products they make and sell.

Product liability refers to manufacturers' and sellers' responsibility for defects in the products they make and sell. It has become a specialized area of law combining aspects of contracts, warranties, torts, and statutory law (at both the state and federal levels). A product-liability suit may be based on negligence or strict liability (both of which are torts) or misrepresentation or breach of warranty (part of contract law).

strict liability
A concept in product-liability law under which a manufacturer or seller is liable for any personal injury or property damage caused by defective products or packaging even though all possible care was used to prevent such defects.

An important concept in product-liability law is **strict liability**. A manufacturer or seller is liable for any personal injury or property damage caused by defective products or packaging—even if all possible care was used to prevent such defects. The definition of defective is quite broad. It includes manufacturing and design defects and inadequate instructions on product use or warnings of danger.

Product-liability suits are very costly. More than 100,000 product-liability suits were filed against hundreds of companies that made or used asbestos, a substance that causes lung disease and cancer but was once used widely in insulation, brake linings, textiles, and other products. Eighteen companies were forced into bankruptcy as a result of asbestos-related lawsuits, and the total cost of asbestos cases to defendants and their insurers exceeds $10 billion (most of which was paid not to the victims but to lawyers and experts).

Bankruptcy Law

bankruptcy
The legal procedure by which individuals or businesses that cannot meet their financial obligations are relieved of their debt.

Congress has given financially distressed firms and individuals a way to make a fresh start. **Bankruptcy** is the legal procedure by which individuals or businesses that cannot meet their financial obligations are relieved of their debts. A bankruptcy court distributes any assets to the creditors.

Bankruptcy can be either voluntary or involuntary. In a *voluntary bankruptcy,* the debtor files a petition with the court, stating that debts exceed assets and asking the court to declare the debtor bankrupt. In an *involuntary bankruptcy,* the creditors file the bankruptcy petition.

The *Bankruptcy Reform Act* of 1978, amended in 1984 and 1986, provides for the resolution of bankruptcy cases. Under this act, two types of bankruptcy proceedings are available to businesses: *Chapter 7* (liquidation) and *Chapter 11* (reorganization). Most bankruptcies, an estimated 70 percent, use Chapter 7. After the sale of any assets, the cash proceeds are given first to secured creditors and then to unsecured creditors. A firm that opts to reorganize under Chapter 11 works with its creditors to develop a plan for paying part of its debts and writing off the rest.

The Bankruptcy Abuse Prevention and Consumer Protection Act went into effect October 17, 2005. Under the new law Americans with heavy debt will find it difficult to avoid meeting their financial obligations. Many debtors will have to work out repayment plans instead of having their obligations erased in bankruptcy court under the new law. "Bankruptcy should always be a last resort in our legal system," President Bush said. "If someone does not pay his or her debts the rest of society ends up paying them. The act will protect those who legitimately need help, stop those who try to commit fraud and bring greater stability and fairness to our financial system."[16]

The new law would require people with incomes above a certain level to pay some or all of their credit-card charges, medical bills, and other obligations under a court-ordered bankruptcy plan. Supporters of the new law argue that bankruptcy frequently is the last refuge of gamblers, impulsive shoppers, the divorced or separated, and fathers avoiding child support. Now there is an objective, needs-based bankruptcy test to determine whether filers should be allowed to cancel their debts or be required to enter a repayment plan. Generally, people with incomes above the state median income would be required to use a plan to repay their debts. People with special circumstances, such as serious medical conditions, would be allowed to cancel debts despite this income level.

Also, companies will need a lot more cash to enter into a bankruptcy than in the past. Before the new law, utilities could not discontinue service as a result of a bankruptcy filing. But under the new act, the filing company must post a cash deposit or equivalent in order to continue their service. Sellers also have priority over other claims with regard to merchandise distributed to the debtor within 20 days prior to the bankruptcy filing.

The act limits the debtor's exclusivity period, which was a real boon of filing for bankruptcy. Past law allowed for indefinite extensions, which served to drag out the time before bondholders and other creditors get any money. But now that period is capped at 18 months, with no room for extension. For large corporations with complicated bankruptcies, such a quick turnaround may not be possible, and if a plan is not filed at the end of 18 months, the company must put itself at the mercy of creditors.

Laws to Promote Fair Competition

antitrust regulation
Laws that prevent companies from entering into agreements to control trade through a monopoly.

Many measures have been taken to try to keep the marketplace free from influences that would restrict competition. These efforts include **antitrust regulation**, laws that prevent companies from entering into agreements to control trade through a monopoly. The first act regulating competition was the *Sherman Antitrust Act*, passed in 1890 to prevent large companies from dominating an industry and making it hard for smaller firms to compete. This broad act banned monopolies and contracts, mergers, or conspiracies in restraint of trade. In 1914 the *Clayton Act* added to the more general provisions of the Sherman Antitrust Act. It outlawed the following:

- *Price discrimination.* Offering a customer discounts that are not offered to all other purchasers buying on similar terms.
- *Exclusive dealing.* Refusing to let the buyer purchase a competitor's products for resale.
- *Tying contracts.* Requiring buyers to purchase merchandise they may not want in order to get the products they do want.
- *Purchase of stock in competing corporations so as to lessen competition.* Buying competitors' stock in such quantity that competition is reduced.

The 1950 *Celler-Kefauver Act* amended the Clayton Act. It bans the purchase of one firm by another if the resulting merger decreases competition within the industry. As a result, all corporate acquisitions are subject to regulatory approval before they can be finalized. Most antitrust actions are taken by the U.S. Department of Justice, based on federal law. Violations of the antitrust acts are punishable by fines, imprisonment, or civil damage payments that can be as high as three times the actual damage amount. These outcomes give defendants an incentive to resolve cases.

The *Federal Trade Commission Act,* also passed in 1914, bans unfair trade practices. This act created the Federal Trade Commission (FTC), an independent five-member board with the power to define and monitor unfair trade practices, such as those prohibited by the Sherman and Clayton Acts. The FTC investigates complaints and can issue rulings called *cease-and-desist orders* to force companies to stop unfair business practices. Its powers have grown over the years. Today the FTC is one of the most important agencies regulating the competitive practices of business.

Regulation of Advertising and Pricing

A number of federal laws directly affect the promotion and pricing of products. The *Wheeler-Lea Act* of 1938 amended the Federal Trade Commission Act and gave the FTC authority to regulate advertising. The FTC monitors companies' advertisements for false or misleading claims.

The most important law in the area of pricing is the *Robinson-Patman Act,* a federal law passed in 1936 that tightened the Clayton Act's prohibitions against price discrimination. An exception is made for circumstances like discounts for quantity purchases, as long as the discounts do not lessen competition. But a manufacturer cannot sell at a lower price to one company just because that company buys all its merchandise from the manufacturer. Also, if one firm is offered quantity discounts, all firms buying that quantity of goods must get the discounts. The FTC and the antitrust division of the Justice Department monitor pricing.

CONCEPT *in Action*

Disgraced author James Frey became an overnight celebrity when Oprah Winfrey selected his harrowing memoir *A Million Little Pieces* for her celebrated book club. The queen of talk hailed *Pieces* as an inspirational tale of addiction and recovery that kept her awake at night, but scandal erupted when the bestseller was found to contain fictitious accounts of Frey's struggle with drugs and incarceration. The controversy escalated when duped readers filed lawsuits against Frey and publisher Doubleday. *Do consumer protection laws protect against publishing fraud?*

consumerism
A social movement that seeks to increase the rights and powers of buyers vis-à-vis sellers.

Consumer Protection Laws

Consumerism reflects the struggle for power between buyers and sellers. Specifically, it is a social movement seeking to increase the rights and powers of buyers vis-à-vis sellers. Sellers' rights and powers include the following:

- To introduce into the marketplace any product, in any size and style, that is not hazardous to personal health or safety, or if it is hazardous, to introduce it with the proper warnings and controls.
- To price the product at any level they wish, provided they do not discriminate among similar classes of buyers.
- To spend any amount of money they wish to promote the product, so long as the promotion does not constitute unfair competition.
- To formulate any message they wish about the product, provided that it is not misleading or dishonest in content or execution.
- To introduce any buying incentives they wish.

Meanwhile, buyers have the following rights and powers:

- To refuse to buy any product that is offered to them.
- To expect products to be safe.
- To expect a product to be essentially as the seller represents it.
- To receive adequate information about the product.

Many laws have been passed to protect consumer rights. Exhibit 3A.2 lists the major consumer protection laws.

Deregulation of Industries

deregulation
The removal of rules and regulations governing business competition.

During the 1980s and 1990s, the U.S. government has actively promoted deregulation, the removal of rules and regulations governing business competition. Deregulation has drastically changed some once-regulated industries (especially the transportation, telecommunications, and financial services industries) and created many new competitors. The result has been entries into and exits from some industries. One of the latest industries to deregulate is the electric power industry. With almost 200 investor-owned electric utilities, it is the largest industry to be deregulated so far.

Consumers typically benefit from deregulation. Increased competition often means lower prices. Businesses also benefit because they have more freedom to operate

Mail Fraud Act (1872)	Makes it a federal crime to defraud consumers through use of the mail.
Pure Food and Drug Act (1906)	Created the Food and Drug Administration (FDA); protects consumers against the interstate sale of unsafe and adulterated foods and drugs.
Food, Drug, and Cosmetic Act (1938)	Expanded the power of the FDA to cover cosmetics and therapeutic devices and to establish standards for food products.
Flammable Fabrics Act (1953)	Prohibits sale or manufacture of clothing made of dangerously flammable fabric.
Child Protection Act (1966)	Prohibits sale of harmful toys and gives the FDA the right to remove dangerous products from the marketplace.
Cigarette Labeling Act (1965)	Requires cigarette manufacturers to put labels warning consumers about health hazards on cigarette packages.
Fair Packaging and Labeling Act (1966)	Regulates labeling and packaging of consumer products.
Consumer Credit Protection Act (Truth-in-Lending Act) (1968)	Requires lenders to fully disclose to borrowers the loan terms and the costs of borrowing (interest rate, application fees, etc.).
Fair Credit Reporting Act (1971)	Requires consumers denied credit on the basis of reports from credit agencies to be given access to their reports and to be allowed to correct inaccurate information.
Consumer Product Safety Act (1972)	Created the Consumer Product Safety Commission, an independent federal agency, to establish and enforce consumer product safety standards.
Equal Credit Opportunity Act (1975)	Prohibits denial of credit on the basis of gender, marital status, race, religion, age, or national origin.
Magnuson-Moss Warranty Act (1975)	Requires that warranties be written in clear language and that terms be fully disclosed.
Fair Debt Collection Practice Act (1978)	Makes it illegal to harass or abuse any person, to make false statements, or to use unfair methods when collecting a debt.
Alcohol Labeling Legislation (1988)	Provides for warning labels on liquor saying that women shouldn't drink when pregnant and that alcohol impairs our abilities.
Nutrition Labeling and Eduction Act (1990)	Requires truthful and uniform nutritional labeling on every food the FDA regulates.
Children's Television Act (1990)	Limits the amount of advertising to be shown during children's television programs to not more than 10.5 minutes per hour on weekends and not more than 12.0 minutes per hour on weekdays.
Americans with Disabilities Act (ADA) (1990)	Protects the rights of people with disabilities; makes discrimination against the disabled illegal in public accommodations, transportation, and telecommunications.
Brady Law (1998)	Imposes a 5-day waiting period and a background check before a gun purchaser can take possession of the gun.
Children's Online Privacy Protection Act (2002)	Regulates the collection of personally identifiable information (name, address, e-mail address, phone number, hobbies, interests, or other information collected through cookies) online from children under age 13.
Can-Spam Anti-Spam Law (2004)	Requires marketers to remove customers from their lists when requested, and provide automated opt-out methods as well as complete contact information (address and phone) with alternate means of removal. It also bans common practices such as false headers and e-mail harvesting (the use of software that spies on Web sites to collect e-mail addresses). Subject lines must be truthful and contain a notice that the message is an ad.

and can avoid the costs associated with government regulations. But more competition can also make it hard for small or weak firms to survive.

Regulation of the Internet

Although over 200 million Americans are signing onto the Web regularly, only a minority do so to purchase products. The majority of electronic commerce remains business-to-business transactions. Americans are still far more likely to get the latest news, rather than the latest fashions, in cyberspace. Yet there are clear successes: Amazon.com is America's biggest bookstore. EBay is a hugely successful auction site.

Piracy of music through peer-to-peer networks is now a major problem for some artists and corporations. The Justice Department has seized computers and software in raids on homes and businesses. These actions have targeted the illegal distribution of copyright-protected movies, software, games, and music. In addition to actions by the federal government, the Recording Industry Association of America has filed lawsuits against a number of individuals who were sharing music illegally.

The government has also become concerned over losing control over telecommunications services (and resultant revenue) because of VOIP (voice over Internet protocol). VOIP is simply using the Internet to transfer voice messages through services such as SKYPE. Some legislators are calling for VOIP taxes to fund E-911 (emergency 911 for cell phones) and CELA (Communications Assistance for Law Enforcement). The Internet environment is extremely dynamic, so what, if any, taxation and further regulation of VOIP occurs remains to be seen.

Taxation of Business

 8 What are the most common taxes paid by businesses?

Taxes are sometimes seen as the price we pay to live in this country. Taxes are assessed by all levels of government on both business and individuals, and they are used to pay for the services provided by government. The federal government is the largest collector of taxes, accounting for 54 percent of all tax dollars. States are next, followed closely by local government taxes. The average American family pays about 37 percent of its income for taxes, 28 percent to the federal government and 9 percent to state and local governments.

Income Taxes

income taxes
Taxes that are based on the income received by businesses and individuals.

Income taxes are based on the income received by businesses and individuals. The income taxes paid to the federal government are set by Congress, regulated by the Internal Revenue Code, and collected by the Internal Revenue Service. These taxes are *progressive*, meaning that rates increase as income increases. Most of the states and some large cities also collect income taxes from individuals and businesses. The state and local governments establish their own rules and tax rates.

Other Types of Taxes

property taxes
Taxes that are imposed on real and personal property based on the assessed value of the property.

payroll taxes
The employer's share of Social Security taxes and federal and state unemployment taxes.

Besides income taxes, individuals and businesses pay a number of other taxes. The four main types are property taxes, payroll taxes, sales taxes, and excise taxes.

Property taxes are assessed on real and personal property, based on the assessed value of the property. They raise quite a bit of revenue for state and local governments. Most states tax land and buildings. Property taxes may be based on fair market value (what a buyer would pay), a percentage of fair market value, or replacement value (what it would cost today to rebuild or buy something like the original). The value on which the taxes are based is the assessed value.

Any business that has employees and meets a payroll must pay **payroll taxes**, the employer's share of Social Security taxes and federal and state unemployment taxes.

sales taxes
Taxes that are levied on goods when they are sold; calculated as a percentage of the price.

excise taxes
Taxes that are imposed on specific items such as gasoline, alcoholic beverages, airline tickets, and guns.

These taxes must be paid on wages, salaries, and commissions. State unemployment taxes are based on the number of employees in a firm who have become eligible for unemployment benefits. A firm that has never had an employee become eligible for unemployment will pay a low rate of state unemployment taxes. The firm's experience with employment benefits does not affect federal unemployment tax rates.

Sales taxes are levied on goods when they are sold and are a percentage of the sales price. These taxes are imposed by states, counties, and cities. They vary in amount and in what is considered taxable. Some states have no sales tax. Others tax some categories (such as appliances) but not others (such as clothes). Still others tax all retail products except food, magazines, and prescription drugs. Sales taxes increase the cost of goods to the consumer. Businesses bear the burden of collecting sales taxes and sending them to the government.

Excise taxes are placed on specific items, such as gasoline, alcoholic beverages, cigarettes, airline tickets, cars, and guns. They can be assessed by federal, state, and local governments. In many cases, these taxes help pay for services related to the item taxed. For instance, gasoline excise taxes are often used to build and repair highways. Other excise taxes—like those on alcoholic beverages, cigarettes, and guns—are used to control practices that may cause harm.

CHAPTER 4

Competing in the Global Marketplace

Learning Goals

After reading this chapter, you should be able to answer these questions:

1 Why is global trade important to the United States and how is it measured?

2 Why do nations trade?

3 What are the barriers to international trade?

4 How do governments and institutions foster world trade?

5 What are international economic communities?

6 How do companies enter the global marketplace?

7 What threats and opportunities exist in the global marketplace?

8 What are the advantages of multinational corporations?

9 What are the trends in the global marketplace?

Exploring Business Careers
Mike Lawton
Domino's Pizza

Domino's Pizza has more than 8,000 stores worldwide. As executive vice president of Domino's International division, Mike Lawton is in charge of every store outside of the United States. In 1983, Domino's opened its first international store in Canada and by the time Lawton joined Domino's in 1999, there were over 1,500 stores beyond the U.S. borders. Today, there are over 3,000 stores in over 55 countries, almost half of all that Domino's operates. Given that Domino's delivers more 400 million pizzas a year, that's a lot of dough he's responsible for!

Such an international scope might seem unusual for someone who has spent much of his life in a single state: Lawton was born in Michigan, went to school at Michigan State University, and today lives in Ann Arbor, Michigan. However, he was never one to turn down an opportunity. A broad base of accounting and financial skills opened a chance early in his career to work on some international projects, and he took it. "Since the work interested me, I jumped into international business." And from there, he's never looked back. "My career goal has always been to hold interesting and challenging positions. I never focused on attaining a particular level or position in a company, but sought to broaden my experiences so I was prepared when opportunities arose." Along with a strong financial and business background, he has direct international experience in Europe, Latin America, and Asia—experience that he is able to bring to his work heading Domino's International division.

Luckily, too, he doesn't have to do it alone. As he readily admits, "When we look at what has created success in our markets, we have to credit the people who take the responsibility of running our stores with excellence very seriously."

The people Lawton refers to are the master franchisees (see Chapter 5) of Domino's international business. In this case, master franchisees are individuals or entities who, under a specific licensing agreement with Domino's, control all operations within the country. They operate their own stores, set up a distribution infrastructure to transport materials into and throughout the country, and create sub-franchisees. One particular benefit of master franchisees is their local knowledge. As discussed in this chapter, a major challenge when opening a business on foreign soil is negotiating the political, cultural, and economic differences of that country. According to Lawton, master franchisees allow Domino's, and the franchisee, to "take advantage of their local expertise in dealing with marketing, political, and regulatory issues, as well as the local labor markets." It takes local experience to know, for example, that only 30 percent of the people in Poland have phones, so carryout needs to be the focus of the business; or that Turkey has changed their street names three times in the past 30 years so delivery is much more challenging; or even that, in Japanese, there is no word for pepperoni, the most popular topping worldwide. These are just a few of the challenges that Domino's has had to overcome on the road to becoming the worldwide leader in the pizza delivery business. Under the leadership of people like Lawton and with the help of dedicated, local master franchisees, Domino's has been able to not only compete in but lead the global pizza delivery market.

Chapter 4 examines the business world of the global marketplace. It focuses on the processes of taking a business global—such as licensing agreements and franchisees—the challenges that are encountered, and the regulatory systems governing the world market of the 21st century.

global vision
The ability to recognize and react to international business opportunities, be aware of threats from foreign competition, and effectively use international distribution networks to obtain raw materials and move finished products to customers.

Today, global revolutions are under way in many areas of our lives: management, politics, communications, technology. The word *global* has assumed a new meaning, referring to a boundless mobility and competition in social, business, and intellectual arenas. No longer just an option, having a global vision has become a business imperative. Having a **global vision** means recognizing and reacting to international business opportunities, being aware of threats from foreign competitors in all markets, and effectively using international distribution networks to obtain raw materials and move finished products to the customer.

U.S. managers must develop a global vision if they are to recognize and react to international business opportunities, as well as remain competitive at home. Often a U.S. firm's toughest domestic competition comes from foreign companies. Moreover, a global vision enables a manager to understand that customer and distribution networks operate worldwide, blurring geographic and political barriers and making them increasingly irrelevant to business decisions. The purpose of this chapter is to explain how global trade is conducted. We also discuss the barriers to international trade and the organizations that foster global trade. The chapter concludes with trends in the global marketplace.

Global Trade in the United States

1 Why is global trade important to the United States and how is it measured?

Over the past two decades, world trade has climbed from $200 billion a year to more than $8 trillion. U.S. companies play a major role in this growth in world trade. Gillette, for example, derives two-thirds of its revenue from its international division.

Starbucks Corp. is among the fastest growing global consumer brands and one of the most visible emblems of U.S. commercial culture overseas. Starbucks' 2,573 international stores now contribute a small portion of the company's revenue. But Chief Executive Orin Smith says overseas outlets will eventually outnumber domestic stores. One day, Starbucks expects to operate at least 18,000 outlets abroad, more than twice the 9,000 stores it now operates worldwide.

Go into a Paris McDonald's and you may not recognize where you are. There are no Golden Arches or utilitarian chairs and tables and other plastic features. The restaurants have exposed brick walls, hardwood floors, and armchairs. Some French McDonald's even have faux marble walls. Most restaurants have TVs with continuous music videos. You can even order an espresso, beer, and chicken on focaccia bread sandwich. It's not America.[1]

Global business is not a one-way street, where only U.S. companies sell their wares and services throughout the world. Foreign competition in the domestic market used to be relatively rare but now occurs in almost every industry. In fact, U.S. makers of electronic goods, cameras, automobiles, fine china, tractors, leather goods, and a host of other consumer and industrial products have struggled to maintain their domestic market shares against foreign competitors. Toyota now has 15 percent of the U.S. auto market followed by Honda at 10 percent and Nissan with 7 percent.[2] Nevertheless, the global market has created vast, new business opportunities for many U.S. firms.

The Importance of Global Business to the United States

Many countries depend more on international commerce than the United States does. For example, France, Great Britain, and Germany all derive more than 19 percent of their gross domestic product (GDP) from world trade, compared to about 12 percent for the United States. Nevertheless, the impact of international business on the U.S. economy is still impressive:

- The United States exports about a fifth of its industrial production and a third of its farm products.
- One of every 10 jobs in the United States is directly or indirectly supported by exports.[3]

- U.S. businesses export over $800 billion in goods to foreign countries every year, and almost a third of U.S. corporate profits is derived from international trade and foreign investment.
- Exports account for almost 25 percent of America's economic growth.

These statistics might seem to imply that practically every business in the United States is selling its wares throughout the world, but most is accounted for by big business. About 85 percent of all U.S. exports of manufactured goods are shipped by 250 companies. Yet, 97 percent of all exporters are small- and medium-size firms.[4]

The Impact of Terrorism on Global Trade

The terrorist attacks on America on September 11, 2001, changed forever the way the world conducts business. The immediate impact was a short-term shrinkage of global trade. Globalization will continue because the world's major markets are too vitally integrated for globalization to stop. Nevertheless, terrorism caused the growth to be slower and costlier.

Companies are paying more for insurance and to provide security for overseas staff and property. Heightened border inspections slow movements of cargo, forcing companies to stock more inventory. Tighter immigration policies curtail the liberal inflows of skilled and blue-collar workers that allowed companies to expand while keeping wages in check. Meanwhile, greater concern about political risk (such as multinational petroleum companies in Venezuela) is causing some firms to greatly narrow their horizons when making new investments. The impact of terrorism may lessen over time, but multinational firms will always be on guard.

Measuring Trade Between Nations

International trade improves relationships with friends and allies, helps ease tensions among nations, and—economically speaking—bolsters economies, raises people's standard of living, provides jobs, and improves the quality of life. The value of international trade is over $5 trillion a year and growing. This section takes a look at some key measures of international trade: exports and imports, the balance of trade, the balance of payments, and exchange rates.

Exports and Imports

exports
Goods and services produced in one country and sold to other countries.

imports
Goods and services that are bought from other countries.

The developed nations (those with mature communication, financial, educational, and distribution systems) are the major players in international trade. They account for about 70 percent of the world's exports and imports. Exports are goods and services made in one country and sold to others. Imports are goods and services that are bought from other countries. The United States is both the largest exporter and the largest importer in the world.

Each year the United States exports more food, animal feed, and beverages than the year before. A third of U.S. farm acreage is devoted to crops for export. The United States is also a major exporter of engineering products and other high-tech goods, such as computers and telecommunications equipment. For more than 40,000 U.S. companies (the majority of them small), international trade offers exciting and profitable opportunities. Among the largest U.S. exporters are Boeing Co., General Motors Corp., General Electric Co., Ford Motor Co., and IBM.

Despite our impressive list of resources and great variety of products, imports to the United States are also growing. Some of these imports are raw materials that we lack, such as manganese, cobalt, and bauxite, which are used to make airplane parts, exotic metals, and military hardware. More modern factories and lower labor costs in other countries make it cheaper to import industrial supplies (like steel) and production equipment than to produce them at home. Most of Americans' favorite hot beverages—coffee, tea, and cocoa—are imported. Lower manufacturing costs have resulted in huge increases in imports from China.

Balance of Trade

balance of trade
The difference between the value of a country's exports and the value of its imports during a specific time.

trade surplus
A favorable balance of trade that occurs when a country exports more than it imports.

trade deficit
An unfavorable balance of trade that occurs when a country imports more than it exports.

The difference between the value of a country's exports and the value of its imports during a specific time is the country's **balance of trade**. A country that exports more than it imports is said to have a *favorable* balance of trade, called a **trade surplus**. A country that imports more than it exports is said to have an *unfavorable* balance of trade, or a **trade deficit**. When imports exceed exports, more money from trade flows out of the country than flows into it.

Although U.S. exports have been booming, we still import more than we export. We have had an unfavorable balance of trade throughout the 1990s and 2000s. In 2004, our exports totaled $795 billion, yet our imports were $1.47 trillion. Thus, the United States had a trade deficit again in 2004 of $675 billion. The estimated deficit for 2006 was slightly over $700 billion.[5] America's exports continue to grow but just not as fast as our imports: The export of goods, such as computers, trucks, and airplanes, is very strong. The sector that is lagging in significant growth is the export of services. Although America exports many services—ranging from airline trips to international phone calls to movie royalties, tourism in the United States by foreigners, education of foreign students, and legal advice—part of the problem is due to piracy. Hollywood estimates that it loses about $3 billion a year from international movie piracy.[6]

Balance of Payments

balance of payments
A summary of a country's international financial transactions showing the difference between the country's total payments to and its total receipts from other countries.

Another measure of international trade is called the **balance of payments**, which is a summary of a country's international financial transactions showing the difference between the country's total payments to and its total receipts from other countries. The balance of payments includes imports and exports (balance of trade), long-term investments in overseas plants and equipment, government loans to and from other countries, gifts and foreign aid, military expenditures made in other countries, and money transfers in and out of foreign banks.

From 1900 until 1970, the United States had a trade surplus, but in the other areas that make up the balance of payments, U.S. payments exceeded receipts, largely due to the large U.S. military presence abroad. Hence, almost every year since 1950, the United States has had an unfavorable balance of payments. And since 1970, both the balance of payments *and* the balance of trade have been unfavorable. What can a nation do to reduce an unfavorable balance of payments? It can foster exports, reduce its dependence on imports, decrease its military presence abroad, or reduce foreign investment. The U.S. balance of payments deficit was over $650 billion in 2005.[7]

The Changing Value of Currencies

The exchange rate is the price of one country's currency in terms of another country's currency. If a country's currency *appreciates*, less of that country's currency is needed to buy another country's currency. If a country's currency *depreciates*, more of that currency will be needed to buy another country's currency.

How do appreciation and depreciation affect the prices of a country's goods? If, say, the U.S. dollar depreciates relative to the Japanese yen, U.S. residents have to pay more dollars to buy Japanese goods. To illustrate, suppose the dollar price of a yen is $0.012 and that a Toyota is priced at 2 million yen. At this exchange rate, a U.S. resident pays $24,000 for a Toyota ($0.012 × 2 million yen = $24,000). If the dollar depreciates to $0.018 to one yen, then the U.S. resident will have to pay $36,000 for a Toyota.

As the dollar depreciates, the prices of Japanese goods rise for U.S. residents, so they buy fewer Japanese goods—thus, U.S. imports decline. At the same time, as the dollar depreciates relative to the yen, the yen appreciates relative to the dollar. This means prices of U.S. goods fall for the Japanese, so they buy more U.S. goods—and U.S. exports rise.

floating exchange rates
A system in which prices of currencies move up and down based upon the demand for and supply of the various currencies.

devaluation
A lowering of the value of a nation's currency relative to other currencies.

Currency markets operate under a system called **floating exchange rates**. Prices of currencies "float" up and down based upon the demand for and supply of each currency. Global currency traders create the supply of and demand for a particular currency based on that currency's investment, trade potential, and economic strength. If a country decides that its currency is not properly valued in international currency markets, the government may step in and adjust the currency's value. In a **devaluation**, a nation lowers the value of its currency relative to other currencies. This makes that country's exports cheaper and should, in turn, help the balance of payments.

In other cases, a country's currency may be undervalued giving its exports an unfair competitive advantage. Many believe that China's huge trade surplus with the United States is partially because China's currency was undervalued. In 2005, a bill was introduced in the United States Senate to place a tariff (tax) of 27.5 percent on all China's exports to the United States if China failed to raise the value of its currency. On July 20, 2005, China said that it would allow its currency to fluctuate and strengthened the yuan's value by 2.1 percent. Since 1995, the yuan had been fixed at 8.11 to the U.S. dollar. Now, the value of the yuan will be fixed against a basket of currencies and not just the dollar.[8]

concept check

What is global vision, and why is it important?

What impact does international trade have on the U.S. economy?

Explain the impact of a currency devaluation.

Why Nations Trade

 Why do nations trade?

One might argue that the best way to protect workers and the domestic economy is to stop trade with other nations. Then the whole circular flow of inputs and outputs would stay within our borders. But if we decided to do that, how would we get resources like cobalt and coffee beans? The United States simply can't produce some things, and it can't manufacture some products, such as steel and most clothing, at the low costs we're used to. The fact is that nations—like people—are good at producing different things: you may be better at balancing a ledger than repairing a car. In that case you benefit by "exporting" your bookkeeping services and "importing" the car repairs you need from a good mechanic. Economists refer to specialization like this as *advantage*.

Absolute Advantage

absolute advantage
The situation when a country can produce and sell a product at a lower cost than any other country or when it is the only country that can provide the product.

A country has an **absolute advantage** when it can produce and sell a product at a lower cost than any other country or when it is the only country that can provide a product. The United States, for example, has an absolute advantage in reusable spacecraft and other high-tech items.

Suppose that the United States has an absolute advantage in air traffic control systems for busy airports and that Brazil has an absolute advantage in coffee. The United States does not have the proper climate for growing coffee, and Brazil lacks the technology to develop air traffic control systems. Both countries would gain by exchanging air traffic control systems for coffee.

Comparative Advantage

principle of comparative advantage
The concept that each country should specialize in the products that it can produce most readily and cheaply and trade those products for those that other countries can produce more readily and cheaply.

Even if the United States had an absolute advantage in both coffee and air traffic control systems, it should still specialize and engage in trade. Why? The reason is the **principle of comparative advantage**, which says that each country should specialize in the products that it can produce most readily and cheaply and trade those products for goods that foreign countries can produce most readily and cheaply. This specialization ensures greater product availability and lower prices.

For example, India and China have a comparative advantage in producing clothing because of low labor costs. Japan has long held a comparative advantage in consumer electronics because of technological expertise. America has an advantage in computer software, airplanes, some agricultural products, heavy machinery, and jet engines.

free trade
The policy of permitting the people and businesses of a country to buy and sell where they please without restrictions.

protectionism
The policy of protecting home industries from outside competition by establishing artificial barriers such as tariffs and quotas.

Thus, comparative advantage acts as a stimulus to trade. When nations allow their citizens to trade whatever goods and services they choose without government regulation, free trade exists. **Free trade** is the policy of permitting the people and businesses of a country to buy and sell where they please without restrictions. The opposite of free trade is **protectionism**, in which a nation protects its home industries from outside competition by establishing artificial barriers such as tariffs and quotas. In the next section, we'll look at the various barriers, some natural and some created by governments, that restrict free trade.

The Fear of Trade and Globalization

The continued protests during meetings of the World Trade Organization and the protests during the convocations of the World Bank and the International Monetary Fund (the three organizations are discussed later in the chapter) show that many people fear world trade and globalization. What do they fear? The negatives of global trade are as follows:

- Millions of Americans have lost jobs due to imports or production shifts abroad. Most find new jobs, but those jobs often pay less.
- Millions of others fear losing their jobs, especially at those companies operating under competitive pressure.
- Employers often threaten to export jobs if workers do not accept pay cuts.
- Service and white-collar jobs are increasingly vulnerable to operations moving offshore.

outsourcing
Sending work functions to another country resulting in domestic workers losing their jobs.

Sending domestic jobs to another country is called **outsourcing**, a topic you will explore more in Chapter 9. Many American companies, such as Dell, IBM, and AT&T have set up call service centers in India, Ireland, and other countries. Now even engineering and research and development jobs are being outsourced. Infineon Technologies recently eliminated 40 high-paying engineering jobs at its San Jose research facility and transferred the work to India.

So is outsourcing good or bad? If you happen to lose your job, it's obviously bad. However, some economists say it leads to cheaper goods and services for U.S. consumers because costs are lower. Also, it should stimulate exports to fast-growing countries. No one knows how many jobs will be lost to outsourcing in coming years. Estimates run as high as 3.3 million jobs by 2015, but most economists think that this is far too high.[9] One study showed that U.S. companies sending computer-systems work abroad yielded

CONCEPT in Action

Anti-globalization groups oppose America's free-trade stance, arguing that corporate interests are hurting the U.S. economy and usurping the power of the American people. The "Stocks and Stripes" flag is a powerful anti-free-trade statement expressing the idea that multinational corporations wield too much power over the United States and its policies. *Are fears expressed by anti-globalization activists and nationalists justified?*

© KENNETH MARTIN/LANDOV

higher productivity that actually resulted in a yearly net increase in U.S. employment of 90,000 jobs.[10]

Benefits of Globalization

A closer look, however, reveals that globalization has been the engine that creates jobs and wealth. Benefits of global trade include the following:

- Productivity grows more quickly when countries produce goods and services in which they have a comparative advantage. Living standards can go up faster.
- Global competition and cheap imports keep prices down, so inflation is less likely to arrest economic growth.
- An open economy spurs innovation with fresh ideas from abroad.
- The United States buys about $2 trillion a year from other countries or 16 percent of the gross domestic product. This is up from 8.5 percent in 1995.[11]
- Since 1997, prices for many heavily traded goods have actually fallen: 86 percent for computers and peripherals, 68 percent for video equipment, 36 percent for toys, 20 percent for women's outerwear, and 17 percent for men's shirts and sweaters. Prices of goods and services not subject to foreign competition have fared less well: college tuition and fees, up 53 percent; cable and satellite television, up 41 percent; dental services, up 38 percent; and prescription drugs and medical supplies, up 37 percent.[12]
- Income from U.S. foreign subsidiaries of firms such as Pepsi, AmericanExpress, and Microsoft is over $200 billion a year, and many are enjoying record profits.[13]

concept check

Describe the policy of free trade and its relationship to comparative advantage.

Why do people fear globalization?

What are the benefits of globalization?

Barriers to Trade

3 What are the barriers to international trade?

International trade is carried out by both businesses and governments—as long as no one puts up trade barriers. In general, trade barriers keep firms from selling to one another in foreign markets. The major obstacles to international trade are natural barriers, tariff barriers, and nontariff barriers.

Natural Barriers

Natural barriers to trade can be either physical or cultural. For instance, even though raising beef in the relative warmth of Argentina may cost less than raising beef in the bitter cold of Siberia, the cost of shipping the beef from South America to Siberia might drive the price too high. *Distance* is thus one of the natural barriers to international trade.

Language is another natural trade barrier. People who can't communicate effectively may not be able to negotiate trade agreements or may ship the wrong goods.

Tariff Barriers

tariff
A tax imposed on imported goods.

A **tariff** is a tax imposed by a nation on imported goods. It may be a charge per unit, such as per barrel of oil or per new car; it may be a percentage of the value of the goods, such as 5 percent of a $500,000 shipment of shoes; or it may be a combination. No matter how it is assessed, any tariff makes imported goods more costly, so they are less able to compete with domestic products.

protective tariffs
Tariffs that are imposed in order to make imports less attractive to buyers than domestic products are.

Protective tariffs make imported products less attractive to buyers than domestic products. The United States, for instance, has protective tariffs on imported poultry, textiles, sugar, and some types of steel and clothing. On the other side of the world, Japan imposes a tariff on U.S. cigarettes that makes them cost 60 percent more than Japanese brands. U.S. tobacco firms believe they could get as much as a third of the Japanese market if there were no tariffs on cigarettes. With tariffs, they have under 2 percent of the market.

Arguments for and against Tariffs Congress has debated the issue of tariffs since 1789. The main arguments *for* tariffs include the following:

- Tariffs protect infant industries. A tariff can give a struggling new domestic industry time to become an effective global competitor.
- Tariffs protect American jobs. Unions, and others, say tariffs keep foreign labor from taking away U.S. jobs.
- Tariffs aid in military preparedness. Tariffs should protect industries and technology during peacetime that are vital to the military in the event of war.

The main arguments *against* tariffs include the following:

- Tariffs discourage free trade and free trade lets the principle of competitive advantage work most efficiently.
  Tariffs raise prices, thereby decreasing consumers' purchasing power. In 1999, President Bush imposed tariffs of 8 percent to 30 percent on a wide variety of steel products. The idea was to give U.S. steel manufacturers time to modernize to better compete in the global marketplace. Within six months of imposing the tariffs, the U.S. price of cold rolled steel jumped from $210 a ton to $350 a ton. The result is that heavy users of steel, such as construction and automobile industries, have seen big increases in their costs of production. By 2004, the U.S. steel industry had rebounded and reorganized since the tariffs were first ordered, and the industry turned a profit for the first time in years. Steelmakers said the tariffs were necessary to ensure their financial viability, implement technological improvements, and fund retiree benefits. Thus, the following year, the tariffs were extended five more years after determining that lifting the tariffs would result in more steel imports from Brazil, Japan, and Russia.[14]

Nontariff Barriers

Governments also use other tools besides tariffs to restrict trade. One type of nontariff barrier is the **import quota** or limits on the quantity of a certain good that can be imported. The goal of setting quotas is to limit imports to the specific amount of a given product. America protects its shrinking textile industry with quotas. In 2005, the United States removed the quotas on clothing coming from China. Eight months after the quotas were lifted, China's apparel exports to the United States jumped 85 percent.[15]

A complete ban against importing or exporting a product is an **embargo**. Often embargoes are set up for defense purposes. For instance, the United States does not allow various high-tech products, such as supercomputers and lasers, to be exported to countries that are not allies. Although this embargo costs U.S. firms billions of dollars each year in lost sales, it keeps enemies from using the latest technology in their military hardware.

Government rules that give special privileges to domestic manufacturers and retailers are called **buy-national regulations**. One such regulation in the United States bans the use of foreign steel in constructing U.S. highways. Many state governments have buy-national rules for supplies and services. In a more subtle move, a country may make it hard for foreign products to enter its markets by establishing customs regulations that are different from generally accepted international standards, such as requiring bottles to be quart size rather than liter size.

Exchange controls are laws that require a company earning foreign exchange (foreign currency) from its exports to sell the foreign exchange to a control agency, usually a central bank. For example, assume that Rolex, a Swiss company, sells 300 watches to Zales Jewelers, a U.S. chain, for $600,000 (U.S.). If Switzerland had exchange controls, Rolex would have to sell its U.S. dollars to the Swiss central bank and would receive Swiss francs. If Rolex wants to buy goods (supplies to make watches)

import quota
A limit on the quantity of a certain good that can be imported.

embargo
A total ban on imports or exports of a product.

buy-national regulations
Government rules that give special privileges to domestic manufacturers and retailers.

exchange controls
Laws that require a company earning foreign exchange (foreign currency) from its exports to sell the foreign exchange to a control agency, such as a central bank.

from abroad, it must go to the central bank and buy foreign exchange (currency). By controlling the amount of foreign exchange sold to companies, the government controls the amount of products that can be imported. Limiting imports and encouraging exports helps a government to create a favorable balance of trade.

Fostering Global Trade

4 How do governments and institutions foster world trade?

dumping
The practice of charging a lower price for a product in foreign markets than in the firm's home market.

Uruguay Round
A 1994 agreement by 117 nations to lower trade barriers worldwide.

World Trade Organization (WTO)
An organization established by the Uruguay Round in 1994 to oversee international trade, reduce trade barriers, and resolve disputes among member nations.

CONCEPT *in Action*

The selection of Beijing to be the host city of the 2008 Summer Olympics was emblematic of China's increasing participation in the global marketplace. America's top businesses make huge investments in the Games, snapping up sponsorships and licensing agreements to promote their brands in some of the world's most populous regions. *In what ways do the Olympic Games foster world trade and provide businesses with an opportunity to gain advantage in global markets?*

© PR NEWSWIRE BURSON-MARSTELLER BEIJING

Antidumping Laws

U.S. firms don't always get to compete on an equal basis with foreign firms in international trade. To level the playing field, Congress has passed antidumping laws. **Dumping** is the practice of charging a lower price for a product (perhaps below cost) in foreign markets than in the firm's home market. The company might be trying to win foreign customers, or it might be seeking to get rid of surplus goods.

When the variation in price can't be explained by differences in the cost of serving the two markets, dumping is suspected. Most industrialized countries have antidumping regulations. They are especially concerned about *predatory dumping,* the attempt to gain control of a foreign market by destroying competitors with impossibly low prices.

The United States recently imposed tariffs on frozen and canned shrimp from Brazil, Ecuador, India, and Thailand. The four countries were found guilty of pricing shrimp at up to 68 percent below their costs. U.S. shrimpers from eight southern states filed a complaint, arguing that increased imports of farm-raised shrimp are depressing prices and putting the shrimpers out of business.[16]

From our discussion so far, it might seem that governments act only to restrain global trade. On the contrary, governments and international financial organizations work hard to increase it, as this section explains.

The Uruguay Round and the World Trade Organization

The **Uruguay Round** of trade negotiations is an agreement that dramatically lowers trade barriers worldwide. Adopted in 1994, the agreement has been now signed by 148 nations. The most ambitious global trade agreement ever negotiated, the Uruguay Round reduced tariffs by one-third worldwide, a move that is expected to increase global income by $235 billion annually. Perhaps the most notable aspect of the agreement is its recognition of new global realities. For the first time, an agreement covers services, intellectual-property rights, and trade-related investment measures such as exchange controls.

The **World Trade Organization (WTO)** replaces the old General Agreement on Tariffs and Trade (GATT), which was created in 1948. The GATT contained extensive loopholes that enabled countries to evade agreements to reduce trade barriers. Today, all WTO members must fully comply with all agreements under the Uruguay Round. The WTO also has an effective dispute settlement procedure with strict time limits to resolve disputes.

The WTO has emerged as the world's most powerful institution for reducing trade barriers and opening markets. The advantage of WTO membership is that member countries lower trade barriers among themselves. Countries that don't belong must negotiate trade agreements individually with all their trading partners. To date, Russia is the largest country that has not qualified for WTO membership.

CONCEPT *in Action*

Based in Toulouse, France, Airbus is one of the world's top commercial aircraft manufacturers, operating design and manufacturing facilities in Europe, Japan, China, and the United States. The airliner's current product line-up of 12 jet-aircraft types ranging from 100 seats to 555 seats is heavy competition for Boeing, a top U.S. airline firm with which Airbus has ongoing subsidy-related disputes. *What is the World Trade Organization's role in settling disputes between competing multinational corporations?*

The United States has had mixed results in bringing disputes before the WTO. To date, it has won slightly less than half of the cases it has presented to the WTO. America has also won about one-third of the cases brought against it by other countries. One of America's biggest losses came when a WTO panel ruled that the Japanese government's attempt to protect Fuji Film from competition by Kodak was not illegal. Recently, the United States targeted Europe, India, South Korea, Canada, and Argentina to file cases against. The disputes ranged from European aviation practices to Indian barriers affecting U.S. automakers. One of the biggest disputes before the WTO involves the United States and the European Union. The United States claims that Europe has given Airbus $15 billion in aid to develop airplanes. The European Union claims that the U.S. government has provided $23 billion in military research that has benefited Boeing's commercial aircraft business. It also claimed that Washington state (the home of Boeing manufacturing) has given the company $3.2 billion in unfair tax breaks.[17]

The first negotiating round since the Uruguay Round started in the capital of Qatar in 2001 is called the Doha Round. To date, the round has shown little progress in advancing free trade. Developing nations are pushing for the reduction of farm subsidies in the United States, Europe, and Japan. Poor countries say that the subsidies stimulate overproduction, which drives down global agricultural prices. Because developing nations' primary exports are agricultural commodities, low prices mean that they cannot compete in the global marketplace. On the other hand, the United States and Europe are interested in bringing down trade barriers in services and manufacturing. At this point, little progress has been made in the Doha Round. The continuing talks have served as a lightning rod for protesters who claim that the WTO serves the interests of multinational corporations, promotes trade over preserving the environment, and treats poor nations unfairly.[18]

The World Bank and International Monetary Fund

Two international financial organizations are instrumental in fostering global trade. The World Bank offers low-interest loans to developing nations. Originally, the purpose of the loans was to help these nations build infrastructure such as roads, power plants, schools, drainage projects, and hospitals. Now the World Bank offers loans to help developing nations relieve their debt burdens. To receive the loans, countries must pledge to lower trade barriers and aid private enterprise. In addition to making loans, the World Bank is a major source of advice and information for developing nations. The United States has granted the organization millions to create knowledge

World Bank
An international bank that offers low-interest loans, as well as advice and information, to developing nations.

databases on nutrition, birth control, software engineering, creating quality products, and basic accounting systems.

The **International Monetary Fund (IMF)** was founded in 1945, one year after the creation of the World Bank, to promote trade through financial cooperation and eliminate trade barriers in the process. The IMF makes short-term loans to member nations that are unable to meet their budgetary expenses. It operates as a lender of last resort for troubled nations. In exchange for these emergency loans, IMF lenders frequently extract significant commitments from the borrowing nations to address the problems that led to the crises. These steps may include curtailing imports or even devaluing the currency.

International Monetary Fund (IMF)
An international organization, founded in 1945, that promotes trade, makes short-term loans to member nations, and acts as a lender of last resort for troubled nations.

Some global financial problems do not have a simple solution. One option would be to pump a lot more funds into the IMF, giving it enough resources to bail out troubled countries and put them back on their feet. In effect, the IMF would be turned into a real lender of last resort for the world economy.

The danger of counting on the IMF, though, is the "moral hazard" problem. Investors would assume that the IMF would bail them out and would therefore be encouraged to take bigger and bigger risks in emerging markets, leading to the possibility of even deeper financial crises in the future.

---

concept check

Describe the purpose and role of the WTO.

What are the roles of the World Bank and the IMF in world trade?

International Economic Communities

 5 **What are international economic communities?**

preferential tariff
A tariff that is lower for some nations than for others.

free-trade zone
An area where the nations allow free, or almost free, trade among each other while imposing tariffs on goods of nations outside the zone.

North American Free Trade Agreement (NAFTA)
A 1993 agreement creating a free-trade zone including Canada, Mexico, and the United States.

Nations that frequently trade with each other may decide to formalize their relationship. The governments meet and work out agreements for a common economic policy. The result is an economic community or, in other cases, a bilateral trade agreement (an agreement between two countries to lower trade barriers). For example, two nations may agree upon a **preferential tariff**, which gives advantages to one nation (or several nations) over others. When members of the British Commonwealth trade with Great Britain, they pay lower tariffs than do other nations. In other cases, nations may form free-trade associations. In a **free-trade zone**, few duties or rules restrict trade among the partners, but nations outside the zone must pay the tariffs set by the individual members.

North American Free Trade Agreement (NAFTA)

The **North American Free Trade Agreement (NAFTA)** created the world's largest free-trade zone. The agreement was ratified by the U.S. Congress in 1993. It includes Canada, the United States, and Mexico, with a combined population of 360 million and an economy of over $6 trillion.

Canada, the largest U.S. trading partner, entered a free-trade agreement with the United States in 1988. Thus, most of the new long-run opportunities opened for U.S. business under NAFTA are in Mexico, America's third largest trading partner. Before NAFTA, tariffs on Mexican exports to the United States averaged just 4 percent, and most goods entered the United States duty-free, so NAFTA's primary impact was to open the Mexican market to U.S. companies. When the treaty went into effect, tariffs on about half the items traded across the Rio Grande disappeared. Since NAFTA came into effect, U.S.–Mexican trade has increased from $80 billion to $275 billion annually. The pact removed a web of Mexican licensing requirements, quotas, and tariffs that limited transactions in U.S. goods and services. For instance, the pact allows U.S. and Canadian financial-services companies to own subsidiaries in Mexico for the first time in 50 years.

The real test of NAFTA will be whether it can deliver rising prosperity on both sides of the Rio Grande. For Mexicans, NAFTA must provide rising wages, better benefits, and an expanding middle class with enough purchasing power to keep buying goods from the United States and Canada. That scenario seems to be working. At the Delphi

© JEFF TOPPING/REUTERS/LANDOV

Mercosur
Trade agreement between Peru, Brazil, Argentina, Uruguay, and Paraguay.

Corp. auto parts plant in Ciudad Juárez, just across the border from El Paso, Texas, the assembly line is a cross section of working-class Mexico. In the years since NAFTA lowered trade and investment barriers, Delphi has significantly expanded its presence in the country. Today it employs 70,000 Mexicans, who every day receive up to 70 million U.S.-made components to assemble into parts. The wages are modest by U.S. standards—an assembly line worker with two years' experience earns about $1.90 an hour. But that's triple Mexico's minimum wage, and Delphi jobs are among the most coveted in Juárez.[19]

The largest new trade agreement is **Mercosur**, which includes Peru, Brazil, Argentina, Uruguay, and Paraguay. The elimination of most tariffs among the trading partners has resulted in trade revenues that currently exceed $16 billion annually. Recent recessions in Mercosur countries have limited economic growth, even though trade among Mercosur countries has continued to grow.

Central America Free Trade Agreement

The newest free trade agreement is the Central America Free Trade Agreement (CAFTA) passed in 2005. Besides the United States, the agreement includes Costa Rica, the Dominican Republic, El Salvador, Guatemala, Honduras, and Nicaragua. The United States is already the principal exporter to these nations, so economists don't think that it will result in a major increase in U.S. exports. It will, however, reduce tariffs on exports to CAFTA countries. Already, some 80 percent of the goods imported into the United States from CAFTA nations are tariff-free. CAFTA countries may benefit from the new permanent trade deal if U.S. multinational firms deepen their investment in the region.

The European Union

In 1993, the member countries of the European Community (EC) ratified the Maastricht Treaty, which proposed to take the EC further toward economic, monetary, and political union. Although the heart of the treaty deals with developing a unified European Market, Maastricht was also intended to increase integration among **European Union (EU)** members.

The EU has helped increase this integration by creating a borderless economy for the 25 European nations, shown on the map in Exhibit 4.1:

European Union
Trade agreement among 25 European nations.

EU25 Member States:		Candidate Countries:	Application Pending:
• Austria	• Latvia	• Bulgaria	• Former Yugoslav
• Belgium	• Lithuania	• Croatia	Republic of Macedonia
• Cyprus	• Luxembourg	• Romania	
• Czech Republic	• Malta	• Turkey	
• Denmark	• The Netherlands		
• Estonia	• Poland		
• Finland	• Portugal		
• France	• Slovakia		
• Germany	• Slovenia		
• Greece	• Spain		
• Hungary	• Sweden		
• Ireland	• United Kingdom		
• Italy			

European integration
The delegation of limited sovereignty by European Union member states to the EU so that common laws and policies can be created at the European level.

European Union member states have set up common institutions to which they delegate some of their sovereignty so that decisions on specific matters of joint interest can be made democratically at the European level. This pooling of sovereignty is also called **European integration**.

One of the principal objectives of the European Union is to promote economic progress of all member countries. The EU has stimulated economic progress by

Exhibit 4.1 > The European Union

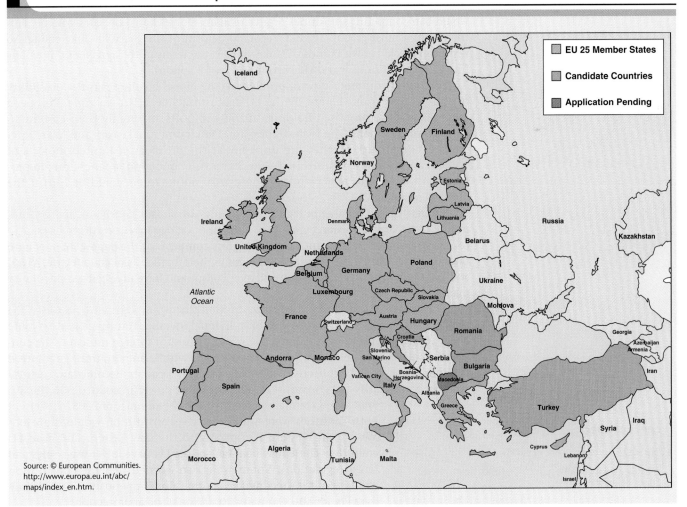

Source: © European Communities. http://www.europa.eu.int/abc/maps/index_en.htm.

eliminating trade barriers, differences in tax laws, and differences in product standards, and by establishing a common currency. A new European Community Bank was created along with a common currency called the euro. The European Union's single market has created 2.5 million new jobs since it was founded and generated more than $1 trillion in new wealth.[20] The opening of national EU markets has brought down the price of national telephone calls by 50 percent since 1998. Under pressure of competition, the prices of airfares in Europe have fallen significantly. The removal of national restrictions has enabled more than 15 million Europeans to go to another EU country to work or spend their retirement.

The EU is a very tough antitrust enforcer; some would say tougher than the United States. The EU, for example, blocked a merger between General Electric and Honeywell (both American companies) even after U.S. regulators had approved the deal! Unlike in the United States, the EU can seal off corporate offices for unspecified periods to prevent destruction of evidence and enter the homes, cars, yachts, and other personal property of executives suspected of abusing their companies' market power or conspiring to fix prices. In 2005, the European offices of Intel were raided by EU antitrust officials seeking information about monopoly power abuse. Advanced Micro Devices (AMD) claimed that Intel had achieved its 90 percent of global market share through threats and kickbacks.[21]

Microsoft has been fighting the European Court since 2002, with no quick end in sight. The Court fined Microsoft for monopolizing Internet access by offering Internet Explorer with its Windows software. The company is also appealing a Court decision requiring it to share code with "open source" companies. Another big U.S. company, Coca-Cola, settled a six-year antitrust dispute with the European Court by agreeing to strict limits on its sales tactics. Coke can't sign exclusive agreements with retailers that would ban competing soft drinks or give retailers rebates based on sales volume. Furthermore, it must give rivals, like Pepsi, 20 percent of the space in Coke coolers so Pepsi can stock its own brands. If Coke violates the terms of the agreement, it will be fined 10 percent of its worldwide revenue (over $2 billion).[22]

An entirely different type of problem facing global businesses is the possibility of a protectionist movement by the EU against outsiders. For example, European automakers have proposed holding Japanese imports at roughly their current 10 percent market share. The Irish, Danes, and Dutch don't make cars and have unrestricted home markets; they are unhappy at the prospect of limited imports of Toyotas and Hondas. Meanwhile France has a strict quota on Japanese cars to protect its own Renault and Peugeot. These local automarkers could be hurt if the quota is raised at all.

Interestingly, a number of big U.S. companies are already considered more "European" than many European companies. Coke and Kellogg's are considered classic European brand names. Ford and General Motors compete for the largest share of auto sales on the continent. IBM and Dell dominate their markets. General Electric, AT&T, and Westinghouse are already strong all over Europe and have invested heavily in new manufacturing facilities there.

The European Union proposed a constitution that would centralize powers at the Union level and decrease the powers of individual member countries. It also would create a single voice in world affairs by creating a post of foreign minister. The constitution also gave the EU control over political asylum, immigration, guaranteed freedom of speech, and collective labor bargaining. In order to become law, each EU country had to ratify the constitution. The two most powerful countries in the EU, France and Germany, voted "no" in the summer of 2005. Citizens of both countries were afraid that the constitution would draw jobs away from Western Europe and to the new Eastern European EU countries. These new members of the EU have lower wage rates and fewer regulations. Voters were also worried that the constitution would result in free-market reforms along American or British lines over France and Germany's traditional social protections.

concept check

Explain the pros and cons of NAFTA.

What is the European Union? Will it ever be a United States of Europe?

Participating in the Global Marketplace

6 How do companies enter the global marketplace?

Companies decide to "go global" for a number of reasons. Perhaps the most urgent reason is to earn additional profits. If a firm has a unique product or technological advantage not available to other international competitors, this advantage should result in major business successes abroad. In other situations, management may have exclusive market information about foreign customers, marketplaces, or market situations not known to others. In this case, although exclusivity can provide an initial motivation for going global, managers must realize that competitors will eventually catch up. Finally, saturated domestic markets, excess capacity, and potential for cost savings can also be motivators to expand into international markets. A company can enter global trade in several ways, as this section describes.

Exporting

exporting
The practice of selling domestically produced goods to buyers in another country.

When a company decides to enter the global market, usually the least complicated and least risky alternative is exporting, or selling domestically produced products to buyers in another country. A company, for example, can sell directly to foreign importers or buyers. Exporting is not limited to huge corporations such as General Motors or Westinghouse. Indeed, small companies typically enter the global marketplace by exporting.[23] The United States is the world's largest exporter. Many small businesses claim that they lack the money, time, or knowledge of foreign markets that exporting requires. The U.S. Small Business Administration (SBA) now offers the Export Working Capital Program, which helps small and medium-size firms obtain working capital (money) to complete export sales. The SBA also provides counseling and legal assistance for small businesses that wish to enter the global marketplace. Companies such as American Building Restoration Products of Franklin, Wisconsin, have benefited tremendously from becoming exporters. American Building is now selling its chemical products to building restoration companies in Mexico, Israel, Japan, and Korea. Exports account for more than 5 percent of the firm's total sales.

Plenty of governmental help is available when a company decides to begin exporting. Export Assistance Centers (EAC) provide a one-stop resource place for help in exporting. Over 700 EACs are placed strategically around the country. Often the Small Business Administration (SBA) is located in the same building as the EAC. The SBA can guarantee loans of $50,000 to $100,000 to help an exporter grow its business. Online help is also available at **http://www.usatrade.gov**. The site lists international trade

CONCEPT *in Action*

The Frisbee is going global. The flying saucer-like disc soared overseas when a Hong Kong distributor purchased American vintage toymaker Wham-O, Inc. Although Wham-O is internationally known, its products have not sold well outside the United States. The company's new Chinese owners believe increased production and distribution in markets like Brazil and South Africa could double Wham-O's sales. *Can vintage American toys like the Frisbee, Hula Hoop, and Slip'N Slide succeed in foreign markets? Why?*

events, offers international marketing research, and has practical tools to help with every step of the exporting process. Companies considering exporting for the first time can go to **http://www.export.gov** and have questions such as "What's in it for me?" "Am I ready for this?" "What do I have to do?" answered. The site also provides a huge list of resources for the first-time exporter.

Licensing and Franchising

licensing
The legal process whereby a firm agrees to allow another firm to use a manufacturing process, trademark, patent, trade secret, or other proprietary knowledge in exchange for the payment of a royalty.

Another effective way for a firm to move into the global arena with relatively little risk is to sell a license to manufacture its product to a firm in a foreign country. **Licensing** is the legal process whereby a firm (the *licensor*) agrees to let another firm (the *licensee*) use a manufacturing process, trademark, patent, trade secret, or other proprietary knowledge. The licensee, in turn, agrees to pay the licensor a royalty or fee agreed on by both parties.

International licensing is a multibillion dollar a year industry. Entertainment and character licensing, such as DVD movies and characters such as Batman, is the largest single category. Trademarks is the second largest source of licensing revenue. Caterpillar licenses its brand for both shoes and clothing, which is very popular in Europe.

U.S. companies have eagerly embraced the licensing concept. For instance, Philip Morris licensed Labatt Brewing Company to produce Miller High Life in Canada. The Spalding Company receives more than $2 million annually from license agreements on its sporting goods. Fruit-of-the-Loom lends its name through licensing to 45 consumer items in Japan alone, for at least 1 percent of the licensee's gross sales.

The licensor must make sure it can exercise sufficient control over the licensee's activities to ensure proper quality, pricing, distribution, and so on. Licensing may also create a new competitor in the long run, if the licensee decides to void the license agreement. International law is often ineffective in stopping such actions. Two common ways that a licensor can maintain effective control over its licensees are by shipping one or more critical components from the United States and by locally registering patents and trademarks in its own name.

Franchising, covered in Chapter 5, is a form of licensing that has grown rapidly in recent years. Over 350 U.S. franchisors operate more than 32,000 outlets in foreign countries, bringing in sales of $6 billion. More than half of the international franchises are for fast-food restaurants and business services. McDonald's international division is responsible for over 50 percent of the chain's sales and 60 percent of its profits.

Having a big name franchise doesn't always guarantee success or mean that the job will be easy. In China, franchises such as A&W, Chili's Grill and Bar, Dunkin Donuts, and Rainforest Café closed up shop.[24] When Subway opened its first sandwich shop, locals stood outside and watched for a few days. Patrons were so confused that the franchisee had to print signs explaining how to order. They didn't believe the tuna salad was made from a fish because they couldn't see the head or tail. And they didn't like the idea of touching their food, so they would hold the sandwich vertically, peel off the paper wrap, and eat it like a banana. Most of all, the Chinese customers didn't want sandwiches.

It's not unusual for Western food chains to have trouble selling in China. McDonald's, aware that the Chinese consume more chicken than beef, offered a spicy chicken burger. KFC got rid of coleslaw in favor of seasonal dishes such as shredded carrots, fungus, or bamboo shoots.

Contract Manufacturing

contract manufacturing
The practice in which a foreign firm manufactures private-label goods under a domestic firm's brand name.

In **contract manufacturing,** a foreign firm manufactures private-label goods under a domestic firm's brand. Marketing may be handled by either the domestic company or the foreign manufacturer. Levi Strauss, for instance, entered into an agreement with the French fashion house of Cacharel to produce a new Levi's line called "Something New" for distribution in Germany.

The advantage of contract manufacturing is that it lets a company "test the water" in a foreign country. By allowing the foreign firm to produce a certain volume of products to specification, and put the domestic firm's brand name on the goods, the domestic firm can broaden its global marketing base without investing in overseas plants and equipment. After establishing a solid base, the domestic firm may switch to a joint venture or direct investment, explained below.

Joint Ventures

joint venture
An agreement in which a domestic firm buys part of a foreign firm or joins with a foreign firm to create a new entity.

Joint ventures are somewhat similar to licensing agreements. In a **joint venture**, the domestic firm buys part of a foreign company or joins with a foreign company to create a new entity. A joint venture is a quick and relatively inexpensive way to enter the global market. It can also be very risky. Many joint ventures fail. Others fall victim to a takeover, in which one partner buys out the other.

Sometimes countries have required local partners in order to establish a business in their country. China, for example, had this requirement in a number of industries until recently. Thus, a joint venture was the only way to enter the market. Joint ventures help reduce risks by sharing costs and technology. Often joint ventures will bring different strengths together from each member. In the General Motors–Suzuki joint venture in Canada, for example, both parties have contributed and gained. The alliance, CAMI Automotive, was formed to manufacture low-end cars for the U.S. market. The plant, which is run by Suzuki management, produces the Chevrolet Equinox and the Pontiac Torrent as well as the new Suzuki SUV. Through CAMI, Suzuki has gained access to GM's dealer network and an expanded market for parts and components. GM avoided the cost of developing low-end cars and obtained models it needed to revitalize the lower end of its product line and its average fuel economy rating. The CAMI factory may be one of the most productive plants in North America. There GM has learned how Japanese automakers use work teams, run flexible assembly lines, and manage quality control.

Direct Foreign Investment

direct foreign investment
Active ownership of a foreign company or of manufacturing or marketing facilities in a foreign country.

Active ownership of a foreign company or of overseas manufacturing or marketing facilities is **direct foreign investment**. Direct investors have either a controlling interest or a large minority interest in the firm. Thus, they stand to receive the greatest potential reward but also face the greatest potential risk. A firm may make a direct foreign investment by acquiring an interest in an existing company or by building new facilities. It might do so because it has trouble transferring some resources to a foreign operation or obtaining that resource locally. One important resource is personnel, especially managers. If the local labor market is tight, the firm may buy an entire foreign firm and retain all its employees instead of paying higher salaries than competitors.

Sometimes firms make direct investments because they can find no suitable local partners. Also, direct investments avoid the communication problems and conflicts of interest that can arise with joint ventures. IBM, in the past, insisted on total ownership of its foreign investments because it did not want to share control with local partners.

General Motors has done very well by building a $5,000 minivan, in China, that gets 43 miles to the gallon in city driving. The minivans have a quarter the horsepower of American minivans, weak acceleration, and a top speed of 81 miles per hour. The seats are only a third of the thickness of seats in Western models but look plush compared to similar Chinese cars. The minivans have made GM the largest automotive seller in China and the biggest center of profit for GM in the world.[25]

Wal-Mart now has over 2,000 stores located outside the United States. In 2006, international sales were over $60 billion. About one-third of all new Wal-Mart stores are opened in global markets.

Not all of its global investments have been successful. In Germany, Wal-Mart bought the 21-store Wertkauf hypermarket chain and then 74 unprofitable and often decrepit Interspar stores. Problems in integrating and upgrading the stores resulted in at least $200 million in losses. Like all other German stores, Wal-Mart stores in Germany are required by law to close at 8 P.M. on weekdays and 4 P.M. on Saturdays and they cannot open at all on Sundays. And costs were astronomical. In 2006, Wal-Mart left the German market.

Wal-Mart, however, seems to be turning the corner on its international operations. It is pushing operational authority down to country managers in order to respond better to local cultures. Wal-Mart enforces certain core principles such as "everyday low prices," but country managers handle their own buying, logistics, building design, and other operational decisions.

Global firms change their strategies as local market conditions evolve. Dell Computer didn't think that it could sell computers online in China. And then it uncovered an amazing statistic. Dell's story unfolds in the Managing Change box.

Countertrade

countertrade
A form of international trade in which part or all of the payment for goods or services is in the form of other goods and services.

International trade does not always involve cash. Today, countertrade is a fast-growing way to conduct international business. In **countertrade**, part or all of the payment for goods or services is in the form of other goods or services. Countertrade is a form of barter (swapping goods for goods), an age-old practice whose origins have been traced back to cave dwellers. The U.S. Commerce Department says that roughly 30 percent of all international trade involves countertrade. Each year about 300,000 U.S. firms engage in some form of countertrade. American companies, including General Electric, Pepsi, General Motors, and Boeing, barter billions of goods and services every year. Recently, the Malaysian government bought 20 diesel-powered locomotives from China and paid for them with palm oil.

The Atwood Richards Co. is the world's largest countertrade organization. Atwood reviews a client's unsold products and issues trade credits in exchange. The credits can be used to obtain other products and services Atwood has acquired—everything from hotel rooms and airline tickets to television advertising time, forklift trucks, carpeting, pulp, envelopes, steel castings, or satellite tracking systems.

concept check

Discuss several ways that a company can enter international trade.

Explain the concept of countertrade.

MANAGING CHANGE

Dell's Success in China Tells Tale of a Maturing Market

In 2003, Dell Inc. rejected a plan to sell computers online in China. The personal-computer giant worried that most Chinese consumers didn't use credit cards and were too poor to become big Web shoppers.

In 2004, Dell executives in China showed their bosses a startling statistic: More than 90 million people in the country's coastal cities have access to the Internet at home or work. "We're missing a great opportunity," William J. Amelio, Dell's top executive in Asia, recalls thinking.

Today, online sales account for about 6 percent of Dell's orders in China and are becoming a big part of the company's push to shake up the Chinese computer industry the way it did in the United States a decade ago. In China, Dell faced repeated warnings that its strategy—which relies on sophisticated computer buyers willing to purchase a product sight unseen—wouldn't work. But by first going after business customers and then pushing into the consumer market, Dell has become China's third-largest seller of PCs, behind two Chinese rivals, with an 8 percent market share.

Dell has learned some new tricks in China. Rather than create a joint venture with a Chinese firm, it waited to form a wholly owned subsidiary that cultivated close ties with a regional government. And it boosted its reputation in the region by teaching quality-checking and just-in-time manufacturing skills to locals.

Dell stuck to its playbook, concentrating initially on business and institutional buyers, who are most familiar with PCs and tend to be the most profitable clients. In China as in Europe, it started out selling high-margin products, such as server computers, and gradually added less pricey desktop and notebook PCs. Most of its orders are taken by telephone sales representatives who work at a call center in Xiamen, a city bigger than Dallas, Texas, on China's southeast coast. In nine other Chinese cities, Dell has sales representatives who visit large business and government customers, sending orders back to colleagues in Xiamen.[26]

Critical Thinking Questions
- Do you think that Dell would have been more successful if it had entered into a joint venture with a Chinese company? Why?
- Do you think that Dell should open a sales force to call on businesses in the United States?

Threats and Opportunities in the Global Marketplace

7 | What threats and opportunities exist in the global marketplace?

To be successful in a foreign market, companies must fully understand the foreign environment in which they plan to operate. Politics, cultural differences, and the economic environment can represent both opportunities and pitfalls in the global marketplace.

Political Considerations

We have already discussed how tariffs, exchange controls, and other governmental actions threaten foreign producers. The political structure of a country may also jeopardize a foreign producer's success in international trade.

nationalism
A sense of national consciousness that boosts the culture and interests of one country over those of all other countries.

Intense nationalism, for example, can lead to difficulties. **Nationalism** is the sense of national consciousness that boosts the culture and interests of one country over those of all other countries. Strongly nationalistic countries, such as Iran and New Guinea, often discourage investment by foreign companies. In other, less radical forms of nationalism, the government may take actions to hinder foreign operations. France, for example, requires that pop music stations play at least 40 percent of their songs in French. This law was enacted because the French love American rock and roll. Without airtime, American CD sales suffer. In another example of nationalism, it was rumored that Pepsico was planning a takeover of the French food and drink company Danone. There was a chorus of opposition from French politicians to the idea of a foreign takeover of Danone, the bottler of Evian water and Danone yogurts. The government warned that it would move to defend Danone from a hostile takeover attempt. Pepsico later denied that it was even interested in Danone. A week later Pernod Ricard, the French beverage company, bought British rival Allied Domecq. The head of Pernod Ricard strongly criticized the French government. He said, "You cannot be pleased when Pernod Ricard buys a British company, but then say that the foreigners do not have the right to take over French companies."[27] By fall 2005, the French government had announced ten industries that it would protect from foreign takeover, including casino gambling and biotechnology.

In a hostile climate, a government may *expropriate* a foreign company's assets, taking ownership and compensating the former owners. Even worse is *confiscation*, when the owner receives no compensation. This happened during rebellions in several African nations during the 1990s and 2000s.

CONCEPT *in Action*

Google's foray into China's lucrative search engine market involved important political considerations. To gain access to the sleeping giant's over 100 million Internet users, Google executives agreed to make censorship concessions, including blocking search results of politically sensitive terms like "democracy" and "Tibet." Free-speech advocates say Google is supporting China's human rights abuses just to make a buck; other critics note the irony that Google refuses to filter children's access to pornographic content in the United States. *Should companies make concessions to nationalism?*

CONCEPT *in Action*

Overcoming language barriers can be tricky. International marketers must be careful to ensure that the promotional messages they send do not convey the wrong meaning to audiences. Advertisers behind the ever-popular "Got Milk?" campaign were forced to drop a Spanish-language version of the slogan because the translation posed the odd question, "Are you lactating?" *What can global marketers do to avoid cross-cultural blunders?*

SERENA WILLIAMS © AMERICA'S MILK PROCESSORS

Cultural Differences

Central to any society is the common set of values shared by its citizens that determine what is socially acceptable. Culture underlies the family, educational system, religion, and social class system. The network of social organizations generates overlapping roles and status positions. These values and roles have a tremendous effect on people's preferences and thus on marketers' options. In China Wal-hart holds live fishing contests on the premises, and in Korea the firm hosts a food competition with variations on a popular dish, kimchee.

Language is another important aspect of culture. Marketers must take care in selecting product names and translating slogans and promotional messages so as not to convey the wrong meaning. For example, Mitsubishi Motors had to rename its Pajero model in Spanish-speaking countries because the term refers to a sexual activity. Toyota Motors's MR2 model dropped the number 2 in France because the combination sounds like a French swearword. The literal translation of Coca-Cola in Chinese characters means "bite the wax tadpole." Perdue Farms' translation of its slogan "It takes a tough man to make a tender chicken" into Spanish means "It takes a sexually aroused man to make a chicken affectionate."

Each country has its own customs and traditions that determine business practices and influence negotiations with foreign customers. For example, attempting to do business in Western Europe during the first two weeks in August is virtually impossible. Businesses close and everyone goes on vacation at the same time. In many countries, personal relationships are more important than financial considerations. For instance, skipping social engagements in Mexico may lead to lost sales. Negotiations in Japan often include long evenings of dining, drinking, and entertaining; only after a close personal relationship has been formed do business negotiations begin. Exhibit 4.2 presents some cultural "dos and don'ts."

Exhibit 4.2 > Cultural Dos and Don'ts

DO:

- Always present your business card with both hands in Asian countries. It should also be right-side up and print-side showing so that the recipient can read it as it is being presented. If you receive a business card, accept it with gratitude and examine it carefully. Don't quickly put it into your pocket.
- Dress to the culture. If you are in Switzerland, always wear a coat and tie. In other countries, a coat and tie may be viewed as overdressing and snobbish.
- Use a "soft-sell" and subtle approach when promoting a product in Japan. Japanese do not feel comfortable with America's traditional hard-selling style.
- Understand the role of religion in business transactions. In Muslim countries, Ramadan is a holy month when most people fast. During this time everything slows down, particularly business.
- Have a local person available to culturally and linguistically interpret any advertising that you plan to do. When American Airlines wanted to promote its new first-class seats in the Mexican market, it translated the "Fly In Leather" campaign literally, which meant "Fly Naked" in Spanish.

DON'T:

- Glad-hand, back-slap, and use first names on your first business meeting in Asia. If you do, you will be considered a lightweight.
- Fill a wine glass to the top if dining with a French businessperson. It is considered completely uncouth.
- Begin your first business meeting in Asia talking business. Be patient. Let your clients get to know you first.
- Kiss someone on the cheek or pat them on the shoulder in Spain before you get to know them. In Chile, expect women to greet you with a kiss on the cheek even if you are a stranger. Do offer a kiss on both cheeks after you become friends with a French woman (even if you are a woman). In Switzerland, offer three kisses.
- Be on time for your appointment in some Latin American countries, but always be on time in Germany.

Economic Environment

The level of economic development varies considerably, ranging from countries where everyday survival is a struggle, such as the Sudan and Eritrea, to countries that are highly developed, such as Switzerland and Japan. In general, complex, sophisticated industries are found in developed countries, and more basic industries are found in less developed nations. Average family incomes are higher in the more developed countries than in the least developed markets. Larger incomes mean greater purchasing power and demand not only for consumer goods and services but also for the machinery and workers required to produce consumer goods. Exhibit 4.3 provides a glimpse of global wealth.

Business opportunities are usually better in countries that have an economic infrastructure in place. **Infrastructure** is the basic institutions and public facilities upon which an economy's development depends. When we think about how our own economy works, we tend to take our infrastructure for granted. It includes the money and banking system that provides the major investment loans to our nation's businesses; the educational system that turns out the incredible varieties of skills and basic research that actually run our nation's production lines; the extensive transportation and communications systems—interstate highways, railroads, airports, canals, telephones,

infrastructure
The basic institutions and public facilities upon which an economy's development depends.

concept check

Explain how political factors can affect international trade.

Describe several cultural factors that a company involved in international trade should consider.

How can economic conditions affect trade opportunities?

Exhibit 4.3 > Where the Money Is

The Top 20	Gross National Income Per Capita* $
Luxembourg	43,940
Norway	43,350
Switzerland	39,880
United States	37,610
Japan	34,510
Denmark	33,750
Iceland	30,810
Sweden	28,840
United Kingdom	28,350
Finland	27,020
Ireland	26,960
Austria	26,720
Netherlands	26,310
Belgium	25,820
Hong Kong, China	25,430
Germany	25,250
France	24,770
Canada	23,930
Australia	21,650
Singapore	21,230
The Bottom Five	
Sierra Leone	150
Liberia	130
Burundi	100
Congo, Democratic Republic	100
Ethiopia	90

* Gross National Income is the value of the final goods and services produced by a country (Gross Domestic Product) together with its income received from other countries (like interest and dividends) less similar payments made to other countries.

Final goods are the goods that are ultimately consumed rather than used in the production of another good. For example, a car sold to a consumer is a final good; the components such as tires sold to the car manufacturer are not; they are intermediate goods used to make the final good. The same tires, if sold to a consumer, would be a final good.

Source: http://www.answers.com
(June 1, 2006).

Internet sites, postal systems, television stations—that link almost every piece of our geography into one market; the energy system that powers our factories; and, of course, the market system itself, which brings our nation's goods and services into our homes and businesses.

The Impact of Multinational Corporations

multinational corporations
Corporations that move resources, goods, services, and skills across national boundaries without regard to the country in which their headquarters are located.

8 What are the advantages of multinational corporations?

Corporations that move resources, goods, services, and skills across national boundaries without regard to the country in which their headquarters are located are **multinational corporations**. Some are so rich and have so many employees that they resemble small countries. For example, the sales of both Exxon and Wal-Mart are larger than the GDP of all but a few nations in the world. Multinational companies are heavily engaged in international trade. The successful ones take political and cultural differences into account.

Many global brands sell much more outside the United States than at home. Coca-Cola has 80 percent of its sales outside the United States; Philip Morris' Marlboro brand 67 percent; Pepsi, 42 percent; Kellogg, 50 percent; Pampers, 65 percent; Nescafe, 50 percent; and Gillette, around 62 percent.[28]

U.S. multinationals made over $340 billion in profit in 2006. In slow-growing, developed economies like Europe and Japan, a weaker dollar helps, because it means cheaper products to sell into those markets, and profits earned in those markets translate into more dollars back home. Meanwhile, emerging markets in Asia, Latin America, and Eastern Europe are growing steadily. General Electric expects 60 percent of its revenue growth to come from emerging markets over the next decade. For Brown-Forman, the spirits company, a fifth of its sales growth of Jack Daniels, the Tennessee whiskey, is coming from developing markets like Mexico and Poland. IBM had rapid sales growth in emerging markets such as Russia, India, and Brazil.[29]

The largest multinational corporations in the world are shown in Exhibit 4.4.

Despite the success of American multinationals abroad, there is some indication that preference for American brands may be slipping. The growth of competing global brands is discussed in the Customer Satisfaction and Quality box.

CONCEPT *in Action*

As overseas investment grows, so does the need for global branding. After a worldwide talent search, McDonald's picked NBA star Yao Ming to be the face of its global marketing effort. Recognizable to sports fans the world over, the 7-foot-5 Ming personifies a youthful, dynamic spirit that transcends cultural and geographic boundaries. *Why is it increasingly important that multinational advertisers identify and sign celebrity spokespersons capable of bridging the East and West?*

© ASSOCIATED PRESS, AP

The Multinational Advantage

Large multinationals have several advantages over other companies. For instance, multinationals can often overcome trade problems. Taiwan and South Korea have long had an embargo against Japanese cars for political reasons and to help domestic automakers. Yet Honda USA, a Japanese-owned company based in the United States, sends Accords to Taiwan and Korea. In another example, when the environmentally conscience Green movement challenged the biotechnology research conducted by BASF, a major German chemical and drug manufacturer, BASF moved its cancer and immune-system research to Cambridge, Massachusetts.

Another advantage for multinationals is their ability to sidestep regulatory problems. U.S. drugmaker SmithKline and Britain's Beecham decided to merge in part so that they could avoid licensing and regulatory hassles in their largest markets. The merged company can say it's an insider in both Europe and the United States. "When we go to Brussels, we're a member state [of the European Union]," one executive explains. "And when we go to Washington, we're an American company."

Multinationals can also shift production from one plant to another as market conditions change. When European demand for a certain

Exhibit 4.4 > The World's Largest Multinational Corporations

Rank		Home Country
1	Exxon Mobil	United States
2	Wal-Mart Stores	United States
3	Royal Dutch/Shell Group	Netherlands
4	BP	Britain
5	General Motors	United States
6	Chevron	United States
7	DaimlerChrysler	Germany
8	Toyota Motor	Japan
9	Ford Motor	United States
10	ConocoPhillips	United States
11	General Electric	United States
12	Total	France
13	ING Group	Netherlands
14	Citigroup	United States
15	AXA	France
16	Allianz	Germany
17	Volkswagen	Germany
18	Fortis	Belgium/Netherlands
19	Crédit Agricole	France
20	American International Group	United States
21	Assicurezioni Generali	Italy
22	Siemens	Germany
23	Sinopec	China
24	Nippon Telegraph & Telephone	Japan
25	Carrefour	France
26	HSBC Holdings	Britain
27	ENI	Italy
28	Aviva	Britain
29	International Business Machines	United States
30	McKesson	United States

Source: "The World's Largest Corporations," *Fortune* (July 24, 2006), p. 113.

solvent declined, Dow Chemical instructed its German plant to switch to manufacturing a chemical that had been imported from Louisiana and Texas. Computer models help Dow make decisions like these so it can run its plants more efficiently and keep costs down.

CONCEPT *in Action*

Japan's Matsushita Electric Industrial is a leading manufacturer of giant plasma-screen TVs. The maker of Panasonic-branded products, Matsushita is engaged in a neck-and-neck competition with Samsung to produce the largest screens for the worldwide home-theater market. Matsushita's monster 103-inch plasma display is among the world's largest such screens, though current retail models are significantly smaller. Unfortunately for most of the world's consumers, giant plasma-screen TVs can cost up to $100,000. *How does being a multinational corporation enable Matsushita to succeed in the high-end electronics market?*

© AFP/GETTY IMAGES

American Brands Face Global Competition

America is the cradle of the consumer goods brand. Here, a free-spending and marketing-saturated public nurtured Coca-Cola, McDonald's, Tide, Calvin Klein, Ford, Dell, and countless others to maturity. Many of those brands grew up to conquer other societies, as well.

But American brands' domination in the global marketplace is eroding. From Nokia to Toyota to LG and Li Ning, companies in Europe and Asia are turning out top-quality goods and selling them as such rather than competing on price. "There are longer-term trends toward greater competition. The United States was the only global brand country [but] that's no longer the case," says Earl L. Taylor, chief marketing officer of the Marketing Science Institute. "Consumers prefer brands that they take to be of higher quality" regardless of the country of origin, he notes. "Increasingly, there will be other successful global brands in the U.S. (market)."

The brands at the top of Interbrand's list of the world's most valuable still originate in the United States; the five most valuable are Coca-Cola, Microsoft, IBM, General Electric, and Intel. American companies have lost the most ground in the middle tier of recognizable brand names, says George T. Haley, professor of marketing at the University of New Haven's School of Business.

One area from which U.S. brands are feeling the pressure is the Asia-Pacific region, which harbors the fastest-growing emerging markets today. In the appliance category, two Chinese companies, Haier and Kelon, are becoming top competitors for well-known U.S. brands General Electric, Whirlpool, and Maytag. Today Haier dominates the dorm refrigerator markets. Nor is the Chinese branding trend confined only to hard goods. Sporting goods and sportswear brand Li Ning, well-known within China, is building its international profile. While the Chinese basketball team wore Nike uniforms in the 2004 Athens Olympic Games, the Spanish team wore Li Ning. The threat to U.S. brands is not confined to China, however. South Korean brands, such as Samsung and LG, also are emerging on the global stage in specific categories, such as electronics, chemicals, and automobiles.

The animosity that many Europeans feel toward the United States is translated into a preference for European or even Asian brands at the expense of U.S. brands. Plus, experts say, European brands are simply becoming stronger and more consistent.

Meanwhile, European brands are gaining momentum in the areas of white goods and consumer goods, putting the pressure on such well-known U.S. brands as Bissell and Hoover, experts say. For instance, Gaggenau is a popular, high-end European kitchen appliance brand, along with Bosch and Dyson. Dyson introduced a high-end vacuum cleaner into the U.S. market. Other European brands maintaining cache—if not always the allure of luxury—include Absolut, Virgin, Mini (as in Cooper), Red Bull, and Ikea.[30]

Critical Thinking Questions

- What can American multinational firms do to regain and maintain their leadership in global branding?
- Do you think that the quality of American products and services is declining, or that the rest of the world is just getting better? Explain your answer.

Multinationals can also tap new technology from around the world. Xerox has introduced some 80 different office copiers in the United States that were designed and built by Fuji Xerox, its joint venture with a Japanese company. Versions of the super-concentrated detergent that Procter & Gamble first formulated in Japan in response to a rival's product are now being sold under the Ariel brand name in Europe and under the Cheer and Tide labels in the United States. Also, consider Otis Elevator's development of the Elevonic 411, an elevator that is programmed to send more cars to floors where demand is high. It was developed by six research centers in five countries. Otis's group in Farmington, Connecticut, handled the systems integration, a Japanese group designed the special motor drives that make the elevators ride smoothly, a French group perfected the door systems, a German group handled the electronics, and a Spanish group took care of the small-geared components. Otis says the international effort saved more than $10 million in design costs and cut the process from four years to two.

Finally, multinationals can often save a lot in labor costs, even in highly unionized countries. For example, when Xerox started moving copier-rebuilding work to Mexico to take advantage of the lower wages, its union in Rochester, New York, objected because it saw that members' jobs were at risk. Eventually, the union agreed to change work styles and to improve productivity to keep the jobs at home.

concept check

What is a multinational corporation?

What are the advantages of multinationals?

Trends in Global Competition

 What are the trends in the global marketplace?

In this section we will examine several underlying trends that will continue to propel the dramatic growth in world trade. These trends are market expansion, resource acquisition, and the emergence of China and India.

Market Expansion

The need for businesses to expand their markets is perhaps the most fundamental reason for the growth in world trade. The limited size of domestic markets often motivates managers to seek markets beyond their national frontiers. The economies of large-scale manufacturing demand big markets. Domestic markets, particularly in smaller countries like Denmark and the Netherlands, simply can't generate enough demand. Nestlé was one of the first businesses to "go global" because its home country, Switzerland, is so small. Nestlé was shipping milk to 16 different countries as early as 1875. Today, hundreds of thousands of businesses are recognizing the potential rich rewards to be found in international markets.

Resource Acquisition

More and more companies are going to the global marketplace to acquire the resources they need to operate efficiently. These resources may be cheap or skilled labor, scarce raw materials, technology, or capital. Nike, for example, has manufacturing facilities in many Asian countries in order to use cheap labor. Honda opened a design studio in southern California to put that "California flair" into the design of some of its vehicles. Large multinational banks such as Bank of New York and Citigroup have offices in Geneva, Switzerland. Geneva is the private banking center of Europe and attracts capital from around the globe.

The Emergence of China and India

China and India—two of the world's hottest economic powerhouses—are impacting businesses around the globe, in very different ways. The boom in China's worldwide exports—up 125 percent in four years—has left few sectors unscathed, be they garlic growers in California, jeans makers in Mexico, or plastic-mold manufacturers in South Korea. India's impact has altered how hundreds of service companies from Texas to Ireland compete for billions of dollars in contracts.

The causes and consequences of each nation's growth are somewhat different. China's exports have boomed largely thanks to foreign investment: Lured by low labor costs, big manufacturers have surged into China to expand their production base and push down prices globally. Now manufacturers of all sizes, making

CONCEPT *in Action*

Giant-screen movie exhibitor Imax is taking its trademark big film presentations to an even bigger market: India. The Canadian theater chain recently expanded into Mumbai and New Delhi where it is dazzling Indian audiences with mega-screen adaptations of today's blockbuster movies. With crystal clear images up to eight stories high and rumbling digital surround sound, the Imax system delivers an unparalleled film experience. *What factors make India an attractive market for Imax?*

everything from windshield wipers to washing machines to clothing, are scrambling either to reduce costs at home or to outsource more of what they make in cheaper locales.[31]

Indians are playing invaluable roles in the global innovation chain. Motorola, Hewlett-Packard, Cisco Systems, and other tech giants now rely on their Indian teams to devise software platforms and multimedia features for next-generation devices. Google principal scientist Krishna Bharat is setting up a Bangalore lab complete with colorful furniture, exercise balls, and a Yamaha organ—like Google's Mountain View (Calif.) headquarters—to work on core search-engine technology. Indian engineering houses use 3-D computer simulations to tweak designs of everything from car engines and forklifts to aircraft wings for such clients as General Motors Corp. and Boeing Co.[32] Barring unforeseen circumstances, within three decades India should have vaulted over Germany as the world's third-biggest economy. By mid-century, China should have overtaken the United States as No. 1. By then, China and India could account for half of global output.[33]

An accelerating trend is that technical and managerial skills in both China and India are becoming more important than cheap assembly labor. China will stay dominant in mass manufacturing and is one of the few nations building multibillion-dollar electronics and heavy industrial plants. India is a rising power in software, design, services, and precision industry.

Today some American entrepreneurs are overcoming cultural, regulatory, and other barriers to build fortunes in the booming Chinese economy. One such example is discussed in the Catching the Entrepreneurial Spirit box.

concept check

What trends will foster continued growth in world trade?

Describe some of the ways businesses can take advantage of these trends to "go global."

CATCHING THE ENTREPRENEURIAL SPIRIT

Making It in China

Today there are thousands of Americans who, through courage, ingenuity, and perseverance, have managed to decode the mysteries of Chinese capitalism. They are creating their own businesses at a furious pace, and some aren't simply surviving: They're getting rich.

Some of the entrepreneurs immerse themselves deeply in Chinese culture and language, while others learn most of what they know from reading Lonely Planet books on the flight over. Some are transplanting American consumer culture, from coffee to hip-hop clubs, while others are inventing entirely new products, like the perfect clothing hanger.

The business education of Chris Barclay took 11 years. It started unfavorably, shortly after Barclay arrived in Beijing in 1994. China wasn't as alien to him as it is to some Americans—he spoke good Mandarin and had lived in Taiwan. But he didn't have much of a clue about Chinese business. One of his first local acquaintances was an American who wanted to make a speedy killing by becoming the hot dog king of China. The guy got a license from Beijing officials to sell wieners from street carts. He bought 1,000 carts and one morning unleashed an army of hot dog peddlers. Within a few hours, the police had impounded his carts. "I have a permit," the American protested. The police laughed. "You have one permit," a police official told him. "You need one for each cart." The would-be hot dog king was 999 permits short, and the dream died then and there.

Barclay took many lessons from the episode, but one stood out: Don't try to get rich quick in China. Sure, it happens. "But longevity is key," he says. "You've got to survive your failures." He endured several himself, including an ill-fated attempt to sell basketballs, before arriving at an insight that has proven valuable for many American entrepreneurs. The easiest way to make money in China today, Barclay says, is to serve the thousands of large American and European corporations flooding into the country. In 1995, with $10,000 in cash, Barclay started a company that offers management training for local Chinese employees of Adidas, Coca-Cola, ConocoPhillips, Sun Microsystems, and other multinationals. To enhance his training business, he opened a hotel on a mountainside near the southern city of Guangzhou, where he supplements workshops with outdoor activities like rock climbing and hiking. Together, the ventures bring in about $2 million a year and earn about $400,000 in profit. Barclay has 30 full-time employees. He's the lone foreigner. He recently received a seven-figure offer from a U.S. consulting firm for his training business alone, and he's considering selling that branch of his business.[34]

Critical Thinking Questions
- What are three important skills and/or knowledge sets that an American entrepreneur needs in China?
- Will America be able to compete in the global marketplace over the next 30 years? If so, what will have to change, if anything?

Summary of Learning Goals

1 **Why is global trade important to the United States and how is it measured?**

International trade improves relations with friends and allies, eases tensions among nations, helps bolster economies, raises people's standard of living, and improves the quality of life. The United States is still the largest importer and exporter in the world. We export a fifth of our industrial production and about a third of our farm crops. One out of every 10 jobs in the United States is supported by exports.

Two concepts important to global trade are the balance of trade (the difference in value between a country's exports and its imports over some period) and the balance of payments (the difference between a country's total payments to other countries and its total receipts from other countries). The United States now has both a negative balance of trade and a negative balance of payments. Another import concept is the exchange rate, which is the price of one country's currency in terms of another country's currency. Currencies float up and down based upon the supply of and demand for each currency. Sometimes a government steps in and devalues its currency relative to the currencies of other countries.

2 **Why do nations trade?**

Nations trade because they gain by doing so. The principle of comparative advantage states that each country should specialize in the goods it can produce most readily and cheaply and trade them for those that other countries can produce most readily and cheaply. The result is more goods at lower prices than if each country produced by itself everything it needed. Free trade allows trade among nations without government restrictions.

3 **What are the barriers to international trade?**

The three major barriers to international trade are natural barriers, such as distance and language; tariff barriers, or taxes on imported goods; and nontariff barriers. The nontariff barriers to trade include import quotas, embargoes, buy-national regulations, and exchange controls. The main argument against tariffs is that they discourage free trade and keep the principle of comparative advantage from working efficiently. The main argument for using tariffs is that they help protect domestic companies, industries, and workers.

4 **How do governments and institutions foster world trade?**

The World Trade Organization created by the Uruguay Round has dramatically lowered trade barriers worldwide. For the first time, a trade agreement covers services, intellectual property rights, and exchange controls. The World Bank makes loans to developing nations to help build infrastructures. The International Monetary Fund makes loans to member nations that cannot meet their budgetary expenses. Despite efforts to expand trade, terrorism can have a negative impact on trade growth.

5 **What are international economic communities?**

International economic communities reduce trade barriers among themselves while often establishing common tariffs and other trade barriers toward nonmember countries. The best-known economic communities are the European Union, NAFTA, CAFTA, and Mercosur.

6 **How do companies enter the global marketplace?**

There are a number of ways to enter the global market. The major ones are exporting, licensing, contract manufacturing, joint ventures, and direct investment.

7 **What threats and opportunities exist in the global marketplace?**

Domestic firms entering the international arena need to consider the politics, economies, and culture of the countries where they plan to do business. For example, government trade policies can be loose or restrictive, countries can be nationalistic, and governments can change. In the area of culture, many products fail because companies don't understand the culture of the country where they are trying to sell their products. Some developing countries also lack an economic infrastructure, which often makes it very difficult to conduct business.

8 **What are the advantages of multinational corporations?**

Multinational corporations have several advantages. First, they can sidestep restrictive trade and licensing restrictions because they frequently have headquarters in more than one country. Multinationals can also move their operations from one country to the next depending on which location offers more favorable economic conditions. In addition, multinationals can tap into a vast source of technological expertise by drawing upon the knowledge of a global workforce.

9 **What are the trends in the global marketplace?**

Global business activity will continue to escalate due to several factors. Firms that desire a larger customer base or need additional resources will continue to seek opportunities outside their country's borders. China and India are emerging as global economic powerhouses.

Key Terms

absolute advantage 137	infrastructure 153
balance of payments 136	International Monetary Fund (IMF) 143
balance of trade 136	joint venture 149
buy-national regulations 140	licensing 148
contract manufacturing 148	Mercosur 144
countertrade 150	multinational corporations 154
devaluation 137	nationalism 151
direct foreign investment 149	North American Free Trade Agreement (NAFTA) 143
dumping 141	outsourcing 138
embargo 140	preferential tariff 143
European Integration 145	principle of comparative advantage 137
European Union (EU) 144	protectionism 138
exchange controls 140	protective tariffs 139
exporting 147	tariff 139
exports 135	trade deficit 136
floating exchange rates 136	trade surplus 136
free trade 138	Uruguay Round 141
free-trade zone 143	World Bank 142
global vision 134	World Trade Organization (WTO) 141
import quota 140	
imports 135	

Preparing for Tomorrow's Workplace: SCANS

1. How can a country's customs create barriers to trade? Ask foreign students to describe such barriers in their country. American students should give examples of problems that foreign businesspeople might experience with American customs. (Information)
2. Should Great Britain be admitted to NAFTA? Why might Britain not wish to join? (Systems)
3. Do you think that CAFTA will have a major impact on the U.S. economy? Why? (Systems)

4. What do you think is the best way for a small company to enter international trade? Why? (Information)
5. How can America compete against China and India in the long run? (Information)
6. Identify some U.S. multinational companies that have been successful in world markets. How do you think they have achieved their success? (Information)
7. **Team Activity** Divide the class into teams. Each team should choose a country and research its infrastructure to determine how it will help or hinder trade. Include a variety of countries, ranging from the most highly developed to the least developed. (Resources, Interpersonal, Information, Technology)

Ethics Activity

The executives of a clothing manufacturer want to outsource some of their manufacturing to more cost-efficient locations in Indonesia. After visiting several possible sites, they choose one and begin to negotiate with local officials. They discover that it will take about six months to get the necessary permits. One of the local politicians approaches the executives over dinner and hints that he can speed up the process, for an advisory fee of $5,000.

Using a Web search tool, locate articles about this topic and then write responses to the following questions. Be sure to support your arguments and cite your sources.

Ethical Dilemma: Is paying the advisory fee a bribe or an acceptable cost of doing business in that area of the world? What should the executives do before agreeing to pay the fee?

Sources: Jane Easter Bahls, "Illicit Affairs? If You Do Business Overseas, Be Certain Your 'Administrative Fees' Aren't Really Illegal Bribes," *Entrepreneur*, September 2004, p. 80; Paul Burnham Finney, "Shaking Hands, Greasing Palms," *New York Times*, May 17, 2005, p. C10; Phelim Kyne, "Freeport-McMoRan Indonesia Payments Not Graft: Official," *FWN Financial News*, January 18, 2006.

Working the Net

1. Go to the Trade Compliance Center site at **http://tcc.mac.doc.gov**. Click on "Research Your Country Market" and then "Search Reports." Pick a country that interests you from the index, and read the most current available reports for that country. Would this country be a good market for a small U.S. motor scooter manufacturer interested in expanding internationally? Why or why not? What are the main barriers to trade the company might face?
2. While still at the Trade Compliance site, **http://tcc.mac.doc.gov**, click on "Trade Agreements" and then "List All Agreements." Select one that interests you and summarize what you learn about it.
3. Review the historical data about exchange rates between the U.S. dollar and the Japanese yen available at **http://www.x-rates.com**. Pull up charts comparing the yen to the dollar for several years. List any trends you spot. What years would have been best for a U.S. company to enter the Japanese marketplace? Given current exchange rate conditions, do you think Japanese companies are increasing or decreasing their exporting efforts in the United States?
4. Visit Foreign Trade Online, **http://www.foreign-trade.com**, and browse through the resources of this international business-to-business trade portal. What types of information does the site provide? Which would be most useful to a company looking to begin exporting? To a company who already exports and wants to find new markets? Rate the usefulness of the site and the information it offers.
5. Go to **http://www.fita.org** which is the Federation of International Trade Associations. Click on "Really Useful Links for International Trade." Follow five of those links and explain how they would help an American manufacturer that wanted to "go global."
6. Go to the World Trade Organization site **http://www.wto.org**. Next, click on "WTO News." Inform the class on current activities and actions at the WTO.
7. Go to **http://www.worldbank.org** and then to **http://www.imf.org**. Compare the types of information available on each Web site. Pick one example from each site and report your findings to the class.

We Want Our MTV (International)

MTV, a mainstay of American pop culture, is just as popular in Shanghai as it is in Seattle and Sydney, Australia, or in Lagos (Nigeria) as it is in Los Angeles. London-based MTV Networks International (MTVNI), the world's largest global network, has taken its winning formula to 167 foreign markets on six continents, including urban and rural areas. It broadcasts in 18 languages to 430 million homes, or about 1.3 billion people, through locally programmed and operated TV channels and Web sites. While the United States currently generates about 80 percent of MTV's profits, 80 percent of the company's subscriber base lives outside the U.S. "Now a large part of our future will be what happens outside the United States, and that is exciting," says Tom Freston, co-president of parent company Viacom and head of MTV Networks.

The MTV brand has evolved beyond its music television roots into a multimedia lifestyle entertainment and culture brand for all ages. In addition to MTV and MTV2, its channel lineup includes Nickelodeon, VH1, Comedy Central, LOGO, TMF (The Music Factory), Game One, and several European music, comedy, and lifestyle channels. Adding to the complexity is MTV's multimedia and interactive nature, with gaming, texting, and Web sites as well as television. Another challenge is integrating acquisitions of local companies such as European competitor Viva, which it purchased in 2004.

The company prefers to hire local employees rather than import staff. According to Brent Hansen, president and chief executive of MTV Networks Europe, getting the local perspective is invaluable in helping the network understand its markets, whether in terms of musical tastes or what children like. For example, Alex Okosi, a Nigerian who went to college in the United States, is chief executive for MTV Base, which launched in sub-Saharan Africa in 2005. Okosi recommended that MTV consider each country as an individual market, rather than blending them all together.

One reason for MTVNI's success is "glocalization"—its ability to adapt programs to fit local cultures while still maintaining a consistent, special style. "When we set a channel up, we always provide a set of parameters in terms of standards of things we require," Hansen explains. "Obviously an MTV channel that doesn't look good enough is not going to do the business for us, let alone for the audience. There's a higher expectation." Then the local unit can tailor content to its market. MTV India conveys a "sense of the colorful street culture," explains Bill Roedy, MTV International's president, while MTV Japan has "a sense of technology edginess; MTV Italy, style and elegance." In Africa, MTV Base will feature videos from top African artists as well as from emerging African music talent. The goal, according to Brent Hansen, is to "provide a unique cultural meeting point for young people in Africa, using the common language of music to connect music fans from different backgrounds and cultures."

Critical Thinking Questions

- Do you agree with Tom Freston that MTV's future lies mostly in its international operations, and why?
- What types of political, economic, and competitive challenges does MTV Networks International face by operating worldwide?
- How has MTVNI overcome cultural differences to create a world brand?

Sources: *MTV International* Web site, http://www.mtv.com/international/ (January 18, 2006); "Now, Africa Gets MTV Base," *Africa News Service*, February 25, 2005, http://www.comtexnews.com; Johnnie L. Roberts, "World Tour," *Newsweek*, June 6, 2005, pp. 34–35; and Robin D Rusch, "MTV Networks Internationally," *Brandchannel.com*, July 26, 2004, http://www.brandchannel.com.

ESPN—Winning the Global Race

If your passion is Indian cricket, Argentinian soccer, or Scottish links golf, tune to ESPN International's programming for live coverage of these and other global sporting events. A division of ESPN Inc., ESPN International has grown to include ownership—in whole or in part—of 29 television networks outside the United States, as well as a variety of brand extension businesses that allow ESPN programming to reach fans in 194 countries and territories.

ESPN International's business entities include television, radio, print, Internet, wireless, consumer products, and event management. ESPN and its holdings maintain offices in such key locations around the world as Beijing, Buenos Aires, Delhi, Hong Kong, Japan, London, Mexico City, Miami, Mumbai, Paris, Sao Paulo, Shanghai, Singapore, Taiwan, and Toronto. The television networks of ESPN International are enjoyed on all seven continents in 11 languages (Arabic, Cantonese, English, French, Hindi, Italian, Japanese, Korean, Mandarin, Portuguese, and Spanish). Program syndication covers over 130 events with broadcast partners in 200 countries. ESPN radio broadcasts can be heard in 13 countries, and offer a combination of live events, sports news, information, and talk. ESPN and X Games branded consumer products include apparel, bikes, skateboards, backpacks, books, and DVDs.

As the worldwide leader in global sports entertainment, ESPN recognized the need to identify, even create, trends in the world of sports. The company produces its own events, most notably the phenomenally successful X Games. The world's premier action sport competition is staged throughout the world, with competitions held annually in the United States, Asia, and Latin America. The games feature edgy "evolving sports"—snow and water sports, as well as skateboard and stunt bike events.

The company's initial 1989 foray into international sports broadcasting was in South America. Minimal data was then available on such basic demographics as household cable penetration, markets, or advertising. Despite this, ESPN followed pioneers CNN and HBO into the international broadcast arena, convinced that sporting events would carry the same global appeal for viewers as news and movies. Its goal was to bring quality programming and journalistic integrity in American sports to a global audience.

ESPN International generates two revenue streams: from cable operators and the companies who buy ESPN advertising airtime. Initially ESPN's advertising was designed to promote viewer tune-in for specific events, with little focus on building the ESPN brand or image. Later, company ads in its own airtime helped build ESPN International brand awareness, which the company hopes worldwide sports viewers will continue to see as synonymous with excellence in sports broadcasting.

Critical Thinking Questions

Using information from the case and the video, answer the following critical thinking questions:

- Why did ESPN take the risk of expanding into the international broadcast arena without having solid data available?
- What is the secret of ESPN's success in bringing American and international sporting events to the global market?
- Why did ESPN create the X Games, and how have the games contributed to the company's global presence?

Source: Adapted from material contained in the video ESPN International; Corporate Web site http://www.espn.com (November 9, 2005).

Hot Links Address Book

A good starting place for help in doing business in foreign markets is the U.S. government's export portal. Here you will find links to export basics, regulations, exchange rates, country and industry research, and much more. http://www.export.gov

For links to a wealth of statistics on world trade, go to the U.S. International Trade Administration's (ITA) Office of Trade and Economic Analysis Web site, http://www.ita.doc.gov

Check out the current U.S. balance of trade with various countries at http://www.bea.doc.gov

Get up-to-the-minute exchange rates at http://www.xe.com

The World Trade Organization tracks the latest trade developments between countries and regions around the world. For the most recent global trading news, visit the WTO's Web site at http://www.wto.org

Gain additional insight into the workings of the International Monetary Fund at http://www.imf.org

For the latest information about NAFTA, visit http://www.nafta-customs.org

Think you'd like to work overseas? For information about jobs in foreign countries, visit http://www.internationaljobs.com

>> continuing case on Apple, Inc.

Part 1 • The Evolution of Apple, Inc.

In the 1970s, the United States business environment was volatile with unpredictable swings in inflation and recession. The political and social environments were unstable due largely to the country's continued presence in Vietnam. Price controls, oil embargos, high unemployment, highly publicized labor disputes, and rapid rates of change in consumer prices all contributed to a decade of pessimism. Such economic issues contributed to the productivity slowdown of the 1970s. The largest slowdowns were in pipelines, motor vehicles, oil/gas extraction, utilities, and air transportation— all industries affected by the energy crisis of the 1970s. Interestingly, this environment proved ripe for innovation and was the backdrop for the inception of Apple, Inc. and a new product category that would ultimately become a way of life in society.

Apple created a new product category when it offered the first personal computer to truly meet the market's needs. This new product category was the result of a unique combination of entrepreneurial energy, innovative technical skills, and financial wizardry. Steve Jobs provided the entrepreneurial energy, Stephen Wozniak imparted the innovative technical skills, and Mike Markkula bestowed his financial expertise upon the product effort. As Apple Computer, these three individuals started an evolution from hobbyist to technical hacker to a mass consumer-marketed personal computer.

A frequently overlooked precursor of Apple's start, however, was the creation and later miniaturization of integrated circuits. The first integrated circuit was introduced in the early 1960s at Texas Instruments and led to the invention of the handheld calculator. The ability to miniaturize electronic circuitry and a group of "geeks" who could foresee a computer revolution are key components in the development of our computerized society.

THE HOMEBREW COMPUTER CLUB

In March 1975, the Homebrew Computer Club met for the first time in one of the member's garages. Members of the club were hobbyists who had electrical engineering or programming backgrounds. Initially, the typical discussion centered around the Altair 8800, a personal computer based on the Intel 8080 microprocessor. But the real intent of the club meetings was for attendees to trade parts, devices, and information. According to Stephen Wozniak, the Apple I was designed for fun to take to the Homebrew Computer Club meeting, not to be a product for a company. Diagrams of the Apple I were shared at the club meetings. Thus, the Apple computer was being demonstrated as it was being developed. In this manner, the product was receiving critical technical review from experts who were dabbling in computers as a hobby. The Homebrew Computer Club was one of the first steps in the development of today's multibillion dollar personal computer industry.

THE WOZNIAK AND JOBS DUO

Stephen Wozniak and Steve Jobs met in 1969 and developed their first commercial product in 1971. Unfortunately, their first invention was not a viable product offering. The two had developed and packaged a "blue box" that could hack into the phone system. Product development was shut down, however, when the developer of the original phone hacking concept was convicted in 1972 of phone fraud charges.

Wozniak was employed at Hewlett-Packard in the mid-1970s when he was developing the early stages of the computer product that was shown regularly at the Homebrew Computer Club meetings. He discussed the computer with his employers at Hewlett-Packard, but they had no interest in the personal computer marketplace and provided him with a legal release. This legal release provided Wozniak ownership rights to the computer he was building while still employed at Hewlett-Packard. Whereas Wozniak was interested in the technical development of the computer, Jobs was more interested in its commercialization. This combination of technical and commercial expertise enabled the two entrepreneurs to begin developing and selling the Apple I computer on a very small scale.

THE RAPID GROWTH OF THE PC INDUSTRY

Intel was the first company to use miniaturization in the development of a microprocessor in 1971. This particular microprocessor was intended for calculators and watches. The Altair 8800, the first personal computer, was introduced in 1975, and the now famous Bill Gates got his start by writing the software for the Altair. Wozniak and Jobs introduced the Apple II, an improved prototype of the Apple I, in 1977.

When International Business Machines released the IBM PC in 1981, the world of the personal computers truly began to open up. IBM used its established brand name to capture a huge chunk of the evolving PC marketplace. In the early 1980s, Apple Computer introduced its MacIntosh. This user-friendly computer had a mouse that allowed users to point and click on icons to execute demands. Although there were several early computer manufacturers, such as Commodore, Atari, and Radio Shack, the battle for market share tended to be fought between IBM and Apple Computer. Because Apple was so user friendly, it found a natural niche as a home and educational computer. IBM's PC, on the other hand, was considered to be the more serious computer for business and computer enthusiasts. In this rapidly expanding marketplace, Apple was the only first generation personal computer manufacturer in the United States to survive against the IBM PC.

By the beginning of 2000, the PC industry was exhibiting signs of maturation. This led to less distinction among competitors and price competition, with Dell Computer at the forefront of the pricing battle. Just as Apple had revolutionized desktop publishing, it was also an early pioneer in the use of electronic communications with its proprietary online services, and it opted to innovate along these communications lines rather than fight a head-to-head battle with Dell. Innovating along the company's strengths with its MacIntosh, Apple focused on its digital communications hub. This focus on communications brought the world the iPod and the iTunes Music Store. By the start of the 21st century, Apple remained at the forefront of electronic communications. Throughout its company life cycle, Apple has helped transform the personal computer industry from a hobby marketplace to a necessity in day-to-day living— this necessity in the worldwide marketplace for flash-based and hard disk drive–based MP3 players is expected to jump from 140 million units in 2005 to 286 million by 2010.

Critical Thinking Questions

- How was the development of the Apple computer different from traditional product development? What are the risks inherent in this type of development process?
- What was technology's role in the development of the personal computer marketplace?
- What market segments existed in the personal computer marketplace, and who were the dominant product providers to these segments?
- What social trends are likely to impact Apple in the future?
- How has Apple been an innovator in the communications marketplace?

Sources: Roy A. Allan, *A History of the Personal Computer*, London, Ontario, Canada: Allan Publishing, 2001; Anonymous, "MP3 Player Market to Reach 286 Million Units by 2010, say In-Stat," *Portable Design*, May 1, 2006, downloaded from http://pd.pennnet.com, accessed on May 31, 2006; DigiBarn Computer Museum, http://www.digibarn.com; IEEE Virtual Museum, http://www.ieee-virtual-museum.org; Carlos Lozada, "The Productivity Slowdown of the 1970s," *National Bureau of Economic Research*, June 2005, downloaded from http://nber.org; Steve Ranger, "IPod and MP3 Player Ownership Soars," *Personal Computer World*, February 17, 2005, downloaded from http://www.pcw.co.uk; Thomas R. Schori and Michael L. Garee, "Does your Company make Things Happen?" *Marketing News*, January 5, 1998, p. 4; Albert Schwenk, "Compensation in the 1970s," *Compensation and Working Conditions Online*, January 30, 2003, downloaded from http://stats.bls.gov; Jason Snell, Steven Levy, Guy Kawasaki, Adam Engst, Roger Ebert, Andy Ihnatko, John Dvorak, and Pamela Pfiffner, "20 Years of the Mac," *Macworld*, February 2004, pp. 68–72; Joel West, "Apple Computer: The iCEO Seizes the Internet," Center for Research on Information Technology and Organizations, Paper 348, 2002, downloaded from http://repositories.cdlib.org; Stephen Wozniak, "Homebrew and How the Apple came to be," downloaded from http://atariarchives.org.

PART 2

Business Ownership

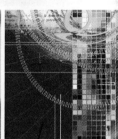

| CHAPTER 5 | Forms of Business Ownership > |
| CHAPTER 6 | Entrepreneurship: Starting and Managing Your Own Business > |

CHAPTER 5

Forms of Business Ownership

Learning Goals

After reading this chapter, you should be able to answer these questions:

1 What are the advantages and disadvantages of the sole proprietorship form of business organization?

2 What are the advantages of operating as a partnership, and what downside risks should partners consider?

3 How does the corporate structure provide advantages and disadvantages to a company, and what are the major types of corporations?

4 What other options for business organization does a company have in addition to sole proprietorships, partnerships, and corporations?

5 What makes franchising an appropriate form of organization for some types of business, and why does it continue to grow in importance?

6 Why are mergers and acquisitions important to a company's overall growth?

7 What current trends will affect the business organizations of the future?

Exploring Business Careers
Jessica MacLean
Sole Proprietor

In most any elementary school classroom, at least one child's answer to the question, "What do you want to do with your life?" will be, "A lawyer." One of the most popular careers, lawyers are powerful figures in society, shaping our laws and ensuring that we adhere to them. Their prominence and power have led to the stereotype of rich, career-driven lawyers, often leaving no room in our minds for those who truly want to bring justice to the world. However, Jessica MacLean, a lawyer focusing primarily on women's rights, is quick to say that, as with many stereotypes, that is only one side of the story. "I know because I lived that—I was on my way to being a successful corporate lawyer. But I realized what I was doing and how different that was from why I'd started practicing. So I walked away from it all to start my own practice."

Nervous about the prospect of private practice, she has chosen to operate as a sole proprietorship for now. Sole proprietorships are easy to set up for people who want to work on their own, prefer direct control of the business, and desire the flexibility to sell the business or close the doors at any time. "For me, it's the best choice because I am not responsible for or to anyone else. I can easily dissolve the business if I find it is not proceeding how I'd planned. More positively, too, if it does succeed, I know that success is due to my hard work.

Indeed MacLean's law career was not always in corporate law. She turned her sights toward law after a Gender and Communications professor at DePaul University suggested her argumentative style might be an asset in that profession. "She said I needed to

tone it down for class—that the other students seemed afraid to speak up—but then asked if I'd ever considered being a lawyer." MacLean, who had always been interested in issues of justice and legality surrounding women, took her professor's advice and made the leap into law.

While in law school, she clerked for the City of Chicago in their Department of Personnel's Sexual Harassment Office and volunteered for the Cook County State's Attorney's Office in the Domestic Violence Division. The cases she worked on were emotionally trying. Despite the difficulty of the cases, she was drawn to them, compelled by the people she helped and the change she was able to affect. After school, she continued in related practice, working first for the Cook County State's Attorney's Office.

After several years with the State's Attorney's Office, she needed a change. It was then that MacLean decided to work for a corporation, a form of business that you will learn about in this chapter. "Why did I switch to corporate law? I think I was burnt out, to some extent. It's so hard to work on those cases, day after day. I needed to see if I would be better somewhere else."

Today, MacLean enjoys the rewards of being a sole proprietor. As the needs of her business change, the form of business ownership may change also. In the meantime, the sole proprietorship structure is ideal for fulfilling her career goals.

Chapter 5 discusses sole proprietorships, as well as several other forms of business ownership, including partnerships and corporations, and compares the advantages and disadvantages of each.

With a good idea and some cash in hand you decide to start a business. But before you get going you need to ask yourself some questions that will help you decide what form of business organization will best suit your needs.

Would you prefer to go it alone as a *sole proprietorship*, or do you want others to share your burdens and challenges in a *partnership*? Or would the limited liability protection of a *corporation*, or perhaps the flexibility of a *limited liability company (LLC)*, make more sense?

There are other questions you need to consider too: Will you need financing? How easy will it be to obtain? Will you attract employees? How will the business be taxed, and who will be liable for the company's debts? If you choose to share ownership with others, how much operating control would they want, and what costs would be associated with that?

As Exhibit 5.1 illustrates, sole proprietorships are the most popular form of business ownership, accounting for 72 percent of all businesses, compared with 8 percent for partnerships and 20 percent for corporations. Because most sole proprietorships and partnerships remain small, corporations generate approximately 84 percent of total business revenues and 53 percent of total profits.

Most start-up businesses select one of these major ownership forms. In the following pages we will discover the advantages and disadvantages of each form of business ownership and the factors that may make it necessary to change from one form of organization to another, as the needs of the business change. As a company expands from small to midsize or larger, the form of business structure selected in the beginning may no longer be appropriate.

Going It Alone: Sole Proprietorships

1 What are the advantages and disadvantages of the sole proprietorship form of business organization?

sole proprietorship
A business that is established, owned, operated, and often financed by one person.

Jeremy Shepherd was working full-time for an airline when, at the age of twenty-two, he wandered into an exotic pearl market in China, searching for a gift for his girlfriend. The strand of pearls he handpicked by instinct was later valued by a jeweler back in the States at twenty times what he paid for them. Jeremy cashed his next paycheck and hurried back to Asia, buying every pearl he could afford, and in 2000 his company Pearl Paradise was born. Shepherd chose the **sole proprietorship** form of business organization—a business that is established, owned, operated, and often financed by one person—because it was the easiest to set up. He did not want partners, and low liability exposure made incorporating unnecessary.

Fluent in Mandarin Chinese, Japanese, and Spanish, and immersed in Asian culture, Shepherd believed the Internet was the way to market his pearls (**http://www.pearlparadise.com**). Offering a wide range of pearl jewelry through fourteen Web sites worldwide, his company sells as many as one thousand items per day. The recent addition of an exclusive Los Angeles showroom allows celebrity customers to shop by appointment. With $5 million in sales last year, and the needs of his business continuing to grow and change, Shepherd concedes he may choose to incorporate the company sometime in the future.[1]

Exhibit 5.1 > Comparison of Forms of Business Organization

Source: Internal Revenue Service, as reported in Table 72, U.S. Bureau of the Census, *Statistical Abstract of the United States, 2006*, 125th ed. (Washington, DC: U.S. Government Printing Office, 2006), p. 504.

Form	Number	Sales	Profits
Sole Proprietorships	72 percent	5 percent	21 percent
Partnerships	8 percent	11 percent	26 percent
Corporations	20 percent	84 percent	53 percent

Advantages of Sole Proprietorships

Sole proprietorships have several advantages that make them popular:

- *Easy and inexpensive to form.* As Jeremy Shepherd discovered, sole proprietorships have few legal requirements (local licenses and permits) and are not expensive to form, making them the business organization of choice for many small companies and start-ups.
- *Profits all go to the owner.* The owner of a sole proprietorship obtains the start-up funds and gets all the profits earned by the business. The more efficiently the firm operates, the higher the company's profitability.
- *Direct control of the business.* All business decisions are made by the sole proprietorship owner without having to consult anyone else.
- *Freedom from government regulation.* Sole proprietorships have more freedom than other forms of business with respect to government controls.
- *No special taxation.* Sole proprietorships do not pay special franchise or corporate taxes. Profits are taxed as personal income as reported on the owner's individual tax return.
- *Ease of dissolution.* With no co-owners or partners the sole proprietor can sell the business or close the doors at any time, making this form of business organization an ideal way to test a new business idea.

Disadvantages of Sole Proprietorships

Along with the freedom to operate the business as they wish, sole proprietors face several disadvantages:

- *Unlimited liability.* From a legal standpoint, the sole proprietor and the company he or she owns is one and the same, making the business owner personally responsible for all debts the company incurs, even if they exceed the company's value. The owner may need to sell other personal property—his or her car, home, or other investments—to satisfy claims against his business.
- *Difficulty raising capital.* Business assets are unprotected against claims of personal creditors, so business lenders view sole proprietorships as high risk due to the owner's unlimited liability. Owners must often use personal funds—borrowing on credit cards, second-mortgaging their homes, or selling investments—to finance their business. Expansion plans can also be affected by an inability to raise additional funding.
- *Limited managerial expertise.* The success of a sole proprietorship rests solely with the skills and talents of the owner, who must wear many different hats and make all decisions. Owners are often not equally skilled in all areas of running a business. A graphic designer may be a wonderful artist but not know bookkeeping, how to manage production, or how to market his or her work.
- *Trouble finding qualified employees.* Sole proprietors often cannot offer the same pay, fringe benefits, and advancement as larger companies, making them less attractive to employees seeking the most favorable employment opportunities.
- *Personal time commitment.* Running a sole proprietorship business requires personal sacrifices and a huge time commitment, often dominating the owner's life with 12-hour workdays and 7-day workweeks.
- *Unstable business life.* The life span of a sole proprietorship can be uncertain. The owner may lose interest, experience ill health, retire, or die. The business will cease to exist unless the owner makes provisions for it to continue operating, or puts it up for sale.
- *Losses are the owner's responsibility.* The sole proprietor is responsible for all losses, although tax laws allow these to be deducted from other personal income.

The sole proprietorship may be a suitable choice for a one-person start-up operation with no employees and little risk of liability exposure. For many sole

Work-Life Balance Important in Small Business

According to a recent survey released by the Wells Fargo/Gallup Small Business Index, about two-thirds of small business owners are satisfied with how they balance their personal lives and work schedules, despite the fact that they work an average 52 hours a week. The survey also found that over half of small business owners work six days a week, with more than 20 percent working all seven. Fourteen percent reported taking zero vacation days in a year, and almost 40 percent of those who do take personal time off said they still answer work-related phone calls and emails while on vacation.

Nonetheless, 67 percent of small business owners said they were satisfied with their personal life-work balance and almost 90 percent said they were satisfied with being a small business owner in general.

It's "not just a willingness" to work more hours, said Laine Caspi, who regularly logs in about 50 hours a week at work as owner of Parents of Invention (**http://www.parentsofinvention.com**), a manufacturer of baby accessories. "It's more like you want to do it. It's a choice, as opposed to someone else saying that you have to be there." Dennis Jacobe, chief economist at the Gallup Organization, agrees. "People see the benefits more closely tied to them when they're the owner," he says. "Working hard and long is a natural aspect of the kind of people willing to start their own business."

But if employees have trouble balancing work and life, odds are they will have less confidence in you as a leader, a recent study shows. The study, which polled more than 50,000 U.S. workers from various markets including professional services, consumer goods, and financial services, found that employees who strike a positive balance between home and work were 11 percent more likely to praise their leaders' ability to set a clear direction.

The Society for Human Resource Management's (SHRM) research also shows work-life balance has a great impact on how employees feel about their leaders. Jennifer Schramm, a manager in SHRM's workplace trends and forecasting research department, predicts that as companies try to maximize the productivity of each employee, work-life balance will become increasingly more important.

"As other factors that contribute to job satisfaction become harder for employees to control—health care benefits, job security, and feeling safe in the work place—work-life balance is something the business owner can offer," Schramm said. "Understanding your work force is key to ensuring employee satisfaction." And research shows that happy employees can yield happy returns for businesses.[2]

Critical Thinking Questions

- Many small business owners expect their employees to be as committed and to work as hard as they do. How would you avoid falling into that trap while still demanding the best from your workers?
- As a small business owner consider some strategies to ensure an appropriate work-life balance for your employees.

> ### concept check
>
> What is a sole proprietorship?
>
> Why is this a popular form of business organization?
>
> What are the drawbacks to being a sole proprietor?

proprietors, however, this is a temporary choice and as the business grows the owner may be unable to operate with limited financial and managerial resources. At this point he or she may decide to take in one or more partners to ensure that the business continues to flourish.

As you will see from the Catching the Entrepreneurial Spirit box, small business owners must work hard at balancing their professional and personal lives.

Partnerships: Sharing the Load

 2 **What are the advantages of operating as a partnership, and what downside risks should partners consider?**

partnership
An association of two or more individuals who agree to operate a business together for profit.

Can **partnerships**, an association of two or more individuals who agree to operate a business together for profit, be hazardous to a business's health? Let's assume partners Ron and Liz own a stylish and successful beauty salon. After a few years of operating the business they find they have contrasting visions for their company. Liz is happy with the status quo, while Ron wants to expand the business by bringing in investors and opening salons in other locations.

How do they resolve this impasse? By asking themselves some tough questions. Whose view of the future is more realistic? Does the business actually have the expansion potential Ron believes it does? Where will he find investors to make his dream of multiple locations a reality? Is he willing to dissolve the partnership and start over again on his own? And who would have the right to their clients?

Ron realizes that expanding the business in line with his vision would require a large financial risk, and that his partnership with Liz offers many advantages he would miss in a sole proprietorship form of business organization. After much consideration he decides to leave things as they are.

CONCEPT *in Action*

Kurt Cobain's soaring posthumous legacy hit turbulence in 2006 when eccentric widow Courtney Love formed a business partnership with music publisher Larry Mestel to co-manage her deceased husband's legendary estate. Although Love asserted that Mestel is the right partner to take Cobain's music to the next generation, fans worry that the former Virgin exec's 25 percent stake in the publishing catalog might land Nirvana's generation-defining songs in deodorant ads and action-movie soundtracks. *What potential conflicts can arise in partnerships?*

general partnership
A partnership in which all partners share in the management and profits. Each partner can act on behalf of the firm and has unlimited liability for all its business obligations.

limited partnership
A partnership with one or more *general partners* who have unlimited liability, and one or more *limited partners* whose liability is limited to the amount of their investment in the company.

general partners
Partners who have unlimited liability for all of the firm's business obligations and who control its operations.

limited partners
Partners whose liability for the firm's business obligations is limited to the amount of their investment. They help to finance the business, but do not participate in the firm's operations.

For those individuals who do not like to "go it alone," a partnership is relatively simple to set up. Offering a shared form of business ownership, it is a popular choice for professional-service firms such as lawyers, accountants, architects, stockbrokers, and real estate companies.

The parties agree, *either orally or in writing,* to share in the profits and losses of a joint enterprise. A *written partnership agreement,* spelling out the terms and conditions of the partnership, *is recommended* to prevent later conflicts between the partners. Such agreements typically include the name of the partnership, its purpose, and the contributions of each partner (financial, asset, skill/talent). It also outlines the responsibilities and duties of each partner and their compensation structure (salary, profit sharing, etc.). It should contain provisions for the addition of new partners, the sale of partnership interests, and procedures for resolving conflicts, dissolving the business, and distributing the assets.

There are two basic types of partnerships: *general and limited*. In a **general partnership**, all partners share in the management and profits. They co-own the assets and each can act on behalf of the firm. Each partner also has unlimited liability for all the business obligations of the firm. A **limited partnership** has two types of partners: one or more **general partners** who have unlimited liability, and one or more **limited partners** whose liability is limited to the amount of their investment. In return for limited liability, limited partners agree not to take part in the day-to-day management of the firm. They help to finance the business but the general partners maintain operational control.

Advantages of Partnerships

Some advantages of partnerships come quickly to mind:

- *Ease of formation.* Like sole proprietorships, partnerships are easy to form. The partners agree to do business together and draw up a *partnership agreement.* For most partnerships, applicable state laws are not complex.
- *Availability of capital.* Because two or more people contribute financial resources, partnerships can raise funds more easily for operating expenses and business expansion. The partners' combined financial strength also increases the firm's ability to raise funds from outside sources.

- *Diversity of skills and expertise.* Partners share the responsibilities of managing and operating the business. Combining partner skills to set goals, manage the overall direction of the firm, and solve problems increases the chances for the partnership's success. To find the right partner you must examine your own strengths and weaknesses, and know what you need from a partner. Ideal partnerships bring together people with complementary backgrounds rather than those with similar experience, skills, and talents. In Exhibit 5.2 you'll find some advice on choosing a partner.
- *Flexibility.* General partners are actively involved in managing their firm and can respond quickly to changes in the business environment.
- *No special taxes.* Partnerships pay no income taxes. A partnership must file a partnership return with the Internal Revenue Service, reporting how profits or losses were divided among the partners. Each partner's profit or loss is then reported on the partner's personal income tax return, with any profits taxed at personal income tax rates.
- *Relative freedom from government control.* Except for state rules for licensing and permits, the government has little control over partnership activities.

Disadvantages of Partnerships

Business owners must consider the following disadvantages of setting up their company as a partnership:

- *Unlimited liability.* All general partners have unlimited liability for the debts of the business. In fact, any one partner can be held personally liable for all partnership debts and legal judgments (like malpractice)—regardless of who caused them. As with sole proprietorships, business failure can lead to a loss of the general partners' personal assets. To overcome this problem many states now allow the formation of *limited liability partnerships (LLPs)*, which protect each individual partner from responsibility for the acts of other partners, and limit their liability to harm resulting from their own actions.

Exhibit 5.2 > Perfect Partners

Picking a partner is both an art and a science. Someone may have all the right credentials on paper, but does that person share your vision and the ideas you have for your company? Are they a straight shooter? Honesty, integrity, and ethics are important, because you may be liable for what your partner does. Be prepared to talk about everything and trust your intuition and your gut feelings—they're probably right. Ask yourself and your potential partner the following questions—then see how well your answers match up:

1. Why do you want a partner?
2. What characteristics, talents, and skills does each person bring to the partnership?
3. How will you divide responsibilities—from long-range planning to daily operations? Who will handle such tasks as marketing, sales, accounting, customer service?
4. What is your long-term vision for the business—its size, life span, financial commitment, etc.?
5. What are your personal reasons for forming this company? Are you looking to create a small company, or build a large one: are you seeking a steady paycheck, or financial independence?
6. Will all parties put in the same amount of time, or is there an alternative arrangement that is acceptable to everyone?
7. Do you have similar work ethics and values?
8. What requirements will be in the partnership agreement?

- *Potential for conflicts between partners.* Partners may have different ideas about how to run their business, which employees to hire, how to allocate responsibilities, and when to expand. Differences in personalities and work styles can cause clashes or breakdowns in communication, sometimes requiring outside intervention to save the business.
- *Complexity of profit-sharing.* Dividing the profits is relatively easy if all partners contribute equal amounts of time, expertise, and capital. But if one partner puts in more money and others more time it might be more difficult to arrive at a fair profit-sharing formula.
- *Difficulty exiting or dissolving a partnership.* As a rule partnerships are easier to form than to leave. When one partner wants to leave, the value of his or her share must be calculated. To whom will that share be sold and will that person be acceptable to the other partners? If a partner who owns more than 50 percent of the entity withdraws, dies, or becomes disabled, the partnership must reorganize or end. To avoid these problems most partnership agreements include specific guidelines for transferring partnership interests, and buy–sell agreements that make provision for surviving partners to buy a deceased partner's interest. Partners can also purchase special life insurance policies designed to fund such a purchase.

Business partnerships are often compared to marriages. As with a marriage, choosing the right partner is critical. So if you are considering forming a partnership, allow plenty of time to evaluate your and your potential partner's goals, personality, expertise, and working style before joining forces.

> **concept check**
>
> How does a partnership differ from a sole proprietorship?
>
> Describe the three main types of partnerships and explain the difference between a limited partner and a general partner.
>
> What are the main advantages and disadvantages of a partnership?

Corporations: Limiting Your Liability

3 How does the corporate structure provide advantages and disadvantages to a company, and what are the major types of corporations?

corporation
A legal entity with an existence and life separate from its owners, who are not personally liable for the entity's debts. A corporation is chartered by the state in which it is formed and can own property, enter into contracts, sue and be sued, and engage in business operations under the terms of its charter.

When people think of corporations they typically think of major, well-known companies like IBM, Microsoft, and General Electric. But corporations range in size from large multinationals with thousands of employees and billions of dollars in sales, to midsize or even smaller firms with few employees and revenues under $25,000.

A **corporation** is a legal entity subject to the laws of the state in which it is formed, where the right to operate as a business is issued by state charter. A corporation can own property, enter into contracts, sue and be sued, and engage in business operations under the terms of its charter. Unlike sole proprietorships and partnerships, corporations are taxable entities with a life separate from its owners, who are not personally liable for its debts.

When launching her company, Executive Property Management Services, Inc., 32-year-old Linda Ravden realized she needed the liability protection of the corporate form of business organization. Her company specialized in providing customized property management services to mid- and upper-level corporate executives on extended work assignments abroad, often for three to five years or longer. Taking care of substantial properties in the $1 million dollar range and above was no small responsibility for Ravden's company. Therefore the protection of a corporate business structure, along with carefully detailed contracts outlining the company's obligations, were crucial in providing Ravden with the liability protection she needed—and the peace of mind to focus on running her business without constant worry.[3]

As Pacific Sunwear's business grew, its form of business organization needed to adjust, too. In the following Managing Change box you'll learn how it managed a very successful transition from single tiny surf shop into mega mall retailer.

MANAGING CHANGE

Pacific Sun's Golden Glow

It all started as a little surf shop in 1980 in Newport Beach, California. It wasn't called PacSun then. It wasn't even all that different from other shops carrying surfboards and wax, except for one thing. The founders had a better idea.

During southern California's wet, cool winters the beaches got empty and the surf store business went dry. Where did everyone go? To the mall, of course. Their idea—to be the first surf shop to move into California's popular mall locations—worked. The company soon grew to 21 stores, selling such popular name brands as Billabong, Gotcha, CatchIt, Stussy, and Quiksilver, as well as its own private-label brands.

What began as a little surf shop is today a leading mall-based specialty retailer in the fast-growing surf, skate, and hip-hop apparel markets. With close to a thousand stores in the United States and Puerto Rico and sales now topping $1 billion, how did the founders make the leap from selling and waxing surfboards to being a major player in the youth apparel market? How has Pacific Sunwear of California, Inc. (http://www.pacsun.com) succeeded when thousands of other clothing companies failed?

"We listen and we change," says the CEO of Pacific Sun. "The kids have the answers, so we listen to get the trends, the solutions, and find out what we are doing right." To remain on the cutting edge of teen tastes, the company hosts an open house every Wednesday at its corporate headquarters in Anaheim, California, where vendors present their wares to PacSun's savvy team of buyers. Being able to distinguish

between short-lived fads and actual trends is important when making merchandise choices. The company's focus on "active brand management" is what keeps its sales climbing.

The founders' philosophy has served their business well. In 1993 the 60-store company sold stock to the public. It now has 786 PacSun and 91 PacSun Outlet stores, plus 186 d.e.m.o. hip-hop apparel stores, for a total of 1,063 stores in 50 states and Puerto Rico, with 12,000 employees. The company's PacSun stores cater to a completely different customer than its d.e.m.o. hip-hop stores. In April 2006, PacSun launched its third concept, One Thousand Steps, a footwear store.

Future plans include a four-year expansion to add 244 new PacSun stores and 279 new d.e.m.o. stores in the United States. The new chain will sell brand-name casual and fashion shoes and accessories. PacSun's projections show this brand growing to 800 stores.

As its business took off, PacSun successfully made the leap from the small sole proprietorship form of business organization to corporate retailing giant. The company is indeed a thousand steps away from its humble beginnings.[4]

Critical Thinking Questions
- How did PacSun manage its evolution from a small, local business to a leading mall-based specialty retailer?
- What form of business organization might PacSun have chosen when it started, and what might have prompted it to change as it grew?

Corporations play an important role in the U.S. economy. As Exhibit 5.1 demonstrated, corporations account for only 20 percent of all businesses, but generate 84 percent of all revenues and 53 percent of all profits. A list of the 10 largest U.S corporations shown in Exhibit 5.3 includes many familiar names that impact our daily lives.

The Incorporation Process

Setting up a corporation is more complex than starting a sole proprietorship or partnership. Most states base their laws for chartering corporations on the Model Business Corporation Act of the American Bar Association, although registration procedures, fees, taxes, and laws that regulate corporations vary from state to state.

Exhibit 5.3 > The 10 Largest U.S. Corporations (ranked by 2005 sales)

	Company	Revenues ($ millions)
1	ExxonMobil	339,938
2	Wal-Mart Stores	315,654
3	General Motors	192,604
4	ChevronTexaco	189,481
5	Ford Motor	177,210
6	ConocoPhillips	166,683
7	General Electric	157,153
8	Citigroup	131,045
9	American International Group	108,905
10	International Business Machines	91,134

Source: "The 2006 Fortune 500," *Fortune,* http://www.fortune.com (May 22, 2006). © 2006 Time Inc. All rights reserved.

CONCEPT *in Action*

Incorporated in 1902, the Target Corporation is one of America's most popular retail stores. Known early on as Goodfellows and the Dayton Dry Goods Company, Target launched into discount retailing in the 1960s and quickly established a strong brand image. Today, youthful shoppers seek out fashionably affordable merchandise at the company's more than 1,300 stores, and the Target bullseye is among the most recognizable trademarks in all of business—more recognizable than even the Nike swoosh. *What steps must companies take to become incorporated?*

A firm does not have to incorporate in the state where it is based and may benefit by comparing the rules of several states before choosing a state of incorporation. Although Delaware is a small state with few corporations actually based there, its pro-corporate policies make it the state of incorporation for many companies, including about half the Fortune 500. Incorporating a company involves five main steps:

- Selecting the company's name
- Writing the *articles of incorporation* (see Exhibit 5.4) and filing them with the appropriate state office, usually the secretary of state
- Paying required fees and taxes
- Holding an organizational meeting
- Adopting bylaws, electing directors, and passing the first operating resolutions

The state issues a corporate charter based on information in the articles of incorporation. Once the corporation has its charter it holds an organizational meeting to adopt bylaws, elect directors, and pass initial operating resolutions. Bylaws provide legal and managerial guidelines for operating the firm.

Exhibit 5.4 > Articles of Incorporation

Articles of incorporation are prepared on a form authorized or supplied by the state of incorporation. Although they may vary slightly from state to state, all articles of incorporation include the following key items:

- Name of corporation
- Company's goals
- Types of stock and number of shares of each type to issue
- Life of the corporation (usually "perpetual," meaning with no time limit)
- Minimum investment by owners
- Methods for transferring shares of stock
- Address of the corporate office
- Names and addresses of the first board of directors

The Corporate Structure

As Exhibit 5.5 shows, corporations have their own organizational structure with three important components: stockholders, directors, and officers.

stockholders (or *shareholders*)
The owners of a corporation who hold shares of stock that carry certain rights.

Stockholders (or shareholders) are the owners of a corporation, holding shares of stock that provide them with certain rights. They may receive a portion of the corporation's profits in the form of dividends, and they can sell or transfer their ownership in the corporation (represented by their shares of stock) at any time. Stockholders can attend annual meetings, elect the board of directors, and vote on matters that affect the corporation in accordance with its charter and bylaws. Each share of stock generally carries one vote.

board of directors
A group of people elected by the stockholders to handle the overall management of a corporation, such as setting major corporate goals and policies, hiring corporate officers, and overseeing the firm's operations and finances.

The stockholders elect a **board of directors** to govern and handle the overall management of the corporation. The directors set major corporate goals and policies, hire corporate officers, and oversee the firm's operations and finances. Small firms may have as few as 3 directors, whereas large corporations usually have 10 to 15.

The boards of large corporations typically include both corporate executives and outside directors (not employed by the organization) chosen for their professional and personal expertise. Outside directors often bring a fresh view to the corporation's activities because they are independent of the firm.

Hired by the board, the *officers* of a corporation are its top management, and include the president and chief executive officer (CEO), vice presidents, treasurer, and secretary, who are responsible for achieving corporate goals and policies. Officers may also be board members and stockholders.

CONCEPT *in Action*

When Walt Disney cast his now-famous mouse as Steamboat Willie back in the 1920s, he had little idea that his animation project would turn into one of the largest entertainment companies in the world. The house that Walt built, with its magical theme parks, movie studios, and product lines, is overseen today by visionary directors with accomplished backgrounds in media, technology, and government. *What important tasks and responsibilities are entrusted to Disney's board of directors?*

© BETH A. KEISER/CORBIS

Advantages of Corporations

The corporate structure allows companies to merge financial and human resources into enterprises with great potential for growth and profits:

- *Limited liability.* A key advantage of corporations is that they are separate legal entities that exist apart from their owners. An owner's (stockholder's) liability for the obligations of the firm is limited to the amount of the stock he or she owns. If the corporation goes bankrupt, creditors can look only to the assets of the corporation for payment.
- *Ease of transferring ownership.* Stockholders of public corporations can sell their shares at any time without affecting the status of the corporation.
- *Unlimited life.* The life of a corporation is unlimited. Although corporate charters specify a life term, they also include rules for renewal. Because the corporation is an entity separate from its owners, the death or withdrawal of an owner does not affect its existence, unlike a sole proprietorship or partnership.
- *Tax deductions.* Corporations are allowed certain tax deductions, such as operating expenses, which reduces their taxable income.
- *Ability to attract financing.* Corporations can raise money by selling new shares of stock. Dividing ownership into smaller units makes it affordable to more investors, who can purchase one or several thousand shares. The large size and stability of corporations also helps them get bank financing. All these financial resources allow corporations to invest in facilities and human resources and expand beyond the scope of sole proprietorships or partnerships. It would be impossible for a sole proprietorship or partnership to make automobiles, provide nationwide telecommunications, or build oil or chemical refineries.

Exhibit 5.5 > Organizational Structure of Corporations

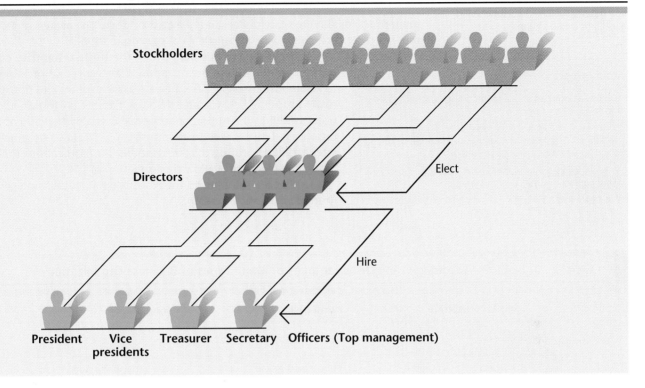

Stockholders

Directors

Elect

Hire

President Vice Treasurer Secretary Officers (Top management)
presidents

Disadvantages of Corporations

Although corporations offer companies many benefits, they have some disadvantages:

- *Double taxation of profits.* Corporations must pay federal and state income taxes on their profits. In addition, any profits (dividends) paid to stockholders are taxed as personal income, although at a somewhat reduced rate.
- *Cost and complexity of formation.* As outlined earlier, forming a corporation involves several steps, and costs can run into thousands of dollars, including state filing, registration, and license fees, as well as the cost of attorneys and accountants.
- *More government restrictions.* Unlike sole proprietorships and partnerships, corporations are subject to many regulations and reporting requirements. For example, corporations must register in each state where they do business, and must also register with the Securities and Exchange Commission (SEC) before selling stock to the public. Unless it is closely held (owned by a small group of stockholders), a firm must publish financial reports on a regular basis, and file other special reports with the SEC and state and federal agencies. These reporting requirements can impose substantial costs, and published information on corporate operations may also give competitors an advantage.

C corporation
A conventional or basic form of corporate organization.

S corporation
A hybrid entity that is organized like a corporation, with stockholders, directors, and officers, but taxed like a partnership, with income and losses flowing through to the stockholders and taxed as their personal income.

Types of Corporations

Three types of corporate business organization provide limited liability:

The C corporation is the conventional or basic form of corporate organization. Small businesses may achieve liability protection through S corporations or limited liability companies (LLCs).

An S corporation is a hybrid entity, allowing smaller corporations to avoid double taxation of corporate profits as long as they meet certain size and ownership

limited liability company (LLC)
A hybrid organization that offers the same liability protection as a corporation but may be taxed as either a partnership or a corporation.

requirements. Organized like a corporation with stockholders, directors, and officers, an S corporation is taxed like a partnership. Income and losses flow through to the stockholders and are taxed as personal income. S corporations are allowed a maximum of 100 qualifying shareholders and one class of stock. The owners of an S corporation are not personally liable for the debts of the corporation.

A newer type of business entity, the **limited liability company** (**LLC**), is also a hybrid organization. Like S corporations they appeal to small businesses because they are easy to set up and not subject to many restrictions. LLCs offer the same liability protection as corporations as well as the option of being taxed as a partnership or a corporation. First authorized in Wyoming in 1977, LLCs became popular after a 1988 tax ruling that treats them like partnerships for tax purposes. Today all states allow the formation of LLCs.

Exhibit 5.6 summarizes the advantages and disadvantages of each form of business ownership.

> **concept check**
>
> What is a corporation? Describe how corporations are formed and structured.
>
> Summarize the advantages and disadvantages of corporations. Which features contribute to the dominance of corporations in the business world?
>
> Why do S corporations and limited liability companies (LLCs) appeal to small businesses?

Exhibit 5.6 > Advantages and Disadvantages of Major Types of Business Organization

	Sole Proprietorship	Partnership	Corporation
Advantages			
	Owner receives all profits.	More expertise and managerial skill available.	Limited liability protects owners from losing more than they invest.
	Low organizational costs.	Relatively low organizational costs.	Can achieve large size due to marketability of stock (ownership).
	Income taxed as personal income of proprietor.	Income taxed as personal income of partners.	Receives certain tax advantages.
	Independence.	Fundraising ability is enhanced by more owners.	Greater access to financial resources allows growth.
	Secrecy.		Can attract employees with specialized skills.
	Ease of dissolution.		Ownership is readily transferable.
			Long life of firm (not affected by death of owners).
Disadvantages			
	Owner receives all losses.	Owners have unlimited liability; may have to cover debts of other, less financially sound partners.	Double taxation because both corporate profits and dividends paid to owners are taxed, although the dividends are taxed at a reduced rate.
	Owner has unlimited liability; total wealth can be taken to satisfy business debts.	Dissolves or must reorganize when partner dies.	More expensive and complex to form.
	Limited fundraising ability can inhibit growth.	Difficult to liquidate or terminate.	Subject to more government regulation.
	Proprietor may have limited skills and management expertise.	Potential for conflicts between partners.	Financial reporting requirements make operations public.
	Few long-range opportunities and benefits for employees.	Difficult to achieve large-scale operations.	
	Lacks continuity when owner dies.		

Specialized Forms of Business Organization

 4 What other options for business organization does a company have in addition to sole proprietorships, partnerships, and corporations?

In addition to the three main forms, several specialized types of business organization also play an important role in our economy. We will look at cooperatives and joint ventures in this section and take a detailed look at franchising in the following section.

Cooperatives

cooperatives
A legal entity typically formed by people with similar interests, such as suppliers or customers, to reduce costs and gain economic power. A cooperative has limited liability, an unlimited life span, an elected board of directors, and an administrative staff; all profits are distributed to the member-owners in proportion to their contributions.

When you eat a Sunkist orange or spread Land O' Lakes butter on your toast you are consuming foods produced by cooperatives. A **cooperative** is a legal entity with several *corporate features,* such as limited liability, an unlimited life span, an elected board of directors, and an administrative staff. Member-owners pay annual fees to the cooperative and share in the profits, which are distributed to members in proportion to their contributions. Because they do not retain any profits, cooperatives are not subject to taxes.

There are currently 750,000 cooperatives with 760 million members in more than 100 countries worldwide.[5] Cooperatives operate in every industry including agriculture, childcare, energy, financial services, food retailing and distribution, health care, insurance, housing, purchasing and shared services, and telecommunications, among others. They range in size from large enterprises like Fortune 500 companies to small local storefronts, and fall into four distinct categories: consumer, producer, worker, and purchasing/shared services.

Cooperatives are autonomous businesses owned and democratically controlled by their members—the people who buy their goods or use their services—not by investors. Unlike investor-owned businesses, cooperatives are organized solely to meet the needs of the member-owners, not to accumulate capital for investors. As democratically controlled businesses, many cooperatives practice the principle of "one member, one vote," providing members with equal control over the cooperative.

buyer cooperative
A group of cooperative members who unite for combined purchasing power.

There are two types of cooperatives. **Buyer cooperatives** combine members' purchasing power. Pooling buying power and buying in volume increases purchasing power and efficiency, resulting in lower prices. At the end of the year members get shares of the profits based on how much they bought. Obtaining discounts to lower costs gives the corner Ace Hardware store the chance to survive against retailing giants like Home Depot Inc. and Lowe's.

Founded in 1924, Ace Hardware is one of the nation's largest cooperatives and is wholly owned by its independent hardware retailer members in stores spanning all 50 states and 68 countries. The typical Ace store consistently outperforms its non-Ace competitors with annual sales that are 85 percent higher, net profits before taxes that are 146 percent higher, and a return on investment that is 42 percent greater.[6]

seller cooperative
Individual producers who join together to compete more effectively with large producers.

Seller cooperatives are popular in agriculture, wherein individual producers join to compete more effectively with large producers. Member dues support market development, national advertising, and other business activities. In addition to Sunkist and Land O'Lakes, other familiar cooperatives are Calavo (avocados), Ocean Spray (cranberries and juices), and Blue Diamond (nuts). Farmland Industries, the largest cooperative in the United States, sells feed, fertilizer, petroleum, and grain.

Cooperatives empower people to improve their quality of life and enhance their economic opportunities through self-help. Throughout the world, cooperatives are providing members with credit and financial services, energy, consumer goods, affordable housing, telecommunications, and other services that would not otherwise be available to them. Exhibit 5.7 on the next page outlines the basic principles of operation cooperatives follow.

- Voluntary and open membership
- Democratic member control
- Member economic participation
- Autonomy and independence
- Education, training, and information
- Cooperation among cooperatives
- Concern for community

Source: "What are Cooperatives," *Press Kit,
National Cooperative Business Association,*
http://www.ncba.coop. Copyright © NCBA.
All rights reserved. Reproduced by permission.

Joint Ventures

joint venture
Two or more companies that form an alliance to pursue a specific project usually for a specified time period.

In a **joint venture** two or more companies form an alliance to pursue a specific project, usually for a specified time period. There are many reasons for joint ventures. The project may be too large for one company to handle on its own, and joint ventures also afford companies access to new markets, products, or technology. Both large and small companies can benefit from joint ventures.

Recently Hyundai Motor Company announced it signed a $1.24 billion deal to form a joint venture with China's Guangzhou Motor Group. The arrangement will give the South Korean automaker access to the commercial vehicle market in China, where its passenger cars are already the top selling foreign brand. Each side will hold equal stakes in the new entity, tentatively named Guangzhou Hyundai Motor Company. The new plant, scheduled to begin production in 2007 with an annual capacity of 200,000 units, will produce small to large trucks and buses as well as commercial vehicles.[7]

concept check

Describe the two types of cooperatives and the advantages of each.

What are the benefits of joint ventures?

CONCEPT *in Action*

Bad Boy Records got its start by producing emerging artists like Faith Evans and The Notorious B.I.G. But company sales dropped after B.I.G., aka Christopher Wallace, was killed in 1997, and other acts soon left the label. More recently, Bad Boy founder Sean "Diddy" Combs inked a 50/50 joint venture with Big-Four record label Warner Music Group to turn things around. *How might this joint venture enable Bad Boy to regain footing and become a force in the music industry again?*

© AP PHOTO/JENNIFER GRAYLOCK

Franchising: A Popular Trend

When Shep Bostin decided to buy a franchise, he researched the usual suspects: Jiffy Lube, McDonald's, and Quiznos Subs. Bostin, then 38, was a top executive at a dying Gaithersburg, Maryland, technology firm, but instead of becoming another McDonald's franchisee, Bostin chose to remain a geek, albeit one who wheeled around in the signature black PT Cruiser of Geeks on Call. Bostin has now been making residential and commercial "house calls" for two years as a Geeks on Call franchisee. The company provides on-site computer assistance via a large pool of disenfranchised techies. He recently expanded his franchise ownership to cover three Maryland territories.[8]

Choosing the right franchise can be challenging. Franchises come in all sizes and demand different skills and qualifications. And with somewhere around 2,500 different franchised businesses in the United States, Bostin had a lot to choose from—from cookie-bouquet peddlers and dog trainers to acupuncture specialists. Exhibit 5.8 shows *Entrepreneur* magazine's top ten franchises for 2006.

Looking at these franchise start-up costs, it is easy to see that an important factor in picking a franchise is money. Bostin paid $60,000 in upfront costs which included the purchase of his PT Cruiser and pays 11 percent of his gross annual sales in royalties. He also pays $250 a week for national advertising, as well as doing his own marketing at local office parks and networking events.

Exhibit 5.8 > Top 10 Franchises for 2006

Franchise Name	Total Investment
1. Subway (sandwiches and salads)	$70,000–220,000
2. Quiznos (sandwiches, soups, salads)	$71,700–251,100
3. Curves (women's fitness/weight loss centers)	$38,400–53,500
4. The UPS Store (business communications and postal services)	$160,900–266,500
5. Jackson Hewitt Tax Service (tax preparation services)	$49,800–94,000
6. Dunkin' Donuts (donuts and baked goods)	$179,000–1,600,000
7. Jani-King (commercial cleaning)	$11,300–34,100
8. RE/MAX Inc. (real estate)	$20,000–200,000
9. 7-Eleven Inc. (convenience store)	Varies
10. Liberty Tax Service (tax preparation services)	$42,300–52,400

Source: "Top 10 Lists for 2006, Entrepreneur's Franchise 500," *Franchise Zone,* http://www. entrepreneur.com/franzone (May 31, 2006). Reprinted with permission of *Entrepreneur Magazine,* Franchise 500 2006.

5 **What makes franchising an appropriate form of organization for some types of business, and why does it continue to grow in importance?**

franchising
A form of business organization based on a business arrangement between a *franchisor,* which supplies the product or service concept, and the *franchisee,* who sells the goods or services of the franchisor in a certain geographic area.

franchisor
In a franchising arrangement, the company that supplies the product or service concept to the *franchisee.*

franchisee
In a franchising arrangement, the individual or company that sells the goods or services of the *franchisor* in a certain geographic area.

franchise agreement
A contract setting out the terms of a franchising arrangement, including the rules for running the franchise, the services provided by the franchisor, and the financial terms. Under the contract, the franchisee is allowed to use the franchisor's business name, trademark, and logo.

Chances are you recognize some of the names listed above and deal with franchise systems in your neighborhood every day. When you have lunch at Taco Bell or Jamba Juice, make copies at Kinko's, change your oil at Jiffy Lube, buy candles at Wick's 'n' Sticks, or mail a package at The UPS Store, you are dealing with a franchised business. These and other familiar name brands mean quality, consistency, and value to consumers. Franchised businesses provided about 10 million jobs with a $229.1 billion payroll, accounting for about 7.5 percent of all private-sector jobs and 5.0 percent of all private-sector payrolls.[9]

Franchising is a form of business organization that involves a **franchisor,** the company supplying the product or service concept, and the **franchisee,** the individual or company selling the goods or services in a certain geographic area. The franchisee buys a package that includes a proven product or service, proven operating methods, and training in managing the business. Offering a way to own a business without starting it from scratch, and to expand operations quickly into new geographic areas with limited capital investment, franchising is one of the fastest growing segments of the economy. Food companies represent the largest number of franchises, as the industry segmentation in Exhibit 5.9 on the next page shows.

A **franchise agreement** is a contract that allows the franchisee to use the franchisor's business name, trademark, and logo. The agreement also outlines rules for running the franchise, services provided by the franchisor, and financial terms. The franchisee agrees to follow the franchisor's operating rules by keeping inventory at certain levels, buying a standard equipment package, keeping up sales and service levels, taking part in franchisor promotions, and maintaining a relationship with the franchisor. In return, the franchisor provides the use of a proven company name and symbols, help in finding a site, building plans, guidance and training, management assistance, managerial and accounting systems and procedures, employee training, wholesale prices for supplies, and financial assistance.

Advantages of Franchises

Like other forms of business organization, franchising offers some distinct advantages:

- *Increased ability for franchisor to expand.* Because franchisees finance their own units, franchisors can grow without making a major investment.
- *Recognized name, product, and operating concept.* Consumers know they can depend on products from franchises like Pizza Hut, Hertz, and Holiday Inn. As a result, the franchisee's risk is reduced and the opportunity for success increased. The franchisee gets a widely known and accepted business with a proven track record, as well as operating procedures, standard goods and services, and national advertising.
- *Management training and assistance.* The franchisor provides a structured training program that gives the new franchisee a crash course in how to start and operate

Exhibit 5.9 > Franchises by Industry Segment

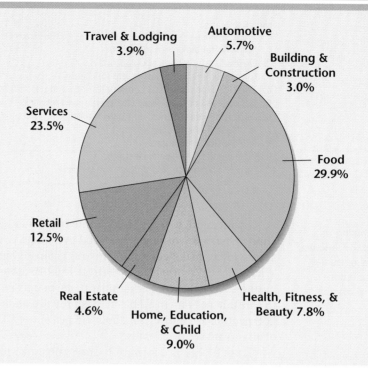

Travel & Lodging
3.9%

Automotive
5.7%

Building &
Construction
3.0%

Services
23.5%

Food
29.9%

Retail
12.5%

Real Estate
4.6%

Home, Education,
& Child
9.0%

Health, Fitness, &
Beauty 7.8%

Source: Statistics provided by FRANdata, a franchise information and research firm based in Arlington, VA, June 1, 2006.

their business. Ongoing training programs for managers and employees are another plus. In addition, franchisees have a peer group for support and sharing ideas.

- *Financial assistance.* Being linked to a nationally known company can help a franchisee obtain funds from a lender. Also, the franchisor typically gives the franchisee advice on financial management, referrals to lenders, and help in preparing loan applications. Many franchisors also offer short-term credit for buying supplies, payment plans, and loans to purchase real estate and equipment. Although franchisors give up a share of profits to their franchisees, they receive ongoing revenues in the form of royalty payments.

CONCEPT *in Action*

Countless franchise opportunities exist for entrepreneurs with access to start-up capital. Despite the broad range of franchise opportunities available, lists of the fastest-growing franchises are heavily weighted with restaurant chains and cleaning services. Start-up costs for a Quiznos franchise can be pricey; expenses associated with opening a Jani-King or a CleanNet cleaning service are significantly lower. *How do entrepreneurs evaluate which franchising opportunity is right for them?*

© TERRI MILLER/E-VISUAL COMMUNICATIONS INC.

CONCEPT *in Action*

Since launching its first franchise in 2001, Norfolk, Virginia's Geeks On Call has seen increasing demand for its mobile tech-support services. Today the company boasts over 300 independently owned and operated units throughout the United States. Instantly recognizable in their geek-marked blue Chrysler PT Cruisers, Geeks On Call certified technicians dutifully drive to anywhere PCs are in need of repair. *How does franchising enable businesses to grow rapidly?*

Disadvantages of Franchises

Franchising also has some disadvantages:

- *Loss of control.* The franchisor has to give up some control over operations and has less control over its franchisees than over company employees.
- *Cost of franchising.* Franchising can be a costly form of business. Costs will vary depending on the type of business, and may include expensive facilities and equipment. The franchisee also pays fees and/or royalties, which are usually tied to a percentage of sales. Fees for national and local advertising and management advice may add to a franchisee's ongoing costs.
- *Restricted operating freedom.* The franchisee agrees to conform to the franchisor's operating rules and facilities design, as well as inventory and supply standards. Some franchises require franchisees to purchase from only the franchisor or approved suppliers. The franchisor may also restrict the franchisee's territory or site, which could limit growth. Failure to conform to franchisor policies could mean the loss of the franchise.

Franchise Growth

Many of today's major franchise brands, such as McDonald's and KFC, started in the 1950s. Through the 1960s and 1970s with more types of businesses—clothing, convenience stores, business services, and many others—using franchising to distribute their goods and services. Growth comes from expansion of established franchises—for example, Subway, Pizza Hut, and Curves, as well as new entrants such as those in Exhibit 5.10 on the next page.

Changing demographics drive franchise industry growth, in terms of who, how, and what experiences the most rapid growth. The continuing growth and popularity of technology and personal computing is responsible for the rapidly multiplying number of eBay drop-off stores, and tech consultants like Geeks on Call are in greater demand than ever. Other growth franchise industries are the specialty coffee market, children's enrichment and tutoring programs, senior care, weight control, and fitness franchises.

And the savviest franchisees see multiunit development as a great way to further expand franchise systems and increase profits. Multiunit buyers tend to be white-collar workers who have been laid off from middle management jobs. They are well qualified financially, and bring management skills, financial resources, business acumen, and a lot of drive to their franchise ventures.

Exhibit 5.10 > Fast Growing and Top New Franchises, 2006

Rank	Fastest Growing Franchises, 2006	Top New Franchises, 2006
1	Subway (fast food)	Geeks On Call America (computer services)
2	Pizza Hut Inc. (fast food)	Moe's Southwest Grill (quick-service restaurant)
3	Quiznos (fast food)	EmbroidMe (embroidery and screen printing, ad specialties)
4	Jan-Pro Franchising Int'l. Inc. (commercial cleaning)	Chester's Int'l. (quick-service restaurant)
5	Curves (women's fitness centers)	ISold It (eBay drop-off stores)
6	Jani-King (commercial cleaning)	United Shipping Solutions (transportation services)
7	Jackson Hewitt Tax Service (tax preparation services)	Super Wash (automated self-service car wash)
8	The UPS Store (business and communication services)	Handyman Matters (handyman services)
9	Coverall Cleaning Concepts (commercial cleaning)	Robeks Fruit Smoothies & Healthy Eats (fast food)
10	CleanNet USA Inc. (commercial cleaning)	1-800-Water Damage (water-damage restoration services)

Source: "Fastest Growing Franchises" and "Top New Franchises," *Franchise Zone*, http://www.entreprenuer.com/franzone/ (May 31, 2006).

CONCEPT *in Action*

Fast-growing franchises are often based around a trendy idea, like a 30-minute workout for women or diet-friendly fast food. But today's hot trends can be tomorrow's outdated fashions. Krispy Kreme experienced frenzied expansion after going public in 2000, but later when the company was hit by accounting troubles and low-carb diet fads, franchisees shut down operations in spades. *How can entrepreneurs protect against investing in short-term fads and ill-managed franchises?*

© AP PHOTO/NELL REDMOND

The Next Big Thing in Franchising

All around you people are talking about the next big thing—Subway is the new miracle weight-loss solution, the half hour workout at Curves the answer to America's fitness needs—and you are ready to take the plunge and buy a trendy franchise. But consumers' desires can change with the tide, so how do you plan an entrance—and exit—strategy when purchasing a franchise that's a big hit today but could be old news by tomorrow? Exhibit 5.11 outlines some tips offered by Michael H. Seid, managing director of Michael H. Seid & Associates, a West Hartford, Connecticut–based management consulting firm specializing in the franchise industry.

International Franchising

Like other forms of business, franchising is part of our global marketplace economy. As international demand for all types of goods and services grows, most franchise systems are already operating internationally or planning to expand overseas. Restaurants, hotels, business services, educational products, car rentals, and nonfood retail stores are popular international franchises.

Franchisors in foreign countries face many of the same problems as other firms doing business abroad. In addition to tracking markets and currency changes, franchisors must understand local culture, language differences, and the political environment. Franchisors in foreign countries also face the challenge of aligning their business operations with the goals of their franchisees, who may be located half a globe away. In the following Expanding Around the Globe box, you will learn about a hugely successful American company that attempted to replicate its success in the Chinese fast food market, with mixed results.

Exhibit 5.11 > Franchise Purchase Tips

Act fast, yet proceed with caution. Normal trends tend to have a five-year life span, so it's important to get in early. Commit to a shorter term when the investment is not so secure.

Put the franchisor to the test. When you get into a franchise system that needs to be nimble, make certain it can respond quickly to change.

Know what you're getting into. Ask the franchisor what product(s) they plan to add if trends change. If they don't have an answer or aren't talking about research and development you still might be able to buy into the trend but not with that franchisor.

Don't invest more than you can afford to lose. Bank your money and look at other investments.

Don't fall in love with a trend. Trends are fickle. Adored one day, they can become one-hit wonders the next. Buy on business sense not on emotions.

Source: Sara Wilson, "All the Rage," *Entrepreneur,* January 2005, http://www.entrepreneur.com.

Is Franchising in Your Future?

Are you ready to be a franchisee? Before taking the plunge ask yourself some searching questions: Are you excited about a specific franchise concept? Are you willing to work hard and put in long hours? Do you have the necessary financial resources? Do you have prior business experience? Do your expectations and personal goals match the franchisors?

Qualities that rank high on franchisors' lists are passion about the franchise concept, desire to be your own boss, willingness to make a substantial time commitment, assertiveness, optimism, patience, and integrity. Prior business experience is also a definite plus, and some franchisors prefer or require experience in their field.

EXPANDING AROUND THE GLOBE

Setting Up (Sandwich) Shop in China

Lured by China's fast-food industry, estimated at $15 billion, Jim Bryant, 50, was not the only entrepreneur to discover it is hard to do business in China. In ten years Bryant has opened 19 Subway stores in Beijing—only half the number he was supposed to have by now—while other companies like Chili's and Dunkin' Donuts have given up their Chinese operations altogether.

Subway, or Sai Bei Wei (Mandarin for "tastes better than others"), is now the third-largest U.S. fast-food chain in China, right behind McDonald's and KFC, and all its stores are profitable. Although Bryant had never eaten a Subway sandwich before, Jana Brands, the company Bryant worked for in China, sold $20 million in crab to Subway annually, so he knew it was big business. When Subway founder Fred DeLuca visited Beijing in 1994, Bryant took him to a place not on the official tour: McDonald's. It was Sunday night and the place was packed. "We could open 20,000 Subways here and not scratch the surface," Bryant remembers De Luca saying.

Two weeks later Bryant called Subway's headquarters in Milford, Connecticut, and asked to be the company representative in China. He would recruit local entrepreneurs, train them to become franchisees, and act as a liaison between them and the company. He would receive half the initial $10,000 franchise fee and one-third of their 8 percent royalty fees. He could also open his own Subway restaurants. Steve Forman, the founder of Jana Brands, invested $1 million in return for a 75 percent stake.

All foreign businesses in China had to be joint ventures with local partners, so Bryant used the Chinese business practice of relying on local relationships to find a manager for his first restaurant in Beijing. The project ran into problems immediately. Work on the store was delayed and construction costs soared. It didn't take Bryant long to realize that he and Forman had been swindled out of $200,000.

When it finally opened, the restaurant was a hit among Americans in Beijing, but the locals weren't sure what to make of it. They didn't know how to order and didn't like the idea of touching their food, so they held the sandwich vertically, peeled off the paper, and ate it like a banana. Most of all, the Chinese didn't seem to want sandwiches.

But Subway did little to alter its menu—something that still irks some Chinese franchisees. "Subway should have at least one item tailored to Chinese tastes to show they respect local culture," says Luo Bing Ling, a Beijing franchisee. Bryant thinks that with time sandwiches will catch on in China. Maybe he's right: Tuna salad, which he couldn't give away at first, is now the number one seller.[10]

Critical Thinking Questions
- What are some of the main problems U.S. franchisors encounter when attempting to expand their business in a country like China?
- What steps can franchisors take to ensure a smooth and successful launch of a new franchise business in a foreign country?

So what can you do to prepare when considering the purchase of a franchise? When evaluating franchise opportunities, professional guidance can prevent expensive mistakes so interview advisers to find those that are right for you. Selecting an attorney with franchise experience will hasten the review of your franchise agreement. Getting to know your banker will speed up the loan process if you plan to finance your purchase with a bank loan, so stop by and introduce yourself. The proper real estate is a critical component for a successful retail franchise, so establish a relationship with a commercial real estate broker to begin scouting locations. Doing your homework can spell the difference between success and failure, and some early preparation can help lay the groundwork for the successful launch of your franchised business.

If the franchise route to business ownership seems right for you, begin educating yourself on the franchise process by investigating various franchise opportunities. You should research a franchise company thoroughly before making any financial commitment. Once you've narrowed your choices, ask for the *Uniform Franchise Offering Circular (UFOC)* for that franchisor, and read it thoroughly. The Federal Trade Commission (FTC) requires franchisors to prepare this document, which provides a wealth of information about the franchisor including its history, operating style, management, past or pending litigation, the franchisee's financial obligations, and any restrictions on the sale of units. Interviewing current and past franchisees is another essential step. And most franchise systems use computers so if you are not computer literate, take a class in the basics.

Would-be franchisees should also check recent issues of small-business magazines such as *Franchise Zone, Entrepreneur, Inc., Business Start Ups,* and *Success* for industry trends, ideas on promising franchise opportunities, and advice on how to choose and run a franchise. The International Franchise Association Web site at **http://www.franchise.org** has links to *Franchise World Magazine* and other useful sites. (For other franchise-related sites, see the "Working the Net" questions.)

> **concept check**
>
> Describe franchising and the main parties to the transaction.
>
> Summarize the major advantages and disadvantages of franchising.
>
> Why has franchising proved so popular?

Mergers and Acquisitions

 6 Why are mergers and acquisitions important to a company's overall growth?

merger
The combination of two or more firms to form one new company.

A **merger** occurs when two or more firms combine to form one new company. For example, in 2005 Bank of America acquired MBNA, one of the largest issuers of credit cards and payment products, for $35 billion. The transaction gives the bank access to MBNA's large customer base, to which it can now offer its many deposit, lending, and investment products and services. The acquisition creates one of the world's largest card providers. "It's really a much larger story about two companies with complementary strengths," says Bank of America Chairman and CEO Kenneth D. Lewis. "The result will be the country's top retailer of financial services with the size and scale to drive distribution and marketing efficiencies." Mergers like this one, in a well-established industry, can produce winning results in terms of improved efficiency and cost savings.[11]

acquisition
The purchase of a target company by another corporation or by an investor group typically negotiated with the target company board of directors.

In an **acquisition**, a corporation or investor group finds a target company and negotiates with its board of directors to purchase it. In Procter & Gamble's recent $57 billion acquisition of Gillette, P & G was the acquirer, Gillette the target company.[12]

Worldwide merger activity in 2005 exceeded $2.7 trillion for both completed and announced deals, an increase of 38 percent compared to 2004. This trend continued into 2006, with first quarter merger transactions totaling $923 billion.[13] Exhibit 5.12 lists the top 10 U.S. merger deals in 2005. We will discuss the increase in international mergers later in this chapter.

horizontal merger
A merger of companies at the same stage in the same industry; done to reduce costs, expand product offerings, or reduce competition.

Types of Mergers

The three main types of mergers are horizontal, vertical, and conglomerate. In a **horizontal merger**, companies at the same stage in the same industry merge to reduce

CONCEPT *in Action*

Media mogul Rupert Murdoch, formerly an Internet naysayer, now believes the Web is the future of media. The News Corporation CEO and wizard behind Fox News acquired the social networking site MySpace in 2005 and has committed billions for additional Net-targeted purchases. Murdoch claims to be shopping for "sticky" sites—ones with popular features such as community networking, music file sharing, instant messaging, and photo publishing. *What factors are driving the new wave of Internet-based acquisitions?*

---

costs, expand product offerings, or reduce competition. Many of the largest mergers are horizontal mergers to achieve economies of scale. Its $1.25 billion acquisition of trucking company Overnite, allows UPS, the world's largest shipping carrier, to step up expansion of its heavy freight–delivery business, thus expanding its product offerings.[14]

vertical merger
A merger of companies at different stages in the same industry; done to gain control over supplies of resources or to gain access to different markets.

In a **vertical merger**, a company buys a firm in its same industry, often involved in an earlier or later stage of the production or sales process. Buying a supplier of raw materials, a distribution company, or a customer, gives the acquiring firm more control. A good example of this is Google's acquisition of Urchin Software Corp., a San Diego–based company that sells "Web analytics," software and services that help companies track the effectiveness of their Web sites and online advertising. The move enables Google to bolster the software tools it provides to its advertisers.[15]

conglomerate merger
A merger of companies in unrelated businesses; done to reduce risk.

A **conglomerate merger** brings together companies in unrelated businesses to reduce risk. Combining companies whose products have different seasonal patterns or respond differently to business cycles can result in more stable sales. The Philip Morris Company, now called Altria, started out in the tobacco industry but diversified as early as the 1960s with the acquisition of Miller Brewing Company. It diversified into the food industry with its subsequent purchase of General Foods, Kraft

---

Exhibit 5.12 > Largest U.S. Merger Deals, 2005

Acquirer	Target	Deal Value in Billions
Procter & Gamble (U.S)	Gillete (U.S.)	$54.9
Bank of America (U.S.)	MBNA (U.S.)	35.8
ConocoPhillips (U.S.)	Burlington Resources (U.S.)	35.4
Boston Scientific (U.S.)	Guidant (U.S.)*	24.9
Investor Group (U.S.)	Adelphia Commun (U.S.)*	17.6
ChevronTexaco (U.S.)	Unocal (U.S.)	17.1
SBC Communications (U.S.)	AT&T (U.S.)	14.7
Koch Forest Products (U.S.)	Georgia-Pacific (U.S.)	12.6
MetLife (U.S.)	Travelers (U.S.)	11.7
FPL Group (U.S.)	Constellation Energy (U.S.)*	11.3

Source: Thomson Financial, cited in "Biggest World-Wide Deals," *Wall Street Journal*, January 3, 2006, p. R3.

Note: Excludes spinoffs, withdrawn deals, and open-market purchases *Pending transactions

Foods, and Nabisco, among others. Current product categories include confectionery, cookies, snack foods, powdered soft drinks, convenience foods, cheese, and coffee.

A specialized, financially motivated type of merger, the **leveraged buyout (LBO)**, became popular in the 1980s but is less common today. LBOs are corporate takeovers financed by large amounts of borrowed money—as much as 90 percent of the purchase price. LBOs can be started by outside investors or the corporation's management. For example, the Dolan family, founders of Cablevision Systems Corp., announced plans to privatize the cable company. The proposed $7.9 billion transaction will enable Cablevision to be more nimble as it contends with phone company Verizon Communications Inc.'s preparation to launch television service in its service area.[16]

Often a belief that a company is worth more than the value of all its stock is what drives an LBO. They buy the stock and take the company private, expecting to increase cash flow by improving operating efficiency or selling off units for cash to pay off debt. Although some LBOs do improve efficiency, many do not live up to investor expectations or generate enough cash to pay their debt.

leveraged buyout (LBO)
A corporate takeover financed by large amounts of borrowed money; can be started by outside investors or the corporation's management.

Merger Motives

Although headlines tend to focus on mega-mergers, "merger mania" affects small companies too, and motives for mergers and acquisitions tend to be similar regardless of the company's size. The goal is often strategic: to improve overall performance of the merged firms through cost savings, elimination of overlapping operations, improved purchasing power, increased market share, or reduced competition. Oracle Corp. recently announced it will pay $5.85 billion to acquire Siebel Systems, it largest competitor in the sales automation programs market.[17]

Company growth, broadening product lines, acquiring technology or management skills, and the ability to quickly acquire new markets, are other motives for acquiring a company. Yahoo Inc.'s $1 billion cash purchase of a 40 percent stake in China's biggest online commerce firm, Alibaba.com, instantly strengthens its ties to the world's second largest Internet market.[18]

Purchasing a company can also offer a faster, less risky, less costly option than developing products or markets in-house, or expanding internationally. eBay's purchase of Skype Technologies, an Internet phone provider based in Luxembourg, for $2.6 billion in cash and stock, is a move to boost trading on its online auction site.[19]

Another motive for acquisitions is financial restructuring—cutting costs, selling off units, laying off employees, and refinancing the company to increase its value to stockholders. Financially motivated mergers are based not on the potential to achieve economies of scale, but rather on the acquirer's belief that the target has hidden value to be unlocked through restructuring. Most financially motivated mergers involve larger companies. Financier Eddie Lampert nursed ailing retailer Kmart out of bankruptcy before orchestrating its recent acquisition of retailing giant Sears for $11 billion.[20]

Emerging Truths

Along with the technology boom of the late 1990s, merger activity also soared. Total annual transactions averaged $1.6 trillion a year. Companies were using their stock, which had been pushed to unrealistically high levels, to buy each other. When the technology bubble burst in 2000, the level of merger activity dropped as well. It fell even further after the United States was attacked September 11, 2001. Then massive corporate wrongdoing began to surface. Stocks plummeted in reaction to these events, and merger transactions, which generally track stock market movements, fell as a result.

But merger activity is once again on the rise. Propelled by a strong economy, low interest rates, good credit, rising stock prices, and stockpiles of cash, U.S. merger activity reached $1.3 trillion in 2005, up 56 percent from the year before. Companies that

CONCEPT *in Action*

Although the motives for mergers and acquisitions range from cutting costs and increasing market share to broadening product lines, some mergers have unintended negative consequences. The disastrous merger of AOL and Time Warner wiped out more than $200 million in shareholder value. Kmart's acquisition of Sears, although creating the nation's third largest retailer, caused discounter-shy Nike to pull shoes from Sears stores. *Why do mergers often fail to meet expectations?*

had postponed looking for acquisition targets reentered the merger market, and strong merger activity continued into 2006.[21]

Size is definitely an advantage when competing in the global marketplace, but bigger does not always mean better in the merger business. Study results show that heady mega-mergers can, in fact, be a bust for investors who own those shares. So companies are wise to consider their options before stuffing their dollars in the biggest merger slot machine they can find. In their eagerness to snare a deal, many buyers pay a premium that wipes out the merger's entire potential economic gain. Often managers envision grand synergies that prove illusory or unworkable, or buy a company that isn't what it seems—not fully understanding what they are getting.

Integrating acquisitions is both an art and a science. Acquirers often underestimate the costs and logistical nightmare of consolidating the operations of merged companies with very different cultures. As a result, they may fail to keep key employees aboard, keep sales forces selling, and customers happy.

Companies will always continue to seek out acquisition candidates, but the fundamental business case for merging will have to be strong. So what should companies look for to identify mergers with a better-than-even chance of turning out well?

- A purchase price that is low enough—a 10 percent premium over market as opposed to 50 percent—so the buyer doesn't need heroic synergies to make the deal work.
  - A target that is significantly smaller than the buyer—and in a business the buyer understands. The more "transformational" the deal, such as entering a new business arena, the bigger the risk.
  - A buyer who pays in cash and not overinflated stock.
  - Evidence that the deal makes both business and financial sense and isn't purely the brainchild of an empire-building CEO. Mergers are tough—culturally, commercially, and logistically. The most important quality a company can bring to a merger may be humility.

concept check

Differentiate between a merger and an acquisition.

What are the most common motives for corporate mergers and acquisitions?

Describe the different types of corporate mergers.

Trends in Business Ownership

7 What current trends will affect the business organizations of the future?

As we learned in Chapter 1, an awareness of trends in the business environment is critical to business success. Many social, demographic, and economic factors affect how businesses organize. When reviewing options for starting or organizing a business or choosing a career path, consider the following trends.

"Baby Boomers" Drive Franchise Trends

We all hear and read a great deal about the "graying of America," which refers to the "Baby Boomer" generation heading towards retirement age. As we learned in Chapter 1, this unprecedented demographic phenomenon—in 2006 the first of 78 million members of the Baby Boom generation turned 60—is driving the ongoing battle to stay young, slim, and healthy. Boomers have transformed every life stage they've touched so far, and their demographic weight means that business opportunities are created wherever they go.

With their interest in staying fit, Boomers are contributing to the growth of fitness and weight-loss franchises. In just the past year, this category in *Entrepreneur's* Franchise 500 has grown from 8 to 17 franchisors. And according to the International Health, Racquet & Sportsclub Association, 39.4 million Americans belong to a health club—up from 24.1 million 10 years ago—so there are plenty of consumers feeding this growing trend. Among the over-55 age group, about one-quarter belong to health clubs.[22]

Another area of Boomer-driven franchise growth is elder care. Founded in 1994, Home Instead Senior Care is recognized as one of the world's fastest growing franchise companies in the eldercare market, with a network of over 600 independently owned and operated franchises in six countries. And as the world's population continues to age, the need for its unique services will continue to increase.

Home Instead Senior Care provides a meaningful solution for the elderly who prefer to remain at home. Compared with the annual cost for a nursing home placement ($60,000), home care at around $45,000 a year is somewhat more affordable. Elder quality of life is enhanced by Home Instead Senior Care's part-time, full-time, and around-the-clock services, designed for people who are capable of managing their physical needs but require some assistance and supervision. Home Instead Senior Care provides meal preparation, companionship, light housekeeping, medication reminders, incidental transportation, and errands. These services make it possible for the elderly to remain in the familiar comfort of their own homes for a longer period of time.[23]

But the best deal yet may be adult day services, one of the top 10 fastest-growing franchises and "still one of the best-kept secrets around" according to *Entrepreneur* magazine. Based on the concept of day care services for children, Sarah Adult Day Services, Inc. offers a franchising opportunity that meets the two criteria for a successful and socially responsible business: a booming demographic market with great potential for growth, and excellent elder care. Programs like SarahCare centers are highly affordable for its clients, ranging from $10,000 to $15,000 a year. The SarahCare franchise allows entrepreneurs to become part of an expanding industry while restoring a sense of dignity and vibrancy to the lives of older adults.[24]

Boomers Rewrite the Rules of Retirement

At age 64, Bob Drucker could be the poster child for retirement except that the concept makes him recoil. Drucker is living his dream. He and his wife have a large house on Long Island where Drucker kicks back by floating in his pool when he's not spoiling his granddaughters with trips to Disneyland.

"The only way you can get me out of here is to carry me out," Drucker says, referring to RxUSA, the online pharmacy he founded and runs in Port Washington, New York. "I love my work and I cannot imagine sitting home and doing nothing."

CONCEPT *in Action*

Baby Boomers racing into their 60s and beyond continue to exhibit the free-spirited and independent tendencies that marked their youth. Yet as they age, numerous eldercare services are coming alongside to provide a little extra help as needed. Among the fastest-growing eldercare businesses are those that specialize in non-medical services. Such services can range from illness recovery and emergency monitoring to helping with errands. *What other services might have popular appeal with aging Baby Boomers?*

© AP PHOTO/CHARLIE NEIBERGALL

Drucker is not alone. Today's Boomers are working longer at their jobs and embracing post-retirement second careers, which often means starting their own small business.[25] As retirees opt to go into business for themselves, they are choosing different forms of business organizations depending on their needs and goals. Some may start small consulting businesses using the simple sole proprietorship form of business organization, while couples or friends might choose to become partners in a retail or franchise venture.

The more healthy and energetic the Baby Boomer generation remains, the more interested it is in staying active and engaged—and that may mean postponing retirement or not retiring at all. A 2004 American Association of Retired Persons (AARP) report found that as this record number of Americans approaches retirement age many are not slowing down. In fact, 79 percent of Boomers plan to work in some capacity during their retirement years, and many of these will start their own small businesses.[26]

Mergers and Foreign Investment Boom, Too

After shunning big deals for more than three years, corporate America has launched a new merger wave. From January 2005 through March 2006, U.S. companies announced deals totaling more than $1.6 trillion. Many of these deals were large ones, with 20 U.S. acquisitions exceeding $10 billion. The largest deal, announced in March 2006, was AT&T's acquisition of BellSouth for $66.7 billion. In addition, foreign merger activity has reached a new high. Worldwide deal volume for just the first quarter of 2006 was $923 billion, the third highest quarter in history. The two quarters that surpassed this figure, however, were in 1999 and 2000, when the stock market reached all-time highs before the bubble burst. European companies announced more than $1.7 trillion in deals from January 2005 through March 2006. The increase is the result of improving economic growth and better stock prices.[27]

This current boom in mergers feels different from earlier mergermania, however. New players are entering the arena, and the number of U.S. and foreign companies making cross-border acquisitions has increased. Whether these new mergers will be good for the global economy remains to be seen. Transactions that lead to cost savings, streamlined operations, and more funding for research and capital investment in new facilities will have positive affects on profitability. Many deals, however, may fail to live up to the acquirers' expectations.

Foreign investment in U.S. companies has also increased dramatically. Between 1985 and 2004, annual foreign direct investment climbed from $185 billion to almost $1.5 trillion.[28] The jump is the result of a worldwide boom in mergers and acquisitions and the need to finance America's growing trade deficit, as well as the continued attraction of the U.S. economy to investors worldwide.

And what about American investment in foreign economies? It is skyrocketing as U.S. businesses seek out opportunities in developing countries. The U.S. Department of Commerce reports that outflows from the United States into foreign countries now exceeds $2 trillion a year.[29] In addition to the attraction of cheap labor and resources, American companies of all sizes are beginning to tap the intellectual capital of developing economies such as China and India, outsourcing such functions as payroll, information technology (IT), Web/e-mail hosting, customer relationship management (CRM), and human resources (HR) to keep costs under control and enhance profitability.

concept check

What are some of the demographic trends currently impacting American business?

As a prospective business owner what could you do to capitalize on these trends?

What other economic trends are influencing today's business organizations?

Summary of Learning Goals

1 **What are the advantages and disadvantages of the sole proprietorship form of business organization?**

The advantages of sole proprietorships include ease and low cost of formation, the owner's rights to all profits, the owner's control of the business, relative freedom from government regulation, absence of special taxes, and ease of dissolution. Disadvantages include owner's unlimited liability for debts and personal absorption of all losses, difficulty in raising capital, limited managerial expertise, difficulty in finding qualified employees, large personal time commitment, and unstable business life.

2 **What are the advantages of operating as a partnership, and what downside risks should partners consider?**

The advantages of partnerships include ease of formation, availability of capital, diversity of managerial skills and expertise, flexibility to respond to changing business conditions, no special taxes, and relative freedom from government control. Disadvantages include unlimited liability for general partners, potential for conflict between partners, sharing of profits, and difficulty exiting or dissolving the partnership. Partnerships can be formed as either general or limited partnerships. In a general partnership the operations of the business are controlled by one or more general partners with unlimited liability. The partners co-own the assets and share the profits. Each partner is individually liable for all debts and contracts of the partnership. In a limited partnership the limited partners are financial partners whose liability is limited to their investment; they do not participate in the firm's operations.

3 **How does the corporate structure provide advantages and disadvantages to a company, and what are the major types of corporations?**

A corporation is a legal entity chartered by a state. Its organizational structure includes stockholders who own the corporation, a board of directors elected by the stockholders to govern the firm, and officers who carry out the goals and policies set by the board. Stockholders can sell or transfer their shares at any time, and are entitled to receive profits in the form of dividends. Advantages of corporations include limited liability, ease of transferring ownership, unlimited life tax deductions, and the ability to attract financing. Disadvantages include double taxation of profits, the cost and complexity of formation, and government restrictions.

4 **What other options for business organization does a company have in addition to sole proprietorships, partnerships, and corporations?**

Businesses can also organize as limited liability companies, cooperatives, joint ventures, and franchises. A limited liability company (LLC) provides limited liability for its owners, but is taxed like a partnership. These two features make it an attractive form of business organization for many small firms. Cooperatives are collectively owned by individuals or businesses with similar interests that combine to achieve more economic power. Cooperatives distribute all profits to their members. Two types of cooperatives are buyer and seller cooperatives. A joint venture is an alliance of two or more companies formed to undertake a special project. Joint ventures can be set up in various ways, through partnerships or special-purpose corporations. By sharing management expertise, technology, products, and financial and operational resources, companies can reduce the risk of new enterprises.

5 **What makes franchising an appropriate form of organization for some types of business, and why does it continue to grow in importance?**

Franchising is one of the fastest-growing forms of business ownership. It involves an agreement between a franchisor, the supplier of goods or services, and a franchisee, an individual or company that buys the right to sell the franchisor's products in a specific area. With a franchise the business owner does not have to start from scratch, but buys a business concept with a proven product or service and operating methods. The franchisor provides use of a recognized brand-name product and operating concept, as well as management training and financial assistance. Franchises can be costly to start, and operating freedom is restricted because the franchisee must conform to the franchisor's standard procedures. The growth in franchising is attributed to its ability to expand business operations quickly into new geographic areas with limited capital investment.

6 Why are mergers and acquisitions important to a company's overall growth?

In a merger, two companies combine to form one company. In an acquisition, one company or investor group buys another. Companies merge for strategic reasons to improve overall performance of the merged firm through cost savings, eliminating overlapping operations, improving purchasing power, increasing market share, or reducing competition. Desired company growth, broadened product lines, and the rapid acquisition of new markets, technology, or management skills are other motives. Another motive for merging is financial restructuring—cutting costs, selling off units, laying off employees, and refinancing the company to increase its value to stockholders.

There are three types of mergers. In a horizontal merger, companies at the same stage in the same industry combine for more economic power, to diversify, or to win greater market share. A vertical merger involves the acquisition of a firm that serves an earlier or later stage of the production or sales process, such as a supplier or sales outlet. In a conglomerate merger, unrelated businesses come together to reduce risk through diversification.

7 What current trends will affect the business organizations of the future?

Americans are getting older but continue to open new businesses, from sole proprietorships to partnerships, corporations to franchise operations. The service sector is booming in efforts to meet the demand for fitness, health, and elder care.

Other key trends include an escalation of worldwide foreign investment through the number of mergers taking place. All forms of business organization can benefit from outsourcing, tapping into the intellectual capital of developing countries.

Key Terms

acquisition   188
board of directors   178
buyer cooperative   181
conglomerate merger   189
cooperative   181
corporation   175
C corporation   179
franchise agreement   183
franchisee   183
franchising   183
franchisor   183
general partners   173
general partnership   173

horizontal merger   188
joint venture   182
leveraged buyout (LBO)   190
limited liability company (LLC)   180
limited partners   173
limited partnership   173
merger   188
partnership   172
S corporation   179
seller cooperative   181
sole proprietorship   170
stockholders (or shareholders)   178
vertical merger   189

Preparing for Tomorrow's Workplace: SCANS

1. Suppose you are considering two job offers for a computer programming position at: a two-year-old consulting firm with 10 employees owned by a sole proprietor, or a publicly traded software developer with sales of $500 million. In addition to comparing the specific job responsibilities, consider the following:
   - Which company offers better training? Do you prefer the on-the-job training you'll get at the small company, or do you want formal training programs as well?

- Which position offers the chance to work on a variety of assignments?
- What are the opportunities for advancement? Employee benefits?
- What happens if the owner of the young company gets sick or decides to sell the company?
- Which company offers a better working environment for you?

Answering these and similar questions will help you decide which job meets your particular needs. (Resources, Information)

2. Before starting your own company you should know the legal requirements in your area. Call the appropriate city or county departments, such as licensing, health, and zoning, to find out what licenses and permits you need, and any other requirements you must meet. Do the requirements vary depending on the type of company? Are there restrictions on starting a home-based business? Contact your secretary of state or other agency that handles corporations to get information on how to incorporate. (Information)

3. Bridget Jones wants to open her own business selling her handmade chocolates over the Internet. Although she has some money saved and could start the business on her own, she is concerned about her lack of bookkeeping and management experience. A friend mentions he knows an experienced businessman seeking involvement with a start-up company. As Bridget's business consultant, prepare recommendations for Bridget regarding an appropriate form of business organization, outlining the issues she should consider and the risks involved, supported by reasons for your suggestions. (Interpersonal, Information)

4. You and a partner co-own Swim-Clean, a successful pool supply and cleaning service. Because sales have tapered off, you want to expand your operations to another town 10 miles away. Given the high costs of expanding, you decide to sell Swim-Clean franchises. The idea takes off and soon you have 25 units throughout the region. Your success results in an invitation to speak at a local Rotary Club luncheon. Prepare a brief presentation describing how you evaluated the benefits and risks of becoming a franchisor, the problems you encountered, and how you established good working relationships with your franchisees. (Information)

5. Do you have what it takes to be a successful franchisee? Start by making a list of your interests and skills, and do a self-assessment using some of the suggestions in this chapter. Next you need to narrow the field of thousands of different franchise systems. At Franchise Handbook Online (**http://www.franchise1.com**), you'll find articles with checklists to help you thoroughly research a franchise and its industry, as well as a directory of franchise opportunities. Armed with this information, develop a questionnaire to evaluate a prospective franchise. (Resources, Interpersonal, Information)

6. Find news of a recent merger using an online search or a business periodical like *Business Week, Fortune,* or the *Wall Street Journal.* Research the merger using a variety of sources including the company's Web site and news articles. Discover the motives behind the merger, the problems facing the new entity, and the company's progress toward achieving its objectives. (Information)

7. **Team Activity** After pulling one too many all-nighters, you realize your college needs an on-campus coffee/food delivery service, and decide this might be a good business opportunity for you and some friends. Split the class into small groups. Start by outlining the management, technical, and financial resources that are needed to start this company. Then evaluate what resources your group brings to the table, and what you will need from partners. Using Exhibit 5.2 as a guide, develop a list of questions for potential partners. After each group presents its findings to the class, it should pair up with another group that seems to offer additional resources. Interview the other group's members using your questions to decide if the teams could work together and if you would proceed with this venture. (Resources, Interpersonal)

Ethics Activity

After seeing a Quiznos franchise recruitment infomercial to recruit franchisees, you are tempted to apply to open your own Quiznos sub shop. However, your research on the company turns up some disturbing information. Many current franchisees are unhappy with the company's management and practices, among them excessive food costs, lack of promised support, and selling new franchise locations that are too close to existing stores. A group of New Jersey franchisees has sued Quiznos for selling them franchises but not providing locations 18 months after taking their franchise fees. Some franchise owners question Quiznos' purchasing tactics, choosing food and beverage suppliers based on the referral fees it receives instead of the lowest cost provider. Other franchisees have suffered major financial losses.

Quiznos, which owns or operates more than 4,000 sub shops, disputes the various claims. President Steve Shaffer points out that in a franchise operation, there will always be unhappy franchisees and those who can't make a success of their units. Besides, Quiznos' franchise offering materials clearly state that the company may open stores in any locations it selects.

Using a Web search tool, locate articles about this topic and then write responses to the following questions. Be sure to support your arguments and cite your sources.

Ethical Dilemma: What are Quiznos' obligations to its franchisees? Is it ethical for the company to open new franchises very close to existing units and to choose vendors based on fees to the parent company rather than the cost to franchisees?

Sources: Kristi Arellano, "Quiznos' Success Not without Problems," *Denver Post,* June 19, 2005, p. K1; Dina Berta, "Quiznos Denies Franchisees' Charges of Cost Gouging, Encroachment Problems," *Nation's Restaurant News,* June 20, 2005, P. 1+; "Quiznos Denies Fraud Suit Charges by 17 Franchisees," *Nation's Restaurant News,* May 16, 2005, p. 102; Quiznos' Web site, http://www.quiznos.com (May 23, 2006).

Working the Net

1. Consult Entrepreneur.com at **http://www.entrepreneur.com**. Click on Business Structure to read articles about S corporations and LLCs. If you were starting a company, which would you choose, and why?

2. Research how to form a corporation and LLC in your state using search engines to find relevant sites. Here are two to get you started: **http://www.corporate.com** and **http://www.usa-corporate.com**. Find out what steps are necessary to set up a corporation in your state. How do the fees compare with other states? If you were incorporating a business, what state would you choose and why?

3. The Federal Trade Commission is the government agency that monitors and regulates franchises. Visit the FTC site (**http://www.ftc.gov**) and explore the links to its resources on franchising, including details on the legal responsibilities of franchisors and franchisees. What kinds of problems should a prospective franchisee look out for when considering a franchise? What kinds of scams are typical in the franchise industry?

4. Go to **http://www.entrepreneur.com/franzone** and enter Franchise Quiz as the search term. In the article, "Are You Suited to Be a Franchisee?" at *Entrepreneur's FranchiseZone,* take the first section (questions 1–33) of the quiz. What did you discover about yourself? Were you surprised at the results?

5. Select three franchises that interest you. Research them at sites such as the Franchise Handbook Online (**http://www.franchise1.com**), *Entrepreneur* magazine's Franchise 500 (**http://www.entrepreneur.com**), and Be the Boss (**www.betheboss.com**). Prepare a chart comparing your selections, including history, number and location of units, financial requirements (initial franchise fee, other start-up costs, royalty and advertising fees), and any other information that would help you evaluate the franchises.

6. *Inc.* Magazine (**http://www.inc.com**) has many franchising articles in its section on Buying a Business or Franchise. They offer insights into how franchisors and franchisees can better manage their businesses. Using the site's resources, discuss ways the owner of a franchise can motivate employees. What specific revenue items and expenses should you monitor daily in a franchise restaurant business to insure that you are profitable?

Organic Farmers Protect Their Turf

With more and more small family farms being threatened with extinction, a group of seven farmers decided in 1988 to create a solution, one which has grown into the largest organic farming cooperative in America, and one of the largest organic brands in the nation. Under the leadership of George Siemon, the farmers founded Organic Valley, a farming cooperative wholly owned and operated by organic farmers who shared a belief that a sustainable approach to agriculture could help rural farm communities survive.

Over the years, those original founding farmers have been joined by 682 others in states ranging from California to Maine—producing milk, eggs, meat, soy, juice, and produce—and the cooperative continues to grow, family farm by family farm. As a result, Organic Valley has become the most successful organic farmer-owned cooperative in the world.

What attracts these farmers to the cooperative style of doing business? First, the support and resources of a large and successful farming cooperative comes in handy in an industry where large corporations have swallowed over 600,000 family farms since 1960. Second, it provides its farmer-owners with independence for their families and their way of life because the farmers know they can rely on a stable income.

The farmers participate in all aspects of the production process, such as selecting the plants, testing the quality and flavor of their products, and approving packaging and transportation. They also decide how to allocate profits and, most important, establish pricing. A quarterly newsletter makes sure members are kept informed and up to date on legislative and other changes affecting the organic food industry. Organic farmers are required by law to manage their property in an environmentally conscious manner. Crops and animals are isolated from pesticides and herbicides, and land and livestock health is enhanced by means of natural inputs. They shun antibiotics, growth hormones, and steroids in favor of other more holistic methods of managing crops and animals.

So why pay more for organic food products? You are contributing to something that is once again a viable part of the American landscape and culture—small family farms and sustainable rural farming communities in America. When you buy from the Organic Valley Farming Cooperative, more of your dollar goes directly to the farming families who are bringing pure high-quality products to market, farmers who might not otherwise be able to continue farming with their commitment to humane animal treatment, responsible stewardship of the environment, and the safeguarding of our critically important natural resources—soil, air, and water.[30]

Critical Thinking Questions

- Why is the cooperative form of business organization appropriate for Organic Valley?
- Describe how the Organic Valley Farming Cooperative has impacted America's small farmers. What effect has it had on the American cultural landscape?
- Is it worth paying more for organic products so that small family farmers can continue to focus on environmentally conscious and socially responsible farming? Why is this important?

Geeks Rule

"I always wanted to be James Bond," says Robert Stephens, talking about the showmanship that shapes his company's unique corporate culture, and the branding that makes it stand out from its competitors. Stephens originally chose the name Geek Squad to suggest an "army" of employees and disguise the fact that his business originally consisted of just one person—himself.

Who hasn't been in the middle of a project with a looming deadline when the computer crashes and all your files are lost? You would be just one of many individuals happy to see someone from the Geek Squad walk through your door. A quick phone call to 1-800-GEEK-SQUAD answers three important questions—can they fix it, when can they be there, what it will cost—and mobilizes a techie in a distinctively painted black, orange, and white "geekmobile." This uniformed, badge-toting "special agent" visits your home or office site to survey the "crime scene," either fixing the problem on-site, or taking the computer away for repair. Either way, your computer problem is solved. The company prides itself on rapid response times and reasonable rates. Clients are billed on a flat-fee basis rather than an hourly rate and receive a follow-up phone call to make sure everything is working and they are happy.

The company's highly trained techie team makes house calls 365 days a year, providing emergency computer support to panicked cranky clients. These special agents have helped out the likes of rockers U2, Ozzy Osbourne, and the Rolling Stones, even getting to attend their concerts for free.

Started by Stephens in 1994 with $200 and a bicycle, Geek Squad now boasts 5 million customers and 700 locations. Acquired by Best Buy in 2002, Geek Squad now has "precincts" in all Best Buy locations nationwide, in addition to Geek Squad stores in selected cities. The company also operates in Alaska, Hawaii, and Canada.

Even though Stephens set up the business as a corporation, he originally believed it would continue to work best if kept small, and had no interest in franchising the company. "There is always the temptation to expand into other services, through boredom or greed or fear, but I would rather be great at one thing than mediocre at several," he said. Stephens has stayed true to his original vision albeit on a grander scale.[31]

Critical Thinking Questions

Using information from the case and the video, answer the following critical thinking questions:

- Why did Robert Stephens set up his company as a corporation even though he wanted to keep it small?
- What was his goal in establishing such a unique identity for his company?
- What benefits does each party gain from Best Buy's acquisition of Geek Squad? Are there potential disadvantages?

Hot Links Address Book

Which Fortune 500 company had the biggest revenue increase? The highest profits? The highest return to investors? What is the largest entertainment company? Get all the details on U.S. companies at http://www.fortune.com/fortune500

Confused about the differences between regular corporations, S corporations, and LLCs? Compare these three business structures at http://www.4inc.com

Did you know U.S. cooperatives serve some 120 million members, or 4 in 10 Americans? For more co-op statistics, check the National Cooperative Business Association Web site at http://www.ncba.org

Combine your sweet tooth with your good business sense by owning a candy franchise. Indulge yourself by finding out the requirements for owning a Rocky Mountain Chocolate Factory franchise at http://www.rmcf.com

Get an international perspective on mergers and acquisitions in health care, media, and information technology at http://www.broadview.com

Want to know what's hot and what's not in franchising? Improve your chances for success at http://www.entrepreneur.com/franchisezone

CHAPTER 6

Entrepreneurship: Starting and Managing Your Own Business

Learning Goals

After reading this chapter, you should be able to answer these questions:

1. Why do people become entrepreneurs, and what are the different types of entrepreneurs?

2. Which characteristics do successful entrepreneurs share?

3. How do small businesses contribute to the U.S. economy?

4. What are the first steps to take if you are starting your own business?

5. Why does managing a small business present special challenges for the owner?

6. What are the advantages and disadvantages facing owners of small businesses?

7. How does the Small Business Administration help small businesses?

8. What trends are shaping entrepreneurship and small-business ownership?

Exploring Business Careers
Natalie Tessler
Spa Space

If you happen to catch her, Natalie Tessler will be trying simultaneously to find the company checkbook, prepare for a 100-person party, and talk to several employees about clients they are assisting. Her first career, as a lawyer for some of the country's most prestigious firms, required a great deal of educational training. None of that training, however, prepared her for running her own business. "People think that, owning a spa, I'm able to live this glamorous lifestyle," she laughs. "Owning a spa is nothing like going to one—my nails always are broken from fixing equipment; my back is usually in pain from sitting hunched over a computer trying to figure out the budget or our next marketing promotion." President and founder of Spa Space, Tessler is a true entrepreneur, embodying the spirit and drive necessary to see her vision become a reality.

She always knew she wanted to start her own business, a place where she could express herself and highlight her own interests. Not until one night, though, when she was having dinner with a friend, who recently had begun a writing career, did she realize it was time. "I was listening to her talk about how much she loved her job. Her passion and excitement—I wanted that. I wanted something that grabbed me and propelled me through the day—and being a lawyer wasn't it."

She began searching for what "it" was. Although she didn't see herself as an artistically creative person, she did find that she had a tremendous passion and talent for hospitality, entertaining others, and

presentation. Seeking an outlet for that flair, she found the spa industry, an industry where attending to the client is key to success. And after much research, the idea for Spa Space was born.

Tessler wanted to design a spa that focused on something new: creating a comfortable, personalized environment of indulgence while not neglecting the medical technology of proper skin care. "My father's a dermatologist, so we discussed the importance of making this more than a spa where you can get a frou-frou, smell-good treatment that might actually harm your skin. We both thought it was important to create an experience that is as beneficial for people's skin as it is for their emotional well-being." To address this need, Spa Space has a medical advisory board that helps with product selection, treatment design, and staff training.

Armed with a vision and a plan, Tessler turned her sights toward making it a reality. Spa Space opened in 2001 and has received a great deal of national recognition for its service excellence and unique treatments. Today, Tessler speaks of where she wants to take the business next. She has ideas of expanding to other locations and focusing on specific aspects that have proven successful, such as catering to women *and* men and providing a range of group services. Wherever she takes Spa Space next, however, one thing is certain. Through persevering entrepreneurship, she has found her passion and is able to live it every day.

This chapter examines the characteristics and potential of entrepreneurship in the business world.

Typical of many who catch the entrepreneurial bug, Natalie Tessler had a vision and pursued it single-mindedly. She is just one of thousands of entrepreneurs from all age groups and backgrounds. Teenagers are starting fashion-clothing companies (see Catching the Entrepreneurial Spirit) and high-tech firms. College graduates are shunning the "jacket and tie" corporate world to head out on their own. Downsized employees, mid-career executives, and retirees who have worked for others all their lives are forming the companies they have always wanted to own.

Companies started by entrepreneurs and small-business owners make significant contributions to the U.S. and global economies. Hotbeds of innovation, they take leadership roles in technological change and the development of new goods and services. Just how important are small businesses (for our purposes, those with fewer than 500 employees) to our economy? Exhibit 6.1 provides insight into the role of small business in today's economy.

You may be one of the millions of Americans who's considering joining the ranks of business owners. As you read this chapter, you'll learn why entrepreneurship continues to be one of the hottest areas of business activity. Then you'll get the information and tools you need to help you decide whether owning your own company is the right career path for you. Next you'll discover what characteristics you'll need to become a successful entrepreneur. Then we'll look at the importance of small businesses in the economy; guidelines for starting and managing a small business; the many reasons small businesses continue to thrive in the United States; and the role of the Small Business Administration. Finally, the chapter explores the trends that shape entrepreneurship and small-business ownership today.

Entrepreneurship Today

1 Why do people become entrepreneurs, and what are the different types of entrepreneurs?

Brothers Fernando and Santiago Aguerre exhibited entrepreneurial tendencies at an early age. At 8 and 9 years old respectively, they sold strawberries and radishes from a vacant lot near their parents' home in Plata del Mar on the Atlantic coast of Argentina. At 11 and 12 they provided a surfboard repair service from their garage. As teenagers, Fer and Santi, as they call one another, opened Argentina's first surf shop, which led to their most ambitious entrepreneurial venture of all.

The flat-footed brothers found that traipsing across hot sand in flip-flops was uncomfortable, so in 1984 they sank their $4,000 savings into manufacturing their own

---

Exhibit 6.1 > The Economic Impact of Small Business

Today's small businesses:

- Total approximately 25 million in the United States with roughly 75 percent having no employees
- Represent 99.7 percent of all employer firms
- Employ half of all private sector employees and 41 percent of high-tech workers
- Pay 45 percent of the total U.S. private payroll
- Generate 60–80 percent of net new jobs annually
- Are 53 percent home-based and 3 percent franchises
- Create more than 50 percent of non-farm private gross domestic product (GDP)
- Produce 26 percent of known export value

Source: "Frequently Asked Questions," *U.S. Small Business Administration, Office of Advocacy,* http://www.sbu.gov./advo. (May 31, 2006).

All Tied up with Success

Baruch Shemtov channeled his annoyance with his school dress code into a thriving business making neckties—by the time he turned 16 years old. The concept came to him after shedding his own tie—mandatory attire required by his school—and spotting a bandana across the room. "I looked at it and thought it would make a great tie," he recalled. He spent the next five hours crafting a thin tie he wore to class the next day. "People loved it and wanted me to make them one."

With his parents' support, he fashioned a few prototype ties, ultimately hiring a New York manufacturer to produce them in bulk. Each tie is handmade in a very painstaking process, Shemtov says, "But one that makes for a much more luxurious necktie." Why ties, you may ask? "People don't see the tie as something fresh, fun, and fashionable, so I decided I would try to reinvent it. I think the necktie is really the only way men can spice up their wardrobes in the traditional workplace," he says.

What makes Shemtov's designs different? The products feature rare fabrics and patterns and a blend of exotic colors and textures that often can't be reproduced. The result is a tie that is both a fashion statement and a collector's item. "Many end up being limited editions," Shemtov says, "which ensures that no one else is going to have what you're wearing." Selling for around $100 each, the Baruch Shemtov line of bold luxury neckwear has found an eager audience in department stores such as Japanese-based chain Takashimaya, on New York's Fifth Avenue.

Starting and running a business as a teen is one thing, but not the only thing for Shemtov, now only 17 years old. His schoolwork, social life, and extracurricular activities also fill his time. The recent high school graduate has also caught the acting bug, adding that he would like to continue performing and "combine television and design in some way."

But the business won't be neglected, he vowed, even after he entered Harvard University. Shemtov commuted between Massachusetts and New York—visiting his factory, exhibiting his wares, and designing new products—while juggling his studies. "I really began to design and manufacture without the objective of money in mind," Shemtov said. "I do this for my own expression. I want to get my designs out there."[1]

Critical Thinking Questions

- What do you think enabled Baruch Shemtov to start and grow a successful business at such a young age?
- What personal characteristics and skills will he need to continue running his business while also attending college full-time?

---

line of beach sandals. Now offering 119 styles, which retail between $14 and $40, Reef Brazil sandals have become the world's trendiest beach footwear, with a presence in nearly every surf shop in the United States. Reef (they dropped Brazil from the name), also makes regular shoes, purses, and apparel.

The leading manufacturer of beach sandals, the company produces 25,000 pairs a day with distribution in more than 100 countries, generating $100 million in revenues by 2004. Christy Glass Lowe, who monitors surf apparel for USBX Advisory Services, notes, "They (Reef) built a brand from nothing and now they're the dominant market share leader."

The Aguerres, who currently live two blocks from one another in La Jolla, California, sold Reef to VF Corporation for more than $100 million in September 2005. In selling Reef, "We've finally found our freedom," Fernando says. "We traded money for time," adds Santiago. Fernando, 47, remains active with surfing organizations, serving as president of the International Surfing Association, among others. Santi, 45, raises funds for his favorite not-for-profit, SurfAid. Both brothers are enjoying serving an industry that has served them so well.[2]

The United States is blessed with a wealth of entrepreneurs such as the Aguerres. According to research by the Small Business Administration, two-thirds of college students intend to be entrepreneurs at some point in their careers, aspiring to become the next Bill Gates or Jeff Bezos, founder of Amazon.com. But before you put out any money or expend energy and time, you'd be wise to check out Exhibit 6.2 on the next page for some preliminary advice.

The desire to be one's own boss cuts across all age, gender, and ethnic lines. Results of a 2002 U.S. Census Bureau survey of business owners released on July 28, 2005, shows that minority groups and women are becoming business owners at a much higher rate than the national average. Exhibit 6.3 on the next page demonstrates these minority-owned business demographics.

Why has entrepreneurship remained such a strong part of the foundation of the U.S. business system for so many years? Because today's global economy rewards innovative, flexible companies that can respond quickly to changes in the business environment. Such companies are started by **entrepreneurs**, people with vision, drive,

entrepreneurs
People with vision, drive, and creativity who are willing to take the risk of starting and managing a business to make a profit, or greatly changing the scope and direction of an existing firm.

Exhibit 6.2 > Innovator's Inventory

Here are some questions would-be entrepreneurs should ask themselves:

1. What is new and novel about your idea?
2. Are there similar products/services out there? If so, what makes yours better?
3. Who is your target market? How many people would use your product or service?
4. What about production costs? How much do you think the market will pay?
5. How defensible is the concept? Is there good intellectual property?
6. Is this innovation strategic to my business?
7. Is the innovation easy to communicate?
8. How might this product evolve over time? Would it be possible to expand it into a product line? Can it be updated/enhanced in future versions?
9. Where would someone buy this product?
10. What are the challenges involved in developing this product?

Source: Adapted from Mike Collins, "Before You Start–Innovator's Inventory," *Wall Street Journal*, May 9, 2005, p. R4. Copyright © Dow Jones and Company, Inc. All rights reserved. Reproduced by permission.

Exhibit 6.3 > Increases in Minority-Owned Businesses

A recent survey shows minority-owned businesses increasing at a rapid rate from 1997 to 2002:

- 1.2 million black-owned businesses in 2002 represents an increase of 45 percent from l997.
- 1.6 million Hispanic-owned businesses in 2002 represents an increase of 31 percent from 1997.
- 1.1 million Asian-owned businesses in 2002 represents an increase of 24 percent from 1997.
- 32,299 Hawaiian/Pacific Islander–owned businesses in 2002 represents an increase of 67 percent from 1997.
- 6.5 million women-owned businesses in 2002 represents an increase of 20 percent from 1997.

Source: "Minority Groups Increasing Business Ownership at Higher Rate than National Average," *U.S. Census Bureau*, July 28, 2005, http://www.census.gov.

and creativity, who are willing to take the risk of starting and managing a business to make a profit.

Entrepreneur or Small-Business Owner?

The term *entrepreneur* is often used in a broad sense to include most small-business owners. The two groups share some of the same characteristics, and we'll see that some of the reasons for becoming an entrepreneur or a small-business owner are very similar. But there is a difference between entrepreneurship and small-business management. Entrepreneurship involves taking a risk, either to create a new business or to greatly change the scope and direction of an existing one. Entrepreneurs typically are innovators who start companies to pursue their ideas for a new product or service. They are visionaries who spot trends.

Although entrepreneurs may be small-business owners, not all small-business owners are entrepreneurs. Small-business owners are managers, or people with technical expertise, who started a business or bought an existing business and made a conscious decision to stay small. For example, the proprietor of your local independent bookstore is a small-business owner. Jeff Bezos, founder of Amazon.com, also sells books. But Bezos is an entrepreneur: He developed a new model—a Web-based book retailer—that revolutionized the bookselling world and then moved on to change

CONCEPT *in Action*

If there is one person responsible for the mainstream success of everything hip-hop in the past 25 years, it's Russell Simmons, founder and CEO of Rush Communications. Since the 1980s when he founded Def Jam Records and launched the careers of the Beastie Boys, LL Cool J, and Run-DMC, Simmons has pioneered countless urban companies and brands from Phat Farm apparel and DefCon3 energy drink to the *Russell Simmons Presents Yoga Live* video series. *What entrepreneurial type best describes Russell Simmons?*

intrapreneurs
Entrepreneurs who apply their creativity, vision, and risk-taking within a large corporation, rather than starting a company of their own.

retailing in general. Entrepreneurs are less likely to accept the status quo and generally take a longer-term view than the small-business owner.

Types of Entrepreneurs

Entrepreneurs fall into several categories: classic entrepreneurs, multipreneurs, and intrapreneurs.

Classic Entrepreneurs *Classic entrepreneurs* are risk takers who start their own companies based on innovative ideas. Some classic entrepreneurs are *micropreneurs* who start small and plan to stay small. They often start businesses just for personal satisfaction and the lifestyle. Miho Inagi is a good example of a micropreneur. On a visit to New York with college friends in 1998 Inagi fell in love with the city's bagels. "I just didn't think anything like a bagel could taste so good," she said. Her passion for bagels led the young office assistant to quit her job and pursue her dream of one day opening her own bagel shop in Tokyo. Although her parents tried to talk her out of it, and bagels were virtually unknown in Japan, nothing deterred her. Other trips to New York followed, including an un-paid six-month apprenticeship at Ess-a-Bagel, where Inagi took orders, cleared trays, and swept floors. On weekends owner Florence Wilpon let her make dough.

In August 2004, using $20,000 of her own savings and a $30,000 loan from her parents, Inagi finally opened tiny Maruichi Bagel. The timing was fortuitous as Japan was about to experience a bagel boom. After a slow start, a favorable review on a local bagel Web site brought customers flocking for what are now considered the best bagels in Tokyo. Inagi earns only about $2,300 a month after expenses, the same amount she was making as a company employee. "Before I opened this store I had no goals," she says, "but now I feel so satisfied."[3]

In contrast, *growth-oriented entrepreneurs* want their business to grow into a major corporation. Most high-tech companies are formed by growth-oriented entrepreneurs. Jeff Bezos recognized that with Internet technology he could compete with large chains of traditional book retailers. Bezos's goal was to build his company into a high-growth enterprise—and he chose a name that reflected his strategy: Amazon.com. Once his company succeeded in the book sector, Bezos applied his online retailing model to other product lines, from toys and house and garden items to tools, apparel, music, and services. In partnership with other retailers, Bezos is well on his way to making Amazon's motto—"Earth's Biggest Selection"—a reality.[4]

Multipreneurs Then there are *multipreneurs,* entrepreneurs who start a series of companies. They thrive on the challenge of building a business and watching it grow. In fact, over half of the chief executives at *Inc.* 500 companies say they would start another company if they sold their current one. Brothers Jeff and Rich Sloan are a good example of multipreneurs, having turned numerous improbable ideas into successful companies. Over the past fifteen years they have renovated houses, owned a horse breeding and marketing business, invented a device to prevent car batteries from dying, and so on. Their latest venture, a multimedia company called StartupNation helps individuals realize their entrepreneurial dreams. And the brothers know what company they want to start next: yours.[5]

Intrapreneurs Some entrepreneurs don't own their own companies but apply their creativity, vision, and risk-taking within a large corporation. Called **intrapreneurs,** these employees enjoy the freedom to nurture their ideas and develop new products,

CONCEPT *in Action*

As a young girl, Helen Greiner loved tech gadgets. But when a spunky droid named R2-D2 helped Luke Skywalker stick it to the Empire in the movie *Star Wars*, Greiner's love became an obsession. Today, Greiner is the cofounder and chairman of iRobot Corporation, a multimillion-dollar robotics firm that creates real-life R2-D2s that do everything from vacuuming household floors to sniffing out terrorist bombs. *How might a person's interests and passions lead to a life of successful entrepreneurship?*

while their employers provide regular salaries and financial backing. Intrapreneurs have a high degree of autonomy to run their own mini-companies within the larger enterprise. They share many of the same personality traits as classic entrepreneurs but take less personal risk. According to Gifford Pinchot, who coined the term *intrapreneur* in his book of the same name, large companies provide seed funds that finance in-house entrepreneurial efforts. These include Intel, IBM, Texas Instruments (a pioneering intrapreneurial company), Eastman Kodak, and Xerox.

Why Become an Entrepreneur?

As the examples in this chapter show, entrepreneurs are found in all industries and have different motives for starting companies. The most common reason cited by CEOs of the *Inc.* 500, the magazine's annual list of fastest-growing private companies, is the challenge of building a business, followed by the desire to control their own destiny. Other reasons include financial independence and frustration working for someone else. Two important motives mentioned in other surveys are a feeling of personal satisfaction with your work, and creating the lifestyle that you want. Do entrepreneurs feel that going into business for themselves was worth it? The answer is a resounding yes. Most say they would do it again.

concept check

Describe several types of entrepreneurs.

What differentiates an entrepreneur from a small-business owner?

What are some major factors that motivate entrepreneurs to start businesses?

Characteristics of Successful Entrepreneurs

2 Which characteristics do successful entrepreneurs share?

Do you have what it takes to become an entrepreneur? Having a great concept is not enough. An entrepreneur must be able to develop and manage the company that implements his or her idea. Being an entrepreneur requires special drive, perseverance, passion, and a spirit of adventure, in addition to managerial and technical ability. Entrepreneurs *are* the company; they tend to work longer hours, take fewer vacations, and cannot leave problems at the office at the end of the day. They also share other common characteristics as described in the next section.

The Entrepreneurial Personality

Studies of the entrepreneurial personality find that entrepreneurs share certain key traits. Most entrepreneurs are:

- *Ambitious*. They are competitive and have a high need for achievement.
- *Independent*. They are individualists and self-starters who prefer to lead rather than follow.
- *Self-confident*. They understand the challenges of starting and operating a business, and are decisive and confident in their ability to solve problems.
- *Risk taking*. Although they are not averse to risk, most successful entrepreneurs favor business opportunities that carry a moderate degree of risk where they can better control the outcome—over highly risky ventures where luck plays a large role.
- *Visionary*. Their ability to spot trends and act upon them sets entrepreneurs apart from small-business owners and managers.
- *Creative*. To compete with larger firms entrepreneurs need to have creative product designs, bold marketing strategies, and innovative solutions to managerial problems.
- *Energetic*. Starting and operating a business takes long hours. Even so, some entrepreneurs start their companies while still employed elsewhere full-time.
- *Passionate*. Entrepreneurs love their work, as Miho Inagi demonstrated by opening a bagel shop in Tokyo despite the odds against it being a success.
- *Committed*. Because they are so committed to their companies, entrepreneurs are willing to make personal sacrifices to achieve their goals. As the Customer Satisfaction and Quality box on the next page describes, Apollonia Poilane makes huge sacrifices to maintain her family's business after tragedy struck.

Most entrepreneurs combine many of the above characteristics. Sarah Levy, 23, loved her job as a restaurant pastry chef but not the low pay, high stress, and long hours of a commercial kitchen. So she found a new one—in her parents' home—and launched Sarah's Pastries and Candies. Part-time staffers now help her fill pastry and candy orders to the soothing sounds of music videos playing in the background. Cornell University graduate Conor McDonough started his own Web design firm, OffThePathMedia.com, after becoming disillusioned with the rigid structure of his job. "There wasn't enough room for my own expression," he says. "Freelancing keeps

CONCEPT *in Action*

Celebrity super-twins Mary-Kate and Ashley Olsen are more than just a couple of pretty faces. The actors-cum-media-moguls are co-owners of Dualstar Entertainment Group, operating a Mary-Kate-and-Ashley entertainment empire estimated in the billions of dollars. From hawking their teen adventures in movies and books to creating grown-up lines of perfume and fashion apparel, the twins know how to mature their brand with their ever-maturing fan base. *What personality traits are common to successful young entrepreneurs like the Olsens?*

© PAUL McCONNELL/GETTY IMAGES

Let Them Eat Bread

How does Harvard University student Apollonia Poilane spend her time between classes? Running one of the best French bakeries in the world—in Paris. When people asked her father, baker Lionel Poilane, what his daughter wanted to do when she grew up, Apollonia would announce she planned to take over the bakery. Then when her parents were killed in a 2002 helicopter crash, France lost its most celebrated baker, and Poilane did just that. Because the name Poilane has earned a place with a very small group of prestige bakers, the 18-year-old determined to continue the tradition of customer satisfaction and quality her grandfather established in 1932.

With organization and determination Poilane, who is studying economics, manages the Paris-based business from her apartment in Cambridge, Massachusetts. "I usually wake up an extra two hours before my classes so I can make sure I get all the phone calls done for work. After classes I check on any business regarding the company and then do my homework," she says. "Before I go to bed I call my production manager in Paris to check the quality of the bread." In fact, she receives a shipment of fresh Poilane bread each week as a flavorful and welcome change from cafeteria food.

"Apollonia is definitely passionate about her job," says Juliette Sarrazin, manager of the successful Poilane Bakery in London, the only Poilane shop outside of Paris. "She really believes in the work of her father and the company, and she is looking at the future, which is very good."

Experiments with sourdough distinguished Poilane products from bread produced by Paris's other bakers and it soon evolved into the crusty loaf that has remained the company's signature product. It is baked with a "P" carved into the crust, a throwback to the days when the use of communal ovens forced bakers to identify their loaves. But it was her father, Lionel Poilane, who turned the family's scrumptious bread into a globally recognized brand, shipped daily via FedEx to upscale restaurants and wealthy clients in the United States, Japan, and elsewhere.

Poilane has retained control of important decisions, strategy, and business goals, describing herself as the "commander of the ship," determining the company's overall direction. Each day is a juggling act, with Poilane solving problems in Paris while other students sleep. Is it worth it? After surviving numerous changes in consumer tastes over the years, the company is now profiting from a growing interest in healthy eating. "More people understand what makes the quality of the bread, what my father spent years studying, so I am thrilled about that," she says. And this young woman understands the importance of keeping customers happy, albeit from a long way away.[6]

Critical Thinking Questions
- What type of entrepreneur is Apollonia Poilane?
- How does she ensure that customer satisfaction and quality are being maintained after her parents' death?

me on my toes," says busy graphic artist Ana Sanchez. "It forces me to do my best work because I know my next job depends on my performance."[7]

Managerial Ability and Technical Knowledge

A person with all the characteristics of an entrepreneur might still lack the necessary business skills to run a successful company. Entrepreneurs need the technical knowledge to carry out their ideas and the managerial ability to organize a company, develop operating strategies, obtain financing, and supervise day-to-day activities. Jim Crane, who built Eagle Global Logistics from a startup into a $250 million company, addressed a group at a meeting saying, "I have never run a $250 million company before so you guys are going to have to start running this business."[8]

Good interpersonal and communication skills are important in dealing with employees, customers, and other business associates such as bankers, accountants, and attorneys. As we will discuss later in the chapter, entrepreneurs believe they can learn these much needed skills. When Jim Steiner started his toner cartridge remanufacturing business, Quality Imaging Products, in 1995, his initial investment was $400. He spent $200 on a consultant to teach him the business and $200 on materials to rebuild his first printer cartridges. He made sales calls from 8.00 a.m. to noon, and made deliveries to customers from noon until 5:00 p.m. After a quick dinner, he moved to the garage, where he filled copier cartridges until midnight, when he collapsed into bed, sometimes covered with carbon soot. And this was not something he did for a couple of months until he got the business off the ground—this was his life for eighteen months.[9] But entrepreneurs usually soon learn that they can't do it all themselves. Often they choose to focus on what they do best and hire others to do the rest.

concept check

Describe the personality traits and skills characteristic of successful entrepreneurs.

What does it mean when we say that an entrepreneur should work on the business, not in it?

Small Business: Driving America's Growth

 3 **How do small businesses contribute to the U.S. economy?**

Although large corporations dominated the business scene for many decades, in recent years small businesses have once again come to the forefront. Corporate greed and fraud have given large corporations a bad name. Downsizings that accompany economic downturns have caused many people to look toward smaller companies for employment, and they have plenty to choose from. Small businesses play an important role in the U.S. economy, representing about half of U.S. economic output, employing about half the private sector workforce, and giving individuals from all walks of life a chance to succeed.

What Is a Small Business?

How many small businesses are there in the United States? Estimates range from 5 million to over 22 million, depending on the size limits government agencies and other groups use to define a small business. So what makes a business "small"? The Small Business Administration classifies all companies with under 500 employees as a small business. In addition, a **small business** has the following characteristics. It is:

small business
A business with under 500 employees that is independently managed, is owned by an individual or a small group of investors, is based locally, and is not a dominant company in its industry.

- Independently managed
- Owned by an individual or a small group of investors
- Locally based (although the market it serves may be widespread)
- Not a dominant company (thus it has little influence in its industry)

Exhibit 6.4 provides a more detailed look at small business owners.

Small businesses in the United States can be found in almost every industry including services, retail, construction, wholesale, manufacturing, finance and insurance, agriculture and mining, transportation, and warehousing. Home-based businesses represent 53 percent of the small-business population. Of these, 91 percent have no paid employees. About two-thirds of all sole proprietorships, partnerships, and S corporations are home-based. They, too, represent a broad range of industries, as shown in Exhibit 6.5 on the next page.

Stephen McDonnell stays home six days a week because "it's good management," not only because he wants to spend time with his wife and three daughters at their restored 200-year-old stone farmhouse in Bucks County, Pennsylvania. McDonnell wanted Applegate Farms, his organic meat company, to be a business that could grow and thrive on its own steam, so he made a radical decision early on. He would limit

---

Exhibit 6.4 > Snapshot of Small Business Owners

Recent data provides a look at small business owners:

- 10.1 million adults are attempting to create new businesses at any one time, about 5.6 million potential new businesses
- Two-thirds of owners reported their business as their primary source of income
- African Americans are 50 percent more likely to engage in start-up activities than whites
- 14 percent are veterans
- 49 percent spend more than 40 hours per week managing or working in their business, with 19 percent devoting 60 hours or more
- 74 percent of businesses with employees are owned by men, 26 percent by women
- 24 percent of small business owners have a bachelor's degree and 19 percent have a graduate degree

Source: "Census Bureau Provides First Glimpse at the Characteristics of U.S. Business Owners," February 2, 2005, http://www.census.gov; "Panel Study on Entrepreneurial Dynamics," *Ewing Marion Kauffman Foundation Entrepreneurial Research Portal 2005,* http://www.research. kauffman.org. Copyright © Ewing Marion Kauffman Foundation. All rights reserved. Reproduced by permission.

Exhibit 6.5 > **Home-based Businesses, by Industry**

Industry	Percentage of Home-based Businesses
Services	60%
Construction	16
Retail	14
Manufacturing, finance, transportation, communications, wholesale	10

Source: "The Small Business Economy 2004," *United States Government Printing Office,* http://www.sbaonline.sba.gov (March 21, 2006).

his physical presence at company headquarters to one day a week—and he has continued to do so for 17 years.

"I don't do this so I can be at home and have a perfect life," he says. "I do it so the company can grow. I'm a controlling boss who has anxiety." McDonnell concedes he can be "hot-blooded," and believes that staying away from the office protects the company from his tendency to micromanage. Sophisticated information systems keep him in touch with his fifty-four employees. "At 5:00 p.m. on a Friday I know more about my business than most CEO's," he says. Applegate has been profitable from the beginning, with revenues increasing 30 percent a year, proving that working from home works.[10]

concept check

What are the criteria the Small Business Administration uses to define a small business?

What social and economic factors have prompted the rise in small business?

Ready, Set, Start Your Own Business

 4 What are the first steps to take if you are starting your own business?

You have decided that you'd like to go into business for yourself. What is the best way to go about it? Start from scratch? Buy an existing business? Or buy a franchise? About 75 percent of business start-ups involve brand-new organizations, with the remaining 25 percent representing purchased companies or franchises. Franchising was discussed in Chapter 5, so we'll cover the other two options in this section.

Getting Started

The first step in starting your own business is a self-assessment to determine whether you have the personal traits you need to succeed and, if so, what type of business would be best for you. Exhibit 6.6 provides a checklist to consider before starting your business.

Finding the Idea Entrepreneurs get ideas for their businesses from many sources. It is not surprising that about 80 percent of *Inc.* 500 executives got the idea for their com-

Exhibit 6.6 > **Checklist for Starting a Business**

Before you start your own small business, consider the following checklist:

- Identify your reasons
- Self-analysis
- Personal skills and experience
- Finding a niche
- Market analysis
- Planning your start-up
- Finances

Source: "Checklist for Starting a Business," http://www.sba.gov/survey/checklist/ (March 20, 2006).

CONCEPT *in Action*

For Steve Jobs, creator of iMac and iPod, the quest for innovation means looking ahead and never resting on one's laurels. Learn more about Steve Jobs and his role at Apple, Inc. by reading the Continuing Case at the end of this chapter. The ingenious Apple co-founder and CEO has displayed remarkable entrepreneurial versatility throughout his career, using time off at Apple to start up Pixar studios, maker of magical computer-animated blockbusters such as *Finding Nemo* and *Monsters, Inc.* How did Jobs' experience at Apple prepare him for success with Pixar?

pany while working in the same or a related industry. Starting a firm in a field where you have experience improves your chances of success. Other sources of inspiration are personal experiences as a consumer; hobbies and personal interests; suggestions from customers, family, and friends; and college courses or other education.

An excellent way to keep up with small-business trends is by reading entrepreneurship and small-business magazines and visiting their Web sites. With articles on everything from idea generation to selling a business, they provide an invaluable resource. Check out Exhibit 6.7 for some of the entrepreneurs who made *Entrepreneur.com*'s

Exhibit 6.7 > *Entrepreneur's* Young Millionaires

Name and Age	Company and Description	Sales
Mike Domek, 36	TicketsNow (world's largest online secondary marketplace for event tickets)	$120 million
Joseph Semprevivo, 34	Joseph's Lite Cookies (sugar- and fat-free cookies)	$100 million
Andrew Fox, 33	Clubplanet.com (online nightlife destination service)	$22 million
Emily Mange, 39 Doug Zell, 39	Intelligentsia Coffee & Tea (coffee roaster, retailer, and wholesaler)	$12 million
Amy Katz, 39 Donna Slavitt, 38	World Packaging Corp. (manufacturer/distributor–promotional, private-label, and licensed items)	$9 million
Ryan Duques, 29 James Warner, 29	Shore Publishing (community newspaper publisher)	$7.5 million
Chris Griffiths, 32	Garrison Guitars (acoustic guitar manufacturer)	$7 million
Darrin King, 34 Jeff King, 38	Clubfurniture.com (online furniture retailer)	$5 million
Joel Boblit, 29	BigBadToyStore (online retailer–collectible toy action figures)	$4 million
Shawn Prez, 34	Power Moves, Inc. (marketing and event planning)	$3 million

(http://www.entrepreneur.com) 2005 list of young millionaires. These dynamic individuals, who are already so successful in their 20s and 30s, came up with unique ideas and concepts and found the right niche for their businesses.

Interesting ideas are all around you. Many successful businesses get started because someone identifies a need and then finds a way to fill it. Do you have a problem that you need to solve? Or a product that doesn't work as well as you'd like? Raising questions about the way things are done, and seeing opportunity in adversity is a great way to generate ideas.

When Mort Rosenthal realized that buying a wireless plan had become nearly as complicated and time-consuming as shopping for a house, he saw a business opportunity. "Every time I've purchased a wireless phone I've experienced frustration," he says. Rosenthal, the founder of Corporate Software, at one time the world's largest PC software distributor, had a simple idea: offer customers a one-stop retail outlet for all their wireless needs. His new company, called "imo" (short for independent mobile), sells all U.S. carrier's plans and phones in one store. The company began rolling out its stores in 2005, with the goal of taking the business nationwide.[11]

Choosing a Form of Business Organization A key decision for a person starting a new business is whether it will be a sole proprietorship, partnership, corporation, or limited liability company. As discussed in Chapter 5, each type of business organization has advantages and disadvantages. The choice depends on the type of business, number of employees, capital requirements, tax considerations, and level of risk involved.

Developing the Business Plan Once you have the basic concept for a product or service, you must develop a plan to create the business. This planning process, culminating in a sound **business plan**, is one of the most important steps in starting a business. It can help to attract appropriate loan financing, minimize the risks involved, and be a critical determinant in whether a firm succeeds or fails. Many people do not venture out on their own because they are overwhelmed with doubts and concerns. A comprehensive business plan lets you run various "what if" analyses and "operate" your business as a dry-run, without any financial outlay or risk. You can also develop strategies to overcome problems—well before the business actually opens.

Taking the time to develop a good business plan pays off. A venture that seems sound at the idea stage may not look so good on paper. A well-prepared, comprehensive, written business plan forces entrepreneurs to take an objective and critical look at their business venture and analyze their concept carefully; make decisions about marketing, production, staffing, and financing; and set goals that will help them manage and monitor its growth and performance.

The business plan also serves as the initial operating plan for the business and writing a good business plan can take several months. But many businesspeople neglect this critical planning tool in their eagerness to begin doing business, getting caught up in the day-to-day operations instead.

The key features of a business plan are a general description of the company, the qualifications of the owner(s), a description of the product or service, an analysis of the market (demand, customers, competition), and a financial plan. The sections should work together to demonstrate why the business will be successful, while focusing on the uniqueness of the business and why it will attract customers. Exhibit 6.8 provides an outline of what to include in each section of a business plan.

The most common use of a business plan is to persuade lenders and investors to finance the venture. The detailed information in the plan helps them assess whether to invest. Even though a business plan may take months to write, it must capture potential investors' interest within minutes. For that reason, the basic business plan should be written with a

---

business plan
A formal written statement that describes in detail the idea for a new business and how it will be carried out; includes a general description of the company, the qualifications of the owner(s), a description of the product or service, an analysis of the market, and a financial plan.

CONCEPT *in Action*

Each year, *Fortune Small Business* holds a national business plan competition to engage the growing number of college students starting their own businesses. One group of students wowed judges with their online SAT-preparation startup, PrepMe. Seeking a piece of the $6 billion online education market, PrepMe offers test-prep tools and Web-based tutoring services that significantly increase students' SAT scores. Shown here is Karel Goel, CEO of PrepMe.com. *What research goes into a winning business plan?*

COURTESY OF PREPME CORPORATION

Exhibit 6.8 > Outline for a Business Plan

Title page: Provides names, addresses, and phone numbers of the venture and its owners and management personnel; date prepared; copy number; and contact person.

Table of contents: Provides page numbers of the key sections of the business plan.

Executive summary: Provides a one- to three-page overview of the total business plan. Written after the other sections are completed, it highlights their significant points and, ideally, creates enough excitement to motivate the reader to continue reading.

Vision and mission statement: Concisely describes the intended strategy and business philosophy for making the vision happen.

Company overview: Explains the type of company, such as manufacturing, retail, or service; provides background information on the company if it already exists; and describes the proposed form of organization—sole proprietorship, partnership, or corporation. This section should be organized as follows: company name and location, company objectives, nature and primary product or service of the business, current status (start-up, buyout, or expansion) and history (if applicable), and legal form of organization.

Product and/or service plan: Describes the product and/or service and points out any unique features; explains why people will buy the product or service. This section should offer the following descriptions: product and/or service; features of the product or service that provide a competitive advantage; available legal protection—patents, copyrights, and trademarks; and dangers of technical or style obsolescence.

Marketing plan: Shows who the firm's customers will be and what type of competition it will face; outlines the marketing strategy and specifies the firm's competitive edge. This section should offer the following descriptions: analysis of target market and profile of target customer; methods of identifying and attracting customers; selling approach, type of sales force, and distribution channels; types of sales promotions and advertising; and credit and pricing policies.

Management plan: Identifies the key players—active investors, management team, and directors—citing the experience and competence they possess. This section should offer the following descriptions: management team, outside investors and/or directors and their qualifications, outside resource people and their qualifications, and plans for recruiting and training employees.

Operating plan: Explains the type of manufacturing or operating system to be used; and describes the facilities, labor, raw materials, and product-processing requirements. This section should offer the following descriptions: operating or manufacturing methods, operating facilities (location, space, and equipment), quality-control methods, procedures to control inventory and operations, sources of supply, and purchasing procedures.

Financial plan: Specifies financial needs and contemplated sources of financing; and presents projections of revenues, costs, and profits. This section should offer the following descriptions: historical financial statements for the last three to five years or as available; pro forma financial statements for three to five years, including income statements, balance sheets, cash flow statements, and cash budgets (monthly for first year and quarterly for second year); breakeven analysis of profits and cash flows; and planned sources of financing.

Appendix of supporting documents: Provides materials supplementary to the plan. This section should offer the following descriptions: management team biographies, any other important data that support the information in the business plan, and the firm's ethics code.

Source: From *ACP-ECollege—Small Business Management: An Entrepreneurial Emphasis,* 13th edition, by Longenecker/Moore/Petty/Palich. © 2006. Reprinted with permission of South-Western, a division of Thomson Learning: http://www.thomsonrights.com, Fax 800-730-2215.

particular reader in mind. Then you can fine-tune and tailor it to fit the investment goals of the investor(s) you plan to approach.

But don't think you can set aside your business plan once you obtain financing and begin operating your company. Entrepreneurs who think their business plan is only for raising money make a big mistake. Business plans should be dynamic documents, reviewed and updated on a regular basis—monthly, quarterly, or annually, depending on how the business progresses and the particular industry changes.

Owners should adjust their sales and profit projections up or down as they analyze their markets and operating results. Reviewing your plan on a constant basis will help you identify strengths and weaknesses in your marketing and management strategies, and help you evaluate possible opportunities for expansion in light of both your original mission and current market trends.

CONCEPT *in Action*

FUBU started when a young entrepreneur from Hollis, Queens began making tie-top skullcaps at home with some friends. With funding from a $100,000 mortgage and a later investment from the Samsung Corporation, CEO Daymond John turned his home into a successful sportswear company. The FUBU brand tops the list for today's fashionistas who don everything from FUBU's classic Fat Albert line to swanky FUBU suits and tuxedos. *How do start-ups obtain funding?*

© GETTY IMAGES

debt
A form of business financing consisting of borrowed funds that must be repaid with interest over a stated time period.

equity
A form of business financing consisting of funds raised through the sale of stock (i.e., ownership) in a business.

angel investors
Individual investors or groups of experienced investors who provide financing for start-up businesses by investing their own funds.

venture capital
Financing obtained from *venture capitalists,* investment firms that specialize in financing small, high-growth companies and receive an ownership interest and a voice in management in return for their money.

Many resources are available to help you prepare your business plan. Later in the chapter we will examine the role of one of these, the Small Business Administration (SBA), which offers sample business plans and online guidance for business plan preparation.

Financing the Business

Once the business plan is complete, the next step is to obtain financing to set up your company. The funding required depends on the type of business and the entrepreneur's own investment. Businesses started by lifestyle entrepreneurs require less financing than growth-oriented businesses, and manufacturing and high-tech companies generally require a large initial investment.

Who provides start-up funding for small companies? Like Miho Inagi and her Tokyo bagel shop, 94 percent of business owners raise start-up funds from personal accounts, family, and friends. Personal assets and money from family and friends are important for new firms, whereas funding from financial institutions may become more important as companies grow. Three-quarters of *Inc.* 500 companies have been funded on $100,000 or less.[12]

The two forms of business financing are **debt**, borrowed funds that must be repaid with interest over a stated time period, and **equity**, funds raised through the sale of stock (i.e., ownership) in the business. Those who provide equity funds get a share of the business's profits. Because lenders usually limit debt financing to no more than a quarter to a third of the firm's total needs, equity financing often amounts to about 65 to 75 percent of total start-up financing.

Two sources of equity financing for young companies are angel investors and venture-capital firms. **Angel investors** are individual investors or groups of experienced investors who provide financing for start-up businesses by investing their own funds. This gives them more flexibility on what they can and will invest in, but because it is their own money angels are careful. Angel investors often invest early in a company's development and they want to see an idea they understand and can have confidence in. In 2004, almost 20 percent of angel deals got funded, almost double the 2003 number. Exhibit 6.9 offers some guidelines on how to attract angel financing.

Venture capital is financing obtained from *venture capitalists,* investment firms that specialize in financing small, high-growth companies. Venture capitalists receive an ownership interest and a voice in management in return for their money. They typically invest at a later stage than angel investors. We'll discuss venture capital in greater detail in Chapter 19.

Buying a Small Business

Another route to small-business ownership is buying an existing business. Although this approach is less risky, many of the same steps for starting a business from scratch apply to buying an existing company. It still requires careful and thorough analysis. The potential buyer must answer several important questions: Why is the owner selling? Does he or she want to retire or move on to a new challenge, or are there problems with the business? Is the business operating at a profit? If not, can this be corrected? On what basis has the owner valued the company, and is it a fair price? What are the owner's plans after selling the company? Will he or she be available to provide assistance through the change of ownership of the business? And depending on the type of business it is, will customers be more loyal to the owner than to the product or service being offered? They could leave the firm if the current owner decides to open a similar business. To protect against this, many purchasers include a "noncompete clause" in the contract of sale.

Exhibit 6.9 > **Making a Heavenly Deal**

You need financing for your start-up business. How do you get angels interested in investing in your business venture?

- Show them something they understand, ideally a business from an industry they've been associated with.
- Have respect for your prospective investors. They know things you don't.
- Hone your vision. Be able to describe your business—what it does and who it sells to—in less than a minute.
- Angels can always leave their money in the bank, so an investment must interest them. It should be something they're passionate about. And timing is important—knowing when to reach out to an angel can make a huge difference.
- They need to see management they trust, respect, and like. Present a mature management team with a strong, experienced leader who can withstand the scrutiny of the angel's inquiries.
- Angels prefer something they can bring added value to. Those who invest could be involved with your company for a long time, or perhaps take a seat on your board of directors.
- They are more partial to deals that don't require huge sums of money or additional infusions of angel cash.
- Emphasize the likely exits for investors and have a handle on who the competition is, why your solution is better, and how you are going to gain market share.

Source: Rhonda Abrams, "What Does it Take to Impress an Angel Investor?" *Inc.com*, http://www.inc.com, March 2001. Copyright © *Inc.com*, Stacy Zhao, "9 Tips for Winning Over Angels," http://www.inc.com, June 2005. Copyright © *Inc.com*.

You should prepare a business plan that thoroughly analyzes all aspects of the business. Get answers to all your questions, and determine, via the business plan, whether the business is a sound one. Then you must negotiate the price and other terms of purchase and obtain appropriate financing. This can be a complicated process, and may require the use of a consultant or business broker.

Risky Business

Running your own business may not be as easy as it sounds. Despite the many advantages of being your own boss, the risks are great as well. About a half a million small businesses fail every year, according to data from the Small Business Administration (SBA) and the Census Bureau.[13]

CONCEPT *in Action*

With over 9,500 locations, Curves International is the fastest growing fitness franchise in the world. The club's all-female clientele and trademark 30-minute workout have generated astounding membership growth in little over a decade. But success didn't come easy for Curves founder Gary Heavin. The pre-med dropout launched a conventional fitness chain during his twenties, became a millionaire by age 30, and soon thereafter declared bankruptcy when his gym business imploded. Undaunted, Heavin went on to launch Curves. *Why do small businesses often fail?*

© CURVES INTERNATIONAL INC.

Businesses close down for many reasons—and not all are failures. Some businesses that close are financially successful and close for nonfinancial reasons. But the causes of business failure can be interrelated. For example, low sales and high expenses are often directly related to poor management. Some common causes of business closure are:

- Economic factors—business downturns and high interest rates
- Financial causes—inadequate capital, low cash balances, and high expenses
- Lack of experience—inadequate business knowledge, management experience, and technical expertise
- Personal reasons—the owners may decide to sell the business or move on to other opportunities

Inadequate early planning is often at the core of later business problems. As described earlier, a thorough feasibility analysis, from market assessment to financing, is critical to business success. Yet even with the best plans, business conditions change and unexpected challenges arise. An entrepreneur may start a company based on a terrific new product only to find that a larger firm with more marketing, financing, and distribution clout introduces a similar item.

The stress of managing a business can also take its toll. The business can consume your whole life. Owners may find themselves in over their heads and unable to cope with the pressures of business operations, from the long hours to being the main decision maker. Even successful businesses have to deal with ongoing challenges. Growing too quickly can cause as many problems as sluggish sales. Growth can strain a company's finances when additional capital is required to fund expanding operations, from hiring additional staff to purchasing more raw material or equipment. Successful business owners must respond quickly and develop plans to manage its growth.

So how do you know when it is time to quit? "Never give up" may be a good motivational catchphrase but it is not always good advice for a small-business owner. Yet some small business owners keep going no matter what the cost. Ian White's company is trying to market a new kind of city map. White, 34, has maxed out 11 credit cards and run up $100,000 in debt since starting Urban Mapping in 2001. He recently declared personal bankruptcy and has been forced to find a job so he can pay his bills.

Maria Martz didn't realize her small business would become a casualty until she saw her 2004 tax return showing her company's losses in black and white—for the second year in a row. It convinced her that enough was enough and she gave up her gift-basket business to become a full-time homemaker. But once the decision is made it may be tough to stick to. "I got calls from people asking how come I wasn't in business anymore. It was tempting to say I'd make their basket but I had to tell myself it is finished now."[14]

concept check

How can potential business owners find new business ideas?

Why is it important to develop a business plan? What should such a plan include?

What financing options do small-business owners have? What risks do they face?

Managing a Small Business

 5 Why does managing a small business present special challenges for the owner?

Managing a small business is quite a challenge. Whether you start a business from scratch or buy an existing one you must be able to keep it going. The small-business owner must be ready to solve problems as they arise and move quickly if market conditions change. In the following Managing Change box, you will see how one company adapted to dramatic shifts in the music industry.

A sound business plan is key to keeping the small-business owner in touch with all areas of his or her business. Hiring, training, and managing employees is another important responsibility because over time the owner's role may change. As the company grows, others will make many of the day-to-day decisions while the owner focuses on managing employees and planning for the firm's long-term success. The owner must constantly evaluate company performance and policies in light of changing market

MANAGING CHANGE

If You Can't Beat 'Em, Make 'Em Happy

Times were tough at Scotti's Record Shops. Customers weren't coming in—they were staying home downloading music onto their MP3 players. And co-owners Jeff and Gary Scotti would hear those who did show up whisper to each other, "Don't buy that. I can burn it for you." "We didn't want to butt heads with iPod owners," Jeff Scotti decided. "We had to embrace them."

Music stores have been getting hammered on all fronts, the most obvious challenges coming from digital downloads and file sharing, both legal and illegal. Stores like Scotti's have also lost CD business to online sellers and other retailers like Abercrombie & Fitch, which attracts teens and college kids shopping for a retail experience with ambiance—and the right crowd.

When Scotti's sales fell to $4.5 million in 2004, from $4.7 million a year earlier, instead of ignoring the changes digital music was forcing on their business, the four-store New Jersey-based chain announced a radical new policy. Buy It, Burn It, Return It. Customers buy a new or used CD, take it home, listen and, if they want, burn a copy to a computer. Within 10 days, they can return the CD for 70 percent store credit. Customers love the policy, says 44-year-old Jeff Scotti. "Now kids are saying, 'Wow, I love it. I'm going to tell all my friends.'"

This is just one of the ways the brothers are changing the way they do business to keep their customers happy and keep pace with the constantly evolving music and retail industry. Choosing from a growing range of clothing, accessories, and music-themed products, the Scottis have updated their merchandise mix, as well as the look of their stores. Body glitter, AC/DC flip-flops, headphones and other equipment for MP3 players, Jimi Hendrix candles, as well as licensed clothing and accessories like Bruce Springsteen T-shirts and Kiss belt buckles, help draw customers. And a growing business in vintage vinyl attracts collectors from as far away as Japan. To further enhance their bottom line, the Scottis closed a fifth store in 2005 when they got a good offer for the remainder of its 10-year lease.

Scotti's has also joined the Music Monitor Network, a consortium of independent stores and distributors that do marketing and other ventures together. Each store in the network has a Monitor This! kiosk, where shoppers can sample new music, get customized CDs, and enter contests. The Scottis also plan to upgrade their Web site and add in-store technology to sell music for cell-phone ring tones and allow online and on-site downloading. All this should keep Scotti's cash registers singing.[15]

Critical Thinking Questions

- How did Scotti's change the way it did business to keep up with a changing music industry and keep their customers happy?
- What approach is the company taking to protect its bottom line into the future?

---

and economic conditions and develop new policies as required. He or she must also nurture a continual flow of ideas to keep the business growing. The types of employees needed may change too as the firm grows. For instance, a larger firm may need more managerial talent and technical expertise.

Using Outside Consultants

One way to ease the burden of managing a business is to hire outside consultants. Nearly all small businesses need a good certified public accountant (CPA) who can help with financial record keeping and decision making, and tax planning. An accountant who works closely with the owner to help the business grow is a valuable asset. An attorney who knows about small-business law can provide legal advice and draw up essential contracts and documents. Consultants in areas such as marketing, employee benefits, and insurance can be used on an as-needed basis. Outside directors with business experience are another way for small companies to get advice. Resources like these free the small-business owner to concentrate on medium- and long-range planning, and day-to-day operations.

Some aspects of business can be outsourced or contracted out to specialists. Among the more common departments that use outsourcing are information technology, customer service, order fulfillment, payroll, and human resources. Hiring an outside company—in many cases another small business—can save money because the purchasing firm buys just the services it needs and makes no investment in expensive technology. Management should review outsourced functions as the business grows because at some point it may be more cost effective to bring them in-house.

Hiring and Retaining Employees

It is important to identify all the costs involved in hiring an employee to make sure your business can afford it. Help-wanted ads, extra space, taxes, and employee benefits will easily add about 10 to 15 percent to their salary. And having an employee may mean more work for you in terms of training and management. It's a catch-22: To grow you need to hire more people, but making the shift from solo worker to boss can be stressful.

Attracting good employees is more difficult for a small firm, which may not be able to match the higher salaries, better benefits, and advancement potential offered by larger firms. Small companies need to be creative to attract the right employees and convince applicants to join their firm. Once they hire an employee, small-business owners must make employee satisfaction a top priority in order to retain good people. Comfortable working conditions, flexible hours, employee benefit programs, opportunities to help make decisions, and a share in profits and ownership are some ways to do this.

Duane Ruh, 49, figured out how to build a $1.2 million business in a town with just 650 residents. It's all about treating employees right. The log birdhouse and bird feeder manufacturer, Little Log Co., located in Sargent, Nebraska, boasts employee-friendly policies you read about but rarely see put into practice. Ruh offers his 32 employees a flexible schedule that gives them plenty of time for their personal lives. During a slow period last summer, Ruh cut back on hours rather than lay anyone off. There just aren't that many jobs in that part of Nebraska that his employees could go to, so when he received a buyout offer that would have closed his facility but kept him in place with an enviable salary, he turned it down. Ruh also encourages his employees to pursue side or summer jobs if they need to make extra money, assuring them that their Little Log jobs are safe.[16]

Going Global with Exporting

More and more small businesses are discovering the benefits of looking beyond the United States for markets. As we learned in Chapter 4, the global marketplace represents a huge opportunity for U.S. businesses, both large and small. Small businesses' decision to export is driven by many factors, one of which is the desire for increased sales and higher profits. U.S. goods are less expensive for overseas buyers when the value of the U.S. dollar declines against foreign currencies, and this creates opportunities for U.S. companies to sell globally. In addition, economic conditions such as a domestic recession, foreign competition within the United States, or new markets opening up in foreign countries may also encourage U.S. companies to export.

Like any major business decision, exporting requires careful planning. Small businesses may hire international-trade consultants to get started selling overseas. These specialists have the time, knowledge, and resources that most small businesses lack. Export trading companies (ETCs) buy goods at a discount from small businesses and resell them abroad. Export management companies (EMCs) act on a company's behalf. For fees of 5 to 15 percent of gross sales and multiyear contracts, they handle all aspects of exporting, including finding customers, billing, shipping, and helping the company comply with foreign regulations.

Many online resources are also available to identify potential markets for your goods and services, and decipher the complexities of preparing to sell in a foreign country. The Small Business Association's Office of International Trade (**http://www.sba.gov/oit**) has links to many valuable sites. The Department of Commerce offers services for small businesses that want to sell abroad. Contact its Trade Information Center (**http://www.trade.gov/td/tic**), or 1-800-USA-TRADE, or its Export Center (**http://www.export.gov**).

concept check

How does the small business owner's role change over time?

How does managing a small business contribute to its growth?

What are the benefits to small firms of doing business internationally, and what steps can small businesses take to explore their options?

Small Business, Large Impact

 6 **What are the advantages and disadvantages facing owners of small businesses?**

An uncertain economy has not stopped people from starting new companies. The National Federation of Independent Businesses reports that 85 percent of Americans view small businesses as a positive influence on American life. This is not surprising when you consider the many reasons why small businesses continue to thrive in the United States:

- *Independence and a better lifestyle.* Large corporations no longer represent job security or offer the fast-track career opportunities they once did. Mid-career employees leave the corporate world—either voluntarily or as a result of downsizing—in search of new opportunities that self-employment provides. Many new college and business school graduates shun the corporate world altogether to start their own companies or look for work in smaller firms.
- *Personal satisfaction from work.* Many small-business owners cite this as one of the primary reasons for starting their companies. They love what they do.
- *Best route to success.* Business ownership provides greater advancement opportunities for women and minorities, as we will discuss later in this chapter. It also offers small business owners the potential for profit.
- *Rapidly changing technology.* Technology advances and decreased costs provide individuals and small companies with the power to compete in industries that were formerly closed to them.
- *Major corporate restructuring and downsizing.* These force many employees to look for other jobs or careers. They may also provide the opportunity to buy a business unit that a company no longer wants.
- *Outsourcing.* As a result of downsizing, corporations may contract with outside firms for services they used to provide in-house. "Outsourcing" creates opportunities for smaller companies that offer these specialized goods and services.
- *Small businesses are resilient.* They are able to respond fairly quickly to changing economic conditions by refocusing their operations.

Pack your bags! Exhibit 6.10 lists the ten hottest cities for entrepreneurs.

Why Stay Small?

Owners of small businesses recognize that being small offers special advantages. Greater flexibility and an uncomplicated company structure allows small businesses to react more quickly to changing market forces. Innovative product ideas can be developed and brought to market more quickly, using fewer financial resources and personnel than would be needed in a larger company. And operating more efficiently keeps costs down as well. Small companies can also serve specialized markets that may not be cost effective for large companies. Another feature is the opportunity to provide a higher level of personal service. Such attention brings many customers back to small businesses like gourmet restaurants, health clubs, spas, fashion boutiques, and travel agencies.

Steve Niewulis played in baseball's minor leagues before an injury to his rotator cuff cut short his career. Niewulis, 32, decided to combine his love of the game with a clever idea that has elevated him to the big leagues. The fact that players had trouble keeping their hands dry while batting inspired his big idea, a sweat-busting rosin bag

---

Exhibit 6.10 > The Ten Hottest Cities for Entrepreneurs

1. Phoenix-Mesa, Arizona
2. Charlotte-Gastonia-Rock Hill, North Carolina-South Carolina
3. Raleigh-Durham-Chapel Hill, North Carolina
4. Las Vegas, Nevada-Arizona
5. Indianapolis, Indiana
6. Washington-Baltimore, District of Columbia, Maryland
7. Atlanta, Georgia
8. Nashville, Tennessee
9. Austin-San Marcos, Texas
10. Memphis, Tennessee

Source: "Hot Cities for Entrepreneurs," *Entrepreneur*, October 2005, http://www.entrepreneur.com. Copyright © *Entrepreneur Magazine*. All rights reserved. Reproduced by permission.

attached to a wristband so a player can dry the bat handle between pitches. In less than two years, Niewulis's Fort Lauderdale, Florida, company, Tap It! Inc., has sold thousands of Just Tap It! wristbands. The product, which retails for $12.95, is used by baseball players, basketball players, tennis players, golfers, even rock climbers. His secret to success? Find a small distribution network that allows small companies, with just one product line, to succeed.[17]

On the other hand, being small is not always an asset. The founders may have limited managerial skills, or encounter difficulties obtaining adequate financing, both potential obstacles to growing a company. Complying with federal regulations is also more expensive for small firms. Those with fewer than 20 employees spend about twice as much per employee on compliance than do larger firms. In addition, starting and managing a small business requires a major commitment by the owner. Long hours, the need for owners to do much of the work themselves, and the stress of being personally responsible for the success of the business can take a toll.

But managing your company's growing pains doesn't need to be a one-person job. Four years after he started DrinkWorks, a company that makes custom drinking cups, Richard Humphrey was logging 100-hour weeks. "I was concerned that if I wasn't there every minute, the company would fall apart." Humphrey got sick, lost weight, and had his engagement fall apart. When forced by a family emergency to leave the company in the hands of his five employees Humphrey was amazed at how well they managed in his absence. "They stepped up to the plate and it worked out," he says. "After that the whole company balanced out."[18]

> **concept check**
>
> Why are small businesses becoming so popular?
>
> Discuss the major advantages and disadvantages of small businesses.

The Small Business Administration

 How does the Small Business Administration help small businesses?

Small Business Administration (SBA)
A government agency that speaks on behalf of small business; specifically it helps people start and manage small businesses, advises them in the areas of finance and management, and helps them win federal contracts.

Many small-business owners turn to the **Small Business Administration (SBA)** for assistance. The SBA's mission is to speak on behalf of small business, and through its national network of local offices it helps people start and manage small businesses, advises them in the areas of finance and management, and helps them win federal contracts. Its toll-free number—1-800-U-ASK-SBA (1-800-827-5722)—provides general information, and its Web site at **http://www.sba.gov** offers details on all its programs.[19]

Financial Assistance Programs

The SBA offers financial assistance to qualified small businesses that cannot obtain financing on reasonable terms through normal lending channels. This assistance takes the form of guarantees on loans made by private lenders. (The SBA no longer provides direct loans.) These loans can be used for most business purposes, including purchasing real estate, equipment, and materials. The SBA has been responsible for a significant amount of small-business financing in the United States. In the fiscal year ended September 30, 2005, the SBA backed more than $19 billion in loans to almost 98,000 small businesses, including about $6 billion to minority-owned firms and $3.3 billion in loans to businesses owned by women. It also provided more than $9 billion in rebuilding loans for victims of the fall 2005 Gulf Coast hurricanes Katrina, Rita, and Wilma—a new record for SBA disaster relief loans.[20]

Other SBA programs include the New Markets Venture Capital Program, which promotes economic development and job opportunities in low-income geographic areas, while other programs offer export financing and assistance to firms that suffer economic harm after natural or other disasters.

Small Business Investment Company (SBIC)
Privately owned and managed investment companies that are licensed by the *Small Business Administration* and provide long-term financing for small businesses.

More than 300 SBA-licensed **Small Business Investment Companies (SBICs)** provide about $2.5 billion each year in long-term financing for small businesses. The SBA's Angel Capital Electronic Network (ACE-Net, **http://acenet.csusb.edu**) offers an Internet-based matching service for small businesses seeking funding of up to $5 million from individual investors. These privately owned and managed investment companies hope to earn a substantial return on their investments as the small businesses grow.

SCORE-ing with Management Assistance Programs

The SBA also provides a wide range of management advice. Its Business Development Library has publications on most business topics. Its "Starting Out" series offers brochures on how to start a wide variety of businesses—from ice-cream stores to fish farms.

Business development officers at the Office of Business Development and local Small Business Development Centers counsel many thousands of small-business owners each year, offering advice, training, and educational programs. The SBA also offers free management consulting through two volunteer groups, the Service Corps of Retired Executives (SCORE), and the Active Corps of Executives (ACE). Executives in these programs use their own business backgrounds to help small-business owners. SCORE has expanded its outreach into new markets by offering e-mail counseling through its Web site (**http://www.score.org**). The SBA also offers free online resources and courses for small-business owners and aspiring entrepreneurs in its E-Business Institute, (**http://www.sba.gov/training**).

Assistance for Women and Minorities

The SBA is committed to helping women and minorities increase their business participation. It offers a minority small-business program, micro-loans, and the publication of Spanish-language informational materials. It has increased its responsiveness to small businesses by giving regional offices more decision authority and creating high-tech tools for grants, loan transactions, and eligibility reviews.

The SBA offers special programs and support services for socially and economically disadvantaged persons, including women, Native Americans, and Hispanics through its Office of Minority Enterprise Development. It also makes a special effort to help veterans go into business for themselves.

> **concept check**
>
> What is the Small Business Administration (SBA)?
>
> Describe the financial and management assistance programs offered by the SBA.

Trends in Entrepreneurship and Small-Business Ownership

8 What trends are shaping entrepreneurship and small-business ownership?

Entrepreneurship has changed since the heady days of the late 1990s, when starting a dot-com while still in college seemed a quick route to riches and stock options. Much entrepreneurial opportunity comes from major changes in demographics, society, and technology, and at present there is a confluence of all three. A major demographic group is moving into a significantly different stage in life, and minorities are increasing their business ownership in remarkable numbers. We have created a society in which we expect to have our problems taken care of, and the technological revolution stands ready with already-developed solutions. Evolving social and demographic trends, combined with the challenge of operating in a fast-paced technology-dominated business climate, are changing the face of entrepreneurship and small-business ownership.

Into the Future: Start-ups Drive the Economy

Did new business ventures drive the economic recovery from the 2001–2002 recession, and are they continuing to make significant contributions to the U.S. economy? The economists who review Department of Labor employment surveys and SBA statistics think so. In recent years, more and more Americans have been going off to work on their own. "Small business drives the American economy," says Dr. Chad Moutray, chief economist for the SBA's Office of Advocacy. "Main Street provides the jobs and spurs our economic growth. American entrepreneurs are creative and productive." Numbers alone do not tell the whole story, however. Are these newly self-employed workers profiting from their ventures or just biding their time during a period of unemployment?

Investment strategist Kenneth Safian, president of Safian Investment Research Inc. based in White Plains, New York, is one of many small-business experts who believe

CONCEPT *in Action*

Rapper by night, entrepreneur by day, Shawn Carter possesses an equal amount of street smarts and business savvy. Narrowly escaping gang-related violence during his teen years, Carter turned to music, founding Roc-a-Fella Records to promote his alter ego, Jay-Z. Multiple Grammys and a dozen hit songs later, Jay-Z is one of the most recognized names in music. Today, Carter heads up Def Jam Records and juggles outside ventures ranging from luxury watches to high-end clothing. *What factors are driving the rapper-as-entrepreneur phenomenon?*

© GETTY IMAGES

that small enterprises are playing an important role in the U.S. economy. Income earned by individuals and partnerships running their own businesses is surging, increasing almost 9 percent a year since 2003. And SBA loans to start-up companies more than doubled from 2000 to 2005. "The economy is becoming more entrepreneurial," Safian says.

These trends show that more workers are striking out on their own and earning money doing it. It has become very clear that encouraging small business activity leads to continued strong overall economic growth.[21]

Changing Demographics Create Entrepreneurial Diversity

As we have seen in Chapters 1 and 5, today's baby boomers will indulge in much less knitting and golf. The AARP predicts silver-haired entrepreneurs will rise in the coming years. According to outplacement specialist John Challenger, the number of over-55 entrepreneurs has grown to about 27 percent of all self-employed workers. This will create a ripple effect in the way we work. Boomers will accelerate the growing acceptance of working from home, adding to the 25 million Americans already showing up to work in their slippers. In addition, the corporate brain drain discussed in Chapter 1 could mean that small businesses will be able to tap into the expertise of seasoned free agents at less-than-corporate prices—and that seniors themselves will become independent consultants to businesses of all sizes.[22]

The growing numbers of baby boomer entrepreneurs has prompted some forward-thinking companies to recognize business opportunities in technology. At one time there was a concern that the aging of the population would create a drag on the economy. Conventional wisdom said that the early parenthood years were the big spending years. As we aged, we spent less, and because boomers are such a big demographic group this was going to create a long-term economic decline. Not true, it now appears. The boomer generation has built sizable wealth, and they are not afraid to spend it to make their lives more comfortable.

"In the future, everything from cell phones to computers will be redesigned for users with limited manual dexterity, poor eyesight, and compromised hearing. Intel, MIT, and other research centers are working on sensor-rich environments that can monitor inhabitants, helping people remember to complete tasks, and watching for sudden behavioral or physical changes," says Jeff Cornwall, who holds the Jack C. Massey Chair in Entrepreneurship at Belmont University in Nashville, Tennessee. "This could be a huge entrepreneurial pot of gold for the next forty years."[23]

Minorities are also adding to the entrepreneurial mix. As we saw in Exhibit 6.3, minority groups and women are increasing business ownership at a much faster rate than the national average, reflecting their confidence in the U.S. economy. These overwhelming increases in minority business ownership paralleled the demand for U.S. Small Business Administration loan products. Loans to minorities increased by 27 percent in 2005 compared to 2004, and loans to women in 2005 jumped almost 50 percent. The SBA loan budget for 2006 included more than $21 billion available to small businesses, which turned to the SBA in record numbers throughout 2005.[24]

The latest Kauffman Foundation Index of Entrepreneurial Activity found that immigrants and Latinos have swelled the growing numbers of self-employed Americans in recent years, increasing the diversity of the country's entrepreneurial class. The SBA notes that the number of Latino-owned businesses has increased 400 percent since 1979 to more than 1 million and now represents about 7 percent of the total U.S. workforce.[25]

"These newly released census estimates and our own loan figures validate what I see in the communities I have visited all across the country," said SBA administrator Hector V. Barreto. "Minority and women entrepreneurs are leading the way in business

CONCEPT *in Action*

The popularity of eBay and other e-commerce sites has given rise to a new kind of entrepreneur: the "mompreneur." Typically ex-corporate professionals, these Web-driven women launch home businesses specializing in the sale of antiques, jewelry, thrift-store fashions, and other items. Aided by digital photography, wireless technology, and friendly postal workers, these savvy moms are the fastest-growing segment of entrepreneurs building successful businesses on eBay. *Why are many professional women leaving the workplace to start entrepreneurial ventures online?*

growth and are making important contributions to [the] nation's economic strength."[26]

The Growth of "Web-Driven Entrepreneurs"

Technology, of course, plays a large role in the U.S. economy, and a recent study found that a new generation of American businesses, "Web-driven entrepreneurs," now make up 25 percent of all U.S. small businesses. According to a survey of 400 small businesses conducted by MasterCard International and Warrillow & Co., a small-business consulting firm, Web-driven entrepreneurs are 25 percent more likely to be women and 25 percent more likely to be university educated.

The study found that Web-savvy companies are also more focused on expansion than their traditional counterparts. "Web-driven entrepreneurs are more growth-focused," said Yoela Harris, director of the Small Business Advisors System at Warrillow & Co. "Internet-based small businesses have a 14 percent growth rate and are 10 years old on average, while traditional small businesses have a 7 percent growth rate and are 14 years old on average."

Over the next five years, 54 percent of Web-driven entrepreneurs plan to access new domestic markets, versus 36 percent of traditional small businesses, 52 percent versus 38 percent plan to introduce new products or services, and 18 percent versus 8 percent plan to access international markets. Thanks to these Web-driven entrepreneurs, the technology growth trend doesn't look ready to slow down anytime soon.[27]

How Far Will You Go to Get Rich?

With enough intelligence and determination, people can get rich almost anywhere in the United States. Whether you own chains of dry cleaners in Queens, car dealerships in Chicago, or oil wells in West Texas, fortunes have been made in every state in the Union. There are some places, however, where the chances of creating wealth are much greater than others.

That is the reason why people who hope to strike it rich move to places like Manhattan or Palo Alto. It's not because the cost of living is low, or the quality of life as a struggling entrepreneur is fun. Whether starting a software or soft-drink company, entrepreneurs know they have to follow the money.

CONCEPT *in Action*

Paying for long-distance calls is so last century. With Skype's proprietary peer-to-peer Internet telephony network, callers can talk to anyone, anywhere for free. Founded in 2003 by Niklas Zennström and Janus Friis, creators of KaZaA, Skype works using a simple software program available for download on almost any computer. Skype's service is so hot that eBay bought the company in 2005 for $2.6 billion. *Why do investors often pay enormous sums to purchase small Web-based companies?*

So where should they go? About $18.2 billion in venture capital was invested last year, according to PricewaterhouseCoopers' quarterly venture capital study, the MoneyTree Survey, so an analysis of the most active venture capital firms provided a partial roadmap. But Kirk Walden, national director of Venture Capital Research of PricewaterhouseCoopers, says, "In general, venture capitalists tend to invest in companies nearby. If a VC is based in Colorado, he's probably going to invest in companies based in Colorado." Other criteria used in the study focused on access to an educated local workforce, proximity to a major university or research center, and—in the belief that like follows like—an analysis of the number of local billionaires in the area.

The winners were Menlo Park/Palo Alto, California, followed by San Francisco, California, and Waltham, Massachusetts. Other hot spots on the list were Boston/Cambridge, Massachusetts; Redwood City, California; New York City; Lexington, Massachusetts; Cupertino, California; Princeton, New Jersey; and Wellesley, Massachusetts. Since those billionaires are not going to leave their homes any time soon, pack your ideas, skills, energy, drive, and creativity, and follow your dreams.[28]

concept check

What significant trends are occurring in the small business arena?

How is entrepreneurial diversity impacting small business and the economy?

How is technology affecting small business?

Summary of Learning Goals

1 **Why do people become entrepreneurs, and what are the different types of entrepreneurs?**

Entrepreneurs are innovators who take the risk of starting and managing a business to make a profit. Most want to develop a company that will grow into a major corporation. People become entrepreneurs for four main reasons: the opportunity for profit, independence, personal satisfaction, and lifestyle. Classic entrepreneurs may be micropreneurs, who plan to keep their businesses small, or growth-oriented entrepreneurs. Multipreneurs start multiple companies, while intrapreneurs work within large corporations.

2 **Which characteristics do successful entrepreneurs share?**

Successful entrepreneurs are ambitious, independent, self-confident, creative, energetic, passionate, and committed. They have a high need for achievement and a willingness to take moderate risks. Good managerial, interpersonal, and communication skills, as well as technical knowledge are important for entrepreneurial success.

3 **How do small businesses contribute to the U.S. economy?**

Small businesses play an important role in the economy. They account for over 99 percent of all employer firms and produce about half of U.S. economic output. Most new private-sector jobs created in the United States over the past decade were in small firms. The Small Business Administration defines a small business as independently owned and operated, with a local base of operations, and not dominant in its field. It also defines small business by size, according to its industry. Small businesses are found in every field, but they dominate the service, construction, wholesale, and retail categories.

4 **What are the first steps to take if you are starting your own business?**

After finding an idea that satisfies a market need, the small-business owner should choose a form of business organization. Preparing a formal business plan helps the business owner analyze the feasibility of his or her idea. The written plan describes in detail the idea for the business and how it will be implemented and operated. The plan also helps the owner obtain both debt and equity financing for the new business.

5 **Why does managing a small business present special challenges for the owner?**

At first, small-business owners are involved in all aspects of the firm's operations. Hiring and retaining key employees and the wise use of outside consultants can free up an owner's time to focus on planning, strategizing, and monitoring market conditions, in addition to overseeing day-to-day operations. Expanding into global markets can be a profitable growth strategy for a small business.

6 **What are the advantages and disadvantages facing owners of small businesses?**

Because of their streamlined staffing and structure, small businesses can be efficiently operated. They have the flexibility to respond to changing market conditions. Small firms can serve specialized markets more profitably than large firms, and provide a higher level of personal service. Disadvantages include limited managerial skill, difficulty in raising capital needed for start-up or expansion, the burden of complying with increasing levels of government regulation, and the major personal commitment that is required by the owner.

7 **How does the Small Business Administration help small businesses?**

The Small Business Administration is the main federal agency serving small businesses. It provides guarantees of private-lender loans for small businesses. The SBA also offers a wide range of management assistance services, including courses, publications, and consulting. It has special programs for women, minorities, and veterans.

8 **What trends are shaping entrepreneurship and small-business ownership?**

Changes in demographics, society, and technology are shaping the future of entrepreneurship and small business in America. More than ever, opportunities exist for entrepreneurs of all ages and backgrounds. The numbers of women and minority business owners continues to rise, and older entrepreneurs are changing the small business landscape. Catering to the needs of an older population and a surge in "Web-based" companies, fuel continued technology growth. An in-depth analysis shows that the best places to start your own small business are those with an educated workforce, a major university or research center, and many local billionaires.

Key Terms

angel investors   214
business plan   212
debt   214
entrepreneurs   203
equity   214
intrapreneurs   205

small business   209
Small Business Administration (SBA)   220
Small Business Investment Company
   (SBIC)   220
venture capital   214

Preparing for Tomorrow's Workplace: SCANS

1. After working in software development with a major food company for twelve years, you are becoming impatient with corporate "red tape" (regulations and routines). You have an idea for a new snack product for nutrition-conscious consumers and are thinking of starting your own company. What entrepreneurial characteristics do you need to succeed? What other factors should you consider

before quitting your job? Working with a partner, choose one to be the entrepreneurial employee and one to play the role of his or her current boss. Develop notes for a script. The employee will focus on why this is a good idea, reasons he or she will succeed, and the employer will play devil's advocate to convince him or her that staying on at the large company is a better idea. Then switch roles and repeat the discussion. (Information, Interpersonal)

2. What does it really take to become an entrepreneur? Find out by interviewing a local entrepreneur, or researching an entrepreneur you've read about in this chapter or in the business press. Get answers to the following questions, as well as any others you'd like to ask:
   - How did you research the feasibility of your idea?
   - How did you develop your vision for the company?
   - How long did it take you to prepare your business plan?
   - Where did you obtain financing for the company?
   - Where did you learn the business skills you needed to run and grow the company?
   - What are the most important entrepreneurial characteristics that helped you succeed?
   - What were the biggest challenges you had to overcome?
   - What are the most important lessons you learned by starting this company?
   - What advice do you have for would-be entrepreneurs?
   (Information, Interpersonal, Systems)

3. A small catering business in your city is for sale for $150,000. The company specializes in business luncheons and small social events. The owner has been running the business for four years from her home but is expecting her first child and wants to sell. You will need outside investors to help you purchase the business. Develop questions to ask the owner about the business and its prospects, and a list of documents you want to see. What other types of information would you need before making a decision to buy this company? Summarize your findings in a memo to a potential investor that explains the appeal of the business for you and how you plan to investigate the feasibility of the purchase. (Information, Interpersonal)

4. Research various types of assistance available to women and minority business owners. Call or visit the nearest SBA office to find out what services and resources it offers. Contact trade associations such as the National Foundation for Women Business Owners (NFWBO), the National Alliance of Black Entrepreneurs, the U.S. Hispanic Chamber of Commerce, and the U.S. Department of Commerce Minority Business Development Agency (MBDA). Call these groups or use the Web to develop a list of their resources and how a small-business owner could use them. (Information, Interpersonal, Technology)

5. Do you have what it takes to be an entrepreneur or small-business owner? You can find many online quizzes to help you figure this out. The *Wall Street Journal* Startup Journal site offers the Entrepreneurial Motivation Quiz at **http://www. startupjournal.com**. What did your results tell you, and were you surprised by what you learned? (Information, Technology)

6. **Team Activity** Your class decides to participate in a local business plan competition. Divide the class into small groups and choose one of the following ideas:
   - A new computer game based on the stock market
   - A company with an innovative design for a skateboard
   - Travel services for college and high school students
   Prepare a detailed outline for the business plan, including the objectives for the business and the types of information you would need to develop product, marketing, and financing strategies. Each group will then present its outline for the class to critique. (Information, Interpersonal, Systems)

As the owner of a small factory that makes plastic sheeting you are constantly seeking ways to increase profits. As the new year begins, one of your goals is to find additional funds to offer annual productivity and/or merit bonuses to your loyal hardworking factory personnel.

Then a letter from a large national manufacturer of shower curtains seems to provide an answer. As part of a new "supplier diversity" program it is putting in place, it is offering substantial purchase contracts to minority-owned suppliers. Even though the letter clearly states that the business must be *minority owned* to qualify for the program, you convince yourself to apply for it based on the fact that all your employees are Latino. You justify your decision by deciding they will benefit from the increased revenue a larger contract will bring, some of which you plan to pass on to them in the form of bonuses later in the year.

Using a Web search tool, locate articles about this topic and then write responses to the following questions. Be sure to support your arguments and cite your sources.

Ethical Dilemma: Is it wrong for this business owner to apply for this program even though it will end up benefiting his employees as well as his business?

Sources: "Kodak Achieves Supplier Diversity Goals," *M2 Presswire,* April 28, 2005, http://www.Kodak.com (May 22, 2006); "Xerox Supplier Diversity Program Celebrates 20 Years of Success," *M2 Presswire,* Dec 12, 2005, http://www.galenet.thomsonlearning.com.

Working the Net

1. Visit Sample Business Plans at **http://www.bplans.com** to review examples of all types of business plans. Select an idea for a company in a field that interests you, and using information from the site, prepare an outline for its business plan.

2. Find a business idea you like or dislike at the American Venture Capital Exchange site, **http://www.avce.com**. Explain why you think this is a good business idea or not. List additional information the entrepreneur should have to consider for this business and research the industry on the Web using a search engine.

3. Evaluate the export potential of your product idea at the Small Business Exporters Network Web site, **http://www.exporters.sbdc.com.** Explore three information areas, including market research, export readiness, and financing. Select a trade link site from government, university, or private categories. Compare them in terms of the information offered to small businesses that want to venture into overseas markets. Which is the most useful, and why?

4. Explore the SBA Web site at **http://www.sba.gov**. What resources are available to you locally? What classes does the E-Business Institute offer? What about financing assistance? Do you think the site lives up to the SBA's goal of being a one-stop shopping resource for the small-business owner? Why or why not?

5. You want to buy a business but don't know much about valuing small companies. Using the "Business for Sale" column available online at **http://www.inc.com**, develop a checklist of questions to ask when buying a business. Also summarize several ways that businesses arrive at their sale price ("Business for Sale" includes the price rationale for each profiled business).

Creative Thinking Case >

180s Gives Old Products New Spin

People laughed when Ron Wilson and Brian Le Gette quit solid investment banking jobs with six-figure salaries to build a better earmuff. The buddies, both engineers, shared a vision based on a simple strategy: to innovate mundane products with redefined style and function.

It all started with the humble earmuff. Walking across campus at Virginia Tech in two feet of snow, Ron Wilson mused about keeping his ears warm without looking like a dork, conceptualizing what would later become the company's signature product, the Ear Warmer. Seven years later he and Wharton Business School buddy, Brian Le Gette (they both earned MBAs in Entrepreneurial Management), designed and developed prototypes of an expandable, collapsible, fleece-covered ear warmer that wraps around the back of the head.

They charged $7,500 in start-up expenses to credit cards, and the following fall sold their first ear warmers on the University of Pennsylvania campus—for $20 a piece. Two classmates interning at QVC persuaded Wilson and Le Gette to hawk their product on the home shopping network, and the rest, as they say, is history. Their QVC debut sold 5,000 Ear Warmers in 8.5 minutes, and three years later home shoppers had bought 600,000 Ear Warmers. Their product was a winner.

Launched by this momentum, their business quickly grew into a booming product design and development company, a creator and marketer of innovative performance wear with 71 employees worldwide. The company's headquarters, known as the 180s Performance Lab, is situated on Baltimore's Inner Harbor and includes an interactive storefront where consumers can test new products. The building's architecture—"floating" conference rooms, a sailcloth roof, four huge windows to the sky—inspires the creative process taking place inside. World-class product design and development teams are constantly working on new innovations, the very core of the 180s culture. And nearly every product has multiple design and utility patents that reflect the unique design solutions the company creates.

Although both founders have now left the company to pursue other interests, it was recently named one of America's Most Innovative Companies by *Inc.* magazine, earned *Fortune's* award for Top Outdoor Products of 2003 for its Exhale gloves, and is number nine on the 2005 *Inc. 500* list of fastest growing private companies. 180s products posted record sales of over $45 million in 2004, and its products are now available through 18,000 retail stores in more than 40 countries. Wilson and Le Gette are the ones laughing now—all the way to the bank.

Critical Thinking Questions

- What characteristics made Ron Wilson and Brian Le Gette successful entrepreneurs?
- How did their partnership and shared vision serve their business goals?
- Is their departure from the company likely to affect its growth? Why or why not?

Sources: Julekha Dash, "180s CEO Le Gette Departs," *Baltimore Business Journal,* July 15, 2005, http://www.bizjournals.com; "Winners Announced for Maryland's Business International Leadership Awards," *World Trade Center Institute* press release, March 9, 2004, "Brian Le Gette, CEO and co-founder, and Tim Hodge, Chief Legal Officer, of 180s, LLC," *World Trade Center Institute,* www.wtci.org/events/awards/leadership2004/legette.htm (November 9, 2005); 180s corporate Web site http://www.180s.com (March 15, 2006).

Video Case >

Healthy Treats Annie's Way

When Annie Withey's first husband suggested she create a snack food to go into the resealable bag he'd invented, the 21-year-old newlywed developed an all natural, cheddar cheese flavored popcorn. The bag never made it to market, but Annie's popcorn, called Smartfood, became one of the fastest selling snack foods in U.S. history—so much so that in 1989 Pepsico Inc.'s Frito-Lay division bought it for about $15 million.

Withey then cashed out stock worth $1 million and created all natural white-cheddar macaroni and cheese, which she and her husband initially marketed by knocking on supermarket doors. They also hit ski lodges, outdoor folk concerts, store parking lots—wherever people gathered. That is how Annie's Homegrown (**http://www.annies.com**), a pioneering company in the natural and organic food industry, was born.

The company now offers 80 natural and organic pasta and canned products, as well as snack crackers and a microwaveable version of its famous mac and cheese, designed for college dorm room convenience. Its products are found in Costco and Target, as well as 18,000 grocery and 6,000 natural food stores nationwide. Yet it still has only 3 percent of the macaroni and cheese market compared with the leader, Kraft, with 80 percent.

"We could never compete directly," says current CEO, John Foraker. "We appeal to a consumer who is less price conscious and willing to pay more to feel good about what they eat." Because Annie's mac and cheese costs 30 percent more than Kraft's, the company's marketing focuses on product attributes.

The nation's leading brand of organic and natural pasta meals and snacks, Annie's Homegrown generated revenues of $34 million in 2004, a 25 percent increase over the previous twelve months, driven by increasing consumer acceptance and demand for high-quality great-tasting organic and natural foods. Organic food sales overall were estimated at $12.25 billion for 2004, and are expected to nearly double to $23.75 billion by 2008, according to an Organic Trade Association's Manufacturer Survey, which predicts 18 percent annual growth for that period.

But for Withey, becoming successful meant taking risks. She had to personally guarantee all loans to her company early on. In 1998 a capital infusion from two small food companies, Consorzio and Fantastic Foods, helped fuel growth, but choosing the right investment company would become critical to the company's long-term expansion goals.

CEO Foraker says Solera Capital LLC, a $250 million private-equity firm run by women, was looking to enter the fast-growing organic food market and took a majority stake in the company with an initial $20 million investment in 2002. "It's a perfect fit says Molly Ashby, Solera's chief executive officer. "It's a great brand, very authentic, with tremendous crossover into both mainstream and natural markets. The remaining interest in the company is held by Withey, current management, and a small group of founding investors. Last year Solera bought Consorzio and Fantastic Foods and combined them with Annie's Homegrown to form Homegrown Naturals Inc. based in Napa, California.

As founder, Annie Withey has assumed the role of "inspirational president." She still writes the text on every product box, and Bernie the Bunny, inspired by her brother's illustration, still appears on every package. As she continues to fill the role of creative and inspirational leader of the company she started, Withey has been described as its "quality gatekeeper" and "moral compass," a humble person whose creative instincts are "right on." When customers write to suggest new products, each idea is still considered, and the "real" Annie never gets tired of hearing how much people enjoy her products.

Critical Thinking Questions

Using information from the case and the video, answer the following critical thinking questions:

- What kind of entrepreneur is Annie Withey? What personal traits does she exhibit that entrepreneurs need to succeed? How have her personal characteristics helped shape the success of her business?
- How did the company evolve from a small business into a multimillion dollar leader in the natural organic food industry? What long-term growth strategies is the company pursuing as it moves into the future under Solera's stewardship?
- Explore the Annie's Web site at **http://www.annies.com**. What unique features did you find? How does this Web site support Annie's mission?

Sources: Adapted from material contained in the video; "Annie's Homegrown"; Tara Siegel Bernard, "Winning a Place on Grocery Store Shelves Annie's Homegrown Finds Some Room as Market for Organic Food Grows," *Wall Street Journal,* March 29, 2005, http://www.w5j.com; "Leading Us All Into Temptation—In a Healthy Way," *Organic Style,* May 2005, http://www.annies.com; corporate Web site, http://www.annie's.com, (March 7, 2006).

Hot Links Address Book

Do you have a great business idea? Taking the quiz at **http://www.edwardlowe.org**, the Edward Lowe Foundation's Web site, will help you determine how feasible the idea is.

At the *Wall Street Journal's* Startup Journal, **http://www.startupjournal.com**, you'll find everything you need to know about starting, financing, and running a business, as well as a searchable database of businesses for sale.

What makes you think you'll be a successful entrepreneur? Taking the Entrepreneurial Test at http://www.sba/gov will help you determine the strength of your entrepreneurial qualities.

Before your business travels to foreign shores, pay a visit to the SBA's Office of International Trade to learn the best ways to enter global markets at http://www.sbaonline.sba.gov/oit

How can you find qualified overseas companies to buy your products? Find out how BuyUSA.com can help you become part of an e-marketplace at http://www.buyusa.com

If you are considering starting a business at home, you'll find tips and advice at the American Association of Home-Based Businesses Web site, http://www.aahbb.org

To learn about the services the U.S. Department of Commerce's Minority Business Development Agency provides for small-business owners, check out http://www.mbda.gov

Part 2 • Ownership at Apple, Inc.

The Apple computer was the brainchild of two people—Stephen Wozniak and Steve Jobs. Wozniak was the self-taught master of electronics, and Jobs was the master of cross-functionality who intertwined electronics expertise with business skills. They needed a third party in the relationship, someone who would bring the money to the venture. This third party was A. C. "Mike" Markkula. Who were these three men, and why did it take all three of them to found Apple?

THE APPLE I – THE INITIAL PARTNERSHIP

Stephen Wozniak

Born with a keen interest in anything electronic and nurtured at the GTE Sylvania computer facility, Wozniak was a student at the University of Colorado in Boulder for only one year. While a student, he polished his FORTRAN and ALGOL programming skills using the university's computer. But he failed to meet the academic requirements of the university and returned home to California. In 1969, Wozniak and friend Bill Fernandez scavenged computer parts from a variety of sources and built the "Cream Soda Computer," named because of the amount of cream soda consumed during the development of the machine. At that time, Wozniak worked as an engineer for Hewlett-Packard on the HP 35 calculator. While he worked for Hewlett-Packard, he became a member of the Homebrew Computer Club.

Using a large employee discount from Hewlett-Packard, Wozniak purchased a Motorola MC6800 microprocessor from HP. He used this microprocessor to develop the first prototype of the Apple I board that he was constantly taking to the computer club meetings. In March 1976, Wozniak had built a computer board that he could interface with his video terminal and a keyboard. Wozniak was the sole designer of the computer part that led to the Apple computer. Although he was working at Hewlett-Packard at the time of the design, HP had relinquished any hold on what Wozniak was doing in his free time.

Steve Jobs

Although Steve Jobs had an interest in electronics, this interest was along the lines of commercialization rather than technical development. He was essentially obsessed with the user's experience with products, always trying to determine what captivated consumers. Jobs pursued this interest at Atari Computer, where he worked on their video games. After meeting Wozniak in the late 1960s and staying in close contact with him throughout the subsequent years, it was Jobs' drive and vision that convinced Wozniak of the commercial viability of his microcomputer board.

Essentially, it was Steve Jobs who made the key decisions that shaped Apple Computer and, because of those decisions, the launch of the personal computer industry. It was Jobs who wanted to name the product (and company) after a fruit, just as it was Jobs who wanted world-class public relations and marketing firms to represent the company. Jobs took personal responsibility for what Apple was making and for how the product felt to the user. Some have described Jobs as a master of hardware (not software), a trailblazer (not follower), a creator (not cloner), and an iconoclast (not an adherer to industry standards). He has been referred to as a perpetual innovation machine, a cultural inspiration, and an entrepreneurial icon.

When Wozniak and Jobs formed a partnership, they had to select a name for their partnership. As entrepreneurs in the heart of a countercultural time period, they thought that "Apple" was a fun and interesting name. Their vision for the company was that people would find their computer useful at home, using it for things such as balancing checkbooks, keeping address lists, and typing letters. An apple was the perfect fruit, representing something found in the home and the company's personal and healthy environment. The partnership gave Wozniak and Jobs equal ownership of 90 percent of Apple Computer. The remaining 10 percent went to Ron Wayne who drew the diagrams of the Apple I board and designed the company logo. Fifty boards were sold to a local retailer and the commercial enterprise began in 1975. As the company sought financing to build more boards in 1976, Ron Wayne ended his relationship with the company due to concerns about his financial obligations. At the same time, Wozniak was improving on the Apple I and moving toward the Apple II.

Before the Apple II was introduced to the market, Wozniak and Jobs showed a prototype to Commodore Computer. Commodore had announced plans to enter the microcomputer market, and the Apple II would have eased the company's entry. However, Commodore and Jobs could not agree on the terms of the sale. Thus, Wozniak and Jobs continued to search for funding to bring the Apple II to market.

THE APPLE II – EXPANDING THE OWNERSHIP TEAM

A. C. "Mike" Markkula

An electrical engineer by training, Markkula retired from Intel when he was in his late 30s. As marketing manager at Intel, he had accumulated stock options that made him a multimillionaire. Markkula agreed to provide the early funding for the Apple II. In addition to securing a $250,000 line of credit for the company, Markkula invested around $90,000 of his own money into the business. He bought one-third of Apple Computer, with Wozniak and Jobs having equal one-third shares of the business. One stipulation by Markkula was that Wozniak leave his job at Hewlett-Packard and devote full-time to the Apple II, something that Wozniak had been hesitant to do. Apple Computer, Inc. was thus created in early 1977. Wozniak was the computer designer, Jobs focused on product appearance and presentation to the public, and Markkula was in charge of marketing and business affairs.

INITIAL PUBLIC OFFERING

By the end of 1979, Apple Computer had net sales of close to $50 million and was the dominant player in the personal computer marketplace. The initial founders had maintained tight control over the company's shares. But in December of 1980, 4.5 million shares of Apple common stock were offered at $22. By the end of that year, each of the original investors of the company was a multimillionaire.

Critical Thinking Questions

- Describe the entrepreneurial styles of Wozniak, Jobs, and Markkula.
- What role did each of the three founders play in the development of Apple Computer?
- Why didn't Commodore Computer want to buy the Apple II from Wozniak and Jobs?
- Ron Wayne resigned from his role as one of the original Apple partners, forgoing millions in earnings as the company grew. Why do you think he hesitated to make the long-term commitment to Apple? What advice would you have given him at the time? What would you say to him today?
- What form(s) of business ownership existed at Apple Computer?

Sources: Anonymous, "A Design, a Dream," *U.S. News & World Report,* October 13, 2005, p. 54; http://www.woz.org, accessed on 3/21/06; Roy A. Allan, *A History of the Personal Computer,* London, Ontario, Canada: Allan Publishing, 2001; Robert X. Cringely, "Because We Like to be Seduced," *Inc. Magazine,* April, 2004, p. 122; Phillip Elmer-DeWitt, "Steve Jobs: Apple's Anti-Gates," *Time,* December 7, 1998, p. 205; Terry Semel, "Steve Jobs," *Time,* April 18, 2005, p. 78; Stephen Wozniak, "Homebrew and How the Apple Came to Be," http://www.woz.org, accessed on 3/21/06; Steve Wozniak, "How We Failed Apple," *Newsweek,* February 1996, http://www.woz.org, accessed on 3/21/06; Jason Zasky, "The Failure Interview: Apple Computer Co-Founder Steve Wozniak," http://www.failuremag.com, accessed on 3/21/06.

PART 3

Managing Organizations

CHAPTER 7

Management and Leadership in Today's Organizations

Learning Goals

After reading this chapter you should be able to answer these questions:

1. What is the role of management?

2. What are the four types of planning?

3. What are the primary functions of managers in organizing activities?

4. How do leadership styles influence a corporate culture?

5. How do organizations control activities?

6. What roles do managers take on in different organizational settings?

7. What set of managerial skills is necessary for managerial success?

8. What trends will affect management in the future?

Exploring Business Careers
Jalem Getz
BuyCostumes.com

You might ask, "How does one come to work in the world of online costume retail?" A passion for holiday make-believe and dress-up? A keen eye for business potential? The drive to capitalize on a competitive advantage? If you're Jalem Getz, the answer is: all of these. Getz is the founder and CEO of BuyCostumes.com, the world's largest online costume and accessories retailer.

As with most business, BuyCostumes.com is the result of careful planning. It is a response to what Getz saw as inherent flaws of resource allocation with the business model of brick-and-mortar costume retailers. "As a brick-and-mortar business, we were the gypsies of retail, which caused scale problems since we started over every year. Because we only were in a mall four or five months a year, locations we had one year often were rented the next. So we had to find new stores to rent each year. Then we had to find management to run the stores, and train employees to staff them. We also had to shuffle the inventory around each year to stock them. It's almost impossible to grow a business like that." By turning to the Internet, however, Getz was able to bypass all of those issues. The virtual "space" was available year-round, and inventory and staff were centralized in a single warehouse location.

Today, BuyCostumes.com is a $30 million a year business that continues to grow with each passing holiday season. It has about 600 employees during its peak season. It carries over 10,000 Halloween items and has upwards of 20 million visitors each holiday season. Last year, they shipped over 1 million costumes across the world, including 45 countries outside the United States. "We say that our goal is to ensure that anytime anyone buys a costume anywhere in the world, it will be from BuyCostumes.com. And, although to some extent we're kidding, we're also very serious."

To keep track of all this action, Getz mixes ideals of a strong work ethic, a willingness to take risks, and an interest in having fun while making a profit. Given the size of the company, BuyCostumes.com organizes its management to help keep the company focused on the corporate goal of continued growth. For Getz, his role in the management hierarchy is to "hire excellent people who have similar goals and who are motivated the same way I am and then put them in a position where they can succeed." Beyond that? "Inspect what you expect." This maxim is a concise way that, although he does not believe in constantly watching over his employees' shoulders, he does believe in periodically checking in with them to ensure that both he and they are on the same page. By considering the process of management a conversation between himself and his employees, he exhibits a strong participative leadership style.

Getz will joke that he wishes he could say that he spent his childhood dreaming of the day he could work with costumes. The truth, though, is that he saw an opportunity, grabbed it, and hasn't let go since. And sometimes, especially during Halloween, truth can be even more satisfying than fiction.

Today's companies rely on managers to guide daily operations using human, technological, financial, and other resources to create a competitive advantage. For many beginning business students, being in "management" is an attractive, but somewhat vague, future goal. This vagueness is due in part to an incomplete understanding of what managers do and how they contribute to organizational success or failure. This chapter introduces the basic functions of management and the skills managers need to drive an organization toward its goals. We will also discuss how leadership styles influence a corporate culture and highlight the trends that are shaping the future role of managers.

The Role of Management

 1 **What is the role of management?**

management
The process of guiding the development, maintenance, and allocation of resources to attain organizational goals.

Management is the process of guiding the development, maintenance, and allocation of resources to attain organizational goals. Managers are the people in the organization responsible for developing and carrying out this management process. Management is dynamic by nature and evolves to meet needs and constraints in the organization's internal and external environments. In a global marketplace where the rate of change is rapidly increasing, flexibility and adaptability are crucial to the managerial process. This process is based in four key functional areas of the organization: planning, organizing, leading, and controlling. Although these activities are discussed separately in the chapter, they actually form a tightly integrated cycle of thoughts and actions.

From this perspective, the managerial process can be described as (1) anticipating potential problems or opportunities and designing plans to deal with them, (2) coordinating and allocating the resources needed to implement plans, (3) guiding personnel through the implementation process, and (4) reviewing results and making any necessary changes. This last stage provides information to be used in ongoing planning efforts, and thus the cycle starts over again. The four functions are highly interdependent, with managers often performing more than one of them at a time and each of them many times over the course of a normal workday.

efficiency
Using the least amount of resources to accomplish the organization's goals.

effectiveness
The ability to produce the desired result or good.

The four management functions can help managers increase organizational efficiency and effectiveness. **Efficiency** is using the least possible amount of resources to get work done, whereas **effectiveness** is the ability to produce a desired result. Managers need to be both efficient and effective in order to achieve organizational goals. For example, JetBlue is the most efficient U.S. airline, operating at under 5 cents per

CONCEPT *in Action*

To create greater collaboration between the visual-effects and computer-gaming divisions of LucasFilm Ltd., film producer and company chairman George Lucas built a $350 million digital-arts studio in Presidio Park to house the creative geniuses behind *Star Wars: Episode III* and *Star Wars Galaxies*. The two divisions' animators and interactive designers now share not only the same office space, but also the same technological design tools and corporate culture. *How do Lucas' planning and organizing decisions increase organizational efficiency and effectiveness at LucasFilm?*

Exhibit 7.1 > What Managers Do and Why

Good management consists of these four activities:		Which results in	And leads to
Planning • Set objectives and state mission • Examine alternatives • Determine needed resources • Create strategies to reach objectives **Organizing** • Design jobs and specify tasks • Create organizational structure • Staff positions • Coordinate work activities • Set policies and procedures • Allocate resources	**Leading** • Lead and motivate employees to accomplish organizational goals • Communicate with employees • Resolve conflicts • Manage change **Controlling** • Measure performance • Compare performance to standards • Take necessary action to improve performance	Organizational efficiency and effectiveness →	Achievement of organizational mission and objectives

seat-mile, which is the cost the company incurs to take one seat (occupied or not) the distance of one mile. No other airline comes close to operating this efficiently: Southwest flies seats at 6.3 cents a mile, and the big airlines like Delta, American, and United average 8.4 cents per seat-mile.[1] That means JetBlue is able to do the same work—or more—with fewer people and less money. JetBlue's efficiency allows the company to sell fares priced up to 65 percent lower than competing airlines, and its growth has skyrocketed.[2]

To meet the demands of such rapid growth, JetBlue increased the number of managers from 115 to 506 over a four-year period by promoting scores of middle managers. But newly promoted managers did not receive proper training (poor *planning* and *organizing*), and so were not as effective as the company needed them to be. CEO David Neeleman said, "They became little dictators, and favoritism started to creep in."[3] The managers, whose job it was to motivate and lead employees to accomplish organizational objectives, were instead rankling their employees and not effective in their new positions (poor *leadership*). In response, top management created a mandatory training program for middle managers (good *controlling*). The result was happier workers, which led to happier customers and the best service rating of any U.S. carrier in an industry quality ranking survey. As this example and Exhibit 7.1 show, good management uses the four management functions to increase a company's efficiency and effectiveness, which leads to the accomplishment of organizational goals and objectives. Let's look more closely at what each of the management functions entails.

concept check

Define the term *management*.

What are the four key functions of managers?

What is the difference between efficiency and effectiveness?

Planning

 What are the four types of planning?

planning
The process of deciding what needs to be done to achieve organizational objectives; identifying when and how it will be done; and determining by whom it should be done.

Planning begins by anticipating potential problems or opportunities the organization may encounter. Managers then design strategies to solve current problems, prevent future problems, or take advantage of opportunities. These strategies serve as the foundation for goals, objectives, policies, and procedures. Put simply, planning is deciding what needs to be done to achieve organizational objectives, identifying when and how it will be done, and determining by whom it should be done. Effective planning requires extensive information about the external business environment in which the firm competes, as well as its internal environment.

CONCEPT *in Action*

Barry Diller not only survived the dot-com crash of 2001, he came out on top. While CEOs of hundreds of poorly planned Internet start-ups sat in stunned amazement as their stocks plummeted from triple-digit valuations to zero, the chairman and CEO of IAC/InterActiveCorp was busy acquiring sensible Web-based businesses like Citysearch and Match that make daily life easier for people all over the world. *What planning activities may have helped Diller and IAC/InterActiveCorp succeed where other dot-coms failed?*

© JOE TABACCA/BLOOMBERG/LANDOV

strategic planning
The process of creating long-range (one to five years), broad goals for the organization and determining what resources will be needed to accomplish those goals.

There are four basic types of planning: strategic, tactical, operational, and contingency. Most of us use these different types of planning in our own lives. Some plans are very broad and long term (more strategic in nature), such as planning to attend graduate school after earning a bachelor's degree. Some plans are much more specific and short term (more operational in nature), such as planning to spend a few hours in the library this weekend. Your short-term plans support your long-term plans. If you study now, you have a better chance of achieving some future goal, such as getting a job interview or attending graduate school. Like you, organizations tailor their plans to meet the requirements of future situations or events. A summary of the four types of planning appears in Exhibit 7.2.

Strategic planning involves creating long-range (one to five years), broad goals for the organization and determining what resources will be needed to accomplish those goals. An evaluation of external environmental factors such as economic, technological, and social issues is critical to successful strategic planning. Strategic plans, such as the organization's long-term mission, are formulated by top-level managers and put into action at lower levels in the organization. For example, when Mickey Drexler took over as CEO of J. Crew, the company was floundering and had been recently purchased by a private equity group.[4] One of Drexler's first moves was to change the strategic direction of the company by moving it out of the crowded trend-following retail segment, where it was competing with stores like Gap, American Eagle, and Abercrombie, and back into the preppie, luxury segment where it began. Rather than trying to sell abundant inventory to a mass market, J. Crew now cultivates scarcity, making sure items sell out early rather than hit the sale rack later in the season. The company is also limiting the number of new stores it opens for the next two years, but planning to double the number of stores in the next five to six years. Drexler is even entertaining the idea of an initial public offering of stock (IPO) if

Exhibit 7.2 > Types of Planning

Type of Planning	Time Frame	Level of Management	Extent of Coverage	Purpose and Goal	Breadth of Content	Accuracy/ Predictability
Strategic	1–5 years	Top management (CEO, vice presidents, directors, division heads)	External environment and entire organization	Establish mission and long-term goals	Broad and general	High degree of uncertainty
Tactical	Less than 1 year	Middle management	Strategic business units	Establish mid-range goals for implementation	More specific	Moderate degree of certainty
Operational	Current	Supervisory management	Geographic and functional divisions	Implement and activate specific objectives	Specific and concrete	Reasonable degree of certainty
Contingency	When an event occurs or a situation demands	Top and middle management	External environment and entire organization	Meet unforeseen challenges and opportunities	Both broad and detailed	Reasonable degree of certainty once event or situation occurs

Changing Strategy Can Change Your Opportunities

For more than 50 years, Gordon Bernard, a printing company in Milford, Ohio, has focused exclusively on printing fundraising calendars for a variety of clients, like cities, schools, scout troops, and fire departments. The company's approximately 4,000 clients nationwide, 10 percent of which have been with the company for over 50 years, generated $4 million in revenue in 2006. In order to better serve customers, company president Bob Sherman invested $650,000 in the purchase of a Xerox iGEN3 digital color press so that the company could produce in-house a part of its calendar product that had been outsourced. The high-tech press has done more for the company than simply reduce costs, however.

The new press gives the company four-color printing capability for the first time in its history, and that has led the management of Gordon Bernard to rethink the company's strategy. The machine excels at short runs, which means that small batches of an item can be printed at a much lower cost than on a traditional press. The press also has the capability to customize every piece that rolls off the machine. For example, if a pet store wants to print 3,000 direct mail pieces, every single postcard can have a personalized greeting and text. Pieces targeted to bird owners can feature pictures of birds, whereas the dog owners' brochure will contain dog pictures. Text and pictures can be personalized for owners of show dogs or overweight cats or iguanas.

Bob Sherman has created a new division to oversee the implementation, training, marketing, and creative aspects of the new production process. The company has even changed how it thinks of itself. No longer does Gordon Bernard consider itself a printing firm, but as a marketing services company with printing capabilities. That change in strategy is prompting the company to seek more commercial work. For example, Gordon Bernard will help clients of its new services develop customer databases from their existing information, and identify additional customer information they might want to collect. Even though calendar sales account for 97 percent of the firm's revenues, that business is seasonal and leaves large amounts of unused capacity in the off-peak periods. Managers hope to see the new division contribute 10 percent of total revenue in the next couple of years.[5]

Critical Thinking Questions
- What type of planning do you think Gordon Bernard is doing?
- Because Gordon Bernard's strategy changed only after it purchased the iGEN3, does the shift constitute strategic planning? Why or why not?

---

mission
An organization's purpose and reason for existing; its long-term goals.

mission statement
A formal document that states an organization's purpose and reason for existing and describes its basic philosophy.

revenues continue to soar. Strategic planning is not only for large companies, however. Learn how one small company changed its strategy and opened up a world of opportunity, described in "Catching the Entrepreneurial Spirit."

An organization's **mission** is formalized in its **mission statement**, a document that states the purpose of the organization and its reason for existing. For example, Ben & Jerry's mission statement addresses three fundamental issues and states the basic philosophy of the company (see Exhibit 7.3).

Exhibit 7.3 > Ben & Jerry's Mission Statement

"Ben & Jerry's is founded on and dedicated to a sustainable corporate concept of linked prosperity. Our mission consists of three interrelated parts:

Product Mission
To make, distribute and sell the finest quality all natural ice cream & euphoric concoctions with a continued commitment to incorporating wholesome, natural ingredients and promoting business practices that respect the Earth and the environment.

Economic Mission
To operate the Company on a sustainable financial basis of profitable growth, increasing value for our stakeholders and expanding opportunities for development and career growth for our employees.

Social Mission
To operate the Company in a way that actively recognizes the central role that business plays in society by initiating innovative ways to improve the quality of life locally, nationally and internationally.

Central to the mission of Ben & Jerry's is the belief that all three parts must thrive equally in a manner that commands deep respect for individuals in and outside the Company and supports the communities of which they are a part."

Source: "Our Mission Statement" http://www.benjerry.com/our_company/our_mission. Copyright © Ben & Jerry's Homemade Inc. All rights reserved. Reproduced by permission.

tactical planning
The process of beginning to implement a strategic plan by addressing issues of coordination and allocating resources to different parts of the organization; has a shorter time frame (less than one year) and more specific objectives than strategic planning.

In all organizations, plans and goals at the tactical and operational levels should clearly support the organization's mission statement.

Tactical planning begins the implementation of strategic plans. Tactical plans have a shorter (less than one year) time frame than strategic plans and more specific objectives designed to support the broader strategic goals. Tactical plans begin to address issues of coordinating and allocating resources to different parts of the organization.

Under Mickey Drexler, many new tactical plans were implemented to support J. Crew's new strategic direction. For example, he severely limited the number of stores opened each year, with only nine new openings in the first two years of his tenure (he closed seven). Instead, he is investing the company's resources in developing a product line that communicates J. Crew's new strategic direction. Drexler has dumped trend-driven apparel because it did not meet the company's new image. He even cut some million-dollar volume items. In their place, he has created limited editions of a handful of garments that he thinks will be popular, many of which fall into his new luxury strategy. For example, J. Crew now buys shoes directly from the same shoe manufacturers that produce footwear for designers like Prada and Gucci. In general, J. Crew has drastically tightened inventories, a move designed to keep reams of clothes from ending up on sale racks and to break its shoppers' habit of waiting for discounts.

This part of the plan is generating great results. Prior to Drexler's change in strategy, half of J. Crew's clothing sold at a discount. After implementing tactical plans aimed to change that situation, only a small percentage now does. The shift to limited editions and tighter inventory controls has not reduced the amount of new merchandise, however. On the contrary, Drexler has created a J. Crew bridal collection, a jewelry line, and Crew Cuts, a line of kids' clothing. The results of Drexler's tactical plans have been impressive. J. Crew saw same-store sales rise 17 percent in one year.[6]

operational planning
The process of creating specific standards, methods, policies, and procedures that are used in specific functional areas of the organization; helps guide and control the implementation of tactical plans.

Operational planning creates specific standards, methods, policies, and procedures that are used in specific functional areas of the organization. Operational objectives are current, narrow, and resource focused. They are designed to help guide and control the implementation of tactical plans. In an industry where new versions of software have widely varying development cycles, Autodesk, maker of software tools for designers and engineers, has implemented new operational plans that are dramatically increasing profits. CEO Carol Bartz shifted the company away from the erratic release schedule it had been keeping to regular, annual software releases. By releasing upgrades on a defined and predictable schedule, the company is able to use annual-subscription pricing, which is more affordable for small and mid-size companies. The new schedule keeps Autodesk customers on the most recent versions of popular software and has resulted in an overall increase in profitability.[7]

The key to effective planning is anticipating future situations and events. Yet even the best-prepared organization must sometimes cope with unforeseen circumstances such as a natural disaster, an act of terrorism, or a radical new technology. Therefore, many companies have developed **contingency plans** that identify alternative courses of action for very unusual or crisis situations. The contingency plan typically stipulates the chain of command, standard operating procedures, and communication channels the organization will use during an emergency.

contingency plans
Plans that identify alternative courses of action for very unusual or crisis situations; typically stipulate the chain of command, standard operating procedures, and communication channels the organization will use during an emergency.

An effective contingency plan can make or break a company. Consider the example of Northwest Airlines. Anticipating a strike by its mechanics, Andy Roberts, Northwest's executive vice president of operations, was the architect of the company's strike contingency plan, a key part of which was finding replacement workers. Managers developed and offered a six-week training seminar to veteran aviation mechanics who had been laid off during the recent industry downturn. Outside contractors were eligible as well. Northwest had no trouble lining up the 1,200 replacement mechanics the company estimated it would require to keep operating during a strike.[8] The company achieved its goal of being able to continue operations if its mechanics walked off the job, which did occur in August 2005. During the initial days of the strike, over half of Northwest flights

MANAGING CHANGE

Boeing Takes Off in New Direction

Boeing and Airbus have been locked in fierce competition for the world's airplane business for decades. What characterized most of that time period was a focus on designing larger and larger airplanes. Since its development in the 1970s, Boeing revamped its pioneering B747 numerous times, and by 2006 boasted over 1,300 of the jumbo jets in operation around the world. As part of this head-to-head competition for bragging rights to the largest jet in the air, Boeing was working on a 747X, a super-jumbo jet designed to hold 525 passengers. In what seemed to be an abrupt change of strategy, Boeing conceded the super-jumbo segment of the market to its rival and killed plans for the 747X. Instead of trying to create a plane with more seats, Boeing engineers began developing planes to fly fewer people at higher speeds. Then, as the rising price of jet fuel surpassed the airlines' ability to easily absorb its increasing cost, Boeing again changed its strategy, this time focusing on developing jets that use less fuel. In the end, Boeing's strategy changed from plane capacity to jet efficiency.

The new strategy required new plans. Boeing managers identified gaps in Airbus' product line and immediately set out to develop planes to fill them. Boeing announced the new 787 "Dreamliner," which boasts better fuel efficiency thanks to lightweight composite materials and next-generation engine design. Even though the 787 has less than half the seating of the Airbus A380, Boeing's Dreamliner is a hit in the market. Orders for the new plane were stronger than anticipated, forcing Boeing to changes its production plans to meet demand. The company

decided to accelerate by four months its planned 787 production rate buildup. The new plan means that seven 787s will roll off the production line every month by 2009, allowing delivery of 444 aircraft by 2012. But that's only 21 aircraft more than previously planned. So in addition, Boeing and its partners began a detailed study of a much more dramatic ramp-up that would see the rate increase gradually from 7 per month to 14 per month by the spring of 2011. If implemented, Boeing will be able to deliver 554 aircraft by the end of 2012. That means a new jet will roll out every day and a half.

Airbus should be so lucky. The company spent so much time and energy on its super-jumbo that its A350 (the plane designed to compete with Boeing's 787) suffered. The 787 uses 15 percent less fuel than the A350, can fly nonstop from Beijing to New York, and is one of the fastest-selling commercial planes ever. By summer 2006, Boeing had orders for over 400 of its 787 Dreamliners; Airbus had yet to announce a major deal for its competing A350. Meanwhile, the A380's order book stalled at around 150 planes.[9]

Critical Thinking Questions
- What seems to be the difference in how Boeing and Airbus have approached planning in recent years?
- Do you think Airbus should change its strategic plans to meet Boeing's or stick with its current plans? Explain.

---

concept check

What is the purpose of planning, and what is needed to do it effectively?

Identify the unique characteristics of each type of planning.

---

continued to arrive on time, and the airline reported only minor glitches.[10] One month into the strike, the company began offering permanent jobs to its replacement workers.[11]

Planning is especially important for companies competing in the global arena. Read "Managing Change" to see how planning is helping Boeing get ahead in a decades-long battle with Airbus Industrie, the European aviation conglomerate.

Organizing

 What are the primary functions of managers in organizing activities?

organizing
The process of coordinating and allocating a firm's resources in order to carry out its plans.

A second key function of managers is **organizing**, which is the process of coordinating and allocating a firm's resources in order to carry out its plans. Organizing includes developing a structure for the people, positions, departments, and activities within the firm. Managers can arrange the structural elements of the firm to maximize the flow of information and the efficiency of work processes. They accomplish this by doing the following:

- Dividing up tasks (*division of labor*)
- Grouping jobs and employees (*departmentalization*)
- Assigning authority and responsibilities (*delegation*)

These and other elements of organizational structure are discussed in detail in Chapter 8. In this chapter, however, you should understand the three levels of a managerial hierarchy. This hierarchy is often depicted as a pyramid as in Exhibit 7.4. The fewest managers are found at the highest level of the pyramid. Called **top management**, they are the small group of people at the head of the organization (such as the CEO, president, and vice president). Top-level managers develop *strategic plans* and address long-range issues such as which industries to compete in, how to capture market share, and what to do with profits. These managers design and approve the firm's basic policies and represent the firm to other organizations. They also define the company's values

top management
The highest level of managers; includes CEOs, presidents, and vice presidents, who develop strategic plans and address long-range issues.

Exhibit 7.4 > The Managerial Pyramid

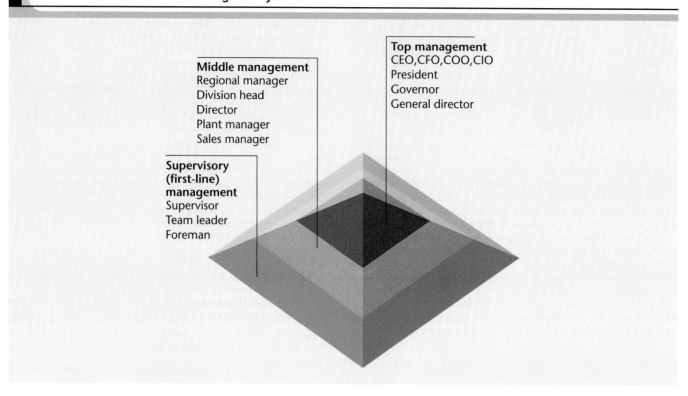

Top management
CEO, CFO, COO, CIO
President
Governor
General director

Middle management
Regional manager
Division head
Director
Plant manager
Sales manager

**Supervisory
(first-line)
management**
Supervisor
Team leader
Foreman

and ethics and thus set the tone for employee standards of behavior. For example, Jack Welch, the former CEO of General Electric, was a role model for his managers and executives. Admirers say that he had an extraordinary capacity to inspire hundreds of thousands of people in many countries and he could change the direction of a huge organization like General Electric as if it were a small firm. Following his leadership, General Electric's executives turned in impressive results. During his tenure, General Electric's average annual shareholder return was 25 percent.[12]

The second and third tiers of the hierarchy are called **middle management** and **supervisory (first-line) management**, respectively. Middle managers (such as division heads, departmental managers, and regional sales managers) are responsible for beginning the implementation of strategic plans. They design and carry out *tactical plans* in specific areas of the company. They begin the process of allocating resources to meet organizational goals, and they oversee supervisory managers throughout the firm. Supervisors, the most numerous of the managers, are at the bottom of the managerial pyramid. These managers design and carry out *operational plans* for the ongoing daily activities of the firm. They spend a great deal of their time guiding and motivating the employees who actually produce the goods and services.

middle management
Managers who design and carry out tactical plans in specific areas of the company.

supervisory (first-line) management
Managers who design and carry out operation plans for the ongoing daily activities of the firm.

concept check

Explain the managerial function of organizing.

What is the managerial pyramid?

Leading, Guiding, and Motivating Others

4 **How do leadership styles influence a corporate culture?**

leadership
The process of guiding and motivating others toward the achievement of organizational goals.

Leadership, the third key management function, is the process of guiding and motivating others toward the achievement of organizational goals. Managers are responsible for directing employees on a daily basis as the employees carry out the plans and work within the structure created by management. Organizations need strong effective leadership at all levels in order to meet goals and remain competitive.

power
The ability to influence others to behave in a particular way.

legitimate power
Power that is derived from an individual's position in an organization.

reward power
Power that is derived from an individual's control over rewards.

coercive power
Power that is derived from an individual's ability to threaten negative outcomes.

expert power
Power that is derived from an individual's extensive knowledge in one or more areas.

referent power
Power that is derived from an individual's personal charisma and the respect and/or admiration the individual inspires.

leadership style
The relatively consistent way that individuals in leadership positions attempt to influence the behavior of others.

CONCEPT *in Action*

Recently topping a *Forbes* list of the world's most powerful women was Condoleezza Rice, the United States secretary of state and oft-mentioned presidential hopeful. The Birmingham, Alabama, native and former Stanford University provost has the distinction of being the first African-American woman to become secretary of state. She is a cabinet-level advisor to the world's leading superpower and the federal government's expert spokesperson on United States foreign policy. *What are Secretary Rice's primary sources of power?*

To be effective leaders, managers must be able to influence others' behaviors. This ability to influence others to behave in a particular way is called power. Researchers have identified five primary sources, or bases, of power:

- Legitimate power, which is derived from an individual's position in an organization
- Reward power, which is derived from an individual's control over rewards
- Coercive power, which is derived from an individual's ability to threaten negative outcomes
- Expert power, which is derived from an individual's extensive knowledge in one or more areas
- Referent power, which is derived from an individual's personal charisma and the respect and/or admiration the individual inspires

Many leaders use a combination of all of these sources of power to influence individuals toward goal achievement. A. G. Lafley gets his legitimate power from his position as CEO of Procter & Gamble. His reward power comes from reviving the company and making the stock more valuable. Also, raises and bonus for managers who meet their goals is another form of reward power. Lafley is also not hesitant to use his coercive power. He has eliminated thousands of jobs, sold underperforming brands, and killed weak product lines. With nearly 30 years of service to the company, Lafley has a unique authority when it comes to P&G's products, markets, innovations, and customers. He has captained the purchase of Clairol, Wella AG, IAMS, as well as the multibillion dollar merger with Gillette. As a result, Lafley has a substantial amount of referent power. Lafley is also widely respected, not only by people at P&G, but by the general business community as well. Ann Gillen Lefever, a managing director at Lehman Brothers, said, "Lafley is a leader who is liked. His directives are very simple. He sets a strategy that everybody understands, and that is more difficult than he gets credit for."[13]

Leadership Styles

Individuals in leadership positions tend to be relatively consistent in the way they attempt to influence the behavior of others, meaning that each individual has a tendency to react to people and situations in a particular way. This pattern of behavior is referred to as leadership style. As Exhibit 7.5 shows, leadership styles can be placed on a continuum that encompasses three distinct styles: autocratic, participative, and free rein.

Autocratic leaders are directive leaders, allowing for very little input from subordinates. These leaders prefer to make decisions and solve problems on their own and expect subordinates to implement solutions according to very specific and detailed instructions. In this leadership style, information typically flows in one direction, from manager to subordinate. The military, by necessity, is generally autocratic. When autocratic leaders treat employees with fairness and respect, they may be considered knowledgeable and decisive. But often autocrats are perceived as narrow-minded and heavy-handed in their unwillingness to share power, information, and decision making in the organization. The trend in organizations today is away from the directive, controlling style of the autocratic leader.

Instead, U.S. businesses are looking more and more for participative leaders, meaning leaders who share decision making with group members and encourage discussion of issues and alternatives. Participative leaders use a democratic, consensual, consultative style. One CEO known for his participative leadership style is Dieter Zetsche of DaimlerChrylser. When he took over at Chrysler it was to turn around an ailing company.

Exhibit 7.5 > **Leadership Styles of Managers**

Amount of authority held by the leader

Autocratic Style	Participative Style (democratic, consensual, consultative)	Free-Rein (laissez-faire) Style
• Manager makes most decisions and acts in authoritative manner. • Manager is usually unconcerned about subordinates' attitudes toward decisions. • Emphasis is on getting task accomplished. • Approach is used mostly by military officers and some production line supervisors.	• Manager shares decision making with group members and encourages teamwork. • Manager encourages discussion of issues and alternatives. • Manager is concerned about subordinates' ideas and attitudes. • Manager coaches subordinates and helps coordinate efforts. • Approach is found in many successful organizations.	• Manager turns over virtually all authority and control to group. • Members of group are presented with task and given freedom to accomplish it. • Approach works well with highly motivated, experienced, educated personnel. • Approach is found in high-tech firms, labs, and colleges.

Amount of authority held by group members

autocratic leaders
Directive leaders who prefer to make decisions and solve problems on their own with little input from subordinates

participative leaders
A leadership style in which the leader shares decision making with group members and encourages discussion of issues and alternatives; includes democratic, consensual, and consultative styles.

He started by interviewing the company's veteran executives to find out why current strategies weren't working. That simple move set him apart from past executives. The low-key Zetsche has been willing to listen and learn from Chrysler's veterans and depends on a team to make decisions.[14] The Customer Satisfaction and Quality box details more of Zetsche's unique leadership style and the impact it is having on Chrysler's overall performance.

CONCEPT *in Action*

The Walt Disney Company's famous 1990s turnaround—one characterized by blockbuster animations like *The Lion King* and mega-acquisitions of ABC and ESPN—is widely credited to the leadership of former-CEO Michael Eisner. But by 2004, Disney's prince charming was butting heads with shareholders and Disney relatives alike, as power struggles surfaced over stalled momentum and Eisner's alleged micromanagement and autocratic leadership style. Mired in controversy, Eisner resigned in 2005, severing all ties with the company. *Under what conditions can autocratic leadership become detrimental?*

© JIM RUYMEN/UPI/LANDOV

Working in Crisis Mode

Dieter Zetsche, CEO of DaimlerChrysler, is known for his participative leadership style, the hallmark of which is listening to the company's employees. But Zetsche also pays very close attention to what the customer is saying. When he became CEO of Chrysler shortly after the company merged with Daimler Benz, Zetsche was charged with turning around the faltering Detroit automaker. During crisis years, the company had historically turned to design as a way to emerge from the brink of disaster. Zetsche, however, knew that design was only part of the solution. He wanted the company to apply its crisis-driven intensity to quality.

Zetsche began by importing the quality-control measures used at Mercedes. If Chrysler's designs and prototypes did not meet quality standards and pass quality checks, the car would not be allowed to move to the next stage of development. Zetsche showed up at test drives for the Chrysler 300, recommended changes and improvements, solicited feedback, and then returned to the test-track to see the results of the changes. He praised the improvements and the engineers' motivation to create the best-quality car the company had ever made. Chrysler sold 120,857 300s in 2004 and received a slew of awards, not to mention rave reviews.

Zetsche paired his focus on quality with a renewed focus on customers—not competitors. Although Chrysler was the originator of the minivan in 1979, the company let its competitive advantage slip away. Twenty years after the first minivans were introduced to the market,

Chrysler faced dozens of competitors, including the tremendously successful Honda Odyssey and Toyota Sienna. Management took its eyes off what consumers wanted and spent billions of dollars to keep up with innovations by its Japanese rivals. Chrysler's dominance in the minivan market eroded.

Recognizing a misplaced focus, Zetsche pointed his designers back toward the customer. What did minivan drivers want out of their vans? Engineers identified a common problem: Drivers wanted to be able to reconfigure their vans for more parcels or people on a moment's notice. Other companies were working on this problem as well, but their solutions were difficult to use and their seats were heavy, some weighing over 50 pounds. Chrysler's solution was "Stow and Go" seating that allowed the driver to transform a minivan with seating for eight to a vehicle that could carry two passengers up front and a full-size motorcycle in the back—in less than one minute! As a result, sales of Chrysler minivans began booming, up 20 percent for its flagship Dodge Caravan and Chrysler Town & Country models.[15]

Critical Thinking Questions
* Do you think Chrysler could have achieved its innovation breakthroughs if Dieter Zetsche had been an autocratic leader? Why or why not?
* What kind of participative leader does Zetsche seem to be? Explain your choice.

---

democratic leaders
Leaders who solicit input from all members of the group and then allow the members to make the final decision through a vote.

consensual leaders
Leaders who encourage discussion about issues and then require that all parties involved agree to the final decision.

consultative leaders
Leaders who confer with subordinates before making a decision, but who retain the final decision-making authority.

free-rein (laissez-faire) leadership
A leadership style in which the leader turns over all authority and control to subordinates.

Participative leadership has three types: democratic, consensual, and consultative. **Democratic leaders** solicit input from all members of the group and then allow the group members to make the final decision through a voting process. This approach works well with highly trained professionals. The president of a physicians' clinic might use the democratic approach. **Consensual leaders** encourage discussion about issues and then require that all parties involved agree to the final decision. This is the general style used by labor mediators. **Consultative leaders** confer with subordinates before making a decision, but retain the final decision-making authority. This technique has been used to dramatically increase the productivity of assembly-line workers.

The third leadership style, at the opposite end of the continuum from the autocratic style, is **free-rein** or **laissez-faire** (French for "leave it alone") **leadership**. Managers who use this style turn over all authority and control to subordinates. Employees are assigned a task and then given free rein to figure out the best way to accomplish it. The manager doesn't get involved unless asked. Under this approach, subordinates have unlimited freedom as long as they do not violate existing company policies. This approach is also sometimes used with highly trained professionals as in a research laboratory.

Although one might at first assume that subordinates would prefer the free-rein style, this approach can have several drawbacks. If free-rein leadership is accompanied by unclear expectations and lack of feedback from the manager, the experience can be frustrating for an employee. Employees may perceive the manager as being uninvolved and indifferent to what is happening or as unwilling or unable to provide the necessary structure, information, and expertise.

There is no one best leadership style. The most effective style for a given situation depends on elements such as the characteristics of the subordinates, the complexity of the task, the source of the leader's power, and the stability of the environment.

Employee Empowerment

Participative and free-rein leaders use a technique called empowerment to share decision-making authority with subordinates. **Empowerment** means giving employees increased autonomy and discretion to make their own decisions, as well as control over the resources needed to implement those decisions. When decision-making power is shared at all levels of the organization, employees feel a greater sense of ownership in, and responsibility for, organizational outcomes.

Management use of employee empowerment is on the rise. This increased level of involvement comes from the realization that people at all levels in the organization possess unique knowledge, skills, and abilities that can be of great value to the company. For example, when hurricane Katrina hit the Gulf Coast, five miles of railroad tracks were ripped off a bridge connecting New Orleans to Slidell, Louisiana. Without the tracks, which fell into Lake Ponchartrain, Norfolk Southern Railroad couldn't transport products between the East and West Coasts. Before the storm hit, however, Jeff McCracken, a chief engineer at the company, traveled to Birmingham with equipment he thought he might need and then to Slidell with 100 employees. After conferring with dozens of company engineers and three bridge companies, McCracken decided to try to rescue the miles of track from the lake. (Building new tracks would have taken several weeks at the least.) To do so, he gathered 365 engineers, machine operators, and other workers, who lined up eight huge cranes and over the course of several hours, lifted the five miles of sunken tracks in one piece out of the lake and bolted it back on the bridge.[16] By giving employees the autonomy to make decisions and access to required resources, Norfolk Southern was able to avoid serious interruptions in its service.

Corporate Culture

The leadership style of managers in an organization is usually indicative of the underlying philosophy, or values, of the organization. The set of *attitudes, values,* and *standards of behavior* that distinguishes one organization from another is called **corporate culture**. A corporate culture evolves over time and is based on the accumulated history of the organization, including the vision of the founders. It is also influenced by the dominant leadership style within the organization. Evidence of a company's culture is seen in its

ALAN LEVENSON/TIME LIFE PICTURES/GETTY IMAGES

CONCEPT *in Action*

Like other Big Three automakers, Ford Motor Company is losing market share and hemorrhaging layoffs in the face of Toyota's astounding ascendancy. According to Chairman Bill Ford Jr., a thorough greening of Ford's corporate culture is the company's only hope. The famously granola-crunching CEO is pouring billions of dollars into eco-friendly factories and institutionalizing innovation-oriented processes around hybrids, biodegradable materials, and hydrogen-powered cars. *Is a "greener" culture fronted by spokes-Muppet Kermit the Frog compatible with Ford's tradition-rich heritage that dates back to the Model T?*

heroes (e.g., Andy Grove of Intel), myths (stories about the company that are passed from employee to employee), symbols (e.g., the Nike swoosh), and ceremonies. The culture at J. M. Smucker, the largest producer of jams and jellies in the United States and makers of Crisco, Jif, and Pillsbury products, is well known for being family-oriented. When the company claimed the top spot on *Fortune's* list of the "100 Best Companies to Work For," list compilers describe the company this way: "It's a 107-year-old, family-controlled business that is run by two brothers who tend to quote the New Testament and Ben Franklin. It's a throwback to a simpler time. If Norman Rockwell were to design a corporation, this would be it."[17] Since the company was founded in 1897, Smucker has adhered to an extremely simple code of conduct: Listen with your full attention, look for the good in others, have a sense of humor, and say thank you for a job well done. Those core corporate values have created a distinctive culture and are embraced by employees. "At first I was skeptical," says director of operations Brian Kinsey, who spent ten years at P&G. "But this family feel is for real." And Tonie Williams, director of marketing for peanut butter, says she's been thanked more in her two years at Smucker than she was in her nine years at Nestlé, Kraft, and P&G combined.[18]

Although culture is intangible and its rules are often unspoken (not the case at Smucker), it can have a strong impact on a company's success. For example, in 2004, Smucker received 6,700 applications for the 80 new jobs it created (total number of employees is approximately 4,700). In that same time period, voluntary employee turnover was only 3 percent.[19] The following year, when it was named to *Fortune's* "Best of the Best" list, for appearing on the list of "Best Companies to Work For" every year since the list began, Smucker received 8,500 applications to fill 752 new job openings and held voluntary turnover to 4 percent. Clearly, a positive, strong culture is a critical success factor for J. M. Smucker.[20]

concept check

How do leaders influence other people's behavior?

How can managers empower employees?

What is corporate culture?

Controlling

5 How do organizations control activities?

The fourth key function that managers perform is **controlling**. Controlling is the process of assessing the organization's progress toward accomplishing its goals. It includes monitoring the implementation of a plan and correcting deviations from that plan. As Exhibit 7.6 shows, controlling can be visualized as a cyclical process made up of five stages:

Exhibit 7.6 > The Control Process

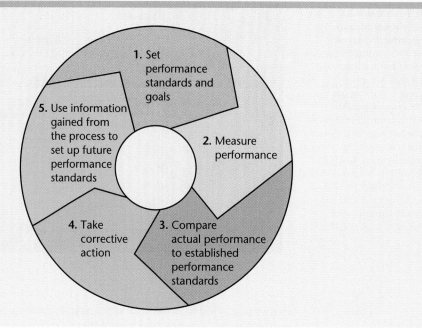

1. Set performance standards and goals

2. Measure performance

3. Compare actual performance to established performance standards

4. Take corrective action

5. Use information gained from the process to set up future performance standards

controlling
The process of assessing the organization's progress toward accomplishing its goals; includes monitoring the implementation of a plan and correcting deviations from the plan.

1. Setting performance standards (goals)
2. Measuring performance
3. Comparing actual performance to established performance standards
4. Taking corrective action (if necessary)
5. Using information gained from the process to set future performance standards

Performance standards are the levels of performance the company wants to attain. These goals are based on its strategic, tactical, and operational plans. The most effective performance standards state a measurable behavioral objective that can be achieved in a specified time frame. For example, the performance objective for the sales division of a company could be stated as "$100,000 in gross sales for the month of January." Each individual employee in that division would also have a specified performance goal. Actual firm, division, or individual performance can be measured against desired performance standards to see if a gap exists between the desired level of performance and the actual level of performance. If a performance gap does exist, the reason for it must be determined and corrective action taken.

Feedback is essential to the process of control. Most companies have a reporting system that identifies areas where performance standards are not being met. A feedback system helps managers detect problems before they get out of hand. If a problem exists, the managers take corrective action. Toyota uses a simple but effective control system on its automobile assembly lines. Each worker serves as the customer for the process just before his or hers. Each worker is empowered to act as a quality control inspector. If a part is defective or not installed properly, the next worker won't accept it. Any worker can alert the supervisor to a problem by tugging on a rope that turns on a warning light (i.e., feedback). If the problem isn't corrected, the worker can stop the entire assembly line.

Why is controlling such an important part of a manager's job? First, it helps managers to determine the success of the other three functions: planning, organizing, and leading. Second, control systems direct employee behavior toward achieving organizational goals. Third, control systems provide a means of coordinating employee activities and integrating resources throughout the organization.

concept check

Describe the control process.

Why is the control process important to the success of the organization?

Managerial Roles

 6 What roles do managers take on in different organizational settings?

informational roles
A manager's activities as an information gatherer, an information disseminator, or a spokesperson for the company.

interpersonal roles
A manager's activities as a figurehead, company leader, or liaison.

decisional roles
A manager's activities as an entrepreneur, resource allocator, conflict resolver, or negotiator.

programmed decisions
Decisions made in response to frequently occurring routine situations.

nonprogrammed decisions
Responses to infrequent, unforeseen, or very unusual problems and opportunities where the manager does not have a precedent to follow in decision making.

In carrying out the responsibilities of planning, organizing, leading, and controlling, managers take on many different roles. A role is a set of behavioral expectations, or a set of activities that a person is expected to perform. Managers' roles fall into three basic categories: *informational roles, interpersonal roles,* and *decisional roles*. These roles are summarized in Exhibit 7.7. In an **informational role**, the manager may act as an information gatherer, an information distributor, or a spokesperson for the company. A manager's **interpersonal roles** are based on various interactions with other people. Depending on the situation, a manager may need to act as a figurehead, a company leader, or a liaison. When acting in a **decisional role**, a manager may have to think like an entrepreneur, make decisions about resource allocation, help resolve conflicts, or negotiate compromises.

Managerial Decision Making

In every function performed, role taken on, and set of skills applied, a manager is a decision maker. Decision making means choosing among alternatives. Decision making occurs in response to the identification of a problem or an opportunity. The decisions managers make fall into two basic categories: programmed and nonprogrammed. **Programmed decisions** are made in response to routine situations that occur frequently in a variety of settings throughout an organization. For example, the need to hire new personnel is a common situation for most organizations. Therefore, standard procedures for recruitment and selection are developed and followed in most companies.

Infrequent, unforeseen, or very unusual problems and opportunities require **nonprogrammed decisions** by managers. Because these situations are unique and

---

Exhibit 7.7 > The Many Roles That Managers Play in an Organization

Role	Description	Example
Informational Roles		
Monitor	Seeks out and gathers information relevant to the organization.	Finding out about legal restrictions on new product technology.
Disseminator	Provides information where it is needed in the organization.	Providing current production figures to workers on the assembly line.
Spokesperson	Transmits information to people outside the organization.	Representing the company at a shareholders' meeting.
Interpersonal Roles		
Figurehead	Represents the company in a symbolic way.	Cutting the ribbon at ceremony for the opening of a new building.
Leader	Guides and motivates employees to achieve organizational goals.	Helping subordinates to set monthly performance goals.
Liaison	Acts as a go-between among individuals inside and outside the organization.	Representing the retail sales division of the company at a regional sales meeting.
Decisional Roles		
Entrepreneur	Searches out new opportunities and initiates change.	Implementing a new production process using new technology.
Disturbance handler	Handles unexpected events and crises.	Handling a crisis situation such as a fire.
Resource allocator	Designates the use of financial, human, and other organizational resources.	Approving the funds necessary to purchase computer equipment and hire personnel.
Negotiator	Represents the company at negotiating processes.	Participating in salary negotiations with union representatives.

© STEFAN ZAKLIN/GETTY IMAGES

complex, the manager rarely has a precedent to follow. The earlier example of the Norfolk Southern employee, who had to decide the best way to salvage a five-mile-long piece of railroad track from the bottom of Lake Ponchartrain, is an example of a nonprogrammed decision. Likewise, when Hurricane Katrina was forecasted to make landfall, Thomas Oreck, CEO of the vacuum manufacturer that bears his name, had to make a series of nonprogrammed decisions. Oreck's corporate headquarters were in New Orleans and its primary manufacturing facility was in Long Beach, Mississippi. Before the storm hit, Oreck transferred its computer systems and call-center operations to backup locations in Colorado and planned to move headquarters to Long Beach. The storm, however, brutally hit both locations. Oreck executives began searching for lost employees, tracking down generators, assembling temporary housing for workers, and making deals with UPS to begin distributing its product (UPS brought food and water to Oreck from Atlanta and took vacuums back to the company's distribution center there). All of these decisions were made in the middle of a very challenging crisis environment.

Whether a decision is programmed or nonprogrammed, managers typically follow five steps in the decision-making process, as illustrated in Exhibit 7.8:

1. Recognize or define the problem or opportunity. Although it is more common to focus on problems because of their obvious negative effects, managers who do not take advantage of new opportunities may lose competitive advantage to other firms.
2. Gather information so as to identify alternative solutions or actions.
3. Select one or more alternatives after evaluating the strengths and weaknesses of each possibility.
4. Put the chosen alternative into action.
5. Gather information to obtain feedback on the effectiveness of the chosen plan.

It can be easy (and dangerous) for managers to get stuck at any stage of the decision-making process. For example, managers can become paralyzed evaluating the options. For the United States Marines Corps (USMC), massaging the data too long can be risky—even deadly. To avoid "analysis paralysis," the USMC uses the 70 percent solution: If you have 70 percent of the information, have done 70 percent of the analysis, and feel 70 percent confident, then move.[21]

Exhibit 7.8 > The Decision-Making Process

5. Follow up to see if the problem has been solved

4. Put the plan into action

3. Select one or more alternatives

2. Identify possible solutions

1. Define the problem

Managerial Skills

7 What set of managerial skills is necessary for managerial success?

In order to be successful in planning, organizing, leading, and controlling, managers must use a wide variety of skills. A *skill* is the ability to do something proficiently. Managerial skills fall into three basic categories: technical, human relations, and conceptual skills. The degree to which each type of skill is used depends upon the level of the manager's position as seen in Exhibit 7.9. Additionally, in an increasingly global marketplace, it pays for managers to develop a special set of skills to deal with global management issues.

CONCEPT *in Action*

If executive headhunters get their way, David Calhoun will soon be head honcho of a leading Fortune 500 company. The 49-year-old president of General Electric's transportation division has held leadership posts with increasing responsibility throughout his career and is a No. 1 draft pick of many recruiters. In his nearly three decades with GE, Calhoun has overseen a range of products, from locomotives and jet engines to lighting. *Which managerial skills are of greatest importance to professionals seeking top management and why?*

	Conceptual Skills	Human Skills	Technical Skills
Top Management			
Middle Management			
Supervisory Management			

Very important   Not as important

Technical Skills

Specialized areas of knowledge and expertise and the ability to apply that knowledge make up a manager's **technical skills**. Preparing a financial statement, programming a computer, designing an office building, and analyzing market research are all examples of technical skills. These types of skills are especially important for supervisory managers because they work closely with employees who are producing the goods and/or services of the firm.

Human Relations Skills

Human relations skills are the interpersonal skills managers use to accomplish goals through the use of human resources. This set of skills includes the ability to understand human behavior, to communicate effectively with others, and to motivate individuals to accomplish their objectives. Giving positive feedback to employees, being sensitive to their individual needs, and showing a willingness to empower subordinates are all examples of good human relations skills. Identifying and promoting managers with human relations skills are important for companies. A manager with little or no people skills can end up using an authoritarian leadership style and alienating employees.

Conceptual Skills

Conceptual skills include the ability to view the organization as a whole, understand how the various parts are interdependent, and

technical skills
A manager's specialized areas of knowledge and expertise, as well as the ability to apply that knowledge.

human relations skills
A manager's interpersonal skills that are used to accomplish goals through the use of human resources.

conceptual skills
A manager's ability to view the organization as a whole, understand how the various parts are interdependent, and assess how the organization relates to its external environment.

concept check

Define the basic managerial skills.

How important is each of these skill sets at the different levels of the management pyramid?

assess how the organization relates to its external environment. These skills allow managers to evaluate situations and develop alternative courses of action. Good conceptual skills are especially necessary for managers at the top of the management pyramid where strategic planning takes place.

Trends in Management and Leadership

8 **What trends will affect management in the future?**

Four important trends in management today are: crisis management, outside directors, the growing use of information technology, and the increasing need for global management skills.

Crisis Management

Crises, both internal and external, can hit even the best-managed organization. Sometimes organizations can anticipate crises, in which case managers develop contingency plans, and sometimes they can't. Take, for example, the sudden death of McDonald's CEO Jim Cantalupo. The company had a solid succession plan in place and immediately named Charlie Bell as new CEO. Only a few months later, Bell announced that he had terminal cancer. Even though the company had prepared for the event of its leader's untimely death, surely it couldn't have anticipated that his successor would also be stricken by a terminal illness at almost the same time. Likewise, consider the devastation caused by hurricanes Katrina and Rita. Harrah's Entertainment had a three-story barge the length of a football field docked in the Gulf of Mexico which was a casino. The hurricane dislodged the barge and threw it overland across U.S. highway 90. Eight thousand Harrah employees were affected by the hurricanes, many of whom were rendered homeless by the storms.[22]

Neither of these crises can be fully anticipated, but managers can develop contingency plans to help navigate through the aftermath of a disaster. Recall the earlier example of Oreck, the vacuum manufacturer that worked quickly after Hurricane Katrina to house its employees and restart its production. What made the company's efforts successful was planning. "We had contingency plans," Thomas Oreck said, adding that the enormity of the storm "caught us a little by surprise."[23] Even though the company had contingency plans, its managers still needed to make dozens of nonprogrammed decisions to get the company back on its feet. Oreck was the first company to reopen in the Mississippi gulf region, sending 500 employees back to work at its Gulfport plant.[24]

No manager or executive can be completely prepared for these types of unexpected crises. However, how a manager handles the situation could mean the difference between disaster, survival, or even financial gain. No matter what the crisis, there are some basic guidelines that managers should follow to minimize the negative outcomes. Managers should not become immobilized by the problem nor ignore it. Managers should face the problem head on. Managers should always tell the truth about the situation and then put the best people on the job to correct the problem. Managers should ask for help if they need it, and finally, managers must learn from the experience to avoid the same problem in the future.[25] Exhibit 7.10 shows what CEOs learned about crisis management in the aftermath of Katrina.

Managers and Information Technology

The second trend having a major impact on managers is the proliferation of information technology. An increasing number of organizations are selling technology, and an increasing number are looking for cutting-edge technology to make and

Howard Schultz Chairman, Starbucks	**Learn from one crisis at a time.** After the Seattle earthquake of 2001, the company invested in a notification system that could handle text messaging. The night before Katrina hit, Starbucks sent out 2,300 phone calls to associates in the region, telling them about available resources.
Gary Loveman CEO, Harrah's Entertainment	**Make life easier for your employees.** Before the storm hit, Harrah's management announced that in the event of total disaster, employees would be paid for at least 90 days. The decision was meant to provide employees with some certainty during a very uncertain time.
J. W. Marriott CEO, Marriott International	**Communicate for safety.** Marriott moved its e-mail system out of New Orleans before Katrina hit. As a result, employees were able to communicate with each other and vendors to get food and water to affected areas. A massive publicity campaign (Dial 1-800-Marriott) helped the company find 2,500 of its 2,800 people in the region.
Bob Nardelli CEO, Home Depot	**Prepare for the next big one.** After each catastrophic event, Home Depot does a postmortem on its response efforts so that employees and managers can become more experienced and better prepared. Before Katrina hit, the company prestaged extra supplies and generators, sent 1,000 relief associates to work in the stores in the Gulf Region, and made sure that area stores were overstocked with first-response items like insecticides, water, and home generators.
Scott Ford CEO, Alltel	**Take care of everybody.** When Katrina hit, Alltel was missing 35 employees. When the company had found all but one, managers used the company's network infrastructure to track her phone activity, contact the last person she had called, and work with the army to find her.
Paul Pressler CEO, Gap	**Empower the workforce.** Gap had 1,300 employees affected by Katrina, and one of the biggest problems the company faced was getting people their paychecks. The company, which had extended payroll by 30 days to affected employees, now encourages all employees to use direct deposit as a means to ensure access to their pay.
Jim Skinner CEO, McDonald's	**Be flexible with company assets.** McDonald's had 280 restaurants close in the immediate aftermath of the storm, but shortly afterward, 201 were already open. During the crisis, McDonald's converted its human resource service center into a crisis command center. The quickly formed help center fielded 3,800 calls.

market the products and services they sell. One particularly useful type of technology is dashboard software. Much like the dashboard in a car, dashboard software gives managers a quick look into the relevant information they need to manage their companies. Most large companies are organized in divisions (which you'll learn about in more detail in Chapter 8), and often each division relies on a particular type of application or database software. Dashboard software allows employees to access information from software they don't routinely use, for example, from an application used by a different division from their own. More important, however, is the ability of a dashboard to show up-to-the-minute information and to allow employees to see all the information they need—like financial and performance data—on a single screen.

CONCEPT *in Action*

Marketing and sales professionals are increasingly turning to advanced software programs called "dashboards" to monitor business and evaluate performance. These computer tools help managers identify valuable customers, track sales, and align plans with company objectives—all in real time. A typical dashboard might include sales and bookings forecasts, monthly close data, customer satisfaction data, and employee training schedules. *How does information technology effect managerial decision making?*

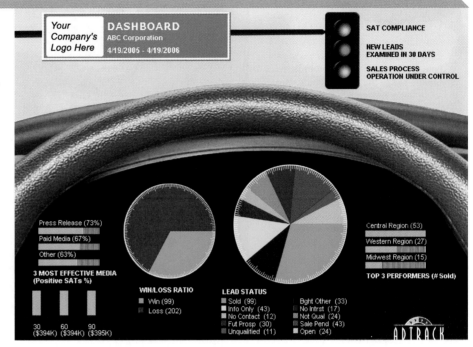

Such integrated functionality is making dashboards extremely popular. A recent poll conducted by Riley Research Associates found that 35 percent of U.S. companies are already running dashboard software, and of those that aren't, 25 percent planned to buy dashboard software that year.[26] Despite the increasing popularity of dashboard technology, the control tool has some drawbacks, like focusing too intently on short-term results and ignoring the overall progress toward long-term goals. And some employees might bristle at being monitored as closely as dashboard tools allow.

Nonetheless, companies are seeing real results from implementing dashboard software. At Capital One Financial Corp., Matt Schuyler, executive vice president in charge of human resources, uses dashboards to track headcount, attrition, and employment needs, so at any given time, his staff knows exactly which positions the company is looking to fill and the qualifications needed for each position. On a recruiting trip to Pennsylvania State University, Schuyler was able to give specific information to potential candidates, not just offer generalities like his competitors. As a result, Schuyler says, "we got a lot of résumés that night."[27]

Managing Multinational Cultures

global management skills
A manager's ability to operate in diverse cultural environments.

The increasing globalization of the world market, as discussed in Chapter 4, has created a need for managers who have **global management skills**, that is, the ability to operate in diverse cultural environments. With more and more companies choosing to do business in multiple locations around the world, employees are often required to learn the geography, language, and social customs of other cultures. It is expensive to train employees for foreign assignments and pay their relocation costs; therefore, choosing the right person for the job is especially important. Individuals who are open-minded, flexible, willing to try new things, and comfortable in a multicultural setting are good candidates for international management positions.

As companies expand around the globe, managers will face the challenges of directing the behavior of employees around the world. They must recognize that

CONCEPT *in Action*

South by Southwest Music Festival (SXSW) began in 1987 as a grassroots concert series for unsigned indie-rock bands. Today the Austin, Texas, music-and-media conference showcases nearly 1500 of the world's best-loved and emerging acts, from Arctic Monkeys and Spoon to Neko Case and the Flaming Lips. Coordination for the festival's international booking and promotions is handled through SXSW, Inc., a management company with offices in the U.S., Europe, Asia, Australia, and New Zealand. *What global management skills do the organizers of SXSW need to be successful?*

because of cultural differences, people respond to similar situations in very different ways. The burden, therefore, falls on the manager to produce results while adapting to the differences among the employees he or she manages.

How a manager gets results, wins respect, and leads employees varies greatly among countries, cultures, and individuals. For example, a *Fortune* 500 retailer based in the United States became frustrated with its Japanese division due to delays implementing a new computer system. When the division finally rolled out the new technology, it was overwhelmingly more effective than the average 65 percent success rate the retailer achieved elsewhere. U.S. management learned that the extra time the Japanese took was for developing internal ownership of the project among employees before executing it—quite a bit different from the "pull-the-trigger" approach used by many U.S. firms.[28] Despite differences like that (examples of which can be cited for every country in the world), managing within a different culture is only an extension of what managers do every day. That is working with differences in employees, processes, and projects.

concept check

How can information technology aid in decision making?

What are three principles of managing multinational cultures?

Describe several guidelines for crisis management.

Summary Of Learning Goals

1 What is the role of management?

Management is the process of guiding the development, maintenance, and allocation of resources to attain organizational goals. Managers are the people in the organization responsible for developing and carrying out this management process. The four primary functions of managers are planning, organizing, leading, and controlling. By using the four functions, managers work to increase the efficiency and effectiveness of their employees, processes, projects, and organizations as a whole.

2 What are the four types of planning?

Planning is deciding what needs to be done, identifying when and how it will be done, and determining by whom it should be done. Managers use four different types of planning: strategic, tactical, operational, and contingency planning. Strategic planning involves creating long-range (one to five years), broad goals and determining the necessary resources to accomplish those goals. Tactical planning has a shorter time frame (less than one year) and more specific objectives that support the broader strategic goals. Operational planning creates specific standards, methods, policies, and procedures that are used in specific functional areas of the organization. Contingency plans identify alternative courses of action for very unusual or crisis situations.

3 What are the primary functions of managers in organizing activities?

Organizing involves coordinating and allocating a firm's resources in order to carry out its plans. It includes developing a structure for the people, positions, departments, and activities within the firm. This is accomplished by dividing up tasks (division of labor), grouping jobs and employees (departmentalization), and assigning authority and responsibilities (delegation).

4 How do leadership styles influence a corporate culture?

Leading is the process of guiding and motivating others toward the achievement of organizational goals. Managers have unique leadership styles that range from autocratic to free-rein. The set of attitudes, values, and standards of behavior that distinguishes one organization from another is called corporate culture. A corporate culture evolves over time and is based on the accumulated history of the organization, including the vision of the founders.

5 How do organizations control activities?

Controlling is the process of assessing the organization's progress toward accomplishing its goals. The control process is as follows: (1) set performance standards (goals), (2) measure performance, (3) compare actual performance to established performance standards, (4) take corrective action (if necessary), and (5) use information gained from the process to set future performance standards.

6 What roles do managers take on in different organizational settings?

In an informational role, the manager may act as an information gatherer, an information distributor, or a spokesperson for the company. A manager's interpersonal roles are based on various interactions with other people. Depending on the situation, a manager may need to act as a figurehead, a company leader, or a liaison.

7 **What set of managerial skills is necessary for managerial success?**

Managerial skills fall into three basic categories: technical, human relations, and conceptual skills. Specialized areas of knowledge and expertise and the ability to apply that knowledge make up a manager's technical skills. Human relations skills include the ability to understand human behavior, to communicate effectively with others, and to motivate individuals to accomplish their objectives. Conceptual skills include the ability to view the organization as a whole, understand how the various parts are interdependent, and assess how the organization relates to its external environment.

8 **What trends will affect management in the future?**

Three important trends in management today are: preparing for crises management, the increasing use of information technology, and the need to manage multinational cultures. Crisis management requires quick action, telling the truth about the situation, and putting the best people on the task to correct the situation. Finally, management must learn from the crisis in order to prevent it from happening again. Using the latest information technology, like dashboard software, managers can make quicker, better-informed decisions. As more companies "go global," the need for multinational cultural management skills is growing. Managers must set a good example, create personal involvement for all employees, and develop a culture of trust.

Key Terms

autocratic leaders 244
coercive power 243
conceptual skills 252
consensual leaders 245
consultative leaders 245
contingency plans 240
controlling 248
corporate culture 246
decisional roles 249
democratic leaders 245
effectiveness 236
efficiency 236
empowerment 246
expert power 243
free-rein (laissez-faire) leadership 245
global management skills 255
human relations skills 252
informational roles 249
interpersonal roles 249
leadership 242

leadership style 243
legitimate power 243
management 236
middle management 242
mission 239
mission statement 239
nonprogrammed decisions 249
operational planning 240
organizing 241
participative leadership 244
planning 237
power 243
programmed decisions 249
referent power 243
reward power 243
strategic planning 238
supervisory (first-line) management 242
tactical planning 240
technical skills 252
top management 241

1. Would you be a good manager? Do a self-assessment that includes your current technical, human relations, and conceptual skills. What skills do you already possess, and which do you need to add? Where do your strengths lie? Based on this exercise, develop a description of an effective manager. (Resources, Information)

2. Successful managers map out what they want to do with their time (planning), determine the activities and tasks they need to accomplish in that time frame (organizing), and make sure they stay on track (controlling). How well do you manage your time? Do you think ahead, or do you tend to procrastinate? Examine how you use your time and identify at least three areas where you can improve your time management skills. (Resources)

3. Often researchers cast leadership in an inspirational role in a company and management in more of an administrative role. That tendency seems to put leadership and management in a hierarchy. Do you think one is more important than the other? Do you think a company can succeed if it has bad managers and good leaders? What about if it has good managers and bad leaders? Are managers and leaders actually the same? (Systems)

4. Today's managers must be comfortable using all kinds of technology. Do an inventory of your computer skills and identify any gaps. After listing your areas of weakness, make a plan to increase your computer competency by enrolling in a computer class on or off campus. You may want to practice using common business applications like Microsoft Excel by building a spreadsheet to track your budget, PowerPoint by creating slides for your next class project, and Outlook by uploading your semester schedule. (Information, Technology)

5. **Team Activity** One of the most common types of planning that managers do is operational planning, or the creation of policies, procedures, and rules and regulations. Assemble a team of three classmates and work as a team to draft an operational plan that addresses employee attendance (or absenteeism). (Interpersonal, Systems)

Ethics Activity

Are top executives paid too much? A study of CEO compensation revealed that CEO bonuses rose considerably—from 20 percent to 30 percent—even at companies whose revenues or profits dropped or those that reported significant employee layoffs. Such high pay for CEOs at underperforming companies, as well as CEO compensation at companies with stellar results, has raised many questions from investors and others. CEO pay has risen considerably in recent years; in 2004, for example, the average pay for a CEO at a public company was $11.4 million— versus just $27,000 for an average nonsupervisory production worker's pay. Under proposed regulations, the Securities and Exchange Commission (SEC) would require public companies to disclose full details of executive compensation, including salaries, bonuses, pensions, benefits, stock options, and severance and retirement packages.

Even some CEOs question the high levels of CEO pay. Edgar Woolard, Jr., former CEO and chairman of DuPont, thinks so. "CEO pay is driven today primarily by outside consultant surveys," he says. Companies all want their CEOs to be in the top half, and preferably the top quarter, of all CEOs. This leads to annual increases. He also criticizes the enormous severance packages that company boards give to CEOs that fail. For example, Carly Fiorina of Hewlett-Packard received $20 million when she was fired.

Using a Web search tool, locate articles about this topic and then write responses to the following questions. Be sure to support your arguments and cite your sources.

Ethical Dilemma: Are CEOs entitled to increases in compensation when their company's financial situation worsens, because their job becomes more challenging? If they fail, are they entitled to huge severance packages for their efforts? Should companies be required to divulge all details of compensation for their highest top managers, and what effect is such disclosure likely to have on executive pay?

Sources: "CEOs are Overpaid, Says Former DuPont CEO Edgar Woolard Jr.," *PR Newswire*, February 9, 2006, http://proquest.umi.com; Elizabeth Souder, "Firm Questions Exxon CEO's Pay." *Dallas Morning News*, December 15, 2005, http://galenet.thomsonlearning.com; "Weaker Company Performance Does Not Seem to Slow CEO Pay Increases," *Corporate Board*, September-October 2005, p. 27, http://galenet.thomsonlearning.com; "What price CEO pay?" *The Blade* (Toledo, Ohio), January 20, 2006, http://www.toledoblade.com.

Working The Net

1. Are you leadership material? See how you measure up at Magno Consulting, **http://www.magnoconsulting.com**. Click on "leadership" for a punch list of attributes for business leaders of the 21st century. Study the list and provide an example of how you would put each item into action.

2. Strategic Advantage, **http://www.strategy4u.com** offers many reasons why companies should develop strategic plans, as well as a strategy tip of the month, assessment tools, planning exercises, and resource links. Explore the site to learn the effect of strategic planning on financial performance and present your evidence to the class. Then select a planning exercise and, with a group of classmates, perform it as it applies to your school.

3. Congratulations! You've just been promoted to your first supervisory position. However, you are at a loss as to how to actually manage your staff. About.com's guide to general management, **http://www.management.about.com**, brings together a variety of materials to help you. Check out the Essentials links such as Management 101 and How To Manage, as well as other resources. Develop a plan for yourself to follow.

4. How do entrepreneurs develop the corporate culture of their companies? Do a search of the term "corporate culture" on *Inc.* **http://www.inc.com**, *Entrepreneur* **http://www.entrepreneur.com**, or *Fast Company* **http://www.fastcompany.com**. Prepare a short presentation for your class that explains the importance of corporate culture and how it is developed in young firms.

5. Good managers and leaders know how to empower their employees. The Business e-Coach at **http://www.1000ventures.com** explains why employee empowerment is so important in today's knowledge economy. After reviewing the information at this site, prepare a brief report on the benefits of employee empowerment. Include several ideas you would like a manager to use to empower you.

6. Get some leadership tips from 7 Steps to Closure at the Learning Center, **http://www.learningcenter.net**. Complete the Closure Planning Form to develop your own personal Success-Oriented Action Plan.

Creative Thinking Case >

Managing an Extreme Makeover

During a tour of a Toyota Corolla assembly plant located near their headquarters in Bangalore, India, executives of Wipro Ltd. hit on a revolutionary idea—why not apply Toyota's successful manufacturing techniques to managing their software development and clients' back-office operations business.

"Toyota preaches continuous improvement, respect for employees, learning, and embracing change," says T. K. Kurien, 45, head of Wipro's 13,600-person business-process outsourcing unit. "What we do is apply people, technology, and processes to solve a business problem."

Among the problems spotted early on by Kurien? Cubicles. They're normal for programmers but interrupt the flow for business-process employees. Deciding to position people side by side at long tables assembly-line style "was a roaring disaster," admits Kurien. "The factory idea concerned people." So based on feedback from his middle managers, Kurien arranged classes to explain his concepts and how they would ultimately make life easier for employees.

Wipro also adopted Toyota's *kaizen* system of soliciting employee suggestions. Priya, 28, who has worked for Wipro for nearly seven years, submitted several *kaizen* and was delighted when her bosses responded promptly to her suggestions. "Even though it's something small, it feels good. You're being considered," she says. Empowerment in the workplace washed over into her private life. As the first woman in her family to attend college she told her parents they may arrange her marriage only to a man who will not interfere with her career.

Kurien and his managers work hard at boosting employee morale, offering rewards—pens, caps, or shirts—to employees who submit suggestions to *kaizen* boxes. And each week a top-performing employee receives a cake. Murthy, 25, an accountant who hopes to be Wipro's chief financial officer some day, spearheaded an effort to cut government import approval times from 30 to 15 days. He got a cake with his name written on it in honey. "I was surprised management knew what I was doing," he says. "Now I want to do more projects."

With $1.7 billion in revenues, 42,000 employees, and a U.S.-traded stock that has advanced 230 percent in two years, Wipro is a star of India's burgeoning information technology industry. Today, the company's paperwork processing operations in Pune, Bangalore, and Chennai bear a clear resemblance to a Toyota plant. Two shifts of young men and women line long rows of tables. At the start of each shift team leaders discuss the day's goals and divide up tasks. And just like in a Toyota factory, electronic displays mounted on the walls shift from green to red if things get bogged down.

This obsession with management efficiency has helped India become the back office operation for hundreds of Western companies, resulting in the transfer of many thousands of jobs offshore. "If the Indians get this right, in addition to their low labor rates, they can become deadly competition," says Jeffrey K. Liker, a business professor at the University of Michigan and author of *The Toyota Way*, a book about Toyota's lean manufacturing techniques. If Kurien's management initiatives succeed, experts may soon be extolling the Wipro way.

Critical Thinking Questions

- What type of manager is T. K. Kurien? How would you characterize his leadership style?
- What managerial role does T. K. Kurien assume in his approach to attaining his division's goal of improved customer service?
- What management skill sets does he exhibit?

Sources: Steve Hamm, "Taking a Page from Toyota's Playbook," BusinessWeek Online http://www.businessweek.com August 22, 2005; Theodore Forbath, "Developing an Effective Global Sourcing Strategy," CIO Update, July 22, 2005, http://www.cioupdate.com; Toyota company Web site http://www.toyota.com December 29, 2005; Wipro company Web site http://www.wipro.com December 29, 2005.

Video Case >

Keeping Employees the SAS Way

If you treat employees as if they make a difference to the company, they *will* make a difference to the company. Satisfied employees create satisfied customers. That's been the employee-focused corporate culture at SAS (**http://www.sas.com**), the world's largest privately held software company and leader in e-business solutions since the company was founded in 1976. With employee turnover consistently and significantly below the industry average, SAS reaps the benefits of the most talented minds in the software business.

What would it take to keep *you* happy on the job? A 35-hour work week? A health and recreation center with Olympic-size pool, gym with personal trainers, basketball court, dance and yoga studio, pool and ping-pong tables? How about an on-site masseuse and free daily laundering of your workout clothes? Or a pianist in the atrium-style dining room where employees enjoy subsidized lunches with their children, picked up from the company's on-site day-care facility? Or unlimited sick days, free comprehensive health insurance, and access to on-site health care at a company-run clinic? Your own private office, a fully stocked break room, discounted membership to the local country club, a week off between Christmas and New Year, even free M & M's on Wednesdays? And of course there are the usual financial rewards of a competitive salary, bonus, and profit sharing plan.

Insanity Inc.? "It's been called worse," says James H. Goodnight, CEO, of the company he helped cofound. "If you treat people right they will make a difference. What we do here makes good business sense." Thanks to an employee defection rate of less than 4 percent, SAS saves $50 to $70 million annually, rewarding its employees by creating a work environment that no one wants to leave.

SAS employs nearly 10,000 people in more than 300 offices spanning the globe, and every day is a dress-down day for the 4,100 people working at the company's 200-acre campus located in Cary, North Carolina. SAS "hires hard and manages easy." It makes sure employees have the technical and intellectual skills for the job and then lets them get on with it. It does not micromanage employees. "We are not into 'face time' here," says Goodnight, "if you need to leave at 4:00 pm on Wednesday to watch your child's soccer game, we trust that you will get your work done." SAS believes in the importance of a life outside work, that people need to recharge their batteries.

And developing its employees' intellectual prowess makes them increasingly valuable to the company. "SAS is in the intellectual property business and our employees work on cutting-edge products. It is not a disgrace to fail, as long as they learn something from it and share the information so we can all learn," says Goodnight. "Our people are our assets and we believe in taking good care of our assets."

This approach has earned SAS many accolades, including eight consecutive years on *Fortune's 100 Best Companies to Work for in America*, recognized 13 times by *Working Mother* as one of the 100 Best Companies for Working Mothers, and featured as the Best Place to Work on the *Oprah* show.

Critical Thinking Questions

- What type of management skills does Jim Goodnight exhibit?
- How does the corporate culture at SAS differ from that of other companies?
- Would a company like SAS appeal to you as a prospective employee? Why or why not?

Sources: Adapted from material in the video, "Work Hard, Play Hard, and Have a Nice Lunch: Corporate Culture at SAS," company Web site http://www.sas.com December 29, 2005; 100 Best Companies to Work For 2005, *Fortune*, http://www.fortune.com December 31, 2005; "SAS' Dr. James Goodnight Named Ernst & Young Entrepreneur of the Year 2005 In Technology Category," Ernst & Young, http://www.ey.com, December 31, 2005.

Hot Links Address Book

How does a company translate its mission statement into company action? Find out at Ben & Jerry's home page at http://www.benjerry.com

Visit the International Business Leaders Forum (IBLF) at http://www.iblf.org to discover what today's international business leaders are focusing on.

To learn more about how firms develop contingency plans for all sorts of crises, visit *Contingency Planning* magazine's Web site at http://www.contingencyplanning.com

Who are the leaders of this year's *Inc.* 500, and what do they have to say about their success? Find out at the *Inc.* 500 site at http://www.inc.com

Want to learn more about Bill Gates' management style? Go to his personal Web site, http://www.microsoft.com/billgates to read his official biography, speeches, and other information.

Learn all about the greatest American business leaders of the 20th century at Harvard Business School's Web site, http://www.hbs.edu

Most successful managers work hard at continually updating their managerial skills. One organization that offers many ongoing training and education programs is the American Management Association. Visit its site at http://www.amanet.org

Search Questia's online library http://www.questia.com for leadership resources. You'll be able to preview a wide variety of books, journals, and other materials.

CHAPTER 8

Designing Organizational Structures

Learning Goals

After reading this chapter, you should be able to answer these questions:

1 What are the five traditional forms of departmentalization?

2 What contemporary organizational structures are companies using?

3 Why are companies using team-based organizational structures?

4 What tools do companies use to establish relationships within their organizations?

5 How can the degree of centralization/decentralization be altered to make an organization more successful?

6 How do mechanistic and organic organizations differ?

7 How does the informal organization affect the performance of the company?

8 What trends are influencing the way businesses organize?

Exploring Business Careers
Karen Denning
Navistar International Corporation

As director of corporate communications for Navistar International Corporation, Karen Denning's role in the structuring of the organization might not be apparent initially. After all, you might ask, doesn't communication typically involve marketing? And what does that have to do with organizational structure? As it turns out, quite a bit.

Named to the *Fortune* 500 Hall of Fame, Navistar's history extends back over 175 years when Cyrus Hall McCormick invented the mechanical reaper in 1831 and decided he needed a way to advertise his new invention. Today, it is a $12 billion corporation whose principal activities are divided into three separate industry segments: truck, engine, and financial services. Accounting for almost 70 percent of the corporation's revenues, the truck segment manufactures and distributes a full line of diesel-powered trucks and school buses. The engine segment, approximately 25 percent of Navistar's revenue, designs and manufactures diesel engines for use in selected vehicles produced by the truck industry segment. It also sells engines for industrial, agricultural, and marine applications. The financial services segment, which accounts for the remaining 5 percent of revenue, provides retail, wholesale, and lease financing of products sold by the truck segment and its dealers within the United States and Mexico. Each segment operates as a separate business and is structured to reflect that independence, with its own marketing, manufacturing, engineering, and finance departments. This separation enables each segment to specialize in its own market and to be able to focus on that market's unique challenges and opportunities.

Denning's role, in large part, is to bring these three segments together in a unified "strategic story" and single corporate culture. Despite the separation between its three segments, Navistar maintains a relatively centralized decision-making process. In part, this is due to the nature of manufacturing, an industry with high capital investments and long product development timetables. Decisions made today have the potential to significantly affect outcomes several months or years down the line, and how issues are handled in one segment can easily impact the entire organization. Even management issues that seem simple, such as those involving hourly workers, are sensitive—in this case, due to the workers' union representation by the United Auto Workers. Thus, each decision needs the careful attention of the management that oversees the whole corporation, and these decisions need to be communicated to the rest of the corporation in a way that ensures the successful execution of a unified vision. "As director of corporate communication, I work with the CEO and executive council to craft the strategic story and communicate where they want to take the company both to those internally and externally. Additionally, I help them communicate with the board of directors and shareholders who are influential in approving and directing where the company is going strategically. In this way, I facilitate the smooth use of the organizational structure by ensuring communication between all levels of Navistar."

This chapter focuses on the different types of organizational structure, the reasons an organization might prefer one structure over another, and how the choice of an organizational structure ultimately can impact that organization's success.

In today's dynamic business environment, organizational structures need to be designed so that the organization can quickly respond to new competitive threats and changing customer needs. Future success for companies will depend on their ability to be flexible and respond to the needs of customers. In this chapter, we'll look first at how companies build organizational structures by implementing traditional, contemporary, and team-based models. Then, we'll explore how managers establish the relationships within the structures they have designed, including determining lines of communication, authority, and power. Finally, we'll examine what managers need to consider when designing organizational structures and the new trends that are changing the choices companies make about organizational design.

Departmentalization—Building Organizational Structures

1 **What are the five traditional forms of departmentalization?**

As you learned in Chapter 7, the key functions that managers perform include planning, organizing, leading, and controlling. This chapter focuses specifically on the organizing function. *Organizing* involves coordinating and allocating a firm's resources so that the firm can carry out its plans and achieve its goals. This organizing, or structuring, process is accomplished by:

- determining work activities and dividing up tasks *(division of labor)*
- grouping jobs and employees *(departmentalization)*
- assigning authority and responsibilities *(delegation)*

formal organization
The order and design of relationships within a firm; consists of two or more people working together with a common objective and clarity of purpose.

The result of the organizing process is a formal organizational structure. A **formal organization** is the order and design of relationships within the firm. It consists of two or more people working together with a common objective and clarity of purpose. Formal organizations also have well-defined lines of authority, channels for information flow, and means of control. Human, material, financial, and information resources are deliberately connected to form the business organization. Some connections are long lasting, such as the links among people in the finance or marketing department. Others can be changed at almost any time, as when a committee is formed to study a problem.

Every organization has some kind of underlying structure. Traditional structures are more rigid and group employees by function, products, processes, customers, or

CONCEPT *in Action*
Founded in 1943, IKEA has grown from a small mail-order operation into an international home-furnishings retailer with over 230 stores in 33 countries throughout Europe, North America, and Asia. Best known for its intriguing modern furniture designs, highly trafficked store openings, and quirky advertising, the IKEA Group consists of multiple corporate divisions corresponding to the company's retail, purchasing, sales, and design and manufacturing functions. *What factors likely influenced the development of IKEA's organizational structure as the company changed over the years?*

regions, as described in the next section. Contemporary and team-based structures are more flexible and assemble employees to respond quickly to dynamic business environments. Regardless of the structural skeleton a company chooses to implement, all managers must first consider what kind of work needs to be done within the firm.

Division of Labor

division of labor
The process of dividing work into separate jobs and assigning tasks to workers.

specialization
The degree to which tasks are subdivided into smaller jobs.

The process of dividing work into separate jobs and assigning tasks to workers is called **division of labor**. In a fast-food restaurant, for example, some employees take or fill orders, others prepare food, a few clean and maintain equipment, and at least one supervises all the others. In an auto assembly plant, some workers install rearview mirrors, whereas others mount bumpers on bumper brackets. The degree to which the tasks are subdivided into smaller jobs is called **specialization**. Employees who work at highly specialized jobs, such as assembly-line workers, perform a limited number and variety of tasks. Employees who become specialists at one task, or a small number of tasks, develop greater skill in doing that particular job. This can lead to greater efficiency and consistency in production and other work activities. However, a high degree of specialization can also result in employees who are disinterested or bored due to the lack of variety and challenge. In Chapter 10, we will discuss ways managers can mitigate the disadvantages of a highly specialized workforce.

Traditional Structures

departmentalization
The process of grouping jobs together so that similar or associated tasks and activities can be coordinated.

organization chart
A visual representation of the structured relationships among tasks and the people given the authority to do those tasks.

After a company divides into jobs the work it needs to do, managers then group the jobs together so that similar or associated tasks and activities can be coordinated. This grouping of people, tasks, and resources into organizational units is called **departmentalization** and facilitates the planning, leading, and control processes.

An **organization chart** is a visual representation of the structured relationships among tasks and the people given the authority to do those tasks. In the organization chart in Exhibit 8.1, each figure represents a job, and each job includes several tasks.

Exhibit 8.1 > Organization Chart for a Typical Appliance Manufacturer

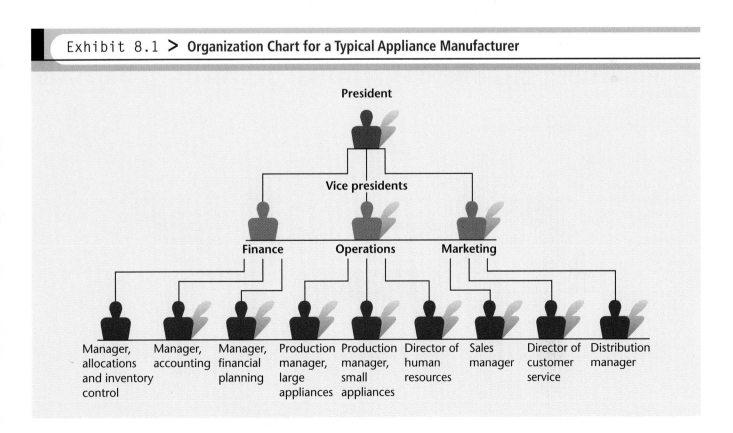

President

Vice presidents

Finance | Operations | Marketing

Manager, allocations and inventory control | Manager, accounting | Manager, financial planning | Production manager, large appliances | Production manager, small appliances | Director of human resources | Sales manager | Director of customer service | Distribution manager

The sales manager, for instance, must hire salespeople, establish sales territories, motivate and train the salespeople, and control sales operations. The chart also indicates the general type of work done in each position. As Exhibit 8.2 shows, five basic types of departmentalization are commonly used in organizations:

functional departmentalization
Departmentalization that is based on the primary functions performed within an organizational unit.

1. *Functional departmentalization*, which is based on the primary functions performed within an organizational unit (marketing, finance, production, sales,

Exhibit 8.2 > Five Traditional Ways to Organize

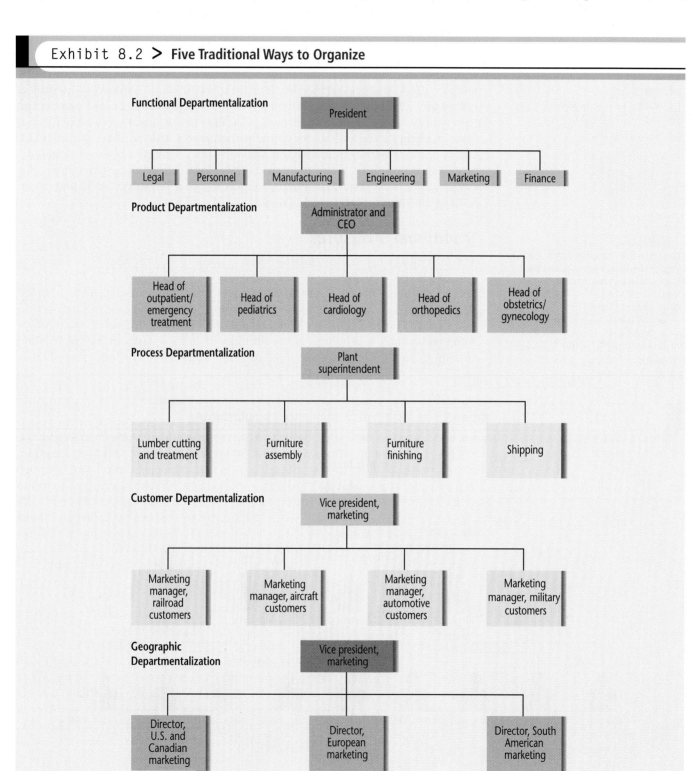

and so on). Ethan Allen Interiors, a vertically integrated furniture manufacturer, switched to functional departmentalization when it reorganized into three functional subsidiaries: retail, operations and marketing, and financial reporting.[1]

2. *Product departmentalization*, which is based on the goods or services produced or sold by the organizational unit (such as outpatient/emergency services, pediatrics, cardiology, and orthopedics). For example, ITT Industries is organized into four product divisions: A Fluid Technology (pumps and wastewater treatment equipment), Defensive Electronics and Services, Motion and Flow Control products (like shock absorbers, pumps for Whirlpool spas, and beverage dispensers), and Electronic Components (like electromechanical switches, keypads, and more).[2]

3. *Process departmentalization*, which is based on the production process used by the organizational unit (such as lumber cutting and treatment, furniture finishing, and shipping). For example, the organization of Sibneft, a Russian oil company, reflects the activities the company needs to perform to extract oil from the ground and turn it into a final product: exploration and research, production (drilling), refining, and marketing and distribution.[3] Pixar, the animated-movie company, is divided into three parallel yet interactive process-based groups: technology development, which delivers computer-graphics tools; creative development, which concocts stories and characters and animates them; and production, which coordinates the film-making process.[4]

4. *Customer departmentalization*, which is based on the primary type of customer served by the organizational unit (such as wholesale or retail purchasers). In 2005, PNC Bank restructured several lines of business within its banking operation. Now the company's banking business is divided into two units to reflect the customers it serves: consumer banking and institutional banking.

5. *Geographic departmentalization*, which is based on the geographic segmentation of organizational units (such as U.S. and Canadian marketing, European marketing, and South American marketing).

People are assigned to a particular organizational unit because they perform similar or related tasks, or because they are jointly responsible for a product, client, or market. Decisions about how to departmentalize affect the way management assigns authority, distributes resources, rewards performance, and sets up lines of communication. Many large organizations use several types of departmentalization. For example, Procter & Gamble (P&G), the multibillion dollar consumer-products company, integrates four different types of departmentalization, which the company refers to as "four pillars." First, the Global Business Units (GBUs) divide the company according to products (baby care/family care, beauty care/feminine care, fabric and home care, snacks and beverages, and health care). Then, P&G uses a geographical approach, creating business units to market its products around the world. There are Market Development Organizations (MDOs) for North America; Asia, India, and Australia; Northeast Asia; Greater China; Central-Eastern Europe, the Middle East, and Africa; Western Europe; and Latin America. P&G's third pillar is Global Business Services division (GBS), which also uses geographic departmentalization (Americas; Asia; and Europe, Middle East, and Africa). GBS groups support their regional MDOs in the areas of accounting, employee benefits and payroll, order management and product logistics, and systems operations. Finally, the divisions of the Corporate Functions pillar provide a safety net to all the other pillars, comprised of functional specialties like customer business development; external relations; finance and accounting; human resources; information technology; legal, marketing, consumer, and market knowledge; product supply; research and development; and workplace services.[5]

---

product departmentalization
Departmentalization that is based on the goods or services produced or sold by the organizational unit.

process departmentalization
Departmentalization that is based on the production process used by the organizational unit.

customer departmentalization
Departmentalization that is based on the primary type of customer served by the organizational unit.

geographic departmentalization
Departmentalization that is based on the geographic segmentation of the organizational units.

---

concept check

How does specialization lead to greater efficiency and consistency in production?

What are the five types of departmentalization?

Line-and-Staff Organization

line organization
An organizational structure with direct, clear lines of authority and communication flowing from the top managers downward.

line-and-staff organization
An organizational structure that includes both line and staff positions.

line positions
All positions in the organization directly concerned with producing goods and services and that are directly connected from top to bottom.

staff positions
Positions in an organization held by individuals who provide the administrative and support services that line employees need to achieve the firm's goals.

The **line organization** is designed with direct, clear lines of authority and communication flowing from the top managers downward. Managers have direct control over all activities, including administrative duties. An organization chart for this type of structure would show that all positions in the firm are directly connected via an imaginary line extending from the highest position in the organization to the lowest (where production of goods and services takes place). This structure with its simple design and broad managerial control is often well suited to small, entrepreneurial firms.

As an organization grows and becomes more complex, the line organization can be enhanced by adding staff positions to the design. Staff positions provide specialized advisory and support services to line managers in the **line-and-staff organization**, shown in Exhibit 8.3. In daily operations, individuals in **line positions** are directly involved in the processes used to create goods and services. Individuals in **staff positions** provide the administrative and support services that line employees need to achieve the firm's goals. Line positions in organizations are typically in areas such as production, marketing, and finance. Staff positions are found in areas such as legal counseling, managerial consulting, public relations, and human resource management.

Contemporary Structures

 What contemporary organizational structures are companies using?

Although traditional forms of departmentalization still represent how many companies organize their work, newer, more flexible organizational structures are in use at many firms. Let's look at matrix and committee structures, and how those two types of organizations are helping companies better leverage the diverse skills of their employees.

Matrix Structure

The **matrix structure** (also called the *project management* approach) is sometimes used in conjunction with the traditional line-and-staff structure in an organization. Essentially, this structure combines two different forms of departmentalization, functional and

---

Exhibit 8.3 > Line-and-Staff Organization

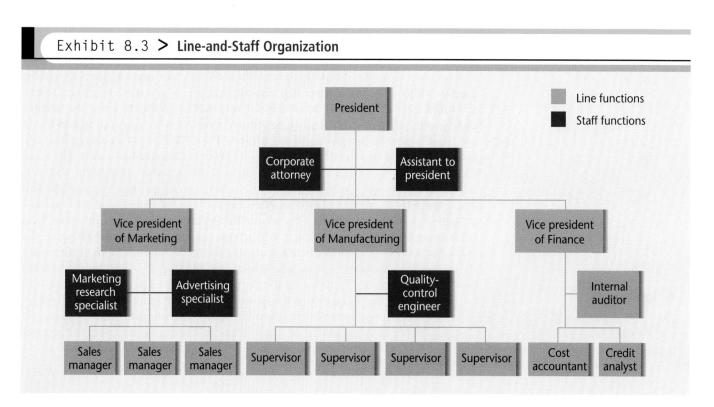

CONCEPT *in Action*

Like the futuristic characters trapped in a dizzying web of confusion in the movie *The Matrix Revolutions*, some managers experience chaos within a contemporary organizational structure known as the matrix. Advocates of matrix structures claim that combining the functional and product forms of departmentalization leads to greater innovation and responsiveness to markets, but others say having multiple supervisors and hierarchies invariably leads to power struggles and confusion among team members. *Are workers capable of serving two masters?*

matrix structure (project management)
An organizational structure that combines functional and product departmentalization by bringing together people from different functional areas of the organization to work on a special project.

product, that have complementary strengths and weaknesses. The matrix structure brings together people from different functional areas of the organization (such as manufacturing, finance, and marketing) to work on a special project. Each employee has two direct supervisors: the line manager from her or his specific functional area and the project manager. Exhibit 8.4 shows a matrix organization with four special project groups (A, B, C, D), each with its own project manager. Because of the dual chain of command, the matrix structure presents some unique challenges for both managers and subordinates.

Advantages of the matrix structure include:

- *Teamwork.* By pooling the skills and abilities of various specialists, the company can increase creativity and innovation and tackle more complex tasks.

Exhibit 8.4 > Matrix Organization

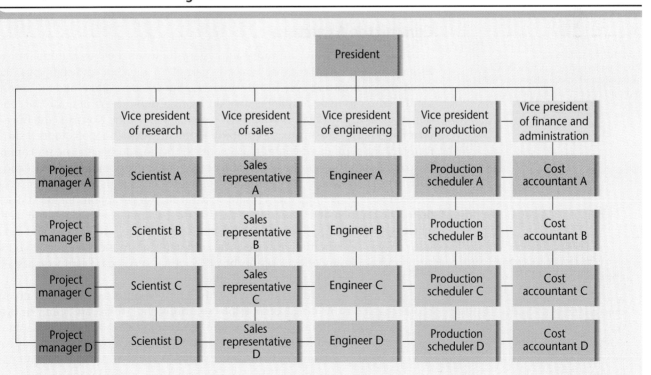

- *Efficient use of resources.* Project managers use only the specialized staff they need to get the job done, instead of building large groups of underused personnel.
- *Flexibility.* The project structure is flexible and can adapt quickly to changes in the environment; the group can be disbanded quickly when it is no longer needed.
- *Ability to balance conflicting objectives.* The customer wants a quality product and predictable costs. The organization wants high profits and the development of technical capability for the future. These competing goals serve as a focal point for directing activities and overcoming conflict. The marketing representative can represent the customer, the finance representative can advocate high profits, and the engineers can push for technical capabilities.
- *Higher performance.* Employees working on special project teams may experience increased feelings of ownership, commitment, and motivation.
- *Opportunities for personal and professional development.* The project structure gives individuals the opportunity to develop and strengthen technical and interpersonal skills.

Disadvantages of the matrix structure include:

- *Power struggles.* Functional and product managers may have different goals and management styles.
- *Confusion among team members.* Reporting relationships and job responsibilities may be unclear.
- *Lack of cohesiveness.* Team members from different functional areas may have difficulty communicating effectively and working together as a team.

Although project-based matrix organizations can improve a company's flexibility and teamwork, some companies are trying to unravel complex matrix structures that create limited accountability. For example, during the first year as Hewlett-Packard CEO, Mark Hurd worked diligently to untangle the complex matrix structure implemented by his predecessor, Carly Fiorina. The reason Hurd gave for tossing out Fiorina's matrix management structure, which muddied responsibilities, was to give business heads more control of their units. "The more accountable I can make you, the easier it is for you to show you're a great performer," says Hurd. "The more I use a matrix, the easier I make it to blame someone else."[6]

Committee Structure

committee structure
An organizational structure in which authority and responsibility are held by a group rather than an individual.

In **committee structure**, authority and responsibility are held by a group rather than an individual. Committees are typically part of a larger line-and-staff organization. Often the committee's role is only advisory, but in some situations the committee has the power to make and implement decisions. Committees can make the coordination of tasks in the organization much easier. For example, Novartis, the huge Swiss pharmaceutical company, has a committee structure, which reports to its board of directors. Four permanent committees report to the board: the chairman's committee, the compensation committee, the audit and compliance committee, and a corporate governance committee. The chairman's committee deals with business matters arising between board meetings and is responsible for high-level appointments and acquisitions. The compensation committee looks at the pay-and-expenses of board members, whereas the audit and compliance committee oversees accounting and financial reporting practices. The corporate governance committee's duties include focusing on board nominations, board performance evaluations, and possible conflicts of interest.[7]

Committees bring diverse viewpoints to a problem and expand the range of possible solutions, but there are some drawbacks. Committees can be slow to reach a decision and are sometimes dominated by a single individual. It is also more difficult to hold any one individual accountable for a decision made by a group. Committee meetings can sometimes go on for long periods of time with little seemingly being accomplished.

concept check

Why does the matrix structure have a dual chain of command?

How does a matrix structure increase power struggles or reduce accountability?

What are advantages of a committee structure? Disadvantages?

Using Teams to Enhance Motivation and Performance

 3 Why are companies using team-based organizational structures?

One of the most apparent trends in business today is the use of teams to accomplish organizational goals. Using a team-based structure can increase individual and group motivation and performance. This section gives a brief overview of group behavior, defines work teams as specific types of groups, and provides suggestions for creating high-performing teams.

Understanding Group Behavior

Teams are a specific type of organizational group. Every organization contains *groups,* social units of two or more people who share the same goals and cooperate to achieve those goals. Understanding some fundamental concepts related to group behavior and group processes provides a good foundation for understanding concepts about work teams. Groups can be formal or informal in nature. Formal groups are designated and sanctioned by the organization; their behavior is directed toward accomplishing organizational goals. Informal groups are based on social relationships and are not determined or sanctioned by the organization.

Formal organizational groups, like the sales department at Dell Computers, must operate within the larger Dell organizational system. To some degree, elements of the larger Dell system, such as organizational strategy, company policies and procedures, available resources, and the highly motivated employee corporate culture, determine the behavior of smaller groups, like the sales department, within Dell. Other factors that affect the behavior of organizational groups are individual member characteristics (e.g., ability, training, personality), the roles and norms of group members, and the size and cohesiveness of the group. Norms are the implicit behavioral guidelines of the group, or the standards for acceptable and nonacceptable behavior. For example, a Dell sales manager may be expected to work at least two Saturdays per month without extra pay. Although this isn't written anywhere, it is the expected norm.

group cohesiveness
The degree to which group members want to stay in the group and tend to resist outside influences.

Group cohesiveness refers to the degree to which group members want to stay in the group and tend to resist outside influences (such as a change in company policies). When group performance norms are high, group cohesiveness will have a positive impact on productivity. Cohesiveness tends to increase when the size of the group is small, individual and group goals are similar, the group has high status in the organization, rewards are group based rather than individual based, and the group competes with other groups within the organization. Work group cohesiveness can benefit the organization in several ways including increased productivity, enhanced worker self-image because of group success, increased company loyalty, reduced employee turnover, and reduced absenteeism. Southwest Airlines is known for its work group cohesiveness. On the other hand, cohesiveness can also lead to restricted output, resistance to change, and conflict with other work groups in the organization.

The opportunity to turn the decision-making process over to a group with diverse skills and abilities is one of the arguments for using work groups (and teams) in organizational settings. For group decision making to be most effective, however, both managers and group members must understand its strengths and weaknesses (see Exhibit 8.5).

Work Groups versus Work Teams

work groups
The groups that share resources and coordinate efforts to help members better perform their individual jobs.

work teams
Like a work group but also requires the pooling of knowledge, skills, abilities, and resources to achieve a common goal.

We have already noted that teams are a special type of organizational group, but we also need to differentiate between work groups and work teams. **Work groups** share resources and coordinate efforts to help members better perform their individual duties and responsibilities. The performance of the group can be evaluated by adding up the contributions of the individual group members. **Work teams** require not only coordination but also *collaboration,* the pooling of knowledge, skills, abilities, and resources in a collective effort to attain a common goal. A work team creates *synergy,* causing the performance of the team as a whole to be greater than the sum of team members' individual contributions. Simply assigning employees to groups and labeling

Exhibit 8.5 > Strengths and Weakneses of Group Decision Making

Strengths	Weaknesses
• Groups bring more information and knowledge to the decision process.	• Groups typically take a longer time to reach a solution than an individual takes.
• Groups offer a diversity of perspectives and, therefore, generate a greater number of alternatives.	• Group members may pressure others to conform, reducing the likelihood of disagreement.
• Group decision making results in a higher-quality decision than does individual decision making.	• The process may be dominated by one or a small number of participants.
• Participation of group members increases the likelihood that a decision will be accepted.	• Groups lack accountability, because it is difficult to assign responsibility for outcomes to any one individual.

them a team does not guarantee a positive outcome. Managers and team members must be committed to creating, developing, and maintaining high-performance work teams. Factors that contribute to their success are discussed later in this section.

Types of Teams

problem-solving teams
Usually members of the same department who meet regularly to suggest ways to improve operations and solve specific problems.

The evolution of the team concept in organizations can be seen in three basic types of work teams: problem solving, self-managed, and cross-functional. **Problem-solving teams** are typically made up of employees from the same department or area of expertise and from the same level of the organizational hierarchy. They meet on a regular basis to share information and discuss ways to improve processes and procedures in specific functional areas. Problem-solving teams generate ideas and alternatives and may recommend a specific course of action, but they typically do not make final decisions, allocate resources, or implement change.

Many organizations that experienced success using problem-solving teams were willing to expand the team concept to allow team members greater responsibility in making decisions, implementing solutions, and monitoring outcomes. These highly autonomous groups are called **self-managed work teams**. They manage themselves without any formal supervision, taking responsibility for setting goals, planning and scheduling work activities, selecting team members, and evaluating team performance.

self-managed work teams
Teams without formal supervision that plan, select alternatives, and evaluate their own performance.

In 2006, over 70 percent of production workers were members of an empowered or self-directed work team.[8] One example is at Chrysler's pickup truck assembly plant in Saltillo, Mexico, where self-directed work teams comprised of 10 to 12 employees take on a set of tasks and tools, including specified maintenance, quality control, and productivity and safety jobs. Team members rotate among different tasks every few hours and are encouraged to find ways to cut time and wasted effort. Those whose jobs become redundant as a result are reassigned. Production has increased to about 38 vehicles an hour from 30, all without additional hiring or overtime.[9] A more extreme version of self-managing teams can be found at W. L. Gore, the company that invented Gore-Tex fabric and Glide dental floss. The three employees who invented Elixir guitar strings contributed their spare time to the effort and persuaded a handful of colleagues to help them improve the design. After working three years *entirely* on their own—without asking for any supervisory or top management permission or being subjected to any kind of oversight—the team finally sought the support of the

Harnessing Talent to Harness the Wind

Many companies boast a global workforce, but few are as skilled at mobilizing experts from diverse disciplines and locales in pursuit of a common goal. At General Electric, executives are encouraged to think beyond the boundaries of their particular business. They come together frequently for training or joint projects. Executives are apt to move among units several times in their careers, letting them build up a rich network of internal contacts. There's also a tradition of plucking people from their day jobs for other projects. At any given time, thousands of GE employees are on so-called bubble assignments—lending their skills to another function or business that pays their salaries for the duration of the project.

James Lyons, a chief engineer at the GE Global Research Center in upstate New York, is the fulcrum for GE's Wind Energy project. The 30-year veteran has brought in engineers from other units and navigated cultural hurdles worldwide. He has recruited materials experts from down the hall who developed the composites for the fan blades of the GE90 aircraft engine; design teams in South Carolina and Salzbergen, Germany; engineers from Ontario, who are tackling the generators; Bangalore researchers who are drafting analytical models and turbine system design tools; and Shanghai engineers who conduct high-end simulations. Chinese researchers design the microprocessors that control the pitch of the blade. And technicians in Munich have created a smart turbine that can calculate wind speeds and signal other turbines to pitch their blades for maximum electricity

production. Lyons keeps his global team focused with e-mails, teleconferences, and clear deadlines.

One way he builds team spirit is to foster familiarity. In addition to regular teleconferences, engineers take stints working in other parts of the operation. That has meant trading engineers from Bangalore and Salzbergen, for example, for a week or two at a time. Along with learning about the core design tools being created in Bangalore or the actual products being made in Salzbergen, they establish better lines of communication. With its $2 billion in annual revenues, the far-flung Wind Energy team is getting results. Among the innovations so far is a new generation of land-based wind turbines with new blade and advanced control technologies for customers who want to generate energy on sites where space is limited. One unit designed for offshore locations sits 30 stories above the ocean, has turbine blades each longer than a football field, and can power 1,400 average American homes a year. Current projects range from a wind farm in Inner Mongolia to working on smaller turbines that could help provide clean water to villages in developing countries.[10]

Critical Thinking Questions

- What challenges do you think face James Lyons in managing his global Wind Energy team?
- Would you be interested in participating in such a geographically widespread team? Why or why not?

---

cross-functional team
Members from the same organizational level but from different functional areas.

concept check

What is the difference between a work team and a work group?

Identify and describe three types of work teams.

What are some ways to build a high-performance team?

larger company, which they needed to take the strings to market. Today, W. L. Gore's Elixir has a 35 percent market share in acoustic guitar strings.[11]

An adaptation of the team concept is called a **cross-functional team**. These teams are made up of employees from about the same hierarchical level, but different functional areas of the organization. Many task forces, organizational committees, and project teams are cross-functional. Often the team members work together only until they solve a given problem or complete a specific project. Cross-functional teams allow people with various levels and areas of expertise to pool their resources, develop new ideas, solve problems, and coordinate complex projects. Both problem-solving teams and self-managed teams may also be cross-functional teams. Read the Expanding around the Globe box for an example of how General Electric is implementing—and succeeding with—global cross-functional teams.

Building High-Performance Teams

A great team must possess certain characteristics, so selecting the appropriate employees for the team is vital. Employees who are more willing to work together to accomplish a common goal should be selected, rather than employees who are more interested in their own personal achievement. Team members should also possess a variety of skills. Diverse skills strengthen the overall effectiveness of the team, so teams should consciously recruit members to fill gaps in the collective skill set. To be effective, teams must also have clearly defined goals. Vague or unclear goals will not provide the necessary direction or allow employees to measure their performance against expectations. Next, high-performing teams need to practice good communication. Team members need to communicate messages and give appropriate feedback

that seeks to correct any misunderstandings. Feedback should also be detached, that is team members should be careful to critique ideas rather than criticize the person who suggests them. Nothing can degrade the effectiveness of a team like personal attacks. Lastly, great teams have great leaders. Skilled team leaders divide work up so that tasks are not repeated, help members set and track goals, monitor their team's performance, communicate openly, and remain flexible to adapt to changing goals or management demands.

Authority—Establishing Organizational Relationships

Once companies choose a method of departmentalization, they must then establish the relationships within that structure. In other words, the company must decide how many layers of management it needs and who will report to whom. The company must also decide how much control to invest in each of its managers and where in the organization decisions will be made and implemented.

Managerial Hierarchy

Managerial hierarchy (also called the *management pyramid*) is defined by the levels of management within an organization. Generally, the management structure has three levels: top, middle, and supervisory management. These three levels were introduced in Chapter 7. In a managerial hierarchy, each organizational unit is controlled and supervised by a manager in a higher unit. The person with the most formal authority is at the top of the hierarchy. The higher a manager, the more power he or she has. Thus, the amount of power decreases as you move down the management pyramid. At the same time, the number of employees increases as you move down the hierarchy.

Not all companies today are using this traditional configuration. One company that has eliminated hierarchy altogether is 5.11 Tactical, a Modesto, California, company that makes law enforcement uniforms. Like nearly every business around the world, 5.11 has a CEO and managers. Unlike nearly every business in the world, they are all on the same organizational line. The owner, Dan Costa, says, "Our management philosophy is that, unlike other management charts, our management is all on one line. I'm the CEO, and I am on that line. We don't have vice presidents, and we don't have directors. We have managers. There isn't a hierarchy in our company. Everybody feels very good and open about their positions and where they are within the company."[12]

An organization with a well-defined hierarchy has a clear **chain of command**, which is the line of authority that extends from one level of the organization to the next, from top to bottom, and makes clear who reports to whom. The chain of command is shown in the organization chart and can be traced from the CEO all the way down to the employees producing goods and services. Under the *unity of command* principle, everyone reports to and gets instructions from only one boss. Unity of command guarantees that everyone will have a direct supervisor and will not be taking orders from a number of different supervisors. Unity of command and chain of command give everyone in the organization clear directions and help coordinate people doing different jobs.

Matrix organizations automatically violate the unity of command principle because employees report to more than one boss, if only for the duration of a project. For example, Unilever, the consumer-products company that makes Dove soap, Surf

CONCEPT *in Action*

Fans of NBC's *The Apprentice* know all about the rewards of effective teamwork—and about the consequences of failure. Each season, millions tune in to watch teams of enterprising protégés compete for the approval of iconic real-estate tycoon Donald Trump. To the group demonstrating the best cohesiveness, collaboration, and resourcefulness, Trump offers beaucoup perks; but to the nonperformers, The Donald offers his trademark "You're fired!" during the dramatic final boardroom scene. *What are common characteristics of high-performance teams?*

4 **What tools do companies use to establish relationships within their organizations?**

managerial hierarchy
The levels of management within an organization; typically, includes top, middle, and supervisory management.

chain of command
The line of authority that extends from one level of an organization's hierarchy to the next, from top to bottom, and makes clear who reports to whom.

detergent, and Country Crock margarine, used to have a matrix structure with one CEO for North America and another for Europe. But employees in divisions that operated in both locations were unsure about which CEO's decisions took precedence.[13] Companies like Unilever and Hewlett-Packard tend to abandon matrix structures because of problems associated with unclear or duplicate reporting relationships, in other words with a lack of unity of command.

Individuals who are part of the chain of command have authority over other persons in the organization. **Authority** is legitimate power, granted by the organization and acknowledged by employees, that allows an individual to request action and expect compliance. Exercising authority means making decisions and seeing that they are carried out. Most managers *delegate*, or assign, some degree of authority and responsibility to others below them in the chain of command. The **delegation of authority** makes the employees accountable to their supervisor. *Accountability* means responsibility for outcomes. Typically, authority and responsibility move downward through the organization as managers assign activities to, and share decision making with, their subordinates. Accountability moves upward in the organization as managers in each successively higher level are held accountable for the actions of their subordinates.

Span of Control

Each firm must decide how many managers are needed at each level of the management hierarchy to effectively supervise the work performed within organizational units. A manager's **span of control** (sometimes called *span of management*) is the number of employees the manager directly supervises. It can be as narrow as two or three employees or as wide as 50 or more. In general, the larger the span of control, the more efficient the organization. As Exhibit 8.6 shows, however, both narrow and wide spans of control have benefits and drawbacks.

If hundreds of employees perform the same job, one supervisor may be able to manage a very large number of employees. Such might be the case at a clothing plant, where hundreds of sewing machine operators work from identical patterns. But if employees perform complex and dissimilar tasks, a manager can effectively supervise only a much smaller number. For instance, a supervisor in the research and development area of a pharmaceutical company might oversee just a few research chemists due to the highly complex nature of their jobs.

authority
Legitimate power, granted by the organization and acknowledged by employees, that allows an individual to request action and expect compliance.

delegation of authority
The assignment of some degree of authority and responsibility to persons lower in the chain of command.

span of control
The number of employees a manager directly supervises; also called span of management.

concept check

How does the chain of command clarify reporting relationships?

What is the role of a staff position in a line-and-staff organization?

What factors determine the optimal span of control?

Exhibit 8.6 > Narrow and Wide Spans of Control

	Advantages	Disadvantages
Narrow span of control	• High degree of control. • Fewer subordinates may mean manager is more familiar with each individual. • Close supervision can provide immediate feedback.	• More levels of management, therefore more expensive. • Slower decision making due to vertical layers. • Isolation of top management. • Discourages employee autonomy.
Wide span of control	• Fewer levels of management means increased efficiency and reduced costs. • Increased subordinate autonomy leads to quicker decision making. • Greater organizational flexibility. • Higher levels of job satisfaction due to employee empowerment.	• Less control. • Possible lack of familiarity due to large number of subordinates. • Managers spread so thin that they can't provide necessary leadership or support. • Lack of coordination or synchronization.

The optimal span of control is determined by the following five factors:

1. *Nature of the task.* The more complex the task, the narrower the span of control.
2. *Location of the workers.* The more locations, the narrower the span of control.
3. *Ability of the manager to delegate responsibility.* The greater the ability to delegate, the wider the span of control.
4. *Amount of interaction and feedback between the workers and the manager.* The more feedback and interaction required, the narrower the span of control.
5. *Level of skill and motivation of the workers.* The higher the skill level and motivation, the wider the span of control.

5 How can the degree of centralization/decentralization be altered to make an organization more successful?

Degree of Centralization

centralization
The degree to which formal authority is concentrated in one area or level of an organization. Top management makes most of the decisions.

decentralization
The process of pushing decision-making authority down the organizational hierarchy.

The Honorable
Michael Brown

© WIN MCNAMEE/GETTY IMAGES

CONCEPT *in Action*

The Federal Emergency Management Agency (FEMA), the United States agency responsible for responding to floods, hurricanes, and other natural disasters, was once an independent agency with a cabinet-level officer directly accountable to the president. But after 9/11, FEMA was placed under the Department of Homeland Security—a move that former director Michael D. Brown said interfered with communication, planning, and coordination breakdowns during Hurricane Katrina. *What degree of centralization is desirable for an emergency-response organization?*

concept Check

What are the characteristics of a centralized organization?

What are the benefits of a decentralized organization?

What factors should be considered when choosing the degree of centralization?

The final component in building an effective organizational structure is deciding at what level in the organization decisions should be made. **Centralization** is the degree to which formal authority is concentrated in one area or level of the organization. In a highly centralized structure, top management makes most of the key decisions in the organization, with very little input from lower-level employees. Centralization lets top managers develop a broad view of operations and exercise tight financial controls. It can also help to reduce costs by eliminating redundancy in the organization. But centralization may also mean that lower-level personnel don't get a chance to develop their decision-making and leadership skills and that the organization is less able to respond quickly to customer demands.

Decentralization is the process of pushing decision-making authority down the organizational hierarchy, giving lower-level personnel more responsibility and power to make and implement decisions. Benefits of decentralization can include quicker decision making, increased levels of innovation and creativity, greater organizational flexibility, faster development of lower-level managers, and increased levels of job satisfaction and employee commitment. But decentralization can also be risky. If lower-level personnel don't have the necessary skills and training to perform effectively, they may make costly mistakes. Additionally, decentralization may increase the likelihood of inefficient lines of communication, competing objectives, and duplication of effort.

Several factors must be considered when deciding how much decision-making authority to delegate throughout the organization. These factors include the size of the organization, the speed of change in its environment, managers' willingness to give up authority, employees' willingness to accept more authority, and the organization's geographic dispersion.

Decentralization is usually desirable when the following conditions are met:

- The organization is very large, like ExxonMobil, Ford, or General Electric.
- The firm is in a dynamic environment where quick, local decisions must be made, as in many high-tech industries.
  - Managers are willing to share power with their subordinates.
  - Employees are willing and able to take more responsibility.
  - The company is spread out geographically, such as JC Penney, Caterpillar, or Ford.

As organizations grow and change, they continually reevaluate their structure to determine whether it is helping the company to achieve its goals.

Organizational Design Considerations

6 How do mechanistic and organic organizations differ?

You are now familiar with the different ways to structure an organization, but as a manager, how do you decide which design will work the best for your business? What works for one company may not work for another. In this section, we'll look at two generic models of organizational design and briefly examine a set of contingency factors that favor each.

Mechanistic versus Organic Structures

mechanistic organization
An organizational structure that is characterized by a relatively high degree of job specialization, rigid departmentalization, many layers of management, narrow spans of control, centralized decision making, and a long chain of command.

organic organization
An organizational structure that is characterized by a relatively low degree of job specialization, loose departmentalization, few levels of management, wide spans of control, decentralized decision making, and a short chain of command.

Structural design generally follows one of the two basic models described in Exhibit 8.7: mechanistic or organic. A **mechanistic organization** is characterized by a relatively high degree of job specialization, rigid departmentalization, many layers of management (particularly middle management), narrow spans of control, centralized decision making, and a long chain of command. This combination of elements results in what is called a tall organizational structure. The U.S. Army and the United Nations are typical mechanistic organizations.

In contrast, an **organic organization** is characterized by a relatively low degree of job specialization, loose departmentalization, few levels of management, wide spans of control, decentralized decision making, and a short chain of command. This combination of elements results in what is called a flat organizational structure. Colleges and universities tend to have flat organizational structures, with only two or three levels of administration between the faculty and the president. Exhibit 8.8 shows examples of flat and tall organizational structures.

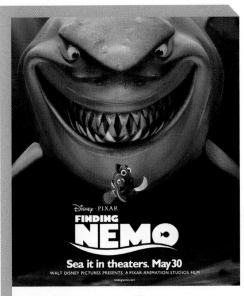

CONCEPT *in Action*

The Walt Disney Company expanded its entertainment empire in 2006 by acquiring Pixar studios, the animation powerhouse behind such blockbusters as *Finding Nemo, The Incredibles,* and *Toy Story.* The $7.4 billion purchase absorbed Pixar into the Disney Studio Entertainment division, one of Disney's four operating units, alongside Parks and Resorts, Consumer Products, and Media Networks. *Why do some analysts believe that Disney's colossal organizational structure could engulf the smaller Pixar operation and stifle its creative output?*

Factors Influencing the Choice Between Mechanistic Versus Organic Structures

Although few organizations are purely mechanistic or purely organic, most organizations tend more toward one type or the other. The decision to create a more mechanistic or a more organic structural design is based on factors such as the firm's overall strategy, the size of the organization, and the stability of its external environment, among others.

A company's organizational structure should enable it to achieve its goals, and because setting corporate goals is part of a firm's overall strategy-making process, it follows that a company's structure depends on its *strategy*. Recall the example of how Hewlett-Packard's CEO, Mark Hurd, is working to untangle the unwieldy organizational structure put in place by his predecessor. Hurd has flattened H-P's 14 layers of management to have more executive vice presidents reporting directly to the CEO. Business units will have more autonomy to execute their plans combined with increased accountability for their results. H-P has simply aligned its structure with its strategy.[14]

That alignment can be challenging for struggling companies trying to accomplish multiple goals. For example, a company with an innovation strategy will need the flexibility and fluid movement of information that an organic organization provides. But a company using a cost-control strategy will require the efficiency and tight control of a mechanistic organization. Often, struggling companies try to simultaneously increase innovation and reign in costs, which can be organizational challenges for managers. Such is the case at Sony, whose CEO, Howard Stringer, cut 10,000 jobs, closed factories, and shuffled management in an attempt to control costs and improve efficiency. At the same time, he is also trying to encourage cross-divisional communication (like between the music and electronics divisions) and increase the pace of innovation.

Exhibit 8.7 > **Mechanistic versus Organic Structure**

Structural Characteristic	Mechanistic	Organic
Job specialization	High	Low
Departmentalization	Rigid	Loose
Management hierarchy (levels of management)	Tall (many levels)	Flat (few levels)
Span of control	Narrow	Wide
Decision-making authority	Centralized	Decentralized
Chain of command	Long	Short

Exhibit 8.8 > **Flat versus Tall Organizational Structures**

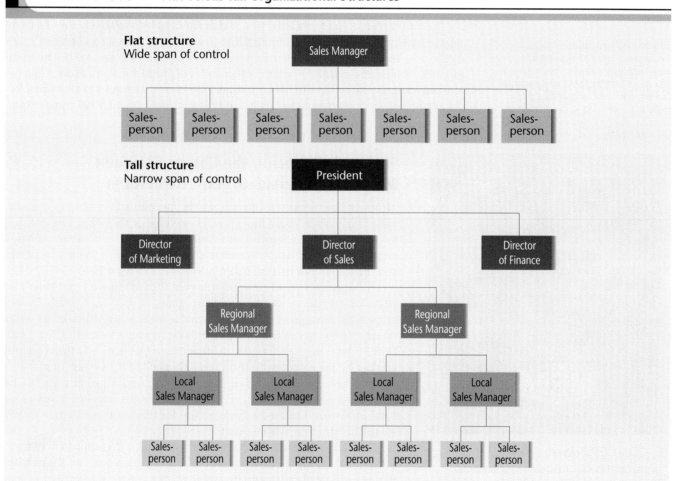

Stringer will need to balance these two strategies regardless of which organizational model he relies on most.[15]

Another factor that affects how mechanistic or organic a company's organizational structure is *size*. Much research has been conducted that shows a company's size has a significant impact on its organizational structure.[16] Smaller companies tend to follow the more organic model, in part because they can. It's much easier to be successful with decentralized decision making, for example, if you have only 50 employees. A company with that few employees is also more likely, by virtue of its size, to have a lesser degree of employee specialization. That's because when there are fewer people to do the work, those people tend to know more about the entire process. As a company grows, it becomes more mechanistic, as systems are put in place to manage the greater number of employees. Procedures, rules, and regulations replace flexibility, innovation, and independence. That isn't always the case, however. W. L. Gore has 6,300 employees and $1.58 billion in annual revenues, but, as noted earlier, uses an extremely organic organizational structure. Employees have no bosses, participate on teams, and often create roles for themselves to fill functional gaps within the company.[17] Read the Managing Change box to find out how Google is trying to maintain its organic feel as it grows, both in revenues and number of employees.

Lastly, the business in which a company operates has a significant impact on its organizational structure. In complex, dynamic, and unstable environments, companies need to organize for flexibility and agility. That is, their organizational structures need to respond to rapid and unexpected changes in the business environment. For companies operating in stable environments, however, the demands for flexibility and agility are not so great. The environment is predictable. In a simple, stable environment, therefore, companies benefit from the efficiencies created by a mechanistic organizational structure.

concept check

Compare and contrast mechanistic and organic organizations.

What factors determine whether an organization should be mechanistic or organic?

MANAGING CHANGE

The Growth of Google

In just seven years, Google Inc. has grown from two founders to over 4,200 employees and, because of its shareholders' enthusiasm, has a market capitalization of over $7 billion. That kind of growth has not come without difficulties. Until just recently, employees, suppliers, and even job applicants were sour on how the company was run. Some customers went so far as to describe the company as "a disorganized madhouse run by people too arrogant to be interested in fixing the problems." Doing a simple deal with Google was more difficult than executing a complex deal with Microsoft. Some predicted the company would implode from a lack of formal organization.

Cultural informality, however, is what fueled Google's creativity and gave it the flexibility to beat its competitors in many areas. Founders Sergey Brin and Larry Page share an office that looks like a college dorm room. Skateboards, hockey gear, scooters, remote-controlled airplanes, and beanbag chairs complement the traditional desks, couch, and computers. Brin and Page aren't the only employees to share an office; to encourage collaboration, sometimes up to four people use a single office. For lunch and dinner each day, Google employees are served a free organic all-you-can-eat buffet that has a reputation for one of the best places to eat in Northern California. The company also provides free laundry and banking at its campus, called the "Googleplex," the centerpiece of which is a sand volleyball court.

Fueled by market growth and an intensely competitive business environment, Google has been adding 4 to 5 employees to the payroll each day, which puts a strain on its informal organization. At the same time, Google needs to retain its flexible, innovative culture if it is to continue to thrive in its dynamic industry.

To balance the seemingly opposite needs of encouraging creativity and implementing controls on a rapidly growing organization, Google has added two levels of management to its organizational structure, for a total of three. Brin and Page hired an outside CEO, Eric Schmidt, who hired a human resources manager. Schmidt also subdivided employees into teams based on product or function. That rudimentary organizational structure has caused some of those previously dissatisfied customers to notice a difference. Whereas before, teams of continuously changing members took care of a single customer, today, each customer has one contact at Google. Issues get dealt with immediately and professionally.

Despite a focus on professionalism, Google still manages to hold onto its entrepreneurial spirit. All engineers are given a day a week to work on their own pet projects, and an ideas mailing list allows employees to circulate innovative ideas and get feedback from across the company. Top managers consult the board regularly to make sure that promising ideas are developed. Google's blend of organic and mechanistic models must be working. Its latest offering of stock generated $4 billion, and roughly 1,500 people apply for those 4 to 5 daily job openings.[18]

Critical Thinking Questions

- Would you be comfortable working in a hyper-flexible organization like Google, or do you prefer a more structured environment?
- Do you think Google will be able to retain its organizational informality at 10,000 employees? 20,000? (Microsoft has 61,000 employees.)

The Informal Organization

7 How does the informal organization affect the performance of the company?

informal organization
The network of connections and channels of communication based on the informal relationships of individuals inside an organization.

Up to this point in the chapter, we have focused on formal organizational structures that can be seen in the boxes and lines of the organization chart. Yet many important relationships within an organization do not show up on an organization chart. Nevertheless, these relationships can affect the decisions and performance of employees at all levels of the organization.

The network of connections and channels of communication based on the informal relationships of individuals inside the organization is known as the **informal organization**. Informal relationships can be between people at the same hierarchical level or between people at different levels and in different departments. Some connections are work related, such as those formed among people who carpool or ride the same train to work. Others are based on nonwork commonalties such as belonging to the same church or health club or having children who attend the same school.

Functions of the Informal Organization

The informal organization has several important functions. First, it provides a source of friendships and social contact for organization members. Second, the interpersonal relationships and informal groups help employees feel better informed about and connected with what is going on in their firm, thus giving them some sense of control over their work environment. Third, the informal organization can provide status and recognition that the formal organization cannot or will not provide employees. Fourth, the network of relationships can aid the socialization of new employees by informally passing along rules, responsibilities, basic objectives, and job expectations. Finally, the organizational grapevine helps employees to be more aware of what is happening in their workplace by transmitting information quickly and conveying it to places that the formal system does not reach.

CONCEPT *in Action*

Smart managers understand that not all of a company's influential relationships appear on the organization chart. Off the chart there exists a web of informal personal connections between workers, across which vital information and knowledge pass constantly. Using social network analysis software and communication-tracking tools, managers are able to map and quantify the normally invisible relationships that form between employees. *How might identifying a firm's informal organization aid managers in fostering teamwork, motivating employees, and boosting productivity?*

© IMAGES.COM/CORBIS

Informal Communication Channels

The informal channels of communication used by the informal organization are often referred to as the *grapevine*, the *rumor mill*, or the *intelligence network*. Managers need to pay attention to the grapevines in their organization, because their employees increasingly put a great deal of stock in the information that travels along it. A recent survey found that many business leaders have their work cut out for them in the speeches and presentations they give employees. Survey participants were asked if they would believe a message delivered in a speech by a company leader or one that they heard over the grapevine. Forty-seven percent of those responding said they would put more credibility in the grapevine. Only 42 percent said they would believe senior leadership, and another 11 percent indicated they would believe a blend of elements from both messages.[19] Perhaps even more interesting is how accurate employees perceive their company grapevine to be: Fifty-seven percent gave it favorable ratings. "The grapevine may not be wholly accurate, but it is a very reliable indicator that something is going on," said one survey respondent.[20]

With this in mind, managers need to learn to use the existing informal organization as a tool that can potentially benefit the formal organization. An excellent way of putting the informal organization to work for the good of the company is to bring informal leaders into the decision-making process. That way, at least the people who use and nurture the grapevine will have more accurate information to send it.

concept check

What is the informal organization?

How can informal channels of communication be used to improve operational efficiency?

Trends In Organizational Structure

8 **What trends are influencing the way businesses organize?**

To improve organizational preformance and achieve long-term objectives, some organizations seek to reengineer their business processes or adopt new technologies that open up a variety of organizational design options such as virtual corporations and virtual teams. Other trends that have strong footholds in today's organizations include outsourcing and managing global businesses.

Reengineering Organizational Structure

reengineering
The complete redesign of business structures and processes in order to improve operations.

virtual corporation
A network of independent companies linked by information technology to share skills, costs, and access to one another's markets; allows the companies to come together quickly to exploit rapidly changing opportunities.

Periodically, all businesses must reevaluate the way they do business. This includes assessing the effectiveness of the organizational structure. To meet the formidable challenges of the future, companies are increasingly turning to **reengineering**—the complete redesign of business structures and processes in order to improve operations. An even simpler definition of reengineering is "starting over." In effect, top management asks, "If we were a new company, how would we run this place?" The purpose of reengineering is to identify and abandon the outdated rules and fundamental assumptions that guide current business operations. Every company has many formal and informal rules based on assumptions about technology, people, and organizational goals that no longer hold. Thus, the goal of reengineering is to redesign business processes to achieve improvements in cost control, product quality, customer service, and speed. The reengineering process should result in a more efficient and effective organizational structure that is better suited to the current (and future) competitive climate of the industry.

The Virtual Corporation

CONCEPT *in Action*

Many leading corporations are going back to the drawing board to address major inefficiencies in their organizations. From General Motors and Volkswagen to Mattel and Six Flags, some of the world's best-known companies are reengineering in hopes of attaining greater profitability through leaner, more efficient organizational structures. Avon's recent $500 million restructuring eliminated multiple layers of management and produced layoffs, but the move is expected to spark a turnaround and save $300 million annually. *What changes are common during reengineering?*

One of the biggest challenges for companies today is adapting to the technological changes that are affecting all industries. Organizations are struggling to find new organizational structures that will help them transform information technology into a competitive advantage. One alternative that is becoming increasingly prevalent is the **virtual corporation**, which is a network of independent companies (suppliers, customers, even competitors) linked by information technology to share skills, costs, and access to one another's markets. This network structure allows companies to come together quickly to exploit rapidly changing opportunities. The key attributes of a virtual corporation are:

- *Technology.* Information technology helps geographically distant companies form alliances and work together.
- *Opportunism.* Alliances are less permanent, less formal, and more opportunistic than in traditional partnerships.
- *Excellence.* Each partner brings its core competencies to the alliance, so it is possible to create an organization with higher quality in every functional area and increase competitive advantage.
- *Trust.* The network structure makes companies more reliant on each other and forces them to strengthen relationships with partners.
- *No borders.* This structure expands the traditional boundaries of an organization.

In the concept's purest form, each company that links up with others to create a virtual corporation is stripped to its essence. Ideally, the virtual corporation has neither central office nor organization chart, no hierarchy, and no vertical integration. It contributes to an alliance only its core competencies, or key capabilities. It mixes and matches what it does best with the core competencies of other companies and entrepreneurs. For example, a manufacturer would only manufacture, while relying on a product design firm to decide what to make and a marketing company to sell the end result.

Although firms that are purely virtual organizations are still relatively scarce, many companies are embracing several characteristics of the virtual structure. One great example is Cisco Systems. Cisco has 34 plants that produce its products, but the company owns only 2 of them. Human hands touch only 10 percent of customer orders. Less than half of all orders are processed by a Cisco employee. To the average customer, the interdependency of Cisco's suppliers and inventory systems makes it look like one huge, seamless company. Virtual companies are not just for big entities like Cisco, however. Read the Catching the Entrepreneurial Spirit box to find out how one member of the new generation of U.S. manufacturers built a company with millions of dollars in revenue with a bare-bones organizational structure.

Virtual Teams

Technology is also enabling corporations to create virtual work teams. Geography is no longer a limitation when employees are considered for a work team. Virtual teams mean reduced travel time and costs, reduced relocation expenses, and utilization of specialized talent regardless of employee's location.

When managers need to staff a project, all they need to do is make a list of required skills and a general list of employees who possess those skills. When the pool of employees is known, the manager simply chooses the best mix of people and creates the virtual team. Special challenges of virtual teams include keeping team members focused, motivated, and communicating positively despite their location. If feasible, at least one face-to-face meeting during the early stages of team formation will help with these potential problems.

CATCHING THE ENTREPRENEURIAL SPIRIT

Instant Companies—Keen!

Footwear companies can spend up to ten months designing new styles, which retailers expect to see and touch long before stocking them. But just eight weeks before they would need samples for their summer line, Jim Van Dine and his three partners were still debating the merits of Mary Janes.

The four men were banging out the concept for Keen Footwear, their new shoe company. Everyone agreed on the core product, an athletic sandal with a protective cap at the toe. Van Dine, hoping to make Keen more than a one-shoe wonder, argued for a broader array of styles, including clogs, slip-ons, and the strap-and-buckle design known as a Mary Jane. "We had one shot to get it right," he says. "I didn't want to just be a sandal company."

Rolling out so many shoes at such a late date would have been unthinkable for an established shoemaker, let alone a brand-new one. Keen, however, had at its disposal resources far more powerful than what has traditionally been available to a start-up. One partner had already reserved capacity in two Chinese factories for massive production runs. Van Dine himself knew there were plenty of freelance shoe designers who could quickly translate his team's vision in to manufacturing specifications. And he believed that Keen could make its brand practically a household name while spending virtually nothing on advertising. In sum, four guys with a great idea, some good contacts, and a loan to cover initial inventory figured they could go head-to-head with Nike in just 60 days.

Two months later, a factory in China was churning out Keen clogs, slip-ons, and yes, Mary Janes—16 styles in all. Keen sold $30 million worth of shoes in its first year—around 700,000 pairs—with Mary Janes and other nonsandals accounting for 45 percent of the total. (It took Teva three years to reach just $1 million in annual sales.) Keen's overnight rise reflects marketing strength, but the company's swift transformation is just one of many product-oriented start-ups going from concept to contender at warp speed.

In every industry you can think of, small, savvy new companies are wedging themselves into established industries unburdened by the fixed costs of an organizational infrastructure. Resources like outsourced manufacturing, Internet-powered publicity, and robust design tools have never before been available so cheaply to start-ups. To get to market fast, these virtual organizations farm out everything they can, from logistics and billing to sales and support. "This," says Timothy Faley, managing director of the University of Michigan's Institute for Entrepreneurial Studies, "is how the manufacturing moguls of the future are getting started."[21]

Critical Thinking Questions
- Do you think Keen's business model is sustainable? In other words, do you think virtual corporations can have long-term success? Why or why not?
- Can any type of company use the virtual corporation model? Explain your answer.

CONCEPT *in Action*

In today's high-tech world, teams can exist anyplace where there is access to a wireless network. With globalization and outsourcing on the rise, organizations from IBM to the United States Defense Department are increasingly utilizing virtual teams to coordinate people and projects—often from halfway around the world. Unlike coworkers in traditional teams, members of virtual teams rarely meet in person, working from different locations and even from different continents. *What practical benefits do virtual teams offer to businesses and employees?*

Outsourcing

Another organizational trend that continues to influence today's managers is outsourcing. For decades, companies have outsourced various functions. For example, payroll functions like recording hours, benefits, wage-rates, and issuing paychecks, have been handled for years by third-party providers. Today, however, outsourcing includes a much wider array of business functions: customer service, production, engineering, information technology, sales and marketing, janitorial services, maintenance, and more. Outsourcing is evolving from a trend to a way of doing business.

Companies outsource for two main reasons: cost reduction and labor needs. Often, to satisfy both requirements, companies will outsource work to firms in foreign countries. It seems that nearly every day an article in the business press mentions global outsourcing. That is because more and more companies are integrating global outsourcing into their business strategy. A recent survey conducted by Archstone, a Connecticut consulting firm, found that 73 percent of the *Fortune* 500 and *Forbes* 2000

CONCEPT *in Action*

Outsourcing has become a popular way for American businesses to lower costs and reorganize labor. While opponents of outsourcing say the practice hurts American workers by shifting jobs overseas, proponents point out that companies engaged in offshoring grow and create new job opportunities that more than make up for the ones moved outside the country. *How might the outsourcing of certain jobs actually contribute to increased job growth and stability in the United States?*

companies it polled, with average annual revenues of $25 billion, see global outsourcing as an important part of their growth strategy and a way to cut administrative costs.[22] In addition, more than 65 percent of the companies in the Archstone survey indicated that their primary reason for outsourcing was labor needs.[23]

The attractiveness of outsourcing should not blind managers to its real challenges and limits. Companies in growing numbers are turning to offshore service providers as a way to cut costs, but a survey of more than 5,000 executives worldwide shows that savings aren't as high as typically expected. "Most people across the board think they're going to cut a third or half of their costs," says Phillip Hatch, president of offshoring consulting and market research firm Ventoro. "That simply isn't realistic."[24] Hatch found that companies achieve only a little better than 9 percent savings as a result of sending work overseas. Weeding out catastrophic failures increases the savings to only 19 percent.[25]

Another misconception about outsourcing is the size of the talent pool in developing nations. Shockingly enough, it isn't as large as you might think. Due to inadequate foreign language proficiency, lack of practical skills, unwillingness to move for a job, and limited or no access to airports and other transportation networks, only a fraction of those dirt-cheap engineers, financiers, accountants, scientists, and other professionals in China, India, and elsewhere can be put to effective use by multinational corporations anytime soon.[26] Only 14 percent of the 33 million university graduates in low-wage countries who have up to seven years experience are ready to work for multinational companies. That compares to 15 million young professionals in higher-wage nations.[27]

Despite the challenges, global outsourcing programs can be effective. To be successful in outsourcing efforts, managers must do the following:

- identify a specific business problem
- consider all possible solutions
- decide whether sending work offshore is the appropriate answer to the problem
- look for offshore providers that have high-caliber systems in place that will push clients to optimize their own internal processes
- find an offshore provider that understands their business.[28]

Companies that follow these basic steps and manage their offshore projects well could surpass the average and realize savings of as much as 30 percent.[29]

Structuring for Global Mergers

Recent mergers creating mega firms (such as eBay and Skype, Procter & Gamble and Gilette, Sprint and Nextel, and Sanofi and Aventis) raise some important questions regarding corporate structure. How can managers hope to organize the global pieces of these huge, complex new firms into a cohesive, successful whole? Should decision making be centralized or decentralized? Should the firm be organized around geographic markets or product lines? And how can managers consolidate distinctly different corporate cultures? These issues and many more must be resolved if mergers of global companies are to succeed.

Beyond designing a new organizational structure, one of the most difficult challenges when merging two large companies is uniting the cultures and creating a single business. The recent merger between Pfizer and Pharmacia, makers of Dramamine and Rogaine, is no exception. Failure to effectively merge cultures can have serious effects on organizational efficiency.

In a plan scheduled to last three years, Pfizer put together 14 groups that would make recommendations concerning finances,

CONCEPT *in Action*

Communication-services firm WebEx helps business professionals get on the same page, even when they're miles apart. As the global leader in applications for collaborative business on the Web, the Santa Clara–based company enables clients to conduct meetings and share documents and presentations—all over the Internet. Using standard devices such as Web cameras and browsers, WebEx clients collaborate on sales, training, and product-design tasks from remote locations. *How might new technologies such as WebEx facilitate global mergers?*

WEBEX COMMUNICATIONS, INC.

concept check

How does technology enable firms to organize as virtual corporations?

What are some organizational issues that must be addressed when two large firms merge?

human resources, operation support, capital improvements, warehousing, logistics, quality control, and information technology. An outside consultant was hired to facilitate the process. One of the first tasks for the groups was to deal with the conqueror (Pfizer) versus conquered (Pharmacia) attitudes. Company executives want to make sure all employees know that their ideas are valuable and they are listening.

Summary of Learning Goals

1   What are the five traditional forms of departmentalization?

To build an organizational structure, companies first must divide the work into separate jobs and tasks. Managers then group related jobs and tasks together into departments. Five basic types of departmentalization (see Exhibit 8.2) are commonly used in organizations:

- *Functional.* Based on the primary functions performed within an organizational unit.
- *Product.* Based on the goods or services produced or sold by the organizational unit.
- *Process.* Based on the production process used by the organizational unit.
- *Customer.* Based on the primary type of customer served by the organizational unit.
- *Geographic.* Based on the geographic segmentation of organizational units.

2   What contemporary organizational structures are companies using?

In recent decades, companies have begun to expand beyond traditional departmentalization methods and use matrix, committee, and team-based structures. Matrix structures combine two types of traditional organizational structures (for example, geographic and functional). Matrix structures bring together people form different functional areas of the organization to work on a special project. As such, matrix organizaitons are more flexible, but because employees report to two direct supervisors, managing matrix structures can be extremely challenging. Committee structures give authority and responsibility to a group rather than to an individual. Committees are part of a line-and-staff organization and often fulfill only an advisory role. Team-based structures also involve assigning authority and responsibility to groups rather than individuals, but different from committees, team-based structures give these groups autonomy to carry out their work.

3   Why are companies using team-based organizational structures?

Work groups share resources and coordinate efforts to help members better perform their individual duties and responsibilities. The performance of the group can be evaluated by adding up the contributions of the individual group members. Work teams require not only coordination but also *collaboration,* the pooling of knowledge, skills, abilities, and resources in a collective effort to attain a common goal. Four types of work teams are used: problem solving, self-managed, cross-functional, and virtual teams. Companies are using teams to improve individual and group motivation and performance.

4 What tools do companies use to establish relationships within their organizations?

The managerial hierarchy (or the *management pyramid*) comprises the levels of management within the organization, and the managerial span of control is the number of employees the manager directly supervises. In daily operations, individuals in line positions are directly involved in the processes used to create goods and services. Individuals in staff positions provide the administrative and support services that line employees need to achieve the firm's goals. Line positions in organizations are typically in areas such as production, marketing, and finance. Staff positions are found in areas such as legal counseling, managerial consulting, public relations, and human resource management.

5 How can the degree of centralization/ decentralization be altered to make an organization more successful?

In a highly centralized structure, top management makes most of the key decisions in the organization with very little input from lower-level employees. Centralization lets top managers develop a broad view of operations and exercise tight financial controls. In a highly decentralized organization, decision-making authority is pushed down the organizational hierarchy, giving lower-level personnel more responsibility and power to make and implement decisions. Decentralization can result in faster decision making and increased innovation and responsiveness to customer preferences.

6 How do mechanistic and organic organizations differ?

A mechanistic organization is characterized by a relatively high degree of work specialization, rigid departmentalization, many layers of management (particularly middle management), narrow spans of control, centralized decision making, and a long chain of command. This combination of elements results in a tall organizational structure. In contrast, an organic organization is characterized by a relatively low degree of work specialization, loose departmentalization, few levels of management, wide spans of control, decentralized decision making, and a short chain of command. This combination of elements results in a flat organizational structure.

7 How does the informal organization affect the performance of a company?

The informal organization is the network of connections and channels of communication based on the informal relationships of individuals inside the organization. Informal relationships can be between people at the same hierarchical level or between people at different levels and in different departments. Informal organizations give employees more control over their work environment by delivering a continuous stream of company information throughout the organization, thereby helping employees stay informed.

8 What trends are influencing the way businesses organize?

Reengineering is a complete redesign of business structures and processes in order to improve operations. The goal of reengineering is to redesign business processes to achieve improvements in cost control, product quality, customer service, and speed.

The virtual corporation is a network of independent companies (suppliers, customers, even competitors) linked by information technology to share skills, costs, and access to one another's markets. This network structure allows companies to come together quickly to exploit rapidly changing opportunities.

Many companies are now using technology to create virtual teams. Team members may be down the hall or across the ocean. Virtual teams mean that travel time and expenses are eliminated and the best people can be placed on the team regardless of where they live. Sometimes, however, it may be difficult to keep virtual team members focused and motivated.

Outsourcing business functions—both globally and domestically—is evolving from trend to regular business practice. Companies choose to outsource either as a cost-saving measure or as a way to gain access to needed human resource talent. To be successful, outsourcing must solve a clearly articulated business problem, and managers must closely match third-party providers with their company's actual needs.

Large global mergers raise important issues in organizational structure. The ultimate challenge for management is to take two huge global organizations and create a single, successful, cohesive organization.

Key Terms

authority 277
centralization 278
chain of command 276
committee structure 272
cross-functional team 275
customer departmentalization 269
decentralization 278
delegation of authority 277
departmentalization 267
division of labor 267
formal organization 266
functional departmentalization 268
geographic departmentalization 269
group cohesiveness 273
informal organization 282
line-and-staff organization 270
line organization 270
line positions 270

managerial hierarchy 276
matrix structure (project management) 271
mechanistic organization 279
organic organization 279
organization chart 267
problem-solving teams 274
process departmentalization 269
product departmentalization 269
reengineering 283
self-managed work teams 274
span of control 277
specialization 267
staff positions 270
virtual corporation 283
work groups 273
work teams 273

Preparing for Tomorrow's Workplace: *SCANS*

1. When people talk of climbing the corporate ladder, they are referring to moving vertically upward through the organizational structure. Many employees plot career paths that will take them to increasingly higher levels of management. Do you think you would be more interested in climbing higher in an organization, or being a middle-management bridge between the employees who do the work and the executives who set the strategy? Explain the reasons for your choice. (Resources, Interpersonal)

2. Teams are an increasingly popular method of organizing corporations, but not all people are suited for teamwork. As a manager, what do you do with employees who are talented but unapproachable? Can you think of a way to involve people who are uncomfortable in team settings so that your teams have the perspective of these employees as well? (Interpersonal)

3. Think about how gossip and rumors travel through a grapevine. Draw as many grapevines as you can think of that reflect the different ways rumors move through an organization. Can you think of information that a manager would want to disseminate through the grapevine? Is there information that is inappropriate to disseminate through informal channels? What? (Information)

4. Do you think that companies that outsource will inevitably become virtual corporations? Why or why not? (Resources, Systems)

5. It used to be that only high-level executives and CEOs were able to work on the road. Mobile corporate computing, however, is trickling down the organizational chart. In your opinion, is there a point in the organizational structure at which working remotely (at home, on the road) should stop? Should all employees in the hierarchy be allowed to work in a virtual environment, or should there be limits? Explain your reasoning. (Technology, Systems)

6. **Team Activity** Have you ever worked on a team with an underperforming member, like a slacker, a complainer, or a critic? Assemble a team of three to five students and brainstorm a list of "bad" team members you have experience working

with. Once you have a list of types, discuss how that person affected the work of the team and the outcome the team produced. Brainstorm ways to better manage and mitigate the negative effects of "bad" team members. Share your results with the class. (Interpersonal, Systems)

Ethics Activity

In January 2006, St. Paul Travelers Insurance announced that it would lay off more than 100 technology employees and outsource their jobs to Indian workers. This change is part of a larger plan to increase its technology outsourcing. Currently the company outsources about 500 jobs and intends to double that number by 2008. As the insurer shifts responsibilities to the Indian contractors, it has asked its own employees to help with training. "We're sitting here training our India (counterparts) in what we do," said one St. Paul employee who no longer is employed. "The gall of the company. It's insulting."

According to company spokesman Shane Boyd, the main reason for outsourcing the technology jobs is to improve efficiency by using temporary workers for short-term projects or to find specially trained workers, rather than for cost savings. "We're going to use outsourcing when it makes sense for our business," he said.

Using a Web search tool, locate articles about this topic and then write responses to the following questions. Be sure to support your arguments and cite your sources.

Ethical Dilemma: Is St. Paul Travelers justified in outsourcing technology jobs to India? Does it have any obligation to find other jobs or provide training for its displaced employees? Should it ask employees who were being laid off to train the contract labor?

Sources: Pete Engardio, "The Future of Outsourcing," *Business Week*, January 30, 2006, p. 50+; "Global Experts Favour Outsourcing of Jobs," *Press Trust of India Ltd.*, January 26, 2006, http://galenet.thomsonlearning.com; Sheryl Jean, "Travelers Outsources IT Jobs," *Saint Paul Pioneer Press* (St. Paul, Minnesota), January 27, 2006, http://galenet.thomsonlearning.com; Bernadette Starzee, "How to Decide Whether and What to Outsource," *Daily Record* (Kansas City, MO), February 9, 2006, http://galenet.thomsonlearning.com.

Working the Net

1. Using a search engine like Google or Yahoo! to search for the term "company organizational charts," find at least three examples of organizational charts for corporations, not-for-profits, or government agencies. Analyze each entity's organizational structure. Is it organized by function, product/service, process, customer type, or geographic location?

2. Search the archives at the *Business Week* (**http://www.businessweek.com**), *Fortune* (**http://www.fortune.com**), or *Forbes* (**http://www.forbes.com**) Web site for stories about companies that have reorganized. Pick two examples and prepare a summary of their reorganization efforts, including the underlying reasons the company chose to reorganize, the key elements of the reorganization plan, and if possible, how successful it has been.

3. Visit the *Inc.* magazine Web site, **http://www.inc.com**, and use the search engine to find articles about virtual corporations. Using a search engine, find the Web site of at least one virtual corporation and look for information about how the company uses span of control, informal organization, and other concepts from this chapter.

4. What are the challenges of being part of a virtual team, for both the leader and the participants? The Virtual Collaboration Research Group of the University of North Texas' Center for Collaborative Organizations, **http://www.workteams.unt.edu/vcrg/index.html**, has a links section with many resources on this topic. Explore the links to find articles about virtual collaboration and select two that interest you. Share your findings with your classmates and lead a discussion about the characteristics of a successful virtual team.

5. Managing change in an organization is no easy task, as you've discovered in your new job with a consulting firm that specializes in change management. To get up to speed, go to Bpubs.com, the Business Publications Search Engine, **http://www.bpubs.com**, and navigate to the Change Management section of the Management Science category. Select three articles that discuss how companies approached the change process and summarize their experiences.

6. After managing your first project team, you think you might enjoy a career in project management. The Project Management Institute is a professional

organization for project managers. Its Web site, **http://www.pmi.org**, has many resources about this field. Start at the Professional Practices section to learn what project management is, then go to the professional Development and Careers pages. What are the requirements to earn the Project Management Professional designation? Explore other free areas of the site to learn more about the job of project manager. Prepare a brief report on the career and its opportunities. Does what you've learned make you want to follow this career path?

7. Many companies are outsourcing portions of their information technology (IT) departments. Should they, and why? Develop a position on this issue using the resources at *NetworkWorld's* Outsourcing Research Center, **http://www. network world.com/topics/outsourcing.html**, and at *InformationWeek's* Outsourcing Tech Center, **http://www.informationweek.com/outsourcing/**. Then divide the class into two groups, those that support outsourcing and those that oppose it, and have a debate on this subject.

Creative Thinking Case >

Meet the Gore Family

Imagine an organization with more than 7,000 employees working at 45 facilities around the world—with no hierarchy structure. W. L. Gore & Associates, headquartered in Newark, Delaware, is a model of unusual business practices. Wilbert Gore, who left Dupont to explore new uses for Teflon, started the company in 1958. Best known for its breathable, weatherproof Gore-Tex fabric, Glide dental floss, and Elixir guitar strings, the company has no bosses, no titles, no departments, and no formal job descriptions. There is no managerial hierarchy at Gore, and top management treats employees, called associates, as peers.

In April 2005, the company named 22-year associate Terri Kelly its new chief executive officer. Unlike large public corporations, Gore's announcement was made without much fanfare. "It's never about the CEO," she says. "You're an associate, and you just happen to be the CEO. We don't like anyone to be the center of attention. She considers the idea that the CEO of W. L. Gore manages the company a misperception. "My goal is to provide the overall direction. I spend a lot of time making sure we have the right people in the right roles. . . . We empower divisions and push out responsibility. We're so diversified that it's impossible for a CEO to have that depth of knowledge—and not even practical."

The company focuses on its products and company values rather than individuals. Committees, comprised of employees, make major decisions such as hiring, firing, and compensation. They even set top executives' compensation. Employees work on teams, which are switched around every few years. In fact, all employees are expected to make minor decisions instead of relying on the "boss" to make them. "We're committed to how we get things done," Kelly says. "That puts a tremendous burden on leaders because it's easier to say, 'Just do it' than to explain the rationale. But in the long run, you'll get much better results because people are making a commitment."

The company tries to maintain a family-like atmosphere by dispersing its employees into 60 buildings, with no more than 200 employees in any one place. Because no formal lines of authority exist, employees can speak to anyone in the company at any time. This arrangement also forces employees to spend considerable time developing relationships. As one employee described it, instead of trying to please just one "boss," you have to please everyone.

The informal organizational structure is working well. With revenues of almost $2 billion, the company produces thousands of advanced technology products for the electronics, industrial, fabrics, and medical markets. Its corporate structure fosters innovation and has been a significant contributor to associate satisfaction. Employee turnover is a low 5 percent a year, and the company can choose new associates from the 38,000 job applications it receives annually. For the ninth consecutive year, W. L. Gore was near the top of the list of *Fortune's* "100 Best Companies to Work For."

Critical Thinking Questions

- Given the lack of formal structure, how important do you think the informal structure becomes? Does Gore's reliance on committee work slow processes down?
- Is W. L. Gore a mechanistic or an organic organization? Support your answer with examples from the case.
- How do you think Gore's organizational structure affects the division of labor?

Sources: Alan Deutschman, "What I Know Now: Terri Kelly, CEO, W. L. Gore & Associates," *Fast Company*, September 2005, p. 96; "Gore Marks 9th Year as One of Nation's Best, Company Earns #5 Position on FORTUNE Magazine '100 Best Companies to Work For' List," *W. L. Gore & Associates*, press release, January 9, 2006, http://www.gore.com; Robert Levering and Milton Moskowitz, "And the Winners Are …," *Fortune*, January 23, 2006, p. 89; Sara J. Welch, "GORE The Fabric of Success," *Successful Meetings*, May 2005, p. 49–51; and W. L. Gore & Associates Web site, http://www.gore.com (February 10, 2006).

Video Case >

Lonely Planet Travels the Globe

With offices on three continents and a distribution center in a fourth, Lonely Planet is as global as its travel books. A leading publisher of guides for free-spirited, independent travelers, the company started in the early 1970s, when founders Tony and Maureen Wheeler wrote the first guidebook, *Across Asia*, at their kitchen table. Today Lonely Planet publishes more than 650 books in multiple languages that cover every area of the world, from Antarctica to Greenland and the Arctic, Belize to Sri Lanka— and all points in between. Travelers turn to its guidebooks, Web site, and the Lonely Planet *Six Degrees* television series on the Discovery Channel for high quality, accurate, and insightful travel information. "We tell it like it is, we try to raise a smile, and we never take ourselves too seriously," says Lonely Planet's Travel Information Manager, Tom Hall. "Our pioneering spirit keeps us searching for new experiences to offer our readers and it's obviously paying off."

Headquartered in Melbourne, Australia, the company also has offices in Oakland, California; London; and Paris. The editors who commission guides are responsible for a specific region and based in the appropriate office. This allows them to acquire in-depth expertise on their areas and follow the latest local trends. Production is centralized at the Melbourne headquarters, and its centralized distribution center is located in Singapore, near its printers. This provides greater control, reduces redundancy on a worldwide basis, and saves money. In addition to its 400 regular employees, Lonely Planet contracts with about 250 professional authors worldwide who provide an insider's perspective on their countries.

This global workforce presents challenges in structuring the company. "Lonely Planet is a very flat organization . . . a very lean organization," says Vice President Robin Goldberg, who heads up marketing and business development. "When you're lean, you need to allow everyone to grow to their greatest potential, to make decisions, to make them fast. If we had too much hierarchy, it would slow us down dramatically." Lonely Planet is structured as a global company and consolidates publishing, information technology, and distribution functions across locations to avoid duplication of efforts. At the same time, Lonely Planet acknowledges the need to customize its products to meet the needs of regional markets, which many have different retailers, languages, and images to appeal to local audiences.

Although its multinational nature makes operations more complex, from time zone changes to cultural differences, it also brings advantages. Authors can get answers from staff members during their work day, regardless of where they happen to be traveling. With information technology personnel based on three continents, the company can offer 24-hour global technical support. Teams can collaborate on projects, handing off their work when they go home for the day to colleagues in another time zone, shortening time to completion. Working with people in other countries provides fresh ideas and different perspectives.

Critical Thinking Questions

- Describe Lonely Planets' organizational structure. Does it support the company's goals?
- How does Lonely Planet incorporate teams into its organizational structure? Suggest other areas where the company could use teamwork effectively.
- Is Lonely Planet a mechanistic or an organic organization? Support your answer with examples from the case and video.

Sources: Adapted from Daft Video Series, Chapter 10, "Lonely Planet: Designing Adaptive Organizations;" Lonely Planet corporate Web site, http://www.lonelyplanet.com (February 11, 2006); "Lonely Planet Publications," Hoover's Inc., http://www.hoovers.com (February 1, 2006); "Lonely Planet voted best guidebook series," Lonely Planet press release, February 10, 2006, http://www.lonelyplanet.com; and "Tony and Maureen Wheeler Honored with Lifetime Achievement Award," Lonely Planet press release, September 20, 2005, http://www.lonelyplanet.com.

Hot Links Address Book

Like corporations, government agencies have organization charts, too. Learn how the Department of Health and Human Services is structured at **http://www.hhs.gov/about/orgchart.html**

Evaluate your own leadership skills by taking several of the management quizzes at HumanLinks.com, **http://www.humanlinks.com**

Find teambuilding resources galore, from team building activities and training exercises to guidance in solving team problems, at Teambuilding, Inc.'s supersite, **http://www.teambuildinginc.com**

To read articles on current best practices in outsourcing for both buyers and providers, and find other outsourcing resources, visit **http://www.outsourcing.com**

What benefits can a company gain by using Web-based organizational charting software? Check out the features Peopleboard.com offers companies at **http://www.people board. com**

How can your organization develop better group skills? A good place to start is Management Help's Group Skills page. Go to **http://www.managementhelp.org** and click on "Group Skills" for links to resources on many topics, including Self-Directed and Self-Managed Work Teams and virtual teams.

MouseTech LLC takes a novel approach to the virtual corporation concept, as you will see from its Web site, **http://www.moustech.net**. Read its company profile at the page about virtual corporations.

CHAPTER 9

Managing Human Resources and Labor Relations

Learning Goals

After reading this chapter, you should be able to answer these questions:

1. What is the human resource management process, and how are human resource needs determined?

2. How do firms recruit applicants?

3. How do firms select qualified applicants?

4. What types of training and development do organizations offer their employees?

5. How are performance appraisals used to evaluate employee performance?

6. What are the types of compensation and methods for paying workers?

7. What is a labor union and how is it organized?

8. What is collective bargaining, and what are some of the key negotiation issues?

9. How are grievances between management and labor resolved, and what tactics are used to force a contract settlement?

10. What are the key laws and federal agencies affecting human resource management and labor relations?

11. What trends and issues are affecting human resource management and labor relations?

Exploring Business Careers
Andrea Herran
Human Resources Consultant

In college, Andrea Herran studied business administration and minored in psychology. Always interested in a business career, she initially took psychology simply because it was interesting. Little did she know how applicable that minor would become. As a human resources (HR) consultant, she often benefits from her psychology background. "Studying human behavior really gave me the background necessary to put myself in the position of others, to see things from their point of view, which has definitely been helpful in my career in human resources."

Herran started out as an administrative assistant in the HR department of a hotel, and her career has run the gamut of human resources over the 17 years since she graduated from college. She has been an employment coordinator, focusing on employee recruitment and selection, and personnel manager, where she learned the skills necessary to maintain and evaluate employees. As a training manager, she sharpened her talent for developing, coordinating, and even administering staff training. Eventually, she became the director of human resources for companies both in the United States and abroad. Indeed, beyond the United States, she has worked in Mexico, Argentina, and South Africa. Today, she sees her varied employment history as key to her success. "Anyone interested in this field should experience as many possibilities within human resources as possible. You leave school with the theory, but only through experience do you really get to see what the potential of such a career is."

Consistent with her desire for a fast-paced, changing environment, both in terms of what she does and who she works with, she has made the move to consulting. "Consulting allows me to draw upon all my human resources skills. I have opened five HR departments in my career, so I bring my full experience to bear on the challenges each company has."

Herran has been working for about six months with her first client, Aquion Water Treatment Products (AWTP), which produces commercial and individual water treatment products such as water softeners and purifiers. She was brought on to update their department, which oversees 138 employees. The department has been using many of the same policies and practices for several years. For example, their performance reviews were very task-oriented. Performance reviews, however, have become much more behavior-oriented in the past 30 years. Instead of determining whether a task was completed, today's performance reviews seek to evaluate not only whether the person completed the task but also how he or she did so, especially examining the interactions involved in the task. Is an employee punctual at returning consumer request calls? How does he or she relate to customers? As a manager, does he or she express thoughts clearly? "By evaluating specific behaviors, you create an environment with clearly set qualifications for advancement and opportunities for targeted employee development. Without this, the *human* aspect of human resources can be overlooked."

This chapter looks at the role of human resources within an organization, from the general processes of developing and planning to the more specific tasks of employee evaluation and compensation.

Human resources management and labor relations involve acquisition, development, use, and maintenance of a human resource mix (people and positions) to achieve strategic organizational goals and objectives. Successful human resource management is based on a company's ability to attract and hire the best employees, equip them with the knowledge and skills they need to excel, compensate them fairly, and motivate them to reach their full potential and perform at high levels. Today's business environment presents numerous challenges to effectively managing employees:

- Technology continues to advance, which places great importance on knowledge workers, especially when demand outstrips the supply of high talent individuals.
- Global business operations involve rapid data transfer and necessitate accelerated decision making by executive and technical employees.
- The workforce is increasingly more diversified and multicultural, which places increased emphasis on communication and cultural understanding.
- Work life and family priorities are more difficult to balance as dual worker families populate the labor force.
- Employment and labor laws continue to greatly influence employee recruitment and hiring, compensation decisions, and employee retention and turnover in both union and nonunion organizations.

Each day, human resource experts and front-line supervisors deal with these challenges while sharing responsibility for attracting and retaining skilled, motivated employees. Whether faced with a large or small human resource problem, supervisors need some understanding of difficult employee relations issues, especially if there are legal implications.

In this chapter, you will learn about the elements of the human resource management process, including human resource planning and job analysis and design, employee recruitment and selection, training and development of employees, performance planning and evaluation, and compensation of the workforce. The chapter also describes labor unions and their representation of millions of American workers in construction, manufacturing, transportation, and service-based industries.

Achieving High Performance Through Human Resource Management

1 **What is the human resource management process, and how are human resource needs determined?**

human resource (HR) management
The process of hiring, developing, motivating, and evaluating employees to achieve organizational goals.

Human resource (HR) management is the process of hiring, developing, motivating, and evaluating employees to achieve organizational goals. The goals and strategies of the firm's business model form the basis for making human resource management decisions. HR practices and systems comprise the firm's human resource decision support system that is intended to make employees a key element for gaining competitive advantage. To this end, the HR management process contains the following sequenced activities:

- Job analysis and design
- Human resource planning and forecasting
- Employee recruitment
- Employee selection
- Training and development
- Performance planning and evaluation
- Compensation and benefits

The human resource management process shown in Exhibit 9.1 encourages the development of high performance employees. The process is sequential because employees can't be trained and paid until selected and placed in jobs, which follows recruitment, which is preceded by human resource planning and job analysis and design. Good HR practices used along this sequence foster performance improvement, knowledge and skill development, and loyal employees who desire to remain with the organization.

CONCEPT *in Action*

The number of illegal immigrants competing for low-wage jobs in the United States continues to grow, placing lawmakers and business leaders at odds over immigration policy. Leaders in the agribusiness, construction, and restaurant sectors say their businesses are dependent on migrant workers. Congressional action dealing with America's estimated 12 million undocumented workers could range from amnesty and guest worker programs to deportation. *What opportunities and challenges do millions of unauthorized workers present to the labor force in the United States?*

HR Planning and Job Analysis and Design

Two important, and somewhat parallel, aspects of the human resource management process are determining employee needs of the firm and the jobs to be filled. When Alcon Labs gained approval from the Food and Drug Administration for sales of a new contact lens disinfectant solution in its Opti-Free product line, it had to determine if additional sales representatives were needed and whether new sales positions with different knowledge and skill requirements should be established.[1] **Human resources planning** at Alcon means having the right number of people, with the

human resources planning
Creating a strategy for meeting current and future human resource needs.

Exhibit 9.1 > Human Resource Management Process

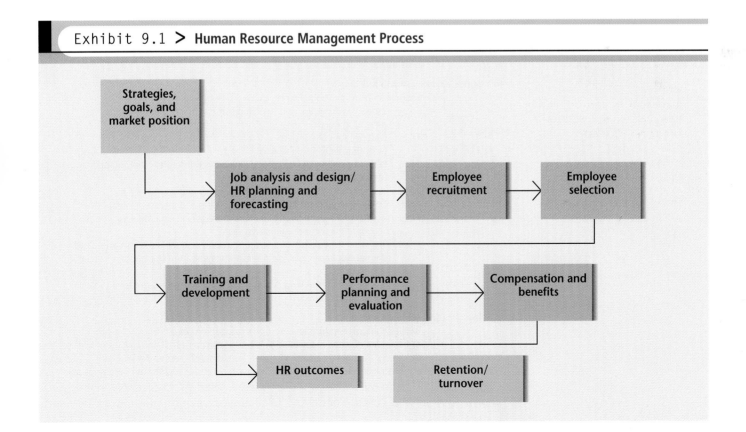

right training, in the right jobs, to meet its sales goals for the new product. Once the need for sales representatives is determined, human resource specialists assess the skills of the firm's existing employees to see whether new people must be hired or current ones trained.

Human resource planners must know what skills different jobs require. Information about a specific job typically begins with a **job analysis**, which is a study of the tasks required to do a job well. This information is used to specify the essential skills, knowledge, and abilities required for the job. Each year HR executives at Kraft Food engage in Kraft's Advancement Planning, which involves reviewing business and market forecasts to determine the number of HR professionals needed by the firm.[2] Also, key HR jobs are examined to make any changes in job duty and task responsibilities. The tasks and responsibilities of a job are listed in a **job description**. The skills, knowledge, and abilities a person must have to fill a job are spelled out in a **job specification**. These two documents help human resource planners find the right people for specific jobs. A sample job description and specification is shown in Exhibit 9.2.

HR Planning and Forecasting

Forecasting an organization's human resource needs, known as an HR *demand forecast,* is an essential aspect of HR planning. This process involves two forecasts:

job analysis
A study of the tasks required to do a particular job well.

job description
The tasks and responsibilities of a job.

job specification
A list of the skills, knowledge, and abilities a person must have to fill a job.

Exhibit 9.2 > **Job Description and Specification**

Position: College Recruiter   **Location: Corporate Offices**
Reports to: Vice President of Human Resources   **Classification: Salaried/Exempt**

Job Summary: Member of HR corporate team. Interacts with managers and department heads to determine hiring needs for college graduates. Visits 20 to 30 college and university campuses each year to conduct preliminary interviews of graduating students in all academic disciplines. Following initial interviews, works with corporate staffing specialists to determine persons who will be interviewed a second time. Makes recommendations to hiring managers concerning best-qualified applicants.

Job Duties and Responsibilities:
Estimated time spent and importance
15%   Working with managers and department heads, determines college recruiting needs.
10%   Determines colleges and universities with degree programs appropriate to hiring needs to be visited.
15%   Performs college relations activities with numerous colleges and universities.
25%   Visits campuses to conduct interviews of graduating seniors.
15%   Develops applicant files and performs initial applicant evaluations.
10%   Assists staffing specialists and line managers in determining who to schedule for second interviews.
5%   Prepares annual college recruiting report containing information and data about campuses, number interviewed, number hired, and related information.
5%   Participates in tracking college graduates who are hired to aid in determining campuses that provide the most outstanding employees.

Job Specification (Qualifications):
Bachelor's degree in human resource management or a related field. Minimum of two years of work experience in HR or department that annually hires college graduates. Ability to perform in a team environment, especially with line managers and department heads. Very effective oral and written communication skills. Reasonably proficient in Excel, Word, and Windows computer environment and familiar with PeopleSoft software.

---

succession planning
Examination of current employees to identify people who can fill vacancies and be promoted.

contingent worker
Person who prefers temporary employment, either part-time or full-time.

---

concept check

Define human resource management.

Distinguish between job analysis, job description, and the job specification.

Describe the human resource management process.

---

(1) determining the number of people needed by some future time (in one year, for example), and (2) estimating the number of people currently employed by the organization who will be available to fill various jobs at some future time; this is an *internal supply forecast.*

The Advancement Planning process at Kraft Foods involves comparing human resource demand and supply forecasts that will reveal whether a surplus or shortage of HR talent exists and the actions required to match demand with the internal supply of HR professionals. The performance of HR professionals at Kraft is reviewed to identify people who can fill vacancies and be promoted, a process known as **succession planning**. According to Thomas Thurman, Kraft's Senior VP of Human Resources, "this process allows us to identify who is ready now for a position of higher responsibility, who will be ready in one to three years, and who will be ready in three to five years."[3] If Kraft has a temporary shortage of HR professionals, it can hire an experienced but possibly semiretired person as a temporary or **contingent worker**, someone who wants to work but not on a permanent, continuous basis. Exhibit 9.3 summarizes the process of planning and forecasting an organization's personnel needs.

Exhibit 9.3 **> Human Resource Planning Process**

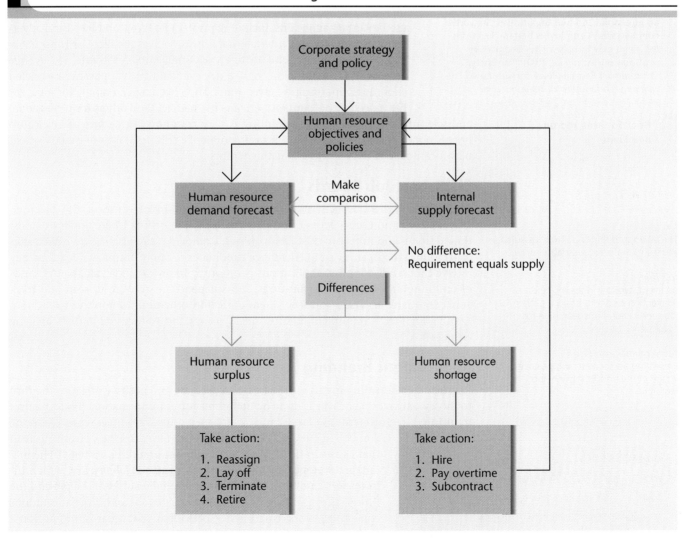

Employee Recruitment

When a firm creates a new position or an existing one becomes vacant, it starts looking for people with qualifications that meet the requirements of the job. Two sources of job applicants are the internal and external labor markets. The internal labor market consists of employees currently employed by the firm; the external labor market is the pool of potential applicants outside the firm.

Internal Labor Market

Internal recruitment can be greatly facilitated by using a human resource information system containing a skills inventory, or computerized employee database of information about an employee's previous work experience, education and certifications, job and career preferences, performance, and attendance. Promotions and job transfers are the most common results of internal recruiting. Burlington Northern Santa Fe Railway, Wal-Mart, Boeing Aircraft, Ritz-Carlton Hotels, and most other firms, large and small, promote from within and manage the upward mobility of their employees.

External Labor Market

The external labor market consists of prospects to fill positions that cannot be filled from within the organization. **Recruitment** is the process of attracting qualified people to form an applicant pool. Numerous methods are used to attract applicants, including print, radio, Web, and television advertising. Hospitality and entertainment firms, such as the Ritz-Carlton and Six Flags, frequently use job fairs to attract applicants. A **job fair**, or *corporate open house*, is usually a one- or two-day event at which applicants are briefed about job opportunities, given tours, and encouraged to apply for jobs. For firms needing accountants, engineers, chemists, and others for professional and scientific positions, college recruiting is very common. These firms (PricewaterhouseCoopers, Cisco Systems, Intel, Texas Instruments, and thousands of others) schedule on-campus interviews with graduating seniors.

Electronic Job Boards

Two relatively new aspects of employee recruitment involve use of the Internet. Monster.com and Career Mosaic.com are electronic job boards where applicants post their résumés and firms can post job openings. Companies can also use their Web sites to announce job openings and encourage candidates to apply online. Large firms may receive thousands of online applications per month. To review and evaluate thousands of online résumés and job applications, firms depend on software to scan and track applicant materials and glean from them critical information for applicant selection. Another high-tech recruitment method, social networking, is discussed in the Managing Change box.

Recruitment Branding

Recruitment branding involves presenting an accurate and positive image of the firm to those being recruited. This is done by including current information about the firm in printed recruitment materials and Web-based job announcements. Carbone Smolan Agency (CSA) is a New York-based image consulting firm that assists in developing a recruitment branding strategy.[4] The materials developed by CSA comprise a *realistic job preview*, which informs job candidates about organizational realities of the job and the firm so they can more accurately evaluate jobs and firm expectations concerning work assignments, performance standards, promotional opportunities and many other characteristics of the job.

CONCEPT *in Action*

Each year, the Council of Hotel and Restaurant Trainers bestows its "Commitment to People" award to one CEO dedicated to developing employees within an organization. The group's 2005 award went to Julia Stewart, the CEO of IHOP Restaurants. Aside from dishing up more than 16 kinds of pancakes, Stewart's company offers employees best-in-class training, from new franchisee development to continuous learning at "IHOP University." *What impact does employee training have on a company's internal recruitment process?*

© FRANK POLICH/REUTERS/LANDOV

2 How do firms recruit applicants?

recruitment
The attempt to find and attract qualified applicants in the external labor market.

job fair
An event, typically one day, held at a convention center to bring together job seekers and firms searching for employees.

recruitment branding
Presenting an accurate and positive image of the firm to those being recruited.

concept check

What are the two sources of job applicants?

What are some methods firms use to recruit applicants?

What is meant by recruitment branding?

MANAGING CHANGE

Social Networking and Employee Recruitment

Referrals and professional networking are commonly used methods of identifying job prospects, particularly for managerial, professional, and technical positions. Several software firms have devised social networking technology, or Web-based services, that technologically facilitate employee referrals, reference checking, and hiring based on networks of personal relationships. Visible Path analyzes company e-mail accounts to determine the strength of professional relationships between and among people. LinkedIn.com assesses the degree of separation that exists between potential job candidates. Monster Networking allows members to search for contacts in their professional fields from the millions of Monster.com users.

LinkedIn is a giant electronic Rolodex or business card file. Membership involves online registering and providing basic information about one's professional experience, contact information, and current employment. A member can search through an extended network of contacts based on his or her professional acquaintances. The basis for a search can be job, company, zip code, or membership in a professional organization. LinkedIn uses the concept that there are no more than six degrees of separation between two people, or one person can be linked to any other individual through no more than six other people. With approximately 2 million members in 120 industries, LinkedIn has opened its database to HR professionals for purposes of posting job notices and searching for candidates.

Visible Path software searches employee e-mail transactions and numerically calculates the strength of personal contacts. HR professionals can then assess the relationships employees have outside the company. Essentially, employee social networks are mapped to assist in recruiting, referencing, and hiring new employees. The customer of Visible Path is the firm that allows employees to include contacts of his or her own choosing. Connections can then be determined between employees and their extended networks of people they know.

LinkedIn and Visible Path operate their systems based on voluntary participation, and members consent to being networked. Nevertheless, important questions can be raised regarding privacy concerns and use of one's social network.[5]

Critical Thinking Questions

- Social networking technology can easily generate a name for an HR recruiting target, but how can the hiring firm convert the target into a candidate who is interested in the job?
- A firm could post a job in LinkedIn for the purpose of seeing whether any of its employees are searching for a new job and planning to leave. Is this appropriate? Why or why not?

---

3 How do firms select qualified applicants?

CONCEPT *in Action*

Online recruiting is among the top Internet success stories of the past decade. Monster and CareerBuilder are hotspots for job hunters and recruiters seeking to establish a working relationship, while other sites like Netshare and JobCentral have a reputation for executive-level opportunities as well as ties to corporations that invest heavily in online recruitment. *What are the advantages and disadvantages of online recruiting compared to traditional forms of recruitment?*

Employee Selection

After a firm has attracted enough job applicants, employment specialists begin the selection process. **Selection** is the process of determining which people in the applicant pool possess the qualifications necessary to be successful on the job. The steps in the employee selection process are shown in Exhibit 9.4 An applicant who can jump over each step, or hurdle, will very likely receive a job offer; thus, this is known as the successive hurdles approach to applicant screening. Alternatively, an applicant can be rejected at any step or hurdle. Selection steps or hurdles are described below:

1. *Initial screening.* During initial screening, an applicant completes an application form, and/or submits a résumé, and has a brief interview of 30 minutes or less. The job application includes information about educational background, previous work experience, and job duties performed. The short, structured interview contains specific questions, such as "Do you have a valid diver's license for operating company vehicles? How many employees were in your work team? How many days did you miss work for illness last year?"

2. *Employment testing.* Following initial screening, the applicant may be asked to take one or more tests such as the Wonderlic Personnel Test, a mental-ability test. Tests can measure special job skills (typing and data entry), aptitudes (numeric and spatial dimensions), and even personality characteristics.

HR Senior VP Martha LaCroix of the Yankee Candle Company uses personality assessments to make sure that prospective employees will fit the firm's culture. LaCroix was helped by Predictive Index (PI) Worldwide in determining Yankee Candle's best and worst-performing store managers for developing a best practice behavioral profile of a top-performing store manager.[6] The profile was used for personality

Exhibit 9.4 > **Steps of the Employee Selection Process**

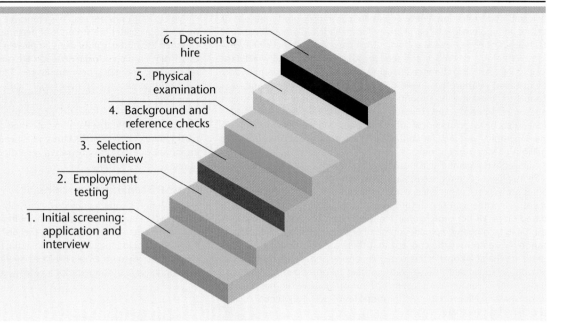

6. Decision to hire

5. Physical examination

4. Background and reference checks

3. Selection interview

2. Employment testing

1. Initial screening: application and interview

selection
The process of determining which persons in the applicant pool possess the qualifications necessary to be successful on the job.

selection interview
An in-depth discussion of an applicant's work experience, skills and abilities, education, and career interests.

testing and to develop interview questions that reveal how an applicant may behave in certain work situations.

3. *Selection interview.* The tool most widely used in making hiring decisions is the **selection interview,** an in-depth discussion of an applicant's work experience, skills and abilities, education, and career interests. For managerial and professional positions, an applicant may be interviewed by several persons, including the line manager for the position to be filled. This interview is designed to determine a person's communication skills and motivation. During the interview, the applicant may be presented with realistic job situations, such as dealing with a disgruntled customer, and asked to describe how she would handle the problem. Carolyn Murray of Gore-Tex listens for casual remarks that may reveal the reality behind applicant answers to her questions. Using a baseball analogy, Carolyn gives examples of how three job candidates struck out in Exhibit 9.5 with her questions.[7]

Exhibit 9.5 > **Striking Out with Gore-Tex**

The Pitch (Question to Applicant)	The Swing (Applicant's Response)	The Miss (Interviewer's Reaction to Response)
"Give me an example of a time when you had a conflict with a team member."	"Our leader asked me to handle all of the FedExing for our team. I did it, but I thought that FedExing was a waste of my time."	"At Gore, we work from a team concept. Her answer shows that she won't exactly jump when one of her teammates needs help."
"Tell me how you solved a problem that was impeding your project."	"One of the engineers on my team wasn't pulling his weight, and we were closing in on a deadline. So I took on some of his work."	"The candidate may have resolved the issue for this particular deadline, but he did nothing to prevent the problem from happening again."
"What's the one thing that you would change about your current position?"	"My job as a salesman has become boring. Now I want the responsibility of managing people."	"He's probably not maximizing his current territory, and he is complaining. Will he find his next role 'boring' and complain about that role, too?"

4. *Background and reference check.* If applicants pass the selection interview, most firms examine their background and check their references. In recent years an increasing number of employers such as American Airlines, Disney, and Microsoft are carefully researching applicants' backgrounds, particularly their legal history, reasons for leaving previous jobs, and even creditworthiness. Retail firms, where employees have extensive contact with customers, tend to be very careful about checking applicant backgrounds.

5. *Physical exams and drug testing.* A firm may require an applicant to have a medical checkup to ensure he or she is physically able to perform job tasks. Drug testing is common in the transportation and health care industries. Southwest Airlines, BNSF Railway, Texas Health Resources, and the U.S. Postal Service use drug testing for reasons of workplace safety, productivity, and employee health.

6. *Decision to hire.* If an applicant progresses satisfactorily through all the selection steps (or jumps all of the selection hurdles), a decision to hire the person is made; however, the job offer may be contingent on passing a physical exam and/or drug test. The decision to hire is nearly always made by the manager of the new employee.

concept check

Describe the employee selection process.

What are some of the ways that prospective employees are tested?

An important aspect of employee recruitment and selection involves treating job applicants as valued customers; in fact, some applicants may be customers of the firm. Read about job applicant customer satisfaction in the Customer Satisfaction and Quality box.

CUSTOMER SATISFACTION AND QUALITY

Puttin' on the Ritz—For Potential Employees

Interviewing for a job can be a nerve-wracking experience. You show up on time in your interview suit expecting to meet someone equally prepared. But that is not always the case. One hears plenty of horror stories of personnel recruiters keeping interviewees waiting while they nonchalantly carry out some unimportant task, like watering their plants. Your meeting with a human resource representative is often your first exposure to the company you are applying to work for, and nothing is more demeaning than to be shown a lack of respect. Firms need to provide good customer service to applicants if they expect to hire the most qualified employees.

The following are further examples of poor customer service when dealing with job applicants:

- A firm reschedules your interview but doesn't let you know about the change
- A firm fails to acknowledge receiving your job application or résumé
- The interviewer eats his or her lunch during your job interview
- The interviewer interrupts the interview to answer cell phone calls that are clearly personal
- The firm fails to contact you for several weeks after your interview
- The interviewer is obviously not prepared to conduct the interview

Firms have several opportunities to create a positive impression of their organization during these key points in the employee selection process. These include a variety of communication channels, such as:

- In-person greetings at a job fair or at the interview itself
- Phone calls to a prospective employee from a human resource professional to set up the interview and any follow-up conversations between human resources and the applicant

- E-mail correspondence to acknowledge receipt of an application and to thank applicants for submitting their job application
- Information packets given to the applicant
- A thank-you note from the employer following the second interview

A firm that is recognized for treating prospective employees especially well is the Ritz-Carlton Hotel, a subsidiary of Marriott International. Ritz managers want to make a good impression, because an applicant could be a future Ritz-Carlton hotel guest. A department head or hotel executive greets each attendee personally at Ritz-Carlton job fairs. Every applicant receives a personal, formal thank-you note for coming to the job fair, and those who are considered for positions but later rejected receive another note. All job fair applicants complete a behavioral questionnaire and are briefly interviewed.

"The Ritz-Carlton knows how to take care of its employees and customers and the upshot is that it has amazing customer service," says David Saxby, president of Phoenix-based Measure-X, a company that specializes in helping utilities improve their customer service and sales. "Ritz-Carlton officials know their efforts create a win-win-win situation. Employees feel good about themselves, guests are happy and the company stays in business."[8]

Critical Thinking Questions

- What are the benefits of an employer treating a job applicant like a customer? Are there costs associated with treating applicants poorly?
- Assume you are a hiring manager, what things can you do to insure that applicants develop a favorable impression of your firm?

Employee Training and Development

 What types of training and development do organizations offer their employees?

training and development
Activities that provide learning situations in which an employee acquires additional knowledge or skills to increase job performance.

orientation
Presentation to get the new employee ready to perform his or her job.

To ensure that both new and experienced employees have the knowledge and skills to perform their jobs successfully, organizations invest in training and development activities. **Training and development** involves learning situations in which the employee acquires additional knowledge or skills to increase job performance. Training objectives specify performance improvements, reductions in errors, job knowledge to be gained, and/or other positive organizational results. The process of creating and implementing training and development activities is shown in Exhibit 9.6. Training is done either on the job or off the job.

On-the-Job Training

New employee training is essential and usually begins with **orientation**, which entails getting the new employee ready to perform on the job. Formal orientation (often a

---

Exhibit 9.6 > **Employee Training and Development Process**

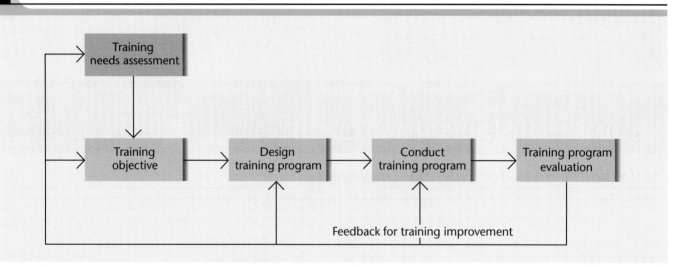

CONCEPT *in Action*

With over 15 manufacturing plants and 38,000 employees in North America, Toyota is becoming as American as baseball and apple pie. Bolstering the Japanese automaker's "American made" image is a new multimillion dollar training center in Georgetown, Kentucky, that serves the company's North American plants. The 98,000-square-foot facility offers hands-on training simulations of Toyota manufacturing processes including production, maintenance, and supervisory management. *How is technology helping companies develop skilled workers both on and off the job?*

TOYOTA MOTOR ENGINEERING & MANUFACTURING NORTH AMERICA, INC. (TEMA)

half-day classroom program) provides information about company policies, salary and benefits, and parking. More important, however, is the specific job orientation by the new employee's supervisor concerning work rules, equipment, and performance expectations. This second briefing tends to be more informal and may last for several days or even weeks.

Beyond employee orientation, job training takes place at the job site or workstation and is directly related to the job. This training involves specific job instruction, coaching (guidance given to new employees by experienced ones), special project assignments, or job rotation. **Job rotation** is the reassignment of workers to several different jobs over time. At Sears and Wal-Mart, management trainees rotate through three or more merchandising departments, customer service, credit, and even the human resource department during the first year or two on the job.

Two other on-the-job forms of training are apprenticeship and mentoring. An **apprenticeship** usually combines specific on-the-job instruction with classroom training. It may last as long as four years and can be found in the skilled trades of carpentry, plumbing, and electrical work. **Mentoring** involves a senior manager or other experienced employee providing job- and career-related information to a mentee. Inexpensive and providing instantaneous feedback, mentoring is becoming increasingly popular with many firms, including FedEx, Merrill Lynch, Dow Chemical, and Bank of America. Whereas mentoring is typically conducted through ongoing face-to-face interactions between mentor and mentee, technology now allows for a long-distance mentoring relationship. Dow Chemical uses e-mail and video conferencing to facilitate long-distance mentoring between persons who are working in different countries. For a mentee whose second language is English, writing e-mail messages in English helps the individual become fluent in English, which is a requirement of all Dow Chemical employees regardless of location and country of origin.[9] For an example of mentoring for cultural orientation, explore Expanding Around the Globe.

Off-the-Job Training

Even with the advantages of on-the-job training, many firms recognize that it is often necessary to train employees away from the workplace. With off-the-job training, employees learn the job away from the job. There are numerous popular methods of off-the-job training. Frequently, it takes place in a classroom where cases, role-play exercises, films, videos, lectures, and computer demonstrations are used to develop workplace skills.

Web-based technology is being increasingly used along with more traditional off-the-job training methods. E-learning *and e-training* involve online computer presentation of information for learning new job tasks. Union Pacific Railroad has tens of thousands of its employees widely dispersed across much of the United States so it delivers training materials electronically to save time and travel costs. Technical and safety training at Union Pacific are made available as **programmed instruction**, a computer-assisted, self-paced, and highly structured training method that presents trainees with concepts and problems using a modular format. Software provided by Plateau Systems can make sure that employees receive, undergo, and complete, as well as sign off on, various training modules.[10]

Computer-assisted training can also be done using a **simulation**, a scaled-down version of a manufacturing process or even a mock cockpit of a jet airplane. American Airlines uses a training simulator for pilots to practice hazardous flight maneuvers or learn the controls of a new aircraft in a safe, controlled environment with no passengers. The simulator allows for more direct transfer of learning to the job.

---

job rotation
Reassignment of workers to several different jobs over time so that they can learn the basics of each job.

apprenticeship
A form of on-the-job training that combines specific job instruction with classroom instruction.

mentoring
A form of on-the-job training in which a senior manager or other experienced employee provides job- and career-related information to a mentee.

programmed instruction
A form of computer-assisted off-the-job training.

simulation
A scaled down version or mock-up of equipment, process, or work environment.

---

concept check

Describe several types of on-the-job training.

What are the advantages of simulation training?

How is technology impacting off-the-job training?

EXPANDING AROUND THE GLOBE

Employees on the (International) Move

Is an international job assignment a step up the ladder to a more rewarding career path or a potential mine-field of professional and family risk? The answer depends as much on an employee's family situation as their ambition, according to a new survey that explores worldwide employee-relocation trends. And it also depends on how well their company supports and handles a transfer to an international location.

Working abroad at one of the thousands of American or foreign multinational firms can be exciting and look good on your résumé. Increasing numbers of recent college graduates and experienced professionals are offered opportunities for overseas work assignments ranging from a few days, to 24 months, or longer. But acclimating to a new country and culture, as well as a new work environment, can be daunting and involves some unique challenges. According to GMAC Global Relocation Services (http://www.gmacglobalrelocation.com), an assignment and mobility consulting service that helps employees settle in a foreign country, retaining expatriate talent remains an enormous challenge for companies. With attrition rates at least double that of nonexpatriate employees, about 21 percent of overseas employees left their companies during an international assignment.

Other challenges face expatriates aside from the demands of work:

- Choosing schools for children
- Securing housing
- Finding medical facilities
- Opening bank accounts
- Finding transportation and obtaining a driver's license
- Completing government forms
- Locating food stores
- Learning about community and entertainment offerings

With 1,200 to 1,500 employees working outside of their home countries at any given time, KPMG International, one of the world's largest public accounting firms with a presence in 144 countries, attempts to deal with employee relocation adjustment issues by utilizing a "buddy" system. At work, the KPMG Global Code of Conduct, entitled "Performance with Integrity," sets out guidelines of ethical conduct that KPMG requires of all its employees worldwide. The code applies equally to partners and employees of all KPMG member firms regardless of their title or position.

To ease the social and cultural burden for new expatriates, the firm links the employee to a buddy for one-on-one support during the length of their assignment, which is typically 24 months. Timothy Dwyer, national director for international human resource advisory services at KPMG, points out that buddies—who usually do not have a direct working relationship with the new expatriate—function in a social role outside of work. They help the new employee and his family resolve the myriad of problems that can arise.

KPMG places a high value on the buddy support role, which is taken into account when performance evaluations are conducted each year. By creating a sense of shared identity within and outside of the organization, KPMG's international employees are more likely to stay on the job.[11]

Critical Thinking Questions

- The buddy system at KPMG is a value-added human resource service that is intangible and difficult to assess; nevertheless, it is important to identity and measure its benefits and costs. What do you think these are and how would you measure them?
- What are the top four or five job qualifications an employee should have to be considered for an overseas assignment?

Performance Planning and Evaluation

 5 **How are performance appraisals used to evaluate employee performance?**

performance appraisal
A comparison of actual performance with expected performance to assess an employee's contributions to the organization.

Along with employee orientation and training, new employees learn about performance expectations through performance planning and evaluation. Managers provide employees with expectations about the job. These are communicated as job objectives, schedules, deadlines, and product and/or service quality requirements. As an employee performs job tasks, the supervisor periodically evaluates the employee's efforts. A **performance appraisal** is a comparison of actual performance with expected performance to determine an employee's contributions to the organization and to make decisions about training, compensation, promotion, and other job changes. The performance planning and appraisal process is shown in Exhibit 9.7 and described below.

1. The manager establishes performance standards.
2. The employee works to meet the standards and expectations.
3. The employee's supervisor evaluates the employee's work in terms of quality and quantity of output and various characteristics such as job knowledge, initiative, relationships with others, and attendance and punctuality.
4. Following the performance evaluation, reward (pay raise) and job change (promotion) decisions can be made.
5. Rewards are positive feedback and provide reinforcement, or encouragement, for the employee to work harder in the future.

Information for performance appraisals can be assembled using rating scales, supervisor logs of employee job incidents, and reports of sales and production

Exhibit 9.7 > **Performance Planning and Evaluation**

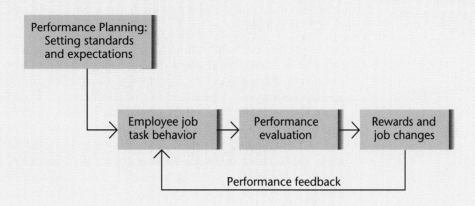

concept check

What are the steps in the performance planning and appraisal process?

What purposes do performance appraisals serve?

Describe some sources of information for the performance appraisal.

statistics. Regardless of the source, performance information should be accurate and a record of the employee's job behavior and efforts. Exhibit 9.8 illustrates a rating scale for one aspect of a college recruiter's job. A rating of "9" is considered outstanding job behavior and performance; a rating of "1" is viewed as very poor to unacceptable.

Exhibit 9.8 > **Example of Behavior-Based Rating Scale for Performance Appraisal**

Position: College Recruiter
Job Description: Visits campuses and conducts interviews of graduating seniors

Explanation of Rating	Performance Rating	Explanation of Rating
Plans and organizes spring semester college recruiting schedule to minimize travel expenses and maximize the number of colleges visited and students interviewed.	9	
	8	Even with tight travel schedules between campuses, this recruiter completes each campus report before arrival at next campus.
	7	In making plans to visit a new campus, this recruiter might not have identified two or three faculty
	6	members for obtaining pre-visit information about degree programs.
Occasionally does not check with college placement office to request student résumés two days before arrival.	5	
	4	Sometimes this recruiter's notes are incomplete concerning a student's response to interview question.
	3	
	2	This recruiter is often several minutes late in starting interviews.
Frequently late in sending thank-you letters to students interviewed.	1	Recruiter is always late completing campus recruiting reports.

Employee Compensation and Benefits

Compensation, which includes both pay and benefits, is closely connected to performance appraisal. Employees who perform better tend to get bigger pay raises. Several factors affect an employee's pay:

1. *Pay structure and internal influences.* Wages, salaries, and benefits usually reflect the importance of the job. The jobs that management considers more important are compensated at a higher rate; president, chief engineer, and chief financial officer are high-paying jobs. Likewise, different jobs of equal importance to the firm are compensated at the same rate. For instance, if a drill-press operator and a lathe operator are considered of equal importance, they may both be paid $21 per hour.

2. *Pay level and external influences.* In deciding how much to pay workers, the firm must also be concerned with the salaries paid by competitors. If competitors are paying higher wages, a firm may lose its best employees. Larger firms conduct salary surveys to see what other firms are paying. Wage and salary surveys conducted by the Chamber of Commerce and the U.S. Department of Labor can also be useful.

An employer can decide to pay at, above, or below the going rate. Most firms try to offer competitive wages and salaries within a geographic area or an industry. If a company pays below-market wages, it may not be able to hire skilled people. The level of a firm's compensation is determined by the firm's financial condition (or profitability), efficiency, and employee productivity, as well as the going rates paid by competitors. Miller Brewing Co. is considered a high-paying firm ($25–28 per hour for production employees).

incentive pay
Additional pay for attaining a specific goal.

Farcus by David Waisglass / Gordon Coulthart

"I'd say your best bet is in Las Vegas."

CONCEPT *in Action*

Since their heyday in World War II, pensions have increasingly placed financial burdens on corporations seeking to reward employees with the promise of big payouts upon retirement. With multinational businesses like IBM, Verizon, and Alcoa now freezing pension benefits, some analysts predict that this once-popular form of indirect pay may be headed for its own retirement. *How might companies respond to employee dissatisfaction over suspended or discontinued retirement pension programs?*

Types of Compensation or Pay

There are two basic types of compensation: direct and indirect. Direct pay is the wage or salary received by the employee; indirect pay consists of various employee benefits and services. Employees are usually paid directly on the basis of the amount of time they work, the amount they produce, or some combination of time and output. An hourly rate of pay or a monthly salary are considered base pay, or an amount of pay received by the employee regardless of output level. In many jobs, such as sales and manufacturing, an employee can earn additional pay as a result of an **incentive pay** arrangement. The accelerated commission schedule for a salesperson shown below indicates that as sales increases, the incentive becomes increasingly more attractive and rewarding, and therefore, pay can function as a powerful motivator. In this example, a salesperson receives a base monthly salary of $1,000, then earns 3 percent on the first $50,000 of product sold, 4 percent on the next $30,000, and 5 percent on any sales beyond $80,000.

Base pay	$1,000
3% × 50,000	1,500
4% × 30,000	1,200
5% × 20,000	1,000
	$4,700

Two other incentive pay arrangements are bonuses and profit sharing. Employees may be paid bonuses for reaching certain monthly or annual performance goals or achieving a specific cost-saving objective. In this instance, employees are rewarded some portion of the amount of cost savings.

In a profit sharing plan, employees may receive some portion of the firm's profit. Employee profit shares are usually based on annual financial performance and therefore are paid once a year. With either a bonus or a profit share, an important incentive pay consideration is whether the bonus or profit share is the same for all employees or whether it is differentiated by level in the organization, base pay, or some other criterion. Choice Homes, a large-scale builder of starter homes, pays an annual incentive share that is the same for everyone; the president receives the same profit share or bonus as the lowest-paid employee.

Indirect pay includes pensions, health insurance, vacations, and many others. Some forms of indirect pay are required by law: unemployment compensation, worker's compensation, and Social Security, which are all paid in part by employers. **Unemployment compensation** provides former employees with money for a certain period while they are unemployed. To be eligible, the employee must have worked a minimum number of weeks, be without a job, and be willing to accept a suitable position offered by the state Unemployment Compensation Commission. Some state laws permit payments to strikers. **Worker's compensation** pays employees for lost work time caused by work-related injuries and may also cover rehabilitation after a serious injury. Social Security is mainly a government pension plan, but it also provides disability and survivor benefits and benefits for people undergoing kidney dialysis and transplants. Medicare (health care for the elderly) and Medicaid (health care for the poor) are also part of Social Security.

unemployment compensation
Government payment to unemployed former workers.

worker's compensation
Pay for lost work time due to employment–related injuries.

Many employers also offer benefits not required by law. Among these are paid time off (vacations, holidays, sick days, even pay for jury duty), insurance (health and hospitalization, disability, life, dental, vision, and accidental death and dismemberment), pensions and retirement savings accounts, and stock purchase options.

Some firms with numerous benefits allow employees to mix and match benefit items or select items based on individual needs. This is a cafeteria-style benefit plan. A younger employee with a family may desire to purchase medical, disability, and life insurance, whereas an older employee may want to put more benefit dollars into a retirement savings plan. All employees are allocated the same number of benefit dollars, but can spend these dollars on different items and in different amounts.

Pay and benefits are obviously important elements of human resource management and are frequently studied as aspects of employee job satisfaction. Pay can be very satisfactory or it can be a point of job dissatisfaction. In a study of job satisfaction conducted by the Society for Human Resource Management and CNN financial news, benefits and direct compensation were ranked one and two respectively as very important elements of job satisfaction by employees from various companies.[12] Employee job satisfaction at Analytical Graphics is discussed in the Catching the Entrepreneurial Spirit box.

concept check

How does a firm establish a pay scale for its employees?

What is the difference between direct and indirect pay?

Explain the concept of a cafeteria-style benefit plan.

The Labor Relations Process

 7 **What is a labor union and how is it organized?**

labor union
An organization that represents workers in dealing with management.

collective bargaining
Negotiating a labor agreement.

Tens of thousands of American firms are unionized and millions of American workers belong to unions. Historically, the mining, manufacturing, construction, and transportation industries have been significantly unionized, but in recent years service-based firms, including health care organizations, have been unionized.

A **labor union**, such as the International Brotherhood of Teamsters, is an organization that represents workers in dealing with management over disputes involving wages, hours, and working conditions. The labor relations process that produces a union-management relationship consists of three phases; union organizing, negotiating a labor agreement, and administering the agreement. In phase one, a group of employees within a firm may form a union on their own, or an established union (United Auto Workers, for example) may target an employer and organize many of the firm's workers into a local labor union. The second phase constitutes **collective bargaining**, which is the process of negotiating a labor agreement that provides for compensation

Analytical Graphics Shoots for the Moon

Have you ever wondered where the best place is to work? The Great Place to Work Institute believes that any company can create a great workplace. According to its Best Companies lists published on its Web site, (http://www.greatplacetowork.com), Analytical Graphics (AGI) of Exton, Pennsylvania, has done just that. The company was listed as the best small company to work for in both 2004 and 2005, based on employee responses to a detailed survey and employer responses to a separate questionnaire.

Founded in his living room by Paul L. Graziani with two colleagues in 1989, the company has put work practices in place that has earned it local, state and national recognition for its innovative work environment. Chief Executive Officer (CEO) Graziani knows every one in the company personally and tries to greet each employee every day—whether at a meeting, lunch, working out in the company fitness center, or in the on-site laundry room. The corporate culture is open, friendly, and supportive of its high performance employees—aerospace, electrical, and software engineers who produce high-tech navigation software for jet planes, missiles, rockets and satellites—the proverbial "rocket scientists."

According to human resources director, Lisa Velte, the management style is "high touch" as well as high tech. Maintaining AGI's friendly atmosphere despite rapid growth is "a personal mission," says Velte. "That is one of my key areas of focus—to make sure that we are doing everything we can to retain the culture," a culture which employees describe as "like a family," characterizing management as "relaxed," "laid back" and "easy to talk to."

Shortly after being hired new employees are appointed "buddies" and rotated through all departments for half-day orientation sessions. At the weekly Friday buffet luncheon, employees are briefed about company performance, new projects, and projected expansion plans. Analytical Graphics is also viewed as a great place to work due to its generous portfolio of employee benefits and services, which include daily breakfasts, lunches, and evening meals for those working into the night on various projects. The firm offers above-average salaries, pays 100 percent of employee health insurance premiums, and provides employees with 40 hours of training each year at an average cost of $2,000 per employee. And for nominal fees employees can utilize other services such as dry cleaning, oil changes, car washes, flower delivery, and shoe-shines.

Graziani cites staff productivity to justify the generous perks—3 million total lines of net computer code written and current sales per employee of $260,000. The fact that its workforce has increased by 39 percent since 2004 proves the point—Analytical Graphics' corporate culture and human resource practices create an appealing place to work and a highly satisfied and productive workforce. [13]

Critical Thinking Questions

- How can a company like Analytical Graphics sustain its "high touch" employee culture and continue to grow rapidly?
- Can a firm give its employees too much in terms of benefits and services? Explain.

and working arrangements mutually acceptable to the union and to management. Finally, the third phase of the labor relations process involves the daily administering of the labor agreement primarily through handling worker grievances and other workforce management problems that require interaction between managers and labor union officials.

The Modern Labor Movement

The basic structure of the modern labor movement consists of three parts: local unions, national and international unions, and union federations. There are approximately 60,000 local unions, 75 national and international unions, and 2 federations. Union membership has been declining for about three decades. Currently, about 12.5 percent of the American labor force are union members, or approximately 14.5 million workers.

local union
Branch of a national union that represents workers in a specific plant or geographic area.

A **local union** is a branch or unit of a national union that represents workers at a specific plant or over a specific geographic area. Local 276 of the United Auto Workers represents assembly employees at the General Motors plant in Arlington, Texas. A local union (in conformance with its national union rules) determines the number of local union officers, procedures for electing officers, the schedule of local meetings, financial arrangements with the national organization, and the local's role in negotiating labor agreements.

The three main functions of the local union are collective bargaining, worker relations and membership services, and community and political activities. Collective bargaining takes place every three or four years. Local union officers and shop stewards in the plant oversee labor relations on a day-to-day basis. A **shop steward** is an elected union official who represents union members to management when workers

shop steward
An elected union official that represents union members to management when workers have complaints.

have complaints. For most union members, his or her primary contact with the union is through union officials at the local level.

A national union can range in size from a few thousand members (Screen Actors Guild) to more than a million members (Teamsters). A national union may have a few to as many as several hundred local unions. The number of national unions has steadily declined since the early 20th century. Much of this decline has resulted from union mergers. In 1999, for example, the United Papermakers International Union (UPICU) and the Oil, Chemical and Atomic Workers Union (OCAW) agreed to merge under the new name of PACE or Paper, Allied-Industrial, Chemical and Energy International Union. PACE has about 320,000 members.

For 50 years, one union federation (the American Federation of Labor-Congress of Industrial Organization, or AFL-CIO) dominated the American labor movement. A **federation** is a collection of unions banded together to further organizing, public relations, political, and other mutually agreed upon purposes of the member unions. In the summer of 2005, several unions (Teamsters, Service Employees International Union, Laborers' International Union, United Farm Workers, Carpenters and Joiners, Unite Here, and the United Food and Commercial Workers Union) split from the AFL-CIO and formed a new federation named the Change to Win Coalition.[14] The new federation and its member unions represent more than five million union members. Change to Win Coalition member unions left the AFL-CIO over leadership disagreements and ineffective organizing strategies of the AFL-CIO; one of its primary goals is to strengthen union organizing drives and reverse the decline in union membership.[15]

federation
A collection of unions banded together to achieve common goals.

Union Organizing

A nonunion employer becomes unionized through an organizing campaign. The campaign is started either from within, by unhappy employees, or from outside, by a union that has picked the employer for an organizing drive. Once workers and the union have made contact, a union organizer tries to convince all the workers to sign authorization cards. These cards prove the worker's interest in having the union represent them. In most cases, employers resist this card-signing campaign by speaking out against unions in letters, posters, and employee assemblies. However, it is illegal for employers to interfere directly with the card-signing campaign or to coerce employees into not joining the union.

Once the union gets signed authorization cards from at least 30 percent of the employees, it can ask National Labor Relations Board (NLRB) for a union certification election. This election, by secret ballot, determines whether the workers want to be represented by the union. The NLRB posts an election notice and defines the bargaining unit—employees who are eligible to vote and who will be represented by the particular union if it is certified. Supervisors and managers cannot vote. The union and the employer then engage in a preelection campaign conducted through speeches, memos, and meetings. Both try to convince workers to vote in their favor. Exhibit 9.9 lists benefits usually stressed by the union during a campaign and common arguments employers make to convince employees a union is unnecessary.

The election itself is conducted by the NLRB. If a majority vote for the union, the NLRB certifies the union as the exclusive bargaining agent for all employees who had been designated as eligible voters. The employer then has to bargain with the union over wages, hours, and other terms of employment. The complete organizing process is summarized in Exhibit 9.10.

In some situations, after one year, if the union and employer don't reach an agreement, the workers petition for a decertification election which is similar to the certification election but allows workers to vote out the union. Decertification elections are also held when workers become dissatisfied with a union that has represented them for a longer time. In recent years, the number of decertification elections has increased to several hundred per year.

Exhibit 9.9 > Benefits Stressed by Unions in Organizing Campaigns and Common Arguments Against Unions

Benefits Stressed by Unions:

Almost Always Stressed	Often Stressed	Seldom Stressed
Grievance procedures	More influence in decision making	Higher-quality products
Job security	Better working conditions	Technical training
Improved benefits	Lobbying opportunities	More job satisfaction
Higher pay		Increased production

Employer Arguments Against Unionization:

- An employee can always come directly to management with a problem; a third party (the union) isn't necessary.
- As a union member, you will pay monthly union dues of $15 to $30.
- Merit-based decisions (promotions) are better than seniority-based.
- Pay and benefits are very similar to the leading firms in the industry.
- We meet all health and safety standards of the Federal Occupational Safety and Health Administration.
- Performance and productivity are more important than union representation in determining pay raises.

Exhibit 9.10 > Union Organizing Process and Election

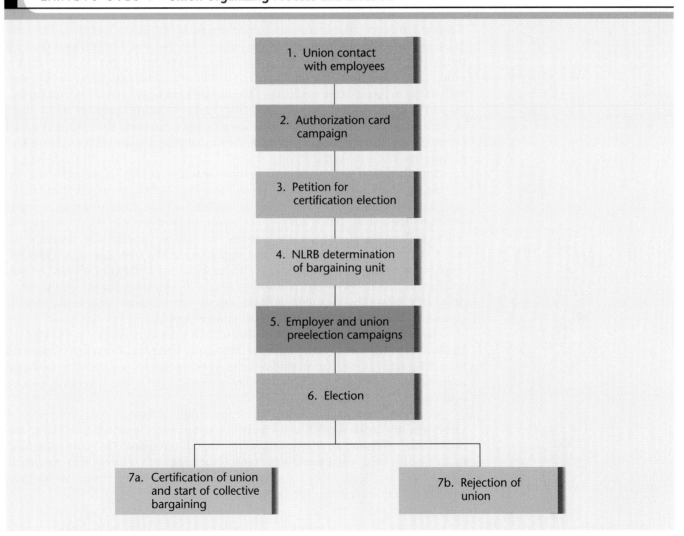

1. Union contact with employees
2. Authorization card campaign
3. Petition for certification election
4. NLRB determination of bargaining unit
5. Employer and union preelection campaigns
6. Election
7a. Certification of union and start of collective bargaining
7b. Rejection of union

Negotiating Union Contracts Through Collective Bargaining

8 What is collective bargaining, and what are some of the key negotiation issues?

A labor agreement, or union contract, is created through *collective bargaining*. Typically, both management and union negotiation teams are made up of a few people. One person on each side is the chief spokesperson. Bargaining begins with union and management negotiators setting a list of contract issues that will be discussed. Much of the bargaining over specific details takes place through face-to-face meetings and the exchange of written proposals. Demands, proposals, and counterproposals are exchanged during several rounds of bargaining. The resulting contract must be approved by top management and ratified by the union members. Once both sides approve, the contract is a legally binding agreement that typically covers such issues as union security, management rights, wages, benefits, and job security. The collective bargaining process is shown in Exhibit 9.11. We will explore some of the bargaining issues below.

Exhibit 9.11 > The Process of Negotiating Labor Agreements

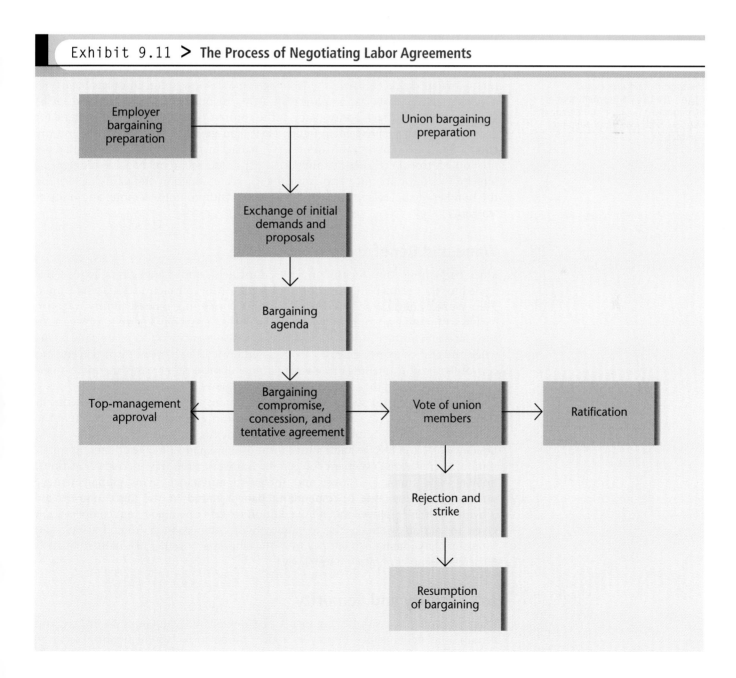

Union Security

union shop
Nonunion workers can be hired but must join the union later.

agency shop
Workers don't have to join a union but must pay union dues.

right-to-work law
State laws that an employee does not have to join a union.

open shop
Workers do not have to join the union or pay union dues.

management rights clause
Clause in a labor agreement that gives management the right to manage the business except as specified in the contract.

A union wants all employees to be union members. This can be accomplished by negotiating a union security clause. The most common union security arrangement is the **union shop** whereby nonunion workers can be hired by the firm, but then they must join the union, normally within 30 to 60 days. An **agency shop** does not require employees to join the union, but to remain employees, workers must pay the union a fee (known as the agency fee) to cover the union's expenses in representing them. The union must fairly represent all workers, including those in the bargaining unit who do not become members.

Under the Taft-Hartley Act of 1947, a state can make any and all forms of union security illegal by enacting a **right-to-work law**. In the 21 states that have these laws, employees can work at a unionized company without having to join the union. This arrangement is commonly known as an **open shop**. Workers don't have to join the union or pay dues or fees to the union.

Management Rights

When a company becomes unionized, management loses some of its decision-making abilities. But management still has certain rights that can be negotiated in collective bargaining. One way to resist union meddling in management matters is to put a **management rights clause** in the labor agreement. Most union contracts have one. A typical clause gives the employer all rights to manage the business except as specified in the contract. For instance, if the contract does not specify the criteria for promotions, with a management rights clause managers will have the right to use any criteria they wish. Another way to preserve management rights is to list areas that are not subject to collective bargaining. This list might secure management's right to schedule work hours, hire and fire workers, set production standards, determine the number of supervisors in each department, and promote, demote, and transfer workers.

Wage and Benefits

Much bargaining effort focuses on wage adjustments and changes in benefits. Once agreed to, they remain in effect for the length of the contract. In 2003, the United Auto Workers negotiated a four-year contract containing modest hourly wage increases with American car manufacturers; pay hikes were about 3 percent each year for the four-year contract. Hourly rates of pay can also increase under some agreements when the cost of living increases above a certain level each year, say 4 percent. No cost-of-living adjustment is made when annual living cost increases are under 4 percent, which has been the experience for the early years of the 21st century.

In addition to requests for wage increases, unions usually want better benefits. In some industries, such as steel and auto manufacturing, benefits are 40 percent of the total cost of compensation. Benefits may include higher wages for overtime work, holiday work, and less desirable shifts; insurance programs (life, health and hospitalization, dental care); payment for certain nonwork time (rest periods, vacations, holiday, sick time); pensions; and income-maintenance plans. Supplementary unemployment benefits (income-maintenance) found in the auto industry are provided by the employer and are in addition to state unemployment compensation given to laid-off workers. The unemployment compensation from the state and supplementary unemployment pay from the employer, together maintain as much as 80 percent of an employee's normal pay.

Job Security and Seniority

Wage adjustments, cost-of-living increases, supplementary unemployment pay, and certain other benefits give employees under union contracts some financial security.

But most financial security is directly related to job security—the assurance, to some degree, that workers will keep their jobs. Of course, job security depends primarily on the continued success and financial well-being of the company. As mentioned earlier, thousands of airline employees lost their jobs after the 9/11 event in 2001; these were employees with the least seniority.

Seniority, the length of an employee's continuous service with a firm, is discussed in about 90 percent of all labor contracts. Seniority is a factor in job security; usually, unions want the workers with the most seniority to have the most job security.

concept check

Discuss the modern labor movement.

What are the various topics that may be covered during collective bargaining?

Explain the differences among a union shop, agency shop, and an open shop.

Managing Grievances and Conflicts

9 **How are grievances between management and labor resolved, and what tactics are used to force a contract settlement?**

In a unionized work environment, employees follow a step-by-step process for handling grievances or disputes between management and labor. Conflicts over contracts, however, are far more challenging to resolve and may result in the union or employer imposing economic pressure as described in this section.

Grievance Handling and Arbitration

grievance
A formal complaint by a union worker that management has violated the contract.

The union's main way of policing the contract is the grievance procedure. A **grievance** is a formal complaint, by an employee or the union, that management has violated some part of the contract. Under a typical contract, the employee starts by presenting the grievance to the supervisor, either in person or in writing. The typical grievance procedure is illustrated in Exhibit 9.12. An example grievance is a situation in which an employee is disciplined with a one-day suspension (and loss of pay) for being late for work several times in one month.

If the problem isn't solved, the grievance is put in writing. The employee, one or more union officials, the supervisor, and perhaps the plant manager then discuss the grievance. If the matter still can't be resolved, another meeting takes place with higher-level representatives of both parties present. If top management and the local union president can't resolve the grievance, it goes to arbitration.

arbitration
Settling labor–management disputes through a third party. The decision is final and binding.

Arbitration is the process of settling a labor-management dispute by having a third party—a single arbitrator or a panel—make a decision. The decision is final and binding on the union and employer. The arbitrator reviews the grievance at a hearing

CONCEPT *in Action*

Terrell Owens is a Dallas Cowboy—at least for now. The controversial NFL wide receiver lost a highly publicized arbitration case with former team the Philadelphia Eagles in which arbitrator Richard Bloch ruled Owens' behavior was destructive and a continuing threat to the organization. Despite protests from player agent Drew Rosenhaus, Bloch ruled that the Eagles' decision to suspend Owens did not violate the labor agreement. *What options did Owens have after losing arbitration?*

Exhibit 9.12 > **Typical Grievance Procedure**

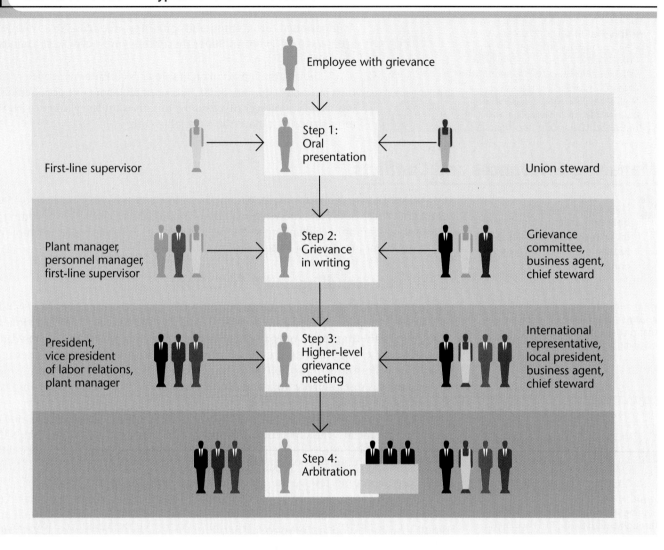

Employee with grievance

First-line supervisor → Step 1: Oral presentation ← Union steward

Plant manager, personnel manager, first-line supervisor → Step 2: Grievance in writing ← Grievance committee, business agent, chief steward

President, vice president of labor relations, plant manager → Step 3: Higher-level grievance meeting ← International representative, local president, business agent, chief steward

Step 4: Arbitration

and then makes the decision, which is presented in a document called the award. In the one-day suspension mentioned above, the arbitration might rule that the discipline was improperly made because the employee's attendance record for the month was not accurately maintained by the firm.

Tactics for Pressuring a Contract Settlement

Virtually all labor agreements specify peaceful resolution of conflicts, usually through arbitration. However, when a contract expires and a new agreement has not been reached, the union is free to strike or engage in other efforts to exert economic pressure on the employer. A *strike* occurs when employees refuse to work. The United Auto Workers union has used a **selective strike strategy** against General Motors, a strategy of conducting a strike at a critical plant that supplies parts to other plants. The union conducted its strike at a stamping and parts facility in Flint, Michigan, which supplied critical parts to other plants. The 54-day strike caused the company to stop production at many of its assembly plants because parts were not available from the Flint plant. General Motors lost approximately $2.2 billion during this dispute. Likewise, the employer can put pressure

selective strike strategy
Strike at a critical plant that typically stops operations system wide.

concept check

Describe the grievance procedure.

In what ways do arbitrators act like judges?

What are some tactics for pressuring for a contract settlement?

CONCEPT *in Action*

New York City's 30,000 public-transit workers walked off the job in 2005 when a labor dispute between the Local 100 chapter of the Transport Workers Union and the Metropolitan Transit Authority turned into a high-stakes showdown. The strike cut short holiday shopping and forced millions of city residents to walk to work, resulting in a virtual shutdown of the Big Apple a week before Christmas. *Why do unions strike?*

on the union through a lockout or hiring strike replacements if the union has called a strike. During the summer 2005 strike of mechanics at Northwest Airlines, the company hired *substitute* or *replacement* mechanics. Exhibit 9.13 provides a summary of union and employer pressure strategies for forcing a contract settlement.

Legal Environment of Human Resources and Labor Relations

10 **What are the key laws and federal agencies affecting human resource management and labor relations?**

Federal laws help ensure that job applicants and employees are treated fairly and not discriminated against. Hiring, training, and job placement must be unbiased. Promotion and compensation decisions must be based on performance. These laws help all Americans who have talent, training, and the desire to get ahead. The key laws that currently impact human resource management and labor relations are listed in Exhibit 9.14.

Several laws govern wages, pensions, and unemployment compensation. For instance, the Fair Labor Standards Act sets the minimum wage, which is periodically raised by Congress. Many minimum-wage jobs are found in service firms, such as McDonald's and car washes. The Pension Reform Act protects the retirement income

---

Exhibit 9.13 > Strategies of Unions and Employers

Union Strategies		Employer Strategies	
Strike:	Employees refuse to work.	**Lockout:**	Employer refuses to let employees enter plant to work.
Boycott:	Employees try to keep customers and others from doing business with employer.	**Strike replacements:**	Employer uses nonunion employees to do jobs of striking union employees.
Picketing:	Employees march near entrance of firm to publicize their view of dispute and discourage customers.	**Mutual-aid pact:**	Employer receives money from other companies in industry to cover some of income lost because of strikes.
Corporate campaign:	Union disrupts stockholder meetings or buys company stock to have more influence over management.	**Shift production:**	Employer moves production to nonunion plant or out of country.

CONCEPT *in Action*

For some occupations, danger is part of the job description. Tallies of work-related casualties routinely identify loggers, pilots, commercial fishermen, and steel workers as holding the most deadly jobs in industry. Job fatalities are often linked to the use of heavy or outdated equipment. However, many work-related deaths also happen in common highway accidents or as homicides. *What laws and agencies are designated to improve occupational safety?*

© NATALIE FOBES/CORBIS

Exhibit 9.14 > Laws Impacting Human Resource Management

Law	Purpose	Agency of Enforcement
Social Security Act (1935)	Provides for retirement income and old age health care	Social Security Administration
Wagner Act (1935)	Gives workers the right to unionize and prohibits employer unfair labor practices	National Labor Relations Board
Fair Labor Standards Act (1938)	Sets minimum wage, restricts child labor, sets overtime pay	Wage and Hour Division, Department of Labor
Taft-Hartley Act (1947)	Obligates the union to bargain in good faith and prohibits union unfair labor practices	Federal Mediation and Conciliation Service
Equal Pay Act (1963)	Eliminates pay differentials based on gender	Equal Employment Opportunity Commission
Civil Rights Act (1964), Title VII	Prohibits employment discrimination based on race, color, religion, gender, or national origin	Equal Employment Opportunity Commission
Age Discrimination Act (1967)	Prohibits age discrimination against those over 40 years of age	Equal Employment Opportunity Commission
Occupational Safety and Health Act (1970)	Protects worker health and safety, provides for hazard-free workplace	Occupational Safety and Health Administration
Vietnam Veterans' Readjustment Act (1974)	Requires affirmative employment of Vietnam War veterans	Veterans Employment Service, Department of Labor
Employee Retirement Income Security Act (1974)—also called Pension Reform Act	Establishes minimum requirements for private pension plans	Internal Revenue Service, Department of Labor, and Pension Benefit Guaranty Corporation
Pregnancy Discrimination Act (1978)	Treats pregnancy as a disability, prevents employment discrimination based on pregnancy	Equal Employment Opportunity Commission
Immigration Reform and Control Act (1986)	Verifies employment eligibility, prevents employment of illegal aliens	Employment Verification Systems, Immigration and Naturalization Service
Americans with Disabilities Act (1990)	Prohibits employment discrimination based on mental or physical disabilities	Department of Labor
Family and Medical Leave Act (1993)	Requires employers to provide unpaid leave for childbirth, adoption, or illness	Equal Employment Opportunity Commission

of employees and retirees. Federal tax laws also affect compensation, including employee profit-sharing and stock purchase plans.

Employers must also be aware of changes to laws concerning employee safety, health, and privacy. The Occupational Safety and Health Act (OSHA) requires employers to provide a workplace free of health and safety hazards. For instance, manufacturers must require their employees working on loading docks to wear steel-toed shoes so their feet won't be injured if materials are dropped. Drug and AIDS testing are also governed by federal laws.

Another employee law that continues to affect the workplace is the Americans with Disabilities Act. To be considered disabled, a person must have a physical or mental impairment that greatly limits one or more major life activities. More than 54 million Americans fall into this category. Employers may not discriminate against disabled persons. They must make "reasonable accommodations" so that qualified employees can perform the job, unless doing so would cause "undue hardship" for the business. Altering work schedules, modifying equipment so a wheelchair-bound person can use it, and making buildings accessible by ramps and elevators are considered reasonable. Two companies often praised for their efforts to hire the disabled are McDonald's and DuPont.

The Family and Medical Leave Act went into effect in 1993. The law applies to employers with 50 or more employees. It requires these employers to provide unpaid leave of up to 12 weeks during any 12-month period to workers who have been employed for at least a year and work a minimum of 25 hours a week. The reasons for the leave include the birth or adoption of a child; the serious illness of a child, spouse, or parent; or a serious illness that prevents the worker from doing the job. When the employee returns, he or she must be given his or her former job back.

The Wagner and Taft-Hartley Acts govern the relationship between an employer and union. Employees have the right to unionize and bargain collectively with the company. The employer must deal with the union fairly, bargain in good faith, and not discriminate against an employee who belongs to the union. The union must also represent all employees covered by a labor agreement fairly and deal with the employer in good faith.

Several federal agencies oversee employment, safety, compensation, and related areas. The **Occupational Safety and Health Administration** (OSHA) sets workplace safety and health standards, provides safety training, and inspects places of work (assembly plants, construction sites, and warehouse facilities, for example) to determine employer compliance with safety regulations.

The Wage and Hour division of the Department of Labor enforces the federal minimum-wage law and overtime provisions of the Fair Labor Standards Act. Employers covered by this law must pay certain employees a premium rate of pay (or time and one-half) for all hours worked beyond 40 in one week.

The **Equal Employment Opportunity Commission** (EEOC) was created by the 1964 Civil Rights Act. It is one of the most influential agencies responsible for enforcing employment laws. The EEOC has three basic functions: processing discrimination complaints, issuing written regulations, and information gathering and dissemination. An employment discrimination complaint can be filed by an individual or a group of employees who work for a company. The group may comprise a **protected class**, such as women, African Americans, or Hispanic Americans. The protected group may pursue a class action complaint that may eventually become a lawsuit. As a measure to prevent employment discrimination, many employers set up **affirmative action programs** to expand job opportunities for women and minorities.

Even with affirmative action and other company efforts to follow the law, each year the EEOC receives tens of thousands of complaints from current or former employees. The monetary benefits that the EEOC wins for employees has grown substantially during the past 10 years. Large monetary settlements often occur when the EEOC files a class action suit against an employer. For example, the $34 million paid by Mitsubishi Motor Manufacturing to settle several sexual harassment cases

Occupational Safety and Health Administration (OSHA)
Sets workplace safety and health standards and assures compliance.

Equal Employment Opportunity Commission (EEOC)
Processes discrimination complaints, issues regulations regarding discrimination, and disseminates information.

protected classes
The specific groups who have legal protection against employment discrimination; include women, African Americans, Native Americans, and others.

affirmative action programs
Programs established by organizations to expand job opportunities for women and minorities.

conciliation
Specialist in labor-management negotiations that acts as a go-between for management and the unions and helps focus on the problems.

mediation
Specialist that facilitates labor-management contract discussions and suggests compromises.

was distributed to nearly 500 former and current female employees (in addition to the lawyers). Also, Sears, Motorola, and AT&T have had to make large back-pay awards and to offer special training to minority employees after the court found they had been discriminated against.

The National Labor Relations Board (NLRB) was established to enforce the Wagner Act. Its five members are appointed by the president; the agency's main office is in Washington, DC, and regional and field offices are scattered throughout the United States. NLRB field agents investigate charges of employer and union wrongdoing (or unfair labor practices) and supervise elections held to decide union representation. Judges conduct hearings to determine whether employers and unions have violated the law.

The Federal Mediation and Conciliation Service helps unions and employers negotiate labor agreements. Agency specialists, who serve as impartial third parties between the union and company, use two processes: conciliation and mediation, both of which require expert communication and persuasion. In **conciliation** the specialist assists management and the union to focus on the issues in dispute and acts as a go-between, or communication channel through which the union and employer send messages to and share information with each other. The specialist takes a stronger role in **mediation** by suggesting compromises to the disputing organizations.

> ## concept check
>
> Discuss the laws that govern wages, pensions, and employee compensation.
>
> Describe the Americans with Disabilities Act.
>
> How do the Wagner and Taft-Hartley Acts impact labor-management relations?

Trends in Human Resource Management and Labor Relations

11 **What trends and issues are affecting human resource management and labor relations?**

Some of today's most important trends in human resource management are using employee diversity as a competive advantage, improving efficiency through outsourcing and technology, and hiring employees who fit the organizational culture. Although overall labor union enrollment continues to decline, a possible surge in membership in service unions is anticipated.

Employee Diversity and Competitive Advantage

competitive advantage
A set of unique features of an organization that are perceived by customers and potential customers as significant and superior to the competition.

American society and its workforce are becoming increasingly more diverse in terms of racial and ethnic status, age, educational background, work experience, and gender. A company with a demographic employee profile that looks like its customers may be in a position to gain a **competitive advantage**, which is a set of unique features of a company and its product or service that are perceived by the target market as superior to those of the competition. Competitive advantage is the factor that causes customers to patronize a firm and not the competition. Many things can be a source of competitive advantage: for Southwest Airlines it is route structure and high asset utilization; for the Ritz-Carlton it is very high quality guest services; for Toyota it is manufacturing efficiency and product durability; and for Starbucks it is location, service, and outstanding coffee products. For these firms, a competitive advantage is also created by their HR practices. Many firms are successful because of employee diversity which can produce more effective problem solving, a stronger reputation for hiring women and minorities, greater employee diversity, quicker adaptation to change, and more robust product solutions because a diverse team can generate more options for improvement.[16]

In order for an organization to use employee diversity for competitive advantage, top management must be fully committed to hiring and developing women and minority individuals. An organization that highly values employee diversity is the United States Postal Service (USPS). In 1992 the Postal Service launched a diversity development program to serve as the organization's "social conscience and to increase employees' awareness of and appreciation for ethnic and cultural diversity both in the postal workplace and among customers." Within about ten years, 36 percent of postal service employees were minority persons: 21.1 percent black, 7.6 percent Hispanic, and nearly 8.0 other minorities. Nearly 25 percent of the organization's highest paid executives, and 32 percent of other managers, were minorities, and more than 40 percent of line supervisors were women.[17]

Outsourcing HR and Technology

The role of the HR professional has changed noticeably over the past 20 years. One significant change has been the use of technology in handling relatively routine HR tasks, such as payroll processing, initial screening of applicants, and benefits enrollments. Large firms such as Nokia and Lockheed Martin purchase specialized software (SAP and Oracle/PeopleSoft) to perform the information processing aspects of many HR tasks. Other firms such as Carter and Burgress (a large engineering firm) outsource, or contract out these tasks to HR service providers, such as Hewitt Associates and Workforce Solutions.

HR outsourcing is done when another firm can perform a task better and more efficiently, thus saving costs. Sometimes HR activities are outsourced because HR requirements are extraordinary and too overwhelming to execute in-house in a timely fashion. Frequently, HR activities are simply outsourced because a provider has greater expertise. Blue Cross and Blue Shield of South Carolina outsourced management of their pension and employee 401(K) savings accounts to Fidelity Investments, a large-scale financial services firm that specializes in investment management.[18]

Organizational Culture and Hiring for Fit

Regardless of general business and economic conditions, many firms are expanding operations and hiring additional employees. For many growing firms, corporate culture can be a key aspect of developing employees into a competitive advantage for the firm. Corporate culture refers to the core values and beliefs that support the mission and business model of the firm and guide employee behavior. Companies such as JetBlue, Ritz-Carlton, and Cypress frequently hire for fit with their corporate cultures. This necessitates recruitment and selection of employees who exhibit the values of the firm. Ritz-Carlton and Cypress use carefully crafted applicant questionnaires to screen for values and behaviors that support corporate culture. JetBlue uses behavioral-based interview questions derived from its corporate values of safety, integrity, caring, fun, and passion. Southwest Airlines has non-HR employees (flight attendants, gate agents, and pilots) and even frequent flyer passengers interview applicants to screen for cultural fit as well as strong customer service orientation.

In addition to cultural fit, firms are increasingly hiring for technical knowledge and skills fit to the job. Sandia National Laboratories, Ratheon, and Lockheed Martin must also find new employees who can pass very detailed background investigations for federal security clearance. In April of 2005, Wabtec Corporation needed a mechanical engineer to work on a very specialized element of locomotive design; the firm would consider only people who had experience with Pro/Engineer Wildfire, a new 3-D computer-aided design package. With very tight technical hiring requirements, Microsoft hires only one out of 100 recent college graduate applicants. During most of 2005, Microsoft received 60,000 résumés per month of every kind and posted only 2,000, openings for software development jobs.[19]

More Service Workers Joining Labor Unions

Organized labor has faced tumultuous times during the last several decades due to declining union membership, loss of factory jobs, dwindling political clout, and the shifting of jobs outside the United States. With union membership now down to 12.5 percent of the U.S. workforce, some wonder if labor unions, who organize as a

CONCEPT *in Action*

Companies are rethinking their rewards for top management, especially in light of the Enron CEO scandal and other instances of sensational executive wrongdoing. Today's top brass are being compensated less through exorbitant salaries and cash bonuses and more through the issuance of restricted stock. While some groups say stock incentives link pay with performance, others deride the compensation as "pay for pulse" and "show-up pay." *Who is right, and what are pros and cons of compensation tied to performance?*

united front against poor working conditions, still have a place in America.[20] Andrew Stern, president of Service Employees International Union (SEIU), is optimistic that unions are capable of resurgence by organizing the growing number of service workers into labor unions. The SEIU is the fastest growing union in the nation—having jumped to 1.8 million members from 1.1 million a decade ago.[21]

Stern's goal is to focus on recruiting the millions of low-wage service workers that are filled by the bulk of the country's working poor. These workers are disproportionately women, immigrants, and members of minority groups that have all been traditionally more open to unionization.[22] If successful at recruiting these workers to the SEIU, Sterns believes that their wages and benefits would increase in much the same way unions brought factory workers into the middle class in the 1930s.[23]

The SEIU believes that the service industry provides a target of opportunity, with the largest expected employment growth through 2012 in low-paid local services:

Job	Projected Growth[24]
Cashier	13%
Customer Service	24%
Food preparation	23%
Janitorial	18%
Nursing aide	25%

In January of 2006, more than 500 nursing, service, and technical workers at North Shore Medical Center in Miami voted to join the SEIU; this was the sixth hospital in the South Florida region to go union in recent years. The newly formed SEIU Nurse Alliance claims approximately 100,000 nurse members in numerous states across the country. SEIU nurses are members of each SEIU local union at a health care facility as well as automatically members of the Alliance, which provides these nurses with a national voice to focus on various challenges and problems emerging in the ever changing health care industry.

Many believe that the future of labor lies primarily in the success of recruitment efforts and enrolling the massive numbers of employees who are in the fast-growing, low-wage service jobs. The SEIU was successful in unionizing 8,000 janitors in Houston, bumping their hourly wage from $5.25 an hour without health benefits to rates comparable to unionized janitors in New York, Chicago, and San Francisco who earn $15 per hour with health benefits. Reversing labor's decline will be challenging, but the SEIU look positively toward the future.[25]

concept check

How can employee diversity give a company a competitive advantage?

Explain the concept of hiring for fit.

Why does the service industry provide an opportunity for labor union growth?

Summary of Learning Goals

1 **What is the human resource management process, and how are human resource needs determined?**

The human resource management process consists of a sequence of activities that begins with the job analysis and HR planning; progresses to employee recruitment and selection; then focuses on employee training, performance appraisal, and compensation; and ends when the employee leaves the organization.

Creating a strategy for meeting human resource needs is called human resource planning, which begins with the job analysis. Job analysis is a process of studying a job to determine its tasks and duties for setting pay, determining employee job performance, specifying hiring requirements, and designing training programs. Information from the job analysis is used to prepare a job description, which lists the tasks and responsibilities of the job. A job specification describes the skills, knowledge, and abilities a person needs to fill the job described in the job description. By examining the human resource demand forecast and the internal supply forecast, human resource professionals can determine if the company faces a personnel surplus or shortage.

2 **How do firms recruit applicants?**

When a job vacancy occurs, most firms begin by trying to fill the job from within the ranks of its own employees, known as the internal labor market. If a suitable internal candidate is not available, the firm turns to the external labor market. Firms use local media to recruit nontechnical, unskilled, and nonsupervisory workers. To locate highly trained recruits, employers use college recruiters, executive search firms, job fairs, and company Web sites to promote job openings. During the job search process, firms present an accurate and positive image of the company to those being recruited, called recruitment branding.

3 **How do firms select qualified applicants?**

The selection process helps identify the candidates in the applicant pool who possess the best qualifications for the open position. Typically, an applicant submits an application, or résumé, and then receives a short, structured interview. If an applicant makes it past the initial screening, he or she may be asked to take an aptitude, personality, or skills test. The next step is the selection interview, which is an in-depth discussion of the applicant's work experience, skills and abilities, education, and career interests. If the applicant passes the selection interview, most firms conduct background checks and talk with their references. Physical exams and drug testing may also be part of the selection process.

4 **What types of training and development do organizations offer their employees?**

Training and development programs are designed to increase employees' knowledge, skills, and abilities in order to foster job performance improvements. Formal training (usually classroom in nature and off-the-job) takes place shortly after being hired. Development programs prepare employees to assume positions of increasing authority and responsibility. Job rotation, executive education programs, mentoring, and special-project assignments are examples of employee development programs.

5 **How are performance appraisals used to evaluate employee performance?**

A performance appraisal compares an employee's actual performance with the expected performance. Performance appraisals serve several purposes but are typically used to determine an employee's compensation, training needs, and advancement opportunities.

6 **What are the types of compensation and methods of paying workers?**

Direct pay is the hourly wage or monthly salary paid to an employee. In addition to the base wage or salary, direct pay may include bonuses and profit shares. Indirect pay consists of various benefits and services. Some benefits are required by law and include unemployment compensation, worker's compensation, and Social Security. Many employers also offer benefits not required by law. These include paid vacations and holidays, pensions, health and other insurance, employee wellness programs, and college tuition reimbursement.

7 **What is a labor union and how is it organized?**

A labor union is an organization that represents workers in dealing with management over disputes involving wages, hours, and working conditions. A company is unionized through an organizing drive that begins either inside, with a small group of existing employees, or outside, with an established union that targets the employer. When the union gets signed authorization cards from 30 percent of the firm's employees, the NLRB conducts a union certification election. A majority vote is needed to certify the union as the exclusive bargaining agent. The union and the employer then begin collective bargaining and have one year in which to reach an agreement.

8 **What is the collective bargaining process, and what are some of the key negotiation issues?**

Collective bargaining is the process of negotiating, administering, and interpreting labor agreements. Both union and management negotiators prepare a bargaining proposal. The two sides meet and exchange demands and ideas. Bargaining consists of compromises and concessions that lead to a tentative agreement. Top management then approves or disapproves the agreement for the management team. Union members vote to either approve or reject the contract. The key issues included in a union contract are wage increases, fringe benefits, and job security.

9 **How are grievances between management and labor resolved, and what tactics are used to force a contract settlement?**

In most labor agreements the grievance procedure consists of three or four steps. In the initial step, the employee files a grievance; this is an oral and/or written presentation to the supervisor and may involve a union steward as representative of the grievant. Steps two and three involve meetings of the employee and one or more union officials and the appropriate supervisor and one or more management officials. If the grievance is not resolved at step three, either party (union or management) can request that an arbitrator, or neutral third party, hear and decide the grievance. The arbitrator reviews the grievance at a hearing and then makes the decision, which is presented in a document called the award.

When a union contract expires and a new agreement has not been reached, the union may impose economic pressure on the firm. These tactics may take the form of strikes, boycotts, picketing, or corporate campaigns. Similarly, employers may implement lockouts, hire replacements, or move production to another facility to place pressure on a union to accept a new contract.

10 **What are the key laws and federal agencies affecting human resource management and labor relations?**

A number of federal laws (listed in Exhibit 9.14) affect human resource management. Federal law prohibits discrimination based on age, race, gender, color, national origin, religion, or disability. The Americans with Disabilities Act bans discrimination against disabled workers and requires employers to change the work environment to accommodate the disabled. The Family and Medical Leave Act requires employers, with certain exceptions, to provide employees up to 12 weeks of unpaid leave a year. The leave can be for the birth or adoption of a child or due to serious illness of a family member.

Federal agencies that deal with human resource administration are the Equal Employment Opportunity Commission (EEOC), the Occupational Safety and Health Administration (OSHA), the Office of Federal Contract Compliance Programs (OFCCP), and the Wage and Hour Division of the Department of Labor. The EEOC and OFCCP are primary agencies for the enforcement of employment discrimination laws; OSHA enforces safety regulation; and the Wage and Hour Division enforces the minimum wage and related laws. Many companies employ affirmative action and safety officers to ensure compliance with antidiscrimination and workplace safety laws. The Wagner and Taft-Hartley Acts govern the union-management relationship, in part through the functions performed by the National Labor Relations Board. The law gives workers the right to form and join labor unions and obligates the employer to deal with the union fairly.

11 **What trends and issues are affecting human resource management and labor relations?**

Human resource managers recognize that diverse workforces create an environment that nurtures creative decision-making, effective problem solving, more agility in adapting to change, and a strong competitive advantage. Therefore, firms are becoming committed to recruiting and hiring a diverse workforce. To maximize efficiency, many firms are outsourcing HR functions and using technology to reduce costs and improve efficiency. Firms are also striving to hire employees that possess qualities that match those of the corporate culture. Although labor unions have faced declining membership in the last several decades, enrollment of service workers into labor unions may increase as low-wage earners seek improved working conditions, pay, and health benefits.

Key Terms

affirmative action programs   319
agency shop   314
apprenticeship   305
arbitration   315
collective bargaining   309
competitive advantage   320
conciliation   320
contingent worker   299
Equal Employment Opportunity
   Commission (EEOC)   319
federation   311
grievance   315
human resource (HR) management   296
human resource (HR) planning   297
incentive pay   308
job analysis   298
job description   298
job fair   300
job rotation   305
job specification   298
labor union   309
local union   310
management rights clause   314

mediation   320
mentoring   305
Occupational Safety and Health
   Administration (OSHA)   319
open shop   314
orientation   304
performance appraisal   306
programmed instruction   305
protected classes   319
recruitment branding   300
recruitment   300
right-to-work law   314
selection interview   302
selection   302
selective strike strategy   316
shop steward   310
simulation   305
succession planning   299
training and development   304
unemployment compensation   309
union shop   314
worker's compensation   309

Preparing for Tomorrow's Workplace: *SCANS*

1. Would an overseas job assignment be good for your career development? If you think so, what country would you prefer to live and work in for two or three years, and what type of job would you like to have in that country? (Resources)

2. The fringe benefit package of many employers includes numerous items such as health insurance, life insurance, pension plan, paid vacations, tuition reimbursement, employee price discounts on products of the firm, and paid sick leave. At your age, what are the three or four most important benefits? Why? Twenty years from now, what do you think will be your three or four most important benefits? Why? (Resources)

3. Assume you have been asked to speak at a local meeting of human resource and labor relations professionals. The topic is whether union membership will increase or decline in the next 50 years. Take either the increase or the decline position and outline your presentation. (Information)

4. Go to the government documents section in your college or university library and inspect publications of the Department of Labor (DOL), including *Employment and Earnings, Compensation and Working Conditions, Monthly Labor Review, Occupational Outlook Handbook,* and *Career Guide to Industries.* Alternatively, go to the DOL, Bureau of Labor Statistics Web site at **http://stats.bls.gov.** Access the most recent DOL publications and locate the following information. (Information)
   - Number of persons in the American workforce
   - Unemployment rate for last year
   - Demographic characteristics of the American workforce: race, ethnic status, age, marital status, and gender.
   - Occupations where there are projected shortages for the next 5 or 10 years.
   - Union membership by major industry category: manufacturing, banking and finance, health care, business and personal services, sports and entertainment, and any other area of interest to you.

5. Assume you are a director of labor relations for a firm faced with a union certification election in 30 days. Draft a letter to be sent to your employees in which you urge them to vote "no union"; be persuasive in presenting your arguments against the union. (Information)

6. Using BCRC, research articles featuring a recent strike or a labor contract settlement. Report to your class the specifics of the strike or settlement. (Technology, Resources)

7. **Team Activity** Select two teams of five. One team will take the position that employees are simply a business expense to be managed. The second team will argue that employees are an asset to be developed to enable the firm to gain a competitive advantage. The remainder of the class will judge which team provided the stronger argument. (Interpersonal)

8. Have you or a family member ever been a union member? If so, name the union and describe it in terms of membership size, membership characteristics, strike history, recent bargaining issues, and employers under union contracts. (Information)

9. **Team Activity** Divide the class into two groups. One group will take the position that workers should be required to join unions and pay dues. The other group will take the position that workers should not be required to join unions. Hold a debate in which a spokesperson from each group is given 10 minutes to present the group's arguments. (Interpersonal)

Ethics Activity

More companies are installing global positioning systems (GPS), which send location information to satellites that transmit the data to receivers at a computer at the company, in company vehicles, and cell phones. As the cost of GPS drops and the number of mobile workers rises—an estimated 105 million in 2006—companies are depending on GPS to monitor the movement of personnel and products. Companies find it improves customer service and helps with time management. "I wanted to see how much time was spent on each job," says one small business owner with a fleet of seven service vehicles. "We've had a few problems in the past—people weren't where they said they'd be. With GPS, we can defend ourselves to the customers. We know how fast the drivers drove, what route they took, and how long they spent on each job."

Many employees don't like the idea of Big Brother following their every move. In 2003, Boston road maintenance drivers demonstrated against the Massachusetts Highway Department, which was using their required GPS-enabled cell phones to measure employee productivity. Does it invade employee privacy, though? "It's a receive-only system. It just tells you a position. What the recipient wants to do with the information is another ballgame," says Michael Swiek, executive director of the U.S. GPS Industry Council.

Using a Web search tool, locate articles about this topic and then write responses to the following questions. Be sure to support your arguments and cite your sources.

Ethical Dilemma: Do GPS devices constitute an invasion of employee privacy? Are there guidelines companies can develop for appropriate GPS use?

Sources: Diane Cadrain, "GPS on Rise; Workers' Complaints May Follow," *HR*, April 2005, pp. 32–33; and Cindy Waxer, "Navigating Privacy Concerns to Equip Workers with GPS," *Workforce Management*, August 1, 2005, p. 71.

Working The Net

1. Go to the JobWeb site of the National Association of Colleges and Employers, **http://www.jobweb.com**, and click on Resumes & Interviews. Read the relevant articles to learn how to prepare an electronic résumé that will get results. Develop a list of rules for creating effective electronic résumés, and revise your résumé into electronic format. Now read about how to apply for a job online. What tips were the most useful to you?

2. Working as a contingent employee can help you explore your career options. Visit the Manpower Web site at **http://www.manpower.com**, and use the Job Search feature to look for several types of jobs that interest you. Choose your current city and one where you would like to live, either in the United States or abroad. What are the advantages of being a temporary worker? What other services does Manpower offer job seekers?

3. As a corporate recruiter, you must know how to screen prospective employees. The Integrity Center Web site at **http://www.integctr.com** offers a brief tutorial on pre-employment screening, a glossary of key words and phrases, and related information. Prepare a short report that tells your assistant how to go about this process.

4. You've been asked to give a speech about the current status of affirmative action and equal employment to your company's managers. Starting with the Web site of the American Association for Affirmative Action (**http://www.affirmativeaction.org**) and its links to related sites, research the topic and prepare an outline for your talk. Include current legislation and recent court cases.

5. Web-based training is becoming popular at many companies as a way to bring a wider variety of courses to more people at lower costs. The Web-Based Training Information Center site at **http://www.webbasedtraining.com** provides a good introduction. Learn about the basics of online training at its Primer page. Then link to the Resources section, try a demo, and explore other areas that interest you. Prepare a brief report on your findings, including the pros and cons of using the Web for training, to present to your class.

6. What are the key issues facing labor unions today? Visit the AFL-CIO Web site, **http://www.aflcio.org** and Labornet, **http://www.labornet.org**. Select three current topics and summarize the key points for the class.

7. Not everyone believes that unions are good for workers. The National Right to Work Legal Defense Foundation offers free legal aid to employees whose "human and civil rights have been violated by compulsory unionism abuses." Read the materials on its site (**http://www.nrtw.org**) and prepare a short report on its position regarding the disadvantages of labor unions.

8. Although we tend to think of labor unions as representing manufacturing employees, many office and service industry employees, teachers, and professional belong to unions. Visit the Web sites of two of the following nonmanufacturing unions and discuss how they help their members: the Office and Professional Employees International Union (**http://www.opeiu.org**), the American Federation of State, County, and Municipal Employees (**http://www.afscme.org**), the National Education Association (**http://www.nea.org**), the Actor's Equity Association (**http://www.actorsequity.org**), and the American Federation of Musicians (**http://www. afm.org**). What are the differences, if any, between these unions and those in other industries?

Creative Thinking Case >

Diversity and Discrimination in the Workplace

Although we live in enlightened times, a recent Gallup Poll found that 15 percent of American workers still experienced some form of workplace discrimination. The study was conducted to mark the anniversary of the Civil Rights Act of 1964, and the creation of the Equal Employment Opportunity Commission (EEOC). It was carried out in conjunction with the EEOC, and partially sponsored by Kaiser-Permanente, the Society for Human Resource Management (SHRM), and United Parcel Service (UPS).

The poll found that the two most frequently cited types of discrimination are gender (26 percent), and race/ethnicity (23 percent). Also mentioned were age, disability, sexual orientation, and religion. The work areas found to be most susceptible to discrimination are promotion and pay. Being selected for a job, and treatment in the workplace, were also cited.

The study discovered that women are twice as likely to report that they have been discriminated against, than men. Among racial and ethnic groups, Asians (31 percent) and blacks (26 percent) are most likely to report experiences of discrimination, followed by Hispanics (18 percent) and whites (12 percent).

"We are grateful to The Gallup Organization and its sponsors for this important information," said EEOC chair, Cari M. Dominguez. "At the Commission we deal with concrete charges of discrimination that workers file, and this insight into the perceptions of discrimination by a sampling of the workforce will aid us as we continue our emphasis on proactive prevention, outreach, and law enforcement."

The survey, conducted via telephone interviews with 1,252 adults, measured employees' evaluation of their companies' efforts to provide diversity and protect against employee discrimination. The results show that employees' satisfaction with their company, their likelihood of retention, and their loyalty, are all highly related to their companies' Diversity Policy Scores. The Gallup Organization's Government Division Partner, Max Larsen, observes, "These data make it pretty clear that it makes good business sense to have operable diversity efforts in organizations."

"The survey results underscore the importance of Kaiser-Permanente's historical commitment to diversity and inclusion, to cultural competence in healthcare, and to the clear articulation of the business imperative that demands workforce diversity," said Kaiser-Permanente vice president and chief diversity officer, Ron Knox. "The survey strengthens Kaiser-Permanente's determination to make workplace discrimination a thing of the past."

"In today's global marketplace, workforce diversity is not a politically or morally correct obligation—it is also a business imperative," said Society for Human Resource Management (SHRM) president and CEO, Susan R. Meisinger, SPHR. "It simply makes good business sense to use the talents of all workers."

Critical Thinking Questions

- Why is workplace diversity so important in today's business environment?
- What are the major sources of workplace discrimination? Cite specific examples from the case.
- What steps are companies taking to ensure that employees are not discriminated against?

Sources: Frank Scanlan, Eric Nielsen, "Almost One in Six Americans Report Discrimination at Workplace in Past Year," SHRMOnline, http://www.shrm.org December 8, 2005; Robyn D. Clarke, "Workplace bias abounds: new study confirms the American workplace has much farther to go to achieve true diversity," *Black Enterprise*, September 2005, http://www.findarticles.com; Francis Lora, "Diversity in the workplace: How much have things really changed?" *Latino Leaders: The National Magazine of the Successful American Latino*, August-September 2005, http://www.findarticles.com.

Video Case >

PepsiCo: More Than Just Personnel

How does a company with a massive international presence, doing business in multiple time zones and languages, manage its employees? PepsiCo does it with a Values Statement and Code of Conduct that spells out what the company stands for, the rules it lives by—and Strategic Human Resources Management. The Values Statement—which reflects the company's aspirations—and the Code of Conduct—which provides the operating principles to achieve those goals—apply to every PepsiCo (**http://www. pepsico.com**) employee and to every business transaction the company makes worldwide. Chairman and chief executive officer Steven S. Reinemund believes the company's continued success comes from its employees' dedication to these principles.

At PepsiCo, Strategic Human Resources Management (SHRM) develops strategies that contribute to company expansion and innovation. It is fully integrated into the organization, "partnering" with every division of PepsiCo's business, and must produce hard line results.

One mode of SHRM divides the work into four "quadrants":

- *Administrative Experts* manage basic human resource functions like paying employees, dealing with their benefits, ensuring they are treated fairly, and more
- *Employee Champions* represent the employees' perspective to management with a view to maximizing their contribution to the company
- *Change Agents* develop systems and processes to facilitate change within the organization
- *Strategic Business Partners* devise strategies for growth in the organization.

Let's look at SHRM in action. Darryl Claiborne, a human resources director for Frito-Lay, a PepsiCo snack division, sometimes heads out on field trips. "There's times that I actually jump on a route truck and spend a day with an employee. As we ride we talk about understanding the business and how to drive the numbers," he says.

In a conventional company, human resource personnel rarely leave their offices. But PepsiCo believes that it is important for HR managers to achieve a more complete integration into the organization's various departments, to everyone's benefit. For example, employee retention has improved as a result of this type of direct communication between managers and employees in the trenches.

When a sales rep asks Darryl about career advancement, Darryl suggests he first meet the obligations of his current job—improving sales figures and establishing a rapport with his customers—before taking advantage of the company's self-nomination procedure which allows employees to inform management they are interested in promotion. In some cases it could mean following an established progression of advancement before moving into management.

PepsiCo recognizes the value of a human resource function that goes beyond the basics to delivers strategies and measurable hard-line results that contribute to the company's success.

It judges employee performance according to the person's contribution to company results and is committed to equal opportunity for all employees and job applicants. PepsiCo's focus on SHRM helps the company grow and innovate—keys to flourishing in today's competitive corporate environment.

Critical Thinking Questions

- What challenges do human resource organizations face in today's competitive business environment? How is PepsiCo meeting those challenges?
- Strategic Human Resources Management refers to an integrated personnel/human resource function. Describe the components of the SHRM planning process and how each one contributes to PepsiCo's corporate development and growth.
- PepsiCo believes in an integrated human resource function, even sending senior human resource personnel out into the field. What important benefits have resulted from this unusual activity?

Sources: Adapted from the video case, "Human Resources Management—PepsiCo"; Society for Human Resource Management (SHRMOnline) http://www.shrm.org; (October 15, 2005); Lin Grensing-Pophal, "First Day Impressions Set Stage for Retention," White Paper for The Society for Human Resources Management, *CareerJournal.com,* http://www.careerjournal.com (October 15, 2005); PepsiCo corporate Web site, http://www.pepsico.com (October 15, 2005).

Hot Links Address Book

Does TeamStaff, a professional employer organization, live up to its motto "Simply a better way to employ people"? Find out at http://www.teamstaff.com

Search the extensive job database of CareerBuilder.com (http://www.careerbuilder.com) for a job in a new city.

Get advice for brushing up your interview skills at the Job Hunting Advice page of the *Wall Street Journal's* Career site, http://careers.wsj.com

How does the Equal Employment Opportunity Commission promote equal opportunity in employment? Visit http://www.eeoc.gov to learn what the agency does.

For the latest news in the human resources field, visit the Web site of the Society for Human Resource Management at http://www.shrm.org

Many companies are using the Web to help manage employees. Visit ADP, http://www.adp.com, to learn how online services can streamline their HR tasks.

At the NLRB Web site, http://www.nlrb.gov, you'll learn about the agency's many activities and how it protects workers' rights.

Visit the Social Security Administration site to track the latest cost-of-living adjustment at http://www.ssa.gov. You'll find it in the publications section.

CHAPTER 10

Motivating Employees

Learning Goals

After reading this chapter, you should be able to answer these questions:

1 What are the basic principles of Frederick Taylor's concept of scientific management?

2 What did Elton Mayo's Hawthorne studies reveal about worker motivation?

3 What is Maslow's hierarchy of needs, and how do these needs relate to employee motivation?

4 How are McGregor's Theories X and Y and Ouchi's Theory Z used to explain worker motivation?

5 What are the basic components of Herzberg's motivator-hygiene theory?

6 What four contemporary theories on employee motivation offer insights into improving employee performance?

7 How can managers redesign existing jobs to increase employee motivation and performance?

8 What initiatives are organizations using today to motivate and retain employees?

Exploring Business Careers
Ed Liddie
British Petroleum (BP)

At first glance, Ed Liddie might seem like a typical guy. A family man, he will tell you about his kids: four of them, ranging in ages from 8 to 16. Shift supervisor of the British Petroleum (BP) Carson refinery in California, he works hard and has been with BP for almost twenty years. He likes rock 'n roll and might tell you he even plays bass guitar occasionally. Oh, and did he mention he's played in the Rock and Roll Hall of Fame? How many "typical" people can say that?

Liddie is a member of the band OVP, along with fellow BP employees Hugh Parsons, Maribel Pegler, Lonnie Sumrall, and Mark and Elaine Rongers. The band formed after some of the members met in 2000 at Operation People, a global BP conference to foster employee motivation in their refineries. In an effort to increase employee satisfaction and retention, BP wanted to hear from the employees about the realities of the day-to-day work. "After all, petroleum is not always pretty," Liddie notes. Following days of intense discussions during the conference, a small group of people would gather in the evening to talk and to relax. "Soon we discovered no matter where we were from—California, Chicago, Scotland, London—we all loved music. It was a great barrier-breaker." Indeed, music was such a common theme, on a whim they decided to form a band to play at the next Operation People conference.

Considering the members of OVP were spread out across the globe, preparation for the conference proved a bit tricky. The group compiled a song list over e-mail, and each member rehearsed alone. "It was scary at first because we had to rely on each other so heavily. It forced us to really trust each other,

though, which probably helped us even more. So that, even though we first met to practice the night before the conference, after the first song, we felt and sounded like we'd been together much longer." And apparently they weren't the only ones who thought they could really rock. Their performance the next night was a huge success, both musically and as an icebreaker for the conference participants. "After we played that night, you could just tell: For the rest of the conference, everyone was a lot more comfortable together and open with each other."

Looking back, Liddie views the performance as a very motivational event for both band members and conference participants. Indeed, the band itself came together as a team, inspired by the goal of sharing great music and helping others to open up. And at the conference, they were able to create a corporate culture in which people felt safe enough to share. BP had allowed OVP a space to flex their musical muscles, and the synergy that the band helped spark carried well past the end of the conference.

In 2004, the band had the opportunity to participate in a competition, the Fortune Battle of the Corporate Bands, at the Rock and Roll Hall of Fame. They competed alongside bands from Nextel and Wells-Fargo, among others, and walked away with the Best Lead Guitarist award. After their success as a band, a team, and a motivating force within BP, though, this almost pales in comparison. Did they make petroleum prettier?

This chapter details motivational theory, both historically and currently, and applies that theory to the business world, where motivation, whether in the form of a rock band or not, is key to success.

motivation
Something that prompts a person to release his or her energy in a certain direction.

need
The gap between what is and what is required.

want
The gap between what is and what is desired.

People can be a firm's most important resource. They can also be the most challenging resource to manage well. Employees who are motivated and work hard to achieve personal and organizational goals can become a crucial competitive advantage for a firm. The key then is understanding the process of motivation, *what* motivates individuals, and *how* an organization can create a workplace that allows people to perform to the best of their abilities. Motivation is the set of forces that prompt a person to release energy in a certain direction. As such, motivation is essentially a need- and want-satisfying process. A **need** is best defined as the gap between what is and what is *required*. Similarly, a **want** is the gap between what is and what is *desired*. Unsatisfied needs and wants create a state of tension that pushes (motivates) individuals to practice behavior that will result in the need being met or the want being fulfilled. That is, motivation is what pushes us to move from where we are to where we want to be because expending that effort will result in some kind of reward.

Rewards can be divided into two basic categories: intrinsic and extrinsic. Intrinsic rewards come from within the individual, things like satisfaction, contentment, sense of accomplishment, confidence, and pride. By contrast, extrinsic rewards come from outside the individual and include things like pay raises, promotions, bonuses, prestigious assignments, and so forth. Exhibit 10.1 illustrates the motivation process.

Successful managers are able to marshal the forces to motivate employees to achieve organizational goals. And just as there are many types of gaps between where organizations are and where they want to be, there are many motivational theories from which managers can draw to inspire employees to bridge those gaps. In this chapter, we will first examine motivational theories that grew out of the industrial revolution and early ideas of organizational psychology. Then we will examine needs-based theories and more contemporary ideas about employee motivation like equity, expectancy, goals, and reinforcement theories. Finally, we will show you how managers are applying these theories in real-world situations.

Early Theories of Motivation

How can managers and organizations promote enthusiastic job performance, high productivity, and job satisfaction? Many studies of human behavior in organizations have contributed to our current understanding of these issues. A look at the evolution of management theory and research shows how managers have arrived at the practices

CONCEPT *in Action*

Danica Patrick is on a roll. The American racecar driver began racing go-karts at age 10 and quickly zoomed her way to multiple national championships. By the time she was old enough to obtain a state driver's license, Patrick was determined to make it in professional racing. In 2005, she became the first woman to ever lead the pack in the Indianapolis 500 and was named the IndyCar Series Rookie of the Year. *What motivates people to achieve their personal best?*

© ASSOCIATED PRESS, AP

Exhibit 10.1 > **Model of Motivation**

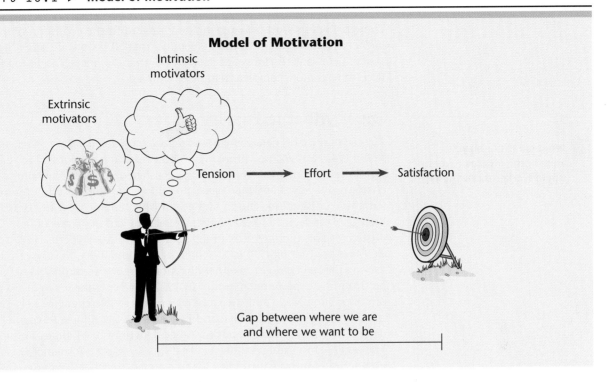

Model of Motivation

Intrinsic motivators

Extrinsic motivators

Tension → Effort → Satisfaction

Gap between where we are and where we want to be

used today to manage human behavior in the workplace. A sampling of the most influential of these theorists and research studies are discussed in this section.

Frederick Taylor's Scientific Management

1 What are the basic principles of Frederick Taylor's concept of scientific management?

scientific management
A system of management developed by Frederick W. Taylor and based on four principles: developing a scientific approach for each element of a job, scientifically selecting and training workers, encouraging cooperation between workers and managers, and dividing work and responsibility between management and workers according to who can better perform a particular task.

One of the most influential figures of the *classical era* of management, which lasted from about 1900 to the mid-1930s, was Frederick W. Taylor, a mechanical engineer sometimes called the "father of **scientific management**." Taylor's approach to improved performance was based on economic incentives and the premise that there is "one best way" to perform any job. As a manager at the Midvale and Bethlehem Steel companies in Philadelphia in the early 1900s, Taylor was frustrated at the inefficiency of the laborers working in the mills.

Convinced that productivity could be improved, Taylor studied the individual jobs in the mill and redesigned the equipment and the methods used by workers. Taylor timed each job with a stopwatch and broke down every task into separate movements. He then prepared an instruction sheet telling exactly how each job should be done, how much time it should take, and what motions and tools should be used. Taylor's ideas led to dramatic increases in productivity in the steel mills and resulted in the development of four basic principles of scientific management:

1. Develop a scientific approach for each element of a person's job.
2. Scientifically select, train, teach, and develop workers.
3. Encourage cooperation between workers and managers so that each job can be accomplished in a standard, scientifically determined way.
4. Divide work and responsibility between management and workers according to who is better suited to each task.

Taylor published his ideas in *The Principles of Scientific Management*. His pioneering work vastly increased production efficiency and contributed to the specialization of labor and the assembly-line method of production. Taylor's approach is still being used nearly a century later in companies such as United Parcel Service (UPS), where industrial engineers maximize efficiency by carefully studying every step of the delivery process looking for the quickest possible way to deliver packages to customers. Though Taylor's work was a giant step forward in the evolution of management, it had a fundamental flaw in that it assumed that all people are primarily motivated by economic means. Taylor's successors in the study of management found that motivation is much more complex than he envisioned.

The Hawthorne Studies

2 What did Elton Mayo's Hawthorne studies reveal about worker motivation?

The classical era of management was followed by the *human relations era,* which began in the 1930s and focused primarily on how human behavior and relations affect organizational performance. The new era was ushered in by the Hawthorne studies, which changed the way many managers thought about motivation, job productivity, and employee satisfaction. The studies began when engineers at the Hawthorne Western Electric plant decided to examine the effects of varying levels of light on worker productivity—an experiment that might have interested Frederick Taylor. The engineers expected brighter light to lead to increased productivity, but the results showed that varying the level of light in either direction (brighter or dimmer) led to increased output from the experimental group. In 1927, the Hawthorne engineers asked Harvard professor Elton Mayo and a team of researchers to join them in their investigation.

From 1927 to 1932, Mayo and his colleagues conducted experiments on job redesign, length of workday and workweek, length of break times, and incentive plans. The results of the studies indicated that increases in performance were tied to a complex set of employee attitudes. Mayo claimed that both experimental and control groups from the plant had developed a sense of group pride because they had been selected to participate in the studies. The pride that came from this special attention motivated the workers to increase their productivity. Supervisors who allowed the employees to have some control over their situation appeared to further increase the workers' motivation. These findings gave rise to what is now known as the **Hawthorne effect,** which suggests that employees will perform better when they feel singled out for special attention or feel that management is concerned about employee welfare. The studies also provided evidence that informal work groups (the social relationships of employees) and the resulting group pressure have positive effects on group productivity. The results of the Hawthorne studies enhanced our understanding of what motivates individuals in the workplace. They indicate that in addition to the personal economic needs emphasized in the classical era, social needs play an important role in influencing work-related attitudes and behaviors.

Hawthorne effect
The phenomenon that employees perform better when they feel singled out for attention or feel that management is concerned about their welfare.

Maslow's Hierarchy of Needs

3 What is Maslow's hierarchy of needs, and how do these needs relate to employee motivation?

Another well-known theorist from the behavioral era of management history, psychologist Abraham Maslow, proposed a theory of motivation based on universal human needs. Maslow believed that each individual has a hierarchy of needs, consisting of physiological, safety, social, esteem, and self-actualization needs, as shown in Exhibit 10.2.

Maslow's theory of motivation contends that people act to satisfy their unmet needs. When you're hungry, for instance, you look for and eat food, thus satisfying a basic physiological need. Once a need is satisfied, its importance to the individual diminishes, and a higher level need is more likely to motivate the person.

According to **Maslow's hierarchy of needs,** the most basic human needs are physiological needs, that is, the needs for food, shelter, and clothing. In large part, it is the physiological needs that motivate a person to find a job. People need to earn money to provide food, shelter, and clothing for themselves and their families. Once people have met these basic needs, they reach the second level in Maslow's hierarchy, which is safety needs. People need to feel secure, to be protected from physical harm,

Maslow's hierarchy of needs
A theory of motivation developed by Abraham Maslow; holds that humans have five levels of needs and act to satisfy their unmet needs. At the base of the hierarchy are fundamental physiological needs, followed in order by safety, social, esteem, and self-actualization needs.

Exhibit 10.2 > Maslow's Hierarchy of Needs

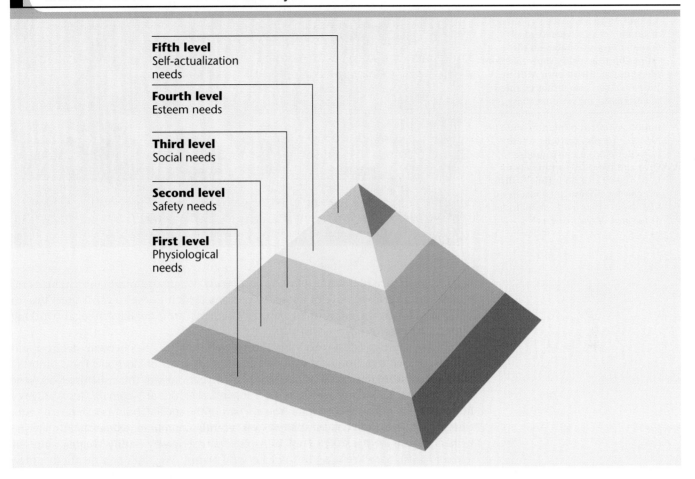

Fifth level
Self-actualization
needs

Fourth level
Esteem needs

Third level
Social needs

Second level
Safety needs

First level
Physiological
needs

and to avoid the unexpected. In work terms, they need job security and protection from work hazards.

Physiological needs and safety are physical needs. Once these are satisfied, individuals focus on needs that involve relationships with other people. At Maslow's third level are social needs, or needs for belonging (acceptance by others) and for giving and receiving friendship and love. Informal social groups on and off the job help people satisfy these needs. At the fourth level in Maslow's hierarchy are esteem needs, which are needs for the respect of others and for a sense of accomplishment and achievement. Satisfaction of these needs is reflected in feelings of self-worth. Praise and recognition from managers and others in the firm contribute to the sense of self-worth. Finally, at the highest level in Maslow's hierarchy are self-actualization needs, or needs for fulfillment, for living up to one's potential, and for using one's abilities to the utmost. In order to give you a better understanding of how Maslow's hierarchy applies in the real business world, let's look at a detailed example about Wegmans supermarkets. When you think of your first-choice job, you probably aren't thinking about working in a supermarket. With grueling hours, low pay, and annual turnover often approaching 100 percent, supermarkets are generally not considered the best places to work—unless you work at Wegmans, which was named one of the top two firms on *Fortune's* "Best Company to Work For" in 2006. Part of what makes Wegmans successful is the company's attention to its employees' needs at all levels of Maslow's hierarchy. The company pays above-market wages (the sous-chef at a Pittsburgh store used to work for Thomas Keller's French Laundry in Napa Valley, and talent like that doesn't come cheap) and until 2003, Wegmans paid 100 percent of its employees'

CONCEPT *in Action*

Simon Cowell has made a career out of snubbing vocally-challenged Mariah Carey wannabes on the ratings-busting reality show *American Idol*. But the British-born A&R rep-turned-TV star also produces a slew of entertainment ventures that are turning heads and shaping the industry. *American Inventor* and *The X-Factor* are his creations, as are Cowell-produced music groups Il Divo and Westlife. Fortunately for fans, Cowell still finds time to dish out cheeky, disgust-filled insults on *Idol*. *What needs motivate individuals at the peak of their careers?*

medical insurance premiums (*physiological needs*). Wegmans' most comparable competitor has a turnover rate of about 19 percent, which doesn't even come close to Wegmans' 6 percent. More than half of Wegmans' store managers began working there in their teens (*safety needs*).

Because employees stay so long, the Wegmans culture has become stronger and more ingrained over time. Edward McLaughlin, director of Cornell's Food Industry Management Program, says "When you're a 16-year-old kid, the last thing you want to do is wear a geeky shirt and work for a supermarket. But at Wegmans, it's a badge of honor. You are not a geeky cashier. You are part of the social fabric" (*social needs*).[1] Sara Goggins, a 19-year-old college student, was recently complimented on the display she helped prepare for the store's French-inspired patisserie—by Danny Wegman himself (*esteem needs*). Sara keeps a photo of her and Danny Wegman behind the counter. Maria Benjamin used to bake "chocolate meatball cookies" to celebrate coworkers' birthdays. They were so popular that she asked Danny Wegman if the store would sell them in the bakery department. He said yes, and it did. Employees like Sara and Maria are routinely recognized for their contributions to the company (*esteem needs*). Wegmans has spent over $54 million for college scholarships to more than 17,500 full- and part-time employees over the past 20 years. Top management thinks nothing of sending store department managers on training expeditions. A cheese manager might take a ten-day trip to visit and study cheesemakers in London, Paris, and Italy; a wine manager might take a company-sponsored trip through the Napa Valley (*self-actualization needs*).[2] As you can see from this extended example, Wegmans works hard to meet its employees' needs at all levels.

Maslow's theory is not without criticism, however. Maslow claimed that a higher-level need was not activated until a lower-level need was met. He also claimed that a satisfied need is not a motivator. A farmer who has plenty to eat is not motivated by more food (the physiological hunger need). Research has not verified these principles in any strict sense. The theory also concentrates on moving up the hierarchy without fully addressing moving back down the hierarchy. Despite these limitations, Maslow's ideas are very helpful for understanding the needs of people at work and for determining what can be done to satisfy them.

McGregor's Theories X and Y

4 How are McGregor's Theories X and Y and Ouchi's Theory Z used to explain worker motivation?

Douglas McGregor, one of Maslow's students, influenced the study of motivation with his formulation of two contrasting sets of assumptions about human nature—Theory X and Theory Y.

Theory X
A management style, formulated by Douglas McGregor, that is based on a pessimistic view of human nature and assumes that the average person dislikes work, will avoid it if possible, prefers to be directed, avoids responsibility, and wants security above all.

The **Theory X** management style is based on a pessimistic view of human nature and assumes the following:

- The average person dislikes work and will avoid it if possible.
- Because people don't like to work, they must be controlled, directed, or threatened with punishment to get them to make an effort.
- The average person prefers to be directed, avoids responsibility, is relatively unambitious, and wants security above all else.

This view of people suggests that managers must constantly prod workers to perform and must closely control their on-the-job behavior. Theory X managers tell people what to do, are very directive, like to be in control, and show little confidence in employees. They often foster dependent, passive, and resentful subordinates.

In contrast, a **Theory Y** management style is based on a more optimistic view of human nature and assumes the following:

Theory Y
A management style, formulated by Douglas McGregor, that is based on a relatively optimistic view of human nature; assumes that the average person wants to work, accepts responsibility, is willing to help solve problems, and can be self-directed and self-controlled.

- Work is as natural as play or rest. People want to and can be self-directed and self-controlled and will try to achieve organizational goals they believe in.
- Workers can be motivated using positive incentives and will try hard to accomplish organizational goals if they believe they will be rewarded for doing so.
- Under proper conditions, the average person not only accepts responsibility but seeks it out. Most workers have a relatively high degree of imagination and creativity and are willing to help solve problems.

Managers who operate on Theory Y assumptions recognize individual differences and encourage workers to learn and develop their skills. An administrative assistant might be given the responsibility for generating a monthly report. The reward for doing so might be recognition at a meeting, a special training class to enhance computer skills, or a pay increase. In short, the Theory Y approach builds on the idea that worker and organizational interests are the same. It is not difficult to find companies that have created successful corporate cultures based on Theory Y assumptions. In fact, *Fortune*'s list of "100 Best Companies to Work For" and the Society for Human Resource Management's list of "Great Places to Work" are full of companies that operate using a Theory Y management style. Starbucks, J. M. Smucker, SAS Institute, Valassis, Whole Foods Market, and Wegmans are all examples of companies that encourage and support their workers. Genencor, a biotechnology firm named the Best Place to Work by the Society for Human Resource Management in 2005, has a culture that celebrates success in all aspects of its business. Employees can reward colleagues with on-the-spot awards for extraordinary effort. According to the company's CEO, Robert Mayer, "Genencor is truly unique among U.S. companies of any size. It is a model for innovation, teamwork, and productivity—and a direct result of our 'work hard, play hard, change the world' philosophy. Investing in our employees has always been good business for Genencor."[3]

Theory Z

Theory Z
A theory developed by William Ouchi that combines U.S. and Japanese business practices by emphasizing long-term employment, slow career development, moderate specialization, group decision making, individual responsibility, relatively informal control over the employee, and concern for workers.

William Ouchi (pronounced O Chee), a management scholar at the University of California, Los Angeles, has proposed a theory that combines U.S. and Japanese business practices. He calls it **Theory Z**. Exhibit 10.3 on the next page compares the traditional U.S. and Japanese management styles with the Theory Z approach. Theory Z emphasizes long-term employment, slow career development, moderate specialization, group decision making, individual responsibility, relatively informal control over the employee, and concern for workers. Theory Z has many Japanese elements. But it reflects U.S. cultural values.

In the past decade, admiration for Japanese management philosophy that centers on creating long-term relationships has declined. The cultural beliefs of groupthink, not taking risks, and employees not thinking for themselves are passé. Such conformity has limited Japanese competitiveness in the global marketplace. Today there is a realization

Exhibit 10.3 > Differences in Management Approaches

Factor	Traditional U.S. Management	Japanese Management	Theory Z (Combination of U.S. and Japanese Management)
Length of employment	Relatively short term; worker subject to layoffs if business is bad	Lifetime; layoffs never used to reduce costs	Long term but not necessarily lifetime; layoffs "inappropriate"; stable, loyal workforce; improved business conditions don't require new hiring and training
Rate of evaluation and promotion	Relatively rapid	Relatively slow	Slow by design; manager thoroughly trained and evaluated
Specialization in a functional area	Considerable; worker acquires expertise in single functional area	Minimal; worker acquires expertise in organization instead of functional areas	Moderate; all experience various functions of the organization and have a sense of what's good for the firm rather than for a single area
Decision making	On individual basis	Input from all concerned parties	Group decision making for better decisions and easier implementation
Responsibility for success or failure	Assigned to individual	Shared by group	Assigned to individual
Control by manager	Very explicit and formal	More implicit and informal	Relatively informal but with explicit performance measures
Concern for workers	Focuses on work-related aspects of worker's life	Extends to whole life of worker	Is relatively concerned with worker's whole life, including the family

Source: Comparison of traditional U.S. and Japanese management styles with the Theory Z approach. Based on information from Jerry D. Johnson, Austin College. Dr. Johnson was a research assistant for William Ouchi.

that Japanese firms need to be more proactive and nimble in order to prosper. It was that realization that led Japanese icon Sony to name a foreigner as the CEO of Japan's most famous company. Over the years, Sony's performance has declined until in April 2005, the company posted its biggest loss ever: Nobuki Idei, the former CEO who inherited Sony's massive debts and stagnant product lines, realized his strategy wasn't working, so he determined to appoint a successor who would be able to transform Sony from the lumbering giant it had become back into the forward-thinking company it had been. Idei tapped Sir Howard Stringer, a Welsh-born American who had been running Sony's U.S. operations. In doing so, Idei hoped to shock company insiders and industry analysts alike. "It's funny, 100 percent of the people around here agree we need to change, but 90 percent of them don't really want to change themselves," he says. "So I finally concluded that we needed our top management to quite literally speak another language."[4]

Herzberg's Motivator–Hygiene Theory

5 **What are the basic components of Herzberg's motivator-hygiene theory?**

Another important contribution to our understanding of individual motivation came from Frederick Herzberg's studies, which addressed the question, "What do people really want from their work experience?" In the late 1950s Herzberg surveyed numerous employees to find out what particular work elements made them feel

CONCEPT *in Action*

Being square has been a hip competitive advantage for on-site tech-support firm Geek Squad since 1994. The company's 24-hour computer-support taskforce consists of uniformed double agents in squad-car-painted geekmobiles on a critical mission: to save frantic customers from computer viruses, crashes, and the blue screen of death. *According to Herzberg's Motivator-Hygiene theory what effect might Geek Squad's artfully geeky work environment have on employee satisfaction?*

motivating factors
Intrinsic job elements that lead to worker satisfaction.

hygiene factors
Extrinsic elements of the work environment that do not serve as a source of employee satisfaction or motivation.

exceptionally good or bad about their jobs. The results indicated that certain job factors are consistently related to employee job satisfaction while others can create job dissatisfaction. According to Herzberg, **motivating factors** (also called *job satisfiers*) are primarily intrinsic job elements that lead to satisfaction. **Hygiene factors** (also called *job dissatisfiers*) are extrinsic elements of the work environment. A summary of motivating and hygiene factors appears in Exhibit 10.4.

One of the most interesting results of Herzberg's studies was the implication that the opposite of satisfaction is not dissatisfaction. Herzberg believed that proper management of hygiene factors could prevent employee dissatisfaction, but that these factors could not serve as a source of satisfaction or motivation. Good working conditions, for instance, will keep employees at a job but won't make them work harder. But poor working conditions, which are job dissatisfiers, may make employees quit. According to Herzberg, a manager who wants to increase employee satisfaction needs to focus on the motivating factors, or satisfiers. A job with many satisfiers will usually motivate workers, provide job satisfaction, and prompt effective performance. But a lack of job satisfiers doesn't always lead to dissatisfaction and poor performance; instead, a lack of job satisfiers may merely lead to workers doing an adequate job, rather than their best.

Although Herzberg's ideas have been widely read and his recommendations implemented at numerous companies over the years, there are some very legitimate concerns about Herzberg's work. Although his findings have been used to explain

Exhibit 10.4 > Herzberg's Motivating and Hygiene Factors

Motivating Factors	Hygiene Factors
Achievement	Company policy
Recognition	Supervision
Work itself	Working conditions
Responsibility	Interpersonal relationships at work
Advancement	Salary and benefits
Growth	Job security

employee motivation, in fact his studies focused on job satisfaction, a different (though related) concept from motivation. Other criticisms focus on the unreliability of Herzberg's methodology, the fact that the theory ignores the impact of situational variables, and the assumed relationship between satisfaction and productivity. Nevertheless, the questions raised by Herzberg about the nature of job satisfaction and the effects of intrinsic and extrinsic factors on employee behavior have proved a valuable contribution to the evolution of theories of motivation and job satisfaction.

Contemporary Views on Motivation

6 **What four contemporary theories on employee motivation offer insights into improving employee performance?**

The early management scholars laid a foundation that enabled managers to better understand their workers and how best to motivate them. Since then, new theories have given us an even better understanding of worker motivation. Three of these theories are explained in this section: the expectancy theory, the equity theory, and the goal-setting theory.

Expectancy Theory

expectancy theory
A theory of motivation that holds that the probability of an individual acting in a particular way depends on the strength of that individual's belief that the act will have a particular outcome and on whether the individual values that outcome.

One of the best-supported and most widely accepted theories of motivation is expectancy theory, which focuses on the link between motivation and behavior. According to expectancy theory, the probability of an individual acting in a particular way depends on the strength of that individual's belief that the act will have a particular outcome and on whether the individual values that outcome. The degree to which an employee is motivated depends on three important relationships, shown in Exhibit 10.5.

1. The link between *effort and performance*, or the strength of the individual's expectation that a certain amount of effort will lead to a certain level of performance.
2. The link between *performance and outcome*, or the strength of the expectation that a certain level of performance will lead to a particular outcome.
3. The link between *outcomes and individual needs*, or the degree to which the individual expects the anticipated outcome to satisfy personal needs. Some outcomes have more valence, or value, for individuals than others do.

CONCEPT *in Action*

Between 1993 and 2005, retired CEO Lee Raymond transformed Exxon-Mobil into a profit-generating powerhouse. During this time, Exxon's market value increased to over $350 billion—overtaking BP as the largest oil company—and workers enjoyed higher wages with no layoffs. In 2005, Raymond's 43-year career with Exxon was rewarded with a retirement package estimated at nearly $400 million—one of the largest in history. *What are the benefits of linking employee pay and incentives to company performance?*

Exhibit 10.5 > How Expectations Can Lead to Motivation

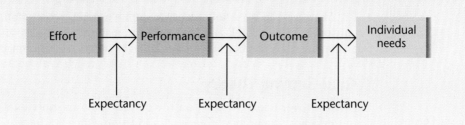

Effort → Performance → Outcome → Individual needs

Expectancy   Expectancy   Expectancy

Based on the expectancy theory, managers should do the following to motivate employees:

● Determine the rewards valued by each employee.
● Determine the desired performance level and then communicate it clearly to employees.
● Make the performance level attainable.
● Link rewards to performance.
● Determine what factors might counteract the effectiveness of an award.
● Make sure the reward is adequate for the level of performance.

equity theory
A theory of motivation that holds that worker satisfaction is influenced by employees' perceptions about how fairly they are treated compared with their coworkers.

Equity Theory

Another contemporary explanation of motivation, **equity theory** is based on individuals' perceptions about how fairly they are treated compared with their coworkers. Equity means justice or fairness, and in the workplace it refers to employees' perceived fairness of the way they are treated and the rewards they earn. For example, imagine that after graduation you were offered a job that paid $55,000 a year and had great benefits. You'd probably be ecstatic. Even more so if you discovered that the coworker in the next cubicle was making $45,000 for the same job. But what if that same colleague were making $59,000 for the same job? You'd probably think it unfair, particularly if the coworker had the same qualifications and started at the same time as you did. Your determination of the fairness of the situation would depend on how you felt you compared to the other person, or referent. Employees evaluate their own *outcomes* (e.g., salary, benefits) in relation to their *inputs* (e.g., number of hours worked, education, and training) and then compare the outcomes-to-inputs ratio to one of the following: (1) the employee's own past experience in a different position in the current organization, (2) the employee's own past experience in a different organization, (3) another employee's experience inside the current organization, or (4) another employee's experience outside the organization.

According to equity theory, if employees perceive that an inequity exists, they will make one of the following choices:

● *Change their work habits* (exert less effort on the job).
● *Change their job benefits and income* (ask for a raise, steal from the employer).
● *Distort their perception of themselves* ("I always thought I was smart, but now I realize I'm a lot smarter than my coworkers").
● *Distort their perceptions of others* ("Joe's position is really much less flexible than mine").

CONCEPT *in Action*

Ben & Jerry's founders Ben Cohen and Jerry Greenfield firmly believe the maxim that companies "do well by doing good." This idealism led the founders to once famously swear that no Ben & Jerry's executive would ever make more than seven times the lowliest worker's wage. But when growth required attracting exceptional top-level management, the company eventually abandoned its self-imposed ratio between its lowest and highest compensation rates. *How might perceived inequities in pay affect worker satisfaction and motivation?*

- *Look at the situation from a different perspective* ("I don't make as much as the other department heads, but I make a lot more than most graphic artists").
- *Leave the situation* (quit the job).

Managers can use equity theory to improve worker satisfaction. Knowing that every employee seeks equitable and fair treatment, managers can make an effort to understand an employee's perceptions of fairness and take steps to reduce concerns about inequity.

Goal-Setting Theory

goal-setting theory
A theory of motivation based on the premise that an individual's intention to work toward a goal is a primary source of motivation.

Goal-setting theory is based on the premise that an individual's intention to work toward a goal is a primary source of motivation. Once set, the goal clarifies for the employee what needs to be accomplished and how much effort will be required for completion. The theory has three main components: (1) specific goals lead to a higher level of performance than do more generalized goals ("do your best"); (2) more difficult goals lead to better performance than do easy goals (provided the individual accepts the goal); and (3) feedback on progress toward the goal enhances performance. Feedback is particularly important because it helps the individual identify the gap between the *real* (the actual performance) and the *ideal* (the desired outcome defined by the goal). Given the trend toward employee empowerment in the workplace, more and more employees are participating in the goal-setting process.

To help employees at the Columbus, Ohio, distribution center for Essilor of America acclimate to the fast work pace, managers develop five goals each year for every employee in the center. Then four times during the year, employees have to provide hard evidence to their managers that they are meeting those goals. Careful goal-setting and feedback helped employees pick and ship 72 million eyeglass lenses to fill half a million orders in 2004. Shipment accuracy was 99.997 percent, and the company kept alive a two-year performance streak.[5]

Reinforcement Theory

reinforcement theory
People do things because they know that certain consequences will follow.

reward
Anything that increases a specific behavior.

punishment
Anything that decreases a specific behavior.

Reinforcement theory says that behavior is a function of its consequences. In other words, people do things because they know other things will follow. So, depending on what type of consequences follows, people will either practice a behavior or refrain from it. There are three basic types of consequences: positive, negative, and none. In general, we think of positive consequences as rewards, but a **reward** is anything that increases the particular behavior. By contrast, **punishment** is anything that decreases the behavior.

CONCEPT *in Action*

With employees clocking longer hours at work, office romances have become more frequent and less taboo than in the past. Regular collaboration between dedicated colleagues can very easily spill over into lunch breaks, happy hour, or even after-hours work assignments. While such tight teamwork raises fewer eyebrows today, companies concerned about workplace distractions and dramatic breakups often frown upon inter-office dating. *How might managers utilize reinforcement theory to discourage employees from pursuing office trysts?*

© IMAGE SOURCE/JUPITER IMAGES

Motivating with the reinforcement theory can be tricky because the theory is functional. All of its components are defined by their function rather than their structure. That is, consequences can operate differently for different people and in different situations. What is considered a punishment by one person may, in fact, be a reward for another. Nonetheless, managers can successfully use reinforcement theory to motivate workers to practice certain behaviors and avoid others. Often, managers use both rewards and punishment to achieve the desired results.

For example, hospitals have long offered surgeons the precious perk of scheduling elective surgeries in the middle of the week so that they can attend conferences, teach medical students, and leave early for the weekend. Although convenient for the surgeons, this scheduling system translates into overcrowding in hospital operating rooms and late starts that accrue throughout the day, causing patients' surgeries to be bumped for hours or even days. St. John's Regional Health Center in Springfield, Missouri, now spreads out its elective surgery schedule to cover five days instead of two. It wasn't easy, however, to convince surgeons to give up their long weekends or to start on time. To help change the pattern of late starts and bumped patient schedules, managers at St. John's used reinforcement theory to ease patient congestion in operating rooms. Now, doctors who are more than 10 minutes late 10 percent of the time are fined a portion of their fee (*punishment* for being late). Fines go into a kitty to reward those who are the best on-time performers (*reward* for being on time). Two years after the program was started, late starts for surgeries dropped from 16 percent to less than 1 percent.[6]

concept check

Discuss the three relationships central to expectancy theory.

Explain the comparison process that is a part of equity theory.

How does goal-setting theory contribute to our understanding of motivation?

What are the main elements of reinforcement theory?

EXPANDING AROUND THE GLOBE

Motivation Is Culture Bound

Most motivation theories in use today were developed in the United States by Americans and about Americans. Of those that were not, many have been strongly influenced by American theories. But several motivation theories do not apply to all cultures. For example, Maslow's theory does not often hold outside the United States. In countries higher on uncertainty avoidance (such as Greece and Japan) as compared with those lower on uncertainty avoidance (such as the United States), security motivates employees more strongly than does self-actualization. Employees in high-uncertainty-avoidance countries often consider job security and lifetime employment more important than holding a more interesting or challenging job. Also contrasting with the American pattern, social needs often dominate the motivation of workers in countries such as Denmark, Norway, and Sweden that stress the quality of life over materialism and productivity.

When researchers tested Herzberg's theory outside the United States, they encountered different results. In New Zealand, for example, supervision and interpersonal relationships appear to contribute significantly to satisfaction and not merely to reducing dissatisfaction. Similarly, researchers found that citizens of Asia, Canada, Europe, Latin America, the Republic of Panama, and the West Indies cited certain extrinsic factors as satisfiers with greater frequency than did their American counterparts. In other words, the factors that motivate U.S. employees, summarized in Exhibit 10.4, may not spark the same motivation in employees in other cultures. Some of the major differences among the cultural groups include the following:

1. English-speaking countries rank higher on individual achievement and lower on the desire for security.
2. French-speaking countries, although similar to the English-speaking countries, give greater importance to security and somewhat less to challenging work.
3. Northern European countries have less interest in "getting ahead" and work recognition goals and place more emphasis on job accomplishment. In addition, they have more concern for people and less for the organization as a whole (it is important that their jobs not interfere with their personal lives).
4. Latin American and Southern European countries find individual achievement somewhat less important; Southern Europeans place the highest emphasis on job security, whereas both groups of countries emphasize fringe benefits.
5. Germany ranks high on security and fringe benefits and among the highest on "getting ahead."
6. Japan, although low on advancement, also ranks second highest on challenge and lowest on autonomy, with a strong emphasis on good working conditions and a friendly working environment.[7]

Critical Thinking Questions

- In today's global business environment, with its diversity of perspectives, can a manager ever successfully use equity theory? Why or why not?
- What impact, if any, do these cultural differences have on managers managing an entirely American workforce? Explain.

From Motivation Theory to Application

 7 How can managers redesign existing jobs to increase employee motivation and performance?

The material presented thus far in this chapter demonstrates the wide variety of theorists and research studies that have contributed to our current understanding of employee motivation. Now we turn our attention to more practical matters, to ways that these concepts can be applied in the workplace to meet organizational goals and improve individual performance.

Motivational Job Design

How might managers redesign or modify existing jobs to increase employee motivation and performance? The following three options have been used extensively in the workplace:

job enlargement
The horizontal expansion of a job by increasing the number and variety of tasks that a person performs.

- *Job Enlargement.* The horizontal expansion of a job, increasing the number and variety of tasks that a person performs, is called **job enlargement**. Increasing task diversity can enhance job satisfaction, particularly when the job is mundane and repetitive in nature. A potential drawback to job enlargement is that employees may perceive that they are being asked to work harder and do more with no change in their level of responsibility or compensation. This can cause resentment and lead to dissatisfaction.

job enrichment
The vertical expansion of a job by increasing the employee's autonomy, responsibility, and decision-making authority.

- *Job Enrichment.* **Job enrichment** is the vertical expansion of an employee's job. Whereas job enlargement addresses the breadth or scope of a job, enrichment attempts to increase job depth by providing the employee with more autonomy, responsibility, and decision-making authority. In an enriched job, the employee can use a variety of talents and skills and has more control over the planning, execution, and evaluation of the required tasks. In general, job enrichment has been found to increase job satisfaction and reduce absenteeism and turnover.

job rotation
The shifting of workers from one job to another; also called *cross-training*.

- *Job Rotation.* Also called *cross-training*, **job rotation** is the shifting of workers from one job to another. This may be done to broaden an employee's skill base or because an employee has ceased to be interested in or challenged by a particular job. The organization may benefit from job rotation because it increases flexibility in scheduling and production, because employees can be shifted to cover for absent workers or changes in production or operations. It is also a valuable tool for training lower-level managers in a variety of functional areas. Drawbacks of job rotation include an increase in training costs and decreased productivity while employees are getting "up to speed" in new task areas.

Work-Scheduling Options

As companies try to meet the needs of a diverse workforce and retain quality employees, while remaining competitive and financially prosperous, managers are challenged to find new ways to keep workers motivated and satisfied. Increasingly popular are alternatives to the traditional work schedule, such as the compressed workweek, flextime, telecommuting, and job sharing.

One option for employees who want to maximize their leisure hours, indulge in three-day weekends, and avoid commuting during morning and evening rush hours is the *compressed workweek*. Employees work the traditional 40 hours, but fit those hours into a shorter workweek. Most common is the 4-40 schedule, where employees work four 10-hour days a week. Organizations that offer this option claim benefits ranging from increased motivation and productivity to reduced absenteeism and turnover. According to the Society for Human Resource Management, in 2006, over 32 percent of U.S. companies offer employees a compressed workweek.[8]

Another scheduling option, flextime, is even more popular, in use at 55 percent of U.S. companies.[9] Flextime allows employees to decide what their work hours will be. Employees are generally expected to work a certain number of hours per week, but have some discretion as to when they arrive at work and when they leave for the day.

CONCEPT *in Action*

Many organizations consider job sharing a sensible way to accommodate part-time workers and yield full-time results. Schools often allow teachers to split classroom duties so they may have time at home with their children. Restaurants use the scheduling option to keep aging veterans in management. Even the NFL's Indianapolis Colts mulled job sharing as a possible way to remedy the publicized burnout and departure of ex-Indianapolis Colt running back Edgerrin James. *What challenges are involved in job sharing?*

job sharing
A scheduling option that allows two individuals to split the tasks, responsibilities, and work hours of one 40-hour-per-week job.

Telecommuting is a work-scheduling option that allows employees to work from home via a computer that is linked with their office, headquarters, or colleagues. Often employers will use a mix of these scheduling options depending on the situation. Jacqueline Pawela-Crew is a group leader in Intel's management engineering unit who works a compressed schedule. She works Monday through Thursday, and on two of those days she telecommutes from her home. On the other two days, she works a flexible schedule, sometimes getting to the office at 6 a.m., so she can be home when her children get home from school. Her manager, Dan Enloe, is a U.S. Navy reservist and divorced dad, so he also uses Intel's flexible schedule to meet his military and family needs.[10] He sees the flexible scheduling as a key motivator for Intel's employees. "I've had workers tell me flat out, they were going to leave Intel if they didn't have the option of some flexibility with their schedules," he says.[11] Richard Semler, CEO of Semco, a Brazilian conglomerate with 3,000 employees, sums up flexible work schedules this way: "The essence to us [at Semco] was that people who are free people, who [can act] based on self-interest, who can balance their own lives, are much happier, more productive people. If you take a business call on a Sunday afternoon, for instance, why not go to the movies on a Monday?" Semco's employees not only choose their own schedules, they often choose which part of the business to work for and even how much they'll be paid.[12]

Job sharing is a scheduling option that allows two individuals to split the tasks, responsibilities, and work hours of one 40-hour-per-week job. Though used less frequently than flextime and the compressed workweek, this option can also provide employees with job flexibility. The primary benefit to the company is that it gets "two for the price of one"—the company can draw on two sets of skills and abilities to accomplish one set of job objectives. Charlotte Schutzman and Sue Manix share the job of vice president of public affairs and communications at Verizon Communications. They have been a job-sharing team for an astonishing 16 years. Each woman works two days a week and on alternate Wednesdays. They talk by phone at least twice a week, and their close partnership has enabled them to stay on track professionally while raising their children—Manix has three, Schutzman has two. "It's been good for us; it's been good for the company," says Schutzman. "If we didn't job-share, we might have left." Charlie Bowman, who oversees work-life programs for Verizon's 212,000 employees, says the biggest benefit in job sharing is that "it allows highly skilled, motivated employees to stay on when they want to work part time but their job must be done full time."[13]

Although each of these work-scheduling options may have some drawbacks for the sponsoring organizations, the benefits far outweigh the problems. For this reason, not only are the number of companies offering compressed work increasing, but so are the number of companies offering other options. Today, over 87 percent of the top companies are offering telecommuting programs, 72 percent offer job sharing, and 70 percent offer flexible schedules. All of these figures are growing, and this trend is expected to continue.

Recognition and Empowerment

All employees have unique needs that they seek to fulfill through their jobs. Organizations must devise a wide array of incentives to ensure that a broad spectrum of employee needs can be addressed in the work environment, thus increasing the likelihood of motivated employees. A sampling of these motivational tools is discussed here.

Formal recognition of superior effort by individuals or groups in the workplace is one way to enhance employee motivation. Recognition serves as positive feedback and reinforcement, letting employees know what they have done well and that their contribution is valued by the organization. Recognition can take many forms, both formal and informal. Some companies use formal awards ceremonies to acknowledge and celebrate their employees' accomplishments. Others take advantage of informal interaction to congratulate employees on a job well done and offer encouragement for the future. Recognition can take the form of a monetary reward, a day off, a congratulatory e-mail, or a verbal "pat on the back." Recognition does not have to come from superiors to be meaningful, however. At Panzano's, a fine-dining Italian restaurant in Denver's Hotel Monaco, employees tack complimentary notes to a bulletin board to recognize the contributions of their coworkers. The board, called the Kudos board, is covered with dozens of anonymous notes saying things like, "Jorge is always a delight to work with. He consistently has a positive attitude and works hard and also he entertains me when I'm bored."[14] Each time a person receives a compliment, his or her name is entered in a monthly drawing for a prize like a Best Buy, Starbucks, or Barnes & Noble gift card.

Employee empowerment, sometimes called employee involvement or participative management, involves delegating decision-making authority to employees at all levels of the organization. Employees are given greater responsibility for planning, implementing, and evaluating the results of decisions. Empowerment is based on the premise that human resources, especially at lower levels in the firm, are an underutilized asset. Employees are capable of contributing much more of their skills and abilities to organizational success if they are allowed to participate in the decision-making process and are given access to the resources needed to implement their decisions. Alberto-Culver, maker of haircare products, looked to its employees for help improving the safety record at one of its manufacturing plants. A Safety Action Team of six members was created and given a small budget. Management provided the team with computers, e-mail, and meeting rooms. Employees on the team were charged with collecting and analyzing safety-related data and working with all employees to find solutions to safety problems. The results were undeniable. In the first year, the recordable injury rate in the plant dropped 44 percent, lost time shrunk by 70 percent, and there were 67 percent less employee grievances. Alberto-Culver then expanded its use of empowered teams to solve problems in areas like quality and productivity. As a result of giving its employees the authority to identify and solve problems in critical operational areas, the company realizes an annual savings of roughly $2 million.[15]

Economic Incentives

Any discussion of motivation has to include the use of monetary incentives to enhance performance. Currently, companies are using a variety of variable-pay programs such as piece-rate plans, profit sharing, gain sharing, stock options, and bonuses to encourage employees to be more productive. Unlike the standard salary or hourly wage, variable pay means that a portion of an employee's pay is directly linked to an individual or organizational performance measure. In *piece-rate pay plans,* for example, employees are paid a given amount for each unit they produce, directly linking the amount they earn to their productivity. *Profit-sharing plans* are based on overall company profitability. Using an established formula, management distributes some portion of company profits to all employees. *Gain-sharing plans* are incentive programs based on group productivity. Employees share in the financial gains attributed to the increased productivity of their group. This encourages employees to increase productivity within their specific work area regardless of the overall profit picture for the organization as a whole.

One well-known approach to monetary incentives is the award of *stock options*, or giving employees the right to purchase a given amount of stock at below-market prices. Stock can be a strong motivator because those who receive the options have the chance to make a lot of money. Lately companies have reduced the amount of equity (stock) they give to employees annually from 7 percent to roughly 2 percent, indicating that stock options are declining in popularity.[16]

One increasingly popular incentive is the bonus. A *bonus* is simply a one-time lump-sum monetary award. In many cases, employees receive bonuses for achieving a particular performance level, such as meeting or exceeding a sales quota, and it is not uncommon for bonuses to be substantial. The two winners of Google's 2005 Founders' Award, a huge spot bonus for great work on a project, split $12 million. For line and staff employees, bonuses can add up to 3 to 5 percent of their annual pay; for middle managers, that figure rises to 10 to 15 percent. Upper managers receive 15 to 25 percent of their base pay as a bonus, and for executives, bonuses can comprise 30 to 50 percent of their annual compensation![17] That's not to say that small bonuses aren't good motivators. George Zimmer, CEO of Men's Wearhouse, gives employees small bonuses for meeting inventory-loss targets (i.e., curtailing shoplifting and employee theft). He thinks financial incentives should be large enough to confer recognition and celebrate accomplishments, but not so large that they distort behavior.[18]

Regardless of their size, bonuses are replacing the raise as the way companies compensate employees for a job well done and motivate them to perform at even higher levels. That is because bonuses can vary according to outcomes. Financial incentives that allow variability in compensation to reflect an individual employee's contribution are generally known as *pay-for-performance* programs. One of the many companies that use pay-for-performance programs is Allstate, which assigns employees' individual performance one of five grades. The size of an employee's bonus depends on his or her grade. For example, one worker may receive a bonus of 5.5 percent of her annual pay, but the worker in the next cubicle doing the exact same job—though less efficiently or productively—may receive only 2 percent. "This allows us to attract better performers and keep the good talent that we have," says Steve Scholl, Allstate's assistant vice president of human resources.[19] In 1991, companies committed 3.8 percent of their annual payroll to pay-for-performance bonuses. Today that figure is over 10 percent.[20]

> **concept check**
>
> Explain the difference between job enlargement and job enrichment.
>
> What are the four work-scheduling options that can enhance employee performance?
>
> Are all employees motivated by the same economic incentives? Explain.

Trends in Employee Motivation

 8 **What initiatives are organizations using today to motivate and retain employees?**

This chapter has focused on understanding what motivates people and how employee motivation and satisfaction affect productivity and organizational performance. Organizations can improve performance by investing in people. In reviewing the ways companies are currently choosing to invest in their human resources, we can spot four positive trends: (1) education and training, (2) employee ownership, (3) work–life benefits, and (4) nurturing knowledge workers. All of the companies making the *Fortunes'* annual list of the "100 Best Companies to Work For" know the importance of treating employees right. They all have programs that allow them to invest in their employees through programs such as these and many more. Today's businesses also face the challenge of increased costs of absenteeism. This section discusses each of these trends in motivating employees.

Education and Training

Companies that provide educational and training opportunities for their employees reap the benefits of a more motivated, as well as a more skilled, workforce. Employees who are properly trained in new technologies are more productive and less resistant to job change. Education and training provide additional benefits by increasing

Everyone's a CFO

Andrew Levine, president of DCI, a New York public relations firm, wanted to implement a more open management style at his company, so he added a financial segment to monthly staff meetings, during which he would share results and trends with his employees. Much to his surprise, employees seemed bored. During one staff meeting he asked his employees how to calculate a profit, and only the receptionist, Sergio Barrios, knew how. Levine was astounded, both at his employees' general deficit in math concepts and at Barrios' knack for figures. Levine then decided to require employees to present the financial reports themselves.

For the next staff meeting, Levine appointed Barrios the Chief Financial Officer (CFO) of the day. Barrios explained the terminology in ways laymen could understand. Since then, Levine has watched his employees become financial whizzes. Each CFO of the day meets with DCI's real CFO for only one day before the meeting. They review income, expenses, and all manner of financial ratios and statements. They discuss revenue projections and general financial trends. The CFO of the day then presents this information at the monthly staff meeting. Maria Mantz, a junior employee, thinks the training is extremely beneficial. "I'm a new, young employee, and I'm being trained not only as a PR executive, but also as a business executive." When Mantz's turn came

around, she stood before 30 of her colleagues and began detailing accounts and asking her audience to refer to the revenue table in their handouts. She asked if anyone know what the five clients who showed an increase in activity had in common, and awarded the coworker who knew the answer (they were all performance-based accounts) with a gift card to a local sandwich shop. Then she opened the floor for debate by asking, "Is that a good thing or a bad thing?"

CFO-of-the-day has definitely been a good thing for DCI, which has been profitable ever since Levine instituted the program. Employees stay an average of five years, up from two-and-a-half years before the program. And customers are also sticking around longer—the length of the client relationship has doubled to over four years. And employees are no longer bored during the financial review section of the monthly meeting.[21]

Critical Thinking Questions
- Do you think a CFO-of-the-day program is a good idea for all companies? Why or why not?
- How comfortable would you be leading the financial discussion at a monthly staff meeting? What could you do to improve your skills in this area?

CONCEPT *in Action*

Companies sometimes create unusual perks to help attract and retain talented workers. Timberland employees receive a $3,000 subsidy to buy a hybrid automobile. Worthington Industries offers workers onsite haircuts for just $4. And at SC Johnson, retirees receive a lifetime membership to the company fitness center. *What trends are emerging in the ways companies seek to motivate workers and keep them happy on the job?*

© THINKSTOCK IMAGES/JUPITER IMAGES

employees' feelings of competence and self-worth. When companies spend money to upgrade employee knowledge and skills, they convey the message "we value you and are committed to your growth and development as an employee." Read about one small company's innovative employee training in the Catching the Entrepreneurial Spirit box.

Employee Ownership

A recent trend that seems to have leveled off is employee ownership, most commonly implemented as employee stock ownership plans, or *ESOPs*. ESOPs are not the same as stock options, however. In an ESOP, employees receive compensation in the form of company stock. Recall that stock options give employees the opportunity to purchase company stock at a set price, even if the market price of the stock increases above that point. Because employees are compensated with stock, over time they can become the owners of the company. Behind employee ownership programs is the belief that employees who think like owners are more motivated to take care of customers' needs, reduce unnecessary expenses, make operations smoother, and stay with the company longer.

According to the National Center for Employee Ownership, there are roughly 11,500 ESOPs in the United States, for a total of 10 million participants.[22] Despite changes in tax laws that resulted in a decrease in the number of publicly traded companies with ESOPs, the amount of stock held by ESOPs has actually increased.[23] In a recent survey of 1,400 corporate ESOPs, 82 percent of respondents reported that the ESOP improved motivation and productivity at their company.[24]

ESOPs, however, also have drawbacks. For example, employees in privately held ESOPs are not able to check the value of their stock on a daily basis and may have to wait a year or more between appraisals.[25] Likewise, some employees—of public and private companies alike—have so much of their nest eggs tied to their company's ESOP that if their company's performance starts to decline, they risk losing a significant portion of their wealth. Such was the case for United Airlines employees when the company declared bankruptcy in 2002. Ironically, almost a decade earlier, the company handed employees half ownership of the airlines as a move to improve overall performance.

Still, many companies successfully implement ESOPs. SAIC, a government contractor based in San Diego, grew to a $7 billion company with a place on the Fortune 500 as a result of its ESOP. SAIC honed its employee-ownership strategy under the hand of J. Robert Beyster, a nuclear physicist who founded the company in 1969. From the beginning, Beyster offered ownership in the business to the scientists who joined him, and over the years SAIC devised various retirement plans, stock incentives, and option grants to encourage employees to buy in.[26]

So what enables one company with an ESOP, like SAIC, to completely outperform another, like United? According to Doug Kruse, an economist at Rutgers University's School of Management and Labor Relations, "It has a lot to do with the way companies treat employees. You can't just call an employee an owner and expect them to respond positively. You have to do something to make them feel like an owner. United Airlines illustrates that employee ownership is not a magic elixir. It takes a lot of finesse to do it right, finesse that SAIC seems to have."[27]

Work–Life Benefits

In another growing trend in the workplace, companies are helping their employees to manage the numerous and sometimes competing demands in their lives. Organizations are taking a more active role in helping employees achieve a balance between their work responsibilities and their personal obligations. The desired result is employees who are less stressed, better able to focus on their jobs, and, therefore, more productive. One increasingly popular tool companies are using to help their employees achieve work-life balance is the paid sabbatical. Sabbaticals can be traced back to the need for an incentive that would attract potential faculty members to Harvard University in the late 1800s. Today, sabbaticals can mean paid time off anywhere from a month to a couple of years.[28] In today's business environment, companies are trying to juggle cutting costs, increasing profits, while simultaneously battling to keep employees motivated and positive about work. Sabbaticals can be an important tool to help managers achieve this balancing act.

Nearly half of the companies on Fortune's 2000 list of the 100 Best Companies to Work For offer paid sabbaticals for their employees. Once reason for the growing popularity of sabbaticals is the increased pressures facing today's workforce. When companies have several rounds of layoffs, for example, fewer employees are left to take care of business, and those employees often feel the need to continually go above and beyond the call of duty in order to avoid receiving a pink slip themselves. About 75 percent of office employees feel that work has infiltrated their private lives. With more and more professions requiring 60-plus-hour workweeks, it is no wonder that there is a growing epidemic of work-related stress.[29] Another factor is the tremendous influx of women into the workforce in the past two decades. More than 45 percent of all employees are women, and 70 percent of married women with children under the age of 18 work outside the home.[30] A working mother often finds herself in a tight balancing act of handling the responsibilities of her family and career, and any unexpected problem can wreak havoc on her situation. And in general, a growing number of employees are already tired and depleted.

In that business environment, sabbaticals are an attractive option for companies hoping to rejuvenate their workforce. For example, Microsoft employees are eligible for a paid sabbatical every five years. Smaller companies also offer sabbaticals, although not as many. Only 2 percent of companies with fewer than 100 employees offer paid sabbaticals.[31] Fred Crosetto, the founder of Ammex, a Seattle-based distributor of disposable gloves, gives his employees a three-week paid sabbatical every five years—on top of the usual vacation and personal time. The only requirement is that employees take all three weeks at once. "We want people to do whatever they want," says Crosetto. "You can see that they're rejuvenated."[32] Likewise, to bolster creativity, the Johnsson Group, a financial services company in Chicago, lets any employee—from an administrative assistant to a vice president—take a two-week sabbatical every three years. The company also chips in $1,000 in spending money for the getaway. As at Ammex, employees must take the entire sabbatical at once, but at Johnsson Group, employees must also agree to go out of town.[33]

Nurturing Knowledge Workers

Most organizations have specialized workers, and managing them all effectively is a big challenge. In many companies, knowledge workers (now two-fifths of the workforce) may have a supervisor, but they are not "subordinates." They are "associates." Within their area of knowledge, they are supposed to do the telling. Because knowledge is effective only if specialized, knowledge workers are not homogeneous, particularly the fast-growing group of knowledge technologists such as computer systems specialists, lawyers, programmers, and others. And because knowledge work is specialized, it is deeply splintered.

A knowledge-based workforce is qualitatively different from a less skilled workforce. True, knowledge workers are still a minority, but they are fast becoming the largest single group. And they have already become the major creator of wealth. Increasingly the success, indeed the survival, of every business will depend on the performance of its knowledge workforce. The challenging part of managing knowledge workers is finding ways to motivate proud, skilled professionals to share expertise and cooperate in such a way to advance the frontiers of their knowledge to the benefit of the shareholders and society in general. To achieve that auspicious goal, several companies have created what they call "communities of practice." Read the Managing Change box to find out how Schlumberger Limited, an oil-field-services company, uses this innovative tool to motivate its highly technical knowledge workers.

Coping with the Rising Costs of Absenteeism

With today's companies trying to do more work with fewer employees, managers must be attentive to two major trends that affect the performance and morale of their employees: absenteeism and turnover. According to a survey published by Harris Interactive in 2005, workplace absenteeism was at a five-year high, during which time some 2.4 percent of workers at 305 for-profit and nonprofit entities nationwide called in sick each day. That amounted to a 50 percent increase over the same period the year before.[34]

The drastic rise in absenteeism is attributed to changes in workplace policies that made sick time a use-it-or-lose-it commodity. Another predictable factor behind all the absences: morale. The survey found that absenteeism rates were 35 percent higher at companies with poor or fair morale than at companies with good or very good morale.[35] Another survey showed that work-life programs that give employees more control over their schedules are the most successful in stemming unscheduled absences. The top four are alternative work arrangements, the ability to leave for children's school functions, telecommuting, and compressed work weeks.[36] See Exhibit 10.6 for a breakdown of the reasons employees give for unscheduled absences.

MANAGING CHANGE

Using Communities of Practice to Motivate Knowledge Workers

Communities of practice (CoPs) have been so named since they early 1990s, but recently they are gaining popularity as a way to motivate knowledge workers. One company that has experienced tremendous success with CoPs is Schlumberger Limited, an oil-field-services company with nearly $11.5 billion in annual revenue. As with all CoPs, what Schlumberger calls Eureka groups are comprised of similar professional employees from across the entire organization. More than 11,750 of the company's 52,000 employees participate in one or more of 23 Eureka groups ranging from chemistry to oil-well engineering.

Before the establishment of the communities, Schlumberger's engineers, physicists, and geologists worked well on individual projects, but the company was ignorant of how to help its employees develop the professional sides of their lives. Since the company sells services and expertise, motivating and cultivating its knowledge workers was a critical success factor. Former CEO Euan Baird felt he had tried everything to manage and motivate the company's technical professionals—and failed. That's when he decided to let them manage themselves. He ordered Schulmberger veteran Henry Edmundson to implement communities of practice.

Schlumberger's Eureka communities have been a tremendous success and helped the company leverage its knowledge assets. Today, more than 50,000 self-created CVs are posted on the company's internal Web site, allowing employees across the 80 countries where the company operates to consult the résumé of nearly every company employee to find someone with a particular area of knowledge or expertise. Another reason the Eureka groups are so successful is that they are completely democratic. Participating employees vote on who will lead each community. An employee who is backed by his or her manager and at least one other community member can run for a term of office that lasts one year. More than 275 employees serve as elected leaders of Schlumberger's Eureka communities, which cost the company about $1 million a year. "Compared with other knowledge initiatives, it's a cheapie," says Edmundson.

John Afilaka, a geological engineer who is a Schlumberger business-development manager in Nigeria, stood for election to the head of the company's rock-characterization community, a group of more than 1,000 people expert in determining what might be in an underground reservoir. He beat an opponent and now spends 15 to 20 percent of his time organizing the group's annual conference and occasional workshops, overseeing the group's Web site, coordinating subgroups, and so forth.

The company's current CEO, Andrew Gould, says the self-governing feature is crucial to the Eureka communities' success. Technical professionals are often motivated by peer review and peer esteem, he says, implying that stock options and corner offices aren't sufficient. The election of leaders, he says, "Ensures the integrity of peer judgments."[37]

Critical Thinking Questions

- How do you think communities of practice help companies like Schlumberger manage in dynamic business environments?
- Although communities of practice are commonly thought of in regard to knowledge workers, could they successfully motivate other employees as well? Why do you think as you do?

Another trend related to employee morale and absenteeism is turnover. After years of stability, the number of employees who are job-searching is on the rise. A survey from the Society of Human Resources Management and CareerJournal.com, 2004 U.S. Job Recovery and Retention, found that 35 percent of current employees are actively seeking a new job, and another 40 percent are passively looking for one.[38] Those figures are great cause for concern. A high rate of turnover can be expensive and dampen the morale of other employees who watch their colleagues leave the

Exhibit 10.6 > Reasons for Unscheduled Absences

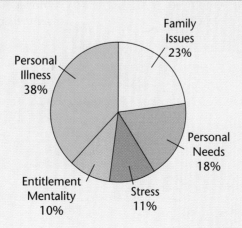

Source: Maggie Raunch, "Strong Relationship Shown between Morale, Absenteeism: Survey Shows Unhappy Employees Use More Sick Days," *Incentive*, May 2005, p. 8. Copyright © *Incentive* magazine. All rights reserved. Reproduced by permission.

Family Issues 23%

Personal Illness 38%

Personal Needs 18%

Stress 11%

Entitlement Mentality 10%

CONCEPT *in Action*

Employers seeking to stem the rising tide of absenteeism are developing innovative, flexible benefits for their employees. SC Johnson offers workers on-site childcare, an in-house doctor, and paternity leave. Prudential allows employees to take time off to care for sick children and elderly parents. Hewlett-Packard boasts a range of flexible work options to fit employees' hectic lives. *Do flexible options and benefits adequately address the root causes of absenteeism?*

company. Both employees and human resource professionals agree on the biggest reasons behind increasing turnover rates: (1) better compensation elsewhere, (2) career opportunities elsewhere, and (3) dissatisfaction with potential for career development at the current organization. Whereas human resource professionals think that burnout and feeling unappreciated are also major causes for leaving, employees cited "readiness for a new experience," boredom, and better benefits elsewhere as more pressing reasons.[39]

High rates of turnover (or absenteeism) at the management level can be destabilizing for employees, who need to develop specific strategies to manage a steady flow of new bosses. High rates of turnover (or absenteeism) at the employee level compromises the company's ability to perform at its highest levels. In order to stay competitive, companies need to have programs in place to motivate employees to come to work each day and to stay with the company year after year.

concept check

What benefits can an organization derive from training and educational opportunities, and stock ownership programs?

Why are sabbaticals growing in popularity as work-life balance tools?

How are knowledge workers different from traditional employees?

Why are absenteeism and turnover rates increasing and what is the impact on companies?

CONCEPT *in Action*

While turnover is an ongoing concern for most businesses, Costco Wholesale Corporation has one of the most loyal, productive workforces in all of retailing—a distinction undoubtedly related to its higher-wage policy. The average full-time Costco worker makes nearly $17 an hour; pays less than 10 percent of the cost of health-insurance premiums; and outsells Wal-Mart employees by hundreds of dollars per square-foot of retail space. Once hired, Costco employees rarely leave. *How might investing in worker satisfaction pay off for companies?*

Summary of Learning Goals

1 **What are the basic principles of Frederick Taylor's concept of scientific management?**

Scientific management is based on the belief that employees are motivated by economic incentives and that there is "one best way" to perform any job. The four basic principles of scientific management developed by Taylor are as follows:

1. Develop a scientific approach for each element of a person's job.
2. Scientifically select, train, teach, and develop workers.
3. Encourage cooperation between workers and managers so that each job can be accomplished in a standard, scientifically determined way.
4. Divide work and responsibility between management and workers according to who is better suited to each task.

2 **What did Elton Mayo's Hawthorne studies reveal about worker motivation?**

The pride that comes from special attention motivates workers to increase their productivity. Supervisors who allow employees to have some control over their situation appeared to further increase the workers' motivation. The Hawthorne effect suggests that employees will perform better when they feel singled out for special attention or feel that management is concerned about employee welfare.

3 **What is Maslow's hierarchy of needs, and how do these needs relate to motivation?**

Maslow believed that each individual has a hierarchy of needs, consisting of physiological, safety, social, esteem, and self-actualization needs. Managers who accept Maslow's ideas attempt to increase employee motivation by modifying organizational and managerial practices to increase the likelihood that employees will meet all levels of needs. Maslow's theory has also helped managers understand that it is hard to motivate people by appealing to already satisfied needs.

4 **How are McGregor's Theories X and Y and Ouchi's Theory Z used to explain worker motivation?**

Douglas McGregor influenced the study of motivation with his formulation of two contrasting sets of assumptions about human nature—designated Theory X and Theory Y. Theory X says people don't like to work and will avoid it if they can. Because people don't like to work, they must be controlled, directed, or threatened to get them to make an effort. Theory Y says that people want to be self-directed and will try to accomplish goals that they believe in. Workers can be motivated with positive incentives. McGregor personally believed that Theory Y assumptions describe most employees and that managers seeking to motivate subordinates should develop management practices based on those assumptions.

William Ouchi's Theory Z combines U.S. and Japanese business practices. Theory Z emphasizes long-term employment, slow career development, and group decision making. The long-term decline of the Japanese economy has resulted in most U.S. firms moving away from Japanese management practices.

5 **What are the basic components of Herzberg's motivator–hygiene theory?**

Frederick Herzberg's studies indicated that certain job factors are consistently related to employee job satisfaction whereas others can create job dissatisfaction. According to Herzberg, motivating factors (also called satisfiers) are primarily intrinsic job elements that lead to satisfaction, such as achievement, recognition, the (nature of) work itself, responsibility, advancement, and growth. What Herzberg termed hygiene factors (also called dissatisfiers) are extrinsic elements of the work environment such as company policy, relationships with supervisors, working conditions, relationships with peers and subordinates, salary and benefits, and job security. These are factors that can result in job dissatisfaction if not well managed. One of the most interesting results of Herzberg's studies was the implication that the opposite of satisfaction is not dissatisfaction. Herzberg believed that proper management of hygiene factors could prevent employee dissatisfaction, but that these factors could not serve as a source of satisfaction or motivation.

6 What four contemporary theories on employee motivation offer insights into improving employee performance?

According to expectancy theory, the probability of an individual acting in a particular way depends on the strength of that individual's belief that the act will have a particular outcome and on whether the individual values that outcome. Equity theory is based on individuals' perceptions about how fairly they are treated compared with their coworkers. Goal-setting theory states that employees are highly motivated to perform when specific goals are established and feedback on progress is offered. Reinforcement theory states that behavior is a function of consequences; that is, people do things because they know other things will follow.

7 How can managers redesign existing jobs to increase employee motivation and performance?

The horizontal expansion of a job by increasing the number and variety of tasks that a person performs is called job enlargement. Increasing task diversity can enhance job satisfaction, particularly when the job is mundane and repetitive in nature. Job enrichment is the vertical expansion of an employee's job to provide the employee with more autonomy, responsibility, and decision-making authority. Other popular motivational tools include work-scheduling options, employee recognition programs, empowerment, and variable-pay programs.

8 What initiatives are organizations using today to motivate and retain employees?

Today firms are using several key tactics to motivate and retain workers. First, companies are investing more in employee education and training, which makes employees more productive and confident in their jobs. Second, managers are giving employees the opportunity to participate in the ownership of the company, which can strongly increase employee commitment. Employers are providing more work-life benefits to employees, and a small but growing percentage of companies is offering employees paid sabbaticals in addition to regular vacation and sick time. As the composition of the workforce changes, it is becoming increasingly important for companies to understand how to manage knowledge workers. One method of doing this is establishing communities of practice that enable workers to share expertise across the organization. Finally, managers in today's business environment need to pay special attention to managing absence rates and employee (and management) turnover.

Key Terms

equity theory   343
expectancy theory   342
goal-setting theory   344
Hawthorne effect   336
hygiene factors   341
job enlargement   346
job enrichment   346
job rotation   346
job sharing   347
Maslow's hierachy of needs   336
motivating factors   341

motivation   334
need   334
punishment 344
reinforcement theory   344
reward   344
scientific management   335
Theory X   339
Theory Y   339
Theory Z   339
want   334

Preparing for Tomorrow's Workplace: SCANS

1. Are you motivated more by intrinsic rewards (satisfaction, sense of accomplishment, etc.) or by extrinsic rewards (money, bonuses, etc.)? Interview some friends and classmates to find out what motivates them. Discuss your differences in perspective. (Interpersonal, Information)

2. Think of a task or project you have completed recently that required a great deal of effort. What motivated you to exert so much energy to complete the task or project? Describe your motivation in terms of the theories presented in the chapter. (Systems)

3. Not all jobs are intrinsically motivating. For example, many entry-level jobs often involve repetitive and simple tasks that can become rapidly boring. (You may have worked a job that fits that description.) How can managers motivate front-line employees (like fast-food cashiers, trash collectors, supermarket cashiers, etc.) to perform at high-levels? (Systems, Interpersonal)

4. If you were offered the opportunity to job share, would you need to have a partner who was motivated by the same things as you are? Why or why not? (Interpersonal)

5. **Team Activity** Assemble a team of three to five students. Imagine that you are the management team for a start-up business with limited resources but a need for a highly motivated, skilled workforce. Brainstorm ways you could motivate your employees other than large bonuses and high salaries. (Resources)

Ethics Activity

You join a large bank that encourages and promotes employee volunteerism, allowing employees one day a month, or up to 12 days a year, to volunteer for a cause of their choosing. Shortly after you start working there as a junior teller your boss's wife is diagnosed with a particularly aggressive form of breast cancer which carries a very poor prognosis. Realizing it will win you kudos with your boss, you choose the local chapter of the Susan B. Komen Foundation—a breast cancer charity that sponsors an annual Race for the Cure—for your company-sponsored volunteer work.

In addition to working at the foundation's office one day a month, you spend your own time actively soliciting other staffers at your firm to sign up for the charity walk in a few month's time. Impressed with your qualities of tireless dedication, your boss puts your name forward for promotion to junior bank officer, well before the customary two years of service normally required for being considered for promotion.

Using a Web search tool, locate articles about this topic and then write responses to the following questions. Be sure to support your arguments and cite your sources.

Ethical Dilemma: Your company is generous in its approach to employee volunteerism. It gives you paid time off and you acquire enhanced job skills through your volunteer activities. Have you just been smart in recognizing the value of volunteering for a charity that you know will earn your boss's personal appreciation? Or are you taking unfair advantage of your boss's vulnerability and manipulating the situation?

Sources: Margarita Bauza, "Companies Find Volunteering Makes Good Business Sense," *Detroit Free Press*, November 20, 2005, http://galenet.thomsonlearning.com; "Deloitte Volunteer IMPACT Survey Reveals Link Between Volunteering and Professional Success," Internet Wire, June 3, 2005, http://galenet.thomsonlearning.com; Charley Hannagan, "Can Work Help?" *Post-Standard (Syracuse, NY)*, September 30, 2005, p. C1.

Working the Net

1. Looking for 1,001 ways to motivate or reward your employees? Bob Nelson can help. Visit his Nelson Motivation site at **http://www.nelson-motivation.com** to get some ideas you can put to use to help you do a better job, either as a manager or as an employee.

2. More companies are offering their employees stock ownership plans. To learn the differences between an employee stock ownership plan (ESOP) and stock options, visit the National Center for Employee Ownership (NCEO) at **http://www.nceo.org** and the Foundation for Enterprise Development (FED) at **http://www.fed.org**. Which stock plan would you rather have? Why?

3. Open-book management is one of the better-known ways to create a participatory work environment. Over 2,000 companies have adopted this practice, which involves sharing financial information with nonmanagement employees and training them to understand financial information. Does it really motivate employees and improve productivity? The National Center for Employee Ownership (NCEO) Web site, **http://www.nceo.org** has a number of articles on Open Book Management in its "Ownership Culture" section. Read several of the articles to get more insight into this practice and then develop your answers to these questions.

4. You've been asked to develop a staff recognition program for your company but don't have a clue where to start! Three sites with articles and other useful information are *Incentive* magazine, **http://www.incentivemag.com**, the National Association for Employee Recognition, **http://www.recognition.org**, and the U.S. Office of Personnel Management, **http://www.opm.gov/perform/reward.html**. Using the material you'll find there, outline the plan you would recommend for your company.

5. You have two great job opportunities. Both are equally attractive in terms of job content and offer the same salary. However, one offers year-end bonuses, whereas the other includes stock options for employees. How do you compare the offers? Learn how to evaluate stock options at the Money section of How Stuff Works, **http://money.howstuffworks.com/question436.htm**. Prepare a comparison of bonuses versus stock options and determine which appeals to you more. Explain your reasons.

6. Use a search engine to find companies that offer "work–life benefits." Link to several companies and review their employee programs in this area. How do they compare? Which benefits would be most important to you if you were job hunting, and why?

Creative Thinking Case >

Motivating Employees: A Monster of a Problem

As mentioned in earlier chapters, American businesses will face a decrease in the available workforce due in part to a smaller generation of talented workers replacing retiring Baby Boomers. "Our study reveals that recruiters and hiring managers are not only cognizant of the issue but are concerned about its current and future impact on organizational growth," said Dr. Jesse Harriott, vice president of research at monster.com (**http://www.monster.com**), the leading global online career and recruitment resource. "Businesses of all sizes and across all industries must develop and implement creative programs and strategies to attract and hire top candidates while retaining and motivating current employees. As the talent pool shrinks, it is imperative that immediate action is taken to ensure businesses are properly prepared and staffed for the future."

In a sampling of over 600 human resource managers, Monster's survey showed that over 75 percent believe compensation is one of the top three motivators that prevent employees from leaving their job. The fact that money motivates top-performing employees is supported by almost half the human resources professionals surveyed for the 2005 Rewards Program and Incentive Compensation Survey released by the Society of Human Resource Management. The survey also found that neither monetary nor non-monetary rewards were effective motivators for underperformers.

While compensation is clearly a significant issue, not all companies can offer this advantage. Other strategies that motivate employee loyalty and commitment are necessary. Some of these include making supervisors more accountable for worker retention; promoting work/life balance for employees; fostering a workplace where employee expectations are clearly articulated; learning and development programs that groom employees for future management roles; performance-based systems that identify and proactively manage top employees and when possible to promote from within; mentoring programs that match new employees with seasoned veterans; monitoring sentiment throughout the employee lifecycle; creating an employment brand "experience" that not only motivates and energizes employees, but can be used to attract new talent.

Diana Pohly, president and owner of The Pohly Company, keeps vigilant watch over the morale of the office, ensuring that employees are satisfied. "Business owners of growing companies must possess strong leadership and management skills in order to solidify the foundation of their business," said Pohly. "Effective team leadership is imperative to sustain efficient team workflows and contribute to employee morale."

"Employees are the lifeblood of any organization. Building a positive work environment is an important strategy in attracting, retaining and motivating a team," says Michelle Swanda, corporate marketing manager of The Principal. Improving employee morale with creative and effective management tactics ultimately boosts employee productivity, and that goes straight to the bottom line.

Critical Thinking Questions

- How are social and economic factors influencing companies' approach to hiring, motivating, and retaining employees?
- What are some of the non-monetary strategies companies must develop to attract, reward, and keep employees motivated?
- What "reward factors" would be important to you when working for a company? List at least five in order of importance and your reasons for each.

Sources: "70 Percent of HR Managers Concerned about Workforce Retention, According to Monster Study," *Business Wire,* Jan 9, 2006, http://www.findarticles.com; "Poll Says Top-Performing Workers Motivated By Money," *Nation's Restaurant News,* April 25, 2005, http://www.findarticles.com. "Team Motivation: Women Business Owners Increase Productivity Through Effective Leadership," *Business Wire,* Oct 27, 2005, http://www.findarticles.com.

Video Case >

Cooking Up Success at P. F. Chang's

What makes a restaurant experience memorable? Great food, ambiance, and attentive service all combine to create an enjoyable dining experience. P. F. Chang's China Bistro's unique blend of traditional Chinese cuisine and contemporary American hospitality sets the stage for the company's mission—to provide guests with exceptional food and service each time they walk through its doors.

P. F. Chang's success depends on attracting and retaining employees who maintain consistency in the quality and atmosphere of its restaurants, so the company seeks individuals who don't just understand exceptional guest service but have a passion for providing it day in and day out. Whether answering patrons' menu questions, recommending additional dishes to round out a meal, or making special sauces tableside, P. F. Chang's dedicated staff pays attention to every detail.

Founded in 1993, the Scottsdale, Arizona, headquartered company has over 115 bistro restaurants and employs 18,600 people. About 200 are executive office personnel, 1,200 are unit management personnel, and the remainder are hourly restaurant personnel. The staff of a typical Bistro restaurant consists of a general manager, three or four managers, an executive chef, one or two sous chefs, and approximately 125 hourly employees. All management and culinary personnel complete a comprehensive 13-week training program and must successfully complete a certification exam. Hourly staff must also complete training programs, which last from one to two weeks and focus on both technical and cultural knowledge.

So what is P. F. Chang's recipe for employee motivation and retention? The company offers a partnership or management equity participation program that allows regional managers, certain general managers, and certain executive chefs to become partners and participate in the profitability of their restaurants. These programs facilitate the development, leadership, and operations of the restaurants. In return for a cash payment to the partnership, the partner receives an ownership interest in a specific restaurant or region, generally ranging from 2 to 7 percent. Partners then share in the income or loss of this restaurant or region.

Operating partner Mark Millor was initially unsure whether he should buy into the partnership and get involved in management. "I was doing very well as a server and had all the free time I wanted, but my friends, my family convinced me, so finally I bought in," he says. "The minute I did, I wanted to become an Operating Partner. In essence I would be running my own business but with a lot less risk involved. I think that is the greatest part of the partnership perspective; when P. F. Chang wins, I win. Hire the right people and then catch them doing something right. Allow them to be successful. . . . Reinforce the behaviors you want to see. When you empower people, everybody wins." By respecting its employees and giving them a high degree of autonomy, P. F. Chang's creates a sense of ownership that motivates employees to perform at the highest levels.

Critical Thinking Questions

- P. F. Chang's is committed to providing guests with a superior dining experience. What role does its employees play in helping the company achieve that goal?
- What key strategy does the company use to motivate its employees? How does personal empowerment influence employee performance?
- Discuss the role employee training and education plays in the company's ongoing quest to distinguish its restaurants from the competition.

Sources: Adapted from the Daft Video Series, Chapter 16: "P. F. Chang's: Motivation in Organizations;" P. F. Chang's corporate Web site http://www.pfchangs.com (October 15, 2005); Tiffany Montgomery, "Scottsdale Arizona Restaurant Chains Eye Orange County, California, for Expansion," *The Orange County Register,* November 14, 2005, http://ocregister.com; and Nation's Restaurant News Web site http://www.nrn.com (January 2, 2006).

Hot Links Address Book

What makes a company a good place to work? Find out by reading about the companies on *Fortune* magazine's "100 Best Companies to Work For" by visiting **http://www.fortune.com**

Expand your knowledge about motivation in the workplace at Accel-Team's site, **http://www.accel-team.com/motivation/index.html**

How do you keep employees satisfied? The Business Research Lab has a series of tips and articles, which you'll find at **http://busreslab.com**

For many resources to help motivate, reward, and retain employees, visit About.com's page, **http://humanresources.about.com/od/motivationrewardretention**

Wish you could have flexible hours? For advice on making this wish come true, visit About.com's Career Planning page on flextime, **http://careerplanning.about.com/od/flextime**

ASTD is a professional association and leading resource on workplace learning and performance issues. Visit its site, **http://www.astd.org**, to learn more about these topics.

How does the Good-Buy network help companies offer work-life benefits? Find out at **http://www.goodbuynetwork.com/aboutus.html**

CHAPTER 11

Achieving World-Class Operations Management

Learning Goals

After reading this chapter, you should be able to answer these questions:

1 Why is production and operations management important in both manufacturing and service firms?

2 What types of production processes do manufacturers and service firms use?

3 How do organizations decide where to put their production facilities? What choices must be made in designing the facility?

4 Why are resource-planning tasks like inventory management and supplier relations critical to production?

5 How do operations managers schedule and control production?

6 How can quality management and lean-manufacturing techniques help firms improve production and operations management?

7 What roles do technology and automation play in manufacturing and service industry operations management?

8 What key trends are affecting the way companies manage production and operations?

Exploring Business Careers
Deborah Butler
Caterpillar

Deborah Butler is a certified Master Black Belt, but don't expect to see her working with Jet Li anytime soon. In fact, her job has little to do with martial arts. Employed by Caterpillar, "the world's leading manufacturer of construction and mining equipment, diesel and natural gas engines, and industrial gas turbines," Butler's Master Black Belt status reflects her expertise in 6 Sigma: the process Cat employees use to continually manage, improve, and create processes, products, and services. "Sigma" refers to the maximum number of defects tolerated in production or service delivery; 6 Sigma is the highest level of quality control, demanding no more than 3.4 defects per million parts. That means if you were to use 6 Sigma in your college career, you would miss only *one half of a single question* in over four years of test taking!

Caterpillar was the first corporation to take 6 Sigma global, deploying it corporate-wide in 2001 not only to its almost 300 facilities, but also eventually to every dealer and over 400 key suppliers throughout the world. The corporation hails the process as a key element of its overall operations management, attributing increased profits, improved customer service, and supply chain efficiency to 6 Sigma.

Caterpillar's more than 300 Master Black Belts lead projects that use 6 Sigma and train the company's approximately 3,300 Black Belts in the principles of the process. Butler is currently in charge of updating and implementing *Our Values in Action: Caterpillar's Worldwide Code of Conduct*. Outlining the four core values of Integrity, Excellence, Teamwork, and Commitment, the updated code of conduct embodies two important aspects of Caterpillar's philosophy on 6 Sigma.

First, Caterpillar recognizes that employees are the heart of any operation. Therefore, Caterpillar employees use 6 Sigma to improve as people and workers, as much as to improve the products they produce. The core values, reflected in a series of action statements such as "We put Integrity in action when we compete fairly," are the product of a year-long development process involving Butler's global team. As part of the project research, the team interviewed thousands of Caterpillar employees, from officers of the company to production and hourly workers, for the purpose of, as Butler says, "bringing to the surface the values that have made Caterpillar a successful enterprise, enhancing behavioral expectations, and accurately expressing Caterpillar's corporate culture."

Caterpillar is not content simply to produce Our Values in Action and leave it at that, however, and the second aspect of its 6 Sigma philosophy is that employees must bring the process to their lives. Butler has worked to inject the code of conduct's values into employee's day-to-day work. If an employee writes about safety-related changes, for example, she would not just list the changes. Instead, she might write first: "According to Our Values In Action, we put Commitment in action when we protect the health and safety of others and ourselves. As such, we are implementing the following changes...." In this way, the code becomes a living part of corporate culture, a critical component of operations management.

Chapter 11 discusses how companies achieve world-class operations management, detailing the processes of production and operations management from planning to quality control.

Nearly every type of business organization needs to find the most efficient and effective methods of producing the goods or services it sells to its customers. Technological advances, ongoing competition, and consumer expectations force companies to rethink where, when, and how they will produce products or services.

Manufacturers have discovered that it is no longer enough to simply push products through the factory and onto the market. Consumers demand high quality at reasonable prices. They also expect manufacturers to deliver products in a timely manner. Firms that can't meet these expectations often face strong competition from businesses that can. To compete, many manufacturers are streamlining how they make their products—by automating their factories, developing new production processes, focusing on quality control techniques, and improving relationships with suppliers.

Service organizations also face challenges. Their customers are demanding better service, shorter waiting periods, and more individualized attention. Like manufacturers, service companies are using new methods to deliver what their customers need and want. Banks, for example, are using technology such as ATMs and the Internet to make their services more accessible to customers. Colleges offer evening, weekend, and online courses to accommodate the schedules of working students. Tax services file tax returns via computer.

This chapter examines how manufacturers and service firms manage and control the creation of products and services. We'll discuss production planning, including the choices firms must make concerning the type of production process they will use; the location where production will occur; the design of the facility; and the management of resources needed in production. Next, we'll explain routing and scheduling, two critical tasks for controlling production and operations efficiency. Then we will look at how firms can improve production and operations by employing quality management and lean manufacturing techniques. Finally we will review some of the trends affecting production and operations management.

Production and Operations Management—An Overview

1 Why is production and operations management important in both manufacturing and service firms?

Production, the creation of products and services, is an essential function in every firm. Production turns inputs, such as natural resources, raw materials, human resources, and capital, into outputs, which are products and services. This process is shown in Exhibit 11.1. Managing this conversion process is the role of operations management.

The goal of customer satisfaction is an important part of effective production and operations. In the past, the manufacturing function in most companies was

CONCEPT in Action

With oil reserves second only to Saudi Arabia, Canada's Alberta province is set to become a vast supplier of crude oil worldwide. Unlike the smooth petroleum that gushes from Arabian wells, however, Alberta's black gold has to be mined from oil-rich sands. The process is rigorous: 400-ton trucks transport excavated bitumen to crushers and mixers that separate the sands from the oil and the resulting slurry travels miles of pipeline to North American refineries. *What are key inputs in the mining of oil sands?*

© NORM BETTS/BLOOMBERG NEWS/LANDOV

Exhibit 11.1 > Production Process for Products and Services

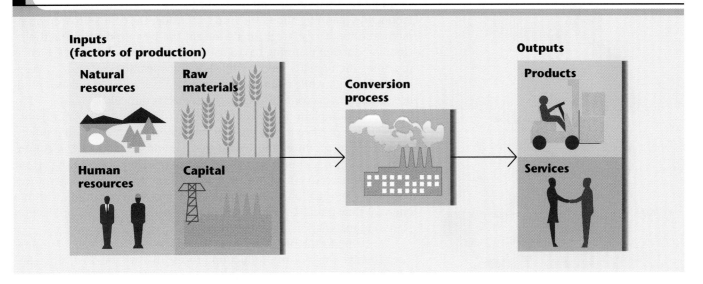

Inputs (factors of production)
- Natural resources
- Raw materials
- Human resources
- Capital

Conversion process

Outputs
- Products
- Services

production
The creation of products and services by turning inputs, such as natural resources, raw materials, human resources, and capital, into outputs, which are products and services.

operations management
Management of the production process.

inwardly focused. Manufacturing had little contact with customers and didn't always understand their needs and desires. In the 1980s, many U.S. industries, such as automotive, steel, and electronics, lost customers to foreign competitors because their production systems could not provide the quality customers demanded. As a result, today most American companies, both large and small, consider a focus on quality to be a central component of effective operations management.

Stronger links between marketing and manufacturing also encourage production managers to be more outwardly focused and to consider decisions in light of their effect on customer satisfaction. Service companies find that making operating decisions with customer satisfaction in mind can be a competitive advantage.

Operations managers, the personnel charged with managing and supervising the conversion process, play a vital role in today's firm. They control about three-fourths of a firm's assets, including inventories, wages, and benefits. They also work closely with other major divisions of the firm, such as marketing, finance, accounting, and human resources, to ensure that the firm produces its goods profitably and satisfies its customers. Marketing personnel help them decide which products to make or which services to offer. Accounting and human resources help them face the challenge of combining people and resources to produce high-quality goods on time and at reasonable cost. They are involved in the development and design of goods and determine what production processes will be most effective.

Production and operations management involve three main types of decisions, typically made at three different stages:

1. *Production planning.* The first decisions facing operations managers come at the *planning stage.* At this stage, managers decide where, when, and how production will occur. They determine site locations and obtain the necessary resources.
2. *Production control.* At this stage, the decision-making process focuses on controlling quality and costs, scheduling, and the actual day-to-day operations of running a factory or service facility.
3. *Improving production and operations.* The final stage of operations management focuses on developing more efficient methods of producing the firm's goods or services.

All three decisions are ongoing and may occur simultaneously. In the following sections, we will take a closer look at the decisions and considerations firms face in each stage of production and operations management.

Gearing Up: Production Planning

An important part of operations management is **production planning**. Production planning allows the firm to consider the competitive environment and its own strategic goals to find the best production methods. Good production planning has to balance goals that may conflict, such as providing high-quality service while keeping operating costs low, or keeping profits high while maintaining adequate inventories of finished products. Sometimes accomplishing all these goals is difficult.

Production planning involves three phases. Long-term planning has a time frame of three to five years. It focuses on which goods to produce, how many to produce, and where they should be produced. Medium-term planning decisions cover about two years. They concern the layout of factory or service facilities, where and how to obtain the resources needed for production, and labor issues. Short-term planning, within a one-year time frame, converts these broader goals into specific production plans and materials management strategies.

Four important decisions must be made in production planning. They involve the type of production process that will be used, site selection, facility layout, and resource planning.

The Production Process: How Do We Make It?

In production planning, the first decision involves which type of **production process**—the way a good or service is created—best fits with company goals and customer demand. An important consideration is the type of good or service being produced because different goods may require different production processes. In general, there are three types of production: mass production, mass customization, and customization. In addition to production type, operations managers also classify production processes in two ways: (1) how inputs are converted into outputs and (2) the timing of the process.

One for All: Mass Production Mass production, manufacturing many identical goods at once, was a product of the Industrial Revolution. Henry Ford's Model-T automobile is a good example of early mass production. Each car turned out by Ford's factory was identical, right down to its color. If you wanted a car in any color except black, you were out of luck. Canned goods, over-the-counter drugs, and household appliances are other examples of goods that are mass-produced. The emphasis in mass production is on keeping manufacturing costs low by producing uniform products using repetitive and standardized processes. As products became more complicated to produce, mass production also became more complex. Automobile manufacturers, for example, must now incorporate more sophisticated electronics into their car designs. As a result, the number of assembly stations in most automobile manufacturing plants has increased.

Just for You: Customizing Goods In mass customization, goods are produced using mass-production techniques, but only up to a point. At that point, the product or service is custom tailored to the needs or desires of individual customers. American Leather, a leather-furniture manufacturer, uses mass customization to produce couches and chairs to customer specifications within 30 days. The basic frames in the furniture are the same, but automated cutting machinery precuts the color and type of leather ordered by each customer. Using mass-production techniques, they are then added to each frame.

Customization is the opposite of mass production. In customization, the firm produces goods or services one at a time according to the specific needs or wants of individual customers. Unlike mass customization, each product or service produced is

CONCEPT *in Action*

From its storied creation in post-war Italy to its big-screen immortalization in movies like *Roman Holiday* and *Quadrophenia*, the Vespa scooter has a reputation for romance, rebellion, and style. Manufactured by Italy's Piaggio, the Vespa's svelte, stainless-steel chassis and aeronautic-inspired designs are seen everywhere in Europe and more and more in the United States. The Piaggio Group presently operates factories in Italy, Spain, India, and China. *What important production-planning decisions does Piaggio need to make as it considers expanding into overseas markets?*

© SUNSET BOULEVARD/CORBIS SYGM

2 What types of production processes do manufacturers and service firms use?

production planning
The aspect of operations management in which the firm considers the competitive environment and its own strategic goals in an effort to find the best production methods.

production process
The way a good or service is created.

mass production
The manufacture of many identical goods at once.

mass customization
A manufacturing process in which goods are mass-produced up to a point and then custom tailored to the needs or desires of individual customers.

customization
The production of goods or services one at a time according to the specific needs or wants of individual customers.

Exhibit 11.2 > **Classification of Production Types**

Mass Production	Mass Customization	Customization
Highly uniform products or services. Many products made sequentially.	Uniform standardized production to a point, then unique features added to each product.	Each product or services produced according to individual customer requirements.
Examples: Breakfast cereals, soft drinks, and computer keyboards.	**Examples:** Dell Computers, tract homes, and Taylor Made Golf clubs.	**Examples:** Custom homes, legal services, and haircuts.

unique. For example, a print shop may handle a variety of projects, including newsletters, brochures, stationery, and reports. Each print job varies in quantity, type of printing process, binding, color of ink, and type of paper. A manufacturing firm that produces goods in response to customer orders is called a **job shop**.

Some types of service businesses also deliver customized services. Doctors, for instance, must consider the illnesses and circumstances of each individual patient before developing a customized treatment plan. Real estate agents may develop a customized service plan for each customer based on the type of house the person is selling or wants to buy. The differences between mass production, mass customization, and customization are summarized in Exhibit 11.2.

job shop
A manufacturing firm that produces goods in response to customer orders.

process manufacturing
A production process in which the basic input is broken down into one or more outputs (products).

Converting Inputs to Outputs As previously stated, production involves converting *inputs* (natural resources, raw materials, human resources, capital) into *outputs* (products or services). In a manufacturing company, the inputs, the production process, and the final outputs are usually obvious. Harley-Davidson, for instance, converts steel, rubber, paint, and other inputs into motorcycles. But the production process in a service company involves a less obvious conversion. For example, a hospital converts the knowledge and skills of its medical personnel, along with equipment and supplies from a variety of sources, into health care services for patients. Exhibit 11.3 on the next page provides examples of the inputs and outputs used by various other businesses.

There are two basic processes for converting inputs into outputs. In **process manufacturing**, the basic input (natural resources, raw materials) is broken down into one or more outputs (products). For instance, bauxite (the input) is processed to extract aluminum (the output). The **assembly process** is just the opposite. The basic inputs, like natural resources, raw materials, or human resources, are either *combined* to create the output or *transformed* into the output. An airplane, for example, is created by assembling thousands of parts which are its raw material inputs. Steel manufacturers use heat to transform iron and other materials into steel. In services, customers may play a role in the transformation process. For example, a tax preparation service combines the knowledge of the tax preparer with the client's information about personal finances in order to complete the tax return.

Production Timing A second consideration in choosing a production process is timing. A **continuous process** uses long production runs that may last days, weeks, or months without equipment shutdowns. This is

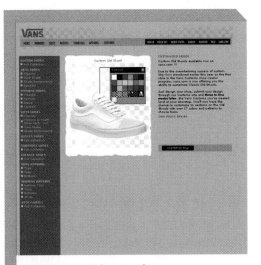

CONCEPT *in Action*

Mass customization has produced a thriving build-to-order society. This revolution in manufacturing is fueled, in part, by pop culture, where the compulsion to parade individuality is a hot commodity. Expressing oneself has never been easier. Consumers can design a new pair of sneakers with Vans Customs, build their own bags at Timbuk2, and customize a snowboard using the Burton Series 13 customization program—all while munching a pack of personalized M&M's candies. *What developments have made mass customization a viable method of production?*

Exhibit 11.3 > Converting Inputs to Outputs

Type of Organization	Input	Output
Airline	Pilots, crew, flight attendants, reservations system, ticketing agents, customers, airplanes, maintenance crews, ground facilities	Movement of customers and freight
Grocery store	Merchandise, building, clerks, supervisors, store fixtures, shopping carts, customers	Groceries for customers
High school	Faculty, curriculum, buildings, classrooms, library, auditorium, gymnasium, students, staff, supplies	Graduates, public service
Manufacturer	Machinery, raw materials, plant, workers, managers	Finished products for consumers and other firms
Restaurant	Food, cooking equipment, serving personnel, chefs, dishwashers, host, patrons, furniture, fixtures	Meals for patrons

assembly process
A production process in which the basic inputs are either combined to create the output or transformed into the output.

continuous process
A production process that uses long production runs lasting days, weeks, or months without equipment shutdowns; generally used for high-volume, low-variety products with standardized parts.

intermittent process
A production process that uses short production runs to make batches of different products; generally used for low-volume, high-variety products.

3 How do organizations decide where to put their production facilities? What choices must be made in designing the facility?

best for high-volume, low-variety products with standardized parts, such as nails, glass, and paper. Some services also use a continuous process. Your local electric company is an example. Per-unit costs are low and production is easy to schedule.

In an **intermittent process**, short production runs are used to make batches of different products. Machines are shut down to change them to make different products at different times. This process is best for low-volume, high-variety products such as those produced by mass customization or customization. Job shops are examples of firms using an intermittent process.

Although some service companies use continuous processes, most service firms rely on intermittent processes. For instance, a restaurant preparing gourmet meals, a physician performing physical examinations or surgical procedures, and an advertising agency developing ad campaigns for business clients, all customize their services to suit each customer. They use the intermittent process. Note that their "production runs" may be very short—one grilled salmon or one eye exam at a time.

Location, Location, Location: Where Do We Make It?

A big decision that managers must make early in production and operations planning is where to put the facility, be it a factory or a service office. The facility's location affects operating and shipping costs and, ultimately, the price of the product or service and the company's ability to compete. Mistakes made at this stage can be expensive, because moving a factory or service facility once production begins is difficult and costly. Firms must weigh a number of factors to make the right decision.

Availability of Production Inputs As we discussed earlier, organizations need certain resources to produce products and services for sale. Access to these resources, or inputs, is a huge consideration in site selection. Executives must assess the availability of raw materials, parts, equipment, and available manpower for each site under consideration. The cost of shipping raw materials and finished goods can be as much as 25 percent of a manufacturer's total cost, so locating a factory where these and other costs are as low as possible can make a major contribution to a firm's success.

CONCEPT *in Action*

Facing stiff competition from rival domestic breweries and sagging demand among Japanese consumers, Japan's Asahi Breweries recently opened its fifth beer plant in neighboring China. In 2003, China overtook the United States as the largest beer market in the world, and the opening of Asahi's new brewing facility is seen as a bid to obtain greater market share in an area of the world where beer consumption is expanding 10 percent annually. *What factors determine where brewing companies locate their operations?*

Companies that use heavy or bulky raw materials, for example, may choose to be located close to their suppliers. Mining companies want to be near ore deposits, oil refiners near oil fields, paper mills near forests, and food processors near farms. Bottlers are discovering that rural Western communities in need of an economic boost make rich water sources. In Sitka, Alaska, it made sense for True Alaska Bottling Company to produce glacier-fed bottled water on the grounds of a closed pulp sawmill. And the San Manuel Bottled Water Group bottles Big Bear Premium Spring Water from springs on the reservation of the San Miguel Band of Mission Indians located in the desert outside San Bernardo, California. The business helps diversify the tribe's revenue beyond casino gambling.[1]

The availability and cost of labor are also critical to both manufacturing and service businesses, and the unionization of local labor is another point to consider in many industries. Payroll costs can vary widely from one location to another due to differences in the cost of living, the number of jobs available, and the size, skills, and productivity of the local workforce. In the case of both water-bottling companies, a ready pool of relatively inexpensive labor was available due to high unemployment in the areas.

Marketing Factors Businesses must evaluate how their facility location will affect their ability to serve their customers. For some firms it may not be necessary to be located near customers. Instead, the firm will need to assess the difficulty and costs of distributing its goods to customers from its chosen location. Other firms may find that locating near customers can provide marketing advantages. When a factory or service center is close to customers, the firm can often offer better service at a lower cost. Other firms may gain a competitive advantage by locating their facilities so that customers can easily buy their products or services. The location of competitors may also be a consideration. And businesses with more than one facility may need to consider how far to spread their locations in order to maximize market coverage.

Manufacturing Environment Another factor to consider is the manufacturing environment in a potential location. Some localities have a strong existing manufacturing base. When a large number of manufacturers in a certain industry are already located in an area, that area is likely to offer greater availability of resources, such as manufacturing workers, better accessibility to suppliers and transportation, and other factors that can increase a plant's operating efficiency.

CONCEPT *in Action*

The $253 million incentives package that Vance, Alabama, offered to Mercedes-Benz in the 1990s to build its M-Class assembly plant there is paying huge dividends for the tiny Tuscaloosa County town. In addition to employing thousands of Alabamians at wages twice the state average, Mercedes-Benz sponsors Vance Elementary School, donates SUVs to local services, attracts suppliers to the area, and is sparking a town makeover with new subdivisions and economic development. *What incentives do states and municipalities offer to attract manufacturers to their region?*

Nestlé is proposing to open a fourth bottled water plant at the foot of Mount Shasta, California, where three other companies have located plants in the past few years. The plants have provided much needed employment to replace logging jobs that are disappearing due to increased restrictions on cutting trees in the surrounding national forests.[2]

Local Incentives Incentives offered by countries, states, or cities may also influence site selection. Tax breaks are a common incentive. A locality may reduce the amount of taxes a firm must pay on income, real estate, utilities, or payroll. Local governments may offer financial assistance and/or exemption from certain regulations to attract or keep production facilities in their area. For example, several companies have relocated to Manatee County, Florida, to receive its Qualified Target Industry Tax Refund. Gammerler Corp., a German company that makes finishing equipment for commercial printers and newspapers, moved its North American headquarters to Palmetto, Florida, from Chicago. By adding new manufacturing jobs that pay at least 115 percent more than the current average to the county's economic base, Gammerler will achieve tax savings of $280,000 a year.[3]

International Location Considerations There are often sound financial reasons for considering a foreign location. Labor costs are considerably lower in countries like Singapore, China, India, and Mexico. Foreign countries may also have fewer regulations governing how factories operate. A foreign location may also move production closer to new markets. As we learned in Chapter 1, automobile manufacturers such as Toyota, BMW, and Hyundai are among many that build plants in the United States to reduce shipping costs.

Designing the Facility

After the site location decision has been made, the next focus in production planning is the facility's layout. The goal is to determine the most efficient and effective design for the particular production process. A manufacturer might opt for a U-shaped production line, for example, rather than a long, straight one, to allow products and workers to move more quickly from one area to another.

Service organizations must also consider layout, but they are more concerned with how it affects customer behavior. It may be more convenient for a hospital to place its freight elevators in the center of the building, for example, but doing so may block the flow of patients, visitors, and medical personnel between floors and departments.

There are three main types of facility layouts: process, product, and fixed-position. All three layouts are illustrated in Exhibit 11.4 on the next page. Cellular manufacturing is another type of facility layout.

process layout
A facility arrangement in which work flows according to the production process. All workers performing similar tasks are grouped together, and products pass from one workstation to another.

Process Layout: All Welders Stand Here The process layout arranges workflow around the production process. All workers performing similar tasks are grouped together. Products pass from one workstation to another (but not necessarily to every workstation). For example, all grinding would be done in one area, all assembling in another, and all inspection in yet another. The process layout is best for firms that produce small numbers of a wide variety of products, typically using general-purpose machines that can be changed rapidly to new operations for different product designs. For example, a manufacturer of custom machinery would use a process layout.

product (or assembly-line) layout
A facility arrangement in which workstations or departments are arranged in a line with products moving along the line.

Product Layout: Moving Down the Line Products that require a continuous or repetitive production process use the **product (or assembly-line) layout**. When large quantities of a product must be processed on an ongoing basis, the workstations or departments are arranged in a line with products moving along the line. Automobile and appliance manufacturers, as well as food-processing plants, usually use a product layout. Service companies may also use a product layout for routine processing operations. For example, overnight film processors use assembly-line techniques.

fixed-position layout
A facility arrangement in which the product stays in one place and workers and machinery move to it as needed.

Fixed-Position Layout: Staying Put Some products cannot be put on an assembly line or moved about in a plant. A **fixed-position layout** lets the product stay in one place while workers and machinery move to it as needed. Products that are impossible to move—ships, airplanes, and construction projects—are typically produced using a fixed-position layout. Limited space at the project site often means that parts of the product must be assembled at other sites, transported to the fixed site, and then assembled. The fixed-position layout is also common for on-site services like housecleaning services, pest control, and landscaping.

cellular manufacturing
Production technique that uses small, self-contained production units, each performing all or most of the tasks necessary to complete a manufacturing order.

Cellular Manufacturing: A Start-to-Finish Focus **Cellular manufacturing** combines some aspects of both product and fixed-position layout. Work cells are small, self-contained production units that include several machines and workers arranged in a compact, sequential order. Each work cell performs all or most of the tasks necessary to complete a manufacturing order. There are usually five to ten workers in a cell, and they are trained to be able to do any of the steps in the production process. The goal is to create a team environment wherein team members are involved in production from beginning to end.

Pulling It Together: Resource Planning

4 Why are resource-planning tasks like inventory management and supplier relations critical to production?

As part of the production-planning process, firms must ensure that the resources needed for production—such as raw materials, parts, equipment, and labor—will be available at strategic moments in the production process. This can be a huge challenge. The components used to build just one Boeing airplane, for instance, number in the millions. Cost is also an important factor. In many industries, the cost of materials and supplies used in the production process amounts to as much as half of sales revenues. Resource planning is therefore a big part of any firm's production strategy.

bill of material
A list of the items and the number of each required to make a given product.

purchasing
The process of buying production inputs from various sources; also called procurement.

Resource planning begins by specifying which raw materials, parts, and components will be required, and when, to produce finished goods. To determine the amount of each item needed, the expected quantity of finished goods must be forecast. A **bill of material** is then drawn up that lists the items and the number of each required to make the product. **Purchasing**, or *procurement*, is the process of buying production inputs from various sources.

Exhibit 11.4 > Facility Layouts

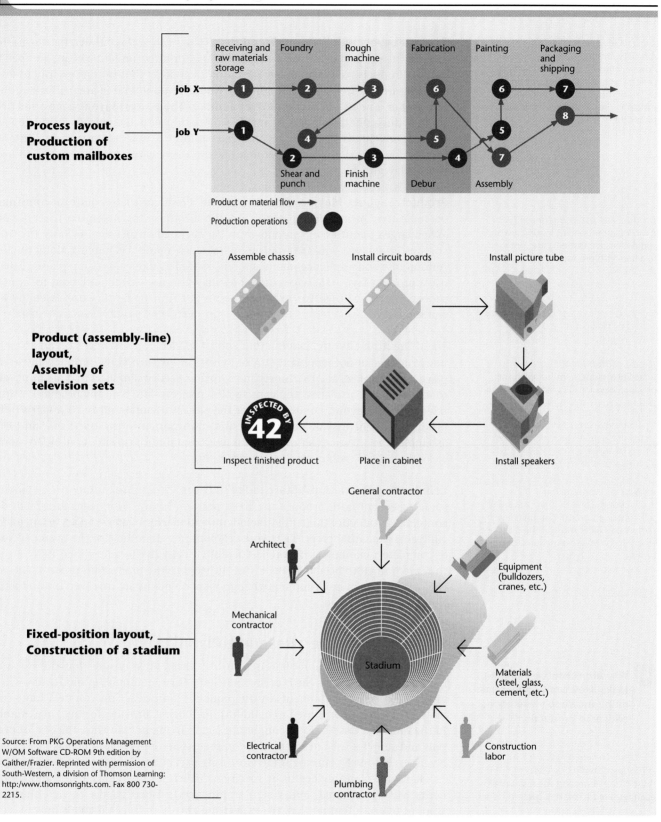

Process layout, Production of custom mailboxes

Receiving and raw materials storage

Foundry

Rough machine

Fabrication

Painting

Packaging and shipping

job X

job Y

Shear and punch

Finish machine

Debur

Assembly

Product or material flow →

Production operations

Product (assembly-line) layout, Assembly of television sets

Assemble chassis

Install circuit boards

Install picture tube

Inspect finished product

Place in cabinet

Install speakers

INSPECTED BY 42

Fixed-position layout, Construction of a stadium

General contractor

Architect

Equipment (bulldozers, cranes, etc.)

Mechanical contractor

Stadium

Materials (steel, glass, cement, etc.)

Electrical contractor

Construction labor

Plumbing contractor

Source: From PKG Operations Management W/OM Software CD-ROM 9th edition by Gaither/Frazier. Reprinted with permission of South-Western, a division of Thomson Learning: http://www.thomsonrights.com. Fax 800 730-2215.

make-or-buy decision
The determination by a firm of whether to make its own production materials or to buy them from outside sources.

outsourcing
The purchase of items from an outside source rather than making them internally.

inventory
The supply of goods that a firm holds for use in production or for sale to customers.

inventory management
The determination of how much of each type of inventory a firm will keep on hand and the ordering, receiving, storing, and tracking of inventory.

Make or Buy? The firm must decide whether to make its own production materials or buy them from outside sources. This is the **make-or-buy decision**. The quantity of items needed is one consideration. If a part is used in only one of many products, buying the part may be more cost-effective than making it. Buying standard items, such as screws, bolts, rivets, and nails, is usually cheaper and easier than producing them internally. Purchasing larger components from another manufacturer can be cost-effective as well. When items are purchased from an outside source instead of being made internally, it is called **outsourcing**. Harley-Davidson, for example, purchases its tires, brake systems, and other motorcycle components from manufacturers that make them to Harley's specifications. However, if a product has special design features that need to be kept secret to protect a competitive advantage, a firm may decide to produce all parts internally.

In deciding whether to make or buy, a firm must also consider whether outside sources can provide the high-quality supplies it needs in a reliable manner. Having to shut down production because vital parts aren't delivered on time can be a costly disaster. Just as bad are inferior parts or materials, which can damage a firm's reputation for producing high-quality goods. Therefore, firms that buy some or all of their production materials from outside sources should make building strong relationships with quality suppliers a priority.

Inventory Management: Not Just Parts A firm's **inventory** is the supply of goods it holds for use in production or for sale to customers. Deciding how much inventory to keep on hand is one of the biggest challenges facing operations managers. On the one hand, with large inventories, the firm can meet most production and customer demands. Buying in large quantities can also allow a company to take advantage of quantity discounts. On the other hand, large inventories can tie up the firm's money, are expensive to store, and can become obsolete.

Inventory management involves deciding how much of each type of inventory to keep on hand and the ordering, receiving, storing, and tracking of it. The goal of inventory management is to keep down the costs of ordering and holding inventories while maintaining enough on hand for production and sales. Good inventory management enhances product quality, makes operations more efficient, and increases profits. Poor inventory management can result in dissatisfied customers, financial difficulties, and even bankruptcy.

One way to determine the best inventory levels is to look at three costs: holding inventory, frequent reordering, and not keeping enough inventory on hand. Managers must measure all three costs and try to minimize them.

CONCEPT *in Action*

Wal-Mart's retail dominance is built upon advanced logistics and inventory management. The company's vendor-managed inventory system puts the burden on suppliers to maintain stock until needed in stores and radio frequency identification tags (RFID) help automate the flow of goods. Wal-Mart's remarkable 2:1 sales-to-inventory ratio is expected to shrink further to a theoretical "zero inventory" state in which it won't pay for products until they're purchased by consumers. *What costs are associated with keeping too much or too little inventory?*

© DAVID MCNEW/GETTY IMAGES

perpetual inventory
A continuously updated list of inventory levels, orders, sales, and receipts.

materials requirement planning (MRP)
A computerized system of controlling the flow of resources and inventory. A master schedule is used to ensure that the materials, labor, and equipment needed for production are at the right places in the right amounts at the right times.

manufacturing resource planning II (MRPII)
A complex computerized system that integrates data from many departments to allow managers to more accurately forecast and assess the impact of production plans on profitability.

enterprise resource planning (ERP)
A computerized resource-planning system that incorporates information about the firm's suppliers and customers with its internally generated data.

To control inventory levels, managers often track the use of certain inventory items. Most companies keep a **perpetual inventory**, a continuously updated list of inventory levels, orders, sales, and receipts, for all major items. Today, companies mostly use computers to track inventory levels, calculate order quantities, and issue purchase orders at the right times.

Computerized Resource Planning Many manufacturing companies have adopted computerized systems to control the flow of resources and inventory. **Materials requirement planning (MRP)** is one such system. MRP uses a master schedule to ensure that the materials, labor, and equipment needed for production are at the right places in the right amounts at the right times. The schedule is based on forecasts of demand for the company's products. It says exactly what will be manufactured during the next few weeks or months and when the work will take place. Sophisticated computer programs coordinate all the elements of MRP. The computer comes up with materials requirements by comparing production needs to the materials the company already has on hand. Orders are placed so items will be on hand when they are needed for production. MRP helps ensure a smooth flow of finished products.

Manufacturing resource planning II (MRPII) was developed in the late 1980s to expand on MRP. It uses a complex computerized system to integrate data from many departments, including finance, marketing, accounting, engineering, and manufacturing. MRPII can generate a production plan for the firm, as well as management reports, forecasts, and financial statements. The system lets managers make more accurate forecasts and assess the impact of production plans on profitability. If one department's plans change, the effects of these changes on other departments are transmitted throughout the company.

Whereas MRP and MRPII systems are focused internally, **enterprise resource planning (ERP)** systems go a step further and incorporate information about the firm's suppliers and customers into the flow of data. ERP unites all of a firm's major departments into a single software program. For instance, production can call up sales information and know immediately how many units must be produced to meet customer orders. By providing information about the availability of resources, including both the human resources and materials needed for production, the system allows for better cost control and eliminates production delays. The system automatically notes any changes, such as the closure of a plant for maintenance and repairs on a certain date or a supplier's inability to meet a delivery date, so that all functions adjust accordingly. Both large and small organizations use ERP to improve operations.

Keeping the Goods Flowing: Supply Chain Management

In the past, the relationship between purchasers and suppliers was often competitive and antagonistic. Businesses used many suppliers and switched among them frequently. During contract negotiations, each side would try to get better terms at the expense of the other. Communication between purchasers and suppliers was often limited to purchase orders and billing statements.

Today, however, many firms are moving toward a new concept in supplier relationships. The emphasis is increasingly on developing a strong **supply chain**. The supply chain can be thought of as the entire sequence of securing inputs, producing goods, and delivering goods to customers. If any links in this process are weak, chances are customers—the end point of the supply chain—will end up dissatisfied.

CONCEPT *in Action*

Manufacturing product labels for over 9,000 Estée Lauder cosmetics products would be impossible without enterprise resource planning (ERP). A daily data feed between ERP systems at Estée Lauder and label-supplier Topflight ensures that machines produce only the labels necessary for the next production run. The data-transfer link is flexible enough to accommodate dynamic design changes to colors and label copy while eliminating purchase orders, invoices, and price negotiations. *What quality and cost benefits does ERP deliver to manufacturers and their customers?*

© TERRI MILLER/E-VISUAL COMMUNICATIONS, INC.

Effective supply chain strategies reduce costs. For example, integration of the shipper and customer's supply chains allows companies to automate more processes and save time. Technology also improves supply chain efficiency by tracking goods through the various supply chain stages and also helping with logistics. With better information about production and inventory, companies can order and receive goods at the optimal point to keep inventory holding costs low.

Companies also need contingency plans for supply chain disruptions. Is there an alternative source of supply if a blizzard closes the airport so that cargo planes can't land or a drought causes crop failures in the Midwest? By thinking ahead, companies can avert major losses. The length and distance involved in a supply line is also a consideration. Importing parts from or outsourcing manufacturing to Asia creates a long supply chain for a manufacturer in Europe or the United States. Perhaps there are closer suppliers or manufacturers who can meet a company's needs at a lower overall cost. Companies should also reevaluate outsourcing decisions periodically.

Strategies for Supply Chain Management

Ensuring a strong supply chain requires that firms implement supply chain management strategies. **Supply chain management** focuses on smoothing transitions along the supply chain, with the ultimate goal of satisfying customers with quality products and services. A critical element of effective supply chain management is to develop tight bonds with suppliers. This may mean reducing the number of suppliers used and asking them to offer more services or better prices in return for an ongoing relationship.

Ford Motor Company plans to pare the number of its suppliers to give larger, longer-term contracts to a strategically selected group, providing the company with access to new technology and supplier expertise. Ford will involve its suppliers in the early stages of vehicle design, giving them money up front for engineering and development. And longer contracts mean suppliers can invest more and not worry that Ford will takes its business elsewhere. "I think we'll put ourselves in a much better position to be successful than the position we're in today," said Tony Brown, Ford's senior vice president for global purchasing.[4]

Instead of being viewed as "outsiders" in the production process, many suppliers play an important role in supporting the operations of their customers. They are expected to meet high quality standards, offer suggestions that can help reduce production costs, and even contribute to the design of new products. The Expanding

supply chain
The entire sequence of securing inputs, producing goods, and delivering goods to customers.

supply chain management
The process of smoothing transitions along the supply chain so that the firm can satisfy its customers with quality products and services; focuses on developing tight bonds with suppliers.

CONCEPT *in Action*

Managing an efficient supply chain is critical for businesses, especially when the product being delivered is a bouquet of fresh-cut flowers. To ensure that only the freshest, most colorful floral arrangement arrives for that special someone, Internet florist ProFlowers ships directly from the flower fields, bypassing the middleman. This direct-from-the-grower strategy, combined with coordinated carrier scheduling and a 100 percent product-inspection policy, enables ProFlowers to deliver flowers twice as fresh as the competition. *What strategies help businesses create and maintain an effective supply chain?*

Sophisticated Supply-Chain Strategies Keep Products on the Move

Headquartered in Tokyo but with offices around the world, shipping company MOL is taking integrating with its customers to new levels. It is joining its customers in a series of joint ventures to build and operate dedicated vessels for as long as 25 years. One such joint venture teamed MOL with a Chinese steel mill, to build and sail ships bringing Brazilian iron ore and coal across the Pacific Ocean for processing.

Sophisticated supply-chain systems that control every aspect of production and transportation are the key to making offshore manufacturing work. Supply-chain software that monitors operations and continually makes adjustments ensures that all processes are running at peak efficiency. By tightly mapping an entire sequence—from order to final delivery—and by automating it as much as possible, supply-chain management can deliver products from across the world while at the same time cutting costs. Companies that can carry a small inventory and get paid faster improve their cash flow and profitability.

Acer, a $7 billion Taiwanese computer and electronics maker, brings components from around the world and assembles them at factories in Taiwan and mainland China—into everything from PC notebooks to TVs. It then reverses the flow by shipping these products to international buyers. "In 2004 Acer sold 4 million portable systems. Without a solid supply-chain infrastructure behind us we couldn't hope to do it," says Sumit Agnihotry, Acer's American director of notebook product marketing.

The synchronizing of trade is essential. If goods don't get into the stores in time, sales might be lost or the company might have to carry larger inventories to avoid sell-outs, which would cut into its profits.

Companies need to continually monitor demand and react quickly by adjusting production. "This gets increasingly difficult when the supply chain stretches across thousands of miles and a dozen time zones," says David Bovet, managing director of Mercer Management Consulting, a Boston-based firm that advises on business tactics. "There are strategies that smart companies are using to bring costs down to earth. Getting the most of lower labor costs overseas requires an emphasis on transportation, and supply-chain skills are a required core competency," he says. His advice to global manufacturers: Cooperate with shippers and integrate supply chains into one cohesive system.

The acknowledged master of supply-chain dynamics is Dell, with its global logistics control room lined with big screens that monitor its shipping lanes at all times. Alongside Dell executives are representatives of its logistics suppliers for guidance and quick action if anything goes wrong.

Risk is the name of the game when it comes to international trade, and companies need to decide whether to play it safe with extra inventory or scramble if a disaster like a port strike occurs. Either way, they need to have contingency plans and be ready to react, and solid supply-chain strategies will ensure they are prepared for any eventuality.[5]

Critical Thinking Questions
- Why are solid supply-chain strategies so important?
- What problems is a company likely to experience without such strategies in place?

Around the Globe box shows the critical role of supply-chain management for global companies.

Talk to Us: Improving Supplier Communications Effective supply chain management depends on strong communications with suppliers. Technology, particularly the Internet, is providing new ways to do this. **E-procurement**, the process of purchasing supplies and materials online, is booming. Some manufacturing firms use the Internet to keep key suppliers informed about their requirements. Intel, for example, has set up a special Web site for its suppliers and potential suppliers. Would-be suppliers can visit the site to get information about doing business with Intel; once they are approved, they can access a secure area to make bids on Intel's current and future resource needs.

The Internet also streamlines purchasing by providing firms with quick access to a huge database of information about the products and services of hundreds of potential suppliers. Many large companies now participate in *reverse auctions* online, which can slash procurement costs. In a reverse auction, the manufacturer posts its specifications for the materials it requires. Potential suppliers then bid against each other to get the job. However, there are risks with reverse auctions. It can be difficult to establish and build ongoing relationships with specific suppliers using reverse auctions because the job ultimately goes to the lowest bidder. Therefore, reverse auctions may not be an effective procurement process for critical production materials. Other types of corporations can use these auctions as well. UMB Bank, headquartered in Kansas City, Missouri, began in 2002 to use this strategy for a variety of products, from paper to computers. Costs dropped by 15 percent to 50 percent, depending on the item. Only prequalified vendors are allowed to bid. "It isn't exclusively about lowest price," says the bank's chairman and CEO Peter deSilva. "We look for service after the sale. We look at shipping costs. We look at maintenance costs."[6]

Another communications tool is **electronic data interchange (EDI)**, in which two trading partners exchange information electronically. EDI can be conducted via

e-procurement
The process of purchasing supplies and materials online using the Internet.

electronic data interchange (EDI)
The electronic exchange of information between two trading partners.

a linked computer system or over the Internet. The advantages of exchanging information with suppliers electronically include speed, accuracy, and lowered communication costs. EDI plays a critical role in Ford Motor Company's efforts to produce and distribute vehicles worldwide. Ford and its major North American logistics partner, Penske Logistics, rely on EDI transmissions from its auto carriers for status updates as they strive to meet strict delivery schedules.[7]

Production and Operations Control

 5 How do operations managers schedule and control production?

Every company needs to have systems in place to see that production and operations are carried out as planned and to correct errors when they are not. The coordination of materials, equipment, and human resources to achieve production and operating efficiencies is called *production control*. Two of its key aspects are routing and scheduling.

Routing: Where to Next?

routing
The aspect of production control that involves setting out the work flow—the sequence of machines and operations through which the product or service progresses from start to finish.

Routing is the first step in production control. It sets out a work flow, the sequence of machines and operations through which a product or service progresses from start to finish. Routing depends on the type of goods being produced and the facility layout. Good routing procedures increase productivity and cut unnecessary costs.

value-stream mapping
Routing technique that uses simple icons to visually represent the flow of materials and information from suppliers through the factory to customers.

One useful tool for routing is **value-stream mapping**, whereby production managers "map" the flow from suppliers through the factory to customers. Simple icons represent the materials and information needed at various points in the flow. Value-stream mapping can help identify where bottlenecks may occur in the production process and is a valuable tool for visualizing how to improve production routing.

Electronics manufacturer Rockwell Collins used value-stream mapping to automate more of its purchasing operations. The company evaluated 23 areas to identify where process changes would improve efficiency. Based on the study, managers decided to automate three steps: request for quote, quote receipt and total purchase cost, and automated purchase order. The company implemented a new system that automatically sends requests for quotes to appropriate suppliers and evaluates the responses to determine which best meets Rockwell Collins' requirements. Once in place, the new systems allowed purchasing professionals to focus on strategic rather than routine activities.[8]

Scheduling: When Do We Do It?

scheduling
The aspect of production control that involves specifying and controlling the time required for each step in the production process.

Closely related to routing is **scheduling**. Scheduling involves specifying and controlling the time required for each step in the production process. The operations manager prepares timetables showing the most efficient sequence of production and then tries to ensure that the necessary materials and labor are in the right place at the right time.

Scheduling is important to both manufacturing and service firms. The production manager in a factory schedules material deliveries, work shifts, and production processes. Trucking companies schedule drivers, clerks, truck maintenance, and repairs in accordance with customer transportation needs. Scheduling at a college entails deciding when to offer which courses, in which classrooms, with which instructors. A museum must schedule special exhibits, ship works to be displayed, market its offerings, and conduct educational programs and tours. Scheduling can range from simple to complex. Giving numbers to customers waiting to be served in a bakery and making interview appointments with job applicants are examples of simple scheduling. Organizations that must produce large quantities of products or services, or service a diverse customer base, face more complex scheduling problems.

Three common scheduling tools used for complex situations are Gantt charts, the critical path method, and PERT.

Gantt charts
Bar graphs plotted on a time line that show the relationship between scheduled and actual production.

Tracking Progress with Gantt Charts Named after their originator, Henry Gantt, Gantt charts are bar graphs plotted on a time line that show the relationship between scheduled and actual production.

In the example shown in Exhibit 11.5, the left side of the chart lists the activities required to complete the job or project. Both the scheduled time and the actual time required for each activity are shown, so the manager can easily judge progress.

Gantt charts are most helpful when only a few tasks are involved, when task times are relatively long (days or weeks rather than hours), and when job routes are short and simple. One of the biggest shortcomings of Gantt charts is that they are static. They also fail to show how tasks are related. These problems can be solved, however, by using two other scheduling techniques, the critical path method and PERT.

The Big Picture: Critical Path Method and PERT To control large projects, operations managers need to closely monitor resources, costs, quality, and budgets. They also must be able to see the "big picture"—the interrelationships of the many different tasks necessary to complete the project. Finally, they must be able to revise scheduling and divert resources quickly if any tasks fall behind schedule. The critical path method (CPM) and the program evaluation and review technique (PERT) are related project management tools that were developed in the 1950s to help managers accomplish this.

critical path method (CPM)
A scheduling tool that enables a manager to determine the critical path of activities for a project—the activities that will cause the entire project to fall behind schedule if they are not completed on time.

critical path
In a critical path method network, the longest path through the linked activities.

In the critical path method (CPM), the manager identifies all of the activities required to complete the project, the relationships between these activities, and the order in which they need to be completed. Then, the manager develops a diagram that uses arrows to show how the tasks are dependent on each other. The longest path through these linked activities is called the critical path. If the tasks on the critical path are not completed on time, the entire project will fall behind schedule.

To better understand how CPM works, look at Exhibit 11.6, which shows a CPM diagram for constructing a house. All of the tasks required to finish the house and an estimated time for each have been identified. The arrows indicate the links between the various steps and their required sequence. As you can see, most of the jobs to be done can't be started until the house's foundation and frame are completed. It will

Exhibit 11.5 > A Typical Gantt Chart

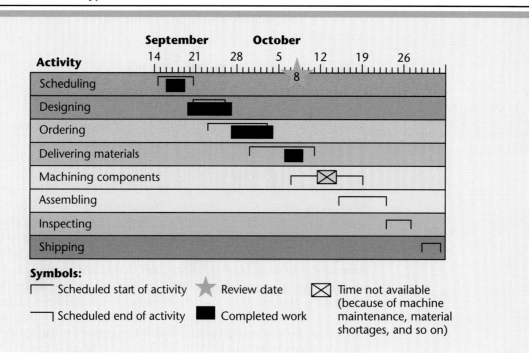

Symbols:
- ⌐ Scheduled start of activity
- ⌐⌐ Scheduled end of activity
- ★ Review date
- ■ Completed work
- ⊠ Time not available (because of machine maintenance, material shortages, and so on)

Exhibit 11.6 > A CPM Network for Building a House

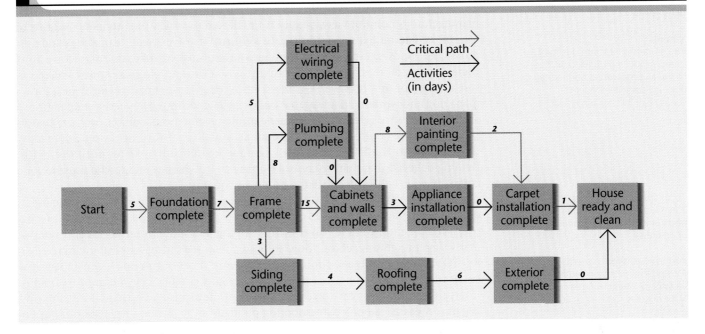

program evaluation and review technique (PERT)
A scheduling tool that is similar to the CPM method but assigns three time estimates for each activity (optimistic, most probable, and pessimistic); allows managers to anticipate delays and potential problems and schedule accordingly.

take five days to finish the foundation and another seven days to erect the house frame. The activities linked by brown arrows form the critical path for this project. It tells us that the fastest possible time the house can be built is 38 days, the total time needed for all of the critical path tasks. The noncritical path jobs, those connected with black arrows, can be delayed a bit or done early. Short delays in installing appliances or roofing won't delay construction of the house because these activities don't lie on the critical path.

Like CPM, **program evaluation and review technique (PERT)** helps managers identify critical tasks and assess how delays in certain activities will affect operations or production. In both methods, managers use diagrams to see how operations and production will flow. PERT differs from CPM in one important respect. CPM assumes that the amount of time needed to finish a task is known with certainty; therefore, the CPM diagram shows only one number for the time needed to complete each activity. In contrast, PERT assigns three time estimates for each activity: an optimistic time for completion, the most probable time, and a pessimistic time. These estimates allow managers to anticipate delays and potential problems and schedule accordingly.

concept check

What is production control, and what are its key aspects?

How can value-stream mapping improve routing efficiency?

Identify and describe three commonly used scheduling tools.

Looking for a Better Way: Improving Production and Operations

6 How can quality management and lean-manufacturing techniques help firms improve production and operations management?

Competing in today's business world is challenging. To compete effectively, firms must keep production costs down. At the same time, however, it's becoming increasingly complex to produce and deliver the high-quality goods and services customers demand. Methods to help meet these challenges include quality management techniques, lean manufacturing, and technology and automation.

Putting Quality First

Successful businesses recognize that quality and productivity must go hand in hand. Quality goods and services meet customer expectations by providing reliable

quality
Goods and services that meet customer expectations by providing reliable performance.

quality control
The process of creating quality standards, producing goods that meet them, and measuring finished goods and services against them.

Total Quality Management (TQM)
The use of quality principles in all aspects of a company's production and operations.

continuous improvement
A commitment to constantly seek better ways of doing things in order to achieve greater efficiency and improve quality.

Six Sigma
A quality control process that relies on defining what needs to be done to ensure quality, measuring and analyzing production results statistically, and finding ways to improve and control quality.

Malcolm Baldrige National Quality Award
An award given to recognize U.S. companies that offer goods and services of world-class quality; established by Congress in 1987 and named for a former secretary of commerce.

performance. Defective products waste materials and time, increasing costs. Worse, poor quality causes customer dissatisfaction, which usually results in lost sales.

A consumer measures quality by how well a product serves its purpose. From the manufacturer's point of view, quality is the degree to which the product conforms to a set of predetermined standards. **Quality control** involves creating quality standards, producing goods that meet them, and measuring finished goods and services against them. It takes more than just inspecting goods at the end of the assembly line to ensure quality control, however. Quality control requires a company-wide dedication to managing and working in a way that builds excellence into every facet of operations.

Dr. W. Edwards Deming, an American management consultant, was the first to say that quality control should be a company-wide goal. His ideas were adopted by the Japanese in the 1950s but largely ignored in the United States until the 1970s. Deming believed that quality control starts with top management, who must foster a company-wide culture dedicated to producing quality.

Deming's concept of **Total Quality Management (TQM)** emphasizes the use of quality principles in all aspects of a company's production and operations. It recognizes that all employees involved with bringing a product or service to customers—marketing, purchasing, accounting, shipping, manufacturing—contribute to its quality. TQM focuses on **continuous improvement**, a commitment to constantly seek better ways of doing things in order to achieve greater efficiency and improve quality. Company-wide teams work together to prevent problems and systematically improve key processes instead of troubleshooting problems only as they arise. Continuous improvement continually measures performance using statistical techniques and looks for ways to apply new technologies and innovative production methods.

Another quality control method is the Six Sigma quality program. Six Sigma is a company-wide process that focuses on measuring the number of defects that occur and systematically eliminating them in order to get as close to "zero defects" as possible. In fact, Six Sigma quality aims to have every process produce no more than 3.4 defects per million. Six Sigma focuses on designing products that not only have fewer defects but that also satisfy customer needs. A key process of Six Sigma is called *DMAIC*. This stands for Define, Measure, Analyze, Improve, and Control. Employees at all levels define what needs to be done to ensure quality, then measure and analyze production results using statistics to see if standards are met. They are also charged with finding ways to improve and control quality.

General Electric was one of the first companies to institute Six Sigma throughout the organization. All GE employees are trained in Six Sigma concepts, and many analysts believe this has given GE a competitive manufacturing advantage. Service firms and government entities have applied Six Sigma to their quality initiatives as well.

Malcolm Baldrige National Quality Award Named for a former secretary of commerce, the **Malcolm Baldrige National Quality Award** was established by the U.S. Congress in 1987 to recognize U.S. companies that offer goods and services of world-class quality. The award promotes awareness of quality and allows the business community to assess which quality control programs are most effective.

Administered by the U.S. Department of Commerce's National Institute of Standards and Technologies (NIST), the award's most important criterion is a firm's effectiveness at meeting customer expectations, as well as demonstrating that it offers quality goods and services. To qualify for the award, a company must also show continuous improvement in internal operations. Company leaders and employees must be active participants in the firm's quality program and they must respond quickly to data and analysis.

Organizations in a wide variety of industries have won the Baldrige Award since it was first presented in 1987. In 2005, for example, the Baldrige Award winners were Sunny Fresh Foods, Inc., a Monticello, Minnesota, food company (manufacturing); DynMcDermott Petroleum Operations, New Orleans, Louisiana (service); Park Place Lexus, Plano, Texas (small business); Richland College, Dallas, Texas, (education); Jenks

Public Schools, Jenks, Oklahoma (education); and Bronson Methodist Hospital, Kalamazoo, Michigan (health care). This was the first year that winners included an automotive dealership, an oil industry business, and a community college. [9]

Worldwide Excellence: International Quality Standards The International Organization for Standardization (ISO), located in Belgium, is an industry organization that has developed standards of quality that are used by businesses around the world. ISO 9000, introduced in the 1980s, is a set of five technical standards designed to offer a uniform way of determining whether manufacturing plants and service organizations conform to sound quality procedures. To register, a company must go through an audit of its manufacturing and customer service processes, covering everything from how it designs, produces, and installs its products, to how it inspects, packages, and markets them. Over 500,000 organizations worldwide have met ISO 9000 standards.

ISO 14000, launched after ISO 9000, was designed in response to environmental issues like global warming and water pollution, and promotes clean production processes. To meet ISO 14000 standards, a company must commit to continually improving environmental management and reducing pollution resulting from its production processes.

Lean Manufacturing Trims the Fat

Manufacturers are discovering that they can better respond to rapidly changing customer demands, while keeping inventory and production costs down, by adopting lean-manufacturing techniques. **Lean manufacturing** streamlines production by eliminating steps in the production process that do not add benefits customers want. In other words, *non-value-added production processes* are cut so that the company can concentrate its production and operations resources on items essential to satisfying customers. Toyota was a pioneer in developing these techniques, but today manufacturers in many industries have adopted the lean-manufacturing philosophy.

Another Japanese concept, **just-in-time (JIT)**, goes hand in hand with lean manufacturing. JIT is based on the belief that materials should arrive exactly when they are needed for production, rather than being stored on site. Relying closely on computerized systems such as MRP, MRPII, and ERP, manufacturers determine what parts will be needed and when, and then order them from suppliers so they arrive "just in time." Under the JIT system, inventory and products are "pulled" through the production process in response to customer demand. JIT requires close teamwork between

ISO 9000
A set of five technical standards of quality management created by the International Organization for Standardization to provide a uniform way of determining whether manufacturing plants and service organizations conform to sound quality procedures.

ISO 14000
A set of technical standards designed by the International Organization for Standardization to promote clean production processes to protect the environment.

lean manufacturing
Streamlining production by eliminating steps in the production process that do not add benefits that customers want.

just-in-time (JIT)
A system in which materials arrive exactly when they are needed for production, rather than being stored on site.

CONCEPT *in Action*

The Hummer H2 plant in Mishawaka, Indiana, is a lean, mean manufacturing machine. Since time is of the essence in the production process, Hummer's AM General assembly plant employs a wireless monitoring system that streamlines parts replenishment and vehicle tracking throughout the 673,000 square-foot facility. When part supplies are low, team members at hundreds of stations along the assembly line may simply push a button and the precise parts and quantities are replenished in minutes. *How do lean manufacturing practices save automakers time and money?*

vendors and purchasing and production personnel because any delays in deliveries of supplies could bring JIT production to a halt.

Unexpected events like the September 11 terrorist attacks or the shutdown of ports due to Hurricane Katrina can cause chaos in the supply chains of manufacturers, resulting in problems for firms relying on JIT. But if employed properly, and in spite of these risks, a JIT system can greatly reduce inventory-holding costs and smooth production highs and lows.

Transforming the Factory Floor with Technology

Technology is helping many firms improve their operating efficiency and ability to compete. Computer systems in particular are enabling manufacturers to automate factories in ways never before possible. Among the technologies helping to automate manufacturing are computer-aided design and manufacturing systems, robotics, flexible manufacturing systems, and computer-integrated manufacturing.

Computer-Aided Design and Manufacturing Systems Computers have transformed the design and manufacturing processes in many industries. In **computer-aided design** **(CAD)**, computers are used to design and test new products and modify existing ones. Engineers use these systems to draw products and look at them from different angles. They can analyze the products, make changes, and test prototypes before manufacturing a single item. **Computer-aided manufacturing (CAM)** uses computers to develop and control the production process. These systems analyze the steps required to make the product, then automatically send instructions to the machines that do the work. **CAD/CAM systems** combine the advantages of CAD and CAM by integrating design, testing, and manufacturing control into one linked computer system. The system helps design the product, control the flow of resources needed to produce the product, and operate the production process.

Cardianove Inc., a Montreal-based manufacturer of medical and surgical equipment, used CAD software to develop the world's smallest heart pump. The company says using computer-aided design shaved two years off the normal design time for cardiac devices. The company's CAD program ran complex three-dimensional simulations to confirm that the design would function properly inside the human body. Using CAD software, Cardianove tested over 100 virtual prototypes before the top three designs were produced for real-life testing.

CONCEPT *in Action*

When commercial-mower specialist Ferris—maker of Ferris, Simplicity, and Snapper zero-turn-radius lawn mowers—needed a more flexible assembly process, production planners installed an in-floor towline conveyor system, which cut lawnmower assembly time in half. The conveyor carries parts down the line in an index-and-dwell pattern, allowing temporary workstation stops and four-way access to the product. Ergonomic fixtures rotate the mowers to proper assembly angles, relieving workers of stressful bending and stretching. *What new technologies are transforming manufacturing?*

PHOTO COURTESY OF FERRIS INDUSTRIES – MUNNSVILLE OPERATION

robotics
The technology involved in designing, constructing, and operating computer-controlled machines that can perform tasks independently.

Robotics *Robots* are computer-controlled machines that can perform independently. **Robotics** is the technology involved in designing, constructing, and operating robots. The first robot, or "steel-collar worker," was used by General Motors in 1961. Robots can be mobile or fixed in one place. Fixed robots have an arm that moves and does what the computer instructs. Some robots are quite simple, with limited movement for a few tasks such as cutting sheet metal and spot welding. Others are complex, with hands or grippers that can be programmed to perform a series of movements. Some robots are even equipped with sensing devices for sight and touch.

Robots usually operate with little or no human intervention. Replacing human effort with robots is most effective for tasks requiring accuracy, speed, or strength. Although manufacturers like Harley-Davidson are most likely to use robots, some service firms are also finding them useful. Hospitals, for example, may use robots to sort and process blood samples, freeing medical personnel from a tedious, sometimes hazardous, repetitive task. The Customer Satisfaction and Quality box describes other ways automation leads to better health care.

Adaptable Factories: Flexible and Computer Integrated Manufacturing Systems
A **flexible manufacturing system (FMS)** automates a factory by blending computers, robots, machine tools, and materials-and-parts-handling machinery into an integrated system. These systems combine automated workstations with computer-controlled transportation devices. Automatic guided vehicles (AGVs) move materials between workstations and into and out of the system.

flexible manufacturing system (FMS)
A system that combines automated workstations with computer-controlled transportation devices—automatic guided vehicles (AGVs)—that move materials between workstations and into and out of the system.

CUSTOMER SATISFACTION AND QUALITY

Can Technology Save Your Life?

Using robots to perform surgery once seemed like a futuristic fantasy, but not anymore. An estimated 36,600 robotic procedures were performed in 2005—from heart by-pass surgeries to kidney transplants—an increase of nearly 50 percent over 2004, and analysts predict this number will double in 2006 to more than 70,000 procedures.

So what accounts for the surge in robotic surgeries? Some preliminary studies suggest improved outcomes for patients. Surgeons who use the da Vinci robotic system find that patients have less blood loss and pain, lower risks of complications, shorter hospital stays, and quicker recovery times than those who have open surgery—or even, in some cases, laparoscopic procedures which are also performed through multiple small incisions.

In October 2005, Dr. Francis Sutter, chief of cardiology at the Heart Center at Lankenau Hospital near Philadelphia, did the first da Vinci double bypass. His patient, a 65-year-old man, had just a single two-inch incision on the left side of his chest and was walking 30 minutes a day just a week and a half after surgery. Tests show his heart function to be normal again.

So what are the downsides? At a price of $1.3 million each, the cost of the robots can be a barrier. Because insurance companies pay a fixed amount for a procedure regardless of how it is performed, the hospital is left to pick up the tab for the more expensive robotic surgeries. Sutter's center held fundraisers to help pay for the da Vinci. And some surgeons are reluctant to commit the time necessary to learn robotic techniques. There is also a concern that once a hospital invests in such an expensive system, surgeons may feel pressured to use it and steer patients towards surgery over other treatment options.

Other types of technology also improve health care. At Aurora St. Luke's Medical Center in Milwaukee, intensive care nurse Brenda Coulter checks a patient coming out of heart-bypass surgery—from a building several miles away. This is the Aurora eICU, from which a team of doctors and nurses keep constant watch on more than ten intensive care units in four different hospitals spread across eastern Wisconsin. "The idea is not to make care more remote," says David Rein, the unit's medical director, "but to bring expertise to the patient's bedside faster than we ever could before."

Monitors display vital signs and the patient's electronic chart, with details on medications, lab tests and X-ray results, and notes on the patient's condition. Cameras can zoom in so closely that monitoring staff can see the capillaries in a patient's eyes.

A survey recently found that patient mortality was 7.2 percent lower in hospitals that were "wired," which has a lot of health care researchers excited. Although the survey doesn't prove that technology *causes* better patient outcomes, it does show there is a strong connection.[10]

Critical Thinking Questions
- How is technology being used to streamline hospital operations, improve the quality of patient care, and provide better outcomes for patients?
- What criteria should hospitals use to evaluate whether these expensive technologies are worthwhile investments?

computer-integrated manufacturing (CIM)
The combination of computerized manufacturing processes (like robots and flexible manufacturing systems) with other computerized systems that control design, inventory, production, and purchasing.

Flexible manufacturing systems are expensive. But once in place a system requires little labor to operate and provides consistent product quality. It can also be adjusted easily and inexpensively. FMS equipment can quickly be reprogrammed to perform a variety of jobs. These systems work well when small batches of a variety of products are required or when each product is made to individual customer specifications. The Managing Change box provides an example.

Computer-integrated manufacturing (CIM) combines computerized manufacturing processes (like robots and flexible manufacturing systems) with other computerized systems that control design, inventory, production, and purchasing. With CIM, when a part is redesigned in the CAD system, the changes are quickly transmitted both to the machines producing the part and to all other departments that need to know about and plan for the change.

Technology and Automation at Your Service

Manufacturers are not the only businesses benefiting from technology. Nonmanufacturing firms are also using automation to improve customer service and productivity. Banks now offer services to customers through automated teller machines (ATMs), via automated telephone systems, and even over the Internet. Retail stores of all kinds use point-of-sale (POS) terminals that track inventories, identify items that need to be reordered, and tell which products are selling well. Wal-Mart, the leader in retailing automation, has its own satellite system connecting POS terminals directly to its distribution centers and headquarters.

concept check

Describe total quality management and the role that Six Sigma, ISO 9000, and ISO14000 play in it.

How can lean manufacturing and just-in-time inventory management help a firm improve its production and operations?

How are both manufacturing and nonmanufacturing firms using technology and automation to improve operations?

MANAGING CHANGE

Factory Flexibility Means Improved Efficiency and Quality

In today's auto manufacturing environment it is difficult to "sell out" a plant that is dedicated to making just one or two vehicle models. Intense price wars, a surge in overseas competition, and steadily increasing manufacturing costs have drained U.S. automaker profits since 2001, forcing some in the industry to rethink their basic assumptions about making cars and trucks. Some auto companies see the need to end the cycle of over-production and binge-discounting that has come to characterize the U.S. auto market and to better match production to shifting consumer demand.

In the hope that it will shave billions of dollars off the cost of producing cars, Daimler-Chrysler AG's Chrysler Group, headquartered in Auburn Hills, Michigan, plans a major revamp of its manufacturing process by improving factory flexibility to build three or more different vehicle models at a single plant. The idea behind the retooling is to improve the odds of a plant operating at close to maximum capacity, a key to profitability in a capital-intensive industry like automobiles. "This environment requires people to do things differently," said Frank Ewasyshyn, senior vice president of manufacturing at Chrysler. "You have to find ways that you never thought of before to reduce your costs and pass that on to the consumer."

Relatively high turnover among assembly workers can mean workers are not as familiar with a company's manufacturing systems—leading to increased labor costs and expensive mistakes. At the Toyota plant in Georgetown, Kentucky, which builds roughly one Camry or Avalon per minute, operators had to make multiple decisions, such as choosing from among 24 kinds of visors and nine different types of seatbelts, depending on which vehicle model was coming down the line.

Toyota, the fourth largest automaker in North America with 12 manufacturing plants that produced 1.44 million vehicles in 2004, began working to improve its flexible-manufacturing systems in Japan, where some Toyota and Honda plants produce as many as six different models per assembly line. In an effort to stabilize quality, the company implemented a new in-plant method to simplify production systems and eliminate as many errors as possible. Known internally as "kitting," workers synchronize packages of parts with the order of vehicle models heading along the assembly line, placing the part kits inside the vehicles under construction. The aim is to limit the number of decisions an hourly worker will make to two or less per vehicle, thus reducing the complexity of their task and improving the quality of the finished product. With the help of manufacturing improvements like this one, the company projects an annual capacity of 1.81 million cars and trucks by 2008.[11]

Critical Thinking Questions

- What combination of factors has forced American automakers to rethink the manufacturing process?
- What steps are they taking to revamp auto manufacturing in the United States, and what specific gains do they anticipate from these changes?

Trends in Production and Operations Management

8 What key trends are affecting the way companies manage production and operations?

What trends will impact U.S. production and operations management both now and in the future? Manufacturing employment stabilized after losing 3 million factory jobs over 43 consecutive months, down to a level of 14.3 million in February 2004. The economy has created 2.1 million new jobs, with unemployment in 2005 standing at 5 percent—the lowest level since September 2001. The pace of production has averaged 4.2 percent growth since the first quarter of 2004, and productivity has grown an even more impressive 4.9 percent. These statistics portray a U.S. economy steaming steadily ahead.[12]

Yet rapid changes in technology and intense global competition—particularly from Asia—create anxiety about the future. Is technology replacing too many jobs? Or with qualified workers predicted to be in short supply, is the increased reliance on technology imperative to the United States' ability to compete in a global marketplace? Will the United States lose its edge in the ongoing war for leadership in innovation? And what should it be doing to ensure that today's students are tomorrow's innovators and scientists?

Recent surveys show finding qualified workers is a major concern facing U.S. industry today. If the United States is to maintain its competitive edge, more federal investment is needed for science and research. And what of the increasingly crucial role of technology? These are some of the trends facing companies today that we will examine.

Americans no longer compete simply against one another but against workers in less developed countries with lower wages and increasing access to modern technology and production techniques. This is particularly true for American manufacturers who account for the bulk of U.S. exports and compete directly with most imports. A more integrated global economy with more import competition and more export opportunities offers both new challenges and opportunities to the United States and its workforce. To maintain its position as the world's leading innovator, it is essential that the United States remain committed to innovation and the concerted development of a more highly educated and skilled workforce.

Looming Workforce Crisis Threatens U.S. Competitiveness

According to the latest National Association of Manufacturers Skills Gap Report, manufacturing executives rank a "high-performing workforce" as the most important factor in their firms' future success. This finding concurs with a recent study by the U.S. Department of Labor, which concluded that 85 percent of future jobs in the United States will require advanced training, an associate degree, or a four-year college degree. Minimum skills will be adequate for only 15 percent of future jobs.

But results of the 2005 NAM Small Manufacturers Operating Survey conducted in July 2005 show that companies are already having trouble finding qualified workers. When asked to identify the most serious problem for their company, survey respondents ranked "finding qualified employees" above high-energy costs and the burdens of taxes, federal regulations, and litigation. Only the cost of health insurance and import competition ranked as more pressing concerns.

As demand for better-educated and more highly skilled workers begins to grow, troubling trends project a severe shortage of such workers. U.S. employers already struggling to find qualified workers will face an increasing shortage of such workers in coming years. To make matters worse, trends in U.S. secondary education suggest that even those future workers who stay in school to study math and science may not receive globally competitive educations.[13]

American Innovation Leadership at Risk

A recently released report shows that America is in danger of losing its global lead in science and innovation for the first time since World War II. The report was prepared by the Task Force on the Future of American Innovation, a coalition of leaders from industry, science, and higher education. Although the United States is still out front of the world's innovation curve, competing countries are climbing the technology ladder quickly, and the only way the United States can continue to create high-wage, value-added jobs is to climb the innovation ladder faster than the rest of the world.

The task force identified dwindling federal investment in science and research as a root cause of the problem. Federal research as a share of GDP has declined 37 percent over the past 30 years. The U.S. share of worldwide high-tech exports has been in a 20-year decline, from 31 percent in 1980 to 18 percent in 2001. Similarly, graduate science and engineering enrollment is declining in the United States while on the rise in China, India, and elsewhere. In addition, retirements from science and engineering jobs here at home could lead to a critical shortage of U.S. talent in these fields in the very near future.[14]

So what needs to be done to reverse this alarming trend? More robust investment is part of the solution because federally funded, peer reviewed, and patented scientific advances are essential to innovation. Such basic research helped bring us lasers, the World Wide Web, magnetic resonance imaging (MRI), and fiber optics. Intel Corporation CEO Craig Barrett noted that, "U.S. employers are being forced to look overseas as they face shortages of qualified, technically trained talent in the U.S. As research goes, so goes the future. If this trend continues, new technologies and the constellation of support industries surrounding them will increasingly develop overseas, not here."[15]

Business Process Management (BPM)—The Next Big Thing?

The 21st century is the age of the scattered corporation. With an assortment of partners and an army of suppliers often spread across thousands of miles, many companies find themselves with global design, supply, and logistics chains stretched to the breaking point. Few firms these days can afford to go it alone—with their own raw materials, in–house production processes, and exclusive distribution systems.[16]

business process management (BPM)
A unified system that has the power to integrate and optimize a company's sprawling functions by automating much of what it does.

"Business Process Management (BPM) is the glue to bind it all together," says Eric Austvold, research director at AMR Research. "It provides a unified system for business." This new and exciting technology has the power to integrate and optimize a company's sprawling functions by automating much of what it does. The results speak for themselves. BPM has saved U.S. firms $117 billion a year on inventory costs alone. Defense contractor Lockheed Martin recently used a BPM system to resolve differences among the hundreds of businesses that it acquired, unifying them into a whole and saving $50 million per year by making better use of existing resources and data.

BPM is the key to the success of such corporate high-flyers as Wal-Mart and Dell, which collect, digest, and utilize all sorts of production, sales, and shipping data to continually hone their operations. So how does BPM actually work? When a Dell system is ordered online, rather than waiting for a person to get the ball rolling, a flurry of electronic traffic flows back and forth between suppliers so that every part arrives within a few hours and that the computer's assembly, as well as software loading and testing, are scheduled. Production runs like a well-oiled clock so customers get their computers quickly, and Dell can bill them on shipment. A well-thought-through BPM system can even reschedule production runs, reroute deliveries, or shift work to a plant out of harm's way if a typhoon off the coast of Thailand threatens freight shipments in and out of your factory.[17]

The amount of available data—business intelligence (BI), enterprise resource planning (ERP), customer relationship management (CRM), and other systems—is staggering. "Companies are flooded with information," says Jeanne Baker, director and chair of the industry support group, Business Process Management Initiative (BPMI), and vice president of technology at Sterling Commerce. "The challenge is to make sense of it all. How you leverage the value chain is the true competitive advantage of the 21st century."[18]

concept check

Describe the impact of the anticipated worker shortage on U.S. business.

How are today's educational trends affecting the future of manufacturing?

What is business process management (BPM) and how do businesses use it to improve operations management?

Summary of Learning Goals

1 Why is production and operations management important in both manufacturing and service firms?

In the 1980s, many U.S. manufacturers lost customers to foreign competitors because their production and operations management systems did not support the high-quality, reasonably priced products consumers demanded. Service organizations also rely on effective operations management in order to satisfy consumers. Operations managers, the personnel charged with managing and supervising the conversion of inputs into outputs, work closely with other functions in organizations to help ensure quality, customer satisfaction, and financial success.

2 What types of production processes do manufacturers and service firms use?

Products are made using one of three types of production processes. In mass production, many identical goods are produced at once, keeping production costs low. Mass production, therefore, relies heavily on standardization, mechanization, and specialization. When mass customization is used, goods are produced using mass-production techniques up to a point, after which the product or service is custom tailored to individual customers by adding special features. When a firm's production process is built around customization, the firm makes many products one at a time according to the very specific needs or wants of individual customers.

3 How do organizations decide where to put their production facilities? What choices must be made in designing the facility?

Site selection affects operating costs, the price of the product or service, and the company's ability to compete. In choosing a production site, firms must weigh the availability of resources—raw materials, manpower, and even capital—needed for production, as well as the ability to serve customers and take advantage of marketing opportunities. Other factors include the availability of local incentives and the manufacturing environment. Once a site is selected, the firm must choose an appropriate design for the facility. The three main production facility designs are process, product, and fixed-position layouts. Cellular manufacturing is another type of facility layout.

4 Why are resource-planning tasks like inventory management and supplier relations critical to production?

Production converts input resources, such as raw materials and labor, into outputs, finished products and services. Firms must ensure that the resources needed for production will be available at strategic moments in the production process. If they are not, productivity, customer satisfaction, and quality may suffer. Carefully managing inventory can help cut production costs while maintaining enough supply for production and sales. Through good relationships with suppliers, firms can get better prices, reliable resources, and support services that can improve production efficiency.

5 How do operations managers schedule and control production?

Routing is the first step in scheduling and controlling production. Routing analyzes the steps needed in production and sets out a workflow, the sequence of machines and operations through which a product or service progresses from start to finish. Good routing increases productivity and can eliminate unnecessary cost. Scheduling involves specifying and controlling the time and resources required for each step in the production process. Operations managers use three methods to schedule production: Gantt charts, the critical path method, and program evaluation and review technique.

6 How can quality management and lean-manufacturing techniques help firms improve production and operations management?

Quality and productivity go hand in hand. Defective products waste materials and time, increasing costs. Poor quality also leads to dissatisfied customers. By implementing quality control methods, firms can reduce these problems and streamline production. Lean manufacturing also helps streamline production by eliminating unnecessary steps in the production process. When activities that don't add value for customers are eliminated, manufacturers can respond to changing market conditions with greater flexibility and ease.

7 What roles do technology and automation play in manufacturing and service industry operations management?

Many firms are improving their operational efficiency by using technology to automate parts of production. Computer-aided design and manufacturing systems, for example, help design new products, control the flow of resources needed for production, and even operate much of the production process. By using robotics, human time and effort can be minimized. Factories are being automated by blending computers, robots, and machinery into flexible manufacturing systems that require less labor to operate. Service firms are automating operations too, using technology to cut labor costs and control quality.

8 What key trends are affecting the way companies manage production and operations?

Data show the U.S. economy steaming steadily ahead, but dramatic advances in technology, predicted worker shortages, and global competition create challenges for the future. How will companies balance their technology and workforce needs? Will the U.S. maintain its lead in the ongoing war for leadership in innovation? And what should it be doing to convert today's students into tomorrow's innovators and scientists? Surveys indicate that finding qualified workers is a major concern facing U.S. industry today. If the U.S. is to maintain its competitive edge, more federal investment is needed for science and research. And what of the increasingly crucial role of technology? These are some of the trends facing companies today that we will examine.

Key Terms

assembly process   368
bill of material   371
business process management (BPM)   386
CAD/CAM systems   382
cellular manufacturing   371
computer-aided design (CAD)   382
computer-aided manufacturing (CAM)   382
computer-integrated manufacturing (CIM)   384
continuous improvement   380
continuous process   368
critical path   378
critical path method (CPM)   378
customization   366
electronic data interchange (EDI)   376
e-procurement   376
enterprise resource planning (ERP)   374
fixed-position layout   371
flexible manufacturing system (FMS)   383
Gantt charts   378
intermittent process   368
inventory   373
inventory management   373
ISO 9000   381
ISO 14000   381
job shop   367
just-in-time (JIT)   381
lean manufacturing   381

make-or-buy decision   373
Malcolm Baldrige National Quality Award   380
manufacturing resource planning II (MRPII)   374
mass customization   366
mass production   366
materials requirement planning (MRP)   374
operations management   365
outsourcing   373
perpetual inventory   374
process layout   371
process manufacturing   367
product (or assembly-line) layout   371
production   365
production planning   366
production process   366
program evaluation and review technique (PERT)   379
purchasing   371
quality   380
quality control   380
robotics   383
routing   377
scheduling   377
Six Sigma   380
supply chain   375
supply chain management   375
Total Quality Management (TQM)   380
value-stream mapping   377

1. Tom Lawrence and Sally Zickle are co-owners of L-Z Marketing, an advertising agency. Last week, they landed a major aerospace manufacturer as a client. The company wants the agency to create its annual report. Tom, who develops the art for the agency, needs about a week to develop the preliminary report design, another two weeks to set the type, and three weeks to get the report printed. Sally writes the material for the report and doesn't need as much time: two days to meet with the client to review the company's financial information and about three weeks to write the report copy. Of course, Tom can't set type until Sally has finished writing the report. Sally will also need three days to proofread the report before it goes to the printer. Develop either a Gantt chart or a critical path diagram for Tom and Sally to use in scheduling the project. Explain why you chose the method you did. How long will it take Tom and Sally to finish the project if there are no unforeseen delays? (Resources, Systems)

2. Look for ways that technology and automation are used at your school, in the local supermarket, and at your doctor's office. As a class, discuss how automation affects the service you receive from each of these organizations. Does one organization use any types of automation that might be effectively used by one of the others? Explain. (Interpersonal, Information)

3. Pick a small business in your community. Make a list of the resources critical to the firm's production and operations. What would happen if the business suddenly couldn't acquire any of these resources? Divide the class into small groups and discuss strategies that small businesses can use to manage their supply chain. (Resources, Information, Interpersonal)

4. Broadway Fashions is a manufacturer of women's dresses. The company's factory has 50 employees. Production begins when the fabric is cut according to specified patterns. After being cut, the pieces for each dress style are placed into bundles, which then move through the factory from worker to worker. Each worker opens each bundle and does one assembly task, such as sewing on collars, hemming dresses, or adding decorative items like appliqués. Then, the worker puts the bundle back together and passes it on to the next person in the production process. Finished dresses are pressed and packaged for shipment. Draw a diagram showing the production process layout in Broadway Fashion's factory. What type of factory layout and process is Broadway using? Discuss the pros and cons of this choice. Could Broadway improve production efficiency by using a different production process or factory layout? How? Draw a diagram to explain how this might look. (Resources, Systems)

5. As discussed in this chapter, many American firms have moved their manufacturing operations to overseas locations in the past decade. Although there can be sound financial benefits to this choice, moving production overseas can also raise new challenges for operations managers. Identify several of these challenges and offer suggestions for how operations managers can use the concepts in this chapter to minimize or solve them. (Resources, Information)

6. **Team Exercise** Reliance Systems, headquartered in Oklahoma City, is a manufacturer of computer keyboards. The company plans to build a new factory and hopes to find a location with access to low-cost but skilled workers, national and international transportation, and favorable government incentives. Working in teams, assign tasks and use the Internet and your school library to research possible site locations, both domestic and international. Choose a location you feel would best meet the company's needs. Make a group presentation to the class explaining why you have chosen this location. Include information about the location's labor force, similar manufacturing facilities already located there, availability of resources and materials, possible local incentives, political and economic environment in the location, and any other factors you feel make this an attractive location. After all teams have presented their proposed locations, as a

class rank all of the locations and decide the top two Reliance should investigate further. (Interpersonal, Information)

7. Your teacher has just announced a huge assignment, due in three weeks. Develop a Gantt chart to plan and schedule more effectively:

- Break the assignment down into smaller tasks: Pick a topic, conduct research at the library or on the Internet, organize your notes, develop an outline, and write, type, and proofread the paper.
- Estimate how much time each task will take.
- Across the top of a piece of paper list all the days until the assignment is due. Along the side of the paper list all the tasks you've identified in the order they need to be done.
- Starting with the first task, block out the number of days you estimate each task will take. Include days that you won't be able to work on the project.
- Track the actual time spent on each task.

After you complete and submit your assignment, compare your time estimates to the actual time each task took. How can these findings help you with future assignments? (Resources, Systems)

Ethics Activity

A recent spate of mine disasters that caused numerous fatalities refocused national attention on the question: Is management doing enough to protect employees on the job? Recent serious OSHA (Occupational Safety and Health Administration) violations resulting in the deaths of two workers, from falls due to the lack of harnesses or guardrails, suggest there is still a long way to go.

Companies are responsible for providing a safe workplace for employees. So why do accidents like these continue to happen? In a word—money. It takes money to purchase harnesses, install guardrails, and otherwise ensure a safe and healthy work environment. And even more is needed to employ the staff necessary to enforce company safety policies. It is often less costly for a company to just pay the fines that are levied for violations.

As a supervisor at a company with frequent violations of OSHA regulations, you worry about your employees' safety. But each time your company needs to implement a new safety feature, end-of-year employee bonuses get smaller. The money has to come from somewhere, management claims.

Using a Web search tool, locate articles about this topic and then write responses to the following questions. Be sure to support your arguments and cite your sources.

Ethical Dilemma: Do you report safety violations to management in the hope they will be corrected before someone gets hurt, or do you stage a total work stoppage to force management's hand, knowing that either way you risk losing popularity at every level, and very possibly your job? Or, of course, you could say nothing and hope for the best. It is not a problem you created and you're just there to do a job after all.

Sources: Susanne Nadeau, "Company Fined Thousands for Trench Collapse: Minnesota Contractor Fights OSHA Fine," *Grand Forks Herald* (Grand Forks, North Dakota), January 12, 2006, http://galenet.thomsonlearning.com; Jacqueline Seibel, "OSHA Fines 2 Firms in Pair of Workplace Deaths," *Milwaukee Journal Sentinel,* February 2, 2006, http://galenet.thomsonlearning.com; John J. Steuby, "Company Cited for Alleged Workplace Safety, Health Violations," *America's Intelligence Wire,* January 13, 2006, http://galenet.thomsonlearning.com.

Working the Net

1. Use the Google search engine, **http://www.google.com**, to conduct a search for "supplier information" and visit the Web sites of several firms (for example, Motorola, Northrop Grumman, Verizon, etc.). Compare the requirements companies set for their suppliers. How do they differ? How are they similar?

2. Visit *Site Selection* magazine, **http://www.siteselection.com**. Click on Area Demographics for information about the manufacturing environment in various U.S. locations. Pick three to four areas to read about. Using this information, what locations would you recommend for firms in the following industries: general services, telecommunications, automotive manufacturing, and electronics manufacturing. Explain.

3. Manufacturers face many federal, state, and local regulations. Visit the National Association of Manufacturers at **http://www.nam.org**. Pick two or three legislative or regulatory issues discussed under the "policy" sections and use a search engine like Yahoo (**http://www.yahoo.com**) to find more information.

4. Using a search engine like Excite (**http://www.excite.com**) or Info Seek (**http://www.infoseek.com**) search for information about technologies such as ERP, CAD/CAM systems, or robotics. Find at least three suppliers for one of these technologies. Visit their Web sites and discuss how their clients are using their products to automate production.

5. Research either the Malcolm Baldrige National Quality Award or the ISO 9000 Quality Standards program on the Internet. Write an executive summary that explains the basic requirements and costs of participating. What are the benefits of participating? Include a brief example of a company that has participated and their experiences. Include a list of relevant Web site links for further reading.

Creative Thinking Case >

Innovation Labs Spark Creativity

With sales of 12.5 million units in less than a year, no one is questioning why designers of the sleek new Razr, Motorola's ultra-light, half-inch-thick cell phone, broke some internal rules in bringing the phone to market. Leaving their cubicles at the company's traditional research facility in suburban Libertyville, Illinois, Motorola engineers joined with designers and marketers at the company's downtown Chicago innovation lab known as Moto City. Open space and waist-high cubicles—for even senior executives—fostered team spirit and a breaking down of barriers, which contributed to the project's success. Customary practices like running new product ideas past regional managers were bypassed. "We did not want to be distracted by the normal inputs we get," says Gary R. Weis, senior director of mechanical engineering. "It would not have allowed us to be as innovative."

Innovation labs are fast becoming a key element in the effort to revamp old-style research and development (R&D). In the past, scientists and engineers toiled away for years in pursuit of patents, then handed their work over to product developers and marketers for eventual shipment to consumers. But today's sophisticated production and operations technology, as well as ferocious competition, can mean new innovations grow old quickly, so companies must work fast to get products to market. To keep pace with consumer demand, Motorola has already introduced new colors for the Razr, as well as follow-on phones like the candy-bar shaped Slvr and the rounded Pebl.

But the need for speed in innovation stretches beyond high-tech companies. Businesses as varied as Mattel, Boeing, Wrigley, Procter & Gamble, and even the Mayo Clinic also use such labs to shatter the bureaucratic barriers that existed among inventors, engineers, researchers, designers, marketers, and others. Now teams of people from different disciplines gather to focus on a problem—brainstorming, tinkering, and toying with different approaches—and generate answers to test on customers. Successful products are then sped to the market.

Although innovation labs are typically created to generate new product ideas, they are also used to improve manufacturing processes. Large organizations have discovered that innovation labs can be a powerful tool for cutting through bureaucratic bloat. At Boeing Company, for instance, nearly 3,000 engineers and finance and program management staffers from scattered locations in the Renton, Washington, area were moved last year to the factory that assembles 737 jetliners. To urge people to mingle, Boeing created common break areas where mechanics and engineers could talk shop over coffee or a snack, building informal relationships that improved both daily working processes and innovations.

But innovation labs are not panaceas. If ideas that emerge from these facilities are flawed, the products will undoubtedly be failures. And some older workers, especially baby boomers, may have a hard time giving up cherished perks such as private offices. Yet for companies in a creative rut, innovation labs can be places where something magical gets started.

Critical Thinking Questions

- How do innovation labs contribute to successful production and operations management?
- In what significant ways do they differ from a more traditional research and development approach?
- What market conditions lead companies to use innovation labs?

Sources: Joseph Weber, Stanley Holmes, and Christopher Palmieri, "'Mosh Pits' of Creativity," *Business Week*, November 7, 2005, http://www.businessweek.com; Rebecca Fannin, "Unlocking Innovation: CEOs Are Learning How to Better Tap University R & D," *The Chief Executive*, June 2005, http://www.findarticles.com; Innovation Labs Web site, http://www.innovationlabs.com (May 22, 2006).

Video Case >

Peapod—Driven to be the Best

Founded in 1989 by brothers Andrew and Thomas Parkinson, Peapod is one of America's leading Internet grocers—and one of the successes in this industry. Anxious to convince customers that they could shop online and still control the quality of their selection, the brothers picked and packed and made deliveries in their own vehicles. "Today, busy customers see us as a lifestyle solution," says company president Andrew Parkinson.

Perhaps the change in attitude was brought about by Peapod's well-priced, diverse product selection, combined with the ease and convenience of their user-friendly Web site. Peapod has more than 8,000 offerings, and the customer's online shopping experience is further enhanced by such features as saved shopping lists, express shopping, weekly specials, recipes, and more.

Now a wholly owned subsidiary of Royal Ahold, an international food retail and service company from The Netherlands, Peapod serves 15 U.S. markets and delivers to more than 235,000 customers each year. Through its expanded partnerships with Ahold U.S.A. stores (Peapod by Stop & Shop and Peapod by Giant), Peapod employs a more integrated bricks-and-clicks business strategy, leveraging the buying power of Ahold to make higher volume, lower-priced purchases; lowering distribution and transportation costs (we'll see more on this later); and boosting inventory management. It's a strategy, Andrew Parkinson says, that holds much promise for the future. "The increasing use of high-speed broadband, advances in portable technologies, and the growing numbers of women doing online shopping will spur the industry to maturity," he says.

Michael Brennan, senior vice president of marketing and product development, explained other operational efficiencies. The company's largest cost component, transportation/delivery, is a crucial aspect of operational management. "A truck and driver is a fixed cost, so whether he delivers one order or twenty the cost remains about the same," Brennan says. Orchestrating customer demand with delivery options to maximize truck/driver usage is key to building "density of delivery," a technique the company calls Smart Mile, to make sure full trucks keep costs per order down. Smart Mile matches customer demand with available delivery options, which are based on where the customer lives. Customers are offered incentives in the form of merchandise discounts to select a delivery time that fits in with other deliveries in their neighborhood.

Lead driver Jeff Frank says that his in-town driving routes are often designed with "hardly a mile between stops." Frank also focuses on getting orders delivered right the first time. That means checking everything thoroughly before leaving the warehouse. "Pickers" use a system of barcode scans to ensure the correct items go into each order. Picked orders are then sent to "shipping lanes," where they are readied for the delivery trucks.

Peapod prides itself on delivering only the freshest produce to customers and monitors customers' satisfaction levels on an ongoing basis. Its mission is "to amaze and delight its customers," and with over 6 million orders under its belt, it looks as though it is doing just that.

Critical Thinking Questions

- What roles do quality and productivity play in a service company like Peapod, and how do they differ from a manufacturing company?
- What impact did Peapod's acquisition by food retailer Ahold have on its operations?
- How does the company manage transportation, its largest cost?

Sources: Adapted from the Peapod video, "The Importance of Control," (October 31, 2005); and Peapod corporate Web site, http://www.peadpod.com (May 31, 2006).

Hot Links Address Book

See how American Leather brings it all together to create beautiful customized couches at http://www.americanleather.com

What characteristics contribute to a city's manufacturing climate? Find out by reading more at *Industry Week's* Web site: http://www.industryweek.com

How do companies decide whether to make or buy? Find out more at the Outsourcing Institute, a professional association where buyers and sellers network and connect: http://www.outsourcing.com

Learn how to build your own Gantt Chart at http://www.mindtools.com/pages/article/newPPM_03.htm

What does it take to win the Malcolm Baldrige National Quality Award? Get the details at http://www.quality.nist.gov

Want to know more about how robots work? Find out at http://electronics.howstuffworks.com/robot.htm

Part 3 • Managing the Business of Apple, Inc.

Apple has experienced a tumultuous life. Its periods of boom or bust have made Apple one of the most talked-about and written-about companies in history. At the beginning of the 1980 banner years, Apple offered its first sale of stock to the public. Other significant events in the 1980s included the introduction of the Macintosh (1984), and the move to desktop publishing with the Mac Plus and the LaserWriter (1986). Jumping ahead to the 21st century, the world is awash with Apple's iPod and iTunes. In between, there were the somewhat abysmal bust periods in which the Lisa flopped (1983) and ten years later when the company experienced an 84 percent drop in earnings. A major player in the management of business at Apple has been Steve Jobs. However, the company did experience a rash of CEOs in its attempt to pull itself out of the mid-1990s slump.

FRAGMENTED LEADERSHIP

In the formative years, Apple was led by Steve Jobs, Steve Wozniak, and Mike Markkula. Not particularly interested in the corporate world and worth more than $100 million, Wozniak left the company around 1985 and discovered a new calling—educating youth. While remaining active in the corporate world, Mike Markkula has focused considerable energy on the world of ethics. Markkula and his wife provided the seed funding and endowment for the Markkula Center for Applied Ethics at Santa Clara University in California. Of the three, Jobs is the only one who remained active in the company.

Jobs led the company until 1985. At that time, the board replaced him with John Sculley. Jobs went on to found NeXT and Pixar. Sculley remained as Apple's CEO until 1993. In 1993, the board appointed Michael Spindler as CEO. Spindler held the position for two years, and then the board appointed Gilbert Amelio to the position. Amelio's term lasted until mid-1997, and Steve Jobs again took the helm. After regaining the leadership position at Apple, Jobs reinvigorated the company and led it to a worldwide competitive position in music, movies, and technology.

The board of directors at Apple is a showcase of prominent individuals, including former United States vice-president Al Gore. In 2004, however, the company was noted as one of 27 California-based Fortune 500 companies that did not have a woman on its board. The company did, however, fare well on the Corporate Equality Index. This index rates large corporations on the basis of policies that affect gay, lesbian, bisexual, and transgender employees. Apple scored perfectly on this index.

MIXED EMPLOYEE SATISFACTION

As the company experienced its roller coaster ride in the product and financial markets, the same appeared to be happening internally. In a 2005 survey conducted by the New York–based research firm Vault, Apple employees expressed mixed reactions to their workplace experiences. Vault conducted interviews of Apple employees in four major areas:

- Workplace (e.g., corporate culture, diversity, hours, dress code, opportunities for advancement),
- Interview and recruiting (e.g., number of rounds of interviews, who conducts interviews, interview questions),
- Salary and compensation (e.g., base salary, signing bonus, year-end bonuses, stock options, vacation time, perks, reimbursements), and
- Business outlook (e.g., competition, distribution channels, products and services, morale).

Responses to the survey were generally positive, except with respect to salary and compensation. Passion, which has always been a hallmark at Apple, was evident in the findings. This passion was exemplified in responses about the company culture, particularly with respect to the dress code, diversity issues, task variety, and belief in the company's products. Findings from those surveyed suggested that employees (e.g., product managers) were less than pleased with the lack of bonuses, raises, and stock options, as well as the inherent difficulties of climbing the corporate ladder. Findings from the Vault survey tended to corroborate a 2003 news story that reported on an incentive bonus program for executives at the director level or higher. This report noted that, although the company failed to reach its stated objectives, a special recognition bonus was approved for 230 executives (director level or higher, but excluding senior executive officers). The failure to meet the stated objectives was attributed to external economic and business conditions rather than employee performance. It was reported that lower-ranking employees were also eligible for bonuses, but within a reduced pool because the company had missed its companywide targets.

OPERATIONS STRATEGIES

Apple Computer was generally known for its lenient business philosophy which included a hands-off approach exemplified in all aspects of its operations. However, this operational style did not match the management philosophies of either Spindler or Amelio who were both considered to be no-nonsense operational managers. As operational managers, Spindler and Amelio focused on cost cutting measures and simplification.

Although Spindler and Amelio attempted operational savings, it was only after Jobs reclaimed the helm that true operational savings were achieved. Jobs recognized that he was not the person to oversee a much-needed operational overhaul, so he brought in an operations expert who had considerable experience at Compaq Computer. In the second half of the 1990s, the company decided to hire outside organizations to perform many of its major business functions that had originally been performed by Apple employees. Called *outsourcing*, these agreements were made with SCI Systems (USA), Quanta (Taiwan), LG (Korea, Mexico, Wales), Alpha Top/GVC (Taiwan), and Hon Hai/Foxconn (China, Czech Republic). With these outsourcing agreements in place, purchased parts, work in progress, and finished goods inventories were reduced dramatically.

In late 1998, to facilitate a new supply chain that involved both build-to-order systems and outsourcing, Apple began using i2 Technologies' Rhythm software to help improve sales forecasting, optimize production, and reduce costs. Additionally, the company adopted an *ERP (enterprise resource planning)* system from SAP, a computerized resource-planning system that incorporates information about the firm's suppliers and customers with its internally generated data. An ERP would allow the company to further reduce operational costs while improving customer service and ultimately increasing revenue. These systems enabled Apple to better link daily production to weekly sales forecasts and provide employees with clear goals and measures for evaluation.

Critical Thinking Questions

* Describe the tumultuous environment as related to CEO turnover at Apple.
* What was Steve Jobs' role during both stints as CEO?
* Why do people enjoy working at Apple even with the apparent compensation problems revealed in the 2005 employee survey?
* Why was Apple hesitant to outsource and install supply chain systems?
* What is an ERP?

Sources: "Apple's Steve Wozniak Is Reprogrammed—As a Grade School Teacher," http://www.woz.org, accessed on March 21, 2006; David Bovet and Joseph Martha, "Change at the Core," *Business 2.0*, November 28, 2000, pp. 278–279; Elizabeth Brown, "California Leads Nation in Naming Women to Boards," *San Francisco Business Times*, February 26, 2004, http://www.bizjournals.com, accessed on February 6, 2006; Peter Burrows and Ronald Grover, "Steve Jobs' Magic Kingdom," *BusinessWeek*, February 6, 2006, pp. 63–69; Peter Cohen, "Gay Advocacy Group gives Apple Perfect Score," *Macworld*, August 14, 2002, http://www.macworld.com, accessed on February 6, 2006; Ian Fried, "Top Apple Employees Take Home Bonuses," *CNET News*, March 24, 2003, http://www.news.com, accessed on February 6, 2006; http://www.scu.edu/ethics, accessed on March 21, 2006; http://www.vault.com, accessed on March 21, 2006; Kasper Jade and Katie Marsal, "Employees Offer Mixed Reactions to Apple Corporate Life," *AppleInsider*, March 30, 2005, http://www.appleinsider.com, accessed on February 6, 2006; Jenny C. McCune, "Polishing the Apple," *Management Review*, September 1996, pp. 43–48; Joel West, "Apple Computer: The iCEO Seizes the Internet," Center for Research on Information Technology and Organizations, Paper 348, 2002, http://repositories.cdlib.org, accessed on December 6, 2005; David B. Yoffie and Yusi Wang, "Apple Computer 2002," Harvard Business School Publishing, Boston, MA, HBS 9-792-469, October 2005.

PART 4

Marketing Management

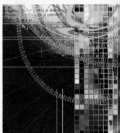

CHAPTER 12

Creating Marketing Strategy to Meet Customers' Needs

Learning Goals

After reading this chapter, you should be able to answer these questions:

1 What are the marketing concept and relationship building?

2 How do managers create a marketing strategy?

3 What is the marketing mix?

4 How do consumers and organizations make buying decisions?

5 What are the five basic forms of market segmentation?

6 How is marketing research used in marketing decision making?

7 What are the trends in understanding the consumer?

Exploring Business Careers
Steve Piehl
Harley Davidson

A road not taken is the next adventure waiting. Live to ride; ride to live. These are just a few of the creeds that Harley riders live by. Whether it's the vision of the open road, the shine of chrome, or the smell of dust mixed with exhaust, people are drawn to Harley Davidson motorcycles. How often do you see someone with "Honda" tattooed on their chest? Harleys are the stuff that dreams and identities are made of.

Steve Piehl, the Director of Communications at Harley Davidson, has been shaping people's dreams for over 25 years. He uses traditional marketing channels such as print, radio, and television advertising; however Harley also, understandably, approaches marketing nontraditionally.

The focus of Harley marketing is not selling a product, but selling an experience. Piehl explains, "The difference of that experience is what has given us success. We don't categorize what that experience is. We leave it up to people to make it their own." For some, a Harley is a ticket to freedom, for others it is a knockout ride to work. Harley's promotion of accessories supports this idea. As Piehl says, "No two Harleys on the street are the same." A part of the purchasing process is a meeting with a "chrome consultant" who can help with customizing and accessorizing your bike. In this way, the bike becomes part of one's identity.

Part of Harley's focus on experience is its support of motorcycle riding as a sport. On their Web site and at the dealerships, they provide tips and classes for rider improvement. Through the Harley Owner's Group (HOG), a membership group of Harley owners, Harley promotes events and rallies where owners can get together and ride. They form what Piehl calls "brothers and sisters of the road."

It is with this focus on the "sport" that Harley creates its most powerful marketing tool: the motorcycle mentor. Through the nature of the Harley community, previous owners coach new owners on buying a more advanced bike, taking an overnight trip, or packing for long-distance rides. Piehl says, "We would be doing a disservice if we said we reach everyone with our product announcements. But when we put it out, it works its way through the customer base. Our owners sell our products. They encourage people to get more involved in the sport." And tools like chat rooms on the Harley Web site or magazines like *HOGtales or Motorcycle Enthusiast* facilitate that sharing.

So how does Harley Davidson measure its marketing success? They participate in Customer Satisfaction Index studies to measure satisfaction for people who purchase new motorcycles. But it is the statistic that over 90% of Harley owners will repurchase a Harley that carries the weight. Piehl laughs, "When we get a customer, we can pretty much keep them. Our marketing is to get new customers and to keep existing [customers] happy."

It is just another part of Harley's creed: We believe life is what you make it, and we make it one hell of a ride.

Chapter 12 examines the role of the consumer in the production of a marketing concept and campaign. As seen in examples like Harley Davidson, although not traditionally thought of as an active component, customers are critical to shaping successful marketing.

Marketing plays a key role in the success of businesses. It is the task of marketing to generate sales for the firm. Sales revenue, in turn, pays workers' salaries, buys supplies, covers the costs of new buildings and equipment, and hopefully, enables the company to earn a profit. If marketing efforts are unsuccessful, there is no need for managers, engineers, production workers, and so forth because the firm will go out of business due to a lack of sales! Now let's look, in depth, at this important business function called *marketing*.

Marketing Creates Revenue—The Lifeblood of the Firm

marketing
The process of discovering the needs and wants of potential buyers and customers and then providing goods and services that meet or exceed their expectations.

exchange
The process in which two parties give something of value to each other to satisfy their respective needs.

Marketing is the process of getting the right goods or services to the right people at the right place, time, and price, using the right promotion techniques. This concept is referred to as the *"right" principle*. We can say that **marketing** is finding out the needs and wants of potential buyers and customers and then providing goods and services that meet or exceed their expectations. Marketing is about creating exchanges. An **exchange** takes place when two parties give something of value to each other to satisfy their respective needs. In a typical exchange, a consumer trades money for a good or service.

To encourage exchanges, marketers follow the "right" principle. If your local Avon rep doesn't have the right lipstick for you when you want it, at the right price, you will not exchange money for a new lipstick from Avon. Think about the last exchange (purchase) you made: What if the price had been 30 percent higher? What if the store or other source had been less accessible? Would you have bought anything? The "right" principle tells us that marketers control many factors that determine marketing success. In this chapter, you will learn about the marketing concept and how organizations create a marketing strategy. You will learn how the marketing mix is used to create sales opportunities. Next, we examine how and why consumers and organizations make purchase decisions. Then, we discuss the important concept of market segmentation, which helps marketing managers focus on the most likely purchasers of their wares. We conclude the chapter by examining how marketing research and decision support systems help guide marketing decision making.

The Marketing Concept

 What are the marketing concept and relationship building?

marketing concept
Identifying consumer needs and then producing the goods or services that will satisfy them while making a profit for the organization.

production orientation
An approach in which a firm works to lower production costs without a strong desire to satisfy the needs of customers.

If you study today's best organizations, you'll see that they have adopted the **marketing concept**, which involves identifying consumer needs and then producing the goods or services that will satisfy them while making a profit. The marketing concept is oriented toward pleasing consumers by offering value. Specifically, the marketing concept involves the following:

- Focusing on customer wants so the organization can distinguish its product(s) from competitors' offerings.
- Integrating all of the organization's activities, including production, to satisfy these wants.
- Achieving long-term goals for the organization by satisfying customer wants and needs legally and responsibly.

Today, companies of every size in all industries are applying the marketing concept. Enterprise Rent-A-Car found that its customers didn't want to have to drive to its offices. Therefore, Enterprise began delivering vehicles to customers' homes or places of work. Disney found that some of its patrons really disliked waiting in lines. In response, Disney began offering FastPass at a premium price, which allows patrons to avoid standing in long lines waiting for attractions.

Firms have not always followed the marketing concept. Around the time of the Industrial Revolution in America (1860–1910), firms had a **production orientation**, which meant that they worked to lower production costs without a strong desire to satisfy the needs of their customers. To do this, organizations concentrated on mass production, focusing internally on maximizing the efficiency of operations, increasing output, and ensuring uniform quality. They also asked such questions as: What can we do best? What can our engineers design? What is economical and easy to produce with our equipment? There is nothing wrong with assessing a firm's capabilities. In fact, such assessments are necessary in planning. But the production orientation does not consider whether what the firm produces most efficiently also meets the needs of the marketplace. By implementing the marketing concept, an organization looks externally to the consumers in the marketplace and commits to customer value, customer satisfaction, and relationship marketing as explained in this section.

Customer Value

customer value
The ratio of benefits to the sacrifice necessary to obtain those benefits, as determined by the customer; reflects the willingness of customers to actually buy a product.

customer satisfaction
The customer's feeling that a product has met or exceeded expectations.

Customer value is the ratio of benefits to the sacrifice necessary to obtain those benefits. The customer determines the value of both the benefits and the sacrifices. Creating customer value is a core business strategy of many successful firms. Customer value is rooted in the belief that price is not the only thing that matters. A business that focuses on the cost of production and price to the customer will be managed as though it were providing a commodity differentiated only by price. In contrast, businesses that provide customer value believe that many customers will pay a premium for superior customer service or accept fewer services for a value price. Southwest Airlines doesn't offer assigned seats, meals, or in-flight movies. Instead the budget carrier delivers what it promises: on-time departures. In "service value" surveys, Southwest routinely beats the full-service airlines like American Airlines that actually provide passengers with luxuries like movies and food on selected long-haul flights.

The automobile industry also illustrates the importance of creating customer value. To penetrate the fiercely competitive luxury automobile market, Lexus adopted a customer-driven approach, with particular emphasis on service. Lexus stresses product quality with a standard of zero defects in manufacturing. The service quality goal is to treat each customer as one would treat a guest in one's home, to pursue the perfect person-to-person relationship, and to strive to improve continually. This strategy has enabled Lexus to establish a clear quality image and capture a significant share of the luxury car market.

Customer Satisfaction

Customer satisfaction is a theme that we have stressed throughout the text. **Customer satisfaction** is the customer's feeling that a product has met or exceeded expectations. Lexus consistently wins awards for its outstanding customer satisfaction. JD Powers and Associates surveys car owners two years after they make their purchase. The Customer Satisfaction Survey is made up of four measures that each describe an element of overall ownership satisfaction at two years: vehicle quality/reliability, vehicle appeal, ownership costs, and service satisfaction from a dealer. Lexus continues to lead the industry and has been America's top-ranked vehicle for five years in a row.[1]

Sometimes building customer satisfaction isn't so easy. Starbucks believed that its customers wanted a variety of drinks to choose from when they came into a store. So the company put a lot of effort into developing new beverages. What they missed was the time that it took the workers to make the complicated new drinks. Wait time went up and customer satisfaction went down. Starbucks did extensive marketing research to find out why customers weren't happy. When the problem was finally understood, Starbucks spent $40 million to add new servers to cut wait times.

CONCEPT *in Action*

Geico—the major auto insurer with the scaly mascot—famously boasts a 97 percent customer-satisfaction rating, based on an independent study conducted by Alan Newman Research, 2006. With this claim, communicated through the company's quirky and ubiquitous advertising, consumers get the message that Geico delivers quality insurance coverage at low prices. *What factors do you think impact the customer-satisfaction ratings for an auto insurer like Geico?*

They also created the Starbucks Card to speed payment. The new counter help, a new ordering system, and the Starbucks Card meant most people were served in less than three minutes. Customer satisfaction zoomed!

Relationship Marketing

relationship marketing
A strategy that focuses on forging long-term partnerships with customers by offering value and providing customer satisfaction.

Relationship marketing is a strategy that focuses on forging long-term partnerships with customers. Companies build relationships with customers by offering value and providing customer satisfaction. Companies benefit from repeat sales and referrals that lead to increases in sales, market share, and profits. Costs fall because it is less expensive to serve existing customers than to attract new ones. Keeping a customer costs about one-fourth of what it costs to attract a new customer.[2]

Customers also benefit from stable relationships with suppliers. Business buyers have found that partnerships with their suppliers are essential to producing high-quality products while cutting costs. Customers remain loyal to firms that provide them greater value and satisfaction than they expect from competing firms.

Frequent-buyer clubs are an excellent way to build long-term relationships. All major airlines have frequent-flyer programs. After you fly a certain number of miles you become eligible for a free ticket. Now, cruise lines, hotels, car rental agencies, credit-card companies, and even mortgage companies give away "airline miles" with purchases. Consumers patronize the airline and its partners because they want the free tickets. Thus, the program helps to create a long-term relationship with the customer. Southwest Airlines carries their loyalty program a bit further than most. Members get birthday cards and some even get profiled in the airline's in-flight magazine!

If an organization is to build relationships with customers, its employees' attitudes and actions must be customer oriented. Any person, department, or division that is not customer oriented weakens the positive image of the entire organization. An employee may be the only contact a potential customer has with the firm. In that person's eyes, the employee is the firm. If greeted discourteously, the potential customer may well assume that the employee's attitude represents the whole firm.

Sometimes companies find that they really don't want to build relationships with all of their customers. This paradox is explained in the Managing Change box.

concept check

- Explain the marketing concept.
- Explain the difference between customer value and customer satisfaction.
- What is meant by relationship marketing?

MANAGING CHANGE

Smart Service Calls Bad Customers

Not all customers are created equal. The smartest companies are crunching reams of data from point-of-sale terminals, customer relationship management software, customer-loyalty programs, and elsewhere to target the buyers who spend the most. IBM, for example, is combing through its data to identify which corporate clients to spend marketing dollars on, when, and for how long. (The point is to ensure that the cost of marketing doesn't exceed the predicted lifetime value of the customer.) Mail-order retailer L.L. Bean found that its most profitable customer is the one who buys for the entire household. Rather than peppering each household in its database every year with dozens of its specialized catalogs—for men, women, kids, and home—it's now focusing on those who buy across all its product lines.

L.L. Bean's best customers now get 40 percent fewer mailings, sales are up 8 percent, and customer retention is climbing. ING Direct takes its favoritism even further: The online discount banker actually fires high-maintenance customers who cut into its margins with too many costly phone calls to the help desk. ING Direct's profits are expected to double to an estimated $250 million a year, proving that pickiness can pay off.[3]

Critical Thinking Questions

- Why don't more companies get rid of bad customers?
- Are there really any bad customers? If companies do better marketing, can't all customers be good customers?

Creating a Marketing Strategy

2 How do managers create a marketing strategy?

There is no secret formula for creating goods and services that provide customer value and customer satisfaction. An organization that is committed to providing superior customer satisfaction puts target customers at the very center of its marketing strategy. Creating a customer-focused *marketing strategy* involves four main steps: understanding the external environment, defining the target market, creating a competitive advantage, and developing a marketing mix. This section will examine the first three steps, and the next section will discuss how a company develops a marketing mix.

environmental scanning
The process in which a firm continually collects and evaluates information about its external environment.

Understanding the External Environment

Unless marketing managers understand the external environment, a firm cannot intelligently plan for the future. Thus, many organizations assemble a team of specialists to continually collect and evaluate environmental information, a process called **environmental scanning**. The goal in gathering the environmental data is to identify future market opportunities and threats.

Computer manufacturers understand the importance of environmental scanning to monitor rapidly changing consumer interests. Since the invention of the PC, techies have taken two things for granted: Processor speeds will grow exponentially, and PCs will become indistinguishable from televisions—that there will be, in industry lingo, convergence. The first prediction obviously has come true, and the second is beginning. Consumers may not like to watch movies on their PCs, but they love listening to music on them. They may not like to send e-mail from their couch, but they love having a PC—known as a digital video recorder—attached to the TV to automatically record all their favorite shows. And although they won't buy an old-fashioned TV from Dell or HP, when it comes to flat-screen TVs, they have no problem at all.

For PC makers, it's also good business. Prices and margins for computers keep falling; gross margins in consumer electronics are twice those in the PC world. And now that the music and movies consumers play on those systems are the same zeros and ones that are the foundation of PCs, there is little conversion cost.

The only clear winner in this new world so far is Apple, which has leveraged its computer platform to make it easy and fashionable for consumers to get with the digital-music age. Apple today sells almost as many iPods per quarter as it does Macs. Microsoft wants in on this business badly, but Hewlett-Packard decided to shift its loyalty to Apple, so Microsoft doesn't have much leverage just now. The other company to watch over the next few years is Sony. It misplayed the convergence game but is redoubling efforts to make its PC, consumer electronics, gaming, and entertainment divisions play together.[4]

In general, six categories of environmental data shape marketing decisions:

CONCEPT *in Action*

At the height of the Atkins craze, about 14 percent of all new food products claimed to be low-carb. But a cool down of low-carb mania has led to a dramatic reduction in products based on nutritional systems like the Atkins and South Beach diets. The allure of carb-conscious dieting is that it enables weight-watchers to lose pounds, not portions—a concession to our super-sized culture of consumption. *What changes in the external environment contributed to the meteoric rise and fall of low-carb marketing?*

- *Social forces* such as the values of potential customers and the changing roles of families and women working outside the home.
- *Demographic forces* such as the ages, birth and death rates, and locations of various groups of people.
- *Economic forces* such as changing incomes, inflation, and recession.
- *Technological forces* such as advances in communications and data retrieval capabilities.
- *Political and legal forces* such as changes in laws and regulatory agency activities.
- *Competitive forces* from domestic and foreign-based firms.

Exhibit 12.1 > The Target Markets for Marriott International

	Price Range	Target Market
Fairfield Inn	$45–65	Economizing business and leisure travelers
TownePlace Suites	$55–70	Moderate-tier travelers who stay three to four weeks
SpringHill Suites	$75–95	Business and leisure travelers looking for more space and amenities
Courtyard	$75–105	Travelers seeking quality and affordable accommodations designed for the road warrior
Residence Inn	$85–110	Travelers seeking a residential-style hotel
Marriott Hotels, Resorts, and Suites	$90–235	Grounded achievers who desire consistent quality
Renaissance Hotels and Resorts	$90–235	Discerning business and leisure travelers who seek creative attention to detail
Ritz-Carlton	$175–300	Senior executives and entrepreneurs looking for a unique, luxury, personalized experience

Defining the Target Market

target market
The specific group of consumers toward which a firm directs its marketing efforts.

Managers and employees focus on providing value for a well-defined target market. The **target market** is the specific group of consumers toward which a firm directs its marketing efforts. It is selected from the larger overall market. Quaker Oats targets its grits to blue-collar consumers in the South. The Limited, Inc. has several different types of stores, each for a distinct target market: Express for trendy younger women, Lerner for budget-conscious women, Lane Bryant and Roaman's for full-size women, and Henri Bendel's for upscale, high-fashion women. These target markets are all part of the overall market for women's clothes. In 2005, Gap launched a new chain, Forth & Towne, targeted toward the "urban chic" female who was born between 1946 and 1964.

Identifying a target market helps a company focus its marketing efforts on those who are most likely to buy its products or services. Concentrating on potential customers lets the firm use its resources efficiently. The target markets for Marriott International's lodging alternatives are shown in Exhibit 12.1. The latest in the Marriott family is SpringHill Suites. The SpringHill idea came from another Marriott chain, Fairfield Suites, an offshoot of Marriott's Fairfield Inns. The suites, opened in 1997, were roomy but devoid of most frills: The closets didn't have doors, and the lobby floors were covered with linoleum. Some franchisees complained to Marriott that the suites were *under*priced: Fairfield Suites guests were saying they would pay a little more for a few more frills. So Marriott began planning an upgrade. To create each of the first 20 or so SpringHill locations, Marriott spent $200,000 renovating an existing Fairfield Suites unit, adding ergonomic chairs, ironing boards, and other amenities. Lobbies at SpringHill hotels are fancier than the rooms themselves: The lobbies have fireplaces, breakfast rooms, crown moldings at the ceiling, and granite or ceramic tile floors.

Creating a Competitive Advantage

competitive advantage
A set of unique features of a company and its products that are perceived by the target market as significant and superior to those of the competition; also called *differential advantage*.

cost competitive advantage
A firm's ability to produce a product or service at a lower cost than all other competitors in an industry while maintaining satisfactory profit margins.

A competitive advantage, also called a differential advantage, is a set of unique features of a company and its products that are perceived by the target market as significant and superior to those of the competition. As Andrew Grove, former CEO of Intel, says, "You have to understand what it is you are better at than anybody else and mercilessly focus your efforts on it." Competitive advantage is the factor or factors that cause customers to patronize a firm and not the competition. There are three types of competitive advantage: cost, product/service differential, and niche.

Cost Competitive Advantage A firm that has a cost competitive advantage can produce a product or service at a lower cost than all its competitors while maintaining satisfactory profit margins. Firms become cost leaders by obtaining inexpensive raw materials, making plant operations more efficient, designing products for ease of manufacture, controlling overhead costs, and avoiding marginal customers.

A cost competitive advantage enables a firm to deliver superior customer value. Chapparal Steel, for example, is the leading low-cost U.S. steel producer because it uses only scrap iron and steel and a very efficient continuous-casting process to make new steel. In fact, Chapparal is so efficient that it is the only U.S. steel producer that ships to Japan. Similarly, Fort Howard Paper's competitive advantage lies in its cost-saving manufacturing process. Fort Howard Paper uses only recycled pulp, rather than the more expensive virgin pulp, to make toilet paper and other products. The quality, however, is acceptable only to the commercial market, such as office buildings, hotels, and restaurants. Therefore, the company does not try to sell to the home market through grocery stores.

Over time, the cost competitive advantage may fail. Typically, if one firm is using an innovative technology to reduce its costs, then other firms in the industry will adopt this technology and reduce their costs as well. For example, Bell Labs invented fiber optic cables that reduced the cost of voice and data transmission by dramatically increasing the number of calls that could be transmitted simultaneously through a two-inch cable. Within five years, however, fiber optic technology had spread through the industry and Bell Labs lost its cost competitive advantage. Firms may also lose their cost competitive advantage if competing firms match their low costs by using the same lower-cost suppliers. Therefore, a cost competitive advantage may not offer a long-term competitive advantage.

Product/Service Differentiation Competitive Advantage Because cost competitive advantages are subject to continual erosion, product/service differentiation tends to provide a longer lasting competitive advantage. The durability of a **differential competitive advantage** tends to make this strategy more attractive to many top managers. Common differential advantages are brand names (Tide detergent), a strong dealer network (Caterpillar Tractor for construction equipment), product reliability (Lexus cars), image (Neiman Marcus in retailing), and service (Federal Express). Brand names such as Chanel, BMW, and Cartier stand for quality the world over. Through continual product and marketing innovations and attention to quality and value, managers at these organizations have created enduring competitive advantages. Arthur Doppelmayer, an Austrian manufacturer of aerial transport systems (ski lifts), believes his main differential advantage, besides innovative equipment design, is his service system, which allows the company to come to the assistance of users anywhere in the world within 24 hours. Doppelmayer uses a worldwide system of warehouses and skilled personnel prepared to move immediately in emergency cases.

Niche Competitive Advantage A company with a **niche competitive advantage** targets and effectively serves a single segment of the market. For small companies with limited resources that potentially face giant competitors, "niche-ing" may be the only viable option. A market segment that has good growth potential but is not crucial to the success of major competitors is a good candidate for a niche strategy. Once a potential segment has been identified, the firm needs to make certain it can defend against challengers through its superior ability to serve buyers in the segment. For example, STI Music Private Bank follows a niche strategy with its concentration on country music stars and entertainment industry professionals in Nashville. Its office is in the heart of Nashville's music district. STI has decided to expand its niche strategy to Miami, the "epicenter" of Latin music, and Atlanta. The latter is a longtime rhythm-and-blues capital and now is the center of contemporary

CONCEPT *in Action*

In the race to be America's premier satellite radio provider, two firms lead the pack. XM, the original pioneer of subscriber-based radio, offers listeners the best in entertainment including exclusive digital streams of major league sports and Oprah Winfrey. Rival company Sirius lures subscribers with a programming mix that includes NBA games and edgy adult banter from shock jock Howard Stern. *What factors might constitute a competitive advantage for companies in the satellite radio business?*

differential competitive advantage
A firm's ability to provide a unique product or service with a set of features that the target market perceives as important and better than the competitor's.

niche competitive advantage
A firm's ability to target and effectively serve a single segment of the market within a limited geographic area.

"urban" music. Both new markets have the kinds of music professionals—entertainers, record executives, producers, agents, and others—that have made STI so successful in Nashville.

Many companies using a niche strategy serve only a limited geographic market. Buddy Freddy's is a very successful restaurant chain but is found only in Florida. Migros is the dominant grocery chain in Switzerland. It has no stores outside that small country.

Block Drug Company uses niching by focusing its product line on tooth products. It markets Polident to clean dentures, Poligrip to hold dentures in place, and Sensodyne toothpaste for people with sensitive teeth. The Orvis Company manufactures and sells everything that anyone might ever need for fly fishing. Orvis is a very successful nicher.

A small company, serving a niche market, often views selling to Wal-Mart as "hitting a home run." We discuss the efforts of one such company in the Catching the Entrepreneurial Spirit box.

concept check

What is environmental scanning?

What is a target market, and why should a company have one?

Explain the three types of competitive advantages and provide examples of each.

CATCHING THE ENTREPRENEURIAL SPIRIT

The Long Road to Wal-Mart

Getting into Wal-Mart is an entrepreneur's equivalent of making it to Broadway. Even a short run on the shelves there can help transform an invention from niche product to household name. And although Wal-Mart certainly isn't the only retail path to commercial success, nor the right outlet for every product, for mass-market merchandise at a certain price point no other bricks-and-mortar retailer reaches so many shoppers. Today the company has 5,300 outlets worldwide, and gets more than 138 million customers a week.

But as with Broadway, there's more than enough talent to fill the stage. Last year about 10,000 new suppliers applied to become Wal-Mart vendors. Of those, only about 200, or 2 percent were ultimately accepted. "We just don't have very many empty shelf spaces," says Excell La Fayette, Jr., Wal-Mart's director of supplier development.

Colin Roche's path to Bentonville, Arkansas, and Wal-Mart's headquarters began in 1987 at his Palo Alto, California, high school. On lunch break, Mr. Roche wandered into a flea market where he purchased a toy robot that, when twisted a certain way, doubles as a pen. While fiddling with the robot and a lighter, he burned the writing tip off one leg and reattached it to the robot's head. Writing in that position, with one index finger between the robot's legs, he found he didn't need to grip so tightly because the design supported the natural weight of his hand. "I'd always had horrible writer's cramp, and this helped," he says.

Colin and a college friend, Bobby Ronsse, founded PenAgain by putting in $5,000 each. They created a wishbone design modeled after the robot. Hard work has paid off for the two entrepreneurs. PenAgain has sales of around $2 million and is sold in 5,000 independent stationery and office-supply stores, 200 Staples in Canada, and other chain outlets including Fred Meyer and Hobby Lobby. Mr. Roche's company also does a strong business in the promotional-products industry, has sold 1.2 million units in Europe alone, and sees about $5,000 in Internet business every month.

Even with these pieces in place, Mr. Roche says the pair still wondered, "How the heck do you get into Wal-Mart?" Speaking with local Wal-Mart managers and attending a trade show finally resulted in an invitation to Bentonville. Colin and Bobby were given an 8:00 A.M. appointment and at 8:01 A.M. they were escorted to a small conference room.

Immediately, the buyer delivered bad news upon seeing the PenAgain. "I've seen this design before and passed," she said, mentioning a competitor's product manufactured in Korea with a similar shape.

Mr. Roche kept his game face on, heart racing. "The difference," he said, "is that we are building a brand. Rather than going to you first, we've got a base of independent retailers and distributors worldwide who have already picked us up." He kept talking, showing her the testimonials, media write-ups, product extensions, and everything else he and Mr. Ronsse had assembled over the previous few years. "She kept taking notes and looking really serious and professional," he recalls.

Finally, with their time allotment nearly up, the buyer closed her notebook. "OK, we will give you a trial period for a certain amount of time," Mr. Roche recalls she said. The parameters of the deal were this: Some 500 stores would carry the product for six weeks, with the expectation that PenAgain would sell at least 85 percent of the product displayed in that time to warrant more permanent shelf space. (Mr. La Fayette of Wal-Mart confirms that these are fairly standard terms.)[5]

Critical Thinking Questions
- Should most small businesses that sell consumer goods try to have their products sold at Wal-Mart? Why or why not?
- Wal-Mart doesn't like to account for more than 30 percent of a supplier's total business. Why do you think this is true?

Developing a Marketing Mix

marketing mix
The blend of product offering, pricing, promotional methods, and distribution system that brings a specific group of consumers superior value.

four Ps
Product, price, promotion, and place (distribution), which together make up the marketing mix.

product strategy
Taking the good or service and selecting a brand name, packaging, colors, a warranty, accessories, and a service program.

pricing strategy
Setting a price based upon the demand for and cost of producing a good or service.

distribution strategy
Creating the means by which products flow from the producer to the consumer.

Once a firm has defined its target market and identified its competitive advantage, it can create the **marketing mix**, that is, the blend of product offering, pricing, promotional methods, and distribution system that brings a specific group of consumers superior value. Distribution is sometimes referred to as place, so the marketing mix is based on the **four Ps**: product, price, promotion, and place. Every target market requires a unique marketing mix to satisfy the needs of the target consumers and meet the firm's goals. A strategy must be constructed for each of the four Ps and blended with the strategies for the other elements. Thus, the marketing mix is only as good as its weakest part. An excellent product with a poor distribution system could be doomed to failure. A successful marketing mix requires careful tailoring. For instance, at first glance you might think that McDonald's and Wendy's have roughly the same marketing mix. After all, they are both in the fast-food business. But McDonald's targets parents with young children through Ronald McDonald, heavily promoted children's Happy Meals, and playgrounds. Wendy's is targeted to a more adult crowd. Wendy's has no playgrounds but it does have carpeting in many stores (a more adult atmosphere) and expanded its menu to include items for adult tastes.

Product Strategy

Marketing strategy typically starts with the product. You can't plan a distribution system or set a price if you don't know what you're going to market. Marketers use the term *product* to refer to both *goods,* such as tires, MP3 players, and clothing, and *services,* such as hotels, hair salons, and restaurants. Thus, the heart of the marketing mix is the good or service. Creating a **product strategy** involves choosing a brand name, packaging, colors, a warranty, accessories, and a service program.

Marketers view products in a much larger context than you might imagine. They include not only the item itself but also the brand name and the company image. The names Ralph Lauren and Gucci, for instance, create extra value for everything from cosmetics to bath towels. That is, products with those names sell at higher prices than identical products without the names. We buy things not only for what they do, but also for what they mean. Product strategies are discussed further in Chapter 13.

Pricing Strategy

Pricing strategy is based on demand for the product and the cost of producing it. Some special considerations can also influence the price. Sometimes, for instance, a special introductory price is used to get people to try a new product. Some firms enter the market with low prices and keep them low, such as Carnival Cruise Lines and Suzuki cars. Others enter a market with very high prices and then lower them over time, such as producers of high-definition televisions and personal computers. You can learn more about pricing strategies in Chapter 13.

Distribution Strategy

Distribution strategy is creating the means (the channel) by which a product flows from the producer to the consumer. One aspect of distribution strategy is deciding how many stores and which specific wholesalers and retailers will handle the product in a geographic area. Cosmetics, for instance, are distributed in many different ways. Avon has a sales force of several hundred thousand representatives who call directly on consumers. Clinique and Estée Lauder are distributed through selected department stores. Cover Girl and Del Laboratories use mostly chain drugstores and other mass merchandisers. Redken sells through beauticians. Revlon uses several of these distribution channels. Distribution is examined in detail in Chapter 14.

CONCEPT *in Action*

With their computerized profile-matching capabilities, online dating services are a high-tech way to make a love connection. Today's date-seeking singles want more than automated personals, however. They want advice from experts. At Match.com, popular shrink Dr. Phil guides subscribers towards healthy relationships. At eHarmony.com, Dr. Neil Clark Warren helps the lovelorn find a soul mate. *How do Internet dating services use various elements of the marketing mix to bolster the effectiveness of their product strategies?*

© CBS/LANDOV

Promotion Strategy

promotion strategy
The unique combination of personal selling, advertising, publicity, and sales promotion to stimulate the target market to buy a product or service.

Many people feel that promotion is the most exciting part of the marketing mix. **Promotion strategy** covers personal selling, advertising, public relations, and sales promotion. Each element is coordinated with the others to create a promotional blend. An advertisement, for instance, helps a buyer get to know the company and paves the way for a sales call. A good promotion strategy can dramatically increase a firm's sales. Promotion is the topic of Chapter 15.

Public relations plays a special role in promotion. It is used to create a good image of the company and its products. Bad publicity costs nothing to send out, but it can cost a firm a great deal in lost business. Good publicity, such as a television or magazine story about a firm's new product, may be the result of much time, money, and effort spent by a public-relations department.

Sales promotion directly stimulates sales. It includes trade shows, catalogs, contests, games, premiums, coupons, and special offers. McDonald's discount coupons and contests offering money and food prizes are examples of sales promotions.

Not-for-Profit Marketing

Profit-oriented companies are not the only ones that analyze the marketing environment, find a competitive advantage, and create a marketing mix. The application of marketing principles and techniques is also vital to not-for-profit organizations. Marketing helps not-for-profit groups identify target markets and develop effective marketing mixes. In some cases, marketing has kept symphonies, museums, and other cultural groups from having to close their doors. In other organizations, such as the American Heart Association, marketing ideas and techniques have helped managers do their jobs better. In the private sector, the profit motive is both an objective for guiding decisions and a criterion for evaluating results. Not-for-profit organizations do not seek to make a profit for redistribution to owners or shareholders. Rather, their focus is often on generating enough funds to cover expenses. For example, the Methodist Church does not gauge its success by the amount of money left in offering plates. The Museum of Science and Industry does not base its performance evaluations on the dollar value of tokens put into the turnstile.

One person who understands not-for-profit marketing is the Broadway producer Jeffrey Seller. His use of marketing is shaking up a very stodgy and traditional industry— the Broadway play. When Mr. Seller started producing "Rent," he convinced his partners to institute a policy of offering a limited number of $20 front-row tickets to attract a younger crowd. For his short-lived effort, "La Boheme," he incorporated advertising into the set—a heresy for a "serious theatrical production." Now he's experimenting with airline-style pricing of theater seats to ensure there's always a full house.

By far the most controversial change Mr. Seller has prompted involves Broadway's No. 1 sales tool—the Tony Awards. He created a promotional campaign targeted at the 730 people who vote for the Tonys, including parties, advertising, and gifts. It positioned "Avenue Q" as a quirky little musical up against a glitzy, Hollywood-backed production. "Avenue Q" won the Tony.[6]

social marketing
The application of marketing techniques to social issues and causes.

Not-for-profit marketing is also concerned with social marketing, that is, the application of marketing to social issues and causes. The goals of **social marketing** are to effect social change (for instance, by creating racial harmony), further social causes (by helping the homeless), and evaluate the relationship between marketing and society (by asking whether society should allow advertising on television shows for young children). Individual organizations also engage in social marketing. The Southern Baptist Radio and Television Convention promotes brotherhood and goodwill by promoting religion and good deeds. M.A.D.D. counsels against drunk driving, and the National Wildlife Federation asks your help in protecting endangered animals and birds.

---

concept check

What is meant by the marketing mix?

What are the components of the marketing mix?

How can marketing techniques help not-for-profit organizations?

Define social marketing.

Buyer Behavior

4 **How do consumers and organizations make buying decisions?**

buyer behavior
The actions people take in buying and using goods and services.

An organization cannot reach its goals without understanding buyer behavior. **Buyer behavior** is the actions people take in buying and using goods and services. Marketers who understand buyer behavior, such as how a price increase will affect a product's sales, can create a more effective marketing mix.

To understand buyer behavior, marketers must understand how consumers make buying decisions. The consumer decision-making process has several steps, which are shown in Exhibit 12.2. The entire process is affected by cultural, social, individual, and psychological factors. The buying process starts with need recognition. This may be as simple as running out of coffee. Yes, I need to purchase more coffee. Or perhaps you recently got married and recognize that you need to start building equity instead of paying rent. Perhaps you are also considering starting a family. Therefore, you decide to buy your first home (Step 1 in Exhibit 12.2).

Next, you begin to gather information about financing, available homes, styles, locations, and so forth (Step 2). After you feel that you have gathered enough information, you begin to evaluate alternatives (Step 3). For example, you might eliminate all homes that cost over $150,000 or are more than a 30-minute drive to your work. Then an offer is made and, if it is accepted, a purchase is made (Step 4). Finally, you assess the experience and your level of satisfaction with your new home (Step 5).

Influences on Consumer Decision Making

Cultural, social, individual, and psychological factors have an impact on consumer decision making from the time a person recognizes a need through postpurchase behavior. We will examine each of these in more detail.

culture
The set of values, ideas, attitudes, and other symbols created to shape human behavior.

Culture Purchase roles within the family are influenced by culture. **Culture** is the set of values, ideas, attitudes, and symbols created to shape human behavior. Culture is

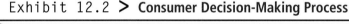
Exhibit 12.2 > Consumer Decision-Making Process

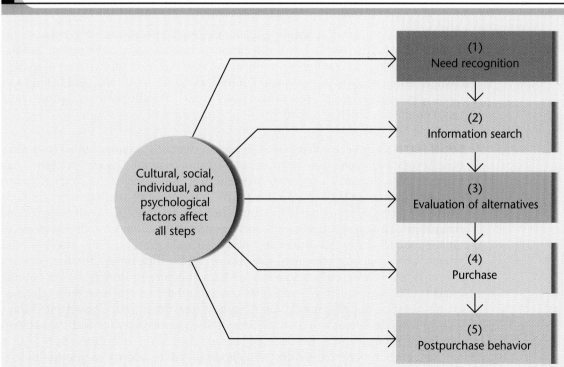

CONCEPT *in Action*

Sarah Jessica Parker is the consummate fashion maven. Adored by fans for her long curly locks and unique sex appeal, she is best known for having played the man-hunting Carrie Bradshaw on HBO's *Sex and the City*. Parker is routinely dubbed "Best Dressed" by glamour magazines and is widely regarded as a style trendsetter. She has been a spokesmodel for Gap and Nutrisse and her Lovely brand perfume is a preferred fragrance of the stars. *How and why do companies choose celebrities to endorse their products?*

environmentally oriented. The nomads of Finland have developed a culture for Arctic survival. Similarly, the natives of the Brazilian jungle have created a culture suitable for jungle living.

Culture by definition is social in nature. It is human interaction that creates values and prescribes acceptable behavior. Thus culture gives order to society by creating common expectations. Sometimes these expectations are codified into law; for example, if you come to a red light, you stop the car. As long as a value or belief meets the needs of society, it will remain part of the culture; if it is no longer functional, the value or belief recedes. The value that very large families are "good" is no longer held by a majority of Americans. Since Americans live in an urban rather than a rural environment, children are no longer needed to perform farm chores.

Culture is not static. It adapts to changing societal needs and evolving environmental factors. The rapid growth of technology has accelerated the rate of cultural change. Inventions such as the elevator made possible modern high-rise cities. Television changed entertainment patterns and family communication flows, and heightened public awareness of political and other news events. The Internet has changed how we communicate and how we work.

Social Factors Most consumers are likely to seek out the opinions of others to reduce their search and evaluation effort or uncertainty, especially as the perceived risk of the decision increases. Consumers may also seek out others' opinions for guidance on new products or services, products with image-related attributes, or products where attribute information is lacking or uninformative. Specifically, consumers interact socially with reference groups, opinion leaders, and family members to obtain product information and decision approval. All the formal and informal groups that influence the buying behavior of an individual are that person's **reference groups**. Consumers may use products or brands to identify with or become a member of a group. They learn from observing how members of their reference groups consume, and they use the same criteria to make their own consumer decisions. A reference group might be a fraternity or sorority, a group you work with, or a club to which you belong.

Reference groups frequently include individuals known as group leaders, or **opinion leaders**—those who influence others. Obviously, it is important for

reference groups
Formal and informal groups that influence buyer behavior.

opinion leaders
Those who influence others.

CONCEPT *in Action*

Since its launching in 2003, MySpace.com has become the Internet's most popular social networking site. The cliquey community portal that "lets you meet your friends' friends," generates more traffic than Google and has ranked among the world's top 20 Web sites. At MySpace, individuals share photos, journals, and interests with an ever-expanding network of mutual acquaintants. The site's connection to the alternative music scene also makes it a haven for the dissemination of youth trends. *How can online communities influence buyer behavior?*

marketing managers to persuade such people to purchase their goods or services. Many products and services that are integral parts of Americans' lives today got their initial boost from opinion leaders. For example, MP3s and flat screen TVs were embraced by opinion leaders well ahead of the general public. Opinion leaders are often the first to try new products and services out of pure curiosity. They are typically self-indulgent, making them more likely to explore unproven but intriguing products and services.

The family is the most important social institution for many consumers, strongly influencing values, attitudes, self-concept—and buying behavior. For example, a family that strongly values good health will have a grocery list distinctly different from that of a family that views every dinner as a gourmet event. Moreover, the family is responsible for the **socialization process**, the passing down of cultural values and norms to children. Children learn by observing their parents' consumption patterns, and so they will tend to shop in a similar pattern.

Marketers should consider family purchase situations along with the distribution of consumer and decision-maker roles among family members. Ordinary marketing views the individual as both decision maker and consumer. Family marketing adds several other possibilities: Sometimes more than one family member or all family members are involved in the decision; sometimes only children are involved in the decision; sometimes more than one consumer is involved; and sometimes the decision maker and the consumer are different people. For example, a parent will select a dentist for a child to visit.

socialization process
The passing down of cultural norms and values to children.

Individual Influences on Consumer Buying Decisions A person's buying decisions are also influenced by personal characteristics that are unique to each individual, such as gender, personality, and self-concept. Individual characteristics are generally stable over the course of one's life. For instance, most people do not change their gender, and the act of changing personality requires a complete reorientation of one's life.

Physiological differences between men and women result in different needs, such as health and beauty products. Just as important are the distinct cultural, social, and economic roles played by men and women and the effects that these have on their decision-making processes. Men and women also shop differently. Studies show that men and women share similar motivations in terms of where to shop—that is, seeking reasonable prices, merchandise quality, and a friendly, low-pressure environment—but they don't necessarily feel the same about shopping in general. Most women enjoy shopping; their male counterparts claim to dislike the experience and shop only out of necessity. Furthermore, men desire simple shopping experiences, stores with less variety, and convenience.

Each consumer has a unique personality. **Personality** is a broad concept that can be thought of as a way of organizing and grouping how an individual typically reacts to situations. Thus, personality combines psychological makeup and environmental forces. It includes people's underlying dispositions, especially their most dominant characteristics. Although personality is one of the least useful concepts in the study of consumer behavior, some marketers believe that personality influences the types and brands of products purchased. For instance, the type of car, clothes, or jewelry a consumer buys may reflect one or more personality traits.

Self-concept, or self-perception, is how consumers perceive themselves. Self-concept includes attitudes, perceptions, beliefs, and self-evaluations. Although self-concept may change, the change is often gradual. Through self-concept, people define their identity, which in turn provides for consistent and coherent behavior.

Self-concept combines the **ideal self-image** (the way an individual would like to be) and the **real self-image** (how an individual actually perceives him or herself). Generally, we try to raise our real self-image toward our ideal (or at least narrow the gap). Consumers seldom buy products that jeopardize their self-image. For example, someone who sees herself as a trendsetter wouldn't buy clothing that doesn't project a contemporary image.

Psychological Influences on Consumer Buying Decisions An individual's buying decisions are further influenced by psychological factors such as perception, and beliefs and attitudes. These factors are what consumers use to interact with their world. They are the tools consumers use to recognize their feelings, gather and analyze information, formulate thoughts and opinions, and take action. Unlike the other three influences on consumer behavior, psychological influences can be affected by a person's environment because they are applied on specific occasions. For example, you will perceive different stimuli and process these stimuli in different ways depending on whether you are sitting in class concentrating on the instructor, sitting outside of class talking to friends, or sitting in your dorm room watching television.

The world is full of stimuli. A stimulus is any unit of input affecting one or more of the five senses: sight, smell, taste, touch, hearing. The process by which we select, organize, and interpret these stimuli into a meaningful and coherent picture is called **perception**. In essence, perception is how we see the world around us and how we recognize that we need some help in making a purchasing decision. People cannot perceive every stimulus in their environment. Therefore, they use **selective exposure** to decide which stimuli to notice and which to ignore. A typical consumer is exposed to more than 250 advertising messages a day but notices only between 11 and 20.

A **belief** is an organized pattern of knowledge that an individual holds as true about his or her world. A consumer may believe that Sony makes the best high definition TVs and has the best picture, greatest selections, and is reasonably priced. These beliefs may be based on knowledge, faith, or hearsay. Consumers tend to develop a set of beliefs about a product's attributes and then, through these beliefs, a *brand image*—a set of beliefs about a particular brand. In turn, the brand image shapes consumers' attitudes toward the product.

An **attitude** is a learned tendency to respond consistently toward a given object, idea, or concept, such as a brand. Attitudes rest on an individual's value system, which represents personal standards of good and bad, right and wrong, and so forth; therefore, attitudes tend to be more enduring and complex than beliefs. For an

personality
A way of organizing and grouping how an individual reacts to situations.

self-concept
How people perceive themselves.

ideal self-image
The way an individual would like to be.

real self-image
How an individual actually perceives him- or herself.

perception
The process by which we select, organize, and interpret stimuli into a meaningful and coherent picture.

selective exposure
The process of deciding which stimuli to notice and which to ignore.

belief
An organized pattern of knowledge that an individual holds as true about the world.

attitude
Learned tendency to respond consistently toward a given object, idea, or concept.

example of the nature of attitudes, consider the differing attitudes of consumers around the world toward the practice of purchasing on credit. Americans have long been enthusiastic about charging goods and services and are willing to pay high interest rates for the privilege of postponing payment. To many European consumers, doing what amounts to taking out a loan—even a small one—to pay for anything seems absurd.

Types of Consumer Buying Decisions

All consumer buying decisions generally fall along a continuum of three broad categories: routine response behavior, limited decision making, and extensive decision making (see Exhibit 12.3). Goods and services in these three categories can best be described in terms of five factors: level of consumer involvement, length of time to make a decision, cost of the good or service, degree of information search, and the number of alternatives considered. The level of consumer involvement is perhaps the most significant determinant in classifying buying decisions. **Involvement** is the amount of time and effort a buyer invests in the search, evaluation, and decision processes of consumer behavior.

Frequently purchased, low-cost goods and services are generally associated with **routine response behavior**. These goods and services can also be called low-involvement products because consumers spend little time on search and decision before making the purchase. Usually, buyers are familiar with several different brands in the product category but stick with one brand. Consumers engaged in routine response behavior normally don't experience need recognition until they are exposed to advertising or see the product displayed on a store shelf.

Limited decision making typically occurs when a consumer has previous product experience but is unfamiliar with the current brands available. Limited decision making is also associated with lower levels of involvement (although higher than routine decisions) because consumers do expend moderate effort in searching for information or in considering various alternatives. Suppose the children's usual brand of cereal, Kellogg's Corn Flakes, is unavailable in the grocery store. Completely out of cereal at home, the parent now must select another brand. Before making a final selection, he or she may pull from the shelf several brands similar to Kellogg's Corn Flakes, such as Corn Chex and Cheerios, to compare their nutritional value and calories and to decide whether the children will like the new cereal.

Consumers practice **extensive decision making** when buying an unfamiliar, expensive product or an infrequently bought item. This process is the most complex type of consumer buying decision and is associated with high involvement on the part of the consumer. This process resembles the model outlined in Exhibit 12.2.

involvement
The amount of time and effort a buyer invests in the search, evaluation, and decision processes of consumer behavior.

routine response behavior
Purchase of low-cost, frequently bought items with little search or decision making.

limited decision making
Consumer has previous product experience but is unfamiliar with the current brands available.

extensive decision making
Purchasing an unfamiliar, expensive, infrequently bought item.

Exhibit 12.3 > Continuum of Consumer Buying Decisions

	Routine Response Behavior	Limited Decision Making	Extensive Decision Making
Consumer Involvement	low	low to moderate	high
Time Required to Make Decision	short	short to moderate	long
Cost	low	low to moderate	high
Information Search	internal only	mostly internal	internal and external
Number of Alternatives	one	few	many

These consumers want to make the right decision, so they want to know as much as they can about the product category and available brands. Buyers use several criteria for evaluating their options and spend much time seeking information. Buying a home or a car, for example, requires extensive decision making.

Business-to-Business Purchase Decision Making

Business buyer behavior and business markets are different from consumer markets. Business markets include institutions such as hospitals and schools, manufacturers, wholesalers and retailers, and various branches of government. The key difference between a consumer product and a business product is the intended use. If you purchase a certain model Dell computer for your home so you can surf the Internet, it is a consumer good. If a purchasing agent for MTV buys exactly the same computer for an MTV script writer, it is a business good. Why? The reason is that MTV is a business, so the computer will be used in a business environment.

Characteristics of the Business-to-Business Market The main differences between consumer markets and business markets are as follows:

1. *Purchase volume.* Business customers buy in much larger quantities than consumers. Think how many truckloads of sugar Mars must purchase to make one day's output of M&Ms. Imagine the number of batteries Sears buys each day for resale to consumers. Think of the number of pens the federal government must use each day.
2. *Number of customers.* Business marketers usually have far fewer customers than consumer marketers. As a result, it is much easier to identify prospective buyers and monitor current needs. Think about how few customers for airplanes or industrial cranes there are compared to the more than 80 million consumer households in the United States.
3. *Location of buyers.* Business customers tend to be much more geographically concentrated than consumers. The computer industry is concentrated in Silicon Valley and a few other areas. Aircraft manufacturing is found in Seattle, St. Louis, and Dallas/Fort Worth. Suppliers to these manufacturers often locate close to the manufacturers to lower distribution costs and facilitate communication.
4. *Direct distribution.* Business sales tend to be made directly to the buyer because such sales frequently involve large quantities or custom-made items like heavy machinery. Consumer goods are more likely to be sold through intermediaries like wholesalers and retailers.

> **concept check**
>
> Explain the consumer decision-making process.
>
> How do business markets differ from consumer markets?

Market Segmentation

 5 **What are the five basic forms of market segmentation?**

market segmentation
The process of separating, identifying, and evaluating the layers of a market in order to identify a target market.

The study of buyer behavior helps marketing managers better understand why people make purchases. To identify the target markets that may be most profitable for the firm, managers use **market segmentation**, which is the process of separating, identifying, and evaluating the layers of a market to identify a target market. For instance, a target market might be segmented into two groups: families with children and families without children. Families with young children are likely to buy hot cereals and presweetened cereals. Families with no children are more likely to buy health-oriented cereals. You can be sure that cereal companies plan their marketing mixes with this difference in mind. A business market may be segmented by large customers and small customers or by geographic area.

The five basic forms of consumer market segmentation are demographic, geographic, psychographic, benefit, and volume. Their characteristics are summarized in Exhibit 12.4 and discussed in the following sections.

Exhibit 12.4 > Forms of Consumer Market Segmentation

Form	General Characteristics
Demographic segmentation	Age, education, gender, income, race, social class, household size
Geographic segmentation	Regional location (e.g., New England, Mid-Atlantic, Southeast, Great Lakes, Plains States, Northwest, Southwest, Rocky Mountains, Far West); population density (urban, suburban, rural); city or county size; climate
Psychographic segmentation	Lifestyle, personality, interests, values, attitudes
Benefit segmentation	Benefits provided by the good or service
Volume segmentation	Amount of use (light versus heavy)

Demographic Segmentation

demographic segmentation
The differentiation of markets through the use of categories such as age, education, gender, income, and household size.

Demographic segmentation uses categories such as age, education, gender, income, and household size to differentiate among markets. This form of market segmentation is the most common. The U.S. Census Bureau provides a great deal of demographic data. For example, marketing researchers can use census data to find areas within cities that contain high concentrations of high-income consumers, singles, blue-collar workers, and so forth.

Many products are targeted to various age groups. Most music CDs, Pepsi, Coke, many movies, the Dodge Neon, and thousands of other products are targeted toward teenagers and persons under 25 years old. In contrast, most cruises, medical products, fine jewelry, vacation homes, Buicks, and denture products are targeted toward people 50 years old and up. An example of how Frito Lay targets various age groups for three of its most popular products is shown is Exhibit 12.5.

CONCEPT in Action

The dirty little secret at Victoria's Secret is that tweens are showing an increasing interest in the company's apparel. Though the lingerie maker strongly denies targeting children ages 8 to 12, it concedes that young girls are buying Victoria's items such as sleepwear from the marketer's tame "Pink" collection. The company's unspoken—but thinly veiled—hope is that tweens will eventually graduate from hearts and glitter to satin and lace. *Can you identify other companies that target teens with their marketing message with hopes of capturing them as loyal users and then turning them into loyal adult users?*

Exhibit 12.5 > Age Segmentation for Fritos, Doritos, and Tostitos

	Name Derivation	Year Introduced	Main Ingredients	Demographic	Snack Niche, According to Frito Lay
Fritos	"Little fried bits" (Spanish)	1932	Corn, vegetable oil, salt	33- to 51-year-old males	"Hunger satisfaction"
Doritos	"Little bits of gold"	1964	Corn, vegetable oil, cheddar cheese, salt	Teens, mostly males	"Bold and daring snacking"
Tostitos	"Little toasted bits" (Spanish)	1981	White corn, vegetable oil, salt	Upscale consumers born between 1946 and 1964	"Casual interaction through friends and family . . .a social food that brings people together"

SOURCE: Frito Lay.

Sometimes several different segmentation criteria are used to precisely pinpoint target markets. For example, Frito Lay can further segment the corn snack products (Fritos, Doritos, and Tostitos) by (A) consumed at work and (B) not consumed at work. Corn snacks consumed at work can be segmented by the type of work and the ability to eat snacks on the job. For example, a factory worker at Ford, an administrative assistant stationed in a cubicle, and an on-the-go nurse at a hospital will each have different snacking habits. As you can see, the type of work a person does can influence when and how the person eats a salty corn snack. This form of segmentation helps Frito Lay develop a promotion campaign, place vending machines, alter package sizes, and even create new products. Ask yourself which type of worker is more likely to have a small bag of Fritos in his/her lunch and which worker is most likely to eat guacamole and Tostitos on the job.

Income is another popular way to segment markets. Income level influences consumers' wants and determines their buying power. Housing, clothing, automobiles, and alcoholic beverages are among the many markets segmented by income. Budget Gourmet frozen dinners are targeted to lower-income groups, whereas the Le Menu line and California Pizza Kitchen frozen pizzas are aimed at higher-income consumers.

Geographic Segmentation

geographic segmentation
The differentiation of markets by region of the country, city or county size, market density, or climate.

Geographic segmentation means segmenting markets by region of the country, city or county size, market density, or climate. *Market density* is the number of people or businesses within a certain area. Many companies segment their markets geographically to meet regional preferences and buying habits. Pizza Hut, for instance, gives Easterners extra cheese, Westerners more ingredients, and Midwesterners both. Both Ford and Chevrolet sell more pickup trucks and truck parts in the middle of the country than on either coast. The well-defined "pickup truck belt" runs from the upper Midwest south through Texas and the Gulf states. Ford "owns" the northern half of this truck belt, and Chevrolet the southern half.

Psychographic Segmentation

Race, income, occupation, and other demographic variables help in developing strategies but often do not paint the entire picture of consumer needs. Demographics pro-

CONCEPT *in Action*

Mindful of America's growing waistline, Nabisco now offers 100-calorie-pack versions of its best-selling food snacks. The snack packs are popular with diet-conscious consumers who have long clamored for food marketers to reduce serving sizes of high-calorie products. Mini and thin-crisp versions of Oreos, Cheese Nips, and other snacks deliver all the taste of their full-sized counterparts, minus the guilt. *How did market segmentation influence the development of Nabisco's 100 Calorie Packs?*

psychographic segmentation
The differentiation of markets by personality or lifestyle.

vide the skeleton, but psychographics add meat to the bones. Psychographic segmentation is market segmentation by personality or lifestyle. People with common activities, interests, and opinions are grouped together and given a "lifestyle name." For example, Harley-Davidson divides its customers into seven lifestyle segments, from "cocky misfits" who are most likely to be arrogant troublemakers, to "laid-back camper types" committed to cycling and nature, to "classy capitalists" who have wealth and privilege.

Benefit Segmentation

benefit segmentation
The differentiation of markets based on what a product will do rather than on customer characteristics.

Benefit segmentation is based on what a product will do rather than on consumer characteristics. For years Crest toothpaste was targeted toward consumers concerned with preventing cavities. Recently, Crest subdivided its market. It now offers regular Crest, Crest Tartar Control for people who want to prevent cavities and tartar buildup, Crest for kids with sparkles that taste like bubble gum, and another Crest that prevents gum disease. Another toothpaste, Topol, targets people who want whiter teeth—teeth without coffee, tea, or tobacco stains. Sensodyne toothpaste is aimed at people with highly sensitive teeth.

Volume Segmentation

volume segmentation
The differentiation of markets based on the amount of the product purchased.

The fifth main type of segmentation is **volume segmentation**, which is based on the amount of the product purchased. Just about every product has heavy, moderate, and light users, as well as nonusers. Heavy users often account for a very large portion of a product's sales. Thus, a firm might want to target its marketing mix to the heavy-user segment. For example, in the fast-food industry, the heavy user (a young, single male) accounts for only one in five fast-food patrons. Yet, this heavy user makes over 60 percent of all visits to fast-food restaurants.

Retailers are aware that heavy shoppers not only spend more, but also visit each outlet more frequently than other shoppers. Heavy shoppers visit the grocery store 122 times per year, compared with 93 annual visits for the medium shopper. They visit discount stores more than twice as often as medium shoppers, and they visit convenience/gas stores more than five times as often. On each trip, they consistently spend more than their medium-shopping counterparts.

concept check

Define market segmentation.

List and discuss the five basic forms of market segmentation.

Using Marketing Research to Serve Existing Customers and Find New Customers

 How is marketing research used in marketing decision making?

marketing research
The process of planning, collecting, and analyzing data relevant to a marketing decision.

How do successful companies learn what their customers value? Through marketing research, companies can be sure they are listening to the voice of the customer. **Marketing research** is the process of planning, collecting, and analyzing data relevant to a marketing decision. The results of this analysis are then communicated to management. The information collected through marketing research includes the preferences of customers, the perceived benefits of products, and consumer lifestyles. Research helps companies make better use of their marketing budgets. Marketing research has a range of uses from fine-tuning existing products to discovering whole new marketing concepts.

For example, everything at the Olive Garden restaurant chain from the décor to the wine list is based on marketing research. Each new menu item is put through a series of consumer taste tests before being added to the menu. Hallmark Cards uses marketing research to test messages, cover designs, and even the size of the cards. Hallmark's experts know which kinds of cards will sell best in which places. Engagement cards, for instance, sell best in the Northeast, where engagement parties are popular. Birthday cards for "Daddy" sell best in the South because even adult southerners tend to call their fathers Daddy.

This section examines the marketing research process, which consists of the following steps:

1. Define the marketing problem.
2. Choose a method of research.
3. Collect the data.
4. Analyze the research data.
5. Make recommendations to management.

Define the Marketing Problem

The most critical step in the marketing research process is defining the marketing problem. This involves writing either a problem statement or a list of research objectives. If the problem is not defined properly, the remainder of the research will be a waste of time and money. Two key questions can help in defining the marketing problem correctly:

1. Why is the information being sought? By discussing with managers what the information is going to be used for and what decisions might be made as a result, the researcher can get a clearer grasp of the problem.
2. Does the information already exist? If so, money and time can be saved and a quick decision can be made.

Choose a Method of Research

survey research
A marketing research method in which data is gathered from respondents, either in person, by telephone, by mail, at a mall, or through the Internet to obtain facts, opinions, and attitudes.

observation research
A marketing research method in which the investigator monitors respondents' actions without interacting directly with the respondents; for example, by using cash registers with scanners.

After the problem is correctly defined, a research method is chosen. There are three basic research methods: survey, observation, and experiment.

With **survey research**, data is gathered from respondents, either in person or at a mall, or through the Internet, by telephone, or mail, to obtain facts, opinions, and attitudes. A questionnaire is used to provide an orderly and structured approach to data gathering. Face-to-face interviews may take place at the respondent's home, in a shopping mall, or at a place of business.

Observation research is research that monitors respondents' actions without direct interaction. In the fastest-growing form of observation research, researchers use cash registers with scanners that read tags with bar codes to identify the item being purchased. Technological advances are rapidly expanding the future of observation research. Arbitron research has developed a portable people meter, P.P.M., about the size of a cell phone, that research participants clip to their belts or any article of clothing. They agree to wear it during all waking hours. Before the study participants go to sleep, they put the P.P.M. in a cradle that automatically sends data back to Arbitron. The P.P.M. will tell the market research company exactly which television programs the person watched and for how long. It also records radio programs listened to, any Web streaming, supermarket Muzak, or any other electronic media that the research participant encountered during the day.

In the third research method, **experiment**, the investigator changes one or more variables—price, package, design, shelf space, advertising theme, or advertising expenditures—while observing the effects of those changes on another variable (usually sales). The objective of experiments is to measure causality. For example, an experiment may reveal the impact that a change in package design has on sales.

Collect the Data

Two types of data are used in marketing research: **primary data**, which are collected directly from the original source to solve a problem; and **secondary data**, which is data previously collected for any purpose other than the one at hand. Secondary data can come from a number of sources, among them government agencies, trade associations, research bureaus, universities, the Internet, commercial publications, and internal company records. Company records include sales invoices, accounting records, data from previous research studies, and historical sales data.

Primary data are usually gathered through some form of survey research. As described earlier, survey research often relies on interviews. See Exhibit 12.6 for the different types of surveys. Today, conducting surveys over the Internet is the fastest growing form of survey research.

experiment
A marketing research method in which the investigator changes one or more variables—price, packaging, design, shelf space, advertising theme, or advertising expenditures—while observing the effects of these changes on another variable (usually sales).

primary data
Information collected directly from the original source to solve a problem.

secondary data
Information that has already been collected for any purpose other than the one at hand.

Exhibit 12.6 > Common Types of Survey Research

Internet surveys	Conducted on the Internet, often using respondents from huge Internet panels (persons agreeing to participate in a series of surveys).
Executive surveys	Interviews of professionals (e.g., engineers, architects, doctors, executives) or decision makers are conducted at their place of business.
Mall-intercept surveys	Interviews with consumers are conducted in a shopping mall or other high-traffic location. Interviews may be done in a public area of the mall, or respondents may be taken to a private test area.
Central-location telephone surveys	Interviews are conducted from a telephone facility set up for that purpose. These facilities typically have equipment that permits supervisors to unobtrusively monitor the interviewing while it is taking place. Many of these facilities do national sampling from a single location. An increasing number have computer-assisted interviewing capabilities. At these locations, the interviewer sits in front of a computer terminal attached to a mainframe or a personal computer. The questionnaire is programmed into the computer, and the interviewer uses the keyboard to directly enter responses.
Self-administered questionnaires	Self-administered questionnaires are most frequently employed at high-traffic locations such as shopping malls or in captive audience situations such as classrooms and airplanes. Respondents are given general information on how to fill out the questionnaire and are expected to fill it out on their own. Kiosk-based point-of-service touch screens provide a way to capture information from individuals in stores, health clinics, and other shopping or service environments. Sometimes software-driven questionnaires on diskettes are sent to individuals who have personal computers.
One-time mail surveys	Questionnaires are mailed or e-mailed to a sample of consumers or industrial users, without prior contact by the researcher. Instructions are included; respondents are asked to fill out the questionnaire and return it. Sometimes a gift or monetary incentive is provided.
Mail panels	Questionnaires are mailed to a sample of individuals who have been precontacted. The panel concept has been explained to them, and they have agreed to participate for some period of time, in exchange for gratuities. Mail panels typically generate much higher response rates than do one-time mail surveys.

Analyze the Data

After the data have been collected, the next step in the research process is data analysis. The purpose of this analysis is to interpret and draw conclusions from the mass of collected data. Many software statistical programs such as SAS and SPSS are available to make this task easier for the researcher.

Make Recommendations to Management

After completing the data analysis, the researcher must prepare the report and communicate the conclusions and recommendations to management. This is a key step in the process because marketing researchers who want their conclusions acted upon must convince the manager that the results are credible and justified by the data collected. Today, presentation software like PowerPoint and Astound provides easy-to-use tools for creating reports and presentations that are more interesting, compelling, and effective than was possible just a few years ago.

concept check

Define marketing research.

Explain the marketing research process.

What are the three basic marketing research methods?

Trends in Marketing

 7 **What are the trends in understanding the consumer?**

To discover exactly what customers value most, organizations are using innovative techniques for collecting customer information. Some of the more sophisticated marketing research techniques that are growing in popularity are the use of the Internet, scanner-based research, loyalty cards, and one-to-one marketing.

Internet Marketing Research

In the United States the online population is nearly equivalent to the U.S. population in most key demographic areas. In 2006, over 170 million Americans logged on each month to shop, e-mail, find information, visit in chat rooms, and so forth.[7] This phenomena has resulted in more and more marketing research being conducted on the Internet. Today, about half of all marketing research expenditures will be for Internet-based marketing research. Current methods of conducting some types of research

CONCEPT *in Action*

Businesses seeking up-to-the-minute feedback on brands are increasingly looking to the blogosphere to learn what customers like and dislike. Online buzz-tracking firms such as Umbria and Factvia traverse millions of blogs, wikis, message boards, and Web sites to analyze consumer opinions on everything from what cars are hot to which *American Idol* performer is popular with viewers. *What makes the blogosphere a useful resource for tracking the latest buzz about brands?*

© ASSOCIATED PRESS, AP

soon may seem as quaint as a steam-engine train. New techniques and strategies for conducting traditional marketing research are appearing online in increasing numbers every day. The growth of Internet marketing research is being fueled because the Internet:

- Provides more rapid access to business intelligence and thus allows for better and faster decision making.
- Improves a firm's ability to respond quickly to customer needs and market shifts.
- Facilitates conducting follow-up studies and longitudinal research.
- Slashes labor- and time-intensive research activities (and associated costs), including mailing, telephone solicitation, data entry, data tabulation, and reporting.

Internet surveys have several specific advantages:

- *Rapid development, real-time reporting.* Internet surveys can be broadcast to thousands of potential respondents simultaneously. The results can be tabulated and posted for corporate clients to view as the returns arrive. Thus, Internet survey results can be in a client's hands in significantly less time than traditional survey results.
- *Dramatically reduced costs.* The Internet can cut costs by 25 to 40 percent while providing results in half the time it takes to do a traditional telephone survey. Data-collection costs account for a large proportion of any traditional market research budget. Telephone surveys are labor-intensive efforts incurring training, telecommunications, and management costs. Using the Internet eliminates these costs completely.
- *Personalization.* Internet surveys can be highly personalized for greater relevance to each respondent's own situation, thus speeding the response process. Respondents enjoy answering only pertinent questions, being able to pause and resume the survey as their schedule allows, and having the ability to see previous responses and correct inconsistencies.
- *Higher response rates.* Busy respondents are growing increasingly intolerant of "snail mail" or telephone-based surveys. Internet surveys take half the time to complete than phone interviews do, can be accomplished at the respondent's convenience (after work hours), and are much more stimulating and engaging. Graphics, interactivity, links to incentive sites, and real-time summary reports make Internet surveys more enjoyable. This results in much higher response rates.
- *Ability to contact the hard-to-reach.* Busy professionals—doctors, engineers, and top management in Global 2000 firms—are the most difficult to reach through traditional survey methods. Many of these groups are well represented online. Internet surveys provide convenient anytime/anywhere access that makes it easy for busy professionals to participate.[8]

Conducting Internet marketing research is possible only in countries that have a high Internet penetration rate such as in Western Europe. When marketing researchers "go global" they face many challenges, as discussed in the Expanding Around the Globe box.

Scanner-Based Research

scanner-based research
System for gathering information from a single group of respondents by continuously monitoring the advertising, promotion, and pricing they are exposed to and the things that they buy.

Scanner-based research is a system for gathering information from a single group of respondents by continuously monitoring the advertising, promotion, and pricing they are exposed to and the things they buy. The variables measured are advertising campaigns, coupons, displays, and product prices. The result is a huge database of marketing efforts and consumer behavior. Scanner-based research is bringing ever closer the Holy Grail of marketing research: an accurate, objective picture of the direct causal relationship between different kinds of marketing efforts and actual sales.

The two major scanner-based suppliers are Information Resources, Inc. (IRI) and the A.C. Nielsen Company. Each has about half the market. However, IRI is the founder of scanner-based research.

Challenges of Conducting Global Marketing Research

Global companies, like Procter & Gamble, McDonald's, and 3M, want global marketing research to help them make good strategic marketing decisions around the world. Yet, doing marketing research in some countries is not easy.

For example, using the same questionnaire asking "How did you like the taste of the new Pizza Hut crust?" might be followed with a scale that goes (1) excellent through (7) poor. Americans might rank the new crust at 3.3 and Asians at 1.7. Thus, the conclusion is that the Asians prefer the new crust more than the Americans. The answer would be wrong! Asians don't like to offend others and therefore rate the new crust higher. In fact, they both liked the new crust the same!

There are many other problems in conducting global research. Cultural habits in some countries virtually prohibit communication with a stranger, particularly for women. For example, a researcher simply may not be able to speak on the phone with a housewife in an Islamic country to find out what she thinks of a particular brand. Second, in many societies, such matters as preferences for hygienic products are too personal to be shared with an outsider. In many Latin American countries, a woman may feel ashamed to talk with a researcher about her choice of a brand of sanitary pad, hair shampoo, or perfume. Third, respondents in many cases may be unwilling to share their true feelings with interviewers because they suspect the interviewers may be agents of the government (for example, seeing information for imposition of additional taxes). Fourth, middle-class people, in developing countries in particular, are reluctant to accept their status and may make false claims to reflect the lifestyle of wealthier people. For example, in a study on the consumption of tea in India, more than 70 percent of the respondents from middle-income families claimed they used one of the several national brands of tea. This finding could not be substantiated because more than 60 percent of the tea sold nationally in India is unbranded, generic tea sold unpackaged. Fifth, many respondents, willing to cooperate, may be illiterate, so that even oral communication may be difficult.[9]

Critical Thinking Questions

- What cultural factors (values, attitudes, ideas, and symbols) may influence the market research conducted in a third-world country?
- How can market researchers improve the accuracy and quality of market research conducted in a foreign country?

IRI's first product is called *BehaviorScan*. A household panel (a group of 3,000 long-term participants in the research project) has been recruited and maintained in each BehaviorScan town. Panel members shop with an ID card, which is presented at the checkout in scanner-equipped grocery stores and drugstores, allowing IRI to track electronically each household's purchases, item by item, over time. It uses microcomputers to measure TV viewing in each panel household and can send special commercials to panel member television sets. With such a measure of household purchasing, it is possible to manipulate marketing variables, such as TV advertising or consumer promotions, or to introduce a new product and analyze real changes in consumer buying behavior.

IRI's most successful product is *InfoScan*—a scanner-based sales-tracking service for the consumer packaged-goods industry. Retail sales, detailed consumer purchasing information (including measurement of store loyalty and total grocery basket expenditures), and promotional activity by manufacturers and retailers are monitored and evaluated for all bar-coded products. Data are collected weekly from more than 31,000 supermarkets, drugstores, and mass merchandisers.

Loyalty Cards

loyalty cards
Cards issued by a manufacturer, service organization, or retailer that give discounts to loyal and frequent shoppers.

Just swipe the card at the checkout register and get a discount on tomatoes, toothpaste, or other specials. You save money, and the store builds a record that lets it know how to serve its best customers. **Loyalty cards** are cards issued by a service organization, retailer, or manufacturer that give discounts to loyal and frequent shoppers. Most companies require the shopper to fill out a demographic profile questionnaire before the card is issued.

Loyalty cards have been around for a few years now, and supermarket and drugstore chains are beginning to reap the benefits. With a huge amount of data being collected on shoppers, from the types of soda they buy to whether they like to shop late at night, merchants are getting smarter at tracking consumer trends. And they're changing their merchandise, store layout, and advertising accordingly to keep their most loyal customers spending. A few examples:

- CVS Corp. launched its loyalty-card program and discovered that cosmetics buyers are its best customers. So beauty products have been put up front in a third of the stores, instead of being relegated to the back corners.

- Food Lion started offering loyalty cards a few years ago and now is stocking up on peppers, cactus leaves, and plantains in its Charlotte, North Carolina, stores to better serve Hispanic customers from the Caribbean.
- Winn-Dixie Stores, which began rolling out a loyalty-card program in March 2002, can now measure the effectiveness of ads on top customers and knows the 25 items that attract the most loyal shoppers.

Retailers estimate that 20 percent of their shoppers account for 80 percent of store sales, so finding out what their best customers want is essential. By simply scanning purchases, stores track what's selling, but when that information is tied to loyalty cards, merchants obtain richer information on who is buying what. This is the prized asset of supermarkets' future.

One-to-One Marketing

one-to-one marketing
Creating a unique marketing mix for every customer.

marketing database
Computerized file of customers' and potential customers' profiles and purchase patterns.

One-to-one marketing is creating a unique marketing mix for every consumer. The key to creating one-to-one marketing is a good marketing database. The information contained in a marketing database helps managers know and understand customers, and potential customers, on an individual basis. A **marketing database** is a computerized file of customers' and potential customers' profiles and purchase patterns.

In the 1960s, network television enabled advertisers to "get the same message to everyone simultaneously." Database marketing can get a customized, individual message to everyone simultaneously through direct mail. This is why database marketing is sometimes called *micromarketing*. Database marketing can create a computerized form of the old-fashioned relationship that people used to have with the corner grocer, butcher, or baker. "A database is sort of a collective memory," says Richard G. Barlow, president of Frequency Marketing, Inc., a Cincinnati-based consulting firm. "It deals with you in the same personalized way as a mom-and-pop grocery store, where they knew customers by name and stocked what they wanted."

The size of some databases is impressive: Ford Motor Company's is about 50 million names; Kraft General Foods, 30 million; Citicorp, 30 million; and Kimberly Clark, maker of Huggies diapers, 10 million new mothers. American Express can pull from its database all cardholders who made purchases at golf pro shops in the past six months, who attended symphony concerts, or who traveled to Europe more than once in the past year, as well as the very few people who did all three.

Companies are using their marketing databases to implement one-to-one marketing. For example, Novartis Seeds, Inc., a Minneapolis-based agriculture business, produces individually customized, full-color brochures for 7,000 farmers. Each piece features products selected by Novartis dealers specifically for the farmer based on information collected about the farm operation and the types of crops grown. Instead of the 30-page catalog Novartis traditionally sent, these customers get a 1-page brochure with only the five or six products they need, plus other complementary products dealers feel they should consider.

concept check

Describe how scanner-based research helps measure the effectiveness of marketing.

Explain how loyalty cards are of benefit to manufacturers and retailers.

Describe one-to-one marketing and the role of marketing databases.

Summary of Learning Goals

1 What are the marketing concept and relationship building?

Marketing includes those business activities that are designed to satisfy consumer needs and wants through the exchange process. Marketing managers use the "right" principle—getting the right goods or services to the right people at the right place, time, and price, using the right promotional techniques. Today, many firms have adopted the marketing concept. The marketing concept involves identifying consumer needs and wants and then producing goods or services that will satisfy them while making a profit. Relationship marketing entails forging long-term relationships with customers, which can lead to repeat sales, reduced costs, and stable relationships.

2 How do managers create a marketing strategy?

A firm creates a marketing strategy by understanding the external environment, defining the target market, determining a competitive advantage, and developing a marketing mix. Environmental scanning enables companies to understand the external environment. The target market is the specific group of consumers toward which a firm directs its marketing efforts. A competitive advantage is a set of unique features of a company and its products that are perceived by the target market as significant and superior to those of the competition.

3 What is the marketing mix?

To carry out the marketing strategy, firms create a marketing mix—a blend of products, distribution systems, prices, and promotion. Marketing managers use this mix to satisfy target consumers. The mix can be applied to nonbusiness as well as business situations.

4 How do consumers and organizations make buying decisions?

Buyer behavior is what people and businesses do in buying and using goods and services. The consumer decision-making process consists of the following steps: recognizing a need, seeking information, evaluating alternatives, purchasing the product, judging the purchase outcome, and engaging in postpurchase behavior. A number of factors influence the process. Cultural, social, individual, and psychological factors have an impact on consumer decision making. The main differences between consumer and business markets are purchase volume, number of customers, location of buyers, direct distribution, and rational purchase decisions.

5 What are the five basic forms of market segmentation?

Success in marketing depends on understanding the target market. One technique used to identify a target market is market segmentation. The five basic forms of segmentation are demographic (population statistics), geographic (location), psychographic (personality or lifestyle), benefit (product features), and volume (amount purchased).

6 How is marketing research used in marketing decision making?

Much can be learned about consumers through marketing research, which involves collecting, recording, and analyzing data important in marketing goods and services and communicating the results to management. Marketing researchers may use primary data, which are gathered through door-to-door, mall-intercept, telephone, the Internet, and mail interviews. The Internet is becoming a quick, cheap, and efficient way to gather primary data. Secondary data are available from a variety of sources including government, trade, and commercial associations. Secondary data save time and money, but they may not meet researchers' needs. A huge amount of secondary data is available on the Internet. Both primary and secondary data give researchers a better idea of how the market will respond to the product. Thus, they reduce the risk of producing something the market doesn't want.

7 What are the trends in understanding the consumer?

Due to the proliferation of Internet users, about half of all marketing research expenditures will be for Internet-based marketing research. BehaviorScan uses scanners and television meters to measure the impact of marketing on sales of specific products. BehaviorScan panels can also measure the impact of coupons, free samples, store displays, new packaging, and pricing. Another trend is retailers capitalizing on shopper loyalty cards. These enable managers to track customer shopping patterns. A final trend is the growing use of one-to-one marketing by using databases to better target the needs of customers and noncustomers.

Key Terms

attitude   412
belief   412
benefit segmentation   417
buyer behavior   409
competitive advantage   404
cost competitive advantage   404
culture   409
customer satisfaction   401
customer value   401
demographic segmentation   415
differential competitive advantage   405
distribution strategy   406
environmental scanning   403
exchange   400
experiment   419
extensive decision making   413
four Ps   407
geographic segmentation   416
ideal self-image   412
involvement   413
limited decision making   413
loyalty cards   422
market segmentation   414
marketing   400
marketing concept   400
marketing database   423
marketing mix   407

marketing research   418
niche competitive advantage   405
observation research   418
one-to-one marketing   423
opinion leader   410
perception   412
personality   412
pricing strategy   406
primary data   419
product strategy   406
production orientation   400
promotion strategy   408
psychographic segmentation   417
real self-image   412
reference groups   410
relationship marketing   402
routine response behavior   413
scanner-based research   421
secondary data   419
selective exposure   412
self-concept   412
social marketing   408
socialization process   411
survey research   418
target market   404
volume segmentation   417

1. Can the marketing concept be applied effectively by a sole proprietorship, or is it more appropriate for larger businesses with more managers? Explain. (Information)
2. Before starting your own business, you should develop a marketing strategy to guide your efforts. Choose one of the business ideas listed below and develop a marketing strategy for the business. Include the type of market research (both primary and secondary) you will perform and how you will define your target market. (Information, Systems)
   - Crafts store to capitalize on the renewed interest in knitting and other crafts
   - Online corporate-training company
   - Ethnic restaurant near your campus
   - Another business opportunity that interests you
3. "Market segmentation is the most important concept in marketing." Why do you think some marketing professionals make this statement? Give an example of each form of segmentation. (Systems)
4. Pick a specific product that you use frequently, such as a cosmetic or toiletry item, a snack food, article of clothing, book, computer program, or music CD. What is the target market for this product, and does the company's marketing strategy reflect this? Now consider the broader category of your product. How can this product be changed and/or the marketing strategy adjusted to appeal to other market segments? (Systems)
5. Can marketing research be carried out in the same manner all over the world? Why or why not? (Technology)
6. **Team Activity** Divide the class into two groups. Debate the following propositions: (1) business buyer behavior can be just as emotional as consumer buyer behavior; (2) consumer buyer behavior can be just as rational as business buyer behavior. (Interpersonal)

Ethics Activity

As a marketing manager at a beverage company, you are always looking for new products to offer—especially in the under-18 market where you are weak. A hot new drink has been a hit with kids in Japan—sales were up to 75,000 bottles a month—and is making its way to Europe. Kidsbeer is a cola-like soft drink that is packaged to look like beer. The same color as lager beer, the drink is formulated to pour with a beer-like foam. It includes guarana, a South American plant extract used in energy drinks. Tomomasu, the Japanese bottler, markets it with the slogan "Even kids cannot stand life unless they have a drink."

The impending arrival of such a drink has raised the ire of consumer groups outside Japan. They are alarmed that any company would glamorize drinking. Already beer drinking is showing up in movies that target kids and teens—for example, *DodgeBall* and *HellBoy*. Says Amon Rappaport of the Marin Institute, a California-based alcohol industry watchdog group, "The last thing we need is another product that introduces kids to drinking when the alcohol industry already spends billions doing that."

Nonetheless, you are intrigued and begin to investigate. Besides, several companies still sell candy cigarettes to kids in the United States (although other countries have banned them).

Using a Web search tool, locate articles about this topic and then write responses to the following questions. Be sure to support your arguments and cite your sources.

Ethical Dilemma: Kidsbeer would boost your company's revenues, because kids love to mimic their parents' behavior. Do you recommend it to top management?

Sources: "Beer-Flavored Soda Headed for Europe," *UPI NewsTrack*, September 19, 2005; "Here's Looking at You, Kid," *Food Management*, October 2005, p. 104; Andrew Adam Newman, "If the Children Can Drink Uncola, What about Unbeer?" *New York Times*, September 19, 2005, p. C8(L); Andrew Adam Newman, "Youngsters Enjoy Beer Ads, Arousing Industry's Critics," *New York Times*, February 13, 2006, p. C15(L); "Drink That Looks Like Beer Getting Popular with Kids, *Kyodo News International*, August 5, 2005.

Working the Net

1. You've been hired by a snack food manufacturer that is interested in adding popcorn snacks to its product line. First, however, the company asks you to find some secondary data on the current market for popcorn. Go to the Dogpile Search Engine (**http://www.dogpile.com**) and do a search for "popcorn consumption." Can you find how much popcorn is sold annually? The geographic locations with the highest popcorn sales? The time of the year when the most popcorn is sold? What are the limitations of doing research like this on the Internet?

2. You and a friend want to start a new magazine for people who work at home. Do a search of the U.S. Census database at **http://www.census.gov** to get information about the work-at-home market. Then visit **http://www.jbsba.com** to expand your research. Summarize your findings.

3. Visit the SRI Consulting site, **http://www.sric-bi.com** and click on the VALS Survey link. First read about VALS survey and how marketers can use it. Describe its value. Then take the survey to find out which psychographic segment you're in. Do you agree or disagree with the results? Why or why not?

4. How good was the marketing strategy you developed in Question 2 of Preparing for Tomorrow's Workplace? Using advice from the marketing section of *Entrepreneur* (**http://www.entrepreneur.com**) or other resources, revisit your marketing strategy for the business you selected and revise the plan accordingly. (*Entrepreneur*'s article "Write a Simple Marketing Plan" is a good place to start.) What did you overlook? (If you didn't do this exercise, pick one of the businesses and draft a marketing strategy using online resources to guide you.)

5. As the number of people online continues to grow, more of the Web surfers are also buying products online. What do researchers say about the characteristics of the online market? What market segments are appearing? Visit several sites to research this topic and then prepare a report on the demographics of online markets and other key considerations for marketers. A good place to start is **http://www.worldopinion.com.** This site contains a lot of information about the marketing research industry. From there, you can link to the sites of market research companies. (Many research company sites require registration or subscriptions; however, you can check press releases for summaries of research findings.) Also search for "Internet marketing" or "online marketing" using search engines and business publication sites like *Business Week, Entrepreneur,* and *Quirks Marketing Research Review.*

Creative Thinking Case >

Panera Rises Above the Competition

Was the concept of a "healthy sandwich" an oxymoron in the 1980s? If you believe Ronald M. Shaich, chief executive officer (CEO) of Panera Bread Company, the fast-food chains of the 1980s were "self-serve gasoline stations for the body."

After earning his MBA from Harvard Business School in 1978, Shaich first attempted making dough with Au Bon Pain, a bakery-café chain he built into 265 locations in eight countries. He acquired the St. Louis Bread Company, a chain of 20 bakery-cafés in 1993, ultimately changing its name to Panera (**http://www.panera.com**) as the company expanded across the United States. Today there are more than 850 Panera bakery-cafés in 36 states, baking fresh bread and pastries daily at each site—with dough that contains no unhealthy trans fats. New offerings are added to Panera's menu to keep regular customers coming back.

Attracting an upscale young demographic, Shaich knew what his customers wanted—fresh, healthy, artisan breads and sandwiches. And, he theorized, they would be willing to pay more for an upscale product in a pleasing setting. His theory proved correct. Chicken sandwiches made with 100 percent hormone-and-antibiotic-free birds pushed sandwich prices up by 7 percent—to $4.99-plus—to cover the increased cost. Although this brought the lunch price for an average Panera patron to $8.51 versus the industry average of $4.55, its loyal customers didn't flinch. "The prices are a little more expensive than fast food, but it's well worth it," says Cynthia Wood, a graphic design teacher who will not take her daughters to other fast-food restaurants.

Panera's higher prices do have an upside, providing patrons with superior quality food, ambience, and service. Unlike other fast-food chains, the company uses china and stainless steel utensils, boasts wood furniture, and has carpeted floors. Its employee benefit package helps keep annual turnover at 60 percent, well below the industry average of 190 percent, ensuring an enhanced level of service.

Listed 37th on *Business Week*'s 2005 Hot Growth ranking of small companies, the chain's sales and net income have risen as fast as its trademark dough over the past five years. Sales increased by 33 percent, and net income is up an average annual of 50 percent. Happy customers give Panera high marks—in 2006 the company won top honors for quality, cleanliness, and order accuracy, the three main criteria on which people base their restaurant choices—and it ranks first or second in fast-food chains. These top ratings from customers are expected to hike Panera's revenues to $1 billion in 2007.

To maintain its competitive edge, Shaich keeps extending Panera's offerings, recently adding breakfast soufflés to bring in morning customers, and free wireless Internet to draw customers after lunch. Shaich is also trying flat-bread pizza and drive-through lanes to entice the dinner crowd. His ability to spot trends early and his acute understanding of what customers want will ensure that Panera continues to lead the dough-making pack.

Critical Thinking Questions

- What accounts for Panera's huge success in the highly competitive fast-food market?
- What unique marketing strategies are contributing to the company's ongoing growth?
- Why has charging higher prices helped, rather than hurt, Panera Bread?

Source: Andy Ford, "Following The Story on Panera's Breakfast!" The Food Channel, August 3, 2005, http://www.foodchannel.com; Andy Ford, "Panera's Semi-Super Souffle and Starbucks Backorder on Bars," The Food Channel, June 28, 2005, http://www.foodchannel.com; "Giving Fast Food a Run For its Money," *BusinessWeek Online—Hot Growth Companies*, April 17, 2006, http://www.businessweek.com, Panera corporate Web site, http://www.panera.com, April 22, 2006.

Video Case >

Teen Power: A Force to be Reckoned With

Cell phones, surfing gear, X-treme sports, video games—these are just some of the lucrative markets where companies focus major marketing dollars on some very important consumers—teenagers. Understanding youth trends and dynamics in the constantly changing teen market remains an ongoing challenge for companies needing to know how best to spend those dollars.

That's where Teen Research Unlimited (TRU) comes in. Started by youthful entrepreneur Peter Zollo in 1982, TRU was the first company to specialize in teen-focused market research. It keeps companies in touch with teen thinking, making it possible for them to forecast trends and remain a step ahead of the competition. Based in Northbrook, Illinois, TRU has worked closely with many of the world's leading youth brands and advertising agencies, playing a key role in groundbreaking advertising and marketing campaigns, and the development of successful products and services. TRU has worked with over half a million teenagers nationwide to assemble data for use in advertising campaigns, product development, store designs, and other strategic business activities. Last year TRU conducted more than 1,000 focus groups and personal in-depth interviews in addition to several major quantitative studies. TRU also applies its expertise to teen advocacy on important social issues and high-risk youth behaviors such as anti-tobacco and drug use, sexual assault, life safety, education, crisis management, and skin cancer.

So how does TRU gather its data and help its clients create effective marketing strategies? When a burgeoning fashion retailer needed ethnographic research to learn more about their target consumer, they asked TRU to help them. TRU spent months scouring malls, sitting down with shoppers, and carrying out a comprehensive national quantitative analysis to gain a well-rounded view of the client and its competitors. At project completion, TRU was able to provide its client with a strategically sound, actionable plan that built on previous strengths, addressed areas requiring improvement, and set a benchmark for future measurements.

In another study a leading manufacturer of backpacks and luggage hired TRU to explore "personal carrying device" trends. To meet the client's research objective, TRU devised a series of in-home interviews focused on which bags people own, when they use them, and what they use them for. These interviews, as well as "intercepts" on snowy Chicago train platforms and the sunny Santa Monica pier, were videotaped to reveal an "on-the-street" take on emerging trends.

The only full-service marketing-research firm dedicated solely to understanding teens, TRU's initial vision remains in place today: *to develop an unparalleled expertise in the teenage market, and to offer clients virtually unlimited methods for researching teens.* And with more businesses than ever focused on marketing to teenage consumers—Abercrombie & Fitch, PepsiCo, Nintendo, and Nokia are just some of TRU's prestigious clients—companies count on TRU's research to remain in touch with what teenagers want.

Critical Thinking Questions

- What makes TRU's research so important?
- In what way is the company unique?
- How does TRU help its customers understand their target market and create effective marketing strategies?

Sources: Adapted from the video "Teenage Research Unlimited," http://www.swlearning.com; Parija Bhatnagar, "More Cheese for the 'Mall Rats,'" *CNN/Money,* February 4, 2005; Ruth Laferla, "Teenagers Shop for Art of the Deal," *New York Times,* September 22, 2005; Mary Ellen Podmolik, "Teen Stores Leading the Herd," *Chicago Tribune,* January 14, 2006, p. 1; TRU corporate Web site http://www.teenresearch.com, April 26, 2006.

Hot Links Address Book

What's the latest in customer loyalty programs? For the answer, do a search for "loyalty programs" at SearchCRM.com, **http://searchcrm.techtarget.com**

Considering a career in marketing? Read articles about different marketing topics of interest and visit the Marketing Jobs and Career Services and Student Resources areas at the American Marketing Association site, **http://www.marketingpower.com**

What's different about business-to-business marketing? Find out at the Business Marketing Association site, **http://www.marketing.org**

How satisfied are American consumers today? The American Customer Satisfaction Index (ACSI) is an economic indicator based on modeling of customer evaluations. Find the latest survey results at **http://www.theacsi.org**

A good place to learn more about marketing research is Quirks Marketing Research Review, where you'll find articles and links to major marketing research firms: **http://www.quirks.com**

For links to numerous marketing research sites, start at ResearchInfo.com: **http://www. researchinfo.com**

For a quick demographic overview of your home state, check out the Quick Facts page of the U.S. Census Bureau, **http://quickfacts.census.gov/qfd/**, after which you can click through to the main Census site to access a vast array of census data: **http://www.census.gov**

CHAPTER 13

Developing Quality Products at the Right Price

Exploring Business Careers
August Schaefer
Underwriters Laboratories, Inc.

August Schaefer, public safety officer for Underwriters Laboratories Inc. (UL), describes his company as "a neat place to work." Not the most exciting description from someone who enjoys his work so much that he has stayed at UL for over 30 years. However, as he says this, he *is* in a laboratory where employees test protective equipment like bullet-resistant vests. In another testing facility, engineers try to break into a safe—by dropping it, smashing into it, and blowing it up. In fact, UL engineers test everything from flat-screen televisions to roofing shingles to drinking water in Iraq. All told, UL tests over 19,000 different products made in over 70,000 factories throughout the world, ensuring that each one conforms to quality and safety standards. The average American household has more than 125 UL-safety-certified products. As Schaefer says, "UL is all around us. We affect everybody's life, every single day."

Originally Underwriters' Electrical Bureau, UL was started in 1894 by William Henry Merrill, who was inspired to start the company after investigating a rash of fires caused by Thomas Edison's light bulb exhibit at the World's Columbian Exposition in Chicago. Today, UL refers to itself as "an independent, not-for-profit product safety certification organization." Being independent and not-for-profit allows them to focus on the safety standards—standards they both develop and test products against—instead of on corporate profits, shareholder interests, or other outside influences. The tests UL engineers conduct vary according to the standards developed for the product being tested, taking into account its

intended use, potential misuses, and other possible dangers. Carrying out the rigorous testing each product undergoes makes UL as much a playground as a place of employment for engineers like Schaefer.

However, the product safety testing that UL conducts is not all fun and games, especially for the manufacturers whose products are tested. Although not required, UL certification has become a vital part of many products' development and often is a critical component of their successful introduction to the marketplace. Manufacturers strive for certification for several reasons: It is a mark of trust and integrity, assuring that a product has been tested thoroughly and that the manufacturer cares not only about the quality of its product but also the safety of its consumer. Beyond this, people interested in the product look for UL safety certification. When a consumer—whether a wholesaler, retailer, or end-user—sees the UL label, he or she can be confident that the product has been tested thoroughly and is compliant with the highest standards.

Ultimately, UL product safety certification provides peace of mind for both manufacturers and consumers. As Schaefer says, "When they buy a product, . . . they don't have to worry, 'Is it going to be a safe product?' They can expect it to be safe when they see the UL mark." And that makes both manufacturers and consumers happy—a "neat" concept, indeed.

This chapter looks at products—what they are, how they are developed and presented to the consumer, and what their role is within an organization and the marketplace as a whole.

The creation of a marketing mix normally begins with the first of the four Ps, product. Only when there is something to sell can marketers create a promotional theme, set a price, and establish a distribution channel (place). Organizations prepare for long-term success by creating and packaging products that add value and pricing them to meet the organization's financial objectives. In addition, organizations respond to changing customer needs by creating new products. This chapter will examine products, brands, and the importance of packaging. We discuss how new products are created and how they go through periods of sales growth and then decline. Next, you will discover how managers set prices to reach pricing goals. Alternative pricing strategies used to reach specific target markets are then discussed. We conclude with a look at trends in products and pricing.

What Is a Product?

 What is a product, and how is it classified?

product
In marketing, any good or service, along with its perceived attributes and benefits, that creates value for the customer.

In marketing, a **product** is any good or service, along with its perceived attributes and benefits, that creates value for the customer. Attributes can be tangible or intangible. Among the tangible attributes are packaging and warranties as illustrated in Exhibit 13.1. Intangible attributes are symbolic, such as brand image. People make decisions about which products to buy after considering both tangible and intangible attributes of a product. For example, when you buy a pair of jeans, you consider price, brand, store image, and style before you buy. These factors are all part of the marketing mix.

Products are often a blend of goods and services as shown in Exhibit 13.2. For example, Honda Civic Hybrid (a good) would have less value without Honda's maintenance agreement (a service). Although Burger King sells such goods as sandwiches and french fries, customers expect quality service as well, including quick food preparation and cleanliness. When developing a product, an organization must consider how the combination of goods and services will provide value to the customer.

Exhibit 13.1 > **Tangible and Intangible Attributes of a Product Create Value for the Buyer**

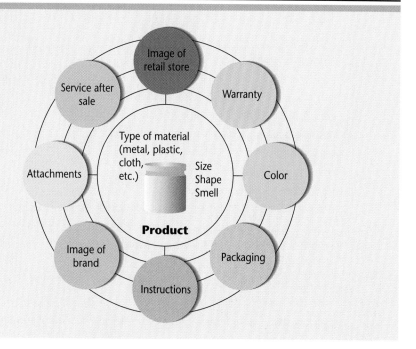

Exhibit 13.2 > Products Are Typically a Blend of Goods and Services

All goods	Both goods and services	All services
Pepper	Restaurants	Dental care
Wrench	Auto repairing	Counseling

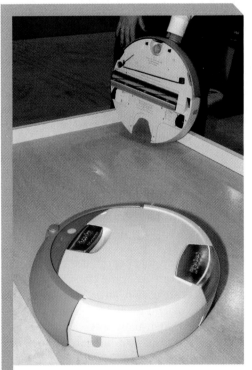

CONCEPT *in Action*

After seeing the Scooba floor-washing robot in action, consumers may never want to touch a mop again. The self-propelled circular bot navigates around hard surfaces, washing and scrubbing floors so they shine like new. A follow-up to the popular Roomba vacuum, Scooba sweeps loose debris, sprays cleaning solution, scrubs surfaces with a brush, and sucks up dirty water—all on its own. *How do marketers classify products like the Scooba floor-cleaning robot?*

Classifying Consumer Products

Because most things sold are a blend of goods and services, the term *product* can be used to refer to both. After all, consumers are really buying packages of benefits that deliver value. The person who buys a plane ride on Continental Airlines is looking for a quick way to get from one city to another (the benefit). Providing this benefit requires goods (a plane, food) and services (ticketing, maintenance, piloting).

Marketers must know how consumers view the types of products their companies sell so that they can design the marketing mix to appeal to the selected target market. To help them define target markets, marketers have devised product categories. Products that are bought by the end user are called *consumer products*. They include electric razors, sandwiches, cars, stereos, magazines, and houses. Consumer products that get used up, such as Nexxus shampoo and Lay's potato chips, are called *consumer nondurables*. Those that last for a long time, such as Whirlpool washing machines and computers, are *consumer durables*.

Another way to classify consumer products is by the amount of effort consumers are willing to make to acquire them. The four major categories of consumer products are unsought products, convenience products, shopping products, and specialty products, as summarized in Exhibit 13.3.

Unsought products are products unknown to the potential buyer or known products that the buyer does not actively seek. New products fall into this category until advertising and distribution increase consumer awareness of them. Some goods are always marketed as unsought items, especially products we do not like to think about or care to spend money on. Life insurance, cemetery plots, time-share condos, and similar items require aggressive personal selling and highly persuasive advertising. Salespeople actively seek leads to potential buyers. Because consumers usually do not seek out this type of product, the company must go directly to them through a salesperson, direct mail, Internet ads, or direct-response advertising.

Convenience products are relatively inexpensive items that require little shopping effort. Soft drinks, candy bars, milk, bread, and small hardware items are examples. We buy them routinely without much planning. This does not mean that such products are unimportant or obscure.

Consumer Product	Examples	Degree of Effort Expended by Consumer
Unsought products	Life insurance Burial plots Time-share condos	No effort
Convenience products	Soft drinks Bread Milk Coffee	Very little or minimum effort
Shopping products	Automobiles Homes Vacations	Considerable effort
Specialty products	Expensive jewelry Gourmet restaurants Limited-production automobiles	Maximum effort

unsought products
Products that either are unknown to the potential buyer or are known but the buyer does not actively seek them.

convenience products
Relatively inexpensive items that require little shopping effort and are purchased routinely without planning.

shopping products
Items that are bought after considerable planning, including brand-to-brand and store-to-store comparisons of price, suitability, and style.

specialty products
Items for which consumers search long and hard and for which they refuse to accept substitutes.

capital products
Large, expensive items with a long life span that are purchased by businesses for use in making other products or providing a service.

expense items
Items, purchased by businesses, that are smaller and less expensive than capital products and usually have a life span of less than one year.

Many, in fact, are well known by their brand names—such as Pepsi-Cola, Pepperidge Farm breads, Domino's pizza, Sure deodorant, and UPS shipping.

In contrast to convenience products, **shopping products** are bought only after a brand-to-brand and store-to-store comparison of price, suitability, and style. Examples are furniture, automobiles, a vacation in Europe, and some items of clothing. Convenience products are bought with little planning, but shopping products may be chosen months or even years before their actual purchase.

Specialty products are products for which consumers search long and hard and for which they refuse to accept substitutes. Expensive jewelry, designer clothing, state-of-the-art stereo equipment, limited-production automobiles, and gourmet restaurants fall into this category. Because consumers are willing to spend much time and effort to find specialty products, distribution is often limited to one or two sellers in a given region, such as Neiman-Marcus, Gucci, or the Porsche dealer.

Some specialty products are, in fact, quite special as discussed in the Customer Satisfaction and Quality box.

Classifying Business Products

Products bought by businesses or institutions for use in making other products or in providing services are called *business* or *industrial products*. They are classified as either capital products or expense items. **Capital products** are usually large, expensive items with a long life span. Examples are buildings, large machines, and airplanes. **Expense items** are typically smaller, less expensive items that usually have a life span of less than a year. Examples are printer ribbons and paper. Industrial products are sometimes further classified in the following categories:

1. *Installations.* These are large, expensive capital items that determine the nature, scope, and efficiency of a company. Capital products like General Motors' Saturn assembly plant in Tennessee represent a big commitment against future earnings and profitability. Buying an installation requires longer negotiations, more planning, and the judgments of more people than buying any other type of product.

2. *Accessories.* Accessories do not have the same long-run impact on the firm as installations, and they are less expensive and more standardized. But they are still capital products. Minolta copy machines, IBM personal computers (PCs), and smaller machines such as Black & Decker table drills and saws are typical accessories. Marketers of accessories often rely on well-known brand names and extensive advertising as well as personal selling.

Being a Winner Sells Used Ferraris

Kevin Crowder walked onto the famed Monza, Italy race track, climbed into a Ferrari F2000 racer, and circled the course with a Grand Prix champion. Mr. Crowder, a Texas businessman who earned more than $20 million when he sold a software company he cofounded, isn't himself a professional driver. He's a customer for one of Ferrari's latest marketing concoctions: the F-1 Clienti program, under which Ferrari resurrects old race cars that would otherwise be headed for the scrap heap. Instead it sells them for $1 million or more, along with the chance to drive them with a professional pit crew's help.

Ferrari has long built its business around exclusivity. It limits production to around 4,500 to 5,000 cars a year at around $180,000 and up. Some customers pay further to race these street cars against fellow owners at company-sponsored "Ferrari Challenge" events. The four-year-old F-1 Clienti adds a superpremium service by giving people a chance to drive the same Ferraris used in Formula One, a series of auto races that are especially popular among Europeans.

The program gives customers "an experience they can't get elsewhere," says Ferrari spokesman Jeffrey Ehoodin. Mr. Ehoodin says the chance to buy an old race car is a reward for loyal customers such as Mr. Crowder, who "worked his way through the ranks" by owning a string of contemporary and vintage Ferraris and participating in Ferrari Challenge.

"I think Ferrari prefers to do F-1 Clienti with its most established customers, and I like that," says Mr. Crowder. "It's nice to know that you can't just walk in with a big wad of cash, plunk it down and necessarily get the car you want. There has to be a real relationship there."[1]

Critical Thinking Questions
- For Mr. Crowder, the F-1 is a specialty good. What kind of product is it for you? Why?
- Do you think that Ferrari has done a good job of building brand loyalty? Could Ford do the same thing?

3. *Component parts and materials.* These are expense items that are built into the end product. Some component parts are custom-made, such as a drive shaft for an automobile, a case for a computer, or a special pigment for painting U.S. Navy harbor buoys; others are standardized for sale to many industrial users. Intel's Pentium chip for PCs and cement for the construction trade are examples of standardized component parts and materials.

4. *Raw materials.* Raw materials are expense items that have undergone little or no processing and are used to create a final product. Examples include lumber, copper, and zinc.

5. *Supplies.* Supplies do not become part of the final product. They are bought routinely and in fairly large quantities. Supply items run the gamut from pencils and paper to paint and machine oil. They have little impact on the firm's long-run profits. Bic pens, Champion copier paper, and Pennzoil machine oil are typical supply items.

6. *Services.* These are expense items used to plan or support company operations; for example, janitorial cleaning and management consulting.

> **concept check**
>
> What is a product?
>
> What are the classes of consumer goods?
>
> Explain how business products are classified.

Building Brand Equity and Master Brands

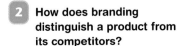
How does branding distinguish a product from its competitors?

brand
A company's product identifier that distinguishes the company's products from those of its competitors.

trademark
The legally exclusive design, name, or other identifying mark associated with a company's brand.

Most industrial and consumer products have a brand name. If everything came in a plain brown wrapper, life would be less colorful and competition would decrease. Companies would have less incentive to put out better products because consumers would be unable to tell one company's products from those of another.

The product identifier for a company is its **brand**. Brands appear in the form of words, names, symbols, or designs. They are used to distinguish a company's products from those of its competitors. Examples of well-known brands are Kleenex tissues, Jeep automobiles, and IBM computers. A **trademark** is the legally exclusive design, name, or other identifying mark associated with a company's brand. No other company can use that same trademark.

Benefits of Branding

Branding has three main purposes: product identification, repeat sales, and new-product sales. The most important purpose is *product identification*. Branding allows marketers to distinguish their products from all others. Exhibit 13.4 identifies the

Exhibit 13.4 > Characteristics of Effective Brand Names

- Easy to pronounce (by both domestic and foreign buyers)
- Easy to recognize
- Easy to remember
- Short
- Distinctive, unique
- Describes the product
- Describes the product's use
- Describes the product's benefits
- Has a positive connotation
- Reinforces the desired product image
- Is legally protectable in home and foreign markets of interest

brand equity
The value of company and brand names.

master brand
A brand so dominant that consumers think of it immediately when a product category, use, attribute, or customer benefit is mentioned.

characteristics of an effective brand name. Brand names can be arbitrary, such as Google, or descriptive, such as Mop-n-Glo. When you mop your floors you will have floors that glow. Coming up with new brand names isn't easy. For example, JetBlue decided that it wanted a real word but not something that sounded like an airline.

The airline came up with early naming candidates such as Fresh Air, Taxi, Egg, and It. But the name Blue—with its simple evocation of clear skies and serenity—emerged a finalist. After trademark lawyers pointed out that it would be impossible to protect the name Blue without a distinctive qualifier, TrueBlue emerged. But that name was already held by a car-rental agency. Eventually, JetBlue was born.[2]

Many brand names are familiar to consumers and indicate quality. The term **brand equity** refers to the value of company and brand names. A brand that has high awareness, perceived quality, and brand loyalty among customers has high brand equity. Brand equity is more than awareness of a brand—it is the personality, soul, and emotion associated with the brand. Think of the feelings you have when you see the brand name Harley-Davidson, Nike, or even Microsoft. A brand with strong brand equity is a valuable asset. Some brands such as Coke, Kodak, Marlboro, and Chevrolet are worth hundreds of millions of dollars.

A brand so dominant in consumers' minds that they think of it immediately when a product category, use, attribute, or customer benefit is mentioned is a **master brand**. Scotch tape and Kleenex tissues are examples of master brands. Exhibit 13.5 lists some of America's master brands in several product categories.

U.S. master brands command substantial premiums in many places around the world. Band-Aids command a 500 percent premium in China.

Exhibit 13.5 > America's Master Brands

Product Category	Master Brand
Adhesive bandages	Band-Aid
Antacids	Alka-Seltzer
Baking soda	Arm & Hammer
Cellophane tape	Scotch Tape
Fast food	McDonald's
Gelatin	Jell-O
Rum	Bacardi
Salt	Morton
Soft drinks	Coca-Cola
Soup	Campbell's

MANAGING CHANGE

American Express Searches for Youth

American Express Co., the 155-year-old financial-services firm long known for catering to gray-haired executives with expense accounts, is offering its customers some unusual new perks: free chocolate martinis, discount passes to New York's head-thumpingly loud Crobar, and the chance to be a disc jockey at a dance club overlooking Times Square.

The offers are part of an ambitious effort by American Express to tackle a serious problem at the core of its business. The U.S. market is saturated with nearly 900 million credit, charge and debit cards. The glut has started to slow several years of rapid industry growth.

More alarming for American Express: Young shoppers are shifting to debit cards. Particularly popular among people on a budget, debit cards draw directly from a person's bank account, with no annual fees or monthly balances. Debit-card charges now represent 60 percent of transactions processed by Visa USA Inc. But American Express has never offered a debit card, and executives say it doesn't plan to.

So now American Express is on a high-stakes hunt for young customers, forcing the company to learn the byways of an unfamiliar new marketplace. At the center of its quest is a new series of no-fee credit cards for urbanites who are single, age 25 to 35, dine out often, like to drink, and aspire to be hip. In ads, American Express dubs this "the über-glam lifestyle you'll easily become accustomed to." In 2005, it launched the first city card, dubbed "In:NYC," and aimed at New Yorkers. Later, it followed with "In:Chicago," and "In:LA."

To develop the cards, American Express's executives have been scouring city hotspots trying to divine the tastes of the often fickle urban crowd. They grilled company interns about what restaurants and trends were cool, and found themselves soliciting customers well after midnight on Manhattan's streets.

The result is a card promising "access" to a lifestyle American Express hopes is desirable. Instead of earning golf clubs or frequent-flier miles, points accumulated on the In:NYC card can be redeemed for a private booth at Underbar, a candle-lit lounge below Union Square's W Hotel, or to get discounts at Suba, a tapas restaurant where diners sit surrounded by a pool of rippling water.[3]

Critical Thinking Question

- Do you think that the "In" card will prove successful outside of major urban areas?
- Do you think that the "In" cards will cause young adults to quit using debit cards? Why?

Building Repeat Sales with Brand Loyalty

brand loyalty
A consumer's preference for a particular brand.

A consumer who tries one or more brands may decide to buy a certain brand regularly. The preference for a particular brand is **brand loyalty**. It lets consumers buy with less time, thought, and risk. Brand loyalty ensures future sales for a firm. It can also help protect a firm's share of the market, discourage new competitors, and thus prolong the brand's life. Brand loyalty even allows companies to raise prices. Quaker Oats Co., maker of Cap'n Crunch, Life, and Quaker oatmeal, raised its prices 3.8 percent. Analysts said that Quaker could do this, even though other cereal makers didn't raise prices, because of the strong consumer loyalty to Quaker products.

Brand loyalty typically builds over time. The first level is *brand recognition,* in which consumers recall having seen or heard of the brand. Companies often spend millions on promotion for new products to achieve brand recognition. A product may then achieve *brand preference* where a consumer prefers a certain brand like the Spin-Brush but may buy an alternative due to lack of availability of the SpinBrush, price, or effective promotion by a competing product. The ultimate for any product manager is *brand insistence* where consumers will buy only that brand. Lexus, for example, has reached this level among some car purchasers.

Whereas Lexus may have reached brand insistence with many of its customers, American Express has done so only with its older, traditional customers. Realizing that its customer base was rapidly graying, American Express is using a new branding strategy to attract a more youthful customer. The new strategy is explained in the Managing Change box.

Facilitating New-Product Sales

The third main purpose of branding is to facilitate *new-product sales.* Let's assume that your class forms a company to market frozen tarts and pies under the name "University Frozen Desserts." Now, assume that Pepperidge Farm develops a new line of identical frozen tarts and pies. Which ones will consumers try? The Pepperidge Farm

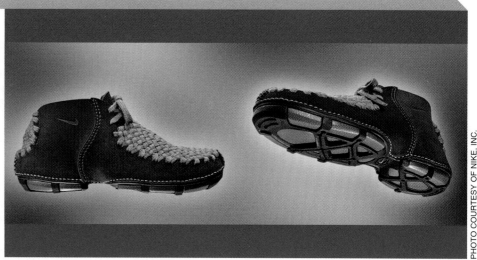

PHOTO COURTESY OF NIKE, INC.

products, without doubt. Pepperidge Farm is known for its quality frozen bakery products. Consumers assume that its new tarts and pies will be of high quality and are therefore willing to give them a try. The well-known Pepperidge Farm brand is facilitating new-product introduction.

Types of Brands

manufacturer brands
Brands that are owned by national or regional manufacturers and widely distributed; also called *national brands*.

Brands owned by national or regional manufacturers and widely distributed are **manufacturer brands**. (These brands are sometimes called national brands, but since some of the brands are not owned by nationwide or international manufacturers, *manufacturer brands* is a more accurate term.) A few well-known manufacturer brands are Ford, Swatch, Nike, and Sony.

Manufacturer brands can bring new customers and new prestige to small retailers. For instance, a small bicycle repair shop in a Midwestern college town got the franchise to sell and repair Trek bicycles. The shop's profits grew quickly, and it became one of the most successful retail businesses in the university area. Because manufacturer brands are widely promoted, sales are often high. Also, most manufacturers of these brands offer frequent deliveries to their retailers. Thus, retailers can carry less stock and have less money tied up in inventory.

dealer brands
Brands that are owned by the wholesaler or retailer rather than the name of the manufacturer.

Brands that are owned by the wholesaler or retailer, rather than that of the manufacturer, are **dealer brands**. Sears has several well-known dealer (or private) brands, including Craftsman, Diehard, and Kenmore. The Independent Grocers Association (IGA), a large wholesale grocery organization, uses the brand name Shurfine on its goods. Dealer brands tie consumers to particular wholesalers or retailers. If you want a Kenmore washing machine, you must go to Sears.

Although profit margins are usually higher on dealer brands than on manufacturer brands, dealers must still stimulate demand for their products. Sears's promotion of its products has made the company one of the largest advertisers in the United States. But promotion costs can cut heavily into profit margins. And if a dealer-brand item is of poor quality, the dealer must assume responsibility for it. Sellers of manufacturer brands can refer a disgruntled customer to the manufacturer.

generic products
Products that carry no brand name, come in plain containers, and sell for much less than brand-name products.

Some consumers don't want to pay the costs of manufacturer or dealer brands. One popular way to save money is to buy **generic products**. These products carry no brand name, come in plain containers, and sell for much less than brand-name products. They are typically sold in black-and-white packages with such simple labels as "liquid bleach" or "spaghetti." Generic products are sold by 85 percent of U.S. supermarkets. Sometimes manufacturers simply stop the production line and substitute a generic package for a brand package, though the product is exactly the same. The most popular generic products are garbage bags, jelly, paper towels, coffee cream substitutes, cigarettes, and paper napkins.

Cobranding

cobranding
Placing two or more brand names on a product or its package.

Cobranding entails placing two or more brand names on a product or its package. Three common types of cobranding are ingredient branding, cooperative branding, and complementary branding. *Ingredient branding* identifies the brand of a part that makes up the product. Examples of ingredient branding are Intel (a microprocessor) in a personal computer, such as Dell, or a premium leather interior (Coach) in an automobile (Lincoln). *Cooperative branding* occurs when two brands receiving equal treatment (in the context of an advertisement) borrow on each other's brand equity. A promotional contest jointly sponsored by Ramada Inns, American Express, and Continental Airlines is an example of cooperative branding. Guests at Ramada who paid with an American Express card were automatically entered in the contest and were eligible to win more than a hundred getaways for two at any Ramada in the continental United States and round-trip airfare from Continental. Finally, with *complementary branding*, products are advertised or marketed together to suggest usage, such as a spirits brand (Seagram's) and a compatible mixer (7-Up).

Cobranding is a useful strategy when a combination of brand names enhances the prestige or perceived value of a product or when it benefits brand owners and users. Starbucks' deal with United Airlines put Starbucks coffee on United flights worldwide and allowed both companies to achieve important brand objectives.

Cobranding may be used to increase a company's presence in markets where it has little or no market share. For example, Disney is attempting to increase its share of the food and beverage market by developing cobranding deals with Minute Maid for an 18-variety line of Disney Xtreme! Disney is also developing coolers based on Mickey and Friends and with Kellogg for cobranded cereals. Georgia-Pacific's Dixie unit has teamed up with Coca-Cola to make a new line of Coke-themed cups. Dixie's marketing group has succeeded in placing the products in the soft-drink section of supermarkets, which could be important in the fight for shelf space and marketing allies. Coca-Cola also has customers that Dixie wants, such as McDonald's, which will sell Coke fountain drinks in a Dixie collectible cup similar to a glass bottle.[4]

> **concept check**
>
> Define the terms *brand* and *trademark*.
>
> Explain the differences between manufacturer brands and dealer brands.
>
> What are the benefits of cobranding?

The Importance of Packaging in a Self-Service Economy

 3 **What are the functions of packaging?**

Just as a brand gives a product identity, its packaging also distinguishes it from competitors' products and increases its customer value. When you go to the store and reach for a bottle of dishwashing detergent, the package is the last chance a manufacturer has to convince you to buy its brand over a competitor's. A good package may cause you to reach for Joy rather than Palmolive.

The Functions of a Package

A basic function of packaging is to protect the product from breaking or spoiling and thus extend its life. A package should be easy to ship, store, and stack on a shelf and convenient for the consumer to buy. Many new packaging methods have been developed recently. Aseptic packages keep foods fresh for months without refrigeration. Examples are Borden's "'sipp' packs" for juices, the Brik Pak for milk, and Hunt's/Del Monte's aseptic boxes for tomato sauce. Some package developers are creating "microatmospheres," which allow meat to stay fresh in the refrigerator for weeks.

A second basic function of packaging is to help promote the product by providing clear brand identification and information about the product's features. For example, Ralston Purina Co.'s Dog Chow brand, the leading dog food, was losing market share. The company decided that the pictures of dog breeds on the package were too old-fashioned and rural. With a new package featuring a photo of a dog and a child, sales have increased.

Labeling

An integral part of any package is its label. Labeling generally takes one of two forms: persuasive or informational. **Persuasive labeling** focuses on a promotional theme or logo, and consumer information is secondary. Cheetos Crunchy, for example, features Chester Cheetah throwing a switch from "cheesy" to "dangerously cheesy." As Frito-Lay notes, "it's the taste against which all other crunchy cheese-flavored snacks are measured by." Note that the standard promotional claims—such as "new," "improved," and "super"—are no longer very persuasive. Consumers have been saturated with "newness" and thus discount these claims.

Informational labeling, in contrast, is designed to help consumers make proper product selections and lower their cognitive dissonance after the purchase. Sears attaches a "label of confidence" to all its floor coverings. This label gives such product information as durability, color, features, cleanability, care instructions, and construction standards. Most major furniture manufacturers affix labels to their wares that explain the products' construction features, such as type of frame, number of coils, and fabric characteristics. The Nutritional Labeling and Education Act of 1990 mandated detailed nutritional information on most food packages and standards for health claims on food packaging. An important outcome of this legislation is guidelines from the Food and Drug Administration for using terms like *low fat, light, reduced cholesterol, low sodium, low calorie,* and *fresh.*

Recently, the Food and Drug Administration called for better nutritional labeling. Kraft Foods has decided to heed the call. Kraft makes a wide range of such products, from Planters Peanuts to Chips Ahoy cookies to Life Savers. The FDA wants the specific calorie count and fat grams, among other items, for the entire package, rather than the single-serve details that packages now carry. By doing so, the FDA believes consumers will have a better idea of just how fattening all those cookies and candy can be if the entire bag is eaten in one sitting. Kraft said its labels will do just that on snacks and beverages that contain two to four servings. If it's likely that more than one person will be eating, say, Cracker Barrel cheese sticks, the package will include single-serve data as well as the full package and will note how many servings are included.

Virtually all consumer packaged goods, as well as many other products, have bar codes to simplify inventory control and checkout. The key to understanding bar codes is shown in Exhibit 13.6.

Adding Value through Warranties

A **warranty** guarantees the quality of a good or service. An **implied warranty** is an unwritten guarantee that the product is fit for the purpose for which it was sold. All sales have an implied warranty under the Uniform Commercial Code (a law that applies to commercial dealings in most states). An **express warranty** is made in writing. Express warranties range from simple statements, such as "100 percent cotton" (a guarantee of raw materials) and "complete satisfaction guaranteed" (a statement of performance), to extensive documentation that accompanies a product.

In 1975, Congress passed the Magnuson-Moss Warranty–Federal Trade Commission Improvement Act to help consumers understand warranties and to help them get action from manufacturers and dealers. A **full warranty** means the manufacturer must meet certain minimum standards, including repair of any defects "within a reasonable time and without charge" and replacement of the merchandise or a full refund if the product does not work "after a reasonable number of attempts" at repair.

CONCEPT *in Action*

The switch to inverted plastic squeeze bottles may be the biggest revolution to hit the condiments industry since the invention of the bottle itself. Perfectly designed for outdoor picnics or in-home use, upside-down squeeze bottles dispense just the right amount of dressings, jams, and syrups—without the mess of ordinary bottles. Their patented silicone valves direct sauces to the intended target every time. *What factors inspire new innovations in packaging?*

© TERRI MILLER / E-VISUAL COMMUNICATIONS INC.

persuasive labeling
A type of product label that reinforces or repeats a promotional theme or logo.

informational labeling
A type of product label that provides product information to aid consumers in making product selections and minimize cognitive dissonance after the purchase.

warranty
A guarantee of the quality of a good or service.

implied warranty
An unwritten guarantee that a product is fit for the purpose for which it is sold.

express warranty
A written guarantee about a product, such as that it contains certain materials, will perform a certain way, or is otherwise fit for the purpose for which it was sold.

full warranty
The manufacturer's guarantee to meet certain minimum standards, including repair or replacement of the product or refunding to the customer if the product does not work.

Exhibit 13.6 > How to Understand a Bar Code

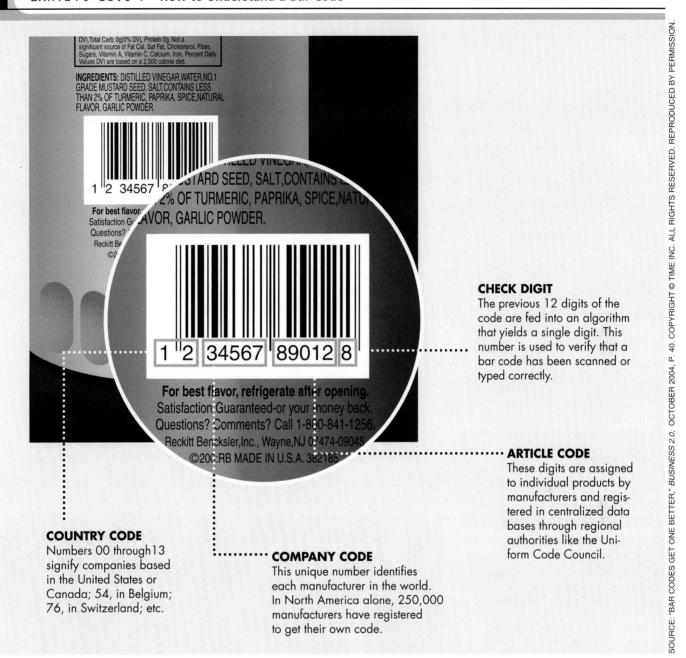

CHECK DIGIT
The previous 12 digits of the code are fed into an algorithm that yields a single digit. This number is used to verify that a bar code has been scanned or typed correctly.

ARTICLE CODE
These digits are assigned to individual products by manufacturers and registered in centralized data bases through regional authorities like the Uniform Code Council.

COUNTRY CODE
Numbers 00 through 13 signify companies based in the United States or Canada; 54, in Belgium; 76, in Switzerland; etc.

COMPANY CODE
This unique number identifies each manufacturer in the world. In North America alone, 250,000 manufacturers have registered to get their own code.

Under the law, any warranty that does not live up to this tough standard must be "conspicuously" promoted as a limited warranty.

Service warranties, such as those sold by Best Buy and Circuit City, are extremely high profit items for the companies. In fact, one analyst found that profit margins on service warranties were 18 times the margins on the goods themselves![5] They account for virtually all of Circuit City's profits and about 45 percent of Best Buy's profit. Before buying a service warranty, remember that many credit cards double the manufacturer's warranty for free. Also, ask yourself "how likely is the equipment to break?" and "how much will it cost to replace?"

concept check

What are the functions of a package?

Explain the differences between an implied warranty, an express warranty, and a full warranty.

Creating Products That Deliver Value

4 **How do organizations create new products?**

line extension
A new flavor, size, or model using an existing brand name in an existing category.

New products pump life into company sales, enabling the firm not only to survive but also to grow. Companies like Allegheny Ludlum (steel), Dow (chemicals), Samsung (electronics), Campbell Soup (foods), and Stryker (medical products) get most of their profits from new products. Companies that lead their industries in profitability and sales growth get 49 percent of their revenues from products developed within the last five years. A recent survey found that 87 percent of top executives in the United States believed that their companies' success depended upon new products.[6]

Marketers have several different terms for new products, depending on how the product fits into a company's existing product line. When a firm introduces a product that has a new brand name and is in a product category new to the organization, it is classified as a new product.

A new flavor, size, or model using an existing brand name in an existing category is called a **line extension**. Diet Cherry Coke and caffeine-free Coke are line extensions. The strategy of expanding the line by adding new models has enabled companies like Seiko (watches), Kraft (cheeses), Oscar Mayer (lunch meats), and Sony (consumer electronics) to tie up a large amount of shelf space and brand recognition in a product category. Crayola now offers Crayola bubble bath shampoo.

Organizing the New-Product Effort

In large organizations, such as Procter & Gamble and Kraft General Foods, new-product departments are responsible for generating new products. The department typically includes people from production, finance, marketing, and engineering. In smaller firms, committees perform the same functions as a new-product department.

For major new-product development tasks, companies sometimes form venture teams. IBM, for example, formed a venture group to create the first PC. Like a new-product department, a venture team includes members from most departments of the company. The idea, however, is to isolate the team members from the organization's day-to-day activities so that they can think and be creative. IBM is headquartered in New York, but the PC venture team was located in Florida.

CONCEPT *in Action*

Iconic jeans-maker Levi Strauss & Co., targets the digital set with a line of denims specially designed for carrying iPod media players. Dubbed Red-Wire, the premium jeans have a built-in docking cradle that houses the iPod safely in a stealth side pocket, virtually eliminating bulge. The trendy duds are a recent extension of the classic Levi's brand, merging fashion and technology in a way that enhances consumers' portable digital lifestyles. *What factors contribute to the success or failure of line extensions?*

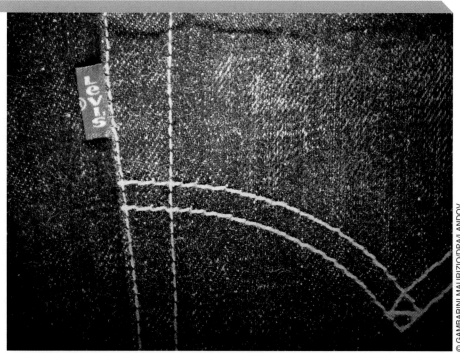

© GAMBARINI MAURIZIO/DPA/LANDOV

CONCEPT *in Action*

The air travel of tomorrow may have little in common with today's passenger flights. Aerospace defense contractors have long tinkered with massive airships for potential military use, but now the private firm Worldwide Aeros Corporation plans to make its Aeroscraft cruise-liner the preferred travel of the future. Spanning two football fields and touted as a flying luxury hotel, Aeroscraft will ferry pampered passengers around the world with unprecedented comfort and style. *At what stage of product development is the Aeroscraft airship?*

© JOHN MACNEILL

focus group
A group of 8 to 12 participants led by a moderator in an in-depth discussion on one particular topic or concept.

brainstorming
A method of generating ideas in which group members suggest as many possibilities as they can without criticizing or evaluating any of the suggestions.

How New Products Are Developed

Developing new products is both costly and risky. New-product failure rates for household and grocery products approach 80 percent. The overall failure rate is approximately 60 percent.[7] Industrial goods failure rates tend to be lower than those for consumer goods. To increase their chances for success, most firms use the following product development process, which is also summarized in Exhibit 13.7.

1. *Set new-product goals.* New-product goals are usually stated as financial objectives. For example, a company may want to recover its investment in three years or less. Or it may want to earn at least a 15 percent return on the investment. Nonfinancial goals may include using existing equipment or facilities.

2. *Develop new-product ideas.* Smaller firms usually depend on employees, customers, investors, and distributors for new ideas. Larger companies use these sources and more structured marketing research techniques, such as focus groups and brainstorming. A **focus group** consists of 8 to 12 participants led by a moderator in an in-depth discussion on one particular topic or concept. The goal of focus group research is to learn and understand what people have to say and why. The emphasis is on getting people talking at length and in detail about the subject at hand. The intent is to find out how they feel about a product, concept, idea, or organization, how it fits into their lives, and their emotional involvement with it. Focus groups often generate excellent product ideas. A few examples of focus group–influenced products are the interior design of the Toyota Rav4, Stick-Up room deodorizers, Swiffer WetJet, and Wendy's Salad Sensations. In the industrial market, machine tools, keyboard designs, aircraft interiors, and backhoe accessories evolved from focus groups.

   Brainstorming is also used to generate new-product ideas. With **brainstorming**, the members of a group think of as many ways to vary a product or solve a problem as possible. Criticism is avoided, no matter how ridiculous an idea seems at the time. The emphasis is on sheer numbers of ideas. Evaluation of these ideas is postponed to later steps of development.

3. *Screen ideas and concepts.* As ideas emerge, they are checked against the firm's new-product goals and its long-range strategies. Many product concepts are rejected because they don't fit well with existing products, needed technology is not available, the company doesn't have enough resources, or the sales potential is low.

4. *Develop the concept.* Developing the new-product concept involves creating a prototype of the product, testing the prototype, and building the marketing strategy. The type and amount of product testing vary, depending on such factors as the company's experience with similar products, how easy it is to make the item, and how easy it will be for consumers to use it. Suppose that Seven Seas is developing a new salad dressing flavor. The company already has a lot of experience in this area, so the new dressing will go directly into advanced taste tests and perhaps home-use tests. To develop a new line of soft drinks, however, Seven Seas would most likely do a great deal of testing. It would study many aspects of the new product before actually making it.

   While the product is tested, the marketing strategy is refined. Channels of distribution are selected, pricing policies are developed and tested, the target market is further defined, and demand for the product is estimated. Management also continually updates the profit plan.

   As the marketing strategy and prototype tests mature, a communication strategy is developed. A logo and package wording are created. As part of the communication strategy, promotion themes are developed, and the product is introduced to the sales force.

Exhibit 13.7 > **Steps to Develop New Products That Satisfy Customers**

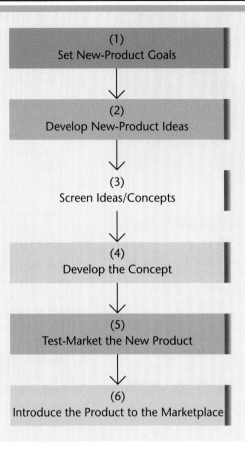

test-marketing
The process of testing a new product among potential users.

5. *Test-market the new product.* **Test-marketing** is testing the product among potential users. It allows management to evaluate various strategies and to see how well the parts of the marketing mix fit together. Few new-product concepts reach this stage. For those that pass this stage, the firm must decide whether to introduce the product on a regional or national basis.

Companies that don't test-market their products run a strong risk of product failure. In essence, test-marketing is the "acid test" of new-product development. The product is put into the marketplace and then the manufacturer can see how it performs against the competition.

6. *Introduce the product.* A product that passes test-marketing is ready for market introduction, called *rollout,* which requires a lot of logistical coordination. Various divisions of the company must be encouraged to give the new item the attention it deserves. Packaging and labeling in a different language may be required. Sales training sessions must be scheduled, spare parts inventoried, service personnel trained, advertising and promotion campaigns readied, and wholesalers and retailers informed about the new item. If the new product is to be sold internationally, it may have to be altered to meet the requirements of the target countries. For instance, electrical products may have to run on different electrical currents.

The Role of the Product Manager

product manager
The person who develops and implements a complete strategy and marketing program for a specific product or brand.

When a new product enters the marketplace in large organizations, it is often placed under the control of a product or brand manager. A **product manager** develops and implements a complete strategy and marketing program for a specific product or

concept check

How do companies organize for new-product development?

What are the steps in the new-product development process?

Explain the role of the product manager.

brand. Product management first appeared at Procter & Gamble in 1929. A new company soap, Camay, was not doing well, so a young Procter & Gamble executive was assigned to devote his exclusive attention to developing and promoting this product. He was successful, and the company soon added other product managers. Since then, many firms, especially consumer products companies, have set up product management organizations.

The Product Life Cycle

5 **What are the stages of the product life cycle?**

product life cycle
The pattern of sales and profits over time for a product or product category; consists of an introductory stage, growth stage, maturity, and decline (and death).

Product managers create marketing mixes for their products as they move through the life cycle. The **product life cycle** is a pattern of sales and profits over time for a product (Ivory dishwashing liquid) or a product category (liquid detergents). As the product moves through the stages of the life cycle, the firm must keep revising the marketing mix to stay competitive and meet the needs of target customers.

Stages of the Life Cycle

As illustrated in Exhibit 13.8, the product life cycle consists of the following stages:

1. *Introduction.* When a product enters the life cycle, it faces many obstacles. Although competition may be light, the *introductory stage* usually features frequent product modifications, limited distribution, and heavy promotion. The failure rate is high. Production and marketing costs are also high, and sales volume is low. Hence profits are usually small or negative.

2. *Growth.* If a product survives the introductory stage, it advances to the *growth stage* of the life cycle. In this stage, sales grow at an increasing rate, profits are healthy, and many competitors enter the market. Large companies may start to acquire small pioneering firms that have reached this stage. Emphasis switches from primary demand promotion to aggressive brand advertising and communicating the differences between brands. For example, the goal changes from convincing people to buy compact plasma TVs to convincing them to buy Sony versus Panasonic or Sharp.

   Distribution becomes a major key to success during the growth stage, as well as in later stages. Manufacturers scramble to acquire dealers and distributors and to build long-term relationships. Without adequate distribution, it is impossible to establish a strong market position.

   Toward the end of the growth phase, prices normally begin falling and profits peak. Price reductions result from increased competition and from cost reductions from producing larger quantities of items (economies of scale). Also, most firms have recovered their development costs by now, and their priority is in increasing or retaining market share and enhancing profits.

3. *Maturity.* After the growth stage, sales continue to mount—but at a decreasing rate. This is the *maturity stage.* Most products that have been on the market for a long time are in this stage. Thus, most marketing strategies are designed for mature products. One such strategy is to bring out several variations of a basic product (line extension). Kool-Aid, for instance, was originally offered in three flavors. Today there are more than 10, as well as sweetened and unsweetened varieties.

4. *Decline (and death).* When sales and profits fall, the product has reached the *decline stage.* The rate of decline is governed by two

CONCEPT *in Action*

Each year Coca-Cola adds new drinks to its product portfolio. While some of these new beverages are close relatives of the original Coca-Cola Classic, others like Coca-Cola Blak constitute entirely new categories of soft drink. A recent cola-coffee invention, Blak has a java-like quality that includes a rich smooth texture and a coffee-like froth when poured. *What challenges do new products like Blak face during the introduction phase of the product life cycle?*

Exhibit 13.8 > Sales and Profits during the Product Life Cycle

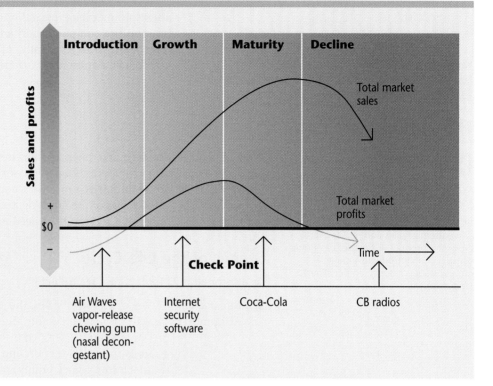

factors: the rate of change in consumer tastes and the rate at which new products enter the market. Sony VCRs are an example of a product in the decline stage. The demand for VCRs has now been surpassed by the demand for DVDs.

The Product Life Cycle as a Management Tool

The product life cycle may be used in planning. Marketers who understand the cycle concept are better able to forecast future sales and plan new marketing strategies. Exhibit 13.9 is a brief summary of strategic needs at various stages of the product life

Exhibit 13.9 > Strategies for Success at Each Stage of the Product Life Cycle

Category	Introduction	Growth	Maturity	Decline
Marketing objectives	Encourage trial, establish distribution	Get triers to repurchase, attract new users	Seek new users or uses	Reduce marketing expenses, keep loyal users
Product	Establish competitive advantage	Maintain product quality	Modify product	Maintain product
Distribution	Establish distribution network	Solidify distribution relationships	Provide additional incentives to ensure support	Eliminate trade allowances
Promotional	Build brand awareness	Provide information	Reposition product	Eliminate most advertising and sales promotions
Pricing	Set introductory price (skimming or penetration pricing)	Maintain prices	Reduce prices to meet competition	Maintain prices

concept check

What is the product life cycle?

Describe each stage of the product life cycle.

What are the marketing strategies for each stage of the product life cycle?

cycle. Marketers must be sure that a product has moved from one stage to the next before changing its marketing strategy. A temporary sales decline should not be interpreted as a sign that the product is dying. Pulling back marketing support can become a self-fulfilling prophecy that brings about the early death of a healthy product.

Pricing Products Right

6 **What is the role of pricing in marketing?**

An important part of the product development process is setting the right price. Price is the perceived value that is exchanged for something else. Value in our society is most commonly expressed in dollars and cents. Thus, price is typically the amount of money exchanged for a good or service. Note that *perceived value* refers to the time of the transaction. After you've used a product you've bought, you may decide that its actual value was less than its perceived value at the time you bought it. The price you pay for a product is based on the *expected satisfaction* you will receive and not necessarily the *actual satisfaction* you will receive.

Although price is usually a dollar amount, it can be anything with perceived value. When goods and services are exchanged for each other, the trade is called *barter*. If you exchange this book for a math book at the end of the term, you have engaged in barter.

Pricing Objectives

Price is important in determining how much a firm earns. The prices charged customers times the number of units sold equals the *gross revenue* for the firm. Revenue is what pays for every activity of the company (production, finance, sales, distribution, and so forth). What's left over (if anything) is profit. Managers strive to charge a price that will allow the firm to earn a fair return on its investment.

The chosen price must be neither too high nor too low. And the price must equal the perceived value to target consumers. If consumers think the price is too high, sales opportunities will be lost. Lost sales mean lost revenue. If the price is too low, consumers may view the product as a great value, but the company may not meet its

CONCEPT *in Action*

With its line of colorful makeup products priced at $1 apiece, Eyes Lips Face Cosmetics (e.l.f.) helps women look great at low prices. The e.l.f. brand, while cheap, is anything but chintzy. Comparisons show that e.l.f. competes with prestige brands on quality, and the product's proposition that beauty need not break the bank has attracted entertainment luminaries including pop icon Hilary Duff and desperate housewife Eva Longoria. *How does e.l.f. overcome the perception that low-dollar cosmetics are low quality?*

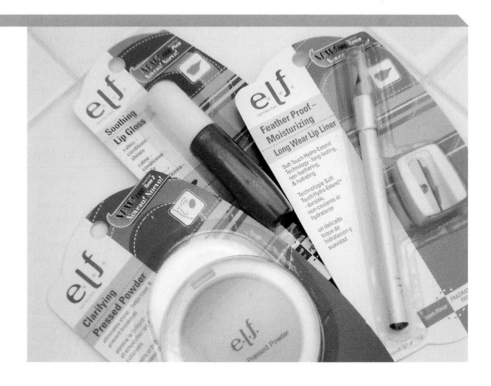

profit goals. Three common pricing objectives are maximizing profits, achieving a target return on the investment, and offering good value at a fair price.

Maximizing Profits

profit maximization
A pricing objective that entails getting the largest possible profit from a product by producing the product as long as the revenue from selling it exceeds the cost of producing it.

Profit maximization means producing a product as long as the revenue from selling it exceeds the cost of producing it. In other words, the goal is to get the largest possible profit from the product. For example, suppose Carl Morgan, a builder of houses, sells each house for $300,000. His revenue and cost projections are shown in Exhibit 13.10. Notice in column 3 that the cost of building each house drops for the second through the fifth house. The lower cost per house results from two things: First, by having several houses under construction at the same time, Morgan can afford to hire a full-time crew. The crew is more economical than the independent contractors to whom he would otherwise subcontract each task. Second, Morgan can order materials in greater quantities than usual and thus get quantity discounts on his orders.

Morgan decides that he could sell 15 houses a year at the $300,000 price. But he knows he cannot maximize profits at more than seven houses a year. Inefficiencies begin to creep in at the sixth house. (Notice in column 3 that the sixth house costs more to build than any of the first five houses.) Morgan can't supervise more than seven construction jobs at once, and his full-time crew can't handle even those seven. Thus, Morgan has to subcontract some of the work on the sixth and seventh houses. To build more than seven houses, he would need a second full-time crew.

The exhibit also shows why Morgan should construct seven houses a year. Even though the profit per house is falling for the sixth and seventh houses (column 4), the total profit is still rising (column 5). But at the eighth house, Morgan would go beyond profit maximization. That is, the eighth unit would cost more than its selling price. He would lose $15,000 on the house, and total profit would fall to $154,000 from $169,000 after the seventh house.

Achieving a Target Return on Investment

target return on investment
A pricing objective where the price of a product is set so as to give the company the desired profitability in terms of return on its money.

Another pricing objective used by many companies is **target return on investment** where a price is set to give the company the desired profitability in terms of return on its money. Among the companies that use target return on investment as their main pricing objective are 3M, Procter & Gamble, General Electric, and DuPont.

To get an idea of how target return works, imagine that you are a marketing manager for a cereal company. You estimate that developing, launching, and marketing a new hot cereal will cost $2 million. If the net profit for the first year is $200,000, the return on investment will be $200,000 ÷ $2,000,000, or 10 percent. Let's say that top management sets a 15 percent target return on investment. (The average target return

---

Exhibit 13.10 > Revenue, Cost, and Profit Projections for Morgan's Houses

(1) Unit of Output (House)	(2) Selling Price (Revenue)	(3) Cost of Building House	(4) Profit on House	(5) Total Profit
1st	$ 300,000	$ 276,000	$ 24,000	$ 24,000
2nd	300,000	275,000	25,000	49,000
3rd	300,000	273,000	27,000	76,000
4th	300,000	270,000	30,000	106,000
5th	300,000	270,000	30,000	136,000
6th	300,000	277,000	23,000	159,000
7th	**300,000**	**290,000**	**10,000**	**169,000**
8th	300,000	315,000	(15,000)	154,000

on investment for large corporations is now about 14 percent.) Since a net profit of $200,000 will yield only a 10 percent return, one of two things will happen: either the cereal won't be produced, or the price and marketing mix will be changed to yield the 15 percent target return.

Value Pricing

value pricing
A pricing strategy in which the target market is offered a high-quality product at a fair price and with good service.

Value pricing has become a popular pricing strategy. **Value pricing** means offering the target market a high-quality product at a fair price and with good service. It is the notion of offering the customer a good value. Value pricing doesn't mean high quality that's available only at high prices. Nor does it mean bare-bones service or low-quality products. Value pricing can be used to sell a variety of products, from a $30,000 Jeep Grand Cherokee to a $12.99 package of L'eggs Sheer Energy hosiery.

A value marketer does the following:

- *Offers products that perform.* This is the price of entry because consumers have lost patience with shoddy merchandise.
- *Gives consumers more than they expect.* Soon after Toyota launched Lexus, the company had to order a recall. The weekend before the recall, dealers phoned every Lexus owner in the United States and arranged to pick up their cars and provide replacement vehicles.
- *Gives meaningful guarantees.* Hyundai offers a 100,000-mile power train warranty. Michelin recently introduced a tire warranted to last 80,000 miles.
- *Gives the buyer facts.* Today's sophisticated consumer wants informative advertising and knowledgeable salespeople.
- *Builds long-term relationships.* American Airlines' Advantage program, Hyatt's Passport Club, and Whirlpool's 800-number hotline all help build good customer relations.

How Managers Set Prices

7 **How are product prices determined?**

After establishing a pricing objective, managers must set a specific price for the product. Two techniques that are often used to set a price are markup pricing and breakeven analysis.

CONCEPT *in Action*

Gas prices have soared in recent years, triggering consumer outrage and congressional hearings over alleged price gouging by the oil industry. As energy firms continue to report record profits, lawmakers stage routine inquisitions of Big Oil CEOs and seek to get in on the action through a proposed "windfall profits" tax. Top producers like ExxonMobile and Shell have defended their pricing methods, citing global demand and political instability as causes of pain at the pump. *What are some reasons gas prices rise and fall?*

© KIM KULISH/CORBIS

markup pricing
A method of pricing in which a certain percentage (the markup) is added to the product's cost to arrive at the price.

breakeven point
The price at which a product's costs are covered, so additional sales result in profit.

fixed costs
Costs that do not vary with different levels of output; for example, rent.

variable costs
Costs that change with different levels of output; for example, wages and cost of raw materials.

fixed-cost contribution
The selling price per unit (revenue) minus the variable costs per unit.

total revenue
The selling price per unit times the number of units sold.

total cost
The sum of the fixed costs and the variable costs.

total profit
Total revenue minus total cost.

Markup Pricing

One of the most common forms of pricing is **markup pricing**. In this method, a certain dollar amount is added to a product's cost to arrive at the retail price. (The retail price is thus *cost plus markup*.) The cost is the expense of manufacturing the product or acquiring it for resale. The markup is the amount added to the cost to cover expenses and leave a profit. For example, if Banana Boat suntan cream costs Walgreen's drugstore $5 and sells for $7, it carries a markup of 29 percent:

Cost	$5	Cost to Walgreen's
Markup	+ 2	Walgreen's markup to cover expenses (utilities, wages, etc.)
Retail	$7	Banana Boat suntan cream price paid by the consumer price

$$\text{Walgreen's markup percentage} = \frac{\text{Markup}}{\text{Retail price}}$$
$$= \frac{\$2}{\$7}$$
$$= 29\%$$

Several elements influence markups. Among them are tradition, the competition, store image, and stock turnover. Traditionally, department stores used a 40 percent markup. But today competition has forced retailers to respond to consumer demand and meet competitors' prices. A department store that tries to sell household appliances at a 40 percent markup would lose customers to such discounters as Wal-Mart and Target. However, a retailer trying to develop a prestige image will use markups that are much higher than those used by a retailer trying to develop an image as a discounter.

Breakeven Analysis

Manufacturers, wholesalers (companies that buy from manufacturers and sell to retailers and institutions), and retailers (firms that sell to end users) need to know how much of a product must be sold at a certain price to cover all costs. The point at which the costs are covered and additional sales result in profit is the **breakeven point**.

To find the breakeven point, the firm measures the various costs associated with the product:

- **Fixed costs** do not vary with different levels of output. The rent on a manufacturing facility is a fixed cost. It must be paid whether production is one unit or a million units.
- **Variable costs** change with different levels of output. Wages and expenses of raw materials are considered variable costs.
- The **fixed-cost contribution** is the selling price per unit (revenue) minus the variable costs per unit.
- **Total revenue** is the selling price per unit times the number of units sold.
- **Total cost** is the total of the fixed costs and the variable costs.
- **Total profit** is total revenue minus total cost.

Knowing these amounts, the firm can calculate the breakeven point:

$$\text{Breakeven point in units} = \frac{\text{Total fixed cost}}{\text{Fixed-cost contribution}}$$

Let's see how this works: Grey Corp., a man-ufacturer of aftershave lotion, has variable costs of $3 per bottle and fixed costs of $50,000. Grey's management believes the company can sell up to 100,000 bottles of aftershave at $5 a bottle without having to lower its price. Grey's fixed-cost contribution is $2 ($5 selling price per bottle minus

$3 variable costs per bottle). Therefore, $2 per bottle is the amount that can be used to cover the company's fixed costs of $50,000.

To determine its breakeven point, Grey applies the previous equation:

$$\text{Breakeven point in bottles} = \frac{\$50,000 \text{ fixed cost}}{\$2 \text{ fixed-cost contribution}}$$

$$= 25,000 \text{ bottles}$$

Grey Corp. will therefore break even when it sells 25,000 bottles of aftershave lotion. After that point, at which the fixed costs are met, the $2 per bottle becomes profit. If Grey's forecasts are correct and it can sell 100,000 bottles at $5 a bottle, its total profit will be $150,000 ($2 per bottle 75,000 bottles).

By using the equation, Grey Corp. can quickly find out how much it needs to sell to break even. It can then calculate how much profit it will earn if it sells more units. A firm that is operating close to the breakeven point may change the profit picture in two ways. Reducing costs will lower the breakeven point and expand profits. Increasing sales will not change the breakeven point, but it will provide more profits.

concept check

Explain how markups are calculated.

Describe breakeven analysis.

What does it mean to "break even"?

Product Pricing

8 **What strategies are used for pricing products?**

Managers use various pricing strategies when determining the price of a product, as this section explains. Price skimming and penetration pricing are strategies used in pricing new products; other strategies such as leader pricing and bundling may be used for established products as well.

Price Skimming

price skimming
The strategy of introducing a product with a high initial price and lowering the price over time as the product moves through its life cycle.

The practice of introducing a new product on the market with a high price and then lowering the price over time is called **price skimming**. As the product moves through its life cycle, the price usually is lowered because competitors are entering the market. As the price falls, more and more consumers can buy the product.

Price skimming has four important advantages. First, a high initial price can be a way to find out what buyers are willing to pay. Second, if consumers find the

CONCEPT *in Action*

Online DVD rental services such as Netflix are changing the way America watches movies. With Netflix, film buffs select their favorite DVD movies online and receive them through the mail in about one business day. In contrast to traditional rental services, Netflix offers over 60,000 titles with no due dates or late fees. *What is Netflix's pricing model and what advantages does it have over traditional movie rental fees?*

© ASSOCIATED PRESS, AP

introductory price too high, it can be lowered. Third, a high introductory price can create an image of quality and prestige. Fourth, when the price is lowered later, consumers may think they are getting a bargain. The disadvantage is that high prices attract competition.

Price skimming can be used to price virtually any new products such as high-definition televisions, new cancer drugs, and color computer printers. For example, the Republic of Tea has launched new Imperial Republic White Tea, which it says is among the rarest of teas. Because it is minimally processed, white tea is said to retain the highest level of antioxidants and has a lower caffeine content than black and green teas. The company says the tea is picked only a few days each year, right before the leaf opens, yielding a small harvest. The product retails for $14 per tin of 50 bags. Products don't have to cost hundreds of dollars to use a skimming strategy.

Penetration Pricing

penetration pricing
The strategy of selling new products at low prices in the hope of achieving a large sales volume.

A company that doesn't use price skimming will probably use **penetration pricing.** With this strategy, the company offers new products at low prices in the hope of achieving a large sales volume. Procter & Gamble did this with the SpinBrush toothbrush. Penetration pricing requires more extensive planning than skimming does because the company must gear up for mass production and marketing. When Texas Instruments entered the digital-watch market, its facilities in Lubbock, Texas, could produce 6 million watches a year, enough to meet the entire world demand for low-priced watches. If the company had been wrong about demand, its losses would have been huge.

Penetration pricing has two advantages. First, the low initial price may induce consumers to switch brands or companies. Using penetration pricing on its jug wines, Gallo has lured customers away from Taylor California Cellars and Inglenook. Second, penetration pricing may discourage competitors from entering the market. Their costs would tend to be higher, so they would need to sell more at the same price to break even.

Penetration pricing is not just a common strategy in the United States. In fact, some of the most successful penetration strategies have been implemented in other countries as the Expanding Around the Globe box explains.

Leader Pricing

leader pricing
The strategy of pricing products below the normal markup or even below cost to attract customers to a store where they would not otherwise shop.

loss leader
A product priced below cost as part of a leader pricing strategy.

Pricing products below the normal markup or even below cost to attract customers to a store where they wouldn't otherwise shop is **leader pricing.** A product priced below cost is referred to as a **loss leader.** Retailers hope that this type of pricing will increase their overall sales volume and thus their profit.

Items that are leader priced are usually well known and priced low enough to appeal to many customers. They also are items that consumers will buy at a lower price, even if they have to switch brands. Supermarkets often feature coffee and bacon in their leader pricing. Department stores and specialty stores also rely heavily on leader pricing.

Bundling

bundling
The strategy of grouping two or more related products together and pricing them as a single product.

Bundling means grouping two or more related products together and pricing them as a single product. Marriott's special weekend rates often include the room, breakfast, and one night's dinner. Department stores may offer a washer and dryer together for a price lower than if the units were bought separately.

The idea behind bundling is to reach a segment of the market that the products sold separately would not reach as effectively. Some buyers are more than willing to buy one product but have much less use for the second. Bundling the second product to the first at a slightly reduced price thus creates some sales that otherwise would not be made. Aussie 3-Minute Miracle Shampoo is typically bundled with its conditioner

Easy Does It All

It's just after midnight on the French Riviera, and while the rich and famous sip champagne in Cannes at the annual film festival, something unsightly and orange cruises into the harbor and plops down its anchor among the majestic yachts. An enormous "EasyCruise.com" logo runs down the length of the ship, with all the subtlety of a flashing neon sign. This is the maiden voyage of a new concept in budget cruising, the 14ᵗʰ venture of low-cost superbrand EasyGroup.

The Easy empire was built on experiments in low-cost living like EasyCruise, and life on the inside is a study in value trumping aesthetics. The company is the brainchild of 38-year-old Greek shipping heir Stelios Haji-Ioannou, who popped up on the international radar screen in 1995 when he founded budget airline EasyJet at the tender age of 28. Now, he is merrily slapping the Easy brand on an almost unlimited array of discount products and services, many of which seem to have little in common. There are Easy movie rentals and an Easy shaving cream. There are Easy Internet cafes, Easy pizzas, and an Easy hotel. There's even an Easy wristwatch. "In an industry where consumers are being ripped off, if I can find a way to give them real value, I'm going to do it," he says.

It's an audacious—some would say delusional—notion. But then, nobody thought Stelios had much of a chance with his low-cost debut, the airline. The airline is now fourth only to Lufthansa, Air France, and KLM in the number of passengers carried within Europe. And although it's true that 11 of the other 14 Easy companies have yet to turn an annual profit, they're still young—half have existed for less than a year.

Competitors, however, often feel threatened by Easy's incursions. Stelios starts price wars almost everywhere he goes, and that has earned him plenty of detractors across many industries. "His assumption that he can take any idea and just slap his brand on it is somewhat arrogant," says Paolo Pescatore, a wireless analyst with research firm IDC. Easy's mobile-phone venture, launched in March, illustrates the typical pattern. It sells SIM cards that can be put into existing handsets and then charges for service. Its debut prices were as much as 40 percent below prevailing norms, and rival Carphone Warehouse countered with deep discounts of its own. Orange, a heavyweight in the United Kingdom, sued Easy—for using orange, the same color that Orange uses in its ads.[8]

Critical Thinking Questions

- With 15 Easy brands on the market, in many different industries, do you think that Stelios has diversified too much? Is he destroying the mystique of the brand?
- Stelios says the United States will be "Easy pickings" for the Easy Group. Do you agree? Why or why not?

---

because many people use shampoo more than conditioner so they don't need a new bottle of conditioner.

Odd-Even Pricing

odd-even (psychological) pricing
The strategy of setting a price at an odd number to connote a bargain and at an even number to suggest quality.

prestige pricing
The strategy of increasing the price of a product so that consumers will perceive it as being of higher quality, status, or value.

Psychology often plays a big role in how consumers view prices and what prices they will pay. **Odd-even pricing (or psychological pricing)** is the strategy of setting a price at an odd number to connote a bargain and at an even number to imply quality. For years, many retailers have priced their products in odd numbers—for example, $99.95 or $49.95—to make consumers feel that they are paying a lower price for the product.

Some retailers favor odd-numbered prices because they believe that $9.99 sounds much less imposing to customers than $10.00. Other retailers believe that an odd-numbered price signals to consumers that the price is at the lowest level possible, thereby encouraging them to buy more units. Neither theory has ever been conclusively proved, although one study found that consumers perceive odd-priced products as being on sale.[9] Even-numbered pricing is sometimes used to denote quality. Examples include a fine perfume at $100 a bottle, a good watch at $500, or a mink coat at $3,000.

Prestige Pricing

The strategy of raising the price of a product so consumers will perceive it as being of higher quality, status, or value is called **prestige pricing**. This type of pricing is common where high prices indicate high status. In the specialty shops on Rodeo Drive in Beverly Hills, which cater to the super-rich of Hollywood, shirts that would sell for $15 elsewhere sell for at least $50. If the price were lower, customers would perceive them as being of low quality.

concept check

What is the difference between penetration pricing and price skimming?

Explain the concept of price bundling.

Describe odd-even pricing and prestige pricing.

Trends in Developing Products and Pricing

 What trends are occurring in products and pricing?

As customer expectations increase and competition becomes fiercer, perceptive managers will find innovative strategies to satisfy demanding consumers and establish unique products in the market. Satisfying customers requires the right prices. The Internet has delivered pricing power to both buyers and sellers. Two other significant trends are the use of yield management systems to maximize revenues and the growing importance of color in packaging and product design.

The Impact of the Internet on Pricing[10]

The Internet, corporate networks, and wireless setups are linking people, machines, and companies around the globe—and connecting sellers and buyers as never before. This link is enabling buyers to quickly and easily compare products and prices, putting them in a better bargaining position. At the same time, the technology enables sellers to collect detailed data about customers' buying habits, preferences, and even spending limits so that they can tailor their products and prices. For a time, all of these developments raised hopes of a more efficient marketplace.

Unfortunately, the promise of pricing efficiencies for Internet retailers and lower costs for consumers has run headlong into reality. Flawed pricing strategies have taken much of the blame for the implosion of many dot-coms. Too many merchants offered deep discounts that made profits all but impossible to achieve. Other e-retailers have felt the consumer backlash against price discrimination, because the Internet has given shoppers the ability to better detect price discrepancies and bargains. The e-retailers must now figure out how to take advantage of the Internet's unique capabilities to set dynamic prices, which would better reflect a customer's willingness to pay more under different circumstances.

Setting prices on the Internet was expected to offer retailers a number of advantages. To begin with, it would be far easier to raise or lower prices in response to demand, without the need for a clerk to run through a store with a pricing gun. Online prices could be changed in far smaller increments—even by just a penny or two—as frequently as a merchant desired, making it possible to fine-tune pricing strategies.

But the real payoff was supposed to be better information on exactly how price-conscious customers are. For instance, knowing that customer A doesn't care whether an Oscar-nominated DVD in her shopping basket costs $21.95 or $25.95 would leave an enterprising merchant free to charge the higher price on the spot. By contrast, knowing that customer B is going to put author John Le Carré's latest thriller back on the shelf unless it's priced at $20, instead of $28, would open an opportunity for a bookseller to make the sale by cutting the price in real time.

The idea was to charge exactly what the market will bear. But putting this into practice online has turned out to be exceptionally difficult, in part because the Internet has also empowered consumers to compare prices to find out if other merchants are offering a better deal or if other consumers are getting a bigger break. And the Internet has also made it easier for consumers to complain.

For example, Amazon.com faced a problem when customers learned they had paid different prices for the same DVD movies as a result of a marketing test in which the retailer varied prices to gauge the effect on demand. After complaints from irate consumers, who learned from online chat boards that they had paid higher prices, Amazon announced it would refund the difference between the highest and lowest prices in the test.

Although the Internet helps drive down prices by making it easier for consumers to shop for the best bargain, it also makes it possible for online merchants to monitor each other's prices—whether higher or lower—and to adjust them in concert without overtly colluding. As long as the number of retailers in a given market is relatively small, it is now much simpler for merchants to signal each other by changing prices for short periods—long enough for their competitors to notice, but not so long that consumers do. Airlines have long used online reservation systems to signal fare changes to each other.

Online price-comparison engines, know as shopbots, are continuing to add new features. Smarter.com now includes coupons and additional retailer discounts in its price results. In the past, consumers would have had to click deep into a retailer's site to find out about these additional savings. Vendio Services Inc. recently introduced a toolbar that people can download. If a person is on the Web page of a particular product—whether it's an iPod or a Canon digital camera—the toolbar flashes a blinking alert when it finds a lower price for that same item somewhere else. The person can then open a window on the side of the site to learn details of the cheaper price—or, simply ignore the alert. BuySafe Inc. introduced a Web site last month that lets consumers search among about 1.5 million products that are backed by antifraud guarantees. If a buyer purchases one of the items and the seller fails to deliver, the buyer can get reimbursed for the full cost up to $25,000. Merchants on the site include those that sell on eBay and Overstock.com.

Use of these sites has boomed in the past few years as people have become more reliant on the Web both as a research tool and as a place to shop. About 60 percent of consumers have used a comparison-shopping Web site.[11] Much of the growth has come from the more-established sites such as Shopzilla, Bizrate, and Nextag as well as the shopping sections of Yahoo Inc., Microsoft Corp.'s MSN, and Google. The big attraction with shopping comparison services, of course, is the hunt for a better bargain. Consumers save 18 to 20 percent on average by using comparison-shopping sites to buy products on the Web.

Merchants like the sites because they help drive consumer spending. Consumers who use comparison-shopping sites spend 25 to 30 percent more on the Web than those who don't, estimates market research firm Forrester Research.[12]

Another area where the Internet is having, and will continue to have, a major impact on pricing is the bargaining power between buyers and sellers. For example, a group of 40-plus retailers, with nearly three and a half times the buying power of Wal-Mart, have formed the WorldWide Retail Exchange. On the manufacturing side, Procter & Gamble, Kraft Foods, and 50 others have invested more than $250 million to build business-to-business (B2B) megamarket Transora. Whatever the outcome of these markets, suppliers will soon be facing a world in which there are no more weak customers. Every buyer will wield Wal-Mart's bargaining power.

Yield Management Systems Help Companies Maximize Their Revenues

yield management systems (YMS)
Mathematical software that helps companies adjust prices to maximize revenue.

When competitive pressures are high, a company must know when it can raise prices to maximize its revenues. More and more companies are turning to yield management systems to help adjust prices. First developed in the airline industry, **yield management systems (YMS)** use complex mathematical software to profitably fill unused capacity. The software employs techniques such as discounting early purchases, limiting early sales at these discounted prices, and overbooking capacity. YMS now are appearing in other services such as lodging, other transportation forms, rental firms, and even hospitals. A key factor in Easy Group's success (see the Expanding Around the Globe box) is its use of YMS.

Yield management systems are spreading beyond service industries as their popularity increases. The lessons of airlines and hotels aren't entirely applicable to other industries, however, because plane seats and hotel beds are perishable—if they go empty, the revenue opportunity is lost forever. So it makes sense to slash prices to move toward capacity if it's possible to do so without reducing the prices that other customers pay. Cars and steel aren't so perishable. Still, the capacity to make these goods is perishable. An underused factory or mill is a lost revenue opportunity. So it makes sense to cut prices to use up capacity if it's possible to do so while getting other customers to pay full price.

Already, the technology has attracted some of the biggest names in the business, from Ann Taylor to Gap to American Eagle, as well as J. C. Penney, Sears, and Home Depot. The software, which can cost a retailer as much as $10 million, can assign different prices to the same item in different stores depending on local demand—it's no accident that a "vintage flower skirt" costs $44 at an American Eagle in St. Cloud, Minnesota, but just $39.95 at an American Eagle in Birmingham, Alabama. Retailers can even predict the demand for particular colors and sizes, and price them accordingly. Supermarkets use the technology to predict how a loss-leading sale on one item, like chips, will spur shoppers to load up on higher-margin products, like salsa.[13]

Color Moves to the Forefront

In the past, color was viewed as just another design element in a package or a product. Today marketers know that colors have the power to create brand imagery and convey moods. They also know it's essential to take demographic differences into account when selecting a brand's plumage, because colors are accepted by different ages, genders, and ethnic groups in different ways.

Traditionally, men and women have had different tastes in color, with women drawn to brighter tones and more sensitive to subtle shadings and patterns. The differences are attributed in part to biology, since females see color better than males do (color blindness is 16 times more prevalent in men), and in part to socialization, with girls more likely to be steered toward coloring books and art supplies. Color is a key consideration when making many buying decisions. For example, one study found 86 percent claiming color to be an important factor when selecting clothes. Seventy-six percent said that it had an effect on car and motorcycle purchases, and 72 percent also said that color impacted their selection of kitchen appliances.[14]

Finding the "right" color for a package or logo is not always easy. Each color can send a different message. Red is an attention-getting color. It promises excitement or hotness, but it may also be a warning, such as a stop sign or fire truck. Red can also indicate sensuality such as for Elizabeth Arden's Red Door fragrance. Focus on hot pink and the message is one of youth and child-like vigor. Mattel's Barbie doll lines have signature bright pint packaging. Orange is a high-energy color that has been shown to stimulate appetite and is often associated with fast food. U-Haul uses the color to reflect visibility. Tide, on the other hand, uses orange to represent energy and cleaning power.

The color brown signifies strength, stability, and dependability. UPS asks, "What can brown do for you?" Brown also is associated with natural. Many organic and natural products are packaged in brown. Green means rejuvenation, refreshment, and the color of nature. Shampoos, with herbal qualities, often have green packaging. Green has also come to mean low-fat or healthy products such as the Healthy Choice brand.[15]

> **concept check**
>
> What benefits do consumers experience when using online price-comparison engines?
>
> Provide one example of how service firms use Yield Management Systems to maximize revenue.
>
> What does color communicate about a package or product?

Summary of Learning Goals

1 **What is a product, and how is it classified?**

A product is any good or service, along with its perceived attributes and benefits, that creates customer value. Tangible attributes include the good itself, packaging, and warranties. Intangible attributes are symbolic like a brand's image. Products are categorized as either consumer products or industrial products. Consumer products are goods and services that are bought and used by the end users. They can be classified as unsought products, convenience products, shopping products, or specialty products, depending on how much effort consumers are willing to exert to get them.

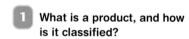

Industrial products are those bought by organizations for use in making other products or in rendering services and include capital products and expense items.

2 **How does branding distinguish a product from its competitors?**

Products usually have brand names. Brands identify products by words, names, symbols, designs, or a combination of these things. The two major types of brands are manufacturer (national) brands and dealer (private) brands. Generic products carry no brand name. Branding has three main purposes: product identification, repeat sales, and new-product sales. Cobranding entails placing two or more brand names on a product or its package.

3 **What are the functions of packaging?**

Often the promotional claims of well-known brands are reinforced in the printing on the package. Packaging is an important way to promote sales and protect the product. A package should be easy to ship, store, and stack on a store shelf. Companies can add value to products by giving warranties. A warranty guarantees the quality of a good or service.

4 **How do organizations create new products?**

To succeed, most firms must continue to design new products to satisfy changing customer demands. But new-product development can be risky. Many new products fail. To be successful, new-product development requires input from production, finance, marketing, and engineering personnel. In large organizations, these people work in a new-product development department. The steps in new-product development are setting new-product goals, exploring ideas, screening ideas, developing the concept (creating a prototype and building the marketing strategy), test-marketing, and introducing the product. When the product enters the marketplace, it is often managed by a product manager.

5 **What are the stages of the product life cycle?**

After a product reaches the marketplace, it enters the product life cycle. This cycle typically has four stages: introduction, growth, maturity, and decline (and possibly death). Profit margins usually are small in the introductory phase, reach a peak at the end of the growth phase, and then decline. Marketing strategies for each stage are listed in Exhibit 13.9.

6 **What is the role of pricing in marketing?**

Price indicates value, helps position a product in the marketplace, and is the means for earning a fair return on investment. If a price is too high, the product won't sell well and the firm will lose money. If the price is too low, the firm may lose money even if the product sells well. Prices are set according to pricing objectives. Among the most common objectives are profit maximization, target return on investment, and value pricing.

7 **How are product prices determined?**

A cost-based method for determining price is markup pricing. A certain percentage is added to the product's cost to arrive at the retail price. The markup is the amount added to the cost to cover expenses and earn a profit. Breakeven analysis determines the level of sales that must be reached before total cost equals total revenue. Breakeven analysis provides a quick look at how many units the firm must sell before it starts earning a profit. The technique also reveals how much profit can be earned with higher sales volumes.

8 **What strategies are used for pricing products?**

The two main strategies for pricing a new product are price skimming and penetration pricing. Price skimming involves charging a high introductory price and then, usually, lowering the price as the product moves through its life cycle. Penetration pricing involves selling a new product at a low price in the hope of achieving a large sales volume.

Pricing tactics are used to fine-tune the base prices of products. Sellers that use leader pricing set the prices of some of their products below the normal markup or even below cost to attract customers who might otherwise not shop at those stores. Bundling is grouping two or more products together and pricing them as one. Psychology often plays a role in how consumers view products and in determining what they will pay. Setting a price at an odd number tends to create a perception that the item is cheaper than the actual price. Prices in even numbers denote quality or status. Raising the price so an item will be perceived as having high quality and status is called prestige pricing.

9 **What trends are occurring in products and pricing?**

The Internet has given pricing power to both buyers and sellers. A second trend is that many service businesses and other companies have turned to yield management systems to maximize their revenues. Finally, color is playing a key role in packaging and product design strategies.

Key Terms

Preparing for Tomorrow's Workplace: SCANS

1. Write an e-mail explaining how most products are a combination of goods and services; provide examples. (Information)
2. Your company plans to start selling gourmet frozen foods through the Internet. You are chairing a team to name this new service. Write an e-mail to team members suggesting things that they should consider in creating a brand name. (Interpersonal)
3. Divide the class into two groups. Have the two groups debate whether consumers will readily accept the following products as generic products: automobile tires,

ice cream, staples, scientific calculators, running shoes, panty hose, gasoline, and men's briefs. (Interpersonal)

4. Under what circumstances would a jeans maker market the product as a convenience product? A shopping product? A specialty product? (Information)

5. Go to the library and look through magazines and newspapers to find examples of price skimming, penetration pricing, and value pricing. Make copies and show them to the class. (Information)

6. Write down the names of two brands to which you are loyal. Indicate the reasons for your loyalty. (Information)

7. Explain how something as obvious as a retail price can have a psychological dimension. (Information)

8. **Team Activity** Divide the class into teams. Create a single market list of products. Each team should go to a different supermarket chain store or an independent supermarket and write down the prices of the goods selected. Report your findings to the class. (Interpersonal)

9. How does the stage of a product's life cycle affect price? Give some examples. (Informational)

10. Why is it important for managers to understand the concept of the breakeven point? (Systems)

Ethics Activity

As cosmetics companies roll out line after line of products to satisfy consumers' quest for youth, the shelves are getting crowded. How can a company stand out? The new Cosmedicine line from Klinger Advanced Aesthetics, introduced at Sephora cosmetics stores in February 2006, promoted its affiliation with the prestigious Johns Hopkins Medicine to distinguish itself from its competition. Hopkins' professors worked with Klinger on product design and reviewed research. In return, Hopkins would receive fees (which could be sizable), Klinger stock, and a seat on Klinger's board. Klinger would be able to use the Johns Hopkins name in advertising and promotional materials. For example, the Sephora Web site displayed this ad: "Truth is, it will achieve your highest skin health possible. . . . Truth is, its performance is confirmed by Johns Hopkins Medicine." Other ads claimed that Cosmedicine was the only skin-care line tested "in consultation with Johns Hopkins Medicine."

Immediately, medical ethicists criticized Johns Hopkins for this arrangement. Hopkins defended its position, claiming that its consulting work does not imply any endorsement of Cosmedicine. "We have been pretty clear about our role," said Hopkins CEO Edward Miller. "We are reporting on the scientific validity of studies that were done by outside testing agencies." And Cosmedicine packaging includes a disclaimer that discloses the nature of the research and financial relationship between Hopkins and Klinger. Others, such as Mildred Cho, associate director of the Stanford Center for Biomedical Ethics; Dr. Peter Lurie of the Public Citizen Health

Research Group; and Dr. Marcia Angell, a former editor of *The New England Journal of Medicine*, believed the promotional materials could mislead consumers. "You can't evaluate the product that's made by a manufacturer that's hired you," said Dr. Angell. "The thing is riddled with conflict of interest."

The uproar caused Johns Hopkins Medicine to acknowledge that its role could be viewed as an endorsement and to refuse an equity position in or a board seat at Klinger. Klinger and Sephora removed references to Hopkins from future advertising and promotional materials.

Using a Web search tool, locate articles about this topic and then write responses to the following questions. Be sure to support your arguments and cite your sources.

Ethical Dilemma: Johns Hopkins Medicine hoped to gain funds for research and teaching with its arrangement with Klinger Advanced Aesthetics. Was it wrong to enter into the relationship with Klinger? Should it have backed down? Could it have structured the deal differently to avoid a conflict of interest? What is an appropriate relationship between academic medical centers and private sector companies?

Sources: Julie Bell and Frank D. Roylance, "Hopkins Assailed for Tie to Product," *Baltimore Sun*, April 6, 2006, http://galenet.thomsonlearning.com; "COSMEDICINE™ in Sephora Stores Now," *PR Newswire*, February 21, 2006, http://galenet.thomsonlearning.com; "Klinger Advanced Aesthetics CEO Details Johns Hopkins Medicine's Consulting Role," *Business Wire*, April 13, 2006, http://galenet.thomsonlearning.com; Rhonda L. Rundle, "A New Name in Skin Care: Johns Hopkins," *Wall Street Journal*, April 5, 2006, p. B1; Rhonda L. Rundle, "Johns Hopkins Backs Off Pact for Skin Care," *Wall Street Journal*, April 11, 2006, p. B1.

Working the Net

1. Thousands of new products are introduced each year, but many don't stay on store shelves for long. NewProductWorks, a new-product development consulting firm, uses its collection of over 70,000 new and once-new products as the foundation for its services. The site also has an online poll that gives you a chance to vote on proposed new products. Go to **http://www.newproductworks.com** and click on "Poll: Hits or Misses?" Read the descriptions of new products, rate them, and then see how your view compares to the composite rating of the product so

far. Summarize your experience. Then click on "Hits & Misses." In this section you'll find products that the NPW experts expect to succeed and those that won't. Pick a product from the "We Expect Them to be Successes" or "Jury Is Out" category and find out where it currently stands.

2. You're working for a company that plans to introduce gourmet treats for pets. Your job is to determine the market for this new product and the marketing issues that may need to be addressed. Do a search online for articles on pet ownership, pet food, and pet products. In addition to search engines, include marketing magazine sites such as *Adweek* and *Brandweek* (**http://www.adweek.com** and **http://www.brandweek.com**) and an online database such as InfoTrak. Write a short report to your manager based on your research.

3. Visit an online retailer such as Amazon.com (**http://www.amazon.com**), PCConnection.com (**http://www.pcconnection.com**), or Drugstore.com (**http://www.drugstore.com**). At the site, try to identify examples of leader pricing, bundling, odd-even pricing, and other pricing strategies. Do online retailers have different pricing considerations than "real-world" retailers? Explain.

4. Do a search on Yahoo (**http://www.yahoo.com**) for online auctions for a product you are interested in buying. Visit several auctions and get an idea of how the product is priced. How do these prices compare with the price you might find in a local store? What pricing advantages or disadvantages do companies face in selling their products through online auctions? How do online auctions affect the pricing strategies of other companies? Why?

5. Pick a new consumer electronic product such as a digital camera, HDTV, or laptop computer. Then go to the following shopping bots: **http://www.dealio.com**, **http://www.become.com**, **http://www.smarter.com**, and **http://brilliantshopper.com**. Compare prices, information, and ease-of-use of the sites. Report your findings to the class.

Creative Thinking Case >

Monster Energy Is Out There

Coca-Cola is promoting its new Full Throttle energy drink, PepsiCo Inc. is marketing energy drinks under its SoBe and Mountain Dew brands, and smaller companies are challenging the soft drink giants with products like Rockstar and FUZE Mega Energy.

But South African Rodney C. Sacks, chairman and chief executive of Hansen's Natural Corporation, believes there's plenty of room for all comers in the booming energy drink market. "These are the new soft drinks of the world," he declares. Sacks and Hansen president and chief financial officer, Hilton H. Schlosberg, raised $6 million from family and friends and bought Hansen, which was doing about $17 million in sales, for $14.5 million in 1992.

The California-based company made wholesome beverages such as preservative-free natural sodas, low-carb peach smoothies, and fruit flavored iced teas—until Sacks and Schlosberg decided to give Red Bull a run for its money. They had seen the product in Europe and timed the launch of Hansen's Energy to coincide with Red Bull's appearance on American store shelves in 1997. Carbonated, citrusy, heavy on sugar and caffeine, Hansens's Energy failed to strike any sparks with its target market of college students, truckers, and sports fans.

So Sacks and Schlosberg added even more sugar and caffeine to a new mixture they marketed as Monster. They sold for the same price as Red Bull but in big black cans twice the size, decorated with neon-colored "claw M" logos. Monster's slogan, "Unleash the beast," its eye-catching packaging, and extreme-sports sponsorships quickly made it a force in the fast-growing $2 billion a year energy-drink market.

Hansen supported the Monster brand with clever marketing. Teams of Monster "ambassadors" distribute samples at concerts, beach parties, and other events. The company sponsors high profile sporting events like motocross, surfing, and skateboarding competitions. Hansen representatives in black Monster vans help assemble store displays and restock racks in convenience store coolers. "A lot of companies say they will do that; [Hansen] really delivers," says Daniel R. Perry, senior vice-president of All-American Bottling Corporation, a Monster distributor based in Oklahoma City.

Sales of $248 million earned Hansen's the top spot on *Forbes'* "Top 200 Best Small Companies in 2005." Hansen's energy-drink sales increased 162 percent last year, three times Red Bull's growth, earning it the number 26 spot on *Business Week's* annual ranking of Hot Growth Companies. But even though Hansen's sales growth gave it an 18 percent share of the energy-drink market, Red Bull still leads with nearly half the market.

Undaunted, Sacks and Schlosberg are fighting back. "A small subset of consumers is going wild over these drinks," says *Beverage Digest* editor and publisher John Sicher. "Hansen is really riding a tiger." The company launched Joker, an energy drink sold exclusively in Circle K convenience stores; Rumba, a morning pick-me-up, caffeine-laced juice drink; and Monster Assault, which comes in a black-and-gray camouflage can that says "Declare war on the ordinary!" It is a catchphrase that captures the high-energy tactics of a formerly low-energy player.

Critical Thinking Questions

- Hansen's Natural made a bold move in developing a product that was the opposite of what the company was known for. What accounts for Monster's huge success?
- What types of unique marketing support helped to sustain the product's tremendous growth?
- How powerful a role did pricing play in pitting Monster against its competition?

Sources: Andrew Murr, "Monster vs. Red Bull," *Newsweek*, March 20, 2006, p. E22; Christopher Palmeri, "Hansen Natural: Charging at Red Bull with a Brawny Energy Brew," *Business Week*, June 6, 2005; Christopher Palmeri, "Online Extra: Fruitful Energy," *Business Week*, June 6, 2005: Hansen's Natural corporate Web site http://www.hansens.com, April 29, 2006.

Video Case >

The (Original) Penguin Marches Again

Chris Kolbe, head of the men's division at lifestyle retailer Urban Outfitters, had fond memories of seeing his dad and grandfather wearing golf shirts and cardigan sweaters carrying a penguin logo. Made by Munsingwear, the brand was the first to use a visible logo as part of its marketing strategy—a move that was later copied by Lacoste with its alligator, Ralph Lauren with its polo player, and others. Although older consumers still bought Penguin products, the brand was largely unknown to younger generations.

Perry Ellis International acquired the brand along with its acquisition of Munsingwear in 1996. As the new owner focused primarily on Munsingwear's other product lines, such as underwear and socks, it pretty much ignored the Penguin brand and its knit shirts.

Aware that young buyers liked retro fashions, Kolbe wanted to relaunch the Penguin brand. He asked Perry Ellis to produce a new version of Penguin golf shirts for Urban Outfitters. The shirts flew off the shelves, and Perry Ellis executives saw an opportunity to enter the 18- to 30-year-old demographic, one that was underserved by Perry Ellis's more mature brand line-up. As Kolbe told Oscar Feldenkreis, Perry Ellis president and COO, "Fashion is a young business. It's young in attitude. It's about having fresh, new ideas." Feldenkreis agreed and hired Kolbe as president and brand manager for the revitalized Penguin.

Kolbe renamed the brand Original Penguin to link it to its past and decided to gear the classic yet trendy line to buyers aged 17 to 30 instead of its older customers. At the same time, he retained the "suburban golfer" look but updated it to appeal to the more fashionable "preppy chic" crowd. Clever ad campaigns attracted attention to the 2003 revival of Original Penguin clothing. It recruited Brad Pitt, Jake Gyllenhaal, Courteney Cox, and the cast of The OC television show to wear its fashions. Sales took off, doubling in each year, and Penguin is now the fastest growing brand for Perry Ellis. In 2004, *Advertising Age* named Original Penguin to its list of the top 50 brand success stories.

The brand now includes not only a complete men's line but also women's and children's clothes, fashion eyewear, footwear, watches, and other accessories. "In order to make it a brand, you have to sell everything," says Feldenkreis. "Otherwise when the polo goes out of fashion, you don't have a business anymore."

In addition to selling through upscale department stores and specialty retailers such as Bloomingdale's, Saks Fifth Avenue, Fred Siegel, Barneys New York, and Urban Outfitters, Original Penguin has its own stores. Its flagship Manhattan store was joined recently by Miami Beach, Florida, and Newport Beach, California. "The stores are the strongest marketing vehicle," says creative director David Bedwell. "We try to create an environment that our clothes live well in. They educate the end consumer and can act as the ultimate showcase for the Original Penguin lifestyle."

Creative Thinking Questions

- How did Chris Kolbe rebuild the Original Penguin brand?
- What type of brand is Original Penguin, and why was branding an important part of the marketing strategy for Original Penguin? Give some specific examples of how branding can create advantages for Penguin and Perry Ellis, its owner.
- Explain how Original Penguin fulfills the characteristics of an effective brand name, as summarized in Exhibit 13.4.

Sources: Adapted from the video, "Managing Change and Innovation: Original Penguin," http://www.swlearning.com/management/video/daft_7e_videos.htm l; "Original Penguin Enters Next Phase of Retail Expansion," *Business Wire*, September 20, 2005, www.findarticles.com; Original Penguin Web site, www.originalpenguin.com, May 2, 2006; Stephanie Thompson, "March of the Original Penguin," *Advertising Age*, August 8, 2005, pp. 4, 23; Elaine Walker, "Penguin Is Back on Cool Customers," *Miami Herald*, December 16, 2005, http://galenet.thomsonlearning.com.

Hot Links Address Book

Learn more about branding products and building brand equity at AllAboutBranding.com, http://www.allaboutbranding.com

See how one consulting firm helps clients pick the right name by pointing your Web browser to http://www.namebase.com

At Brandchannel.com, an online exchange, you'll find branding success stories, failures, debates, and more: http://www.brandchannel.com

Find out how to trademark a design, name, or other identifying mark by visiting the U.S. Patents and Trademark Office at http://www.uspto.gov

Curious about how generic and private label products are manufactured? Visit the Private Label Manufacturers Association at http://www.plma.com

Protect yourself! The Federal Trade Commission has more information about warranties at http://www.ftc.gov

For the latest trends in packaging, visit the Packaging Digest site, http://www.packagingdigest.com

Companies are turning to smart-pricing software to improve margins on products. Find out how one company's software works at Zilliant's Web site, http://www.zilliant.com

If you have ever wondered how manufacturers make certain types of products, this is the site for you! At How Products Are Made, you can find the details on everything from accordians and action figures to zippers, and everything in between: http://www.madehow.com

CHAPTER 14

Distributing Products in a Timely and Efficient Manner

Learning Goals

After reading this chapter, you should be able to answer these questions:

1. What is the nature and function of distribution?

2. When would a marketer use exclusive, selective, or intensive distribution?

3. What is wholesaling, and what are the types of wholesalers?

4. What are the different kinds of retail operations and the components of a successful retailing strategy?

5. How can supply chain management increase efficiency and customer satisfaction?

6. What are the trends in distribution?

Exploring Business Careers
John Pearson
DHL

John Pearson knows distribution. As the executive vice president of commercial for DHL's U.S. operations, he seeks to bring the company's efficient, reliable product distribution to every corner of the United States. Started in 1969 by Adrian **D**alsey, Larry **H**illblom, and Robert **L**ynn to ship documents between San Francisco and Honolulu, DHL has grown into a leader in the international shipping industry.

Delivering 1 billion shipments annually to over 200 countries and territories, DHL plays a critical role in more than 4.2 million customers' distribution channels, providing vital linkages between manufacturers, wholesalers, retailers, and end users. To deliver the quality of service customers expect from DHL, the company's domestic operations rely on many of the same distribution processes that have brought them success internationally. DHL provides door-to-door service for both pickups and deliveries to maximize efficiency for the customer. Every package the company delivers can be tracked throughout its shipment, making the delivery process as transparent to the customer as if they delivered the package themselves. In addition, DHL's domestic operations offer a variety of specialized services such as DHL Same Day, which is available 24 hours a day, offers pickup within one hour, and guarantees that the customer's package will be on the next available flight to its destination. Organizations such as America's Blood Centers, which provides half the

nation's volunteer blood supply, use DHL Same Day to quickly deliver time-sensitive blood products across the country.

DHL takes a number of steps to ensure efficiency and quality in the services it offers. DHL runs operations through its own hubs, gateways, and service facilities. It owns over 72,000 vehicles to complete shipments. In Pearson's eyes, one key to their success is the fact that they do not outsource customer service to agents. Instead, the company has its own offices, staffed by DHL employees, who are able to convey to the customer DHL's commitment to quality service. "The ability for us to service our customers with our own offices, as opposed to agents, is critical." Another example of DHL's corporate distribution system is its agreement with U.S. Customs. The quantity of packages DHL was sending through the customs agency in Miami, either leaving or entering the United States, was slowing down service for both customs and DHL. To solve this problem, they reached an agreement whereby DHL has its own customs agencies within its Miami facility. DHL's system allows the company to concentrate on its goal: effectively meeting and exceeding the distribution needs of others.

Chapter 14 details the importance of effective product and service distribution for a company, examining the importance of distribution channels, wholesaling, retailing, and supply chain management to the success of a company.

This chapter explores how organizations use a distribution system to enhance the value of a product and examines the methods they use to move products to locations where consumers wish to buy them. First, we'll discuss the functions and members of a distribution system. Next, we'll explore the role of wholesalers and retailers in delivering products to customers. We'll also discuss how supply chain management increases efficiency and customer satisfaction. Finally, we'll look at trends in distribution.

The Nature and Functions of Distribution

1 What is the nature and function of distribution?

distribution (logistics)
Efficiently managing the acquisition of raw materials to the factory and the movement of products from the producer to industrial users and consumers.

manufacturer
A producer; an organization that converts raw materials to finished products.

distribution channel
The series of marketing entities through which goods and services pass on their way from producers to end users.

marketing intermediaries
Organizations that assist in moving goods and services from producers to end users.

Distribution (or logistics) is efficiently managing the acquisition of raw materials to the factory and the movement of products from the producer or **manufacturer** to industrial users and consumers. Logistics activities are usually the responsibility of the marketing department and are part of the large series of activities included in the supply chain. As discussed in Chapter 11, a supply chain is the system through which an organization acquires raw material, produces products, and delivers the products and services to its customers. Exhibit 14.1 illustrates a supply chain. Supply chain management helps increase the efficiency of logistics service by minimizing inventory and moving goods efficiently from producers to the ultimate users.

On their way from producers to end users and consumers, goods and services pass through a series of marketing entities known as a **distribution channel**. We will look first at the entities that make up a distribution channel and then will examine the functions that channels serve.

Marketing Intermediaries in the Distribution Channel

A distribution channel is made up of **marketing intermediaries**, or organizations that assist in moving goods and services from producers to end users and consumers. Marketing intermediaries are in the middle of the distribution process

Exhibit 14.1 > Supply Chain

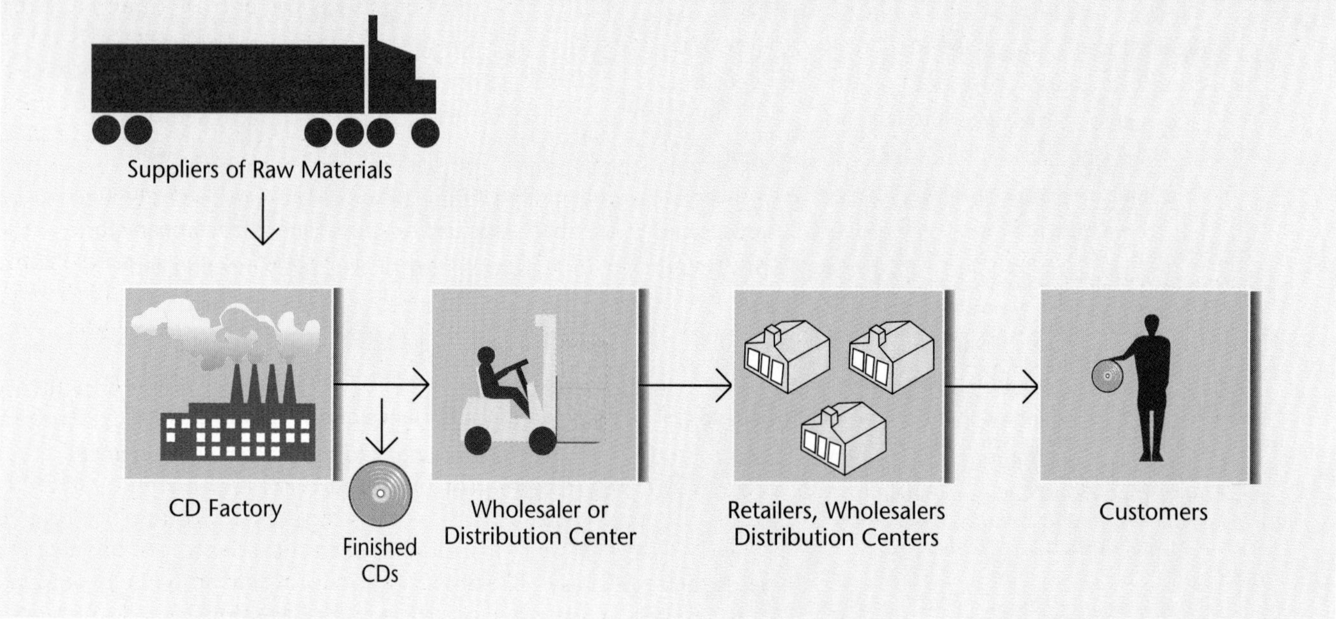

Suppliers of Raw Materials → CD Factory / Finished CDs → Wholesaler or Distribution Center → Retailers, Wholesalers Distribution Centers → Customers

agents
Sales representatives of manufacturers and wholesalers.

brokers
Go-betweens that bring buyers and sellers together.

industrial distributors
Independent wholesalers that buy related product lines from many manufacturers and sell them to industrial users.

wholesalers
Firms that sell finished goods to retailers, manufacturers, and institutions.

retailers
Firms that sell goods to consumers and to industrial users for their own consumption.

dual distribution (or multiple distribution)
Two or more channels that distribute the same product to target markets.

CONCEPT *in Action*

The "Big Four" networks and their local TV affiliates are scrambling to stave off the end of television as we know it, as a new generation of viewers has taken to watching streaming Internet video on computers, mobile phones, and iPods. Consumer migration to video download services such as YouTube, In2TV, and iTunes has the networks rushing to create multiformat distribution systems that can deliver Internet TV programming. *How might direct digital distribution upset network television's traditional distribution channel?*

between the producer and the end user. The following marketing intermediaries most often appear in the distribution channel:

- *Agents and brokers.* **Agents** are sales representatives of manufacturers and wholesalers, and **brokers** are entities that bring buyers and sellers together. Both agents and brokers are usually hired on commission basis by either a buyer or a seller. Agents and brokers are go-betweens whose job is to make deals. They do not own or take possession of goods.
- *Industrial distributors.* **Industrial distributors** are independent wholesalers that buy related product lines from many manufacturers and sell them to industrial users. They often have a sales force to call on purchasing agents, make deliveries, extend credit, and provide information. Industrial distributors are used in such industries as aircraft manufacturing, mining, and petroleum.
- *Wholesalers.* **Wholesalers** are firms that sell finished goods to retailers, manufacturers, and institutions (such as schools and hospitals). Historically, their function has been to buy from manufacturers and sell to retailers.
- *Retailers.* **Retailers** are firms that sell goods to consumers and to industrial users for their own consumption.

At the end of the distribution channel are final consumers, like you and me, and industrial users. Industrial users are firms that buy products for internal use or for producing other products or services. They include manufacturers, utilities, airlines, railroads, and service institutions, such as hotels, hospitals, and schools.

Exhibit 14.2 shows various ways marketing intermediaries can be linked. For instance, a manufacturer may sell to a wholesaler that sells to a retailer that in turn sells to a customer. In any of these distribution systems, goods and services are physically transferred from one organization to the next. As each takes possession of the products, it may take legal ownership of them. As the exhibit indicates, distribution channels can handle either consumer products or industrial products.

Alternative Channel Arrangements

Rarely does a producer use just one type of channel to move its product. It usually employs several different or alternative channels, which include multiple channels, nontraditional channels, and strategic channel alliances.[1]

Multiple Channels When a producer selects two or more channels to distribute the same product to target markets, this arrangement is called **dual distribution** (or **multiple distribution**). For example, since Sears took over Lands' End (a traditional direct business-to-consumer clothing manufacturer), Sears stores sell Lands' End products, and Sears credit cards are accepted on the Lands' End Web site. Avon, a direct supplier of health and beauty products for women, offers consumers four alternatives for purchasing products. They can contact a representative in person (the original business model), purchase on the Web, order direct from the company, or pick up products at an Avon Salon & Spa. With both Sears/Lands' End and Avon, identical products are being distributed to existing markets using more than one channel of distribution.

Dual channels don't always work out as planned. Tupperware finally stopped a 15-year slide in sales with new booths at shopping malls and a push onto the Internet. New buzz led to more Tupperware parties where salespeople set up shop in people's living rooms to show off plastic food storage containers and such. Then the company decided to place Tupperware in all Target stores with salespeople in the aisles to demonstrate the merchandise. It looked like the answer to a chronic problem: how to sell face-to-face in an era when shoppers don't have time for a door-to-door

Consumer products channels

Manu-facturer	Manu-facturer	Manu-facturer	Farmer	Service company
↓	↓	↓	↓	↓
Wholesaler	Retailer	Consumer	Broker	Agent/broker
↓	↓		↓	↓
Retailer	Consumer		Retailer	Consumer
↓			↓	
Consumer			Consumer	

Consumer (col 1): Common for cosmetics, small hardware items, novelties, groceries

Consumer (col 2): Used for large appliances, cars, furniture, and by large retailers such as Wal-Mart for all inventory needs. Also, a growing Internet retailing channel (biggest dollar volume consumer channel)

Consumer (col 3): Used by some direct-mail manu-facturers, craftspeople, farmers' markets. Also used for Internet direct sales

Consumer (col 4): Common for many food items, such as fruits and produce

Consumer (col 5): Popular for such services as insurance, stocks and bonds, real estate. The Internet is having a big impact here

Industrial products channels

Manu-facturer	Manu-facturer	Manu-facturer
↓	↓	↓
Industrial user	Agent/broker	Industrial distributor
	↓	↓
	Industrial user	Industrial user

Industrial user (col 1): Common for overhead cranes, metal buildings, business aircraft, other custom or expensive products. A growing Internet channel (biggest dollar volume industrial channel)

Industrial user (col 2): Popular with smaller manu-facturers (agent acts as manu-facturer's sales force)

Industrial user (col 3): Used for less expensive industrial products and parts. More and more volume is moving through the Internet and sold directly to the user

CONCEPT *in Action*

Cabela's started as a two-person, direct-mail operation in the early 1960s. Today, the Sidney, Nebraska–based outdoor outfitter is the world's largest direct marketer and specialty retailer of hunting, fishing, and related merchandise. In addition to operating its famed catalog business, Cabela's now sells goods to customers through the Internet and at retail superstores. Cabela's showrooms bring the outdoors inside—the stores' museum-quality displays of wildlife, fishing ponds, and mountain replicas are veritable tourist attractions. *What logistical challenges arise from using multiple distribution channels?*

sales pitch. Tupperware also figured the move would give it a stream of potential party hosts and sales-force recruits.

But moving into Target turned out to be one of the worst disasters ever at Tupperware. It was so easy to find the company's products that interest in its parties plummeted. Fewer parties meant fewer chances to land other parties and new salespeople—which Tupperware needs to offset turnover that often hits 100 percent a year.

In nine months, sales fell 17 percent and Tupperware then decided to pull its products from Target. A year later, in 2005, sales had still not recovered.[2]

Nontraditional Channels Often nontraditional channel arrangements help differentiate a firm's product from the competition. For example, manufacturers may decide to use nontraditional channels such as the Internet, mail-order channels, or infomercials to sell products instead of going through traditional retailer channels. Although nontraditional channels may limit a brand's coverage, they can give a producer serving a niche market a way to gain market access and customer attention without having to establish channel intermediaries. Nontraditional channels can also provide another avenue of sales for larger firms. For example, a London publisher sells short stories through vending machines in the London Underground. Instead of the traditional book format, the stories are printed like folded maps making them an easy-to-read alternative for commuters.

Kiosks, long a popular method for ordering and registering for wedding gifts, dispersing cash through ATMs, and facilitating airline check-in, are finding new uses. Ethan Allen furniture stores use kiosks as a product locator tool for consumers and salespeople. Kiosks on the campuses of Cheney University allow students to register for classes, see their class schedule and grades, check account balances, and even print transcripts. The general public, when it has access to the kiosks, can use them to gather information about the university.

Small- and medium-sized Louisiana food and beverage companies banded together to sell their goods over the Internet at **http://www.shoppinglouisiana.com**. They also have found that they can successfully sell their offerings through the QVC Shopping Network. With electronic media rapidly evolving, downloading first-run movies to cell phones may not be too far off! The changing world of electronics technology opens many doors for new, nontraditional channels.

strategic channel alliances
One manufacturer using another manufacturer's previously established channel to distribute its goods.

CONCEPT *in Action*

A shared-distribution agreement between Hansen Natural Corporation and Anheuser-Busch has provided a burst of adrenaline to Monster Energy, a popular energy drink and rival of worldwide category leader Red Bull. By sharing the brewing company's first-class network of wholesalers, Hansen can deliver Monster to more customers than ever before. The partnership likewise enables Anheuser-Busch and its channel partners to profit from the fast-growing energy-beverage category. *Why do companies like Hansen Natural form strategic channel alliances instead of developing and expanding their own distribution networks?*

Strategic Channel Alliances Producers often form **strategic channel alliances** which enable the producers to deliver products and services using another manufacturer's already-established channel. Alliances are used most often when the creation of marketing channel relationships may be too expensive and time-consuming. Amazon and Circuit City have a multiyear agreement to expand the selection of electronics available on Amazon.com. Under the agreement, Amazon.com customers have the option of purchasing items from Amazon's inventory of electronic items or from the broader selection offered by Circuit City. The arrangement benefits both companies: It allows Amazon.com to deepen its selection without increasing its own inventory expense, and it increases sales for Circuit City. Similarly, Amazon.com and Target formed an alliance involving the customer service and distribution operations for Target.com. The deal increases Target's online selection of books, music, and entertainment while adding clothing, jewelry, and other products to Amazon's selection.

Strategic channel alliances are proving to be more successful for growing businesses than mergers and acquisitions. This is especially true in global markets where cultural differences, distance, and other barriers can prove challenging. For example, Heinz has a strategic alliance with

Kagome, one of Japan's largest food companies. The companies are working together to find ways to reduce operating costs while expanding both brands' market presence globally.

The Functions of Distribution Channels

Why do distribution channels exist? Why can't every firm sell its products directly to the end user or consumer? Why are go-betweens needed? Channels serve a number of functions.

Channels Reduce the Number of Transactions Channels make distribution simpler by reducing the number of transactions required to get a product from the manufacturer to the consumer. Assume for the moment that only four students are in your class. Also assume that your professor requires five textbooks, each from a different publisher. If there were no bookstore, 20 transactions would be necessary for all students in the class to buy the books, as shown in Exhibit 14.3. If the bookstore serves as a go-between, the number of transactions is reduced to nine. Each publisher sells to one bookstore rather than to four students. Each student buys from one bookstore instead of from five publishers.

Dealing with channel intermediaries frees producers from many of the details of distribution activity. Producers are traditionally not as efficient or as enthusiastic about selling products directly to end users as channel members are. First, producers may wish to focus on production. They may feel that they cannot both produce and

Exhibit 14.3 **> How Distribution Channels Reduce the Number of Transactions**

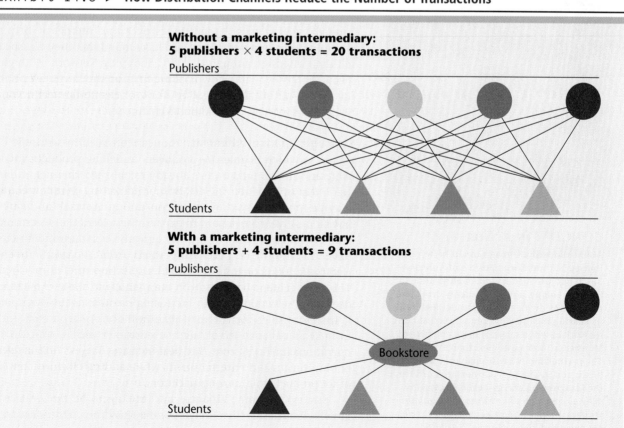

distribute in a competitive way. On the other hand, manufacturers are eager to deal directly with giant retailers, such as Wal-Mart. Wal-Mart offers huge sales opportunities to producers.

Channels Ease the Flow of Goods Channels make distribution easier in several ways. The first is by *sorting,* which consists of the following:

- *Sorting out.* Breaking many different items into separate stocks that are similar. Eggs, for instance, are sorted by grade and size.
- *Accumulating.* Bringing similar stocks together into a larger quantity. Twelve large grade A eggs could be placed in some cartons and 12 medium grade B eggs in other cartons.
- *Allocating.* Breaking similar products into smaller and smaller lots. (Allocating at the wholesale level is called **breaking bulk**.) For instance, a tank-car load of milk could be broken down into gallon jugs. The process of allocating generally is done when the goods are dispersed by region and as ownership of the goods changes.

breaking bulk
The process of breaking large shipments of similar products into smaller, more usable lots.

Without the sorting, accumulating, and allocating processes, modern society would not exist. We would have home-based industries providing custom or semicustom products to local markets. In short, we would return to a much lower level of consumption.

A second way channels ease the flow of goods is by locating buyers for merchandise. A wholesaler must find the right retailers to sell a profitable volume of merchandise. A sporting-goods wholesaler, for instance, must find the retailers who are most likely to reach sporting-goods consumers. Retailers have to understand the buying habits of consumers and put stores where consumers want and expect to find the merchandise. Every member of a distribution channel must locate buyers for the products it is trying to sell.

Channel members also store merchandise so that goods are available when consumers want to buy them. The high cost of retail space often means that many goods are stored by the wholesaler or the manufacturer.

Channels Perform Needed Functions The functions performed by channel intermediaries help increase the efficiency of the channel. Yet consumers sometimes feel that the go-betweens create higher prices. They doubt that these intermediaries perform useful functions. Actually, however, if channel intermediaries did not perform important and necessary functions at a reasonable cost, they would cease to exist. If firms could earn a higher profit without using certain channel members, they would not use them.

Channel intermediaries perform three general functions: transactional, logistical, and facilitating. We have already discussed logistics. Transactional functions involve contacting and communicating with prospective buyers to make them aware of goods and services that are available. Sellers attempt to explain why their offerings provide more features, benefits, and value than the competition. The third function is facilitating, which includes financing and market research. Research answers questions such as who is buying the products, where do they like to buy the items, and what are the characteristics of the users. The three basic functions that channel intermediaries perform are summarized in Exhibit 14.4.

A useful rule to remember is that, although channel intermediaries can be eliminated, their functions cannot. The manufacturer must either perform the functions of the intermediaries itself or find new ways of getting them carried out. Publishers can bypass bookstores, for instance, but the function performed by the bookstores then has to be performed by the publishers or by someone else.

concept check

List and define the marketing intermediaries that make up a distribution channel.

Provide an example of a strategic channel alliance.

How do channels reduce the number of transactions?

Exhibit 14.4 > Marketing Channel Functions Performed by Intermediaries

Type of Function	Description
Transaction Functions	**Contacting and promoting:** Contacting potential customers, promoting products, and soliciting orders
	Negotiating: Determining how many goods or services to buy and sell, type of transportation to use, when to deliver, and method and timing of payment
	Risk taking: Assuming the risk of owning inventory
Logistical Functions	**Physically distributing:** Transporting and sorting goods
	Storing: Maintaining inventories and protecting goods
	Sorting out: Breaking down a heterogeneous supply into separate homogeneous stocks
	Accumulation: Combining similar stocks into a larger homogeneous supply
	Allocation: Breaking a homogeneous supply into smaller and smaller lots ("breaking bulk")
	Assortment: Combining products into collections or assortments that buyers want available at one place
Facilitating Function	**Researching:** Gathering information about other channel members and consumers
	Financing: Extending credit and other financial services to facilitate the flow of goods through the channel to the final consumer

The Intensity of Market Coverage

When would a marketer use exclusive, selective, or intensive distribution?

exclusive distribution
A distribution system in which a manufacturer selects only one or two dealers in an area to market its products.

selective distribution
A distribution system in which a manufacturer selects a limited number of dealers in an area (but more than one or two) to market its products.

All types of distribution systems must be concerned with market coverage. How many dealers will be used to distribute the product in a particular area? As Exhibit 14.5 shows, the three degrees of coverage are exclusive, selective, and intensive. The type of product determines the intensity of the market coverage.

When a manufacturer selects one or two dealers in an area to market its products, it is using **exclusive distribution.** Only items that are in strong demand can be distributed exclusively because consumers must be willing to travel some distance to buy them. If Wrigley's chewing gum were sold in only one drugstore per city, Wrigley's would soon be out of business. However, Bang and Olufsen stereo components, Jaguar automobiles, and Adrienne Vittadini designer clothing are distributed exclusively with great success.

A manufacturer that chooses a limited number of dealers in an area (but more than one or two) is using **selective distribution.** Since the number of retailers handling the product is limited, consumers must be willing to seek it out. Timberland boots, a high-quality line of footwear, are distributed selectively. So are Sony televisions, Maytag

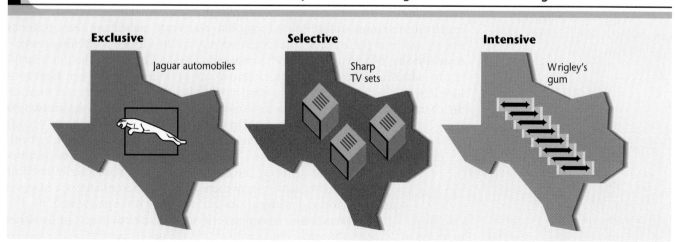

Exclusive — Jaguar automobiles

Selective — Sharp TV sets

Intensive — Wrigley's gum

Save-A-Lot Chooses Selective Distribution

James Arbertha spent 15 years trying to persuade grocers to open a store in his poor, urban neighborhood in Wichita, Kansas. Wal-Mart Stores Inc., Kroger Co., and others turned him down, leaving residents to travel several miles for bread and milk.

Most supermarkets "just weren't interested in coming to the inner city," says Mr. Arbertha, who runs a not-for-profit group that builds affordable housing. He says the neighborhood's crime-ridden history might have turned grocers away.

Recently, Mr. Arbertha found a taker. Save-A-Lot, a unit of grocery retailer and wholesaler Supervalu Inc., signed an agreement to open a 15,300-square-foot store that will sell fresh produce, meat, and other staples at what it promises will be about 40 percent less than the nearest Kroger, and also cheaper than Wal-Mart.

Save-A-Lot has quietly become one of the nation's most successful grocery chains by courting a demographic supermarkets have long ignored: the poor. The Earth City, Missouri, chain is blanketing the country with tiny, inexpensive stores catering to households earning less than $35,000 a year, generating higher profits than most grocers while doing so.

Save-A-Lot undercuts other grocers by stocking mostly its own brands of goods, displaying products in cardboard boxes, and charging customers a dime for bags. Its stores don't have bakeries, pharmacies, or grocery baggers. To keep operating costs down, Save-A-Lot franchises many locations, so that 75 percent of its stores are run by licensees. Its stores stock less than 2,800 high-turnover items, a fraction of the 32,000 found in most supermarkets. Whereas the average grocer offers more than 60 sizes, flavors, and brands of mustard, Save-A-Lot sells just two under its own brand: brown and yellow, in one size each.[3]

Critical Thinking Questions

- Do you think that Save-A-Lot would be successful on most college campuses? Is this a growth opportunity?
- Why do you think that big discounters like Wal-Mart don't serve much of the inner city market?

---

intensive distribution
A distribution system in which a manufacturer tries to sell its products wherever there are potential customers.

concept check

Name the three degrees of market coverage.

Describe the types of products that are distributed using intensive distribution.

washers, Waterford crystal, and Tommy Hilfiger clothing. When choosing dealers, manufacturers look for certain qualities. Sony may seek retailers that can offer high-quality customer service. Tommy Hilfiger may look for retailers with high-traffic locations in regional shopping malls. All manufacturers try to exclude retailers that are a poor credit risk or that have a weak or negative image.

A manufacturer that wants to sell its products everywhere there are potential customers is using **intensive distribution**. Such consumer goods as bread, tape, and lightbulbs are often distributed intensively. Usually, these products cost little and are bought frequently, which means that complex distribution channels are necessary. Coca-Cola is sold in just about every type of retail business, from gas stations to supermarkets.

One firm, Save-A-Lot, uses selective distribution to bring customer satisfaction to a target market that other retailers have ignored. The story is explained in the Customer Satisfaction and Quality box.

Wholesaling

 3 **What is wholesaling, and what are the types of wholesalers?**

Wholesalers are channel members that buy finished products from manufacturers and sell them to retailers. Retailers in turn sell the products to consumers. Manufacturers that use selective or exclusive distribution normally sell directly to retailers. Manufacturers that use intensive distribution often rely on wholesalers.

Wholesalers also sell products to institutions, such as manufacturers, schools, and hospitals, for use in performing their own missions. A manufacturer, for instance, might buy computer paper from Nationwide Papers, a wholesaler. A hospital might buy its cleaning supplies from Lagasse Brothers, one of the nation's largest wholesalers of janitorial supplies.

Sometimes wholesalers sell products to manufacturers for use in the manufacturing process. A builder of custom boats, for instance, might buy batteries from a battery wholesaler and switches from an electrical wholesaler. Some wholesalers even sell to other wholesalers, creating yet another stage in the distribution channel.

About half of all wholesalers offer financing for their clients. They sell products on credit and expect to be paid within a certain time, usually 60 days. Other wholesalers

CONCEPT *in Action*

If diamonds are a girl's best friend, then women can find plenty of friends at Sam's and Costco. The two leading membership-warehouse chains recently entered the luxury market, offering expensive diamond rings at steeply discounted prices. At Sam's, a 3.74-carat pink diamond pendant was reportedly priced 25 percent below its $750,000 valuation. At Costco, a 10.6-carat yellow-diamond ring valued at $264,765 listed for $180,000. *Why do cash-and-carry wholesalers offer jewelry for considerably lower prices than those offered by high-end retailers like Tiffany and Neiman Marcus?*

© BLEND IMAGES/JUPITER IMAGES

merchant wholesaler
An institution that buys goods from manufacturers (takes ownership) and resells them to businesses, government agencies, other wholesalers, or retailers.

full-service merchant wholesalers
Wholesalers that provide many services for their clients, such as providing credit, offering promotional and technical advice, storing and delivering merchandise, or providing installation and repairs.

limited-service merchant wholesalers
Wholesalers that typically carry a limited line of fast-moving merchandise and do not offer many services to their clients.

cash and carry wholesaler
A limited-service merchant wholesaler that does not offer credit or delivery services.

manufacturers' representatives
Salespeople who represent noncompeting manufacturers; function as independent agents rather than as salaried employees of the manufacturers.

operate like retail stores. The retailer goes to the wholesaler, selects the merchandise, pays cash for it, and transports it to the retail outlet.

Because wholesalers usually serve limited areas, they are often located closer to retailers than the manufacturers are. Retailers can thus get faster delivery at lower cost from wholesalers. A retailer who knows that a wholesaler can restock store shelves within a day can keep a low level of inventory on hand. More money is then available for other things because less cash is tied up in items sitting on the shelves or in storerooms.

Types of Wholesaler Intermediaries

The two main types of wholesalers are merchant wholesalers and agents and brokers, as shown in Exhibit 14.6. Merchant wholesalers take title to the product (ownership rights); agents and brokers simply facilitate the sale of a product from producer to end user.

Merchant Wholesalers Merchant wholesalers make up 80 percent of all wholesaling establishments and conduct slightly under 60 percent of all wholesale sales. A **merchant wholesaler** is an institution that buys goods from manufacturers and resells them to businesses, government agencies, other wholesalers, or retailers. All merchant wholesalers take title to the goods they sell. Most merchant wholesalers operate one or more warehouses where they receive goods, store them, and later reship them. Customers are mostly small or moderate-size retailers, but merchant wholesalers also market to manufacturers and institutional clients. Merchant wholesalers can be categorized as either full-service or limited-service wholesalers, depending on the number of channel functions they perform.

Full-service merchant wholesalers perform many functions. They assemble an assortment of products for their clients, provide credit, and offer promotional help and technical advice. In addition, they maintain a sales force to contact customers, store and deliver merchandise, and perhaps offer research and planning support. Depending on the product line, full-service merchant wholesalers sometimes provide installation and repair as well. Full service also means "going the extra mile" to meet special customer needs, such as offering fast delivery in emergencies.

As the name implies, **limited-service merchant wholesalers** perform only a few of the full-service merchant wholesaler's activities. Generally, limited-service merchant wholesalers carry a limited line of fast-moving merchandise. They do not extend credit or supply market information. One type of limited-service merchant wholesaler is the **cash and carry wholesaler**. This wholesaler doesn't offer credit or delivery, hence the term "cash and carry" wholesaler. Sam's Clubs and Costco are nationally known cash and carry wholesalers. About 60 percent of Sam's volume is done with small businesses. These companies are unique because they are not only wholesalers but also do business with consumers. Government employees, credit union members, and employees of large corporations, among others, can pay an annual fee (usually $35) and shop at Costco or Sam's. Retail customers typically pay a 5 percent markup as well. Exhibit 14.7 lists additional types of limited-service merchant wholesalers.

Agents and Brokers As mentioned earlier, agents represent manufacturers and wholesalers. **Manufacturers' representatives** represent noncompeting manufacturers. These salespeople function as independent agents rather than as salaried employees of manufacturers. They do not take title to or possession of merchandise. They get commissions if they make sales—and nothing if they don't. They are found in a variety of industries, including electronics, clothing, hardware, furniture, and toys.

Exhibit 14.6 > The Two Categories of Wholesalers

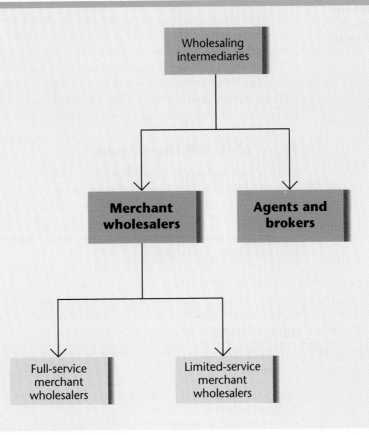

Brokers bring buyers and sellers together. Like agents, brokers do not take title to merchandise, they receive commissions on sales, and they have little say over company sales policies. They are found in markets where the information that would join buyers and sellers is scarce. These markets include real estate, agriculture, insurance, and commodities.

Exhibit 14.7 > Limited-Service Merchant Wholesalers

Cash and carry wholesalers:	Have a limited line of fast-moving goods and sell to small retailers for cash. Normally do not deliver.
Truck wholesalers:	Perform primarily a selling and delivery function. Carry a limited line of semiperishable merchandise (such as milk, bread, snack foods), which they sell for cash as they make their rounds of supermarkets, small groceries, hospitals, restaurants, factory cafeterias, and hotels.
Drop shippers:	Operate in bulk industries, such as coal, lumber, and heavy equipment. Do not carry inventory or handle the product. Upon receiving an order, they select a manufacturer, who ships the merchandise directly to the customer on the agreed-upon terms and time of delivery. The drop shipper assumes title and risk from the time the order is accepted to its delivery to the customer.
Rack jobbers:	Serve grocery and drug retailers, mostly in the area of nonfood items. They send delivery trucks to stores, and the delivery people set up toys, paperbacks, hardware items, health and beauty aids, and so on. They price the goods, keep them fresh, set up point-of-purchase displays, and keep inventory records. Rack jobbers retain title to the goods and bill the retailers only for the goods sold to consumers. They do little promotion because they carry many branded items that are highly advertised.
Producers' cooperatives:	Owned by farmer members and assemble farm produce to sell in local markets. The co-op's profits are distributed to members at the end of the year. Co-ops often attempt to improve product quality and promote a co-op brand name, such as Sun Maid raisins, Sunkist oranges, or Diamond walnuts.

The Competitive World of Retailing

 4 What are the different kinds of retail operations and the components of a successful retailing strategy?

Some 30 million Americans are engaged in retailing. Of this number, almost 16 million work in service businesses like barber shops, lawyers' offices, and amusement parks. Although most retailers are involved in small businesses, most sales are made by the giant retail organizations, such as Sears, Wal-Mart, Target, and JCPenney. Half of all retail sales come from fewer than 10 percent of all retail businesses. This small group employs about 40 percent of all retail workers. Retailers feel the impact of changes in the economy more than many other types of businesses. Survival depends on keeping up with changing lifestyles and customer shopping patterns.

Types of Retail Operations

There is a great deal of variety in retail operations. The major types of retailers are described in Exhibit 14.8, which divides them into two main categories: in-store and nonstore retailing. Examples of *in-store retailing* include Sears, Wal-Mart, Target, Macy's, and Neiman Marcus. These retailers get most of their revenue from people who come to the store to buy what they want. Many in-store retailers also do some catalog and telephone sales.

Exhibit 14.8 > Retailing Takes Many Forms

Types of In-Store Retailing	Description	Examples
Department store	Houses many departments under one roof with each treated as a separate buying center to achieve economies of buying, promotion, and control	JCPenney, Saks Bloomingdale's, Macy's
Specialty store	Specializes in a category of merchandise and carries a complete assortment	Toys "R" Us, Radio Shack, Zales Jewelers
Convenience store	Offers convenience goods with long store hours and quick checkout	7-Eleven, Circle K
Supermarket	Specializes in a wide assortment of food, with self-service	Safeway, Kroger, Winn-Dixie
Discount store	Competes on the basis of low prices and high turnover; offers few services	Wal-Mart, Target
Off-price retailer	Sells at prices 25 percent or more below traditional department store prices in spartan environment	Robs, T.J. Maxx, Clothestime
Factory outlet	Owned by manufacturer; sells close-outs, factory seconds, and canceled orders	Levi Strauss, Ship 'n Shore, Dansk
Catalog store	Sends catalogs to customers and displays merchandise in showrooms where customers can order from attached warehouse	Best, Lurias
Hypermart	Offers huge selection of food and general merchandise with very low prices; sometimes called "mall without a wall"	Hypermart USA, American Fare
Types of Nonstore Retailing	**Description**	**Examples**
Vending machine	Sells merchandise by machine	Canteen
Direct selling	Sells face-to-face, usually in the person's home	Fuller Brush, Avon, Amway
Direct-response marketing	Attempts to get immediate consumer sale through media advertising, catalogs, pop-up ads or direct mail	K-Tel, L.L. Bean, Ronco
Home shopping networks	Selling via cable television	Home Shopping Network, QVC
Internet retailing (e-retailing)	Selling over the Internet	Bluefly.com, landsend.com, gap.com, Amazon.com, Cheapstuff.com, Dell.com

---

CONCEPT *in Action*

Urban Outfitters has cornered the market on fashionable apparel for style-conscious teens. Hipsters browsing the racks at the Philadelphia-based retailer's over 100 stores find an array of vintage tennis shoes, trendy pants, and retro sweaters. The retailer's kitschy t-shirts feature ironically humorous messages that mock stereotypes and prejudices by reiterating them. *How can Urban Outfitters maximize the elements of a successful retail strategy to attract its target market of bohemian, pop-culture-obsessed youth?*

Nonstore retailing includes vending, direct selling, direct-response marketing, home shopping networks, and Internet retailing. Vending uses machines to sell food and other items, usually as a convenience in institutions like schools and hospitals.

Direct selling involves face-to-face contact between the buyer and seller, but not in a retail store. Usually, the seller goes to the consumer's home. Sometimes contacts are made at the place of work. Mary Kay Cosmetics, Avon, Herbalife, and Amway each employ over 100,000 direct salespeople. Some companies, such as Longaberger baskets, specialize in parties in a person's home. Most parties are a combination social affair and sales demonstration. The hostess usually gets a discount and a special gift for rounding up a group of friends. Such parties seem to be replacing door-to-door canvassing. The sales of many direct-sales companies have suffered, however, as women continue to enter the workforce on a full-time basis.

Direct-response marketing is conducted through media that encourage a consumer to reply. Popular direct-response media are catalogs, direct mail, television, pop-up ads, newspapers, and radio. The ads invite a person to "call the toll-free number now" or to fill out an order blank. Direct-response marketing includes K-Tel selling "golden oldies" and an ex-racecar driver touting herbal baldness remedies. It also includes the catalogs sent out by Land's End, L. L. Bean, J. Crew, Nordstrom's, and countless others.

Components of a Successful Retailing Strategy

Retailing is a very competitive business. Managers have to develop an effective strategy to survive. The key tasks in building a retail strategy are defining a target market, developing a product offering, creating an image and a promotional strategy, choosing a location, and setting prices.

Defining a Target Market The first and foremost task in developing a retail strategy is to define the target market. This process begins with market segmentation, the topic of an earlier chapter, and the determination of a target market. For example, Target's merchandising approach for sporting goods is to match its product assortment to the demographics of the local store and region. Target stores in the Northeast stock a variety of ski equipment to satisfy the local interest in downhill and cross-country skiing. The amount of space devoted to sporting goods, as well as in-store promotions, also varies according to each store's target market.

Target markets in retailing are often defined by demographics. Dollar General and Family Dollar stores target households earning less than $25,000 per year. Eddie Bauer targets suburban 25- to 45-year-olds. Claire's, a retailer selling inexpensive costume jewelry, such as Y-shaped necklaces, wire tricep bracelets, and headbands, targets 12- to 14-year-old girls.

Sometimes retail stores and chains are created to reach a new target market. Gap, for example, realized that it wasn't reaching women 35 years and older. Gap decided to design an all new chain just for this target market. It is called Forth & Towne and is designed for "social shopping." The design places in the middle of each store a grand round "salon" of fitting rooms, furnished like a little hotel lobby. At its center are comfortable chairs and a "style table" laid out with fashion magazines, fresh flowers, and bottles of water. Forth & Towne's success will largely depend on whether women in its target demographic choose to linger in that salon.

Developing the Product Offering The second element in determining a retail strategy is the product offering, also called the product assortment or merchandise mix.

Retailers decide what to sell on the basis of what their target market wants to buy. They can base their decision on market research, past sales, fashion trends, customer requests, and other sources. For example, after more companies began promoting office casual days, Brooks Brothers, the upscale retailer of men's and women's conservative business wear, updated its product line with khaki pants, casual shirts, and a selection of brightly colored shirts and ties.

After determining what products will satisfy target customers' desires, retailers must find sources of supply and evaluate the products. When the right products are located, the retail buyer negotiates a purchase contract. The buying function can be performed in-house or delegated to an outside firm. The goods must then be moved from the seller to the retailer, which means shipping, storing, and stocking the inventory. The trick is to manage the inventory by cutting prices to move slow goods and by keeping adequate supplies of hot-selling items in stock.

One of the more efficient new methods of managing inventory and streamlining the way products are moved from supplier to distributor to retailer is called **efficient consumer response** (ECR). At the heart of ECR is **electronic data interchange** (EDI), the computer-to-computer exchange of information, including automatic shipping notifications, invoices, inventory data, and forecasts. In a full implementation of ECR, products are scanned at the retail store when purchased, which updates the store's inventory lists. Headquarters then polls the stores to retrieve the data needed to produce an order. The vendor confirms the order, shipping date, and delivery time, then ships the order, and transmits the invoice electronically. The item is received at the warehouse, scanned into inventory, and then sent to the store. The invoice and receiving data are reconciled, and payment via an electronic transfer of funds completes the process. Many retailers are experimenting with or have successfully implemented ECR and EDI. Dillard's, one of the fastest-growing regional department store chains, has one of the most technologically advanced ECR systems in the industry.

The pioneer and market leader in ECR systems is Wal-Mart. Now, the retailing giant is carrying ECR a step further with radio ID tags (RFID), discussed later in the chapter.

Creating an Image and Promotional Strategy The third task in developing a retail strategy is to create an image and a promotional strategy. Promotion combines with the store's merchandise mix, service level, and atmosphere to make up a retail image.

efficient consumer response (ECR)
A method of managing inventory and streamlining the movement of products from supplier to distributor to retailer; relies on electronic data interchange to communicate information such as automatic shipping notifications, invoices, inventory data, and forecasts.

electronic data interchange (EDI)
Computer-to-computer exchange of information, including automatic shipping notifications, invoices, inventory data, and forecasts; used in efficient consumer response systems.

CONCEPT *in Action*

Whether peering through department store windows, buying holiday gifts, or going on a spending spree, people love to shop. Shopping makes people feel good and a growing body of research suggests that shopping activates key areas of the brain, boosting one's mood—at least until the bill arrives. Feelings of pleasure and satisfaction derived from a buying binge may be linked to brain chemicals that produce a "shopping high." *How might retailers use atmosphere to stimulate consumers' natural impulse to shop?*

© ASSOCIATED PRESS, AP

We will discuss promotion in more detail in the next chapter. *Atmosphere* refers to the physical layout and décor of the store. They can create a relaxed or busy feeling, a sense of luxury, a friendly or cold attitude, and a sense of organization or clutter.

These are the most influential factors in creating a store's atmosphere:

- *Employee type and density.* Employee type refers to an employee's general characteristics—for instance, neat, friendly, knowledgeable, or service oriented. Density is the number of employees per 1,000 square feet of selling space. A discounter such as Target has a low employee density that creates a "do-it-yourself" casual atmosphere.
- *Merchandise type and density.* The type of merchandise carried and how it is displayed add to the atmosphere the retailer is trying to create. A prestigious retailer such as Saks or Bergdorf Goodman carries the best brand names and displays them in a neat, uncluttered arrangement.
- *Fixture type and density.* Fixtures can be elegant (rich woods), trendy (chrome and smoked glass), or old, beat-up tables, as in an antique store. The fixtures should be consistent with the general atmosphere the store is trying to create. By displaying its merchandise on tables and shelves rather than on traditional pipe racks, the Gap creates a relaxed and uncluttered atmosphere that enables customers to see and touch the merchandise more easily. In addition to traditional display racks, Bass Pro Shops feature shooting and archery ranges, 64,000 gallon aquariums stocked with trophy bass and other fish, huge rock fireplaces with trophy mounts, numerous ponds, and waterfalls. A typical Bass Pro Shop has several million customers a year. It is not unusual for someone to drive over 100 miles to get to a Bass Pro Shop.[4]
- *Sound.* Sound can be pleasant or unpleasant for a customer. Classical music at a nice Italian restaurant helps create ambiance, just as country and western music does at a truck stop. Music can also entice customers to stay in the store longer and buy more or encourage them to eat quickly and leave a table for others.
- *Odors.* Smell can either stimulate or detract from sales. The wonderful smell of pastries and breads entices bakery customers. Conversely, customers can be repulsed by bad odors, such as cigarette smoke, musty smells, antiseptic odors, and overly powerful room deodorizers.

Choosing a Location The next task in creating a retail strategy is figuring out where to put the store. First, a community must be chosen. This decision depends on the strength of the local economy, the nature of the competition, the political climate, and so forth. Then a specific site must be selected. One important decision is whether to locate in a shopping center. Large retailers and sellers of shopping goods like furniture and cars can use a free-standing store because customers will seek them out. Such a location also has the advantages of low-cost land or rent and perhaps no direct competitors close by. It may be harder to attract customers to a free-standing location, however. Another disadvantage is that the retailer can't share costs for promotion, maintenance, and holiday decorating, as do stores in a mall.

Setting Prices Another strategic task of the retail manager is to set prices. The strategy of pricing was presented in Chapter 13. Retailing's goal is to sell products, and the price is critical in ensuring that sales take place.

Price is also one of the key elements in the store's image and positioning strategy. Higher prices often imply quality and help support the prestige image of such retailers as Lord & Taylor, Saks Fifth Avenue, Coach, Cartier, and Neiman Marcus. On the other hand, discounters and off-price retailers offer good value for the money.

One of the world's best retailers at creating a great atmosphere for its customers is Selfridges in London. We explain why in the Expanding Around the Globe box.

concept check

Describe at least five types of in-store retailing and four forms of nonstore retailing.

Discuss the components of a successful retail strategy.

Creative Retailing at Selfridges

To steer traffic to its flagship store in London, Selfridges sought divine intervention—that is, a 50-foot statue of Jesus. The small-scale replica of Rio de Janeiro's famous monument gazed down on shoppers during a month-long Brazilian-themed promotion.

Combined with a radical redesign of the retail space that makes each of Selfridges' four outlets feel more like a collection of quirky boutiques than one gargantuan marketplace, stunts like the Brazil 40° celebration have transformed the once-staid 95-year-old British retail chain into a premier arbiter of hip. Selfridges' success has spurred retailers worldwide to take a closer look. "A department store chief who has not made his way to Selfridges to study its operation," says Arnold Aronson, former CEO of Saks Fifth Avenue, "is an executive not doing his job."

Typically, department stores develop their own merchandising strategies, resulting in a retail space crowded with Tommy Hilfiger, Ralph Lauren, and other predictable names arranged in displays that rarely vary from one chain to the next. Selfridges, however, operates on the theory that no one understands a product better than the designer or vendor that created it. So individual designers are allotted space in Selfridges and asked to create in-store displays that highlight their work. Traditional "departments" such as shoes, cosmetics, and men's business wear have been organized by lifestyle—youth, sports, or women's contemporary. This helps expose customers to merchandise they might not otherwise see.

Recently, Selfridges asked a tattoo and body-piercing parlor called Metal Morphosis to set up shop next to some women's fashion vendors. Metal Morphosis was such a huge hit with shoppers en route to the clothing racks that it will soon expand to other Selfridges outlets.

Selfridges is also known for its "happenings." Recently, a group of 100 "Elvises" gathered to sing *Viva Las Vegas* in an attempt to enter the *Guinness Book of World Records*. One bizarre happening was called Body Craze. Selfridges had hundreds of folks in its London store pose in the buff as part of an exhibit by New York photographer Spencer Tunick. In part by heavily promoting its gala happenings, the retailer has been able to cycle more than 10 million browsers through its stores each year.[5]

Critical Thinking Questions

- Selfridges has opened a new store described as a "silver blob" or "spaceship." The building has no straight lines and is covered with 15,000 anodized aluminum disks. The atrium is an array of high-gloss white elevators and balconies that are all slanted to avoid "the atrium look." Do you think Selfridges is becoming too cool or hip? What impact will this have on sales?
- Would Selfridges be successful in America? Why or why not?

Using Supply Chain Management to Increase Efficiency and Customer Satisfaction

5 How can supply chain management increase efficiency and customer satisfaction?

Distribution is an important part of the marketing mix. Retailers don't sell products they can't deliver, and salespeople don't (or shouldn't) promise deliveries they can't make. Late deliveries and broken promises may mean loss of a customer. Accurate order filling and billing, timely delivery, and arrival in good condition are important to the success of the product.

The goal of supply chain management is to create a satisfied customer by coordinating all of the activities of the supply chain members into a seamless process. Therefore, an important element of supply chain management is that it is completely customer driven. In the mass-production era, manufacturers produced standardized products that were "pushed" down through the supply channel to the consumer. In contrast, in today's marketplace, products are being driven by customers, who expect to receive product configurations and services matched to their unique needs. For example, Dell only builds computers according to its customers' precise specifications, such as the amount of RAM memory; type of monitor, modem, or CD drive; and amount of hard-disk space. The process begins by Dell purchasing partly built laptops from contract manufacturers. The final assembly is done in Dell factories in Ireland, Malaysia, or China where microprocessors, software, and other key components are added. Those finished products are then shipped to Dell-operated distribution centers in the United States where they are packaged with other items and shipped to the customer.

Through the channel partnership of suppliers, manufacturers, wholesalers, and retailers along the entire supply chain who work together toward the common goal of creating customer value, supply chain management allows companies to respond with the unique product configuration and mix of services demanded by the customer. Today, supply chain management plays a dual role: first, as a *communicator* of customer demand that extends from the point of sale all the way back to the supplier, and second, as a *physical flow process* that engineers the timely and cost-effective movement of goods through the entire supply pipeline.

Accordingly, supply chain managers are responsible for making channel strategy decisions, coordinating the sourcing and procurement of raw materials, scheduling production, processing orders, managing inventory, transporting and storing supplies and finished goods, and coordinating customer service activities. Supply chain managers are also responsible for the management of information that flows through the supply chain. Coordinating the relationships between the company and its external partners, such as vendors, carriers and third-party companies, is also a critical function of supply chain management. Because supply chain managers play such a major role in both cost control and customer satisfaction, they are more valuable than ever.

Managing the Logistical Components of the Supply Chain

Logistics, discussed earlier, is a term borrowed from the military that describes the process of strategically managing the efficient flow and storage of raw materials, in-process inventory, and finished goods from the point of origin to point of consumption. The supply chain team manages the logistical flow. Key decisions in managing the logistical flow are: finding and procuring raw materials and supplies, production scheduling, choosing a warehouse location and type, inventory control setting up a materials-handling system, and making transportation decisions.

Sourcing and Procurement

One of the most important links in the supply chain is that between the manufacturer and the supplier. Purchasing professionals are on the front lines of supply chain management. Purchasing departments plan purchasing strategies, develop specifications, select suppliers, and negotiate price and service levels.

The goal of most sourcing and procurement activities is to reduce the costs of raw materials and supplies and to have the items available when they are needed for production or for the office but not before (see just-in-time manufacturing in Chapter 11).

Retailers like 1-800-Flowers.com and FTD use local florists as the backbone of their distribution networks; flowers travel from the farm to a distributor and then to a wholesaler before finally reaching the flower shop. By the time they reach consumers, flowers can be 8 to 12 days old. ProFlowers.com found this procurement system too inefficient and costly. The company developed a network-based system that transforms each domestic flower farm into a self-contained distribution facility. Growers handle everything from receiving real-time flower orders to adding personalized message cards. The company has been profitable since its founding in 1998.[6]

Production Scheduling

In traditional mass-market manufacturing, production begins when forecasts call for additional products to be made or inventory control systems signal low inventory levels. The firm then makes a product and transports the finished goods to its own warehouses or those of intermediaries, where the goods wait to be ordered by retailers or customers. Production scheduling based on pushing a product down to the consumer obviously has its disadvantages, the most notable being that companies risk making products that may become obsolete or that consumers don't want in the first place.

In a customer "pull" manufacturing environment, which is growing in popularity, production of goods or services is not scheduled until an order is placed by the customer specifying the desired configuration. This process, known as *mass customization,* or *build-to-order,* uniquely tailors mass-market goods and services to the needs of the individuals who buy them. Mass customization was explained in Chapter 11. Companies as diverse as BMW, Dell Computer, Levi Strauss, Mattel, and a slew of Web-based businesses are adopting mass customization to maintain or obtain a competitive edge.

CONCEPT *in Action*

Converting quilted cotton fabrics into brightly colored Vera Bradley bags and totes is as much a challenge today as it was when friends Patricia Miller and Barbara Bradley Baekgaard created prototypes from their basement in 1982—only on a much larger scale. Manufacturing and distributing over 9 million uniquely patterned bags annually requires Vera Bradley's state-of-the-art distribution center, a 200,000 square-foot facility that houses manufacturing, distribution, and retail operations operated by computerized planning, racking, and order-picking systems. *How do modern distribution centers differ from traditional warehouses?*

distribution centers
Warehouses that specialize in rapid movement of goods to retail stores by making and breaking bulk.

inventory control system
A system that maintains an adequate assortment of items to meet a user or customer's needs.

Choosing a Warehouse Location and Type

Deciding where to put a warehouse is mostly a matter of deciding which markets will be served and where production facilities will be located. A *storage warehouse* is used to hold goods for a long time. For instance, Jantzen makes bathing suits at an even rate throughout the year to provide steady employment and hold down costs. It then stores them in a warehouse until the selling season.

Distribution centers are a special form of warehouse. They specialize in changing shipment sizes rather than storing goods. Such centers make bulk (put shipments together) or break bulk. They strive for rapid inventory turnover. When shipments arrive, the merchandise is quickly sorted into orders for various retail stores. As soon as the order is complete, it is delivered. Distribution centers are the wave of the future, replacing traditional warehouses. Companies simply can't afford to have a lot of money tied up in idle inventory.

Inventory Control

Closely interrelated with the procurement, manufacturing, and ordering processes is the **inventory control system**—a method that develops and maintains an adequate assortment of materials or products to meet a manufacturer's or customer's demands.

Inventory decisions, for both raw materials and finished goods, have a big impact on supply chain costs and the level of service provided. If too many products are kept in inventory, costs increase—as do risks of obsolescence, theft, and damage. If too few products are kept on hand, then the company risks product shortages and angry customers, and ultimately lost sales.

7-Eleven has used supply-chain technology to control inventories and dramatically raise its profitability. In a matter of seconds, any store manager can tap into 7-Eleven's proprietary computer system and pull up real-time data on what products are selling best at that location or across the country. Instant weather reports, too, can dictate whether more umbrellas are needed for an impending storm or if a store should stock up on a muffin that sells particularly well when the temperature drops below 40 degrees. Employees are trained to stay current on upcoming sporting events or school functions to prepare for a surge in beer runs or notebook purchases. The constant tweaking means that slow-moving items are cleared away, so managers can make room for some of the 50 or so new ones 7-Eleven introduces every week. That leads to fewer overstocks and understocks, which means happier customers.[7]

MANAGING CHANGE

Digital Detectives Not Only Manage Inventories But Will Change Your Life

What do Japanese schoolchildren, Avis rental cars, luggage traveling through an airport, and a palate of Wal-Mart goods have in common? These seemingly disparate people, places, and things all have electronic radio-frequency identification tags to indicate who or what they are. Better known as RFID, this technology is an evolutionary update to the venerable bar code. It broadcasts information about an item continuously instead of waiting for it to be scanned manually.

At their simplest, these tags are basic one-way information devices. By combining a short-range radio with the bare minimum of electronics, RFID tags can do everything from identifying an item in a store for pricing and inventory purposes to spotting luggage on its way through an airport to recording the journey of a shipping container halfway around the world. No bigger than a fingernail, the most common RFID tags hold only rudimentary information, often just a model designation or serial number.

Italian makers of Parmesan cheese have found a use for RFID. The chips are embedded in the crust of many of the freshly made wheels. The tags hold information about where the cheese was made, on what day, even what the milk-producing cows had been eating—all of which can affect the way the cheese looks, how it tastes, and what it will cost. Using the RFID tags is helping to block wheels of counterfeit Parmigiano-Reggiano from Eastern Europe that routinely flood supermarkets around the world.

More complex and expensive tags go a step further: They can read and write data. At up to $10 each, these tags are meant for more valuable items, such as rental cars or shipping containers, and can store as much as 2 megabytes of data. For instance, a refrigerated truck carrying recently packaged chicken parts from a processing plant to a store might have RFID tags that track and record the temperature inside to detect spoilage while it's en route.

Here's a look at some present and contemplated uses of RFID technology.

- **Price Pressure:** In the relentless race to cut costs, RFID price tags can lower overhead in stores by simultaneously reducing shoplifting and automatically reordering inventory. When all items in a store are tagged, consumers simply wheel their carts by an RFID scanner. Their accounts are automatically charged for the purchases.
- **Flashy Passport:** Just wave your RFID passport at the immigration officer's scanner and you're through, but forget about having pages of international entry stamps to show off.
- **Pressure Check:** International tire maker Michelin is considering putting RFID tags inside its tires to hold manufacturing and user information.
- **School's Out:** Some schools have set automatic gates to open only when a valid student's RFID tag is presented. Expelled students can quickly be dropped from the approved list.
- **Gas 'n Go:** ExxonMobil's SpeedPass uses RFID technology to let drivers pay for gas without opening their wallets. Just put the key fob near the gas pump's scanner to charge the fuel to a credit card.
- **Road Tolls:** Probably the biggest use of RFID is in automated toll-collection devices such as E-Z Pass. When you drive by the toll booth scanner, the device identifies you and subtracts the toll from your account, all without you having to come to a complete stop.[8]

Critical Thinking Questions

- What do you see as the basic advantages of RFID over traditional bar codes?
- There is talk about using RFID for tickets to ball games, gambling chips, at airports, and inventory control in your own refrigerator. Explain how these processes might work.

The latest tool that companies are using to manage inventories is the RFID mentioned earlier. The growing popularity of radio-frequency identification tags (RFID) is discussed in the Managing Change box.

Setting Up a Materials-Handling System

A materials-handling system moves and handles inventory. The goal of such a system is to move items as quickly as possible while handling them as little as possible. Rite Aid, the huge drugstore chain, uses bar codes, moving carousels, and eight miles of conveyors to process 60,000 cartons a day in its California distribution center. Its sophisticated materials-handling system provided 99.6 percent accuracy and a 99 percent on-time delivery to its retail drug stores.

Making Transportation Decisions

Transportation typically accounts for between 5 and 10 percent of the price of goods. Physical-distribution managers must decide which mode of transportation to use to move products from producer to buyer. This decision is, of course, related to all other physical-distribution decisions. The five major modes of transportation are railroads,

Exhibit 14.9 > Criteria for Ranking Modes of Transportation

	Highest				Lowest
Relative cost	Air	Truck	Rail	Pipe	Water
Transit time	Water	Rail	Pipe	Truck	Air
Reliability	Pipe	Truck	Rail	Air	Water
Capability	Water	Rail	Truck	Air	Pipe
Accessibility	Truck	Rail	Air	Water	Pipe
Traceability	Air	Truck	Rail	Water	Pipe

motor carriers, pipelines, water transportation, and airways. Distribution managers generally choose a mode of transportation on the basis of several criteria:

- *Cost.* The total amount a specific carrier charges to move the product from the point of origin to the destination.
- *Transit time.* The total time a carrier has possession of goods, including the time required for pickup and delivery, handling, and movement between the point of origin and the destination.
- *Reliability.* The consistency with which the carrier delivers goods on time and in acceptable condition.
- *Capability.* The carrier's ability to provide the appropriate equipment and conditions for moving specific kinds of goods, such as those that must be transported in a controlled environment (for example, under refrigeration).
- *Accessibility.* The carrier's ability to move goods over a specific route or network.
- *Traceability.* The relative ease with which a shipment can be located and transferred.

Using these six criteria, a shipper selects the mode of transportation that will best meet its needs. Exhibit 14.9 shows how the basic modes of transportation rank in terms of these criteria.

> **concept check**
>
> What is the goal of supply chain management?
>
> Describe the key decisions in managing the logistical flow.
>
> What factors are considered when selecting a mode of transportation?

Trends in Distribution

 6 What are the trends in distribution?

Companies are using new distribution strategies to boost their profits and gain a competitive edge. In this section we'll discuss four emerging trends in distribution: category management, outsourcing logistics functions, manufacturers opening retail stores, and Internet retailing.

Category Management

category management
Suppliers manage the inventory of a category of products for a retailer.

Borders Books used to carry more than 10 titles about sushi in its cooking section. Now, it has cut the number to three because HarperCollins, the nation's third-largest publishing house, told Borders to do so. This is the mushrooming trend toward category management. **Category management** is where the nation's largest retailers ask one supplier in a category to determine how the retailer should best stock its shelves. Thus, HarperCollins tells Borders which cookbooks to carry from all cookbook publishers! Category management is becoming standard practice at nearly every U.S. supermarket, convenience store, mass merchant, and drug chain. The reason is that it works. Retailers attribute 14 percent sales growth to category management.

A retailer can increase profits by managing itself not as a collection of products, but product categories. People don't shop for soft drinks the way that they shop for meat. With soft drinks, it may be more effective to group brands (Pepsi, Coke, store brand) together; in another category, freshness is most important. Sophisticated computer programs and marketing research help decide which products and how much should be carried. Manufacturers that supply most of the category management are called captains. Category captains include: soft drinks—Coca-Cola; wine—E&J Gallo; Shaving—Gillette; pet food—Nestlé Purina; and detergent—Procter & Gamble.

The best retailers are far from passive when it comes to accepting category captains' recommendations. Wal-Mart runs the captain's plan by a "validator," which is a second supplier. So Dole, for example, runs a check on what Del Monte proposes.

Outsourcing Logistics Functions

outsourcing (or *contract logistics*)
Turning over all or part of the logistics function to an independent third party.

External partners are becoming increasingly important in the efficient deployment of supply chain management. **Outsourcing**, or **contract logistics**, is a rapidly growing segment of the distribution industry in which a manufacturer or supplier turns over the entire function of buying and managing transportation or another function of the supply chain, such as warehousing, to an independent third party. Many manufacturers are turning to outside partners for their logistics expertise in an effort to focus on the core competencies that they do best. Partners create and manage entire solutions for getting products where they need to be, when they need to be there. Logistics partners offer staff, an infrastructure, and services that reach consumers virtually anywhere in the world. Because a logistics provider is focused, clients receive service in a timely, efficient manner, thereby increasing customers' level of satisfaction and boosting their perception of added value to a company's offerings.

Third-party contract logistics enable companies to cut inventories, locate stock at fewer plants and distribution centers, and still provide the same service level or even better. The companies then can refocus investment on their core business. Toshiba, for example, is handing over its entire laptop repair operation to UPS Supply Chain Solutions, the shipper's $2.4 billion logistics outsourcing division.[9] UPS will send broken Toshiba laptops to its facility in Louisville, Kentucky, where UPS engineers will diagnose and repair defects. Consumers will notice an immediate change: In the past, repairs could take weeks, depending on whether Toshiba needed components from Japan. But because the UPS repair site is adjacent to its air hub, customers should get their machines back, as good as new, in just a matter of days. UPS also recently entered an agreement with Birkenstock Footprint Sandals. UPS contracts with ocean carriers to get shoes made in Germany across the Atlantic to New Jersey ports, instead of routing them through the Panama Canal to the shoemaker's California warehouses. Each incoming shipment is whisked away to a UPS distribution hub and, within hours, to retailers. By handing over its logistics to UPS, Birkenstock has cut the time it takes to get shoes to stores by half, to just three weeks. "Our spring fashion merchandise shipped 100 percent on time—and it was the first time in history I've been able to say that," says Birkenstock's chief operating officer, Gene Kunde.[10]

Manufacturer's Retail Stores

Although many manufacturers have jumped on the e-retailing bandwagon, others are realizing that they need more shelf space than traditional specialty stores and department stores can devote to their brands. Many are using physical stores to connect with consumers. Retail stores enable a manufacturer to control its own destiny, giving it the power to create its own image, train employees, set prices, and decide how and when to run promotions.

It's a strategy that takes finesse, however, because a manufacturer's existing distributors are unlikely to welcome the competition, at least at the beginning. But, like Nike-town, a store can serve as a giant advertising vehicle that showcases a sweeping line of merchandise and spurs sales at other outlets.

© JANA BIRCHUM/GETTY IMAGES

Maybe the best example is our featured running case Apple. Its sleek stores, which offer training sessions, free Internet access, and café-type buzz, have greatly added to the firm's profits. Hershey's has opened a 3,600-square-foot candy store on Chicago's Michigan Avenue. Apparel makers Lacoste and Puma have gone on store-building binges to remake their images, both with great success. Shoemaker Birkenstock sells through its own stores, and Bose has successfully used its branded outlets—complete with home theater demonstration rooms—to showcase its audio gear without getting drowned out by the competition at large electronics retailers.[11]

The Soaring Growth of Internet Retailing (e-retailing)

Estimates by various researchers say that 10 to 12 percent of all retail sales will be online by 2008.[12] Why? One reason is the economics of shopping. Think time spent,

© DES JENSON/BLOOMBERG NEWS/LANDOV

gasoline, finding a parking spot, locating your intended store, and then driving home. Now think a mouse click. Countless small businesses have taken the plunge to serve the growing army of online shoppers. A growing number, including e-jeweler Blue Nile, luggage site eBags, and show retailer Zappos.com, are experiencing sales of $100 million a year or more. The increasing sophistication of search technology and comparison-shopping sites have allowed online businesses cheaply and effectively to market their products to millions of potential customers. Often, these innovations are bringing less-well-known brands and merchants to consumers' attention.

Online merchants can offer a far broader array of merchandise than specialty brick-and-mortar retailers, because they don't have to keep the products on store shelves. Consider eBags Inc., the suburban Denver luggage purveyor. It easily dwarfs the selection a local specialty store can keep in stock. "We carry 12,000 bags; they have 250, most of them black," laughs Peter Cobb, eBags' vice-president for marketing.[13]

After a slow start, the world's largest retailer Wal-Mart has begun moving into e-retailing in a big way. It is now in almost every major category of Web-related consumer commerce. In 2005, the Wal-Mart site had more than 500 million visits. The company has taken some innovative steps to leverage the Web to drive people to its stores. A case in point is the company's online tire service, which allows you to order automobile tires to be picked up and mounted at a Wal-Mart tire center. You can order prescription refills for delivery by mail or for pickup at Wal-Mart's pharmacy department. Wal-Mart's online photo service, which in addition to providing a way to store your pictures on the Web, allows you to send your digital pictures to be printed in a Wal-Mart store of your choice, with a one-hour turnaround. Also, Wal-Mart has launched a service that allows customers to create custom CDs, which are shipped to them by mail, with any of the 500,000 songs on its music site.[14]

concept check

Explain category management and why it is popular.

What are the benefits of outsourcing one or more functions of the supply chain to a third party?

What factors contribute to the Internet's soaring growth in e-retailing?

Summary of Learning Goals

1 What is the nature and function of distribution?

Distribution or logistics is efficiently managing the acquisition of raw materials to the factory and the movement of products from the producer or manufacturer, to industrial users and consumers. Logistics activities are usually the responsibility of the marketing department and are part of the large series of activities included in the supply chain.

Distribution channels are the series of marketing entities through which goods and services pass on their way from producers to end users. Distribution systems focus on the physical transfer of goods and services and on their legal ownership at each stage of the distribution process. Channels (a) reduce the number of transactions, (b) ease the flow of goods, and (c) increase channel efficiency.

2 When would a marketer use exclusive, selective, or intensive distribution?

The degree of intensity depends in part on the type of product being distributed. Exclusive distribution (one or two dealers in an area) is used when products are in high demand in the target market. Selective distribution has a limited number of dealers per area, but more than one or two. This form of distribution is used for consumer shopping goods, some specialty goods, and some industrial accessories. Intensive distribution occurs when the manufacturer sells its products in virtually every store willing to carry them. It is used mainly for consumer convenience goods.

3 **What is wholesaling, and what are the types of wholesalers?**

Wholesalers typically sell finished products to retailers and to other institutions, such as manufacturers, schools, and hospitals. They also provide a wide variety of services, among them storing merchandise, financing inventory, breaking bulk, providing rapid delivery to retailers, and supplying market information. The two main types of wholesalers are merchant wholesalers, and agents and brokers. Merchant wholesalers buy from manufacturers and sell to other businesses. Full-service merchant wholesalers offer a complete array of services to their customers, who are retailers. Limited-service merchant wholesalers typically carry a limited line of fast-moving merchandise and offer few services to their customers. Agents and brokers are essentially independents who provide buying and selling services. They receive commissions according to their sales.

4 **What are the different kinds of retail operations and the components of a successful retailing strategy?**

Some 30 million Americans are engaged in retailing. Retailing can be either in-store or nonstore. In-store retail operations include department stores, specialty stores, discount stores, off-price retailers, factory outlets, and catalog showrooms. Nonstore retailing includes vending machines, direct sales, direct-response marketing, and Internet retailing.

Creating a retail strategy is important in all kinds of retailing and involves defining a target market, developing a product offering, creating an image and a promotional strategy, choosing a location, and setting prices. The most important factors in creating a store's atmosphere are employee type and density, merchandise type and density, fixture type and density, sound, and odors.

5 **How can supply chain management increase efficiency and customer satisfaction?**

The goal of supply chain management is to coordinate all of the activities of the supply chain members into a seamless process, thereby increasing customer satisfaction. The logistical components of the supply chain include: sourcing and procurement, inventory control, production scheduling, choosing a warehouse location and type, setting up a materials-handling system, and making transportation decisions.

6 **What are the trends in distribution?**

Four emerging trends in distribution are category management, outsourcing logistics functions, manufacturers opening retail stores, and Internet retailing. The former is where large retailers ask one supplier in a category of products to determine how the retailer should best stock its shelves. Nearly every supermarket chain, convenience store chain, mass merchant, and drugstore chain uses category management. Vendors use sophisticated computer programs and marketing research to determine which products and how much should be carried. The result is greater sales and higher profits.

Outsourcing or contract logistics is growing very rapidly. This is where all or part of the supply chain function is turned over to a third party. Typically, the manufacturer or supplier saves money and increases customer satisfaction. Another trend is that manufacturers are opening their own retail stores to gain additional shelf space and to increase consumer buzz. A final trend is the huge growth in Internet retailing. The ease of use and ability to comparison shop is driving millions of people to the Internet to purchase goods and services. Huge retailers like Wal-Mart are quickly increasing their Web presence.

Key Terms

Preparing for Tomorrow's Workplace: SCANS

1. **Team Activity** Divide the class into two groups with one taking the "pro" position and the other the "con" position on the following issue: "The only thing marketing intermediaries really do is increase prices for consumers. It is always best to buy direct from the producer." (Interpersonal)

2. Trace the distribution channel for some familiar product. Compose an e-mail that explains why the channel has evolved as it has and how it is likely to change in the future. (Systems)

3. You work for a small chain of department stores (six stores total) located within a single state. Write a memo to the president explaining how e-retailing may affect the chain's business. (Technology)

4. Go to a successful, independent specialty store in your area that has been in business for quite a while. Interview the manager and try to determine how the store successfully competes with the national chains. (Interpersonal)

5. Discuss why innovation is so important in retailing today. Be sure to give examples. (Information)

6. **Team Activity** Divide the class into teams. Each team should select a local manufacturer to visit. The team should interview managers to determine how its supply chain functions. Make a report to the class. (Interpersonal)

7. How does supply chain management increase customer value? (Systems)

8. Give some examples of nontraditional channels and why you think that they are successful. (Systems)

Ethics Activity

As a sales representative for a small regional gourmet food manufacturer, you are excited about the company's launch of a new line of flavored mustards such as raspberry balsamic, horseradish, and curry. Although your products are well received by consumers in smaller retail outlets, one of your biggest challenges is getting the major grocery chains such as Safeway, Giant, and Whole Foods to carry your products and also give you decent shelf space for your products. Your company competes with large food manufacturers like French's and Kraft, who makes the popular Grey Poupon line. Kraft's large product line and huge promotional budget give it incredible marketing clout. It's standard practice for food manufacturers and distributors to pay retailers "slotting fees" for premium shelf position in their stores and even to limit shelf space for competing products.

Until now, your CEO has refused to pay slotting fees and considers them unethical, believing that they ultimately raise prices for consumers and curtail competition. Retailers consider the fees a legitimate promotional expense and compensation for the risk of selling new products—not to mention a revenue source that can range from $5,000 to over $50,000.

Using a Web search tool, locate articles about this topic and then write responses to the following questions. Be sure to support your arguments and cite your sources.

Ethical Dilemma: Your company's two-year sales plan—and your ability to meet your sales quota—depends on getting larger distribution for your new product line. Should your company begin paying slotting fees to get better and more shelf space, or do you agree with your CEO that such fees are unethical?

Sources: "California Legislator Asks for Disclosures on Slotting Fees," *The Food Institute Report*, March 14, 2005, p. 8; "California Mulls Over Slotting Fees," *Supermarket News*, February 14, 2005, p. 6; Mark Hamstra, "Study Sees Purpose in Slotting Fees," *Supermarket News*, April 18, 2005, p. 8; Stephanie Thompson, "No News is Bad News for Food Biz," *Advertising Age*, August 8, 2005, p. 1.

Working the Net

1. Visit *Industry Week*'s Web site at **http://www.industryweek.com.** Under Archives, do a search using the search term "supply chain management." Choose an article from the results that describes how a company has used supply chain management to improve customer satisfaction, performance, or profitability. Give a brief presentation to your class on your findings.

2. What are some of the logistics problems facing firms that operate internationally? Visit the *Logistics Management* magazine Web site at **http://www.logisticsmgmt. com** and see if you can find information about how firms manage global logistics. Summarize the results.

3. Search for information on retail careers at the About.com's retail industry information site, **http://www.retailindustry.about.com.** What types of careers are available in retailing? What skills are needed? Does a career in retailing appeal to you? Why or why not?

4. How does category management help companies? For one view, visit the InfoCenter's Category Management pages of Hershey's Vending division at **http://www.hersheysvending.com.** What benefits does this system claim to offer to owners of vending machines? What are the advantages for Hershey's? Browse the rest of the Web site. What other helpful information does it provide?

5. One of the biggest challenges for retailers is integrating their various channels to provide a seamless experience for customers, regardless of the channel. Pick two of the following companies, explore their Web sites, and compare the channel integration strategies: Staples (**http://www.staples.com**), Gap (**http://www.gap.com**), Wal-Mart (**http://www.walmart.com**), Powell's Books (**http://www.Powells.com**), LLBean (**http://www.llbean.com**), or Target Stores (**http://www.target.com**). In addition to looking at the Web sites from a channel perspective, you may want to look at the company information and news sites.

6. Go to **http://www.woot.com**. Why do you think that this e-retailer is successful? How can it expand its market? Why do you think that the site has such a cult following?

7. A beauty of the Internet is the ability to comparison shop like never before. To compare brands, features, and prices of products, go to three of these sites: **http://www.bottomdollar.com, http://mysimon.com, or http://www.compare. net.** For the best bargains try **http://www.overstock.com, http://www. smartbargains.com, http://www.bluefly.com, http://www.smartshopper.com, http://www.nextag.com,** or **http://www.shopzilla.com.** Which is easiest to use? Hardest? Which provides the most information?

Amway's Distribution Network Helps Company Realize Its Vision

Started more than 40 years ago by the late Jay Van Andel and Rich DeVos, the Amway Corporation grew out of their business selling Nutrilite supplements. Beginning with L.O.C.™ Multi-Purpose Cleaner, an efficient cleaning product that is still part of the Amway product line, Amway expanded rapidly, offering people the chance to become Independent Business Owners (IBO's) selling Amway's growing range of products. The company quickly became a global leader in multilevel marketing—a position it still holds.

From the start, Amway's dedication to providing quality products led the company to invest in state-of-the-art product development processes, supported by the finest quality manufacturing and distribution facilities to be found anywhere in the world. Today the company offers more than 450 company-branded products and services globally, including nutritional supplements, cleaning products, cosmetics, and water treatment. It is part of an international organization with annual sales in excess of $6.2 billion, reaching into more than 80 countries and territories worldwide.

So how does a business so large ensure that its 3 million customers receive quality goods on time? The main manufacturing facilities for Amway products are situated on a 256-acre complex in Ada, Michigan. Nutrilite products are manufactured at Buena Park and Lakeview in California, and additional manufacturing facilities are located at Guangzhou in China. Because cultural preferences and legal requirements vary widely around the world, so does the range of Amway products available in each market. National regulations mean that product offerings are different in Germany and the United Kingdom for example. To cater to its markets' diverse needs, Amway's dispatch and distribution facilities uses the latest technology to ensure that the company delivers.

Products enter the distribution chain from integrated manufacturing and packaging facilities designed to bring you the products you need exactly when you need them. The Central Warehouse at Ada, Michigan, covers more than 680,000 square feet—over 15.6 acres! Here, 95 dedicated staff dispatch more than 30,000 items every day via 49 loading docks. Products are also distributed from 38 additional centers in 31 countries around the world, located in China, Europe, and South Africa, among others. In addition, the company has more than 200 shops in over 100 cities to support Amway sales representatives and their customers. Web stores, where customers can obtain information about products and place online orders, round out the company's product distribution and supply options.

Amway's guiding vision is simple—to make a positive difference to people around the world by helping them live better lives with products and services that offer superior quality and value. By making the Amway shopping experience faster, easier, and more convenient, its state-of-the-art global ordering and distribution network is helping the company realize its vision.

Critical Thinking Questions

- What challenges does Amway face in the global distribution of its products and services?
- How does the company meet those challenges?
- How does Amway's product distribution network contribute to the company's overall vision?

Sources: Amway corporate Web site, http://www.amway.com, April 26, 2006; "Amway Corporation-Overview," Hoovers Web site, http://www.hoovers.com, April 26, 2006.

Success Blooms at 1-800-Flowers

Do you need to send flowers for a relative's birthday in Germany, to celebrate your daughter's first big business presentation in the United Kingdom, or to congratulate your neighbors across the street on the birth of their new baby? One call to 1-800-FLOWERS does it all—floral arrangements individually created by the nation's top floral artists, hand-delivered the same day at the peak of freshness and perfection—whether your loved ones are in Australia, the Philippines, Mexico, Italy, Japan, Hawaii, Alaska, or Puerto Rico.

So how do they do it? After opening his first retail store in 1976, Jim McCann, chief executive officer of 1-800-FLOWERS, built a chain of 14 flower shops in the New York metropolitan area before acquiring the 1-800-FLOWERS telephone number in 1986 and continuing to grow his business under that name. His understanding of his customer base and market helped him create a reliable brand his customers could trust.

He knew that when selling such a perishable product, efficient access and distribution is critical to success. The company's sophisticated fulfillment system includes its BloomNet network of 1,500 florists throughout the United States, including 35 company-operated stores and 85 franchised stores, as well as distribution and warehouse facilities. BloomNet partners are selected based on their commitment to quality and service and strictly monitored by 1-800-FLOWERS—part of its focus on customer service.

McCann extended his business into other channels, going online in 1992 and opening a Web site in 1995. He maintains strategic marketing relationships with a number of online services, including America Online, Microsoft Network (MSN), and Yahoo! The company's third-party vendor-direct program allows for easy and efficient delivery of gourmet foods, candies, and gift baskets, among other items. Its collection of brands includes home décor and garden merchandise sold under Plow & Hearth; premium popcorn and other food gifts sold under The Popcorn Factory; chocolates from Fannie May, Godiva, and others; and baked cookies and desserts from Cheryl & Co.

Headquartered on Long Island, New York, 1-800-FLOWERS, (http://www.1800flowers.com) is today one of the most recognized brands in flower and gift retailing. Available online 24 hours a day, seven days a week, customers can also visit a company-operated or franchised store. The Web site also allows customers to send free *virtual flowers*—building their own virtual bouquet complete with flowers, accents, a beautiful vase, and even a personalized message.

1-800-FLOWERS maintains a comprehensive quality assurance program that incorporates ongoing blind test orders, telephone surveys with customers and recipients, in-store and mail surveys, and customer service reports. With customers assured of a 100 percent satisfaction and freshness guarantee on all products and services, the company's fortunes should continue to blossom.

Critical Thinking Questions

- Describe the unique challenges faced by companies that sell highly perishable products.
- How does 1-800-FLOWERS meet and address those challenges?
- What other types of distribution or product access should the company consider?

Sources: Adapted from the video "1-800 Flowers," http://www.swlearning.com; Tim Beyers, "Budding Growth at 1-800-Flowers?" *The Motley Fool*, http://www.fool.com, August 11, 2005; Tony Goins, "1-800-Flowers to buy Cheryl & Co.," *Business First of Columbus*, March 11, 2005; Rich Smith, "1-800-Flowers Buys Fannie May," *The Motley Fool*, April 10, 2006, http://www.fool.com; 1-800-FLOWERS corporate Web site, http://1800flowers.com; April 29, 2006.

Hot Links Address Book

Consumers can now comparison shop like never before. To compare brands, features, and prices of products, go to one of these sites: http://www.bottomdollar.com, http://www.mysimon.com, or http://www.compare.net

At the National Retail Federation's Web site, you'll find current retail statistics, links to retailing resources, and information about retailing careers: http://www.nrf.com

The American Wholesale Marketers Association is an international trade organization for distributors of convenience products in the United States. Visit its Web site to browse the latest issue of *Distribution Channels* magazine and learn more about this field: http://www.awmanet.org

Want to learn more about direct selling? Learn how people become Amway representatives and find out more about the company by visiting http://www.amway.com

Stores magazine offers hundreds of ideas for putting together a successful retail strategy: http://www.stores.org

Freightworld offers detailed information on various modes of transportation and links to transportation companies: http://www.freightworld.com

For articles on supply chain management along with information on the latest technology in the field, check out The *Supply Chain Management Review,* http://www.manufacturing.net/SCM

CHAPTER 15

Using Integrated Marketing Communications to Promote Products

Learning Goals

After reading this chapter, you should be able to answer these questions:

1. What are the goals of promotional strategy?

2. What are the elements of the promotional mix, and what is integrated marketing communications?

3. What is advertising and what are the different types of advertising?

4. What are the advertising media, and how are they selected?

5. What are the elements of an advertising campaign?

6. What is personal selling?

7. What are the goals of sales promotion, and what are several types of sales promotion?

8. How does public relations fit into the promotional mix?

9. What factors affect the promotional mix?

10. What are three important trends in promotion?

Exploring Business Careers
Kevin Lello
U.S. Music Corporation

The music industry is a tough business—just ask any of the thousands of garage bands, weekend DJs, and shower soul-singers that are struggling to make it. However, musicians are not the only ones fighting for recognition in the music world. Kevin Lello sees the music scene from another side, that of music equipment and instrument manufacturers. Lello is vice president of marketing for US Music Corporation, a company that, along with equipment like amps and home recording technology, makes Washburn guitars. When it comes to guitars, he wants the world to know that Washburn is the best. One of our most important goals now is to raise awareness. Washburn guitars have been around since 1883—that's over a hundred years of guitar-making expertise. Yet, we still have not capitalized on name recognition like some of our competitors. We're going to change that." To do so, Lello and Washburn have moved beyond a solely sales-focused marketing strategy to create a promotional mix that will get their message out, attract customers and drive sales.

Advertising is a main thrust of Washburn's marketing strategy. Print advertisements for Washburn guitars can be seen in guitar magazines such as *Guitar World* and *Guitar Player,* as well as in fanzines (magazines focused on the artists) like *Hit Parader* and *Revolver.* However, Washburn's customers are media-savvy, and their advertising reflects that. "We've really worked to build a strong presence in interactive media, incorporating banner advertisements,

Web sites, and different Flash media advertising. Recently, we started a podcast on iTunes called Chicago Guitar Shop that allows us to bring weekly news to our customers. Right now, it's about the most immediate advertising you can get."

One particularly innovative means of reaching people is through interactive relationship marketing, which connects with people through social networking Web sites like Friendster and Facebook. For those involved in the music business, there is no better Web site than MySpace for communicating with other musicians, agents, record labels, and equipment manufacturers. Washburn uses various advertising media to connect to its customers. However, to build a complete promotional mix, they also rely on a variety of sales promotion activities and public relations. Often, they will coordinate meet-and-greet sweepstakes opportunities, where an artist or band will meet with fans and other musicians at local guitar dealers. In this way, Washburn is able not only to connect with the musicians, but also to strengthen relationships with and stimulate business for the dealers.

Today, Washburn is focused on becoming the most popular brand of guitar in the world. Accomplishing this requires that they leverage every aspect of marketing available to them: personal selling, advertising, sales promotion, and public relations. In this chapter, you will explore how companies decide on their promotional goals and develop marketing strategies to achieve those goals.

495

Very few goods or services can survive in the marketplace without good promotion. Marketers promote their products to build demand. **Promotion** is an attempt by marketers to inform, persuade, or remind consumers and industrial users to influence their opinion or elicit a response. Once the product has been created, promotion is often used to convince target customers that it has a differential advantage over the competition. A *differential competitive advantage,* as explained in Chapter 12, is a set of unique features that the target market perceives as important and better than the competition's features and may result in purchase of the brand. Such features may include high quality, fast delivery, low price, good service, and the like. Lexus, for example, is seen as having a quality differential advantage over other luxury cars. Therefore, promotion for Lexus stresses the quality of the vehicle.

This chapter presents the goals of promotion, the last element of the marketing mix, and explores the elements of the promotional mix. You will also learn about advertising and how personal selling and public relations fit into the promotional mix.

Promotional Goals

1 What are the goals of promotional strategy?

Most firms use some form of promotion. The meaning of the Latin root word is "to move forward." Hence actions that move a company toward its goals are promotional in nature. Because company goals vary widely, so do promotional strategies. The goal is to stimulate action. In a profit-oriented firm, the desired action is for the consumer to buy the promoted item. Mrs. Smith's, for instance, wants people to buy more frozen pies. Not-for-profit organizations seek a variety of actions with their promotions. They tell us not to litter, to buckle up, to join the army, and to attend the ballet.

Promotional goals include creating awareness, getting people to try products, providing information, retaining loyal customers, increasing the use of products, and identifying potential customers. Any promotional campaign may seek to achieve one or more of these goals:

CONCEPT *in Action*

People who had never heard of Carl's Jr. were dramatically introduced to the California-based burger chain in 2005 when a commercial for Carl's Spicy BBQ Burger featured socialite Paris Hilton. In the TV spot, a swimsuit-clad Hilton washes a sleek Bentley before stealing away to take a bite of the hefty sandwich. The $5 million ad generated enormous buzz and garnered millions in controversy-related publicity. *Are risqué ads risky for advertisers?*

© WENN/LANDOV

1. *Creating awareness.* All too often, firms go out of business because people don't know they exist or what they do. Small restaurants often have this problem. Simply putting up a sign and opening the door is rarely enough. Promotion through ads on local radio or television, coupons in local papers, flyers, and so forth can create awareness of a new business or product.

   Large companies often use catchy slogans to build brand awareness. Dodge trucks' wildly successful ads where a guy yells over to another truck at a stoplight, "That thing got a HEMI?" has created a huge number of new customers for Dodge trucks. HEMI has become a brand within a brand. Now, DaimlerChrysler is extending the HEMI engine to the Jeep brand hoping for the same success.

2. *Getting consumers to try products.* Promotion is almost always used to get people to try a new product or to get nonusers to try an existing product. Sometimes free samples are given away. Lever, for instance, mailed over 2 million free samples of its Lever 2000 soap to target households. Coupons and trial-size containers of products are also common tactics used to tempt people to try a product. Celebrities are also used to get people to try products. Beyonce, for example, received $4.7 million from L'Oreal to promote its products. And Catherine Zeta-Jones got $20 million to tout T-Mobile worldwide[1]

3. *Providing information.* Informative promotion is more common in the early stages of the product life cycle. An informative promotion may explain what ingredients (like fiber) will do for your health, tell you

why the product is better (high-definition television versus regular television), inform you of a new low price, or explain where the item may be bought.

People typically will not buy a product or support a not-for-profit organization until they know what it will do and how it may benefit them. Thus, an informative ad may stimulate interest in a product. Consumer watchdogs and social critics applaud the informative function of promotion because it helps consumers make more intelligent purchase decisions. Star-Kist, for instance, lets customers know that its tuna is caught in dolphin-safe nets.

4. *Keeping loyal customers.* Promotion is also used to keep people from switching brands. Slogans such as Campbell's Soups are "M'm! M'm! Good!" and "Intel Inside" remind consumers about the brand. Marketers also remind users that the brand is better than the competition. For years, Pepsi has claimed it has the taste that consumers prefer. Continental Airlines brags of its improvement in on-time ratings. Such advertising reminds customers about the quality of the product.

Firms can also help keep customers loyal by telling them when a product or service is improved. Marriott recently announced that it was spending $190 million on new bedding.[2] It will offer plusher mattresses, softer sheets, more pillows, and a new, fresh look.

5. *Increasing the amount and frequency of use.* Promotion is often used to get people to use more of a product and to use it more often. The National Cattlemen's Beef Association reminds Americans to "Eat More Beef." The most popular promotion to increase the use of a product may be frequent-flyer or -user programs. The Marriott Rewards program awards points for each dollar spent at a Marriott property. At the Platinum level, members receive a guaranteed room, an upgrade to their finest available accommodations, access to the concierge lounge, a free breakfast, free local phone calls, and a variety of other goodies.

6. *Identifying target customers.* Promotion helps find customers. One way to do this is to list a Web site. For instance, the *Wall Street Journal* and *Business Week* include Web addresses for more information on computer systems, corporate jets, color copiers, and other types of business equipment, to help target those who are truly interested. Fidelity Mutual Funds ads trumpet, "Solid investment opportunities are out there," then direct customers to go to **http://www.fidelity.com**. A full-page ad in the *Wall Street Journal* for Sprint unlimited wireless e-mail invites potential customers to visit **http://www.sprint.com**. These Web sites typically will ask for your e-mail address.

> **concept check**
>
> What is the objective of a promotional campaign?
>
> How would the promotional campaigns for a new restaurant and an established brand differ?

The Promotional Mix and Integrated Marketing Communications

2 **What are the elements of the promotional mix, and what is integrated marketing communications?**

promotional mix
The combination of advertising, personal selling, sales promotion, and public relations used to promote a product.

The combination of advertising, personal selling, sales promotion, and public relations used to promote a product is called the **promotional mix**. Each firm creates a unique mix for each product. But the goal is always to deliver the firm's message efficiently and effectively to the target audience. These are the elements of the promotional mix:

- *Advertising.* Any paid form of nonpersonal promotion by an identified sponsor.
- *Personal selling.* A face-to-face presentation to a prospective buyer.
- *Sales promotion.* Marketing activities (other than personal selling, advertising, and public relations) that stimulate consumer buying, including coupons and samples, displays, shows and exhibitions, demonstrations, and other types of selling efforts.
- *Public relations.* The linking of organizational goals with key aspects of the public interest and the development of programs designed to earn public understanding and acceptance.

Ideally, marketing communications from each promotional-mix element (personal selling, advertising, sales promotion, and public relations) should be integrated. That is, the message reaching the consumer should be the same regardless of whether

© FREDERICK M. BROWN/GETTY IMAGES

it comes from an advertisement, a salesperson in the field, a magazine article, or a coupon in a newspaper insert.

This unintegrated, disjointed approach to promotion has propelled many companies to adopt the concept of **integrated marketing communications (IMC)**. IMC involves carefully coordinating all promotional activities—media advertising, sales promotion, personal selling, and public relations, as well as direct marketing, packaging, and other forms of promotion—to produce a consistent, unified message that is customer focused. Following the concept of IMC, marketing managers carefully work out the roles the various promotional elements will play in the marketing mix. Timing of promotional activities is coordinated, and the results of each campaign are carefully monitored to improve future use of the promotional mix tools. Typically, a marketing communications director is appointed who has overall responsibility for integrating the company's marketing communications.

Pepsi relied on IMC to launch Pepsi One. The $100 million program relied on personal selling in the distribution channels, a public-relations campaign with press releases to announce the product, and heavy doses of advertising and sales promotion. The company toured the country's shopping malls setting up Pepsi One "lounges"—inflatable couches with plastic carpeting—for random taste tests. It also produced 11,000 end-cap displays for supermarket aisles and created stand-up displays for 12-packs to spark impulse purchases. It secured Oscar-winning actor Cuba Gooding Jr. as spokesperson for the ad campaign. The ads made their debut during the World Series. The tagline for the ad campaign was "Only One has it all."

The sections that follow examine the elements of the promotional mix in more detail.

integrated marketing communications (IMC)
The careful coordination of all promotional activities—media advertising, sales promotion, personal selling, and public relations, as well as direct marketing, packaging, and other forms of promotion—to produce a consistent, unified message that is customer focused.

The Huge Impact of Advertising

 3 What is advertising and what are the different types of advertising?

advertising
Any paid form of nonpersonal presentation by an identified sponsor.

Most Americans are bombarded daily with advertisements to buy things. **Advertising** is any paid form of nonpersonal presentation by an identified sponsor. It may appear on television or radio; in newspapers, magazines, books, or direct mail; or on billboards, transit cards, or the Internet. In the United States, a child is exposed to more than 30,000 TV commercials a year. Adults are exposed to three times as many—more than 2 million commercials in a lifetime.[3]

The money that big corporations spend on advertising is mind-boggling. Total advertising expenses in this country are estimated to be more than $198 billion in

2007.[4] Global advertising expenditures are approximately $453 billion annually.[5] General Motors is America's largest advertiser, spending over $3.4 billion annually. This is slightly under $400,000 per hour, seven days a week, 24 hours per day. America's biggest global spender on advertising is Procter & Gamble at $5.8 billion.[6]

Volkswagen paid $100 million to be a sponsor of the 2008 Beijing Olympic Games. The NFL and Gatorade signed a deal in 2005 to go through 2011 worth $384 million. Super Bowl games cost about $2.5 million for a 30-second commercial. A "Monday Night Football" commercial costs about $350,000 for 30 seconds.

The Impact of Technology and the Internet on Traditional Advertising

Many new media are not hard-wired or regulated, and digital technology is delivering content any time, anywhere. Cable, satellite, and the Internet have highly fragmented audiences, making them tougher than ever to reach. In the late 1950s, *Gunsmoke* on CBS captured a 65 percent share of the TV audience nearly every Saturday night. Only one event, the Super Bowl, has a chance to do that now.

Traditional forms of entertainment are being rapidly digitized. Magazines, books, movies, shows, and games can be accessed through a laptop or a cell phone. By 2010, 83 million U.S. homes will have broadband connections; nearly as many as the 88 million that now have cable and satellite hookups.[7]

Technology is driving many of the changes, but so is consumer behavior. Advertiser questions abound. How do you market a product to young people when millions of them are glued to video game screens instead of TVs? How do you reach TV audiences when viewers can TiVo their way past your ads? What should you make of blogs? Podcasts? Product placements? We will touch on each of these later in the chapter.

In the next section, you will learn about the different types of advertising, the strengths and weaknesses of traditional advertising media, and the functions of an advertising agency.

Types of Advertising

product advertising
Advertising that features a specific good or service.

comparative advertising
Advertising that compares the company's product with competing, named products.

reminder advertising
Advertising that is used to keep a product's name in the public's mind.

institutional advertising
Advertising that creates a positive picture of a company and its ideals, services, and roles in the community.

advocacy advertising
Advertising that takes a stand on a social or economic issue; also called *grassroots lobbying*.

The form of advertising most people know is **product advertising**, which features a specific good or service. It can take many different forms. One special form is **comparative advertising**, in which the company's product is compared with competing, named products. Coca-Cola and Pepsi often use comparative advertising. Does comparative advertising work? Recent research says that comparative ads grab your attention and increase your purchase intention. Some comparative ads, however, lack believability and are not effective.[8] Another special form is **reminder advertising**, which is used to keep the product name in the public's mind. It is most often used during the maturity stage of the product life cycle. Reminder advertising assumes that the target market has already been persuaded of the product's merits and just needs a memory boost. Miller beer, V8 vegetable juice, and the FTD florist association use reminder promotion.

In addition to product advertising, many companies use **institutional advertising**. This type of advertising creates a positive picture of a company and its ideals, services, and roles in the community. Instead of trying to sell specific products, it builds a desired image and goodwill for the company. For example, Weyerhaeuser ran a full-page ad in a number of publications that says, "There's a reason we'll never run out of trees. We put them back after we use them." The ad goes on to say that Weyerhaeuser plants over 100 million seedlings every year to replenish the forests. Some institutional advertising supports product advertising that targets consumers. Other institutional advertising is aimed at stockholders or the public. **Advocacy advertising** takes a stand on a social or economic issue. It is sometimes called *grassroots lobbying*. Energy companies often use this type of advertising to influence public opinion about regulation of their industry.

Choosing Advertising Media

4 What are the advertising media, and how are they selected?

advertising media
The channels through which advertising is carried to prospective customers; includes newspapers, magazines, radio, television, outdoor advertising, direct mail, and the Internet.

cost per thousand (CPM)
Cost per thousand contacts is a term used in expressing advertising costs; refers to the cost of reaching 1,000 members of the target market.

reach
The number of different target consumers who are exposed to a commercial at least once during a specific period, usually four weeks.

frequency
The number of times an individual is exposed to an advertising message.

audience selectivity
An advertising medium's ability to reach a precisely defined market.

The channels through which advertising is carried to prospective customers are the **advertising media**. Both product and institutional ads appear in all the major advertising media. Exhibit 15.1 indicates where all of the money spent on advertising goes. Exhibit 15.2 summarizes the strengths and weaknesses of these media. Each company must decide which media are best for its products. Two of the main factors in making that choice are the cost of the medium and the audience reached by it.

Advertising Costs and Market Penetration Cost per contact is the cost of reaching one member of the target market. Naturally, as the size of the audience increases, so does the total cost. Cost per contact enables an advertiser to compare media vehicles, such as television versus radio, or magazine versus newspaper, or, more specifically, *Newsweek* versus *Time*. An advertiser debating whether to spend local advertising dollars for TV spots or radio spots could consider the cost per contact of each. The advertiser might then pick the vehicle with the lowest cost per contact to maximize advertising punch for the money spent. Often costs are expressed on a **cost per thousand (CPM)** contacts basis.

Reach is the number of different target consumers who are exposed to a commercial at least once during a specific period, usually four weeks. Media plans for product introductions and attempts at increasing brand awareness usually emphasize reach. For example, an advertiser might try to reach 70 percent of the target audience during the first three months of the campaign. Because the typical ad is short-lived and often only a small portion of an ad may be perceived at one time, advertisers repeat their ads so consumers will remember the message. **Frequency** is the number of times an individual is exposed to a message. Average frequency is used by advertisers to measure the intensity of a specific medium's coverage.

Media selection is also a matter of matching the advertising medium with the product's target market. If marketers are trying to reach teenage females, they might select *Seventeen* magazine. If they are trying to reach consumers over 50 years old, they may choose *Modern Maturity*. A medium's ability to reach a precisely defined market is its **audience selectivity**. Some media vehicles, like general newspapers and network television, appeal to a wide cross section of the population. Others—such as *Brides, Popular Mechanics, Architectural Digest,* MTV, ESPN, and Christian radio stations—appeal to very specific groups.

CONCEPT *in Action*

In addition to listing hundreds of scrumptious menu choices and cheesecakes, the Cheesecake Factory's magazine-sized menus feature a number of full-page glossy ads for Bebe, Macy's, Mercedes-Benz, and more. An increasingly popular media option, menu advertising offers many promotional benefits: huge readership by a captive audience; outstanding demographic selectivity; and great value—less than a penny per exposure. *How do advertisers decide whether or not menu advertising is right for their promotional mixes?*

© TERRI MILLER/E-VISUAL COMMUNICATIONS, INC.

Exhibit 15.1 > Total U.S. Advertising Expenditures by Media Categories—2007*

Broadcast TV	$48,493
Cable TV	24,491
Newspapers	63,497
Radio	25,096
Yellow Pages	18,626
Magazines	14,075
B-to-B magazines	10,706
Internet	15,500
Out-of-home	6,568
Movie screen ads	868

Exhibit 15.2 > Strengths and Weaknesses of Major Media

Medium	Strengths	Weaknesses
Newspapers	Geographic selectivity and flexibility Short-term advertiser commitments News value and immediacy Constant readership High individual market coverage Low cost	Little demographic selectivity Short-lived Low pass-along rate
Magazines	Good reproduction, especially color Message permanence Demographic selectivity (can reach affluent audience) Regionality Local-market selectivity Special-interest possibilities Relatively long advertising life	Long-term advertiser commitments Slow audience buildup Limited demonstration capacities Lack of urgency Long lead time for ad placement May be expensive for national coverage
Radio	Low and negotiable costs High frequency Immediacy of message Relatively little seasonal change in audience Highly portable Short scheduling notice Short-term advertiser commitments Entertainment carryover	No visuals Advertising message short-lived Background sound Commercial clutter (a large number of ads in a short time)
Television	Widely diversified audience Creative visual and audio opportunities for demonstration Immediacy of message Entertainment carryover	High cost Limited demographic selectivity Advertising message short-lived Consumer skepticism about advertising claims
Network	Association with programming prestige	Long-term advertiser commitments
Local	Geographic selectivity Associated with programs of local origin and appeal Short lead time	Narrow audience on independent stations High cost for broad geographic coverage
Outdoor advertising	Repetition possibilities Moderate cost Flexibility	Short messages Lack of demographic selectivity Many distractions when observing the message
Direct mail	Very efficient with good mailing list Can be personalized by computer Can reach very specific demographic market Lengthy message with photos and testimony	Very costly with poor mailing list May never be opened
Internet	Inexpensive global coverage Available at any time Interactive personalized message Ability to reach narrow audience	Advertisers lack familiarity with the media Difficult to measure ad effectiveness Pop-up clutter

Internet Advertising Internet advertising is rapidly becoming a mature and accepted media choice. Advertising revenue is growing about 25 percent a year and should hit $18 billion by 2008. Search advertising on Google and Yahoo account for the bulk of the revenue growth. Big, traditional advertisers are shifting more of their advertising budgets to the Internet. Ford, for example, decided to move 15 percent of its advertising budget to the Internet.

Two growing areas of Internet advertising are behavioral targeting and online video. **Behavioral targeting** allows advertisers to target Web users based upon their surfing habits. If a visitor on **http://www.Cars.com** is researching an Infiniti M45, Tacoda (a provider of behavioral targeting) attaches a cookie representing that consumer with the information that they are shopping for a car. (The cookie data do not include personal information about consumers.) Continuing online browsing, the car shopper may click to his or her local-newspaper site, or the pages of **http://www. SportingNews.com**, where Tacoda can serve an ad for Allstate auto insurance. "We can infer things about the user based on where they go, and when they leave a site and go somewhere else, we can serve them an ad based on their previous behavior," says a spokesman for Tacoda.[9]

Most online video ads run about 20 seconds. If they are any longer, people tend to click off the ads. Say you go to **http://www. CNN.com** and see an interesting headline with a "watch" link next to it. Before you can watch the video clip of the headline story, you may view an online video ad that contains interactive (clickable) features other than the standard play, pause, and stop buttons. These increase the time that viewers will watch the ad.[10]

Advertising Agencies

Advertising agencies are companies that help create ads and place them in the proper media. Many firms rely on agencies to both create and monitor their ad campaigns.

Full-service advertising agencies offer the five services shown in Exhibit 15.3. Members of the creative-services group develop promotional themes and messages, write copy, design layouts, take photos, and draw illustrations. The media-services

behavioral targeting
Targeting individuals based on their click stream.

advertising agencies
Companies that help create ads and place them in the proper media.

CATCHING THE ENTREPRENEURIAL SPIRIT

This Is Your Brain on Advertising

As an attractive Englishwoman in her early 20s wanders the mall with a set of electrodes affixed to her scalp, David Lewis sees the activity of her alpha and beta brain waves—"the stuff of human thought," he calls it—splashing across his computer screen in a zigzagging mass of red and green. "She's alert but not engaged," he explains as his subject saunters into an upscale shoe store. Which is true, until she picks up a pair of pink stilettos. Suddenly a colorful explosion of activity cascades across Lewis's screen. "You can see that beta activity on the left side of the brain—the analytical side—falls away," he explains. "Look how quickly the purchase decision takes place!" And indeed, a few minutes later, the cash register rings and the woman strides back into the mall with the pair of heels in a bag.

As chief scientist at market research company Neuroco of Weybridge, England, founded in 2005, Lewis conducts similar experiments for global players including Bridgestone, Hewlett-Packard, and some in the food, beverage, and cosmetics industries. Neuroco is the United Kingdom's first agency built on the nascent science of neuromarketing. By studying activity in the brain, neuromarketing combines the techniques of neuro-science and clinical psychology to develop insights into how we respond

to products, brands, and advertisements. From this, marketers hope to understand the subtle nuances that distinguish a dud pitch from a successful campaign.

When Neuroco was hired by Royal & SunAlliance, the second-largest U.K. insurance company, Lewis evaluated one of Royal's 30-second television spots by wiring 60 volunteers with electrodes. Then, frame by frame, Lewis examined the subjects' EEG readings as they watched the commercial. He discovered that the viewers' brains were most engaged during the ad's dramatic action scene, but interest flagged significantly at the tagline, "You'd better ring the Royal."

"The results suggested that the catchphrase was unlikely to prove memorable," Lewis concluded. Royal pulled the spot shortly after the experiment.[11]

Critical Thinking Questions
- Do you think that neuromarketing really works? Why or why not?
- Are consumers behaving normally when they know that they are being observed? In this case, when their brain waves are being recorded while wearing a set of electrodes?

Exhibit 15.3 > Functions of an Advertising Agency

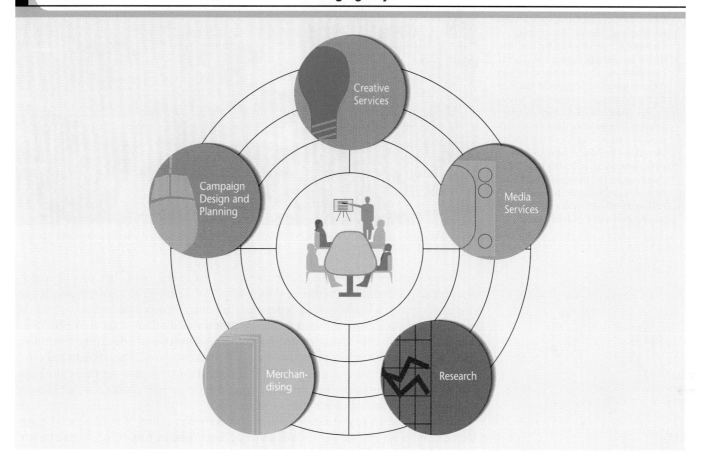

group selects the media mix and schedules advertising. Researchers may conduct market research studies for clients or help develop new products or gauge the firm's or product's image. Merchandising advice may include developing contests and brochures for the sales force. Campaign design and planning are often wholly in the hands of the agency, although some firms prefer to do much of the work in-house, relying on the agency only for scheduling media and evaluating the campaign.

Advertising agencies are always seeking a better way to communicate their messages. Part of this process is understanding how target consumers think. A small British company is using technology to take consumer insights to a new level as explained in the Catching the Entrepreneurial Spirit box.

concept check

Indicate some of the strengths and weaknesses of the eight main advertising media.

Describe cost per contact. How does it help advertisers compare media options?

Creating an Advertising Campaign[12]

 5 **What are the elements of an advertising campaign?**

advertising campaign
A series of related advertisements focusing on a common theme, slogan, and set of advertising appeals.

Advertisements that are seen on television, in magazines, and on the Internet are typically the result of an **advertising campaign**—a series of related advertisements focusing on a common theme, slogan, and set of advertising appeals. It is a specific advertising effort for a particular product that extends for a defined period of time.

Determining the Advertising Objective

Before any creative work can begin on an advertising campaign, it is important to determine what goals or objectives the advertising should achieve. An *advertising*

objective identifies the specific communication task that a campaign should accomplish for a specified target audience during a specified period. The objectives of a specific advertising campaign often depend on the overall corporate objectives and the product being advertised. For example, McIlhenny Company's Tabasco Hot Sauce launched a print advertising campaign with the objective of educating consumers about how to use the product and the variety of flavors offered. The ads featured product information embedded in the label, which was blown up to cover the entire page. The ad copy for the Garlic Pepper Sauce read: "The only one potent enough to ward off both hypothermia and vampires at once."

A new trend in advertising campaign objectives is called "call to action" goals. The idea is to get the viewer to take some action. This, in turn, gives the advertiser measurable results (viewers take action or they don't). A recent call-to-action campaign for the Mini Cooper alerts viewers about the threat from peddlers of counterfeit cars. But for those who care enough to follow the instructions, a miniature adventure awaits. The ads compare the Mini Cooper with other oft-copied status badges—a Rolex watch, a pair of Ray-Bans. Then it urgently warns viewers not to be tricked into buying a fake. "I thought, 'A Mini Cooper for 1,200 bucks? Let's motor, right?'" says a person the spot identifies as a "humiliated victim," whose face is obscured.

"Wrong!" the announcer intones. Then comes the call to action: The spot invites viewers to buy a DVD for $19.99 that tells all about the counterfeit Mini crisis in a 10-minute "program." And it directs viewers to a Web site where they can learn more about the organization and even submit photos of fake Minis they have created.

Mini customers appreciate the joke. The DVD offers about an hour's worth of entertainment.[13] Other call-to-action campaigns are more straightforward. Papa John's Pizzas tells viewers how to order online. A Colgate ad advises viewers to go to a Web site for a rebate offer.

Developing Advertising Appeals and Executing the Message

advertising appeal
An advertising appeal identifies a reason to buy a product or service.

An **advertising appeal** identifies a reason for a person to buy a product. Developing advertising appeals, a challenging task, is typically the responsibility of the creative people in the advertising agency. Advertising appeals typically play off of consumers' emotions, such as fear, vanity, fun, pleasure, or love, or address some need or want the consumer has, such as a need for convenience, profit, or the desire to save money.

Message execution is the way an advertisement portrays its information. Any ad should immediately draw the reader's, viewer's, or listener's attention. The advertiser

Exhibit 15.4 > Common Executional Styles for Advertising

Humor	Uses humor to improve recall: Dodge's "That Thing Got a HEMI?"
Fantasy	Creates a fantasy built around a product: Miller Lite commercials with girls on the beach
Slice-of-life	Displays people in normal settings: McDonald's ads showing young people enjoying fries and a Big Mac
Animation	Uses animation: Budweiser frogs or Charlie tuna
Mood	Shows moods such as peace, romance, and beauty: Chanel perfume
Demonstration	Shows expected benefit: Tide ad showing clothes that are cleaner, whiter, brighter
Musical	Entertains viewers with music: Delicious Curves clothes targeting urban and Latina customers with music sung by Ashanti
Scientific	Uses research or scientific evidence: Pepto-Bismol uses diagram of a stomach to show how the liquid coats and soothes upset stomach

must then use the message to hold consumers' interest, create desire for the good or service, and ultimately motivate action—a purchase.

The style in which the message is executed is one of the most creative elements of an advertisement. Exhibit 15.4 lists some examples of executional styles used by advertisers. Executional styles often dictate what type of media is to be employed to convey the message. Scientific executional styles lend themselves well to print advertising where more information can be conveyed. On the other hand, demonstration and musical styles are more likely found in broadcast advertising and on the Internet.

Executional styles are often quite different in foreign countries. In some countries ads are more sexually suggestive and in others women are very limited as to the role they can play in an advertising campaign. Japanese love of gadgets and technology makes an unusual campaign for Northwest Airlines possible. The story is explained in the Expanding Around the Globe box.

concept check

Before the creative work for an advertising campaign begins, what should be determined?

Why is it challenging to develop an advertising appeal?

EXPANDING AROUND THE GLOBE

Northwest Takes Ads to New Heights

Northwest Airlines is harnessing Japan's love of gadgets to open a new frontier in interactive advertising: tempting consumers to access prizes and games by scanning giant bar codes with their cellphone cameras.

In its latest Tokyo outdoor campaign, Northwest Airlines, the fourth-largest U.S. airline by traffic, is covering the city's billboards and subway stations with ads containing the bar codes, which look like huge geometric Rorschach tests. The ads invite passersby to unlock a message hidden inside the square of black-and-white pixels called a QR code, which requires a special reader to decode.

Sound complicated? Not in Japan, where some 30 million people already carry the special readers around, tucked inside their cellphones. With a snapshot using the cellphone's camera, the information is decoded, directing the phone's Web browser to coupons, games, or further details on a product.

QR codes have grown in popularity in Japan over the past year, showing up thumbnail-size on magazine and newspaper ads as a quick automatic link between print and on-line media that doesn't require the customer to type in an Internet address or remember any special coding. Passersby who snap a photo of the code with their phones are taken to a special, shrunk-down mobile version of Northwest's Web site, which features a game in which players can win coupons for flights.

Critical Thinking Questions
- What do you think were the campaign objectives of Northwest Airlines? Why not just run traditional ads?
- In 2004, more money was spent for online advertising in Japan than on radio advertising. Why is Japan so far ahead of the United States in Internet advertising?

The Importance of Personal Selling

 6 **What is personal selling?**

personal selling
A face-to-face sales presentation to a prospective customer.

Advertising acquaints potential customers with a product and thereby makes personal selling easier. **Personal selling** is a face-to-face sales presentation to a prospective customer. Sales jobs range from salesclerks at clothing stores to engineers with MBAs who design large, complex systems for manufacturers. About 6.5 million people are engaged in personal selling in the United States. Slightly over 45 percent of them are women. The number of people who earn a living from sales is huge compared, for instance, with the half a million workers employed in the advertising industry. Personal selling offers several advantages over other forms of promotion:

- Personal selling provides a detailed explanation or demonstration of the product. This capability is especially desirable for complex or new goods and services.
- The sales message can be varied according to the motivations and interests of each prospective customer. Moreover, when the prospect has questions or raises objections, the salesperson is there to provide explanations. In contrast, advertising and sales promotion can respond only to the objections the copywriter thinks are important to customers.
- Personal selling can be directed only to qualified prospects. Other forms of promotion include some unavoidable waste because many people in the audience are not prospective customers.
- Personal selling costs can be controlled by adjusting the size of the sales force (and resulting expenses) in one-person increments. In contrast, advertising and sales promotion must often be purchased in fairly large amounts.
- Perhaps the most important advantage is that personal selling is considerably more effective than other forms of promotion in obtaining a sale and gaining a satisfied customer.

The Professional Salesperson

Companies that recruit college graduates to enter the field of selling want to develop professional salespeople. A professional salesperson has two main qualities: complete product knowledge and creativity. The professional knows the product line from A to Z and understands what each item can and cannot do. He or she also understands how to apply the product to meet customers' needs. For instance, a sales rep may find a way to install conveyor equipment that will lower the cost of moving products in the prospective customer's plant.

Professional salespeople develop long-term relationships with their clients. Most salespeople rely on repeat business, which depends, of course, on trust and honesty. Most professional selling is not high pressured. Instead, the sales process is more a matter of one professional interacting with another, such as a salesperson working with a purchasing agent. Professional salespeople are largely sources of information and creative problem solvers. They cannot bully a professional buyer into making an unwanted purchase.

Sales Positions

College graduates have many opportunities in sales. Among them are the following:

- *Selling to wholesalers and retailers.* When a firm buys products for resale, its main concerns are buying the right product and getting it promptly. Often retailers expect the manufacturer's salesperson to stock the merchandise on the shelves and to set up promotional materials approved by the store. Sometimes these sales jobs are entry-level training positions that can lead to better opportunities.
- *Selling to purchasing agents.* Purchasing agents are found in government agencies, manufacturing firms, and institutions (hospitals and schools). Purchasing agents look for credibility (Can the salesperson deliver merchandise of the proper quality when needed?), service after the sale, and a reasonable price. The message the salesperson must get across is one of complete dependability and reliability.

• *Selling to committees.* The form of selling that may demand the most professionalism and creativity is selling to a buying committee. When a purchase decision is so important that it will have a big impact on the buyer's long-run success, it is usually made by a committee. When American Airlines decides to order 100 new airplanes, for instance, a committee decides what type of plane to buy. A committee sales presentation requires careful analysis of the potential buyer's needs. It commonly includes an audiovisual display.

The Selling Process

Selling is a process that can be learned. Scholars have spelled out the steps of the selling process, shown in Exhibit 15.5, and professional salespeople use them all the time. These steps are as follows:

1. *Prospecting and qualifying.* To start the process, the salesperson looks for **sales prospects**, those companies and people who are most likely to buy the seller's offerings. This activity is called **prospecting**. Because there are no surefire ways to find prospects, most salespeople try many methods.

For many companies, the inquiries generated by advertising and promotion are the most likely source of prospects. Inquiries are also known as sales leads. Leads usually come in the form of letters, cards, e-mail addresses, or telephone calls. Some companies supply salespeople with prospect lists compiled from external sources, such as Chamber of Commerce directories, newspapers, public records, club membership lists, Internet inquiries, and professional or trade publication subscription lists. Meetings, such as professional conventions and trade shows, are another good source of leads. Sales representatives attend such meetings to display and demonstrate their company's products and to answer the questions of those attending. The firm's files and records can be another source of prospects. Correspondence with buyers can be helpful. Records in the service department can identify people who already own equipment and might be prospects for new models. Finally, friends and acquaintances of salespeople can often supply leads.

sales prospects
The companies and people who are most likely to buy a seller's offerings.

prospecting
The process of looking for sales prospects.

Exhibit 15.5 > Steps in Making a Successful Sale

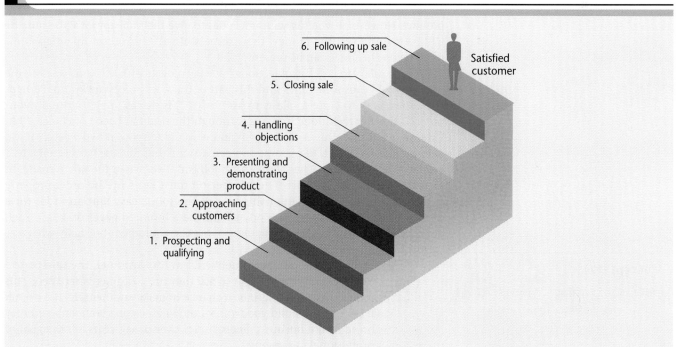

6. Following up sale

5. Closing sale

4. Handling objections

3. Presenting and demonstrating product

2. Approaching customers

1. Prospecting and qualifying

Satisfied customer

qualifying questions
Inquiries used by salespeople to separate prospects from those who do not have the potential to buy.

One rule of thumb is that not all prospects are "real." Just because someone has been referred or has made an inquiry does not mean that the person is a genuine prospect. Salespeople can avoid wasting time and increase their productivity by qualifying all prospects. **Qualifying questions** are used to separate prospects from those who do not have the potential to buy. The following three questions help determine who is a real prospect and who is not:

- Does the prospect have a need for our product?
- Can the prospect make the buying decision?
- Can the prospect afford our product?

2. *Approaching customers.* After identifying a prospect, the salesperson explains the reason for wanting an appointment and sets a specific date and hour. At the same time, the salesperson tries to build interest in the coming meeting. One good way to do this is to impart an interesting or important piece of information—for instance, "I think my product can cut your shipping and delivery time by two days."

3. *Presenting and demonstrating the product.* The presentation and demonstration can be fully automated, completely unstructured, or somewhere in between. In a fully automated presentation, the salesperson shows a movie, slides, or makes a PowerPoint presentation and then answers questions and takes any orders. A completely unstructured presentation has no set format. It may be a casual conversation, with the salesperson presenting product benefits that might interest the potential buyer.

4. *Handling objections.* Almost every sales presentation, structured or unstructured, meets with some objection. Rarely does a customer say "I'll buy it" without asking questions or voicing concerns. The professional salesperson tries to anticipate objections so they can be countered quickly and with assurance.

   Often employed in business, the "higher authority" objection is frequently used when one of the parties says, "This agreement looks good, but I'll have to run it by my committee" (or wife or any other "higher authority"). The result is that that sales presentation turns out to be just a preliminary, nonbinding round. After the higher authority responds, often disapproving the agreement, the sale goes into round two or starts all over again.

   The next time you buy a house, car, or anything expensive, watch carefully how the salesperson will say, "If we find the house (or car) that you really like, is there any reason you could not make the purchase today?" Once they get the green light, the salesperson will spend whatever time it takes to find you the right product. However, if you say your uncle has to give the final approval, because he will be loaning you the money, the salesperson will try and set up an appointment when the uncle can be present.

5. *Closing the sale.* After all the objections have been dealt with, it's time to close the sale. Even old pros sometimes find this part of the sales process awkward. Perhaps the easiest way to close a sale is to ask for it: "Ms. Jones, may I write up your order?" Another technique is to act as though the deal has been concluded: "Mr. Bateson, we'll have this equipment in and working for you in two weeks." If Mr. Bateson doesn't object, the salesperson can assume that the sale has been made.

6. *Following up on the sale.* The salesperson's job isn't over when the sale is made. In fact, the sale is just the start. The salesperson must write up the order properly and turn it in promptly. Often this part of the job is easy. But an order for a complex piece of industrial equipment may be a hundred pages of detail. Each detail must be carefully checked to ensure that the equipment is exactly what was ordered.

   After the product is delivered to the customer, the salesperson must make a routine visit to see that the customer is satisfied. This follow-up call may also be a chance to make another sale. But even if it isn't, it will build goodwill for the salesperson's company and may bring future business. Repeat sales over many years are the goal of professional salespeople.

concept check

What are the advantages of personal selling?

Describe the professional salesperson.

Explain the selling process.

Sales Promotion

7 What are the goals of sales promotion, and what are several types of sales promotion?

sales promotions
Marketing events or sales efforts—not including advertising, personal selling, and public relations—that stimulate buying.

Sales promotion helps make personal selling and advertising more effective. **Sales promotions** are marketing events or sales efforts—not including advertising, personal selling, and public relations—that stimulate buying. Today, sales promotion is a $300 billion industry and growing. Sales promotion is usually targeted toward either of two distinctly different markets. Consumer sales promotion is targeted to the ultimate consumer market. Trade sales promotion is directed to members of the marketing channel, such as wholesalers and retailers.

The goal of many promotion tactics is immediate purchase. Therefore, it makes sense when planning a sales promotion campaign to target customers according to their general behavior. For instance, is the consumer loyal to your product or to your competitor's? Does the consumer switch brands readily in favor of the best deal? Does the consumer buy only the least expensive product, no matter what? Does the consumer buy any products in your category at all?

Procter & Gamble Co. believes shoppers make up their mind about a product in about the time it takes to read this paragraph.

This "first moment of truth," as P&G calls it, is the three to seven seconds when someone notices an item on a store shelf. Despite spending billions on traditional advertising, the consumer-products giant thinks this instant is one of its most important marketing opportunities. It recently created a position entitled Director of First Moment of Truth, or Director of FMOT (pronounced "EFF-mott") to produce sharper, flashier in-store displays. There's a 15-person FMOT department at P&G headquarters in Cincinnati as well as 50 FMOT leaders stationed around the world.[14]

One of P&G's most prominent in-store promotions has been for a new line of Pampers. In the United States, P&G came up with what it calls "a shopper concept"— a single promotional theme that allows it to pitch products in a novel way. The theme for Pampers was: "Babies First." In stores, the company handed out information on childhood immunizations, car-seat safety, and healthy diets while promoting its diapers and wipes in other parts of the store. To market Pampers diapers in the United Kingdom, P&G persuaded retailers earlier this year to put fake doorknobs high up on restroom doors, to remind parents how much babies need to stretch.

The objectives of a promotion depend on the general behavior of target consumers as described in Exhibit 15.6. For example, marketers who are targeting loyal users of their product don't want to change behavior. Instead, they want to reinforce existing behavior or increase product usage. Frequent-buyer programs that reward

CONCEPT *in Action*

Pet lovers want the best for their animals and choosing a proper diet is an essential part of raising happy, healthy pets. That's why Purina offers the Purina ONE 30-Day Challenge. To participate in the sales promotion, animal-lovers transition their pets to Purina ONE premium brand food; track pet performance using an interactive scorecard; and evaluate the "before-and-after" results of their pet's health. *What promotional objectives underlie the Purina ONE 30-Day Challenge?*

© TERRI MILLER/E-VISUAL COMMUNICATIONS, INC.

Exhibit 15.6 > Types of Consumers and Sales Promotion Goals

Type of Behavior	Desired Results	Sales Promotion Examples
Loyal customers: People who buy your product most or all of the time	Reinforce behavior, increase consumption, change purchase timing	Loyalty marketing programs, such as frequent-buyer cards or frequent-shopper clubs
		Bonus packs that give loyal consumers an incentive to stock up or premiums offered in return for proof-of-purchase
Competitor's customers: People who buy a competitor's product most or all of the time	Break loyalty, persuade to switch to your brand	Sweepstakes, contests, or premiums that create interest in the product.
Brand switchers: People who buy a variety of products in the category	Persuade to buy your brand more often	Sampling to introduce your product's superior qualities compared to their brand
Price buyers: People who consistently buy the least expensive brand	Appeal with low prices or supply added value that makes price less important	Trade deals that help make the product more readily available than competing products
		Coupons, cents-off packages, refunds, or trade deals that reduce the price of the brand to match that of the brand that would have been purchased

consumers for repeat purchases can be effective in strengthening brand loyalty. Other types of promotions are more effective with customers prone to brand switching or with those who are loyal to a competitor's product. Cents-off coupons, free samples, or an eye-catching display in a store will often entice shoppers to try a different brand.

Two growing areas of sales promotion are couponing and product placement. American consumers receive over $250 billion worth of coupons each year and redeem about $3 billion.[15] Almost 80 percent of all Americans redeem coupons. Sunday newspaper supplements remain the number one source, but there has been explosive growth of online or "consumer printed" coupons. General Mills, Kimberly-Clark, and General Electric like online coupons because they have a higher redemption rate. Coupons are used most often for grocery shopping. Do they save you money? One study found that people using coupons at the grocery store spent eight percent more than those who didn't.[16]

Product placement is paid inclusion of brands in mass media programming. This includes movies, TV, books, music videos, and video games. So when you see Ford vehicles in the latest James Bond movie or Tom Hanks drinking a Coke on-screen, that

CONCEPT *in Action*

Whether making a cameo appearance or starring in a major role, brands are top talent in the entertainment world. Coca-Cola sits at the judges' table on *American Idol;* Under Armour is the performance apparel of choice for the virtual characters in top-selling computer games like *Tom Clancy's Ghost Recon 2* and *Tiger Woods PGA Tour 2006;* and Reese's Pieces are forever immortalized in *E.T. The Extra-Terrestrial. Does product placement blur the lines between advertising and content and should viewers be concerned?*

© KEVIN WINTER/GETTY IMAGES

is product placement. Product placement has become a huge business. For example, in 2005, there were 8,012 appearances by the top 10 most-placed brands on major TV networks between January 1 and April 26.[17] The top brand placed was Coca-Cola Classic followed by Everlast apparel and Gatorade. Toyota paid several million dollars to have its cars featured on the reality TV show *The Contender.* Many large companies are cutting their advertising budgets to spend more on product placements. One area of product placement that is raising ethical issues is so called "experts" being paid to mention brands on the air. *Child* magazine's technology editor James Oppenheimer went on an ABC station to review educational toys. He praised *My ABCs Picture Book,* a personalized photo album from Eastman Kodak. What he didn't say was that Kodak paid him to mention the photo album. Similarly, Katleen de Monchy talked on *Good Morning America* about clothes worn by the stars at the Golden Globes. She mentioned Faviana, DSW, and retailer David's Bridal. All paid her to mention these products on TV.[18]

> **concept check**
>
> How does sales promotion differ from advertising?
>
> Describe several types of sales promotion.

Public Relations Helps Build Goodwill

 How does public relations fit into the promotional mix?

public relations
Any communication or activity designed to win goodwill or prestige for a company or person.

publicity
Information about a company or product that appears in the news media and is not directly paid for by the company.

Like sales promotion, public relations can be a vital part of the promotional mix. **Public relations** is any communication or activity designed to win goodwill or prestige for a company or person. Its main form is **publicity**, information about a company or product that appears in the news media and is not directly paid for by the company. Publicity can be good or bad. Reports of children overeating fast food leading to obesity is an example of negative publicity.

Naturally, firms' public relations departments try to create as much good publicity as possible. They furnish company speakers for business and civic clubs, write speeches for corporate officers, and encourage employees to take active roles in such civic groups as the United Way and the Chamber of Commerce. The main tool of the public relations department is the *press release,* a formal announcement of some newsworthy event connected with the company, such as the start of a new program, the introduction of a new product, or the opening of a new plant. Public relations departments may perform any or all of the functions described in Exhibit 15.7.

New-Product Publicity

Publicity is instrumental in introducing new products and services. Publicity can help advertisers explain what's different about their new product by prompting free news stories or positive word of mouth about it. During the introductory period, an especially

Exhibit 15.7 > The Functions of a Public Relations Department

Public Relations Function	Description
Press relations	Placing positive, newsworthy information in the news media to attract attention to a product, a service, or a person associated with the firm or institution
Product publicity	Publicizing specific products or services
Corporate communications	Creating internal and external messages to promote a positive image of the firm or institution
Public affairs	Building and maintaining national or local community relations
Lobbying	Influencing legislators and government officials to promote or defeat legislation and regulation
Employee and investor relations	Maintaining positive relationships with employees, shareholders, and others in the financial community
Crisis management	Responding to unfavorable publicity or a negative event

innovative new product often needs more exposure than conventional, paid advertising affords. Public relations professionals write press releases or develop videos in an effort to generate news about their new product. They also jockey for exposure of their product or service at major events, on popular television and news shows, or in the hands of influential people. A rather bizarre form of new product publicity was for an online gambling site, **http://www.GoldenPalace.com.** The company paid $650,000 to have a new monkey species named Golden Palace. The firm also paid a woman $15,000 to have GoldenPalace.com tattooed across her forehead.

Event Sponsorship

Public relations managers may sponsor events or community activities that are sufficiently newsworthy to achieve press coverage; at the same time, these events also reinforce brand identification. Sporting, music, and arts activities remain the most popular choices of event sponsors. For example, almost all of the major college football bowls are sponsored by a product such as the Toyota Gator Bowl, AT&T Cotton Bowl, and the Tostitos Fiesta Bowl. Many sponsors are also turning to more specialized events that have tie-ins with schools, charities, and other community service organizations.

Georgia-Pacific's Quilted Northern Ultra bath tissue competes in what is generally considered a low-interest, commodity category where products traditionally compete on functionality and price. But marketers sought to differentiate the brand, drive sales, and increase market share while striking an emotional chord with consumers through event sponsorship. The bath tissue is the national sponsor of the Race for the Cure, to promote the company's role with the Susan G. Komen Breast Cancer Foundation.

Creating Buzz Much of sales promotion and publicity is about creating buzz. Buzz marketing (or viral marketing) is intense word-of-mouth marketing. Word-of-mouth is essentially a linear process with information passing from one individual to another, then to another. A marketer has successfully created a buzz when the interactions are so intense that the information moves in a matrix pattern rather than a linear one and everyone is talking about the topic. Leading edge firms now feel that they get more bang-for-their-buck using buzz marketing than other forms of promotion. The new technique is discussed in the Managing Change box.

concept check

What are the functions of a public relations department?

Explain the concept of event sponsorship.

CONCEPT *in Action*

The invention of the Taser M26 and X26 nonlethal stun devices has revolutionized global law enforcement, protecting police officers and saving thousands of lives during potentially deadly altercations. While Tasers are out fighting crime, Taser International Inc., fights off dozens of product-liability lawsuits from opponents, winning strings of victories in the courts and trumpeting Taser-gun safety using mountains of expert medical and scientific studies. *What publicity tools can Taser International use to communicate the public-safety benefits of its products?*

© AUSTRALIAN ASSOCIATED PRESS, AAP

MANAGING CHANGE

Buzz Marketing Sparks Conversation and Awareness

Donovan Unks, a 28-year-old biotech researcher at Stanford University, spent valuable minutes every day for three months to follow an Audi marketing campaign. The ads for the new A3 hatchback, appearing in magazines and on TV, billboards, and the Internet, wove a complicated serialized mystery of a stolen car. Some 500,000 people, according to Audi, tracked the story by following online clues. But Unks and his friend Laura Burstein didn't just play the game. They were drafted to be characters in the plot by ad agency McKinney & Silver in Durham, North Carolina, after they answered an encrypted ad in *The Hollywood Reporter* that only solvers of binary code could read. In their Audi roles, the two drove all night to a music festival, crashed a party, were blogged about by fans of the story and Webcast worldwide on the final night of the drama at the Viceroy Hotel in Santa Monica, California. Audi spent $5 million-plus to run "The Art of the Heist" game. The car maker thinks few online gamers will actually buy an A3. The real goal is to generate buzz among the 25-to-35-year-old, upper-income males Audi targets.

In another example of buzz marketing, Google introduced g-mail and created scarcity by giving out g-mail accounts to only a handful of "power users." Other users who aspired to be like these power users "lusted" for a g-mail account and this manifested itself in their bidding for g-mail invites on eBay. Demand was created by limited supply; the cachet of having a g-mail account caused the word of mouth.

Procter & Gamble has a special word-of-mouth department called Tremor. Tremor has identified 250,000 teenagers it calls connectors. They are people who have a social network five to six times the size of a normal person and a deep propensity to talk about ideas to that network. P&G sends the teenagers new products to try out from time to time. Again, the goal is to create buzz.[19]

Critical Thinking Questions

- Think of other techniques that companies can use to create buzz.
- Sony hired 60 actors to hang around tourist attractions and act like tourists. Their job was to ask passersby to take their pictures with the new Sony Ericson camera phone. Hennessy Cognac hired 150 actors to drink at trendy bars and chat with patrons about the cognac. The object was to create buzz. Is this ethical?

Factors That Affect the Promotional Mix

9 What factors affect the promotional mix?

Promotional mixes vary a great deal from product to product and from one industry to the next. Advertising and personal selling are usually a firm's main promotional tools. They are supported by sales promotion. Public relations helps develop a positive image for the organization and its products. The specific promotional mix depends on the nature of the product, market characteristics, available funds, and whether a push or a pull strategy is used.

The Nature of the Product

Selling toothpaste differs greatly from selling overhead industrial cranes. Personal selling is most important in marketing industrial products and least important in marketing consumer nondurables (consumer products that get used up). Broadcast advertising is used heavily in promoting consumer products, especially food and other nondurables. Print media and the Internet are used for all types of consumer products. Industrial products may be advertised through special trade magazines. Sales promotion, branding, and packaging are roughly twice as important (in terms of percentage of the promotional budget) for consumer products as for industrial products.

Market Characteristics

When potential customers are widely scattered, buyers are highly informed, and many of the buyers are brand loyal, the promotional mix should include more advertising and sales promotion and less personal selling. But sometimes personal selling is required even when buyers are well informed and geographically dispersed, as is the case with super computers and airplanes. Industrial installations and component parts may be sold to knowledgeable people with much education and work experience. Yet a salesperson must still explain the product and work out the details of the purchase agreement.

Salespeople are also required when the physical stocking of merchandise—called **detailing**—is the norm. Milk and bread, for instance, are generally stocked by the person who makes the delivery, rather than by store

CONCEPT *in Action*

When it comes to creating buzz, few companies have as much star power in their corner as Teenage Millionaire, the Hollywood-based designer of fashionable D.I.Y-chic T-shirts. Best known for popularizing the "Jesus Is My Homeboy" tops worn by Tinseltown celebs and religious devotees alike, Teenage Millionaire has garnered enormous publicity from fashionistas like Hillary Duff, Jessica Simpson, Brad Pitt, and Ashton Kutcher—all wearers of Teenage Millionaire apparel. *What conditions are necessary for marketing buzz to develop?*

© ADREES LATIF/REUTERS/LANDOV

detailing
The physical stocking of merchandise at a retailer by the salesperson who delivers the merchandise.

personnel. This practice is becoming more common for convenience products as sellers try to get the best display space for their wares.

Available Funds

Money, or the lack of it, is one of the biggest influences on the promotional mix. A small manufacturer with a tight budget and a unique product may rely heavily on free publicity. The media often run stories about new products.

If the product warrants a sales force, a firm with little money may turn to manufacturers' agents. They work on commission, with no salary, advances, or expense accounts. The Duncan Co., which makes parking meters, is just one of the many that rely on manufacturers' agents.

Push and Pull Strategies

push strategy
A promotional strategy in which a manufacturer uses aggressive personal selling and trade advertising to convince a wholesaler or retailer to carry and sell its merchandise.

Manufacturers may use aggressive personal selling and trade advertising to convince a wholesaler or a retailer to carry and sell their merchandise. This approach is known as a **push strategy**. The wholesaler, in turn, must often push the merchandise forward by persuading the retailer to handle the goods. A push strategy relies on extensive personal selling to channel members, or trade advertising, and price incentives to wholesalers and retailers. The retailer then uses advertising, displays, and other promotional forms to convince the consumer to buy the "pushed" products. This approach also applies to services. For example, the Jamaican Tourism Board targets promotions to travel agencies, which are members of its distribution channel.

pull strategy
A promotional strategy in which a manufacturer focuses on stimulating consumer demand for its product, rather than on trying to persuade wholesalers or retailers to carry the product.

At the other extreme is a **pull strategy**, which stimulates consumer demand in order to obtain product distribution. Rather than trying to sell to wholesalers, a manufacturer using a pull strategy focuses its promotional efforts on end consumers. As they begin demanding the product, the retailer orders the merchandise from the wholesaler. The wholesaler, confronted with rising demand, then places an order from the manufacturer. Thus, stimulating consumer demand pulls the product down through the channel of distribution. Heavy sampling, introductory consumer advertising, cents-off campaigns, buzz marketing, and couponing may all be used as part of a pull strategy. For example, using a pull strategy, the Jamaican Tourism Board may entice travelers to come to its island by offering discounts on hotels or airfare. The push and pull promotional strategies are illustrated in Exhibit 15.8.

Rarely does a company use a pull or a push strategy exclusively. Instead, the mix will emphasize one of these strategies. For example, pharmaceutical company Sanofi Aventis uses a push strategy by using personal selling and sampling of Allegra D, the allergy drug, to physicians and pharmacies. The company also uses print ads in consumer magazines, network TV, newspaper ads, and a Web site, **http://www.allegra.com**, aimed at final consumers to pull the product through the channel.

> **concept check**
>
> Explain how the nature of the product, market characteristics, and available funds can affect the promotional mix.
>
> Distinguish between push and pull strategies.

Trends in Promotion

 10 What are three important trends in promotion?

Advances in technology are changing the marketing landscape. As you will see in this section, marketers are harnessing new technology to hone their marketing message and reach more customers.

Promotion through Blogs

Blogs provide marketers with a real-time dialogue with customers and an avenue to promote its products or services. A *blog* is an online journal with regularly updated content. This content is pushed to subscribers by RSS (really simple syndication) or

Exhibit 15.8 > **Push and Pull Promotional Strategies**

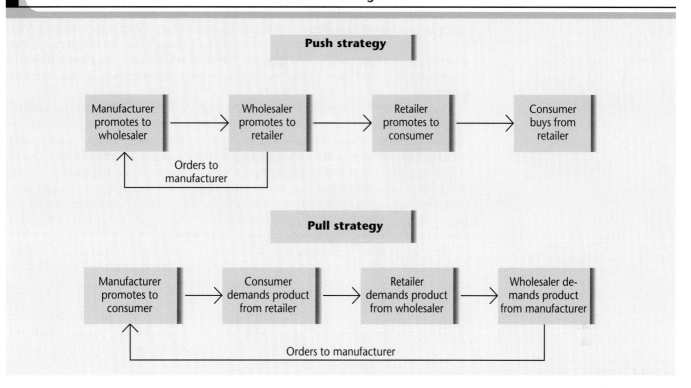

e-mail and allows for response and discussion from site visitors. RSS enables users to automatically gather updates from various Web sites, especially news sites and blogs, and display headlines and a brief summary of those updates in a single location.

Well-run marketing blogs usually focus tightly on one niche area, product line, or vertical market segment. The aim is to provide the blogs' readers with a constantly renewing source of news and insight about that topic. About 70,000 new blogs are created daily; over 1.3 million blog entries are posted daily.[20]

Many companies are setting up their own blogs. A few of the new bloggers are General Motors, Apple, American Cancer Society, and Microsoft, to name a few. These companies blog because they: (1) get real-time input from customers and prospects, (2) create and maintain relationships, (3) can have a dialogue with their clients and prospects, and (4) can focus on specific marketing goals. For example, Jeep can use a blog to show its expertise in off-road adventure driving and develop a perception as a trustworthy authority. In addition to thought leadership blogs, companies have created event blogs, customer relation blogs, advertising blogs, prelaunch of a new product or service blogs, media relation blogs, and crisis management blogs.[21]

Firms can also use emerging search tools like BlogPulse, Feedster, PubSub, and Technorati to monitor conversations about their company and brands. A public relations department might then decide to feed new product information to bloggers who are evangelists for their brand.

Growing Use of Technology in Promotion

All forms of promotion are applying more and more technology to enhance effectiveness. The downtowns of European cities tend to have much greater foot traffic than those of the United States. As a result, street posters tend to be used more often. A typical size might be 12 feet tall and 6 feet wide, with full-color ads. Now, with the application of technology, the posters sing, talk, or even smell. A recent London poster ad for an energy drink called Purdey's played "chilled out" windchimes at bus stops. With the touch of a button on a poster, London pedestrians can get a whiff of Procter & Gamble's new shampoo Head & Shoulders Citrus Smell.

New, full-size digital billboards mean that messages can be changed in an instant. The signs let several companies share one space and target messages based on "day-parts." In the morning a department store could advertise a sale, and in the afternoon a bar might promote happy-hour specials. "We're moving from selling space to selling time," says Michael Hudes, executive VP for corporate development at Clear Channel Outdoor.[22]

"Short codes," a sequence of four or five digits, are another popular new form of text messaging that consumers can key into their cell phones to participate in promotions or get more information about a product. Under Pepsi's "Go Pro" sweepstakes, for example, consumers are no longer required to enter special under-the-cap codes onto a Web site. Instead, they can just punch the codes into their cell phones, type in "G-O-P-R-O" and they are automatically entered to win a sweepstakes for good tickets to major sporting events. Already brands like Claritin are giving consumers the chance to punch in a short code to receive free samples. Close-Up Toothpaste, Icebreakers, Macy's, and Nokia are also running short code promotions.[23]

One of the more interesting new technologies used for promotion is called Hyper-Sonic Sound. Unlike conventional speakers, which project a sound wave that disperses in air, this technology emits a focused wave of ultrasound, using frequencies beyond the range of human hearing. The ultrasound becomes audible as it mixes with air, creating a column of sound with virtually constant volume. No sound is projected behind or to the sides of the emitter. At a Safeway supermarket a shopper was caught off-guard by a subtle voice above the corned beef. Glancing up, she saw a plasma screen bursting with color and seeming to address only her. The voice pitched a special on Sara Lee honey turkeys and brown-sugar hams. In tests at other retail stores, these laserlike sound beams pinpoint individual shoppers to encourage buying with recorded messages. At some Wal-Marts that have in-store McDonald's, for example, shoppers hear messages extolling the fast-food outlet's offerings.[24]

---

concept check

Describe how Toyota may want to use a blog to educate consumers about the hybrid Prius.

How does technology improve the effectiveness of advertising?

CONCEPT *in Action*

Television has jumped on the podcasting craze in recent years, offering digital downloads of top-rated TV shows such as *24, The Tonight Show,* and *Desperate Housewives.* The Big Four networks' venture into podcasting—while delighting consumers—sent shockwaves across the advertising world. Initial podcasts priced at $1.99 generated high margins and talk of eventual subscription and rental pricing models—with no advertising. *How will advertisers pitch brands if ad-free consumer-controlled content eliminates the traditional 30-second commercial?*

Advertisers Jump on Podcasting

Podcasts are basically blogs with an audio element. The trend developed when a new version of iTunes software made it easy for people to create their own podcasts andpost them on a Web site. Other podcasting software can be found at **http://www.podcastingalley.com.** There are over 8,000 podcasters in the United States. Besides individuals, companies are beginning to do their own podcasts. ABC News is now offering a podcast of *Nightline* and other programs. For listeners, the advantage of a podcast is convenience. Their favorite programs download automatically from the Internet, usually free of charge, and they can listen to the programs any time they wish. They can also listen wherever they wish, if they have an iPod or other MP3 player to receive the downloads.

Clear Channel, the nation's largest radio broadcaster, offers material from nearly 40 different stations as podcasts. At first ad-free, Clear Channel's podcasts now include a 15-second advertisement before the programming—short enough that people won't fast-forward through it. Clear Channel plans to begin encouraging listeners who hear a podcast interview or song to visit a station's Web site and buy a full album through a retailing partner. Clear Channel already has a partnership with Amazon.com.[25]

Pet owners can go to **http://www.purina.com** and opt-in to receive Purina's podcasts. The products will offer advice ranging from animal training to pet insurance. Weekly tips will also be sent on things such as how to help your dog lose weight. Owners spend about $13.4 billion a year on pet food. The aim of the podcasts is to build brand loyalty with a soft sell.[26]

concept check

Describe how Toyota may want to use a blog to educate consumers about the hybrid Prius.

How does technology improve the effectiveness of advertising?

Summary of Learning Goals

1 What are the goals of promotional strategy?

Promotion aims to stimulate demand for a company's goods or services. Promotional strategy is designed to inform, persuade, or remind target audiences about those products. The goals of promotion are to create awareness, get people to try products, provide information, keep loyal customers, increase use of a product, and identify potential customers.

2 What are the elements of the promotional mix, and what is integrated marketing communications?

The unique combination of advertising, personal selling, sales promotion, and public relations used to promote a product is the promotional mix. Advertising is any paid form of nonpersonal promotion by an identified sponsor. Personal selling consists of a face-to-face presentation in a conversation with a prospective purchaser. Sales promotion consists of marketing activities—other than personal selling, advertising, and public relations—that stimulate consumers to buy. These activities include coupons and samples, displays, shows and exhibitions, demonstrations, and other selling efforts. Public relations is the marketing function that links the policies of the organization with the public interest and develops programs designed to earn public understanding and acceptance. Integrated marketing communications (IMC) is being used by more and more organizations. It is the careful coordination of all of the elements of the promotional mix to produce a consistent, unified message that is customer focused.

3 What is advertising and what are the different types of advertising?

Institutional advertising creates a positive picture of a company. Advocacy advertising takes a stand on controversial social or economic issues. Product advertising features a specific good or service. Comparative advertising is product advertising in which the company's product is compared with competing, named products. Reminder advertising is used to keep a brand name in the public's mind.

4 What are the advertising media, and how are they selected?

The main types of traditional advertising media are newspapers, magazines, radio, television, outdoor advertising and direct mail. Newspaper advertising delivers a local audience but has a short life span. Magazines deliver special-interest markets and offer good detail and color. Radio is an inexpensive and highly portable medium but has no visual capabilities. Television reaches huge audiences and offers visual and audio opportunities, but it can be very expensive. Outdoor advertising requires short messages but is only moderately expensive. Direct mail can reach targeted audiences, but it is only as good as the mailing list. The Internet is global in scope and can offer a personalized message response. More and more advertising dollars are being shifted to the Internet. Search advertising on Google and Yahoo account for the bulk of the growth. Media are evaluated on a CPM (cost per thousand contacts) basis and by reach and frequency.

5 What are the elements of an advertising campaign?

An advertising campaign is a series of related ads focusing on a common theme, slogan, and set of advertising appeals. Creating a campaign begins with setting advertising objectives. Next, advertising appeals are specified and then message execution strategies are developed.

6 What is personal selling?

About 6.5 million people in the United States are directly engaged in personal selling. Personal selling enables a salesperson to demonstrate a product and tailor the message to the prospect; it is effective in closing a sale. Professional salespeople are knowledgeable and creative. They also are familiar with the selling process, which consists of prospecting and qualifying, approaching customers, presenting and demonstrating the product, handling objections, closing the sale, and following up on the sale.

7 What are the goals of sales promotion, and what are several types of sales promotion?

Immediate purchase is the goal of most sales promotion whether it is aimed at consumers or the trade (wholesalers and retailers). The most popular sales promotions are coupons, samples, product placement, premiums, contests, and sweepstakes. Trade shows, conventions, and point-of-purchase displays are other types of sales promotion.

8 How does public relations fit into the promotional mix?

Public relations is mostly concerned with getting good publicity for companies. Publicity is any information about a company or product that appears in the news media and is not directly paid for by the company. Public relations departments furnish company speakers for business and civic clubs, write speeches for corporate officers, and encourage employees to take active roles in civic groups. These activities help build a positive image for an organization and create buzz, which is a good backdrop for selling its products.

9 What factors affect the promotional mix?

The factors that affect the promotional mix are the nature of the product, market characteristics, available funds, and whether a push or a pull strategy is emphasized. Personal selling is used more with industrial products, and advertising is used more heavily for consumer products. With widely scattered, well-informed buyers and with brand-loyal customers, a firm will blend more advertising and sales promotion and less personal selling into its promotional mix. A manufacturer with a limited budget may rely heavily on publicity and manufacturers' agents to promote the product.

10 What are three important trends in promotion?

The Internet and new technology are having a major impact on promotion and promotion expenditures. Traditional media are losing advertising funds to the Internet. Many companies are now creating blogs to get closer to customers and potential customers. Technology is enabling street posters to sing, talk, and even emit smells. New full-sized digital billboards enable messages to be changed instantly. Entering short codes on cellphones is attracting many young consumers, and HyperSonic Sound enables stores to get audio messages to the customer at the point of purchase. Podcasts offer advertisers a new medium to reach consumers.

Key Terms

Preparing for Tomorrow's Workplace: SCANS

1. Think of a product that you use regularly. Find several examples of how the manufacturer markets this product, such as ads in different media, sales promotions, and publicity. Assess each example for effectiveness in meeting one or more of the six promotional goals described in the chapter. Then analyze them for effectiveness in reaching you as a target consumer. Consider such factors as the media used, the style of the ad, and ad content. Present your findings to the class. (Information)

2. Go to the blogging search sites listed in the text and find personal blogs, both positive and negative, for a brand. Also report on a consumer good manufacturer's blogging site. Was it appealing? Why or why not? (Technology)

3. *The Internet and technology has changed the world of promotion forever.* Explain the meaning of this sentence. (Technology)

4. Explain how different types of promotion can build brand loyalty. What types of promotion can be used to generate impulse buying? (Information)

5. What advantages does personal selling offer over types of promotion? (Information)

6. Choose a current advertising campaign for a beverage product. Describe how the campaign uses different media to promote the product. Which media is used the most, and why? What other promotional strategies does the company use for the product? Evaluate the effectiveness of the campaign. Present your results to the class. (Information)

7. The Promotional Products Association International is a trade association of the promotional-products industry. Its Web site, **http://www.ppa.org**, provides an introduction to promotional products and how they are used in marketing. Read its FAQ page and the Industry Sales Volume statistics (both reached through the Education link). Then go to the Resources and Technology section then case studies and link to the most recent Golden Pyramid Competition. Choose three to four winners from different categories. Now prepare a short report on the role of promotional products in the promotional mix. Include the examples you selected and explain how the products helped the company reach its objective. (Technology)

8. **Team Activity** Apply what you learned in this chapter to a real-world business situation. Divide the class into groups of four or more. Each group will assume the role of the Marketing and Sales Department for Cameron Balloons, a company in Bristol, England. Go to **http://www.cameronballoons.com**, where you will learn

about the company and its major business functions. After familiarizing yourself with the company, focus on the marketing and sales pages. Develop a promotional strategy for the company. Be sure to explain the basis for the strategy, the target market(s), which promotional channels you will use and why (not all may be appropriate), and whether you recommend a push or a pull strategy. (Interpersonal)

Ethics Activity

After working really hard to distinguish yourself, you've finally been promoted to a senior account executive at a major advertising agency and placed in charge of the agency's newest account, a nationally known cereal company. Their product is one you know contains excessive amounts of sugar as well as artificial colorings, and lacks any nutritional value whatsoever. In fact, you have never allowed your own children to eat it.

Your boss has indicated that the cereal company would like to use the slogan, "It's good for you," in their new television and print advertising campaign. You know that a $2 billion lawsuit has been filed against the Kellogg and Viacom corporations for marketing junk food to young children. The suit cited "alluring product packaging, toy giveaways, contests, collectibles, kid-oriented Web sites, magazine ads, and branded toys and clothes." In addition, two consumer groups have brought suit against children's television network, Nickelodeon, for "unfair and deceptive junk-food marketing."

Your new role at the agency will be tested with this campaign. Doing a good job on it will cement your position and put you in line for a promotion to vice president. But as a responsible parent you have strong feelings about misleading advertising targeted at susceptible children.

Using a Web search tool, locate articles about this topic and then write responses to the following questions. Be sure to support your arguments and cite your sources.

Ethical Dilemma: Do you follow your principles and ask to be transferred to another account? Or do you help promote a cereal you know may be harmful to children in order to secure your career?

Sources: Stephanie Thompson, "Standing Still, Kellogg Gets Hit with a Lawsuit," *Advertising Age*, January 23, 2006; Stephanie Thompson, "Kellogg Co. Might as Well Have Painted a Bull's-eye on Itself," *Advertising Age*, January 23, 2006; and Abbey Klaassen, "Viacom Gets Nicked," *Advertising Age*, January 23, 2006 (all from http://galenet.thomsonlearning.com).

Working the Net

1. The Zenith OptiMedia site at **http://www.zenithoptimedia.com** is a good place to find links to Internet resources on advertising. At the site, click on "Leading Corporate and Brand Sites." Pick three of the company sites listed and review them, using the concepts in this chapter.

2. Go to the *Sales and Marketing* magazine site at **http://www.salesandmarketing. com.** Read several of the free recent articles from the magazine as well as online exclusives and prepare a brief report on current trends in one of the following topics: sales strategies, marketing strategies, customer relationships, or training. Also check out their new blog "Soundoff." What is your opinion of this blog?

3. Does a career in marketing appeal to you? Start your journey at Careers in Marketing, **http://www.careers-in-marketing.com**, and explore the five different areas listed there: Advertising & Public Relations, Market Research, Non-Profit, Product Management, and Retailing. Which one appeals to you most, and why? Briefly describe the type of work you would be doing, the career path, and how you will prepare to enter this field (for example, courses, part-time jobs, etc.).

4. Entrepreneurs and small businesses don't always have big sales promotion budgets. The Guerrilla Marketing Web page at **http://www.gmarketing.com** has many practical ideas for those with big ideas but small budgets. After exploring the site, explain the concept of guerrilla marketing. Then list five ideas or tips that appeal to you and summarize why they are good marketing strategies.

5. Press releases are a way to get free publicity for your company and products. Visit several of the following sites to learn how to write a press release: **http://www.press-release-examples.com**, **http://www.publicityinsider.com**, or **http://www.netpress.org/careandfeeding.html.** Which sites were most helpful, and why? Develop a short "how-to" guide on press releases for your classmates. Then write a press release that announces the opening of your new health food restaurant, Zen Foods, located just two blocks from campus.

Advertisers Score with the World Cup

What sporting event is televised in 213 countries and watched by more passionate fans than any other? If you guessed the Olympics, you'd be wrong. It's the World Cup football (soccer) matches, which last a month and are held every four years. An estimated 29 billion people watched the 2002 Cup matches, and Web surfers registered over 2 billion page views at **http://www.FIFAworldcup.com.** Even more viewers tuned in for the June 2006 games, held in Germany. Online venues such as chat rooms, blogs, and discussion boards added another media channel for fans to get more of the action.

Soccer's worldwide popularity makes it a prime advertising buy for many global companies, who want to get their message out to these large audiences. More than 240 million players on 1.4 million teams around the world play the game, supporting its claim to be the world's favorite sport. As the FIFA World Cup Web site explains, "The FIFA World Cup™ reaches an audience of a size and diversity that is unrivalled by any other single-sports body. Add to this a passion for the game found in all corners of the world, and you have a sporting, social, and marketing phenomenon." As a result, companies vie to become Official Partners with global marketing rights as well as custom opportunities. The 2006 FIFA World Cup™ Official Partners were adidas, Avaya, Budweiser, Coca-Cola, Continental, Deutsche Telekom, Emirates, Fujifilm, Gillette, Hyundai, MasterCard, McDonald's, Philips, Toshiba, and Yahoo!.

The World Cup's global nature presents major challenges as well as opportunities for its advertisers. Unlike the Super Bowl, which focuses on the United States, the World Cup requires even greater levels of creativity to produce ads that make a strong connection with soccer fans from very diverse cultures. Ads may have to appeal to viewers in countries as different as Ireland, Mexico, Malaysia, and Bangladesh.

Companies accomplish this task in various ways. They can select the countries that see their ads. Some have one ad for all countries, whereas others customize ads. MasterCard overcame the language barrier by showing soccer fans from many countries cheering. The only words appear at the end with the company logo: "Football fever. Priceless." Anheuser-Busch, which spent more for its 2006 World Cup ads than it did for its Olympics or Super Bowl ads, also opted for a visual rather than verbal ad: People in the stands at a sporting event do the "wave," holding cards that show beer flowing from a Budweiser bottle into a glass, which then empties. "If you get too complicated, you lose people with different cultures and perspectives," says Tony Ponturo, vice president of global sports marketing for the brewer. Gillette starts with the same ad but uses digital techniques so that each ad features the team colors for the country where the spot is showing.

Critical Thinking Questions

- What are some of the challenges global marketers encounter when developing advertising and promotion campaigns? How does the type of product affect the promotional strategies?
- You work for an ad agency that has a World Cup sponsor as a client. What approach would you recommend for your agency as it develops a campaign—universal, customized for each geographical region, or something else, and why?
- What types of companies could benefit from placing ads on the FIFA Web site, and how can they use the Internet effectively to promote their products?

Sources: Adapted from "Marketing & TV," *Fédération Internationale de Football Association,* http://www.fifa.com, May 3, 2006; Aaron O. Patrick, "World Cup's Advertisers Hope One Size Fits All," *Wall Street Journal,* March 28, 2006, p. B7; "The Wave, " TV Commercials, *Budweiser.com,* http://www.Budweiser.com, May 3, 2006; "World Cup Advertising Analysis," *Analyst Wire,* March 3, 2006, http://galenet.thomsonlearning.com.

Jimmy John's Gourmet Sandwich Shops Cut the Mustard

Jimmy John's Gourmet Sandwich Shop is not like any other sub shop. No games or gimmicks—just good old-fashioned, homemade sandwiches from fresh-baked bread, all-natural meats, and vegetables that are sliced daily at each restaurant.

Founded in 1983 in a converted garage in Charleston, Illinois, by 19-year-old Jimmy John Liautaud, the company now boasts more than 395 corporate and franchised locations in more than 34 states and two countries.

How did they come so far in just 23 years? The company is known for its passion for fresh, quality products and high-speed execution. Its rigorous method of sandwich making gives the chain an advantage over others. "When you come to a Jimmy John store, you always know what you are going to get," says Joseph Zammar, a Maryland franchisee. "The sandwiches are very consistent. A menu offering only six meats, one type of cheese, and two types of breads, has to be consistent—and good."

In spite of the simplicity of Jimmy John's ingredients, its menu boasts more than 20 sandwich options as well as Jimmy chips, Jimmy cookies, and Jimmy pickles. Sandwiches can be ordered in 8-inch sub size or club style on thick-sliced seven-grain bread. Zammar trained for seven months before opening his store, learning to make sandwiches the Jimmy John's way. "I was surprised when they said I needed months of training to make a sandwich, but it really took a lot of practice," he says.

The company also takes a novel approach to advertising and promotion, using humor to promote the brand as being "a little fun and a little different," Liautaud says. And Jimmy John's uses aggressive product sampling to expand brand awareness. A recent new franchisee threw a grand-opening party, complete with live local radio coverage—selling award-winning sandwiches for $1.50 each. The company is also trying out TV spots that feature founder, Jimmy John Liautaud, as brand spokesman. Liautaud decided to star in the TV spots because "I'm simple, I'm right to the point, and I'm maniacal about the brand."

But the Champaign, Illinois–based chain is in a highly competitive industry. "I think it is a hard business to be in," says Mark Bomse, vice president of Owings Mills, Maryland–based developer, Greenberg Commercial Corporation. "Quizno's and Subway have the market share. I don't know how many other companies can go head-to-head with two companies that are that big, strong, and consistent." And expanding, according to *Retail Traffic* magazine. Quizno's has 4,400 locations worldwide; Subway, a much larger chain, has nearly 22,000 locations.

Jimmy John's is expanding, too, with more than 200 additional franchise units currently under development. Besides their dining-in option, Jimmy John's offers catering, including party subs, party platters, and box lunches. And they deliver—in every sense of the word.

Critical Thinking Questions

- When developing its integrated marketing campaign, what goals should Jimmy John's have for its advertisements and other promotional strategies?
- What marketing and promotional strategies does the company use to distinguish itself from the competition? How well do they accomplish the company's objectives?
- How effective a marketing tool is it to feature the company's founder in its TV advertising?

Sources: Greg Cebrzynski, "Jimmy John's Tests TV Spots Featuring Jimmy John Himelf," *Nation's Restaurant News,* March 28, 2005; "Jimmy John's Gourmet Sandwich Shops Makes Crystal Lake Debut," May 3, 2006, http://www.jimmyjohns.com; Kara Kridler, "Midwestern Sub Shop, Jimmy John's, to Open More Shops in MD," *Daily Record* (Baltimore, MD), June 21, 2005, http://galenet.thomsonlearning.com; Betsy Malone, "Jimmy John's Gourmet Sandwiches Offers More Than 20 Sandwich Options," *Daily Telegram* (Superior, WI), February 24, 2005, http://galenet.thomsonlearning.com.

Hot Links Address Book

A good site for the latest on interactive and Internet marketing is ClickZ network, where you'll find news, advice from experts, statistics, feature articles, and more: http://www.clickz.com/news

How can you find the right magazine in which to advertise? The MediaFinder Web site has a searchable database of thousands of magazines: http://www.mediafinder.com

Which companies are currently the target of consumer complaints about advertising? You'll find out at the site for the National Advertising Division (NAD) of the Council of Better Business Bureaus, http://www.nadreview.org

Want to avoid legal problems with your sweepstakes promotions? Find detailed information about advertising and trade regulation law at the site for Arent Fox, a law firm that specializes in this area: http://www.arentfox.com

What should a media kit for the press include? 101 Public Relations provides the answer, along with other good information about getting publicity for your company: http://www.101publicrelations.com

Advertising Age magazine has a wealth of information about the latest in advertising, including videos and ratings of new ads: http://www.adage.com

continuing case on Apple, Inc.

Part 4 • Marketing at Apple, Inc.

To marketers, the name "Apple" might seem an odd name for a computer company. But the name represented everything that the company's founders wanted to project—personal, healthy, and in the home. Over time, this storyline led to Apple's lifestyle branding strategy. Another benefit of the name was that *Apple* was always at the top of the alphabetical list when computer magazines identified new microcomputers that were slated to hit the market.

Unfortunately by the mid-1990s, industry experts had begun suggesting that Apple was passive and ignoring the changing business environment. They claimed that Apple did not have a competitive advantage either in its offering or pricing. Essentially, customers began asking, "Why should I pay a higher price for Apple products that only work with each other when the components of competing computers (PCs) work with each other? Astute shoppers could buy the "best" computer, the "best" monitor, the "best" printer, and the "best" software (or even cheapest of any of these) from different vendors and feel assured that they would all work together. This definitely was not the case for Apple products. However, a quick turnaround in perception occurred. By the next decade, Apple was being lauded as one of the most innovative companies in corporate America. Some would suggest that Apple's innovation is driven by the company's product design, that marketing at Apple begins with this innovative product design, and that great business is derived from great product.

PRODUCT MODELS AND TARGET MARKETS

When Apple's sales and market share collapsed in the mid-1990s, Steve Jobs reappeared as its savior. One of his earliest moves was to frame the company's computer product strategy within a two-by-two matrix. Within this matrix, the company would have two different product models (desktop and laptop) for two different market segments (professional and consumer). The professional market would be offered the Power Mac and the PowerBook models, and the consumer market would have the iMac and the iBook. In both markets, these products would come to represent a lifestyle brand, and this lifestyle branding strategy meant that Apple consumers would be offered more than just computers.

Ultimately, Apple crossed professional, consumer, and generational boundaries with iPod, currently the world's best-selling digital audio player. Using its strategy surrounding innovative product design, Apple was able to merge its products into an all-encompassing strategy that hinged on the digital world. The focus on a digital hub took the world into the third phase of personal computing. In the first phase, users were seeking utility (word processing, spreadsheets, and graphics). The second phase was about the Internet. In the third phase, the emphasis is on digital products (cameras, MP3 players, cell phones, and PDAs) that have entered into the mainstream of everyday life.

In this digital environment, Apple introduced the iPod, one of the most significant "disruptive innovations" in history. With the introduction of the iPod, Apple became deeply rooted in consumer lifestyle and become a cultural phenomenon. Whereas competitors were also offering their own versions of portable media players, the iPod quickly became synonymous for MP3 players and a huge success for the company. Within a five-year time period, the company created multiple versions of the iPod, with the iPod Nano introduced in the fall of 2005 amidst much fanfare. By late 2005, estimated quarterly sales of various versions of the iPod were around seven million units.

According to some experts, Apple provided three signature product innovations in its thirty years of existence: the Apple II, the Macintosh, and the iPod. However, Apple also provides a full product offering. The company makes its own hardware (computers), software (Mac OS), and the programs that run on its operating system (iTunes, iMovie); it makes the consumer electronic devices that connect to its hardware, software, and operating system (iPod); and provides the online service for content (iTunes Music Store).

DISTRIBUTION THROUGH RETAIL STORES

When crafting the marketing mix, Apple chose an innovative distribution plan to satisfy the needs of the target consumers and meet the firm's goals. Although Apple did some innovative advertising at various points when promoting its Macintosh computers, its foray into retail stores has been a key driver in generating product interest and sales. But, its retail success did not come without some ups and downs. Originally, the company partnered with retail chains such as BusinessLand, ComputerLand, Sears Business Centers, ComputerWare, Circuit City, and CompUSA. When sales were in the depths of decline in the mid 1990s, the company phased out many of its dealers and focused upon Comp-USA's Apple store-in-a-store concept. This concept was later adopted at other retail chains (e.g., Fry's Electronics and Micro Center). The bottom line was that Apple recognized that it needed to make its products readily available to the mass market if it was to become a branded consumer product.

Much to the disappointment of its Apple resellers, the company announced that it would begin opening and operating its own Apple stores. In doing so, Steve Jobs conveyed his concern that resellers had been unsuccessful at making Apple's stylish products appealing at the consumer level. The first Apple Store opened on May 19, 2001, with well-trained Apple salespeople. Computer and retail experts predicted the failure of the specialty stores, citing that Apple users already knew where to buy Apple products so Apple did not need to invest in retail stores with high fixed costs. They argued that the high-priced Apple products would have limited appeal to the mass consumer, and that a company not known for its customer service would be unable to provide assistance to the average consumer.

Yet, a mere three years after opening its first retail store, Apple was attaining around one-seventh of its revenue from Apple Stores. Interestingly, customers in these Apple Stores were not just current Apple users. Rather, half of the Macs sold at the Apple Stores were to first-time Mac buyers. When the iPod was introduced, consumers could easily visit an Apple Store and make their MP3 purchase.

Additionally, having its own retail outlet made it easy for Apple to offer a variety of iPod accessories such as carrying cases, portable stereos, and adapters. Essentially, Apple was locking consumers into Apple supported add-ons rather than sending consumers to competitors' add-on products. By the end of 2005, Apple operated 116 stores in the United States and eight stores in Canada, Japan, and the United Kingdom.

Critical Thinking Questions

- How was Apple's market segmented?
- Why was the iPod referred to as a disruptive innovation?
- Where did pricing fit into Apple's marketing program?
- Why were channel partners unhappy when Apple opened its own stores?
- Why has the company been more successful attracting new Apple users through its Apple Stores instead of through innovative advertising?

Sources: Peter Burrows, "Can the iPod Keep Leading the Brand?" *BusinessWeek,* November 8, 2004, p. 54; Peter Burrows and Ronald Grover, "Steve Jobs' Magic Kingdom," *BusinessWeek,* February 6, 2006, pp. 63–69; Amanda Cantrell, "Mac Sales May Juice Apple's Earnings," *CNN Money,* October 10, 2005, http://www.cnnmoney.com, accessed on 3/21/06; Alice A. Cuneo, Tobi Elkin, Hank Kim, and T. L. Stanley, "Apple Transcends as Lifestyle Brand," *Advertising Age,* December 15, 2003, pp. S2–S6; Cliff Edwards, "Sorry, Steve: Here's Why it Won't Work," *BusinessWeek,* May 21, 2001, pp. 44–45; Lev Grossman, "How Apple Does It," *Time Canada,* October 24, 2005, pp. 42–46; Carleen Hawn, "If He's So Smart. . . Steve Jobs, Apple, and the Limits of Innovation," *Fast Company,* January 2004, http://pf.fastcompany.com, accessed on 12/6/05; Jenny C. McCune, "Polishing the Apple," *Management Review,* September 1996, pp. 43–48; Gregory Quick, "Apple Blossoming from New Consumer Strategy," *Computer Retail Week,* July 6, 1998, p. 3; Josh Quittner and Rebecca Winters, "Apple's New Core," *Time South Pacific,* January 14, 2002, pp. 46–53; Jason Snell, "Geniuses Behind Bars," *Macworld,* May 2004, p. 9; Stephen Wozniak, "Homebrew and How the Apple Computer Came to Be," http://www.atariarchives.org, accessed on 3/20/06; Joel West, "Apple Computer: The iCEO Seizes the Internet," Center for Research on Information Technology and Organizations, Paper 348, 2002, http://repositories.cdlib.org, accessed on 12/6/05; Tom Yager, "Into the Mac Trap," *Infoworld.com,* January 31, 2005, p. 56; http://finance.yahoo.com/q/pr?s=AAPL, accessed on 2/6/06.

PART 5

Technology and Information

CHAPTER 16

Using Technology to Manage Information

Learning Goals

After reading this chapter, you should be able to answer these questions:

1 How has information technology transformed business and managerial decision making?

2 Why are computer networks an important part of today's information technology systems?

3 What types of systems make up a typical company's management information system?

4 How can technology management and planning help companies optimize their information technology systems?

5 What are the best ways to protect computers and the information they contain?

6 What are the leading trends in information technology?

Exploring Business Careers
Rebekah Krupski
A.G. Edwards

When meeting with an A.G. Edwards (http://www. agedwards.com) financial consultant, most likely you are thinking about money, *your* money. Whether you seek a short-term investment or a retirement nest egg, that will be your focus. You probably will not be thinking about the technological infrastructure required to transmit information throughout a multibillion dollar, nationwide institution like A.G. Edwards—information that often is private and financial in nature. Luckily for you, however, the company employs many people to think about just that—people like Rebekah Krupski, who works in its Information Technology (IT) division.

Starting with A.G. Edwards as a systems analyst eight years ago, Krupski is currently the manager of the IT Vendor Management Office, which focuses on the hardware and software vendors with whom A.G. Edwards does business. Her position involves not only fostering relationships with vendors, but also keeping abreast of the newest IT trends and evaluating cutting-edge products. Additionally, Krupski must ensure that the equipment the company currently uses is performing as promised by the vendors. "One of my main roles is to make sure that A.G. Edwards, and ultimately the client, are getting the IT performance that they expect and that they are paying for."

Given the company's size, A.G. Edwards' management information system (MIS) is necessarily large. The IT Vendor Management Office is located within the IT Business Management department, which oversees the IT division's business aspects. The division includes four other departments that each have a different focus: the division's financial targeting and planning, its human resource management needs, compliance issues related to information sharing and financial regulations; and the training and evaluation of IT division members. Together these five departments manage the company's extensive IT needs.

Computer and Internet technologies have impacted the way financial institutions conduct business. No longer are firms reliant on phone transactions and paper trails. Instead businesses today operate at lightning speed in a real-time environment of electronic transactions and computer-based information storage. At A.G. Edwards, IT is critical for both employees and clients. One of the IT division's most important functions is security. As regulations controlling personal information tighten and the technology to infiltrate security systems evolves, A.G. Edwards' protection of its own information and that of its clients is increasingly a priority. However, that is not it's only function. Internally, the company's MIS provides vital reporting functionality, such as what allows financial consultants to track client interests and needs. Clients rely on the system for financial information, whether they want to access the day's stock quotes as the markets close or their own retirement plan at three in the morning. As Krupski states, "The main factors differentiating any company's IT management are its processes, the services it offers clients and how those services are run, and its time-to-market with any new services." To stay competitive, A.G. Edwards has focused efforts on making its MIS as flexible and responsive as possible. In this way, the company can respond to its own needs, as well as the client's and the market's.

This chapter focuses on IT's role in business, examining the details of MIS organization, as well as the challenges companies encounter in an increasingly technological world.

information technology (IT)
The equipment and techniques used to manage and process information.

As A.G. Edwards' executives learned, harnessing the power of information technology gives a company a significant competitive advantage. **Information technology (IT)** includes the equipment and techniques used to manage and process information.

Information is at the heart of all organizations. Without information about the processes of and participants in an organization—including orders, products, inventory, scheduling, shipping, customers, suppliers, employees—a business cannot operate.

Transforming Businesses through Information

1 How has information technology transformed business and managerial decision making?

In less than 60 years, we have shifted from an industrial society to a knowledge-based economy driven by information. Businesses depend on information technology for everything from running daily operations to making strategic decisions. Computers are the tools of this information age, performing extremely complex operations as well as everyday jobs like word processing and creating spreadsheets. The pace of change has been rapid since the personal computer became a fixture on most office desks. Individual units became part of small networks, followed by more sophisticated enterprise-wide networks. Exhibits 16.1 and 16.2 summarize the types of computer equipment and software, respectively, most commonly used in business management information systems (MIS) today.

Although most workers spend their days at powerful desktop computers, other groups tackle massive computational problems at specialized supercomputer centers. Tasks that would take years on a PC can be completed in just hours on a supercomputer. With their ability to perform complex calculations quickly, supercomputers play a critical role in national security research, such as analysis of defense intelligence; scientific research, from biomedical experiments and drug development to simulations of earthquakes and star formations; demographic studies such as analyzing and predicting voting patterns; and weather and environmental studies. Businesses, too, put supercomputers to work improving inventory and production management and for product design.[1] The speed of these special machines has been rising steadily to meet increasing demands for greater computational capabilities, and the next goal is quadrillions of computations per second, or *petaflops*. Achieving these incredible speeds is critical to future scientific, medical, and business discoveries. Many countries, among them the United States, China, France, and Japan, have made petascale computing a priority.[2]

In addition to a business's own computers and internal networks, the Internet makes it effortless to connect quickly to almost anyplace in the world. As Thomas Friedman points out in his book *The World Is Flat*, "We are now connecting all of the knowledge centers on the planet together into a single global network, which . . . could usher in an amazing era of prosperity and innovation."[3] The opportunities for collaboration on a global scale increase daily. A manager can share information with hundreds of thousands of people worldwide as easily as with a colleague on another floor of the same office building. The Internet and the Web have become indispensable business tools that facilitate communication within companies as well as with customers. The rise of electronic trading hubs, discussed in the Expanding around the Globe box, is just one example of how technology is facilitating the global economy.

Many companies entrust an executive called the **chief information officer (CIO)** with the responsibility of managing all information resources. The importance of

© BOB SCHATZ

CONCEPT *in Action*

In today's high-tech world, CIOs must possess not only the technical smarts to implement global IT infrastructures, integrate communications systems with partners, and protect customer data from insidious hackers, but must also have strong business acumen. FedEx's acclaimed tech chief Rob Carter manages the technology necessary to deliver more than 6 million packages daily, with an eye towards greater business efficiency, growth, and profits. *Why is it important for CIOs to possess both technological and business expertise?*

chief information officer (CIO)
An executive with responsibility for managing all information resources in an organization.

Exhibit 16.1 > Business Computing Equipment

Computer Type	Description	Comments
Desktop personal computers (PCs)	Self-contained computers on which software can reside. These PCs can also be linked into a network over which other programs can be accessed.	Increasing power, speed, memory, and storage make these computers the dominant computer for many business processes. Can handle text, audio, video, and complex graphics.
Laptop computers	Portable computers similar in power to desktop computers.	Smaller size and weight make mobile computing easier for workers.
Minicomputers	Medium-sized computers with multiple processors, able to support from 4 to about 200 users at once.	The distinction between the larger minicomputers and smaller mainframes is blurring.
Mainframe computers	Large machines about the size of a refrigerator; can simultaneously run many different programs and support hundreds or thousands of users. Greatest storage capacity and processing speeds.	Extremely reliable and stable, used by companies and governments to process large amounts of data. More secure than PCs. Not subject to crashes; can be upgraded and repaired while operating.
Supercomputers	Most powerful computers, now capable of operating at speeds of 280 trillion calculations per second.	Companies can rent time to run projects from special supercomputer centers.

this responsibility is immense. As Jerry McElhatton, the retired CIO of MasterCard, points out, "Next to actual cash itself, data is probably the most precious asset a financial institution has. And for good reason." Companies such as MasterCard, banks, and insurance companies don't sell tangible products. "There is nothing to look at in a showroom, nothing to ship, nothing that will make a noise if you drop it. There is

Exhibit 16.2 > Business and Personal Software Applications

Application Type	Description
Word processing software	Used to write, edit, and format documents such as letters and reports. Spelling and grammar checkers, mail merge, tables, and other tools simplify document preparation.
Spreadsheet software	Used for preparation and analysis of financial statements, sales forecasts, budgets, and similar numerical and statistical data. Once the mathematical formulas are keyed into the spreadsheet, the data can be changed and the solution will be recalculated instantaneously.
Database management programs	Serve as electronic filing cabinets for records such as customer lists, employee data, and inventory information. Can sort data based on various criteria to create different reports.
Graphics and presentation programs	Create tables, graphs, and slides for customer presentations and reports. Can add images, video, animation, and sound effects.
Desktop publishing software	Combines word processing, graphics, and page layout software to create documents. Allows companies to design and produce sales brochures, catalogs, advertisements, and newsletters in-house.
Communications programs	Translate data into a form for transmission and transfer it across a network to other computers. Used to send and retrieve data and files.
Integrated software suites	Combine several popular types of programs, such as word processing, spreadsheet, database, graphics presentation, and communications programs. Component programs are designed to work together.
Groupware	Facilitates collaborative efforts of workgroups so that several people in different locations can work on one project. Supports online meetings and project management (scheduling, resource allocation, document and e-mail distribution, etc.).
Financial Software	Used to compile accounting and financial data and create financial statements and reports.

CONCEPT *in Action*

While early Web-based business-productivity tools such as Google Spreadsheets have been characterized by sluggish performance and limited functionality, the technology industry's shift to Internet-based software and services represents a massive change. Use of Internet-based applications is growing so rapidly that even Microsoft is scrambling to produce Web versions of its flagship business application, Microsoft Office. *What advantages do Web-based business applications have over conventional PC software applications?*

knowledge worker
A worker who develops or uses knowledge, contributing to and benefiting from information used to perform planning, acquiring, searching, analyzing, organizing, storing, programming, producing, distributing, marketing, or selling functions.

simply an agreement that something will happen, such as funds will become available if the customer signs on the dotted line. That's what makes data so precious to us and why we're more protective of it than the average mother lioness is with her cubs," McElhatton explains.[4]

Today most of us are **knowledge workers** who develop or use knowledge. Knowledge workers contribute to and benefit from information they use to perform planning, acquiring, searching, analyzing, organizing, storing, programming, producing,

EXPANDING AROUND THE GLOBE

Electronic Hubs Integrate Global Commerce

Thanks to the wonders of technological advancement, global electronic trading now goes far beyond the Internet retailing and trading that we are all familiar with. Special Web sites known as trading hubs, or eMarketplaces, facilitate electronic commerce between businesses in specific industries such as automotive manufacturing, retailing, telecom provisioning, aerospace, financial products and services, and more. In 2005 approximately 6 percent of business-to-business trade in the European Union was done via trading hubs, a level unheard of even several years ago.

The trading hub functions as a means of integrating the electronic collaboration of business services. Each hub provides standard formats for the electronic trading of documents used in a particular industry, as well as an array of services to sustain eCommerce between businesses in that industry. Services include demand forecasting, inventory management, partner directories, and transaction settlement services. And the payoff is significant—lowered costs, decreased inventory levels, and shorter time to market—resulting in bigger profits and enhanced competitiveness. For example, large scale manufacturing procurement can amount to billions of dollars. Changing to "just-in-time purchasing" on the hub can save a considerable percentage of these costs.

Electronic trading across a hub can range from the collaborative integration of individual business processes to auctions and exchanges of goods (electronic barter). Global content management is an essen-

tial factor in promoting electronic trading agreements on the hub. A globally consistent view of the "content" of the hub must be available to all. Each participating company handles its own content, and applications such as *content managers* keep a continuously updated master catalog of the inventories of all members of the hub. The *transaction manager* application automates trading arrangements between companies, allowing the hub to provide aggregation and settlement services.

Ultimately, trading hubs for numerous industries could be linked together in a global eCommerce Web—an inclusive "hub of all hubs." One creative thinker puts it this way: "The traditional linear, one step at a time, supply chain is dead. It will be replaced by parallel, asynchronous, real-time marketplace decision-making. Take manufacturing capacity as an example. Enterprises can bid their excess production capacity on the world eCommerce hub. Offers to buy capacity trigger requests from the seller for parts bids to suppliers who in turn put out requests to other suppliers, and this whole process will all converge in a matter of minutes."[5]

Critical Thinking Questions
- How do companies benefit from participating in an electronic trading hub?
- What impact does electronic trading have on the global economy?

distributing, marketing, or selling functions. We must know how to gather and use information from the many resources available to us.

Because most jobs today depend on information—obtaining, using, creating, managing, and sharing it—this chapter begins with the role of information in decision making and goes on to discuss computer networks and management information systems. The management of information technology—planning and protection—follows. Finally, we'll look at the latest trends in information technology. Throughout the chapter, examples show how managers and their companies are using computers to make better decisions in a highly competitive world.

Data and Information Systems

Information systems and the computers that support them are so much a part of our lives that we almost take them for granted. These **management information systems (MIS)**, methods and equipment that provide information about all aspects of a firm's operations, provide managers with the information they need to make decisions. They help managers properly categorize and identify ideas that result in substantial operational and cost benefits.

Businesses collect a great deal of *data*—raw, unorganized facts that can be moved and stored—in their daily operations. Only through well-designed IT systems and the power of computers can managers process these data into meaningful and useful *information* and use it for specific purposes, such as making business decisions. One such form of business information is the **database**, an electronic filing system that collects and organizes data and information. Using software called a *database management system (DBMS),* you can quickly and easily enter, store, organize, select, and retrieve data in a database. These data are then turned into information to run the business and to perform business analysis.

Databases are at the core of business information systems. For example, a customer database containing name, address, payment method, products ordered, price, order history, and similar data provides information to many departments. Marketing can track new orders and determine what products are selling best; sales can identify high-volume customers or contact customers about new or related products; operations managers need order information to obtain inventory and schedule production of the ordered products; and finance needs sales data to prepare financial statements. "If we can segment and analyze the data properly, we can figure out what customers really want, what original purchases lead to add-on sales, and fill the holes in our customer relationships," says former CIO McElhatton.[6] Later in the chapter we will see how companies use very large databases called data warehouses and data marts.

Companies are discovering that they can't operate well with a series of separate information systems geared to solving specific departmental problems. It takes a team effort to integrate the systems described in Chapter 11 throughout the firm. Company-wide *enterprise resource planning (ERP)* systems that bring together human resources, operations, and technology are becoming an integral part of business strategy. So is managing the collective knowledge contained in an organization, using data warehouses and other technology tools. Technology experts are learning more about the way the business operates, and business managers are learning to use information systems technology effectively to create new opportunities and reach their goals.

Another challenge that businesses face is transforming thousands of paper documents into digital format, to make the information accessible to databases and other information systems. The Catching the Entrepreneurial Spirit box introduces you to a company that built its success on this mundane task.

CATCHING THE ENTREPRENEURIAL SPIRIT

Documenting the Future

Potential customers of Captiva Software didn't share company co-founder and chief executive Reynolds Bish's belief that paper wasn't going away. They held to the idea that personal computers and the Internet would make paper disappear, and they weren't going to invest in software to organize their documents. That almost caused Captiva to go under. "We really were afraid we weren't going to make it," said Jim Berglund, an early investor in Captiva and a former board member.

But Bish asked investors for another $4 million commitment—on a bet that paper was here to stay. Bish recalls a board member telling him, "Five years from now people are going to either think you're a genius or a complete idiot."

That conversation took place six years ago. Captiva Software was recently named one of the fastest-growing technology companies in San Diego by the accounting firm Deloitte & Touche, for its 172 percent increase in revenue between 2000 and 2004. The company was recently acquired by EMC Corp.—the sixth-largest software company in the world and top maker of corporate data-storage equipment, with projected annual revenues of more than $9 billion—for $275 million in cash, rewarding embattled early Captiva investors with 10 times their money back.

Captiva began its journey to the big time in 1989 in Park City, Utah, as TextWare Corp., a small data entry company. Cofounder Steven Burton's technical expertise, Bish's business background, and a credit card, helped them get the business going. "It was pure bootstrapping," Bish said. "We did everything from going without a salary for a year or more to using up our credit cards."

Bish and Burton quickly saw the need for employees to enter data more directly and accurately. The software they developed still required clerks to type information from a paper document, but it could check for inaccuracies, matching zip codes to cities for instance. In 1996 TextWare produced software that could "read" type-written words on a scanned piece of paper, which significantly reduced the number of data entries clerks needed. It found popularity with credit-card processors, insurance companies, shipping companies, and other corporations that handled thousands of forms every day.

TextWare acquired or merged with five firms, went public, changed its name twice, and in 1998 set up its headquarters in San Diego, California, after buying Wheb Systems, which is based there. In 2002, the company merged with publicly held ActionPoint, a San Jose, California, document processing company, and changed its name to Captiva.

An estimated 80 percent of all information is still paper-based, according to market research firm Forrester Research. Captiva's flagship products, InputAccel and FormWare, process over 85 million pieces of paper worldwide every day, leaving no doubt that Bish's vision was on target. Paper is indeed here to stay.[7]

Critical Thinking Questions

- What role did cofounders Reynolds Bish and Steven Burton play in the evolution of tiny TextWare into hugely successful Captiva?
- What other unique factors were responsible for the company's remarkable growth?

Linking Up: Computer Networks

 2 **Why are computer networks an important part of today's information technology systems?**

computer network
A group of two or more computer systems linked together by communications channels to share data and information.

Today most businesses use networks to deliver information to employees, suppliers, and customers. A **computer network** is a group of two or more computer systems linked together by communications channels to share data and information. Today's networks often link thousands of users and can transmit audio and video as well as data.

Networks include clients and servers. The *client* is the application that runs on a personal computer or workstation. It relies on a *server* that manages network resources or performs special tasks such as storing files, managing one or more printers, or processing database queries. Any user on the network can access the server's capabilities.

By making it easy and fast to share information, networks have created new ways to work and increase productivity. They provide more efficient use of resources, permitting communication and collaboration across distance and time. With file sharing, all employees, regardless of location, have access to the same information. Shared databases also eliminate duplication of effort. Employees at different sites can "screen share" computer files, working on data as if they were in the same room. Their computers are connected by phone or cable lines, they all see the same thing on their display, and anyone can make changes that are seen by the other participants. The employees can also use the networks for videoconferencing.

Networks make it possible for companies to run enterprise software, large programs with integrated modules that manage all of the corporation's internal operations. Enterprise resource planning systems run on networks. Typical subsystems include finance, human resources, engineering, sales and order distribution, and order management and procurement. These modules work independently and then automatically exchange information, creating a company-wide system that includes current delivery dates, inventory status, quality control, and other critical information. Let's now look at the basic types of networks companies use to transmit data—local area networks and wide area networks—and popular networking applications like intranets and virtual private networks.

Connecting Near and Far with Networks

Two basic types of networks are distinguished by the area they cover. A **local area network (LAN)** lets people at one site exchange data and share the use of hardware and software from a variety of computer manufacturers. LANs offer companies a more cost-effective way to link computers than linking terminals to a mainframe computer. The most common uses of LANs at small businesses, for example, are office automation, accounting, and information management. LANs can help companies reduce staff, streamline operations, and cut processing costs. LANs can be set up with wired or wireless connections.

A **wide area network (WAN)** connects computers at different sites via telecommunications media such as phone lines, satellites, and microwaves. A modem connects the computer or a terminal to the telephone line and transmits data almost instantly, in less than a second. The Internet is essentially a worldwide WAN. Long-distance telephone companies, such as AT&T, MCI, and Sprint, operate very large WANs. Companies also connect LANs at various locations into WANs. WANs make it possible for companies to work on critical projects around the clock by using teams in different time zones.

Several forms of WANs—intranets, virtual private networks (VPNs), and extranets—use Internet technology. Here we'll look at intranets, internal corporate networks that are widely available in the corporate world, and VPNs. Extranets are discussed in the online enrichment chapter, "Using the Internet for Business Success," at **http://www.thomson.edu.com/introbusiness/gitman.**

Although wireless networks have been around for more than a decade, they are increasing in use because of falling costs, faster and more reliable technology, and improved standards. They are similar to their wired LAN and WAN cousins, except they use radio frequency signals to transmit data. You probably use a wireless WAN (WWAN) regularly when you use your cellular phone. WANs' coverage can span several countries. Telecommunications carriers AT&T Wireless, Cingular Wireless, Sprint PCS, T-Mobile, and Verizon operaters use wireless WANs.

Wireless LANs (WLANs) that transmit data at one site offer an alternative to traditional wired systems. WLANs' reach is a radius of 500 feet indoors and 1,000 feet outdoors and can be extended with antennas, transmitters, and other devices. The wireless devices communicate with a wired access point into the wired network. WLANs are convenient for specialized applications where wires are in the way or when employees are in different locations in a building. Hotels, airports, restaurants, hospitals, retail establishments, universities, and warehouses are among the largest users of WLANs. For example, St. Agnes Hospital in Baltimore, Maryland, recently upgraded its existing WLAN to improve voice quality and reliability. The new WLAN supports many different functions, from better on-site communication among doctors and nurses through both data transmission and voice-over-Internet phone systems to data-centric applications such as its Meditech clinical information system and pharmacy management.[8]

An Inside Job: Intranets

Like LANs, **intranets** are private corporate networks. Many companies use both types of internal networks. However, because they use Internet technology to connect computers, intranets are WANs that link employees in many locations and with different types of computers. Essentially mini-Internets that serve only the company's employees, intranets operate behind a *firewall* that prevents unauthorized access. Employees navigate using a standard Web browser, which makes the intranet easy to use. They are also considerably less expensive to install and maintain than other network types and take advantage of the Internet's interactive features such as chat rooms and team workspaces. Many software providers now offer off-the-shelf intranet

© ASSOCIATED PRESS, MICROSOFT

packages so that companies of all sizes can benefit from the increased access to and distribution of information.

Companies now recognize the power of intranets to connect employers and employees in many ways, promoting teamwork and knowledge sharing. Intranets have many applications, from human resource (HR) administration to logistics. The benefits administration intranet at UnumProvident Corp., a major insurance company, quickly became a favorite with employees. Instead of having to contact a HR representative to make any changes in personnel records or retirement plan contributions or submit time sheets, staff members simply log on to the intranet and update the information themselves. The intranet proved to be especially valuable after a merger in 2001. With more than 9,000 employees in multiple locations, UnumProvident expanded its intranet, which had been used mostly for marketing and client services, to handle more HR functions and improve communications. Managers can now process staffing updates, performance reviews, and incentive payments without filing paperwork with human resources. Employees regularly check an online job board for new positions. Shifting routine administrative tasks to the intranet brought UnumProvident additional benefits: It reduced the size of the HR department by 30 percent, and HR staff members can now turn their attention to more substantive projects.[9]

Enterprise Portals Open the Door to Productivity

enterprise portal
A customizable internal Web site that provides proprietary corporate information to a defined user group, such as employees, supply chain partners, or customers.

Intranets that take a broader view serve as sophisticated knowledge management tools. One such intranet is the **enterprise portal**, an internal Web site that provides proprietary corporate information to a defined user group. Portals can take one of three forms: business to employee (B2E), business to business (B2B), and business to consumer (B2C). Unlike a standard intranet, enterprise portals allow individuals or user groups to customize the portal home page to gather just the information they need for their particular job situations into one place and deliver it through a single Web page. Because of their complexity, enterprise portals are typically the result of a collaborative project that brings together designs developed and perfected through the collaborative effort of HR, corporate communications, and information technology departments.

More companies are turning to portal technology to provide:

- A consistent, simple user interface across the company
- Integration of disparate systems and multiple sets of data and information
- A single source for accurate and timely information that integrates internal and external information

- A shorter time to perform tasks and processes
- Cost savings through the elimination of "information intermediaries"
- Improved communications within the company and with customers, suppliers, dealers, and distributors

At Intercontinental Hotels Group (IHG), a new enterprise portal will connect staff at the group's 3,500 hotels around the world and support marketing, human resources, finance, and IT functions. A major goal is to eliminate duplication of efforts. "All of these departments are tackling similar problems independently," says David House, IHG's senior vice president for global human resources. "For example, you might have marketing efforts going on in one part of the world and someone doing a similar kind of thing in another without knowing it." The portal will facilitate collaboration and teamwork throughout the organization. "We want people to use the intranet to bridge these gaps, to improve availability of information, and to better exploit the intellectual capital in the organization," explains House.[10]

No More Tangles: Wireless Technologies

Wireless technology has become commonplace today. We routinely use devices such as cellular phones, personal digital assistants (PDAs), garage door openers, and television remote controls—without thinking of them as examples of wireless technology. Businesses use wireless technologies to improve communications with customers, suppliers, and employees. You may have seen the term Wi-Fi, which refers to wireless fidelity. When products carry the "Wi-Fi Certified" designation, they have been tested and certified to work with each other, regardless of manufacturer.

Companies in the package delivery industry, such as UPS and FedEx, were among the first users of wireless technology. Delivery personnel use handheld computers to send immediate confirmation of package receipt. You may also have seen meter readers and repair personnel from utility and energy companies send data from remote locations back to central computers.

Bluetooth short-range wireless technology is a global standard that improves personal connectivity for users of mobile phones, portable computers, stereo headsets, and MP3 players. Bluetooth wirelessly connects keyboards and mice to computers and headsets to phones and music players. A Bluetooth-enabled mobile phone, for example, provides safer hands-free cell phone use while driving. The technology is finding many applications in the auto industry as well. "Bluetooth wireless technology will start to become standard in cars in the near future," predicts David McClure,

CONCEPT in Action

Although designing a true mobile replacement for the desktop PC has proved elusive for computer manufacturers, ultramobile PCs offer wireless functions many professionals want—Web browsing, e-mail, Microsoft Office, and telephony. The Samsung Q1 Ultra Mobile PC runs Microsoft Windows XP and Vista, and with its 7-inch LCD touch screen and stylus, the mini-tablet provides the power of a desktop PC with the freedom of pen and paper. *What impact might ultramobile computing have on business?*

head of Telematics Research at SBD automotive technology consultants. Many car and cell phone manufacturers—among them Audi, BMW, DaimlerChrysler, Honda, Saab, Toyota, Volkswagen, Motorola, and Nokia—already offer Bluetooth hands-free solutions. Other uses include simplifying the connection of portable digital music players to the car's audio system and of transferring music to the system.[11]

Private Lines: Virtual Private Networks

virtual private networks (VPNs)
Private corporate networks connected over a public network, such as the Internet. VPNs include strong security measures to allow only authorized users to access the network.

Many companies use **virtual private networks (VPNs)** to connect two or more private networks (such as LANs) over a public network, such as the Internet. VPNs include strong security measures to allow only authorized users to access the network and its sensitive corporate information. Companies with widespread offices may find that a VPN is a more cost-effective option than creating a network using purchased networking equipment and leasing expensive private lines. This type of private network is more limited than a VPN, because it doesn't allow authorized users to connect to the corporate network when they are at home or traveling.

As Exhibit 16.3 shows, the VPN uses existing Internet infrastructure and equipment to connect remote users and offices almost anywhere in the world—without long-distance charges. In addition to saving on telecommunications costs, companies using VPNs don't have to buy or maintain special networking equipment and can outsource management of remote access equipment. VPNs are useful for salespeople and telecommuters, who can access the company's network as if they were on-site at the company's office. On the downside, the VPN's availability and performance, especially when it uses the Internet, depends on factors largely outside of an organization's control.

VPNs are popular with many different types of organizations. Global law firm Baker & McKenzie, with 3,300 attorneys in 38 countries, uses a VPN to connect lawyers and clients. It outsourced the VPN to Equant, a provider that offers service in 145 countries, making it easy to expand into new locations. Equant operates its own private network, which gives Baker & McKenzie a higher level of quality, security, and reliability.[12] The Abilene, Texas, Independent School District developed a cost-effective VPN for distance learning and educational software applications that will save as much as $875,000 over a five-year period. Instead of having to install software on individual computers, the district distributes them to students and teachers through the VPN. Chief Technical Officer Martin Yarborough says that without the system, he would need five more technical support staff to maintain all the computers.[13]

Software on Demand: Application Service Providers

application service providers (ASPs)
A service company that buys and maintains software on its servers and distributes it through high-speed networks to subscribers, for a set period and price.

As software developers release new types of application programs and updated versions of existing ones every year or two, companies have to analyze whether they can justify buying or upgrading to the new software—in terms of both cost and implementation time. **Application service providers (ASPs)** offer a different approach to this problem.

Exhibit 16.3 > Virtual Private Networks (VPNs)

VPN Client — Local ISP — Public network — Internal LAN — VPN Server

CONCEPT *in Action*

Salesforce.com dominates the customer-relationship-management market by offering an on-demand menu of over 250 business-software applications developed by partners like Adobe, Google, Skype, and Business Objects. The company's software-as-a-service platform, AppExchange, is enormously popular with small businesses—and even with big ones like Nokia and Staples—that don't want the IT hassle or expense of buying and maintaining conventional licensed applications. Salesforce.com predicts one million subscribers for 2008. *What are the benefits and risks to using software remotely hosted by ASPs?*

Companies subscribe, usually on a monthly basis, to an ASP and use the applications much like you'd use telephone voice mail, the technology for which resides at the phone company. Other names for ASPs include on-demand software, hosted applications, and software-as-a-service. Exhibit 16.4 shows how the ASP interfaces with software and hardware vendors and developers, the IT department, and users.

The simplest ASP applications are automated—for example, a user might use one to build a simple e-commerce site. ASPs provide three major categories of applications to users:

- Enterprise applications, including customer relationship management, enterprise resource planning (ERP), e-commerce, and data warehousing.
- Collaborative applications for internal communications, e-mail, groupware, document creation, and management messaging.
- Applications for personal use—for example, games, entertainment software, and home-office applications.

According to recent surveys, about one-third of U.S. companies currently use an ASP, and another third indicate that they will take the ASP route by 2007. AMR Research estimates that revenues from subscriptions to on-demand software products were about $2 billion in 2006. Although this represents less than 10 percent of the total software market, this sector is growing much more rapidly—more than 20 percent a year—while traditional software sales are rising at about 6 to 8 percent.[14] As this market grows, more companies are adding on-demand offerings to their traditional software packages. SAP, one of the world's largest software companies, recently joined the ranks of ASPs such as Salesforce.com and Siebel to offer on-demand customer relationship management (CRM) software. CRM has been an especially successful on-demand software category, and SAP hopes that customers who begin with on-demand CRM will buy the software to run in-house once they become familiar with its capabilities.[15]

Until recently, many companies were reluctant to outsource critical enterprise applications to third-party providers. As ASPs improved their technologies

Exhibit 16.4 > Structure of an ASP Relationship

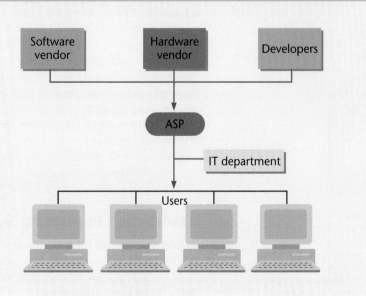

and proved to be reliable and cost-effective, attitudes have changed. Companies, both large and small, that seek cost advantages like the convenience ASPs provide. The basic idea behind subscribing to an ASP is compelling. Users can access any of their applications and data from any computer, and IT can avoid purchasing, installing, supporting, and upgrading expensive software applications. ASPs buy and maintain the software on their servers and distribute it through high-speed networks. Subscribers rent the applications they want for a set period and price. The savings in licensing fees, infrastructure, time, and staff are significant.[16]

managed service providers (MSPs)
Next generation of ASPs, offering customization and expanded capabilities such as business processes and complete management of the network servers.

Managed service providers (MSPs) represent the next generation of ASPs, offering greater customization and expanded capabilities that include business processes and complete management of the network servers. For example, American Airlines decided to outsource its Web site, contact center, and automated voice systems to Totality Corp. rather than hire the specialized engineering staff to develop and manage the sophisticated technology. "We needed the ability to manage not only our infrastructure, but also our customer-facing processes in an integrated fashion," explains Scott Hyden, American's managing director of interactive marketing. With Totality as its MSP partner, the airline improved both the quality and speed of customer service.[17]

concept check

What is a computer network? What benefits do companies gain by using networks?

How do a LAN and a WAN differ? Why would a company use a wireless network?

What advantages do VPNs offer a company? ASPs and MSPs?

Management Information Systems

 What types of systems make up a typical company's management information system?

Whereas individuals use business productivity software such as word processing, spreadsheet, and graphics programs to accomplish a variety of tasks, the job of managing a company's information needs falls to *management information systems:* users, hardware, and software that support decision making. Information systems collect and store the company's key data and produce the information managers need for analysis, control, and decision making.

As we learned in Chapter 11, factories use computer-based information systems to automate production processes and order and monitor inventory. Most companies use them to process customer orders and handle billing and vendor payments. Banks use a variety of information systems to process transactions such as deposits, ATM withdrawals, and loan payments. Most consumer transactions also involve information systems. When you check out at the supermarket, book a hotel room using a toll-free hotel reservations number, or buy CDs over the Internet, information systems record and track the transaction and transmit the data to the necessary places.

Companies typically have several types of information systems, starting with systems to process transactions. Management support systems are dynamic systems that allow users to analyze data to make forecasts, identify business trends, and model business strategies. Office automation systems improve the flow of communication throughout the organization. Each type of information system serves a particular level of decision making: operational, tactical, and strategic. Exhibit 16.5 shows the relationship between transaction processing and management support systems as well as the management levels they serve. Let's now take a more detailed look at how companies and managers use transaction processing and management support systems to manage information.

transaction processing system (TPS)
An information system that handles the daily business operations of a firm. The system receives and organizes raw data from internal and external sources for storage in a database using either batch or online processing.

Transaction Processing Systems

A firm's integrated information system starts with its **transaction processing system (TPS).** The TPS receives raw data from internal and external sources and prepares these data for storage in a database similar to a microcomputer database but vastly larger. In fact, all the company's key data are stored in a single huge database that becomes the

Exhibit 16.5 > A Company's Integrated Information System

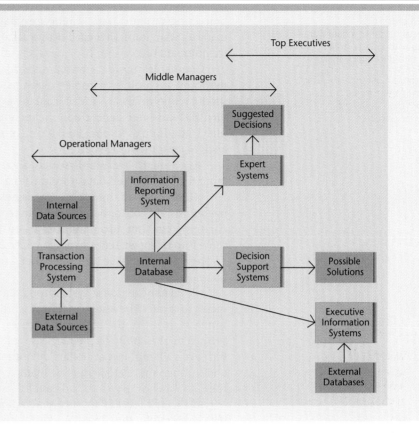

company's central information resource. As noted earlier, the *database management system* tracks the data and allows users to query the database for the information they need.

The database can be updated in two ways: **batch processing**, where data are collected over some time period and processed together, and **online**, or **real-time**, **processing**, which processes data as they become available. Batch processing uses computer resources very efficiently and is well suited to applications such as payroll processing that require periodic rather than continuous processing. Online processing keeps the company's data current. When you make an airline reservation, the agent enters your reservation directly into the airline's computer and quickly receives confirmation. Online processing is more expensive than batch processing, so companies must weigh the cost versus the benefit. For example, a factory that operates round-the-clock may use real-time processing for inventory and other time-sensitive requirements but process accounting data in batches overnight.

Decisions, Decisions: Management Support Systems

Transaction processing systems automate routine and tedious back-office processes such as accounting, order processing, and financial reporting. They reduce clerical expenses and provide basic operational information quickly. **Management support systems (MSSs)** use the internal master database to perform high-level analyses that help managers make better decisions.

Information technologies such as data warehousing are part of more advanced MSSs. A **data warehouse** combines many databases across the whole company into one central database that supports management decision making. With a data warehouse, managers can easily access and share data across the enterprise, to get a broad

batch processing
A method of updating a database in which data are collected over some time period and processed together.

online (real-time) processing
A method of updating a database in which data are processed as they become available.

management support system (MSS)
An information system that uses the internal master database to perform high-level analyses that help managers make better decisions.

data warehouse
An information technology that combines many databases across a whole company into one central database that supports management decision making.

overview rather than just isolated segments of information. Data warehouses include software to extract data from operational databases, maintain the data in the warehouse, and provide data to users. They can analyze data much faster than transaction processing systems. Data warehouses may contain many **data marts**, special subsets of a data warehouse that each deal with a single area of data. Data marts are organized for quick analysis.

Companies use data warehouses to gather, secure, and analyze data for many purposes, including customer relationship management systems, fraud detection, product line analysis, and corporate asset management. Retailers might wish to identify customer demographic characteristics and shopping patterns to improve direct-mailing responses. Banks can more easily spot credit-card fraud, as well as analyze customer usage patterns.

According to Forrester Research, about 60 percent of companies with $1 billion or more in revenues use data warehouses as a management tool. Union Pacific (UP), a $12 billion railroad, turned to data warehouse technology to streamline its business operations. By consolidating multiple separate systems, UP achieved a unified supply chain system that also enhanced its customer service. "Before our data warehouse came into being we had stovepipe systems," says Roger Bresnahan, principal engineer. "None of them talked to each other. . . . We couldn't get a whole picture of the railroad."

UP's data warehouse system took many years and the involvement of 26 departments to create. The results were well worth the effort: UP can now make more accurate forecasts, identify the best traffic routes, and determine the most profitable market segments. The ability to predict seasonal patterns and manage fuel costs more closely has saved UP millions of dollars by optimizing locomotive and other asset utilization and through more efficient crew management. In just three years, Bresnahan reports, the data warehouse system had paid for itself.[18]

At the first level of an MSS is an *information-reporting system,* which uses summary data collected by the TPS to produce both regularly scheduled and special reports. The level of detail would depend on the user. A company's payroll personnel might get a weekly payroll report showing how each employee's paycheck was determined. Higher-level mangers might receive a payroll summary report that shows total labor cost and overtime by department and a comparison of current labor costs with those in the prior year. Exception reports show cases that fail to meet some standard. An accounts receivable exception report that lists all customers with overdue accounts would help collection personnel focus their work. Special reports are generated only when a manager requests them; for example, a report showing sales by region and type of customer can highlight reasons for a sales decline.

Decision Support Systems

A **decision support system (DSS)** helps managers make decisions using interactive computer models that describe real-world processes. The DSS also uses data from the internal database but looks for specific data that relate to the problems at hand. It is a tool for answering "what if" questions about what would happen if the manager made certain changes. In simple cases, a manager can create a spreadsheet and try changing some of the numbers. For instance, a manager could create a spreadsheet to show the amount of overtime required if the number of workers increases or decreases. With models, the manager enters into the computer the values that describe a particular situation, and the program computes the results. Marketing executives at a furniture company could run DSS models that use sales data and demographic assumptions to develop forecasts of the types of furniture that would appeal to the fastest-growing population groups.

Athletic apparel and footwear manufacturer PUMA turned to a predictive analytics program to improve its North American real-time inventory management system. Its existing ERP system lacked the flexibility to provide new types of reports

---

data mart
Special subset of a data warehouse that deals with a single area of data and is organized for quick analysis.

decision support system (DSS)
A management support system that helps managers make decisions using interactive computer models that describe real-world processes.

required by the rapidly changing industry, requiring PUMA to call the vendor to make all changes. With the new software, Karen King, the company's data warehouse specialist, creates and generates the reports she needs, as she needs them. Instead of taking a day or more, she can produce a report in an hour or less.[19]

Executive Information Systems

Although similar to a DSS, an **executive information system (EIS)** is customized for an individual executive. These systems provide specific information for strategic decisions. For example, a CEO's EIS may include special spreadsheets that present financial data comparing the company to its principal competitors and graphs showing current economic and industry trends.

Expert Systems

An **expert system** gives managers advice similar to what they would get from a human consultant. Artificial intelligence enables computers to reason and learn to solve problems in much the same way humans do, using what-if reasoning. Although they are expensive and difficult to create, expert systems are finding their way into more companies as more applications are found. Lower-end expert systems can even run on PDAs like the Palm Pilot. Top-of-the-line systems help airlines appropriately deploy aircraft and crews, critical to the carriers' efficient operations. The cost of hiring enough people to do these ongoing analytical tasks would be prohibitively expensive. Expert systems have also been used to help explore for oil, schedule employee work shifts, and diagnose illnesses. Some expert systems take the place of human experts, whereas others assist them.

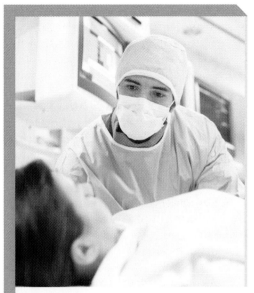

© ROYALTY-FREE/CORBIS

CONCEPT *in Action*

Decision support systems help businesses by providing quantitative data and predictive models that aid problem solving and decision making. Now the health-care industry wants this technology in hospitals to improve the practice of medicine. Spearheading the effort for a clinical decision-support system is the American Medical Informatics Association, which believes a national DSS could help physicians with diagnosing and treating illnesses. *What are the pros and cons to having medical professionals rely on a DSS for help in treating patients?*

executive information system (EIS)
A management support system that is customized for an individual executive; provides specific information for strategic decisions.

expert system
A management support system that gives managers advice similar to what they would get from a human consultant; it uses artificial intelligence to enable computers to reason and learn to solve problems in much the same way humans do.

office automation system
An information system that uses information technology tools such as word processing systems, e-mail systems, cell phones, PDAs, pagers, and fax machines to improve communications throughout an organization.

Office Automation and Communication Systems

Today's **office automation systems** assist all levels of employees and enable managers to handle most of their own communication. Many of the newer devices now combine multiple functions. The key elements, many of which have been around for years and others that are fairly new, include:

- Word processing systems for producing written messages.
- E-mail systems for communicating directly with other employees and customers and transferring computer files.
- Departmental scheduling systems for planning meetings and other activities.
- Cell phones for providing telephone service away from the office, as in cars. Newer models can receive and send e-mail and text messages, graphics, and browse the Web.
- Personal digital assistants (PDAs) such as Palm Pilots that replace paper personal planners and address books; these can also transfer data to and from the user's PC and run some software. Newer models can also handle e-mail and Web browsing, and some include cell phones.
- Wireless e-mail devices, such as the Blackberry.
- Pagers that notify employees of phone calls. Some pagers can display more extensive written messages sent from a computer network.
- Voice-mail systems for recording, storing, and forwarding phone messages.
- Facsimile (fax) systems for delivering messages on paper within minutes.
- Electronic bulletin boards and computer conferencing systems for discussing issues with others who are not present.

CONCEPT *in Action*

While e-mail has long provided professionals with free, instant communication, the standard in office messaging may soon require postage. AOL and Yahoo are testing systems that provide preferential, secure e-mail delivery for companies that pay from one-fourth of a cent to a penny for each message. Providers say pay e-mail will eliminate spam and generate millions in revenues as traffic grows to over 300 billion messages daily by 2009. *Will businesses be willing to pay for e-mail?*

© ICONICA/GETTY IMAGES

concept check

What are the main types of management information systems, and what does each do?

Differentiate between the types of management support systems, and give examples of how companies use each.

How can office automation systems help employees work more efficiently?

Office automation systems also make telecommuting and home-based businesses possible. An estimated 8 million people work at home, using microcomputers and other high-tech equipment to keep in touch with the office. Instead of spending time on the road twice a day, telecommuters work at home two or more days a week. We'll take a closer look at the rising number of mobile workers in the Trends in Information Technology section.

Technology Management and Planning

4   **How can technology management and planning help companies optimize their information technology systems?**

With the help of computers, people have produced more data in the last 30 years than in the previous 5,000 years combined. Companies today make sizable investments in information technology to help them manage this overwhelming amount of data, convert the data into knowledge, and deliver it to the people who need it. In many cases, however, the companies do not reap the desired benefits from these expenditures. Among the typical complaints from senior executives are that the company is spending too much and not getting adequate performance and payoff from IT investments, these investments do not relate to business strategy, the firm seems to be buying the latest technology for technology's sake, and communications between IT specialists and IT users are poor.

Optimize IT!

Managing a company's enterprise-wide IT operations, especially when those often stretch across multiple locations, software applications, and systems, is no easy task. IT managers must deal not only with on-site systems; they must also oversee the networks and other technology, such as PDAs and cell phones that handle e-mail messaging, that connect staff working at locations ranging from the next town to another continent. At the same time, IT managers face time constraints and budget restrictions, making their jobs even more challenging.

Growing companies may find themselves with a decentralized IT structure that includes many separate systems and duplication of efforts. A company that wants to enter or expand into e-commerce needs systems that are flexible enough to adapt to this changing marketplace. Security for equipment and data is another critical area, which we will cover later in the chapter.

The goal is to develop an integrated, company-wide technology plan that balances business judgment, technology expertise, and technology investment. IT planning requires a coordinated effort among a firm's top executives, IT managers, and business-unit managers to develop a comprehensive plan. Such plans must take into account the company's strategic objectives and how the right technology will help managers reach those goals.

Technology management and planning go beyond buying new technology. Today companies are cutting IT budgets so that managers are being asked to do more with less. They are implementing projects that leverage their investment in the technology they already have, finding ways to maximize efficiency and optimize utilization.

Managing Knowledge Resources

As a result of the proliferation of information, we are also seeing a major shift from information management to a broader view that focuses on finding opportunities in and unlocking the value of intellectual rather than physical assets. Whereas *information management* involves collecting, processing, and condensing information, the more difficult task of **knowledge management (KM)** focuses on researching, gathering, organizing, and sharing an organization's collective knowledge to improve productivity, foster innovation, and gain competitive advantage. Some companies are even creating a new position, *chief knowledge officer*, to head up this effort.[20]

Companies use their IT systems to facilitate the physical sharing of knowledge. But better hardware and software are not the answer to KM. KM is not technology based but rather a business practice that uses technology. Technology alone does not constitute KM, nor is it the solution to KM. Rather, it facilitates KM. Executives with successful KM initiatives understand that KM is not a matter of buying a major software application that serves as a data depository and coordinates all of a company's intellectual capital. According to Melinda Bickerstaff, vice president of knowledge management at Bristol-Myers Squibb, any such "leading with technology" approach is a sure path to failure. "Knowledge management has to be perceived as a business problem solver, not as an abstract concept," Bickerstaff explains.

Effective KM calls for an interdisciplinary approach that coordinates all aspects of an organization's knowledge. It requires a major change in behavior as well as technology to leverage the power of information systems, especially the Internet, and a company's human capital resources. The first step is creating an information culture through organizational structure and rewards that promotes a more flexible, collaborative way of working and communicating. However, moving an organization toward KM is no easy task, but well worth the effort in terms of creating a more collaborative environment, reducing duplication of effort, and increasing shared knowledge. The benefits can be significant in terms of growth, time, and money.

At Bristol-Meyers Squibb (BMS), a major pharmaceutical company, Bickerstaff began the KM implementation by looking for specific information-related problems to solve so that the company would save time and/or money. For example, she learned that company scientists were spending about 18 percent of their time searching multiple databases to find patents and other information. Simply integrating the relevant databases gave researchers the ability to perform faster searches. A more complex project involved compiling the best practices of drug development teams with the best FDA approval rates so that other groups could benefit. Rather than send forms that could be easily set aside, Bickenstaff arranged to conduct interviews and lessons-learned sessions. The information was then developed into interesting articles rather than dry corporate reports.[21]

Technology Planning

A good technology plan provides employees with the tools they need to perform their jobs at the highest levels of efficiency. The first step is a general needs assessment, followed by ranking of projects and the specific choices of hardware and software.

knowledge management (KM)
The process of researching, gathering, organizing, and sharing an organization's collective knowledge to improve productivity, foster innovation, and gain competitive advantage.

Exhibit 16.6 > **Questions for IT Project Planning**

- What are the company's overall objectives?
- What problems does the company want to solve?
- How can technology help meet those goals and solve the problems?
- What are the company's IT priorities, both short and long term?
- What type of technology infrastructure (centralized or decentralized) best serves the company's needs?
- Which technologies meet the company's requirements?
- Are additional hardware and software required? If so, will they integrate with the company's existing systems?
- Does the system design and implementation include the people and process changes, in addition to the technological ones?
- Do you have the in-house capabilities to develop and implement the proposed applications, or should you bring in an outside specialist?

concept check

What are some ways a company can manage its technology assets to its advantage?

Differentiate between information management and knowledge management. What steps can companies take to manage knowledge?

List the key questions managers need to ask when planning technology purchases.

Exhibit 16.6 poses some basic questions departmental managers and IT specialists should ask when planning technology purchases.

Once managers identify the projects that make business sense, they can choose the best products for the company's needs. The final step is to evaluate the potential benefits of the technology, in terms of efficiency and effectiveness. For a successful project, you must evaluate and restructure business processes, choose technology, develop and implement the system, and manage the change processes to best serve your organizational needs. Installing a new IT system on top of inefficient business processes is a waste of time and money!

Protecting Computers and Information

 What are the best ways to protect computers and the information they contain?

Have you ever lost a term paper you'd worked on for weeks because your hard drive crashed or you deleted the wrong file? You were upset, angry, and frustrated. Multiply that paper and your feelings hundreds of times over, and you can understand why companies must protect computers, networks, and the information they store and transmit from a variety of potential threats. For example, security breaches of corporate information systems—from human hackers or electronic versions like viruses and worms—are increasing at an alarming rate. The ever-increasing dependence on computers requires plans that cover human error, power outages, equipment failure—and, since September 11, 2001, terrorist attacks. To withstand natural disasters such as major fires, earthquakes, and floods, many companies install specialized fault-tolerant computer systems.

Disasters are not the only threat to data. A great deal of data, much of it confidential, can easily be tapped or destroyed by anyone who knows about computers. Keeping your networks secure from unauthorized access—from internal as well as external sources—requires formal security policies and enforcement procedures. The increasing popularity of mobile devices—laptops, handheld computers, PDAs, and digital cameras—and wireless networks requires calls for new types of security provisions.

In response to mounting security concerns, companies have increased spending on technology to protect their IT infrastructure and data. Along with specialized hardware and software, companies need to develop specific security strategies that take a proactive approach to prevent security and technical problems before they start. However, a recent survey of 8,200 IT executives worldwide revealed that only 37 percent have an information security strategy, whereas about 24 percent of the others plan to develop one by 2007.[22]

Data Security Issues

Unauthorized access into a company's computer systems can be expensive, and not just in monetary terms. The FBI estimates that computer crime cost U.S. businesses

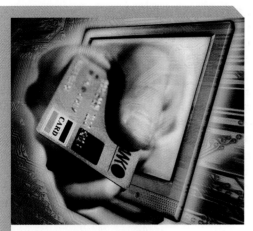

CONCEPT *in Action*

Data security is under constant attack. Almost 40 million Visa and MasterCard accounts were stolen when cybercrooks breached third-party CardSystems Solutions in 2005. MySpace users face personal and data-related peril as the social networking site struggles against online predators. Even the United States military fell victim when information on over 26 million veterans and 2 million troops was temporarily lost in a 2006 data breach. *What impact do identity theft and other data-security issues have on global networking and e-commerce?*

more than $67 billion in 2005, compared to just $450 million in 2001. The most costly categories of threats were worms, viruses, and Trojan horses (defined later in this section); computer theft, financial fraud, and unauthorized network access. The 2005 FBI Computer Crime survey also reports that almost all U.S. businesses reported at least one security issue, and almost 20 percent incurred 20 or more incidents.[23] In the 11-year period from 1995 to 2005, the number of vulnerabilities (susceptibility to security deficiencies) reported to the CERT Coordination center, a federally financed information center for computer security information, has climbed from 171 to almost 6,000 in 2005. Most of the increase occurred since 2000, when the number of vulnerabilities was only 1,090.[24]

Computer crooks are becoming more sophisticated all the time, finding new ways to get into ultrasecure sites. "As companies and consumers continue to move towards a networked and information economy, more opportunity exists for cybercriminals to take advantage of vulnerabilities on networks and computers," says Chris Christiansen, program vice president at technology research firm IDC.[25] Whereas early cybercrooks were typically amateur hackers working alone, the new ones are more professional and often work in gangs to commit large-scale Internet crimes for large financial rewards. The Internet, where criminals can hide behind anonymous screen names, has increased the stakes and expanded the realm of opportunities to commit identity theft and similar crimes. Catching such cybercriminals is difficult, and fewer than 5 percent are caught.[26] (We discuss Internet crime in more detail in the online enrichment chapter, "Using the Internet for Business Success" at **http://www. thomsonedu.com/introbusiness/gitman.**)

Firms are taking steps to prevent these costly computer crimes and problems, which fall into several major categories:

- *Unauthorized access and security breaches.* Whether from internal or external sources, unauthorized access and security breaches are a top concern of IT managers. These can create havoc with a company's systems and damage customer relationships. Unauthorized access also includes employees, who can copy confidential new-product information and provide it to competitors or use company systems for personal business that may interfere with systems operation. About 45 percent of respondents to the 2005 FBI Computer Crime Survey experienced such internal intrusions.[27] Networking links also make it easier for someone outside the organization to gain access to a company's computers.

  One of the latest forms of cybercrime involves secretly installing keylogging software via software downloads, e-mail attachments, or shared files. This software then copies and transmits a user's keystrokes—passwords, PINs, and other personal information—from selected sites, such as banking and credit card sites to thieves. Recently Brazilian police broke up a keylogging scheme that stole about $4.7 million from 200 bank accounts. In Russia, thieves used similar techniques to withdraw more than $1 million from French bank accounts. Keylogging is increasing in the United States as well. The number of such incidents reported in December 2005 was 6,000, up 65 percent from December 2004, and about 10 million computers may be infected with keyloggers.[28]

- *Computer viruses, worms, and Trojan horses.* Computer viruses and related security problems such as worms and Trojan horses are among the top threats to business and personal computer security. A computer program that copies itself into other software and can spread to other computer systems, a **computer virus** can destroy the contents of a computer's hard drive or damage files. Another form is called a *worm* because it spreads itself automatically from computer to computer. Unlike a virus, a worm doesn't require e-mail to replicate and transmit itself into

computer virus
A computer program that copies itself into other software and can spread to other computer systems.

other systems. It can enter through valid access points. In January 2006, for example, two mass-mailing worms were discovered: Email-Worm.Win32.Nyxem.e and Email-Worm.Win32.VB.bi. These worms delete certain types of files and attempt to disable security-related and file sharing software.

Trojan horses are programs that appear to be harmless and from legitimate sources but trick the user into installing them. When run, they damage the user's computer. For example, a Trojan horse may claim to get rid of viruses but instead infects the computer. Other forms of Trojan horses provide a "trapdoor" that allows undocumented access to a computer, unbeknownst to the user. Trojan horses do not, however, infect other files or self-replicate.[29]

Viruses can hide for weeks or months before starting to damage information. A virus that "infects" one computer or network can be spread to another computer by sharing disks or by downloading infected files over the Internet. To protect data from virus damage, virus protection software automatically monitors computers to detect and remove viruses. Program developers make regular updates available to guard against newly created viruses. In addition, experts are becoming more proficient at tracking down virus authors, who are subject to criminal charges.

- *Deliberate damage to equipment or information.* For example, an unhappy employee in the purchasing department could get into the computer system and delete information on past orders and future inventory needs. The sabotage could severely disrupt production and the accounts payable system. Willful acts to destroy or change the data in computers are hard to prevent. To lessen the damage, companies should back up critical information.

- *Spam.* Although you might think that *spam,* or unsolicited and unwanted e-mail, is just a nuisance, it also poses a security threat to companies. Viruses spread through e-mail attachments that can accompany spam e-mails. On most days, spam accounts for 70 to 80 percent of all e-mail sent, according to Postini, a message filtering company. In contrast, mail that carries viruses represents just 1.5 percent of all messages on average. The volume of spam has increased five times since just 2003. Spam is now clogging blogs, instant messages, and cell phone text messages as well as e-mail inboxes. Spam presents other threats to a corporation: lost productivity and expenses from dealing with spam—like opening the messages, searching for legitimate messages that special spam filters keep out. The cost of spam is more than $50 billion worldwide and $17 billion a year for U.S. businesses. Spam filters can greatly reduce the amount of spam that gets through, but spammers continually find new ways to bypass them.[30]

- *Software and media piracy.* The copying of copyrighted software programs, games, and movies by people who haven't paid for them is another form of unauthorized use. Piracy, defined as using software without a license, takes revenue away from the company that developed the program—usually at great cost. It includes making counterfeit CDs to sell as well as personal copying of software to share with friends. The Business Software Alliance estimates that the global software piracy rate is 35 percent and the cost to software manufacturers is more than $33 billion a year worldwide. Of that amount, U.S. firms accounted for $6.6 billion. The highest rates of piracy, ranging from 92 percent to 87 percent, are in Vietnam, Ukraine, China, Indonesia, and Russia. In the United States, it is 21 percent.

Software firms take piracy seriously and go after the offenders. Countries are also becoming more vigilant in cracking down on pirates. In February 2006, 19 people in the United States, Australia, and Barbados were charged with illegally distributing copyrighted computer software, games, and movies valued at more than $6.5 million over the Internet. Microsoft recently filed lawsuits against eight eBay sellers who sold counterfeit versions of Windows and Office.[31] Many also make special arrangements so that large companies can get multiple copies of programs at a lower cost rather than use illegal copies. Companies are continually adding features such as anti-piracy codes and "shells" to limit the use of the software on other computers and prevent unauthorized copying of CDs. Recent

CONCEPT *in Action*

The first computer hackers were mostly harmless techno-geeks and curious experimenters testing the limits of a new electronic medium. Today the world of computing is brimming with cybercriminals—sophisticated computer experts that defraud millions by exploiting network security holes. Cybercrimes may involve phishing, pharming, scumware, spyware, spam, viruses and other threats to sensitive personal and corporate data. *What can businesses and individuals do to avoid becoming victims of cybercrime?*

versions of Microsoft's Windows XP and Office require "activation" to get full use and limit the user in the number of times he or she can start up a system without registering the software. Other companies like Intuit and Adobe require customers to obtain a special product activation number before using their software.

Preventing Problems

Creating formal written information security policies to set standards and provide the basis for enforcement is the first step in a company's security strategy. Unfortunately, a recent survey of 8,200 IT executives worldwide revealed that only 37 percent have such plans, and just 24 percent of the other companies intend to develop one within a year. Without information security strategies in place, companies spend too much time in a reactive mode—responding to crises—and don't focus enough on prevention.[32]

Security plans should have the support of top management, and then follow with procedures to implement the security policies. Because IT is a dynamic field with ongoing changes to equipment and processes, it's important to review security policies often. Some security policies can be handled automatically, by technical measures, whereas others involve administrative policies that rely on humans to perform them. Examples of administrative policies are "Users must change their passwords each quarter" and "End users will update their virus signatures at least once a week." Exhibit 16.7 shows the types of security measures companies use to protect data.

Preventing costly problems can be as simple as regularly backing up applications and data. Companies should have systems in place that automatically back up the company's data every day and store copies of the backups off-site. In addition, employees should back up their own work regularly. Another good policy is to maintain a complete and current database of all IT hardware, software, and user details to make it easier to manage software licenses and updates and diagnose problems. In many cases, IT staff can use remote access technology to automatically monitor and fix problems, as well as update applications and services.

Companies should never overlook the human factor in the security equation. One of the most common ways that outsiders get into company systems is by posing as an employee, first getting the staffer's full name and username from an e-mail message, then calling the help desk to ask for a forgotten password. Crooks can also get passwords by viewing them on notes attached to a desk or computer monitor, using machines that employees leave logged on when they leave their desks, and leaving laptop computers with sensitive information unsecured in public places.

Exhibit 16.7 > Methods Companies Use to Protect Data

Method	Percent Using
Anti-virus software	98%
Firewalls	91
Anti-spyware	75
Spam filters	75
VPNs	46
Intrusion prevention or detection systems	23
Smart cards	7
Biometrics	4

Exhibit 16.8 > Procedures to Protect IT Assets

- Develop a comprehensive plan and policies that include portable as well as fixed equipment.
- Protect the equipment itself with stringent physical security measures to the premises.
- Protect data using special *encryption* technology to encode confidential information so only the recipient can decipher it.
- Stop unwanted access from inside or outside with special authorization systems. These can be as simple as a password or as sophisticated as fingerprint or voice identification.
- Install *firewalls,* hardware or software designed to prevent unauthorized access to or from a private network.
- Monitor network activity with intrusion-detection systems that signal possible unauthorized access, and document suspicious events.
- Conduct periodic IT audits to catalog all attached storage devices as well as computers.
- Use technology that monitors ports for unauthorized attached devices and turn off those that are not approved for business use.
- Train employees to troubleshoot problems in advance, rather than just react to them.
- Hold frequent staff-training sessions to teach correct security procedures, such as logging out of networks when they go to lunch and changing passwords often.
- Make sure employees choose sensible passwords, at least six and ideally eight characters long, containing numbers, letters, and punctuation marks. Avoid dictionary words and personal information.
- Establish a database of useful information and FAQs (frequently asked questions) for employees so they can solve problems themselves.
- Develop a healthy communications atmosphere.

Portable devices, from handheld computers and PDAs to tiny plug-and-play flash drives and other storage devices (including MP3 players) pose security risks as well. They are often used to store sensitive data such as passwords, bank details, and calendars. PDAs can spread viruses when users download virus-infected documents to their company computers. Research firm Gartner Inc. reports that only about 10 percent of companies have policies covering security for these portable devices. "It's actually a fairly big problem," says Eric Ouellet, Gartner's vice president of research for security. "You've got so much space on these things now. You can go for an iPod or MP3 player and you've got 60 GB or more on them. You can put a small database on them. It's just a matter of time before we hear about someone losing data because of this."[33]

Imagine the problems that could arise if an employee saw a calendar entry on a PDA like "meeting re: layoffs," an outsider saw "meeting about merger with ABC Company," or an employee lost a flash drive containing files about marketing plans for a new product. Manufacturers are responding to IT managers' concerns about security by adding password protection and encryption to flash drives. Companies can also use flash drive monitoring software that prevents unauthorized access on PCs and laptops.

Companies have many ways to avoid an IT meltdown, as Exhibit 16.8 demonstrates. Further discussion of protecting confidential data is covered in the online chapter, "Using the Internet for Business Success," at **http://www.thomsonedu.com/introbusiness/gitman.**

Keep IT Confidential: Privacy Concerns

The very existence of huge electronic file cabinets full of personal information presents a threat to our personal privacy. Until recently, our financial, medical, tax, and other records were stored in separate computer systems. Computer networks make it easy to pool these data into data warehouses. Companies also sell the information they collect about you from sources like warranty registration cards, credit-card records, registration at Web sites, personal data forms required to purchase online, and grocery store discount club cards. Telemarketers can combine data from different sources to create fairly detailed profiles of consumers.

The September 11, 2001, tragedy raised additional privacy concerns. In its aftermath, the government began looking for ways to improve domestic-intelligence collection and analyze terrorist threats within the United States. Sophisticated database applications that look for hidden patterns in a group of data, a process called **data mining**, increase the potential for tracking and predicting people's daily activities. Legislators and privacy activists worry that such programs as this and ones that eavesdrop electronically could lead to excessive government surveillance that encroaches on personal privacy. The stakes are much higher as well: Errors in data

data mining
Sophisticated database applications that look for hidden patterns in a group of data to help track and predict future behavior.

CONCEPT *in Action*

At the heart of the computer-privacy dilemma is the tradeoff between confidentiality and convenience. Today's tech-savvy consumers are increasingly willing to give out personal information in exchange for greater shopping, download, and user benefits. Entrusting personal data to online merchants eliminates repeat data entry, enables greater personalization of Web sites, and produces remarkably relevant cross-selling and search results. *Can consumers have both convenience and privacy, or will they ultimately have to choose one or the other?*

© ROYALTY-FREE/CORBIS

mining by companies in business may result in a consumer being targeted with inappropriate advertising, whereas a governmental mistake in tracking suspected terrorists could do untold damage to an unjustly targeted person.

Increasingly, consumers are fighting to regain control of personal data and how that information is used. Privacy advocates are working to block sales of information collected by governments and corporations. For example, they want to prevent state governments from selling driver's license information and supermarkets from collecting and selling information gathered when shoppers use barcoded plastic discount cards. With information about their buying habits, advertisers can target consumers for specific marketing programs.

The challenge to companies is to find a balance between collecting the information they need while at the same time protecting individual consumer rights. Most registration and warranty forms that ask questions about income and interests have a box for consumers to check to prevent the company from selling their names. Many companies now state their privacy policies to ensure consumers that they will not abuse the information they collect. Regulators are taking action against companies that fail to respect consumer privacy. In March 2006, New York State sued Gratis Internet for selling information acquired through site visitor registrations to outside e-mail marketers—despite clearly stating on the site that Gratis "does not . . . sell/rent e-mails." Hundreds of millions of marketing e-mails bombarded those whose information was shared without their knowledge.[34] We'll return to the topic of protecting consumer privacy in the online chapter, "Using the Internet for Business Success," at **http://www.thomsonedu.com/introbusiness/gitman**.

concept check

Describe the different threats to data security.

How can companies protect information from destruction and unauthorized use?

Why are privacy rights advocates alarmed over the use of techniques such as data warehouses and data mining?

Trends in Information Technology

6 What are the leading trends in information technology?

Information technology is a continually evolving field. The fast pace and amount of change, coupled with IT's broad reach, make it especially challenging to isolate industry trends. From the time we write this chapter to the time you read it—as little as six months—new trends will appear and those that seemed important may fade. However, some trends that are reshaping today's IT landscape are digital forensics, the shift to a distributed workforce, and the increasing use of grid computing.

Cyber Sleuthing: A New Style of Crime Busting

What helped investigators bring suit against Enron, Merck's Vioxx, and the BTK killer? Digital evidence taken from an individual's computer or corporate network—Web pages, pictures, documents, and e-mails are part of a relatively new science called *digital forensics*. Digital forensics software safeguards electronic evidence used in investigations by creating a duplicate of a hard drive that an investigator can search by keyword, file type, or access date. Clients can have professional investigators from a firm like Guidance Software access suspect hard drives—Guidance makes EnCase, a forensic software tool used by 17,000 clients including 90 percent of all law-enforcement investigators— or they can buy the software for around $2,400 and do it themselves.[35] The Managing Change Box discusses how companies are using digital forensics today.

But nowadays digital sleuthing is not limited to cops. Companies like Microsoft and J. P. Morgan Chase have their own secret in-house digital forensics teams. And what if you're in New York and need to seize a hard drive in Hong Kong? No problem. Over 75 members of the Fortune 500 now use technology that allows them to search hard drives remotely over their corporate networks. Digital forensics makes it possible to track down those who steal corporate data and intellectual property. Broadcom, a semiconductor chip designer, used computer forensics to investigate and apprehend former employees who were attempting to steal trade secrets. In the process, Broadcom gathered incriminating e-mails, including deleted documents, that gave it solid evidence to use the 1986 Federal Computer Fraud and Abuse Act to stop the former employees from starting up a rival firm.[36]

However, there is a downside to having these advanced capabilities. If this kind of software falls into the wrong hands, sophisticated hackers could access corporate

MANAGING CHANGE

New Software Tool Unearths Your Secrets

Cyber-crimes in our technologically driven world are on the increase— identity theft, pornography, and sexual predator victim access, to name a few. The FBI's computer analysis response team confirms their case-load has tripled to over 5,000 cases in 2005. To keep up with the changing world we live in, law enforcement, corporations, and government agencies have turned to new crime-fighting tools, one of the most effective being digital forensics.

The leader in this new technology is Guidance Software, founded in 1997 to develop solutions that search, identify, recover, and deliver digital information in a forensically sound and cost-effective manner. Headquartered in Pasadena, California, the company employs 285 people at offices and training facilities in Washington, DC; San Francisco, California; Houston, Texas; New York, New York; and Liverpool, England. The company's more than 20,000 high-profile clients include leading police agencies, government investigation and law enforcement agencies, and Fortune 1000 corporations in the financial service, insurance, high-tech and consulting firms, health care, and utility industries.

Guidance Software's suite of EnCase® solutions is the first computer forensics tool able to provide world-class electronic investigative capabilities for large-scale complex investigations. Law enforcement officers, government/corporate investigators, and consultants around the world can now benefit from computer forensics that exceed anything previously available. The software offers an investigative infrastructure that provides network-enabled investigations, enterprise-wide integration with other security technologies, and powerful search and collection tools. With EnCase, clients can conduct digital investigations, handle large-scale data collection needs, and respond to external attacks.

McAfee, a leading developer of security software, achieved significant results almost immediately after implementing EnCase. "EnCase Enterprise saved us more than $1 million in the first six months of its use," says Ted Barlow, McAfee's vice president of risk management. "It also allowed us to complete a critical merger and acquisition discovery issue that would have been impossible with any other software or service options in the market today."

Guidance Software also helps reduce corporate and personal liability when investigating computer-related fraud, intellectual property theft, and employee misconduct. It protects against network threats like hackers, worms, and viruses, and hidden threats such as malicious code.

In response to increases in the number and scope of discovery requests, Guidance Software developed its eDiscovery Suite. The software package dramatically improves the practice of large-scale discovery— the identification, collection, cataloging, and saving of evidence— required in almost every major legal case these days. eDiscovery integrates with other litigation-support software to significantly decrease the time for corporations to accomplish these tasks. At the same time, it improves regulatory compliance and reduces disruption. The result is many millions of dollars in cost savings.[37]

Critical Thinking Questions
- How is Guidance Software responding to and helping to manage changes in our technology-driven world?
- What other types of forensics software do you foresee a need for in the future? Do you think there are ethical issues in using forensics software, and why?

networks and individual computers as easily as taking candy from a baby—and the victims would not even know it was happening. In an age of corporate wrongdoing, sexual predators, and computer porn, your hard drive will tell investigators everything they need to know about your behavior and interests, good and bad. Cyber-sleuthing means we are all potential targets of digital forensics. As evidenced by the huge increase in identity theft, personal privacy—once an unassailable right—is no longer as sacred as it once was.

The Distributed Workforce

In 2003, Agilent Technologies shuttered 48 sales offices. Was this a sign that the company was in trouble? Far from it. Instead of maintaining expensive offices in multiple locations, Agilent sent those employees home to work and adopted a new model for its employees: the distributed workforce. Employees have no permanent office space and work from home or on the road. Now almost three-quarters of Agilent employees work from remote locations part- or full-time. Some have not met in person with their managers for several years. Yet the shift to virtual workers has been a huge success. Not only does Agilent save about 60 percent on its personnel and related costs, but it also has happier, more productive employees.

Agilent is not alone in recognizing the benefits of distributed workers, especially in companies that depend on knowledge workers. According to the Work Design Collaborative LLC in Prescott, Arizona, currently about 12 percent of all workers in the United States fall into this category, and in urban areas the number could be as high as 15 percent. By 2012, it could reach 40 percent overall as long commutes, high gas costs, and better connecting tools and technologies make this an attractive option for many workers who like the flexibility. Already employees use the Internet to conduct videoconferenced meetings and collaborate on teams that span the globe. On the down side, working from home can also mean being available 24/7—although most workers consider the trade-off well worth it.

Remote workers account for about 40 percent of IBM's and 33 percent of AT&T's employees. Intel also has a successful virtual-work program that has been popular with working parents. "Technology allows working remotely to be completely invisible," says Laura Dionne, the company's director of supply-chain transformation. At Boeing, 8,000 employees participate in the virtual-work program, and it has been a critical factor in attracting and retaining younger workers. Almost half of Sun Microsystems' employees are "location-independent," reducing real estate costs by $300 million. Additional benefits for Sun are higher productivity from these workers and the ability to hire the best talent. "Our people working these remote schedules are the happiest employees we have, and they have the lowest attrition rates," says Bill MacGowan, senior vice president for human resources at Sun. "Would I rather settle on someone mediocre in the Bay Area, or get the best person in the country who is willing to work remotely?"[38]

Grid Computing Offers Powerful Solutions

How can smaller companies that occasionally need to perform difficult and large-scale computational tasks find a way to accomplish their projects? They can turn to *grid computing*, also called *utility computing* or *peer-to-peer computing*. Grid technology provides a way to divide the job into many smaller tasks and distribute them to a virtual supercomputer consisting of many small computers linked into a common network. Combining multiple desktop machines results in computing power that exceeds supercomputer speeds. A hardware and software infrastructure clusters and integrates computers and applications from multiple sources, harnessing unused power in existing PCs and networks. The grid structure distributes computational resources but maintains central control of the process. A central server acts as a team leader and traffic monitor. The controlling cluster server divides a task into subtasks, assigns the work to computers on the grid with surplus processing power, combines the results, and moves on to the next task until the job is finished. Exhibit 16.9 shows how a typical grid setup works.

Exhibit 16.9 > How Grid Computing Works

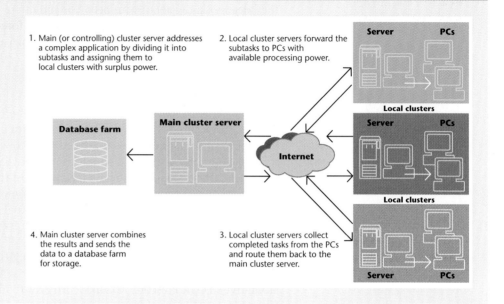

1. Main (or controlling) cluster server addresses a complex application by dividing it into subtasks and assigning them to local clusters with surplus power.

2. Local cluster servers forward the subtasks to PCs with available processing power.

4. Main cluster server combines the results and sends the data to a database farm for storage.

3. Local cluster servers collect completed tasks from the PCs and route them back to the main cluster server.

With utility computing, any company—large or small—can access the software and computer capacity on an as-needed basis. As John Meyer, vice president of brand strategy at software company Computer Associates, asks, "Why should manufacturers pay millions of dollars to run their computer infrastructure, when they can pay on demand for the amount of IT resources they actually consume?"[39]

IBM, Sun Microsystems, and Hewlett-Packard are among the companies providing as-needed grid services. Although grid computing appears similar to outsourcing or on-demand software from ASPs, it has two key differences:

- Pricing is set per-use, whereas outsourcing involves fixed-price contracts.
- Grid computing goes beyond hosted software and includes computer and networking equipment as well as services.

Grids provide a very cost-effective way to provide computing power for complex projects in areas such as weather research and financial and biomedical modeling. Because the computing infrastructure already exists—grids tap into computer capacity that is otherwise unused—the cost is quite low. The increased interest in grid technology will contribute to high growth. In the global financial services sector alone, capital investment in grid computing is projected to rise from about $88 million in 2005 to $1.2 billion by 2010.[40]

Companies are setting up internal grids as well as tapping into the grids of outside companies. Bank of America, for example, uses grid computing to perform hundreds of thousands of complex calculations daily related to derivative trading. The grid efficiently computes profit and loss and runs thousands of market scenarios to analyze risk—tasks it could not complete in time without the grid setup. "We can now more efficiently use the computing power that we have available to us in the bank, and that allows us to scale up considerably," explains Andy Bishop, head of liquid products and technology at the firm. Other uses for grid computing include a global cross-business grid. "Lots of different businesses around the bank can now pitch in and use this capacity to calculate what they need over a 24-hour day, [and be indifferent to and unaware of] the location of the computer power they are accessing. This is particularly helpful when business units are located in different time zones."[41]

concept check

How are companies and other organizations using digital forensics to obtain critical information?

Why do companies find that productivity rises when they offer employees the option of joining the virtual workforce?

What advantages does grid computing offer a company? What are some of the downsides to using this method?

Summary of Learning Goals

1 How has information technology transformed business and managerial decision making?

Businesses depend on information technology (IT) for everything from running daily operations to making strategic decisions. Companies must have management information systems that gather, analyze, and distribute information to the appropriate parties, including employees, suppliers, and customers. These systems are comprised of different types of computers that collect data and process it into usable information for decision making. Managers tap into databases to access the information they need, whether for placing inventory orders, scheduling production, or preparing long-range forecasts. They can compare information about the company's current status to its goals and standards. Company-wide enterprise resource planning systems that bring together human resources, operations, and technology are becoming an integral part of business strategy.

2 Why are computer networks an important part of today's information technology systems?

Today companies use networks of linked computers that share data and expensive hardware to improve operating efficiency. Types of networks include local area networks (LANs), wide area networks (WANs), and wireless local area networks (WLANs). Intranets are private WANs that allow a company's employees to communicate quickly with each other and work on joint projects, regardless of their location. Companies are finding new uses for wireless technologies like handheld computers, cell phones, and e-mail devices. Virtual private networks (VPNs) give companies a cost-effective secure connection between remote locations by using public networks like the Internet.

3 What types of systems make up a typical company's management information system?

A management information system consists of a transaction processing system, management support systems, and an office automation system. The transaction processing system (TPS) collects and organizes operational data on the firm's activities. Management support systems help managers make better decisions. They include an information-reporting system that provides information based on the data collected by the TPS to the managers who need it; decision support systems that use models to assist in answering "what if" types of questions; and expert systems that give managers advice similar to what they would get from a human consultant. Executive information systems are customized to the needs of top management. All employees benefit from office automation systems that facilitate communication by using word processing, e-mail, fax machines, and similar technologies.

4 How can technology management and planning help companies optimize their information technology systems?

To get the most value from IT, companies must go beyond simply collecting and summarizing information. Technology planning involves evaluating the company's goals and objectives and using the right technology to reach them. IT managers must also evaluate the existing infrastructure to get the best return on the company's investment in IT assets. Knowledge management (KM) focuses on sharing an organization's collective knowledge to improve productivity and foster innovation. Some companies establish the position of chief knowledge officer to head up KM activities.

5 What are the best ways to protect computers and the information they contain?

Because companies are more dependent on computers than ever before, they need to protect data and equipment from natural disasters and computer crime. Types of computer crime include unauthorized use and access, software piracy, malicious damage, and computer viruses. To protect IT assets, companies should prepare written security policies. They can use technology such as virus protection, firewalls, and employee training in proper security procedures. They must also take steps to protect customers' personal privacy rights.

6 What are the leading trends in information technology?

IT is a dynamic industry, and companies must stay current on the latest trends to identify ones that help them maintain their competitive edge, such as digital forensics, the distributed workforce, and grid computing. With digital forensics techniques, corporations, government agencies, attorneys, and lawmakers can obtain evidence from computers and corporate networks—Web pages, pictures, documents, and e-mails. Many knowledge workers now work remotely rather than from an office. Companies adopting the distributed workforce model gain many benefits, such as cost savings, more satisfied and productive employees, and increased employee retention. Grid computing harnesses the idle power of desktop PCs and other computers to create a virtual supercomputer. A company can access the grid on an as-needed basis instead of investing in its own supercomputer equipment. Outsourcing a portion of the company's computing needs provides additional flexibility and cost advantages. Companies can also set up internal grids.

Key Terms

application service providers (ASPs)   538
batch processing   541
chief information officer (CIO)   530
computer network   534
computer virus   547
data mart   542
data mining   550
data warehouse   541
database   533
decision support system (DSS)   542
enterprise portal   536
executive information system (EIS)   543
expert system   543
information technology (IT)   530

intranet   535
knowledge management (KM)   545
knowledge worker   533
local area network (LAN)   535
managed service providers (MSPs)   540
management information system (MIS)   533
management support system (MSS)   541
office automation system   543
online (real-time) processing   541
transaction processing system (TPS)   540
virtual private networks (VPNs)   538
wide area network (WAN)   535

Preparing for Tomorrow's Workplace: SCANS

1. How has information technology changed your life? Describe at least three areas (both personal and school/work related) where having access to better information has improved your decisions. Are there any negative effects? What steps can you take to manage information better? (Information, Technology)

2. Visit or conduct a phone interview with a local small-business owner about the different ways her or his firm uses information technology. Prepare a brief report on your findings that includes the hardware and software used, how it was selected, benefits of technology for the company, and any problems in implementing or using it. (Interpersonal, Information)

3. Your school wants to automate the class registration process. Prepare a memo to the dean of information systems describing an integrated information system that would help a student choose and register for courses. Make a list of the different groups that should be involved and questions to ask during the planning process. Include a graphic representation of the system that shows how the data becomes useful information. Indicate the information a student needs to choose courses and its sources. Explain how several types of management support systems could help students make better course decisions. Include ways the school could use the information it collects from this system. Have several students present their plans to the class, which will take the role of university management in evaluating them. (Resources, Systems, Technology)

4. You recently joined the IT staff of a midsized consumer products firm. After a malicious virus destroys some critical files, you realize that the company lacks a security strategy and policies. Outline the steps you'd take to develop a program to protect data and the types of policies you'd recommend. How would you present the plan to management and employees to encourage acceptance? (Resources, Technology)

5. **Team Activity** Should companies outsource IT? Some executives believe that IT is too important to outsource and that application service providers (ASPs) don't have a future. Yet spending for ASP subscriptions, MSPs, and other forms of IT outsourcing continue to grow. What's your position? Divide the class into groups designated "for" or "against" outsourcing and/or ASPs. Have them research the current status of ASPs using publications like *CIO* and *Computerworld* and Web sites like ASPnews.com, **http://www.aspnews.com.** (Interpersonal, Information)

Ethics Activity

As the owner of a small but growing business, you are concerned about employees misusing company computers for personal matters. Not only does this cost the company in terms of employee productivity, but it also ties up bandwidth that may be required for company operations and exposes the firm's networks to increased risks of attacks from viruses, spyware, and other malicious programs. Installing e-mail monitoring and Web security and filtering software programs would allow you to track e-mail and Internet use, develop use policies, block access to inappropriate sites, and limit the time employees can conduct personal online business. At the same time, the software will protect your IT networks from many types of security concerns, from viruses to Internet fraud. You are concerned, however, that employees will take offense and consider such software an invasion of privacy.

Using a Web search tool, locate articles about this topic and then write responses to the following questions. Be sure to support your arguments and cite your sources.

Ethical Dilemma: Should you purchase employee monitoring software for your company, and on what do you base your decision? If you install the software, do you have an obligation to tell employees about it? Explain your answers and suggest ways to help employees understand your rationale.

Sources: Lindsay Gerdes, "You Have 20 Minutes to Surf. Go," *Business Week*, December 26, 2005, p. 16; "Nothing Personal," *Global Cosmetic Industry*, August 2005, p. 19; and "Tips on Keeping Workplace Surveillance from Going to Far," *HR Focus*, January 2006, p. 10.

Working the Net

1. Enterprise resource planning (ERP) is a major category of business software. Visit the site of one of the following companies: SAP (**http://www.sap.com**); Oracle and Peoplesoft, which Oracle acquired, (**http://www.oracle.com**); or SSA Global (**http://www.ssaglobal.com**). Prepare a short presentation for the class about the company's ERP product offerings and capabilities. Include examples of how companies use the ERP software. What are the latest trends in ERP?

2. What can intranets and enterprise portals accomplish for a company? Find out by using such resources as Brint.com's Intranet Portal, **http://www.brint.com/ Intranets.htm**, and *Intranet Journal,* **http://www.intranetjournal.com/.** Look for case studies that show how companies apply this technology. Summarize the different features an intranet or enterprise portal provides.

3. Learn more about the CERT Coordination Center (CERT/CC), which serves as a center of Internet security expertise. Explore its Web site, **http://www.cert.org.**

What are the latest statistics on incidents reported, vulnerabilities, security alerts, security notes, mail messages, and hotline calls? What other useful information does the site provide to help a company protect IT assets?

4. Research the latest developments in computer security at *Computerworld*'s site, **http://computerworld.com/securitytopics/security.** What types of information can you find here? Pick one of the categories in this area (Cybercrime, Encryption, Disaster Recovery, Firewalls, Hacking, Privacy, Security Holes, Viruses and Worms, and VPN) and summarize your findings.

5. How can someone steal your identity? Using information at the Federal Trade Commission's central Web site for information about identity theft, **http://www.consumer.gov/idtheft/**, compile a list of the ways thieves can access key information to use your identity. What steps should you take if you've been a victim of identity theft? Summarize key provisions of federal laws dealing with this crime and the laws in your state.

Creative Thinking Case >

Novartis' Prescription for Invoice Processing

What do you do when you have more than 600 business units operating through 360 independent affiliates in 140 countries around the world—processing complex invoices in various languages and currencies? You seek out the best technology solution to make the job easier.

At global pharmaceutical giant Novartis, the IT department is a strategic resource, a community of 2,000 people serving 63,000 customers in 200 locations and 25 data centers. Because most of the company's invoices come from international suppliers they have differences in design, language, taxes, and currency. Consequently, many ended up as "query items" requiring manual resolution by Novartis accounting staff—which delayed payments and made those invoices extremely costly to process. In fact, finance personnel spent so much of their time resolving queried invoices that other work suffered. A solution was badly needed.

To maximize its investment Novartis needed a flexible solution that would meet its current and future needs and function in other business departments in a variety of geographic locations. It should provide fast accurate document capture, multi-language support, and extend to other types of information—such as faxes and electronic data—in addition to paper documents. Finally, in order to obtain financing for the project, return on investment (ROI) was required within 9 months of project implementation.

Input*Accel* for Invoices from Captiva Software Corporation was the answer. The software extracts data from paper documents, applies intelligent document recognition (IDR) technology to convert them to digital images, and sends relevant data to enterprise resource planning (ERP), accounts payable (A/P), and other back-end management systems. The specialized Input*Accel* server manages output by recognizing and avoiding holdups in the workflow process. It also ensures if a server goes offline, others will carry on functioning, thus avoiding downtime.

Now Novartis scans incoming invoices at a centrally located site, and the images are transmitted to the Input*Accel* for Invoices server for image improvement. Invoice data is then extracted and validated against supplier information. Most invoices are transferred directly for payment, with relatively few invoices requiring transfer to one of three accounts payable clerks who deal with queries manually.

Thanks to IT, overall efficiency has increased, processing errors are reduced, and accounting personnel can use their time and expert knowledge for more meaningful tasks than resolving invoice errors. For Novartis it is "mission accomplished."

Critical Thinking Questions

- What factors contributed to Novartis' invoice processing being so complex?
- How did IT help the company solve that problem?
- What other uses and functions does Input*Accel* serve and how will this be useful to Novartis over the long term? (You may want to visit the Captiva Web site, **http://www.captiva.com**, for more information on Input*Accel*'s capabiities.)

Sources: Adapted from Kathryn Balint, "Captiva's Paper Chase Paying Off," *San Diego Union-Tribune,* December 9, 2005, pp. C1, C5. Captiva corporate Web site, http://www.captivasoftware.com, March 22, 2006; "Processing Invoices From Around the World," *Captiva Software,* http://www.captivasoftware.com, February 2, 2006; Novartis corporate Web site, http://www.novartis.com March 20, 2006.

Video Case >

Big Blue Turns Small Businesses into Large Competitors

"It is like music, once it is in place and working," says Susan Jain, a marketing executive with IBM Global Services. She is talking about Enterprise Resource Planning or ERP, complex software modules that do just about everything to help companies run more efficiently and competitively. Because the old systems were separate and unable to relate one piece of information to another, information systems weren't integrated. Day-to-day operations were cumbersome, and management reporting was often inaccurate. ERP makes information accessible immediately, greatly improving overall operating efficiency, speeding up internal reporting procedures, and reducing the time to bring new products to market.

ERP is a "relational database" that consolidates all aspects of information gathering and dissemination. For example, ERP software modules can receive an order, check raw-material stocks to make sure the order can be produced, order any additional materials that may be needed, place the order in the production schedule, and send it to shipping and invoicing. Its human resources module will even help hire and train the staff needed to produce and fulfill the order.

Companies no longer need to predict way in advance what products customers might want, or keep tons of product on warehouse shelves gathering dust. ERP literally allows companies to "build to order"—in fact IBM has an automobile customer that does just that. It builds to order, one car at a time, eliminating the customary guessing games of what colors or styles may be popular at a given time.

Even small and midsized companies are investing in ERP systems to enable them to grow and compete, despite the substantial investment in time and dollars. The software costs around $1 million, with an equal expenditure required for new hardware. Implementation, training, and education can cost two to three times that amount and take years in the case of very large companies. IBM Global Financing offers a broad array of financing offerings to companies wanting to acquire ERP systems.

In recent years, however, IBM has begun shifting to an "Information as a Service" strategy whereby companies can tap into IBM's resources in numerous areas to transform their businesses. Under this model, customers don't have to make large up-front investments in technology to access cutting edge software but can pay as they go.

Other benefits include quick start-up and enhanced flexibility. IBM sees software-as-a-service as critical to remaining competitive, projecting that this market will grow 25 percent a year through 2010.

For example, high growth at Skyworks Solutions, a Massachusetts telecommunications firm, was outpacing the firm's IT capability. It turned to IBM Global Services for on-demand, hosted ERP applications management services that would provide greater flexibility to respond to marketplace changes and access to high quality IT resources. Along with improved efficiency, the new IT services brought Skyworks cost savings of 18 percent.

Critical Thinking Questions

- As the manager responsible for production-related IT for a large manufacturing company, you recommend the acquisition of ERP software to your bosses. Be specific in describing how such a system would help your company be more competitive and the types of information you would want such a system to integrate.

- Explain how you would propose to track performance to justify the cost of installing such a system. What options do you have other than purchasing the system outright?

- What market and other changes have led to IBM's new emphasis on software-as-a-service? Discuss the implications of this shift, both for IBM and the customers who use IBM's on demand and other services.

Sources: Adapted from material in the video: "Are You Ready for IBM?" and Steve Hamm and Spencer E. Ante, "Beyond Blue," *Business Week*, April 18, 2005, http://www.businessweek.com; "IBM—On Demand Business," *IBM*, http://www-306.ibm.com, April 3, 2006; "Skyworks: Achieving Business and IT Flexibility with Applications on Demand," *IBM*, January 23, 2006, http://www-306.ibm.com; and "Solutions: IBM Software as Services," *IBM*, http://www-304.ibm.com, April 3, 2006.

Hot Links Address Book

If you want to know the definition of a computer term or more about a particular topic, Webopedia has the answer: **http://www.webopedia.com**

Can't tell a LAN from a WAN? Learn more about networking at About.com's Networking pages, **http://www.compnetworking.about.com/mbody.htm**

To find out if that e-mail alerting you to another virus threat is real or a hoax, check out the latest information at **http://www.snopes.com**

How can you "inoculate" your computer against viruses? Symantec's Security Response has the latest details on virus threats and security issues: **http://www.symantec.com/avcenter**

Darwin.com is an online magazine that offers helpful articles and Executive Guides that provide a good introduction to key IT topics: **http://www.darwinmag.com**

Curious about how companies are using on-demand grid computing? Read the Grid FAQ at the Grid Computing Technology Centre, and then check out some of the many links to other resources. **http://www.gridcomputing.com**

CHAPTER 17

Using Financial Information and Accounting

Learning Goals

After reading this chapter, you should be able to answer these questions:

1. Why are financial reports and accounting information important, and who uses them?

2. What are the differences between public and private accountants, and are public accountants subject to new regulations?

3. What are the six steps in the accounting cycle?

4. In what terms does the balance sheet describe the financial condition of an organization?

5. How does the income statement report a firm's profitability?

6. Why is the statement of cash flows an important source of information?

7. How can ratio analysis be used to identify a firm's financial strengths and weaknesses?

8. What major trends affect the accounting industry today?

Exploring Business Careers
Evie Wexler
The Little Guys

Evie Wexler describes the early days of The Little Guys, the home electronics business she and her husband started in the mid-1990s, as "days of rapid weight gain." "We were so busy we didn't lunch until four o'clock. By that time we were starving so, you know, we'd eat like twelve hot dogs. It was crazy hours." Like many entrepreneurs, the Wexlers brought in a few key people early on, and that core group handled every aspect of the fledgling business. From constructing individual "living rooms" that allow their customers to better envision a particular home theater setup in their own homes to raising capital for start-up costs, they soon became experts in all facets of running a business. One area that required expertise, and quickly, was accounting. As you know, without money a business cannot survive, and to prosper, business owners must use that money wisely.

Since the beginning of The Little Guys, the Wexlers, who are both involved in the business's finances, have worked with a public accountant who provides the financial experience. Initially, when they were most concerned with cultivating trust in their manufacturers and the buying public, he gave them the financial tools and background necessary to keep the cash flow steady, making the business a successful venture. As the business developed and they became more comfortable with the workings of the financial world, the accountant's role shifted. Once the Wexlers knew the ins and outs of balance sheets, and assets and liabilities, he became more of a consultant on issues of financial forecasting. Today, they meet with him at least once a quarter to review the

financials. He continues to handle the more complex financial calculations, such as figuring adjustments based on depreciation of their assets; however, much of the time, she laughs, he just "reassures us that we're doing okay," and that their financial decisions are sound.

For the day-to-day bookkeeping, the Wexlers use QuickBooks, a common accounting software package. They use it to prepare the reports that then allow them to conduct daily financial essentials such as paying bills and calculating payroll. In addition, the software has extensive reporting capabilities that provide the Wexlers with an up-to-date snapshot of the business's finances. These reports allow them to evaluate the financial health of the company and make decisions based on that evaluation. They can capture trends and adjust their spending or inventory based on those results. Ultimately, they can be responsive to changes in the business as those changes affect their finances.

In the years since the Wexlers first took The Little Guys from dream to reality, they have grown steadily into one of the most well-known home electronics dealers in the Chicago area. It hasn't always been easy, with many of the early days stretching on more than 16 hours a day. But sound financial practices have made them a success, allowing them to develop relationships with both their suppliers and their customers.

This chapter examines the role of accounting in business, how accounting contributes to a company's overall success, the three primary financial statements, and careers in accounting.

Financial information is central to every organization. To operate effectively, businesses must have a way to track income, expenses, assets, and liabilities in an organized manner. Financial information is also essential for decision-making. Managers prepare financial reports using accounting, a set of procedures and guidelines for companies to follow when preparing financial reports. Unless you understand basic accounting concepts, you will not be able to "speak" the standard financial language of businesses.

Accounting: More than Numbers

1 Why are financial reports and accounting information important, and who uses them?

Prior to 2001, accounting topics rarely made the news. That changed when Enron Corp.'s manipulation of accounting rules to improve its financial statements hit the front pages of newspapers. The company filed bankruptcy in 2001, and its former top executives were charged with multiple counts of conspiracy and fraud. Arthur Andersen, Enron's accounting firm, was indicted and convicted of obstruction of justice and in 2002, the once respected firm went out of business. Soon financial abuses at other well-known companies—among them Tyco, Adelphia, WorldCom, and more recently Krispy Kreme and HealthSouth—surfaced. Top executives at these and other companies were accused of knowingly flouting accepted accounting standards to inflate current profits and increase their compensation. Many were subsequently convicted:

- Andrew Fastow, Enron's former chief financial officer, and Ben Glisan Jr., its former treasurer—Pleaded guilty and received prison terms of 10 and 5 years, respectively. In May 2006, Ken Lay, Enron's former chairman, was convicted of all Enron-related charges. Jeffrey Skilling, the former CEO, was convicted of 19 charges.
- Bernard Ebbers, WorldCom's CEO—25 years in prison for conspiracy, securities fraud, and filing false reports with regulatory agencies—crimes that totaled $11 billion in accounting fraud.
- Adelphia Communications executives John Rigas and Timothy Rigas—Sentenced to 15 and 20 years in prison, respectively, for looting and fraud.
- Tyco's CEO L. Dennis Kozlowski—Fined $70 million and sentenced to 8 to 25 years.[1]

These and other cases raised critical concerns about the independence of those who audit a company's financial statements, questions of integrity and public trust, and issues

CONCEPT *in Action*

The conviction of former Enron executives Kenneth Lay and Jeffrey Skilling closed a chapter on one of the largest accounting scandals in history. The ex-chiefs misled investors and employees about Enron's financial health by fabricating earnings and hiding billions of dollars of debt in off-balance-sheet entities. While tens of thousands of people lost jobs and investment savings during Enron's collapse, the event also sparked a period of reform. *What are the lessons of Enron for executives and accounting professionals?*

© ASSOCIATED PRESS, AP

with current financial reporting standards. Investors suffered as a result, because the crisis in confidence sent stock prices tumbling, and companies lost billions in value.

So it's no surprise that more people are paying attention to accounting topics! We now recognize that accounting is the backbone of any business, providing a framework to understand the firm's financial condition. Reading about accounting irregularities, fraud, audit (financial statement review) shortcomings, out-of-control business executives, and bankruptcies, we have become very aware of the importance of accurate financial information and sound financial procedures.

All of us—whether we are self-employed, work for a local small business or a multinational Fortune 100 firm, or are not currently in the workforce—benefit from knowing the basics of accounting and financial statements. We can use this information to educate ourselves about companies before interviewing for a job or buying a company's stock or bonds. Employees at all levels of an organization use accounting information to monitor operations. They also must decide which financial information is important for their company or business unit, what those numbers mean, and how to use them to make decisions.

This chapter starts by discussing why accounting is important for businesses and for users of financial information. Then it provides a brief overview of the accounting profession and the post-Enron regulatory environment. Next it presents an overview of basic accounting procedures, followed by a description of the three main financial statements—the balance sheet, the income statement, and the statement of cash flows. Using these statements, we then demonstrate how ratio analysis of financial statements can provide valuable information about a company's financial condition. Finally, the chapter explores current trends affecting the accounting profession.

Accounting Basics

accounting
The process of collecting, recording, classifying, summarizing, reporting, and analyzing financial activities.

Accounting is the process of collecting, recording, classifying, summarizing, reporting, and analyzing financial activities. It results in reports that describe the financial condition of an organization. All types of organizations—businesses, hospitals, schools, government agencies, and civic groups—use accounting procedures. Accounting provides a framework for looking at past performance, current financial health, and possible future performance. It also provides a framework for comparing the financial positions and financial performances of different firms. Understanding how to prepare and interpret financial reports will enable you to evaluate two computer companies and choose the one that is more likely to be a good investment.

The accounting system shown in Exhibit 17.1 converts the details of financial transactions (sales, payments, purchases, and so on) into a form that people can use

---

Exhibit 17.1 > The Accounting System

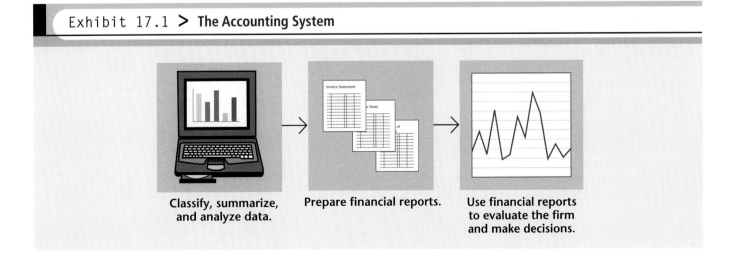

Classify, summarize, and analyze data.

Prepare financial reports.

Use financial reports to evaluate the firm and make decisions.

to evaluate the firm and make decisions. Data become information, which in turn becomes reports. These reports describe a firm's financial position at one point in time and its financial performance during a specified period. Financial reports include *financial statements,* such as balance sheets and income statements, and special reports, such as sales and expense breakdowns by product line.

Who Uses Financial Reports?

The accounting system generates two types of financial reports, as shown in Exhibit 17.2: internal and external. Internal reports are used within the organization. As the term implies, **managerial accounting** provides financial information that managers inside the organization can use to evaluate and make decisions about current and future operations. For instance, the sales reports prepared by managerial accountants show how well marketing strategies are working. Production cost reports help departments track and control costs. Managers may prepare very detailed financial reports for their own use and provide summary reports to top management.

Financial accounting focuses on preparing external financial reports that are used by outsiders, that is, people who have an interest in the business but are not part of management. Although these reports also provide useful information for managers, they are used primarily by lenders, suppliers, investors, and government agencies to assess the financial strength of a business.

To ensure accuracy and consistency in the way financial information is reported, accountants in the United States follow **generally accepted accounting principles (GAAP)** when preparing financial statements. The **Financial Accounting Standards Board (FASB)** is a private organization that is responsible for establishing financial accounting standards in the United States.

At the present time, there are no international accounting standards. Because accounting practices vary from country to country, a multinational company must make sure that its financial statements conform to both its own country's accounting standards and those of the parent company's country. Often another country's standards are quite different from U.S. GAAP. The U.S. Financial Accounting Standards Board (FASB) and the International Accounting Standards Board (IASB) are currently working together to develop global accounting standards that make it easier to compare financial statements of foreign-based companies. The Expanding Around the Globe box discusses the challenges involved in this effort.

managerial accounting
Accounting that provides financial information that managers inside the organization can use to evaluate and make decisions about current and future operations.

financial accounting
Accounting that focuses on preparing external financial reports that are used by outsiders such as lenders, suppliers, investors, and government agencies to assess the financial strength of a business.

generally accepted accounting principles (GAAP)
The financial accounting standards followed by accountants in the United States when preparing financial statements.

Financial Accounting Standards Board (FASB)
The private organization that is responsible for establishing financial accounting standards in the United States.

Exhibit 17.2 > Reports Provided by the Accounting System

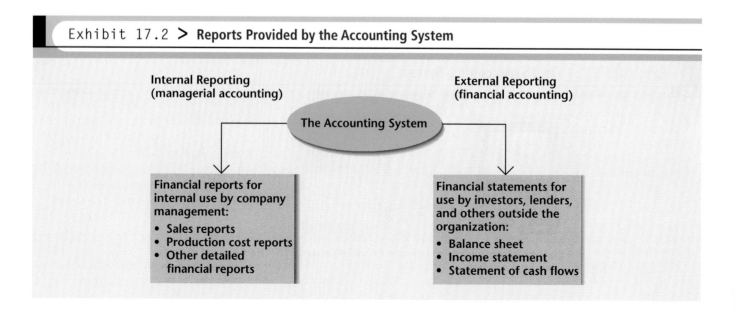

Internal Reporting
(managerial accounting)

External Reporting
(financial accounting)

The Accounting System

Financial reports for internal use by company management:
• Sales reports
• Production cost reports
• Other detailed financial reports

Financial statements for use by investors, lenders, and others outside the organization:
• Balance sheet
• Income statement
• Statement of cash flows

Moving Toward One World of Numbers

Imagine being treasurer of a major multinational company with significant operations in 10 other countries. Because the accounting rules in those countries don't conform to GAAP, your staff has to prepare nine sets of financial reports that comply with the host country's rules—and also translate the figures to GAAP for consolidation into the parent company's statements. It's a massive undertaking.

If the U.S. Financial Accounting Standards Board (FASB) and the International Accounting Standards Board (IASB) have their way, your task will be much easier in years to come. These groups are working together to develop international accounting standards that will remove disparities between national and international standards, improve the quality of financial information worldwide, and simplify comparisons of financial statements across borders for both corporations and investors.

In February 2006, the FASB and the IASB jointly published a Memorandum of Understanding (MOU) reaffirming the two organizations' desire to create uniform global accounting standards. "This document underscores our strong commitment to continue to work together with the IASB to bring about a common set of accounting standards that will enhance the quality, comparability, and consistency of global financial reporting, enabling the world's capital markets to operate more effectively," said Robert Herz, FASB's chairman. Sir David Tweedie, chairman of the IASB, agreed: "The pragmatic approach described in the MOU enables us to provide much-needed stability for companies using IFRS [the IASB's International Financial Reporting Standards] in the near term," he commented. (About 100 countries currently use IFRS, with more signing on each year.)

As they worked toward convergence, the board members decided to develop a new set of common standards, rather than try to reconcile the two standards. These new standards must be better than existing ones, not simply eliminate differences. Merging GAAP and IFRS into a consistent set of international accounting standards has proven to be very difficult because of different approaches used in the two sets.

However, the convergence project is moving ahead more quickly than the sponsoring groups anticipated. Raising capital outside a corporation's home country overseas will be easier for companies, because they will not have to restate their financial reports to conform to either GAAP or IFRS. Because the goal is to develop improved accounting standards, the boards take the big picture view in seeking solutions, regardless of whether they are GAAP or IFRS. Surprisingly—at least to many U.S. corporate executives—many of the new standards may be based on IFRS, not GAAP. "Companies need to pay attention to what's going on at the IASB, even if they operate only in the United States," advises FASB Chairman Herz. "The thinking of one board will influence the thinking of the other."[2]

Critical Thinking Questions

- Is it important to have a single set of international accounting standards for at least publicly owned companies? Defend your answer.
- How close are IASB and FASB to developing uniform global accounting standards? Use a search engine and also the archives of *CFO* magazine, http://www.cfo.com, to research this and summarize your findings.

Financial statements are the chief element of the **annual report**, a yearly document that describes a firm's financial status. Annual reports usually discuss the firm's activities during the past year and its prospects for the future. Three primary financial statements included in the annual report are discussed and shown later in this chapter:

- The balance sheet
- The income statement
- The statement of cash flows

The Accounting Profession

2 **What are the differences between public and private accountants, and are public accountants subject to new regulations?**

annual report
A yearly document that describes a firm's financial status and usually discusses the firm's activities during the past year and its prospects for the future.

When you think of accountants, do you picture someone who works in a back room, hunched over a desk, wearing a green eye shade and scrutinizing pages and pages of numbers? Although today's accountants still must love working with numbers, they now work closely with their clients to not only prepare financial reports but also help them develop good financial practices. Computers have taken the tedium out of the number crunching and data-gathering parts of the job and now offer powerful analytical tools as well. Therefore, accountants must keep up with information technology trends. The accounting profession has grown due to the increased complexity, size, and number of businesses and the frequent changes in the tax laws. Accounting is now a $40-plus billion industry. The more than 1.2 million accountants in the United States are classified as either public accountants or private (corporate) accountants. They work in public accounting firms, private industry, education, and government, and about 10 percent are self-employed.

Public Accountants

Independent accountants who serve organizations and individuals on a fee basis are called **public accountants**. Public accountants offer a wide range of services, including preparation of financial statements and tax returns, independent auditing of financial records and accounting methods, and management consulting. **Auditing**, the process of reviewing the records used to prepare financial statements, is an important responsibility of public accountants. They issue a formal *auditor's opinion* indicating whether the statements have been prepared in accordance with accepted accounting rules. This written opinion is an important part of the annual report.

The largest public accounting firms, called the Big Four, operate worldwide and offer a variety of business consulting services in addition to accounting services. In order of size, they are PricewaterhouseCoopers (PWC), Deloitte & Touche Tohmatsu International (DTT), KPMG International, and Ernst & Young (E&Y). A former member of this group, Arthur Andersen, disbanded in 2002 as a result of the Enron scandal.

To become a **certified public accountant (CPA)**, an accountant must complete an approved bachelor's degree program and pass a test prepared by the American Institute of Certified Public Accountants (AICPA). Each state also has requirements for CPAs such as several years' on-the-job experience and continuing education. Only CPAs can issue the auditor's opinion on a firm's financial statements. Most CPAs first work for public accounting firms and later may become private accountants or financial managers. Of the about 330,000 accountants who belong to the AICPA, 40 percent work in public accounting firms and 43 percent in business and industry.[3]

Private Accountants

Accountants employed to serve one particular organization are **private accountants**. Their activities include preparing financial statements, auditing company records to be sure employees follow accounting policies and procedures, developing accounting systems, preparing tax returns, and providing financial information for management decision making. Whereas some private accountants hold the CPA designation, managerial accountants also have a professional certification program. Requirements to become a **certified management accountant (CMA)** include passing an examination.

public accountants
Independent accountants who serve organizations and individuals on a fee basis.

auditing
The process of reviewing the records used to prepare financial statements and issuing a formal *auditor's opinion* indicating whether the statements have been prepared in accordance with accepted accounting rules.

certified public accountant (CPA)
An accountant who has completed an approved bachelor's degree program, passed a test prepared by the American Institute of Certified Public Accountants, and met state requirements. Only a CPA can issue an auditor's opinion on a firm's financial statements.

private accountants
Accountants who are employed to serve one particular organization.

certified management accountant (CMA)
A managerial accountant who has completed a professional certification program, including passing an examination.

Reconfiguring the Accounting Environment

Although our attention was focused on big-name accounting scandals, an epidemic of accounting irregularities was also taking place in the wider corporate arena. The number of companies restating annual financial statements grew at an alarming rate, tripling from 1997 to 2002. In the wake of the numerous corporate financial scandals, Congress and the accounting profession took major steps to prevent future accounting irregularities. These measures targeted the basic ways, cited by a report from the AICPA, that companies massaged financial reports through creative, aggressive, or inappropriate accounting techniques, including:

- Committing fraudulent financial reporting.
- Unreasonably stretching accounting rules to significantly enhance financial results.
- Following appropriate accounting rules, but using loopholes to manage financial results.

Why did companies willfully push accounting to the edge—and over it—to artificially pump up revenues and profits? Looking at the companies involved in the recent scandals, some basic similarities have emerged:

- A company culture of arrogance and above-average tolerance for risk.
- Interpretation of accounting policies to their advantage and manipulation of the rules to get to a predetermined result and conceal negative financial information.
- Compensation packages tied to financial or operating targets, making executives and managers greedy and pressuring them to find sometimes questionable ways to meet what may have been overly optimistic goals.
- Ineffective checks and balances, such as audit committees, boards of directors, and financial control procedures, that were not independent from management.
- Centralized financial reporting that was tightly controlled by top management, increasing the opportunity for fraud.
- Financial performance benchmarks that were often out of line with the companies' industry.
- Complicated business structures that clouded how the company made its profits.
- Cash flow from operations that seemed out of line with reported earnings. (You'll learn about this important difference between cash and reported earnings in the sections on the income statement and statement of cash flows.)
- Acquisitions made quickly, often to show growth rather than for sound business reasons; management focused more on buying new companies than making the existing operations more profitable.[4]

Companies focused on making themselves look good in the short term, doing whatever was necessary to top past performance and to meet the expectations of investment analysts, who project earnings, and investors, who panic when a company misses the analysts' forecasts. Executives who benefited when stock prices rose had no incentive to question the earnings increases that led to the price gains.

These number games raised serious concerns about the quality of earnings and questions about the validity of financial reports. Investors discovered to their dismay that they could neither assume that auditors were adequately monitoring their clients' accounting methods nor depend on the integrity of published financial information.

Better Numbers Ahead

Since 2002 a number of accounting reforms have been put in place to set better standards for accounting, auditing, and financial reporting. Investors, now aware of the possibility of various accounting shenanigans, are avoiding companies that use complicated financial structures and off-the-books financing.

CONCEPT *in Action*

The Sarbanes-Oxley Act has done much to re-deem store the public's trust in corporate fi-nancial reporting, but it may not do enough to recover bonuses bestowed on CEOs unde-servedly. Because the Act's provision on executive forfeiture of bonuses is vague and doesn't allow shareholder lawsuits, many ex-chiefs like CA's Sanjay Kumar have not been required to pay back multimillion-dollar rewards acquired through fraudulent accounting. *Should the government increase federal regulation of accounting practices, or can business resolve such issues through self-regulation?*

Sarbanes-Oxley Act
Act passed in 2002 that sets new standards for auditor independence, financial disclosure and reporting, and internal controls; establishes an inde-pendent oversight board; and restricts the types of nonaudit services auditors can provide audit clients.

On July 30, 2002, the **Sarbanes-Oxley Act** went into effect. This law, one of the most extensive pieces of business legislation ever passed by Con-gress, was designed to start the economy on the road to recovery and address the investing public's lack of trust in corporate America. It redefines the public corporation–auditor relationship and restricts the types of ser-vices auditors can provide to clients. The Act clarifies auditor-independence issues, places increased accountability on a company's senior executives and management, strengthens disclosure of insider transactions (an em-ployee selling stock based on information not known by the public), and prohibits loans to executives.

A new, independent five-member Public Company Accounting Over-sight Board (PCAOB) was given the authority to set and amend auditing, quality control, ethics, independence, and other standards for audit reports. The Act specifies that all PCAOB members be financially literate. Two members must have their CPA designation, and the other three can-not be or have been CPAs. Appointed and overseen by the Securities and Exchange Commission (SEC), the PCAOB can also inspect accounting firms; investigate breaches of securities law, standards, competency, and conduct; and take disciplinary action. The Board registers public account-ing firms, as the Act now requires. Altering or destroying key audit docu-ments now carries felony charges and increased penalties.

Other key provisions of the Act cover the following areas:

- *Auditing standards.* The Board must include in its standards several requirements, such as maintaining audit work papers and other doc-umentation for audit reports for seven years, the review and ap-proval of audit reports by a second partner, and audit standards for quality control and review of internal control procedures.
- *Financial disclosure.* Companies must clearly disclose all transactions that may have a material current or future effect on their financial condition, including those that are off the books or with unconsoli-dated entities (related companies whose results the company is not required to combine with its own financial statements under current accounting rules). Management and major stockholders must disclose transac-tions such as sales of company stock within two days of the transaction. The company must disclose its code of ethics for senior financial executives. Any significant changes in a company's operations or financial condition must be disclosed "on a rapid and current basis."
- *Financial statement certification.* Chief executive officers and chief financial offi-cers must certify company financial statements, with severe criminal and civil penalties for false certification. If securities fraud results in restatement of finan-cial reports, these executives will lose any stock-related profits and bonuses they received prior to the restatement.
- *Internal controls.* Each company must have appropriate internal control proce-dures in place for financial reporting, and its annual report must include a report on implementation of those controls to assure the integrity of financial reports.
- *Consulting work.* The Act restricts the nonauditing work auditors may perform for an auditing client. In the past, the large accounting firms had expanded their role to include a wide range of advisory services that went beyond their tradi-tional task of validating a company's financial information. Conflicts of interest arose when the same firm earned lucrative fees for both audit and consulting work for the same client.[5]

Other regulatory organizations also took steps to prevent future abuses. In Sep-tember 2002, the AICPA Auditing Standards Board (ASB) issued expanded guidelines to help auditors uncover fraud while conducting audits. The New York Stock Exchange stiffened its listing requirements so that the majority of directors at listed companies must be independent and not employees of the corporation. Nor can auditors serve on clients' boards for five years. Companies listed in the Nasdaq marketplace cannot hire former auditors at any level for three years.

In response to the passage of Sarbanes-Oxley and other regulations, companies implemented new control measures and improved existing ones. The burdens in both cost and time have been considerable. Many companies had to redesign and restructure financial systems to improve efficiency. More than 60 percent of finance executives believe that their investment in increased controls has improved shareholder perceptions of their company's ethics. However, about one-third reported that costs would depress earnings and negatively affect stock prices.[6] The Managing Change box takes a closer look at how companies are responding to the implementation of Sarbanes-Oxley and its changes in audit and reporting requirements.

Has Sarbanes-Oxley been effective in reducing financial statement fraud? Results from a 2005 survey of certified fraud examiners are mixed. In terms of identifying financial statement fraud, 13 percent believe SarbOx has been very effective and another 52 percent consider it somewhat effective. However, they express concern that the immediate changes in corporate culture and attitudes may not last. About one-third believes that the initial high level of interest and oversight of corporate executives is already waning. The best strategies to prevent fraud are executives who promote a top-down tone of integrity, prosecution of those who commit fraud, and implementation of strict internal controls.[7]

> **concept check**
>
> Compare the responsibilities of public and private accountants. How are they certified?
>
> Summarize the major changes affecting accounting and corporate reporting and the reasons for them.

MANAGING CHANGE

SarbOx Gives CFOs a Big Headache

The Sarbanes-Oxley Act (SarbOx) has been a mixed blessing for accountants and financial executives. In addition to adding considerably to the responsibilities of a company's finance managers, compliance with the act has significantly increased the costs of running the finance function. The relationship between corporate financial executives and their external auditors has changed as well.

One of the most commonly voiced concerns is the massive documentation the Act requires, and numerous surveys support this. *CFO* magazine reports that workloads had increased substantially for 75 percent of respondents. The costs of complying are high as well, and according to the Financial Executives Institute, most companies spent more on compliance than expected. AMR Research reports that corporations spent an estimated $20 billion from 2002 to 2006 for SarbOx compliance. Every $1 billion in revenues generates about $1 million in compliance-related costs. The impact on a company's earnings can be quite significant. Companies with revenues over $500 million estimated that SarbOx cut into earnings by about 2 percent; at smaller companies, that figure rose to 4.5 percent. Personnel costs—additional internal auditors and accountants to handle documentation, testing, and certification of internal controls—account for a significant portion of the spending. As Bob Ross, controller of retailer Urban Outfitters, says, SarbOx compliance calls for "documenting countless procedures and processes, which to most employees of this company are second nature. In 2004, such compliance reduced the company's earnings per share at least 1 cent and also made his job "a struggle to explain common sense."

Although finance executives feel that the costs of SarbOx compliance may outweigh the benefits, investors disagree. A critical benefit of

SarbOx—and perhaps one of the most important—is in the area of investor confidence. "Obviously, to the extent 404 [a section of SarbOx] impacts earnings negatively, it's a concern," says Cynthia L. Richson, corporate governance officer for the $64.5 billion Ohio Public Employees Retirement System (OPERS). "On the other hand, who is measuring the cost of corruption and accounting scandals we've been through? Some cite that as contributing to a $7 trillion, even as high as $9 trillion, collapse in the capital markets."

Both financial managers and the PCAOB have called for an evaluation of the new regulations now that they have been in place for several years. Currently, all companies are subject to the same rules, when in fact what is appropriate to assess risks at one company may not be relevant at another. Suggestions to improve the Act include adjusting the level of testing to take risk into account and developing different compliance standards based on a company's size. Opponents of the latter change assert that smaller companies tend to have more problems with internal controls and financial reporting procedures. "The exemption from those rules would create a kind of free-fire zone on investors," said Damon Silvers, associate general counsel of the AFL-CIO.[8]

Critical Thinking Questions
- Should the Sarbanes Oxley Act be amended to provide different levels of compliance for smaller companies? Why or why not?
- What types of trade-offs do companies face in complying with Sarbanes-Oxley?

Basic Accounting Procedures

 What are the six steps in the accounting cycle?

Using generally accepted accounting principles, accountants record and report financial data in similar ways for all firms. They report their findings in financial statements that summarize a company's business transactions over a specified time period. As mentioned earlier, the three major financial statements are the balance sheet, income statement, and statement of cash flows.

People sometimes confuse accounting with bookkeeping. Accounting is a much broader concept. *Bookkeeping,* the system used to record a firm's financial transactions, is a routine, clerical process. Accountants take bookkeepers' transactions, classify and summarize the financial information, and then prepare and analyze financial reports. Accountants also develop and manage financial systems and help plan the firm's financial strategy.

The Accounting Equation

assets
Things of value owned by a firm.

liabilities
What a firm owes to its creditors; also called *debts.*

owners' equity
The total amount of investment in the firm minus any liabilities; also called *net worth.*

The accounting procedures used today are based on those developed in the late 15th century by an Italian monk, Brother Luca Pacioli. He defined the three main accounting elements as assets, liabilities, and owners' equity. **Assets** are things of value owned by a firm. They may be *tangible,* such as cash, equipment, and buildings, or *intangible,* such as a patent or trademarked name. **Liabilities**—also called *debts*—are what a firm owes to its creditors. **Owners' equity** is the total amount of investment in the firm minus any liabilities. Another term for owners' equity is *net worth.*

The relationship among these three elements is expressed in the accounting equation:

$$\text{Assets} - \text{Liabilities} = \text{Owners' equity}$$

The accounting equation must always be in balance (that is, the total of the elements on one side of the equals sign must equal the total on the other side).

Suppose you start a bookstore and put $10,000 in cash into the business. At that point, the business has assets of $10,000 and no liabilities. This would be the accounting equation:

Assets		Liabilities		Owners' equity
$10,000	=	$0	+	$10,000

The liabilities are zero and owners' equity (the amount of your investment in the business) is $10,000. The equation balances.

To keep the accounting equation in balance, every transaction must be recorded as two entries. As each transaction is recorded, there is an equal and opposite event so that two accounts or records are changed. This method is called **double-entry bookkeeping.**

double-entry bookkeeping
A method of accounting in which each transaction is recorded as two entries so that two accounts or records are changed.

Suppose that after starting your bookstore with $10,000 cash, you borrow another $10,000 from the bank. The accounting equation will change as follows:

Assets		Liabilities		Owners' equity	
$10,000	=	$0	+	$10,000	Initial equation
$10,000	=	$10,000	+	$0	Borrowing transaction
$20,000	=	$10,000	+	$10,000	Equation after borrowing

Now you have $20,000 in assets—your $10,000 in cash and the $10,000 loan proceeds from the bank. The bank loan is also recorded as a liability of $10,000 because it's a debt you must repay. Making two entries keeps the equation in balance.

The Accounting Cycle

The *accounting cycle* refers to the process of generating financial statements, beginning with a business transaction and ending with the preparation of the report. Exhibit 17.3 shows the six steps in the accounting cycle. The first step in the cycle is to analyze the data collected from many sources. All transactions that have a financial

Exhibit 17.3 > The Accounting Cycle

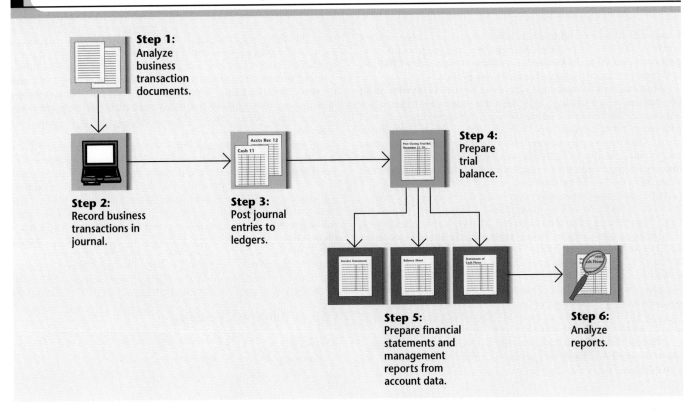

Step 1: Analyze business transaction documents.

Step 2: Record business transactions in journal.

Step 3: Post journal entries to ledgers.

Step 4: Prepare trial balance.

Step 5: Prepare financial statements and management reports from account data.

Step 6: Analyze reports.

impact on the firm—sales, payments to employees and suppliers, interest and tax payments, purchases of inventory, and the like—must be documented. The accountant must review the documents to make sure they're complete.

Next, each transaction is recorded in a *journal*, a listing of financial transactions in chronological order. The journal entries are then recorded in *ledgers*, which show

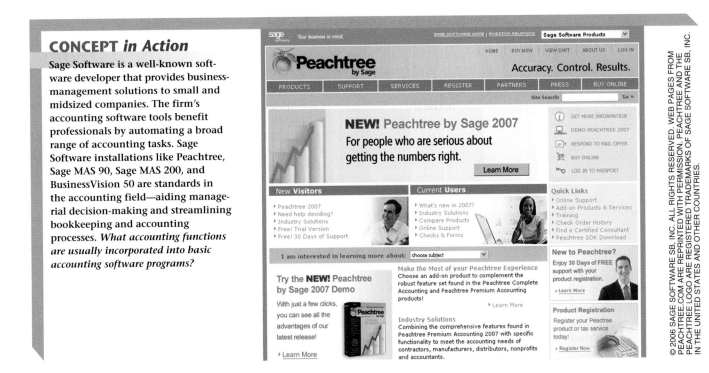

CONCEPT *in Action*

Sage Software is a well-known software developer that provides business-management solutions to small and midsized companies. The firm's accounting software tools benefit professionals by automating a broad range of accounting tasks. Sage Software installations like Peachtree, Sage MAS 90, Sage MAS 200, and BusinessVision 50 are standards in the accounting field—aiding managerial decision-making and streamlining bookkeeping and accounting processes. *What accounting functions are usually incorporated into basic accounting software programs?*

CPAs Dig Deep for Customer Service

Knowledge is power, and understanding what your customers want and how your firm can provide it often differentiates you from the competition. To obtain useful knowledge and outrun rivals, many CPA firms are looking to data mining tools and software systems.

What exactly is data mining? Well, it has nothing to do with going underground. It is a database application that "hunts down patterns in a group of data to predict future behavior," or, alternatively, "a tool with which a user can view specific figures within various company reports." Data mining goes beyond earlier database applications so that accountants can dig more deeply into client financial data, to gain meaningful insight into the company's financial condition and use this information to make better decisions.

In the past, only larger enterprises could afford pricey data mining tools and systems, as well as the database administrators to manage them. Today even small and midsized companies can afford these investigative tools. "We had been seeking a program to assist us in analyzing and reviewing all the results of our practice. . . . something not really report driven, but more on an analytical basis," said Joyce Kelstein, assistant controller at the 75-person, Princeton, New Jersey–based CPA firm, The Mercadien Group. After examining several programs, Kelstein's firm discovered Dynamic Software Solutions International's eAnalytics Portal. "It is state of the art, giving us the ability to manipulate and review and analyze literally any kind of data within our source program," she says.

According to Peter Kaufman, president of DSS International, a financial software reseller, the newest products consolidate several tools into one attractively priced package. "Before, everything was specific to each specific product—you might have an HR (human resources) package, an accounting system, and a time and billing or manufacturing system," he says. "You would have three different reporting tools, one for each. Basically, today, [eAnalytics Portal] will pull into a common desktop reporting . . . all the data together, so it really enhances the user's experience. Now these databases are close to being self-maintained, so it's pretty easy."

So how does this translate into improved customer service? With data mining software, CPAs can drill down into and analyze unstructured data to identify trends and patterns, creating reports that answer critical questions. Many data mining programs integrate with existing software at both CPA and client firms, further simplifying the process. Dashboard and scorecard features give CPAs quick access to required data without having to open the original financial statement or spreadsheet. Clients now want answers based on the most current financial data, and many data mining applications let CPAs access real-time as well as historical data. Such features help CPAs provide better quality advice to their customers and also manage their own practices more efficiently.[9]

Critical Thinking Questions:
- What important functions do data mining software serve for CPA firms?
- How can it become a valuable customer service tool?

---

increases and decreases in specific asset, liability, and owners' equity accounts. The ledger totals for each account are summarized in a *trial balance,* which is used to confirm the accuracy of the figures. These values are used to prepare financial statements and management reports. Finally, individuals analyze these reports and make decisions based on the information in them.

Computers in Accounting

Computerized accounting programs do many different things. Most accounting packages offer six basic modules that handle general ledger, sales order, accounts receivable, purchase order, accounts payable, and inventory control functions. Tax programs use accounting data to prepare tax returns and tax plans. Computerized point-of-sale terminals used by many retail firms automatically record sales and do some of the bookkeeping. The Big Four and many other large public accounting firms develop accounting software for themselves and for clients.

Accounting and financial applications typically represent one of the largest portions of a company's software budget. Accounting software ranges from off-the-shelf programs for small businesses to full-scale customized enterprise resource planning systems for major corporations. As the Customer Satisfaction and Quality box explains, small CPA firms are now using sophisticated IT applications like data mining to provide better service to clients.

> **concept check**
>
> Explain the accounting equation.
>
> Describe the six-step accounting cycle.
>
> What role do computers play in accounting?

The Balance Sheet

 4 In what terms does the balance sheet describe the financial condition of an organization?

The balance sheet, one of three financial statements generated from the accounting system, summarizes a firm's financial position at a specific point in time. It reports the resources of a company (assets), the company's obligations (liabilities), and the difference between what is owned (assets) and what is owed (liabilities), or owners' equity.

CONCEPT *in Action*

Krispy Kreme, the company that gave the world the hot-doughnut experience, hit a financial mudslide in 2004. Revelations of questionable accounting at the doughnut chain triggered SEC investigations, leading to numerous financial restatements and the shuffling of top financial officers. In one instance, the company's multimillion-dollar acquisition expenses landed injudiciously on its balance sheet as intangible assets, skewing earnings. *What items qualify as intangible assets?*

balance sheet
A financial statement that summarizes a firm's financial position at a specific point in time.

liquidity
The speed with which an asset can be converted to cash.

current assets
Assets that can or will be converted to cash within the next 12 months.

fixed assets
Long-term assets used by a firm for more than a year such as land, buildings, and machinery.

depreciation
The allocation of an asset's original cost to the years in which it is expected to produce revenues.

intangible assets
Long-term assets with no physical existence, such as patents, copyrights, trademarks, and goodwill.

The assets are listed in order of their **liquidity**, the speed with which they can be converted to cash. The most liquid assets come first, and the least liquid are last. Because cash is the most liquid asset, it is listed first. Buildings, on the other hand, have to be sold to be converted to cash, so they are listed after cash. Liabilities are arranged similarly: Liabilities due in the short term are listed before those due in the long term.

The balance sheet as of December 31, 2008, for Delicious Desserts, Inc., an imaginary bakery, is illustrated in Exhibit 17.4. The basic accounting equation is reflected in the three totals highlighted on the balance sheet: Assets of $148,900 equal the sum of liabilities and owners' equity ($70,150 + $78,750). The three main categories of accounts on the balance sheet are explained below.

Assets

Assets can be divided into three broad categories: current assets, fixed assets, and intangible assets. **Current assets** are assets that can or will be converted to cash within the next 12 months. They are important because they provide the funds used to pay the firm's current bills. They also represent the amount of money the firm can quickly raise. Current assets include:

- *Cash.* Funds on hand or in a bank.
- *Marketable securities.* Temporary investments of excess cash that can readily be converted to cash.
- *Accounts receivable.* Amounts owed to the firm by customers who bought goods or services on credit.
- *Notes receivable.* Amounts owed to the firm by customers or others to whom it lent money.
- *Inventory.* Stock of goods being held for production or for sale to customers.

Fixed assets are long-term assets used by the firm for more than a year. They tend to be used in production and include land, buildings, machinery, equipment, furniture, and fixtures. Except for land, fixed assets wear out and become outdated over time. Thus, they decrease in value every year. This declining value is accounted for through depreciation. **Depreciation** is the allocation of the asset's original cost to the years in which it is expected to produce revenues. A portion of the cost of a depreciable asset—a building or piece of equipment, for instance—is charged to each of the years in which it is expected to provide benefits. This practice helps match the asset's cost against the revenues it provides. Because it is impossible to know exactly how long an asset will last, estimates are used. They are based on past experience with similar items or IRS guidelines for assets of that type. Notice that, through 2008, Delicious Desserts has taken a total of $16,000 in depreciation on its bakery equipment.

Intangible assets are long-term assets with no physical existence. Common examples are patents, copyrights, trademarks, and goodwill. *Patents* and *copyrights* shield the firm from direct competition, so their benefits are more protective than productive. For instance, no one can use more than a small amount of copyrighted material without permission from the copyright holder. *Trademarks* are registered names that can be sold or licensed to others. One of Delicious Desserts' intangible assets is a trademark valued at $4,500. *Goodwill* occurs when a company pays more for an acquired firm than the value of its tangible assets. Delicious Desserts' other tangible asset is goodwill of $7,000.

Liabilities

Liabilities are the amounts a firm owes to creditors. Those liabilities coming due sooner—current liabilities—are listed first on the balance sheet, followed by long-term liabilities.

Exhibit 17.4 > Balance Sheet for Delicious Desserts

Delicious Desserts, Inc.
Balance Sheet as of December 31, 2008

Assets

Current assets:			
Cash			$15,000
Marketable securities			4,500
Accounts receivable		$45,000	
Less: Allowance for doubtful accounts		1,300	43,700
Notes receivable			5,000
Inventory			15,000
Total current assets			$ 83,200
Fixed assets:			
Bakery equipment		$56,000	
Less: Accumulated depreciation		16,000	$40,000
Furniture and fixtures		$18,450	
Less: Accumulated depreciation		4,250	14,200
Total fixed assets			54,200
Intangible assets:			
Trademark		$ 4,500	
Goodwill		7,000	
Total intangible assets			11,500
Total assets			**$148,900**

Liabilities and Owners' Equity

Current liabilities:			
Accounts payable		$30,650	
Notes payable		15,000	
Accrued expenses		4,500	
Income taxes payable		5,000	
Current portion of long-term debt		5,000	
Total current liabilities			$60,150
Long-term liabilities:			
Bank loan for bakery equipment		$10,000	
Total long-term liabilities			10,000
Total liabilities			**$ 70,150**
Owners' equity:			
Common stock (10,000 shares outstanding)		$30,000	
Retained earnings		48,750	
Total owners' equity			78,750
Total liabilities and owners' equity			**$148,900**

current liabilities
Short-term claims that are due within a year of the date of the balance sheet.

Current liabilities are those due within a year of the date of the balance sheet. These short-term claims may strain the firm's current assets because they must be paid in the near future. Current liabilities include:

- *Accounts payable.* Amounts the firm owes for credit purchases due within a year. This account is the liability counterpart of accounts receivable.
- *Notes payable.* Short-term loans from banks, suppliers, or others that must be repaid within a year. For example, Delicious Desserts has a six-month, $15,000 loan from its bank that is a note payable.

- *Accrued expenses.* Expenses, typically for wages and taxes, that have accumulated and must be paid at a specified future date within the year although the firm has not received a bill.
- *Income taxes payable.* Taxes owed for the current operating period but not yet paid. Taxes are often shown separately when they are a large amount.
- *Current portion of long-term debt.* Any repayment on long-term debt due within the year. Delicious Desserts is scheduled to repay $5,000 on its equipment loan in the coming year.

long-term liabilities
Claims that come due more than one year after the date of the balance sheet.

retained earnings
The amounts left over from profitable operations since the firm's beginning; equal to total profits minus all dividends paid to stockholders.

Long-term liabilities come due more than one year after the date of the balance sheet. They include bank loans (such as Delicious Desserts' $10,000 loan for bakery equipment), mortgages on buildings, and the company's bonds sold to others.

Owners' Equity

Owners' equity is the owners' total investment in the business after all liabilities have been paid. For sole proprietorships and partnerships, amounts put in by the owners are recorded as capital. In a corporation, the owners provide capital by buying the firm's common stock. For Delicious Desserts, the total common stock investment is $30,000. **Retained earnings** are the amounts left over from profitable operations since the firm's beginning. They are total profits minus all dividends (distributions of profits) paid to stockholders. Delicious Desserts has $48,750 in retained earnings.

concept check

What is a balance sheet?

What are the three main categories of accounts on the balance sheet, and how do they relate to the accounting equation?

How do retained earnings relate to owners' equity?

The Income Statement

5 How does the income statement report a firm's profitability?

income statement
A financial statement that summarizes a firm's revenues and expenses and shows its total profit or loss over a period of time.

The balance sheet shows the firm's financial position at a certain point in time. The income statement summarizes the firm's revenues and expenses and shows its total profit or loss over a period of time. Most companies prepare monthly income statements for management and quarterly and annual statements for use by investors, creditors, and other outsiders. The primary elements of the income statement are revenues, expenses, and net income (or net loss). The income statement for Delicious Desserts for the year ended December 31, 2008, is shown in Exhibit 17.5.

CONCEPT *in Action*

Airlines hampered by soaring fuel costs have found it necessary to restructure under Chapter 11 bankruptcy protection. Delta's financial rehabilitation has entailed increasing international routes, raising domestic fares, flying fewer planes, and terminating pensions. The Atlanta-based carrier estimates that it must reduce costs and increase revenue by $3 billion for full recovery. Like other carriers, Delta measures progress by tracking costs- and revenues-per-available-seat mile (RASM). *Which financial statement shows Delta's net profit or net loss?*

© ASSOCIATED PRESS, AP

Exhibit 17.5 > Income Statement for Delicious Desserts

Delicious Desserts, Inc.
Income Statement for the Year Ending December 31, 2008

Revenues		
Gross sales	$275,000	
Less: Sales discounts	2,500	
Less: Returns and allowances	2,000	
Net sales		$270,500
Cost of Goods Sold		
Beginning inventory, January 1	$ 18,000	
Cost of goods manufactured	109,500	
Total cost of goods available for sale	$127,500	
Less: Ending inventory December 31	15,000	
Cost of goods sold		112,500
Gross profit		$158,000
Operating Expenses		
Selling expenses		
Sales salaries	$31,000	
Advertising	16,000	
Other selling expenses	18,000	
Total selling expenses	$ 65,000	
General and administrative expenses		
Professional and office salaries	$20,500	
Utilities	5,000	
Office supplies	1,500	
Interest	3,600	
Insurance	2,500	
Rent	17,000	
Total general and administrative expenses	50,100	
Total operating expenses		115,100
Net profit before taxes		$ 42,900
Less: Income taxes		10,725
Net profit		$ 32,175

Revenues

revenues
The dollar amount of a firm's sales plus any other income it received from sources such as interest, dividends, and rents.

gross sales
The total dollar amount of a company's sales.

net sales
The amount left after deducting sales discounts and returns and allowances from gross sales.

expenses
The costs of generating revenues.

cost of goods sold
The total expense of buying or producing a firm's goods or services.

Revenues are the dollar amount of sales plus any other income received from sources such as interest, dividends, and rents. The revenues of Delicious Desserts arise from sales of its bakery products. Revenues are determined starting with gross sales, the total dollar amount of a company's sales. Delicious Desserts had two deductions from gross sales. *Sales discounts* are price reductions given to customers that pay their bills early. For example, Delicious Desserts gives sales discounts to restaurants that buy in bulk and pay at delivery. *Returns and allowances* is the dollar amount of merchandise returned by customers because they didn't like a product or because it was damaged or defective. Net sales is the amount left after deducting sales discounts and returns and allowances from gross sales. Delicious Desserts' gross sales were reduced by $4,500, leaving net sales of $270,500.

Expenses

Expenses are the costs of generating revenues. Two types are recorded on the income statement: cost of goods sold and operating expenses.

The **cost of goods sold** is the total expense of buying or producing the firm's goods or services. For manufacturers, cost of goods sold includes all costs directly related to production: purchases of raw materials and parts, labor, and factory overhead (utilities, factory maintenance, machinery repair). For wholesalers and retailers, it is the cost of goods bought for resale. For all sellers, cost of goods sold includes all the expenses of preparing the goods for sale, such as shipping and packaging.

Delicious Desserts' cost of goods sold is based on the value of inventory on hand at the beginning of the accounting period, $18,000. During the year, the company spent $109,500 to produce its baked goods. This figure includes the cost of raw materials, labor costs for bakery workers, and the cost of operating the bakery area. Adding the cost of goods manufactured to the value of beginning inventory, we get the total cost of goods available for sale, $127,500. To determine the cost of goods sold for the year, we subtract the cost of inventory at the end of the period:

$$\$127,500 - \$15,000 = \$112,500$$

The amount a company earns after paying to produce or buy its products but before deducting operating expenses is the **gross profit**. It is the difference between net sales and cost of goods sold. Because service firms do not produce goods, their gross profit equals net sales. Gross profit is a critical number for a company because it is the source of funds to cover all the firm's other expenses.

The other major expense category is **operating expenses**. These are the expenses of running the business that are not related directly to producing or buying its products. The two main types of operating expenses are selling expenses and general and administrative expenses. *Selling expenses* are those related to marketing and distributing the company's products. They include salaries and commissions paid to salespeople and the costs of advertising, sales supplies, delivery, and other items that can be linked to sales activity, such as insurance, telephone and other utilities, and postage. *General and administrative expenses* are the business expenses that cannot be linked to either cost of goods sold or sales. Examples of general and administrative expenses are salaries of top managers and office support staff; utilities; office supplies; interest expense; fees for accounting, consulting, and legal services; insurance; and rent. Delicious Desserts' operating expenses totaled $115,100.

Net Profit or Loss

The final figure—or bottom line—on an income statement is the **net profit** (or **net income**) or **net loss**. It is calculated by subtracting all expenses from revenues. If revenues are more than expenses, the result is a net profit. If expenses exceed revenues, a net loss results.

Several steps are involved in finding net profit or loss. (These are shown in the right-hand column of Exhibit 17.5.) First, cost of goods sold is deducted from net sales to get the gross profit. Then total operating expenses are subtracted from gross profit to get the net profit before taxes. Finally, income taxes are deducted to get the net profit. As shown in Exhibit 17.5, Delicious Desserts earned a net profit of $32,175 in 2008.

It is very important to recognize that profit does not represent cash. The income statement is a summary of the firm's operating results during some time period. It does not present the firm's actual cash flows during the period. Those are summarized in the statement of cash flows, which is discussed briefly in the next section.

gross profit
The amount a company earns after paying to produce or buy its products but before deducting operating expenses.

operating expenses
The expenses of running a business that are not directly related to producing or buying its products.

net profit (net income)
The amount obtained by subtracting all of a firm's expenses from its revenues, when the revenues are more than the expenses.

net loss
The amount obtained by subtracting all of a firm's expenses from its revenues, when the expenses are more than the revenues.

statement of cash flows
A financial statement that provides a summary of the money flowing into and out of a firm during a certain period, typically one year.

> **concept check**
>
> What is an income statement? How does it differ from the balance sheet?
>
> Describe the key parts of the income statement. Distinguish between gross sales and net sales.
>
> How is net profit or loss calculated?

The Statement of Cash Flows

 6 Why is the statement of cash flows an important source of information?

Net profit or loss is one measure of a company's financial performance. However, creditors and investors are also keenly interested in how much cash a business generates and how it is used. The **statement of cash flows**, a summary of the money flowing into and out of a firm, is the financial statement used to assess the sources and uses of

CONCEPT *in Action*

Coinstar is a cash cow—literally. The financial-services firm established a niche counting America's loose change at the exits of supermarkets and shopping malls everywhere. For a small fee, Coinstar's coin-counting machines turn penny jars and piggy banks into cash vouchers and gift cards for use at Starbucks and elsewhere. The company recently used its positive cash flow for the all-cash acquisition of money-transfer firm Travelex. *What does the statement of cash flows indicate about a company's financial status?*

cash during a certain period, typically one year. All publicly traded firms must include a statement of cash flows in their financial reports to stockholders. The statement of cash flows tracks the firm's cash receipts and cash payments. It gives financial managers and analysts a way to identify cash flow problems and assess the firm's financial viability.

Using income statement and balance sheet data, the statement of cash flows divides the firm's cash flows into three groups:

- *Cash flow from operating activities.* Those related to the production of the firm's goods or services.
- *Cash flow from investment activities.* Those related to the purchase and sale of fixed assets.
- *Cash flow from financing activities.* Those related to debt and equity financing.

Delicious Desserts' statement of cash flows for 2008 is presented in Exhibit 17.6. It shows that the company's cash and marketable securities have increased over the last year. And during the year the company generated enough cash flow to increase inventory and fixed assets and to reduce accounts payable, accruals, notes payable, and long-term debt.

---

concept check

What is the purpose of the statement of cash flows?

Why has cash flow become such an important measure of a firm's financial condition?

What situations can you cite from the chapter that support your answer?

Exhibit 17.6 > Statement of Cash Flows for Delicious Desserts

Delicious Desserts, Inc.
Statement of Cash Flows for 2008

Cash Flow from Operating Activities		
Net profit after taxes	$27,175	
Depreciation	1,500	
Decrease in accounts receivable	3,140	
Increase in inventory	(4,500)	
Decrease in accounts payable	(2,065)	
Decrease in accruals	(1,035)	
Cash provided by operating activities		$24,215
Cash Flow from Investment Activities		
Increase in gross fixed assets	($ 5,000)	
Cash used in investment activities		($5,000)
Cash Flow from Financing Activities		
Decrease in notes payable	($ 3,000)	
Decrease in long-term debt	(1,000)	
Cash used by financing activities		($4,000)
Net increase in cash and marketable securities		$15,215

Analyzing Financial Statements

 7 How can ratio analysis be used to identify a firm's financial strengths and weaknesses?

ratio analysis
The calculation and interpretation of financial ratios using data taken from the firm's financial statements in order to assess its condition and performance.

Individually, the balance sheet, income statement, and statement of cash flows provide insight into the firm's operations, profitability, and overall financial condition. By studying the relationships among the financial statements, however, one can gain even more insight into a firm's financial condition and performance.

Ratio analysis involves calculating and interpreting financial ratios using data taken from the firm's financial statements in order to assess its condition and performance. A financial ratio states the relationship between financial data on a percentage basis. For instance, current assets might be viewed relative to current liabilities or sales relative to assets. The ratios can then be compared over time, typically three to five years. A firm's ratios can also be compared to industry averages or to those of another company in the same industry. Period-to-period and industry ratios provide a meaningful basis for comparison, so that we can answer questions such as, "Is this particular ratio good or bad?"

It's important to remember that ratio analysis is based on historical data and may not indicate future financial performance. Ratio analysis merely highlights potential problems; it does not prove that they exist. However, ratios can help managers monitor the firm's performance from period to period, to understand operations better and identify trouble spots.

Ratios are also important to a firm's present and prospective creditors (lenders), who want to see if the firm can repay what it borrows and assess the firm's financial health. Often loan agreements require firms to maintain minimum levels of specific ratios. Both present and prospective shareholders use ratio analysis to look at the company's historical performance and trends over time.

Ratios can be classified by what they measure: liquidity, profitability, activity, and debt. Using Delicious Desserts' 2008 balance sheet and income statement (Exhibits 17.4 and 17.5), we can calculate and interpret the key ratios in each group. Exhibit 17.7 summarizes the calculations of these ratios for Delicious Desserts. We'll now discuss how to calculate the ratios and, more important, how to interpret the ratio value.

Liquidity Ratios

liquidity ratios
Ratios that measure a firm's ability to pay its short-term debts as they come due.

current ratio
The ratio of total current assets to total current liabilities; used to measure a firm's liquidity.

acid-test (quick) ratio
The ratio of total current assets excluding inventory to total current liabilities; used to measure a firm's liquidity.

Liquidity ratios measure the firm's ability to pay its short-term debts as they come due. These ratios are of special interest to the firm's creditors. The three main measures of liquidity are the current ratio, the acid-test (quick) ratio, and net working capital.

The **current ratio** is the ratio of total current assets to total current liabilities. Traditionally, a current ratio of 2 ($2 of current assets for every $1 of current liabilities) has been considered good. Whether it is sufficient depends on the industry in which the firm operates. Public utilities, which have a very steady cash flow, operate quite well with a current ratio well below 2. A current ratio of 2 might not be adequate for manufacturers and merchandisers that carry high inventories and have lots of receivables. The current ratio for Delicious Desserts for 2008, as shown in Exhibit 17.7, is 1.4. This means little without a basis for comparison. If the analyst found that the industry average for small bakeries was 2.4, Delicious Desserts would appear to have low liquidity.

The **acid-test (quick) ratio** is like the current ratio except that it excludes inventory, which is the least-liquid current asset. The acid-test ratio is used to measure the firm's ability to pay its current liabilities without selling inventory. The name *acid-test* implies that this ratio is a crucial test of the firm's liquidity. An acid-test ratio of at least 1 is preferred. But again, what is an acceptable value varies by industry. The acid-test ratio is a good measure of liquidity when inventory cannot easily be converted to cash (for instance, if it consists of very specialized goods with a limited market). If inventory is liquid, the current ratio is better. Delicious Desserts' acid-test ratio for 2008 is 1.1. Because the bakery's products are perishable, it does not carry large inventories. Thus, the values of its acid-test and current ratios are fairly close. At a manufacturing company, however, inventory typically makes up a large portion of current assets, so the acid-test ratio will be lower than the current ratio.

Exhibit 17.7 > Ratio Analysis for Delicious Desserts at Year-End 2008

Ratio	Formula	Calculation	Result
Liquidity Ratios			
Current ratio	$\dfrac{\text{Total current assets}}{\text{Total current liabilities}}$	$\dfrac{\$83{,}200}{\$60{,}150}$	1.4
Acid-test (quick) ratio	$\dfrac{\text{Total current assets} - \text{inventory}}{\text{Total current liabilities}}$	$\dfrac{\$83{,}200 - \$15{,}000}{\$60{,}150}$	1.1
Net working capital	Total current assets − Total current liabilities	$\$83{,}200 - \$60{,}150$	$23,050
Profitability Ratios			
Net profit margin	$\dfrac{\text{Net profit}}{\text{Net sales}}$	$\dfrac{\$32{,}175}{\$270{,}500}$	11.9%
Return on equity	$\dfrac{\text{Net profit}}{\text{Total owners' equity}}$	$\dfrac{\$32{,}175}{\$78{,}750}$	40.9%
Earnings per share	$\dfrac{\text{Net profit}}{\substack{\text{Number of shares of}\\ \text{common stock outstanding}}}$	$\dfrac{\$32{,}175}{10{,}000}$	$3.22
Activity Ratio			
Inventory turnover	$\dfrac{\text{Cost of goods sold}}{\text{Average inventory}}$		
	$\dfrac{\text{Cost of goods sold}}{(\text{Beginning inventory} + \text{Ending inventory})/2}$	$\dfrac{\$112{,}500}{(\$18{,}000 + \$15{,}000)/2}$	
		$\dfrac{\$112{,}500}{\$16{,}500}$	6.8 times
Debt Ratio			
Debt-to-equity ratio	$\dfrac{\text{Total liabilities}}{\text{Owners' equity}}$	$\dfrac{\$70{,}150}{\$78{,}750}$	89.1%

net working capital
The amount obtained by subtracting total current liabilities from total current assets; used to measure a firm's liquidity.

Net working capital, though not really a ratio, is often used to measure a firm's overall liquidity. It is calculated by subtracting total current liabilities from total current assets. Delicious Desserts' net working capital for 2008 is $23,050. Comparisons of net working capital over time often help in assessing a firm's liquidity.

Profitability Ratios

To measure profitability, a firm's profits can be related to its sales, equity, or stock value. **Profitability ratios** measure how well the firm is using its resources to generate profit and how efficiently it is being managed. The main profitability ratios are net profit margin, return on equity, and earnings per share.

profitability ratios
Ratios that measure how well a firm is using its resources to generate profit and how efficiently it is being managed.

net profit margin
The ratio of net profit to net sales; also called *return on sales*. It measures the percentage of each sales dollar remaining after all expenses, including taxes, have been deducted.

The ratio of net profit to net sales is the **net profit margin**, also called *return on sales*. It measures the percentage of each sales dollar remaining after all expenses, including taxes, have been deducted. Higher net profit margins are better than lower ones. The net profit margin is often used to measure the firm's earning power. "Good" net profit margins differ quite a bit from industry to industry. A grocery store usually has a very low net profit margin, perhaps below 1 percent, whereas a jewelry store's net profit margin would probably exceed 10 percent. Delicious Desserts' net profit margin for 2008 is 11.9 percent. In other words, Delicious Desserts is earning 11.9 cents on each dollar of sales.

CONCEPT *in Action*

For giant retailers like Macy's, the high expense of operating a store counters the elevated markup on merchandise, resulting in slim profit margins. Since competition forces marketers to keep prices low, it is often a retailer's cost-cutting strategy, not initial markup or sales volume, that determines whether the business will be profitable. *What expenses other than payroll and the cost of merchandise affect a retailer's net profit margin?*

return on equity (ROE)
The ratio of net profit to total owners' equity; measures the return that owners receive on their investment in the firm.

The ratio of net profit to total owners' equity is called **return on equity** (ROE). It measures the return that owners receive on their investment in the firm, a major reason for investing in a company's stock. Delicious Desserts has a 40.9 percent ROE for 2008. On the surface, a 40.9 percent ROE seems quite good. But the level of risk in the business and the ROE of other firms in the same industry must also be considered. The higher the risk, the greater the ROE investors look for. A firm's ROE can also be compared to past values to see how the company is performing over time.

earnings per share (EPS)
The ratio of net profit to the number of shares of common stock outstanding; measures the number of dollars earned by each share of stock.

Earnings per share (EPS) is the ratio of net profit to the number of shares of common stock outstanding. It measures the number of dollars earned by each share of stock. EPS values are closely watched by investors and are considered an important sign of success. EPS also indicates a firm's ability to pay dividends. Note that EPS is the dollar amount earned by each share, not the actual amount given to stockholders in the form of dividends. Some earnings may be put back into the firm. Delicious Desserts' EPS for 2008 is $3.22.

Activity Ratios

activity ratios
Ratios that measure how well a firm uses its assets.

inventory turnover ratio
The ratio of cost of goods sold to average inventory; measures the speed with which inventory moves through a firm and is turned into sales.

Activity ratios measure how well a firm uses its assets. They reflect the speed with which resources are converted to cash or sales. A frequently used activity ratio is inventory turnover. The **inventory turnover ratio** measures the speed with which inventory moves through the firm and is turned into sales. It is calculated by dividing cost of goods sold by the average inventory. (Average inventory is estimated by adding the beginning and ending inventories for the year and dividing by 2.) Based on its 2008 financial data, Delicious Desserts' inventory, on average, is turned into sales 6.8 times each year, or about once every 54 days (365 days ÷ 6.8). The acceptable turnover ratio depends on the line of business. A grocery store would have a high turnover ratio, maybe 20 times a year, whereas the turnover for a heavy equipment manufacturer might be only 3 times a year.

Debt Ratios

debt ratios
Ratios that measure the degree and effect of a firm's use of borrowed funds (debt) to finance its operations.

Debt ratios measure the degree and effect of the firm's use of borrowed funds (debt) to finance its operations. These ratios are especially important to lenders and investors. They want to make sure the firm has a healthy mix of debt and equity. If the firm relies too much on debt, it may have trouble meeting interest payments and repaying loans. The most important debt ratio is the debt-to-equity ratio.

CONCEPT *in Action*

Charter Communications, the country's number four cable-TV provider, has amassed billions in debt in recent years. The firm's interest-payment expense eats up a large portion of revenues and its quarterly losses have been astronomical: Charter's losses per share have often matched its share price. Some investors continue to put confidence in Charter Chairman Paul Allen, legendary cofounder of Microsoft, while others have lost their life's savings in the company's stock. *How can investors use the debt-to-equity ratio to help make investment decisions?*

The **debt-to-equity ratio** measures the relationship between the amount of debt financing (borrowing) and the amount of equity financing (owners' funds). It is calculated by dividing total liabilities by owners' equity. In general, the lower the ratio, the better. But it is important to assess the debt-to-equity ratio against both past values and industry averages. Delicious Desserts' ratio for 2008 is 89.1 percent. The ratio indicates that the company has 89 cents of debt for every dollar the owners have provided. A ratio above 100 percent means the firm has more debt than equity. In such a case, the lenders are providing more financing than the owners.

concept check

How can ratio analysis be used to interpret financial statements?

Name the main liquidity and profitability ratios and explain what they indicate.

What kinds of information do activity ratios give? Why are debt ratios of concern to lenders and investors?

Trends in Accounting

 8   What major trends affect the accounting industry today?

debt-to-equity ratio
The ratio of total liabilities to owners' equity; measures the relationship between the amount of debt financing (borrowing) and the amount of equity financing (owner's funds).

The post Sarbanes-Oxley business environment has brought many changes to the accounting profession. The public accounting industry could no longer regulate itself but instead became subject to formal regulation for the first time. The new regulatory environment set higher standards for audit procedures—and at the same time created uncertainty in how to interpret the rules. Once again the core auditing business, rather than financial advisory and management consulting services, became their primary focus. The relationship between accountants and their clients has changed, and the role of chief audit executive has taken on new visibility. The FASB is pushing for major changes in GAAP, such as the shift to principles-based accounting and separate procedures for private and small companies.

Reevaluating SarbOx

In the period following the enactment of Sarbanes-Oxley, auditors had no experience with how to apply and interpret the Act. Many took a conservative view and went to extremes in following the provisions of Section 404 of the Act (audits of internal controls). The PCAOB subsequently criticized such practices and acknowledged that they unnecessarily raised compliance costs. "The criticisms are valid, and the profession needs to transition to a risk-based, judgment approach," commented Kelly Dreishpoon, manager at Rothstein Kass, a New Jersey CPA firm. "However, a lot of the initial approach [to Section 404] was predicated by the first-time-through nature of the implementation. What other guidance was there outside the strict interpretation of what was written?"

Both the PCAOB and AICPA issued guidance that covered these concerns and helped auditors increase the effectiveness of their audits. In May 2005, the PCAOB released a more flexible policy statement. It provided guidelines to help accountants move to determine what is required to audit and test internal control procedures effectively and at an appropriate cost. Among its recommendations:

- Integrating internal control audits with financial statement audits
- Using judgment as to the risk levels rather than applying standard checklists, to avoid overfocusing on low-risk areas
- Auditing internal controls from the top down to identify relevant processes for further examination, rather than auditing everything
- Applying risk assessment tools to focus on accounts with potential for material misstatements[10]

The AICPA's Auditing Standards Board (ASB) addressed similar issues in its March 2006 Risk Assessment Standards, which included eight Statements on Auditing Standards. "The standards will result in more effective audits as a result of better risk assessments and improved design and performance of audit procedures to respond to the risks," said John Fogarty, ASB chairman.[11]

Accountants Stick to the Numbers

During the 1980s, accountants moved beyond their traditional task of auditing a company's financial information to provide additional services. Their first steps were financial services that were a logical extension of their audit assignments, such as tax, legal, and investment advisory services. As they moved further afield from their core businesses, they developed huge consulting units that provided a wide range of information technology, business strategy, human resources, and similar management services.

Nonaudit fees soon dwarfed revenues from audits. Especially at the largest firms, accountants became more involved in the operations of their clients. This raised the question of potential conflicts of interest: Can auditors serve both the public and the client? Auditors' main purpose is to certify financial statements. Could they maintain sufficient objectivity to raise questions while auditing a client that provides significant consulting revenues? Can they review systems and methods that they designed and implemented?

Sarbanes-Oxley brought an end to the days when accountants could serve as both auditor and advisor to a client. Auditors may no longer provide eight specific types of nonaudit services to their audit clients. These include services (like bookkeeping) related to the client's accounting records or financial statements, design and implementation of financial information systems, internal auditing, management functions, human resources, investment services, and legal services.

The relationship between finance executives and their outside accountants has become increasingly formal, in part because of lawsuits against audit firms as well as the new regulations. "The consultative advice that auditors had been able to provide in the past has now changed to 'You tell me what you think the answer is, and I'll get back to you on that,' " explains Patrick Scannell, CFO at Netezza Corp., a Massachusetts data-warehousing firm. Adds CPA Russell Wieman of Grant Thornton LLP, "We're a lot more cautious than we used to be. In the past, you may have given [a client] the benefit of the doubt. We won't necessarily do that now."

CONCEPT *in Action*

Accounting malfeasance at government-sponsored mortgage giant Fannie Mae led to the ouster of ex-CEO Franklin Raines and raised questions about the firm's internal auditing. Investigations into the lender's $11 billion scandal noted that designated accounting watchdog Sampath Rajappa became a cheerleader for the Raines's plan to boost earnings-per-share targets to which executive bonuses were linked. *Are internal auditors capable of providing objective oversight for their firms' finances and avoiding conflicts of interest?*

In the first year of Sarbanes-Oxley compliance, auditors struggled with how rigidly to apply the new rules. That led to strained relationships between a company's audit committee and its outside CPAs. Accountants were unsure how much advice they could provide with regard to internal controls, so they took few chances. CFOs are increasingly frustrated with the new roles. It takes longer to get answers to questions, and sometimes the response doesn't come at all. "We recently went to our auditor [with a question] and it was like Fear Factor 101," says Leon Level, CFO of Computer Sciences Corp. "They said, 'Where's your white paper?'" Nor could Level obtain written advice at several Big Four firms. "I'm the CFO of a major public company, and I couldn't get an answer." No one is sure what is considered appropriate when it comes to asking questions and getting answers. CFOs are concerned that requests for advice may now be interpreted as not having adequate controls.[12]

Internal Auditors Step Up

Sarbanes-Oxley and other regulatory legislation, such as the Health Insurance Portability and Accountability Act (HIPAA), have increased the visibility and prominence of the internal audit department and the chief audit executive (CAE). No longer relegated to the background, the CAE is working more closely with other corporate executives and board members to educate them on compliance issues and develop strategies to improve overall compliance. "The CAE's role is becoming more visible and more multifaceted, requiring not only technical knowledge and expertise, but also an enormous amount of time, patience, and a heightened sense of responsibility," says Chuck Eldridge, head of the financial officers practice at executive search firm Korn/Ferry International.[13] In addition, companies can no longer use the same firm to perform both the internal and external audits. Many companies are bringing internal audits in-house, which creates high demand for qualified personnel in this area.

Closing the GAAP

Many accounting industry experts place some of the blame for recent accounting fraud on the complexity of GAAP, among them Robert Herz, who is now head of FASB. The FASB supports a shift from rules-based accounting to the principles-based accounting system used by the International Accounting Standards Board. Instead of asking if the accounting follows the rules, executives and auditors would look at how it shows a transaction's underlying economics. "A principles-based system is one where the accounting standard simply lays out objectives of good reporting in an area," explains Herz. Standards would be broader, simpler, and more concise—12 pages instead of 200 pages.

However, Herz anticipates much resistance to such a change. "Fundamental structural, institutional, cultural, and behavioral forces have caused, and continue to cause, complexity in the system and impede transparent financial reporting," he says. These forces include an overemphasis on short-term earnings that leads to using accounting "tricks" to boost quarterly results. Another obstacle is that relying on principles, which are open to interpretation, could lead to problems with regulators. This uncertainty does not exist with standards and rules.

No easy answers are on the horizon. "Everyone is in favor of simplification," says former FASB chairman Dennis Beresford, who currently teaches accounting at the University of Georgia. But "everyone also wants rules—just in case."[14]

Private companies and small businesses are also unhappy with GAAP's complexity. They have asked the FASB to consider a simpler version of GAAP, as the Catching the Entrepreneurial Spirit box explains.

---

concept check

What issues have surfaced since the Sarbanes-Oxley Act went into effect, and how is the accounting industry resolving them?

How has the relationship between public accounting firms and their clients changed in recent years? Why have the internal audit function and the CAE become more important?

What changes is FASB considering for GAAP?

Small Businesses Claim It's Time for "GAAP Lite"

Small companies with perhaps a single bookkeeper find it impossible to keep up with frequent modifications to the GAAP rules. For many years CEOs of privately held companies have complained that rules for larger public companies are inappropriate and burdensome for their smaller companies to follow. "Someone with a $5 million business doesn't have the expertise or time to sit down and say 'I wonder how this new standard will affect me,'" says Eric P. Wallace, partner at Carbis Walker LLP, a small CPA firm based in New Castle, Pennsylvania, serving thousands of small-business clients.

The answer that private business owners have proposed is a greatly simplified version of GAAP, with different rules that focus specifically on their needs. But others insist that a double standard is too cumbersome for small businesses and their CPAs to cope with. Richard Forrestel Jr., a member of the Financial Accounting Standards Board (FASB) Small Business Advisory Committee, and treasurer and secretary of Cold Spring Construction Company located in Akron, New York, says, "It would be chaos in the accounting world."

As Dan Noll, director of accounting standards at the New York City–based American Institute of Certified Public Accountants (AICPA), explains, "The major complaint we were hearing was that people just weren't using the information coming out of GAAP or the resulting financial reporting," says. But with regular GAAP versus "mini GAAP" back in the limelight, the AICPA has decided to get involved—and this time smaller companies may actually see some results.

The FASB sets the standards of financial accounting and reporting in the private sector that are recognized by the SEC and the AICPA. These standards are vital to the performance of the economy because investors, creditors, auditors, and others rely on visible, believable, comparable financial data. In 2004, the FASB established the Small Business Advisory Committee to consider the needs of small companies when developing U.S. accounting standards. "The FASB has always recognized small businesses as an important constituency," commented FASB chairman Robert H. Herz. "Formation of the Small Business Advisory Committee should be a win-win for everyone involved, and the Board looks forward to working with the group."

So does the FASB truly understand what small businesses need? The September 2005 recruitment of a project manager to lead its financial reporting and accounting initiatives for privately held companies suggests it is at least trying. The position was created "to lend further consideration to the real-world differences that exist in financial reporting and accounting between private and public companies," according to the job description.

Russ Golden, senior technical advisor at the FASB, says, "All the options are on the table"—from a separate standard to individual amendments to current GAAP rules. In a less than perfect world, small business may have to be satisfied with the latter. [15]

Critical Thinking Questions

- Why is it important for small, privately held companies to have their own accounting procedures, different from those imposed on larger public companies?
- If you were the CEO of a small business, how would you choose to reduce your company's financial reporting and accounting burden?

Summary of Learning Goals

1 Why are financial reports and accounting information important, and who uses them?

Accounting involves collecting, recording, classifying, summarizing, reporting, and analyzing a firm's financial activities according to a standard set of procedures. The financial reports resulting from the accounting process give managers, employees, investors, customers, suppliers, creditors, and government agencies a way to analyze a company's past, current, and future performance. Financial accounting is concerned with the preparation of financial reports using generally accepted accounting principles. Managerial accounting provides financial information that management can use to make decisions about the firm's operations.

2 What are the differences between public and private accountants, and are public accountants subject to new regulations?

Public accountants work for independent firms that provide accounting services—such as financial report preparation and auditing, tax return preparation, and management consulting—to other organizations on a fee basis. Private accountants are employed to serve one particular organization and may prepare financial statements, tax returns, and management reports.

The bankruptcies of companies like Enron and WorldCom, plus widespread abuses of accounting practices, raised critical issues of auditor independence and the integrity and reliability of financial reports. To set better standards for accounting, auditing, and financial reporting and prevent future accounting irregularities, Congress passed the Sarbanes-Oxley Act in 2002. This Act establishes an independent board to oversee the accounting profession, sets stricter auditing and financial disclosure standards, and places increased accountability on a company's senior executives and management. It restricts auditors from providing certain types of consulting services to clients. Other organizations such as the SEC, the New York Stock Exchange, and accounting industry professional associations issued new regulations and guidelines related to compliance with the Act.

3 What are the six steps in the accounting cycle?

The accounting cycle refers to the process of generating financial statements. It begins with analyzing business transactions, recording them in journals, and posting them to ledgers. Ledger totals are then summarized in a trial balance that confirms the accuracy of the figures. Next the accountant prepares the financial statements and reports. The final step involves analyzing these reports and making decisions. Computers have simplified many of these labor-intensive tasks.

4 In what terms does the balance sheet describe the financial condition of an organization?

The balance sheet represents the financial condition of a firm at one moment in time, in terms of assets, liabilities, and owners' equity. The key categories of assets are current assets, fixed assets, and intangible assets. Liabilities are divided into current and long-term liabilities. Owners' equity, the amount of the owners' investment in the firm after all liabilities have been paid, is the third major category.

5 How does the income statement report a firm's profitability?

The income statement is a summary of the firm's operations over a stated period of time. The main parts of the statement are revenues (gross and net sales), cost of goods sold, operating expenses (selling and general and administrative expenses), taxes, and net profit or loss.

6 Why is the statement of cash flows an important source of information?

The statement of cash flows summarizes the firm's sources and uses of cash during a financial-reporting period. It breaks the firm's cash flows into those from operating, investment, and financing activities. It shows the net change during the period in the firm's cash and marketable securities.

7 How can ratio analysis be used to identify a firm's financial strengths and weaknesses?

Ratio analysis is a way to use financial statements to gain insight into a firm's operations, profitability, and overall financial condition. The four main types of ratios are liquidity ratios, profitability ratios, activity ratios, and debt ratios. Comparing a firm's ratios over several years and comparing them to ratios of other firms in the same industry or to industry averages can indicate trends and highlight financial strengths and weaknesses.

8 What major trends affect the accounting industry today?

Under the more stringent regulations of Sarbanes-Oxley, higher standards applied to audits. However, accountants were unsure of how strictly to interpret the rules. Many were too rigid, and this increased the costs of audits significantly. In response, the PCAOB and AICPA published guidance to help auditors use risk assessments. Accountants returned to their core auditing business, rather than financial advisory and management consulting services. The relationship between accountants and their clients has changed, as the threat of lawsuits made accountants less willing to offer advice. The role of chief audit executive has taken on new visibility. We could also see some major changes in GAAP from a shift to principles-based rather than rules-based accounting. FASB is also considering simplifying GAAP for private and small companies.

Key Terms

accounting 565
acid-test (quick) ratio 581
activity ratios 583
annual report 567
assets 572
auditing 568
balance sheet 575
certified management accountant (CMA) 568
certified public accountant (CPA) 568
cost of goods sold 578
current assets 575
current liabilities 576
current ratio 581
debt ratios 583
debt-to-equity ratio 584
depreciation 575
double-entry bookkeeping 572
earnings per share (EPS) 583
expenses 578
financial accounting 566
Financial Accounting Standards Board (FASB) 566
fixed assets 575
generally accepted accounting principles (GAAP) 566

gross profit 579
gross sales 578
income statement 577
intangible assets 575
inventory turnover ratio 583
liabilities 572
liquidity 575
liquidity ratios 581
long-term liabilities 577
managerial accounting 566
net loss 579
net profit margin 582
net profit (net income) 579
net sales 578
net working capital 582
operating expenses 579
owners' equity 572
private accountants 568
profitability ratios 582
public accountants 568
ratio analysis 581
retained earnings 577
return on equity (ROE) 583
revenues 578
Sarbanes-Oxley Act 570
statement of cash flows 579

Preparing for Tomorrow's Workplace: **SCANS**

1. Your firm has been hired to help several small businesses with their year-end financial statements.

   a. Based on the following account balances, prepare the Marbella Design Enterprises balance sheet as of December 31, 2008:

Cash	$30,250
Accounts payable	28,500
Fixtures and furnishings	85,000
Notes payable	15,000
Retained earnings	64,450
Accounts receivable	24,050
Inventory	15,600
Equipment	42,750
Accumulated depreciation on fixtures and furnishings	12,500
Common shares (50,000 shares at $1)	50,000
Long-term debt	25,000
Accumulated depreciation on equipment	7,800
Marketable securities	13,000
Income taxes payable	7,500

b. The following are the account balances for the revenues and expenses of the Windsor Gift Shop for the year ending December 31, 2008. Prepare the income statement for the shop. (Resources, Information)

Rent	$ 15,000
Salaries	23,500
Cost of goods sold	98,000
Utilities	8,000
Supplies	3,500
Sales	195,000
Advertising	3,600
Interest	3,000
Taxes	12,120

2. During the year ended December 31, 2008, Lawrence Industries sold $2 million worth of merchandise on credit. A total of $1.4 million was collected during the year. The cost of this merchandise was $1.3 million. Of this amount, $1 million has been paid, and $300,000 is not yet due. Operating expenses and income taxes totaling $500,000 were paid in cash during the year. Assume that all accounts had a zero balance at the beginning of the year (January 1, 2008). Write a brief report for the company controller that includes calculation of the firm's (a) net profit and (b) cash flow during the year. Explain why there is a difference between net profit and cash flow. (Information, Systems)

3. A friend has been offered a sales representative position at Draper Publications, Inc., a small publisher of computer-related books, but wants to know more about the company. Because of your expertise in financial analysis, you offer to help analyze Draper's financial health. Draper has provided the following selected financial information:

Account balances on December 31, 2008:	
Inventory	$72,000
Net sales	450,000
Current assets	150,000
Cost of goods sold	290,000
Total liabilities	180,000
Net profit	35,400
Total assets	385,000
Current liabilities	75,000
Other information	
Number of common shares outstanding	25,000
Inventory at January 1, 2008	48,000

Calculate the following ratios for 2008: acid-test (quick) ratio, inventory turnover ratio, net profit margin, return on equity (ROE), debt-to-equity ratio, and earnings per share (EPS). Summarize your assessment of the company's financial performance, based on these ratios, in a report for your friend. What other information would you like to have to complete your evaluation? (Information, Systems)

4. Use the Internet and business periodicals to research how companies and accounting firms are implementing the provisions of the Sarbanes-Oxley Act. What are the major concerns they face? What rules have other organizations issued that relate to Act compliance? Summarize your findings. (Information)

5. **Team Activity** Two years ago, Rebecca Mardon started a computer consulting business, Mardon Consulting Associates. Until now, she has been the only employee, but business has grown enough to support an administrative assistant and another consultant this year. Before she adds staff, however, she wants to hire an accountant and computerize her financial record keeping. Divide the class into small groups, assigning one person to be Rebecca and the others to represent

members of a medium-size accounting firm. Rebecca should think about the type of financial information systems her firm requires and develop a list of questions for the firm. The accountants will prepare a presentation making recommendations to her as well as explaining why their firm should win the account. (Resources, Interpersonal)

6. One of the best ways to learn about financial statements is to prepare them. Put together your personal balance sheet and income statement, using Exhibits 17.4 and 17.5 as samples. You will have to adjust the account categories to fit your needs. Here are some suggestions:
   - Current assets—cash on hand, balances in savings and checking accounts.
   - Investments—stocks and bonds, retirement funds.
   - Fixed assets—real estate, personal property (cars, furniture, jewelry, etc.).
   - Current liabilities—charge-card balances, loan payments due in one year.
   - Long-term liabilities—auto loan balance, mortgage on real estate, other loan balances that will not come due until after one year.
   - Income—employment income, investment income (interest, dividends).
   - Expenses—housing, utilities, food, transportation, medical, clothing, insurance, loan payments, taxes, personal care, recreation and entertainment, and miscellaneous expenses.

   After you complete your personal financial statements, use them to see how well you are managing your finances. Consider the following questions:
   a. Should you be concerned about your debt ratio?
   b. Would a potential creditor conclude that it is safe or risky to lend you money?
   c. If you were a company, would people want to invest in you? Why or why not? What could you do to improve your financial condition? (Information)

Ethics Activity

As the controller of a medium-sized manufacturing company, you take pride in the accounting and internal control systems you have developed for the company. You and your staff have kept up with changes in the accounting industry and been diligent in updating the systems to meet new accounting standards. Your outside auditor, which has been reviewing the company's books for 15 years, routinely complimented you on your thorough procedures.

The passage of the Sarbanes-Oxley Act, with its emphasis on testing internal control systems, has initiated several changes. You have studied the law and made adjustments to ensure you comply with the regulations, even though it has created additional work. Your auditors, however, have chosen to interpret SarbOx very aggressively—too much so, in your opinion. The auditors have recommended that you make costly improvements to your systems and also enlarged the scope of the audit engagement, raising their fees. When you question the partner in charge, he explains that the new-

ness of the law means that it is open to interpretation and it is better to err on the side of caution than risk noncompliance. You are not pleased with this answer, as you believe that your company is in compliance with SarbOx, and consider changing auditors.

Using a Web search tool, locate articles about this topic and then write responses to the following questions. Be sure to support your arguments and cite your sources.

Ethical Dilemma: Should you change auditors because your current one is too stringent in applying the Sarbanes-Oxley Act? What other steps could you take to resolve this situation?

Sources: Laurie Brannen, "Sarbanes-Oxley's Footprint on Finance Deepens," Business Finance, March 2005, http://www.businessfinancemag.com; Eric Krell, "Sarbanes Fatigue Strikes the Boardroom," Business Finance, May 2005, http://www.businessfinancemag.com; Michael Rapoport, "SEC Panel to Turn In Report on Sarbanes Debate," Wall Street Journal, April 17, 2006, p. C3; Tim Reason, "Feeling the Pain," CFO, May 1, 2005, http://www.cfo.com; and Helen Shaw, "Donaldson, Levitt Diverge on Convergence," *Bob* February 22, 2006, http://www.cfo.com.

Working the Net

1. Visit the Web site of one of the following major U.S. public accounting firms: Deloitte & Touche, **http://www.deloitte.com**; Ernst & Young, **http://www.ey.com**; KPMG, **http://www.kpmg.com**; PricewaterhouseCoopers, **http://www.pwcglobal.com**; Grant Thornton, **http://www.grantthornton.com**; or BDO Seidman, **http://www.bdo.com**. Explore the site to learn the services the firm offers. What other types of resources does the firm have on its Web site? How well does the firm communicate via the Web site with existing and prospective clients? Summarize your findings in a brief report.

2. Do annual reports confuse you? Many Web sites can take the mystery out of this important document. See IBM's Guide to Understanding Financials at **http://www. prars.com/ibm/ibmframe.html.** Moneychimp's "How to Read an Annual Report" features an interactive diagram that provides a big picture view of what the report's financial information tells you: **http://www.moneychimp.com/articles/ financials/fundamentals.htm.** Which site was more helpful to you, and why?

3. Corporate reports filed with the SEC are now available on the Web at the EDGAR (Electronic Data Gathering, Analysis, and Retrieval system) Web site, **http:// www.sec.gov/edgar.shtml.** First, read about the EDGAR system; then go to the search page **http://www.sec.gov/edgar/searchedgar/webusers.htm.** To see the type of information that companies must file with the SEC, use the search feature to locate a recent filing by Microsoft. What types of reports did you find, and what was the purpose of each report?

4. Can you judge an annual report by its cover? What are the most important elements of a top annual report? Go to Sid Cato's Official Annual Report Web site, **http://www.sidcato.com,** to find his 15 standards for annual reports and read about the reports that receive his honors. Then get a copy of an annual report and evaluate it using Cato's 135-point scale. How well does it compare to his top picks?

5. Go to the Web site of the company whose annual report you evaluated in Question 4. Find the Web version of its annual report and compare it to the print version. What differences do you find, if any? Do you think companies should put their financial information online? Why or why not?

Creative Thinking Case >

Compliance Conundrum

The Sarbanes-Oxley Act of 2002 placed new compliance and disclosure burdens on corporate executives. Not only must top executives certify their firms' financial statements, but they must also quickly publicize "on a current basis" such matters as insider transactions in the company's stock, events that require certain SEC filings, and "any material changes in their financial condition."

No wonder, then, that a company's Web site has become a critical component of its investor-relations efforts. Both investors and analysts now turn first to corporate Web sites as a major source of information for quarterly earnings releases, press releases other than earnings, annual reports, SEC filings such as the 10K or 10Q, Webcasts of current conference calls with security analysts and archives of past Webcasts, and other financial and investment-related information. Companies often outsource their online investor relations initiatives to specialized companies such as Thomson/CCBN IR Web Hosting and Thomson/CCBN Webcasting.

Because the Web has become such an important way to reach individual and institutional investors, most major companies today also use their corporate Web sites to communicate compliance with the Act and rebuild investor confidence. Their Web sites now include corporate governance information such as composition of the Board of Directors and its committees, governance policies, alerts to changes in corporate governance, and related information. Companies can also set up governance reporting procedures and hotlines to record complaints, as Section 301 of Sarbanes-Oxley requires. An additional benefit of providing ready access to materials on corporate governance and regulatory compliance is an increase in investor confidence in the organization's credibility.

Technology is helping companies with other compliance solutions as well. For example, specialized software from companies such as Compliance 360 and Open-Pages provides corporations with comprehensive governance, risk, and compliance management programs for Sarbanes-Oxley and other regulatory agencies. Together, all compliance-related data streamlines the compliance process across the enterprise, eliminates redundancy, identifies risks, and reduces the cost of compliance. Duke University Hospital implemented Compliance 360's software to track thousands of constantly changing regulations, standards, codes, and accreditations. "Our corporate compliance management solution automates many of those processes and provides an enterprise-wide view of corporate compliance through a single interface," says Steve McGraw, CEO of Compliance 360.

Critical Thinking Questions

- How does the Web help companies manage compliance with the Sarbanes-Oxley Act?
- Why are companies turning to firms like Open Pages and Compliance 360 to improve compliance procedures?
- Visit the investor relations pages of the corporate Web sites for two of the following companies: ExxonMobil, IBM, Dell, Microsoft, Pfizer, Bank of America, AT&T, Verizon, Gilette, or Procter & Gamble. How well does each company use the Web to present information? Where does corporate governance information appear, and what does it tell you about the company?

Sources: Adapted from *Compliance 360* Web site, http://www.compliance360.com, April 16, 2006; "Duke University Hospital Selects Compliance 360 for Regulatory Management," *PR Newswire*, July 27, 2005, http://galenet.thomsonlearning.com; "Multicare Health System Selects Open Pages SOX Express for Sarbones-Oxley Compliance," *Internet Wire*, February 13, 2006, http://galenet.thomsonlearning.com; and "Thomson/CCBN's Corporate Governance Online Disclosure Solution," *Thomson Financial*, 2004, http://www.thomson.com/financial, April 17, 2006.

Video Case >

Uno Corporation Knows Pizza by the Numbers

Aaron Spencer, now Uno Corporation chairman, enjoyed his first Chicago Original Deep Dish Pizza so much that he contacted Ike Sewell, founder of the original Pizzeria Uno restaurants, about expanding to other cities. He formed Uno Corporation in 1979, opening both company-owned and franchise units across the United States. By 1992 there were 100 Pizzeria Uno restaurants. Today the company has more than 200 restaurants in 32 states, the District of Columbia, Puerto Rico, South Korea, and the United Arab Emirates.

As the company grew, so did the restaurant concept and the menu. In 2003 the restaurant name changed from Pizzeria Uno to Uno Chicago Grill to better reflect its Chicago warehouse decor and casual dining menu. Appetizers, ribs, seafood, burgers, steaks, pasta dishes, and desserts joined its signature deep dish pizzas.

A high growth business such as Uno Corporation requires accurate, timely financial data to succeed. "How you manage your financial performance or operating performance on a daily business is very important," says Craig Miller, Uno's chief financial officer. "The margins in the restaurant business average 3 to 4 cents on every dollar." Therefore, accounting for every penny becomes critical to achieving profitability.

Uno Corporation's financial data support decisions ranging from building a new restaurant and allocating funds to planning menus and developing marketing campaigns. Responsibility for data collection rests with the finance, accounting, and analysis people. They test that data against historical performance, evaluate how these decisions affected the company, and then project their impact on Uno's future.

Managing costs is essential to the restaurant business. Uno's restaurant managers keep a close watch on food, labor, repairs and maintenance, and other controllable costs. As Miller explains, "It's a thin profitability, and it doesn't take much to throw it out of whack. . . . If you get a big spike [in cost] in one of your big food items that is out of your control, you can wipe out your profitability pretty quickly. You can't make a profit if you have to turn around and raise prices. It destroys the value equation against some of your competitors."

Accounting for Uno's widespread operations uses a sophisticated computer system to manage the cost structure. Each restaurant has computerized point-of-sale terminals that collect such data as sales figures, what items people buy, inventory replenishment statistics, and hours and wage rates of employees. With this data, Uno Corporation can compare each unit's operating performance against its theoretical food control system. "If you are planning to run a 25 percent cost of sales and it goes to 27 percent, why is that?" says Miller.

In addition to short-term operations, Uno Corporation must manage its balance sheet to permit future growth. The average Uno restaurant requires $1.7 million in up-front capital, excluding land. Uno uses debt to finance its expansion program. The company's goal is to sustain its 20 to 25 percent annual growth in EPS and revenue. "We think we can do that by managing our balance sheet very well and being prudent about our investments," says Miller.

Critical Thinking Questions

- Why is it important for Uno Corporation to have an effective and efficient accounting information system? How does the industry in which a company operates affect its accounting systems?
- What types of accounting reports are likely to be most useful to the restaurant managers, and what areas would be most important to them? Explain your answer. How might this differ from a manufacturing company manager's reports and analysis?
- Describe the different types of ratios that Uno Corporation can use for financial analysis and how they can measure company performance. Which does Miller consider the most critical, and why? How might activity ratios help accountants at Uno assess their company's performance?

Sources: Adapted from the video "Accounting the Uno Way," 2002; and Uno Corporation Web site, http://www.unos.com, May 15, 2006.

Hot Links Address Book

What issues is the FASB working on now? Check it out at **http://www.fasb.org**

Two good sites to learn about the latest news in the accounting industry are Electronic Accountant, **http://www.electronicaccountant.com** and Accounting Web, **http://www.accountingweb.com**

To become more familiar with annual reports and key financial statements, head for IBM's Investment Guides. The material offers a good overview of financial reporting and shows you what to look for when you read these documents: **http://www.ibm.com/investor/tools/financials.phtml**

To find out more about the accounting profession and becoming a CPA, visit the American Institute of Certified Public Accountants' Web site at **http://www.aicpa.org/** and click on "Students."

The Accounting Library site has a virtual consultant to help companies choose the best accounting applications for their needs. Check it out at **http://www.excelco.com/**

A comprehensive site with information about careers in accounting, certification programs, internships, and links to many related Web site can be found at: **http://accountingmajors.com**

At their Web sites, you can learn about the types of services the Big Four accounting firms are now offering their clients: **http://www.deloitte.com http://www.ey.com http://www.kpmg.com** and **http://www.pwcglobal.com**

continuing case on Apple, Inc.

Part 5 • Information Technology at Apple, Inc.

Apple is in the business of information and technology. The company focuses on using innovative technology to improve the way information is accumulated and shared. As one of the earliest entries into the information age, Apple has been at the forefront of technological innovation and one of the leaders in the information age.

EARLY DEVELOPMENTS IN TECHNOLOGICAL INNOVATION

AppleLink was the worldwide computer network that electronically connected Apple's employees, sales force, dealers, and third-party developers. The initial use of AppleLink was for electronic mail. Apple employees were encouraged to use AppleLink at work and at home. Encouraging home usage was a critical step in obtaining buy-in to what Apple executives thought was the future of electronic mail—being in touch regardless of time and location. After going online in 1985, AppleLink opened up a new avenue of communication within the company. As a new phenomenon, Apple employees began to share opinions, ideas, thoughts, and concerns using electronic communication. Employees debated company issues as well as worldwide events in this new format. Some suggest that AppleLink was a precursor to today's e-mail. AppleLink also provided dealers with the ability to quickly and easily communicate with the company. From the perspective of external software developers, AppleLink was a direct connection for internal company support.

Eventually, Apple aligned with Quantum Computer Services to develop AppleLink Personal Edition, which led to the development of e-mail exchanges among personal computer users. Apple Computer, with its AppleLink software, became infamous in 1991 with the first e-mail message from space. On August 28, 1991, the crew of the space shuttle STS-43 *Atlantis* sent e-mail greetings using a Mac Portable and specially configured AppleLink software. *Atlantis* astronauts Shannon Lucid and James C. Adamson sent the message "Hello Earth! Greetings from the STS-43 Crew. This is the first AppleLink from space. Having a GREAT time, wish you were here . . . send cryo and RCS! Hasta la vista, baby . . . we'll be back!"

The AppleLink Personal Edition software was a forerunner for America Online, which was developed by Quantum (Apple retained ownership of the AppleLink name). After Quantum launched the original AOL software, Apple premiered its own eWorld program in 1994. eWorld was to be a competitor to AOL and was developed for Macintosh computer users. However, eWorld was discontinued in 1996 when Apple and America Online, Inc. partnered to distribute AOL to Apple customers.

In its continued quest to develop better internal communication programs, Apple developed AppleTalk. AppleTalk enabled multiple users to share files, applications, and printers. With the introduction of AppleTalk, new computer vocabulary such as "servers" and "clients" became commonplace. The device that allowed users to share services was referred to as the *server,* and the users of the services were called *clients* (for example, a desktop computer was usually the user or client). AppleTalk was one of the earliest uses of a distributed client/server network. AppleTalk Phase 1 was developed in the early 1980s and was for use in local workgroups. AppleTalk Phase 2 was then developed for use in larger Internet workgroups.

ADVANCED TECHNOLOGIES AND LATER DEVELOPMENTS

The rapid rise of the Internet led to massive changes in Apple's internal and external information technology environments. Internally, technological advances inspired new modes of training both for the company workforce and Apple users. The means of reaching current and potential Apple users also changed dramatically. From an external environmental perspective, the products ultimately developed and offered by Apple led to new and intriguing uses of technology.

Apple uses its information technology in its training and development programs. Apple University, home of the company's training and development program, engages executives in interactive electronic forums in which the executives can exchange insight and information about changes in the business environment. The University also uses its vast electronic network as a library of both company- and industry-wide information. This electronic campus allows information to be exchanged quickly among interested parties.

With a twist on training and development, Apple offers programs to professional educators who use Apple computers in the classroom. The intent of the Apple Professional

Development program is to help educators make the best use of classroom technologies and to raise student achievement. The company's online resources are available with a subscription to Apple Digital School Community. The subscription makes available online tutorials, libraries of articles and resources, and an interactive environment for professional development.

Advances in information technology, as well as changes in the competitive environment (particularly involving that of Dell Computer), led to dramatic changes in the way Apple reached it customer base. Apple began phasing out many of its resellers and moved to a more direct, online sales program. In the mid-1990s, the company began using its vast technological resource to debut a Web site that allowed customers to make online purchases. This direct sales model has helped Apple improve its forecasting and became a forerunner to the Apple Stores that began opening in 2001.

Apple's e-commerce strategies evolved into a wide array of product offerings that reached customers around the world. The company developed a set of revolutionary "i" products that essentially changed the way customers thought about products, services, capabilities, and connections. Probably the most popular and revolutionary product has been iTunes—a digital music library for organizing and playing digital music and video files. Used in connection with the iPod and iTunes Music Store, customers can purchase and download songs onto their MP3 players. This product combination has been extremely successful for Apple, with the billionth iTunes song sold in February of 2006. iChat is an instant text messaging application that supports both AOL and Jabber Instant Messenger services, and iChat AV allows ease of use in videoconferencing. iCal is a personal calendar that allows for sharing schedules over the Internet. In conjunction with iSync, the iCal can be synchronized with a mobile phone, PDA, or iPod. Apple tapped into the digital picture marketplace with its iLife series that included iPhoto, iMovie HD, and iDVD. With these types of product development, Apple Computer used advances in information technology to improve internal and external communication and to make revolutionary changes in longstanding product communities—essentially moving normal, everyday aspects of life onto the computer for sharing worldwide.

Critical Thinking Questions

- What early advances in information technology did Apple Computer develop?
- How were these early advances precursors to later developments at Apple?
- What new developments occurred at Apple in response to new advanced technologies, including the Internet?
- Why did AOL survive whereas Apple's electronic programs, such as AppleLink and eWorld, did not?
- How can advances in information technology help employees in different locations and different business units communicate and work together more effectively?

Sources: Anonymous, "Apple Computer Launches eWorld, Its New Online Community," *PR Newswire*, June 20, 1994, http://scottconverse.com/apple's_eworld.htm, accessed on 4/5/06; Anonymous, "Apple PR: Cupertino, CA/Vienna, VA," March 7, 1996, http://scottconverse.com/apple's_eworld.htm, accessed on 4/5/06; Owen Linzmayer and Bryan Chaffin, "This Week in Apple History," *the Mac Observer*, October 31, 2004, http://www.macobserver.com, accessed on 4/6/06; Judy D. Olian, Cathy C. Durham, Amy L. Kristof, Kenneth G. Brown, Richard M. Pierce, and Linda Kunder, "Designing Management Training and Development for Competitive Advantage: Lessons from the Best," *Human Resource Planning* 21 (1), 1998, pp. 20–31; Gregory C. Rogers, "Apple Computer (A) (Abridged): Corporate Strategy and Culture," Harvard Business School Publishing, Boston, MA, HBS 9-495-044, February 1997; Joel West, "Apple Computer: The iCEO Seizes the Internet," Center for Research on Information Technology and Organizations, Paper 348, 2002, http://repositories.cdlib.org, accessed on 12/6/05; http://www.apple.com, accessed on 4/6/06; http://www.cisco.com/univercd/cc/td/doc/cisintwk/ito_doc/ applet.htm, accessed on 4/5/06.

PART 6

Finance

CHAPTER 18

Understanding Money and Financial Institutions

Learning Goals

After reading this chapter, you should be able to answer these questions:

1 What is money, what are its characteristics and functions, and what are the three parts of the U.S. money supply?

2 How does the Federal Reserve manage the money supply?

3 What are the key financial institutions, and what role do they play in the process of financial intermediation?

4 How does the Federal Deposit Insurance Corporation (FDIC) protect depositors' funds?

5 What role do U.S. banks play in the international marketplace?

6 What trends are reshaping financial institutions?

Exploring Business Careers
Michael Cleary
JP Morgan Chase

We live in a world of giants—not of the *Jack and the Beanstalk* variety, but giants who tempt us with fast food, develop our computer technology, or sell us our groceries and just about everything else under one expansive roof. As companies expand, consistency is an issue. A McDonald's hamburger in San Diego needs to taste the same as one in Miami. Along with this, differentiation also becomes more critical. Think about it: When you order a Coke at a restaurant, does it much matter if the waiter asks you, "Is Pepsi alright?" For most people, it doesn't. A company needs to set themselves apart, while maintaining the consistent quality that makes them successful. And financial institutions are no exception.

Therefore, when the directors of JP Morgan Chase decided to revamp their 200-year-old institution, they looked for a dynamic, forward-thinking leader. They found Michael Cleary. A constant innovator, Cleary had cut his teeth in the oil and gas exploration business before moving to banking as president of First Chicago's online banking venture, Wingspan. When JP Morgan Chase bought First Chicago, they were impressed with Cleary's knowledge and ideas about the banking industry and promoted him to chief operating officer of Chase, the brand of their U.S. commercial banking services.

Cleary quickly saw the need to differentiate Chase. Within a nationwide field of banking choices, why would a customer choose Chase? His vision for delineating Chase focused more on customer experience than on who had the best rate. As he says, "This is a commodity industry and you can either differentiate yourself on rate, which I think is a very difficult thing to do, or you can differentiate yourself on customer experience. And we focus on customer experience."

Cleary's strategy is straightforward: Treat each customer as an individual with unique needs that Chase can meet. To do this, he stresses the importance of having all the financial services in one place for the customer to access and providing the trained staff and sophisticated technology to assure that these services efficiently satisfy the customer's financial wants. "That's what we're here to do. Can we help them get their first mortgage? Can we talk to them about consolidating debt with a home equity loan instead of using their credit cards? But it's really about individual answers. And it really is that my needs are very different than someone else's needs."

One simple yet revolutionary change he made was to remove the word "Bank" from their name. The company's commercial banking brand is "Chase." As Cleary explains, the term "bank" is too limiting. People think of it as checking and savings accounts. The new Chase needed to provide the entire gamut of financial services and individualize that service to the needs of each customer.

Chapter 18 focuses on the role of financial institutions in U.S. and international economies. It discusses different types of financial institutions, how they are set up and function internally, and government oversight of their operations.

Advanced technology, globalization of markets, and the relaxation of regulatory restrictions are accelerating the pace of change in the financial services industry. These changes are giving businesses and consumers new options for conducting their financial transactions. The competitive landscape for financial institutions is also changing, creating new ways for these firms to increase their market share and boost profits.

Because financial institutions connect people with money, this chapter begins with a discussion of money, its characteristics and functions, and the components of the U.S. money supply. Next, it explains the role of the Federal Reserve System in managing the money supply. Then it describes different types of financial institutions and their services and the organizations that insure customer deposits. The chapter ends with a discussion of international banking and trends in the financial institutions.

Show Me the Money

1 **What is money, what are its characteristics and functions, and what are the three parts of the U.S. money supply?**

money
Anything that is acceptable as payment for goods and services.

Money is anything that is acceptable as payment for goods and services. It affects our lives in many ways. We earn it, spend it, save it, invest it—and often wish we had more of it. Business and government use money in similar ways. Both require money to finance their operations. By controlling the amount of money in circulation, the federal government can promote economic growth and stability. For this reason, money has been called the lubricant of the machinery that drives our economic system. Our banking system was developed to ease the handling of money.

Characteristics of Money

For money to be a suitable means of exchange, it should have these key characteristics:

- *Scarcity.* Money should be scarce enough to have some value but not so scarce as to be unavailable. Pebbles, which meet some of the other criteria, would not work well as money because they are widely available. Too much money in circulation increases prices (inflation, as discussed in Chapter 2). Governments control the scarcity of money by limiting the quantity of money in circulation.
- *Durability.* Any item used as money must be durable. A perishable item such as a banana becomes useless as money when it spoils. Even early societies used durable forms of money, such as metal coins and paper money, which lasted for a long time.
- *Portability.* Money must be easily moved around. Large or bulky items, such as boulders or heavy gold bars, cannot be transported easily from place to place.
- *Divisibility.* Money must be capable of being divided into smaller parts. Divisible forms of money help make transactions of all sizes and amounts possible.

Exhibit 18.1 provides some interesting facts about our money.

Functions of Money

Using a variety of items as money would be confusing. Thus, societies develop a uniform money system to measure the value of goods and services. For money to be acceptable, it must function as a medium of exchange, as a standard of value, and as a store of value.

As a *medium of exchange,* money makes transactions easier. Having a common form of payment is much less complicated than having a barter system, wherein goods and services are exchanged for other goods and services. Money allows the exchange of products to be a simple process.

Money also serves as a *standard of value.* With a form of money whose value is accepted by all, goods and services can be priced in standard units. This makes it

Exhibit 18.1 > Fantastic Facts About Money

Did you know that:

- Currency paper is composed of 25% linen and 75% cotton.
- About 4,000 double folds (first forward and then backwards) are required before a note will tear.
- The Bureau of Engraving and Printing produces 35 million notes a day with a face value of approximately $635 million.
- 95% of the notes printed each year are used to replace notes already in circulation.
- 45% of the notes printed are $1 notes.
- The largest note ever printed by the Bureau of Engraving and Printing was the $100,000 Gold Certificate, Series 1934.
- During fiscal year 2005, it cost approximately 5.7 cents per note to produce 8.6 billion U.S. paper currency notes.
- A stack of currency one mile high would contain over 14 million notes.
- If you had 10 billion $1 notes and spent one every second of every day, it would require 317 years for you to go broke.

Source: "Money Facts," *Bureau of Engraving and Printing,* http://www.moneyfactory.gov, June 3, 2006.

easy to measure the value of products and allows transactions to be recorded in consistent terms.

As a *store of value,* money is used to hold wealth. It retains its value over time, although it may lose some of its purchasing power due to inflation. Individuals may choose to keep their money for future use rather than exchange it today for other types of products or assets.

The U.S. Money Supply

currency
Cash held in the form of coins and paper money.

The U.S. money supply is composed of currency, demand deposits, and time deposits. Currency is cash held in the form of coins and paper money. Other forms of currency are travelers' checks, cashier's checks, and money orders. The amount of currency in circulation depends on public demand. Domestic demand is influenced primarily by prices for goods and services, income levels, and the availability of alternative payment methods such as credit cards. Until the mid-1980s nearly all U.S. currency circulated only domestically. Today domestic circulation totals only a small fraction of the total amount of U.S. currency in circulation.

CONCEPT *in Action*

United States currency is becoming more colorful and secure, as the Bureau of Engraving and Printing has redesigned $10, $20, and $50 bills with enhanced design and security flourishes. The newest $10 bill issued by the Federal Reserve features the first treasury secretary, Alexander Hamilton, emblazoned in American symbols against a background tinged with orange, yellow, and red. The note's color-shifting ink, watermark, and security thread are especially difficult to counterfeit. *How often does the Fed issue currency and why?*

Exhibit 18.2 > How Long Will Your Money Last?

Have you ever wondered how quickly money wears out from being handled or damaged? Not surprisingly, smaller denominations have a shorter life span.

$1 bill	18 months
$5 bill	15 months
$10 bill	18 months
$20 bill	24 months
$50 bill	5 years
$100 bill	8.5 years
coins	25 years

Source: "Circulation of Money," *Federal Reserve Bank of Atlanta Publications,* http://www.frbatlanta.org, June 5, 2006.

demand deposits
Money kept in checking accounts that can be withdrawn by depositors on demand.

time deposits
Deposits at a bank or other financial institution that pay interest but cannot be withdrawn on demand.

M1
The total amount of readily available money in the system and includes currency and demand deposits.

M2
A term used by economists to describe the U.S. monetary supply. Includes all M1 monies plus time deposits and other money that are not immediately accessible.

In the past twenty years the amount of U.S. currency has grown more than 300 percent to about $760 billion and is now held widely outside the country.[1] Foreign demand is influenced by the political and economic uncertainties associated with some foreign currencies, and recent estimates show that between one-half and two-thirds of the value of currency in circulation is held abroad.[2] Some residents of foreign countries hold dollars as a store of value, whereas others use it as a medium of exchange.

Federal Reserve notes make up more than 99 percent of all U.S. currency in circulation. Each year the Federal Reserve Board determines new currency demand and submits a print order to the Treasury's Bureau of Engraving and Printing (BEP). The order represents the Federal Reserve System's estimate of the amount of currency the public will need in the upcoming year and reflects estimated changes in currency usage and destruction rates of unfit currency. Exhibit 18.2 shows how long we can expect our money to last on average.

Demand deposits consist of money kept in checking accounts that can be withdrawn by depositors on demand. Demand deposits include regular checking accounts as well as interest bearing and other special types of checking accounts. **Time deposits** are deposits at a bank or other financial institution that pay interest but cannot be withdrawn on demand. Examples are certain savings accounts, money market deposit accounts, and certificates of deposit. Economists use two terms to report on and discuss trends in the U.S. monetary system: M1 and M2. M1 (the *M* stands for money) is used to describe the total amount of readily available money in the system and includes currency and demand deposits. As of April 2006, the M1 monetary supply was $1.4 trillion. M2 includes all M1 monies plus time deposits and other money that is not immediately accessible. In April 2006, the M2 monetary supply was $6.8 trillion.[3]

Credit cards, sometimes referred to as "plastic money," are routinely used as a substitute for cash and checks. Credit cards are not money; they are a form of borrowing. When a bank issues a credit card to a consumer, it gives a short-term loan to the consumer by directly paying the seller for the consumer's purchases. The consumer pays the credit card company after receiving the monthly statement. Credit cards do not replace money; they simply defer payment.

concept check

What is money, and what are its characteristics?

What are the main functions of money?

What are the three main components of the U.S. money supply? How do they relate to M1 and M2?

The Federal Reserve System

 How does the Federal Reserve manage the money supply?

Before the 20th century, there was very little government regulation of the U.S. financial or monetary systems. In 1907, however, several large banks failed, creating a public panic that led worried depositors to withdraw their money from other banks. Soon, many other banks had failed and the U.S. banking system was near collapse. The Panic of 1907 was so severe that Congress created the Federal Reserve System in 1913 to provide the nation with a more stable monetary and banking system.

Exhibit 18.3 > **Federal Reserve Districts and Banks**

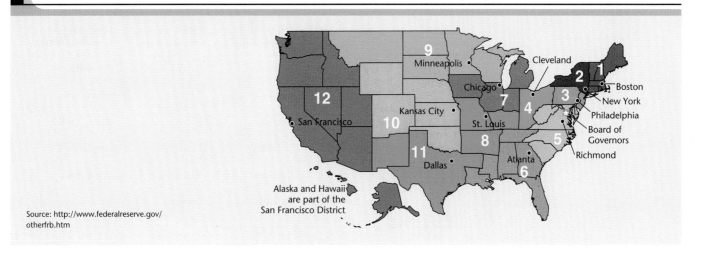

Source: http://www.federalreserve.gov/otherfrb.htm

Federal Reserve System (Fed)
The central bank of the United States; it consists of 12 district banks, each located in a major U.S. city.

open market operations
The purchase or sale of U.S. government bonds by the Federal Reserve to stimulate or slow down the economy.

The **Federal Reserve System** (commonly called the Fed) is the central bank of the United States. The Fed's primary mission is to oversee the nation's monetary and credit system and to support the ongoing operation of America's private-banking system. The Fed's actions affect the interest rates banks charge businesses and consumers, help keep inflation under control, and ultimately stabilize the U.S. financial system. The Fed operates as an independent government entity. It derives its authority from Congress but its decisions do not have to be approved by the president, Congress, or any other government branch. However, Congress does periodically review the Fed's activities and the Fed must work within the economic framework established by the government.

The Fed consists of 12 district banks, each covering a specific geographic area. Exhibit 18.3 shows the 12 districts of the Federal Reserve. Each district has its own bank president who oversees operations within that district.

Originally, the Federal Reserve System was created to control the money supply, act as a borrowing source for banks, hold the deposits of member banks, and supervise banking practices. Its activities have since broadened, making it the most powerful financial institution in the United States. Today, four of the Federal Reserve System's most important responsibilities are carrying out monetary policy, setting rules on credit, distributing currency, and making check clearing easier.

Carrying Out Monetary Policy

The most important function of the Federal Reserve System is carrying out monetary policy. The Federal Open Market Committee (FOMC) is the Fed policy-making body that meets eight times a year to make monetary policy decisions. It uses its power to change the money supply in order to control inflation and interest rates, increase employment, and influence economic activity. Three tools used by the Federal Reserve System in managing the money supply are open market operations, reserve requirements, and the discount rate. Exhibit 18.4 summarizes the short-term effects of these tools on the economy.

Open market operations—the tool most frequently used by the Federal Reserve—involve the purchase or sale of U.S. government bonds. The U.S. Treasury issues bonds to obtain the extra money needed to run the government (if taxes and other revenues aren't enough). In effect, Treasury bonds are long-term loans (five years or longer) made by businesses and individuals to the government. The Federal Reserve buys and sells

CONCEPT *in Action*

The Federal Reserve raised interest rates over a dozen times in the two years prior to Fed Chairman Alan Greenspan's retirement in 2006. Incoming chief Ben Bernanke initially continued the policy, tightening rates further. Raising the interest rate is a favorite Fed strategy for heading off inflation, which is believed to accompany rapid economic growth—although some major United States growth periods, such as the '90s, '50s, and late 1800s, weren't inflationary. *What effect do higher interest rates have on the economy?*

© MARK WILSON/GETTY IMAGES

Tool	Action	Effect on Money Supply	Effect on Interest Rates	Effect on Economic Activity
Open market operations	Buy government bonds	Increases	Lowers	Stimulates
	Sell government bonds	Decreases	Raises	Slows Down
Reserve requirements	Raise reserve requirements	Decreases	Raises	Slows Down
	Lower reserve requirements	Increases	Lowers	Stimulates
Discount rate	Raise discount rate	Decreases	Raises	Slows Down
	Lower discount rate	Increases	Lowers	Stimulates

these bonds for the Treasury. When the Federal Reserve buys bonds, it puts money into the economy. Banks have more money to lend so they reduce interest rates, which generally stimulates economic activity. The opposite occurs when the Federal Reserve sells government bonds.

reserve requirement
Requires banks that are members of the Federal Reserve System to hold some of their deposits in cash in their vaults or in an account at a district bank.

Banks that are members of the Federal Reserve System must hold some of their deposits in cash in their vaults or in an account at a district bank. This **reserve requirement** ranges from 3 to 10 percent on different types of deposits. When the Federal Reserve raises the reserve requirement, banks must hold larger reserves and thus have less money to lend. As a result, interest rates rise and economic activity slows down. Lowering the reserve requirement increases loanable funds, causes banks to lower interest rates, and stimulates the economy; however, the Federal Reserve seldom changes reserve requirements.

discount rate
The interest rate that the Federal Reserve charges its member banks.

The Federal Reserve is called "the banker's bank" because it lends money to banks that need it. The interest rate that the Federal Reserve charges its member banks is called the **discount rate.** When the discount rate is less than the cost of other sources of funds (such as certificates of deposit), commercial banks borrow from the Federal Reserve and then lend the funds at a higher rate to customers. The banks profit from the *spread,* or difference, between the rate they charge their customers and the rate paid to the Federal Reserve. Changes in the discount rate usually produce changes in the interest rate that banks charge their customers. The Federal Reserve raises the discount rate to slow down economic growth and lowers it to stimulate growth.

Setting Rules on Credit

Another activity of the Federal Reserve System is setting rules on credit. It controls the credit terms on some loans made by banks and other lending institutions. This power, called **selective credit controls**, includes consumer credit rules and margin requirements. *Consumer credit rules* establish the minimum down payments and maximum repayment periods for consumer loans. The Federal Reserve uses credit rules to slow or stimulate consumer credit purchases. *Margin requirements* specify the minimum amount of cash an investor must put up to buy securities or investment certificates issued by corporations or governments. The balance of the purchase cost can be financed through borrowing from a bank or brokerage firm. By lowering the margin requirement, the Federal Reserve stimulates securities trading. Raising the margin requirement slows trading.

selective credit controls
The power of the Federal Reserve to control consumer credit rules and margin requirements.

Distributing Currency: Keeping the Cash Flowing

The Federal Reserve distributes the coins minted and the paper money printed by the U.S. Treasury to banks. Most paper money is in the form of Federal Reserve notes. Look at a dollar bill and you'll see "Federal Reserve Note" at the top. The large letter seal on the left indicates which Federal Reserve Bank issued it. For example, bills bearing a *D* seal are issued by the Federal Reserve Bank of Cleveland, and those with an *L* seal are issued by the San Francisco district bank.

Making Check Clearing Easier

Another important activity of the Federal Reserve is processing and clearing checks between financial institutions. When a check is cashed at a financial institution other than the one holding the account on which the check is drawn, the Federal Reserve's system lets that financial institution—even if distant from the institution holding the account on which the check is drawn—quickly convert the check into cash. Checks drawn on banks within the same Federal Reserve district are handled through the local Federal Reserve Bank using a series of bookkeeping entries to transfer funds between the financial institutions. The process is more complex for checks processed between different Federal Reserve districts.

The time between when the check is written and when the funds are deducted from the check writer's account provides float. *Float* benefits the check writer by allowing it to retain the funds until the check clears; that is, when the funds are actually withdrawn from its accounts. Businesses open accounts at banks around the country that are known to have long check-clearing times. By "playing the float," firms can keep their funds invested for several extra days, thus earning more money.

To reduce this practice, in 1988 the Fed established maximum check-clearing times. However, as credit cards and other types of electronic payments have become more popular, the use of checks is declining. Responding to this decline, the Federal Reserve scaled back its check-processing facilities in early 2003, closing five sites and cutting a net of 400 jobs. Current estimates predict that check volume could decline by 9.5 percent per year between 2006 and 2010.[4]

concept check

What are the four key functions of the Federal Reserve System?

What three tools does the Federal Reserve System use to manage the money supply, and how does each affect economic activity?

U.S. Financial Institutions

 What are the key financial institutions, and what role do they play in the process of financial intermediation?

The well-developed financial system in the United States supports our high standard of living. The system allows those who wish to borrow money to do so with relative ease. It also gives savers a variety of ways to earn interest on their savings. For example, a computer company that wants to build a new headquarters in Atlanta might be financed partly with the savings of families in California. The Californians deposit their money in a local financial institution. That institution looks for a profitable and safe way to use the money and decides to make a real estate loan to the computer company. The transfer of funds from savers to investors enables businesses to expand and the economy to grow.

Households are important participants in the U.S. financial system. Although many households borrow money to finance purchases, they supply funds to the financial system through their purchases and savings. Overall, businesses and governments are users of funds. They borrow more money than they save.

Sometimes those who have funds deal directly with those who want them. A wealthy realtor, for example, may lend money to a client to buy a house. Most often, financial institutions act as intermediaries—or go-betweens—between the suppliers and demanders of funds. The institutions accept savers' deposits and invest them in financial products (such as loans) that are expected to produce a return. This process, called **financial intermediation**, is shown in Exhibit 18.5. Households are shown as

financial intermediation
The process in which financial institutions act as intermediaries between the suppliers and demanders of funds.

Exhibit 18.5 > The Financial Intermediation Process*

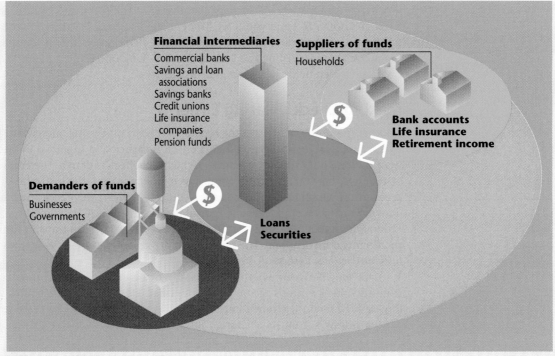

Financial intermediaries
Commercial banks
Savings and loan
associations
Savings banks
Credit unions
Life insurance
companies
Pension funds

Suppliers of funds
Households

Bank accounts
Life insurance
Retirement income

Demanders of funds
Businesses
Governments

Loans
Securities

*Only the dominant suppliers and demanders are shown here. Clearly, a single household, business, or government can be either a supplier or demander, depending on circumstances.

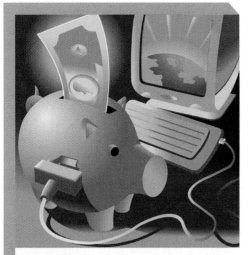

CONCEPT *in Action*

According to the United States Department of the Treasury, nearly three-fourths of senior citizens use direct deposit for receiving Social Security, SSI, and other federal benefits. Baby Boomers are less comfortable with direct deposit services, however, preferring standard paper deposits to their electronic counterpart. Banks promote the electronic transfer of funds because it eliminates paper and mail costs; seniors like the convenience and aren't fretting over cybercrime. *Are electronic banking services the wave of the future?*

© IMAGES.COM/CORBIS (RM)

suppliers of funds, and businesses and governments are shown as demanders. However, a single household, business, or government can be either a supplier or a demander, depending on the circumstances.

Financial institutions are the heart of the financial system. They are a convenient vehicle for financial intermediation. They can be divided into two broad groups: depository institutions (those that accept deposits) and nondepository institutions (those that do not accept deposits).

Depository Financial Institutions

Not all depository financial institutions are alike. Most people call the place where they save their money a "bank." Some of those places are indeed banks, but other depository institutions include thrift institutions and credit unions.

Commercial Banks A commercial bank is a profit-oriented financial institution that accepts deposits, makes business and consumer loans, invests in government and corporate securities, and provides other financial services. Commercial banks vary greatly in size from the "money center" banks located in the nation's financial centers, to smaller regional and local community banks. As a result of consolidations, small banks are decreasing in number. A large share of the nation's banking business is now held by a relatively small number of big banks. There are about 7,527 commercial banks in the United States, accounting for $9 trillion in assets and more than $8 trillion in total liabilities.[5] Banks hold a variety of assets, as shown in the diagram in Exhibit 18.6.

Exhibit 18.7 lists the top 10 insured U.S.-chartered commercial banks, based on their consolidated assets.

Exhibit 18.6 > **Assets of FDIC-Insured Commercial Banks, 2005**

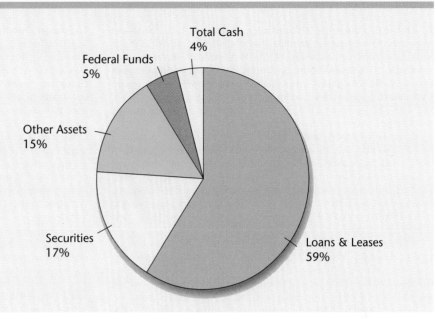

Source: "Financial Services Fact Book," Insurance Information Institute Web site, http://www. financialservices.org, June 3, 2006.

commercial banks
Profit-oriented financial institutions that accept deposits, make business and consumer loans, invest in government and corporate securities, and provide other financial services.

bank charter
An operating license issued to a bank by the federal government or a state government; required for a commercial bank to do business.

thrift institutions
Depository institutions formed specifically to encourage household saving and to make home mortgage loans.

Customers' deposits are a commercial bank's major source of funds, the main use for which is loans. The difference between the interest the bank earns on loans and the interest it pays on deposits, plus fees it earns from other financial services, pays the bank's costs and provide a profit.

Commercial banks are corporations owned and operated by individuals or other corporations. They can be either national or state banks and to do business, they must get a **bank charter**—an operating license—from a state or federal government. *National banks* are chartered by the Comptroller of the Currency, who is part of the U.S. Treasury Department. These banks must belong to the Federal Reserve System and must carry insurance on their deposits from the Federal Deposit Insurance Corporation. *State banks* are chartered by the state in which they are based. Generally, state banks are smaller than national banks, are less closely regulated than national banks, and are not required to belong to the Federal Reserve System.

Thrift Institutions A **thrift institution** is a depository institution formed specifically to encourage household saving and to make home mortgage loans. Thrift

Bank	Consolidated Assets
1. Bank of America Corp.	$1,104,944,000
2. J. P. Morgan Chase & Co.	1,093,394,000
3. Citigroup, Inc.	749,335,000
4. Wachovia Corp.	496,566,000
5. Wells Fargo & Co.	415,802,000
6. U.S. Bancorp	208,940,000
7. SunTrust Bank Inc.	178,282,000
8. HSBC Bank USA NA	158,754,000
9. State Street Bank and Trust Corp.	91,927,000
10. Keybank NA	88,877,000

Source: "Insured U.S.-Chartered Commercial Banks That Have Consolidated Assets of $300 Million or More, Ranked by Consolidated Assets as of December 31, 2005, *Federal Reserve Statistical Release* March 7, 2006 http://www. federal reserve.gov.

Ranking the Banks

Which banks provide the best customer satisfaction? J. D. Power and Associates (JDPA), based in Westlake Village, California, ranked 33 major banks based on Internet surveys of 12,904 households. In the research company's 2006 Retail Banking Satisfaction Study, top performers such as Cherry Hill, New Jersey–based Commerce Bancorp; Newport Beach, California–based Downey Savings and Loan; and online bank ING of the Netherlands received high ratings in convenience, service quality, problem resolution, and image in the marketplace.

Commerce Bancorp was viewed as "customer-focused, providing personal service, and for being an innovative company," writes JDPA authors Jeff Taylor and Gina Pingitore. ING lost points for "impersonal service" but got high marks for "superior online performance, good product and fee offerings, and an image as an innovator," they say. Downey Savings, with more than 50 percent of its branches located in supermarkets, scored well on "convenience and customer focus," according to the survey.

Assessing customer satisfaction is also the goal of the American Customer Satisfaction Index (ACSI), which granted Wachovia Corporation top honors for the fifth straight year. Charlotte-based Bank of America Corporation, New York–based JPMorgan Chase and Company, and San Francisco–based Wells Fargo & Company took the other top spots.

In random-sample telephone interviews carried out in late 2005, Wachovia was awarded 79 out of a possible 100 points. Gwynne Whitley, the bank's head of corporate customer service excellence, ascribes much of Wachovia's achievement to chief executive officer Kenneth

Thompson's monthly meetings to review service quality. The group, which includes business line heads and senior technology executives, examines customer service information from the previous month as well as reports from the bank's regional executives. Information also comes from in-house surveys of service quality that Wachovia carries out quarterly with the Princeton, New Jersey–based Gallup Organization. Whitley says Wachovia was particularly pleased with its accomplishment in 2005 because it integrated Birmingham-based SouthTrust Corp. that year, and notes that customer service often declines after a major bank acquisition.

Translating customer satisfaction into customer loyalty is the name of the game. "Customer satisfaction is great but if you really want organic growth, you need to up this thing to another level," Whitley says. With that in mind, Thompson's group will soon be examining results from a new case management system that Wachovia is putting in place. The system will follow problematic customer service issues to their final outcome, determining Wachovia's capacity to resolve them. With this level of commitment to customer satisfaction and quality, Wachovia could easily top the ACSI survey again in 2006.[6]

Critical Thinking Questions:

- What can banks and financial institutions do to retain their customers and make them feel valued?
- Is there a cost involved in not making customer service a priority? Explain your answer.

---

institutions include *savings and loan associations (S&Ls)* and *savings banks.* S&Ls keep large percentages of their assets in home mortgages. Compared with S&Ls, savings banks focus less on mortgage loans and more on stock and bond investments. Thrifts are declining in number. At their peak in the late 1960s, there were more than 4,800. But a combination of factors has reduced their ranks significantly, including sharp increases in interest rates in the late 1970s and increased loan defaults during the recession of the early 1980s. By year-end 2005, due mostly to acquisitions by or conversions to commercial banks or other savings banks, the number of thrifts had fallen to 1,305.[7]

credit unions
Not-for-profit, member-owned financial cooperatives.

Credit Unions A credit union is a not-for-profit, member-owned financial cooperative. Credit union members typically have something in common: They may, for example, work for the same employer, belong to the same union or professional group, or attend the same church or school. The credit union pools their assets, or savings, in order to make loans and offer other services to members. The not-for-profit status of credit unions makes them tax-exempt, so they can pay good interest rates on deposits and offer loans at favorable interest rates. Like banks, credit unions can have either a state or federal charter.

The approximately 8,700 credit unions in the United States have more than 84 million members and over $678 billion in assets.[8] The five largest credit unions in the United States are shown in Exhibit 18.8. However, recent data from the Credit Union National Association (CUNA) economic forecast indicate that credit union growth rates will decline into 2007. Rising interest rates, high oil prices, low household savings, and record debt levels will slow consumer and business investment spending.[9]

Services offered Commercial banks, thrift institutions, and credit unions offer a wide range of financial services for businesses and consumers. Typical services offered by

Exhibit 18.8 > Five Largest U.S. Credit Unions

Source: "Top 100 Credit Unions—Year-end 2005," Credit Union National Association Web site, http://www.cuna.org, March 2006.

1. Navy Federal Credit Union, Merrifield, Virginia
2. State Employees Credit Union, Raleigh, North Carolina
3. Pentagon Federal Credit Union, Alexandria, Virginia
4. Golden 1 Credit Union, Sacramento, California
5. Boeing Employees Credit Union, Tukwila, Washington

depository financial institutions are listed in Exhibit 18.9. Some financial institutions specialize in providing financial services to a particular type of customer, such as consumer banking services or business banking services. Online banking is one of the top ten Internet activities according to the Center for the Digital Future at the University of Southern California Annenberg School for Communication. However, a study by the Gartner Group found that 28 percent of respondents said online attacks are causing them to reduce their Web banking activity.[10] The Managing Change box describes other ways banks are using technology.

Nondepository Financial Institutions

Some financial institutions provide certain banking services but do not accept deposits. These nondepository financial institutions include insurance companies, pension funds, brokerage firms, and finance companies. They serve both individuals and businesses.

Insurance Companies Insurance companies are major suppliers of funds. Policyholders make payments (called *premiums*) to buy financial protection from the insurance company. Insurance companies invest the premiums in stocks, bonds, real estate, business loans, and real estate loans for large projects. The insurance industry is discussed in detail in the Appendix to Chapter 19, "Managing Risk and Insurance."

Exhibit 18.9 > Services Offered by Depository Financial Institutions

Service	Description
Savings accounts	Pay interest on deposits
Checking accounts	Allow depositors to withdraw any amount of funds at any time up to the amount on deposit
Money market deposit accounts	Savings accounts on which the interest rate is set at market rates
Certificates of deposit (CDs)	Pay a higher interest rate than regular savings accounts, provided that the deposit remains for a specified period
Consumer loans	Loans to individuals to finance the purchase of a home, car, or other expensive items
Business loans	Loans to businesses and other organizations to finance their operations
Money transfer	Transfer of funds to other banks
Electronic funds transfer	Use of telephone lines and computers to conduct financial transactions
Automated teller machine (ATM)	Allows bank customers to make deposits and withdrawals from their accounts 24 hours a day
Debit cards	Allow customers to transfer money from their bank account directly to a merchant's account to pay for purchases
Smart card	Card that stores monetary value and can be used to buy goods and services instead of using cash, checks, and credit and debit cards
Online banking	Allows customers to conduct financial transactions via the Internet or through a dial-in line that operates with a bank's software

© TIM BOYLE/GETTY IMAGES

MANAGING CHANGE

Technology Continues to Change the Face of Banking

In today's highly competitive financial marketplace, both large and small banks face pressure to achieve greater brand differentiation and increased market share, shareholder value, and profitability. Increasingly, they are turning to technology to give them the edge.

For example, Microsoft is partnering with other leading software, hardware, and systems providers to offer "experience Banking, a three-pronged approach to helping banks and other financial services firms change the overall experience they provide to their customers, employees and operations." These technology solutions integrate with banks' existing systems and allow bank employees to easily access data. Benefits include better decision-making, improved cross-selling opportunities, and increased customer satisfaction and loyalty.

All sizes of banking institutions can implement Microsoft's "experience Banking" solutions. "We are thrilled to see that community banks and credit unions are experiencing the same success as the larger banks," said Bill Hartnett, general manager of strategy and solutions for the Financial Services Group at Microsoft.

In their ongoing quest for market domination, leading banks across the globe have adopted the latest technologies to increase return on investment, achieve more streamlined operations, and enhance customer service. Barclays Bank, the world's ninth-largest bank, standardized its desktop computer network to streamline business processes and improve communication without compromising highly sensitive information. The new system enabled employees to quickly respond to customer requests and work collaboratively on data and documents to make business decisions more quickly. Standard Chartered Bank, with more than 30,000 employees in 500 locations in 50 countries worldwide, adopted an instant messaging solution to enable real-time communication and collaboration. The company achieved a revenue boost of 5 percent, increases in produc-

tivity of up to 500 percent, and greater agility to respond to market opportunities.

Community banks are also implementing sophisticated technology. Often their size is an advantage, allowing them to quickly develop the IT systems they need to succeed in niche markets. "Microsoft's 'experience Banking' initiative clearly supports our mission of providing exceptional customer service and personalized experience in a unique environment," says Ray Davis, CEO of Oregon's Umpqua Bank. Woodforest National Bank, with 200 branches in Texas, North Carolina, and Virginia, developed a multilingual telephone banking system that not only decreased call times 50 percent and the need for live operator support by up to 70 percent, but also significantly reduced costs.

"Competition in banking has never been fiercer," says Warren Lewis, managing director of banking, Microsoft Financial Services Group. "With the competition just a mouse click or a street corner away, banks may experience customer attrition rates of 15 percent or higher. Consumers expect seamless customer experiences—at the branch or ATM, through a call center, or via the Internet. Failure to meet customer expectations can result in a customer opening an account across the street. With the cost for acquiring a new customer $3,500, no one can afford to lose a customer." By implementing new and better technology solutions, banks can increase their customer retention rates and improve the overall customer experience.[11]

Critical Thinking Questions

* Describe the basic approach of Microsoft's "experience Banking" initiative. Why have software providers created specialized solutions for banks?
* How has this technology helped banks change the way they do business?

pension funds
Large pools of money set aside by corporations, unions, and governments for later use in paying retirement benefits to their employees or members.

Pension Funds Corporations, unions, and governments set aside large pools of money for later use in paying retirement benefits to their employees or members. These **pension funds** are managed by the employers or unions themselves or by outside managers, such as life insurance firms, commercial banks, and private investment firms. Pension plan members receive a specified monthly payment when they reach a given age. After setting aside enough money to pay near-term benefits, pension funds invest the rest in business loans, stocks, bonds, or real estate. They often invest large sums in the stock of the employer. U.S. pension fund assets total about $2.7 trillion.[12]

Brokerage Firms A *brokerage firm* buys and sells securities (stocks and bonds) for its clients and gives them related advice. Many brokerage firms offer some banking services. They may offer clients a combined checking and savings account with a high interest rate and also make loans, backed by securities, to them. Chapter 20 explains the activities of brokerage firms in more detail.

Finance Companies A *finance company* makes short-term loans for which the borrower puts up tangible assets (such as an automobile, inventory, machinery, or property) as security. Finance companies often make loans to individuals or businesses that cannot get credit elsewhere. Promising new businesses with no track record and firms that can't get more credit from a bank often obtain loans from *commercial finance companies. Consumer finance companies* make loans to individuals, often to cover the lease or purchase of large consumer goods such as automobiles or major household appliances. To compensate for the extra risk, finance companies usually charge higher interest rates than banks.

> **concept check**
>
> What is the financial intermediation process?
>
> Differentiate between the three types of depository financial institutions and the services they offer.
>
> What are the four main types of non-depository financial institutions?

Insuring Bank Deposits

 4 How does the Federal Deposit Insurance Corporation (FDIC) protect depositors' funds?

Federal Deposit Insurance Corporation (FDIC)
An independent, quasi-public corporation backed by the full faith and credit of the U.S. government that insures deposits in commercial banks and thrift institutions for up to a ceiling of $100,000 per account.

The U.S. banking system worked fairly well from when the Federal Reserve System was established in 1913 until the stock market crash of 1929 and the Great Depression that followed. Business failures caused by these events resulted in major cash shortages as people rushed to withdraw their money from banks. Many cash-starved banks failed because the Federal Reserve did not, as expected, lend money to them. The government's efforts to prevent bank failures were ineffective. Over the next two years, 5,000 banks—about 20 percent of the total number—failed.

President Franklin D. Roosevelt made strengthening the banking system his first priority. After taking office in 1933, Roosevelt declared a bank holiday, closing all banks for a week so he could take corrective action. Congress passed the Banking Act of 1933, which empowered the Federal Reserve System to regulate banks and reform the banking system. The act's most important provision was the creation of the **Federal Deposit Insurance Corporation (FDIC)** to insure deposits in commercial banks. The 1933 act also gave the Federal Reserve authority to set reserve requirements, ban interest on demand deposits, regulate the interest rates on time deposits, and prohibit banks from investing in specified types of securities. In 1934 the Federal Savings and Loan Insurance Corporation (FSLIC) was formed to insure deposits at S&Ls. When the FSLIC went bankrupt in the 1980s, the FDIC took over responsibility for administering the fund that insures deposits at thrift institutions.

Today, the major deposit insurance funds include the following:

- *The Bank Insurance Fund (BIF).* Administered by the FDIC, this fund provides deposit insurance to commercial banks.
- *The Savings Association Insurance Fund (SAIF).* Administered by the FDIC, this fund provides deposit insurance to thrift institutions.
- *The National Credit Union Share Insurance Fund.* Administered by the National Credit Union Administration, this fund provides deposit insurance to credit unions.

Role of the FDIC

The FDIC is an independent, quasi-public corporation backed by the full faith and credit of the U.S. government. It examines and supervises about 5,250 banks and savings banks, more than half the institutions in the banking system. It insures about $3 trillion of deposits in U.S. banks and thrift institutions against loss if the financial institution fails.[13] The FDIC insures all member banks in the Federal Reserve System. The ceiling on insured deposits is $100,000 per account. Each insured bank pays the insurance premiums, which are a fixed percentage of the bank's domestic deposits. In 1993, the FDIC switched from a flat rate for deposit insurance to a risk-based premium system because of the large number of bank and thrift failures during the 1980s and early 1990s. Some experts argue that certain banks take too much risk because they view deposit insurance as a safety net for their depositors—a view many believe contributed to earlier bank failures.

Enforcement by the FDIC

To ensure that banks operate fairly and profitably, the FDIC sets guidelines for banks and then reviews the financial records and management practices of member banks at least once a year. Bank examiners perform these reviews during unannounced visits, rating banks on their compliance with banking regulations—for example, the Equal Credit Opportunity Act, which states that a bank cannot refuse to lend money to people because of their color, religion, or national origin. Examiners also rate a bank's overall financial condition, focusing on loan quality, management practices, earnings, liquidity, and whether the bank has enough capital (equity) to safely support its activities.

> ### concept check
>
> What is the FDIC, and what are its responsibilities?
>
> What are the major deposit insurance funds?
>
> What can the FDIC do to help financially troubled banks?

When bank examiners conclude that a bank has serious financial problems, the FDIC can take several actions. It can lend money to the bank, recommend that the bank merge with a stronger bank, require the bank to use new management practices or replace its managers, buy loans from the bank, or provide extra equity capital to the bank. The FDIC may even cover all deposits at a troubled bank, including those over $100,000, to restore the public's confidence in the financial system.

International Banking

 5 **What role do U.S. banks play in the international marketplace?**

The financial marketplace spans the globe, with money routinely flowing across international borders. U.S. banks play an important role in global business by providing loans to foreign governments and businesses. Multinational corporations need many special banking services, such as foreign-currency exchange and funding for overseas investments. U.S. banks also offer trade-related services, like global cash management, that helps firms manage their cash flows, improve their payment efficiency, and reduce their exposure to operational risks. Sometimes consumers in other nations have a need for banking services that banks in their own countries don't provide. Therefore, large banks often look beyond their national borders for profitable banking opportunities.

Many U.S. banks have expanded into overseas markets by opening offices in Europe, Latin America, and Asia. They often provide better customer service than local banks and have access to more sources of funding. Citibank, for example, was the first bank to offer banking-by-phone and 24-hour-a-day ATM service in Japan. It earns approximately 50 percent of its net income from operations outside North America.[14]

For U.S. banks, expanding internationally can be difficult. Banks in other nations are often subject to fewer regulations than U.S. banks, making it easier for them to undercut American banks on the pricing of loans and services. Some governments also protect their banks against foreign competition. The Expanding Around the Globe box illustrates the difficulty Citigroup faced trying to gain a larger share of the lucrative Chinese banking market, only to be foiled by government red tape. The Chinese government imposes high fees and limits the amount of deposits that foreign banks can accept

CONCEPT *in Action*

While world banks play a central role in global economic development, they also play a part in global counter-terrorism. The Society for Worldwide Interbank Financial Telecommunication (SWIFT), an international banking cooperative that oversees financial transactions in more than 200 countries, began monitoring the wire transfers of suspected terrorists after 9/11. SWIFT's financial surveillance, in coordination with United States Treasury Department initiatives, has led to the interruption of terror networks worldwide. *Why do world banks have an interest in combating terrorism?*

from customers. It also controls foreign-bank deposit and loan interest rates, limiting the ability of foreign banks to compete with government-owned Chinese banks.

International banks operating within the United States also have a substantial impact on the economy through job creation—they employ over 120,000 people in the United States and over 90 percent of these are U.S. citizens—operating and

EXPANDING AROUND THE GLOBE

Breaching Banking Barriers in China

If Citigroup's bid to purchase a majority stake in Guangdong Development Bank—with its nationwide network of over 500 branches and booming credit-card business—had been successful, it would have captured the largest ownership stake held by a foreign investor in a Chinese bank and thereby gained full management control. It could have ended regulatory limits on foreign ownership of Chinese financial institutions, overcoming the current regulatory limits of 20 percent ownership for a single foreign investor in a Chinese bank and less than 25 percent for all foreign shareholders.

But the Chinese government refused to put aside the ownership rule, killing Citigroup's bid to be the first foreign firm to surpass the ownership limit in a mainland lender. The government's denial indicates an increasing resistance to state-asset sales in the country. "There's real concern about losing control of the banking system and fears that the local banks have no way to compete with the more sophisticated foreign banks," said Stephan Rothlin, secretary general of the Center for International Business Ethics in Beijing.

So New York city–based Citigroup, the largest lender in the United States, abandoned its larger stake bid in an effort to keep its bid for a smaller stake in the bank alive. China forbids foreign companies from purchasing more than 19.9 percent of a bank. Citigroup wanted 40 percent of Guangdong Development as part of an investment consortium that sought an overall 85 percent stake.

The question of control is vital in China, where banks are striving to introduce modern risk-management systems after decades of uncontrolled lending. "China should pass a law to prevent 'malicious' mergers and acquisitions by overseas companies seeking monopolies," Li Deshu, the former head of the national statistics bureau and a ministerial-level official, said during the National People's Congress in March 2006. Other critics say that foreign companies are profiteering after paying too little for their stakes. "Pricing China's big four banks only on their net assets fails to factor in the value of their brand and customers," said Shi Jianping, dean of the School of Finance at Central University of Finance & Economics. In fact, HSBC made a $4 billion profit on its recent $2.18 billion investment in Bank of Communications, although it cannot sell its stake until August 2008. And Bank of America has a paper return of $5.82 billion on a $3 billion China Construction Bank stake it bought in October 2005, which it also cannot sell until 2008.

Banking forecasters say it is doubtful that authorities will permit any of the "Big Four" state-owned Chinese banks to come under overseas rule any time soon. Any relaxation of the limits is more liable to concern smaller provincial and city banks, which would benefit from foreign investment and expertise.[15]

Critical Thinking Questions
- Why are the Chinese so reluctant to allow foreign companies a major ownership stake in their banks?
- Why are Chinese banks attractive to foreign investors? Explain.

Exhibit 18.10 > The World's Biggest Banks, 2005

UBS	Switzerland
Citigroup	United States
Mizuho Financial Group	Japan
HSBC	United Kingdom
Credit Agricole	France
BNP Paribas	France
ING Group	Netherlands
JPMorgan Chase	United States
Deutsche Bank	Germany

Source: "The World's Biggest Banks 2005," *Global Finance Magazine,* http://www.gfmag.com, May 29, 2006.

capital expenditures, taxes, and other contributions. According to March 2005 Federal Reserve data, the combined banking and non-banking assets of the U.S. operations of international banks totaled $3.63 trillion.[16]

The United States has two banks listed in the top ten world's biggest banks as shown in Exhibit 18.10.

Political and economic uncertainty in other countries can make international banking a high-risk venture. In the late 1990s, for example, Asian banks underwrote loans—to finance highly speculative real estate ventures and corporate expansions that fueled booming economies in several Pacific Rim countries—which attracted many foreign investors. The bank loans and foreign investments made the balance sheets of the Asian banks and their customers look better than they actually were, which encouraged United States, German, French, and other European banks to make billions of dollars worth of loans to Thailand, Indonesia, Malaysia, and Korea. When investors started taking their money out of the Asian banks, the banks' assets plummeted, forcing currency devaluations. The situation severely injured the economies of several Asian countries, resulting in high inflation and deep debt. Lacking capital, Asian banks could not get loans to conduct business, and companies couldn't get loans to finance the production and export of their products. The crisis also hurt many U.S. banks.

> **concept check**
>
> What is the role of U.S. banks in international banking?
>
> What challenges do U.S. banks face in foreign markets?

Trends in Financial Institutions

 6 **What trends are reshaping financial institutions?**

What factors will influence financial institutions in the years ahead? The latest reports claim there will be a continued focus on regulatory and compliance issues, as well as on operational efficiency. Financial institutions will have to fight for their share of the domestic market and seek growth by expanding into emerging markets, and merger activity will continue.

Despite a projected rocky road ahead, banks plan to tackle ambitious marketing and technology initiatives in 2006. According to a report by Boston, Massachusetts-based Aite Group, that forecasts the top ten U.S. banking industry trends for 2006, after three years of booming profits, U.S. commercial banks are thriving. But in 2006, banks have been forced to negotiate an obstacle course of unstable interest rates, defaults on loans, waning demand for mortgage financing, and increases in regulatory compliance requirements. Aite Group predicts U.S. banks will "engage more aggressively in pursuing untapped customer segments, marketing innovative products, refreshing key components of their technology infrastructure, leveraging the Internet better to attract new customers and cross-sell to existing ones, and battling at the point-of-sale to deliver more value to merchants and consumers."[17] The diagram in Exhibit 18.11 demonstrates these trends.

Banks may not have an easy time ahead, but several trends bode well for the future. An exciting new market segment has opened up a world of possibilities for financial firms. Regulators are stepping up controls to prevent money laundering, and branch banking is once again in vogue.

Exhibit 18.11 > Top 10 Banking Industry Trends in 2006

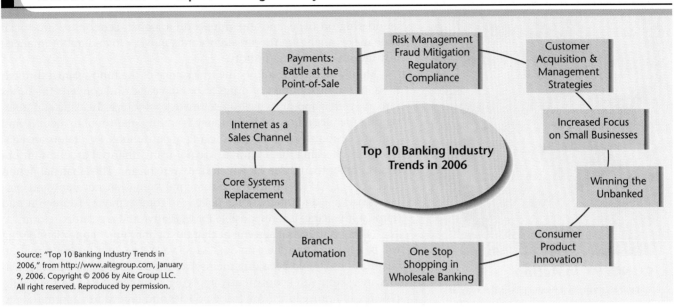

Top 10 Banking Industry Trends in 2006

Payments: Battle at the Point-of-Sale

Risk Management Fraud Mitigation Regulatory Compliance

Customer Acquisition & Management Strategies

Internet as a Sales Channel

Increased Focus on Small Businesses

Core Systems Replacement

Winning the Unbanked

Branch Automation

Consumer Product Innovation

One Stop Shopping in Wholesale Banking

CONCEPT *in Action*

The ongoing campaign against money-laundering touched the entertainment world in 2006 when jeweler Yakov Arabov—aka "Jacob the Jeweler"—was arrested on money-laundering and drug-trafficking charges. Founder of the prestigious luxury brand Jacob & Co., and jeweler of choice among hip-hop artists and Hollywood celebrities, Arabov has famously bedecked stars like Kanye West, Sir Elton John, and Jessica Simpson with his signature bling. *Why is there a renewed push by financial institutions to crack down on money-laundering?*

The "Ivy League Mom"—Hot New Financial Consumer

"Ivy League Moms" are the newest untapped consumer source for financial firms, claims a new report entitled "The Untapped Financial Consumer," released by the Aite Group on May 17, 2006. So why do "Ivy League moms" matter so much to financial institutions? They represent almost 10 million U.S. households, with assets of $6.5 trillion, a market segment with so much profit potential that it is causing the financial industry to sit up and take notice.

"There is a new player in the U.S. consumer market—the 'Ivy League Mom' segment," notes Ekaterina O. Walsh, Ph.D., Research Director with Aite Group and author of the report. "The name reflects the intellectual prowess of these highly educated women. They are unique and demanding—but lucrative for any financial institution. While all marketers must take notice of Ivy League Moms, it's especially important that financial services firms do. These consumers are their dream come true."

Comprised of affluent professionals who have left the workforce to raise children, this group of women makes their own financial decisions, manages investments, and influences their high-net-worth spouses as well. Young and loyal, they are candidates for many financial products and services, and a firm can anticipate having their business for many years into the future. They are also often in a position to refer their similarly well-heeled friends. And when they re-enter the workforce one day, they can anticipate even greater wealth.[18]

Dirty Money—New Focus on Money Laundering

In today's world of international terrorism and the relatively easy and "invisible" electronic transfer of funds, the current focus on money laundering is here to stay says Boston, Massachusetts–based Aite Group, which anticipates increased emphasis on money laundering compliance. The International Monetary Fund (IMF) estimates that *money laundering*, the process drug traffickers use to introduce proceeds gained from the sale or

CONCEPT *in Action*

A retail-banking renaissance is under way as banks invest greater marketing resources in their local branches. While call centers and online-banking are arguably more convenient options for the customer than going to a local bank, local branches offer marketers opportunities for generating revenue, cross-selling financial products, and building long-term relationships through premier customer service. *What can banks do to make their retail branch offices more inviting to customers?*

© PHOTODISC GREEN/GETTY IMAGES

distribution of controlled substances into the legitimate financial market, amounts to between 2 and 5 percent of the world's gross domestic product, or about $600 billion annually.[19] The potential impact of money laundering on firms and individuals on a global, economic, and social scale makes analyzing the stream of funds moving in and out of financial institutions an ongoing priority.

Money laundering allows the true source of the funds gained through the sale and distribution of drugs to be concealed and converts the funds into assets that appear to have a legitimate legal source. Tracking and intercepting the illegal flow of drug money is an important tool to identify and dismantle international drug trafficking organizations. Regulators are continuously checking that criminals are not using financial products for objectives other than those for which they were meant. The Financial Action Task Force (FATF) is an intergovernmental body that develops and promotes national and international policies to combat money laundering and terrorist financing. It is responsible for legislative and regulatory reform.

"There is universal agreement that the fight against money laundering will be a priority from here on out," says Eva Weber, an Aite Group analyst. "Institutions should be asking themselves the same questions that regulators are asking: Am I consistently applying anti-money laundering (AML) policies and procedures? Are those policies and procedures appropriate to the risks my business faces? Can I demonstrate compliance fairly readily?"

AML vendors are offering improved technology in response to financial firms' requirements. Key AML functions are list checking, transaction monitoring, and reporting. Weber observes that there is no "right" answer when it comes to preventing money laundering. "Regulators are unlikely to penalize institutions for isolated oversights, as long as those institutions have given appropriate thought to their anti-money laundering programs."[20]

A Branch Renaissance in Retail Banking

It wasn't that long ago when a bank employee would stop you outside the bank to ask you your business, more often than not directing you to the nearest ATM machine rather than permitting you entry into the bank itself. Bank customers weren't meant to "bother" busy bank employees with such mundane transactions as making deposits, checking balances, paying bills, or withdrawing funds.

Market evolution has transformed what happens in today's branch environment, and those days appear to be over. Banks now recognize that the branch is still the cornerstone of retail banking and the most effective delivery channel for increasing revenues through the sale of higher-margin services and products. The direct personal interaction available at the branch provides the optimum environment for selling these products. The idea of utilizing branches as "stores" instead of "transaction centers" is not new, but today it has gained renewed momentum as banks feel the pressure to produce more profits from their branch network.[21]

According to research conducted by Boston-based Celent Communications, only 45 percent of branch activities are transaction related (deposits, withdrawals, transfers, etc.). But along with the shift to in-branch sales and service, there is a need to better serve customers. At the most basic level, banks lose customers because of poor service. By providing branch employees with the tools and information that enable immediate access to customer information and facilitate real-time issue resolutions, banks are striving to eliminate the delays and frustrations that drive customers to make changes. With the average retail banking customer attrition rate 12 to 15 percent and the cost to acquire a new customer 5 to 10 times more than retaining an existing one, it makes sense for banks to do everything they can to keep their customers, even if it means letting them back inside the bank again—for free.[22]

concept check

What factors are creating a difficult economic environment for banks?

Why are "Ivy League moms" such an attractive market segment to the financial services industry?

What impact has terrorism had on the banking industry?

What is the "retail branch renaissance," and why is it so important to banks?

Summary of Learning Goals

1 **What is money, what are its characteristics and functions, and what are the three parts of the U.S. money supply?**

Money is anything accepted as payment for goods and services. For money to be a suitable means of exchange, it should be scarce, durable, portable, and divisible. Money functions as a medium of exchange, a standard of value, and a store of value. The U.S. money supply consists of currency (coins and paper money), demand deposits (checking accounts), and time deposits (interest-bearing deposits that cannot be withdrawn on demand).

2 **How does the Federal Reserve manage the money supply?**

The Federal Reserve System (the Fed) is an independent government agency that performs four main functions: carrying out monetary policy, setting rules on credit, distributing currency, and making check clearing easier. The three tools it uses in managing the money supply are open market operations, reserve requirements, and the discount rate.

3 **What are the key financial institutions, and what role do they play in the process of financial intermediation?**

Financial institutions can be divided into two main groups: depository institutions and nondepository institutions. Depository institutions include commercial banks, thrift institutions, and credit unions. Nondepository institutions include insurance companies, pension funds, brokerage firms, and finance companies. Financial institutions ease the transfer of funds between suppliers and demanders of funds.

4 **How does the Federal Deposit Insurance Corporation (FDIC) protect depositors' funds?**

The Federal Deposit Insurance Corporation insures deposits in commercial banks through the Bank Insurance Fund and deposits in thrift institutions through the Savings Association Insurance Fund. Deposits in credit unions are insured by the National Credit Union Share Insurance Fund, which is administered by the National Credit Union Administration. The FDIC sets banking policies and practices and reviews banks annually to ensure that they operate fairly and profitably.

5 **What role do U.S. banks play in the international marketplace?**

U.S. banks provide loans and trade-related services to foreign governments and businesses. They also offer specialized services such as cash management and foreign-currency exchange.

6 **What trends are reshaping financial institutions?**

Various economic and social factors mean banks face challenges ahead. Financial institutions continue to face regulatory and compliance issues while striving for their share of the market. Affluent "Ivy League moms" are the latest new market segment for the financial services industry, and other opportunities exist both domestically and internationally to ensure banks' continued growth. Banks and federal agencies are placing greater emphasis on regulations to fight money laundering so that funds do not fall into the wrong hands. The Financial Action Task Force (FATF) is an intergovernmental body that develops and promotes national and international policies to combat the illegal flow of drug money. Banks are adopting a "back-to-basics" approach that is changing the way they do business. The branch bank is once again a focus of customer service efforts.

Key Terms

bank charter   607
commercial banks   607
credit unions   608
currency   601
demand deposits   602
discount rate   604
Federal Deposit Insurance Corporation (FDIC)   611
Federal Reserve System (Fed)   603
financial intermediation   605

M1   602
M2   602
money   600
open market operations   603
pension funds   611
reserve requirement   604
selective credit controls   604
thrift institutions   607
time deposits   602

Preparing for Tomorrow's Workplace: *SCANS*

1. How much does a checking account cost? Call or visit several local banks and weigh prices and services. Take into consideration how you use your checking account, how many checks a month you write, and the average balances you keep. On the Internet, BankRate.com (**http://www.bankrate.com**) lets you digitally compare bank products. Could you pay lower fees elsewhere? Could you earn interest on your checking account at a credit union? Would you be better off paying a monthly fee with unlimited check-writing privileges? Crunch the numbers to find the best deal. (Resources, Information)

2. You are starting a small business selling collectible books over the Internet and need to establish a business banking account that will provide the following services: business checking, credit-card processing, a business savings account, and perhaps a line of credit. Call or visit at least three local banks to gather information about their business banking services, including data about fees, service options, and other features of interest to entrepreneurs. Write a short summary of each bank's offerings and benefits and make a recommendation about which bank you would choose for your new business. (Interpersonal, Information)

3. If you watch the news, you've undoubtedly heard mention that the Fed is going to raise or lower interest rates. What exactly does this mean? Explain how the Fed's decision to raise and lower its discount rate might affect (a) a large manufacturer of household appliances, (b) a midsize software firm, (c) a small restaurant, (d) a family hoping to purchase their first home, and (e) a college student. (Information)

4. Research the banking system of another country and write a report on your findings by answering these questions: Is there a central banking system similar to the U.S. Federal Reserve system in place? Which government agency or department controls it and how does it operate? How stable is the country's central banking system? How does it compare in structure and operation to the Federal Reserve System? How much control does the government have over banks operating in the country? Are there any barriers to entry specifically facing foreign banks? What would this mean to a foreign business attempting to do business in this country? (Information)

5. Banks use databases to identify profitable and unprofitable customers. Bankers say they lose money on customers who typically keep less than $1,000 in their checking and savings accounts and frequently call or visit the bank. Profitable customers keep several thousand dollars in their accounts and seldom visit a teller or call the bank. To turn unprofitable customers into profitable ones, banks have

assessed fees on almost 300 services, including using a bank teller, although many of the fees are waived for customers who maintain high account balances. Bankers justify the fees by saying they're in business to earn a profit. Discuss whether banks are justified in treating profitable and unprofitable customers differently. Defend your answers. (Information, Systems)

6. **Team Activity** During its regular meetings, the Federal Open Market Committee, the Federal Reserve's monetary policy-making body, considers a number of economic indicators and reports before making decisions. The decisions made by the Fed include: whether to sell or purchase Federal treasury bonds, whether to raise or lower bank reserve requirements, and whether to raise or lower the Federal reserve discount rate. Divide your class into groups (if possible, try to use seven members, the size of the FOMC) and assign each group one of these decisions. As a group, identify the types of information used by the Fed in making their assigned decision and how that information is used. Find the most recent information (sources may include newspapers, business publications, online databases, etc.) and analyze it. Based on this information and your group's analysis, what should the Fed do now? Present your findings and recommendations to the class. (Interpersonal, Information)

Ethics Activity

You are a loan officer with Sweet Home Mortgage Company. The senior vice president in charge of your area sets new loan quotas for your group and suggests that courting more subprime borrowers would make the new quotas easier to meet. He reminds you that the company can justifiably charge higher interest rates, loan fees, and servicing costs for these higher-risk loans. He also points out that the loans will earn you and your team larger commissions as well. "Everyone wins," he tells you. "We help people who might otherwise not be able to get the financing they need, the company makes money, and so do you."

But you are uneasy about the company's focus on subprime borrowers, low-income applicants with blemished or limited credit histories, many of whom are also minorities. You suspect the company's tactics could be considered "predatory lending" or "reverse redlining." You are also convinced that the cost of Sweet Home's subprime loans aren't tied to the increased risk factor at all, but to how much profit the company can squeeze from a group of unsophisticated borrowers with few other options.

Using a Web search tool, locate articles about this topic and then write responses to the following questions. Be sure to support your arguments and cite your sources.

Ethical Dilemma: Should you seek out subprime loans, knowing that you will have to charge borrowers the high fees your company demands, while believing they may not be totally justified?

Sources: Kimberly Blanton, "Dark Side of Subprime Loans," *The Boston Globe,* August 3, 2005, http://www.boston.com; Sue Kirchhoff, "Minorities Depend on Subprime Loans," *USA Today,* March 16, 2005, http://www.usatoday.com; "Subprime Lending," HUD Web site, http://www.hud.gov, June 8, 2006.

Working the Net

1. Banking on a great career? Go to **http://www.careerbank.com** to explore what positions are available. Use the Salary Wizard to estimate what you can earn and make a presentation on the type of job you might choose and its location.

2. Visit the International Money Laundering Network Services Association (**http://www.imolin.org**) for the latest information on what organizations are doing to ensure international monetary transfers remain out of terrorists' hands. Summarize your findings.

3. Find out everything you want to know about financial institutions and banking from the latest edition of the U.S. Census Bureau *Statistical Abstract of the United States*. Visit the U.S. Census Bureau Web site at **http://www.census.gov** to access the Banking, Finance, and Insurance Section of this publication. Explain why this information is important to you.

4. Using an Internet search engine such as Google (**http://www.google.com**) or Yahoo (**http://www.yahoo.com**), research information on the bank branch renaissance. Make a presentation describing the merits of this trend to your class.

5. There is a current move to increase the security of financial transactions with credit cards that generate a one-time passcode for every transaction. Go to **http://www.dogpile.com** to research articles on the pros and cons. Write up your findings and recommendations.

6. What are your rights to privacy when dealing with financial institutions? Research the specific privacy provisions related to banking and financial services using the Internet and write a paper on how you can use this information to protect your privacy and financial identity.

Creative Thinking Case >

NetBank's Virtual Service Is Here to Stay

Online banking is flourishing, and most banks offer some Internet services as customers grow more comfortable with the technology. According to Pew Internet's Online Banking 2006 report, about 63 million Americans now do some online banking, making online banking one of the fastest growing Internet activities.

But NetBank (**http://www.netbank.com**) is different. It's a virtual bank only, with no physical location, no branch offices, and no tellers. It operates exclusively on the Internet, yet offers all the services of a regular bank. NetBank customers can open checking accounts, pay bills, get a mortgage loan, apply for credit cards, and even buy insurance, 24 hours a day, 7 days a week through the Internet.

Douglas K. Freeman, NetBank's CEO, believes convenience is the biggest appeal for NetBank's retail and commercial customers. The majority have their paychecks deposited directly into their NetBank accounts and access their funds through ATMs. Although Netbank's 9,700 ATMs accounted for an annual 26.4 million in transactions, NetBank does not charge an ATM access fee. And because NetBank has no tellers or physical locations, it saves on overhead costs and passes those savings on to customers by paying higher interest rates on deposit accounts and charging lower service fees.

"What is attractive about NetBank to our customers is the fact that we save them time and give them control over their finances," Freeman says. "Today, most families are two-income families and people simply do not have enough time to do everything they have to do. People are on the Internet at home anyway and going to a Web site like NetBank to do financial transactions literally takes a tenth of the time it does to get in a car and drive to a bank branch."

Strategic marketing alliances with companies like Quicken helps bring in new customers, as does Internet advertising. "We do very targeted advertising on the Internet as we are trying to attract financially savvy people who are heavy Internet users," says Freeman. And despite a 2005 increase in the bank's overall customer base of 5.6 percent to 285,669, and strong deposit growth of $154 million, an increase of 5.8 percent over 2004, Freeman sees room for even greater expansion in the future.

"No business survives without being innovative, and even though the competition in Internet banking has increased tremendously in the past ten years, we are still setting the standard for the industry. NetBank's tenth anniversary is a testament to our ability to grow successfully into a unique financial services company. With consumers' needs continuing to evolve, we are set to make their preferences a reality. We will be their bridge to the future," he says.

Critical Thinking Questions

- Do you think NetBank's strategy of targeting Internet users only is a sound business plan? Explain.
- Do you agree or disagree with Freeman's definition of banking convenience, and why? What types of banking customers might NetBank not be able to serve effectively?
- What are the advantages and disadvantages of focusing solely on the Internet as a delivery channel? Do you think that NetBank will eventually need to add other types of customer contact points? If so, what types would you recommend and why?

Sources: Susannah Fox and Jean Beier, "Online Banking 2006: Surfing to the Bank," *Pew Internet & American Life Project*, June 14, 2006, http://pewinternet.org; "NetBank Introduces Commercial Loans for Small Businesses," *PrimeZone Newswire*, May 11, 2006, http://www.primezone.com; "NetBank Amends 2005–2006 CRA Strategic Plan; Makes Draft Available for Public Review," *Business Wire*, October 7, 2005, http://www.findarticles.com; and "Ten Successful Years: A Bridge to the Future," Shareholder Letter, *Netbank Annual Report 2005*, http://www.netbankinc.com, June 8, 2006.

Video Case: >

Customers Come First at Firstbank Corporation

Are small, community banks a thing of the past? Not if you live in Michigan, where Firstbank Corporation (**http://www.firstbank-corp.com**) is headquartered. This bank holding company consists of a network of affiliated community banks and bank service companies with 39 offices located throughout the state of Michigan: Firstbank–Alma, Firstbank–Mt. Pleasant, Firstbank–West Branch, Firstbank–Lakeview, Firstbank–St. Johns, and Keystone Community Bank.

Firstbank Corporation was initially established in 1985 as a one-bank holding company for Firstbank–Alma, formerly the Bank of Alma established in 1901. In 1987, Firstbank Corporation expanded into a multibank holding company to allow for new business opportunities and growth. Between 1995 and 2001 Firstbank Corporation developed and/or acquired its armored car, real estate appraisal, title insurance, and real estate brokerage subsidiaries in order to offer a wider array of financial services to its customers. In 2005 it acquired a sixth bank subsidiary, Keystone Financial Corporation and its wholly owned subsidiary Keystone Community Bank.

Offering a full range of deposit and loan products, Firstbank's affiliates seek to differentiate themselves from their banking competition by continuously focusing on exceptional customer service. The banks believe that integrity, customer satisfaction, and trust are the key elements of solid community banking. Each affiliate bank has its own president and board of directors. This helps each bank to make decisions that focus on its local community and local customers.

Firstbank–Mt. Pleasant, for instance, is headed by Thomas R. Sullivan, who is also president and CEO of Firstbank Corporation. He emphasizes that Firstbank customers will have a more personal and flexible banking experience because the bank strives to tailor its services to individual customer needs. The bank offers "a wide variety of checking and savings accounts to fit . . . [customers'] individual or corporate needs, and all types of consumer, mortgage, and commercial loans." The bank also offers its customers access to stocks, bonds, mutual funds, annuities, and insurance products.

Firstbank–Alma emphasizes making banking convenient and knowing its customers so it can recommend appropriate financial solutions whatever a customer's banking needs happen to be. Another unit of Firstbank Corporation is 1st Armored, Inc., which provides armored courier services for financial institutions in Michigan. These include Federal Reserve shipping, individual bank deliveries, coin wrapping, and automated teller machine servicing.

Firstbank Corporation's Code of Business Conduct upholds its core values of honesty, fairness, and integrity. Those may be small town values but they are principles every customer will identify with.

Critical Thinking Questions

- What role does Firstbank Corporation play in the U.S. financial system?
- Why have Firstbank Corporation affiliates been able to keep a strong customer base despite competition from larger banks with a national presence?
- Visit the Firstbank–Alma Web site (**http://www.firstbank-alma.com**). If you were the owner of a small restaurant in Alma, would you bank with Firstbank– Alma? Conversely, if you were the vice president of finance for a $250 million local manufacturing company, what services would you need? Could this bank handle both companies' needs? Explain.

Sources: Adapted from material in the video "Financial Statement Analysis/Creditor and Investor Decisions: Firstbank and Roney & Co.," Firstbank corporate Web site, http://www.firstbank-corp.com, June 4, 2006; "Firstbank Corporation Announces Closing of the Keystone Financial Corporation Acquisition, Firstbank press release, October 3, 2005, http://www.firstbank-corp.com.

Hot Links Address Book

Tour the American Currency Exhibit to learn the history of our nation's money at http://www.frbsf.org/currency

The Web site of the Federal Reserve Bank of St. Louis offers an easy-to-understand explanation of how the Federal Reserve System works, called "In Plain English:" http://www.stls.frb.org/publications/pleng

The FDIC gets so many requests about banks' insurance status that it added an option to determine "Is my bank insured?" on the consumer pages of its Web site. Visit http://www.fdic.gov

What goes on at a Federal Open Market Committee Meeting? Find out by reading the minutes of the Committee's latest meeting at http://www.federalreserve.gov/fomc

Want to know more about the relationship between Congress and the Federal Reserve? Go to http://www.house.gov/jec/fed/fed/fed-impt.htm

Find out what other services the Federal Reserve provides to financial institutions at http://www.frbservices.org

How did Abraham Lincoln do his banking? Take a cyber-tour of American banking history at http://www.occ.treas.gov/occ140th/history.htm

To find out if you're eligible to join a credit union, visit the Credit Union National Administration's credit union locator at http://www.creditunion.coop/cu_locator/index.html

CHAPTER 19

Managing the Firm's Finances

Learning Goals

After reading this chapter, you should be able to answer these questions:

1 What roles do finance and the financial manager play in the firm's overall strategy?

2 How does a firm develop its financial plans, including forecasts and budgets?

3 What types of short-term and long-term expenditures does a firm make?

4 What are the main sources and costs of unsecured and secured short-term financing?

5 How do the two primary sources of long-term financing compare?

6 What are the major types, features, and costs of long-term debt?

7 When and how do firms issue equity, and what are the costs?

8 What trends are affecting the practice of financial management?

APPENDIX: MANAGING RISK AND INSURANCE

9 What is risk and how can it be managed? What makes a risk insurable?

10 What types of insurance coverage should businesses consider?

Exploring Business Careers
Scott Swanson
JP Morgan Chase

Many people dream of working for themselves and owning their own small business. But this involves a large investment of time, dedication, creativity, and money. Even the best ideas fall flat without strong financial backing and fiscal management. Most small businesses don't have a chief financial officer, so a partnership with a reliable financial institution is crucial to ensuring viability.

Scott Swanson, the national executive for Business Bank at JP Morgan Chase, feels strongly about the need to support small businesses. "We have always been an entrepreneurial nation. Small business is the core of our economy. Our Business Bank provides us with an opportunity to support this business segment." Chase helps small business owners by loaning them money or helping them collect money to further invest in the business.

Unlike corporations, small businesses cannot rely on the sale of stock shares to help them raise capitol to purchase equipment, raw materials, real estate, or to pay employees. And often a "time lag" exists between when products are sold and when payments come in. That is where Swanson and Chase come in. "We help bridge that gap between accounts payable and accounts receivable, to help businesses run more smoothly." Chase uses two mechanisms to do this: loans and lines of credit. Long term loans are lump sums that can be used for purchases of buildings, equipment, or inventory. Payments of the loan go towards the interest and the principal. In contrast, lines of credit are sums of money available to the business owner as he or she needs them. Only the interest must be paid off monthly. Lines of credit can be used to smooth out cash flow and pay for daily business needs, such as utilities and wages, until payments for products sold come in. As customers pay the company, those funds are used to pay down the line of credit.

Swanson believes that in order to support small business owners, Chase must develop strong relationships with them. "In order to be an effective partner, we need to share information. We need to understand what a business owner sees as their business's future, so we can be proactive in providing solutions and opportunities to maximize future growth." To achieve this, Swanson ensures his bankers are constantly trained in the services Chase provides and have the necessary resources to best understand their customer's business. In this way, the bankers can adapt as the needs of the company change.

Scott Swanson has a commitment to supporting small businesses. Through Chase's many services and products, Swanson is ensuring that this vital sector of our economy stays vibrant. And he is helping more business owners realize their dream.

This chapter examines the importance of money to the life of a business, examining the role of the financial manager and the basic components of financial planning.

In today's fast-paced global economy, managing a firm's finances is more complex than ever. A thorough command of traditional finance activities—financial planning, investing money, and raising funds—is only part of the job. Financial managers are more than number crunchers. As part of the top-management team, chief financial officers (CFOs) need a broad understanding of their firm's business and industry, as well as leadership ability and creativity. They must never lose sight of the primary goal of the financial manager: to maximize the value of the firm to its owners.

All firms, whether start-up companies with three employees or major multinational corporations with billions of dollars in annual revenue, need to manage their finances efficiently and effectively. Otherwise, the firm will not have the resources it needs to pay its bills and run its daily operations or to make investments in future growth.

Financial management—spending and raising a firm's money—is both a science and an art. The science part is analyzing numbers and flows of cash through the firm. The art is answering questions like these: Is the firm using its financial resources in the best way? Aside from costs, why choose a particular form of financing? How risky is each option?

Whether you are a marketing manager, purchasing agent, or systems analyst, knowledge of finance will help you to do your job better. You'll be able to understand your company's financial statements, its financial condition, and management's investment and financing decisions. Financial information also provides feedback on how well you are doing and identifies problems. On a more practical note, you may be asked to prepare a budget for your department or unit. Employees who understand the financial decision-making process will be able to prepare proposals that address financial concerns. As a result, they will be more likely to get the resources they require to accomplish the firm's goals.

If you own a business, you must pay close attention to financial management. Without financial plans you may find yourself running out of cash. It's easy to get so caught up in growing sales that you neglect your billing and collection methods. In fact, managing accounts receivable is often one of the more challenging aspects of running a young company.

This chapter focuses on the financial management of a firm. We'll start with an overview of the role of finance and of the financial manager in the firm's overall business strategy. Next we consider the basics of financial planning: forecasts and budgets. Discussions of short- and long-term uses of funds and sources of short- and long-term financing follow. Finally, we'll look at key trends affecting financial management. The appendix that follows discusses managing risk and insurance.

The Role of Finance and the Financial Manager

1 What roles do finance and the financial manager play in the firm's overall strategy?

financial management
The art and science of managing a firm's money so that it can meet its goals.

Any company, whether it's a two-attorney law partnership or General Motors, needs money to operate. To make money, it must first spend money—on inventory and supplies, equipment and facilities, and employee wages and salaries. Therefore, finance is critical to the success of all companies. It may not be as visible as marketing or production, but management of a firm's finances is just as much a key to the firm's success.

Financial management—the art and science of managing a firm's money so that it can meet its goals—is not just the responsibility of the finance department. All business decisions have financial consequences. Managers in all departments must work closely with financial personnel. If you are a sales representative, for example, the company's credit and collection policies will affect your ability to make sales. The head of the IT department will need to justify any requests for new systems.

Revenues from sales of the firm's products should be the chief source of funding. But money from sales doesn't always come in when it's needed to pay the bills. Financial managers must track how money is flowing into and out of the firm (see Exhibit 19.1). They work with the firm's other department managers to determine

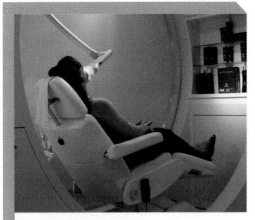

CONCEPT *in Action*

Smile-conscious consumers around the country visit BriteSmile teeth-whitening spas to brighten-up their pearly whites. Yet revenues generated from their hundreds of thousands of customers have proved no match for the California-based dental firm's mounting expenses. To keep operations going, BriteSmile has slashed prices and sold millions of dollars worth of assets. Despite ongoing challenges, the company's rejection of numerous takeover bids may signal plans for a turnaround. *Who is responsible for making key financial decisions for businesses?*

cash flows
The inflows and outflows of cash for a firm.

how available funds will be used and how much money is needed. Then they choose the best sources to obtain the required funding.

For example, a financial manager will track day-to-day operational data such as cash collections and disbursements to ensure that the company has enough cash to meet its obligations. Over a longer time horizon, the manager will thoroughly study whether and when the company should open a new manufacturing facility. The manager will also suggest the most appropriate way to finance the project, raise the funds, and then monitor the project's implementation and operation.

Financial management is closely related to accounting. In most firms both areas are the responsibility of the vice president of finance or the CFO. But the accountant's main function is to collect and present financial data. Financial managers use financial statements and other information prepared by accountants to make financial decisions. Financial managers focus on cash flows, the inflows and outflows of cash. They plan and monitor the firm's cash flows to ensure that cash is available when needed.

The Financial Manager's Responsibilities and Activities

Financial managers have a complex and challenging job. They analyze financial data prepared by accountants, monitor the firm's financial status, and prepare and implement financial plans. One day they may be developing a better way to automate cash collections, the next they may be analyzing a proposed acquisition. The key activities of the financial manager are:

- *Financial planning.* Preparing the financial plan, which projects revenues, expenditures, and financing needs over a given period.

Exhibit 19.1 > How Cash Flows through a Business

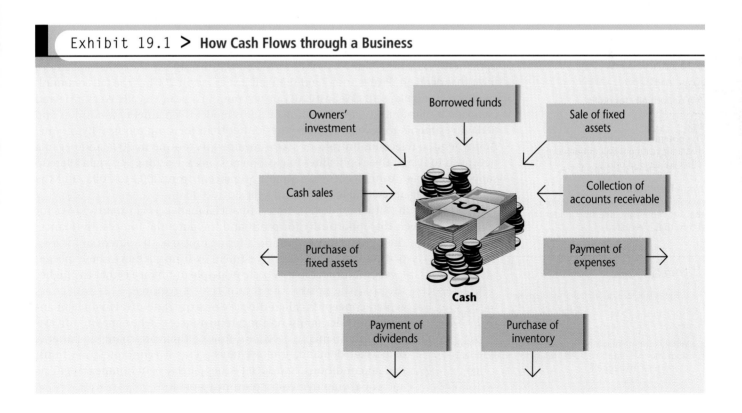

- *Investment (spending money).* Investing the firm's funds in projects and securities that provide high returns in relation to their risks.

- *Financing (raising money).* Obtaining funding for the firm's operations and investments and seeking the best balance between debt (borrowed funds) and equity (funds raised through the sale of ownership in the business).

The Goal of the Financial Manager

How can financial managers make wise planning, investment, and financing decisions? The main goal of the financial manager is *to maximize the value of the firm to its owners.* The value of a publicly owned corporation is measured by the share price of its stock. A private company's value is the price at which it could be sold.

To maximize the firm's value, the financial manager has to consider both short- and long-term consequences of the firm's actions. Maximizing profits is one approach, but it should not be the only one. Such an approach favors making short-term gains over achieving long-term goals. What if a firm in a highly technical and competitive industry did no research and development? In the short run, profits would be high because research and development is very expensive. But in the long run, the firm might lose its ability to compete because of its lack of new products.

This is true regardless of a company's size or point in its life cycle. At Corning, a company founded more than 150 years ago, CEO Wendell Weeks believes in taking the long-term view and not managing for quarterly earnings to satisfy Wall Street's expectations. The company, once known to consumers mostly for kitchen products such as Corelle dinnerware and Pyrex heat-resistant glass cookware, is today a technology company that manufactures specialized glass and ceramic products. It is a leading supplier of flat glass panels for LCD displays used in large-screen televisions and other electronic products and was the inventor of optical fiber and cable for the telecommunications industry. These product lines require large investments during their long research and development (R&D) cycles and for plant and equipment once they go into production.

This can be risky in the short term, but staying the course can pay off. The LCD glass unit reported losses for 14 years. Now it provides 38 percent of total revenues and most of the profits. As major telecommunications companies built up their fiber optic networks in the late 1990s and early 2000s, Corning expanded its capacity to meet that demand. Profits rose—and then fell just as fast in 2001 as the telecommunications sector collapsed. "We lost half our revenues in a year," recalls Weeks. He and company leaders quickly revamped the business model to channel new business and R&D investments to several product lines rather than focusing too heavily on one. And when the telecommunications sector regained its footing in 2004 and began a new push to install fiber optic lines to customers' homes, Corning was right there to supply the cable. Annual sales rose almost 50 percent from 2003 to 2005, and the company was again profitable for the first year since 2000.[1]

As the Corning situation demonstrates, financial managers constantly strive for a balance between the opportunity for profit and the potential for loss. In finance, the opportunity for profit is termed **return**; the potential for loss, or the chance that an investment will not achieve the expected level of return, is **risk**. A basic principle in finance is that the higher the risk, the greater the return that is required. This widely accepted concept is called the **risk-return trade-off**. Financial managers consider many risk and return factors when making investment and financing decisions. Among them are changing patterns of market demand, interest rates, general economic conditions, market conditions, and social issues (such as environmental effects and equal employment opportunity policies).

return
The opportunity for profit.

risk
The potential for loss or the chance that an investment will not achieve the expected level of return.

risk-return trade-off
A basic principle in finance that holds that the higher the risk, the greater the return that is required.

concept check

What is the role of financial management in a firm?

How do the three key activities of the financial manager relate?

What is the main goal of the financial manager? How does the risk-return trade-off relate to the financial manager's main goal?

Financial Planning: Looking Ahead

 2 How does a firm develop its financial plans, including forecasts and budgets?

As we learned in Chapter 7, companies use several types of plans to determine how to achieve organizational objectives. A company's *financial plan* is part of the overall company plan and guides the firm toward its business goals and the maximization of its value. The financial plan enables the firm to estimate the amount and timing of its investment and financing needs. It also gives an organization benchmarks against which to measure its performance.

To prepare a financial plan, the financial manager must first consider existing and proposed products, the resources available to produce them, and the financing needed to support production and sales. Forecasts and budgets are essential to the firm's financial planning. They should be part of an integrated planning process that links them to strategic plans and performance measurement. "To keep your company on a path, it has to have some kind of map," says Paula Brock, CFO of the Zoological Society of San Diego. "The budgeting-and-planning process is that map. I cannot imagine an organization feeling in control if it didn't have that sort of discipline." When she arrived at the Society, the finance arm was not part of the overall strategic planning process. "There was a 10-year plan in a narrative sense, but not in terms of how we were going to make it happen financially," she recalls. She immediately took steps to change that, educating all levels of Society personnel in the importance of forecasting and budgeting and the close link between those plans and the Society's ability to achieve its strategic goals. "That gap [between high-level strategy and budgeting] had to be bridged," explains Brock. It was a goal that "had to be understood at the highest levels of the organization, but also sold to the lowest levels."[2]

Forecasting the Future

The financial-planning process starts with financial forecasts, or projections of future developments within the firm. The estimated demand for the firm's products (the sales forecast) and other financial and operating data are key inputs. At Ford Motor Company, economic analysts estimate expected production and sales for each line of cars and trucks. Then financial analysts prepare detailed short- and long-term financial forecasts based on these assumptions.

short-term forecasts
Projections of revenues, costs of goods, and operating expenses over a one-year period.

Short-term forecasts, or *operating plans,* project revenues, costs of goods, and operating expenses over a one-year period. Using short-term forecasts, Ford's financial managers estimate the next year's expenses for inventory, labor, advertising, and other operating activities. These estimates form the basis for cash budgets, described below, which forecast cash inflows and outflows over the same period.

Caterpillar Inc., a major manufacturer of construction and mining equipment, expects to see continued revenue growth. "Our outlook calls for another 10 percent top-line growth, which will nearly double the company's sales compared to sales and revenues over the last three to four years," says Douglas R. Oberhelman, formerly Caterpillar's CFO and now a group president. Planning for this growth calls for increased attention to short-term planning, cash flow, inventory levels, and asset turnover ratios. "We simply have to work harder than ever to implement improved cash-to-cash cycles," he says.[3]

long-term forecasts
Projections of a firm's activities and the funding for those activities over a period that is longer than 1 year, typically 2 to 10 years.

Long-term forecasts, or *strategic plans,* cover a period that is longer than one year, typically 2 to 10 years, and take a broader view of the firm's financial activities. With these forecasts, management can assess the financial effects of various business strategies: What would be the financial results of investing in new facilities and equipment? Of developing new products? Of eliminating a line of business? Of acquiring other firms? Long-term forecasts also show where the funding for these activities is expected to come from. Corning's long-term forecasts, for example, will show its strategy for funding the company's R&D efforts and for investments in new and existing facilities.

Lenders typically ask potential borrowers for forecasts that cover the period the loan will be outstanding. They use them to evaluate the risk of the loan and to see that adequate cash flow will be available to pay off the borrowing. Then they structure loan terms and covenants (requirements that the company comply with certain operating and financial measures during the loan period) based on those statements.

Budgets

Firms prepare **budgets** to plan and control their future financial activities. Budgets are formal written forecasts of revenues and expenses that set spending limits based on operational forecasts. All budgets begin with forecasts. Budgets provide a way to control expenses and compare the actual performance to the forecast. By monitoring actual revenues and expenses and comparing them to budgets on a regular basis, companies gain critical information about operations. When variances to the budget occur, managers can analyze them to determine if they need to take steps to correct them. Suppose the owner of a small printing company sees that May sales are down and expenses are over budget because a major press broke down and the company was unable to fulfill many orders on time. This situation would require asking such questions as: How old is the press, has it broken down before, should the company continue to repair it or is it time to replace it, can the company afford a new press, and how would it finance the new press? A back-up plan to prevent lost orders would be another possible outcome of this budget review.

Firms use several types of budgets, most of which cover a one-year period:

- **Cash budgets** forecast the firm's cash inflows and outflows and help the firm plan for cash surpluses and shortages. Because having enough cash is so critical to their financial health, many firms prepare annual cash budgets subdivided into months or weeks. Then they project the amount of cash needed in each shorter time period.

- **Capital budgets** forecast outlays for fixed assets (plant and equipment). They usually cover a period of several years and ensure that the firm will have enough funds to buy the equipment and buildings it needs.

CONCEPT in Action

Many people dream of starting a small business. Unfortunately, nearly half of all entrepreneurs watch their dreams fall apart within five years—most often because their new businesses are undercapitalized. Management consultant firms generally advise aspiring small-business owners to budget up to three times the cash they need starting out. *What types of fixed assets would a fast-growing, outdoor-video billboard company include in its capital budget?*

© ALAN SCHEIN PHOTOGRAPHY/CORBIS

operating budgets
Budgets that combine sales forecasts with estimates of production costs and operating expenses in order to forecast profits.

 Operating budgets combine sales forecasts with estimates of production costs and operating expenses in order to forecast profits. They are based on individual budgets for sales, production, purchases of materials, factory overhead, and operating expenses. Operating budgets are then used to plan operations: dollars of sales, units of production, amounts of raw materials, dollars of wages, and so forth.

Budgets are routinely used to monitor and control the performance of a division, a department, or an individual manager. Unexpected expenditures can throw budgets off completely. When actual outcomes differ from budget expectations, management must take action. Several years ago, an outbreak of the deadly bird infection Newcastle Disease in southern California threatened the valuable exotic bird population at the San Diego Zoo and its Wild Animal Park. For the Zoological Society of San Diego, which operates the zoo and park, preventing the disease became a top priority. It incurred enormous unbudgeted expenses to shut all bird exhibits and sanitize shoes and clothing of workers and tires of delivery trucks to keep the disease out of the zoo, as well as close to $500,000 to quarantine birds. These measures were successful in preventing Newcastle Disease from infecting the zoo's birds. The Zoological Society's budget also survived because CFO Brock had instituted a monthly budget reforecast process. "When we get a hit like this, we still have to find a way to make our bottom line," she says. In addition to worrying about the disease, zoo scientists also took steps to reallocate resources to the emergency measures. "Because we had timely awareness, we were able to make adjustments to weather the storm," Brock says.[4]

> **concept check**
>
> What is a financial plan? Name two types of financial planning documents.
>
> Distinguish between short- and long-term forecasts. How are both used by financial managers?
>
> Briefly describe three types of budgets.

How Organizations Use Funds

3 What types of short-term and long-term expenditures does a firm make?

To grow and prosper, a firm must keep investing money in its operations. The financial manager decides how best to use the firm's money. Short-term expenses support the firm's day-to-day activities. For instance, athletic-apparel maker Nike regularly spends money to buy such raw materials as leather and fabric and to pay employee salaries. Long-term expenses are typically for fixed assets. For Nike, these would include outlays to build a new factory, buy automated manufacturing equipment, or acquire a small manufacturer of sports apparel.

Short-Term Expenses

Short-term expenses, often called *operating expenses,* are outlays used to support current selling and production activities. They typically result in current assets, which include cash and any other assets (accounts receivable and inventory) that can be converted to cash within a year. The financial manager's goal is to manage current assets so the firm has enough cash to pay its bills and to support its accounts receivable and inventory.

cash management
The process of making sure that a firm has enough cash on hand to pay bills as they come due and to meet unexpected expenses.

Cash Management: Assuring Liquidity Cash is the lifeblood of business. Without it, a firm could not operate. An important duty of the financial manager is **cash management,** or making sure that enough cash is on hand to pay bills as they come due and to meet unexpected expenses.

Businesses use budgets to estimate the cash requirements for a specific period. Many companies keep a minimum cash balance to cover unexpected expenses or changes in projected cash flows. The financial manager arranges loans to cover any shortfalls. If the size and timing of cash inflows closely match the size and timing of cash outflows, the company needs to keep only a small amount of cash on hand. A company whose sales and receipts are fairly predictable and regular throughout the year needs less cash than a company with a seasonal pattern of sales and receipts. A toy company, for instance, whose sales are concentrated in the fall, spends a great deal

marketable securities
Short-term investments that are easily converted into cash.

commercial paper
Unsecured short-term debt—an IOU—issued by a financially strong corporation.

of cash during the spring and summer to build inventory. It has excess cash during the winter and early spring, when it collects on sales from its peak selling season.

Because cash held in checking accounts earns little, if any, interest, the financial manager tries to keep cash balances low and to invest the surplus cash. Surpluses are invested temporarily in **marketable securities**, short-term investments that are easily converted into cash. The financial manager looks for low-risk investments that offer high returns. Three of the most popular marketable securities are Treasury bills, certificates of deposit, and commercial paper. (**Commercial paper** is unsecured short-term debt—an IOU—issued by a financially strong corporation.) Today's financial managers have new tools to help them find the best short-term investments, such as online trading platforms that save time and provide access to more types of investments. These have been especially useful for smaller companies who don't have large finance staffs. "We don't have enough to invest that we can chase money market [funds] or commercial paper," says Bob DiAntonio of Arbella Insurance Group, a Massachusetts company that provides property and casualty insurance. By using an online money market platform to invest between $20 million and $35 million each day, he has access to about 30 different investments. The portal allows him to move Arbella's cash into the ones offering the highest interest rates in a few minutes. "We don't have to waste half the morning doing short-term investments," he says.[5]

Companies with overseas operations face even greater cash management challenges, as the Expanding Around the Globe box explains. Developing the systems for international cash management may sound simple in theory, but in practice it's extremely complex. In addition to dealing with multiple foreign currencies, treasurers must understand and follow banking practices and regulatory and tax requirements in each country. Regulations may impede their ability to move funds freely across borders. Also, issuing a standard set of procedures for every office may not work because local business practices differ from country to country. Moreover, local managers may resist

EXPANDING AROUND THE GLOBE

Follow the Money

If you think it's hard to balance your checking account, imagine trying to deal with $4 billion or more in 1,400 accounts in 46 different currencies for 233 legal entities, at 145 banks worldwide! That's the job facing Jim Colby, assistant treasurer of Honeywell International Inc., and his counterparts at other multinational companies, who grapple with complex treasury operations like this on a daily basis. With so much at stake, international cash management becomes a priority for financial managers.

Many companies are joining Honeywell in the quest for more efficient global cash management systems. Corporate treasurers want to identify and pool cash from overseas operations so that these cash balances can be put to work. In addition, recent regulatory changes have brought huge amounts of cash back to the United States from overseas operations—and too much cash can be as much of a problem as too little. "Cash is a wonderful thing to have, but when it's yielding 3.5 percent pretax, then it's also a burden. That is not a viable return on a large asset," says David O'Brien, assistant treasurer of EDS Corp.

At Honeywell, Colby and his team turned to a Web-based technology solution to improve its global cash pooling system. Prior to 2002, Honeywell couldn't track its cash, most of which was outside the United States and earning little or no interest. The company launched a centralized

Web portal in 2002, and Honeywell's business units began reporting their cash holdings. By 2005 Honeywell upgraded to an automated treasury platform.

Once Honeywell knew where its cash holdings were, it could manage this cash more efficiently and profitably. Treasury managers developed budgets and goals for interest income that were tied to cash balance forecasts, exchange rates in each country, and other factors. Next, they pooled cash from individual bank accounts and invested it in marketable securities. The interest income goals established performance benchmarks and were factored into incentive compensation. The results were significant. Today most of Honeywell's cash is now actively managed and the interest income is about twice what it was in 2002. The company can also quickly identify which cash reserves are available to make an acquisition or fund a large capital project.[6]

Critical Thinking Questions
* Why is managing cash such an important part of a financial manager's job? Why is having too much cash a problem?
* What were the benefits from Honeywell's new cash management procedures worldwide? For a multinational company? Are there any disadvantages?

the shift to a centralized structure because they don't want to give up control of cash generated by their units. Corporate financial managers must be sensitive to and aware of local customs and adapt the centralization strategy accordingly.

In addition to seeking the right balance between cash and marketable securities, the financial manager tries to shorten the time between the purchase of inventory or services (cash outflows) and the collection of cash from sales (cash inflows). The three key strategies are to collect money owed to the firm (accounts receivable) as quickly as possible, to pay money owed to others (accounts payable) as late as possible without damaging the firm's credit reputation, and to turn inventory quickly in order to minimize the funds tied up in it.

accounts receivable
Sales for which a firm has not yet been paid.

Managing Accounts Receivable Accounts receivable represent sales for which the firm has not yet been paid. Because the product has been sold but cash has not yet been received, an account receivable amounts to a use of funds. For the average manufacturing firm, accounts receivable represent about 15 to 20 percent of total assets.

The financial manager's goal is to collect money owed to the firm as quickly as possible, while offering customers credit terms attractive enough to increase sales. Accounts receivable management involves setting *credit policies,* guidelines on offering credit; and *credit terms,* specific repayment conditions, including how long customers have to pay their bills and whether a cash discount is given for quicker payment. Another aspect of accounts receivable management is deciding on *collection policies,* the procedures for collecting overdue accounts.

Setting up credit and collection policies is a balancing act for financial managers. On the one hand, easier credit policies or generous credit terms (a longer repayment period or larger cash discount) result in increased sales. On the other hand, the firm has to finance more accounts receivable. The risk of uncollectible accounts receivable also rises. Businesses consider the impact on sales, timing of cash flow, experience with bad debt, customer profiles, and industry standards when developing their credit and collection policies.

Companies that want to speed up collections actively manage their accounts receivable, rather than passively letting customers pay when they want to. The Credit Research Foundation reports that companies are improving the efficiency of receivables collection processes, as demonstrated by a decline in median days sales outstanding (DSO), a key measure of accounts receivable performance. From 2001 to 2005, DSO fell 5.1 days to 40.5 days, the lowest since 1995.

CONCEPT *in Action*

Cash is king when it comes to the financial management of an organization. Therefore, smart cash-flow management means delaying payouts while speeding up collection cycles. Strategies for going after overdue accounts range from sending simple past-due e-mail notices to hiring a collection attorney. Implementing technology to automate accounts receivable is also effective—payment tracking software helped Duke University Health System recover $4.5 million in managed care underpayments in one year. *Why is setting collection policies a balancing act for financial managers?*

Technology plays a big role in helping companies improve their credit and collections performance. "Technologies such as improved ERP systems have made the order process better, reducing the errors that result in customer deductions, which lead to extended DSO," says Terry Callahan, president of the Credit Research Foundation.[7] For example, the University of Pittsburgh Medical Center developed its own U-Pay software system to improve collections of small consumer payments from multiple service providers using different billing systems. The new technology became necessary as changes to health insurance increased the amounts the patients had to pay themselves. U-Pay automated the payment and billing processes and now handles most of the center's point-of-sale collections. Collections have increased by 50 percent, bad debt write-offs fell $250,000, and credit card processing costs dropped $100,000 per year.[8]

Other companies chose to outsource financial business processes to specialists rather than develop their own systems, as the Customer Satisfaction and Quality box explains.

Inventory Another use of funds is to buy inventory needed by the firm. In a typical manufacturing firm, inventory is nearly 20 percent of total assets. The cost of inventory includes not only its purchase price, but also ordering, handling, storage, interest, and insurance costs.

Production, marketing, and finance managers usually have differing views about inventory. Production managers want lots of raw materials on hand to avoid production delays. Marketing managers want lots of finished goods on hand so customer orders can be filled quickly. But financial managers want the least inventory possible without harming production efficiency or sales. Financial managers must work closely

CUSTOMER SATISFACTION AND QUALITY

Exporting Applies to Finance, Too

As financial reporting, compliance requirements under Sarbanes-Oxley, and global trade regulations make finance more complex, financial managers are turning over all types of financial and accounting business processes to firms that specialize in those services. The availability of cutting-edge technology and specialized electronic platforms that would be difficult and expensive to develop in-house is winning over firms of all sizes.

Giving up control of finance to a third party has not been easy for CFOs. Clearly, the risks are high when financial and other sensitive corporate data is transferred to an outside computer system; data could be compromised or lost, or rivals could steal corporate data. It's also harder to monitor an outside provider than your own employees. "Finance in most organizations remains a spider's web of connections between different departments, which always makes it complicated," says Anoop Sagoo, vice president of Accenture Finance Solutions in Europe.

One outsourcing area that has attracted many clients is international trade, which has regulations that differ from country to country and requires huge amounts of documentation. With specialized IT systems, providers can track not only the physical location of goods but also all the paperwork associated with shipments. Processing costs for goods purchased overseas are about twice that of domestic goods, so more efficient systems pay off. "People understand that there's no way that they can have all the right expertise internally," says Beth Enslow, vice president at technology consultants Aberdeen Group. "You can have great advice, but you have to get the documents and make sure suppliers fill them out correctly. . . . You need the execution capability in place."

Telecom equipment manufacturer Lucent reduced costs and increased customer satisfaction by outsourcing its global logistics to JP Morgan Chase's Vastera unit. "Vastera gives us a competitive advantage," says Greg Johnston, Lucent's director of supply chain logistics. He praises Vastera's TradeSphere software for its "ability to work across our supply chain and work with our other partners—brokers, forwarders—to ensure that we get material delivered to our customers in a timely and a compliant fashion."

TradeCard, another outsourcer, provides customers with a Web-based platform that automates international trade transactions, from procurement through payment. Burton Snowboards, featured in Chapter 1's video case, uses TradeCard to pay its suppliers electronically. With TradeCard's automated early payment system, Burton pays vendors faster if they accept a discount. Tom D'Urso, Burton's treasurer, considers the program "a zero-risk investment with an above-market rate of return." Vendors like it as well. "They click and [the payment] is there in 24 to 48 hours. The instant nature of it, the fact that it has expanded their [credit] facility, makes us good guys in their eyes," D'Urso says.[9]

Critical Thinking Questions
- If you were a CFO, how much, if any, of your firm's financial and accounting processes would you be willing to outsource, and why? Compare the advantages and disadvantages to the firm of outsourcing versus keeping finance in-house.
- Why do many firms choose to outsource their international trade operations?

with production and marketing to balance these conflicting goals. Techniques for reducing the investment in inventory—inventory management, the just-in-time system, and materials requirement planning—were described in Chapter 11.

For retail firms, inventory management is a critical area for financial managers, who closely monitor inventory turnover ratios. As we learned in Chapter 17, this ratio shows how quickly inventory moves through the firm and is turned into sales. "If the turnover number goes too low, it adversely affects our working capital and we have to borrow money to cover the excess inventory," says Andrew Demott, CFO of Superior Uniform Group, a wholesale apparel company. Holding purchased inventory in the warehouse increases inventory costs and uses financial resources that could be deployed more effectively elsewhere. At the same time, Dermott explains, a high inventory turnover ratio may indicate that goods may not be available for customers, who will take their business to another firm.[10]

Lowe's the home improvement chain, measures inventory turnover weekly. Although its days inventory outstanding (DIO) rose in 2004, the company was not worried. "We manage the business for the long term," explains Robert Hull, Lowe's CFO. "We'll take a short-term blip in a metric." The higher DIO came during the first phase of a "rapid response replenishment" program to hold more safety stock at stores while it built up its regional distribution network. The initiative ultimately shortened the time to refill inventory from these centers so that in 2005, DIO fell.[11]

Long-Term Expenditures

capital expenditures
Investments in long-lived assets, such as land, buildings, machinery, and equipment, that are expected to provide benefits that extend beyond one year.

capital budgeting
The process of analyzing long-term projects and selecting those that offer the best returns while maximizing the firm's value.

A firm also uses funds for its investments in long-lived assets, such items as land, buildings, machinery, equipment, and information systems. These are called **capital expenditures**. Unlike operating expenses, which produce benefits within a year, the benefits from capital expenditures extend beyond one year. For instance, a printer's purchase of a new printing press with a usable life of seven years is a capital expenditure. It appears as a fixed asset on the firm's balance sheet. Paper, ink, and other supplies, however, are expenses. Mergers and acquisitions, discussed in Chapter 5, are also considered capital expenditures.

Firms make capital expenditures for many reasons. The most common are to expand and to replace or renew fixed assets. Another reason is to develop new products. Most manufacturing firms have a big investment in long-term assets. Boeing Company, for instance, puts millions of dollars a year into airplane-manufacturing facilities.

Because capital expenditures tend to be costly and have a major effect on the firm's future, the financial manager must analyze long-term projects and select those that offer the best returns while maximizing the firm's value. This process is called **capital budgeting**. Decisions involving new products or the acquisition of another business are especially important. Managers look at project costs and forecast the future benefits the project will bring—for example, from increased productivity, staff reductions, and other cost savings—to calculate the firm's estimated return on the investment.

concept check

Distinguish between short- and long-term expenses.

What is the financial manager's goal in cash management? List the three key cash management strategies.

Describe a firm's main motives in making capital expenditures.

Obtaining Short-Term Financing

 What are the main sources and costs of unsecured and secured short-term financing?

How do firms raise the funding they need? They borrow money (debt), sell ownership shares (equity), and retain earnings (profits). The financial manager must assess all these sources and choose the one most likely to help maximize the firm's value.

Like expenses, borrowed funds can be divided into short- and long-term loans. A short-term loan comes due within one year; a long-term loan has a maturity greater than one year. Short-term financing is shown as a current liability on the balance sheet, and is used to finance current assets and support operations. Short-term loans can be unsecured or secured.

Unsecured Short-Term Loans

unsecured loans
Loans for which the borrower does not have to pledge specific assets as security.

Unsecured loans are made on the basis of the firm's creditworthiness and the lender's previous experience with the firm. An unsecured borrower does not have to pledge specific assets as security. The three main types of *unsecured short-term loans* are trade credit, bank loans, and commercial paper.

Trade Credit: Accounts Payable When Goodyear sells tires to General Motors, GM does not have to pay cash on delivery. Instead, Goodyear regularly bills GM for its tire purchases, and GM pays at a later date. This is an example of **trade credit**: the seller extends credit to the buyer between the time the buyer receives the goods or services and when it pays for them. Trade credit is a major source of short-term business financing. The buyer enters the credit on its books as an **account payable**. In effect, the credit is a short-term loan from the seller to the buyer of the goods and services. Until GM pays Goodyear, Goodyear has an account receivable from GM, and GM has an account payable to Goodyear.

trade credit
The extension of credit by the seller to the buyer between the time the buyer receives the goods or services and when it pays for them.

accounts payable
Purchases for which a buyer has not yet paid the seller.

Bank Loans Unsecured bank loans are another source of short-term business financing. Companies often use these loans to finance seasonal (cyclical) businesses. For instance, a swimwear manufacturer has strong sales in the spring and summer and lower sales during the fall and winter. It needs short-term bank financing to increase inventories before its strongest selling season and to finance accounts receivable during late winter and early spring, as shown in Exhibit 19.2. The company repays these bank loans when it sells the inventory and collects the receivables.

Unsecured bank loans include lines of credit and revolving credit agreements. A **line of credit** is an agreement between a bank and a business. It specifies the maximum amount of unsecured short-term borrowing the bank will make available to the firm over a given period, typically one year. A line of credit is not a guaranteed loan; the bank agrees to lend funds only if it has money available. Usually, the

line of credit
An agreement between a bank and a business that specifies the maximum amount of unsecured short-term borrowing the bank will make available to the firm over a given period, typically one year.

Exhibit 19.2 > Swimwear Manufacturer's Seasonal Cash Flows

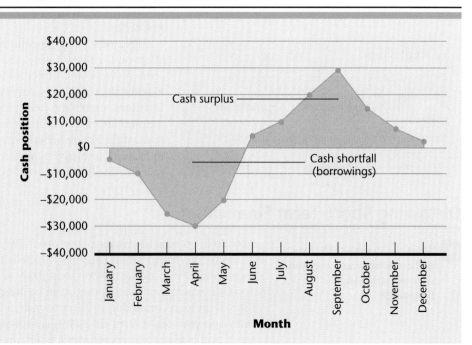

firm must repay any borrowing within a year. It must also either pay a fee or keep a certain percentage of the loan amount (10 to 20 percent) in a checking account at the bank.

revolving credit agreement
A line of credit under which a bank guarantees that a certain amount of money will be available for a business to borrow over a given period.

Another bank loan, the **revolving credit agreement**, is basically a guaranteed line of credit. Because the bank guarantees that a certain amount of money will be available, it charges an extra fee in addition to interest. Revolving credit agreements are often arranged for a 2- to 5-year period. Finance companies as well as banks may provide these credit facilities.

Firms often obtain annual lines of credit based on their expected seasonal needs. Then they can quickly borrow without having to reapply to the bank each time funds are needed. Suppose the swimwear manufacturer projected a cash shortfall of $80,000 for the period from February to June. The financial manager might get a $100,000 line of credit from the bank. (The extra $20,000 would be there to cover any unexpected outlays.) The firm could borrow funds as needed—$10,000 in February, $25,000 in March, $30,000 in April. Then it could gradually repay the loan as it collects cash during the summer months.

Commercial Paper As noted earlier, *commercial paper* is an unsecured short-term debt—an IOU—issued by a financially strong corporation. Thus, it is a short-term investment for firms with temporary cash surpluses, and it is a financing option for major corporations. Corporations issue commercial paper in multiples of $100,000 for periods ranging from 3 to 270 days. Many big companies use commercial paper instead of short-term bank loans because the interest rate on commercial paper is usually 1 to 3 percent below bank rates.

Secured Short-Term Loans

secured loans
Loans for which the borrower is required to pledge specific assets as collateral, or security.

Secured loans require the borrower to pledge specific assets as *collateral,* or security. The secured lender can legally take the collateral if the borrower doesn't repay the loan. Commercial banks and commercial finance companies are the main sources of secured short-term loans to business. Although typically these asset-based loans are popular with borrowers whose credit is not strong enough to qualify for unsecured loans, today many large corporations such as Hartmarx, Goodyear, and Bumble Bee Seafoods also use asset-based loans. Finance executives turn to this type of short-term

CONCEPT *in Action*

For businesses with steady orders but a lack of cash to make payroll or other immediate payments, factoring is a popular way to obtain financing. In factoring, a firm sells its invoices to a third-party funding source for cash. The factor purchasing the invoices then collects on the due payments over time. Trucking companies with voluminous accounts receivable in the form of freight bills are good candidates for factoring. *Why might firms choose factoring instead of loans?*

financing for several reasons. Often these loans have less restrictive loan covenants (financial and operating measures with which the borrower must comply) than unsecured loans. They also give the borrower greater flexibility to finance growth because the amount of the loan rises in step with the levels of receivables and inventory used as collateral. Hartmarx, a $600 million apparel manufacturer, has a $200 million asset-based credit facility that reaches its highest levels in late summer and early fall as retailers buy heavily in anticipation of the holiday season. "It makes sense because we're borrowing based on a specific need," explains Glenn Morgan, Hartmarx executive vice president and CFO.[12]

Typically, the collateral for secured short-term loans is accounts receivable or inventory. Because accounts receivable are normally quite liquid (easily converted to cash), they are an attractive form of collateral. The appeal of inventory—raw materials or finished goods—as collateral depends on how easily it can be sold at a fair price.

factoring
A form of short-term financing in which a firm sells its accounts receivable outright at a discount to a factor.

Another form of short-term financing using accounts receivable is **factoring**. A firm sells its accounts receivable outright to a *factor,* a financial institution (usually a commercial bank or commercial finance company) that buys accounts receivable at a discount. Factoring is widely used in the clothing, furniture, sporting goods, and appliance industries. Factoring allows a firm to turn its accounts receivable into cash without worrying about collections. Because the factor assumes all the risks and expenses of collecting the accounts, firms that factor all of their accounts can reduce the costs of their credit and collection operations. Factoring is more expensive than a bank loan, however, because the factor buys the receivables at a discount from their actual value. But often a company has no choice because it has neither the track record to get unsecured financing nor other collateral to pledge as security for a loan.

Raising Long-Term Financing

A basic principle of finance is to match the term of the financing to the period over which benefits are expected to be received from the associated outlay. Short-term items should be financed with short-term funds, and long-term items should be financed with long-term funds. Long-term financing sources include both debt (borrowing) and equity (ownership). Equity financing comes either from selling new ownership interests or from retaining earnings.

Debt versus Equity Financing

5 **How do the two primary sources of long-term financing compare?**

Say that the Boeing Company plans to spend $2 billion over the next four years to build and equip new factories to make jet aircraft. Boeing's top management will assess the pros and cons of both debt and equity and then consider several possible sources of the desired form of long-term financing.

The major advantage of debt financing is the deductibility of interest expense for income tax purposes, which lowers its overall cost. In addition, there is no loss of ownership. The major drawback is **financial risk**: the chance that the firm will be unable to make scheduled interest and principal payments. The lender can force a borrower that fails to make scheduled debt payments into bankruptcy. Most loan agreements have restrictions to ensure that the borrower operates efficiently.

financial risk
The chance that a firm will be unable to make scheduled interest and principal payments on its debt.

Equity, on the other hand, is a form of permanent financing that places few restrictions on the firm. The firm is not required to pay dividends or repay the investment. However, equity financing gives common stockholders voting rights that provide them with a voice in management. Equity is more costly than debt. Unlike the interest on debt, dividends to owners are not tax-deductible expenses. Exhibit 19.3 summarizes the major differences between debt and equity financing.

Exhibit 19.3 > Major Differences between Debt and Equity Financing

	Debt Financing	Equity Financing
Voice in management	Creditors typically have none, unless borrower defaults on payments. Creditors may be able to place restraints on management in event of default.	Common stockholders have voting rights.
Claim on income and assets	Debt holders rank ahead of equity holders. Payment of interest and principal is a contractual obligation of the firm.	Equity owners have a residual claim on income (dividends are paid only after interest and any scheduled principal) and no obligation to pay dividends.
Maturity	Debt has a stated maturity and requires repayment of principal by a specified maturity date.	The company is not required to repay equity, which has no maturity date.
Tax treatment	Interest is a tax-deductible expense.	Dividends are not tax-deductible and are paid from after-tax income.

Financial managers try to select the mix of long-term debt and equity that results in the best balance between cost and risk. If a company's debt load gets too high, in the view of investors and securities analysts, the costs of borrowing will rise. Company policies about the mix of debt and equity vary. Some companies have high debt compared to equity. Debt as a percentage of equity is 163 percent at International Paper, a capital-intensive manufacturer. Others keep debt to a minimum. The long-term debt-to-equity ratio for Pfizer is about 17 percent; Nike, 12 percent; ExxonMobil, 7 percent; Starbucks, 4 percent; Microsoft, 3 percent; and Apple Computer, 0 percent.

Long-Term Debt Financing

 6 **What are the major types, features, and costs of long-term debt?**

term loan
A business loan with an initial maturity of more than one year; can be unsecured or secured.

bonds
Long-term debt obligations (liabilities) issued by corporations and governments.

Long-term debt is used to finance long-term (capital) expenditures. The initial maturities of long-term debt typically range between 5 and 20 years. Three important forms of long-term debt are term loans, bonds, and mortgage loans.

A **term loan** is a business loan with an initial maturity of more than one year. Term loans generally have 5- to 12-year maturities and can be unsecured or secured. They are available from commercial banks, insurance companies, pension funds, commercial finance companies, and manufacturers' financing subsidiaries. A contract between the borrower and the lender spells out the amount and maturity of the loan, the interest rate, payment dates, purpose of the loan, and other provisions such as operating and financial restrictions on the borrower to control the risk of default. Term loans may be repaid on a quarterly, semiannual, or annual schedule. The payments include both interest and principal, so the loan balance declines over time. Borrowers try to arrange a repayment schedule that matches the forecast cash flow from the project being financed.

Bonds are long-term debt obligations (liabilities) issued by corporations and governments. Like term loans, corporate bonds are issued with formal contracts that set forth the obligations of the issuing corporation and the rights of the bondholders. Most bonds are issued in multiples of $1,000 (par value) with initial maturities of 10 to 30 years. The stated interest rate, or *coupon rate,* is the percentage of the bond's par value that the issuer will pay each year as interest.

A mortgage loan is a long-term loan made against real estate as collateral. The lender takes a mortgage on the property, which lets the lender seize the property, sell it, and use the proceeds to pay off the loan if the borrower fails to make the scheduled payments. Long-term mortgage loans are often used to finance office buildings, factories, and warehouses. Life insurance companies are an important source of these loans. They make billions of dollars' worth of mortgage loans to businesses each year.

Equity Financing

7 **When and how do firms issue equity, and what are the costs?**

Equity is the owners' investment in the business. In corporations, the preferred and common stockholders are the owners. A firm obtains equity financing by selling new ownership shares (external financing), or by retaining earnings (internal financing), or for small and growing, typically high-tech companies through venture capital (external financing).

Selling New Issues of Common Stock

common stock
A security that represents an ownership interest in a corporation.

Common stock is a security that represents an ownership interest in a corporation. The cover of the prospectus for a new issue of common stock is shown in Exhibit 19.4. It shows that in January 2006, Chipotle Mexican Grill offered 7,878,788 shares priced at $22 per share. Underwriters' fees totaled $1.54 per share, leaving $20.46 per share, or a total of $161.2 million. Chipotle received about $124 million and its parent, McDonald's (the selling shareholder), received $37.2 million. The company also incurred several million dollars in issuance costs for printing, legal work, and accounting. Dividends, discussed below, are another potential cost of issuing common stock.

The Chipotle offering is an example of a company *going public*—its first sale of stock to the public. Usually, a high-growth company has an *initial public offering (IPO)* because it needs to raise more funds to finance continuing growth. An IPO often enables existing stockholders, usually employees, family, and friends who bought the stock privately, to earn big profits on their investment. Companies that are already public can issue and sell additional shares of common stock to raise equity funds, called secondary offerings.

The Chipotle IPO was one of the more successful in recent years, with its stock price doubling the first day. In May 2006, the company announced a secondary offering of 4.2 million shares at $61.50 per share.[13]

CONCEPT *in Action*

Under Armour Inc.'s 2005 public-offering under the ticker symbol "UARM" was the hottest IPO for an American company in five years. The company's shares nearly doubled to $25 on the first day of trading and had topped $40 by mid-2006. The compression-apparel leader became a top sports brand by inventing tight-fitting synthetic undergarments that wick sweat away from the body, leaving athletes dryer and more comfortable. *What are pros and cons of going public?*

© PR NEWSWIRE UNDER ARMOUR, INC.

But going public has some drawbacks. For one thing, there is no guarantee an IPO will sell. It is also expensive. Big fees must be paid to investment bankers, brokers, attorneys, accountants, and printers. Once the company is public, it is closely watched by regulators, stockholders, and securities analysts. The firm must reveal such information as operating and financial data, product details, financing plans, and operating strategies. Providing this information is often costly.

IPOs can be successful when a company is well established and market conditions are right. Strong equity markets in the late 1990s and into 2000 prompted many companies to go public, especially very young Internet-related companies. Companies that were only a year or two old rushed to go public to take advantage of market conditions. Their prices popped up to what many believed were unrealistic levels. When the dot-com bubble burst and capital markets dried up, far fewer companies were willing to brave the IPO waters. Instead they turned to other financing sources to tide them over until the market for new issues picked up in 2004. Volatile U.S. stock markets and lower returns caused IPO activity to fall 20 percent in 2005. Worldwide, however, the market for IPOs was strong, with issuance of new equity rising 18 percent. In early 2006, stronger U.S. stock market performance resulted in an increase in IPO announcements. Overseas IPO activity continued strong.[14]

Going public is the dream of many small company founders and early investors, who hope to recoup their investments and become instant millionaires. Google, which went public in 2004 at $85 a share and soared to $475 in early 2006 before settling back to trade in the high-300 range in June 2006, is one of the more successful IPOs. But sometimes the dream turns into a nightmare, as it did for Vonage Holdings, a leading provider of Internet phone service, and its investors. Its May 24, 2006, IPO was a disaster, and by mid-June the stock was more than 40 percent below its $17 offering price. Investors lost interest in Web companies that are big on promises but have yet to show a profit. In the Creative Thinking Case at the end of this chapter, you'll learn more about the problems that plagued the Vonage IPO.

Some companies choose to remain private. Cargill, Hallmark Cards, Levi Strauss, Mars, Publix Super Markets, and Toys "R" Us are among the largest U.S. private companies. Housewares retailer Crate & Barrel is another company that likes its private status. Despite many offers from investment bankers to go public to raise funds for expansion, Crate & Barrel management opted to grow more slowly and use private sources of funding instead.

Dividends and Retained Earnings

dividends
Payments to stockholders from a corporation's profits.

stock dividends
Payments to stockholders in the form of more stock; may replace or supplement cash dividends.

Dividends are payments to stockholders from a corporation's profits. A company does not have to pay dividends to stockholders. But if investors buy the stock expecting to get dividends and the firm does not pay them, the investors may sell their stock. If too many sell, the value of the stock decreases. Dividends can be paid in cash or in stock. **Stock dividends** are payments in the form of more stock. Stock dividends may replace or supplement cash dividends. After a stock dividend has been paid, more shares have a claim on the same company, so the value of each share often declines.

At their quarterly meetings, the company's board of directors (with the advice of its financial managers) decides how much of the profits to distribute as dividends and how much to reinvest. A firm's basic approach to paying dividends can greatly affect its share price. A stable history of dividend payments indicates good financial health. In September 2004, American Express raised its dividend 20 percent and raised it another 25 percent in May 2006. Chief Executive Ken Chenault said that dividend increases represent a good way to deliver value to shareholders.[15]

If a firm that has been making regular dividend payments cuts or skips a dividend, investors start thinking it has serious financial problems. The increased uncertainty often results in lower stock prices. Thus, most firms set dividends at a level they can keep paying. They start with a relatively low dividend payout ratio so that they can maintain a steady or slightly increasing dividend over time.

retained earnings
Profits that have been reinvested in a firm.

Retained earnings, profits that have been reinvested in the firm, have a big advantage over other sources of equity capital: They do not incur underwriting costs. Financial managers strive to balance dividends and retained earnings to maximize the value of the firm. Often the balance reflects the nature of the firm and its industry. Well-established and stable firms and those that expect only modest growth, like public utilities, financial-services companies, and large industrial corporations, typically pay out much of their earnings in dividends. For example, in the year ending March 31, 2006, Altria Group paid dividends of $3.20 per share, Bank of America paid $2.00 per share, ChevronTexaco paid $2.08 per share, Dominion Resources paid $2.76 per share, Merck paid $1.52 per share, and Wachovia Bank paid $2.04 per share.

Most high-growth companies, like those in technology-related fields, finance much of their growth through retained earnings and pay low or no dividends to stockholders. As they mature, many decide to begin paying dividends, as did Microsoft and Qualcomm, in 2003.

Preferred Stock

Another form of equity is **preferred stock**. Unlike common stock, preferred stock usually has a dividend amount that is set at the time the stock is issued. These dividends must be paid before the company can pay any dividends to common stockholders. Also, if the firm goes bankrupt and sells its assets, preferred stockholders get their money back before common stockholders do. Preferred stock is described in greater detail in Chapter 20.

Like debt, preferred stock increases the firm's financial risk because it obligates the firm to make a fixed payment. But preferred stock is more flexible. The firm can miss a dividend payment without suffering the serious results of failing to pay back a debt.

Preferred stock is more expensive than debt financing, however, because preferred dividends are not tax-deductible. Also, because the claims of preferred stockholders on income and assets are second to those of debtholders, preferred stockholders require higher returns to compensate for the greater risk.

Venture Capital

As we learned in Chapter 6, *venture capital* is another source of equity capital. It is most often used by small and growing firms that aren't big enough to sell securities to the public. This type of financing is especially popular among high-tech companies that need large sums of money.

Venture capitalists invest in new businesses in return for part of the ownership, sometimes as much as 60 percent. They look for new businesses with high growth potential, and they expect a high investment return within 5 to 10 years. By getting in on the ground floor, venture capitalists buy stock at a very low price. They earn profits by selling the stock at a much higher price when the company goes public. Venture capitalists generally get a voice in management through a seat on the board of directors. Jobster Inc., an online job advertising service that uses vertical search techniques for targeted matches of employers and job candidates, raised $19.5 million for product development and market expansion. Investors in this second round of financing were Mayfield Fund and previous investors, Ignition Partners and Trinity Ventures. Venture capitalists from all three have seats on Jobster's board.[16]

Getting venture capital is difficult, even though there are hundreds of private venture-capital firms in this country. Most venture capitalists finance only about 1 to 5 percent of the companies that apply. It was harder than usual to get venture capital financing from 2001 through 2003, after the technology bubble burst. By 2004, venture capitalists were once again hungry for deals. During 2004, U.S. venture-capital firms invested $20.4 billion in young companies, an increase of 8 percent over 2003, and 2005 financings reached $22.1 billion. Information technology (IT) companies received 54 percent of the total, followed by health care at 30 percent and retailers and consumer/business products and services at 12 percent. Venture capital firms also were willing to make investments in early stage deals, which represented 35 percent of transactions. These trends continued into 2006; the amount invested during the first quarter was 18 percent higher than the same period in 2005, with IT leading the way.[17]

In addition to venture capital firms, start-up firms can also find equity capital from private foundations, corporations, states, and wealthy individuals (called *angel investors*). Angel investors are motivated by the potential to earn a high return on their investment. Accountants, attorneys, business associates, financial consultants, bankers, and others may help the small firm find an angel. Although it's difficult to accurately estimate the size of this informal market, the Center for Venture Research at the University of New Hampshire estimates that about 225,000 angels

CONCEPT *in Action*

Billionaire financier Philip Anschutz—whose holdings span oil, railroads, movie theaters, and sports—is staking his next fortune on family-friendly cinema. Anschutz bankrolled *Ray*, the Oscar-winning biopic on R&B legend Ray Charles, and backed the remake of E.B. White's *Charlotte's Web*. But it was his investment in the big-screen adaptation of C.S. Lewis's Narnia series that struck gold— *The Lion, the Witch and the Wardrobe* grossed over $291 million domestically. *How do businesses obtain financing from venture capitalists and angel investors?*

invest $22 billion each year, much of which is for the first three stages of funding: seed, start-up, and early stage.[18]

Corporations seeking to gain access to promising new technologies also offer venture funding. Intel, for example, invests through its Intel Capital unit. In April 2006, it was a lead investor in Nanochip, a California company that makes advanced micro-electro-mechanical systems (MEMS) data storage chips. The additional funding will help Nanochip develop a new class of low-power, very high-capacity, and high-performance memory chips for consumer electronics products. Intel also invested in Pipex Wireless, a joint venture with ISP Pipex Communications, to provide WiMax, long-range wireless broadband technology, to major cities in the United Kingdom.[19]

concept check

Compare the advantages and disadvantages of debt and equity to the issuer.

Discuss the costs involved in issuing common stock.

Briefly describe these sources of equity: retained earnings, preferred stock, venture capital.

Trends in Financial Management

8 **What trends are affecting the practice of financial management?**

Many of the key trends shaping the practice of financial management echo those in other disciplines. For example, as we saw in the earlier boxes on global cash management and outsourcing, technology is improving the efficiency with which financial managers run their operations.

Finance has moved from a relatively isolated, inward-looking function to a unit that is heavily involved in shaping and implementing a company's overall strategic objectives. In the post-Sarbanes-Oxley-Act era, CFOs have also taken on responsibility for overseeing corporate compliance with the act. The continued expansion of the financial manager's role in risk management is a natural outgrowth of the new regulations.

The CFO's Role Continues to Expand

During the 1990s, CFOs became more than just numbers people. They joined top management in developing and implementing the firm's strategic direction. Negotiating billion-dollar mergers and finding creative financing vehicles were all part of the day's work. They were the company's face to the Wall Street analysts, who watched to see if the company would meet each quarter's earnings estimates.

In the early 2000s, the financial manipulations of Enron, Tyco, Adelphia, and WorldCom placed all CFOs under a magnifying glass. The Sarbanes-Oxley Act, discussed in detail in Chapter 17, clearly prohibited certain practices and established

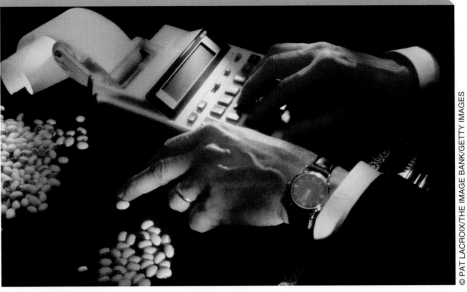

CONCEPT *in Action*
The CFO-as-busy-beancounter image has undergone an extreme makeover, as today's financial chiefs increasingly perform highly visible decision-making roles alongside CEOs. Intense pressure for Sarbanes-Oxley compliance along with expectations of beating the numbers each quarter are major factors behind both the rising prominence and turnover of financial officers. And as responsibility increases, so does pay. In 2005, Intuit Inc. offered incoming CFO Kiran Patel an annual salary 38 percent higher than that of his predecessor. *Have CFOs become chief executive material?*

© PAT LACROIX/THE IMAGE BANK/GETTY IMAGES

more stringent regulations for financial reporting. To avoid any suspicion of wrongdoing, companies often voluntarily ended strategies that were legal but could raise questions. At the same time, Sarbanes-Oxley added corporate governance and greater accountability to the CFO's role, significantly increasing the scope and complexity.

CFOs are more highly visible and active in company management than ever before. They serve as both business partner to the chief executive and a fiduciary to the board. "Today, in what I'll call the post-Enron, post-WorldCom era, there's been a restored emphasis on the fiduciary and control aspects," says Robert Lumpkins, vice chairman and CFO of Cargill Inc., a privately owned international agricultural and industrial products company. "Finance today is well-balanced between what I'll call the value-adding and the value-preservation aspects." In global organizations such as Cargill, with 142,000 employees in 61 countries, finance managers must also be sensitive to cultural differences and different approaches to solving problems.[20]

Finance professionals need to have a broad view of company operations to communicate effectively with business unit managers, board members, creditors, and investors. Douglas Oberheim, a group president at Caterpillar, credits his years as CFO with providing him the broad perspective to see the company from the shareholder's viewpoint and the understanding of the importance of cross-functional activities. In addition to such traditional duties as arranging mergers and acquisitions, raising and allocating capital, and managing treasury operations, CFOs are also key players in matters pertaining to information technology, human resources, and the supply chain. Interpersonal skills are essential because they must motivate employees and encourage a positive environment that promotes accountability and ethical behavior down through the organization. Finance managers must learn to be team players who can work with employees in other functional areas. At times finance and business unit executives have differing positions, and it takes careful negotiation to resolve issues. For example, business units may want to maintain larger cash balances than finance recommends. Educating unit managers about the cost of idle cash and establishing appropriate incentives can change corporate culture.[21]

In the aftermath of the recent accounting scandals, CFOs consider accuracy of financial reporting their top priority, and they also must now provide more detailed explanations of what's behind the numbers to board members and other stakeholders. Rather than showering the board with financial reports and statistics, CFOs are crafting more focused presentations that deal with the company's overall financial health and future prospects.[22] They must also educate board members about the implications of Sarbanes-Oxley and what the company is doing to comply with the Act's provisions. In the Managing Change box, we'll learn more about how today's CFOs are changing the role and perception of the finance function.

Weighing the Risks

The job of managing a company's risk, which became even more difficult after the September 11, 2001 terrorist attacks, continues to be challenging for financial executives. Adding to the complexity are the volatile economy and financial markets at home and abroad. No longer does risk management focus narrowly on buying insurance to protect against loss of physical assets and interruption of business. Instead, more companies now consider **enterprise risk management (ERM)** a priority. ERM goes beyond just identifying, monitoring, and lowering risk to include a strategic approach to defining and managing all elements of a company's risk.

As the risk management function expands beyond its traditional role, companies recognize that ERM can make significant contributions to financial performance and shareholder returns. Because a failure in a company's risk control procedures can lead to substantial financial losses, corporate CFOs and treasurers are taking a proactive, leadership role in ERM. This requires them to get more involved with operations and form partnerships with business unit executives. "Effective risk management requires the ability to walk in the shoes of operations," says David Kelsey, senior vice president

enterprise risk management (ERM)
A company-wide, strategic approach to identifying, monitoring, and managing all elements of a company's risk.

MANAGING CHANGE

Finance Looks Outward

No longer does finance operate in its own little world of spreadsheets and banking relationships. Most CFOs want the finance function to be viewed by their company's business units as a strategic partner who can contribute to their success. "I happen to be a finance practitioner, but I've always been on the strategy side of the business," says Carol Tomé, CFO of Home Depot. "It's really what we can do to influence business that's the exciting part."

Tomé was ahead of her peers in promoting strategic finance. Her efforts to integrate finance into business units began when she became Home Depot's treasurer in 1995. Line managers were wary as she moved finance managers into operational units, but she won them over with patience. "You know what? I wouldn't make a single decision without my finance partner at my side," an executive from a merchandising unit told her. "It was like music to my ears," Tomé says. Bob Nardelli, Home Depot's president and CEO, supported Tomé's vision and worked closely with her to implement her plans. "Bob understands the value of a strong finance organization and the impact a strong finance organization can have on a company," she says.

The globalization of finance also affects the role of the CFO. "The days when the role of the CFO was limited to reporting, bean-counting, and cost cutting are definitely over," says Philippe Blondiaux, Nestlé Group's CFO for Russia. "What is expected from us is to be co-pilots of our business. In a country like Russia, which is set to be one of the growth engines of the Nestlé Group, one of my personal objectives is to see where to invest to get the best possible return."

Prudential Financial Inc. is another company that has changed the way operating units perceive finance. As senior vice president and Treasurer Chuck Chaplin explains, "My contribution, after our IPO, has been to change [treasury's] orientation from inward and functional to outward and business-focused. . . . The businesses need to be market-driven, and treasury needs to help build and channel that drive, but treasury needs to set policy and enforce controls. It takes a delicate balance." Maintaining that balance is difficult but essential. "Without that balance, treasury people could be seen as outsiders, annoying agents from corporate there to keep an eye on them," he explains. "Or else, [the treasury people] could go native and shift their loyalty to the business [unit]," Chaplin says.

For both Tomé and Chaplin, the goal is productive cooperation and teamwork between finance and the business units. The more each function understands the other, the better they can collaborate to meet corporate objectives. "We set an acceptable level of risk at the corporate level, and that level is not flexible," Chaplin says. "We try to be creative in how we help them grow the businesses, but we don't help the businesses fudge that line."[23]

Critical Thinking Questions
- How has the CFO's job changed in recent years, and why?
- What qualifications does today's CFO need, and how can finance managers who want to move into senior management acquire them?

---

and CFO of Sealed Air Corp., a New Jersey packaging products manufacturer. "Risk management can't be perceived as getting in the way of what business wants to do. Risk management needs to manage exposures, but not by creating more work or increasing costs."[24]

Companies face a wide range of financial and other risks, including:

- *Credit risk.* Exposure to loss as a result of default on a financial transaction or a reduction in a security's market value due to decline in the credit quality of the debt issuer.
- *Market risk.* Risk resulting from adverse movements in the level or volatility of market prices of securities, commodities, and currencies.
- *Operational risk.* The risk of unexpected losses arising from deficiencies in a firm's management information, support, and control systems and procedures.

Jennifer Ceran, treasurer of eBay Inc., was an early adopter of ERM. Ceran recognized the need for the finance area to go beyond the traditional risk tasks asssigned to the treasury operation, such as insurance, and take a broader view of all the risks affecting the company. Evaluating all types of risk and their impact on each other is critical to reducing overall risk for any company. As Rossini Zumwalt, assistant treasurer and director of finance at software firm Symantec explains, "We identified the risks we already knew about, but what were we leaving out? It's not just the risk you know. It's the risks you don't know. We forgot the 'E' in ERM. I think that's why companies are challenged. It's important to attach the 'E,' to go beyond traditional risks."[25]

Companies are also using risk management in response to new corporate governance guidelines. Better risk management procedures are important to stockholders in the post-Enron era. They want to know that companies have taken steps to minimize risks that would affect the company's values.

> **concept check**
>
> How has the role of CFO changed since the passage of the Sarbanes-Oxley Act?
>
> Why are improved risk management procedures important to stockholders?

Summary of Learning Goals

1 **What roles do finance and the financial manager play in the firm's overall strategy?**

Finance is the art and science involved in managing the firm's money. The financial manager must decide how much money is needed and when, how best to use the available funds, and how to get the required financing. The financial manager's responsibilities include financial planning, investing (spending money), and financing (raising money). Maximizing the value of the firm is the main goal of the financial manager, whose decisions often have long-term effects.

2 **How does a firm develop its financial plans, including forecasts and budgets?**

Financial planning enables the firm to estimate the amount and timing of the financial resources it needs to meet its business goals. The planning process begins with forecasts based on the demand for the firm's products. Short-term forecasts project expected revenues and expenses for one year. They are the basis for cash budgets, which show the flow of cash into and out of the firm and are used to plan day-to-day operations. Long-term forecasts project revenues and expenses over more than one year, typically 2 to 10 years. These strategic plans allow top management to analyze the impact of different options on the firm's profits.

3 **What types of short-term and long-term expenditures does a firm make?**

A firm invests in short-term expenses—supplies, inventory, and wages—to support current production, marketing, and sales activities. The financial manager manages the firm's investment in current assets so that the company has enough cash to pay its bills and support accounts receivable and inventory. Long-term expenditures (capital expenditures) are made for fixed assets such as land, buildings, machinery, and equipment. Because of the large outlays required for capital expenditures, financial managers carefully analyze proposed projects to determine which offer the best returns.

4 **What are the main sources and costs of unsecured and secured short-term financing?**

Short-term financing comes due within one year. The main sources of unsecured short-term financing are trade credit, bank loans, and commercial paper. Secured loans require a pledge of certain assets, such as accounts receivable or inventory, as security for the loan. Factoring, or selling accounts receivable outright at a discount, is another form of short-term financing.

5 **How do the two primary sources of long-term financing compare?**

Financial managers must choose the best mix of debt and equity for their firm. The main advantage of debt financing is the tax-deductibility of interest. But debt involves financial risk because it requires the payment of interest and principal on specified dates. Equity—common and preferred stock—is considered a permanent form of financing on which the firm may or may not pay dividends. Dividends are not tax-deductible.

6 **What are the major types, features, and costs of long-term debt?**

The main types of long-term debt are term loans, bonds, and mortgage loans. Term loans can be secured or unsecured and generally have 5- to 12-year maturities. Bonds usually have initial maturities of 10 to 30 years. Mortgage loans are secured by real estate. Long-term debt usually costs more than short-term financing because of the greater uncertainty that the borrower will be able to make the scheduled loan payments.

7 **When and how do firms issue equity, and what are the costs?**

The chief sources of equity financing are common stock, retained earnings, and preferred stock. The cost of selling common stock includes issuing costs and potential dividend payments. Retained earnings are profits reinvested in the firm. For the issuing firm, preferred stock is more expensive than debt because its dividends are not tax-deductible and its claims are secondary to those of debt holders, but less expensive than common stock. Venture capital is often a source of equity financing for small and growing, typically high-tech, companies.

8 What trends are affecting the practice of financial management?

The role of the CFO has continued to expand since the passage of the Sarbanes-Oxley Act, with CFOs taking the central role in overseeing corporate compliance with the Act and reestablishing public trust. CFOs must look outward and be business focused. Most CFOs are promoting strategic finance and encouraging finance staff to be team players who work closely with business units to achieve corporate goals. Companies face a wide range of risks, including credit risk, market risk, and operational risk. More companies are adopting enterprise risk management (ERM) to identify and evaluate risks and select techniques to control and reduce risk. Financial executives are taking a leadership role in ERM.

Key Terms

accounts payable 636	line of credit 636
accounts receivable 633	long-term forecasts 629
bonds 639	marketable securities 632
budgets 630	mortgage loan 640
capital budgeting 635	operating budgets 631
capital budgets 630	preferred stock 643
capital expenditures 635	retained earnings 642
cash budgets 630	return 628
cash flows 627	revolving credit agreement 637
cash management 631	risk 628
commercial paper 632	risk-return trade-off 628
common stock 640	secured loans 637
dividends 642	short-term forecasts 629
enterprise risk management (ERM) 645	stock dividends 642
factoring 638	term loan 639
financial management 626	trade credit 636
financial risk 638	unsecured loans 636

Preparing for Tomorrow's Workplace: SCANS

1. The head of your school's finance department has asked you to address a group of incoming business students about the importance of finance to their overall business education. Develop an outline with the key points you would cover in your speech. (Information)

2. As a financial manager at General Foods Company, you are preparing forecasts and budgets for a new line of high-nutrition desserts. Why should the finance department prepare these plans for the product development group? What factors would you consider in developing your projections and assessing their impact on the firm's profits? (Resources, Information)

3. You are the cash manager for a chain of sporting goods stores facing a cash crunch. To date, the chain has always paid accounts payable within the credit period. The CFO wants to consider extending payments beyond the due date. Write a memo that discusses the pros, cons, and ethics of stretching accounts payable as well as other cash-saving options to investigate. (Systems)

4. You are the chief financial officer of Discovery Labs, a privately held, five-year-old biotechnology company that needs to raise $3 million to fund the development of a new drug. Prepare a report for the board of directors that discusses the types of long-term financing available to the firm, their pros and cons, and the key factors to consider in choosing a financing strategy. (Information)

5. **Team Activity** Does paying dividends enhance the value of a company? Some financial experts caution companies to look long and hard before beginning to pay themselves dividends. They believe that committing yourself to a regular dividend curtails financial flexibility and reduces debt capacity. Dividends might

also signal that the company doesn't have good growth opportunities in which to invest its excess cash. Others counter that dividends can help a company's stock by making it less volatile. Standard & Poor's data supports this; typically, dividend-paying stocks in the S&P 500 outperform nonpayers. Divide the class into two teams to debate whether dividends add value to a company's stock. (Interpersonal, Information)

Ethics Activity

When ammunitions manufacturer Allied Defense Group was unable to obtain bank financing to expand one of its plants, CFO Robert Dowski solved the company's cash flow crunch by making a one-month bridge loan of up to $2 million from his personal funds. "We could have gone to other lenders for bridge financing, but it was just too complicated," said Dowski. "It took 15 minutes for me to decide to do it myself. I believe the company has a tremendous future. If I didn't have that confidence, I wouldn't be loaning the money." Allied's general counsel, top executives, and board of directors approved the transaction. Allied disclosed the loan terms—12 percent annual interest and 1,000 shares of Allied stock per $1 million of loan principal—in an SEC filing. Dowski advanced the company $1 million, earning interest of $10,000 and 1,000 shares, which were worth about $22,000 at that time.

Although loans from companies *to* officers are no longer permitted under the Sarbanes-Oxley Act, loans *from* officers are legal. However, Dowski's generosity could also be seen as a conflict of interest, because he might place his personal interests ahead of the company's.

Using a web search tool, locate articles about this topic and then write responses to the following questions. Be sure to support your arguments and cite your sources.

Ethical Dilemma: As a member of Allied Defense Groups' board of directors, would you approve the loan from Dowski? On what do you base your decision? Are there circumstances that would cause you to change your decision and why?

Sources: "Allied Defense Raises Eyebrows with Loan from CFO," *Washington Post*, February 20, 2006, p. D2; Lisa Yoon, "Executive Loans Can Run Both Ways," *CFO.com*, March 06, 2006, http://www.cfo.com.

Working the Net

1. CIT Group (**http://www.cit.com**), a major business and consumer finance company, offers businesses many different products and services. Click on Industry and chose a manufacturing and a service industry. What products does CIT offer each, and how do they differ? Next click on Business Phase and compare the types of products and services CIT has for each stage of a firm's life cycle. Summarize your findings.

2. If factoring accounts receivable is still a mystery to you, visit the 21st Financial Solutions site, **http://www.21stfinancialsolutions.com**. Follow the links on the home page to answer these questions: What are factoring's advantages? What are the additional benefits, and what types of companies can use factoring to their advantage? Then summarize the factoring process.

3. Visit the Wells Fargo Bank site, **http://www.wellsfargo.com**, to learn about the bank's products and services for corporate customers. Under the tab labeled Commercial, link to Business Financing. Describe briefly each type of loan Wells Fargo offers. Then do the same for Treasury Management services. How can the bank's Commercial Electronic Office help financial managers? What other services does the bank offer commercial clients?

4. Use the Venture Capital Resource Directory at vFinance, **http://www.vfinance.com**, to link to three different venture capital firms. Compare the firms' investment strategies (industry specialization, age of companies in which they invest, etc.). Also do an AngelSearch to check out two angel investor firms. How do their requirements differ from the venture firms?

5. For the latest news in risk management, including market, credit, operational, and other types of risk, visit RiskCenter, **http://www.riskcenter.com**. Scan the headlines to identify the latest issues in risk management. What issues seem to be of greatest concern? Select three articles that interest you and prepare brief summaries to share with your classmates.

Investors Hang Up on Vonage

Founded in 2002, Vonage quickly became a major player in Voice over Internet Protocol (VoIP) phone service. Using Internet connections instead of traditional phone lines, it offered customers an attractive flat rate of about $25 a month for calls to the United States, Canada, and many European countries. By its May IPO, Vonage had 1.7 million customers and more than half the U.S. market for Internet phone service. Vonage claimed to be the fastest growing phone company in the United States. Revenues in 2005 were almost triple 2004 levels.

Management thought the time was right to go public and raise funds for expansion. Investors were again interested in IPOs after several years of low demand. So on May 24, 2006, it sold 31.25 million shares and raised $531 million. It also offered its individual customers—usually closed out of high-profile IPOs—the chance to buy 100 shares at the IPO price, an unusual move. So why was the Vonage IPO the worst in two years?

Timing is everything, and Vonage's timing was off. The market fell sharply on inflation concerns. The shares opened on the New York Stock Exchange at $17, fell to $14.85 by the end of the first day, and were trading below $7 by September 2006.

The offer to individual investors worked against Vonage, sending a message to some analysts that institutions were not interested in buying the stock and that Vonage needed help from its customers. Chad Brand of Peridot Capital Management considered this a "huge red flag. . . . If that's not a sign that nobody else wanted their stock, I don't know what is," he posted on his Web site.

Several factors negatively affected the Vonage offering. Increased competition creates pricing pressure. Rivals range from small VoIP players similar to Vonage to Internet powerhouses including Google, Yahoo, and MSN. Cable companies such as Time Warner, that offer phone service bundled with television and broadband services, and Verizon and other traditional providers are lowering prices as well. Vonage's sales are already falling, while costs-per-subscriber are rising. The company's marketing costs are very high, and the per-line cost of providing service is also rising at the same time as customer complaints about service quality are mounting.

Regulatory uncertainty adds another layer of complexity. Telecommunications providers are campaigning to charge for carrying other company's calls. This would add to Vonage's costs. As Vonage grows, it will be required to collect sales tax and other fees, pushing customer bills well above the $25 flat rate they were expecting to pay and removing pricing advantages.

These are just a few of the issues that stand in the way of Vonage's profitability—currently projected for 2009. In fact, Vonage's IPO prospectus says that it will focus on growth rather than profitability and went so far as to say that it might never become profitable. As a public company, Vonage will be under greater pressure to execute its business plan and also face close scrutiny from its investors. Only time will tell if investors hang up when Vonage calls.

Critical Thinking Questions

- What issues should executives of a company such as Vonage consider before deciding to go public? In your opinion, was the company ready for an IPO, and why?
- How else could Vonage have raised funds to continue to grow? Compare the risks of raising private equity to going public.

- Use a search engine and a site such as Yahoo Finance to learn about Vonage's current situation. Prepare a brief summary, including its current financial situation. Is it still a public company, and how has its stock fared?

Sources: David A. Gaffen, "Tale of Two IPOs," *Wall Street Journal Online*, May 24, 2006, http://www.wsj.com; Olga Kharif, "Vonage's Iffy IPO," *Business Week Online*, February 9, 2006, http://www.businessweek.com; Timothy J. Mullaney, "Vonage's Lackluster IPO," *Business Week Online*, May 24, 2006, http://www.businessweek.com; Shawn Young and Li Yuan, "Vonage Faces User Complaints as IPO Looms," *Wall Street Journal*, May 18, 2006, p. B1; Shawn Young and Lynn Cowan, "Vonage Lacks Voltage in Its IPO, with Weakest Debut in 2 Years," *Wall Street Journal*, May 25, 2006, p. C4; Shawn Young and Randall Smith, "How Vonage's High-Profile IPO Stumbled on the Stock Market," *Wall Street Journal*, June 3, 2006, p. A1.

Video Case >

Tweeter Sings a Different Tune

From a single store in Boston in 1972, Tweeter Home Entertainment Group is the parent company for a group of regional specialty consumer electronics retailers with $800 million in revenues in 2005. The company now has 160 stores in 22 states, operating under the names Tweeter, HiFi Buys, Hillcrest High Fidelity, Showcase Home Entertainment, and Sound Advice. Unlike other national electronics chains, the company doesn't try to be all things to all people. It sells only mid- to high-end audio and video equipment—no low-end products, computers, home office equipment, or appliances.

"Tweeter has been successful because we have been true to our niche as a specialty retailer," says Joe McGuire, Tweeter's former CFO who in July 2005 became Tweeter's president and chief operating officer. "We are clear on who we are—and who we are not." Tweeter began an aggressive expansion program of new-store openings and acquisitions in 1996, which continued through 2005. The company went public in July 1998.

"Being CFO of a company that's growing, and getting the chance to take the company public is a lot of fun," McGuire says. He points out that successful growth requires that the "back end of [the] house" is in order. "You cannot grow a company at 50 to 60 percent if you do not have strong financial controls in place, run good management information systems, and provide decision support to people who are running the company."

Tweeter's rapid expansion through acquisitions placed pressure on McGuire to maintain a strong profit picture. Reducing accounts receivable and inventory has been a priority. He also arranged for a larger asset-based bank credit facility in order to give Tweeter greater operating flexibility.

McGuire believes that the most important measure for a public company that wants access to the capital markets is net profits. "We can talk about cash flow or return on assets—and they all have their place in the process. But they must support our decision to grow net income." He continues, "We believe in keeping it simple. We spend a lot of time measuring net margins and knowing the components and also looking at return on equity. Someone who invested in Tweeter last year should be entitled to see that money grow this year."

Changing dynamics in home audio and video sales have affected the company's strategy. The popularity of relatively inexpensive portable digital media products such as MP3 players reduced sales of big ticket stereo systems. Facing increasing competition from big-box electronics chains such as Best Buy, Tweeter retrenched and restructured. It closed 19 stores and placed greater emphasis on home installation and repair services. Business is on the upswing again, however, as more consumers shift to digital and high-definition televisions and upgrade their audio systems to complement the advanced television sets.

Critical Thinking Questions

- Evaluate Joe McGuire's financial management practices based on what you have learned in this chapter about the financial manager's primary goal and key responsibilities.
- What are the general and financial management implications of growing the company through acquisitions compared to opening new stores?
- How does being a public company affect Tweeter's financial management decisions? What advantages does it bring?

Sources: Adapted from material in the video "Financial Management at Tweeter Home Entertainment Group" and Sandra Jones, "Wounded Woofer," *Crain's Chicago Business,* July 18, 2005, p. 3; Tweeter corporate Web site, http://www.twtr.com, June 6, 2006; Jennifer Waters, "Tweeter Ekes Out Profit; Shares Gain," *MarketWatch,* April 27, 2006, http://www.marketwatch.com; Tweeter Annual Report 2005, http://www.twtr.com, June 6, 2006; "Tweeter Home Entertainment Group Reports Results for Its Second Fiscal Quarter Ended March 31, 2006," *Business Wire,* April 27, 2006, http://biz.yahoo.com.

Hot Links Address Book

When you come across a finance term you don't understand, visit the Hypertextual Finance Glossary at **http://www.duke.edu/~charvey/classes/wpg/glossary.htm**

What challenges do today's financial managers face? To find out, browse through recent issues of *CFO* magazine at **http://www.cfo.com**

Find an introduction to the types of cash management services banks offer their customers at Centura Bank's site, **http://www.rbccentura.com/business/cashman/index.html**

Learn about the services and current rates offered by 1st Commercial Credit, a factoring firm, at **http://www.1stcommercialcredit.com**

Which companies are getting funding from venture capital firms? For this and other information, visit vFinance.com at **http://www.vfinance.com**

Learn how Reuters Risk Management Services, at **http://risk.reuters.com** helps companies with global operations identify, measure, and manage financial risk.

A P P E N D I X

Managing Risk and Insurance

Overview

Every day, businesses and individuals are exposed to many different kinds of risk. Investors who buy stocks or speculate in commodities may earn a profit, but they also take the risk of losing all or part of their money. Illness is another type of risk, involving financial loss from not only the cost of medical care but also the loss of income.

Businesses, too, are exposed to many types of risk. Market risks, such as lower demand for a product or worsening economic conditions, can hurt a firm. Other risks involve customers, who could be injured on a company's premises or by a company's product. Like homes and cars owned by individuals, business property can be damaged or lost through fire, floods, and theft. Businesses must also protect themselves against losses from theft by dishonest employees. The loss of a key employee is another risk, especially for small firms.

It is impossible to avoid all risks, but individuals and businesses can minimize risks or buy protection—called insurance—against them. Although some risks are uninsurable, many others are insurable. Let's now look at basic risk concepts and the types of insurance available to cover them.

Risk Management

 What is risk and how can it be managed? What makes a risk insurable?

risk management
The process of identifying and evaluating risks and selecting and managing techniques to adapt to risk exposures.

risk
The chance of financial loss due to a peril.

speculative risk
The chance of either loss or gain, without insurance against the possible loss.

Every business faces risks like the ones listed above. **Risk management** involves analyzing the firm's operations, evaluating the potential risks, and figuring out how to minimize losses in a cost-efficient manner. In today's complex business environment, the concern for public and employee welfare and the potential for lawsuits have both increased. Risk management thus plays a vital role in the overall management of a business.

Types of Risk

Individuals and firms need to protect themselves against the economic effects of certain types of risk. In an insurance sense, **risk** (sometimes called *pure risk*) is the chance of financial loss due to a peril. Insurable risks include fire, theft, auto accident, injury or illness, a lawsuit, or death. **Speculative risk** is the chance of either loss or gain. Someone who buys stock in the hope of later selling it at a profit is taking a speculative risk and cannot be insured against it.

Strategies to Manage Risk

Risk is part of life. Nevertheless, people have four major ways to deal with it:

- *Risk avoidance.* Staying away from situations that can lead to loss. A person can avoid the risk of a serious injury by choosing not to go skydiving. Kinder-Care, a nationwide day-care chain, could avoid risk by not transporting children to and from school or taking them on field trips. Manufacturers who wish to avoid risks could produce only goods that have a proven track record. But these risk-avoidance strategies could stifle growth in the long run. Thus risk avoidance is not good for all risks.

- *Self-insurance.* The willingness to bear a risk without insurance, also called *risk assumption.* This offers a more practical way to handle many types of risks. Many large firms with warehouses or stores spread out over the United States—Sears or Kmart, for instance—may choose not to insure them. They assume that, even if disaster strikes one location, the others won't be harmed. The losses will probably be less than the insurance premiums for all the locations. Many companies self-insure because it is cheaper to assume some risks than to insure against them. Some choose to pay small claims themselves and insure only for catastrophic losses. Others "go naked," paying for all claims from company funds. This is clearly the most risky strategy. A big claim could cripple the firm or lead to bankruptcy.
- *Risk reduction.* Adopting techniques to prevent financial losses. For example, companies adopt safety measures to reduce accidents. Construction workers are required to wear hard hats and safety glasses. Airlines keep their aircraft in good condition and require thorough training programs for pilots and flight attendants. Hotels install smoke alarms, sprinkler systems, and firewalls to protect guests and minimize fire damage.
- *Risk transference.* Paying someone else to bear some or all of the risk of financial loss for certain risks that can't be avoided, assumed, or reduced to acceptable levels. The way to transfer risk is through **insurance**. Individuals and organizations can pay a fee (a *premium*) and get the promise of compensation for certain financial losses. The companies that take on the risks are called *insurance companies.*

insurance
The promise of compensation for certain financial losses.

Insurance Concepts

 10 **What types of insurance coverage should businesses consider?**

insurance policy
A written agreement that defines what the insurance covers and the risks that the insurance company will bear for the insured party.

underwriting
A review process of all insurance applications and the selection of those who meet the standards.

insurable interest
An insurance applicant's chance of loss if a particular peril occurs.

Companies purchase insurance to cover insurable risks. An **insurance policy** is the written agreement that defines what the insurance covers and the risks that the insurance company will bear for the insured party. It also outlines the policy's benefits (the maximum amount that it will pay in the event of a loss) and the premium (the cost to the insured for coverage). Any demand for payment for losses covered by the policy is a *claim.*

Before issuing a policy, an insurance company reviews the applications of those who want a policy and selects those that meet its standards. This **underwriting** process also determines the level of coverage and the premiums. Each company sets its own underwriting standards based on its experience. For instance, a life insurance company may decide not to accept an applicant who has had a heart attack within five years (or to charge a 50 to 75 percent higher premium). A property insurer may refuse to issue a policy on homes near brush-filled canyons, which present above-average fire hazards.

To get insurance, the applicant must have an **insurable interest**: the chance of suffering a loss if a particular peril occurs. In most cases, a person cannot insure the life of a friend, because the friend's death would not be considered a financial loss. But business partners can get life insurance on each other's lives because the death of one of them would have a financial impact on their firm.

insurable risk
A risk that an insurance company will cover. It must meet certain criteria.

Insurable Risks

Insurance companies are professional risk takers, but they won't provide coverage against all types of risk. Some risks are insurable; some are not. For instance, changes in political or economic conditions are not insurable. An **insurable risk** is one that an insurance company will cover. For a risk to be insurable, it must meet these criteria:

- *The loss must not be under the control of the insured.* The loss must be accidental—that is, unexpected and occurring by chance. Insurance companies do not cover losses purposely caused by the insured party. No insurance company will pay for the loss of a clothing store that the insured set on fire. Nor will most companies pay life insurance benefits for a suicide.

law of large numbers
Insurance companies' predictions of the likelihood that a peril will occur in order to calculate premiums.

- *There must be many similar exposures to that peril.* Insurance companies study the rates of deaths, auto accidents, fires, floods, and many other perils. They know about how many of these perils will occur each year. The **law of large numbers** lets them predict the likelihood that the peril will occur and then calculate premiums.

  Suppose that an insurance company has 150 policies in Morton, Iowa. The company knows from past experience that these policyholders are likely to have a total of 12 car accidents a year and that the average payment for a claim in Morton has been $1,000. The total claims for one year's car accidents in Morton would be $12,000 (12 accidents × $1,000). Thus the company would charge each policyholder a premium of at least $80 ($12,000 ÷ 150). Profits and administrative expenses would make the premium somewhat higher.

- *Losses must be financially measurable.* The dollar amount of potential losses must be known so the insurance company can figure the premiums. Life insurance is for a fixed amount specified at the time the policy is bought. Otherwise, the company and the *beneficiary* (the one who gets the funds) would have to agree on the value of the deceased's life at the time of death. Premiums have to be calculated before then, however.

- *The peril must not be likely to affect all the insured parties at the same time.* Insurance companies must spread out their risks by insuring many people and businesses in many locations. This strategy helps minimize the chance that a single calamity will wipe out the insurance company.

deductibles
The amounts that the insured must pay before insurance benefits begin.

- *The potential loss must be significant.* Insurance companies cannot afford to insure trivial things for small amounts. Many policies have **deductibles**, amounts that the insured must pay before insurance benefits begin.

- *The company must have the right to set standards for insurance coverage.* Insurance companies can refuse to cover people with health problems like AIDS, cancer, or heart trouble, a poor driving record, or a dangerous job or hobby. They can also charge higher premiums because of the higher risks they are covering.

Premium Costs

Insurance policies must be economical—relatively low in cost compared to the benefits—so people will want to buy them. Yet the premiums must also cover the risks that the insurance company faces. Insurance companies collect statistics on many perils. Then specially trained mathematicians called *actuaries* use the law of large numbers to develop actuarial tables, which show how likely each peril is. Actuarial tables are the basis for calculating premiums. For example, actuaries use a mortality table showing average life expectancy and the expected number of deaths per 1,000 people at given ages to set life insurance premiums.

Almost every homeowner buys insurance to cover the perils of fire, theft, vandalism, and other home-related risks. With such a large pool of policyholders, homeowners policies are usually inexpensive. Annual premiums are about 0.5 percent (or less) of the value of the home. This low cost encourages people to buy policies and thereby helps spread the insurance companies' risk over many homes throughout the country.

When setting premiums, insurers also look at the risk characteristics of certain groups, in order to assess the probability of loss for those groups. For instance, smokers tend to die younger than nonsmokers do and thus pay higher life insurance premiums. Female drivers under the age of 25 have a lower rate of accidents than male drivers, so their car insurance premiums are lower.

Insurance Providers

Insurers can be either public or private. Public insurance coverage is offered by specialized government agencies. The federal government is in fact the largest single insurer in the United States. Private insurance coverage is provided by privately organized (nongovernment) companies.

Public Insurance Government-sponsored insurance falls into two general categories: social insurance programs and other programs. Social insurance provides protection for problems beyond the scope of private insurers. These programs include:

unemployment insurance
Pays laid-off workers weekly benefits while they seek new jobs.

- *Unemployment insurance.* Every state has an **unemployment insurance** program that pays laid-off workers weekly benefits while they seek new jobs. Persons who terminate their employment voluntarily or are fired for cause are not eligible for unemployment insurance. These programs also provide job counseling and placement services. The benefits usually start a week after a person has lost a job and continue for 26 to 39 weeks, depending on the state. The size of the weekly benefit depends on the workers' previous income and varies from state to state. Unemployment insurance is funded by payroll taxes levied on employers.

workers' compensation
Covers the expenses of job-related injuries and diseases, including medical costs, rehabilitation, and job retraining if necessary.

- *Workers' compensation.* Every state has laws requiring employers to fund **workers' compensation** insurance to cover the expenses of job-related injuries and diseases, including medical costs, rehabilitation, and job retraining if necessary. It also provides disability income benefits (salary and wage payments) for workers who can't perform their job. Employers can buy workers' compensation policies or self-insure. A company's premium is based on the amount of its payroll and the types of risks present in the workplace. For instance, a construction company would pay a higher premium for workers' compensation insurance than would a jewelry store.

Social Security
Insurance that provides retirement, disability, death, and health benefits.

- *Social Security.* **Social Security** insurance provides retirement, disability, death, and health insurance benefits. Social Security is funded by equal contributions from workers and employers. These benefits go mostly to people over 65, although they are available to younger people who are disabled. More than 90 percent of all U.S. workers and their families are eligible to qualify for Social Security benefits.

Medicare
A health insurance program for those over 65.

- *Medicare.* A health insurance program for those over 65, **Medicare** was added to Social Security in 1965 and has two parts: hospital insurance, financed through the Social Security tax, and medical insurance, financed through government contributions and monthly premiums paid by those who want this coverage. Because Medicare pays only part of the insured's medical expenses, many people buy *supplemental insurance* from private insurance companies.

Private Insurance Companies Private insurance companies sell property and liability insurance, health insurance, and life insurance. Life and health insurance companies dominate the industry, accounting for about 70 percent of total assets. Regulation of private insurance companies is under the control of the states and thus varies from state to state.

There are two basic ownership structures for private insurance companies: stockholder and mutual. Just like other publicly owned corporations, *stock insurance companies* are profit-oriented companies owned by stockholders. The stockholders do not have to be policyholders, and the policyholders do not have to be stockholders. Their profits come from insurance premiums in excess of claim payments and operating expenses and from investments in securities and real estate. Metropolitan Life Corporation is the largest stockholder-owned insurance company in the United States, with assets of about $257 billion. Other major stock insurance companies are Aetna, Allstate Insurance, Continental Insurance, Fireman's Fund Insurance, John Hancock, and Prudential. Of about 5,000 insurance companies in the United States, most are stock insurance companies.

The rest are *mutual insurance companies,* which are not-for-profit organizations owned by their policyholders and chartered by each state. Any excess income is returned to the policyholder-owners as dividends, used to reduce premiums, or retained to finance future operations. The policyholders elect the board of directors, who manage the company. Many of the large life insurance companies in the United States are mutuals, including New York Life, Masssachusetts Mutual, and Northwestern Mutual Life. State Farm, one of the largest auto insurers, is also a mutual company.

Types of Insurance

In the Online Enrichment Chapter: Managing Your Personal Finances, we introduce several types of personal insurance coverage: property, liability, health, and life. Businesses also purchase insurance for these risks, but with some differences. Most companies offer group health and life insurance plans for their employees as a fringe benefit. Employers typically pay some of the health insurance premiums, and employees pay the rest. The cost is usually considerably less than for individual policies, although it pays to check before signing up. For example, companies may pay for the entire cost of life insurance equal to one or two times the employee's annual salary, with an option to purchase more under the group plan, but the premiums may be more expensive than buying an individual policy.

Businesses often insure the lives of key employees, such as top executives, salespeople, inventors, and researchers, whose death could seriously limit the income or value of a firm. To protect themselves, businesses buy **key-person life insurance**, a life insurance policy that names the company as beneficiary. In the case of a partnership, which is dissolved when a partner dies, key-person insurance is often bought for each partner, with the other partner named as the beneficiary, so that the surviving partner can buy the partnership interest from the estate of the deceased and continue operating.

key-person life insurance
A term insurance policy that names the company as beneficiary.

Property and Liability Insurance More than 3,500 companies offer property and liability policies. This type of insurance is important for businesses, which wish to protect against losses of property and lawsuits arising from harm to other people. *Property insurance* covers financial losses from damage to or destruction of the insured's assets as a result of specified perils, whereas *liability insurance* covers financial losses from injuries to others and damage to or destruction of others' property when the insured is considered to be the cause. It also covers the insured's legal defense fees up to the maximum amount stated in the policy. Automobile liability insurance, which we will discuss in more detail in the online chapter Managing Your Personal Finances, is an example. It would pay for a fence damaged when the insured person lost control of his or her car. Commercial and product liability insurance also fall into this category.

Commercial liability insurance covers a variety of damage claims, including harm to the environment from pollution. In the case of *product liability,* if a defective furnace exploded and damaged a home, the manufacturer would be liable for the damages. If the manufacturer were insured, the insurance company would cover the losses or pay to dispute the claim in court.

Property and liability insurance is a broad category. Businesses buy many types of property and liability insurance. These protect against loss of property due to fire, theft, accidents, or employee dishonesty, and financial losses arising from liability cases. Landlords and owners of business property buy *building insurance,* a type of property coverage, for protection against both property damage and liability losses. For instance, if a person broke an arm slipping on a wet floor in a hardware store, the business's insurance policy would cover any claim.

coinsurance
Property insurance coverage that is equal to a certain percentage of the property's value.

Property insurance policies usually include a coinsurance clause. **Coinsurance** requires the property owner to buy insurance coverage equal to a certain percentage of the property's value. To cut premium costs, policyholders often insure buildings for less than their full value, in the hope that a fire or other disaster will damage only part of the property. But insurers limit the payout if the property is underinsured. They use coinsurance clauses as an incentive for businesses to maintain full insurance on their buildings. For instance, some fire insurance policies have an 80 percent coinsurance clause. If the owner of a building valued at $400,000 buys a policy with coverage equal to at least $320,000 (80% × $400,000), he or she will collect the full amount of any partial loss. If the owner buys a policy for less coverage, the insurance company will pay for only part of the partial loss.

Special Types of Business Liability Insurance Businesses also purchase several other types of insurance policies, depending on their particular needs:

- *Business interruption insurance.* This optional coverage is often offered with fire insurance. It protects business owners from losses occurring when the business must be closed temporarily after property damage. **Business interruption insurance** may cover such costs as rental of temporary facilities, wage and salary payments to employees, payments for leased equipment, fixed payments (for instance, rent and loans), and profits that would have been earned during the period. *Contingent business interruption insurance* covers losses to the insured in the event of property damage to a major supplier or customer.
- *Theft insurance.* Businesses also want to protect their property against financial losses due to crime. **Theft insurance** is the broadest coverage and protects businesses against losses from an act of stealing. Businesses can also buy more limited types of theft insurance.
- *Fidelity and surety bonds.* What if a firm has a dishonest employee? This situation is covered by a *fidelity bond,* an agreement that insures a company against theft committed by an employee who handles company money. If a restaurant manager is bonded for $50,000 and steals $60,000, the restaurant will recover all but $10,000 of the loss. Banks, loan companies, and retail businesses that employ cashiers typically buy fidelity bonds.
- A *surety bond,* also called a *performance bond,* is an agreement to reimburse a firm for nonperformance of acts specified in a contract. This form of insurance is most common in the construction industry. Contractors buy surety bonds to cover themselves in case the project they are working on is not completed by the specified date or does not meet specified standards. In practice, the insurance company often pays another contractor to finish the job or to redo shoddy work when the bonded contractor fails to perform.
- *Title insurance.* A title policy protects the buyer of real estate against losses caused by a defect in the title—that is, a claim against the property that prevents the transfer of ownership from seller to purchaser. It eliminates the need to search legal records to be sure that the seller was actually the owner of (had clear title to) the property.
- *Professional liability insurance.* This form of insurance covers financial losses (legal fees and court-awarded damages up to specific limits) resulting from alleged malpractice by professionals in fields like medicine, law, architecture, and dentistry. *Directors and officers insurance* is a type of **professional liability insurance** designed to protect top corporate management, who have also been the target of malpractice lawsuits. It pays for legal fees and court-awarded damages up to specific limits.

---

business interruption insurance
Covers such costs as rental of temporary facilities, wage and salary payments to employees, payments for leased equipment, fixed payments, and profits that would have been earned during a period of closure after property damage.

theft insurance
A broad insurance coverage that protects businesses against losses for an act of stealing.

professional liability insurance
Insurance designed to protect top corporate management, who have been the target of malpractice lawsuits.

Summary of Learning Goals

9 What is risk, and how can it be managed? What makes a risk insurable?

Risk is the chance for financial loss due to a peril. Both individuals and businesses need to protect themselves against several types of risks. Many of these—death, poor health, property damage—can be covered by insurance, which pays the insured up to a specified amount in the event of loss from a particular peril. Risk can be managed by avoiding situations known to be risky, by assuming the responsibility for losses due to certain types of risk (called self-insurance), by reducing it through taking safety measures, and by transferring it to an insurance company.

10 What types of insurance coverage should businesses consider?

Property insurance covers losses arising from damage to property owned by the insured person or business. Liability insurance covers losses due to injuries to others or their property determined to be caused by the insured. Other important coverages for businesses include business interruption, automobile, theft, fidelity and surety bonds, personal liability, professional liability, and product liability.

Businesses must also be knowledgeable about health and life insurance, which they typically offer employees as part of fringe benefits packages.

Key Terms

business interruption insurance   658
coinsurance   657
deductibles   655
insurable interest   654
insurable risk   654
insurance   654
insurance policy   654
key-person life insurance   657
law of large numbers   655
Medicare   656

professional liability insurance   658
risk   653
risk management   653
Social Security   656
speculative risk   653
theft insurance   658
underwriting   654
unemployment insurance   656
workers' compensation   656

CHAPTER 20

Understanding Securities and Securities Markets

Exploring Business Careers
Richard L. Sandor
Chicago Climate Exchange
Northwestern University

For someone interested in the world of securities and securities markets, the numerous career possibilities are limited only by imagination. Nowhere is this more clearly seen than in the career of Dr. Richard L. Sandor.

Dr. Sandor is regarded as the "father of financial futures." Futures, are legally binding obligations to buy or sell specified quantities of commodities or financial instruments. When Dr. Sandor first started working, however, the idea of trading financial instruments was still just that—an abstract idea.

He began his career as a student at the City University of New York, Brooklyn College, where he received his Bachelor of Arts degree. In 1967, Dr. Sandor received a Ph.D. in Economics from the University of Minnesota and began teaching at the University of California, Berkeley. While at Berkeley, he also was director of the California Commodity Advisory and Research Project, a project to design and test the feasibility of an all-electronic commodity futures market.

On sabbatical from the University in the early 1970s, Dr. Sandor served as the vice president and chief economist for the Chicago Board of Trade, one of the largest futures and options-futures exchanges in the world. It was during his time at the Chicago Board of Trade that he created what became known as the interest rate derivatives market, where interest rates are the financial commodities traded. At the time, the idea was unheard of—futures trading was done with actual commodities, such as corn, soybeans, or grain, not with something as abstract as financial concepts.

Today, however, over 80 percent of the trading that occurs on the floor of the Chicago Board of Trade involves financial futures such as those that Dr. Sandor helped to develop.

Since the development of financial futures, Dr. Sandor has continued to be creative in his approach to securities markets, shifting his economic expertise to the areas of social and environmental change. Most recently, he has worked to found the Chicago Climate Exchange (CCX), an exchange market that, Dr. Sandor hopes, will decrease overall emissions and potential global warming by providing market-based incentives to companies that reduce their emissions. Based on a successful program designed by Dr. Sandor to combat acid rain, the CCX fuses the economic forces of financial markets with the world's environmental needs, once again proving Dr. Sandor's constant innovation.

Today, Dr. Sandor is chairman and CEO of the Chicago Climate Exchange and a research professor at Northwestern's Kellogg School of Management. Over his four-decade career, Dr. Sandor has never stopped looking for ways to expand the world of securities markets. From his early work at UC Berkeley to his work with the financial futures to his commitment to environmental change, he has been a creative force driving the development of the securities exchange markets.

In Chapter 20 you will learn about different types of securities and the securities markets where they trade.

661

Today, more people have a direct stake in the stock market than ever before. Whereas investing in the stock market was once the province of the wealthy, many smaller investors jumped into buying and selling stock as the markets boomed in the 1990s. About 60 percent of adult Americans now own stocks, compared to just 25 percent in 1981.[1]

The securities markets have a long history of rising and falling and ultimately rising again, affecting both corporate plans and investor pocketbooks. To capitalize on the cyclical nature of the securities markets, both business managers and investors must understand the basics of the securities traded and the securities markets. This chapter begins by describing the different types of securities available to investors: common and preferred stocks, bonds, mutual funds, futures contracts, and options. A discussion of the functions of the securities markets and the professionals that sell securities—investment bankers and stockbrokers—follows. Next, we'll examine the operation and regulation of securities exchanges and other markets. Discussions of the popular sources of investment information and security price quotations follow. Finally, we'll look at some important trends affecting the securities markets today.

Investor's Choice: Stocks and Bonds

securities
Investment certificates issued by corporations or governments that represent either equity or debt.

As we discussed in Chapter 19, a central concern of most businesses is raising capital to finance operations and expansion. Many corporations use securities as a source of long-term financing. **Securities** are investment certificates that represent either equity (ownership in the issuing organization) or debt (a loan to the issuer). Corporations and governments sell securities to investors, who in turn take on a certain amount of risk with the hope of receiving a profit from their investment. Whereas we discussed equity and debt securities from the corporation's perspective in Chapter 19, let's review the advantages of these and other types of securities from an investor's viewpoint.

1 How do common stock and preferred stock differ as investments?

Sharing the Wealth—and the Risk: Stocks

Equity securities, commonly called *stocks,* represent shares of ownership in a corporation. A share of stock is issued for each unit of ownership and the stockholder (owner)

CONCEPT *in Action*

In addition to creating opportunities for wealth, stock ownership grants shareholders the right to vote on numerous business decisions. While typically inconsequential, shareholder resolutions have led to some surprising changes in corporate government and environmental policies. The ouster of former Disney chief Michael Eisner, HP's merger with Compaq, and the creation of Apple's free computer recycling program are high-profile examples of shareholder power. *What are the advantages of owning common stock and preferred stock?*

© ASSOCIATED PRESS, AP

gets a stock certificate to prove ownership. If you own a share of stock in General Electric (GE) Corp., for example, you are a partial owner of GE. Your ownership interest isn't very big, because GE has billions of shares of stock outstanding, but your ownership gives you certain rights and potential rewards. The two types of equity securities are common stock and preferred stock. Each has advantages and disadvantages for investors.

Common Stock *Common stock* is the most widespread form of stock ownership. Common stockholders receive the right to vote on many important corporate decisions, such as who should sit on the company's board of directors and whether the firm should merge with another company. In most cases, common stockholders get one vote for each share of stock they own. Common stock also gives investors the opportunity to share in the company's success, either through dividends or stock price increases.

As discussed in Chapter 19, *dividends* are the part of corporate profits that the firm distributes to shareholders. Dividends for common stock can be paid in either cash or additional shares of stock (called *stock dividends*). Common stock dividends are declared annually or quarterly (four times a year) by a corporation's board of directors. They are typically paid quarterly. However, common stock dividends are paid only after all other obligations of the firm—payments to suppliers, employees, bondholders, and other creditors, plus taxes and preferred stock dividends—have been met. Some firms, especially rapidly growing companies and those in high-technology industries, choose not to pay any dividends on their common stock. Instead, they reinvest their profits in more buildings, equipment, and new products in hope of earning greater profits in the future. As noted in Chapter 17, these reinvested profits are called *retained earnings*.

One advantage of common stock ownership is its liquidity: Many common stocks are actively traded in securities markets and can be quickly bought and sold. An investor can benefit by selling common stock when its price increases, or *appreciates,* above the original purchase price. Investors in FedEx, the worldwide shipper, benefited from the company's early investments in China, which gave it an advantage over its competitors. A jump in new China routes in 2006 pushed stock prices higher as well, from about $76 in September 2005 to $120 in early May 2006.[2]

Although the returns from common stock dividends and price appreciation can be quite attractive, common stockholders have no guarantee that they will get any return on their investment. Stock prices are subject to many risks related to the economy, the industry, and the company. Like any commodity, the price of a specific company's stock is affected by supply and demand. The supply of a stock is limited by the number of shares a company has issued, whereas demand is created by the number of investors who want to buy the stock from those who already own it. Factors that can increase demand for a stock—and its price—include strong financial reports, new product market opportunities, and positive industry trends. However, demand can fall—and a stock's price drop—when negative events occur.

The threat of a lawsuit or increased government regulation of a firm's industry can send stock prices downward. Market conditions can also affect a company's stock price. Factors like these can hold down a common stock's dividends and its price, making it hard to predict the stock's return. For example, Merck & Co., a major pharmaceutical firm, recalled Vioxx after it was revealed that the popular painkiller could increase the risk of heart attacks and strokes. Its stock price fell 38 percent from September to December 2004 and never fully regained lost ground. Merck faced lawsuits that could cost it billions, and the company lost $22 billion in market value since it had to pull Vioxx off the market. Even announcements of promising new drugs and FDA approval of a cancer vaccine in June 2006 failed to return the stock to its 2004 high of $49.[3]

Preferred Stock *Preferred stock* is a second form of corporate ownership. Unlike common stockholders, preferred stockholders do not receive voting rights. However, preferred stock does provide several advantages to investors that common stock does not, specifically in the payment of dividends and the distribution of assets if the firm is liquidated.

The dividend for preferred stock is usually set at the time the stock is issued, giving preferred stockholders a clearer picture of the dividend proceeds they can expect from their investment. This dividend can be expressed either in dollar terms or as a percentage of the stock's par (stated) value. As with common stock, the company's board of directors may decide not to pay dividends if the company encounters financial hardships. However, most preferred stock is *cumulative preferred stock,* which means that preferred stockholders must receive all unpaid dividends before any dividends can be paid to common stockholders. Suppose, for example, that a company with a $5 annual preferred dividend misses its quarterly payment of $1.25 ($5.00 ÷ 4). The following quarter, the firm must pay preferred stockholders $2.50—$1.25 in unpaid preferred dividends from the previous quarter plus the $1.25 preferred dividend for the current quarter—before it can pay any dividends to common stockholders. Similarly, if the company goes bankrupt, preferred shareholders are paid off before common stockholders.

Investors like preferred stock because of the fixed dividend income. Although companies are not legally obligated to pay preferred dividends, most have an excellent record of doing so. However, the fixed dividend can also be a disadvantage because it limits the cash paid to investors. Thus, preferred stock has less potential for price appreciation than common stock.

Cashing In with Bonds

2 What are bonds, and what investment advantages and disadvantages do they offer?

When many people think of financial markets, they picture the equity markets. However, the bond markets are huge—the Bond Market Association estimates that the global bond market is $48 trillion. In the United States, companies and government entities sold about $5.6 trillion in new bond issues in 2005. Average daily trading volume exceeded $900 billion, with U.S. treasury securities accounting for 60 percent of the total.[4]

Bonds are long-term debt obligations (liabilities) of corporations and governments. A bond certificate is issued as proof of the obligation. The issuer of a bond must pay the buyer a fixed amount of money—called **interest,** stated as the *coupon rate*—on a regular schedule, typically every six months. The issuer must also pay the bondholder the amount borrowed—called the **principal,** or *par value*—at the bond's maturity date (due date). Bonds are usually issued in units of $1,000—for instance, $1,000, $5,000, or $10,000. The two sources of return on bond investments are interest income and gains from sale of the bonds. The long-term corporate bond had an average yield of 5.6 percent in 2005, down from 8 percent in 2000.[5]

Unlike common and preferred stockholders, who are owners, bondholders are creditors (lenders) of the issuer. In the event of liquidation, the bondholders' claim on the assets of the issuer comes before that of any stockholders.

Bonds do not have to be held to maturity. They can be bought and sold in the securities markets. However, the price of a bond changes over its life as market interest rates fluctuate. When the market interest rate drops below the fixed interest rate on a bond, it becomes more valuable and the price rises. If interest rates rise, the bond's price will fall. (Bond prices will be discussed in greater depth in the Security Price Quotations section later in the chapter.)

Corporate Bonds *Corporate bonds,* as the name implies, are issued by corporations. They usually have a par value of $1,000. They may be secured or unsecured, include special provisions for early retirement, or be convertible to common stock. About

interest
A fixed amount of money paid by the issuer of a bond to the bondholder on a regular schedule, typically every six months; stated as the *coupon rate*.

principal
The amount borrowed by the issuer of a bond; also called *par value*.

Exhibit 20.1 > **Popular Types of Corporate Bonds**

Bond Type	Characteristics
Collateral trust bonds	Secured by securities (stocks and bonds) owned by the issuer. Value of collateral is generally 25 to 35 percent higher than the bond's par value.
Convertible bonds	Unsecured bonds that can be exchanged for a specified number of shares of common stock.
Debenture	Unsecured bonds typically issued by creditworthy firms.
Equipment trust certificates	Used to finance "rolling stock"—airplanes, ships, trucks, railroad cars. Secured by the assets financed.
Floating-rate bonds	Bonds whose interest rate is adjusted periodically in response to changes in specified market interest rates. Popular when future inflation and interest rates are uncertain.
High-yield (junk) bonds	Bonds rated Ba or lower by Moody's or BB or lower by Standard & Poor's. High-risk bonds with high returns to investors. Frequently used to finance mergers and takeovers.
Mortgage bonds	Secured by property, such as land, equipment, or buildings.
Zero-Coupon Bonds	Issued with no coupon rate and sold at a large discount from par value. "Zeros" pay no interest prior to maturity. Investor's return comes from the gain in value (par value minus purchase price).

high-yield (junk) bonds
High-risk, high-return bonds.

secured bonds
Corporate bonds for which specific assets have been pledged as collateral.

mortgage bonds
Corporate bonds that are secured by property, such as land, equipment, or buildings.

debentures
Unsecured bonds that are backed only by the reputation of the issuer and its promise to pay the principal and interest when due.

convertible bonds
Corporate bonds that are issued with an option that allows the bondholder to convert them into common stock.

$707.5 billion in new corporate bonds were issued in 2005. Exhibit 20.1 summarizes the features of some popular types of corporate bonds.

High-yield, or **junk**, **bonds** are high-risk, high-return bonds that became popular during the 1980s, when they were widely used to finance mergers and takeovers. Today, they are used by companies whose credit characteristics would not otherwise allow them access to the debt markets. Because of their high risk, these bonds generally earn 3 percent or more above the returns on high-quality corporate bonds.

Corporate bonds can be either secured or unsecured. **Secured bonds** have specific assets pledged as collateral, which the bondholder has a right to take if the bond issuer defaults. **Mortgage bonds** are secured by property, such as land, equipment, or buildings. **Debentures** are unsecured bonds. They are backed only by the reputation of the issuer and its promise to pay the principal and interest when due. In general, debentures have a lower risk of default than secured bonds and therefore have lower interest rates. Of course, a debenture issued by a financially shaky firm probably has greater default risk than a mortgage bond issued by a sound one.

Corporate bonds can be issued with an option for the bondholder to convert them into common stock. **Convertible bonds** generally allow the bondholder to exchange each bond for a specified number of shares of common stock. For instance, a $1,000 par value convertible bond can be convertible into 40 shares of common stock—no matter what happens to the market price of the common stock. Because convertible bonds could be converted to stock when the price is very high, these bonds usually have a lower interest rate than nonconvertible bonds.

Government Securities Both the federal government and local government agencies also issue bonds. The U.S. Treasury sells three major types of federal debt securities,

CONCEPT *in Action*

Financial troubles deepened for Ford and GM in 2005, as both Moody's and Standard & Poor's (S&P) downgraded the automakers' credit ratings to junk status. Like a person with bad credit who must pay higher interest on loans, businesses with junk ratings find it expensive to borrow money. Some investors find the high-yield junk bonds attractive, while others are more pessimistic about the automakers' ability to repay. *What are the risks and rewards of buying junk bonds?*

municipal bonds
Bonds issued by states, cities, counties, and other state and local government agencies.

commonly called "governments": Treasury bills, Treasury notes, and Treasury bonds. All three are viewed as risk-free because they are backed by the U.S. government. *Treasury bills* mature in less than a year and are issued with a minimum par value of $1,000. *Treasury notes* have maturities of 10 years or less, and *Treasury bonds* have maturities as long as 25 years or more. Both notes and bonds are sold in denominations of $1,000 and $5,000. The interest earned on government securities is subject to federal income tax but is free from state and local income taxes. According to the Bond Market Association, a total of $746 billion in U.S. treasury securities were issued in 2005, down 12 percent from 2004. Federal agencies also issued $669 billion in debt in 2005, a drop of 24 percent from the 2004 level.[6]

Municipal bonds are issued by states, cities, counties, and other state and local government agencies. This market is very localized, with about 50,000 municipal issuers and 1.5 million issues. Municipalities sold bonds totaling $408 billion in 2005.[7] These bonds typically have a par value of $5,000 and are either general obligation or revenue bonds. *General obligation bonds* are backed by the full faith and credit (and taxing power) of the issuing government. *Revenue bonds,* on the other hand, are repaid only from income generated by the specific project being financed. Examples of revenue bond projects include toll highways and bridges, power plants, and parking structures. Because the issuer of revenue bonds has no legal obligation to back the bonds if the project's revenues are inadequate, they are considered more risky and therefore have higher interest rates than general obligation bonds.

Municipal bonds are attractive to investors because interest earned on them is exempt from federal income tax. For the same reason, the coupon interest rate for a municipal bond is lower than for a similar-quality corporate bond. In addition, interest earned on municipal bonds issued by governments within the taxpayer's home state is exempt from state income tax as well. In contrast, all interest earned on corporate bonds is fully taxable.

Exhibit 20.2 > Moody's and Standard & Poor's Bond Ratings

Moody's Ratings	S & P Ratings	Description
Aaa	AAA	**Prime-quality investment bonds:** Highest rating assigned; indicates extremely strong capacity to pay.
Aa	AA	**High-grade investment bonds:** Also considered very safe bonds, although not quite as safe as Aaa/AAA issues;
A	A	Aa/AA bonds are safer (have less risk of default) than single As.
Baa	BBB	**Medium-grade investment bonds:** Lowest of investment-grade issues; seen as lacking protection against adverse economic conditions.
Ba	BB	**Junk bonds:** Provide little protection against default;
B	B	viewed as highly speculative.
Caa	CCC	**Poor-quality bonds:** Either in default or very close to it.
Ca	CC	
C	C	
	D	

concept check

What are the advantages and disadvantages of common stock for investors and corporations?

What is preferred stock, and how is it different from common stock?

Describe the common features of all bonds and the advantages and disadvantages of bonds for investors.

bond ratings
Letter grades assigned to bond issues to indicate their quality, or level of risk; assigned by rating agencies such as Moody's and Standard & Poor's (S&P).

Bond Ratings Bonds vary in quality, depending on the financial strength of the issuer. Because the claims of bondholders come before those of stockholders, bonds are generally considered less risky than stocks. However, some bonds are in fact quite risky. Companies can *default*—fail to make scheduled interest or principal payments—on their bonds.

Investors can use **bond ratings**, letter grades assigned to bond issues to indicate their quality or level of risk. Ratings for corporate bonds are easy to find. The two largest and best-known rating agencies are Moody's and Standard & Poor's (S&P), whose publications are in most libraries and in stock brokerages. Exhibit 20.2 lists the letter grades assigned by Moody's and S&P. A bond's rating can change if a company's financial condition changes.

Playing the Market with Other Types of Securities

3 What other types of securities are available to investors?

mutual fund
A financial-service company that pools its investors' funds to buy a selection of securities that meet its stated investment goals.

In addition to equity and debt, investors have several other types of securities available to them. The most popular are mutual funds, exchange-traded funds, futures contracts, and options. Mutual funds appeal to a wide range of investors. Futures contracts and options are more complex investments for experienced investors.

Mutual Funds

Suppose that you have $1,000 to invest but don't know which stocks or bonds to buy, when to buy them, or when to sell them. By investing in a mutual fund, you can buy shares in a large, professionally managed *portfolio*, or group, of stocks and bonds. A **mutual fund** is a financial-service company that pools its investors' funds to buy a selection of securities—marketable securities, stocks, bonds, or a combination of securities—that meet its stated investment goals.

Each mutual fund focuses on one of a wide variety of possible investment goals, such as growth or income. Many large financial-service companies, like Fidelity Investments and The Vanguard Group, sell a wide variety of mutual funds, each with a different investment goal. Investors can pick and choose funds that match their particular interests. Some specialized funds invest in a particular type of company or asset: in one industry such as health care or technology, in a geographical region such as Asia, or in an asset such as precious metals. Mutual funds also provide a way to invest in the broad market through *index funds*, which hold stocks in the same weights as the market measure they track.

Mutual funds are one of the most popular investments for individuals today, who can choose from about 8,000 different funds. Investments in mutual funds are almost $18 trillion worldwide, of which U.S. mutual funds hold $9.5 trillion. About 91 million individuals representing almost half of all U.S. households own mutual funds.[8] Mutual funds appeal to investors for three main reasons:

- They are a good way to hold a diversified, and thus less risky, portfolio. Investors with only $500 or $1,000 to invest cannot diversify much on their own. Buying shares in a mutual fund lets them own part of a portfolio that may contain 100 or more securities.
- Mutual funds are professionally managed.
- Mutual funds can offer higher returns than individual investors could achieve on their own.

A MANAGED PORTFOLIO REALLY MAKES A LOT OF SENSE. DEPENDING, OF COURSE, ON WHO'S MANAGING IT.

Fidelity FundsManager Program™ provides you with a model portfolio of mutual funds. It's managed for you on an ongoing basis by experts, based on your investment objectives. Experts can do a lot for you and your peace of mind. Call, click, or visit Fidelity. Because you're not just invested. You're *personally invested.*™

FIDELITY FUNDSMANAGER PROGRAM™
EXPERTLY MANAGED PORTFOLIOS
BASED ON YOUR GOALS
DIVERSIFIED TO HELP REDUCE RISK

CALL TODAY FOR MORE INFORMATION ON FUNDSMANAGER

| 1.800.FIDELITY | FIDELITY.COM | 85 INVESTOR CENTERS | *Fidelity Investments*

Portfolio Advisory Services℠ Fidelity FundsManager Program is a service of Strategic Advisers, Inc., a registered investment adviser and a Fidelity Investments company. Strategic Advisers identifies a model portfolio for each customer based on his/her goals, risk tolerance, and time horizon. Results may vary. Certain restrictions apply. This service provides discretionary money management for a fee.

CONCEPT *in Action*

Mutual funds are a popular way to invest in major markets, especially for people who can't follow stocks on a regular basis. Mutual funds expose investors to a basket of securities managed by a financial-service professional and fund portfolios targeted to different investor interests. *Why are mutual funds so popular with investors?*

Exchange-Traded Funds

exchange-traded fund (ETF)
A basket of stocks in a category, such as industry sector, investment objective, or geographical area, or that track an index. ETFs are similar to mutual funds but trade like stocks.

A relatively new type of investment, the **exchange-traded fund (ETF)**, has become very popular with investors. ETFs are similar to mutual funds because they hold a broad basket of stocks with a common theme, giving investors instant diversification. ETFs trade on stock exchanges (most trade on the American Stock Exchange, AMEX), so its price changes throughout the day, whereas mutual fund net asset values (NAVs) are calculated once a day, at the end of trading. ETF assets have doubled from about $156 billion in 2004 to $313 billion in early 2006.[9]

Investors can choose from more than 200 ETFs that track almost any market sector, from a broad market index such as the S&P 500 (described later in this chapter), industry sectors such as health care or energy, and geographical areas such as a particular country—Japan—or region—Latin America. ETFs have very low expense ratios. However, because they trade as stocks, investors pay commissions to buy and sell these shares.

Futures Contracts

futures contracts
Legally binding obligations to buy or sell specified quantities of commodities or financial instruments at an agreed-on price at a future date.

Futures contracts are legally binding obligations to buy or sell specified quantities of commodities (agricultural or mining products) or financial instruments (securities or currencies) at an agreed-on price at a future date. An investor can buy commodity futures contracts in cattle, pork bellies (large slabs of bacon), eggs, coffee, flour, gasoline, fuel oil, lumber, wheat, gold, and silver. Financial futures include Treasury securities and foreign currencies, such as the British pound or Japanese yen.

Futures contracts do not pay interest or dividends. The return depends solely on favorable price changes. These are very risky investments because the prices can vary a great deal.

Options

options
Contracts that entitle holders to buy or sell specified quantities of common stocks or other financial instruments at a set price during a specified time.

Options are contracts that entitle holders to buy or sell specified quantities of common stocks or other financial instruments at a set price during a specified time. As with futures contracts, they are very risky investments. Investors must correctly guess future price movements in the underlying financial instrument to earn a positive return. Unlike futures contracts, options do not legally obligate the holder to buy or sell and the price paid for an option is the maximum amount that can be lost. However, options have very short maturities so it is easy to quickly lose a lot of money with them.

concept check

Why do mutual funds appeal to investors? Discuss some of the investment goals pursued by mutual funds.

What are futures contracts? Why are they risky investments?

How do options differ from futures contracts?

On the Trading Floor: Securities Markets

 4 **What is the function of the securities markets?**

institutional investors
Investment professionals who are paid to manage other people's money.

Stocks, bonds, and other securities are traded in securities markets. These markets streamline the purchase and sales activities of investors by allowing transactions to be made quickly and at a fair price. They make the transfer of funds from lenders to borrowers much easier. Securities markets are busy places. On an average day, individual and institutional investors trade billions of shares of stock in more than 10,000 companies through securities markets. They also trade bonds, mutual funds, futures contracts, and options. *Individual investors* invest their own money to achieve their personal financial goals. **Institutional investors** are investment professionals who are paid to manage other people's money. Most of these professional money managers work for financial institutions, such as banks, mutual funds, insurance companies, and pension funds. Institutional investors control very large sums of money, often buying stock in 10,000-share blocks. They aim to meet the investment goals of their clients. Institutional investors are a major force in the securities markets, accounting for about half of the dollar volume of equities traded.

Businesses and governments also take part in the securities markets. Corporations issue bonds and stocks to raise funds to finance their operations. They are also among the institutional investors that purchase corporate and government securities. Federal, state, and local governments sell bonds and other debt instruments to finance specific projects and cover budget deficits.

The Role of Investment Bankers and Stockbrokers

investment bankers
Firms that act as intermediaries, buying securities from corporations and governments and reselling them to the public.

underwriting
The process of buying securities from corporations and governments and reselling them to the public, hopefully at a higher price; the main activity of investment bankers.

stockbroker
A person who is licensed to buy and sell securities on behalf of clients.

Two types of investment specialists play key roles in the functioning of the securities markets. **Investment bankers** help companies raise long-term financing. These firms act as intermediaries, buying securities from corporations and governments and reselling them to the public. This process, called **underwriting**, is the main activity of the investment banker, which acquires the security for an agreed-upon price and hopes to be able to resell it at a higher price to make a profit. Investment bankers advise clients on the pricing and structure of new securities offerings, as well as on mergers, acquisitions, and other types of financing. Well-known investment banking firms include Goldman Sachs, Merrill Lynch, Morgan Stanley Dean Witter, Lehman Brothers, Credit Suisse, UBS, and Smith Barney (a division of Citigroup).

A **stockbroker** is a person who is licensed to buy and sell securities on behalf of clients. Also called *account executives,* these investment professionals work for brokerage firms and execute the orders customers place for stocks, bonds, mutual funds, and other securities.

Stockbrokers are the link between public companies and the investors interested in buying their stock. Before investing in securities, investors must select a stock brokerage firm, select a stockbroker at that firm, and open an account. Investors are wise to seek a broker who understands their investment goals and can help them pursue their objectives. We'll discuss how individuals make securities transactions in the Online Enrichment Chapter: Managing Your Personal Finances.

Brokerage firms are paid commissions for executing clients' transactions. Although brokers can charge whatever they want, most firms have fixed commission schedules for small transactions. These commissions usually depend on the value of the transaction and the number of shares involved. There are several categories of stock brokerage firms, from full-service brokerages to various types of discount brokerages to those that operate only online. Discount brokerages can save investors 30 percent or more on securities transactions.

In recent years, the differences between brokerage firms have blurred and the competition has increased. The once bare-bones discount and online brokerage firms have added more products and services, and full-service brokerage firms are courting online investors. Within the discount category, for example, you'll find full-service discount firms offering most of the same services as full-service brokers, such as branch offices, account representatives, and research, whereas others execute only stock and option trades. We'll discuss the changing environment for brokerage firms in the Trends in Securities and Securities Markets section.

CONCEPT *in Action*

Online brokerages like E*Trade and Scottrade have given rise to a new market player: the self-directed investor. These "do-it-yourselfers" take their financial futures into their own hands, buying and selling stocks over the Internet for a fraction of the cost associated with traditional brokerage firms. Online investors pay commission fees as low as $4 while accessing streaming quotes and charts, financial news, and risk analyzers—all on their computer screens. *What are the pros and cons of online investing?*

Online Investing

Improvements in Internet technology have made it possible for investors to research, analyze, and trade securities online. Today almost all brokerage firms offer online trading capabilities. Online brokerages are popular with "do-it-yourself" investors who choose their own stocks and don't want to pay a full-service broker for these services. Lower transaction costs are a major benefit. Fees at online brokerages range from $4 to $20, depending on the number of trades a client makes and the size of a client's account. Although there are many online brokerage firms, the five largest—Charles Schwab, Fidelity Investments, TD Ameritrade, E*Trade, and Scottrade—

account for about 80 percent of all trading volume and about $1.3 trillion in assets in customer accounts.[10] The Internet also offers investors a wealth of investment information, as we will see later in this chapter.

Types of Markets

primary market
The securities market where *new* securities are sold to the public, usually with the help of investment bankers.

secondary market
The securities market where *old* (already issued) securities are bought and sold, or traded, among investors.

Securities markets can be divided into primary and secondary markets. The **primary market** is where *new* securities are sold to the public, usually with the help of investment bankers. In the primary market, the issuer of the security gets the proceeds from the transaction. A security is sold in the primary market just once—the first time it is issued by the corporation or government. The Chipotle IPO we discussed in Chapter 19 represented a primary market offering.

Later transactions take place in the **secondary market**, where *old* (already issued) securities are bought and sold, or traded, among investors. When you place an order to buy or sell 100 shares of Starbucks, you are using the secondary market. The issuing companies generally are not involved in these transactions. The vast majority of securities transactions take place in secondary markets, which include *broker markets* such as the New York Stock Exchange and *dealer markets* such as the NASDAQ market, an electronic trading system, and the over-the-counter (OTC) markets provide a trading market for smaller, unlisted securities. We'll discuss each of these in greater detail in the next section.

concept check

How do securities markets help businesses and investors? How does an investment banker work with companies to issue securities?

How is online investing changing the securities industry?

Distinguish between primary and secondary securities markets.

Buying and Selling at Securities Exchanges

5 **Where can investors buy and sell securities?**

When we think of stock markets, we are typically referring to secondary markets, which handle most of the securities trading activity. The two segments of the secondary markets are broker markets and dealer markets, as Exhibit 20.3 shows. The primary difference between broker and dealer markets is the way each executes securities trades. Securities trades can also take place in alternative market systems and on non-U.S. securities exchanges.

Exhibit 20.3 > The Secondary Markets: Broker and Dealer Markets

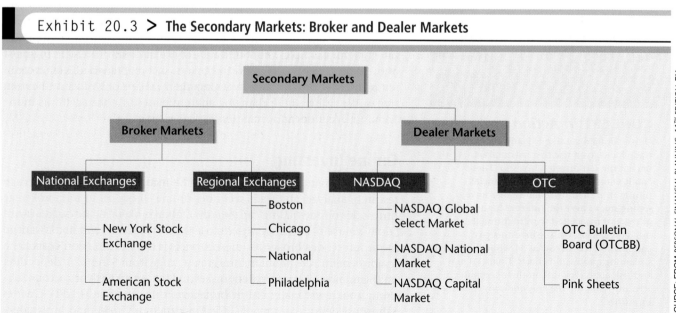

SOURCE: FROM *PERSONAL FINANCIAL PLANNING, 11TH EDITION,* BY GITMAN/JOEHNK; © 2008. REPRINTED WITH PERMISSION OF SOUTH-WESTERN, A DIVISION OF THOMSON LEARNING. HTTP://WWW.THOMSONRIGHTS.COM. FAX 800 730–2215.

CONCEPT *in Action*

The New York Stock Exchange (NYSE) is the largest securities market in the world. Its market capitalization dwarfs foreign and domestic markets. Unlike many newer markets, the NYSE trades mostly through *specialists,* market professionals who match up buyers and sellers of securities, while pocketing the spread between the bid and ask price on market orders. *How does the NYSE's hybrid trading system differ from fully automated, electronic trading?*

The securities markets both in the United States and around the world are in flux and undergoing tremendous changes. We present the basics of securities exchanges in this section and discuss the latest trends in the global securities markets later in the chapter.

Broker Markets

broker markets
National and regional securities exchanges on whose premises securities trading takes place.

The **broker market** consists of national and regional securities exchanges that bring buyers and sellers together through brokers on a centralized trading floor. In the broker market, the buyer purchases the securities directly from the seller through the broker. Broker markets account for about 60 percent of the total dollar volume of all shares traded in the U.S. securities markets.

New York Stock Exchange The oldest and most prestigious broker market is the *New York Stock Exchange (NYSE),* which has existed since 1792. Often called the Big Board, it is located on Wall Street in downtown New York City. The NYSE, which lists the shares of almost 2,800 corporations, had a total domestic market capitalization of $13.3 billion at year-end 2005. (Its total global market capitalization, which includes non-U.S. companies, was about $22 billion.) On a typical day, more than 1.7 billion shares of stock valued at $65 billion are traded on the NYSE.[11] It represents 90 percent of the trading volume in the U.S. broker marketplace. Major companies like IBM, Coca-Cola, AT&T, Procter & Gamble, Ford Motor Co., and Chevron list their shares on the NYSE. In 2005, total share volume on the NYSE was more than 400 billion shares, a record for the exchange. Companies that list on the NYSE must meet stringent listing requirements and annual maintenance requirements, which give them creditability.

The NYSE is also popular with non-U.S. companies. More than 450 foreign companies with a global market capitalization of almost $8 trillion now list their securities on the NYSE.[12]

Until recently, all NYSE transactions occurred on the vast NYSE trading floor. Each company traded at the NYSE is assigned to a trading post on the floor. When an exchange member receives an order to buy or sell a particular stock, the order is transmitted to a floor broker at the company's trading post. The floor brokers then compete with other brokers on the trading floor to get the best price for their customers.

In response to competitive pressures from electronic exchanges, the NYSE created a Hybrid Market that combines features of the floor auction market and automated trading. Its customers will now have a choice of how they execute trades. In the Trends section we'll discuss other changes the NYSE is making to maintain a leadership position among securities exchanges.

Another national stock exchange, the American Stock Exchange (AMEX), lists the securities of about 700 corporations but handles only 4 percent of the annual share volume of shares traded on U.S. securities exchanges. Because the AMEX's rules are less strict than those of the NYSE, most AMEX firms are smaller and less well known than NYSE-listed corporations. Some firms move up to the NYSE once they qualify for listing there. Other companies choose to remain on the AMEX. Companies cannot be listed on both exchanges at the same time. The AMEX has become a major market, however, for exchange-traded funds, very popular securities that are similar to mutual funds, and in options trading.

Regional Exchanges The remaining 6 percent of annual share volume takes place on several regional exchanges in the United States, which list about 100 to 500 securities of firms located in their area. Regional exchange membership rules are much less strict than for the NYSE. The top regional exchanges are the Boston, Chicago, Philadelphia, and National (formerly the Cincinnati) exchanges. An electronic network linking the NYSE and many of the regional exchanges allows brokers to make securities transactions at the best prices.

The regional exchanges, which have struggled to compete, benefited from the passage of the SEC's Regulation National Market System which is scheduled to be in 2007. The new ruling makes price the most important factor in making securities trades, and all orders must go to the trading venue with the best price.[13] As we'll see later in the chapter, the regional exchanges are taking steps to compete more effectively in the U.S. securities arena.

Dealer Markets

Unlike broker markets, **dealer markets** do not operate on centralized trading floors but instead use sophisticated telecommunications networks that link dealers throughout the United States. Buyers and sellers do not trade securities directly, as they do in broker markets. They work through securities dealers called *market makers*, who make markets in one or more securities and offer to buy or sell securities at stated prices. A security transaction in the dealer market has two parts: the selling investor sells his or her securities to one dealer, and the buyer purchases the securities from another dealer (or in some cases, the same dealer).

NASDAQ The largest dealer market is the **National Association of Securities Dealers Automated Quotation system**, commonly referred to as NASDAQ. The first electronic-based stock market, the NASDAQ is a sophisticated telecommunications network that links dealers throughout the United States. Founded in 1971 with origins in the OTC market, today NASDAQ is a separate securities exchange that is no longer part of the OTC market. The NASDAQ lists more companies and trades more shares than the NYSE, but the NYSE still leads in total market capitalization. An average of 1.8 billion shares were exchanged daily in 2005 through NASDAQ, which is now the largest electronic stock market.[14] It provides up-to-date bid and ask prices on about 3,200 of the most active OTC securities. Its sophisticated electronic communication system provides faster transaction speeds than traditional floor markets and is the main reason for the popularity and growth of the OTC market.

In January 2006 the SEC approved NASDAQ's application to operate as a national securities exchange. As a result, the NASDAQ Stock Market LLC will operate independently and no longer be part of the National Association of Securities Dealers, its primary regulator. This removes possible conflicts of interest between the market and its regulatory arm. "NASDAQ will benefit from an enhanced ability to compete with other domestic and foreign exchanges that enjoy the benefits of being fully independent public company exchanges," said Bob Greifeld, NASDAQ president and chief executive officer.[15]

The securities of many well-known companies, some of which could be listed on the organized exchanges, trade on the NASDAQ. Examples include Amazon.com, Apple Computer, Coors, Dell Computer, Google, Intel, Microsoft, Panera Bread, Qualcomm, and Starbucks. The stocks of most commercial banks and insurance companies also trade in this market, as do most government and corporate bonds. About 440 foreign companies also trade on the NASDAQ.

In July 2006, the NASDAQ changed its structure to a three-tier market:

- The NASDAQ Global Select Market, a new tier with "financial and liquidity requirements that are higher than those of any other market," according to NASDAQ. More than 1,000 NASDAQ companies qualify for this group.
- The NASDAQ Global Market (formerly the NASDAQ National Market), which lists abut 1,650 companies.
- The NASDAQ Capital Market replaces the NASDAQ Small Cap Market and lists about 550 companies.

All three market tiers adhere to NASDAQ 's rigorous listing and corporate governance standards.[16]

The Over-the-Counter Market The over-the-counter (OTC) markets refer to those other than the organized exchanges described above. There are two OTC markets: The *Over-the-Counter Bulletin Board (OTCBB)* and the *Pink Sheets*. These markets generally list small companies and have no listing or maintenance standards, making them attractive to young companies looking for funding. OTC companies do not have to file with the SEC or follow the costly provisions of Sarbanes-Oxley. Investing in OTC companies is therefore highly risky and should be for experienced investors only. In the Catching the Entrepreneurial Spirit box, we'll see how new ownership is trying to bring greater respectability to Pink Sheets and transform it into a viable trading platform for small companies.

Alternative Trading Systems

electronic communications networks (ECNs)
Electronic trading networks that allow institutional traders and some individuals to make securities transactions directly.

In addition to broker and dealer markets, alternative trading systems (ATSs) such as electronic communications networks (ECNs) make securities transactions. ECNs are private trading networks that allow institutional traders and some individuals to make direct transactions in what is called the *fourth market*. ECNs bypass brokers and dealers, to automatically match electronic buy and sell orders. They are most effective for high-volume, actively traded stocks. Money managers and institutions such as pension funds and mutual funds with large amounts of money to invest like ECNs because they cost far less than other trading venues.

As ECNs began to compete with the NYSE and NASDAQ, exchanges themselves acquired their own ECNs. Archipelago is now part of the NYSE, and the NASDAQ acquired INET ECN from Instinet Group. As of mid-2006, the five independent ECNs were BATS, DirectEdge, Track, OnTrade, and Bloomberg Tradebook. In addition, advances in technology have made it possible for brokerage firms and other financial institutions to develop their own ECNs.[17]

Global Trading and Foreign Exchanges

Improved communications and the elimination of many legal barriers are helping the securities markets go global. The number of securities listed on exchanges in mor than one country is growing. Foreign securities are now traded in the United Stat Likewise, foreign investors can easily buy U.S. securities.

Stock markets also exist in foreign countries: Over 100 countries operate own securities exchanges. The Tokyo and London Stock Exchanges (LSE) rank b

Many Companies Are "In the Pink"

R. Cromwell Coulson, the chairman of privately held Pink Sheets LLC, refers to his century-old company as the "Las Vegas of Wall Street." Pink Sheets, a stock quotation service that handles high-risk ventures and isn't regulated by the Securities and Exchange Commission (SEC), is named for the pink paper on which company stock prices were once printed and distributed to professional traders.

Companies delisted from the NASDAQ, or in bankruptcy protection like Delta Air Lines, are traded on the Pink Sheets. But so are solid big-name businesses like Deutsche Bank and Loews Cineplex Entertainment. "We are the tier of stuff that can't, won't, or doesn't want to be listed on the exchange," Coulson says.

Other companies use the Pink Sheets as a testing ground before approaching the larger exchanges. "It's like the Minor League for baseball. There are some people who go right up and play for the (New York) Yankees, and others who do a year or two in the Minors," Coulson says. Still, no one denies that the Pink Sheets remain a dicey place to invest. "This is not 'investing,' this is gambling," he says. "But people make money gambling sometimes."

Perhaps the biggest gamble was Coulson's purchase of the company in the late 1990s. At that time investors who wanted stock had to contact their brokers, who called traders for the most up-to-date price. Dishonest traders and non-SEC-regulated companies created an ongoing potential for fraud. Now 40-year-old Coulson, who is partial to "unknown, unloved, unwashed, and out-of-favor stocks," is working hard to differentiate between promising companies and those he calls "dark and dodgy." Questionable businesses have multiplied of late as bogus information travels freely via the Internet and small investors trade for themselves.

Since 2003 new regulations make it more difficult for small businesses to get noticed by Wall Street. So entrepreneurs are turning to the Pink Sheets, where the amount of stock traded has more than doubled—to $50 billion annually. "We need to clean up the Pink Sheets so that small companies have a trading platform that is more viable," says Gerald Laporte, chief of the office of small-business policy at the Securities and Exchange Commission. "Cromwell Coulson is taking the Pink Sheets in the right direction."

Coulson has introduced a "tiering" system to rank companies— from those large enough to be on a major exchange, with audited financial reports and a share price of at least $1—to smaller issuers with audited financial reports. A final group will be small companies with information prepared not by auditors but by "persons with sufficient financial skills"

Coulson has renamed his 35-member firm Pink Sheets LLC. It now posts quotes online and uses "Pink Link," an email service that allows buyers and sellers to communicate electronically. He won't disclose figures but says revenue has grown 300 percent since his purchase, proving that sometimes gambles do pay off.[18]

Critical Thinking Questions
- What function does Pink Sheets LLC serve?
- If Pink Sheets did not exist, what would become of the companies that list on it? Explain.

---

the NYSE and NASDAQ; Exhibit 20.4 lists the world's leading stock exchanges by domestic market capitalization. Other important foreign stock exchanges include those in Toronto, Montreal, Buenos Aires, Zurich, Sydney, Paris, Frankfurt, Hong Kong, and Taiwan. The number of big U.S. corporations with listings on foreign exchanges is growing steadily, especially in Europe. For example, significant activity in NYSE-listed stocks also occurs on the LSE. The LSE also is getting a growing share of the world's IPOs. Emerging markets such as India are also attracting investor attention, as the Expanding Around the Globe box explains.

Exhibit 20.4 > The World's Largest Stock Markets, Year-end 2005

Rank	Exchange Name	Domestic Market Capitalization (U.S. Billions)
1	New York Stock Exchange	$13,311
2	Tokyo	4,573
3	NASDAQ	3,604
4	London	3,058
5	Euronext*	2,707
6	TSX Group (Toronto)	1,482
7	Deutsche Bourse	1,221
8	Hong Kong	1,055
9	BME Spanish Exchanges	960
10	Swiss Exchange	935

Global Stocks—India Leads the Pack

Until relatively recently, foreign investors avoided India because it was considered backward, an uncertain bet. But India has undergone an economic metamorphosis as foreign investors, particularly Americans, rush to participate in one of the world's fastest growing economies. India's economy has grown 6 percent a year during the past decade and was expected to grow a further 7 percent in 2006.

According to data from the Securities and Exchange Board of India, which regulates its stock market, foreigners have invested $7.4 billion in Indian equities, an increase of 61 percent over the same period last year. "India's emergence as a new global economic poster boy is helping the stock market," said Rajeev Malik, a senior economist with JP Morgan Chase and Company in Singapore.

Foreign investors are pumping more than $10 billion a year into Indian stocks the Confederation of Indian Industry said. Fueling investor confidence is the rapid growth of India's top companies—expected to continue at more than 15 percent—and the economy. Farm output has jumped six-fold; the construction industry is responding to increased demand for homes and shopping malls by an expanding consumer middle class—call-center workers, software writers, offshore researchers, and other new-economy workers. Major industrial companies like oil and petrochemicals, steel, automobiles, and software, are flourishing due to increased exports and robust domestic demand. Transporting money in and out of the country, once a complicated exercise, is now fairly straightforward. Regulations governing the size of foreign investment in Indian firms have been relaxed. Indian companies now observe disclosure rules that were frequently previously disregarded.

All these factors have contributed to a 24 percent gain in the benchmark index of the Bombay Stock Exchange, the Sensex, causing some to wonder whether a bubble is in the making. Rising interest rates in the United States and Europe could spell trouble for the Sensex. As Malik observed, "Equity indices have gone up too much too fast." Higher rates, concerns about oil prices, and fears that U.S. consumers may run out of steam, are making some nervous.

So are dark clouds on the horizon? Andy Xie, chief Asia economist for Morgan Stanley, thinks so. "A business cycle usually ends when central banks tighten quickly in response to an inflation problem. The current bubble, just like previous ones, will burst unexpectedly." But Indian Finance Minister P. Chidambaram dismisses talk of a bubble, claiming rocketing share prices signal confidence in India's economy. "Optimism stems from very strong domestic demand, high export growth, and the entrepreneurial skills of our manufacturers and service providers. We can pursue our goals for social justice and equality only if we have high growth," he says.[19]

Critical Thinking Questions

- What factors contribute to the strength of India's robust economy and stock exchange?
- Why do some suspect the Indian stock market may be experiencing a "bubble?" Explain. Using the Internet, research the current situation in the Indian stock market to learn the answer.

Why should U.S. investors pay attention to international stock markets? As we've discussed throughout this book, the worlds' economies are increasingly interdependent. Businesses must look beyond their own national borders to find materials to make their goods and markets for foreign goods and services. The same is true for investors, who may find that they can earn higher returns in international markets. For example, in 2005 gains in the U.S. markets were disappointing. The Dow Jones Industrial Average fell 0.6 percent, and other broad market indexes rose just 1 to 3 percent. Elsewhere, the story was different. The Dow Jones World Index, not including the United States rose 14.4 percent. Individual star performers included Norway, South Korea, Austria, and Pakistan, whose stock exchange indexes posted gains of more than 50 percent.[20] However, buying securities on many foreign exchanges, which may not be as regulated as markets in developed nations, carries much higher risks.

Market Conditions: Bull Market or Bear Market?

bull markets
Markets in which securities prices are rising.

bear markets
Markets in which securities prices are falling.

Two terms that often appear in the financial press are "bull market" and "bear market." Securities prices rise in **bull markets**. These markets are normally associated with investor optimism, economic recovery, and government action to encourage economic growth. In contrast, prices go down for prolonged periods in **bear markets**. Investor pessimism, economic slowdown, and government restraint are all possible causes. As a rule, investors earn better returns in bull markets; they earn low, and sometimes negative, returns in bear markets.

Bull and bear market conditions are hard to predict because they refer to long-term trends. Usually, they can't be identified until after they begin. (A short or small downturn is called a *market correction*.) Over the past 50 years, the stock market has generally been bullish, reflecting general economic growth and prosperity. Bull

CONCEPT *in Action*

Whether dominated by optimistic bulls or pessimistic bears, the market always provides moneymaking opportunities for savvy investors. *Longs* are investors who make money when the market is rising, by buying low and selling high. *Shorts* are investors who make money from the market's decline, borrowing shares to sell high in hopes of buying them back at lower prices. Long or short, the trick is to determine whether market conditions are bearish or bullish. *Why are market trends hard to predict?*

© ASSOCIATED PRESS, AP

concept check

How do the broker markets differ from dealer markets, and what organizations compose each of these two markets?

Why is the globalization of the securities markets important to U.S. investors? What are some of the other exchanges where U.S companies can list their securities?

Differentiate between a bull market and a bear market.

markets tend to last longer than bear markets. The bull market that started in 1982 lasted a full five years, and the bear market that preceded it lasted just over a year and a half. The longest bull market on record began in October 1990 and peaked in early 2000. The last bear market was from June 2002 to February 2003. Markets rose at a reasonably steady pace through mid-2006, when investors began to wonder whether falling markets signaled the start of another bear market or were just going through another correction.

Regulation of Securities Markets

 6 **How are securities markets regulated?**

Securities and Exchange Commission (SEC)
The main federal government agency responsible for regulating the U.S. securities industry.

In the United States, both the federal government and state governments regulate securities markets. The states were the first to pass laws aimed at preventing securities fraud. However, most securities transactions occur across state lines, so federal securities laws are more effective.

In 1934, Congress established the **Securities and Exchange Commission (SEC)**, as the main federal government agency responsible for regulating the U.S. securities industry. The SEC has five commissioners who are appointed by the president of the United States. In order to make sure the SEC remains nonpartisan, no more than three commissioners may belong to the same political party. All commissioners must be approved by a Senate vote. Each year, the SEC files between 400 and 500 civil enforcement actions against individuals and companies that break securities laws. The SEC can also order that the trading of a stock be suspended when a company is under investigation. Recently the Federal National Mortgage Association (Fannie Mae) was sanctioned by the SEC for charges of accounting fraud from 1998 through 2004. Fannie Mae paid $400 million in penalties for accounting irregularities, including manipulating accounting rules to give executives larger bonuses.[21] Exhibit 20.5 highlights some of the common violations that may lead to SEC investigations and punishments.

The SEC also oversees the *Securities Investor Protection Corporation (SIPC)*. The SIPC is a private, not-for-profit corporation that insures the securities and cash in the customer accounts of member brokerage firms in the event those firms fail. However, it's important to keep in mind that investors do not have any insurance against losses due to market conditions or fraud.

Exhibit 20.5 > Securities Industry Violations Leading to SEC Investigations

- Insider trading
- Misrepresenting or omitting important information about securities
- Stealing customer funds or securities
- Violating broker-dealer responsibilities to treat customers fairly
- Selling securities without proper SEC registration

In addition to legislation and government regulation, the securities industry has self-regulatory groups and measures to help protect investors.

Securities Legislation The *Securities Act of 1933* was passed by Congress in response to the 1929 stock market crash and subsequent problems during the Great Depression. It protects investors by requiring full disclosure of information about new securities issues. The issuer must file a *registration statement* with the SEC, which must be approved by the SEC before the security can be sold.

The *Securities Exchange Act of 1934* formally gave the SEC power to control the organized securities exchanges. The act was amended in 1964 to give the SEC authority over the OTC market as well. The amendment included rules for operating the stock exchanges and granted the SEC control over all participants (exchange members, brokers, dealers) and the securities traded in these markets.

The 1934 act also banned **insider trading**, the use of information that is not available to the general public to make profits on securities transactions. Because of lax enforcement, however, several big insider-trading scandals occurred during the late 1980s. The *Insider Trading and Fraud Act of 1988* greatly increased the penalties for illegal insider trading and gave the SEC more power to investigate and prosecute claims of illegal actions. The meaning of insider was expanded beyond a company's directors, employees, and their relatives to include anyone who gets private information about a company.

A recent insider trading scheme involved 13 people in the United States, Germany, and Croatia who used insider information to trade stocks ahead of major

insider trading
The use of information that is not available to the general public to make profits on securities transactions.

CONCEPT *in Action*

In 2006, France's highest court upheld a ruling that billionaire investor and Democratic Party financier George Soros illegally bought and sold shares of Société Générale after receiving information about a planned corporate raid on the bank. In addition to incurring a multimillion dollar fine for Soros, the insider trading conviction expanded the list of billionaires that have unfairly gamed securities markets while cheating ordinary investors. *What regulations help prevent insider trading in the U.S.?*

© DANIEL ACKER/BLOOMBERG NEWS/LANDOV

merger announcements, generating more than $6.4 million on illegal stock trades. Investment banking analysts not only divulged information on upcoming merger transactions, but also placed employees at a *Business Week* printing plant to leak prepublication information from the "Inside Wall Street" column. The SEC cracked the case after noticing very heavy trading in Reebok securities in advance of the announcement of its acquisition by Adidas-Salomon AG. Several of the participants were charged with conspiracy to commit securities fraud and insider trading and six counts of securities fraud.[22]

Other important legislation includes the *Investment Company Act of 1940,* which gives the SEC the right to regulate the practices of investment companies (such as mutual funds), and the *Investment Advisers Act of 1940,* which requires investment advisers to disclose information about their background. The SIPC was established in 1970 to protect customers if a brokerage firm fails by insuring each customer's account for up to $500,000.

In response to corporate scandals that hurt thousands of investors, the SEC passed new regulations designed to restore public trust in the securities industry. It issued **Regulation FD** (for Fair Disclosure) in October 2000. Regulation FD requires public companies to share information with all investors at the same time, leveling the information playing field. The Sarbanes-Oxley Act of 2002, discussed in Chapters 17 and 19, has given the SEC more power when it comes to regulating how securities are offered, sold, and marketed. As a result, the SEC has been undergoing major reform, in both how it operates and its regulatory activities. It issues orders regarding the Public Company Accounting Oversight board and continues to take steps to improve implementation of Sarbanes-Oxley requirements.

In February 2003, the SEC also approved a rule that requires Wall Street analysts to certify the truthfulness of their research reports and public statements. Analysts must also disclose if they've received compensation related to their stock recommendations. The new rules were developed after high-profile analysts at leading investment firms were accused of providing positive research reports even though they didn't favor the stock, in an attempt to win other business for their firms from the subject companies.

Self-Regulation The investment community also regulates itself, developing and enforcing ethical standards to reduce the potential for abuses in the financial marketplace. The individual stock exchanges, such as the NYSE, have established strict rules, policies, and codes of conduct for their members. The National Association of Securities Dealers (NASD) oversees the nation's 5,600 brokerage firms and more than half a million registered brokers. It develops rules and regulations, provides a dispute resolution forum, and conducts regulatory reviews of member activities for the protection and benefit of investors.

In response to "Black Monday"—October 19, 1987, when the Dow Jones Industrial Average (DJIA) plunged 508 points and the trading activity severely overloaded the exchange's computers—and a similar situation in October 1989, the securities markets instituted corrective measures to prevent a repeat of the crisis and reduce market volatility. Now, under certain conditions, **circuit breakers** stop trading for a short cooling-off period to limit the amount the market can drop in one day. These levels are adjusted periodically based on the level of critical market indexes and the time of day. For example as of the second quarter of 2006, a 1,100-point (10 percent) decline in the DJIA that occurs prior to 2 p.m. triggers a one-hour halt in trading; between 2 and 2:30 p.m., it stops trading for 30 minutes; and after 2:30 p.m. it does not stop trading. However, if the DJIA drops 2,250 points (20 percent) before 1 p.m., market activity stops for two hours; between 1 and 2 p.m., activity ceases for one hour; and after 2 p.m., the market closes. Should the DJIA fall 30 percent, or 3,350 points, at any time, the market closes for the day.[23]

Regulation FD
An SEC regulation that requires public companies to share information with all investors at the same time, leveling the information playing field.

circuit breakers
Measures that, under certain conditions, stop trading in the securities markets for a short cooling-off period to limit the amount the market can drop in one day.

concept check

How does the SEC regulate securities markets in the United States?

What is insider trading, and how can it be harmful?

Briefly describe the key provisions of the main federal laws designed to protect securities investors.

Popular Sources of Investment Information

7 Which sources of investment information are the most helpful to investors, and what can investors learn from stock, bond, and mutual fund quotations?

Good information is essential to successful investing. Knowledge of current market conditions and investment options should increase returns. Individual investors can now benefit from the type of information formerly available only to investment professionals. The following sections describe commonly used sources of investment information.

Company Financial Reports

All publicly traded companies are required by the SEC to file regular statements about their current financial conditions. Investors can access these statements by requesting a copy from a company's investor relations office. The SEC also maintains an online database of all company financial statements. The database, called EDGAR, is accessible from the SEC's main Web site. Annual reports are issued each year by publicly traded companies and include an annual financial statement. They usually also provide important information about the company's business strategies and operations. Most firms now publish an online version of their annual report at their corporate Web sites.

Economic and Financial Publications

Two of the best-known publications for economic and financial information are the *Wall Street Journal,* the weekday newspaper providing the most complete and up-to-date coverage of business and financial news, and *Barron's,* a weekly newspaper that carries detailed company analyses. Other excellent sources are magazines such as *Business Week, Kiplinger's Personal Finance, Forbes, Fortune, Smart Money, Worth,* and *Money.* Newspapers in most cities have sections with business news. Subscription advisory services also offer investment information and recommendations. Moody's, Standard & Poor's, Morningstar, and Value Line Investment Survey are among the best known. Each offers a wide range of services. Numerous investment newsletters also give subscribers market analyses and make specific buy and sell recommendations. The major securities brokerage firms have their own analysts who issue reports on the companies they follow. Although in many cases you must be a client of the firm to receive analyst reports, some Web sites have summaries or offer them for sale.

Online Information Resources

There has been a virtual explosion of online investment Web sites during the past five years. New sites appear every day, and many soon disappear. However, do not confuse this volume of information with good information! "Buyer beware" is certainly appropriate advice when using investment information from the Internet. Standards for accuracy and integrity are lax, and conflict-of-interest policies are rare. That glowing report on a stock investment could be written by owners of the stock who will profit by pushing up the price.

Despite these cautions, the Internet has many valuable investment resources, such as those listed in Exhibit 20.6. Most of these offer both information—current economic and business news, and educational articles—and tools that allow you to track investment performance, receive alerts of breaking news and specific stock price changes, and more. Some also provide databases of information that allow investors to screen (filter) vast amounts of information to make stock or mutual fund selections. The business publications mentioned in the preceding section frequently publish investment Web site recommendations and rankings.

CONCEPT *in Action*

The proliferation of online sources has broadened the options available for receiving financial information. Whereas yesterday's investors favored esteemed publications like the *Wall Street Journal,* today's tech-savvy market watchers increasingly turn to more interactive sources such as The Street.com, a Web-based financial clearinghouse founded by eccentric markets commentator Jim Cramer. The famously excitable Cramer entertains Web and broadcast audiences with wide-ranging financial advice interspersed with manic shouts of *boo-yah! How do online investment resources empower investors?*

© ALEX WONG/GETTY IMAGES FOR MEET THE PRESS

Exhibit 20.6 > Online Sources of Investment Information and Education

Popular Information, Education, and Tracking Sites

CBS Marketwatch	http://www.marketwatch.com
CNNMoney	http://money.cnn.com
Excite	http://money.excite.com
FreeEdgar	http://www.freeedgar.com
Investopedia	http://www.investopedia.com
Investor's Clearinghouse	http://www.investoreducation.org
MoneyChimp	http://www.moneychimp.com
Morningstar	http://www.morningstar.com
MSN MoneyCentral Investor	http://moneycentral.msn.com/investor
The Motley Fool	http://www.fool.com
National Association of Investors Corp.	http://www.better-investing.org
Reuters	http://www.reuters.com
The Street.com	http://www.thestreet.com
The Wall Street Journal Interactive Edition	http://www.wsj.com
Yahoo! Finance	http://finance.yahoo.com

Stock and Mutual Fund Screening Sites

CBS Marketwatch	http://www.marketwatch.com
Morningstar	http://www.morningstar.com
MSN MoneyCentral Investor	http://moneycentral.msn.com/investor
Quicken	http://www.quicken.com
SmartMoney	http://www.smartmoney.com
Wall Street City	http://www.wallstreetcity.com
Yahoo! Finance	http://screen.yahoo.com/stocks.html
Zacks Analyst Watch	http://www.zacks.com

They can help you find reliable online information sources and learn more about how to use them wisely.

Security Price Quotations

The security price quotations in the *Wall Street Journal* and other financial media provide a wealth of current information. The quotations typically report the results of the previous day's trading activity. Stock brokerage firms have electronic quotation systems that give up-to-the-minute prices, and investors can subscribe to special online services that also give real-time stock quotations. Many of the sites listed in Exhibit 20.6 also provide real-time quotations for a fee, in addition to free quotes on a delayed basis.

Stock Quotations Prices for NYSE, AMEX, and NASDAQ stocks are all quoted the same way: in decimals. Exhibit 20.7 shows a portion of the June 8, 2006, stock quotations for NYSE-listed stocks, as they appeared in the *Wall Street Journal* on June 7. These quotations show not only the most recent (close) price, but also the highest and lowest price paid for the stock during the previous 52 weeks, the annual dividend, the dividend yield, the price/earnings ratio, the day's trading volume, and the change from the previous day's closing price. The **price/earnings (P/E) ratio** is calculated by dividing the current market price by annual earnings per share. A company's P/E ratio should be compared to those of other companies in the same industry.

To understand how to read stock quotations, follow the listing for the common stock of Disney in Exhibit 20.7, highlighted in orange. Over the previous 52 weeks,

price/earnings (P/E) ratio
The current market price of a stock divided by its annual earnings per share.

Exhibit 20.7 > **Disney Stock Quotation for June 7, 2006**

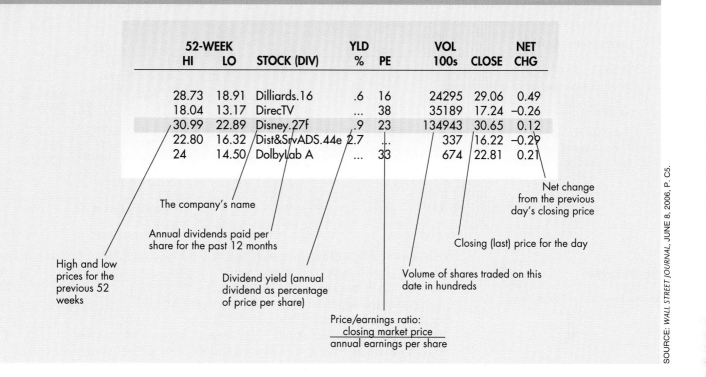

52-WEEK HI	52-WEEK LO	STOCK (DIV)	YLD %	PE	VOL 100s	CLOSE	NET CHG
28.73	18.91	Dilliards.16	.6	16	24295	29.06	0.49
18.04	13.17	DirecTV	...	38	35189	17.24	−0.26
30.99	22.89	Disney.27f	.9	23	134943	30.65	0.12
22.80	16.32	Dist&SrvADS.44e	2.7	...	337	16.22	−0.29
24	14.50	DolbyLab A	...	33	674	22.81	0.21

High and low prices for the previous 52 weeks

The company's name

Annual dividends paid per share for the past 12 months

Dividend yield (annual dividend as percentage of price per share)

Price/earnings ratio:
$$\frac{\text{closing market price}}{\text{annual earnings per share}}$$

Volume of shares traded on this date in hundreds

Closing (last) price for the day

Net change from the previous day's closing price

SOURCE: *WALL STREET JOURNAL*, JUNE 8, 2006, P. C5.

the stock traded at a high of $30.99 and a low of $22.89. It paid annual dividends of $.27, a 0.9 percent dividend yield. (Note that these columns are blank for DirecTV, a firm that doesn't pay a dividend.) On June 7, Disney's P/E ratio was 23 and 13,494,300 shares (134,943 × 100) were traded. The closing price, or last price, of the stock on June 7 was $30.65, a 12-cent positive change from the previous day's closing price.

Preferred stocks are listed separately in the *Wall Street Journal* and many other publications. The letters *pf* or *pr* after the company's name identify a preferred stock. Other abbreviations and symbols, such as the "f" after Disney's dividend, are used by publications like the *Wall Street Journal* to indicate a variety of factors, including stock splits, dividend changes, new 52-week highs or lows, and many other conditions. A key to what these abbreviations mean is usually provided at the beginning of each publication's financial section.

Bond Quotations Bond quotations are also included in the *Wall Street Journal* and other financial publications. Exhibit 20.8 shows the first part of the quotations for the 40 most active fixed-coupon NYSE bonds trading on June 7, 2006. The bonds are listed by trading volume. On this day, the highlighted (in orange) Aetna bond had the highest trading volume: $161,200,000. The bond has a coupon of 6.625 percent and matures June 15, 2036.

Bond prices are expressed as a percentage of the face value (principal). A closing price above 100 means the bond is selling at more than its face value (at a *premium*). A closing price below 100 is less than the face value (the bond is selling at a *discount*). Aetna's bond closed at 99.997, so it is selling at a very slight discount. The estimated spread refers to the difference between this bond and the comparable Treasury security. This Aetna bond is trading at 1.46 percent above the 30-year U.S. Treasury (UST) bond.

Summary listings for other types of bonds, including municipal bonds, high-yield bonds, and Treasury bonds, are also listed in the securities quotations pages. Their quotations are similar to corporate bond listings.

Exhibit 20.8 > Aetna Corporate Bond Quotation for June 7, 2006

Corporate Bonds

Wednesday, June 7, 2006
Forty most active fixed-coupon corporate bonds

COMPANY (TICKER)	COUPON	MATURITY	LAST PRICE	LAST YIELD	*EST SPREAD	UST†	EST $ VOL (000's)
Aetna (AET)	6.625	Jun 15, 2036	99.997	6.625	146	30	161,200
K. Hovnanian Enterprises Inc (HOV)	8.625	Jan 15, 2017	100.250	8.591	357	10	108,800
Sovereign Cap Trust (SCPT)	7.908	Jun 13, 2036	101.631	7.671	250	30	108,400

SOURCE: WALL STREET JOURNAL, JUNE 8, 2006, P. C4.

net asset value
The price at which each share of a mutual fund can be bought or sold.

Mutual Fund Quotations Mutual fund share prices are quoted in dollars and cents and trade at their NAV, or **net asset value**, the price at which each share of the mutual fund can be bought or sold. The mutual fund quotations shown in Exhibit 20.9 are the ones that appear in the *Wall Street Journal*'s Monthly Mutual Fund Review. Less comprehensive quotations that include NAV, net change in NAV from the previous day, and year-to-date percent return appear daily in the *Wall Street Journal* and in most major newspapers. The exhibit explains other items in the quotes, such as fees, returns, and annual expense ratio, for the Fidelity Blue Chip Fund, which is in the Large Cap Core category.

Exhibit 20.9 > Fidelity Blue Chip Mutual Fund Quotation for May 31, 2006

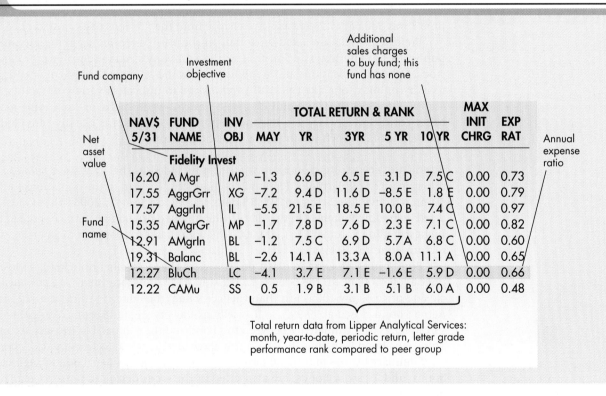

Total return data from Lipper Analytical Services: month, year-to-date, periodic return, letter grade performance rank compared to peer group

SOURCE: WALL STREET JOURNAL, JUNE 5, 2006, P. R3.

CONCEPT *in Action*

Navigating the universe of stocks can be daunting. Fortunately, major indexes make the task easier. The S&P 500, a leading indicator of United States equities, is comprised of giant corporations that reflect the risk-return characteristics of large-cap stocks. The Russell 2000 Index tracks the performance of fast-growing small businesses and is considered to be the benchmark for small-cap stocks and related mutual funds. *How do investors use market averages and indexes to measure the market's movements?*

Market Averages and Indexes

"How's the market doing today?" This question is commonly asked by people interested in the securities market. An easy way to monitor general market conditions is to follow market averages and indexes, which provide a convenient way to gauge the general mood of the market by summarizing the price behavior of securities. **Market averages** use the arithmetic average price of groups of securities at a given point in time to track market movements. **Market indexes** measure the current price behavior of groups of securities relative to a base value set at an earlier point in time. The level of an average or index at any given time is less important than its behavior—its movement up and down over time. The Markets Lineup page of the *Wall Street Journal's* Money and Investing section includes the major market indicators: stock, bond, and mutual fund indexes; most active issues; NYSE volume, interest rates, and selected commodities; and mutual fund prices.

The most widely used market average is the Dow Jones Industrial Average (DJIA). It measures the stock prices of 30 large, well-known corporations, listed along with the original 12 Dow Jones stocks, as shown in Exhibit 20.10. The companies in the DJIA are chosen for their total market value and broad public ownership. It includes both NYSE and NASDAQ stocks. It is calculated by adding the closing price of each of the 30 stocks and dividing by the DJIA divisor, a number that changes over time to adjust for events such as stock splits.

The DJIA changes daily. If the DJIA closes at 9,500 one day and at 9,620 the next, the typical stock in the index would have moved up by about 1.25 percent [(9,620 − 9,500)/9,500]. There are three other Dow Jones averages: a 20-stock transportation average, a 15-stock utility average, and a composite average based on the stocks in all three averages. Dow Jones also has several other indexes such as the Global Titans 50 Index and the broad Dow Jones Wilshire 5000 Composite Index, which represents the performance of all U.S.-headquartered equity securities with readily available price data.

An important market index is the **Standard & Poor's (S&P) 500 stock index**. The S&P 500 is broader than the DJIA. It includes 400 industrial stocks, 20 transportation stocks, 40 public utility stocks, and 40 financial stocks. It includes NYSE, AMEX, and NASDAQ stocks. Many market analysts prefer the S&P 500 index to the DJIA because of

---

market averages
Summarizes the price behavior of securities based on the arithmetic average price of groups of securities at a given point in time; used to monitor general market conditions.

market indexes
Measures of the current price behavior of groups of securities relative to a base value set at an earlier point in time; used to monitor general market conditions.

Dow Jones Industrial Average (DJIA)
The most widely used market average; measures the stock prices of 30 large, well-known corporations that trade on the NYSE and NASDAQ.

Standard & Poor's (S&P) 500 stock index
An important market index that includes 400 industrial stocks, 20 transportation stocks, 40 public utility stocks, and 40 financial stocks; includes NYSE, AMEX, and NASDAQ stocks.

Exhibit 20.10 > **The Dow Jones Industrial Average Then and Now**

The Original 12 Dow Jones Stocks	Today's 30 Dow Jones Stocks
American Cotton Oil	Aluminum Co. of America (ALCOA)
American Sugar Refining Co.	Altria Group
American Tobacco	American Express
Chicago Gas	American International Group
Distilling & Cattle Feeding Co.	AT&T
General Electric Co.	Boeing
Laclede Gas Light Co.	Caterpillar
National Lead	Citigroup
North American Co.	Coca-Cola
Tennessee Coal, Iron & Railroad Co.	Walt Disney
U.S. Leather	DuPont
U.S. Rubber Co.	ExxonMobil
	General Electric
	General Motors
	Hewlett Packard
	Home Depot
	Honeywell
	IBM
	Intel
	Johnson & Johnson
	J. P. Morgan Chase
	McDonald's
	Merck
	Microsoft
	Pfizer
	Procter & Gamble
	3M
	United Technologies
	Verizon
	Wal-Mart Stores

NASDAQ Composite Index
Broad-based market index that measures all NASDAQ domestic- and international-based common stocks listed on the NASDAQ Stock Market.

its broad base. It is calculated by dividing the sum of the closing market prices of the 500 stocks by the sum of the market values of those stocks in the base period and multiplying the result by 10. Like the DJIA, the S&P 500 is meaningful only when compared to index values at other time periods. The S&P has other indexes, such as the MidCap 400 Index that tracks stocks of medium-size companies and a series of global indexes including the S&P Global 1200 and indexes that focus on specific geographic regions.

A third major index is the **NASDAQ Composite Index**, a broad-based index that includes over 3,000 NASDAQ securities. It includes both U.S. and international companies and has joined the DJIA and S&P 500 as the most commonly quoted indexes.

Several indexes track activity in the bond markets. The Lehman Brothers U.S. Aggregate and U.S. Government Credit Indexes and the three Merrill Lynch corporate debt indexes are the most popular.

concept check

What are four popular sources of investment information?

What type of investment information can investors find on the Internet? What are the positive and negative aspects of using Internet sources of investment information?

What roles do market averages and indexes play in the investment process?

Trends in Securities and Securities Markets

8 **What current trends are transforming the securities markets?**

The 1990s were a euphoric time for many investors. Stock prices seemed to be on a never-ending upward spiral, fed by frenzied growth in the economy and the dot-com technology boom. The stock market bubble burst in 2000, and news of corporate scandals brought the securities markets back to earth. In the years that followed, the securities industry focused on rebuilding investor trust. The SEC assumed a stronger role and implemented additional regulations to protect investors from fraud and misinformation. It improved access to investment information by making all SEC filings fully searchable on the Web. It continued to pursue companies that failed to comply with Sarbanes-Oxley and to bring charges against corporate executives for accounting fraud and to sanction brokers and the exchanges themselves when it discovered irregularities. This increased government regulation and enforcement are attempting to provide better protection for investors, while the industry itself is redefining how it serves customer needs.

The securities industry itself and public corporations also took steps to regain investor trust. By 2003, investors were returning to the markets and the securities exchanges shifted their focus to improving their operations and serving investors better. The NYSE and NASDAQ went head to head in the United States. Small companies began to seek out non-U.S. exchanges for their IPOs. A wave of mergermania hit the global securities markets. Stock brokerage firms continued to look for ways to adapt to these and other changes in the securities markets.

Vying for the U.S. Crown

The NYSE and NASDAQ are waging a heated battle for supremacy in the U.S. securities markets. The NYSE was falling behind its more nimble rival, which already had an electronic platform. Its answer, as the Managing Change box explains, was to make sweeping changes in its organizational structure by going public and merging with Archipelago, a major ECN, to enter the electronic marketplace. NASDAQ responded immediately by acquiring another ECN, Instinet's INET. The NYSE then made history by signing an agreement to merge with Euronext and create the first exchange to span the Atlantic. Not to be outdone, the NASDAQ was increasing its ownership of shares in the London Stock Exchange to 25 percent. These transactions reduced the fragmentation in the marketplace and also eliminated many of the differences between the two exchanges. At the same time, the two exchanges emerged stronger and better able to compete with each other.[24] They also turned their attention overseas, as we will see in the following section.

In response, the regional stock exchanges quickly positioned themselves to take full advantage of the changes in trading from Regulation NMS, which gives regional exchanges equal standing in the national market system. They geared up their electronic trading platforms to handle the increased trading volume and formed partnerships with broker-dealers to improve deal flow. "I see a leveling of the playing field—the ability to post a better quote and attract order flow in any market," says Dave Herron, CEO of the Chicago Stock Exchange.[25]

CONCEPT *in Action*

In keeping with its primary responsibility to enforce federal securities laws and regulate the industry, the Securities and Exchange Commission promotes its online EDGAR database as the best way for investors to get access to important financial filings from publicly traded companies. The EDGAR is a searchable version of the SEC's securities regulation information—a vital tool for investors looking to steer clear of businesses with shaky financial dealings. *How does the SEC help foster investor confidence?*

Small Companies Take Their IPOs to London

The London Stock Exchange (LSE) has become home to an increasing share of the world's IPOs. One group that is taking its business to London is small U.S. companies who choose to list their shares on the LSE's Alternative Investment Market (AIM). AIM is currently home to more than 25 U.S. companies who might not otherwise be able to go public.

One of the principal reasons they cite for heading to London is the higher cost of going public in the United States since the passage of Sarbanes-Oxley. The stricter requirements and internal controls provisions are costly for small firms to implement. Many small companies that list with AIM have a significant international business component or cannot

MANAGING CHANGE

The "New" New York Stock Exchange

On March 8, 2006, the New York Stock Exchange (NYSE) welcomed a new company to its listings: itself! Since 1792 the NYSE had operated as a not-for-profit company with members who purchased seats that allowed them to trade securities on the exchange. "The Opening Bell, which has long symbolized the success and vitality of our capital market system, today rings in a new era for the Exchange, our customers, and investors," said John A. Thain, chief executive officer of NYSE Group.

For years the NYSE had experienced increasing competition from the rival NASDAQ Stock Market and other electronic trading platforms. It found the answer to its problems in its acquisition of Archipelago Holdings, one of its major electronic competitors. The merger of the two organizations created a for-profit, publicly traded company named the NYSE Group, Inc., and brought the NYSE a sizable electronic trading platform, which it needed to remain competitive in today's fast-paced securities markets. The new corporation formed two subsidiaries: The New York Stock Exchange, the largest market for listed securities in the world, and NYSE Arca, the former Archipelago Exchange which had itself acquired the Pacific Exchange in early 2005. Through Arca, the NYSE Group could now trade more products, including equities listed on other U.S. stock exchanges, including NASDAQ, over-the-counter equities, fixed-income products, options, and exchange traded funds. NYSE customers now have a choice between the traditional floor-based auction market and high-speed electronic trading.

Soon after it went public, the NYSE Group announced its next step: a merger with Euronext NV, a cross-border European exchange that owns the Paris, Lisbon, Brussels, and Amsterdam stock exchanges and the electronic London International Financial Futures and Options Exchange (LIFFE). "It is not enough to build the best marketplace in the U.S. or a champion of Europe," said Thain. "The challenge is to build

the best marketplace in the world." After it obtains all necessary regulatory approvals, NYSE Euronext will be the first trans-Atlantic stock exchange and the world's largest publicly traded exchange company, with a market capitalization of $20 billion. Headquartered in New York, its shares will be listed in both New York and Paris.

The merger with Euronext would diversify the NYSE Group even further by giving it access to international listings and increase its participation in the high-growth derivatives market through LIFFE. Derivatives are securities contracts whose price depends on an underlying asset, such as stocks, bonds, commodities, currencies, interest rates, and market indexes. The larger company is well positioned to acquire other exchanges. The NYSE and Euronext jointly approached the Bolsa Italiana in Milan—before its own deal had been approved.

More changes lie ahead for the reborn NYSE. Because the Euronext trading system is totally electronic, there could be a shift to more electronic trading and less emphasis on floor trades, although CEO Thain promises to maintain the current hybrid system with both types of trades. The NYSE Group hopes that combining multiple securities trading subsidiaries will lead to lower operating costs and estimates potential cost savings from the Euronext merger at $373 million. Investors, too, could benefit as trading costs drop from greater operating efficiencies and it becomes easier to trade in international markets.[26]

Critical Thinking Questions

- What steps did the NYSE take to improve its ability to compete in the global securities markets, and why?
- What challenges does the NYSE Group face as a public company with several subsidiaries that combine different trading platforms and cross national borders?

---

meet NASDAQ's listing requirements. For others, AIM offers an alternative to private venture financing before they are ready for NASDAQ.

Initial and ongoing listing costs are lower on AIM as well. To list on the NASDAQ, a company must pay an initial fee of about $5 million and incur about $2.3 million per year to maintain the listing. On AIM, the initial cost is about $3.8 million for the AIM, and annual expenses run about $900,000. For companies with market capitalization of about $250 million, these savings add up.[27]

Mergermania in the Global Markets

Mergermania has come to the securities markets themselves, which have begun to consolidate to capture larger shares of the world's trading volume in multiple types of securities. As discussed earlier, the merger of the NYSE and Euronext prompted other securities exchanges to look for new sources of revenue. Until recently, securities exchange partnerships between countries were difficult to arrange. "Historically, exchanges were always a source of national pride," explains Tom Kirchmaier, a corporate governance specialist at the London School of Economics. The NYSE-Euronext deal paved the way for future exchange consolidations.[28]

As in other industries, big is better in financial markets as well. The rise of electronic trading networks facilitates the flow of money across national borders and increases competition from global players. Economies of scale make a big difference in profitability because competition drives down trading fees. As trading volume rises, an exchange can lower the per-trade costs and compete more effectively. This places extreme pressure on the mid-tier European exchanges such as Borsa Italiana and Bolsas y Mercados Espanoles (BME), a holding company for Spain's four regional exchanges, to consider going public and look for their own partnerships.[29]

In addition, many international companies are taking their IPOs to non-U.S. exchanges to avoid the cost of compliance with the additional regulations of Sarbanes-Oxley. This has prompted U.S. exchanges to seek other European partners to recapture the lucrative IPO fees.[30]

Online Brokerage Reinvents Itself

With the rate of online investing rising—most first-time users are either below age 35 or are retirees—online brokerage firms are seeking new ways to capture and keep their customers. One of the ways they're doing it is by broadening the services they offer to investors.

Over the past two years, the online brokerage industry has remade itself, discarding the no-frills business model in exchange for offering customers a broader selection of investment options. The differences between the full-service discounters and the bare-bones rivals have all but disappeared. Despite larger numbers of online investors, competition is fierce and has driven the price of trades down. Commissions at full-service brokers are not that much higher than at basic brokers. Consolidation in the industry has also contributed to lower commissions. TDAmeritrade, created by the merger between TD Waterhouse and Ameritrade, cut the online stock trades to a flat $9.99. E* Trade, which acquired Brown Co., has a tiered fee structure ranging from $6.99 to $12.99 but will let former Brown clients keep their $5 commission. And some new entrants to the online brokerage industry offer commissions below $5. Although this is good for investors, who can focus on features and service rather than pricing, the firms themselves are struggling to differentiate themselves.

At the same time, complicated new trading fee arrangements make comparisons on the cost of a stock trade more difficult, so navigating these new choices can be confusing for online brokerage users. Cheap online stock trades are often obscured by a collection of financial services that includes banking, and savings and credit offerings. The intention is obvious: Online brokerage firms want customers to spend more on these additional services, wherein lie their own profits.

"We will be seeing hybrid services," says Dan Sondhelm, partner and president of SunStar, a financial services industry consulting firm. "Many of the online brokers will offer limited investing advice, and firms will offer flat-fee pricing as well as multiple-call advice packages to be used on an as-needed basis."

What you are seeing is a peek into the future of the online investment industry. Overall, these developments are both good news and bad news for investors with a do-it-yourself style. Better research information is available and more affordable. And cheap stock fees are still around. But they will be based on the number of trades, the amount of your trading account, and the ancillary services you are willing to pay for. In the Creative Thinking Case, we'll see how one of the leading online brokerages, E*Trade, is dealing with these trends.

Some authorities are convinced that online investing's new direction will result in better outcomes for investors. The accent on quick, cheap trades through discount brokers challenged the baseline philosophy of long-term investing—and may have been detrimental to many investors' portfolios. Without a doubt, the "churn rate" (turnover) in the stock market was at its peak during the height of the discount brokerage era. "The goal of investing should be long-term planning, not active trading, so an emphasis on inexpensive trades is just not good business," says Bruce Fenton, president of Norwell, Massachusetts-based Atlantic Financial, a full-service stock brokerage firm.[31]

Summary of Learning Goals

1 **How do common stock and preferred stock differ as investments?**

Common and preferred stocks represent ownership—equity—in a corporation. Common stockholders have voting rights, but their claim on profits and assets ranks behind that of holders of other securities. Preferred stockholders receive a stated dividend. It must be paid before any dividends are distributed to common stockholders.

Common stocks are more risky than preferred stocks. They offer the potential for increased value through growth in the stock price and income through dividend payments. But neither price increases nor dividends are guaranteed. Preferred stocks are usually bought for their dividend income rather than potential price appreciation.

2 **What are bonds, and what investment advantages and disadvantages do they offer?**

Bonds are a form of debt and may be secured or unsecured. Bondholders are creditors of the issuing organization, and their claims on income and assets rank ahead of those of preferred and common stockholders. The corporation or government entity that issues the bonds must pay interest periodically and repay the principal at maturity. Bonds provide a steady source of income and the potential for price appreciation if interest rates fall below the coupon rate. However, investors also bear the risk that rising interest rates may erode the bond's price.

3 **What other types of securities are available to investors?**

Mutual funds are financial-service companies that pool the funds of many investors to buy a diversified portfolio of securities. Investors choose mutual funds because they offer a convenient way to diversify and are professionally managed. Futures contracts are legally binding obligations to buy or sell specified quantities of commodities or financial instruments at an agreed-on price at a future date. They are very risky investments because the price of the commodity or financial instrument may change drastically. Options are contracts that entitle the holder the right to buy or sell specified quantities of common stock or other financial instruments at a set price during a specified time. They, too, are high-risk investments.

4 **What is the function of the securities markets?**

Securities markets allow stocks, bonds, and other securities to be bought and sold quickly and at a fair price. New issues are sold in the primary market. After that, securities are traded in the secondary market. Investment bankers specialize in issuing and selling new security issues. Stockbrokers are licensed professionals who buy and sell securities on behalf of their clients.

5 **Where can investors buy and sell securities?**

Securities are resold in secondary markets, which include both broker markets and dealer markets. The broker market consists of national and regional securities exchanges such as the New York Stock Exchange, that bring buyers and sellers together through brokers on a centralized trading floor. Dealer markets use sophisticated telecommunications networks that link dealers throughout the United States. The NASDAQ and over-the-counter markets are examples of dealer markets. In addition to the U.S. markets, more than 100 countries have securities exchanges. The largest non-U.S. exchanges are the Tokyo, London, Euronext, Deutsche Bourse, and Toronto exchanges.

6 **How are securities markets regulated?**

The Securities Act of 1933 requires disclosure of important information regarding new securities issues. The Securities Exchange Act of 1934 and its 1964 amendment formally empowered the Securities and Exchange Commission and granted it broad powers to regulate the organized securities exchanges and the over-the-counter market. The Investment Company Act of 1940 places investment companies such as mutual funds under SEC control. The securities markets also have self-regulatory groups like the NASD and measures such as "circuit breakers" to halt trading if the Dow Jones Industrial Average drops rapidly.

7 | **Which sources of investment information are the most helpful to investors, and what can investors learn from stock, bond, and mutual fund quotations?**

The most popular sources of investment information are economic and financial publications like the *Wall Street Journal, Barron's, Business Week, Fortune, Smart Money,* and *Money*. The newest sources of information include the numerous Internet sites. Other sources are subscription services, investment newsletters, and security price quotations.

Stock quotations show the percentage change in the stock's price since the beginning of the year, the highest and lowest prices paid for the stock during the previous 52 weeks, the annual dividend, the dividend yield, the price/earnings ratio, the day's trading volume, the closing price, and the change from the previous day's closing price. Bond quotations show the coupon interest rate, maturity date, current yield, trading volume, closing price, and change in closing price from the previous day. Mutual fund quotations provide the fund's net asset value, net change in NAV from the previous day, and year-to-date percent return.

8 | **What current trends are transforming the securities markets?**

Competition among the world's major securities exchanges has changed the composition of the financial marketplace. The NYSE and NASDAQ went head to head in the United States. The NYSE became a for-profit company and acquired Archipelago, an electronic exchange, and merged with Euronext to form the first transatlantic exchange. NASDAQ also expanded by acquiring its own ECN and buying a 25 percent stake in the London Stock Exchange. Small companies turned to the London Stock Exchange for their IPOs. A wave of mergermania hit the global securities markets as economies of scale became more important. As the differences among online stock brokerage firms decreased, many firms merged to increase their market share and began offering other types of financial services.

Key Terms

bear markets 675	municipal bonds 666
bond ratings 667	mutual fund 667
broker markets 671	NASDAQ Composite Index 684
bull markets 675	National Association of Securities Dealers
circuit breakers 678	Automated Quotation (NASDAQ)
convertible bonds 665	system 672
dealer markets 672	net asset value (NAV) 682
debentures 665	options 668
Dow Jones Industrial Average (DJIA) 683	price/earnings (P/E) ratio 680
electronic communications networks	primary market 670
(ECNs) 673	principal 664
exchange-traded fund (ETF) 668	Regulation FD 678
futures contracts 668	secondary market 670
high-yield (junk) bonds 665	secured bonds 665
insider trading 677	securities 662
institutional investors 668	Securities and Exchange Commission
interest 664	(SEC) 676
investment bankers 669	Standard & Poor's (S&P) 500 stock
market averages 683	index 683
market indexes 683	stockbroker 668
mortgage bonds 665	underwriting 668

Preparing for Tomorrow's Workplace: SCANS

1. Research the trends in the IPO marketplace from 1998 to 2006. Then select two IPO success stories and two failures. Prepare a report for the class on their performance. What lessons about the securities markets can you learn from their stories? (Information)

2. While having dinner at a Manhattan restaurant, you overhear two investment bankers at the next table. They are discussing the takeover of Bellamco Industries by Gildmart Corp., a deal that has not yet been announced. You have been thinking about buying Bellamco stock for a while, so the next day you buy 500 shares for $30 each. Two weeks later, Gildmart announces its acquisition of Bellamco at a price of $45 per share. Have you earned a profit fairly, or are you guilty of insider trading? What's wrong with insider trading? (Information)

3. What role do a CEO's actions/strategies have in influencing a company's stock performance? Prepare a class presentation that answers this question using both positive and negative examples from at least three companies covered in recent business news. In your presentation, discuss what your recommendations for each CEO would be. (Information, Systems)

4. Research the job responsibilities of a corporate Investor Relations Officer (IRO). If possible, try to interview an IRO, by either phone or e-mail. The National Investor Relations Institute (**http://www.niri.org**), a trade association for IROs, is an alternate source of information. What types of experience and education does an IRO need in order to perform effectively? How are their roles changing? Write a paper summarizing your findings. Is this a career that interests you? (Interpersonal, Information)

5. **Team Activity** Is joining an investment club be a good way to learn about investing in the stock market? Divide the class into groups of five to eight students to develop a strategy to form their own investment club. Use the National Association of Investors Corporation (NAIC) Web site at **http://www.better-investing. org** to learn how investment clubs operate and the investment strategy the NAIC teaches. Then each group should set up guidelines for their investment club and present their plan to the class. After the presentations, the class members should discuss whether they would prefer to start investing through an investment club or on their own. (Resources, Interpersonal, Information)

Ethics Activity

In June 2006, the SEC opened an investigation into the stock option practices of Cyberonics, a Houston medical devices manufacturer. As defined by the SEC, stock options give a company's employees the right to buy a specific number of shares at a fixed price within a certain period of time. Holders of stock options hope that the price of the stock will rise by the time they exercise their options so that they make a profit. Companies use stock options to compensate, retain, attract, and motivate executives and other employees.

The issue at Cyberonics was the timing of options grants to three executives in 2004, to buy stock at $19.58—the June 14 closing price—just after the company received FDA approval of one of its devices. This positive news was expected to raise its share price and guarantee the executives profits if they exercised the options. On June 16, 2004, the price jumped 62 percent to open at $31.70.

This practice of issuing stock options in advance of good news is called *spring-loading*. Whether spring-loading is illegal is unclear, however, and became the focus of more than 40 SEC inquiries.

Some experts believe that timing options grants in this manner is a form of insider trading, although they concede that proving that the good news would in fact raise the share price could be tricky.

Cyberonics' CFO Pamela B. Westbrook maintained that the options were "properly approved, priced, and granted at fair market value." In addition, the executives receiving the options had not yet exercised the options. At the end of July 2006, Cyberonics shares were trading between $20 and $22.

Using a Web search tool, locate articles about this topic and then write responses to the following questions. Be sure to support your arguments and cite your sources.

Ethical Dilemma: Is it legal for a company to grant stock options to its executives just before it releases good news, or does this constitute insider trading?

Sources: "Dates from Hell: Executive Share Options," *Economist*, July 22, 2006, p. 68; "Employee Stock Options Plans," Securities and Exchange Commission, http://www.sec.gov/answers/empopt.htm; Jane Sasseen, "Another Dodgy Way to Dole Out Options," *Business Week*, June 26, 2006, p. 40; and "SEC Probing Cyberonics Stock Options," *Houston Business Journal*, June 13, 2006, http://biz.yahoo.com.

Working the Net

1. Choose a company currently traded on the NYSE (**http://www.nyse.com**). Find the company's Web site using a search engine such as Google.com. At the Web site, find the firm's investor relations information. Review the information, including, if available, the most recent online annual report. Follow up by researching whether any SEC actions have been taken against the firm at the SEC Web site, **http://www.sec.gov**. Summarize your findings in a brief report that discusses whether you would recommend this company's stock as an investment.

2. Using the same company you researched in Question 1, research the company on several of the online resources discussed in this chapter. Look particularly for any analysts' evaluation of the stock, its potential, and trends in its trading history. Summarize your findings in a brief report. Based on this information would you recommend this stock as an investment? Did your evaluation change from Question 1 after further research? Why or why not?

3. At The Vanguard Group's site, **http://www.vanguard.com**, go to the page for Personal Investors, then to the Planning & Education section. Click on Investment Education and read several of the articles, including How to Select a Mutual Fund. After learning about the fundamentals of mutual funds, prepare a presentation for the class based on the materials.

4. You've been asked to address your investment club on socially responsible investing and how companies qualify as socially responsible. Research this topic at the Web sites of the Social Investment Forum, **http://www.socialinvest.org**, and Co-op America, **http://www.coopamerica.org**. Prepare a detailed outline of the key points you would include in the speech. How can your personal financial decisions have a positive impact on communities and the environment? Do you support socially responsible investing, and why?

5. Using the information and links available at the Bond Market Association's Web site, **http://www.bondmarkets.com**, write a brief paper explaining the pros and cons of investing in corporate bonds. In your paper, provide at least three examples of currently available corporate bonds from a site such as **http://www.investinginbonds.com**, and explain why they would be good investments.

6. Visit the sites of several brokerages that offer online trading capabilities, such as Charles Schwab (**http://www.schwab.com**), E*Trade (**http://www.etrade.com**), TDAmeritrade (**http://www.tdameritrade.com**), Scottrade (**http://www.scottrade.com**), or any others you know. Compare them for ease of use, quality of information, account minimums, and other criteria you select. To check out the firms, look up annual rankings of online investment firms at *Smart Money* (**http://www.smartmoney.com/brokers**) and independent ratings companies such as J. D. Power (**http://www.jdpower.com/finance**). How do the firms you compared rate? Which firm would you prefer to use, and why?

7. Pick a portfolio of five companies in at least three different industries. Choose companies you know, read the financial press to find good candidates, or try one of the stock screening sites in Exhibit 20.6. Set up a table to track the stock prices. Record the end-of-month prices for the past six months and track the daily price movements for at least two weeks (longer is even better!). Visit the Web sites of these companies to view their investor relations information and go to the EDGAR database at the SEC Web site, **http://www.sec.gov**, to review recent company SEC filings. Finally, monitor economic and market trends and other events that affect market conditions. Share the performance of the portfolio with your classmates. Explain your basis for selecting each stock and analyze its price changes.

Discount Brokerage Firms Change Direction

The emphasis on cheap fees and lightning-fast trades seems to be a thing of the past in the discount brokerage industry. Most firms are shifting their focus to an ever-broadening range of services and advice. And defying stock market traditions, some are forming partnerships with banks, airlines, and retailers so their customers can make stock trades from anywhere—their home computer, cell phone, or while on vacation.

E*Trade is a good example of the dramatic changes that have taken place in the discount brokerage marketplace. Founded in 1982 as a straightforward brokerage firm called Trade Plus, it was one of the first firms to offer online trading in 1992, when it assumed its present name. And until a couple of years ago, E*Trade was the alternative to larger firms and inflated costs.

In 2005, the Menlo Park, California-based company purchased two noteworthy online brokerage firms—BrownCo, the online trading arm of J. P. Morgan Chase, for $1.6 billion, and online broker Harrisdirect for $700 million. These acquisitions contributed to E*Trade's increased 2005 revenues of $1.7 billion, up from $1.4 billion in 2004. The firm's net income also increased to $430 million, up from $380 million a year ago, and its share price rose 163 percent between June and December 2005.

"E*Trade no longer wants to be associated with a discount image," says R. Jarrett Lilien, the company's president and chief operating officer. "We're about education, tools, and value now," he says. According to Lilien, a totally automatic, do-it-yourself system isn't ideal either. "It turns out that just about everyone wants to talk to a real person sometimes about their investments—about once a year," he says.

So E*Trade now offers 20 walk-in investment centers where customers can find any type of advice they need. Its goal is to put 80 percent of its customers within 20 miles of human assistance by increasing the number of walk-in centers to 36 over the next couple of years. Its swiftly growing global presence, major home-mortgage operation, and other traditional banking products have turned E*Trade Financial into the nation's eighth-largest savings bank, based on total assets.

"Investing in the future is going to be a mostly online experience, but there will be other options for more direct information and advice if and when you want them," Lilien says. "The online brokerage of the future is the one that can successfully deliver all those combinations of service, at any given time."

Critical Thinking Questions

- Why was discount trading a negative experience for both individual investors and the stock market overall?
- How did companies like E*Trade respond to investor concerns and needs? Do you think the addition of other financial services such as mortgages was a good move, and why?
- If you were an online trader how important would cheap stock trades be? What other services would you look for? Explain.

Sources: Adapted from Jason Brooks, "ETrade Goes into the Great Wide Open," eweek.com, January 29, 2006, http://www.eweek.com; E-*Trade Financial corporate Web site, http://www.us.etrade.com, June 14, 2006; Kate Fitzgerald, "Keying In on the Internet, Better Investing, June 2006, p. 26; "Shares in E*Trade Plunge After Sale," International Herald Tribune—Marketplace by Bloomberg, April 4, 2006, http://www.iht.com.

Morgan Stanley Builds Its Future, One Client at a Time

Founded as an investment bank in 1935, Morgan Stanley has a long history and a strong brand identity, ranking among Wall Street's elite. The company also has a number of securities industry "firsts" to its credit, including the first computer model for financial analysis, the introduction of automated processing for securities trading, and the creation of innovative new types of securities.

In 1997 Morgan Stanley merged with Dean Witter, combining that company's strong retail brokerage services with its own investment banking and institutional securities operations. Today the combined firm is global, with about 54,000 employees in more than 600 offices in 30 countries, and client assets under management totaling more than $622 billion.

Morgan Stanley is highly regarded for its financial advice and market execution, offering clients a wide range of services through four business segments: Institutional Securities (investment banking, institutional sales and trading, research), Individual Investor Group (investor advisory services, wealth management, individual investor services), Investment Management (global asset management products and services for individual and institutional investors), and Credit Services (Discover-branded cards and other consumer finance products and services). The firm continues to be on the cutting edge in its use of technology.

During the high-flying 1990s, Morgan Stanley and its Wall Street peers enjoyed a period of fast growth and increasing profitability as the stock market soared and corporate-financing activity flourished. As the new century started, however, the 10-year bull market ended, bringing very different and volatile economic conditions. Few companies wanted to issue securities, merger activity fell off sharply, and individual investors retreated to the sidelines as stock prices tumbled.

Along with many other financial institutions, Morgan Stanley reduced its staff and closed offices in response to lower revenues from the financial markets. The Institutional Securities unit focused its resources on building stronger relationships with top clients. It developed its own systems to automate its NASDAQ and options trading, which offered clients improved execution at lower cost. The Individual Investor Group began emphasizing fee-based accounts rather than transactional arrangements.

As the markets gradually improved, Morgan Stanley focused on building up relationships "one client at a time." Whether working with large corporations looking to raise financing, or individual investors saving for college or retirement, the people at Morgan Stanley evaluate clients' needs, develop financial plans, and implement strategies to reach objectives.

Current chairman and chief executive officer John J. Mack states. "We have the right team, the right assets, and the right business mix in place. Now we must maintain a relentless focus on one priority: performance. . . . We will tear down any barriers that impede our ability to create a cohesive 'one firm' culture in which every employee acts and feels like an owner of the firm."

It is clear that Morgan Stanley has every intention of maintaining its position at the forefront of the securities industry.

Critical Thinking Questions

- How has Morgan Stanley adapted to the changing climate in the securities industry? Discuss the impact of changes in securities industry regulations and how they affect the competitive environment.
- Explain why it is important for Morgan Stanley's clients to understand their personal investment objectives. What might some of these be for a corporate client? As a potential individual client, list several of your personal financial goals.
- Visit the Morgan Stanley Web site, **http://www.morganstanley.com**, and explore the pages for individual investors. Which of the features and benefits presented on the site appeal to you most? Would you feel comfortable choosing Morgan Stanley as your investment adviser, and why?

Sources: Adapted from material in the video, "Plan Now Pay Later: Financing and Investing at Morgan Stanley"; "Letter to Shareholders," *Morgan Stanley Annual Report 2005*, http://www.morganstanley.com, June 13, 2006; Morgan Stanley corporate Web site, http://www.morganstanley.com, June 12, 2006.

Hot Links Address Book

Start your online exploring at Yahoo! Finance, which offers everything from breaking business and world news to stock research, portfolio tracking tools, and educational articles, at http://finance.yahoo.com

The Motley Fool is a favorite site for both novice and experienced investors. What can you learn at the Fool's School today? Go to its Web site at: http://www.fool.com

You'll find a minicourse on different types of bonds at http://www.investinginbonds.com

What is the current level of outstanding Treasury securities? Find out at the Bureau of the Public Debt site, http://www.publicdebt.treas.gov

How much is currently invested in mutual funds? In ETFs? The Investment Company Institute tracks these figures on a monthly basis at http://www.ici.org

MoneyChimp.com strives to educate investors by offering clear, practical articles on a complete range of finance and investing topics, including investment basics, understanding annual reports, stock valuation, and more: http://www.moneychimp.com

Quickly find the latest news for different stock markets around the world at http://quotes.nasdaq.com/asp/globalmarkets.asp

Thinking of investing in a particular company? Go to the SEC's Web site to access the EDGAR database of the financial reports filed by all public companies with the SEC: http://www.sec.gov

>> continuing case on Apple, Inc.

Part 6 • Financial Management at Apple, Inc.

In the early days of the company's history, Apple's founders and venture capitalists maintained tight control of the company and its shares. As the company began to grow, however, an initial public offering (IPO) was planned. This is an example of a company *going public*—its first sale of stock to the public. The company successfully completed a $96.8 million initial public stock issue in December of 1980. The company went public on December 12, 1980 at $22 per share.

The company experienced a rise of more than 30 percent on its 1980 IPO, a precursor to several boom years. Despite ups and downs, Apple's stock rose continuously between 1985 and 1991. However, 1991 was the beginning of both internal and external problems for Apple. Company stock jumped up and down considerably from 1991 with the company hitting rock bottom in July of 1997, resulting in a profitability crisis and, ultimately, a viability crisis. By March of 2000, however, the stock price had skyrocketed again hit an all-time high. According to some analysts, Apple had pioneered the get rich quick IPO and had also epitomized the boom and bust cycle of technology companies.

Apple's common stock is traded on the NASDAQ Stock Market under the ticker symbol AAPL and on the Frankfurt Stock Exchange under the symbol APCD. The company does not have any preferred stock outstanding, and there have been three stock splits since the company went public in 1980—in May of 1987, June of 2000, and February of 2005. When a company declares a stock split, the price of the stock decreases and the number of shares increases proportionately. By reducing the price of the stock, companies try to make their stock more affordable to these investors. Quarterly financial results are released on the third Wednesday of each quarter, with the fiscal year beginning the first of October.

SHARE PRICES PLUMMET

Apple had steadily taken itself into near oblivion by the mid 1990s. By the beginning of 1996, the company had basically fallen into the category of sad stories about hi-tech companies that had gone broke. At the end of the first quarter in 1996, the company reported a loss of $740 million and its market share had shrunk to 5.4 percent. With cash reserves dwindling, new CEO Gilbert Amelio was seeking additional financing. Rather than continuing to adhere to what was referred to as a developer-led culture, Amelio promised investors that the company was going to concentrate on products with good profit margins (a premium-priced, differentiation strategy). This meant a shift to a competitive market focus, as well as a more structured organization with processes and management systems that enabled checks and balances.

According to Apple's chief financial officer during this time, the company had spent 10 years responding to financial crisis after financial crisis with only short-term solutions. The initial step in finding the cure for such growing pains was to find the cash to keep the company running, followed by adding managerial discipline to all functions of the company. The managerial discipline adhered to by Amelio was that of streamlining the product and reducing the payroll through staff cuts. However, Amelio's high priced, cost-cutting efforts were unsuccessful. Apple's shares hit their all time low and he was forced out in 1997—only one year after taking the company's helm.

JOBS' RETURN AND APPLE'S REBOUND

The July day in 1997 that Amelio left Apple was the same day that Steve Jobs returned. Unlike Amelio, who had attributed Apple's problems to a lax developer-led culture, Jobs attributed Apple's problems to new product development that resulted in products without passion. Thus, Jobs began a drastic turnaround of the company.

This turnaround took Apple from a beleaguered computer company to a top performer in about three years. By 2000, Apple was experiencing notably improved stock performance. While the company did experience a slump in the late 1990s, the slump was industry-wide, and Apple began pulling out of the slump before its competitors. As such, the company's stock was of interest to investors who were focused more on valuation than rapid growth in earnings. These value investors specialize in bargain shopping, purchasing stock at a low point and sticking with it for the longer-term. Apple's stock hit an all-time high of $72.10 in March of 2000.

Five years later, Apple set another new stock market high. The company's stock finished trading on January 31, 2005, at $76.80. This trading price valued the company around $30 billion. In October of 2005, the company reported its highest revenue and earnings in company history.

It shipped around 1.2 million Macintosh computers and 6.5 million iPods during fiscal 2005 fourth quarter. This was a 48 percent increase in Mac sales and a 220 percent increase in iPod sales compared to fiscal 2004 fourth quarter. Key numbers for fiscal 2005 were $14 billion in sales (a 68 percent one-year sales growth), $1.3 billion net income (a 384 percent one-year net income growth), and 13,426 employees (a 23 percent one-year employee growth).

The strength of Macintosh and iPod sales continued into the first quarter of 2006. The company's first quarter profits nearly doubled with iPod quarterly sales of around 14 million units and Macintosh quarterly sales of approximately 1.25 million units. While Mac sales were below analysts' projections, the company had its first $1 billion sales quarter in its retail stores. Net income for the first quarter of 2006 was $565 million or 65 cents per share. Revenue was $5.75 billion, up from $3.49 billion. Within a 12 month period, the company's shares were up more than 140 percent. For the second quarter of 2006, analysts had predicted revenue of $4.83 billion. However, January reporting by Apple placed second quarter 2006 revenue at $4.3 billion. As such, Apple shares, on January 18, 2006, fell $2.22, closing at $82.49 on NASDAQ—down from its $86.40 high on January 12, 2006.

Critical Thinking Questions

- Why did Apple reduce the price of its stocks through stock splits?
- Describe a value investor.
- What was the impact of the revenue increase for the first quarter of 2006?
- Was Apple on target for continued growth in fiscal 2006?
- What was driving 2006 forecast revenue?

Sources: Roy A. Allan, *A History of the Personal Computer*, London, Ontario, Canada: Allan Publishing, 2001; Anonymous, "Apple Seeks Cash," *Information Week*, May 6, 1996, p. 30; Anonymous, "Apple Sells 661 Million Dollars' Worth of Notes, Common Stock," *Agence France-Presse*, June 10, 1996, downloaded from http://global.factiva.com, accessed on 12/6/05; Anonymous, "Buyers Bite at Apple Offer," *Electronic News*, June 17, 1996, p. 12; Peter Burrows and Ronald Grover, "Steve Jobs' Magic Kingdom," *BusinessWeek*, February 6, 2006, pp. 63–69; Thomas Claburn, "Financial Analyst sees Windows Users Going Mac," *InternetWeek*, November 8, 2005, downloaded from http://www.internetweek.com, accessed on 12/6/05; Dow Jones &. Co., Inc., "Apple Computer Shares Sold Out; Nautilus Fund Skids on Sale," *DowJones Newswires*, December 12, 1980, downloaded from http://global.factiva.com, accessed on 12/6/05; Benny Evangelista, "Preaching beyond the Mac Faithful iPod Phenomenon could have Halo Effect on Apple's Mac Products," *San Francisco Chronicle*, December 5, 2004, downloaded from http://www.sfgate.com, accessed on 4/7/06; Robert Paul Leitao, "Welcome," *ATPM*, February 2005, downloaded from http://www.atmp.com, accessed on 4/5/06; Reuters, "Apple Profit Nearly Doubles but Forecast Disappoints," *USA Today*, January 18, 2006, downloaded from http://www.usatoday.com, accessed on 4/7/06; Pui-Wing Tam, "Value Investors Go Apple (Computer) Picking," *Wall Street Journal*, March 29, 2001, p. C1; Chris Ward, "The Apple Crumble that was saved by Dr. Amelio's Recipe," *The Times*, July 31, 1996, downloaded from http://global.factiva.com, accessed on 12/6/05; Joel West, "Apple Computer: The iCEO Seizes the Internet," Center for Research on Information Technology and Organizations, Paper 348, 2002, downloaded from http://repositories.cdlib.org, accessed on 12/6/05; http://www.apple.com/investor, accessed on 4/7/06; http://www.hoovers.com, accessed on 2/6/06.

SCORING GUIDELINES

After you answer the questions in each of the fun self-tests that appear in the "Prologue: A Guide to Your Future Success," determine your score and evaluate your skills using the following scoring guidelines.

Exhibit P.1 Fun Self-Test: Can You Persuade Others?

For questions 1, 2, 4, 8, 10 and 11, use the following to calculate your score:

Strongly Agree	Agree	Neither Agree nor Disagree	Disagree	Strongly Disagree
2 points	1 point	0 points	0 points	0 points

For questions 3, 5, 6, 7, and 9 use the following to calculate your score:

Strongly Agree	Agree	Neither Agree nor Disagree	Disagree	Strongly Disagree
0 points	0 points	0 points	4 points	5 points

If your score is between 40–55 you have an excellent ability to persuade others. A score between 30–39 means you have reasonably good persuasion skills. However, you may need to improve your listening and communicating skills. A score below 30 means that you should consider reading a book or taking a short course on "how to persuade others."

Exhibit P.2 Fun Self-Test: Are You Good at Office Politics?

For questions 1, 3, 4, 7, 8, 10, 12 and 13, give yourself 1 point if you said "true." For questions 2, 5, 6, 9 and 11, give yourself 1 point if you said "false." If your score is 9 or below, you may be good at managing your work, but you need to improve your political skills. Being political means getting along with others in order to move them toward accomplishing a specific goal. If your score is low, consider reviewing the tips offered in the Prologue on how to be an effective political player.

Exhibit P.4 Fun Self-Test: How Well Do You Manage Your Time?

For questions 2, 6, 8, 9, 11, 13, 14 and 15, use the following to calculate your score:

Strongly Disagree	Disagree	Neither Agree nor Disagree	Agree	Strongly Agree
0 points	0 points	0 points	4 points	5 points

For questions 1, 3, 4, 5, 7, 10 and 12, use the following to calculate your score:

Strongly Disagree	Disagree	Neither Agree nor Disagree	Agree	Strongly Agree
5 points	4 points	0 points	0 points	0 points

If your score is 60 or above, you have excellent time management skills. Congratulations—you use your time well! If your score is below 60, consider reading a book on time management, taking a course on time management, or investing in time management tools such as a weekly project planner. The Prologue has additional tips that may be useful in improving your time management skills.

Exhibit P.5 Fun Self-Test: Are You Good at Managing Money?

For questions 2, 3, 5, 6, 10 and 11, use the following to calculate your score:

Strongly Disagree	Disagree	Neither Agree nor Disagree	Agree	Strongly Agree
0 points	0 points	0 points	4 points	5 points

For questions 1, 4, 7, 8 and 9, use the following to calculate your score:

Strongly Disagree	Disagree	Neither Agree nor Disagree	Agree	Strongly Agree
5 points	4 points	0 points	0 points	0 points

If your score is 44 or higher, you are able to manage money while balancing your expenses and income. You will be ready to handle financial emergencies without turning to friends or relatives. If your score is 36–43, your savings habits may be inconsistent. To achieve better savings, control your expenses and avoid unnecessary purchases. If your score is 35 or below, you spend too much! Remember it's a lot more painful to earn money than to spend it. You need to gain control of your finances by limiting your spending, paying off credit cards, or investing in a good personal finance book or course. You may also need to meet with a financial advisor to seek direction on your spending and saving habits.

Exhibit P.6 Fun Self-Test: Do You Have Good Study Habits?

If you answered "yes" to questions 3, 5, 7, 8 and 11, give yourself 1 point for each correct answer.

If you answered "no" to questions 1, 2, 4, 6, 9, 10 and 12, give yourself 1 point for each correct answer.

If your score is 10 or above, congratulations! You have good study habits. If your score is below 10, read the tips offered in the Prologue on improving your study skills. You may also meet with someone at your school to help maximize your study time.

Exhibit P.7 Fun Self-Test: How Assertive Are You?

For questions 1, 3, 4, 7, 9 and 13, use the following to calculate your score:

Strongly Agree	Agree	Neither Agree nor Disagree	Disagree	Strongly Disagree
5 points	4 points	0 points	0 points	0 points

For questions 2, 5, 6, 8, 10, 11 and 12, use the following to calculate your score:

Strongly Agree	Agree	Neither Agree nor Disagree	Disagree	Strongly Disagree
0 points	0 points	0 points	4 points	5 points

If your score is 44 or higher, you stand up for your rights while showing respect for others. You quickly respond to unfair criticism. You should be able to fair well in office politics. If your score is 43 or lower, you may want to consider ways to become more comfortable communicating your ideas and opinions and managing your relationships with others.

Exhibit P.8 Fun Self-Test: Are You A Good Listener?

For questions 3, 4, 8 and 9, use the following to calculate your score:

Strongly Agree	Agree	Neither Agree nor Disagree	Disagree	Strongly Disagree
5 points	4 points	0 points	0 points	0 points

For questions 1, 2, 5, 6, 7 and 10, use the following to calculate your score:

Strongly Agree	Agree	Neither Agree nor Disagree	Disagree	Strongly Disagree
0 points	0 points	0 points	4 points	5 points

Listening is an important communication skill that will help you succeed in your career. By becoming an effective listener, you gain respect from your colleagues, pick up insights and ideas on improving your job performance, and develop a skill that is important in managing others. If you have a score of 32 or above, then you are a good listener. If your score falls below 32, you need to improve your listening skills. Search the Web for articles and ideas on becoming a better listener and begin practicing your new skills with your friends and coworkers.

GLOSSARY

A

absolute advantage The situation when a country can produce and sell a product at a lower cost than any other country or when it is the only country that can provide the product.

accounting The process of collecting, recording, classifying, summarizing, reporting, and analyzing financial activities.

accounts payable Purchase for which a buyer has not yet paid the seller.

accounts receivable Sales for which a firm has not yet been paid.

acid-test (quick) ratio The ratio of total current assets excluding inventory to total current liabilities; used to measure a firm's liquidity.

acquisition The purchase of a target company by another corporation or by an investor group typically negotiated with the target company board of directors.

activity ratios Ratios that measure how well a firm uses its assets.

administrative law The rules, regulations, and orders passed by boards, commissions, and agencies of government (local, state, and federal).

advertising Any paid form of nonpersonal presentation by an identified sponsor.

advertising agencies Companies that help create ads and place them in the proper media.

advertising appeal An advertising appeal identifies a reason to buy a product or service.

advertising campaign A series of related advertisements focusing on a common them, slogan, and set of advertising appeals.

advertising media The channels through which advertising is carried to prospective customers; includes newspapers, magazines, radio, television, outdoor advertising, direct mail, and the Internet.

advocacy advertising Advertising that takes a stand on a social or economic issue; also called grassroots lobbying.

affirmative action programs Programs established by organizations to expand job opportunities for women and minorities.

agency shop Workers don't have to join a union but must pay union dues.

agents Sales representatives of manufacturers and wholesalers.

angel investors Individual investors or groups of experienced investors who provide financing for start-up businesses by investing their own funds.

annual report A yearly document that describes a firm's financial status and usually discusses the firm's activities during the past year and its prospects for the future.

antitrust regulation Laws that prevent companies from entering into agreements to control trade through a monopoly.

appellate courts (courts of appeals) The level of courts above the trial courts; the losing party in a civil case and the defendant in a criminal case may appeal the trial court's decision to an appellate court.

application service providers (ASPs) A service company that buys and maintains software on its servers and distributes it through high-speed networks to subscribers, for a set period and price.

apprenticeship A form of on-the-job training that combines specific job instruction with classroom instruction.

arbitration A method of settling disputes in which the parties agree to present their case to an impartial third party and are required to accept the arbitrator's decision.

assembly process A production process in which the basic inputs are either combined to create the output or transformed into the output.

assets Things of value owned by a firm.

attitude Learned tendency to respond consistently toward a given object, idea, or concept.

audience selectivity An advertising medium's ability to reach a precisely defined market.

auditing The process of reviewing the records used to prepare financial statements and issuing a formal auditor's opinion indicating whether the statements have been prepared in accordance with accepted accounting rules.

authority Legitimate power, granted by the organization and acknowledged by employees, that allows an individual to request action and expect compliance.

autocratic leaders Directive leaders who prefer to make decisions and solve problems on their own with little input from subordinates.

B

Baby Boomers Americans born between 1946 and 1964.

balance of payments A summary of a country's international financial transactions showing the difference between the country's total payments to and its total receipts from other countries.

balance of trade The difference between the value of a country's exports and the value of its imports during a specific time.

balance sheet A financial statement that summarizes a firm's financial position at a specific point in time.

bank charter An operating license issued to a bank by the federal government or a state government; required for a commercial bank to do business.

bankruptcy The legal procedure by which individuals or businesses that cannot meet their financial obligations are relieved of their debt.

barriers to entry Factors, such as technological or legal conditions, that prevent new firms from competing equally with an existing firm.

batch processing A method of updating a database in which data are collected over some time period and processed together.

bear markets Markets in which securities prices are falling.

behavioral targeting Targeting individuals based on their click stream.

belief An organized pattern of knowledge that an individual holds as true about the world.

benefit segmentation The differentiation of markets based on what a product will do rather than on customer characteristics.

bill of material A list of the items and the number of each required to make a given product.

board of directors A group of people elected by the stockholders to handle the overall management of a corporation, such as setting major corporate goals and policies, hiring corporate officers, and overseeing the firm's operations and finances.

bond ratings Letter grades assigned to bond issues to indicate their quality, or level of risk; assigned by rating agencies such as Moody's and Standard & Poor's (S&P).

bonds Long-term debt obligations (liabilities) issued by corporations and governments.

brainstorming A method of generating ideas in which group members suggest as many possibilities as they can without criticizing or evaluating any of the suggestions.

brand A company's product identifier that distinguishes the company's products from those of its competitors.

brand equity The value of company and brand names.

brand loyalty A consumer's preference for a particular brand.

breach of contract The failure by one party to a contract to fulfill the terms of the agreement without a legal excuse.

breakeven point The price at which a product's costs are covered, so additional sales result in profit.

breaking bulk The process of breaking large shipments of similar products into smaller, more usable lots.

broker markets National and regional securities exchanges on whose premises securities trading takes place.

brokers Go-betweens that bring buyers and sellers together.

budgets Formal written forecasts of revenues and expenses that set spending limits based on operational forecasts; include cash budgets, capital budgets, and operating budgets.

bull markets Markets in which securities prices are rising.

bundling The strategy of grouping two or more related products together and pricing them as a single product.

business An organization that strives for a profit by providing goods and services desired by its customers.

business cycles Upward and downward changes in the level of economic activity.

business interruption insurance Covers such costs as rental of temporary facilities, wage and salary payments to employees, payments for leased equipment, fixed payments, and profits that would have been earned during that period.

business law The body of law that governs commercial dealings.

business plan A formal written statement that describes in detail the idea for a new business and how it will be carried out; includes a general description of the company, the qualifications of the owner(s), a description of the product or service, an analysis of the market, and a financial plan.

Business Process Management (BPM) A unified system that has the power to integrate and optimize a company's sprawling functions by automating much of what it does.

buyer behavior The actions people take in buying and using goods and services.

buyer cooperative A group of cooperative members who unite for combined purchasing power.

buy-national regulations Government rules that give special privileges to domestic manufacturers and retailers.

C

C corporation Conventional or basic form of corporate organization.

CAD/CAM systems Linked computer systems that combine the advantages of computer-aided design and computer-aided manufacturing. The system helps design the product, control the flow of resources, and operate the production process.

capital The inputs, such as tools, machinery, equipment, and buildings, used to produce goods and services and get them to the customer.

capital budgeting The process of analyzing long-term projects and selecting those that offer the best returns while maximizing the firm's value.

capital budgets Budgets that forecast a firm's outlays for fixed assets (plant and equipment), typically covering a period.

capital expenditures Investments in long-lived assets, such as land, buildings, machinery, and equipment, that are expected to provide benefits that extend beyond one year.

capital products Large, expensive items with a long life span that are purchased by businesses for use in making other products or providing a service.

capitalism An economic system based on competition in the marketplace and private ownership of the factors of production (resources); also known as the private enterprise system.

cash and carry wholesaler A limited-service merchant wholesaler that does not offer credit or delivery services.

cash budgets Budgets that forecast a firm's cash inflows and outflows and help the firm plan for cash surpluses and shortages.

cash flows The inflows and outflows of cash for a firm.

cash management The process of making sure that a firm has enough cash on hand to pay bills as they come due and to meet unexpected expenses.

category management Suppliers manage the inventory of a category of products for a retailer.

cellular manufacturing Production technique that uses small, self-contained production units, each performing all or most of the tasks necessary to completea manufacturing order.

centralization The degree to which formal authority is concentrated in one area or level of an organization. Top management makes most of the decisions.

certified management accountant (CMA) A managerial accountant who has completed a professional certification program, including passing an examination.

certified public accountant (CPA) An accountant who has completed an approved bachelor's degree program, passed a test prepared by the American Institute of Certified Public Accountants, and met state requirements. Only a CPA can issue an auditor's opinion on a firm's financial statements.

chain of command The line of authority that extends from one level of an organization's hierarchy to the next, from top to bottom, and makes clear who reports to whom.

chief information officer (CIO) An executive with responsibility for managing all information resources in an organization.

circuit breakers Measures that, under certain conditions, stop trading in the securities markets for a short cooling-off period to limit the amount the market can drop in one day.

circular flow The movement of inputs and outputs among households, businesses, and governments; a way of showing how the sectors of the economy interact.

cobranding Placing two or more brand names on a product or its package.

code of ethics A set of guidelines prepared by a firm to provide its employees with the knowledge of what the firm expects in terms of their responsibilities and behavior toward fellow employees, customers, and suppliers.

coercive power Power that is derived from an individual's ability to threaten negative outcomes.

coinsurance Property insurance coverage that is equal to a certain percentage of the property's value.

collective bargaining Negotiating a labor agreement.

commercial banks Profit-oriented financial institutions that accept deposits, make business and consumer loans, invest in government and corporate securities, and provide other financial services.

commercial paper Unsecured short-term debt—an IOU—issued by a financially strong corporation.

committee structure An organizational structure in which authority and responsibility are held by a group rather than an individual.

common law The body of unwritten law that has evolved out of judicial (court) decisions rather than being enacted by a legislature; also called case law.

common stock A security that represents an ownership interest in a corporation.

communism An economic system characterized by government ownership of virtually all resources, government control of all markets, and economic decision making by central-government planning.

comparative advertising Advertising that comparesthe company's product with competing, named products.

competitive advantage A set of unique features of a company and its products that are perceived by the target market as significant and superior to those of the competition; also called differential advantage.

component lifestyle A lifestyle made up of a complex set of interests, needs, and choices.

computer network A group of two or more computer systems linked together by communications channels to share data and information.

computer virus A computer program that copies itself into other software and can spread to other computer systems.

computer-aided design (CAD) The use of computers to design and test new products and modify existing ones.

computer-aided manufacturing (CAM) The use of computers to develop and control the production process.

computer-integrated manufacturing (CIM) The combination of computerized manufacturing processes (like robots and flexible manufacturing systems) with other computerized systems that control design, inventory, production, and purchasing.

conceptual skills A manager's ability to view the organization as a whole, understand how the various parts are interdependent, and assess how the organization relates to its external environment.

conciliation Specialist in labor-management negotiations that acts as a go-between for management and the unions and helps focus on the problems.

conglomerate merger A merger of companies in unrelated businesses; done to reduce risk.

consensual leaders Leaders who encourage discussion about issues and then require that all parties involved agree to the final decision.

consultative leaders Leaders who confer with subordinates before making a decision, but who retain the final decision-making authority.

consumer price index (CPI) An index of the prices of a "marketbasket" of goods and services purchased by typical urban consumers.

consumerism A social movement that seeks to increase the rights and powers of buyers vis-à-vis sellers.

contingency plans Plans that identify alternative courses of action for very unusual or crisis situations; typically stipulate the chain of command, standard operating procedures, and communication channels the organization will use during an emergency.

contingent worker Person who prefers temporary employment, either part-time or full-time.

continuous improvement A commitment to constantly seek better ways of doing things in order to achieve greater efficiency and improve quality.

continuous process A production process that uses long production runs lasting days, weeks, or months without equipment shutdowns; generally used for high-volume, low-variety products with standardized parts.

contract An agreement that sets forth the relationship between parties regarding the performance of a specified action; creates a legal obligation and is enforceable in a court of law.

contract manufacturing The practice in which a foreign firm manufactures private-label goods under a domestic firm's brand name.

contractionary policy The use of monetary policy by the Fed to tighten the money supply by selling government securities or raising interest rates.

controlling The process of assessing the organization's progress toward accomplishing its goals; includes monitoring the implementation of a plan and correcting deviations from the plan.

convenience products Relatively inexpensive items that require little shopping effort and are purchased routinely without planning.

convertible bonds Corporate bonds that are issued with an option that allows the bondholder to convert them into common stock.

cooperatives A legal entity typically formed by people with similar interests, such as suppliers or customers, to reduce costs and gain economic power. A cooperative has limited liability, an unlimited life span, an elected board of directors, and an administrative staff; all profits are distributed to the member-owners in proportion to their contributions.

copyright A form of protection established by the government for creators of works of art, music, literature, or other intellectual property; gives the creator the exclusive right to use, produce, and sell the creation during the lifetime of the creator and for 50 years thereafter.

corporate culture The set of attitudes, values, and standards that distinguishes one organization from another.

corporate philanthropy The practice of charitable giving by corporations; includes contributing cash, donating equipment and products, and supporting the volunteer efforts of company employees.

corporation A legal entity with an existence and life separate from its owners, who are not personally liable for the entity's debts. A corporation is chartered by the state in which it is formed and can own property, enter into contracts, sue and be sued, and engage in business operations under the terms of its charter.

cost competitive advantage A firm's ability to produce a product or service at a lower cost than all other competitors in an industry while maintaining satisfactory profit margins.

cost of goods sold The total expense of buying or producing a firm's goods or services.

cost per thousand (CPM) Cost per thousand contacts is a term used in expressing advertising costs; refers to the cost of reaching 1,000 members of the target market.

cost-push inflation Inflation that occurs when increases in production costs push up the prices of final goods and services.

costs Expenses incurred in creating and selling goods and services.

countertrade A form of international trade in which part or all of the payment for goods or services is in the form of other goods and services.

credit unions Not-for-profit, member-owned financial co-operatives.

critical path method (CPM) A scheduling tool that enables a manager to determine the critical path of activities for a project-the activities that will cause the entire project to fall behind schedule if they are not completed on time.

critical path In a critical path method network, the longest path through the linked activities.

cross-functional team Members from the same organizational level but from different functional areas.

crowding out The situation that occurs when government spending replaces spending by the private sector.

culture The set of values, ideas, attitudes, and other symbols created to shape human behavior.

current assets Assets that can or will be converted to cash within the next 12 months.

current liabilities Short-term claims that are due within a year of the date of the balance sheet.

current ratio The ratio of total current assets to total current liabilities; used to measure a firm's liquidity.

customer departmentalization Departmentalization that is based on the primary type of customer served by the organizational unit.

customer satisfaction The customer's feeling that a product has met or exceeded expectations.

customer value The ratio of benefits to the sacrifice necessary to obtain those benefits, as determined by the customer; reflects the willingness of customers to actually buy a product.

customization The production of goods or services one at a time according to the specific needs or wants of individual customers.

cyclical unemployment Unemployment that occurs when a downturn in the business cycle reduces the demand for labor throughout the economy.

D

data mart Special subset of a data warehouse that deals with a single area of data and is organized for quick analysis.

data mining Sophisticated database applications that look for hidden patterns in a group of data to help track and predict future behavior.

data warehouse An information technology that combines many databases across a whole company into one central database that supports management decision making.

database An electronic filing system that collects and organizes data and information.

dealer brands Brands that are owned by the wholesaler or retailer rather than the name of the manufacturer.

dealer markets Securities markets where buy and sell orders are executed through dealers, or "market makers" linked by telecommunications networks.

debentures Unsecured bonds that are backed only by the reputation of the issuer and its promise to pay the principal and interest when due.

debt A form of business financing consisting of borrowed funds that must be repaid with interest over a stated time period.

debt ratios Ratios that measure the degree and effect of a firm's use of borrowed funds (debt) to finance its operations.

debt-to-equity ratio The ratio of total liabilities to owners' equity; measures the relationship between the amount of debt financing following and the amount of equity financing (owner's funds).

decentralization The process of pushing decision-making authority down the organizational hierarchy.

decision support system (DSS) A management support system that helps managers make decisions using interactive computer models that describe real-world processes.

decisional roles A manager's activities as an entrepreneur, resource allocator, conflict resolver, or negotiator.

deductibles The amounts that the insured must pay before insurance benefits begin.

delegation of authority The assignment of some degree of authority and responsibility to persons lower in the chain of command.

demand The quantity of a good or service that people are willing to buy at various prices.

demand curve A graph showing the quantity of a good or service that people are willing to buy at various prices.

demand deposits Money kept in checking accounts that can be withdrawn by depositors on demand.

demand-pull inflation Inflation that occurs when the demand for goods and services is greater than the supply.

democratic leaders Leaders who solicit input from all members of the group and then allow the members to make the final decision through a vote.

demographic segmentation The differentiation of markets through the use of categories such as age, education, gender, income, and household size.

demography The study of people's vital statistics, such as their age, gender, race and ethnicity, and location.

deontology A person who will follow his or her obligations to an individual or society because upholding one's duty is what is ethically correct.

departmentalization The process of grouping jobs together so that similar or associated tasks and activities can be coordinated.

depreciation The allocation of an asset's original cost to the years in which it is expected to produce revenues.

deregulation The removal of rules and regulations governing business competition.

detailing The physical stocking of merchandise at a retailer by the salesperson who delivers the merchandise.

devaluation A lowering of the value of a nation's currency relative to other currencies.

differential competitive advantage A firm's ability to provide a unique product or service with a set of features that the target market perceives as important and better than the competitor's.

direct foreign investment Active ownership of a foreign company or of manufacturing or marketing facilities in a foreign country.

discount rate The interest rate that the Federal Reserve charges its member banks.

distribution (logistics) Efficiently managing the acquisition of raw materials to the factory and the movement of products from the producer to industrial users and consumers.

distribution centers Warehouses that specialize in rapid movement of goods to retail stores by making and breaking bulk.

distribution channel The series of marketing entities through which goods and services pass on their way from producers to end users.

distribution strategy Creating the means by which products flow from the producer to the consumer.

dividends Payments to stockholders from a corporation's profits.

division of labor The process of dividing work into separate jobs and assigning tasks to workers.

double-entry bookkeeping A method of accounting in which each transaction is recorded as two entries so that two accounts or records are changed.

Dow Jones Industrial Average (DJIA) The most widely used market average; measures the stock prices of 30 large, well-known corporations that trade on the NYSE and Nasdaq.

duel distribution (or **multiple distribution**) Two or more channels that distribute the same product to target markets.

dumping The practice of charging a lower price for a product in foreign markets than in the firm's home market.

E

earnings per share (EPS) The ratio of net profit to the number of shares of common stock outstanding; measures the number of dollars earned by each share of stock.

economic growth An increase in a nation's output of goods and services.

economic system The combination of policies, laws, and choices made by a nation's government to establish the systems that determine what goods and services are produced and how they are allocated.

economics The study of how a society uses scarce resources to produce and distribute goods and services.

effectiveness The ability to produce the desired result or good.

efficiency Using the least amount of resources to accomplish the organization's goals.

efficient consumer response (ECR) A method of managing inventory and streamlining the movement of products from supplier to distributor to retailer; relies on electronic data interchange to communicate information such as automatic shipping notifications, invoices, inventory data, and forecasts.

electronic communications networks (ECNs) Electronic trading networks that allow institutional traders and some individuals to make securities transactions directly.

electronic data interchange (EDI) Computer-to-computer exchange of information, including automatic shipping notifications, invoices, inventory data, and forecasts; used in efficient consumer response systems.

embargo A total ban on imports or exports of a product.

empowerment The process of giving employees increased autonomy and discretion to make decisions, as well as control over the resources needed to implement those decisions.

enterprise portal A customizable internal Website that provides proprietary corporate information to a defined user group, such as employees, supply chain partners, or customers.

enterprise resource planning (ERP) A computerized resource-planning system that incorporates information about the firm's suppliers and customers with its internally generated data.

enterprise risk management (ERM) A company-wide, strategic approach to identifying, monitoring, and managing all elements of a company's risk.

entrepreneurs People who combine the inputs of natural resources, labor, and capital to produce goods or services with the intention of making a profit or accomplishing a not-for-profit goal.

environmental scanning The process in which a firm continually collects and evaluates information about its external environment.

e-procurement The process of purchasing supplies and materials online using the Internet.

Equal Employment Opportunity Commission (EEOC) Processes discrimination complaints, issues regulations regarding discrimination, and disseminates information.

equilibrium The point at which quantity demanded equals quantity supplied.

equity A form of business financing consisting of funds raised through the sale of stock (i.e., ownership) in a business.

equity theory A theory of motivation that holds that worker satisfaction is influenced by employees' perceptions about how fairly they are treated compared with their coworkers.

ethical issue A situation where a person must choose from a set of actions that may be ethical or unethical.

ethics A set of moral standards for judging whether something is right or wrong.

European integration The delegation of limited sovereignty by European Union member states to the EU so that common laws and policies can be created at the European level.

European Union Trade agreement among 25 European nations.

exchange The process in which two parties give something of value to each other to satisfy their respective needs.

exchange controls Laws that require a company earning foreign exchange (foreign currency) from its exports to sell the foreign exchange to a control agency, such as a central bank.

exchange-traded fund (ETF) A basket of stocks in a category, such as industry sector, investment objective, or geographical area, or that track an index. ETFs are similar to mutual funds but trade like stocks.

excise taxes Taxes that are imposed on specific items such as gasoline, alcoholic beverages, airline tickets, and guns.

exclusive distribution A distribution system in which a manufacturer selects only one or two dealers in an area to market its products.

executive information system (EIS) A management support system that is customized for an individual executive; provides specific information for strategic decisions.

expansionary policy The use of monetary policy by the Fed to increase the growth of the money supply.

expectancy theory A theory of motivation that holds that the probability of an individual acting in a particular way depends on the strength of that individual's belief that the act will have a particular outcome and on whether the individual values that outcome.

expense items Items, purchased by businesses, that are smaller and less expensive than capital products and usually have a life span of less than one year.

expenses The costs of generating revenues.

experiment A marketing research method in which the investigator changes one or more variables—price, packaging, design, shelf space, advertising theme, or advertising expenditures—while observing the effects of these changes on another variable (usually sales).

expert power Power that is derived from an individual's extensive knowledge in one or more areas.

expert system A management support system that gives managers advice similar to what they would get from a human consultant; it uses artificial intelligence to enable computers to reason and learn to solve problems in much the same way humans do.

exporting The practice of selling domestically produced goods to buyers in another country.

exports Goods and services produced in one country and sold by other countries.

express warranty A written guarantee about a product, such as that it contains certain materials, will perform a certain way, or is otherwise fit for the purpose for which it was sold.

extensive decision making Purchasing an unfamiliar, expensive, infrequently bought item.

F

factoring A form of short-term financing in which a firm sells its accounts receivable outright at a discount to a factor.

factors of production The resources used to create goods and services.

federal budget deficit The condition that occurs when the federal government spends more for programs than it collects in taxes.

Federal Deposit Insurance Corporation (FDIC) An independent, quasi-public corporation backed by the full faith and credit of the U.S. government that insures deposits in commercial banks and thrift institutions for up to a ceiling of $100,000 per account.

Federal Reserve System (the Fed) The central bank of the United States; it consists of 12 district banks, each located in a major U.S. city.

federation A collection of unions banned together to achieve common goals.

financial accounting Accounting that focuses on preparing external financial reports that are used by outsiders such as lenders, suppliers, investors, and government agencies to assess the financial strength of a business.

Financial Accounting Standards Board (FASB) The private organization that is responsible for establishing financial accounting standards in the United States.

financial intermediation The process in which financial institutions act as intermediaries between the suppliers and demanders of funds.

financial management The art and science of managing a firm's money so that it can meet its goals.

financial risk The chance that a firm will be unable to make scheduled interest and principal payments on its debt.

fiscal policy The government's use of taxation and spending to affect the economy.

fixed assets Long-term assets used by a firm for more than a year such as land, buildings, and machinery.

fixed costs Costs that do not vary with different levels of output; for example, rent.

fixed-cost contribution The selling price per unit (revenue) minus the variable costs per unit.

fixed-position layout A facility arrangement in which the product stays in one place and workers and machinery move to it as needed.

flexible manufacturing system (FMS) A system that combines automated workstations with computer-controlled transportation devices—automatic guided vehicles (AGVs)—that move materials between workstations and into and out of the system.

floating exchange rates A system in which prices of currencies move up and down based upon the demand for and supply of the various currencies.

focus group A group of 8 to 12 participants led by a moderator in an in-depth discussion on one particular topic or concept.

formal organization The order and design of relationships within a firm; consists of two or more people working together with a common objective and clarity of purpose.

four Ps Product, price, promotion, and place (distribution), which together make up the marketing mix.

franchise agreement A contract setting out the terms of a franchising arrangement, including the rules for running the franchise, the services provided by the franchisor, and the financial terms. Under the contract, the franchisee is allowed to use the franchisor's business name, trademark, and logo.

franchisee In a franchising arrangement, the individual or company that sells the goods or services of the franchisor in a certain geographic area.

franchising A form of business organization based on a business arrangement between a franchisor, which supplies the product or service concept, and the franchisee, who sells the goods or services of the franchisor in a certain geographic area.

franchisor In a franchising arrangement, the company that supplies the product or service concept to the franchisee.

free trade The policy of permitting the people and businesses of a country to buy and sell where they please without restrictions.

free-rein (laissez-faire) leadership A leadership style in which the leader turns over all authority and control to subordinates.

free-trade zone An area where the nations allow free, or almost free, trade among each other while imposing tariffs on goods of nations outside the zone.

frequency The number of times an individual is exposed to an advertising message.

frictional unemployment Short-term unemployment that is not related to the business cycle.

full employment The condition when all people who want to work and can work have jobs.

full warranty The manufacturer's guarantee to meet certain minimum standards, including repair or replacement of the product or refunding to the customer if the product does not work.

full-service merchant wholesalers Wholesalers that provide many services for their clients, such as providing credit, offering promotional and technical advice, storing and delivering merchandise, or providing installation and repairs.

functional departmentalization Departmentalization that is based on the primary functions performed within an organizational unit.

futures contracts Legally binding obligations to buy or sell specified quantities of commodities or financial instruments at an agreed-on price at a future date.

G

Gantt charts Bar graphs plotted on a time line that show the relationship between scheduled and actual production.

general partnership A partnership in which all partners share in the management and profits. Each partner can act on behalf of the firm and has unlimited liability for all its business obligations.

general partners Partners who have unlimited liability for all of the firm's business obligations and who control its operations.

generally accepted accounting principles (GAAP) The financial accounting standards followed by accountants in the United States when preparing financial statements.

Generation X Americans born between 1964 and 1977.

Generation Y Americans born between about 1977 and 1997.

generic products Products that carry no brand name, come in plain containers, and sell for much less than brand-name products.

geographic departmentalization Departmentalization that is based on the geographic segmentation of the organizational units.

geographic segmentation The differentiation of markets by region of the country, city or county size, market density, or climate.

global management skills A manager's ability to operate in diverse cultural environments.

global vision The ability to recognize and react to international business opportunities, be aware of threats from foreign competition, and effectively use international distribution networks to obtain raw materials and move finished products to customers.

goal-setting theory A theory of motivation based on the premise that an individual's intention to work toward a goal is a primary source of motivation.

goods Tangible items manufactured by businesses.

grievance A formal complaint by a union worker that management has violated the contract.

gross domestic product (GDP) The total market value of all final goods and services produced within a nation's borders in a year.

gross profit The amount a company earns after paying to produce or buy its products but before deducting operating expenses.

gross sales The total dollar amount of a company's sales.

group cohesiveness The degree to which group members want to stay in the group and tend to resist outside influences.

H

Hawthorne effect The phenomenon that employees perform better when they feel singled out for attention or feel that management is concerned about their welfare.

high-yield (junk) bonds High-risk, high-return bonds.

horizontal merger A merger of companies at the same stage in the same industry; done to reduce costs, expand product offerings, or reduce competition.

human relations skills A manager's interpersonal skills that are used to accomplish goals through the use of human resources.

human resource (HR) management The process of hiring, developing, motivating, and evaluating employees to achieve organizational goals.

human resource planning Creating a strategy for meeting current and future human resource needs.

hygiene factors Extrinsic elements of the work environment that do not serve as a source of employee satisfaction or motivation.

I

ideal self-image The way an individual would like to be.

implied warranty An unwritten guarantee that a product is fit for the purpose for which it is sold.

import quota A limit on the quantity of a certain good that can be imported.

imports Goods and services that are bought from other countries.

incentive pay Additional pay for attaining a specific goal.

income statement A financial statement that summarizes a firm's revenues and expenses and shows its total profit or loss over a period of time.

income taxes Taxes that are based on the income received by businesses and individuals.

industrial distributors Independent wholesalers that buy related product lines from many manufacturers and sell them to industrial users.

inflation The situation in which the average of all prices of goods and services is rising.

informal organization The network of connections and channels of communication based on the informal relationships of individuals inside an organization.

information technology (IT) The equipment and techniques used to manage and process information.

informational labeling A type of product label that provides product information to aid consumers in making product selections and minimize cognitive dissonance after the purchase.

informational roles A manager's activities as an information gatherer, an information disseminator, or a spokesperson for the company.

infrastructure The basic institutions and public facilities upon which an economy's development depends.

insider trading The use of information that is not available to the general public to make profits on securities transactions.

institutional advertising Advertising that creates a positive picture of a company and its ideals, services, and roles in the community.

institutional investors Investment professionals who are paid to manage other people's money.

insurable interest An insurance applicant's change of loss if a particular peril occurs.

insurable risk A risk that an insurance company will cover. It must meet certain criteria.

insurance The promise of compensation for certain financial losses.

insurance policy A written agreement that defines what the insurance covers and the risks that the insurance company will bear for the insured party.

intangible assets Long-term assets with no physical existence, such as patents, copyrights, trademarks, and goodwill.

integrated marketing communications (IMC) The careful coordination of all promotional activities—media advertising, sales promotion, personal selling, and public relations, as well as direct marketing, packaging, and other forms of promotion—to produce a consistent, unified message that is customer focused.

intensive distribution A distribution system in which a manufacturer tries to sell its products wherever there are potential customers.

interest A fixed amount of money paid by the issuer of a bond to the bondholder on a regular schedule, typically every six months; stated as the coupon rate.

intermittent process A production process that uses short production runs to make batches of different products; generally used for low-volume, high-variety products.

International Monetary Fund (IMF) An international organization, founded in 1945, that promotes trade, makes short-term loans to member nations, and acts as a lender of last resort for troubled nations.

interpersonal roles A manager's activities as a figurehead, company leader, or liaison.

intranet An internal corporate-wide area network that uses Internet technology to connect computers and link employees in many locations and with different types of computers.

intrapreneurs Entrepreneurs who apply their creativity, vision, and risk-taking within a large corporation, rather than starting a company of their own.

inventory control system A system that maintains an adequate assortment of items to meet a user or customer's needs.

inventory management The determination of how much of each type of inventory a firm will keep on hand and the ordering, receiving, storing, and tracking of inventory.

inventory turnover ratio The ratio of cost of goods sold to average inventory; measures the speed with which inventory moves through a firm and is turned into sales.

inventory The supply of goods that a firm holds for use in production or for sale to customers.

investment bankers Firms that act as intermediaries, buying securities from corporations and governments and reselling them to the public.

involvement The amount of time and effort a buyer invests in the search, evaluation, and decision processes of consumer behavior.

ISO 14000 A set of technical standards designed by the International Organization for Standardization to promote clean production processes to protect the environment.

ISO 9000 A set of five technical standards of quality management created by the International Organization for Standardization to provide a uniform way of determining whether manufacturing plants and service organizations conform to sound quality procedures.

job enlargement The horizontal expansion of a job by increasing the number and variety of tasks that a person performs.

job enrichment The vertical expansion of a job by increasing the employee's autonomy, responsibility, and decision-making authority.

job fair An event, typically one day, held at a convention center to bring together job seekers and firms searching for employees.

job rotation Reassignment of workers to several different jobs over time so that they can learn the basics of each job.

job sharing A scheduling option that allows two individuals to split the tasks, responsibilities, and work hours of one 40-hour-per-week job.

job shop A manufacturing firm that produces goods in response to customer orders.

job specification A list of the skills, knowledge, and abilities a person must have to fill a job.

joint venture Two or more companies that form an alliance to pursue a specific project usually for a specified time period.

judiciary The branch of government that is responsible for settling disputes by applying and interpreting points of law; consists of the court system.

justice What is considered fair according to the prevailing standards of society; an equitable distribution of the burdens and rewards that society has to offer.

just-in-time (JIT) A system in which materials arrive exactly when they are needed for production, rather than being stored on site.

K

key-person life insurance A term insurance policy that names the company as beneficiary.

knowledge The combined talents and skills of the workforce.

knowledge management (KM) The process of researching, gathering, organizing, and sharing an organization's collective knowledge to improve productivity, foster innovation, and gain competitive advantage.

knowledge worker A worker who develops or uses knowledge, contributing to and benefiting from information used in performing planning, acquiring, searching, analyzing, organizing, storing, programming, producing, distributing, marketing, or selling functions.

J

job analysis A study of the tasks required to do a particular job well.

job description The tasks and responsibilities of a job.

L

labor Economic contributions of people.

labor union An organization that represents workers in dealing with management.

law of large numbers Insurance companies' predictions of the likelihood that a peril will occur in order to calculate premiums.

laws The rules of conduct in a society, created and enforced by a controlling authority, usually the government.

leader pricing The strategy of pricing products below the normal markup or even below cost to attract customers to a store where they would not otherwise shop.

leadership The process of guiding and motivating others toward the achievement of organizational goals.

leadership style The relatively consistent way that individuals in leadership positions attempt to influence the behavior of others.

lean manufacturing Streamlining production by eliminating steps in the production process that do not add benefits that customers are willing to pay for.

legitimate power Power that is derived from an individual's position in an organization.

leveraged buyout (LBO) A corporate takeover financed by large amounts of borrowed money; can be started by outside investors or the corporation's management.

liabilities What a firm owes to its creditors; also called *debts*.

licensing The legal process whereby a firm agrees to allow another firm to use a manufacturing process, trademark, patent, trade secret, or other proprietary knowledge in exchange for the payment of a royalty.

limited decision making Consumer has previous product experience but is unfamiliar with the current brands available.

limited liability company (LLC) A hybrid organization that offers the same liability protection as a corporation but may be taxed as either a partnership or a corporation.

limited partnership A partnership with one or more general partners who have unlimited liability, and one or more limited partners whose liability is limited to the amount of their investment in the company.

limited partners Partners whose liability for the firm's business obligations is limited to the amount of their investment. They help to finance the business, but do not participate in the firm's operations.

limited-service merchant wholesalers Wholesalers that typically carry a limited line of fast-moving merchandise and do not offer many services to their clients.

line extension A new flavor, size, or model using an existing brand name in an existing category.

line of credit An agreement between a bank and a business that specifies the maximum amount of unsecured short-term borrowing the bank will make available to the firm over a given period, typically one year.

line organization An organizational structure with direct, clear lines of authority and communication flowing from the top managers downward.

line positions All positions in the organization directly concerned with producing goods and services and that are directly connected from top to bottom.

line-and-staff organization An organizational structure that includes both line and staff positions.

liquidity ratios Ratios that measure a firm's ability to pay its short-term debts as they come due.

liquidity The speed with which an asset can be converted to cash.

local area network (LAN) A network that connects computers at one site, enabling the computer users to exchange data and share the use of hardware and software from a variety of computer manufacturers.

local union Branch of a national union that represents workers in a specific plant or geographic area.

long-term forecasts Projections of a firm's activities and the funding for those activities over a period that is longer than 1 year, typically 2 to 10 years.

long-term liabilities Claims that come due more than one year after the date of the balance sheet.

loss leader A product priced below cost as part of a leader pricing strategy.

loyalty cards Cards issued by a manufacturer, service organization, or retailer that give discounts to loyal and frequent shoppers.

M

M1 The total amount of readily available money in the system, that includes currency and demand deposits.

M2 A term used by economists to describe the U.S. monetary supply. Includes all M1 monies plus time deposits and other money that are not immediately accessible.

macroeconomics The subarea of economics that focuses on the economy as a whole by looking at aggregate data for large groups of people, companies, or products.

make-or-buy decision The determination by a firm of whether to make its own production materials or buy them from outside sources.

Malcolm Baldrige National Quality Award An award given to recognize U.S. companies that offer goods and services of world-class quality; established by Congress in 1987 and named for a former secretary of commerce.

managed service providers (MSPs) Next generation of ASPs, offering customization and expanded capabilities such as business processes and complete management of the network servers.

management The process of guiding the development, maintenance, and allocation of resources to attain organizational goals.

management information system (MIS) The methods and equipment that provide information about all aspects of a firm's operations.

management rights clause Clause in a labor agreement that gives management the right to manage the business except as specified in the contract.

management support system (MSS) An information system that uses the internal master database to perform high-level analyses that help managers make better decisions.

managerial accounting Accounting that provides financial information that managers inside the organization can use to evaluate and make decisions about current and future operations.

managerial hierarchy The levels of management within an organization; typically, includes top, middle, and supervisory management.

manufacturer A producer; an organization that converts raw materials to finished products.

manufacturer brands Brands that are owned by national or regional manufacturers and widely distributed; also called national brands.

manufacturers' representatives Salespeople who represent noncompeting manufacturers; function as independent agents rather than as salaried employees of the manufacturers.

manufacturing resource planning II (MRPII) A complex computerized system that integrates data from many departments to allow managers to better forecast and assess the impact of production plans on profitability.

market averages Summarize the price behavior of securities based on the arithmetic average price of groups of securities at a given point in time; used to monitor general market conditions.

market indexes Measures of the current price behavior of groups of securities relative to a base value set at an earlier point in time; used to monitor general market conditions.

market segmentation The process of separating, identifying, and evaluating the layers of a market in order to identify a target market.

market structure The number of suppliers in a market.

marketable securities Short-term investments that are easily converted into cash.

marketing The process of discovering the needs and-wants of potential buyers and customers and then providing goods and services that meet or exceed their expectations.

marketing concept Identifying consumer needs and then producing the goods or services that will satisfy them while making a profit for the organization.

marketing database Computerized file of customers' and potential customers' profiles and purchase patterns.

marketing intermediaries Organizations that assist in moving goods and services from producers to end users.

marketing mix The blend of product offering, pricing, promotional methods, and distribution system that brings a specific group of consumers superior value.

marketing research The process of planning, collecting, and analyzing data relevant to a marketing decision.

markup pricing A method of pricing in which a certain percentage (the markup) is added to the product's cost to arrive at the price.

Maslow's hierarchy of needs A theory of motivation developed by Abraham Maslow; holds that humans have five levels of needs and act to satisfy their unmet needs. At the base of the hierarchy are fundamental physiological needs, followed in order by safety, social, esteem, and self-actualization needs.

mass customization A manufacturing process in which goods are mass-produced up to a point and then custom tailored to the needs or desires of individual customers.

mass production The ability to manufacture many identical goods at once.

master brand A brand so dominant that consumers think of it immediately when a product category, use, attribute, or customer benefit is mentioned.

materials requirement planning (MRP) A computerized system of controlling the flow of resources and inventory. A master schedule is used to ensure that the materials, labor, and equipment needed for production are at the right places in the right amounts at the right times.

matrix structure (project management) An organizational structure that combines functional and product departmentalization by bringing together people from different functional areas of the organization to work on a special project.

mechanistic organization An organizational structure that is characterized by a relatively high degree of job specialization, rigid departmentalization, many layers of management, narrow spans of control, centralized decision making, and a long chain of command.

mediation A method of settling disputes in which the parties submit their case to an impartial third party but are not required to accept the mediator's decision.

mediator Specialist that facilitates labor-management contract discussions and suggests compromises.

Medicare A health insurance program for those over 65.

mentoring A form of on-the-job training in which a senior manager or other experienced employee provides job- and career-related information to a mentee.

merchant wholesaler An institution that buys goods from manufacturers (takes ownership) and resells them to businesses, government agencies, other wholesalers, or retailers.

Mercosur Trade agreement between Peru, Brazil, Argentina, Uruguay, and Paraguay.

merger The combination of two or more firms to form one new company.

microeconomics The subarea of economics that focuses on individual parts of the economy such as households or firms.

middle management Managers who design and carry out tactical plans in specific areas of the company.

mission An organization's purpose and reason for existing; its long-term goals.

mission statement A formal document that states an organization's purpose and reason for existing and describes its basic philosophy.

mixed economies Economies that combine several economic systems; for example, an economy where the government owns certain industries but others are owned by the private sector.

monetary policy A government's programs for controlling the amount of money circulating in the economy and interest rates.

money Anything that is acceptable as payment for goods and services.

monopolistic competition A market structure in which many firms offer products that are close substitutes and in which entry is relatively easy.

mortgage bonds Corporate bonds that are secured by property, such as land, equipment, or buildings.

mortgage loan A long-term loan made against real estate as collateral.

motivating factors Intrinsic job elements that lead to worker satisfaction.

motivation Something that prompts a person to release his or her energy in a certain direction.

multinational corporations Corporations that move resources, goods, services, and skills across national boundaries without regard to the country in which their headquarters are located.

municipal bonds Bonds issued by states, cities, counties, and other state and local government agencies.

mutual fund A financial-service company that pools its investors' funds to buy a selection of securities that meet its stated investment goals.

N

NASDAQ Composite Index Broad-based market index that measures all NASDAQ domestic and international based common stocks listed on the NASDAQ Stock Market.

National Association of Securities Dealers Automated Quotation (Nasdaq) system The first electronic-based stock market and the fastest-growing part of the stock market.

national debt The accumulated total of all of the federal government's annual budget deficits.

nationalism A sense of national consciousness that boosts the culture and interests of one country over those of all other countries.

natural resources Commodities that are useful inputs in their natural state.

need The gap between what is and what is required.

net asset value (NAV) The price at which each share of a mutual fund can be bought or sold.

net loss The amount obtained by subtracting all of a firm's expenses from its revenues, when the expenses are more than the revenues.

net profit (net income) The amount obtained by subtracting all of a firm's expenses from its revenues, when the revenues are more than the expenses.

net profit margin The ratio of net profit to net sales; also called return on sales. It measures the percentage of each sales dollar remaining after all expenses, including taxes, have been deducted.

net sales The amount left after deducting sales discounts and returns and allowances from gross sales.

net working capital The amount obtained by subtracting total current liabilities from total current assets; used to measure a firm's liquidity.

niche competitive advantage A firm's ability to target and effectively serve a single segment of the market within a limited geographic area.

nonprogrammed decisions Responses to infrequent, unforeseen, or very unusual problems and opportunities where the manager does not have a precedent to follow in decision making.

North American Free Trade Agreement (NAFTA) A 1993 agreement creating a free-trade zone including Canada, Mexico, and the United States.

not-for-profit organization An organization that exists to achieve some goal other than the usual business goal of profit.

O

observation research A marketing research method in which the investigator monitors respondents' actions without interacting directly with the respondents; for example, by using cash registers with scanners.

Occupational Safety and Health Administration (OSHA) Sets workplace safety and health standards and assures compliance.

odd-even (psychological) pricing The strategy of setting a price at an odd number to connote a bargain and at an even number to suggest quality.

office automation system An information system that uses information technology tools such as word processing systems, e-mail systems, cell phones, PDAs, pagers, and fax machines to improve communications throughout an organization.

oligopoly A market structure in which a few firms produce most or all of the output and in which large capital requirements or other factors limit the number of firms.

one-to-one marketing Creating a unique marketing mix for every customer.

on-line (real-time) processing A method of updating a database in which data are processed as they become available.

open market operations The purchase or sale of U.S. government bonds by the Federal Reserve to stimulate or slow down the economy.

open shop Workers do not have to join the union or pay union dues.

operating budgets Budgets that combine sales forecasts with estimates of production costs and operating expenses in order to forecast profits.

operating expenses The expenses of running a business that are not directly related to producing or buying its products.

operational planning The process of creating specific standards, methods, policies, and procedures that are used in specific functional areas of the organization; helps guide and control the implementation of tactical plans.

operations management Management of the production process.

opinion leaders Those who influence others.

options Contracts that entitle holders to buy or sell specified quantities of common stocks or other financial instruments at a set price during a specified time.

organic organization An organizational structure that is characterized by a relatively low degree of job specialization, loose departmentalization, few levels of management, wide spans of control, decentralized decision making, and a short chain of command.

organization chart A visual representation of the structured relationships among tasks and the people given the authority to do those tasks.

organizing The process of coordinating and allocating a firm's resources in order to carry out its plans.

orientation Presentation to get the new employee ready to perform his or her job.

outsourcing (or contract logistics) Turning over all or part of the logistics function to an independent third party.

owners' equity The total amount of investment in the firm minus any liabilities; also called net worth.

P

participative leadership A leadership style in which the leader shares decision making with group members and encourages discussion of issues and alternatives; includes democratic, consensual, and consultative styles.

partnership An association of two or more individuals who agree to operate a business together for profit.

patent A form of protection established by the government for inventors; gives an inventor the exclusive right to manufacture, use, and sell an invention for 17 years.

payroll taxes The employer's share of Social Security taxes and federal and state unemployment taxes.

penetration pricing The strategy of selling new products at low prices in the hope of achieving a large sales volume.

pension funds Large pools of money set aside by corporations, unions, and governments for later use in paying retirement benefits to their employees or members.

perception The process by which we select, organize, and interpret stimuli into a meaningful and coherent picture.

perfect (pure) competition A market structure in which a large number of small firms sell similar products, buyers and sellers have good information, and businesses can be easily opened or closed.

performance appraisal A comparison of actual performance with expected performance to assess an employee's contributions to the organization.

perpetual inventory A continuously updated list of inventory levels, orders, sales, and receipts.

personal selling A face-to-face sales presentation to a prospective customer.

personality A way of organizing and grouping how an individual reacts to situations.

persuasive labeling A type of product label that reinforces or repeats a promotional theme or logo.

planning The process of deciding what needs to be done to achieve organizational objectives; identifying when and how it will be done; and determining by whom it should be done.

power The ability to influence others to behave in a particular way.

preferential tariff A tariff that is lower for some nations than for others.

preferred stock An equity security for which the dividend amount is set at the time the stock is issued.

prestige pricing The strategy of increasing the price of a product so that consumers will perceive it as being of higher quality, status, or value.

price skimming The strategy of introducing a product with a high initial price and lowering the price over time as the product moves through its life cycle.

price/earnings (P/E) ratio The current market price of a stock divided by its annual earnings per share.

pricing strategy Setting a price based upon the demand for and cost of producing a good or service.

primary data Information collected directly from the original source to solve a problem.

primary market The securities market where new securities are sold to the public, usually with the help of investment bankers.

principal The amount borrowed by the issuer of a bond; also called par value.

principle of comparative advantage The concept that each country should specialize in the products that it can produce most readily and cheaply and trade those products for those that other countries can produce more readily and cheaply.

private accountants Accountants who are employed to serve one particular organization.

problem-solving teams Usually members of the same department who meet regularly to suggest ways to improve operations and solve specific problems.

process departmentalization Departmentalization that is based on the production process used by the organizational unit.

process layout A facility arrangement in which work flows according to the production process. All workers performing similar tasks are grouped together, and products pass from one workstation to another.

process manufacturing A production process in which the basic input is broken down into one or more outputs (products).

producer price index (PPI) An index of the prices paid by producers and wholesalers for commodities such as raw materials, partially finished goods, and finished products.

product In marketing, any good or service, along with its perceived attributes and benefits, that creates value for the customer.

product advertising Advertising that features a specific good or service.

product departmentalization Departmentalization that is based on the goods or services produced or sold by the organizational unit.

product (assembly-line) layout A facility arrangement in which workstations or departments are arranged in a line with products moving along the line.

product liability The responsibility of manufacturers and sellers for defects in the products they make and sell.

product life cycle The pattern of sales and profits over time for a product or product category; consists of an introductory stage, growth stage, maturity, and decline (and death).

product manager The person who develops and implements a complete strategy and marketing program for a specific product or brand.

product strategy Taking the good or service and selecting a brand name, packaging, colors, a warranty, accessories, and a service program.

production The creation of products and services by turning inputs, such as natural resources, raw materials, human resources, and capital, into outputs, which are products and services.

production orientation An approach in which a firm works to lower production costs without a strong desire to satisfy the needs of customers.

production planning The aspect of operations management in which the firm considers the competitive environment and its own strategic goals in an effort to find the best production methods.

production process The way a good is made.

productivity The amount of goods and services one worker can produce.

professional liability insurance Insurance designed to protect top corporate management, who have been the target of malpractice lawsuits.

profit The money left over after all costs are paid.

profit maximization A pricing objective that entails getting the largest possible profit from a product by producing the product as long as the revenue from selling it exceeds the cost of producing it.

profitability ratios Ratios that measure how well a firm is using its resources to generate profit and how efficiently it is being managed.

program evaluation and review technique (PERT) A scheduling tool that is similar to the CPM method but assigns three time estimates for each activity (optimistic, most probable, and pessimistic); allows managers to anticipate delays and potential problems and schedule accordingly.

programmed decisions Decisions made in response to frequently occurring routine situations.

programmed instruction A form of computer-assisted off-the-job training.

promotion The attempt by marketers to inform, persuade, or remind consumers and industrial users to engage in the exchange process.

promotion strategy The unique combination of personal selling, advertising, publicity, and sales promotion to stimulate the target market to buy a product or service.

promotional mix The combination of advertising, personal selling, sales promotion, and public relations used to promote a product.

property taxes Taxes that are imposed on real and personal property based on the assessed value of the property.

prospecting The process of looking for sales prospects.

protected classes The specific groups who have legal protection against employment discrimination; include women, African Americans, Native Americans, and others.

protectionism The policy of protecting home industries from outside competition by establishing artificial barriers such as tariffs and quotas.

protective tariffs Tariffs that are imposed in order to make imports less attractive to buyers than domestic products are.

psychographic segmentation The differentiation of markets by personality or lifestyle.

public accountants Independent accountants who serve organizations and individuals on a fee basis.

public relations Any communication or activity designed to win goodwill or prestige for a company or person.

publicity Information about a company or product that appears in the news media and is not directly paid for by the company.

pull strategy A promotional strategy in which a manufacturer focuses on stimulating consumer demand for its product, rather than on trying to persuade wholesalers or retailers to carry the product.

punishment Anything that decreases a specific behavior.

purchasing power The value of what money can buy.

purchasing The process of buying production inputs from various sources; also called procurement.

pure monopoly A market structure in which a single firm accounts for all industry sales and in which there are barriers to entry.

push strategy A promotional strategy in which a manufacturer uses aggressive personal selling and trade advertising to convince a wholesaler or retailer to carry and sell its merchandise.

Q

qualifying questions Inquiries used by salespeople to separate prospects from those who do not have the potential to buy.

quality Goods and services that meet customer expectations by providing reliable performance.

quality control The process of creating standards for quality, producing goods that meet them, and measuring finished products and services against them.

quality of life The general level of human happiness based on such things as life expectancy, educational standards, health, sanitation, and leisure time.

R

ratio analysis The calculation and interpretation of financial ratios using data taken from the firm's financial statements in order to assess its condition and performance.

reach The number of different target consumers who are exposed to a commercial at least once during a specific period, usually four weeks.

real self-image How an individual actually perceives him- or herself.

recession A decline in GDP that lasts for at least two consecutive quarters.

recruitment The attempt to find and attract qualified applicants in the external labor market.

recruitment branding Presenting an accurate and positive image of the firm to those being recruited.

reengineering The complete redesign of business structures and processes in order to improve operations.

reference groups Formal and informal groups that influence buyer behavior.

referent power Power that is derived from an individual's personal charisma and the respect and/or admiration the individual inspires.

Regulation FD An SEC regulation that requires public companies to share information with all investors at the same time, leveling the information playing field.

reinforcement theory People do things because they know that certain consequences will follow.

relationship management The practice of building, maintaining, and enhancing interactions with customers and other parties to develop long-term satisfaction through mutually beneficial partnerships.

relationship marketing A strategy that focuses on forging long-term partnerships with customers by offering value and providing customer satisfaction.

reminder advertising Advertising that is used to keep a product's name in the public's mind.

reserve requirement Requires banks that are members of the Federal Reserve System to hold some of their deposits in cash in their vaults or in an account at a district bank.

retailers Firms that sell goods to consumers and to industrial users for their own consumption.

retained earnings The amounts left over from profitable operations since the firm's beginning; equal to total profits minus all dividends paid to stockholders.

return The opportunity for profit.

return on equity (ROE) The ratio of net profit to total owners' equity; measures the return that owners receive on their investment in the firm.

revenue The dollar amount of a firm's sales plus any other income it received from sources such as interest, dividends, and rents.

revolving credit agreement A line of credit under which a bank guarantees that a certain amount of money will be available for a business to borrow over a given period.

reward Anything that increases a specific behavior.

reward power Power that is derived from an individual's control over rewards.

right-to-work law State laws that an employee does not have to join a union.

risk The potential for loss or the chance that an investment will not achieve the expected level of return.

risk management The process of identifying and evaluating risks and selecting and managing techniques to adapt to risk exposures.

risk-return trade-off A basic principle in finance that holds that the higher the risk, the greater the return that is required.

robotics The technology involved in designing, constructing, and operating computer-controlled machines that can perform tasks independently.

routine response behavior Purchase of low-cost, frequently bought items with little search or decision making.

routing The aspect of production control that involves setting out the work flow—the sequence of machines and operations through which the product or service progresses from start to finish.

S

S corporation A hybrid entity that is organized like a corporation, with stockholders, directors, and officers, but taxed like a partnership, with income and losses flowing through to the stockholders and taxed as their personal income.

sales promotions Marketing events or sales efforts—not including advertising, personal selling, and public relations-that stimulate buying.

sales prospects The companies and people who are most likely to buy a seller's offerings.

sales taxes Taxes that are levied on goods when they are sold; calculated as a percentage of the price.

Sarbanes-Oxley Act Act passed in 2002 that sets new standards for auditor independence, financial disclosure and reporting, and internal controls; establishes an independent oversight board; and restricts the types of nonaudit services auditors can provide audit clients.

savings bonds Government bonds issued in relatively small denominations.

scanner-based research System for gathering information from a single group of respondents by continuously monitoring the advertising, promotion, and pricing they are exposed to and the things that they buy.

scheduling The aspect of production control that involves specifying and controlling the time required for each step in the production process.

scientific management A system of management developed by Frederick W. Taylor and based on four principles: developing a scientific approach for each element of a job, scientifically selecting and training workers, encouraging cooperation between workers and managers, and dividing work and responsibility between management and workers according to who can better perform a particular task.

seasonal unemployment Unemployment that occurs during specific seasons in certain industries.

secondary data Information that has already been collected for any purpose other than the one at hand.

secondary market The securities market where old (already issued) securities are bought and sold, or traded, among investors.

secured bonds Corporate bonds for which specific assets have been pledged as collateral.

secured loans Loans for which the borrower is required to pledge specific assets as collateral, or security.

Securities and Exchange Commission (SEC) The main federal government agency responsible for regulating the U.S. securities industry.

securities Investment certificates issued by corporations or governments that represent either equity or debt.

selection interview An in-depth discussion of an applicant's work experience, skills and abilities, education, and career interests.

selection The process of determining which persons in the applicant pool possess the qualifications necessary to be successful on the job.

selective credit controls The power of the Federal Reserve to control consumer credit rules and margin requirements.

selective distribution A distribution system in which a manufacturer selects a limited number of dealers in an area (but more than one or two) to market its products.

selective exposure The process of deciding which stimuli to notice and which to ignore.

selective strike strategy Strike at a critical plant that typically stops operations systemwide.

self-concept How people perceive themselves.

self-managed work teams Teams without formal supervision that plan, select alternatives, and evaluate their own performance.

seller cooperative Individual producers who join together to compete more effectively with large producers.

servicemark A symbol, name, or design that identifies a service rather than a tangible object.

services Intangible offerings of businesses that can't be held, touched, or stored.

shop steward An elected union official that represents union members to management when workers have complaints.

shopping products Items that are bought after considerable planning, including brand-to-brand and store-to-store comparisons of price, suitability, and style.

short-term forecasts Projections of revenues, costs of goods, and operating expenses over a one-year period.

simulation A scaled down version or mock-up of equipment, process, or work environment.

Six Sigma A quality control process that relies on defining what needs to be done to ensure quality, measuring and analyzing production results statistically, and finding ways to improve and control quality.

small business A business with under 500 employees that is independently managed, is owned by an individual or a small group of investors, is based locally, and is not a dominant company in its industry.

Small Business Administration (SBA) A government agency that speaks on behalf of small business; specifically it helps people start and manage small businesses, advises them in the areas of finance and management, and helps them win federal contract.

Small Business Investment Company (SBIC) Privately owned and managed investment companies that are licensed by the Small Business Administration and provide long-term financing for small businesses.

social investing The practice of limiting investments to securities of companies that behave in accordance with the investor's beliefs about ethical and social responsibility.

social marketing The application of marketing techniques to social issues and causes.

social responsibility The concern of businesses for the welfare of society as a whole; consists of obligations beyond those required by law or contracts.

Social Security Insurance that provides retirement, disability, death, and health benefits.

socialism An economic system in which the basic industries are owned either by the government itself or by the private sector under strong government control.

socialization process The passing down of cultural norms and values to children.

sole proprietorship A business that is established, owned, operated, and often financed by one person.

span of control The number of employees a manager directly supervises; also called span of management.

specialization The degree to which tasks are subdivided into smaller jobs.

specialty products Items for which consumers search long and hard and for which they refuse to accept substitutes.

speculative risk The chance of either loss or gain, without insurance against the possible loss.

staff positions Positions in an organization held by individuals who provide the administrative and support services that line employees need to achieve the firm's goals.

stakeholders Individuals or groups to whom a business has a responsibility; include employees, customers, the general public, and investors.

Standard & Poor's (S&P) 500 stock index An important market index that includes 400 industrial stocks, 20 transportation stocks, 40 public utility stocks, and 40 financial stocks; includes NYSE, AMEX, and Nasdaq stocks.

standard of living A country's output of goods and services that people can buy with the money they have.

statement of cash flows A financial statement that provides a summary of the money flowing into and out of a firm during a certain period, typically one year.

statutory law Written law enacted by a legislature (local, state, or federal).

stock dividends Payments to stockholders in the form of more stock; may replace or supplement cash dividends.

stockbroker A person who is licensed to buy and sell securities on behalf of clients.

stockholders (or shareholders) The owners of a corporation who hold shares of stock that carry certain rights.

strategic alliance A cooperative agreement between business firms; sometimes called a strategic partnership.

strategic channel alliances One manufacturer using another manufacturer's previously established channel to distribute its goods.

strategic giving The practice of tying philanthropy closely to the corporate mission or goals and targeting donations to regions where a company operates.

strategic planning The process of creating long-range (one to five years), broad goals for the organization and determining what resources will be needed to accomplish those goals.

strict liability A concept in product-liability law under which a manufacturer or seller is liable for any personal injury or property damage caused by defective products or packaging even though all possible care was used to prevent such defects.

structural unemployment Unemployment that is caused by a mismatch between available jobs and the skills of available workers in an industry or region; not related to the business cycle.

succession planning Examination of current employees to identify people who can fill vacancies and be promoted.

supervisory (first-line) management Managers who design and carry out operation plans for the ongoing daily activities of the firm.

supply The quantity of a good or service that businesses will make available at various prices.

supply chain The entire sequence of securing inputs, producing goods, and delivering goods to customers.

supply chain management The process of smoothing transitions along the supply chain so that the firm can satisfy its customers with quality products and services; focuses on developing tighter bonds with suppliers.

supply curve A graph showing the quantity of a good or service that businesses will make available at various prices.

survey research A marketing research method in which data is gathered from respondents, either in person, by telephone, by mail, at a mall, or through the Internet to obtain facts, opinions, and attitudes.

T

tactical planning The process of beginning to implement a strategic plan by addressing issues of coordination and allocating resources to different parts of the organization; has a shorter time frame (less than one year) and more specific objectives than strategic planning.

target market The specific group of consumers toward which a firm directs its marketing efforts.

target return on investment A pricing objective where the price of a product is set so as to give the company the desired profitability in terms of return on its money.

tariff A tax imposed on imported goods.

technical skills A manager's specialized areas of knowledge and expertise, as well as the ability to apply that knowledge.

technology The application of science and engineering skills and knowledge to solve production and organizational problems.

term loan A business loan with an initial maturity of more than one year; can be unsecured or secured.

test-marketing The process of testing a new product among potential users.

theft insurance A broad insurance coverage that protects business against losses for an act of stealing.

Theory X A management style, formulated by Douglas McGregor, that is based on a pessimistic view of human nature and assumes that the average person dislikes work, will avoid it if possible, prefers to be directed, avoids responsibility, and wants security above all.

Theory Y A management style, formulated by Douglas McGregor, that is based on a relatively optimistic view of human nature; assumes that the average person wants to work, accepts responsibility, is willing to help solve problems, and can be self-directed and self-controlled.

Theory Z A theory developed by William Ouchi that combines U.S. and Japanese business practices by emphasizing long-term employment, slow career development, moderate specialization, group decision making, individual responsibility, relatively informal control over the employee, and concern for workers.

thrift institutions Depository institutions formed specifically to encourage household saving and to make home mortgage loans.

time deposits Deposits at a bank or other financial institution that pay interest but cannot be withdrawn on demand.

top management The highest level of managers; includes CEOs, presidents, and vice presidents, who develop strategic plans and address long-range issues.

tort A civil, or private, act that harms other people or their property.

total cost The sum of the fixed costs and the variable costs.

total profit Total revenue minus total cost.

total quality management (TQM) The use of quality principles in all aspects of a company's production and operations.

total revenue The selling price per unit times the number of units sold.

trade credit The extension of credit by the seller to the buyer between the time the buyer receives the goods or services and when it pays for them.

trade deficit An unfavorable balance of trade that occurs when a country imports more than it exports.

trade surplus A favorable balance of trade that occurs when a country exports more than it imports.

trademark The legally exclusive design, name, or other identifying mark associated with a company's brand.

training and development Activities that provide learning situations in which an employee acquires additional knowledge or skills to increase job performance.

transaction processing system (TPS) An information system that handles the daily business operations of a firm. The system receives and organizes raw data from internal and external sources for storage in a database using either batch or online processing.

trial courts The lowest level of courts, where most cases begin; also called courts of general jurisdiction.

U

underwriting The process of buying securities from corporations and governments and reselling them to the public, hopefully at a higher price; the main activity of investment bankers.

unemployment compensation Government payment to unemployed former workers.

unemployment insurance Pays laid-off workers weekly benefits while they seek new jobs.

unemployment rate The percentage of the total labor force that is not working, but actively looking for work.

Uniform Commercial Code (UCC) A model set of rules that apply to commercial transactions between businesses and between businesses and individuals; has been adopted by all states except Louisiana, which uses only part of it.

union shop Non-union workers can be hired but must join the union later.

unsecured loans Loans for which the borrower does not have to pledge specific assets as security.

unsought products Products that either are unknown to the potential buyer or are known but the buyer does not actively seek them.

Uruguay Round A 1994 agreement by 117 nations to lower trade barriers worldwide.

utilitarianism A philosophy that focuses on the consequences of an action to determine whether it is right or wrong; holds that an action that affects the majority adversely is morally wrong.

V

value pricing A pricing strategy in which the target market is offered a high-quality product at a fair price and with good service.

value-stream mapping Routing technique that uses simple icons to visually represent the flow of materials and information from suppliers through the factory and to customers.

variable costs Costs that change with different levels of output; for example, wages and cost of raw materials.

venture capital Financing obtained from venture capitalists, investment firms that specialize in financing small, high-growth companies and receive an ownership interest and a voice in management in return for their money.

vertical merger A merger of companies at different stages in the same industry; done to gain control over supplies of resources or to gain access to different markets.

virtual corporation A network of independent companies linked by information technology to share skills, costs, and access to one another's markets; allows the companies to come together quickly to exploit rapidly changing opportunities.

virtual private networks (VPNs) Private corporate networks connected over a public network, such as the Internet. VPNs include strong security measures to allow only authorized users to access the network.

volume segmentation The differentiation of markets based on the amount of the product purchased.

W

want The gap between what is and what is desired.

warranty A guarantee of the quality of a good or service.

wholesalers Firms that sell finished goods to retailers, manufacturers, and institutions.

wide area network (WAN) A network that connects computers at different sites via telecommunications media such as phone lines, satellites, and microwaves.

work groups The groups that share resources and coordinate efforts to help members better perform their individual jobs.

work teams Like a work group but also requires the pooling of knowledge, skills, abilities, and resources to achieve a common goal.

worker's compensation Covers the expenses of job-related injuries and diseases, including medical costs, rehabilitation, and job retraining if necessary.

World Bank An international bank that offers low-interest loans, as well as advice and information, to developing nations.

World Trade Organization (WTO) An organization established by the Uruguay Round in 1994 to oversee international trade, reduce trade barriers, and resolve disputes among member nations.

Y

yield management systems (YMS)
Mathematical software that helps companies adjust prices to maximize revenue.

ENDNOTES

Prologue

1. Marlene Caroselli, *Interpersonal Skills*, (Thomson South-Western, a part of The Thomson Corportion, 2003), The section "Getting Ahead in Business and Life" is also adapted from the above text.
2. The Persuasion self-test was created by the authors and from the following sources: *Persuade Others to - Follow Your Way of Thinking*, http://www.winstonbrill.com/bril001/html/article_index/articles/251-300/article271_body.html; *Six Unique Ways to Persuade Others*, http://www.micaworld.com/pdfs/Six%20Unique%20%20Ways%20%20Persuade%20Others.pdf; *Strategies of Influence and Persuasion*, Kenrick Cleveland, http://www.maxpersuasion.com; http://www.gowerpub.com/pdf/imppeopleconstch1.pdf; *Power Persuasion—How to Persuade People*, http://www.1000ventures.com/business_guide/crosscutings/persuading_people.html; and *How to Persuade and Influence People*, Wolf J. Rinke, Ph.D., CSP, #554 Innovative Leader Volume 11, Number 6, June 2002, http://www.winstonbrill.com/bril001/html/article_index/articles/551-600/article554_body.html.
3. The Office Politics scale was developed by the authors and from the following sources: *Don't Sabotage Your Success!—Make Office Politics Work*, Karen Ginsburg Wood, http://www.atlasbooks.com/markplc/00492.htm; *Play the Office Politics Game*, Cynthia A. Broderick, http://www.bankrate.com/brm/news/advice/19990914a.asp; *The Fairness of Office Politics . . . Integrity and Political Motivation!* Edward B. Toupin, http://www.hotlib.com/articles/show.php?t=The_Fairness_of_Office_Politics_... Integrity_and_Political_Motivation!; *Fly Under the Radar to Absorb Delicate Office Politics*, Peter Vogt, MonsterTRAK Career Coach, http://content.monstertrak. monster.com/resources/archive/onthejob/politics; *The New Office Politics: We've Seen the Enemy at Work, and Sometimes It's Us,* Audrey Edwards, *Essence*, March 2005, http://www.findarticles.com/p/articles/mi_ml264/is_11_35/ai_n11830673; *Assessment—Office Politics,* First Edition, http://www.course.com/downloads/courseilt/e-assessments/0619254394.pdf; and *Play Office Politics and Keep Your Soul*, http://www.createyourvision.com/playofficepolitics.htm.
4. The section on planning is adapted from: *Investing in Your Future* (Thomson South-Western, a part of The Thomson Corporation, 2007), pp. 1–10.
5. The material on Going to College is adapted from Abby Marks-Beale, *Success Skills: Strategies for Study and Lifelong Learning* (Thomson South-Western, a part of The Thomson Corporation, 2007).
6. The Time Management scale was created by the authors and: *Time Management Quiz,* http://www.nus.edu.sg/osa/guidance/quiz/timemgmtquiz.html; *Manage Your Time in Ten Steps,* http://www.familyeducation.com/article/0,1120,1-263,00.html; *Time Management Quiz,* http://tools.monster.com/quizzes/pareto; *Stress Management, Better Health Channel,* http://www.betterhealth.vic.gov.au/bhcv2/bhcsite.nsf/pages/quiz_manage_stress? *Stress Management Quiz,* http://www.betterhealth.vic.gov.au/bhcv2/bhcsite.nsf/pages/quiz_manage_stress?; *Time Management,* http://uwadmnweb.uwyo.edu/RanchRecr/handbook/time_management.htm; and *Time Management: Importance of Good Practice,* http://www.accel-team.com /techniques/time_management.html.
7. The Ability to Manage Money scale was created by your authors and: *Quiz – Can You Manage Money?,* http://collegeanduniversity.net/collegeinfo/index.cfm?catid=20&pageid=2339&affid=75; *Boston.com/Business/Your Money,* http://www.boston.com/business/personalfinance/articles/2005/04/03can_you_manage_your_own_month?mode=PF; *Psychology of Money Management,* http://www.uwec.edu/counsel/pubs/Money.htm; *Managing Your Money,* http://www.nelliemae.com/managingmoney; *The Importance of Managing Money,* http://www.mtstcil.org/skills/budget-12.html; and *How Do You Rate as a Money Manager?,* http://cahe.nmsu.edu/pubs/_g/G-219.pdf.
8. The self-quiz on How to Study was prepared by the authors using: *EDinformatics – Education for the Information Age,* http://www.edinformatics.com/education/howtostudy.htm; *The Manila Times,* March 20, 2004, http://www.manilatimes.net/national/2004/mar/20/yehey/life/20040320lif2.html; *Ten Traps of Studying—Improving Your Studying Skills—CAPS—UNC—Chapel Hill,* http://caps.unc.edu/TenTraps.html; and *Language Study Skills,* http://www.usingenglish.com/study-skills.html.
9. Julie Griffin Levitt. *Your Career: How to Make It Happen*, 5th edition (Thomson South-Western, a part of The Thomson Corporation, 2006), pp. 2–4.
10. The Assertiveness test was prepared by the authors using: *Test Your Assertive Level,* http://www.hodu.com/assertiveness-skills.shtml; *Assertive Action Plan,* http://www.headinjury.com/assertplan.html; *Assertiveness,* http://www.coping.org/relations/assert.htm; *Perception of Assertiveness as a Function of Tag Questions,* http://www.ycp.edu/besc/Journal2002/paper%201.htm; and *Assertion Training,* http://front.csulb.edu/tstevens/assertion_training.htm.
11. Levitt, p. 36.
12. Ross DeVol and Lorna Wallace, "Best Performing Cities: Where

America's Jobs Are Created and Sustained," *Milken Institute* (November 2004).

13. Pat Criscito, "Electronic Resumes," *Business Know-How* (August 28, 2005).

14. "Using Resume Keywords: An Important Strategy for Your Resume," http://www.bc.edu/offices/careers/skills/resumes/keywords (September 2, 2005).

15. *Ibid.*

16. *Ibid.*

17. Levitt, p. 205.

18. The Are You a Good Listener scale was created by the authors using the following: *American Management Association – Self-Test: Are you a good listener,* http://www.amanet.org/arc_center/archive/quiz_aug2003.htm; *How To Be an Active Listener,* http://techrepublic.com/5102-10878-5054191.html; *Are You a Good Listener?,* http://www.nidoqubein.com/article15.html; *Are You a Good Listener?,* http://www.lwvohio.org/members/postboard/june2004/Are_You_a_Good_Listener.pdf; *Productivity – Are You a Good Listener?,* http://www.effectivemeetings.com/productivity/communication/listener.asp; *Are You a Good Listener?—Listen and Profit,* Mike Kelly, http://www.simplysolo.com/kelly.htm; *Joan Lloyd at Work,* http://www.joanlloyd.com/articles/open.asp?art=026.htm; and *Humanities 2000—Listening Skills,* http://www.h2000.utoledo.edu/hs/clay/ListenSkills.html.

Chapter 1

1. "World-wide Quality of Life Survey," (London: Mercer Consulting Group, press release, March 14, 2005), http://www.mercerhr.com.

2. Phred Dvorak, "Sony to Cut 10,000 Jobs, Reduce Costs by $1.8 Billion," *Wall Street Journal,* September 22, 2005, p. A3; and Adam Lashansky, "Saving Face at Sony," *Fortune,* February 21, 2005, pp. 79–86.

3. Jacob Hale Russell, "Art Museums Debate Skills for Top Post," *Wall Street Journal,* August 18, 2005, pp. B1, B3.

4. Cort Brinkerhoff, "Sundance Gives Artists Sanctuary," *Deseret News* (Salt Lake City), August 14, 2005, http://www.findarticles.com; Dave McNary, "Sundance Back in Loop,"

Variety, May 22, 2005, http://www.variety.com; Sundance Institute Web site, http://institute.sundance.org (May 22, 2006); and Margery Weinstein, "Restoration Founder to Head Sundance," *Catalog Age,* March 1, 2005, http://www.findarticles.com.

5. "The Brains Business," *Economist,* September 10, 2005, pp. 3–4.

6. Allan E. Alter, "Knowledge Workers Need More Supervision," *CIO Insight,* August 5, 2005, http://www.cioinsight.com; and Edward H. Baker, "How to Manage Smart People," *CIO Insight,* August 5, 2005, http://www.cioinsight.com.

7. "In Name Only?" *Economist,* July 9, 2005, p, 58; and "Official: Ready for Privatization," *Forbes.com,* September 29, 2005, http://www.forbes.com.

8. Mark Wilkinson, "U.S. Businesses Largely Unscathed by Rita," Reuters, September 27, http://biz.yahoo.com/rb/050927/hurricane_business.html?.v=1 (October 7, 2005).

9. Lauren Young, "Shelter After The Storm," *Business Week,* October 3, 2005, http://www.businessweek.com.

10. "Search Engine Google Opens Lobbying Office," *Washington Post,* October 6, 2005, http://www.washingtonpost.com.

11. "Generation Y Defined," *On-Point Marketing and Promotions,* http://www.onpoint-marketing.com/generation-y.htm, (May 23, 2006); and "Q&As from Howe and Strauss, authors of Millennials Rising," *MillennialsRising.com,* http://www.millenialsrising.com, (May 23, 2006).

12. Desiree J. Hanford, "Long-Term Success of E-Tailers Will Hinge on 'Echo Boomers'," *Wall Street Journal,* July 27, 2005, p. B3A; and Jilian Mincer, "Generation Y Is New Territory For Financial-Service Marketers," *Wall Street Journal,* September 26, 2005, p. B.5.

13. Hanford, "Long-Term Success of E-Tailers," p. B3A.

14. Caron Alarab, "Generation Y Spending Trends: Gotta Have It," *Detroit Free Press,* August 25, 2005, http://www.freep.com/money/tech/youngcomps25e_20050825.htm.

15. Jilian Mincer, "Generation Y Is New Territory For Financial-Service Marketers," *Wall Street Journal,* September 26, 2005, p. B.5; Robin Sidel, "Hip Check: American Express Tries to Find Its Place with

a Younger Crowd," *Wall Street Journal,* September 22, 2005, pp. A1, A8.

16. Katherine Yung, "Generation Xers Hit Middle Age," *Houston Chronicle,* July 10, 2005, p. 3.

17. Diana Ransom, "Generation X Tops Boomers in Luxury Spending," *New York Daily News,* June 8, 2005, p. 6.

18. Anne D'Innocenzio, "New Gap Brand Caters to Boomers," *San Diego Union-Tribune,* August 24, 2005, pp. C1, C4; and Cheryl V. Jackson, "Generation Gap," *Chicago Sun-Times,* August 25, 2005. pg. 54.

19. Kelly Greene, "When We're All 64," *Wall Street Journal,* September 26, 2005, p. R.1; and Bradley Johnson, "Half of Boomers Hit the 50 Mark, but Spending Not Likely to Slow Down," *Advertising Age,* July 4, 2005, p. 18.

20. Louise Lee, "Love Those Boomers," *Business Week,* October 24, 2005, http://www.businessweek.com.

21. Jeanette Borzo, "Follow the Money: More Businesses Are Starting to Cater to an Affluent—and Discriminating — 'Mature Market'," *Wall Street Journal,* September 26, 2005. p. R9 and Anne D'Innocenzio, "Revlon Targets Older Women to Boost Sales," *Associated Press,* April 10, 2006, http://news.yahoo.com.

22. Greene, "When We're All 64," p. R1; Johnson, "Half of Boomers Hit the 50 Mark," p. 18; and Kevin Kelly, "Aging Buyers Dictate Trends," *Ward's Auto World,* June 2005.

23. Borzo, "Follow the Money," p. R9.

24. Section based on Andrea Coombes, "The Case for Older Workers: Value," *San Diego Union-Tribune,* January 29, 2006, p. H7; Peter Coy, "Old. Smart. Productive." *Business Week,* June 27, 2005, http://www.businessweek.com; Ellen M. Heffes, "Dramatic Workforce Trends Require Planning Now," *Financial Executive,* July/August 2005, pp. 18–21; Patricia Kitchen, "The 4 Generation Workplace, It's Not What It Used to Be," *Newsday,* August 14, 2005, p. A52; and Jennifer J. Salopek, "The New Brain Drain," *T+D,* June 2005, pp. 23–24.

25. Haya El Nasser and Lorrie Grant, "Immigration Causes Age, Race Split," *USA Today,* June 9, 2005, p. 1A; Cynthia Gartman, "Opportunities and Competitive Advantages for the Future," *Franchising World,* June 2005, pp. 27–28;

"Hispanic Population Passes 40 Million, Census Bureau Reports," U.S. Census Bureau press release, June 9, 2005, http://www.census.gov; and "U.S. Interim Projections by Age, Sex, Race, and Hispanic Origin," U.S. Census Bureau, 2004, http://www.census.gov.

26. El Nasser and Grant, "Diversity Tints a New Kind of Generation Gap," *USA Today*, June 9, 2005, p. 4A; and El Nasser and Grant, "Immigration Causes Age, Race Split," p. 1A.

27. Tony Carnevale, "The Coming Labor and Skills Shortage," *T+D*, January 2005, pp. 37–41; Coy, "Old. Smart. Productive." http://www.businessweek.com; "J&J: "Quality of People Is Key to Growth," *Financial Executive*, July/August 2005, p. 19; and Heffes, "Dramatic Workforce Trends Require Planning Now," pp. 18–21.

28. Jeffrey M. Humphreys, "The Multicultural Economy 2004: America's Minority Buying Power," *Georgia Business and Economic Conditions*, Third Quarter 2004, pp. 2, 3, 5, 6.

29. El Nasser and Grant, "Diversity Tints a New Kind of Generation Gap," p. 4A; and Wilson Liévano "Satellite, Cable-TV Companies Target Large Hispanic Market," *Wall Street Journal*, February 21, 2006, p. B4.

30. "Foreign-Born Population Tops 34 Million, Census Bureau Estimates," U.S. Census Bureau press release, February 22, 2005, http://www.census.gov.

31. Jeffrey S. Passel and Roberto Suro "Rise, Peak and Decline: Trends in U.S. Immigration 1992–2004; Executive Summary" (Washington, DC: Pew Hispanic Center, September 27, 2005).

32. Humphreys, "The Multicultural Economy 2004," p. 2; and "Texas Becomes Nation's Newest 'Majority-Minority' State, Census Bureau Announces," U.S. Census Bureau press release, August 11, 2005, http://www.census.gov.

33. "100-Calorie Snack Packs: Fad or Diet Tool?" *San Diego Union-Tribune*, October 12, 2005, pp. E1, E3.

34. "Table A-1. Employment Status of the Civilian Population by Sex and Age" in "Employment Situation Summary, September 2005," *Bureau of Labor Statistics*, October 7, 2005, http://www.bls.gov/; "Employment Characteristics of Families in 2004," *Bureau of Labor Statistics*, June 9, 2005, http://www.bls.gov.

35. "Top Facts About Women-Owned Businesses," *Center for Women's Business Research*, http://www.womensbusinessresearch.org (October 18, 2005).

36. Roger Schilling, "Reaching Those Female Fans," *American Coin-Op*, September 2005, pp. 31–37.

37. "Productivity and Costs: Fourth Quarter and Annual Averages, 2004," *Bureau of Labor Statistics*, March 3, 2005, http://www.bls.gov/lpc.

38. Chris Price, "U.S. Productivity Now Vulnerable to EU Nations," *New Orleans CityBusiness*, March 14, 2005, p. 1.

39. G. Thomas Sims, "Western Europe Shows Slip in Competitiveness," *Wall Street Journal*, September 29, 2005, p. A17.

40. "Developing Countries' Goods Trade Share Surges to 50-Year Peak," *World Trade Organization*, April 14, 2005, http://www.wto.org.

41. "World Economy," *The World Factbook*, Central Intelligence Agency, October 4, 2005, http:// www.cia.gov.

42. Box based on Gina P. Barge, "The New Comfort of Business Travel," *Black Enterprise*, October 2005, p. 157; "On Service, Solutions, and SunChips," *Sky*, September 2005, p. 10; and Evan Perez, "Ramping Up Delta's Global Fare," *Wall Street Journal*, October 18, 2005, p. D3.

43. Royal Ford, "Made in America: In a Fundamental Shift for the Auto Industry, More Foreign Cars Sold in the U.S. Are Being Built Here Rather Than Imported," *Boston Globe*, September 4, 2005, p. D1.

44. Kevin Robinson-Avila, "Workers Reassigned on Farm: Mechanical Thinner Saves Labor in Chili," *Southwest Farm Press*, September 1, 2005, http://www.southwestfarmpress.com.

45. "What Is MEMS?" *MEMS and Nanotechnology Clearinghouse*, http://www.memsnet.org (October 25, 2005).

46. G.S. Early, "Something for Everyone," *High-Tech Bulletin*, KCI Communications, Inc., November 7, 2005, e-mail newsletter, hightechbulletin@kci-com.

47. G. Patrick Pawling, "Fortune Magazine Lists Cisco Systems as One of the Best Places to Work," *News@Cisco*, January 14, 2005, http://newsroom.cisco.com.

48. Matthew Boyle, "The Wegmans Way," *Fortune*, January 24, 2005, p. 64.

49. "The 100 Best Companies to Work For," *Fortune*, January 24, 2005, p. 77.

50. Nanette Byrnes, "What Not To Do," *Business Week*, October 10, 2005, p. 74.

51. Patricia O'Connell, "How HR Can Be 'Actively Harmful'," *BusinessWeek Online*, October 10, 2005.

52. Heffes, "Dramatic Workforce Trends Require Planning Now," pp. 18–21; Kitchen, "The 4 Generation Workplace," p. A52.

53. "Why Study Convergence?" *Center for the Study of Technology and Society*, http://www.tecsoc.org/convergence (May 23, 2006).

54. Kathryn Balint, "Phone Companies Paving a Way to TV Land," *San Diego Union-Tribune*, January 23, 2006, p. A1; Peter Grant, "Telecom Venture to Test Service of Wireless, Cable," *Wall Street Journal*, April 10, 2006, p. B4; and Bruce Meyerson, "4 Top Cable Providers to Branch into Cell Service," *San Diego Union-Tribune*, November 3, 2005, p. C4.

55. Jim Kerstetter, "Homeland Security: A Tech Boom This Time?" *Business Week Online*, May 10, 2005, http://www.businessweek.com; and Sarah Lacy, "Meet The CIA's Venture Capitalist," *Business Week Online*, May 10, 2005, http://www.businessweek.com.

Chapter 2

1. Peter Burrows, "Notebooks without Wide Margins," *Business Week*, September 5, 2005, http://www.businessweek.com, Jason Dean and Pui-Wing Tam, "The Laptop Trail," *Wall Street Journal*, June 9, 2005, pp. B1, B8; and H-P Web site, http://www.hp.com.

2. Michael Mandel, "The Economics Fueling the French Riots," *Business Week Online*, November 7, 2005, http://www.businessweek.com; and Carol Matlack, "Crisis in France," *Business Week*, November 21, 2005, http://www.businessweek.com.

3. Michael Mandel, "The Economics Fueling the French Riots," *Business Week Online*, November 7, 2005, http://www.businessweek.com.

4. Michael Ellis, "Ford Will Cut 4,000 Salaried Jobs," *Detroit Free Press*, November 19, 2005, http://www.freep.com.

5. Statistics from the World Bank, as reported in "Economics and Financial Flows Tables," *Earth Trends*,

http://earthtrends.wri.org (November 20, 2005).

6. Greg Ip, "Fed Raises Rates by 1/4 Point, Hints More May Come," *Wall Street Journal*, March 29, 2006, A1.
7. John J. Fialka, Jackie Calmes, and Jeffrey Ball, "Katrina Reveals U.S. Energy Vulnerability," *Wall Street Journal*, September 2, 2005, p. A5; Marianne Lavelle, "The (Big) Ripple Effect," *U.S. News & World Report*, September 12, 2005, pp. 33–35; "Storm Damage Pushes U.S. Closer to Energy Crisis," *Wall Street Journal*, September 2, 2005, pp. A1, A5.
8. Dean Calbreath, "Top Six for '06," *San Diego Union-Tribune*, January 1, 2006, p. H2.
9. Spencer E. Ante, "Verizon: Stumbling But Unbowed," *Business Week*, November 7, 2005, http://www.businessweek.com; Spencer E. Ante and Roger O. Crockett, "Rewired and Ready for Combat," *Business Week*, November 7, 2005, pp. 110–113; Roger O. Crockett, "At SBC, It's All About 'Scale and Scope,'" *Business Week*, November 7, 2005, http://www.businessweek.com; James S. Granelli, "Phone Carriers Set Sights on Cable Television's Turf," Los Angeles Times, December 10, 2005, p. C.1; Steven Levy, "Would you Buy a Quad from this Man?" *Newsweek*, November 14, 2005, p. E8; Dionne Searcey, "AT&T Rolls Out Net-Based TV," *Wall Street Journal*, January 5, 2006, p. D3; Dionne Searcey, Jesse Drucker, and Sarmad Ali, "As Telecom Shifts, Providers Seek New Connections," *Wall Street Journal*, December 6, 2005, pp. A1, A8; Verizon Corporate Web site, http://www.verizon.com.
10. Jon E. Hilsenrath and Greg Ip, "Economy Shows Resilience in Face of Massive Jolt *Wall Street Journal*, September 6, 2005, pp. A1, A5.
11. Calbreath, "Top Six for '06," p. H1.
12. Nelson D. Schwartz, "Why China Scares Big Oil," *Fortune*, July 25, 2005, p. 33–36; and "The World's Number One: Saudi Oil," *Economist*, November 12, 2005, p. 83.
13. Gregory L. White and Chip Cummins, "Gas Dispute Pinches Europe," *Wall Street Journal*, January 2, 2006, http://www.online.wsj.com.
14. Dennis K. Berman and Russell Gold, "Conoco Sets Pact to Buy Burlington," *Wall Street Journal*, December 13, 2005, p. A3.

15. Pui-Wing Tam and Ann Zimmerman, "Wal-Mart's H-P Elves," *Wall Street Journal*, December 15, 2005, pp. B1, B4.
16. Phred Dvorak and Evan Ramstad, "TV Marriage: Behind Sony-Samsung Rivalry, an Unlikely Alliance Develops," *Wall Street Journal*, January 3, 2006, pp. A1, A6.
17. Marcia Heroux Pounds, "Asian Entrepreneurs on Rise as U.S. Business Creation Drops, Study Says," *South Florida Sun-Sentinel*, June 3, 2005, p. D1.
18. James McGregor, Advantage, China," *Washington Post*, July 31, 2005; Page B1.
19. "One Billion Opportunities?" *Wall Street Journal*, October 18, 2005, pp. B1, B5; and Wu Jiao, "Students Given Helping Hand to Start Businesses," *China Daily*, December 6, 2005, p. 5.
20. Kevin Maney, "Chinese Start-Ups Open Arms to Venture Capital," *USA Today*, May 9, 2005, p. B1; Marko Marschek, "China is Ripe for VCs with the Right Approach," *Venture Capital Journal*, November 2005, pp. 41–43; and Tom Stein, "Globe Trotters: Venture firms Are Increasingly Looking beyond U.S. Shores," *Venture Capital Journal*, May 1, 2005, pp. 38–44.
21. Joellen Perry, "A Challenge to Europe's Economies," *U.S. News & World Report*, November 21, 2005, p. 36.

Chapter 3

1. "Report Shows How Krispy Kreme Sweetened Results," *Wall Street Journal* (August 1, 2005), p. A1, A6.
2. Marianne Moody Jennings, *Case Studies in Business Ethics*, 2nd ed. (St. Paul: West Publishing Company, 1996), pp. xx-xxiii.
3. "Tyco Trial Jurors Say Defendants Weren't Credible," *Wall Street Journal* (June 20, 2005), pp. A1, A10; and "When Charity Begins at Home," *Business Week* (November 9, 2004), p. 76.
4. "100 Best Corporate Citizens," *Business Ethics* (Spring 2006).
5. Stephen Barrett, "Court Dismisses Sharper Image Lawsuit Against Consumers Union," http://www.quackwatch.org (April 19, 2005).
6. http://www.sharperimage.com (September 3, 2006).
7. "We're Good Guys, Buy From Us," *Business Week* (November 22, 2004), p. 74.

8. Sarah Ellison and Eric Bellman, "Clean Water, No Profit," *Wall Street Journal* (February 3, 2005), pp. B1, B2.
9. "The Debate Over Doing Good," p. 77.
10. "CSR Wire Members Contribute More than $100 Million to Hurricane Relief," http://www.csrwire.com (September 2, 2005).
11. Stacy Perman, "Tiny Outfits, Big Hearts," *Business Week Online* (February 7, 2005), http://www.businessweek.com. Copyright © The McGraw-Hill Companies, Inc. All rights reserved. Reproduced by permission.
12. Alan Murray, "Citigroup CEO Pursues Culture of Ethics," *Wall Street Journal*, March 2, 2005, p. A2. Copyright © 2005 by Dow Jones & Company, Inc. All rights reserved. Reproduced by permission.
13. http://www.business-ethics.com.
14. Amy Merrick, "Gap Offers Unusual Look at Factory Conditions," *Wall Street Journal* (May 12, 2004), pp. A1, A12; "Gap Minds Itself," http://www.globalexchange.org (April 1, 2005).
15. *Ibid.*
16. Adapted from "In the Bag," *Fast Company*, March 2005, http://www.fastcompany.com; Andrew Tilin, "Bagging the Right Customers," *Business 2.0*, May 2005, pp. 56–57; Timbuk2 corporate Web Site, http://www.timbuk2.com (November 13, 2005); David Worrell, "Go for the Gold" *Entrepreneur*, July 2005, http://www.entrepreneur.com; and "It's All in the Bag for Timbuk2," *San Francisco Chronicle*, (May 1, 2006).
17. Adapted from Material in the video "The Rewards of Paying Fair: Ethics and Social Responsibility at equal Exchange"; and Equal Exchange Corporate Web Site, http://www.equalexchange.com, (November 10, 2005).

Chapter 4

1. "It's A Grand e-Latte World," *Wall Street Journal* (December 15, 2004), pp. B1, B4; and "Starbucks Outlets," htpp://www.answers.com (September 9, 2005).
2. "Japanese Makers Taking Market Share," htpp://www.edmunds.com (August 18, 2005).
3. http://otrade.businessroundtable.org/trade (September 7, 2005).
4. "Supporting Small Business," http://www.whitehouse.org (June 17, 2005).

5. "Sure, the Trade Deficit Is Scary—But We Can Handle It," *Business Week* (May 23, 2005), p. 41.

6. "The Export Engine Needs a Turbocharge," *Business Week* (February 14, 2005), p. 32.

7. http://www.cosmos-club.org/Journal.

8. "U.S. Welcomes China Currency: Reevaluation," *Voice of America* Press Release (July 21, 2005).

9. "Behind the Outsourcing Debate: Surprisingly Few Hard Numbers," *Wall Street Journal* (April 12, 2004), pp. A1, A7.

10. "Outsourcing May Create U.S. Jobs," *Wall Street Journal* (March 30, 2004), p. A2; and, "Outsourcing Innovation," *Business Week* (March 21, 2005), p. 84.

11. "Protect US from Protectionists," *Wall Street Journal* (April 25, 2005), p. A14.

12. *Ibid.*

13. "Global Market Is Good to U.S. Firms," *Wall Street Journal* (October 8, 2004), p. A14.

14. "Some Steel Tariffs to Remain for Five Years," *Wall Street Journal* (April 15, 2005), p. B3.

15. "Just Try Selling Half a Pantsuit," *Business Week* (August 22, 2005), p. 12.

16. "U.S. Moves Toward Shrimp Levies," *Wall Street Journal* (December 21, 2004), p. A11.

17. "Global Dogfight," *Wall Street Journal* (June 1, 2005), pp. A1, A14.

18. "New WTO Chief Targets Trade Deal," *Wall Street Journal* (May 16, 2005), p. A14.

19. "Mexico, Was NAFTA Worth It?" *Business Week* (January 21, 2005), pp. 66–72.

20. http://europa.eu.int (September 10, 2005).

21. "Intel Raided in EU Antitrust Investigation," *The Globe and Mail* (July 13, 2005), p. B8.

22. "EU Limits Coke's Sales Tactics in Settlement of Antitrust Case," *Wall Street Journal* (June 23, 2005), p. B6.

23. http://www.business.gov (international trade) January 31, 2003.

24. "How China Eats a Sandwich," *Fortune* (March 21, 2005), pg. F210B.

25. "GM Splits with Creator of Its Success in China," *International Herald Tribune* (August 9, 2005), p. 13.

26. Evan Ramstad and Gary McWilliams, "For Dell, Success in China Tells Tale of Maturing Market," *Wall Street Journal,* July 5, 2005, pp. A1, A8. Copyright © 2005 by Dow Jones & Company, Inc. All rights reserved. Reproduced by permission.

27. "Pernod Boss Slams French Protectionism," *Associated Press Newswires* (August 1, 2005).

28. "Does Globalization Have Staying Power?" *Marketing Management* (March/April 2002), pp. 18–22.

29. "U.S. Multinationals Reap Overseas Bounty," *Wall Street Journal* (April 4, 2005), p. A2.

30. Deborah Vence, "Not Taking Care of Business?" *Marketing News,* March 15, 2005, pp. 19–20. Copyright © 2005 American Marketing Association. All rights reserved. Reproduced by permission.

31. Neil King, "A Whole New World," *Wall Street Journal* (September 17, 2004), pp. R1–R2.

32. Pete Engardio, "A New World Economy," *Business Week* (August 22/29, 2005), pp. 52–58.

33. *Ibid.*

34. G. Pascal Zachary, "Making It in China," *Business 2.0,* August 2005, pp. 59–66. Copyright © 2005 by Time, Inc. All rights reserved. Reproduced by permission.

Chapter 5

1. Tara Siegel Bernard, "Building a Luxury Retail Business on the Web," *The Wall Street Journal- Small Business,* July 12, 2005, p. B4; Pearl Paradise corporate Web site, http://www.pearlparadise.com (May 9, 2006).

2. Jena Wuu, "Work-Life Not an Issue for Owners," *Inc. Online,* August 10, 2005, http://www.inc.com; Christina Galoozis, "Employees View Leadership Through Lens of Work-Life Balance," *Inc. Online,* June 8, 2005, http://www.inc.com.

3. Linda Ravden, personal interview by author May 25, 2006.

4. Marie Driscoll, "Pacific Sun's Golden Glow," *Business Week Online,* November 9, 2004, http://www.businessweek.com; Ron Ehlers (VP Information Services, Pacific Sunwear of California, Inc.) "Pacific Sunwear: Maintain a Fresh Brand by Anticipating Consumer Needs," presentation to the Retail Systems MIX Summit, May 25, 2005, http://www.retailsystems.com; "Corporate Profile," Pacific Sun corporate Web site, http://www.pacsun.com.

5. "Definition of Cooperatives" University of Wisconsin Online— Center for Cooperatives, http://www.wisc.edu/uwcc/info/i_pages/prin.html (May 24, 2006).

6. Ace Hardware Web site, http://www.acehardware.com (April 5, 2006).

7. Seon-Jin Cha, "Hyundai Forms China Joint Venture," *The Wall Street Journal,* June 22, 2005, p. B4.

8. Megan Barnett, "Size up a Ready-Made Business," *U.S. News & World Report,* August 2, 2004, p. 69.

9. "The Economic Impact of Franchised Businesses in the United States," *International Franchise Association,* http://www.franchise.org.

10. Carlye Adler, "How China Eats a Sandwich," *Fortune,* March 21, 2005, p. F210-B; Julie Bennett, "Chinese Market Offers Franchise Challenges," *Startup Journal–The Wall Street Journal Online,* http://www.startupjournal.com; Subway corporate Web site, http://www.subway.com (March 25, 2006).

11. "Bank of America to Acquire MBNA," *New Jersey Business,* September 1, 2005, p. 67.

12. Patricia Sellers, "It was a No-Brainer," *Fortune,* February 21, 2005, p. 97.

13. Dennis K. Berman, "Big Deals Put Europe at M&A Center Stage," *Wall Street Journal,* April 3, 2006, p. C9; and Denis K. Berman, "Fistfuls of Dollars Fuel the M&A Engine," *Wall Street Journal,* January 3, 2006, p. R3.

14. Harry R. Webber, "UPS to Buy Trucking Company Overnight for $1.25 Billion to Expand Its Freight Business," *USA Today,* May 17, 2005, p. 6B.

15. Kevin J. Delaney, "Google to Buy Urchin Software, Provider of Data for Advertisers," *The Wall Street Journal,* March 29, 2005, p. B4.

16. Peter Grant, "Cable Systems' New Weapon in Phone Battle: Going Private," *Wall Street Journal–Marketplace,* June 21, 2005, p. B1.

17. Laurie J. Flynn, "Oracle Acquiring Another Big Rival," *San Diego Union–Tribune,* September 13, 2005, p. C1.

18. Joe McDonald, "Yahoo Buys Stake in China's No. 1 Web Shopping Firm," *Associated Press, San Diego Union-Tribune,* August 12, 2005, p. C1.

19. Ken Belson, "eBay to Buy Internet Phone Provider Skype," *San Diego Union-Tribune,* September 13, 2005, p. C1.

20. Andy Serwer, "A Marriage of Inconvenience," *Fortune,* December 13, 2004, p.50.

21. Dennis K. Berman, "Fistful of Dollars Fuel the M&A Engine," p. R3.

22. Jeanette Borzo, "Follow the Money: More Businesses Are Starting to Cater to an Affluent— and Discriminating—'Mature Market'," *Wall Street Journal*, September 26, 2005. p. R9; and Sara Wilson, "All the 'Rage,'" *Entrepreneur*, January 2005, http://www.entrepreneur.com.

23. Home Instead Corporate Web site http://www.homeinstead.com (May 4, 2006).

24. "Sarah Adult Day Services," *Franchise Zone*, http://www.entrepreneur.com/franzone/ (May 31, 2006).

25. Stephanie Clifford, "What You Need To Know Now," *Inc. Magazine*, September 2005, p. 27.

26. James J. L'Allier, PhD, & Kenneth Kolosh, "Preparing for Baby Boomer Retirement," Bellevue University Online, June 2005, http://www.clomedia.com.

27. Berman, "Big Deals Put Europe at M&A Center Stage," p. C9; and Berman, "Fistfuls of Dollars Fuel the M&A Engine," p. R3.

28. Greg Hitt, "U.S. Foreign-Investment Debate Goes Global," *Wall Street Journal*, May 30, 2006, p. A4.

29. *Ibid.*, p. A4.

30. Judy Ettenhofer, "Organic Valley a Big Success," *The Capital Times*, July 29, 2004, http://www.madison.com; Craig Maier, "Duckworths Part of Organic Valley Success Story," *Juneau County Star-Times*, January 22, 2005, http://www.star-times.scwn.com (September 28, 2005); Organic Valley corporate Web site, http://www.organicvalleycoop.com (May 26, 2006).

31. Hilary Potkewitz, "Geek Support: Techies Make House Calls Like Old-Time Docs," *Los Angeles Business Journal*, June 13, 2005, http://www.findarticles.com; "Stand Alone Geek Squads Target Small Business," *DSN Retailing Today*, February 7, 2005, http://www.findarticles.com; corporate Web sites for Geek Squad, http://www.geeksquad.com, and Best Buy, http:www.bestbuy.com, (April 27, 2006).

Chapter 6

1. Rod Kurtz, "Five Ideas to Watch," from *Inc. Magazine*, March 2004, http://www.inc.com (September 29, 2005); Denise Penny, "Isn't He Just To Tie For?" *New York Magazine*, December 7, 2003 and "The Tie Guy," http://www.cnn.com, posted September 27, 2005.

2. Shannon McMahon, "Stepping into a Fortune," *San Diego Union-Tribune*," April 5, 2005, p. C4.

3. Andrew Morse, "An Entrepreneur Finds Tokyo Shares Her Passion for Bagels," *The Wall Street Journal*, October 18, 2005, p. B1.

4. Paul D. Reynolds, Nancy M. Carter, William B. Gartner, Patricia G. Greene, and Larry W. Cox. *The Entrepreneur Next Door: Characteristics of Individuals Starting Companies in America*. (Kansas City, MO: E. M. Kauffman Foundation, 2002).

5. Jim Morrison, "Entrepreneurs," *American Way Magazine*, October 15, 2005, p.94.

6. Martha Irvine, "More 20-Somethings Are Blazing Own Paths in Business," *San Diego Union-Tribune*, November 22, 2004, p. C6.

7. Gregory Katz, "Her Daily Bread," *American Way Magazine*, July 15, 2005, p. 34; Poilane Web site http://www.poilane.com (October 27, 2005).

8. Keith McFarland, "What Makes Them Tick," *Inc. 500*, October 19, 2005, http://www.inc.com.

9. *Ibid.*

10. Donna Fenn, "The Remote Control CEO," *Inc. Magazine*, October 2005, p. 92.

11. Olga Kharif, "A Cellular Call for Simplicity," *Business Week Online*, July 17, 2005, http://www.businessweekonline.com (October 27, 2005).

12. Keith McFarland, "What Makes Them Tick."

13. Andrew Blackman, "Know When To Give Up," *Wall Street Journal*, May 9, 2005, p. R9.

14. *Ibid.*

15. Jolie Solomon, "If You Can't Beat 'Em . . . make 'Em Happy," *The Wall Street Journal Online*, http://www.wsj.com (September 27, 2005); Scotti's corporate Web site http://www.scotticd.com (September 27, 2005).

16. Michelle Prather, "Talk of the Town," *Entrepreneur Magazine*, February 2003, http://www.entrepreneur.com. Little Log Company, Inc. Web site, http://www.littlelog.com (May 31, 2006).

17. Don Debelak, "Rookie Rules," *Business Start-Ups Magazine*, http://www.entrepreneur.com (March 2, 2006).

18. Keith McFarland, "What Makes Them Tick."

19. Much of the statistical information for the SBA section is from the Small Business Administration Web site, http://www.sba.gov.

20. "Small Businesses Receive Nearly 100,000 SBA-Backed Loans in FY 2005, a Fifth Consecutive Record," *Small Business Administration*, press release, October 5, 2005, http://www.sba.gov/news.

21. John A. Challenger, "As Entrepreneurs, Seniors Lead U.S. Start-Ups," *Franchising World*, August 2005, p. 53; Jon E. Hilsenrath, "Self-Employed Boost The Economic Recovery," *Start-Up Journal*, http://www.wsj.com; "Report Documents 2004 As a Good year for Small Business," *Small Business Administration*, press release, January 5, 2006, http://www.sba.gov/news; *The Small Business Economy 2005: A Report to the President* (Washington, D.C.: United States Government Printing Office, 2005); and "Small Businesses Receive Nearly 100,000 SBA-Backed Loans in FY 2005," October 5, 2005.

22. Challenger, p. 53; Coombes, "The case for Older Workers: Value," p. H7; and Maggie Overfelt, "Future Entrepreneurs: Gray Heads," *Fortune Small Business*, December 2004, http://www.fortune.com.

23. Jeff Cornwall, "We Will Not Go Quietly," *The Entrepreneurial Mind*, June 22, 2004, http://www.belmont.edu (October 27, 2005).

24. "Demand for SBA-Backed Loans Continues at Record Pace Through Third Quarter of FY 2005," *SBA News Release*, July 6, 2005, http://www.sba.gov (October 28, 2005).

25. Daniel Del'Re, "Entrepreneurship Grows in All Market Conditions," September, 27, 2005, http://www.inc.com (October 30, 2005).

26. "Minority and Women Business Ownership Increasing Faster than National Average" *SBA News Release*, July 29, 2005, http://www.sba.gov.

27. Stacy Zhao, "Web-Based Companies Significant Part of U.S. Small Business," *Inc.com*, June 7, 2005, http://www.inc.com.

28. Betsy Schiffman, "Best Places to Get Rich," *Forbes.com*, http://www.forbes.com (October 28, 2005).

Chapter 7

1. Barney Gimbel, "Southwest's New Flight Plan," *Fortune*, May 16, 2005, p. 97.

2. Susan Carey, "Amid JetBlue's Rapid Ascent, CEO Adopts Big Rival's Traits," *Wall Street Journal*, August 25, 2005, p. A1.

3. Bridget Finn, "How to Turn Managers into Leaders," *Business 2.0*, September 2004, p. 70.

4. Julia Boorstin. "Mickey Drexler's Second Coming," *Fortune,* May 2, 2005, p. 101.
5. Karen Bells, "Hot Off the Press; Milford Printer Spends Big to Fill New Niche," *Cincinnati Business Courier,* July 15, 2005, pp. 17–18.
6. Boorstin, "Mickey Drexler's Second Coming."
7. David Bank, "Autodesk Stages Revival," *Wall Street Journal,* August 19, 2005, p. B3.
8. Janet Adamy, "One Mechanic's Journey to Aid Northwest Air," *Wall Street Journal,* August 26, 2005, p. B1.
9. Alex Taylor, III, "Boeing Finally Has a Flight Plan," *Fortune,* June 13, 2005, pp. 27–28; J. Lynn Lundsford and Rod Stone, "Boeing Net Falls, but Outlook Is Rosy," *Wall Street Journal,* July 28, 2005, p. A3; Carol Matlack and Stanley Holmes, "Why Airbus Is Losing Altitude," *Business Week,* June 20, 2005, p. 20; J. Lynn Lunsford, "UPS to Buy 8 Boeing 747s, Lifting Jet's Prospects," *Wall Street Journal,* September 18, 2005, p. A2; "Airbus to Launch A350 Jet in October," *Xinhua News Agency,* September 14, 2005, online; "Boeing Plans Major Change," *Performance Materials,* April 30, 2001, p.5."
10. Avery Johnson, Susan Carey, and Chris Maher, "Delays Frustrate Air Travelers, but Carrier Reports Few Glitches," *Wall Street Journal,* August 22, 2005, online.
11. Susan Carey, "With Talks at End, Northwest to Offer Jobs to Stand-Ins," *Wall Street Journal,* September 12, 2005, p. B2.
12. Jeffery Garten, "Jack Welch: A Role Model for Today's CEO," *Business Week* (September 10, 2001).
13. Nancy Brumback, "6. A.G. Lafley, Chairman and CEO, Procter & Gamble Company," *Supermarket News,* July 25, 2005.
14. Fara Warner, "Keeping the Crisis in Chrysler," *Fast Company,* September 2005, pp. 69–73.
15. *Ibid.*
16. Carol Hymowitz, "Middle Managers Are Unsung Heroes on Corporate Stage," *Wall Street Journal,* September 19, 2005, p. B1.
17. Julia Boorstin, "100 Best Companies to Work For," *Fortune,* January 12, 2004, online; Michael Zawacki, "Family Values: Placing Equal Emphasis on Employees and Quality," *Inside Business,* October 2004, p. 98.
18. *Ibid.*
19. *Ibid.*
20. J.M. Smucker corporate summary found in "Best Companies to Work For," *Fortune,* January 24, 2005, online.
21. Michael Useem and Jerry Useem, "Great Escapes: Nine Decision-Making Pitfalls—And Nine Simple Devises to Beat Them," *Fortune,* June 27, 2005, p. 98.
22. "New Lessons to Learn," *Fortune,* October 3, 2005, pp. 87–88.
23. Gerry Beatty, "Oreck Says It's on Road to Recovery as Katrina's Impact Felt on Operations," *HFN The Weekly Newspaper for the Home Furnishing Network,* September 12, 2005, p. 3.
24. "Hurricane Recovery: First Plan in Gulfport, Mississippi Area Re-Opens—Oreck Corporation Puts 500 People Back to Work," *PRNewswire,* September 9, 2005, online.
25. This section is adapted from David Henry, Mike France, and Louis Lavelle, "The Boss on the Sidelines: How Auditors, Directors, and Lawyers Are Asserting Their Power," *Business Week,* April 25, 2005, pp. 88–96.
26. "Dashboard Use Rising," *Intelligent Enterprise,* March 2005, p. 18.
27. Carol Hymowitz, "Dashboard Technology: Is It a Helping Hand or a New Big Brother?" *Wall Street Journal,* September 26, 2005, p. B1.
28. Diane Nilsen, Brenda Kowske, and Kshanika Anthony, "Managing Globally—Managing a Diverse Global Environment Is Critical Today. How You Do It Depends on Where You Are," *HR Magazine,* August 2005, p. 111.

Chapter 8

1. "Ethan Allen Restructures, Creates 3 Subsidiaries," *HFN, the Weekly Newspaper for the Home Furnishing Network,* August 8, 2005, p. 3.
2. ITT Industries Annual Report 2004 Fact Sheet, http://www.itt.com/downloads/ITT_2004_ENGLISH.pdf, October 19, 2005.
3. Sibneft.com, http://www.sibneft.ru/pages.php?lang=1&page=25, October 19, 2005.
4. Brent Schlender, "Incredible: The Man Who Built Pixar's Innovation Machine," *Fortune,* November 15, 2004, p. 212.
5. http://www.pg.com/jobs/corporate_structure/four_pillars.jhtml.
6. Peter Burrows, "HP Says Goodbye to Drama; Five months in, CEO Mark Hurd's no-nonsense approach is being felt in a big way—and the Street has taken notice," *Business Week Online,* September 1, 2005.
7. http://www.novartis.com/about_novartis/ en/board_ directors.shtml.
8. Traci Purdum, "Teaming, Take 2: Once a Buzzword, Teaming Today Is One of the Fundamentals of Manufacturing," *Industry Week,* May 2005, p. 41.
9. Joseph B. White, "LaSorda's Chrysler Challenge," *The Wall Street Journal,* August 15, 2005, p. B5.
10. Diane Brady, "Reaping the Wind: GE's Energy Initiative Is a Case Study in Innovation without Borders," *Business Week,* October 11, 2004, p. 201; Patricia Sellers, "Blowing in the Wind: To Build a Better Wind Turbine, General Electric Built a Global Team of Researchers in Germany, China, India, and the U.S.," *Fortune,* July 25, 2005, p. 130.
11. Alan Deutschman, "The Fabric of Creativity: Pound for Pound, W.L. Gore Just Might Be the Most Innovative Company in America. Here's Why," *Fast Company,* December 2004, pp. 54–60.
12. Kristina Seward, "5.11 Tactical CEO Keeps His Employees Busy," *Modesto Bee,* September 28, 2005.
13. "Unilever UK Gets Its House in Order," *Grocer,* February 12, 2005, p. 8; "From Rivalry to Mergers; Anglo-Dutch Companies," *The Economist (US),* February 12, 2005, p. 61.
14. "Re-Inventing H-P the Hurd Way," *Information Age,* September 10, 2005.
15. Hiroshi Ikematsu, "Sony's Restructuring No Easy Task," *The Yomiuri Shimbun,* September 23, 2005; Cliff Edwards with Tom Lowry, Moon Ihlwan, and Kenji Hall, "The Lessons for Sony at Samsung," *Business Week,* October 10, 2005, p. 37.
16. See R. Z. Gooding and J.A. Wagner III, "A Meta-Analytic Review of the Relationship between Size and Performance: The Productivity and Efficiency of Organizations and Their Subunits," *Administrative Science Quarterly,* December 1985, pp. 462–481.
17. Alan Deutschman, "The Fabric of Creativity: Pound for Pound, W.L. Gore Just Might Be the Most Innovative Company in America.

Here's Why," *Fast Company*, December 2004, pp. 54–60.

18. Michael Liedtke, "Google Morphing into Multifaceted Juggernaut," *Houston Chronicle*, October 2, 2005; Fred Vogelstein, "Google @ $165: Are These Guys for Real?" *Fortune*, December 13, 2004, pp. 106–108; Alan Deutschman, "Can Google Stay Google?" *Fast Company*, August 2005, pp. 62–68.

19. "New Study Shows That Workers Believe the Office Grapevine More Than They Do Management," *M2 Presswire*, September 14, 2005.

20. *Ibid.*

21. Michael V. Copeland and Andrew Tilin, "The New Instant Companies," *Business 2.0*, June 2005, pp. 82–83. Copyright © Time Inc. All rights reserved. Reproduced by permission.

22. Richard Lee, "More Firms Move Manufacturing Overseas, Connecticut Study Shows," *Stamford Advocate*, October 20, 2005.

23. Karin Rives, "Cost, Better Worker Access Drive Companies to Send Jobs Offshore, Survey Shows," *The News & Observer*, October 12, 2005.

24. Jennifer Mears, "Offshore Use on the Rise but Savings Lag," *Network World*, July 25, 2005, p. 13.

25. *Ibid.*

26. Rives, "Cost, Better Worker Access Drive Companies to Send Jobs Offshore."

27. *Ibid.*

28. *Ibid.*

29. *Ibid.*

Chapter 9

1. Maria M. Perotin, "New Alcon Soft Lens Solutions Approved," *Fort Worth Star-Telegram* (October 13, 2005), p.2c.

2. Robert Rodriguez, "Filling the HR Pipeline," *HR Magazine*, vol. 49 (September, 2004), pp.78–84.

3. *Ibid.*

4. Jennifer C. Berkshire, "Social Network Recruiting," *HR Magazine*, vol. 50 (April, 2005), pp. 95–98.

5. Carolyn Brandon, "Truth in Recruitment Branding," *HR Magazine*, vol. 50 (November, 2005), pp. 89–96.

6. Eric Krell, "Personality Counts," *HR Magazine*, vol. 50 (November, 2005), pp. 46–52.

7. "Gore-Tex," *Fast Company* (January, 1999), p. 160.

8. Gene J. Koprowski, "Rude Awakening", *HR Magazine*, vol. 49 (September 2004), pp. 50–55.

9. Stephanie Oferman, "Mentors Without Borders," *HR Magazine*, vol. 49 (March, 2004), pp. 83–86.

10. Eric Krell, "Budding Relationships," *HR Magazine*, vol. 50 (June, 2005), pp. 114–118.

11. Michael A. Tucker, "E-Learning Evolves," *HR Magazine*, vol. 50 (October, 2005), pp.75–78.

12. Pamela Babcock, "Find What Workers Want," *HR Magazine*, vol. 50 (April, 2005), pp. 50–56.

13. Ann Pomeroy, "Great Places, Inspired Employees," *HR Magazine*, vol. 49 (July, 2004), pp. 44–63.

14. Jill Lawrence, "Union's Break off from AFL-CIO," *USA Today* (July 26, 2005), pp. 5A and 6A.

15. Kris Maher, "Breakaway Unions to Organize Themselves First," *Wall Street Journal* (September 26, 2005), p. A6.

16. Taylor Cox and Stacy Blake, "Managing Cultural Diversity: Implications for Organizational Competitiveness," *Academy of Management Executive*, vol. 5 (1991), pp. 45–56.

17. Pamela Babcock, "Diversity Down to the Letter," *HR Magazine*, vol 49 (June, 2004), pp. 90–94.

18. Drew Robb, "Easier Money," *HR Magazine*, vol. 50 (October, 2005), pp. 80–88.

19. Shawn Begley, "Behind 'Shortage' of Engineers: Employers Grow More Choosy," *Wall Street Journal* (November 16, 2005), pp. A1 and A12.

20. Aaron Bernstein and Joseph Weber, "So Long, AFL-CIO. Now What?" *Business Week* (August 8, 2005), p. 35.

21. Steven Greenhouse, "Splintered, but Unbowed," *New York Times* (July 30, 2005), p. C1.

22. Aaron Bernstein and Joseph Weber, "So Long, AFL-CIO. Now What?" *Business Week* (August 8, 2005), p. 35

23. *Ibid.*

24. Projections of job growth from 2002 to 2012 Data: Bureau of Labor Statistics.

25. Steven Greenhouse, "Splintered, but Unbowed," *New York Times* (July 30, 2005), p. C1.

Chapter 10

1. Matthew Boyle, "The Wegmans Way," *Fortune*, January 24, 2005, pp. 62–68.

2. *Ibid.*

3. "Genencor Named Best Place to Work in the U.S.," *PR Newswire*, June 20, 2005.

4. Brent Schlender, "Inside the Shakeup at Sony: The Surprising Selection of Howard Stringer as Sony's CEO Was a Classic Boardroom Tale of Executive Intrigue and Dashed Ambitions," *Fortune*, April 4, 2005, p. 94.

5. Kurt Swank, "60 Seconds with ... Kurt Swank on How to Set Stretch Goals and Meet Them," *Modern Materials Handling*, April 2005, p. 76.

6. Laura Landro, "Unsnarling Traffic Jams in the O.R.," *Wall Street Journal*, August 10, 2005, p. D1.

7. From Nancy J. Adler, *International Dimensions of Organizational Behavior*, 4th ed. (South-Western Thomson Learning, 2002) pp. 174–181.

8. Susan Kelly, "Give Us a Break! The Benefit That Employees Want Most—That Is Besides More Money—Is More Time," *Treasury and Risk Management*, June 2004, online.

9. *Ibid.*

10. Susan Caminiti, "A Champion of Change," *Fortune*, September 20, 2004, p. S10.

11. *Ibid.*

12. Stacy A. Teicher, "On the Frontier of Flexibility; Slowly, Companies Are Offering Flexible Schedules—a Key Demand of Workers," *The Christian Science Monitor*, June 7, 2004, p. 13.

13. Carolyn Hirschman, "Share and Share Alike: Job Sharing Can Boost Productivity and Help Retain Vital Workers, but It Can't Work Effectively without Help from HR," *HRMagazine*, September 2005, p. 52.

14. Dina Berta, "Empowered Staff Thrives at Fine-Dining Panzano," *Nation's Restaurant News*, September 12, 2005, p. 59.

15. James P. Kaletta and Marc Jolley, "Safety Improvement Sparks Organizational Change at Alberto Culver: A Single Effort to Improve Safety through Employee Involvement Spawns a Global Movement That Provides Alberto Culver with a Rich Payback," *Occupational Hazards*, June 2005, pp. 54–57

16. Alan Deutschman, "Can Google Stay Google?" *Fast Company*, August 2005, p.66.

17. Jeff D. Opdyke, "Getting a Bonus Instead of a Raise: More Companies Link Pay to Performance for Broad Range of Employees," *Wall Street Journal*, December 29, 2004, p. D1, D2.

18. Jeffrey Pfeffer, "The Pay-for-Performance Fallacy," *Business 2.0*, July 2005, p. 64.

19. Opdyke, "Getting a Bonus Instead of a Raise."

20. *Ibid.*
21. Nadine Heintz, "Everyone's a CFO," *Inc. Magazine*, September 2005, pp. 42–43.
22. Kathy Bergen, "SmithBucklin Becomes Wholly Owned by Employees," *Chicago Tribune*, June 28, 2005.
23. "The Employee Ownership Foundation and the ESOP Association Release Results of 2005 ESOP Company Survey," *PRNewswire*, September 27, 2005.
24. *Ibid.*
25. Brent Hunsberger, "Counting on the Company," *The Oregonian*, June 5, 2005.
26. Penni Crabtree, "Employees Will Maintain Control at SAIC," *San Diego Union-Tribune*, September 4, 2005.
27. *Ibid.*
28. Andrew E. Carr and Thomas Li-Ping, "Sabbaticals and Employee Motivation: Benefits, Concerns, and Implications," *Journal of Education for Business*, January-February 2005, pp.160–165.
29. *Ibid.*
30. *Ibid.*
31. Nadine Heintz, "Breaking Away: If You Love Your Employees, Set Them Free—With Paid Sabbaticals," *Inc. Magazine*, October 2004, p. 44.
32. *Ibid.*
33. Jennifer Keeney, "Perky Places to Work," *Fortune Small Business*, October 2005, online at http://www.fortune.com/fortune/smallbusiness/managing/articles/0,15114,389898,00.html.
34. David Wessel, "Motivating Workers by Giving Them a Vote," *Wall Street Journal*, August 25, 2005, p. A2. Copyright © Dow Jones & Company, Inc. All rights reserved. Reproduced by permission.
35. "Short Takes," *Crain's Cleveland Business*, August 22, 2005, p. 15.
36. "Sick Puppy," *Training*, January 2005, p. 10.
37. Maggie Raunch, "Strong Relationship Shown between Morale, Absenteeism: Survey Shows Unhappy Employees Use More Sick Days," *Incentive*, May 2005, p. 8.
38. "Surveys Reveal Turnover Rates Are on the Rise," *Report on Salary Surveys*, May 2005, pp. 1–6.
39. *Ibid.*

Chapter 11

1. Jim Carlton, "Can a Water Bottler Invigorate One Town?" *The Wall Street Journal*, June 9, 2005, p. B1.
2. *Ibid.*
3. Tilde Herrera, "Manatee Tax Cuts Lure New Company," *Bradenton Herald* (FL), May 4, 2005, p. 1B.
4. Dee-Ann Durbin, "Ford Announces Plans to Use Fewer Suppliers," *San Diego Union-Tribune,* September 30, 2005, p. C3.
5. Brian Nadel, "Chain and Command," *Fortune,* July 25, 2005; Dell company Web site http://www.dell.com (May 20, 2006); MOL company Web site http://www.mol.com (May 20, 2006); Acer company Web site http://www.global.acer.com (May 20, 2006).
6. Erik Sherman, "Supply Chain Alchemy," *Chief Executive*, March 1, 2005, p. 46.
7. Neil Shister, "Redesigned Supply Chain Positions Ford for Global Competition," *World Trade*, May 2005, p. 20.
8. Maria Varmazis, "Automation Frees Time for Strategic Activities," *Purchasing*, September 2005, p. 40.
9. "Six Organizations to Receive 2005 Presidential Award for Quality and Performance Excellence," National Institute of Standards and Technology, press release, November 22, 2005, http://www.nist.gov.
10. Jennifer Barrett, "Cutting Edge," *Newsweek,* December 12, 2005, p. 52–54; Eric Berger, "A Robot May Have Aided in Your Surgery," *Houston Chronicle*, March 19, 2006, pg. 10. Josh Fishman, "Can High Tech Save Your Life?" *U.S. News & World Report*, August 1, 2005, p. 45–52.
11. Neal E. Boudette and Norihiko Shirouzu, "Amid Price War, Chrysler to Revamp Manufacturing," *The Wall Street Journal*, August 2, 2005, p. A1; Gregory Cancelada, "Chrysler Minivan Plant Here Is Tops in Produtivity," *St. Louis Post-Dispatch*, June 2, 2006, http://www.stltoday.com; "Chrysler Group Announces up to $1 Billion Investment in St. Louis Assembly Plants," DaimerChrysler company press release, http://www.comnetchrysler.com; "Overview of Toyota's North American Manufacturing Operations," Toyota company Web site http://www.toyota.com (May 26, 2006).
12. "2005 Annual Labor Day Report: The Looming Workforce Crisis—Preparing American Workers for 21st Century Competition," National Association of Manufacturers Web site http://www.nam.org (May 30, 2006).
13. "2005 Annual Labor Day Report: The Looming Workforce Crisis—Preparing American Workers for 21st Century Competition," National Association of Manufacturers.
14. "The Knowledge Economy: Is the United States Losing Its Competitive Edge?" Future of Innovation Web site http//:www.futureofinnovation.org.
15. Letter from John Engler, President, National Association of Manufacturers, NAM Web site http://www.nam.org; "New Survey Shows Broadening Skills Gap Threatens Manufacturing Competitiveness," National Association of Manufacturers, press release, November 22, 2005, http://www.nam.org; and "U.S. Manufacturing Innovation Leadership at Risk," National Association of Manufacturers, press release, February 1, 2006, http://www.nam.org.
16. Elizabeth Millard, "Is Your Company Ready for BPM?" *CIO*, May 15, 2006, http://www.ciotoday.com.
17. Hollis Bischoff, "Teetering on the BPM Strategy Edge," http://www.bpminstitute.org (May 29, 2006).
18. 2005 Annual Labor Day Report, "The Looming Workforce Crisis—Preparing American Workers for 21st Century Competition," National Association of Manufacturers.

Chapter 12

1. "Lexus Has Top-Ranked Vehicle for Five Years in a Row," www.lexus.com (May 18, 2005).
2. "The Loyalty Advantage," *Write Stuff*, July 1, 2005.
3. "Operations Lesson 3: Smart Service Begets Customers; Smarter Service Gets Rid of the Bad Ones," *Business 2.0*, December 2004, p. 125. Copyright © Time Inc. All rights reserved. Reproduced by permission.
4. "10 Tech Trends to Bet On," *Fortune*, February 23, 2005, p. 76–88.
5. Gwendolyn Bounds, "The Long Road to Wal-Mart," *Wall Street Journal*, September 19, 2005, p. R1, R4. Copyright © Dow Jones & Company, Inc. All rights reserved. Reproduced by permission.
6. Brooks Barnes, "To Push Musicals, Producer Shakes Up Broadway Tactics," *Wall Street Journal*, March 10, 2005, p. A1, A12.
7. McDaniel, Carl and Roger Gates. Excerpt from *Marketing Research*

Essentials, 5th edition, Hoboken, NJ: John Wiley & Sons, 2005, p. 174. Copyright © 2005 by John Wiley & Sons Inc. All rights reserved. Reproduced by permission.

8. "How Cool Is That," *Smart Money*, June 2005, p. 13.

9. Carl McDaniel and Roger Gates, *Marketing Research Essentials*, 5th ed. (Hoboken, NJ: John Wiley & Sons, 2006), p. 131–133.

Chapter 13

1. Jonathan Welsh, "Checkered-Flag Past Helps Ferrari Unload a Fleet of Used Cars," *Wall Street Journal*, January 11, 2005, p. A1, A10. Copyright © Dow Jones & Company, Inc. All rights reserved. Reproduced by permission.

2. Alex Frankel, "The New Science of Naming," *Business 2.0*, December 2004, p. 53–55.

3. Robin Sidel, "American Express Tries to Find Its Place With a Younger Crowd," *Wall Street Journal*, September 22, 2005, pp. A1, A5.

4. The cobranding material is from: Charles Lamb, Joe Hair, and Carl McDaniel, *Marketing 8th ed.*, (Mason, Ohio: Thomson Publishing, 2006), p. 318–319.

5. "The Warranty Windfall," *Business Week*, December 20, 2004, p. 84–85.

6. "Brand Managers Struggle With Product Launches: Survey," *PROMO Xtra*, July 14, 2005.

7. "High Failure Rates for New Products to be Key Focus of Marketing Summit," *PR Leap*, August 1, 2005.

8. "Easy Does It All," *Business 2.0*, August 2005, p. 69–74. Copyright © Time Inc. All rights reserved. Reproduced by permission.

9. "The Penny Is in the Mind of the Beholder," *Quick's Marketing Research Review,* July/August 2005, p. 8.

10. Part of this section is adapted from: Charles Lamb, Joe Hair, and Carl McDaniel, *Marketing 8th ed.*, (Mason, Ohio: Thomson Publishing, 2006), p. 604–606.

11. "The Next Generation of Price-Comparison Sites," *Wall Street Journal*, September 14, 2005, p. D1, D13.

12. *Ibid.*

13. "The Price is Right," *Smart Money*, December 2004, p. 90–93.

14. "Coloring Your World," *Marketing Management*, July/August 2005, p. 5.

15. "Marketers Ask: Hues On First?" *Marketing News*, February 15, 2004, p. 8.

Chapter 14

1. This section partially adapted from: Charles Lamb, Joe Hair, and Carl McDaniel, *Marketing 8th ed.*, (Mason, Ohio: Thomson Publishing, 2006), p. 402–403.

2. "A Deal with Target Put Lid on Revival at Tupperware," *Wall Street Journal*, February 18, 2004, p. A1, A9; and "Tupperware Announces Second Quarter EPS," news release, http://www.tupperware.com (July 26, 2005).

3. Janet Adamy, "To Find Growth, No-Frills Grocer Goes Where Other Chains Won't," *Wall Street Journal*, August 30, 2005, p. A1, A8. Copyright © Dow Jones & Company Inc. All rights reserved. Reproduced by permission.

4. "Luring 'Em In," *Business 2.0*, March 2005, p. 44–46.

5. Matthew Maier, "The Department Store Rises Again," *Business 2.0*, August 2004, p. 56–57. Copyright © Time Inc. All rights reserved. Reproduced by permission; and "Nice One," MX Australia, news, April 18, 2005, http://www.global.factivia.com, October 20, 2005.

6. "A More Profitable Harvest," *Business 2.0*, May 2005, p. 66–67.

7. "7-Eleven Gets Sophisticated," *Business 2.0*, January/February 2005, p. 93–100.

8. "Who Made My Cheese? Tags Track Parmesan's Age, Origin," *Wall Street Journal*, July 7, 2005, p. B1, B6. Copyright © Dow Jones & Company Inc. All rights reserved. Reproduced by permission.

9. "The Next Delivery? Computer Repairs by UPS," *Business 2.0*, July 2005, p. 30–31.

10. "Big Brown's New Bag," *Business Week*, July 19, 2004, p. 54–56.

11. "Why Some Brands Can Stand Alone," *Business 2.0*, October 2005, p. 49–52.

12. Eric Savitz, "Tech File: Look Who's Storming the Net—Wal-Mart Isn't the First Name that Comes to Mind When You Think Internet Retailing; But Will It Be?" *Smart Money*, June 1, 2005, p. 46–49.

13. "E-Tailing Finally Hits Its Stride," *Business Week*, December 20, 2004, p. 36–37.

14. Savitz, "Tech File: Look Who's Storming the Net—Wal-Mart Isn't the First Name that Comes to Mind When You Think Internet Retailing; But Will It Be?" *Smart Money*, June 1, 2005, p. 47.

Chapter 15

1. "Why the Caveman Loves the Pitchman," *Business 2.0*, April 2005, p. 37–39.

2. "Marriott Hotel Owners and Franchisees Investing $190 Million in New Bedding," *Hotel Online*, January 25, 2005, http://www.hotel-online.com/news/pr2005 (October 22, 2005).

3. Chuck Chakrapani, "From the Editor," *Marketing Research*, Summer 2005, p. 2.

4. "Demand for Traditional Advertising Firm: Internet Up Again," *Zenith Optimedia*, January 2005, http://www.zenithoptimedia.com (October 17, 2005).

5. *Ibid.*

6. *Fast Pack* (Chicago: *Advertising Age*, 2005), p. 3.

7. "Turbulent New World," *Business Week*, March 7, 2005, p. 89–90.

8. "Rational Exuberance," *Media Outlook*, September 26, 2005, p. SR23.

9. "Facing Crunch, Sites Zero In On Targeted Ads," *Advertising Age*, October 10, 2005, p. 31.

10. "Study: Video Keeps Viewers' Attention," *Advertising Age*, October 10, 2005, p. 33.

11. Thomas Mucha, "This Is Your Brain on Marketing," *Business 2.0*, August 2005, p. 35–37. Copyright Time Inc.

12. This section is partially adapted from: Charles Lamb, Joe Hair, and Carl McDaniel, *Marketing 8th ed.* (Mason, Ohio: Thomson Publishing, 2006), p. 515–521.

13. "Call to Action Ads Give Clients Results They Can Measure," *Wall Street Journal*, March 22, 2005, p. B1, B4.

14. "In a Shift, Marketers Beef Up Ad Spending Inside Stores," *Wall Street Journal*, September 21, 2005, p. A1, A8.

15. "Online Coupons: An Engaging Idea," *Brandweek*, May 2, 2005, p. 20.

16. "Those Coupons Are Actually Clipping You," *Money*, May 2005, p. 28.

17. "Small Screen Gets Crowded as Brand Placements Double," *Brandweek*, May 9, 2005, p. 12.

18. "How Companies Pay TV Experts for On-Air Product Mentions," *Wall Street Journal*, April 19, 2005, p. A1, A12.

19. "Getting Buzz Marketers to Fess Up," *Wall Street Journal*, February 9, 2005, p. B9. Copyright © Dow Jones & Company. "P&G Buzz Program Tremor Moving On to Mothers," *Brandweek*, September 26, 2005, p. 15. Copyright © VNU Business Publications USA; and "Advertising Of, By, and For the People," *Business Week*, July 25, 2005, p. 63–64. Copyright © The McGraw-Hill Companies Inc.

20. "Splogs Roil Web, and Some Blame Google," *Wall Street Journal*, October 19, 2005, p. B1, B2.

21. Dana VanDen Heuvel, "Leveraging Blogs and Blogging for Marketing and Promotions," *AMA Blogging Webcast* (July 7, 2005); and "Get Connected: Leverage Blogs as Biz Tool," *Marketing News*, September 1, 2005, p. 7.

22. "The A.M.-P.M. Billboard," *Business 2.0*, June 2005, p. 32.

23. "More Marketers Call on Short Codes," *Brandweek*, June 27, 2005, p. 4.

24. "Hey, You! How About Lunch," *Wall Street Journal*, April 1, 2004, p. B1, B5.

25. "As Podcasts Boom, Big Media Rushes to Stake a Claim," *Wall Street Journal*, October 10, 2005, p. A1, A6.

26. "Purina Marketing Is Going Mobile with Pet Podcasts," *Wall Street Journal*, June 29, 2005, p. B2B.

Chapter 16

1. Bruce Lieberman, "Supercomputing Now Indispensable," *San Diego Union-Tribune*, November 12, 2005, pp. A1, 20.

2. "Solving the Superspeed Dilemma," *Business Week Online*, December 12, 2005, http://www.businessweek.com.

3. Thomas Friedman, *The World Is Flat* (New York: Farrar, Straus and Giroux, 2005) p. 8.

4. "Electronic Trading Hubs," http://www.com-met2005.org.uk April 4, 2006; David Luckham, "The Global Information Society and the Need for New Technology," http://www.informit.com, April 4, 2006; "Trading Hubs," http://www.investni.com April 4, 2006; "Trading Hubs in Asia," *Oikono*, December 6, 2005, http://www.oikono.com.

5. Jerry McElhatton, "Data BPO Can End Restless Nights for CIOs," *Bank Technology News*, February 2006, p.31.

6. *Ibid.*

7. Adapted from Kathryn Balint, "Captiva's Paper Chase Paying Off," *San Diego Union-Tribune*, December 9, 2005, pp. C1, C5; Brian Sherman, "Input Management and Opportunities for the Reseller Channel: An Interview with Wayne Ford, VP of Partner Alliances at Captiva," *ECM Connection*, http://www.ecmconnection.com, December 27, 2005; Captiva Software corporate Web site http://www.captivasoftware.com, March 16, 2006; EMC corporate Web site http://www.emc.com, March 16, 2006.

8. "St. Agnes Hospital Improves Patient Care and Management, Reduces Costs with Pervasive Meru Wireless LAN Deployment," *Meru Networks*, press release, February 13, 2006, http://www.merunetworks.com/news/press_releases/021306.shtml

9. Rita Zeidner, "Building a Better Intranet," *HR Magazine*, November 1, 2005, p. 99.

10. James Brown, "Hotel Group Installs Global Staff Intranet," *Computing*, October 20, 2005, http://www.computing.co.uk.

11. "Bluetooth® Wireless Technology Becoming Standard in Cars," *Bluetooth SIG*, February 13, 2006, http://www.bluetooth.com.

12. "Leading Global Law Firm Extends Contract with Equant to Ensure Seamless Service," *Business Wire*, January 10, 2006, http://galenet.thomsonlearning.com.

13. "Abilene Independent School District Installs AEP Networks' SSL VPN, Saves Up to $875,000 in Tech Support Costs over Five Years," *Internet Wire*, February 14, 2006, http://galenet.thomsonlearning.com.

14. Mitch Betts, "Application Service Providers Are Back for a Second Act," *Computerworld* November 14, 2005, http://computerworld.com; Jeffrey Kaplan, "Software-as-a-Service Myths," *Business Week*, April 17, 2006, http://www.businessweek.com; and Sarah Lacy, "The On-Demand Software Scrum," *Business Week*, April 17, 2006, http://www.businessweek.com.

15. Richard Waters, "SAP Ventures into On-Demand Software Field," *Financial Times*, February 3, 2006, p. 28.

16. Kaplan, "Software-as-a-Service Myths."

17. Stacy Collett, "MSPs: The New Hosts, *Computerworld*, November 14, 2005, http://computerworld.com.

18. Kathleen Hickey, "Data Warehouses Integrate Supply Chains," *World Trade*, February 1, 2006, p. 42.

19. Aaron Dalton, "Better Data with Business Intelligence," *Industry Week*, July 1, 2005, p. 54.

20. Section based on "Executive Guides: Knowledge Management," *Darwin Executive Guides*, http://guide.darwinmag.com/technology/enterprise/knowledge/index.html (April 3, 2006).

21. Jack Gordon, Making Knowledge Management Work, *Training*, August 1, 2005, p. 16+.

22. Scott Berinato, "The Global State of Information Security 2005," *CIO*, September 15, 2005, http://www.cio.com.

23. Joris Evers, "Computer Crime Costs $67 Billion, FBI Says," *CNet News.com*, January 16 2006, http://www.news.com.

24. "Vulnerabilities Reported," *CERT/CC Statistics*, March 31, 2006, http://www.cert.org/stats/cert_stats.html.

25. "Cybercrime Cost about $400 Billion," Computer Crime Research Center, July 6, 2005, http://www.crime-research.org.

26. *Ibid.*

27. Joris Evers, "Computer Crime Costs $67 Billion, FBI Says."

28. Tom Zeiler, Jr., "Keylogging Software Leads Bad Guys to Bank Accounts," *San Diego Union-Tribune*, February 27, 2006, pp. A1, A7.

29. "The Difference Between a Virus, Worm and Trojan Horse?" *Webopedia*, http://www.webopedia.com (April 1, 2006).

30. "Spam Costs World Businesses $50 Billion," *InternetWeek*, February 23, 2005; and "Spam Rates Rebound," *InternetWeek*, March 7, 2006, both from http://galenet.thomsonlearning.com/.

31. "Microsoft Files Piracy Charges Against Eight," *InternetWeek*, March 15, 2006, http://galenet.thomsonlearning.com/; Megan Reichgott, "19 People Indicted in Alleged $6.5 Million Software Piracy Plot," *San Diego Union-Tribune*, February 1, 2006, http://www.signonsandiego.com; and Bill Roberts, "Pirates, Beware: EDA Goes on the Offensive against Software Piracy," *Electronic Business*, March 2006, p. 26.

32. Scott Berinato, "The Global State of Information Security 2005."

33. Lucas Mearian, "IT Managers See Portable Storage Device Security Risk," *Computerworld*, March 17,

2006, http://www.computerworld.com.

34. Michael Gormley, "Spitzer Accuses Web Firm of Breach of Privacy in Sale of E-Mail Addresses," *Buffalo News*, March 24, 2006, http://www.buffalonews.com.

35. Matthew Boyle, "Tech in Action—The Latest Hit: CSI in Your Hard Drive," *Fortune,* November 14, 2005, p. 39.

36. John Patzakis, "Forensics Is Not Just a Word for Cops," *SCMagazine*, September 2005, http://www.scmagazine.com.

37. Matthew Boyle, "Tech In Action—The Latest Hit: CSI in Your Hard Drive."; "Guidance Software Introduces the World's Most Complete and Advanced eDiscovery Solution," Press Release, Guidance Software Corporate Web site, January 30, 2006, http://www.guidancesoftware.com; "Guidance Software, Inc. Ranked 244th Fastest Growing Technology Company in North America for the 2005 Deloitte Technology Fast 500," Guidance Software Corporate Web site, November 30, 2005, http://www.guidancesoftware.com.

38. Michelle Conlin, "The Easiest Commute of All," *Business Week*, December 12, 2005, p. 78.

39. Doug Bartholomew, "IT On Tap?" *Industry Week*, June 1, 2005, p. 64.

40. Maria Wakem, "Spending on Grid Technology to Rise," *Wall Street & Technology* September 1, 2005, http://www.wallstreetandtech.com.

41. Leslie Kramer, "Powering Up the Grid," *Wall Street & Technology*, January 1, 2006, http://www.wallstreetandtech.com.

Chapter 17

1. Alexei Barrionuevo, "Two Enron Chiefs Are Convicted in Fraud and Conspiracy Trial," *New York Times*, May 26, 2006, http://www.nytimes.com; "Events in the Enron Case," *Wall Street Journal*, March 8, 2006, http://www.wsj.com; "Ex-World-Com CEO Receives 25 Years," *San Diego Union-Tribune*, July 14, 2005, p. A1; Daniel Kadlec, "Does Kozlowski's Sentence Fit the Crime?" *Time*, September 20, 2005, http://www.time.com.

2. Glenn Cheney, "FASB, IASB Agree to Push on with Convergence Effort," *Accounting Today* April 3, 2006, http://ask.elibrary.com; "FASB and IASB Reaffirm Commit-

ment to Enhance Consistency, Comparability and Efficiency in Global Capital Markets" *Financial Accounting Standards Board,* February 27, 2006, http://www.fasb.org/news/; "FASB Issues Accounting Standard That Improves the Reporting of Accounting Changes as Part of Convergence Effort with IASB," *Financial Accounting Standards Board*, June 1, 2005, http://www.fasb.org/news/; Tim Reason, "The Narrowing GAAP," *CFO*, December 1, 2005, http://www.cfo.com.

3. "Sources and Occupations of AICPA Membership," *AICPA*, http://www.aicpa.org (April 9, 2006).

4. Robert Durak, "Audit Risk Alert—2002/03: Current Risks" (New York: American Institute of Certified Public Accountants, Inc., 2002), p. 14; Eric Krell, "What Triggers Financial Restatements?" *Business Finance*, October 2005, http://www.businessfinacemag.com.

5. "In the Name of the Dollar: A Closer Look at the Sarbanes-Oxley Act of 2002," *California CPA*, September 2002, http://www.findarticles.com.

6. Laurie Brannen, "Sarbanes-Oxley's Footprint on Finance Deepens," *Business Finance*, March 2005, http://www.businessfinancemag.com; and Laurie Brannen, "Sarbanes-Oxley's Impact on Shareholders," *Business Finance*, February 2005, http://www.businessfinancemag.com.

7. Adapted from John Goff, "Fractured Fraternity," *CFO* September 1, 2005, http://www.cfo.com; David M. Katz, "A Tough Act to Follow," *CFO*, March 15, 2006, http://www.cfo.com; Eric Krell, "Sarbanes Fatigue Strikes the Boardroom Business Finance," May 2005, http://www.businessfinancemag.com; Michael Rapoport, "SEC Panel to Turn In Report on Sarbanes Debate," *Wall Street Journal*, April 17, 2006, p. C3; and Tim Reason, "Feeling the Pain," *CFO*, May 1, 2005, http://www.cfo.com.

8. "The 2005 Oversight Systems Report on Corporate Fraud," *Oversight Systems*, http://www.oversightsystems.com (April 16, 2006).

9. Adapted from L. Gary Boomer, "Technology Strategy for the Future—and Today!" *WebCPA*, http://www.webcpa.com (April 9, 2006); Dynamic Software Solutions

Web site http://www.dssinternational.com (April 5, 2006); "Growing Use of Data Mining in Businesses and Government," *AccountingWEB.com*, September 8, 2005, http://www.accountingweb.com; Lisa Spinelli, "Data Mining Tools Drilling into Small Business Market," *Accounting Today*, September 5, 2005, p. 5.

10. Laurie Brannen, "PCAOB Issues Audit Guidance," *Business Finance*, July 2005, http://businessfinancemag.com.

11. "AICPA Issues New Risk Assessment Auditing Standards," *AICPA* press release, February 22, 2006, http://www.aicpa.org.

12. Goff, "Fractured Fraternity," September 1, 2005.

13. John Cummings, "Chief Audit Execs Come to the Fore," *Business Finance*, May 2005, http://businessfinancemag.com.

14. Marie Leone, "FASB Calls for a Cultural Change," *CFO*, March 7, 2006, http://www.cfo.com; Amey Stone and Robert Herz, "It's Like When Someone Robs a Bank," *Business Week Online*, August 19, 2002, http://www.businessweek.com.

15. Adapted from "The Case For Private Company GAAP," *Journal of Accountancy*, May 2005, http://www.aicpa.org; "Council Approves Moving Forward with Exploring GAAP for Private Companies," AICPA Web site http://www.aicpa.org (April 5, 2006): "FASB Establishes Small Business Advisory Committee," *FASB*, March 18, 2004, http://www.fasb.org; "GAAP For Private Companies," *The Practicing CPA*, March/April 2005, http://www.aicpa.org; and C.J. Prince, "Closing the GAAP" *Entrepreneur*, January 2006, http://www.entrepreneur.com.

Chapter 18

1. The Federal Reserve Board, "U.S. Currency," Remarks by Vice Chairman Roger W. Ferguson, Jr., September 28, 2005, http://www.federalreserve.gov.

2. "United States Dollar," http://en.wikipedia.org. June 3, 2006.

3. "Money Stock Measures," Federal Reserve Statistical Release, June 1, 2006, http://www.federalreserve.gov.

4. Karen Epper Hoffman, "Retailer's Role in the Demise of the Check,"

Bank Administration Institute (BAI) Web site, http://www.bai.org (June 3, 2006).

5. "Financial Services Fact Book-Commercial Banks," Insurance Information Institute Web site, http://www.financialservicesfacts.org (June 3, 2006).

6. American Customer Service Index Web site, http://www.theacsi.com (May 18; 2006); Commerce Bank corporate Web site, http://www.commerceonline.com (May 18, 2006); "Customer Satisfaction and Commitment? J.D. Power and ACSI Rank the Banks," *BAI Resource Directory*, http://www.bai.org (March 1, 2006); Downey Savings Web site http://www.downeysavings.com May 18, 2006; ING Direct Web site, http://www.ingdirect.com (May 18, 2006); J. D. Power and Associates Web site, http://www.jdpower.com (May 18, 2006); and Wachovia Web site, http://www.wachovia.com (May 18, 2006).

7. "Financial Services Fact Book-Thrift Institutions," Insurance Information Institute Web site, http://www.financialservicesfacts.org (June 3, 2006).

8. "Statistics for Federally Insured Credit Unions," National Credit Union Administration Web site, http://www.ncua.gov (June 3, 2006).

9. "2006 & 2007 Forecast," Credit Union National Association Web site, http://www.advice.cuna.org (June 3, 2006).

10. "The World's Best Internet Banks, 2005," http://www.internet.rudecactus.com (May 29, 2006).

11. "Community Banks and Credit Unions Are Realizing Business Success with Microsoft's Experience Banking Initiative," Microsoft press release, November 15, 2005, http://www.microsoft.com; "Delivering on the Promise to Change the Banking Experience," Microsoft press release, November 15, 2005, http://www.microsoft.com; "Microsoft Chooses Umpqua Bank's Pearl District Store to Demonstrate Banking Initiative Vision," *Portland Business News*, July 1, 2005, http://www.portland.dbusinessnews.com; and Ivan Schneider, "Size Matters," *Bank Systems & Technology*, January 31, 2006, http://www.banktech.com.

12. "Reforms to U.S. Pension Funding and Accounting Rules: Their Potential Effect on Equity Values and Interest Rates," Press Room, United States Treasury Web site, http://www.ustreas.gov (May 17, 2006).

13. "Who Is the FDIC?" Federal Deposit Insurance Corporation Web site, http://www.fdic.gov (June 3, 2006).

14. Frederick W. Stakelbeck, Jr., "U.S. Banks Investing in China," *FrontPage*, http://www.frontpagemagazine.com (September 15, 2005).

15. "Overview of Economic Benefits to the United States from the Activities of International Banks," Institute of International Bankers Web site, http://www.iib.org (June 3, 2006).

16. "Bidding Heats Up for Guangdong Bank," *Bobsguide Web site*, May 22, 2006, http://www.bobsguide.com; Andrew Browne and Kate Linebaugh, "A Citigroup Deal in China Could Open New Era," *Wall Street Journal Online*, January 3, 2006, http://www.wsj.com; Cathy Chan, "Citigroup Pulls Back on Guangdong Bank Bid," *International Herald Tribune*, May 10, 2006, http://www.iht.com; and Citigroup corporate Web site, http://www.citigroup.com (May 17, 2006).

17. "Top 10 Banking Industry Trends in 2006," Aite Group, January 9, 2006, http://www.aitegroup.com.

18. Ekaterina O. Walsh, Ph.D., "The Untapped Financial Consumer," May 17, 2006, Aite Group Web site, http://www.aitegroup.com.

19. "Money Laundering," U.S. Drug Enforcement Web site, http://www.dea.gov (June 2, 2006).

20. "Anti-Money Laundering Technology: Automating the Haystack Search," May 12, 2006, Aite Group Web site, http://www.aitegroup.com.

21. Sriram Kannan, "A Look Into Banking Trends for 2006—The Branch Renaissance Continues," *Art & Science of Management*, October 21, 2005, http://ksriram.blogspot.com.

22. "Retail Banking Industry Trends," *Branch Decisions*, http://www.branchdecisions.com (June 2, 2006).

Chapter 19

1. Corning Inc. Web site, http://www.corning.com (June 3, 2006); Jonathan Fahey, "Glass Menagerie," *Forbes*, April 24, 2006, pp. 87–90; and Kevin Maney, "Corning CEO Insists on Keeping His Eye on the Long-Term Ball," *USA Today*, May 11, 2005, p. 3B.

2. Tim Reason, "Budgeting in the Real World," *CFO*, July 1, 2005, http://www.cfo.com.

3. Laurie Brannen, "Leadership Q&A: Finance at the Forefront," *Business-Finance*, April 2006, http://www.businessfinancemag.com.

4. Reason, "Budgeting in the Real World," http://www.cfo.com.

5. Karen M. Kroll, "The Changing Face of Treasury Investments," *Business Finance*, March 2006, http://businessfinancemag.com.

6. Adapted from Richard Gamble, "Got Cash? Who Doesn't?" *Treasury & Risk Management*, December 2005/January 2006, http://www.treasuryandrisk.com; Richard Gamble, Susan Kelly, and John Labate, "The 2005 Alexander Hamilton Award Winners: Cash Management; Bronze Award Winner: Honeywell International," *Treasury & Risk Management*, November 2005, all from http://www.treasuryandrisk.com; and Karen M. Kroll, "Treasury Today: To Centralize or Not?" *Business Finance*, April 2006, http://businessfinancemag.com.

7. John Cummings, "DSO Hits 10-Year Low," *Business Finance*, May 2006, http://businessfinancemag.com.

8. Richard Gamble, Susan Kelly, and John Labate, "Treasury & Risk Management's 10th Annual Alexander Hamilton Awards," *Treasury & Risk Management*, November 2005, http://www.treasuryandrisk.com.

9. John Edwards, "BPO: Is Wider Better?" CFO.com, February 21, 2006, http://www.cfo.com; Susan Kelly, "Up Against Stiff Trade Winds? Boost Your Tech Power," *Treasury & Risk Management*, September 2005, http://www.treasuryandrisk.com; Dave Lindorff, "Trusting Others with Your Data," *Treasury & Risk Management*, May 2006, http://www.treasuryandrisk.com.

10. Helen Shaw, "Trimming Hemlines and Deadlines," *CFO*, April 24, 2006, http://www.cfo.com.

11. Tim Reason, "Capital Ideas: The 2005 Working Capital Survey," *CFO*, September 1, 2005, http://www.cfo.com.

12. Karen M. Kroll, "Asset-Based Lending Goes Mainstream," *Business Finance*, May 2006, http://www.businessfinancemag.com.

13. "Chipotle Mexican Grill Announces Pricing of Secondary

Offering," *Business Wire*, May 19, 2006, http://biz.yahoo. com; Lynn Cowan, "Chipotle Mexican Grill's IPO Sizzles," *Wall Street Journal*, January 27, 2006, p. C3; and Matt Krantz, "Chipotle Rolls a Win as IPO Price Ignites," *USA Today*, January 27, 2006, http://www. usatoday.com.

14. Lynn Cowan, "Foreign Offerings Spice Up the IPO Market," *Wall Street Journal*, January 3, 2006, p. R3; and Lynn Cowan, "The IPO Pop," *Wall Street Journal*, May 16, 2006, p. C4.

15. "American Express Raises Payout, Sets Buyback," *Wall Street Journal*, May 23, 2006, p. B3.

16. Rebecca Buckman, "Silicon Valley Start-Ups See Cash Everywhere," *Wall Street Journal*, March 20, 2006, p. C1; and "Jobster Raises $19.5 Million in Series B Financing Backed by Mayfield Fund, Ignition Partners and Trinity Ventures," Jobster press release, August 30, 2005, http://www.jobster.com.

17. "Equity Financings for U.S. Venture-Backed Companies, by Industry Group (1999–4Q' 2005)," *Dow Jones VentureOne*, http://venturecapital.dowjones.com (June 5, 2006); "Increased U.S. Venture-Capital Investing in Fourth Quarter Drives Annual Total to Highest Level in Four Years," *Dow Jones VentureOne*, January 23, 2006, http://venturecapital.dowjones. com; and "U.S. Venture Capital Investing Tops $6 Billion in First Quarter of 2006, Highest First Quarter Investment Level Since 2001," *Dow Jones VentureOne*, April 24, 2006, http:// venturecapital. dowjones.com.

18. Elaine Pofeldt, "Touched by an Angel," *Fortune*, May 1, 2006, p. 124.

19. Jo Best, "Intel Invests in U.K. WiMax Venture," *News.com*, April 5, 2006, http://news.com.com; and Dawn Kawamoto, "Nanochip Lands Intel Investment," *News.com*, April 18 2006, http://news.com.com.

20. John Cummings, "Guiding the Global Enterprise," *Business Finance*, June 2005, http://www. businessfinancemag.com.

21. Laurie Brannen, "A Bird's Eye View of Finance," *Business Finance*, May 2005; and Laurie Brannen "Finance at the Forefront," *Busi-nessFinance*, April 2006, both from http://www.businessfinancemag. com; and Richard Gamble, "Straddling the Great Divide," *Treasury & Risk Management*, September 2005, http://www. treasuryandrisk.com.

22. Brannen, "Leadership Q&A: Finance at the Forefront," http:// www.businessfinancemag.com; and Marie Leone, "Are You Over-worked?" *CFO*, March 15, 2006, http://www.cfo.com.

23. Adapted from Laurie Brannen, "A Bird's Eye View of Finance," *Business Finance*, May 2005, http:// www.businessfinancemag.com; Richard Gamble, "Straddling the Great Divide," *Treasury & Risk Management*, September 2005, http://www.treasuryandrisk.com; Susan Kelly, "Who Says Women Can't Work With Tools? Not Home Depot," *Treasury & Risk Manage-ment*, November 2005, http:// www.treasuryandrisk.com; and Duncan Wood, "Avoiding the Bad BRICs," *Treasury & Risk Manage-ment*, June 2006, http://www. treasuryandrisk. com.

24. Joanne Sammer, "What CFOs Want From Risk Management," *Business Finance*, April 2006, http:// www.businessfinancemag.com.

25. Ann Lubart, "Saving a Seat at the Table," *Treasury & Risk Management*, March 2005, http://www.treasuryandrisk.com

Chapter 20

1. Finlay Lewis, "Bush to Focus on Healthy Economy in Effort to Recharge His Agenda," *San Diego Union-Tribune*, January 6, 2006, http://www.signonsandiego.com.

2. "FedEx Corporation," *Yahoo! Finance*, http://finance.yahoo.com (June 10, 2006); and Anne Fisher, "America's Most Admired Companies," *Fortune*, March 6, 2006, p. 65, 71.

3. Amy Barrett, "The Pain Is Just Beginning," *Business Week*, September 5, 2005, p. 40; Robert Langreth, "Trouble Breathing," *Forbes*, April 24, 2006, http:// elibrary.bigchalk.com; and "Merck & Co.," *Yahoo! Finance*, http:// finance.yahoo.com (June 10, 2006).

4. Statistics from *The Bond Market Association*, http://www. bondmarket.com (June 6. 2006).

5. "Moody's Corporate Bond Yield Averages, 1980–2006," *The Bond Market Association*, http://www. bondmarket.com (June 6, 2006).

6. "Issuance in the U.S. Bond Mar-kets," *The Bond Market Association*, http://www.bondmarket.com (June 6, 2006).

7. *Ibid*.

8. *2006 Investment Company Fact Book*, 46th Edition (Washington, DC: Investment Company Institute, May 2006).

9. Selena Maranjian, "Are ETFs Getting out of Control?" *Fool.com*, April 12, 2006, http://www.fool.com.

10. Jeff D. Opdyke and Jane J. Kim, "The New Landscape of Online Trading," *Wall Street Journal*, August 9, 2005, pp. D1–2.

11. "NYSE Group and Euronext N.V. Agree to a Merger of Equals," NYSE Group press release, June 1, 2006, http://www.nyse.com.

12. NYSE corporate Web site, http:// www.nyse.com, (June 6, 2006).

13. Tom Groenfeldt, "Gearing Up for Greater Volume," *Institutional Investor*, April 2006, p. 55; and Ivy Schmerken, "Resurrecting the Regionals," *Wall Street & Technology*, November 2005, p. A38.

14. Nasdaq Web site, http://www. nasdaq.com (June 6, 2006).

15. "SEC Approves NASDAQ's Exchange Registration Applica-tion," Nasdaq press release, January 16, 2006, http://www. nasdaq.com.

16. "Nasdaq Creates New Market Tier with Highest Listing Standards in the World," Nasdaq press release, February 15, 2006, http://www. nasdaq.com; and "Nasdaq Global Select Fact Sheet," Nasdaq, http:// www.nasdaq.com (June 12, 2006).

17. Sandeep Junnarkar, "After Delisting Pink Sheets Beckon," *CNET News.com*, March 18, 2001, http:// www.news.com.com; Ianthe Jeanne Dugan, "Pink Sheets Aims for Respectability Under Ex-Trader," *Wall Street Journal*, December 17, 2005, p. B1; Pink Sheets LLC corporate Web site, http://www. pinksheets.com (June 8, 2006).

18. Peter Chapman, "ECNs Packing Their Bags: Saying Sayonara to Nasdaq," *Traders Magazine*, May 2006, http://www.tradersmagazine. com; and Ivy Schmerken, "Reg NMS Turns 1," *Wall Street & Technology*, March 2006, p. 48.

19. Rajesh Mahapatra, "Booming Indian Economy a Boon for Its Stock Market," *Chicago Sun–Times*, September 1, 2005. p. 58; Shefali Anand, "Investors' Challenge: Markets Seem Too Linked," *Wall Street Journal*, June 2, 2006. p. C.1; Craig Karmin, "Year-End Review of Markets & Finance 2005; Surging World Markets Entice U.S. In-vestors," *Wall Street Journal*, January 3, 2006, p. R8.

20. Craig Karmin, "Year-End Review of Markets & Finance 2005; Surging World Markets Entice U.S. Investors," p. R8.
21. James R. Hagerty and John D. McKinnon, "Fannie Mae to Pay $400 Million to Settle Probe," *Wall Street Journal*, May 23, 2006, p. A3.
22. Paul Davies and Susanne Craig, "Insider Mix: Goldman, Business-Week, Croatia," *Wall Street Journal*, April 12, 2006, p. C1.
23. "Circuit Breakers and Trading Collars," NYSE corporate Web site, http://www.nyse.com, (June 12, 2006).
24. Aaron Lucchetti, "Other Exchange Courtships Loom as NYSE and Euronext Near Deal," *Wall Street Journal*, May 22, 2006, p. C1; and Jamie Selway, "The New Exchange Business," *Traders Magazine*, June 2005, http://www.tradersmagazine.com.
25. Schmerken, "Resurrecting the Regionals," p. A38.

26. Jenny Anderson and Heather Timmons, "Big Board's Bid for Euronext Advances," *New York Times*, May 23, 2006, http://www.nytimes.com; "FAQ: NYSE-Euronext," *Wall Street Journal Online*, June 11, 2006, http:// www.onlne.wsj.com; Aaron Lucchetti, Alistair Macdonald, and Kara Scannell, "NYSE, Euronext Set Plan to Form a Markets Giant," *Wall Street Journal*, June 2, 2006, p. A1; Michael J. Martinez, "Big board Envisons Post-Merger Future," *San Diego Union-Tribune*, December 7, 2005, pp. C1, C4; "NYSE 2005 Year-End Review," New York Stock Exchange press release, December 30, 2005, http://www.nyse.com; Jamie Selway, "The New Exchange Business," *Traders Magazine*, June 2005, http://www.tradersmagazine.com; and "Winners and Losers In NYSE-Euronext Deal," *Wall Street Journal Online*, June 2, 2006, http://www.online.wsj.com.

27. Lynn Cowan, "Small U.S. Firms Take AIM in London," *Wall Street Journal*, April 17, 2006, p. C5.
28. Anderson and Timmons, "Big Board's Bid for Euronext Advances," http://www.nytimes.com.
29. "Crowding the Dance Floor," *Economist*, May 20, 2006, p. 93.
30. Anderson and Timmons, "Big Board's Bid for Euronext Advances," http://www.nytimes.com; Lucchetti, "Other Exchange Courtships Loom as NYSE and Euronext Near Deal," p. C1; "NYSEly Does It," *Economist.com*, May 23, 2006, http://www.economist.com;
31. Kate Fitzgerald, "Keying In on the Internet, *Better Investing*, June 2006, p. 26; and Eleanor Laise and William Mauldin, "Hook the Right Broker," *Smart Money*, August 1, 2005, pp. 78–81.

SUBJECT INDEX

A

AARP, 222
Absenteeism
    reasons for unscheduled, 353
    reducing employee, 106
    rising costs of, 352–354
Absolute advantage, 137
Accessories, 434
Accountability, 277
Account executives, 669
Accounting
    computers in, 574
    cycle, 572–574
    environment, reconfiguring, 569
    equation, 572
    explanation of, 565–566
    financial, 566
    irregularities, 569
    managerial, 566
    processes, outsourcing, 634
    profession, 567–571
    reforms, 569–571
    reports provided by, 566
    scandals, 105, 110, 119, 186, 190,
        564–565
    shift from rules-based to
        principles-based, 586
    standards, 566
        desire to create uniform global,
            567
    system, 565
    trends in, 584–586
Accounting cycle, 572–574
    six steps in, 573
Accounts payable, 636
Accounts receivable, 575
    managing, 633–634
Accrued expenses, 577
Acid-test ratio, 581
Acquisitions, 188–189
    integrating, 191
    motives for, 191
Acronyms, 13
Action learning, 54
Active Corps of Executives
    (ACE), 221
Activity ratios, 583
Actual satisfaction, 447
ACT-UP, 112
Administrative agencies, 121
Administrative law, 119
Advertising
    aggressive trade, 514
    appeals, developing, 504–505

choosing media for, 500
common executional styles for, 505
costs and market penetration, 500
defined, 498
expenditures, 498–499
    by media categories, total U.S.—
        2007, 501
to Hispanics, complexity of, 46
impact of technology and the
    Internet on traditional, 499
incorporated into Broadway sets, 408
Internet, 502
menu, 500
messages, typical consumer
    exposure to, 412
objectives, 503–504
and podcasting, 516–517
in promotional mix, 497
regulation of pricing and, 127
types of, 499
Advertising agencies, 502–503
    functions of, 503
Advertising appeals, 504
    message execution for, 504–505
Advertising campaigns, 503
    objectives of, 503–504
Advertising media, 500
Advocacy advertising, 499
Affirmative action programs, 319
Afilaka, John, 353
African Americans
    as protected class, 319
    spending power of, 46
    in U.S. population, 45
Age Discrimination Act (1967), 318
Agency shop, 314
Agents, 467, 474–475
Aguerre, Fernando, 202–203
Aguerre, Santiago, 202–203
AIDS testing, 319
Alcohol labeling legislation
    (1988), 129
Allen, Paul, 584
Alternative trading systems
    (ATSs), 673
Amelio, Gilbert, 394, 395
Amelio, William, 150
American Cancer Society, 32
American Federation of Labor-Congress
    of Industrial Organizations
    (AFL-CIO), 311, 571
American Institute of Certified Public
    Accountants (AICPA), 568, 587
    Auditing Standards Board (ASB),
        570, 585

American Society for the Prevention of
    Cruelty to Animals (ASPCA), 31
American Stock Exchange
    (AMEX), 671
Americans with Disabilities Act (1990),
    318, 319, 324
Angel investors, 214, 643
    getting interest of, 215
Annual reports
    chief element of, 567
    on corporate Web sites, 679
Anschutz, Philip, 643
Antidumping laws, 141
Antitrust regulation, 127
Appellate courts, 121
Application service providers (ASPs),
    538–540
    relationship, structure of, 539
Appreciation, 136, 663
Apprenticeships, 3, 305
Arabov, Yakov, 615
Arbertha, James, 473
Arbitration, 121, 315–316
Aronson, Arnold, 480
Articles of incorporation, 177
ASCII text files, 19
Ashby, Molly, 229
Asians
    spending power of, 46
    in U.S. population, 45
Assembly line, 335
    layout, 371, 372
Assembly process, 367
Assets, 572
    current, 575
    fixed, 575
    intangible, 575
    inventory as, 634–635
    investment in long-lived, 635
    liquid, 575
    procedures to protect IT, 550
Attitudes, 48, 412–413
Audience selectivity, 500
Auditing, 568
Auditors, 568, 571
    ASB guidelines for, 570
    internal, 586
    main purpose of, 585
    new rules for, 586
    restrictions imposed on, 585
Auditor's opinion, 568
Audits, 584
Austvold, Eric, 386
Authority, 276–277
Authorization cards, 311

cash flow through, 627
changes caused by Internet, 53
checklist for starting, 210
closure, common causes of, 216
computing equipment, 531
creating awareness of new, 496
creation of Web sites, 53
decisions affected by tax policies, 75
defined, 30
developing plan for, 212–214
and economies, workings of, 66–68
effect of economy on, 67
environmental protection and, 107
ethnic diversity's impact on, 45–46
expansion needs of, 157
financing, 214
finding idea for, 210–212
global, importance to United States
    of, 134–135
home-based, 544
illegal and irresponsible
    behavior, 105
impact of acts of nature on, 39–40
importance of learning basics of, 3
by industry, home-based, 210
irresponsible but legal behavior, 105
legal and responsible behavior, 106
managing socially responsible,
    104–106
nature of, 30–31
negative effects of inflation on, 73
new focus of, 54
ownership, trends in, 191–193
reaction to business cycles by, 70
reasons for studying, 33
risk, 215–216
social factors affecting, 48–49, 58
starting your own, 210–214
taxation of, 130–131
use of technology to create
    change, 52
Business cycles, 40, 69–70
Business environment
    demographic factors in, 41–48
    dynamics of, 39
    economic forces affecting, 40
    effect of social change on, 48–49
    external, 39, 40
    internal, 39
    political and legal factors affecting,
        40–41
    understanding, 39–40
Business ethics, 98–99
    influence of justice on individual,
        99–100
    negative image created by
        poor, 101
Business interruption insurance, 658
Business law, 120
    contracts in, 122
Business markets, 414
Business organization
    advantages and disadvantages of
        major types of, 180
    choosing form of, 212
    comparison of forms of, 170
    cooperatives, 181

corporations, 175–180. *See also*
    Corporations
    joint ventures, 182
    partnerships, 172–173
    sole proprietorships, 170
    specialized forms of, 181–182
Business plan, 212
    outline for, 213
Business Process Management
    (BPM), 386
Business products, 434
Business-to-business market
    characteristics of, 414
    purchase decision making in, 414
Butler, Deborah, 363
Buyer behavior, 409
Buyer cooperatives, 181
Buy-national regulations, 140
Buzz marketing, 513

C

CAD/CAM systems, 382
Cafeteria-style benefit plan, 309
Calhoun, David, 251
Callahan, Terry, 634
Can-Spam Anti-Spam Act (2004), 129
Cantalupo, Jim, 253
Capacity, 123
Capital, 34, 364
Capital budgeting, 635
Capital budgets, 630
Capital expenditures, 635
Capitalism, 35–36, 66
    global trend toward, 57
Capital products, 434
Capital Research Center, 112
*Career Employment Opportunities
    Directory—Business
    Administration*, 18
Careers
    choosing, 4
    offering job satisfaction and
        financial reward, 3
    self-assessment, to help choose,
        16–17
    transferable competencies for, 17
Carpenters and Joiners, 311
Carter, Rob, 530
Carter, Shawn, 222
Case law, 110
Cash, 575
    inflows and outflows of, 627
Cash and carry wholesalers, 474
Cash budgets, 630
Cash flows, 627
    management of, 633
    through a business, 627
Cash management, 631–633
    challenges for companies with
        overseas operations, 632
Category management, 484–485
C corporation, 179
Cease-and-desist orders, 127
Celler-Kefauver Act (1950), 127
Cellular manufacturing, 371
Center for Venture Research, 643–644

Central America Free Trade Agreement
    (CAFTA), 144
Centralization, 278
Ceran, Jennifer, 646
Certificates of deposit, 632
Certified management accountant
    (CMA), 568
Certified public accountant
    (CPA), 568
Chain of command, 276–277
Challenger, John, 222
Change to Win Coalition, 311
Changing Times Annual Survey, 18
Charities, 32
Checks
    clearing, 605
    declining use of, 605
Chenault, Ken, 642
Chidambaram, P., 675
Chief audit executive (CAE), 586
Chief financial officers (CFOs)
    continued expansion of role of,
        644–645
    effect of globalization of finance
        on, 646
    effect of Sarbanes-Oxley on, 645
    giving up control of finance to third
        party by, 634
Child labor, 113
Child Protection Act (1966), 129
Children's Online Privacy Protection
    Act (2002), 129
Children's Television Act (1990), 129
Childs, Stephanie, 49
Chill, 62
China
    banking in, 613
    booming economy of, 52
    comparative advantage of, 137
    emergence of, 157–158
    energy needs of, 86
    entrepreneurial ventures
        in, 88–89
    growth of GDP in, 69
    joint ventures in, 187
    outsourcing in, 193
    selection for Summer Olympics
        in, 141
    trade surplus of, 137
Christiansen, Chris, 547
Churchill, Winston, 246
Cigarette Labeling Act (1965), 129
Circuit breakers, 678
Circular flow, 67
    economics as, 67–68, 68
Civil Aeronautics Board, 119
Civil Rights Act (1964), Title VII, 318,
    319, 328
Claiborne, Darryl, 329–330
Clark, Gordon "Grubby," 93
Classic entrepreneurs, 205
Clayton Act (1914), 127
Cleary, Michael, 599
Client (network), 534
Cobain, Kurt, 173
Cobb, Peter, 487
Cobranding, 439

cultural differences in, 152
direct foreign investment and, 149–150
economic environment in, 153–154
electronic hubs in, 532
exporting, 147
franchising and, 148
joint ventures and, 149
licensing and, 148
multinational corporations in, 154
political considerations in, 151
Global trade
fostering, 141–143
impact of terrorism on, 135
negative aspects of, 138
in United States, 134–135
Global vision, 134
Glos, Michael, 86
Goal-setting theory, 344
Goggins, Sara, 338
Goldberg, Robin, 292
Golden, Russ, 587
Gooding, Cuba, Jr., 498
Goodnight, James M., 262
Goods, 30
consumer, 153
keeping steady prices for, 72
prices of, in free market, 77–78
products as blends of services and, 433
quality, 379–380
relation of transportation to price of, 483–484
Gore, Al, 394
Gore, Wilbert, 291
Gould, Andrew, 353
Government securities, 665–666
Grapevines, 282
Grassroots lobbying, 499
Graziani, Paul L., 310
Great Depression, 677
Greenfield, Jerry, 343
Green movement, 154
Greenspan, Alan, 74, 603
Greifeld, Bob, 673
Greiner, Helen, 206
Grid computing, 553–554
Grievance
defined, 315
handling and arbitration, 315–316
procedure, typical, 316
Gross domestic product (GDP), 50, 69
Gross National Income, 153
Gross profit, 579
Gross revenue, 447
Gross sales, 578
Gross world product (GWP), 50
Group behavior, understanding, 272–273
Group cohesiveness, 272
Group leaders, 410–411
Groupthink, 339
Grove, Andrew, 247, 404
Growth-oriented entrepreneurs, 205
Guthrie, Hugh, 46

H

Habitat for Humanity, 32
Hackers, 546
Haji-Ioannou, Stelios, 453
Haley, George T., 156
Hand, Learned, 119
Harris, Yoela, 223
Hartnett, Bill, 610
Hawthorne studies, 336
Health insurance, 656
premiums, 657
Health Insurance Portability and Accountability Act (HIPAA), 586
Heavin, Gary, 215
Herran, Andrea, 295
Herron, Dave, 685
Herzberg, Frederick, 340–342
motivating and hygiene factors of, 341
Herz, Robert, 567, 586, 587
High-yield bonds, 665
Hilton, Paris, 496
Hispanics
as protected class, 319
spending power of, 46
in U.S. population, 45
House, David, 537
Howe, Neil, 41
Hull, Robert, 635
Human relations skills, 252
Human resource management. *See also* Management
defined, 296
laws impacting, 318
process, 296, 297
trends in, 320–322
Human resources, 364
outsourcing, 321
Human resources planning, 299
and forecasting, 298–299
and job analysis and design, 297–298
process, 299
Human rights, 100
corporate decisions regarding, 113
Humphrey, Richard, 220
Hurd, Mark, 279
Hurricane Katrina, 253
aid given by small businesses after, 110
corporate philanthropy after, 109
economic predictions related to, 85
effect on economy of, 74
effect on insurance companies of, 610
and FEMA, 278
impact on businesses of, 39–40
impact on U.S. energy prices of, 82
rescue of animals after, 32
Hurricane Rita, 253
Hyden, Scott, 540
Hygiene factors, 341

I

Iacocca, Lee, 4, 504
Ideal self-image, 412

Idei, Nobuki, 340
Image
brand, 412
creating, in retail strategy, 478–479
price, as key element in store's, 479
Immelt, Jeff, 111
Immigration
effect on demographics of, 46–48
policies
conflicts regarding, 297
impact of terrorism on, 135
self-employment and, 222
Immigration Reform and Control Act (1986), 318
Implied contract, 122
Implied warranties, 124, 440
Import quota, 140
Imports, 135
Inagi, Miho, 205, 207
Incentive pay, 308
Income statement, 577
expenses, 578–579
net profit or loss, 579
revenues, 578
sample, 578
Income taxes, 130
payable, 577
Index funds, 667
India
booming economy of, 52
comparative advantage of, 137
emergence of, 157–158
energy needs of, 86
entrepreneurial ventures in, 88
growth of economy in, 675
outsourcing in, 193
service centers for, 138
Indirect pay, 308
components of, 309
Individual investors, 668
Individual rights, 100–101
Industrial distributors, 467
Industrial loan corporation (ILC), 92
Industrial products, 434
advertising for, 513
categories of, 434–435
Industrial Revolution, 400
Inflation
defined, 72
effects of, 72
Fed strategy for heading off, 603
impact of, 73
measuring, 73
types of, 73
Influence buying, 98
Informal organization, 282
communication channels in, 282
functions of, 282
Information
digital sending of, 56
hiding or divulging, 99
jobs dependent on, 533
promotion to provide, 496–497
protection of computers and, 546–549
transforming businesses through, 533

Macenczak, Lee, 46
MacGowan, Bill, 553
Mack, John J., 693
MacLean, Jessica, 169
Macroeconomics
  defined, 67
  economic growth and, 69–70
  employment and, 70–71
  entrepreneurship and, 88–89
  fiscal policy and, 74–77
  importance of price stability to, 72
  monetary policy and, 74
  three main goals of, 68–69
Magnuson-Moss Warranty Act (1975),
  129, 440–441
Mail Fraud Act (1872), 129
Make-or-buy decision, 373
Malcolm Baldrige National Quality
  Award, 380
Malik, Rajeev, 675
Managed service providers (MSPs), 540
Management. *See also* Human resource
  management
  activities of good, 237
  approaches, differences in, 340
  classical era of, 335
  first-line, 242
  functions of, 236
  hierarchy, 241–242
  human relations era of, 336
  and leadership, trends in, 253–256
  making recommendations to, 420
  middle, 242
  participative, 348
  rights in unionized companies, 314
  role of, 236–241
  span of, 277–278
  styles, 339–340
  supervisory, 242
  tool, product life cycle as, 446–447
  top, 241–242
  union-, relationship, 309. *See also*
    Labor unions
Management information systems
  (MIS), 533
  computer equipment used in, 531
  decision support, 542–543
  executive, 543
  expert, 543
  management support, 541–542
  office automation, 543–544
  software used in business, 531
  transaction processing, 540–541
Management pyramid, 276–277
Management rights clause, 314
Management support systems (MSSs),
  541–542
Managerial accounting, 566
Managerial hierarchy, 276–277
Managers
  challenges of globalization to, 256
  decision making requirements of,
    249–250
  delegation of authority and
    responsibility by, 277
  following examples set by, 101
  functions of, 236

and information technology, 255
leadership styles of, 244
need for global vision of U.S., 134
organizing duties of, 241
roles of, 249–250
setting of prices by, 449–451
skills needed by, 251–253
trends for, 53–57
Manix, Sue, 347
Mantz, Maria, 350
Manufacturer brands, 438
Manufacturers, 466
  retail stores of, 485–486
  supplying category
    management, 485
Manufacturers' agents, 474
Manufacturers' representatives, 474
Manufacturing
  cellular, 371
  computer-aided (CAM), 382
  computer-integrated (CIM), 384
  environment, 369–370
  function, in past, 364–365
  just-in-time, 381–382
  lean, 381
  process, 367
Manufacturing resource planning II
  (MRPII), 374
Margin requirements, 604
Marketable securities, 575, 632
Market averages, 683
Market correction, 675
Market density, 416
Market indexes, 683–684
Marketing
  blogs, 515
  channel functions performed by
    intermediaries, 472
  decisions, environmental data
    shaping, 403
  defined, 400
  direct-response, 477
  factors and site selection, 369
  family, 411
  not-for-profit, 408
  one-to-one, 423–424
  social, 408
  trends in, 420–424
Marketing concept
  components of, 400–401
  customer satisfaction and, 401–402
  customer value and, 401
  defined, 400
  relationship building and, 402
Marketing database, 423–424
Marketing intermediaries, 466–467
  channel functions performed
    by, 472
  functions performed by, 471
Marketing mix. *See also* Distribution
  defined, 407
  developing, 407–414
  distribution strategy and, 407
  and not-for-profit
    organizations, 408
  pricing strategy and, 407
  product life cycle and, 445–446

product strategy and, 407
promotion strategy and, 408
Marketing research
  challenges of conducting
    global, 422
  choosing method for, 418–419
  data analysis, 420
  data collection for, 419
  defined, 418
  defining marketing problem
    for, 418
  Internet, 420–421
  process, steps in, 418
Marketing strategy
  defining target market and, 404
  external environment and, 403
Market makers, 672
Market risk, 646
Market segmentation, 414–417
  benefit, 417
  defined, 414
  demographic, 415–416
  forms of consumer, 415
  geographic, 416
  psychographic, 416–417
  volume, 417
Market structures
  comparison of, 83
  defined, 82
  monopolistic competition, 84
  oligopoly, 84
  perfect competition, 82–83
  pure monopoly, 83–84
Markkula, Mike, 165, 232, 394
Markup pricing, 450
Martz, Maria, 216
Maslow, Abraham, 336–338
Maslow's hierarchy of needs,
  336–338, 337
  criticism of, 338
  relation of culture to, 345
Mass customization, 366, 367, 481
Mass production, 366, 367
Master brands, 436
  America's, 436
Master franchisees, 133
Materials-handling system,
  setting up, 483
Materials requirement planning
  (MRP), 374
Matrix structure, 270–272
  advantages of, 271–272
  disadvantages of, 272
Mayo, Elton, 336
McClure, David, 537–538
McCormack, Sean, 86
McCracken, Jeff, 246
McDonnell, Stephen, 209–210
McDonough, Conor, 207
McElhatton, Jerry, 531–532, 533
McGraw, Steve, 592
McGregor, Douglas, 338–339
McGuire, Joe, 651
McLaughlin, Edward, 338
Mechanistic organizations, 279
  versus organic organizations,
    279–281

O

Oberhelman, Douglas R., 629
Observation research, 418–419
Occupational Outlook Handbook, 18
Occupational Safety and Health Act (OSHA) (1970), 318, 319
Occupational Safety and Health Administration (OSHA), 319
O'Connell, Patty, 44–45
Odd-even pricing, 453
Office automation systems, 543–544
Office of Federal Contract Compliance Programs (OFCCP), 324
Off-the-job training, 305
Oil, Chemical and Atomic Workers Union (OCAW), 311
Older Boomers, 43
Oligopoly, 84
Olsen, Ashley, 207
Olsen, Mary-Kate, 207
One-to-one marketing, 423–424
Online processing, 541
Online video, 502
On-the-job training, 304–305
Open market operations, 603–604
Open shop, 314
Operating budgets, 631
Operating expenses, 579, 631
Operating plans, 629
Operational planning, 240
Operational risk, 646
Operations management
    customer satisfaction and, 364–365
    improving, 365, 379–384
    location issues related to, 368–370
    production process and, 366–368
    quality and, 365
    role of, 364–365
    trends in, 385
    types of decisions involving, 365
Opinion leaders, 410–411
Oppenheimer, James, 511
Options, 668
Oreck, Thomas, 250
Organic organizations, 279
    versus mechanistic organizations, 279–281
Organizational structures
    building, 266–272
    committee structure, 272
    degree of centralization in, 278
    division of labor in, 267
    flat versus tall, 280
    formal, 266–267
    impact of company's business on, 281
    line-and-staff organization, 270
    matrix structure, 270–272
    mechanistic versus organic, 279
    reengineering, 283
    relationships in, 276–278
    span of control and, 277–278
    traditional, 267–269
    trends in, 283–289
Organization chart, 267–268
    for typical appliance manufacturer, 267

Organization for Economic Cooperation and Development (OECD), 35
Organization(s)
    chain of command in, 276–277
    design considerations for, 279–281
    identification of trends by, 53
    influence on ethical conduct of, 101–102, 104
    informal, 282
    not-for-profit, 32, 408
    politics in, 5–6
    provision of ethics training programs by, 101
    strategy-making process of, 279
    use of funds by, 631–635
    violating rules of, 99
    virtual, 283–284
Organizing, 237, 241–242
    five traditional ways of, 268
    function, components of, 266
Organizing campaigns, 311
Orientation, 304
Ouchi, William, 339–340
Outputs
    components of, 364
    converting inputs to, 367, 368
Outsourcing, 52, 70, 138, 285–286, 395
    attractiveness of, 286
    in China, 193
    financial and accounting processes, 634
    HR and technology, 321
    in India, 138, 193
    logistics function, 485
    misconceptions about, 286
    opportunities created for small businesses, 219
    reasons for, 285
    of supplies, 373
Over-the-counter (OTC) market, 670, 673
OVP (band), 333
Owners' equity, 572

P

PACE. *See* Paper, Allied-Industrial, Chemical and Energy International Union (PACE)
Packaging
    functions of, 439–440
    importance of, in self-service economy, 439–441
    labels on, 440
Page, Larry, 35, 281
Paper, Allied-Industrial, Chemical and Energy International Union (PACE), 311
Parker, Sarah Jessica, 410
Parkinson, Andrew, 392
Parkinson, Thomas, 392
Parsons, Hugh, 333
Participative leaders, 243–245
Partnerships, 172–173
    advantages of, 173–174
    disadvantages of, 174–175

external, in supply chain management, 485
    finding right person for, 174
Par value, 639, 664
    of Treasury bills, 666
Patel, Kiran, 644
Patents, 124, 148
    as assets, 575
Patrick, Danica, 334
Pawela-Crew, Jacqueline, 347
Pay-for-performance programs, 349
Payment of damages, 123
Payner, Melissa, 42
Payroll taxes, 130
Pearson, John, 465
Peer-to-peer computing, 553–554
Pegler, Maribel, 333
Penetration pricing, 452
Pension funds, 611
Pension Reform Act (1974), 317–318
Pensions, 308
People skills, building, 4
Perceived value, 447
Perception, 412
Perfect competition, 82–83
    characteristics of, 82
Performance
    job design and, 346
    monetary incentives to enhance, 348–349
    planning and evaluation, 306–307
    standards, components of effective, 248
    using teams to enhance, 273–276
Performance appraisal, 306–307
    example of behavior-based rating scale for, 307
Performance bonds, 658
Perpetual inventory, 374
Perry, Daniel R., 461
Perry, David, 110
Personal digital assistants (PDAs), 11, 53, 550
Personality, 412
Personal selling
    advantages of, 506
    aggressive, 514
    employment opportunities in, 506–507
    professionals, 506
    in promotional mix, 497
    steps in process of, 507–508
Persuasion, 4
Pescatore, Paolo, 453
Petaflops, 530
Petascale computing, 530
Peterson's Business and Management Jobs, 18
Pharming, 549
Phishing, 549
Physical exams, 303
Piece-rate pay plans, 348
Pinchot, Gifford, 206

marketing factors related to, 369
production planning and, 368
Six Sigma, 380
Skill assessment, 16–17
Skilling, Jeffrey, 564
Skills
and attitudes, transferable, 17
conceptual, 252–253
developing interpersonal, 4–7
global management, 256
human relations, 252
inventory, 300
job-specific, 17
managerial, 251–253
at different management levels,
importance of, 252
study, 12–13
technical, 252
test-taking, 13–15
Skills inventory, 300
Slander, 125
Sloan, Jeff, 205
Sloan, Rich, 205
Small Business Administration (SBA),
147, 203
assistance for women and
minorities, 221
classification of small business
by, 209
financial assistance programs
of, 220
free online resources and courses for
small-business owners, 221
management assistance programs
of, 221
Small businesses. *See also* Entrepreneurs; Entrepreneurship
advantages of, 219–220
buying, 214–215
characteristics of, 209
difference between entrepreneurs
and owners of, 204–205
disadvantages of, 220
economic impact of, 202
exporting and, 147, 218
hiring and retaining employees,
217–218
impact of, 219
importance of work-life balance
in, 172
Internet-based, 223
keeping up with trends of,
211–212
magazines for, 188
managing, 216–218
relief contributions given by, 110
risk of, 204
snapshot of owners of, 209
trends in ownership of, 221–224
use of outside consultants
by, 217
use of Web sites by, 53
Small Business Investment Companies
(SBICs), 220
Smith, Orin, 134
Snoop Dogg, 504
Social investing, 110

Socialism, 37
dissatisfaction with, in Western
Europe, 89
Socialization process, 411
Social marketing, 408
Social responsibility
corporate, 104
balance of conflicting interests
and, 113
pyramid of, 105
defined, 104
dimensions of, 104–106
global ethics and, 112–113
through corporate philanthropy,
107, 109
trends in ethics and, 111–112
Social Security, 309, 656
direct deposit for, 606
Social Security Act (1935), 318
Society for Human Resource
Management (SHRM), 172, 309,
328, 346, 353
Society, responsibility to, 107, 109
Software
applications, business and
personal, 531
for creating résumés, 18–19
customer relationship management
(CRM), 539–540
dashboard, 255
on demand, 538–540
digital forensics, 552–553
flash drive monitoring, 550
for job training, 305
keeping current database of current
IT, 549
litigation-support, 552
piracy, 548–549
podcasting, 516
presentation, 420
security, 552
social network analysis, 282
statistical programs for data
analysis, 420
technology industry's shift to
Internet-based, 532
Sole proprietorships, 170
advantages of, 171
disadvantages of, 171
Sondhelm, Dan, 687
Soros, George, 677
Sourcing, 481
Spam, 548, 549
Span of control, 277–278
narrow and wide, 277
optimal, 278
Span of management, 277–278
Special-interest groups, targets
of, 112
Specialization, 267
of labor, 335
Specialty products, 434
Speculative risk, 653
Spindler, Michael, 394, 395
Spinella, Art, 44
The Spirit of Liberty (Hand), 119
Spread, 604

Spyware, 549
Staff positions, 270
Stakeholders
balancing conflicting interests of,
113
defined, 106
responsibilities to, 106–107,
109–111
Standard & Poor's (S&P) 50 stock
index, 683–684
Standard of living, 30
improving worldwide, 86
measuring, 57
State banks, 607
Statement of cash flows, 579–580
sample, 580
three groups composing, 580
Statutory law, 119
Steiner, Jim, 208
Stephens, Robert, 198–199
Stern, Andrew, 322
Stern, Howard, 41, 405
Stock, 662–663
common, 640, 663
preferred, 643, 664
quotations, 680–681
Stockbrokers, 669
Stock dividends, 642, 663
Stockholders, 178, 662–663
common, 663
preferred, 664
Stock insurance companies, 656
Stock market crash (1929), 611
Stock markets, 670
effect of business scandals on, 110
world's largest, year-end
2005, 674
Stock options, 348–349
Strategic alliances, 87
Strategic channel alliances, 469–470
Strategic giving, 111
Strategic partnerships, 87
Strategic planning, 238–240
Strategic plans, 241, 629
Strauss, William, 41
Strict liability, 126
Strikes, 316–317
Stringer, Michael, 31
Stringer, Sir Howard, 279–280, 340
Structural unemployment, 71–72
Study skills, 12–13
Succession planning, 299
Successive hurdles approach, 301
Sullivan, Thomas R., 622
Sumrall, Lonnie, 333
Supercomputers, 530
Supervisory management, 242
Supplemental insurance, 656
Supplies, 435
Supply
changes in, 81–82
defined, 78
and demand, price determination
through interaction of, 79
nature of, 78–79
Supply chain, 374, 466
importance of efficient, 375

managing logistical components
of, 481
Supply chain management, 87, 374, 466
choosing warehouse location and
type, 482
critical role of, for global
companies, 376
dual role of, 480
external partners in deployment
of, 485
increasing efficiency and customer
satisfaction through, 480–484
inventory control, 482–483
production scheduling, 481
sourcing and procurement, 481
strategies for, 375–377
Supply curve, 78–79
factors causing shifts in, 81
Surety bonds, 658
Survey research, 418
common types of, 419
Surveys, 419
advantages of Internet, 421
Sutter, Francis, 383
Synergy, 273

T

Tactical planning, 240
Taft-Hartley Act (1947), 314, 318,
319, 324
Target market
defining, 404
in developing retailing strategy,
477
for new products, 443
product categories and, 433
Target return on investment, 448–449
Tariffs, 139
arguments for and against, 140
preferential, 143
Taxes
around the world: percentage of
gross income and GDP, 75
breaks on, as incentive, 370
for corporations, 175, 178
cutting of, 75
excise, 131
income, 130
for partnerships, 174
payroll, 130
property, 130
sales, 131
for sole proprietorships, 171
Taylor, Earl L., 156
Taylor, Frederick W., 335–336
Taylor, Jeff, 608
Team building. *See also* Teams
participating in, 6
retreats for, 54
Teams. *See also* Team building
building high-performance,
275–276
cross-functional, 275
to enhance motivation and
performance, 273–276
problem-solving, 274

self-managed, 274
types of, 273–275
virtual, 284
work groups versus work, 273
Teamsters Union, 311
Teamwork, 46
Technical skills, 252
Technology
advances helpful to small
businesses, 219
boom of late 1990s, 190
changing banking, 610
and China's rapid growth, 69
contributing to increased
productivity, 50
defined, 52
designed to intercept terrorist
attacks, 56–57
impact of, 52–53
on advertising, 499
improving credit and collections
performance using, 634
for improving health care, 383
intelligence-related, 57
multinationals and, 156
nontraditional channels made
available by electronics, 469
outsourcing, 321
planning, 545–546
portal, 536–537
present and contemplated uses of
RFID, 483
in promotion, growing use of, 516
supply-chain, 482
tools of, 52
transforming factory floor with,
382–384
Web-based, 305
wireless, 537–538
Telecommunications, 53
Telecommunications Act of
1996, 40
Telecommuting, 347, 544
Term loans, 639
Terrorism
effect on mergers of, 190
impact of, on global trade, 135
interruption of networks connected
to, 613
Terrorist attacks, 56–57
threats to data from, 546
Tessler, Natalie, 201, 202
Test-marketing, 444
Test-taking skills, 13–15
Thain, John A., 686
Theft insurance, 658
Theory X, 339
Theory Y, 339
Theory Z, 339–340
Thompson, Kenneth, 608
Thrift institutions, 607–608
Thurman, Thomas, 299
Time deposits, 602
Time management, 11
Timoni, Paolo, 43
Title insurance, 658
Tomé, Carol, 646

Top management, 241–242
challenges to, 253–256
Torts, 125
Total cost, 450
Total profit, 450
Total Quality Management (TQM), 380
Total revenue, 450
Trade
barriers to, 139–141
fear of, 138–139
between nations, measuring,
135–141
reasons for, 137–139
Trade credit, 636
Trade deficit, 136
Trademarks, 124, 435
as assets, 575
franchisee use of, 183
recognizable, 177
as source of licensing
revenue, 148
that have become generic, 125
Trade secrets, 148
Trade surplus, 136
Trading hubs, 532
Traditionals, in workforce, 55
Training and development, 304–305
off-the-job training, 305
on-the-job training, 304–305
process, 304
Transaction processing systems,
540–541
Transportation
criteria for ranking modes of, 484
decisions, making, 483–484
five major modes of, 483–484
Transport Workers Union, 317
Treasury bills, 632, 666
Treasury bonds, 603–604, 666
Treasury notes, 666
Trends
ability to spot and act upon, 207
in accounting, 584–586
baby boomers driving
franchise, 192
in business ownership, 191–193
in developing products and pricing,
454–456
in distribution, 484–487
in economics and competition,
85–89
in employee motivation, 349–354
in entrepreneurship and small-business ownership, 221–224
in ethics and social responsibility,
111–112
in financial institutions, 614–616
in financial management, 644–646
focusing on "human" of human
capital, 54–55
franchises as popular, 182. *See also*
Franchises
in global competition, 156–158
in human resource management
and labor relations, 320–322
in information technology,
551–554

crisis, looming U.S., 385
distributed, 553
diversity of, 320–321
four-generation, 55–56
graying, 58
knowledge-based, 352
rejuvenation of, 351–352
women in, 49, 351
Work groups. *See also* Work teams
cohesiveness of, 272
informal, 336
versus work teams, 273
Workplace safety, 113
Work teams. *See also* Work
groups
virtual, 284
versus work groups, 273

World Bank, 142–143
protests aimed at, 138
World Economic Forum (WEF), 50
growth competitive index, 2005, 51
World Trade Organization (WTO), 36,
50, 141–142
Wozniak, Stephen, 165, 231, 394

X

Xie, Andy, 675

Y

Yarborough, Martin, 538
Yield management systems (YMS),
455–456

Young, Andrew, 512
Younger Boomers, 43

Z

Zammar, Joseph, 522
Zennström, Niklas, 223
Zeta-Jones, Catherine, 496
Zetsche, Dieter, 243–244, 245
Zhijun, Gao, 88
Zimmer, George, 349
Zollo, Peter, 428–429
Zumwalt, Rossini, 646

COMPANY INDEX

Motorola, 102, 109, 158, 320, 391, 538
Mrs. Smith's, 496
Munsingwear, 461
Music Monitor Network, 217
MySpace.com, 411

N

Nabisco, 48, 190, 417
National Cattlemen's Beef Association, 497
National Energy Technology Laboratory, 46
National Wildlife Federation, 408
Nationwide Papers, 473
Navistar International Corporation, 265
NEC, 70
Neiman Marcus, 405, 476, 479
Nescafé, 154
Nestlé, 73, 157, 370, 485, 646
NetBank, 620–621
Netezza Corp., 585
Netflix, 451
Netshare, 301
Neuroco, 502
News Corporation, 189
New York Life, 656
Nextel, 286, 333
Nike, 87, 156, 157, 177, 191, 247, 284, 436, 438, 486, 631, 639
Nintendo, 429
Nissan, 134
Nokia, 156, 321, 429, 516, 538, 539
Nordstrom, 61, 477
Norfolk Southern Railroad, 246
Northwest Airlines, 51, 240–241, 505
Northwestern Mutual Life, 656
Novartis Seeds, Inc., 424, 558–559
Nutrisse, 410

O

OAO Gazprom, 86
Ocean Spray, 181
OffThePathMedia.com, 207
Ohio Public Employees Retirement System (OPERS), 571
Olive Garden, 418
1–800-Flowers, 481, 491–492
OpenPages, 592
Oracle Corp., 190
Orange, 453
Oreck, 250, 253
Organic Valley, 198
Orvis Company, 406
Oscar Mayer, 442
Otis Elevator, 156
Overnite, 189
Overstock.com, 455
Owens Cleaners, 110

P

Pacific Sunwear of California, Inc., 176
Palm Harbor Enterprises, 40

Pampers, 154
Panera Bread Company, 427–428, 673
Panzano's, 348
Papa John's Pizzas, 504
Peapod, 392–393
Pearl Paradise, 170
PenAgain, 406
Pennzoil, 435
Penske Logistics, 377
People's Alliance Federal Credit Union, 45
PeopleSoft, 89
PepsiCo, 138, 151, 154, 228, 329–330, 429, 460, 497, 498, 499, 516
Perdue Farms, 152
Pernod Ricard, 151
Perry Ellis International, 461–462
P. F. Chang's, 359–360
Pfizer, 40–41, 104, 110, 286–287, 639
Pharmacia, 286
Philip Morris Company, 148, 154, 189
Philips, 521
Piaggio, 43, 366
Pink Sheets LLC, 674
Pixar Studios, 211, 269, 279
Pizza Hut, 183, 416, 422
Plateau Systems, 305
PNC Bank, 269
Poilane Bakery, 208
Polaroid, 84
The Popcorn Factory, 492
PrepMe, 212
PricewaterhouseCoopers, 104, 224, 300, 568
Procter & Gamble, 50, 52, 109, 156, 243, 247, 269, 286, 391, 422, 442, 445, 448, 455, 485, 499, 509, 513, 516, 671
ProFlowers.com, 481
Prudential, 354, 646, 656
Publix Super Markets, 642
PubSub, 515
PUMA, 486, 542–543

Q

Quaker Oats Co., 404, 437
Qualcomm, 89, 642, 673
Quality Imaging Products, 208
Quanta, 395
Quicken, 620
Quizno's Subs, 182, 184, 522
QVC, 228, 469

R

Radio Shack, 166
Rainforest Café, 148
Ralph Lauren, 407, 461
Ramada Inns, 439
Raytheon, 321
Recreational Equipment Inc. (REI), 108
Reebok, 106
Reef, 203
Research in Motion, 53
Revlon, 44, 407

Riley Research Associates, 255
Rite Aid, 483
Ritz-Carlton Hotels, 300, 303, 320, 321
Roaman's, 404
Roc-a-Fella Records, 222
Rockwell Collins, 377
Rolex, 140–141, 142
Rothstein Kass, 584
Royal & SunAlliance, 502
Rush Communications, 205
RxUSA, 192

S

Saab, 538
Safeway, 44, 516
Safian Investment Research Inc., 221–222
Sage Software, 573
SAIC, 351
Saks Fifth Avenue, 479, 480
Salesforce.com, 102, 539
Sam's Clubs, 474
Samsung Corporation, 87, 156, 214, 442, 537
Sandia National Laboratories, 321
San Manuel Bottled Water Group, 369
Sanofi, 286
Sanofi Aventis, 514
Sarah Adult Day Services, Inc., 192
Sarah's Pastries and Candies, 207
Sara Lee, 516
SAS, 261–262
Save-A-Lot, 473
SBC, 138
Schlumberger Limited, 352, 353
SCI Systems, 395
SC Johnson, 108, 350, 354
Scotti's Record Shops, 217
Scottrade, 669–670
Sealed Air Corp., 646
Sears, 190, 191, 320, 456, 467, 476
Seiko, 442
Selfridges, 479, 480
Semco, 347
7-Eleven, 482
Shanghai Dingjia Ventures, 89
Sharper Image, 105–106
Shell, 86
Siebel Systems, 190, 539
Sirius Satellite Radio, 41, 405
Six Flags, 283, 300
Skype Technologies, 190, 223, 286, 539
Skyworks Solutions, 560
Smarter.com, 455
Smartfood, 228
Smith Barney, 669
SmithKline, 154
Society for Worldwide Interbank Financial Telecommunication (SWIFT), 613
Solera Capital LLC, 229
Sony, 31, 70, 87, 279–280, 340, 442, 446, 472
South Beach Diet, 48
Southern Baptist Radio and Television Convention, 408